ENVIRONMENTAL AND NATURAL RESOURCES LAW

Fourth Edition

ENVIRONMENTAL AND NATURAL RESOURCES LAW

Fourth Edition

Eric Pearson
Associate Dean and Professor of Law
Creighton University School of Law

Casebook ISBN: 978–0–7698–4748–1
Looseleaf ISBN: 978–0–7698–4749–8

Library of Congress Cataloging-in-Publication Data

Pearson, Eric.
Environmental and Natural Resources Law / Eric Pearson.— 4th ed.
p. cm.
Includes index.
ISBN 978-0-7698-4748-1
1. Environmental law — United States. 2. Natural resources — Law and legislation — United States. I. Title.
KF3775.P43 2012
344.7304'6—dc23

2012018932

This publication is designed to provide authoritative information in regard to the subject matter covered. It is sold with the understanding that the publisher is not engaged in rendering legal, accounting, or other professional services. If legal advice or other expert assistance is required, the services of a competent professional should be sought.

Note TO USERS
To ensure that you are using the latest materials available in this area, please be sure to periodically check the LexisNexis Law School web site for downloadable updates and supplements at www.lexisnexis.com/lawschool.

Editorial Offices
121 Chanlon Rd., New Providence, NJ 07974 (908) 464-6800
201 Mission St., San Francisco, CA 94105-1831 (415) 908-3200
www.lexisnexis.com

MATTHEW◆BENDER

DEDICATION

For my wife, Lorraine,
and for our children, Scott and Julia.

PREFACE

Taken in its expansive sense, "environmental and natural resources law" encompasses pollution control law, energy allocation and conservation law, species and habitat protection, common law property rights, regulatory theory, and a host of other areas. In the law school setting, this obviously expansive body of legal material frequently is divided into two courses, an environmental law course focusing mainly on issues of pollution control and a natural resources law course covering the rest. As its title indicates, this textbook combines the two. The combination, I have found, works well, despite the academic challenge a broader examination can portend. For one thing, a panoptic coverage of this sort serves ideally as a platform for students whose plans include future intense study in these areas of law. It goes without saying that providing such a foundation is precisely what an introductory survey course ought to do. Beyond that, exposure to this broad reach of subject matter fosters in students a more rich understanding of generic issues and controversies that animate these areas of law. From the professor's point of view, a major advantage inures at the course design stage. With more to choose from, instructors can supplement or reduce subject matter coverage as best suits their individual circumstances and the needs of their students.

With those considerations in mind, these materials have as a primary goal the examination of the "structure" of environmental and natural resources regulation. The book is organized to demonstrate how regulatory programs work both in the absolute and in relation to each other. In my view, this goal is more achieved more seamlessly if the book is used in conjunction with a statutory supplement.

Chapters 1 through 3 survey what might be thought of as classic "foundational" material. Chapter 1 presents a thumbnail sketch of the environmental movement that has led to the current array of legal controls, and offers a quick look into the world of administrative agencies and how they operate. Chapter 2 examines how the common law has dealt with pollution and resource allocation problems. This foray is important if only because common law mechanisms remain to this day effective tools for resolving environmental disputes. A review of the strengths and weaknesses of the common law as a method to protect the environment also sheds light on why environmental and natural resources law is now dominated by statute and regulation. Chapter 3 introduces the structure of regulation, in particular the significant interplay of the federal government, on the one hand, and the states, on the other, across this spectrum of law. As it turns out, polluters typically have two governmental masters, and in many instances, those masters disagree on what the polluter should or should not do. Chapter 3 ventures into the constitutional law of takings as well: since virtually every environmental protection and resource regulatory initiative burdens the use and value of real property, takings principles are ever relevant.

Chapters 4 through 8 present the natural resource law coverage. Chapter 4 introduces the National Environmental Policy Act, the federal government's effort to put its own house in order. Chapter 5 examines the history of and legal regime governing federal lands and the natural resources they so abundantly contain. This coverage is important because fully one-third of land in this nation is titled in the federal government. Chapter 6 discusses the public trust doctrine, a common law principle rooted in history but continually growing in prominence. Chapter 7 shifts the focus to the Endangered Species

PREFACE

Act, one of the most significant resource protection statutes in world history. Chapter 8 concludes this part of the book with an overview the domestic law of water rights. Issues of rights to water are critical to environmental quality, especially in western states, and students are well served by having some familiarity with these legal principles.

Chapters 9 through 12 present the major federal pollution control and remediation programs. Chapters 9, 10, and 11 review the Clean Air Act, the Clean Water Act, and the Resource Conservation and Recovery Act, respectively. Chapter 12 presents the book's coverage of the significant "Superfund law," formally known as the Comprehensive Environmental Response, Compensation, and Liability Act ("CERCLA"). This statute is the federal government's pathbreaking effort at remediation of hazardous waste contamination. CERCLA has taken on infamous importance in the regulatory world because of its far-reaching liability structure.

This subject matter coverage necessarily brings into play issues of administrative law. Administrative law, briefly described, is the law of government agencies and how they operate. Administrative law is part and parcel of our course; indeed, many of the cases in this book were decided on administrative grounds. As you might expect, administrative law cannot be systematically examined in this course, due to time limitations. (For what is may be worth, administrative law *should not* be finely probed here — an academic discipline in its own right, it is better learned in a separate course devoted exclusively to the topic.) Nonetheless, for purposes of orientation, and to facilitate a better appreciation of the primary course material, this book offers, in addition to the commentary in the introductory chapter, *see supra*, four "Notes on Administrative Law" at various points in the text.

Not covered in the book, obliquely or otherwise, is environmental litigation. Courses on environmental litigation typically deal with an array of issues involving civil procedure, trial tactics, and federal court practice. This material, like administrative law, is essential groundwork for environmental lawyers, or at least those who expect to enter the courtroom, but is best left to a course devoted exclusively to those purposes.

Eric Pearson
May 2012

Table of Contents

Table of Contents

Table of Contents

Table of Contents

Table of Contents

Table of Contents

Table of Contents

Table of Contents

Table of Contents

Chapter 1

INTRODUCTION

"Nothing in the world, not all the armies, is so powerful as an idea whose time has come." *Victor Hugo*

SYNOPSIS

A. SOME BACKGROUND AND PERSPECTIVE

B. ISSUES OF THE REGULATORY STATE

C. ISSUES OF REGULATION

    1. The Regulated Community

    2. Assessing Risk

    3. The Derivative Nature of Environmental and Natural Resources Law

A. SOME BACKGROUND AND PERSPECTIVE

In the 1960s, there was no isolated field of law known as Environmental and Natural Resources Law. There is one now, for reasons of necessity. Why has it become a necessary legal discipline, along with labor law, corporate law, immigration law, and so many others? The answer has everything to do with the relationship between the physical world and its most prominent resident, *homo sapiens*.

In earlier times, before the dawn of "modern" society, human beings lived within the constraints of the physical world. Hunters and gatherers all, they plied the natural world for their sustenance, and lived in fear of its numerous caprices. Their demands on natural resources were modest: humans were simply incapable of subduing the massive carrying capacity of the natural environment.

These conditions, however, no longer obtain. In the current day, but for the occasional eruption, tsunami, earthquake, or atmospheric roil, nature no longer constrains human activity. The reality now is that *homo sapiens* can largely do as it pleases. In significant measure, we have become impervious to weather, disease, and famine. In this revised syndrome, it is nature that genuflects to the human enterprise, not the other way around.

This avulsion in the relationship of humanity with environment has come to pass for easily identifiable reasons. In numerical terms, the human species has thrived, its performance far exceeding that of any other species in the history of the planet. The global human population, which approximated a relatively paltry 2.5 billion in 1950, swelled to comfortably more than 6 billion by 2010, and is projected to exceed 9 billion by 2050. In the United States, the experience is of a kind: while the U.S.

1

population was below 160 million in 1950, it exceeded 300 million in 2010 and is predicted to top 400 million by 2050. This explosion of numbers obviously direly stresses the finite resource base that is Earth.

The way humans beings live their lives has taken a huge environmental toll as well. Simply put, we regard the world as little more than a cookie jar. As the history of the west amply illustrates, natural resources exist in our minds mainly for what they can provide. In North America, for example, early European settlers, unlike the indigenous Indian populations they encountered, viewed the breathtakingly vast frontiers they discovered as essentially unlimited bounty, available for the taking. Without seemingly a non-utilitarian thought, they avidly exploited the resplendent wildlife, foliage, water, and soils arrayed before them. Without pause to reflect, they consumed, and did so rapaciously.[1]

These first immigrants began the adventure by establishing an agrarian society. When farming became the central economic pursuit, the largely untrammeled environment suffered an enormous transmutation. Land was separated out, parcel by parcel, with each controlled by its owner. The owner could, and typically did, plow, clear, drain, and otherwise reconfigure the natural landscape to his liking. The result was abundant harvests and a higher standard of living for the human inhabitants of the continent, to be sure. But other species fared only as well as good fortune might allow.

In the eighteenth and nineteenth centuries, the agrarian society was joined by the Industrial Revolution. This period of national history saw massive numbers of people relocating from rural areas into the great and increasingly crowded cities to take up residence alongside smelters, open hearths, trains, steamboats, and the other machinery of the new age. Smokestacks belched pollution into the air, sewers flushed wastes into rivers, and people went to work. The overtly negative quality-of-life implications brought about by all of this were tolerated without serious complaint. Unclean air and water were seen as unavoidable trade-offs. As stated in a state court decision challenging the burgeoning steel industry of Pittsburgh, Pennsylvania, on common law nuisance grounds, "one's bread is more important than landscape or clear skies." *Versailles Borough v. McKeesport Coal & Coke Co.*, 83 PITT. L.J. 375, 379 (1935).

Indeed, as poignantly encapsulated by the inestimable Pogo (in Walt Kelly's *Earth Day*, 1971, cartoon bearing the same name), "[W]e have met the enemy, and he is us."

Thus arose the need for some remedy, some means by which to arrest this damaging regression. But the remedy proved to be a long time coming. The first awakenings of public awareness to this tragedy-in-the-making came, as often is the case, at the behest of far-thinking individuals. Among these were Henry David Thoreau, an author and naturalist ("In wildness is the preservation of the world."),

---

[1] This anthropogenic perspective finds an ancient root in none other than the Bible. The *Book of Genesis* forthrightly declares that man should have "dominion over the fish and the sea, and over the fowl of the air, and over the cattle, and over all the earth and over every creeping thing that creepeth upon the earth." (I:26). It further instructs that persons should "[B]e fruitful and multiply and replenish the earth and subdue it." *Book of Genesis 1:28.*

John Muir, founder of the Sierra Club ("When one tugs at a single thing in nature, he finds it attached to the rest of the world."), and Gifford Pinchot, the first chief of the United States Forest Service ("Unless we practice conservation, those who come after us will have to pay the price of misery, degradation, and failure for the progress and prosperity of our day."). These individuals, among others, saw nature in a different light. They saw it as holding inherent value, a value separate and distinct from its service as a source of material benefits for humankind. Their vision gave birth to the so-called "Conservation Movement." Early manifestations of this social movement were the setting aside of Central Park in Manhattan in 1853, of Yellowstone National Park in 1872, and of several national forests. The movement became a political *cause celebre* after Muir hosted big-game hunter President Theodore Roosevelt over three nights in Yosemite National Park in 1903. Muir used the occasion to persuade the President to join the cause, something the former Rough Rider was surely predisposed to do. (For a picture of Muir and Roosevelt, see Chapter 5, *infra*.) As students of history know, TR turned out to be a bully good ally — during his Administration, five national parks were established, 148 million acres were added to the national forests, 400,000 acres were added to the wildlife refuges, and 1.4 million acres were designated as national monuments.

Capturing the ethical and moral underpinnings of the Conservation Movement, perhaps more effectively than any other person, was Aldo Leopold, a founder of both the Wilderness Society and the profession of game management. In his book, *A Sand County Almanac*, posthumously published in 1949, Leopold began by bemoaning the abject disregard with which Americans treated the land. Even though the national conversation intoned a reverence for nature, Leopold failed to see any of it in practice:

> Yes, but just what and whom do we love? Certainly not the soil, which we are sending helter-skelter downriver. Certainly not the waters, which we assume have no function except to turn turbines, float barges, and carry off sewage. Certainly not the plants, of which we exterminate whole communities without batting an eye. Certainly not the animals, of which we have already extirpated many of the largest and most beautiful species.

A SAND COUNTY ALMANAC 239–40 (Oxford University Press ed., 1966).

In place of this thoughtlessness, Leopold proposed a new "land ethic" to "affirm the right" of natural resources, both plant and animal, to some "continued existence, and, at least in some locations, their "continued existence in a natural state." *Id.* at 240. The land ethic would "change[ ] the role of Homo sapiens from conqueror of the land-community to plain member and citizen of it. It implies respect by humans for our fellow travelers, as well as a respect for the entire ecological community." *Id.*

Leopold's call for a new land ethic was all the more acute given the much publicized environmental insults of the time. In fact, much seemed to be going wrong with the environment. In October 1948, for example, a temperature inversion in Donora, Pennsylvania (the home town of Stan Musial and the Ken Griffeys, Sr. and Jr.), trapped air pollutants for several days, causing the deaths of 68 people and visiting permanent lung damage on uncounted others. In 1954, residents of Bikini Atoll in the Pacific Ocean were exposed to fallout from a hydrogen bomb test. Many suffered radiation sickness and worse. In the 1960s, oil spills ravaged the shores of

California. And late in that decade, the population witnessed what many had thought could never happen, the ignition and combustion of a major urban waterway. The affected stream was the Cuyahoga River near Cleveland, Ohio. *Time* magazine, among other publications, gave the event prominent coverage. Asserting that the Cuyahoga "oozes rather than flows," *Time* warned that immersion in the waters of the river would cause not drowning, but "decay." *The Cities: The Price of Optimism*, TIME, Jan. 8, 1969. (In reality, the fire was not the catastrophic event it was portrayed to be. *See* Chapter 10, *infra*.)

Yet another publication, Rachel Carson's 1962 book, *Silent Spring*, fueled the "green fire" even more. *Silent Spring* detailed how the profligate use of agricultural pesticides wreaked havoc on avian life. The book brought home the undeniable message that even the routine activities that comprise day-to-day life could produce environmental damage on the grand scale. This sense of urgency only grew more intense when exciting satellite color photography of the day portrayed a lonely Mother Earth both finite and fragile.

All of this eventually convinced the public that something needed to be done. The rise of environmentalism was underway. But, even so, the issue had yet to command the attention of Congress. The environmental movement had not yet taken on a federal political dimension. Congress needed to understand the gravity of the problem and, even more so, the enormity of public support for some address of it. Congress was made finally to understand, and the day of its epiphany was April 22, 1970. Earth Day stands as testimony to the impact a single person with a single idea can work upon an entire nation.

The person was United States Senator Gaylord Nelson of Wisconsin. Born in 1916, Nelson served ten years in the Wisconsin state senate and followed that with two terms as the state's governor. In that latter capacity, he earned his environmental stripes by sponsoring programs to create "green jobs" and by enlarging wilderness areas and public parks. These initiatives, among others, earned him the sobriquet of "Conservation Governor" and paved the way for his election to the United States Senate in 1962.

Nelson began what would ultimately span three terms as a United States Senator by convincing President John F. Kennedy to undertake a national speaking tour to promote conservation, a tour JFK completed less than two months before his assassination in November 1963. To Nelson's disappointment, however, the speaking tour failed to ignite the congressional action he so ardently desired. Indeed, the more pressing issues of the day — the civil rights movement and the war in Vietnam, to name two — were commanding the public stage. Undeterred, Nelson pushed on. In a signal accomplishment, he managed to include a new "Green Thumb" program into President Lyndon Johnson's War on Poverty. The program, which employed low income older Americans in conservation-related jobs, resulted in the planting of thousands of trees, the construction of rest areas and public parks, the restoration of national historic sites, and more.

But still no national political environmental movement was stirring. That all changed when Nelson happened upon a grand idea. While on a flight from Los Angeles to San Francisco, where he was scheduled to address a conservation gathering at the University of California at Berkeley, Nelson happened to read an article about an anti-Vietnam war "teach-in." The idea struck him: why not do a teach-in for the environment? When he formally proposed the idea in September 1969, the telephones started ringing off the hook. The idea caught fire so spontaneously that planning for the event had to be moved out of the Senator's office to larger quarters. As Nelson put it, "I wanted a demonstration big enough to capture the attention of the politicians and force the issue to become part of the political dialogue. It did that. From that day on, it was a political issue. It achieved everything I had hoped for, and more." George Lobsenz, WASHINGTON NEWS (UPI), Apr. 21, 1990.

Earth Day became to environmentalism what Dr. Martin Luther King's "I Have A Dream" oration at the Lincoln Memorial became to civil rights. It demonstrated in undeniable fashion the enormity of political support for environmental protection. Earth Day saw a national outpouring of concern by millions of Americans across the country. On that day, education programs about the environment were presented in thousands of schools, and hundreds of thousands of students took time to collect litter from parks, school grounds, and neighborhoods. Additional thousands of people demonstrated in Philadelphia, Washington, D.C., Chicago, New York City, and other metropolitan areas. Manhattan banned vehicular traffic in part of its downtown area. Not to be left out, Congress adjourned to let its members attend and participate in rallies across the country.

With national attention finally focused on issues of environmental protection and natural resource use, the issue was not whether to do something, but how. As an initial matter, it at least was obvious how not to proceed. For increasingly obvious reasons, the effort could not be left to the states. The few states that had tried to improve environmental quality within their borders had largely failed in their efforts, for reasons of scientific uncertainty and lack of political will. Beyond that, there was the problem of neighbors. Even if one state could clean up, it would still suffer the insults of nearby states whose home-generated air and water pollution would gratuitously stray in. *See, e.g.*, Chapter 2, *infra*. Nor could the effort be left to the courts. Armed only with the common law of nuisance and negligence, judicial tribunals simply are incapable of serving as instruments to promote national political goals. *See, e.g.*, Chapter 2, *infra*. Accordingly, the federal government would necessarily be the prime mover. Congress would have to enact statutes and President Nixon and his successors would have to cobble together the administrative capacity to implement those statutes.

Congress moved with alacrity and, for that reason, the succeeding decennary has come to be known as the "Environmental Decade." The legislation Congress zealously passed in the 1970s endure to this day as the flagships of environmental and natural resources law. Those enactments include: the National Environmental Policy Act (1970); the Clean Air Act (1970); the Clean Water Act (1972); the Federal Insecticide, Fungicide, and Rodenticide Act (1972); the Marine Protection, Research, and Sanctuaries Act (the "Ocean Dumping Act") (1972); the Noise Control Act (1972); the Endangered Species Act (1973); the Forest and Rangeland Renewable Resources Planning Act (1974); the Safe Drinking Water Act (1974); the Federal Land Policy and Management Act (1976); the Resource Conservation and Recovery Act (1976); the Toxic Substances Control Act (1976); the Surface Mining Reclamation and Control Act (1977); and the Comprehensive Environmental

Response, Compensation and Liability Act (the "Superfund" law) (1980). Quite understandably, these legislative enactments could be long on goals but short on details. Congress was, after all, with virtually no experience and only scant information to guide it, forging ahead with a monumental new enterprise. The default solution for this perplexity was to leave a good deal of the heavy lifting to the newly created Environmental Protection Agency. EPA, along with the Department of Interior ("DOI") and a number of sister agencies, was assigned the arduous task of constructing comprehensive and effective regulatory programs to carry out the optimistic statutory goals. Which it has done, some say with a vengeance.

B. ISSUES OF THE REGULATORY STATE

At this juncture, it is advisable to engage an examination, however cursory, of the regulatory state. Indeed, modern environmental and natural resources law is overwhelmingly regulatory; there is little common law here. Accordingly, practitioners in this area of law must be familiar with administrative agencies, how they are empowered, and how they (should) behave. The abbreviated materials that follow supply some rudimentary information of this sort.[2]

What are administrative agencies anyway? They are governmental organizations, typically located in the executive branch of government, that disburse benefits ("entitlement agencies") and/or impose restrictions on private activity ("regulatory agencies"). They can do what they do because they have received authority from a legislative body; in the federal arena, that body is, of course, Congress. Congress enacts statutes which both establish national policy goals and empower agencies to implement those goals. Agencies determine what implementing powers they have, or do not have, by doing what we all do: they read the statutes that authorize the programs they are charged to administer. (Indeed, this assessment is no snapshot endeavor. Much of the litigation with agencies centers on whether they have the powers they purport to exercise.) Agencies need to clearly understand the extent of their powers, for a reason both plain and simple: if an agency has no power to do something, it may not do that something, regardless of how wonderful the something might be. Actions taken by agencies that exceed their powers are *ultra vires*, and of no legal force and effect.

In addition to discerning the reach of subject matter authority, agencies must detail the procedures that will govern exercises of that authority. The agency's authorizing legislation (often referred to as its "organic law") often instructs agencies on these matters. Also in the mix for these purposes are statutes which establish procedural minima for all agencies. (The most significant generally applicable statute governing matters of process in the federal arena is the Administrative Procedure Act.)

In the main, agencies are given procedural powers of two main sorts. The first is the power to make "rules and regulations," which are, in effect, "little statutes" promulgated to add detail to the regulatory program. The second power is the

---

[2] At several points in this book, the reader will come upon "Administrative Law Notes," the purpose of which is to give some additional information about this area of law. Please know that these Notes cannot suffice as a substitute for a more intensive study.

power to adjudicate. Agencies typically have their own "courts" (sometimes referred to as a "tribunal") run by persons known as "administrative law judges." As one might expect, trials before these tribunals need procedural rules to govern them. (As a practical matter, when agencies take other actions, such as inspecting, requiring entities to submit information, and so forth, procedural requirements are slim.) Since rulemaking is categorically the most significant of these agency functions, some attention to it is warranted.

Rulemaking is the major tool by which agencies translate the generalized commands of authorizing legislation into particularized requirements. Agencies use rulemaking routinely. In the environmental and natural resources law context, the result is literally thousands of pages of federal regulations that: constrain or entirely prohibit emissions and discharges of pollutants into the ambient media around us (i.e., the air, water, and land); mandate the protection of flora and fauna on both private and public land; require government to consider the environmental impacts of the actions it takes; determine the societal ends public land shall promote and the availability of natural resources for extraction from that land; and more. Typically, these same regulations allow for substantial penalties for compliance failures. Federal regulations can be found in the Code of Federal Regulations ("C.F.R."); regulations promulgated by state agencies can be found in state law regulatory codes.

Before an agency, federal or state, promulgates a rule, however, it selects the form the rule shall take. There are four major possibilities, and agencies are free to choose any of them — so long as the authorizing legislation permits the choice.

(i) Command and control regulation. This form of regulation is the workhorse of environmental and natural resources law, and the regulatory state generally, perhaps more because of habit than affirmative choice. "Command and control" regulations operate in the straightforward manner their name indicates. They declare as illegal certain actions or omissions and announce penalties for those who fail to abide. An example: assume a statute obligates industrial polluters to reduce emissions of air pollutants so as to achieve the level of air quality that is "requisite to protect the public health." A command and control regulation in place to implement this statutory directive might require, say, coal-fired power plants, to reduce emissions of, say, sulfur dioxide, to no more than, say, ten parts for every million parts of emitted air (i.e., 10 ppm). Complex regulations of this sort, as you may expect, carve qualifiers and exceptions into the fabric of the rule itself; often agency rules are much more opaque than the organic legislation that authorizes those rules.

Have command and control regulations accomplished their goals? In all likelihood, the answer is a resounding "yes," but detractors complain, *inter alia*, of their "one size fits all" character, which can significantly increase costs of compliance. Detractors have a valid point here.

(ii) Market-based regulation. A recent and currently popular variation on command and control regulation is market-based regulation. Market-based regulatory systems impose mandates and penalties, just as do conventional command and control regulatory systems, but are qualitatively different in that they offer at least a limited range of choices to the regulated community. Whereas the typical command and control regulation says, "Do X," market-based regulations say, "Do X, Y, or Z, whatever you wish, so long as in conjunction with others also regulated our overall clean-up target is met." The best known example of market-based regulation is cap and trade regulation, recently and loudly touted as the best way to reduce carbon dioxide emissions widely blamed for global warming. Market-based regulations can be more cost-effective than command and control regulations, but they have been criticized for unevenness in achieved results.

(iii) Taxation. A third regulatory model does not involve compulsion of the same sort. Taxation, when used for regulatory purposes, declines to declare actions to be illegal. Instead, it says, "Do X, Y, Z, or anything else. One caveat, though: if you don't do X, you will have to pay a significantly greater tax than you would if you do do X." When used for regulatory purposes, taxation enjoys the benefits of high compliance rates. This form of regulation also imposes a lesser administrative burden on regulators. Indeed, would we even need an Environmental Protection Agency if the Internal Revenue Service could move in? While the federal government does use taxation to influence private behavior on a common basis — by allowing deductions for favored classes of persons (e.g., those paying mortgage interest, those raising children, and those buying energy-efficient furnaces (in 2010, anyway)), it has rarely used taxation in environmental and natural resources law.

(iv) Voluntary measures. On occasion, an agency will promulgate regulations compliance with which is made voluntary. In this circumstance, the regulation says, "Please do X" and nothing more. This form of regulation boasts the "benefit" of not being compulsory, but the question is whether it works. A gentleman by the name of Garrett Hardin, in a most famous article, *The Tragedy of the Commons*, 162 Science 1234 (1968), made a forceful case that voluntary regulations do not work:

> The tragedy of the commons develops in this way. Picture a pasture open to all. It is to be expected that each herdsman will try to keep as many cattle as possible on the commons. Such an arrangement may work reasonably satisfactorily for centuries because tribal wars, poaching, and disease keep the numbers of both man and beast well below the carrying capacity of the land. Finally, however, comes the day of reckoning, that is, the day when the long-desired goal of social stability becomes a reality. At this point, the inherent logic of the commons remorselessly generates tragedy.

> As a rational being, each herdsman seeks to maximize his gain. Explicitly or implicitly, more or less consciously, he asks, "What is the utility to me of adding one more animal to my herd?"

Id. at 1244.

At this point, Hardin argues, the rational economic choice for each individual is to place as many animals on the commons as she can, for a simple reason. One's own cow on the commons yields to its owner a 100% benefit, while keeping the cow off the commons yields to its owner only a fractional benefit, shared with all other grazers. "[T]herein is the tragedy. Each man is locked into a system that compels him to increase his herd without limit — in a world that is limited. . . . Freedom in a commons brings ruin to all." *Id.* at 1244.

Hardin's argument demonstrates the central deficiency of voluntary controls: individual economic imperatives will produce an over-exploitation of natural resources, precisely the opposite of what voluntary regulations seek to accomplish. Persons acting in their own rational self-interest not only will ignore voluntary admonitions, but will also take for fools those who honor them. What are examples of commonses, that is, resources potentially available to all for use or misuse? To name a few, they include grazing lands (the subject of Hardin's analysis), the high seas, the ambient air, surface and groundwater, wildlife, and on and on. Indeed, the entire physical world is a commons. (Ever go to dinner with someone who routinely orders the most expensive items on the menu but likes to split the bill with you? If you agree to the split, think of the bill as a commons and yourself as the fool).[3]

C. ISSUES OF REGULATION

Once the form of the regulation is decided, the more daunting question of the regulation's content presents itself. The following is intended to familiarize readers with several of the common challenges administrative officials face as they construct regulatory programs. Our brief review addresses three foundational matters. First is a short discussion of the (euphemistically known) "regulated community." Second is an article commenting on what can be the most difficult challenge facing regulators: determining how much risk or harm, if any, a regulatory enterprise shall permit. Last is a reminder that environmental and natural resources law, like all law, is a derivative discipline, dependent on other sciences for its content.

1. The Regulated Community

A prerequisite feature of regulation is the definition of the "regulated community," that is, the assemblage of legal persons who shall be subject to the regulatory program itself. Typically, the regulated community is comprised of those who are causing or have caused the problem for which the statute is a response. Those persons comprise the regulated community, in the common case, because the governing legislation so directs. Statutes so direct, in turn, because asking "wrongdoers" to stop their wrongdoing comports with basic moral

---

[3] How to eliminate the tragedy of the commons? Three approaches have been identified: (a) privatize the commons; (b) unitize the commons (i.e., employ a single operator to manage the commons for the benefit of all); and (c) regulate the commons (i.e., use regulations to restrict access to the commons). *See, e.g.*, Barton H. Thompson, Jr., *Tragically Difficult: The Obstacles to Governing the Commons*, 30 ENVT'L LAW 241 (2000). Notably, all of these approaches implement enforceable mandates.

There has emerged a theory of the anticommons. *See* Michael A. Heller, *The Tragedy of the Anticommons: Property in the Transition fromof Marx to Markets*, 111 HARV. L. REV. 621 (1998). As you might expect, an anticommons is the opposite of a commons. In a commons, the problem is too many persons with rights to use and too few persons with rights to exclude others from use. The result is overexploitation. In an anticommons, the problem is too many persons having rights to exclude. The result is underexploitation — the tragedy of the anticommons. This phenomenon has been seen in Russia, where storefronts have been empty of consumer goods. The problem is that one "owner" might have the right to sell, another the right to revenues from sale, another the right to lease, another to occupy. And any single "owner" can block all others from using the property productively. Anticommonses in property are curable if the prevailing legal system allows individuals to assemble a collection of property rights sufficient to put property to productive use.

standards of morality and ethics. Beyond that, focusing on these persons makes sense for reasons of economics. Fundamental economic theory suggests that persons should not be permitted to "externalize" costs (defined broadly). An entity externalizes a cost when it forces that cost to be borne by a person or persons unassociated with the cost-creating activity and not sharing in the benefits the activity produces. A classic example of an economic externality in the environmental and natural resources context is a factory that pollutes. The factory provides a benefit for its owner — the production of goods results in economic profit for the owner — but by polluting the countryside, the factory imposes an often significant cost on nearby residents, persons external to the actor and not sharing in the profits. The public, in effect, is made to subsidize the production of goods in the form of a reduced quality of life. Such costs should be "internalized" by ceasing the pollution.[4]

Economic theory, however, also can be used to justify the selection of a regulated community on other than fault grounds. The argument was best presented by the famous economist, Ronald Coase, in his pathbreaking article, *The Problem of Social Cost*, 3 J. L. & Econ. 1 (1960). Focusing on the example of a polluting factory, Coase argued for replacing fault as the basis for designating the regulated community with economic utility:

> The question is commonly thought of as one in which A inflicts harm on B and what has to be decided is: how should we restrain A? But this is wrong. We are dealing with a problem of a reciprocal nature. To avoid the harm to B would inflict harm on A. The real question that has to be decided is: should A be allowed to harm B or should B be allowed to harm A? The problem is to avoid the more serious harm.

Id. at 1. The Coasean approach has been followed by some courts in common law nuisance cases, *see, e.g.*, Chapter 2, *infra*, but has generally been eschewed by agencies. Do you find this approach to be sensible?

2. Assessing Risk

When agencies such as the EPA set regulatory standards to protect public health and the environment, they face the persistent question of how much to regulate. Should the agency ban all emissions of pollutants? If it does so, it will

---

[4] Externalities are objectionable as well for their effect on resource use and allocation. Externalities tend to discourage the optimal use of natural resources. One who can externalize costs may well make different choices about how to use resources than one who cannot. She might be willing, for example, to use land for a minimal personal gain, even if the use imposes a substantial burden on others, simply because the burden is, in fact, imposed on others. Alternatively, she might be unwilling to change a current land use to a more benign form because the benefit of the change inures to the public, not to her.

Notably, an externality can exist not only when an economic *burden* is exported to a third person, but also when a *benefit* is exported. Suppose, for example, that an individual constructs a residence of high artistic and architectural value, so that the residence becomes a landmark attraction enjoyed by the public at large. In such a circumstance, the builder has externalized an aesthetic, and perhaps even a monetary, benefit to the public and has received no compensation for doing so. As you are likely aware, circumstances such as these can prompt the enactment of landmark preservation legislation, which delimits the rights of the benefit-exporting property owner to alter the structure. Unlike pollution control legislation, landmark preservation legislation perpetuates, rather than removes, externalities.

reduce health risks from exposure to the airborne pollutants to zero. But if it does so, it might bankrupt the industries subject to the regulation. If it allows some emissions, the question becomes how much.

EPA addresses these problems with a two-step approach. First, it attempts to understand the problem. To do this, the agency must assemble a massive amount of scientific information, much of which will likely be internally conflicting. This is the risk assessment phase of EPA's standard-setting enterprise. Then, being careful to factor in a margin of safety, the agency must translate the raw data into a single numerical standard that supposedly represents an optimal condition of environmental quality for public health and welfare. This is the risk management phase of standard-setting. How well the agency undertakes both phases is, in reality, the grist of every lawsuit that challenges on the merits a health-based regulation. The following thoughtful article, written by a two-time, former Administrator of the EPA, sheds some light on these complex matters.

William D. Ruckelshaus, *Risk, Science and Democracy*
ISSUES IN SCIENCE AND TECHNOLOGY, 19-38 (Spring 1985)[5]

"Risk" is the key concept here. It was hardly mentioned in the early years of EPA, and it does not have an important place in the Clean Air or Clean Water Acts passed in that period. Of the events that contributed to this change, the most important were the focus of public attention on PCBs and asbestos (two substances that are ubiquitous in the American environment and that are capable of causing cancer) and the realization that exposure to a very large number of unfamiliar and largely untested chemicals is universal. The discovery by cancer epidemiologists that cancer rates vary with environment suggested that pollution might play a role in causing this disease. And finally, the cancer risk was pushed to the forefront by the emergence of abandoned dumps of toxic chemicals as a consuming public issue. As a direct result of this shift in attention, the relation of EPA to its science base was altered; the problem of uncertainty was moved from the periphery to the center.

This shift occurred because the risks of effects from typical environmental exposures to toxic substances — unlike the touchable, visible, and malodorous pollution that stimulated the initial environmental revolution — are largely constructs or projections based on scientific findings. We would know nothing at all about chronic risk attributable to most toxic substances if scientists had not detected and evaluated them. Our response to such risks, therefore, must be based on a set of scientific findings. Science, however, is hardly ever unambiguous or unanimous, especially when the data on which definitive science must be founded scarcely exist. The toxic effects on health of many of the chemicals EPA considers for regulation fall into this class.

"Risk assessment" is the device that government agencies such as EPA have adopted to deal with this quandary. It is the attempt to quantify the degree of hazard that might result from human activities — for example, the risks to human health and the environment from industrial chemicals. Essentially, it is a kind of

---

[5] Reprinted with permission of the author. Copyright © William D. Ruckelshaus, 2006.

pretense; to avoid the paralysis of protective action that would result from waiting for "definitive" data, we assume that we have greater knowledge than scientists actually possess and make decisions based on those assumptions.

Of course, not all risk assessment is on the controversial outer edge of science. We have been looking at the phenomenon of toxic risk from environmental levels of chemicals for a number of years, and as evidence has accumulated for certain chemicals, controversy has diminished and consensus among scientists has become easier to obtain. For other substances — and these are the ones that naturally figure most prominently in public debate — the data remain ambiguous.

In such cases, risk assessment is something of an intellectual orphan. Scientists are uncomfortable with it when the method must use scientific information in a way that is outside the normal constraints of science. They are encroaching on political judgments and they know it. As Alvin Weinberg has written:

> Attempts to deal with social problems through the procedures of science hang on the answers to questions that can be asked of science and yet which cannot be answered by science. I propose the term *trans-scientific* for these questions. . . . Scientists have no monopoly on wisdom where this kind of trans-science is involved; they shall have to accommodate the will of the public and its representatives.

However, the representatives of the public, in this instance policy officials in protective agencies, have their problems with risk assessment as well. The very act of quantifying risk tends to reify dreaded outcomes in the public mind and may make it more dif cult to gain public acceptance for policy decisions or push those decisions in unwise directions. It is hard to describe, say, one cancer case in 70 years among a population of a million as an "acceptable risk" when such a description may too easily summon up for any individual the image of some close relative on his deathbed. Also, the use of risk assessment as a policy basis inevitably provokes endless arguments about the validity of the estimates, which can seriously disrupt the regulatory timetables such officials must live by.

Despite this uneasiness, there appears to be no substitute for risk assessment, in that some sort of risk finding is what tells us that there is any basis for regulatory action in the first place. The alternative to not performing risk assessment is to adopt a policy of either reducing all *potentially* toxic emissions to the greatest degree technology allows (of which more later) or banning all substances for which there is any evidence of harmful effect, a policy that no technological society could long survive. Beyond that, risk assessment is an irreplaceable tool for setting priorities among the tens of thousands of substances that could be subjects of control actions — substances that vary enormously in their apparent potential for causing disease. In my view, therefore, we must use and improve risk assessment with full recognition of its current shortcomings.

This accommodation would be much easier from a public policy viewpoint were it possible to establish for all pollutants the environmental levels that present zero risk. This is prevented, however, by an important limitation of the current technique; the difficulty of establishing definitive no-effect levels for exposure to most carcinogens. Consequently, whenever there is any exposure to such substances, there is a calculable risk of disease. The environmentalist ethos, which is reflected in many of our environmental laws, and which requires that zero-risk levels of pollutant exposure be established, is thus shown to be an impossible goal for an industrial society, as long as we retain the no-threshold model for carcinogenesis. . . .

This situation has given rise to two conflicting viewpoints on protection. The first, usually proffered by the regulated community, argues that regulation ought not to be based on a set of unprovable assumptions but only on connections between pollutants and health effects that can be demonstrated under the canons of science in the strict sense. It points out that for the vast majority of chemical species, we have no evidence at all that suggests effects on human health from exposures at environmental levels. Because many important risk assessments are based on assumptions that are scientifically untestable, the method is too susceptible to manipulation for political ends and, the regulated community contends, it has been so manipulated by environmentalists.

The second viewpoint, which has been adopted by some environmentalists, counters that waiting for firm evidence of human health effects amounts to using the nation's people as guinea pigs, and that is morally unacceptable. It proposes that far from overestimating the risks from toxic substances, conventional risk assessments underestimate them, for there may be effects from chemicals in combination that are greater than would be expected from the sum effects of all chemicals acting independently. While approving of risk assessment as a priority-setting tool, this viewpoint rejects the idea that we can use risk assessment to distinguish between "significant" and "insignificant" risks. Any identifiable risk ought to be eliminated up to the capacity of available technology to do so.

It is impossible to evaluate the merits of these positions without first drawing a distinction between the assessment of risk and the process of deciding what to do about it, which is "risk management." The arguments in the form sketched here are really directed at both these processes, a common confusion that has long stood in the way of sensible policymaking.

Risk assessment is an exercise that combines available data on a substance's potency in causing adverse health effects with information about likely human exposure, and through the use of plausible assumptions, it generates an estimate of human health risk. Risk management is the process by which a protective agency decides what action to take in the face of such estimates. Ideally the action is based on such factors as the goals of public health and environmental protection, relevant legislation, legal precedent, and application of social, economic, and political values. *Risk Assessment in the Federal Government*, a National Research Council (NRC) document, recommends that regulatory agencies establish a strict distinction between the two processes, to allay any confusion between them. In my view Congress should do the same in all statutes seeking to deal with risk.

Returning now to the opposing viewpoints we see that both reflect the fear that risk assessment may be imbued with values repugnant to one or more of the parties involved. That is, some people in the regulated community believe that the structure of risk assessment inherently exaggerates risk, while many environmentalists believe that it will not capture all the risk that may actually exist. As we have seen, this disagreement is not resolvable in the short run through recourse to science. Risk assessment is necessarily dependent on choices made among a host of assumptions, and these choices will inevitably be affected by the values of the choosers, whether they be scientists, civil servants, or politicians.

The NRC report suggests that this problem can be substantially alleviated by the establishment of formal public rules guiding the necessary inferences and assumptions. These rules should be based on the best available information concerning the underlying scientific mechanisms. Adoption of such guidelines reduces the possibility that an EPA administrator may manipulate the findings of some risk assessment so as to avoid making the difficult, and perhaps politically unpopular, choices involved in a risk-management decision. Both industry and environmentalists fear this manipulation — from different brands of administrator, needless to say. Although we cannot remove values from risk assessment, we can and should keep those values from shifting arbitrarily with the political winds.

The explicit and open codification suggested by the NRC will also ensure that the assumptions used in risk assessment will at least be uniform among all agencies that adopt them, will be plausible scientifically, and will reflect a predictable and relatively constant policy amid this complex and chaotic hybrid discipline. It also offers the possibility that one day all the protective agencies of the government will speak with one voice when they address risks, so that estimates of risk will be comparable among agencies and the public at last will be able to make a fair comparison of the individual risk-management decisions of separate agencies.

The remaining points of both positions are really about risk management and on this issue both are awed. At its extreme, the first position — that regulation should be based solely on scientifically provable connections between pollutants and health effects — would allow the release of unlimited quantities of substances that cause cancer in animals, on the assumption that there will be no analogous effect on people and that there must be thresholds for carcinogenesis. I expect that most Americans would reject that assumption as imprudent, given our current knowledge about carcinogenesis (for example, the similarity of cancer causing genes across species). At some level we have to regard the possibility that we are controlling somewhat in excess of the true risk as a kind of insurance, with the cost of control as its premium. The effort to reduce apprehension, even so-called unreasonable apprehension, about the future results of current practices is a valid social function. Risk-management agencies such as EPA could be chartered to do precisely that. If so, we had better make clear what we are doing, and establish rules for doing it.

The weakness of the second viewpoint, that any identifiable risk ought to be eliminated up to the capacity of available technology to do so, lies in the concept of a best available technology that must invariably be applied where risk is discovered. "Best" and "available" are terms as infinitely debatable as the assumptions of risk assessment. There is always a technology conceivable that is an improvement on a previous one, and as the last increments of pollution are removed, the cost of each successive x goes up very steeply. Because, according to the no-threshold assumption, even minute quantities of carcinogens can be projected out to cause cases of disease, arguments about technology reduce in the end to arguments about risk and cost: technology A allows a residual risk of 10-5 and costs $1 million; technology B allows a residual risk of 10-6 and costs $10 million, and soon ad infinitum. It is specious to pretend that costs do not matter, because it is always possible to show that a certain level of removal, costs in fact do matter: technology Z allows residual risks of 10-15 and costs $1 trillion.

Once this is admitted, as it almost always is when we come down to debating actual regulations, the position is reduced to arguments about affordability. This too is treacherous ground. Firms vary in their ability to pay, and what is affordable for one may bankrupt another. If requirements are adjusted so as not to cripple the poorest firms, the policy amounts to an environmental subsidy to the less efficient players in our economy. . . .

My point is that in confronting any risk there is no way to escape the question "Is controlling it worth it?" We must ask this question not only in terms of the relationship of the risk reduced and the cost to the economy but also as it applies to the resources of the agency involved. Policy attention is the most precious commodity in government, and a regulation that marginally protects only 20 people may take up as much attention as a regulation that surely protects a million.

"Is it worth it?" That this question must be asked and asked carefully is a token of how the main force of the environmental idea has been modified by the recent focus on toxic risk to human health. In truth this question should always have been asked, but because the early goals of environmentalism were so obviously good, the requirement to ask, "Is it worth it?" was not firmly built into all our environmental laws. Who would dare to question the worth of saving Lake Erie? Environmentalism at its inception was a grand vision, one that nearly all Americans willingly shared. Somehow that vision of the essential unity of nature and of the need for bringing industrial society into harmony with it has been lost among the parts per billion, and with it we have lost the capacity to reach social consensus on environmental policy.

———

The Ruckelshaus article proffers for consideration, among other ideas, the prospect that regulation might issue forth even before the science underlying the regulatory initiative is complete. This notion is known as the "precautionary principle." At the core of the principle is the old adage, "better safe than sorry." The principle announces that "regulation is required whenever there is a possible risk to health, safety, or the environment, even if the supporting evidence is speculative and even if the economic costs of regulation are high." Cass R. Sunstein, *The Paralyzing Principle: Does the Precautionary Principle Point us in any Helpful Direction?* REGULATION 32, 33 (Winter 2002–03). The precautionary principle is especially applicable, the argument goes, in circumstances involving potential serious or irreversible harm facing the public. In such cases, the principle calls for a shift in the burden of proof on whether and how to go forward with regulation away from where the burden usually lies, on those who would impose regulation, to those who stand in opposition to the regulatory effort. The principle enjoys traction across the specter of environmental and natural resources law, as well as in other areas of law and policy. Do you view the precautionary principle as common sense or nonsense?

3. The Derivative Nature of Environmental and Natural Resources Law

We conclude with a reminder of the *realpolitik* of environmental and natural resources law — that it is a derivative science. By this is meant that the content of environmental and natural resources law necessarily depends upon information secured from external sources. In this area of law, the various disciplines from which content is drawn include the health sciences, geology, hydrology, engineering, economics, psychology, physics, and a host of others. Accordingly, as the Ruckelshaus article, *supra*, intimates, practitioners must assemble a working command of the underlying science that drives the regulatory effort.

Unfortunately, as also mentioned in the Ruckelshaus article, the underlying science is rarely consistent and clear. Indeed, there is intense disagreement on even overarching issues. Consider in this regard the ongoing debate on the gravity of the climate change phenomenon. In the view of some, the extant science demonstrates incontrovertibly that the planet is poised for destruction. As long ago as 1992, then-Vice-President Al Gore made the case famously, in his book, EARTH IN THE BALANCE — ECOLOGY AND THE HUMAN SPIRIT (1992). Gore argued in that publication that "[H]uman civilization is now the dominant cause of change in the global environment. Yet we resist this truth and find it hard to imagine that our effect on the earth must now be measured by the same yardstick used to calculate the strength of the moon's pull on the oceans or the force of the wind against the mountains." *Id.* at 30. (In the years following the publication of EARTH IN THE BALANCE, Gore undertook a crusade to end global warming, and received a Nobel Peace Prize for his efforts.)

On the other side of the issue are the "ecorealists," who are often heard to argue that the problems of environmental degradation are typically drastically overstated. In the words of one: "in almost every ecological category, nature has for millions of centuries been generating worse problems than any created by people." GREGG EASTERBROOK, A MOMENT ON THE EARTH — THE COMING AGE OF ENVIRONMENTAL OPTIMISM, at xvii (1995). Agreeing with this perspective is Bjørn Lomborg, a professor of statistics in Denmark who has described himself as an "old left-wing Greenpeace member." Lomborg is the author of a quite sensational book called THE SKEPTICAL ENVIRONMENTALIST — MEASURING THE REAL STATE OF THE WORLD (2001). In his book, Lomborg painstakingly reviewed hard data on both the state of the physical world and the prospects for continued human survival. Comparing that data with what Lomborg called the "litany" (i.e., the conventional wisdom of doom and gloom), the author concluded the environment is getting better, not worse. Complete with a bibliography seventy-one pages in length, the book called into question the rigor and urgency of environmental protection regulation. Not unexpectedly, the publication engendered a firestorm of controversy. *See, e.g.,* Bruce Yandle, *Symposium on Bjørn Lomborg's "The Skeptical Environmentalist"*, 53 CASE W. RES. L. REV. 285 (2002). (Lomborg reprised his book with another focused on the science underlying climate change: BJØRN LOMBORG, COOL IT — THE SKEPTICAL ENVIRONMENTALIST'S GUIDE TO GLOBAL WARMING (2008)).

Ecorealists would rather see governments address the "truly murderous," if more mundane, problems of our time, such as dirty water, which kills thousands of people across the globe every day. *See, e.g.*, CHRISTOPHER D. STONE, THE GNAT IS OLDER THAN MAN — GLOBAL ENVIRONMENT AND THE HUMAN AGENDA, at xviii (1993) (arguing that in the 1990s about 27,000 people, mostly children, would die each day from treatable diseases).

There are no indications that the science underlying environmental and natural resources law will harden at any time soon. Nor should anyone expect the debates will cease.

Chapter 2

COMMON LAW CONSIDERATIONS

"[The American lawyer] . . . views the great judge as one who has the intelligence to discern the best rule of law for the case at hand and then the skill to perform the broken-field running through earlier cases that leaves him free to impose that rule: distinguishing one prior case on the left, straight-arming another one on the right, high-stepping away from another precedent about to tackle him from the rear, until (bravo!) he reaches the goal — good law." ANTONIN SCALIA, MATTER OF INTERPRETATION 9 (1997)

SYNOPSIS

A. INTRODUCTION

We begin coverage of substantive legal materials with a look at the common law. Both property and tort law can serve to address disputes over environmental degradation and resource use. We should pay attention to these areas of law for several reasons. First, much of the regulatory regime we will examine finds its underlying rationale in common law theory. Second, even in these days of high profile and comprehensive regulation, environmental and natural resource lawyers continue to employ common law theories in litigation, sometimes successfully, *see, e.g., Wood v. Picillo*, 443 A.2d 1244 (R.I. 1982) (finding a nuisance to result from maintenance of a sometimes explosive hazardous waste dump on a farm) and sometimes unsuccessfully, (*see, e.g., North Carolina v. Tennessee Valley Authority*, 615 F.3d. 291 (4th Cir. 2010) (dismissing nuisance action against public utility for prudential reasons and because compliance with statutory standards indicated defendant's conduct did not rise to the level of a nuisance). Last, the manifest inadequacy of common law to serve as a vehicle to effect social change helps to explain why this field of law has been overtaken by statutory and regulatory controls.

B. PROPERTY LAW

1. The Law of Waste

One area of common law that can address environmental and natural resource issues is the law of waste. Narrow in application, this is the area of law that determines rights of persons who share title to the same parcel of land. In the typical scenario, the plaintiff in a "waste case" is a future interest holder who objects to "waste" of a parcel by a present possessor defendant. The question in these cases invariably is how much the present use of land should be restricted, if at all, for the benefit of holders of future interests.

The matter is not always simple. "Waste" can be "voluntary" (i.e., caused by actions which are deliberate) or "permissive" (i.e., caused by a failure to act). "Waste" can also be "innocent" (i.e., caused by acts of a third person when the possessory tenant is without fault), although liability for innocent waste is rarely found in the present day.

With respect to voluntary waste, the old English approach was quite solicitous of the rights of the future interest holder. The party in possession was prohibited from cutting timber, for example, except as needed for necessities, such as repairs or fuel. Similarly, she or he was not permitted to mine the land, unless the mine was in operation when the possession began, in which case the possessor could extract minerals without restriction. Furthermore, possessors were not to demolish any structures on the land, even if the demolition would increase land value.

In this country, while this rigid approach may still be followed in some instances with respect to mining rights, it has largely been replaced by a test of reasonableness. Present possessors may use land so long as the use is "reasonable." Predictably, what constitutes "reasonable use" of land is debatable.

Various factors bear on the determination whether a person's use of land is reasonable vis á vis the remainderman or reversioner. The character and intensity of the possessor's use is obviously relevant. Also relevant is whether the use is a one commonly pursued in the area. The use's impact on the market value of the affected parcel is important as well. In assessing reasonableness, moreover, courts are often inclined to compare the current use to that which the future interest holder would devote the property upon assuming possession. By this measure, for example, a proposed demolition of a building might be allowed because the future interest holder's intention is to construct a new residence. Finally, the likelihood of the plaintiff's securing possession of the parcel in the future is significant. A plaintiff with only a remote chance of securing a possessory title in the future has a similarly remote chance of prevailing in a waste case.

With respect to permissive waste, persons in possession have the duty to make repairs and pay all charges on the property, including property taxes, as failure to pay these could result in forfeiture of the estate. The person in possession typically must pay amounts due on outstanding mortgages as well, at least if the mortgage was taken out by that person; if the mortgage predated the possession, its payment might be apportioned between the parties. The possessor must pay special assessments for public improvements to the extent that the benefit of the public improvements are enjoyed by that person. Generally, the possessor is under no burden to assume costs of this sort to the extent those costs exceed the economic benefits supplied by the land itself.

When waste has occurred, and the plaintiff is a proper party to sue, available remedies include damages and injunctive relief. In some cases, courts have placed property in receivership to assure that repairs are made and that moneys received are devoted to such repairs.

2. Conservation and Preservation Servitudes

A person holding a possessory estate in real property, such as the fee simple absolute, has a variety of rights with respect to that property. He can occupy the land, build on it, sell or donate it, and so forth. In addition, he can exclude others from doing the same. This right of exclusion brings with it the prospect of keeping the land in its existing natural condition.

Thus, it is clear that property rights can contribute to environmental protection. But how can this protection be made permanent? Suppose you live on a beautiful tract of land that serves as a habitat for animals and plants, and you would like to maintain the land for those purposes. You fear that when you pass the scene, the next holder of fee simple title would develop the land for residential use. What can you do to assure the land remains in its natural state? One possible solution would be to donate your fee simple title to an organization pledged to conservation purposes. The downside to this is palpable, however — after the donation, you would no longer have the right to live on the land. Alternatively, you could donate it to the organization in your will, but this would mean your family members or other loved ones would lose all claim to the parcel.

Perhaps the best solution for you would be the use of a conservation or preservation servitude. These property rights were first created in the 1880s to protect parkways in and around Boston. They are commonly used in the current day, in good measure because of the federal Tax Reform Act of 1976, which made them tax-deductible. Conservation and preservation servitudes protect environmental quality by restricting possessors of property from taking actions that would compromise that quality. Many states have enacted statutes to ratify the use of such servitude interests. A typical provision can be found in the statutory code of Nebraska, which defines a conservation easement as:

> a right, whether or not stated in the form of an easement, restriction, covenant, or condition in any deed, will, agreement, or other instrument executed by or on behalf of the owner of an interest in real property imposing a limitation upon the rights of the owner or an affirmative obligation upon the owner appropriate to the purpose of retaining or protecting the property in its natural, scenic, or open condition, assuring its availability for agricultural, horticultural, forest, recreational, wildlife habitat, or open space use, protecting air quality, water quality, or other natural resources, or for such other conservation purpose as may qualify as

a charitable contribution under the Internal Revenue Code of 1954, as amended.

R.R.S. Neb. § 762, 111(1).

That same code defines a preservation easement as:

> a right, whether stated in the form of an easement, restriction, covenant, or condition in any deed, will, agreement, or other instrument executed by or on behalf of the owner of an interest in real property imposing a limitation upon the rights of the owner or an affirmative obligation upon the owner appropriate to the purpose of preserving the historical, architectural, archaeological, or cultural aspects of real property, or for such other historic preservation purpose as may qualify as a charitable contribution under the Internal Revenue Code of 1954, as amended.

R.R.S. Neb. § 762, 111(2).

In order to "minimize conflicts with land use planning," these easements must be approved by the appropriate governing body. Once created, they may be released to the holder of the servient estate, if approved. R.R.S. Neb. § 762, 113. However, they can also be assigned to any governmental body or charitable corporation or to a trust authorized to secure such an easement. They can be modified or terminated upon a showing that they are no longer "in the public interest" or no longer serve the conservation or preservation purpose for which they were created. R.R.S. Neb. § 762, 114.

On August 17, 2006, President George W. Bush signed into law an expansion of federal tax incentives for conservation-related donations. Specifically, the new statute raised the deduction a landowner can take for donating a conservation easement from 30 percent of his or her income to 50 percent. For qualifying ranchers and farmers, the law raised the deduction to 100 percent. The law also extended the carryforward period for the donor to take the deduction from 5 to 15 years. The value of the donated servitude for tax purposes is its fair market value, typically the difference between the land's fair market value with and without the servitude.

The increasingly popular use of conservation and preservation servitudes has encouraged a proliferation of "land trusts." Land trusts are not "trusts" in the conventional sense of the term. Rather, they are organizations, funded primarily by private donations, that protect land and water by buying or accepting donations of land or development rights in land. The majority of the more than 1,200 land trusts in existence, more than a third of which are located in New England, are local and run by volunteers. Local and regional land trusts have protected approximately five million acres around the country. An organization known as the Nature Conservancy is the largest land trust in the country. Founded in 1951 and supported financially by more than one million members and 1,900 foundations and corporations, this nonprofit organization has protected more than 119 million acres of land and 5,000 miles of rivers around the world. It currently manages about 1,400 preserves, the largest system of private nature sanctuaries in the world. It has chapters in all 50 states. The Nature Conservancy can be found on the web at www.nature.org.

In place to lend assistance to the many land trusts and to act as an umbrella organization for them is an entity known as the Land Trust Alliance. Founded in 1982, the Land Trust Alliance may be found on the web at www.lta.org.

C.   TORT LAW: THE LAW OF NUISANCE

More important than property law in these respects is tort law. The areas of tort theory most closely related to environmental and natural resources law are strict liability, negligence, trespass, and nuisance. The law of *strict liability* applies when a defendant engages in ultrahazardous activity. In such cases, defendants are held liable for injuries regardless of considerations of proximate cause — the simple fact of injury to a plaintiff is sufficient for a *prima facie* case. The law of *negligence* assesses liability upon a finding of (a) a standard of care (b) breached by a defendant so as to (c) proximately cause (d) an injury to a plaintiff (subject to defenses such as contributory negligence and assumption of risk). Negligence law addresses the legal sufficiency of actions that produce unintended consequences. Negligence law reaches a wide range of disputes, the vast majority of which have nothing to do with environmental and natural resources law. The law of *trespass* comes into play when a defendant intends an act that interferes with another's possessory rights in land. A technical trespass is deemed to occur even when the intended act causes no harm or damage to the land.

The most significant common law theory for our purposes, and the one which will command our attention, is the law of nuisance. "There is perhaps no more impenetrable jungle in the entire law than that which surrounds the word 'nuisance.' " WILLIAM L. PROSSER, THE LAW OF TORTS 592 (1964). "Nuisance" is defined as the actionable interference with the use and enjoyment of rights in land. Like strict liability, negligence, and trespass, the law of nuisance springs from tort concepts (although early judicial opinions often characterized nuisance in terms of property rights). Nuisances are divisible into two types, public and private. As one might expect, public nuisances are those that interfere with rights of the public. Cases involving air and water pollution, slaughterhouses, hazardous or combustible materials storage so to create undue risk, operation of gambling establishments and the like are often common law public nuisance cases. Private nuisances are those that affect persons in their individual capacities. Cases involving dust, smoke, odors, noise, light, and electromagnetic fields are often common law private nuisance cases. A single pattern of conduct can qualify as both a public and private nuisance.

MORGAN v. HIGH PENN OIL CO.
238 N.C. 185, 77 S.E.2d 682 (1953)

[This case was a civil action to recover damages and injunctive relief for a private nuisance. Plaintiffs owned a nine-acre tract of residential land upon which was located their dwelling house, a restaurant, and accommodations for thirty-two trailers. About one thousand feet away, the defendant operated an oil refinery. The evidence showed that the refinery emitted "nauseating gases and odors . . . in such amounts and densities as to render persons of ordinary sensibilities uncomfortable and sick; that the operation of the oil refinery thus substantially impaired the use and enjoyment of the nine acres by the plaintiffs and their renters; and that the defendants failed to put an end to the atmospheric pollution arising out of the operation of the oil refinery after notice and demand from the plaintiffs to abate it." The jury found the refinery to be a nuisance. Entering a judgment to that effect, the trial judge awarded damages in the amount of $2,500 and issued an injunction.]

ERVIN, J.

. . . .

The High Penn Oil Company contends that the evidence is not sufficient to establish either an actionable or an abatable private nuisance. This contention rests on a twofold argument somewhat alternative in character. The High Penn Oil Company asserts primarily that private nuisances are classified as nuisances per se or at law, and nuisances per accidens or in fact; that when one carries on an oil refinery upon premises in his rightful occupation, he conducts a lawful enterprise, and for that reason does not maintain a nuisance per se or at law; that in such case the oil refinery can constitute a nuisance per accidens or in fact to the owner of neighboring land if, and only if, it is constructed or operated in a negligent manner; that there was no testimony at the trial tending to show that the oil refinery was constructed or operated in a negligent manner; and that consequently the evidence does not suffice to establish the existence of either an actionable or an abatable private nuisance. The High Penn Oil Company insists secondarily that the plaintiffs in a civil action can recover only on the case presented by their complaint; that the complaint in the instant action states a cause of action based solely on negligence; that there was no testimony at the trial indicating that the oil refinery was constructed or operated in a negligent manner; and that consequently the evidence is not sufficient to warrant the relief sought and obtained by the plaintiffs, even though it may be ample to establish a nuisance.

The case on appeal discloses some substantial reasons for contesting the soundness of the thesis of the High Penn Oil Company that there was no testimony at the trial tending to show that the oil refinery was constructed or operated in a negligent manner. Even expert witnesses for the defendants testified in substance on cross-examination that the oil refinery would not emit gases or odors in annoying quantities if it were "operated properly." We would be compelled, however, to reject the argument of the High Penn Oil Company on the present aspect of the appeal even if we should accept at face value its thesis that there was no testimony at the trial tending to show that the oil refinery was constructed or operated in a negligent manner.

The High Penn Oil Company asserts with complete correctness that private nuisances may be classified as nuisances per se or at law, and nuisances per accidens or in fact. A nuisance per se or at law is an act, occupation, or structure which is a nuisance at all times and under any circumstances, regardless of location or surroundings. . . . Nuisances per accidens or in fact are those which become nuisances by reason of their location, or by reason of the manner in which they are constructed, maintained, or operated. . . . The High Penn Oil Company also asserts with complete correctness that an oil refinery is a lawful enterprise and for that reason cannot be a nuisance per se or at law. . . . The High Penn Oil Company falls into error, however, when it takes the position that an oil refinery cannot become a nuisance per accidens or in fact unless it is constructed or operated in a negligent manner.

Negligence and nuisance are distinct fields of tort liability. . . . While the same act or omission may constitute negligence and also give rise to a private nuisance per accidens or in fact, and thus the two torts may coexist and be practically inseparable, a private nuisance per accidens or in fact may be created or maintained without negligence. . . . Most private nuisances per accidens or in fact are intentionally created or maintained, and are redressed by the courts without allegation or proof of negligence.

The law of private nuisance rests on the concept embodied in the ancient legal maxim *Sic utere tuo ut alienum non laedas*, meaning, in essence, that every person should so use his own property as not to injure that of another. . . . As a consequence, a private nuisance exists in a legal sense when one makes an improper use of his own property and in that way injures the land or some incorporeal right of one's neighbor. . . .

Much confusion exists in respect to the legal basis of liability in the law of private nuisance because of the deplorable tendency of the courts to call everything a nuisance, and let it go at that. . . . The confusion on this score vanishes in large part, however, when proper heed is paid to the sound propositions that private nuisance is a field of tort liability rather than a single type of tortious conduct; that the feature which gives unity to this field of tort liability is the interest invaded, namely, the interest in the use and enjoyment of land; that any substantial non-trespassory invasion of another's interest in the private use and enjoyment of land by any type of liability-forming conduct is a private nuisance; that the invasion which subjects a person to liability for private nuisance may be either intentional or unintentional; that a person is subject to liability for an intentional invasion when his conduct is unreasonable under the circumstances of the particular case; and that a person is subject to liability for an unintentional invasion when his conduct is negligent, reckless or ultra hazardous.

An invasion of another's interest in the use and enjoyment of land is intentional in the law of private nuisance when the person whose conduct is in question as a basis for liability acts for the purpose of causing it, or knows that it is resulting from his conduct, or knows that it is substantially certain to result from his conduct. . . . A person who intentionally creates or maintains a private nuisance is liable for the resulting injury to others regardless of the degree of care or skill exercised by him to avoid such injury. . . . One of America's greatest jurists, the late Benjamin N. Cardozo, made this illuminating observation on this aspect of the law: "Nuisance as a concept of the law has more meanings than one. The primary meaning does not involve the element of negligence as one of its essential factors. One acts sometimes at one's peril. In such circumstances, the duty to desist is absolute whenever conduct, if persisted in, brings damage to another. Illustrations are abundant. One who emits noxious fumes or gases day by day in the running of his factory may be liable to his neighbor though he has taken all available precautions. He is not to do such things at all, whether he is negligent or careful." *McFarlane v. City of Niagara Falls*, 247 N.Y. 340, 160 N. E. 391.

When the evidence is interpreted in the light most favorable to the plaintiffs, it suffices to support a finding that in operating the oil refinery the High Penn Oil Company intentionally and unreasonably caused noxious gases and odors to escape onto the nine acres of the plaintiffs to such a degree as to impair in a substantial manner the plaintiffs' use and enjoyment of their land. This being so, the evidence is ample to establish the existence of an actionable private nuisance, entitling the plaintiffs to recover temporary damages from the High Penn Oil Company. . . . When the evidence is taken in the light most favorable to the plaintiffs, it also suffices to warrant the additional inferences that the High Penn Oil Company intends to operate the oil refinery in the future in the same manner as in the past; that if it is permitted to carry this intent into effect, the High Penn Oil Company will hereafter cast noxious gases and odors onto the nine acres of the plaintiffs with such recurring frequency and in such annoying density as to inflict irreparable injury upon the plaintiffs in the use and enjoyment of their home and their other adjacent properties; and that the issuance of an appropriate injunction is necessary to protect the plaintiffs against the threatened irreparable injury. This being true, the evidence is ample to establish the existence of an abatable private nuisance, entitling the plaintiffs to such mandatory or prohibitory injunctive relief as may be required to prevent the High Penn Oil Company from continuing the nuisance. . . .

The contention of the High Penn Oil Company that the complaint states a cause of action based solely on negligence is untenable. To be sure, the plaintiffs assert that the defendants were "negligent and careless" in specified particulars in constructing and operating the oil refinery. When the complaint is construed as a whole, however, it alleges facts which show a private nuisance resulting from an intentional and unreasonable invasion of the plaintiffs' interest in the use and enjoyment of their land. . . .

For the reasons given, the evidence is sufficient to withstand the motion of the High Penn Oil Company for a compulsory nonsuit. . . .

NOTES

1. **Sam Ervin.** The judge who decided *High Penn* was Sam Ervin, later to represent North Carolina in the United States Senate and best known for his major role in the Watergate investigations of President Richard Nixon.

2. **Unreasonableness.** For an actionable nuisance, the harm visited upon the plaintiff must be unreasonable. Unreasonableness depends less on the conduct of the defendant than upon the harm that conduct causes. Accordingly, socially acceptable conduct, such as manufacturing, may be viewed as unreasonable for nuisance purposes if it causes an undue harm to the land of a plaintiff. To be unreasonable, a harm must be more than minimal (in *High Penn*, the defendant had "impair[ed] in a *substantial* manner the plaintiffs' use and enjoyment of their land") (emphasis added). Other factors that influence the determination of reasonableness of harm include the character of the neighborhood, the intensity and duration of the interference, and prevailing customary uses of land.

In some cases, the social utility of a defendant's activities may have a significant bearing on choices of remedy and determinations of liability. *See, e.g., Kuper v. Lincoln-Union Elec. Co.*, 557 N.W.2d 748 (S.D. 1996) (suggesting that the emanation of stray voltage from a public utility that substantially interfered with a nearby dairy operation cannot be a nuisance).

WEINHOLD v. WOLFF
555 N.W.2d 454 (Iowa 1996)

JUDGES: ANDREASEN, J., concurred in part and dissented in part with NEUMAN and TERNUS, JJ., joining the concurrence and dissent.

OPINION: Considered en banc.

Landowners in close proximity to a commercial hog feeding and hog confinement facility sued the owner of the facility. The landowners alleged nuisance and negligence and prayed for damages and injunctive relief. The facility owner answered, asserted affirmative defenses, and counterclaimed. The parties tried the case to the court solely on the landowners' nuisance claim. Following trial, the district court concluded the landowners had proven the facility was a temporary nuisance.

Iowa Code section 352.11(1) (1993) grants a defense against nuisance suits to owners of farmland approved as agricultural land. The district court refused to apply section 352.11(1) to the unique facts of this case. The court concluded that section 352.11(1) would work an unconstitutional taking of the landowners' preexisting nuisance claim. . . .

The court awarded the landowners $45,000 in damages for their pain and suffering, but refused to grant them injunctive relief. The damage award was in two parts. In part one, the court awarded the landowners $9,000 for pain and suffering that occurred before the county approved the facility's land as an agricultural area. In part two, the court awarded the landowners $36,000 for pain and suffering that occurred after approval and through the end of trial. The facility owners appealed, and the landowners cross-appealed.

As discussed in detail in the analysis of these issues, we affirm as modified in part, reverse in part, and remand for further proceedings.

Background Facts.

In 1977 Dennis and Ruth Weinhold purchased about four acres of real property in Buena Vista County for $8,000. They have lived on this acreage since the purchase.

They raise various breeds of alternative livestock such as deer, emu, rhea, antelope, and occasionally elk.

In February 1974 Norman and Pam Wolff purchased an eightyacre tract of land approximately onehalf mile directly south of the Weinholds' land. The Wolffs originally planted all the land with grain. Since November 1990 the Wolffs have operated a commercial hog feeding and confinement facility on part of this land, which they commute to from their home located about two and onehalf miles away.

The facility is substantial and occupies about four acres of the eightyacre tract.

The Wolffs have run the facility at full capacity since its inception and finish about 2,080 hogs per year. The building used to house the hogs is approximately fortyone feet by one hundred sixtyone feet. About 6256 square feet are devoted to hog production. The building runs east and west.

An integral part of the facility is a 500,000 gallon, uncovered, earthen, waste collection basin. The basin is located to the east of the building used to house the hogs. The basin is 130feet long, 110feet wide, and 14.5-feet deep.

The hogs are kept within pens located over a slatted floor. The waste falls through the slats and into twofoot pits underneath the hog confinement building. When waste accumulation in the pits reaches sixteen inches, a plug is pulled. The waste flows through an eightinch diameter underground pipe east to the outside of the building where the waste enters the bottom of the earthen basin.

The pits are emptied every four weeks on an alternating basis. Each time the pits are emptied, about 10,000 to 15,000 gallons of waste are deposited into the basin. Twice a year, the waste is emptied from the basin and applied to area fields as fertilizer. This waste is often applied to fields near the Weinholds' property.

In the fall of 1991, the Wolffs and several farmers neighboring the facility applied for an "agricultural area" designation for the land on which the facility sits. The Wolffs filed the application with the Buena Vista County Board of Supervisors pursuant to what is now Iowa Code section 352.6. The board approved the application on October 8. This was about a year after the Wolffs began the hog feeding and confinement operation.

Background Proceedings.

On July 29, 1992, the Weinholds filed a twocount petition at law. Count I alleged the Wolffs' commercial hog feeding and confinement operation was a nuisance because it created noxious and offensive odors that pervaded the Weinholds' property. The Weinholds asked for money damages and injunctive relief to abate the nuisance. Count II alleged the noxious odors emanating from the Wolffs' hog feeding and confinement operation were the proximate result of the Wolffs' negligence. In this count, the Weinholds asked for money damages.

The Wolffs answered, denied liability, asserted an affirmative defense, and counterclaimed. The Wolffs asserted the affirmance [sic] defense under what is now Iowa Code section 352.11.

The Wolffs' counterclaim alleged the Weinholds' suit was frivolous and caused the Wolffs' mental anguish, inconvenience, and expense. The Wolffs asked for damages that would fairly compensate them for the harm resulting from the Weinholds' actions.

Although the case contained both legal and equitable issues, the parties agreed before trial to try the case in equity. During trial, the Weinholds withdrew their negligence claim. The Wolffs withdrew their counterclaim at the close of the evidence.

In their appeal, the Wolffs challenge the district court's finding that the facility

(1) constituted a nuisance and (2) did not have the section 352.11 defense against nuisance suits. The Wolffs also challenge the damage award.

The Weinholds challenge the district court's finding that the nuisance was temporary and not permanent. The Weinholds also complain because the court did not award for (1) the diminished market value of their real property, (2) special damages occurring after trial, and (3) injunctive relief to abate the nuisance. . . .

The Issues.

Nuisance. The first issue we consider is whether the Wolffs' hog feeding and confinement operation was a nuisance.

Applicable law. Under Iowa Code section 657.1,

> *whatever* is injurious to health, indecent, or *offensive to the senses*, or an obstruction to the free use of property, so *as essentially to interfere with the comfortable enjoyment of life or property, is a nuisance*, and a civil action by ordinary proceedings may be brought to enjoin and abate the same and to recover damages sustained on account thereof.

(Emphasis added.)

Additionally, under Iowa Code section 657.2,

> the following are nuisances: . . . using any building or other place for the exercise of any trade, . . . which, by occasioning noxious exhalations, offensive smells, or other annoyances, becomes injurious and dangerous to the health, comfort, or property of individuals. . . .

These statutory provisions do not modify the common-law's application to nuisances. *Bates v. Quality Ready Mix Co.*, 261 Iowa 696, 703, 154 N.W.2d 852, 857 (1967). These provisions are skeletal in form, and the courts look to the common law to fill in the gaps.

A private nuisance is "an actionable interference with a person's interest in the private use and enjoyment of the person's land." *Id.* Parties must use their own property in such a manner that they will not unreasonably interfere with or disturb their neighbor's reasonable use and enjoyment of the neighbor's property. *Id.*

> Whether a lawful business is a nuisance depends on the reasonableness of conducting the business in the manner, at the place, and under the circumstances in question. *Id.* Thus the existence of a nuisance does not depend on the intention of the party who created it. *Patz. v. Farmegg Prods.,Inc.*, 196 N.W.2d 557, 561 (Iowa 1972). Rather, it depends on the following three factors: priority of location, the nature of the neighborhood, and the wrong complained of. *Id.* From this discussion it is clear that whether a party has created and maintained a nuisance is ordinarily a factual question. *Bates*, 261 Iowa at 704, 154 N.W.2d at 857.

> A fact finder uses the normal person standard to determine whether a nuisance involving personal discomfort or annoyance is significant enough to constitute a nuisance. *Pat.*, 196 N.W.2d at 561. The normal-person

standard is an objective standard and is explained in comment d to section 821F of the Restatement (Second) of Torts (1977):

> When [an invasion] involves . . . personal discomfort or annoyance, it is sometimes difficult to determine whether the invasion is significant [enough to constitute a nuisance]. The standard for the determination of significant character is the standard of normal persons or property in the particular locality. If normal persons living in the community would regard the invasion in question as definitely offensive, seriously annoying or intolerable, then the invasion is significant. If normal persons in that locality would not be substantially annoyed or disturbed by the situation, then the invasion is not a significant one, even though the idiosyncracies of the particular plaintiff may make it unendurable to him.

The Merits.

[The court noted that for a three year period, the hog confinement operation caused a significant burden on nearby residents. The smells were distinguishable and substantially more intrusive than those from a "more traditional hog operation." The court reviewed three factors to determine the presence of an actionable nuisance: (a) the nature of the neighborhood (here, the neighborhood, while agricultural, was also residential); (b) the wrong complained-of (here, the odors were persistent and "close to intolerable to a person of ordinary or normal sensibility"); and (c) priority of location (here, the plaintiffs had acquired their farm and had taken up occupancy before the offending sewage lagoon was constructed. The court found this latter factor "weighed heavily in favor of the [plaintiff] on the nuisance issue.").]

Defense to nuisance suits provided by Iowa Code section 352.11(1).A

Applicable law. Iowa Code section 352.11(1) provides:

> *Nuisance restriction. A farm or farm operation located in an agricultural areas hall not be found to be a nuisance regardless of the established date of operation or expansion of the agricultural activities of the farm or farm operation. The subsection does not apply if the nuisance results from the negligent operation of the farm or farm operation. This subsection does not apply to actions or proceedings arising from injury or damage to person or property caused by the farm or farm operation before the creation of the agricultural area.*

(Emphasis added.)

Under Iowa Code section 352.6, an agricultural area is created by the owner submitting a proposal to the county board for the creation of an agricultural area within the county. . . . The proposal shall include a description of the proposed area, including its boundaries. The territory shall be as compact and as nearly adjacent as feasible. Land shall not be included in an agricultural area without the consent of the owner. Agricultural areas shall not exist within the corporate limits of the city. . . . Agricultural areas may be created in a county which has adopted zoning ordinances. Except as provided in this section, the use of the land in agricultural areas is limited to farm operations.

The Merits.

The Wolffs maintain that the language of section 352.11(1) is clear on its face and requires no interpretation by us. The statute, they say, prohibits any award for damages for nuisance actions after the affected property has been included in an agricultural area as defined by section 352.6.

The Wolffs do not dispute that the district court's $9,000 award to the Weinholds for special damages occurring before October 8, 1991, was proper. (On October 8, 1991, the county board of supervisors approved the Wolffs' property as an agricultural area.)

The Wolffs do, however, contend the $36,000 award for special damages occurring on and after October 8, 1991, was improper. The $36,000 award is improper, the Wolffs assert, because those damages occurred after the county had approved the Wolffs' property as an agricultural area. The Wolffs insist the legislature intended that a party should not recover for nuisance damages which occur after the county has approved the property as an agricultural area.

The Weinholds agree section 352.11(1) is clear on its face, but they argue the statute plainly favors their claim. The Weinholds contend their nuisance action arose out of "injury created and damage sustained" before the county approved the Wolffs' property as an agricultural area. In short, the Weinholds rely on the following language in section 352.11(1): "This subsection does not apply to actions or proceedings arising from injury or damage to person or property caused by the farm or farm operation before the creation of the agricultural area."

Section 352.11(1) is a "right to farm" law designed to protect agricultural operations by giving those operations meeting the statutory requirements a defense to nuisance actions. *See* Neil D. Hamilton, *A Livestock Producer's Legal Guide to: Nuisance, Land Use Control, and Environmental Law* 21 (1992). All fifty states have enacted right to farm laws in various forms. *Id.*

Negligent operation of the farm resulting in the nuisance defeats the defense. Additionally, the defense does not apply to actions or proceedings arising from injury or damage to property caused by the farm operation before the agricultural area is established.

Our interpretation suggests that the legislature has determined that farming operations like the Wolffs' are sufficiently important to the state to warrant protective state laws like section 352.11(1). The practical effect of these laws, of course, is to limit the ability of persons affected by the operation to sue operators for nuisance.

The purpose clause of Iowa Code chapter 352 supports our interpretation. *See* Iowa Code § 352.1. Section 352.1 states in pertinent part:

> *The general assembly recognizes the importance of preserving the state's finite supply of agricultural land.* Conversion of farmland to urban

development, and other nonfarm uses, reduces future food production capabilities and may ultimately undermine agriculture as a major economic activity in Iowa. *It is the intent of the general assembly to provide local citizens and local governments the means by which agricultural land may be protected from nonagricultural development pressures.* This may be accomplished by . . . establishment of agricultural areas in which substantial agricultural activities are encouraged, so that land inside these areas . . . is conserved for the production of food, fiber, and livestock, *thus assuring the preservation of agriculture as a major factor in the economy of this state.*

(Emphasis added.)

The problem in this case is that the Wolffs started their operation about a year before their land was approved as an agricultural area. As we see it, the parties' contentions are resolved by whether the nuisance was permanent or temporary. Before beginning our analysis, we need to distinguish between these types of nuisances.

The distinction has been explained this way:

An action in damages may be maintained for the creation of a nuisance and a subsequent and separate action may be maintained for the continuance of such nuisance. The determination of whether a single right of action or successive rights are created by a nuisance for damages depends primarily upon whether the cause of injury is permanent or temporary. The nature of the damages, as being temporary or permanent, is determined by the character of the nuisance to which the land is subjected and not by the quantity of resultant damages. The question generally is one of fact for the jury. If injuries from a nuisance are of a permanent character and go to the entire value of the estate, there can be but one action, and all damages — past, present, and future — are recoverable therein; in such a case, one recovery is a grant or license to continue the nuisance, and there can be no second recovery for its continuance. Stated otherwise, damages for permanent nuisances are not dependent upon any subsequent use of the property but are complete when the nuisance comes into existence. . . . Where the injury from the alleged nuisance is temporary in its nature, or is of a continuing or recurring character, the damages are ordinarily regarded as continuing, and one recovery against the wrongdoer is not a bar to successive actions for damages thereafter accruing from the same wrong. In such a case, every day's continuance is a new nuisance. That is, each repetition of the nuisance creates further liability, and gives rise to a new cause of action. If the nuisance does not involve the entire destruction of the estate or its beneficial use, but may be apportioned from time to time, separate actions must be brought for each recurring injury, and recovery may be had for damages sustained within the period of the statute of limitations applicable to the action. That is, where a nuisance is temporary, damages to property affected by the nuisance are recurrent and may be recovered from time to time until the nuisance is abated. A temporary nuisance may in some circumstances give rise to permanent damages, as well as temporary damages. . . . The rule applicable where the nuisance is permanent has been applied in cases where the court does not deem it just and equitable to order the thing which causes the injury to be removed, although it is removable, since, under such circumstances, the plaintiff must in one action recover his damages and the defendant must pay all the damages suffered, both past and present, unless the defendant removes the thing before the time of trial, in which case damages are recoverable only up to the time of such removal.

58 Am. Jur. 2d Nuisances §§ 273–75 (1989).

For reasons that follow, we think — contrary to the district court — the uniquefacts of this case dictate that we consider the nuisance permanent. We characterize the facts here as unique to emphasize that

> the terms "permanent" and "temporary" are somewhat nebulous in that they have practical meaning only in relation to particular fact situations and can change in characterization from one set of facts to another.

Mel Foster Co. Properties v. American Oil Co., 427 N.W.2d 171, 175 (Iowa 1988) (quoting Note, *Stream Pollution — Recovery of Damages*, 50 Iowa L. Rev. 141, 153 (1964); holding that chemical contamination of land encompassed aspects of both a temporary and permanent nuisance; injury was temporary in the sense that the cause of pollution had been discovered and abated, and harmful effects would eventually dissipate; injury was permanent in the sense that it constituted damage to ground itself and would continue for an indefinite but significant period of time; court used measure of damages applicable to permanent nuisance).

First, there is no record evidence that, short of shutting down the operation, the Wolffs can or will abate the nuisance in the future. The district court speculated that technology would eventually solve the odor problem. There was, however, no record evidence that odor control breakthroughs were near. A knowledgeable expert in this area testified that more research was necessary on how to detect and control odor.

Mr. Wolff testified he used an odor control additive in the waste basin. He also testified, however, that he stopped using the additive because the additive was ineffective.

The engineer who designed the waste system for the Wolffs offered no evidence that there were any technological breakthroughs on the horizon to control odor.

We agree with the Weinholds' assessment of the district court's finding on this issue: "The court's rationale that the nuisance was not permanent due to rapidly developing technology that would 'hopefully' aid in the control of odor was unsupported by anything other than wishful thinking."

Moreover, the Wolffs offered no evidence that they intended to cease the operation in the foreseeable future. The evidence, in fact, points the other way because the Wolffs built the waste basin with the capacity to double its current holdings. *See Mel Foster Co. Properties*, 427 N.W.2d at 175 (permanent in legal sense does not mean forever — indefinitely long is sufficient); Patz, 196 N.W.2d at 562 (permanent easement is one of such character that it will be reasonably certain to continue in the future).

Second, we can abate the odor by ordering closure of the earthen basin. This is not an equitable and practical solution because our closure order would result in closing the whole operation. See 58 Am. Jur. 2d *Nuisances* § 275 ("The rule applicable where the nuisance is permanent has been applied in cases where the court does not deem it just and equitable to order the thing which causes the injury to be removed, although it is removable."). In addition, such a result would be contrary to the spirit and purpose of chapter 352.

Last, without the removal order, the Wolffs would have, in effect, a license to continue the nuisance. See 58 Am. Jur. 2d *Nuisances* § 274. Because of the section 352.11(1) defense against nuisance suits, the Weinholds would have no corresponding right to recover for the continuing nuisance. In these unique circumstances, equity dictates that the Weinholds recover in this action all of their past, present, and future damages. See *Wesley v. City of Waterloo*, 232 Iowa 1299, 1303, 8 N.W.2d 430, 432 (1943) (in the case of a permanent nuisance, plaintiff may maintain only one action; plaintiff is therefore allowed to recover all damages — past, present, and future — in the one action).

We reach the critical issue in this case: Did the legislature intend to cut off the Weinholds' cause of action to recover damages because of a permanent nuisance? We think not. Our conclusion is borne out by the plain language of section 352.11(1). As mentioned, section 352.11(1) gives owners of operations within approved agricultural areas a defense against nuisance suits. The defense does not, however, "apply to actions or proceedings arising from injury or damages to person or property caused by the . . . farm operation before the creation of the agricultural area." Iowa Code § 352.11(1).

Iowa Code section 352.2(9) defines "nuisance action or proceeding" to mean "an *action*, claim, or proceeding, whether brought at law, in equity, or as an administrative proceeding, which is based on nuisance." (Emphasis added.) An "action" in its usual legal sense means "a lawsuit brought in a court; . . . the legal and formal demand of one's right from another person or party made and insisted on in a court of justice." BLACK'S LAW DICTIONARY 28 (6th ed. 1990). The Weinholds' lawsuit meets the definition of "nuisance action" in section 352.2(9). This lawsuit is an action because they brought it in a court and are demanding their right to relief for damages from the Wolffs. Additionally, the Weinholds' lawsuit is based on nuisance.

Under Iowa law, causes of actions accrue when the wrongful act produces loss or damage to the claimant. *McKiness Excavating & Grading, Inc. v. Morton Bldgs., Inc.*, 507 N.W.2d 405, 408 (Iowa 1993). Here the nuisance created by the Wolffs' operation caused the Weinholds damage long before the county approved the Wolffs' land as an agricultural area. Because the nuisance is a permanent one, the Weinholds' damages were complete at the time the nuisance arose. This is so because a permanent nuisance "contemplates that [the nuisance] is at once necessarily productive of all the damages that can ever result from it." Patz, 196 N.W.2d at 562 (citation omitted). *See also Wesley*, 232 Iowa at 1303, 8 N.W.2d at 432 (in the case of a permanent nuisance, plaintiff may maintain only one action; plaintiff is therefore allowed to recover all damages — past, present, and future — in one action).

We have held that we should not construe a statute "as taking away common law rights existing at the time of enactment unless that result is imperatively required." *Ford v. Venard*, 340 N.W.2d 270, 273 (Iowa 1983) (citation omitted). Our interpretation that section 352.11(1) does not take away the Weinholds' nuisance action is consistent with this rule of statutory construction.

Moreover, we see evidence in Iowa Code chapter 352 to support our interpretation. Iowa Code section 352.6(1)(a) provides that "nonconforming preexisting residences may be continued in residential use" in an approved agricultural area. So not only was the legislature concerned about conserving farmland for agricultural purposes, it was also concerned about preserving private residential property. Our interpretation allowing the Weinholds to recover all of the damages they are entitled to strikes a balance between these two competing interests. Finally, our interpretation would not affect the overall legislative scheme in chapter 352 because, as the Weinholds point out, it is unlikely that many hog farms are nuisances before farmland is approved as an agricultural area.

We hold therefore that section 352.11(1) did not afford the Wolffs a defense to the Weinholds' nuisance action for past, present, and future damages.

[The portion of the opinion dealing with calculations of damages is omitted.]

Injunctive relief: whether the district court should have granted injunctive relief and ordered abatement of the nuisance.

Applicable Law.

In determining whether to grant injunctive relief to abate a nuisance, courts employ a balancing test incorporating the following factors: (a) the character of the interest to be protected, (b) the relative adequacy to the plaintiff of injunction and of other remedies, (c) plaintiff's delay in bringing suit, (d) plaintiff's misconduct, (e) the relative hardship likely to result to defendant if injunction is granted and to plaintiff if it is denied, (f) the interests of third persons and of the public, and (g) the practicality of framing and enforcing the order or judgment. *Helmkamp v. Clark Ready Mix Co.*, 214 N.W.2d 126, 130 (Iowa 1974). The decision is a judgment call. Id.

The Merits on the Injunctive Relief Issue.

The final issue concerns whether the district court should have granted the Weinholds injunctive relief and ordered an abatement of the nuisance. The Weinholds contend the court should have. The Wolffs, of course, contend otherwise.

In applying the balancing factors in Helmkamp, we conclude we should deny the Weinholds injunctive relief. We do so for the following reasons.

First, we have already determined that the Weinholds should have special damages. Additionally, the district court may on remand award damages to the Weinholds for diminution of the market value of their property. We think such damages provide the Weinholds an adequate remedy.

Second, as we mentioned, to abate the nuisance, we would need to order removal or closure of the basin. As we also mentioned, this is not an equitable and practical solution because such relief would result in closing the operation. Closing the operation would be contrary to the spirit and purpose of Iowa Code chapter 352.

Last, because closing the operation would be contrary to the legislature's goal of protecting farming operations, the public's interest is directly implicated.

Disposition.

In summary, we conclude as follows. First, the Wolffs' facility constitutes a nuisance. Second, contrary to the district court's finding, the nuisance is permanent rather than temporary. Third, Iowa Code section 352.11(1) afforded the Wolffs no defense to the Weinholds' nuisance action. Fourth, we award the Weinholds $45,000 for all past, present, and future special damages. This is in contrast to the district court's award of $45,000 for such damages through the trial date. Fifth, the district court on remand shall determine on the record the amount, if any, the Weinholds shall receive for diminution in market value of their land. Last, we refuse to grant the Weinholds any injunctive relief.

In view of the above conclusions, we need not address other issues raised by the parties.

We therefore affirm as modified in part, reverse in part, and remand for further proceedings.

Affirmed As Modified In Part; Reversed In Part; Remanded For Further Proceedings.

All justices concur except Andreasen, Neuman, and Ternus, JJ., who concur in part and dissent in part.

[Additional opinions omitted.]

NOTES AND QUESTIONS

1. ***The Role of Statutes.*** As *Weinhold* shows, Iowa has enacted statutes to address the problem of nuisance. In fact, all states have done so. Statutes interact with the common law in various ways. In some cases, statutes replace and make null and void the common law. The federal Clean Water Act, for example, was found to have displaced the federal common law of nuisance for water pollution in certain respects. *Milwaukee v. Illinois*, 451 U.S. 304, 101 S. Ct. 1784 (1981). For a quite important recent example of this, see *American Electric Power v. Connecticut*, 131 S. Ct. 2527, 180 L. Ed. 2d 435 (2011) (the *AEP* decision is set forth in Chapter 9, *infra*). Federal statutes can preempt state common law as well. For that matter, federal law has preemptive capacity over state statutory law as well. *See, e.g., International Paper Co. v. Ouellette*, 479 U.S. 481, 107 S. Ct. 805 (1987) (discussing the Clean Water Act's preemption of state law); *San Diego Gas & Elec. Co. v. Superior Court*, 13 Cal. 4th 893, 920 P.2d 669 (1996) (declaring a nuisance claim to be inconsistent with an agency regulation). For more on preemption, see Chapter 3, *infra*. As you know, statutes also can create independent causes of action unrelated to the common law. Thus, objectionable behavior might qualify both as a statutory nuisance and as a common law nuisance. A plaintiff in a statutory nuisance

case need only show the defendant has violated the statute to make a *prima facie* case (e.g., defendant ran a brothel); no showing of specific harm to the plaintiff is necessary. In yet other instances, statutes can codify common law. Such is the case with Iowa's § 657.1; when a statute codifies common law, plaintiffs still must prove harm under common law standards to prevail. In still other instances, statutes can modify the common law. Because it supplies a defense unavailable at common law, Iowa's § 352.11(1) (the "right-to-farm law") is an example of this type of provision.

Notably, statutes can affect common law in other ways as well. In *Weinhold*, the court used the right-to-farm statute as a partial justification for its decision to deny injunctive relief. Even though inapplicable to the merits of the case, the court found the statute influential on the issue of remedy.

2. *Balancing the Equities.* To determine the availability of equitable relief, the court in *Weinhold* engaged in the longstanding practice of "balancing the equities." Balancing the equities is a highly subjective weighing process designed to find a remedy that will occasion the least overall harm. The idea is to avoid a ruling that harms the defendant more than it helps the plaintiff. The result of this exercise can be the award of complete or limited injunctive relief, or, alternatively, a complete denial of any relief. For a famous case in which the court allowed permanent damages in lieu of injunctive relief, see *Boomer v. Atlantic Cement Co.*, 26 N.Y.2d 219, 257 N.E.2d 870 (1970). In an arguably even more famous case, a court ordered a defendant to relocate, so its nuisance behavior would no longer interfere with the plaintiff (plaintiff won?), but the plaintiff was ordered to pay for the relocation (defendant won?). *Spur Industries, Inc. v. Del E. Webb Dev't Co.*, 108 Ariz. 178, 494 P.2d 700 (1972).

There are several arguments against balancing the equities. First is the simple observation that persons should not be forced to endure significant burdens simply because the cure may be even more burdensome. Should not tortfeasors be required to cease their nuisance behaviors, regardless of other considerations? Second is the matter of legitimization: a judicial refusal to order abatement of a nuisance can be seen as a *de facto* licensing of that behavior. Third is the matter of equality: balancing equities often results in different actors receiving disparate judicial treatment for what is essentially the same behavior. Thus, for example, when engaging in balancing, a court may be more willing to shut down a mom-and-pop operation than a major employer. Last, as noted above, judicial refusals to enjoin nuisance behavior can disincline tortfeasors from curing the problems they cause, even if a cost-effective solution becomes available.

Proponents of balancing, however, argue its propriety because much so-called nuisance behavior is not tortious at all, at least not in the classic sense. Rather, pursuits once perfectly valid become "incompatible land uses," and thereby are characterized as nuisances, only because greater numbers of people have taken up residence at locations proximate to the uses. Since there is no "wrongdoer" in the classic sense, the theory continues, courts should accommodate as much as possible the interests of all contestants in a lawsuit.

How would Aldo Leopold, Garrett Hardin, and Ronald H. Coase (*see* Ch. 1, *supra*) view the practice of "balancing the equities"?

3. *The Moving to the Nuisance Defense.* In *Weinhold*, the plaintiffs had acquired their farm before the defendants began their hog feeding operation, a fact the court found "weighed heavily in favor of the [plaintiff]." Suppose the converse were true, that plaintiffs had moved in *after* the hog feeding operation began? Logically, this fact should weigh heavily in favor of the defendant. Should whether the plaintiff "moved to the nuisance" bear on the issue of liability?

In some states, the moving to the nuisance defense has been enshrined by statute. See, for example, Nebraska's version of a right-to-farm law:

> A farm or farm operation shall not be found to be a public or private nuisance if the farm or farm operation existed before a change in the land use or occupancy of land in and about the locality of such farm or farm operation and before such change in land use or occupancy of land the farm or farm operation would not have been a nuisance.

Neb. Rev. Stat. § 24-403.

4. *Permanent Nuisances.* Damages are the only available remedy in permanent nuisance cases. A typical measure of damages is the diminution in market value of the burdened land. Is this an appropriate measurement?

Continuing nuisances may be abated, but it is the plaintiffs' burden to prove that abatement is possible at some reasonable cost by some reasonable means. This can be a difficult burden. For a case in which the court determined that the nuisance was not continuing because it was not reasonably abatable, see *Mangini v. Aerojet General*, 40 Cal. App. 4th 303 (1994).

Did the finding of a permanent nuisance in *Weinhold* determine the available remedy, or did the available remedy determine the finding of a permanent nuisance? Note that the permanent nuisance determination in *Weinhold* was important for reasons other than remedy: the statutory defense was deemed inapplicable because the nuisance was a permanent one.

The distinction between permanent and continuing nuisance can be critical with respect to the statute of limitations. For permanent nuisances, persons are generally required to bring a single lawsuit for all injuries, past, present, and future, within a time certain after the permanent nuisance commences. Failure to bring suit in a timely manner precludes relief. By contrast, with a continuing nuisance, lawsuits for damages can be brought successively until abatement is secured. *See, e.g., Baker v. Burbank Glendale Pasadena Airport Authority*, 39 Cal. 3d 862, 705 P.2d 866 (1985). When the nuisance is permanent, the damages are deemed complete at the time the interference began.

A NOTE ON RESERVE MINING

Since the law of strict liability, negligence, trespass, and nuisance are available to injured litigants in every state, why is it that federal and state statutes have so permeated environmental and natural resources law? The famous *Reserve Mining v. Herbst*, 256 N.W.2d 808 (Minn. 1977), sheds light on this issue. The Reserve Mining Company operated a taconite mining and processing operation from the mid 1940s into the 1970s at a site along Lake Superior near Silver Bay, Minnesota.

Taconite is a substance marketable for its iron ore content, but processing the material results in the generation of waste material known as "tailings." For many years, Reserve disposed of tailings by dumping them into Lake Superior. So much entered the lake that an enormous delta formed. The delta was visible even on the relatively crude satellite photography of the time.

While this disposal activity was ongoing, the thought was that the tailings would sink to the bottom of a 900-foot trough in the Lake and be forever gone. In the 1960s, however, it was determined that fibers from the tailings in the Lake were making their way into the drinking water of the residents of Silver Bay, and that fibers from the Reserve site itself, blown by the wind, were lodging in the breathing passages of those same residents. The fight was on.

The case was litigated in a variety of courts, state and federal, and on a variety of issues, including whether Reserve's mining operation should cease, whether the tailings were dangerous to health and, if so, how much exposure to tailings was tolerable, and whether Reserve should dispose of its tailings on land rather than into the Lake. Finally, in 1977, fully 30 years after Reserve had first been granted permission by the State of Minnesota to dump into the Lake, the formal legal battles drew to a close with a final judicial opinion issued by the Minnesota Supreme Court. Requiring Reserve to dispose of its tailings in a land site known as Mile Post 7, the court paused to reflect on the lessons of the case.

This case should serve as an example to future generations for several lessons:

(1) Man has been a wasteful user of natural resources. He has been the most rapacious animal ever to walk the face of the earth. Greater controls must be exercised in the future in selecting the location for large industrial complexes.

(2) There is an absolute necessity that there be established uniform national air and water quality standards, and that those standards be uniformly enforced throughout the nation to prevent industry from blackmailing one state into lowering its standards with the threat it will move elsewhere if the state fails to comply.

(3) A decision other than that made in this case would not penalize Reserve as much as the public in general. If Reserve left the state, how would the lake cleanup begin? With the taxpayers footing the costs? Reserve is paying a heavy price for its past practices. It is being compelled to spend hundreds of millions of dollars for tailings disposal and to cease the use of Lake Superior as a dumping area. It can be forced to pay damages for any violation of its permits. It has had to accept a site originally strongly opposed by it and has had conditions imposed on its use of Mile Post 7 which are very stringent and will be constantly monitored. Their permit is for an initial 5-year period only.

This is the fourth time in the past 5 years that the Reserve problem has been before this court. . . . This court has been briefed on the facts in dispute and on the issues raised by all appeals since the initial stages of the appeal from the administrative agencies in the summer of 1976. Due to the time limitations decreed in Federal orders, a large portion of the physical resources of this court has been diverted from our regular calendar to this case for a period of over 9 months so that we would be fully cognizant of all facets of the case prior to oral argument . . . and be able to make an early decision. This court has done all that it can to apply law and reason to find a solution to this long drawn out and acrimonious dispute. In the clouds of smoke generated by all of the litigation, it appears at times that many have forgotten that the objective of getting Reserve out of Lake Superior onto a suitable on-land disposal site is within reach. I believe this decision is consistent with that objective.

Reserve Mining Co. v. Herbst, 256 N.W.2d 808, 852 (Minn. 1977) (Yetka, J., concurring).

Do you think the Minnesota Supreme Court was accurate in its view that uniform regulatory standards are necessary to arrest humankind's "rapacious" waste of natural resources? Is the court accurate in thinking common law nuisance doctrine is an insufficient tool to address and resolve environmental disputes? Why, for example, could not public nuisance theory be employed in the battle to end global warming? Consider: many scientists contend that anthropogenic (i.e., human-caused) emissions of carbon dioxide into the air are a major cause of global warming. Global warming, as you know, is perceived to be a life-threatening environmental crisis in the making. Curbing carbon dioxide emissions, accordingly, ought to alleviate warming. Would not a public nuisance cause of action filed against the nation's power companies to force them to reduce their carbon dioxide emissions be a worthwhile step in the fight against global warming? Perhaps another worthwhile step would be a cause of action against automobile manufacturers to force them to either stop producing vehicles that emit carbon dioxide or, failing that, to pay damages for some of the injuries global warming causes.

For that matter, did not the plaintiffs prevail in *Weinhold*?

A worthwhile exercise for you: assemble a list of reasons why public nuisance theory ought to play a greater role in environmental and natural resources law, or ought not.

Chapter 3

CONSTITUTIONAL CONSIDERATIONS

"[T]he Framers split the atom of sovereignty. It was the genius of their idea that our citizens would have two political capacities, one state and one federal, each protected from incursion by the other." *U.S. Term Limits, Inc. v. Thornton*, 514 U.S. 779, 838, 115 S. Ct. 1842, 1872 (1995) (Kennedy, J., concurring).

A. INTRODUCTION

Common law shines as a mechanism to solve narrow disputes between small numbers of persons, primarily because it can focus on the peculiarities of each dispute and craft precisely tailored remedies to resolve those disputes. But common law does not shine when called upon to advance a social agenda. The same feature that allows common law to excel in more narrow contexts — its decentralized, case-by-case approach to dispute resolution — largely disables it as a tool to promote a public cause. This shortcoming became starkly clear in the 1950s and 1960s with respect to environmental protection and natural resource conservation. In those decades, America was rapidly getting unhealthier, dirtier, and less pleasant to live in. Common law mechanisms, primarily the law of nuisance, was not arresting this slide.

What was needed was a uniform and rigorous federal and state commitment to clean the environment and deter wasteful resource use. That commitment, moreover, would have to take the form of statute, ordinance, and regulation. In the 1970s, the "environmental decade," that is precisely what happened. Legislated into existence during that time was what endure to this day as the flagships of environmental and natural resources law, including: the National Environmental Policy Act (1970); the Clean Air Act (1970); the Clean Water Act (1972); the Federal Insecticide, Fungicide, and Rodenticide Act (1972); the Marine Protection, Research, and Sanctuaries Act (the "Ocean Dumping Act") (1972); the Noise Control Act (1972); the Endangered Species Act (1973); the Forest and Rangeland Renewable Resources Planning Act (1974); the Safe Drinking Water Act (1974); the Federal Land Policy and Management Act (1976); the Resource Conservation and Recovery Act (1976); the Toxic Substances Control Act (1976); the Surface Mining Reclamation and Control Act (1977); and the Comprehensive Environmental Response, Compensation and Liability Act (the "Superfund" law) (1980). We will begin reviewing much of this statutory material soon, but as a prelude to that endeavor, it is well to first examine the foundational issues raised by the emergence of a two-tiered regulatory state.

We begin, as we must, by reviewing the relationship between the federal and state governments as established by the Federal Constitution. This area of law is loosely referred to as the law of federalism. First, we will look at the constitutional authorities vested in the federal and state governments respectively. Then, we will examine the problems that can arise when those powers are exercised. The subject areas reviewed are: the Tenth Amendment to the Federal Constitution, which comes into play when the exercise of federal power interferes with state interests; preemption issues, which come into play when both federal and state powers are exercised to the same end; and the dormant Commerce Clause, which comes into play when the exercise of state power interferes with federal interests. Understanding the allocation and interplay of federal and state power is essential because environmental and natural resources law implicates both federal and state law.

Thereafter, we turn to the rights of the individual, who, we should not forget, is the focus of this vast regulatory enterprise. We will limit our review to an examination of rights of the individual in her or his capacity as a holder of property rights, for the reason that a great deal of resource protection regulation impedes such property rights. This inquiry starts with a look at eminent domain authority and concludes with a review of the Takings Clause of the Federal Constitution.

B. ENUMERATED AND SOVEREIGN POWERS

As every law student knows, both the federal and state governments enjoy substantial constitutional power. Federal power is best exemplified by the far-reaching Commerce Clause of the Federal Constitution. U.S. CONST., art I, § 8, cl. 3. State authority is found in what is known as the "police power." (Note that, except for "home rule" municipalities, which secure authority directly from state constitutions, local governments typically have no constitutional power. Typically, their authorities derive from delegations from legislatures of the states in which they are located. Local governments, therefore, are largely irrelevant for constitutional federalism purposes.)

The bedrock of the federalism relationship is state sovereignty. States are the constitutional true sovereigns. This means that states are clothed with a broad and generally undifferentiated police power, which allows them to regulate the broad sweep of matters that affect life within their borders. States have police power simply because they exist. In fact, it is this amorphous and all-consuming authority that itself defines a state as a state: any entity without such a power cannot lay claim to that status. This inherent power stems from a general grant of authority from the governed to the state government. The federal government, by contrast, is not a true sovereign despite the tendency of some courts and commenters to speak of a "federal police power," which does not exist. Justice Powell explains in the case below.

GARCIA v. SAN ANTONIO METROPOLITAN TRANSIT AUTHORITY
469 U.S. 528, 570–72, 105 S. Ct. 1005, 1027–28 (1985)

POWELL, J. (dissenting):

The Framers had definite ideas about the nature of the Constitution's division of authority between the Federal and State Governments. In The Federalist No. 39, for example, Madison explained this division by drawing a series of contrasts between the attributes of a "national" government and those of the government to be established by the Constitution. While a national form of government would possess an "indefinite supremacy over all persons and things," the form of government contemplated by the Constitution instead consisted of "local or municipal authorities [which] form distinct and independent portions of the supremacy, no more subject within their respective spheres to the general authority, than the general authority is subject to them, within its own sphere." *Id.*, at 256 (J. Cooke ed. 1961). Under the Constitution, the sphere of the proposed government extended to jurisdiction of "certain enumerated objects only, . . . [leaving] to the several States a residuary and inviolable sovereignty over all other objects." *Ibid.*

Madison elaborated on the content of these separate spheres of sovereignty in THE FEDERALIST No. 45:

> The powers delegated by the proposed Constitution to the Federal Government, are few and defined. Those which are to remain in the State Governments are numerous and indefinite. The former will be exercised principally on external objects, as war, peace, negotiation, and foreign commerce. . . . The powers reserved to the several States will extend to all the objects, which, in the ordinary course of affairs, concern the lives, liberties and properties of the people; and the internal order, improvement, and prosperity of the State.

Id. at 313 (J. Cooke ed. 1961).

Madison considered that the operations of the federal government would be "most extensive and important in times of war and danger; those of the state governments in times of peace and security." *Ibid.* As a result of this division of powers, the state governments generally would be more important than the federal government. *Ibid.*

The framers believed that the separate sphere of sovereignty reserved to the States would ensure that the States would serve as an effective "counterpoise" to the power of the federal government. The States would serve this essential role because they would attract and retain the loyalty of their citizens. The roots of such loyalty, the founders thought, were found in the objects peculiar to state government. For example, Hamilton argued that the States "[regulate] all those personal interests and familiar concerns to which the sensibility of individuals is more immediately awake." The Federalist No. 17, p. 107 (J. Cooke ed. 1961). Thus, he maintained that the people would perceive the States as "the immediate and visible guardian of life and property," a fact which "contributes more than any other circumstance to impressing upon the minds of the people affection, esteem and reverence towards the government." *Ibid.* Madison took the same position, explaining that "the people will be more familiarly and minutely conversant" with the business of state governments, and "with the members of these, will a greater proportion of the people have the ties of personal acquaintance and friendship, and of family and party attachments." The Federalist No. 46, p. 316 (J. Cooke ed. 1961). Like Hamilton, Madison saw the States' involvement in the everyday concerns of the people as the source of their citizens' loyalty. *Ibid. See also* Nagel, *Federalism as a Fundamental Value:* National neLeague of Cities *in Perspective*, 1981 Sup. Ct. Rev. 81.

NOTES AND QUESTIONS

1. ***Federal and State Power.*** Thus, states have inherent authorities while the federal government has enumerated powers, themselves voluntarily relinquished to the federal government by the people. Enumerated powers are external to the federal government and are textually narrow in reach. By comparison, the state police power is internal to state governments and is broad in reach. For obvious reasons, the federal government could lose its constitutional authority. An amendment to the Federal Constitution would accomplish that. It would seem axiomatic, however, that a state could not lose its police power by any mechanism for any reason. If it did, the state would cease to be a state.

Might a state, however, resolve that its police power is of lesser reach than that of a neighbor state? For that matter, what entity ought to determine the reach of the police power? The United States Supreme Court? In this regard, see, e.g., *Berman v. Parker*, 348 U.S. 26, 75 S. Ct. 98 (1954).

2. ***Abdication of Federal Power.*** Could the federal government voluntarily abdicate an enumerated power? In *Zabel v. Tabb*, 430 F.2d 199 (5th Cir. 1970), the issue was whether Congress's enactment of the Submerged Lands Act of 1953 ("SLA") accomplished that result. The SLA transferred title to submerged coastal lands from the federal government to the states. *See* Chapter 5, *infra.* The statute contained the following express language: "[subject to certain exceptions] the right and power to manage, administer, lease, develop, and use the [transferred] lands and natural resources all in accordance with applicable State law [shall] be, and they are . . . recognized, confirmed, established, and vested in and assigned to the respective States." 43 U.S.C.A. § 1311(a). Based on this text, the argument was made that Congress had stripped itself of powers to regulate the use of the

transferred property. Examining the text and legislative history, the Fifth Circuit Court of Appeals found that what was lost to the federal government was title, not power. Notably, however, the Court did not object to the idea that, had the facts been different, an abdication could have taken place.

Of all the enumerated powers supplied to the federal government in the United States Constitution, surely the most important in terms of raw empowerment is the "affirmative" Commerce Clause (so called to distinguish it from the "dormant" Commerce Clause). The Clause provides that "The Congress shall have Power . . . [t]o regulate Commerce with foreign Nations, and among the several States, and with the Indian Tribes." U.S. Const., art. I, § 8, cl. 3. As you know, Congress has relied on this Clause more than any other as authority for its regulatory activity.

When examining the question of the reach of the Commerce Clause, courts used to issue the equivalent of a blank check. They routinely found the Clause to justify federal regulation in areas only distantly related to interstate commerce. In more recent times, however, the courts have begun to focus on the issue.

GIBBS v. BABBITT
214 F.3d 483 (4th Cir. 2000)

Judges: Before Wilkinson, Chief Judge, and Luttig and Michael, Circuit Judges. Chief Judge Wilkinson wrote the majority opinion, in which Judge Michael joined. Judge Luttig wrote a dissenting opinion.

Wilkinson, Chief Judge:

In this case we ask whether the national government can act to conserve scarce natural resources of value to our entire country. Appellants challenge the constitutionality of a Fish and Wildlife Service regulation that limits the taking of red wolves on private land. The district court upheld the regulation as a valid exercise of federal power under the Commerce Clause. We now affirm because the regulated activity substantially affects interstate commerce and because the regulation is part of a comprehensive federal program for the protection of endangered species. Judicial deference to the judgment of the democratic branches is therefore appropriate.

I.

A.

In response to growing concern over the extinction of many animal and plant species, Congress enacted the Endangered Species Act of 1973 (ESA), Pub. L. 93-205, 81 Stat. 884 (codified as amended at 16 U.S.C. §§ 1531–44 (1994 & Supp. III 1997)). Congress found that many of the species threatened with extinction are of "esthetic, ecological, educational, historical, recreational, and scientific value to the Nation and its people." 16 U.S.C. § 1531(a)(3) (1994). Congress also found that "various species of fish, wildlife, and plants in the United States have been rendered extinct as a consequence of economic growth and development untempered by adequate concern and conservation." *Id.* § 1531(a)(1). To address these national concerns, the ESA sets forth a comprehensive regulatory scheme to conserve these species and the ecosystems upon which they depend. The Act provides, inter alia, for the listing of "endangered" and "threatened" species, *id.* § 1533, and various recovery plans for the "conservation and survival" of listed species, *id.* § 1533(f).

The cornerstone of the statute is section 9(a)(1), which prohibits the taking of any endangered species without a permit or other authorization. *Id.* § 1538(a)(1)(B). The term "take" is defined as "to harass, harm, pursue, hunt, shoot, wound, kill, trap, capture, or collect, or to attempt to engage in any such conduct." *Id.* § 1532(19). . . .

B.

[This case dealt with the red wolf, Canis rufus, an endangered species, an "experimental" population of which was reintroduced into the wild by the FWS. By regulation, the protections of the ESA extended to this experimental population. The specific regulation at issue was Section 17.84(c), which prohibited the taking of red wolves on private land unless the taking "is not intentional or willful, or is in defense of that person's own life or the lives of others." 50 C.F.R. § 17.84(c)(4)(i).

In October, 1990, plaintiff Richard Lee Mann shot and killed a red wolf on his private land because he feared the wolf would harm his cattle. The federal government prosecuted Mann, who pled guilty. Thereafter came this challenge to the federal government's authority to protect red wolves on private land.]

C.

. . . .

II.

We consider this case under the framework articulated by the Supreme Court in *United States v. Lopez*, 514 U.S. 549, 115 S. Ct. 1624, 131 L. Ed. 2d 626 (1995), and *United States v. Morrison*, 120 S. Ct. 1740, 146, L. Ed. 2d 658 (2000), *aff'g Brzonkala v. Virginia Polytechnic Institute and State University*, 169 F.3d 820 (4th Cir. 1999). While Congress's power to pass laws under the Commerce Clause has been interpreted broadly, both Lopez and Morrison reestablish that the commerce power contains "judicially enforceable outer limits." *See Lopez*, 514 U.S. at 566; *Morrison*, 2000 WL 574361, at 6. It is essential to our system of government that the commerce power not extend to effects on interstate commerce that are so remote that we "would effectually obliterate the distinction between what is national and what is local." *National Labor Relations Board v. Jones & Laughlin Steel Corp.*, 301 U.S. 1, 37, 57 S. Ct. 615, 81 L. Ed. 893 (1937). Indeed, the judiciary has the duty to ensure that federal statutes and regulations are promulgated under one of the enumerated grants of constitutional authority. It is our further duty to independently evaluate whether "a rational basis exists for concluding that a regulated activity sufficiently affects interstate commerce." *Lopez*, 514 U.S. at 557. . . .

The *Lopez* Court recognized three broad categories of activity that Congress may regulate under its commerce power. 514 U.S. at 558. "First, Congress may regulate the use of the channels of interstate commerce. Second, Congress is empowered to regulate and protect the instrumentalities of interstate commerce, or persons or things in interstate commerce, even though the threat may come only from intrastate activities. Finally, Congress' commerce authority includes the power to regulate those activities having a substantial relation to interstate commerce, i.e., those activities that substantially affect interstate commerce." *Id. at* 558–59 (citations omitted).

Section 17.84(c) is "not a regulation of the use of the channels of interstate commerce, nor is it an attempt to prohibit the interstate transportation of a commodity through the channels of commerce." *Lopez*, 514 U.S. at 559. The term "channel of interstate commerce" refers to, inter alia, "navigable rivers, lakes, and canals of the United States; the interstate railroad track system; the interstate highway system; . . . interstate telephone and telegraph lines; air traffic routes; television and radio broadcast frequencies." *United States v. Miles*, 122 F.3d 235, 245 (5th Cir. 1997). This regulation of red wolf takings on private land does not target the movement of wolves or wolf products in the channels of interstate commerce.

This case also does not implicate *Lopez*'s second prong, which protects things in interstate commerce. Although the Service has transported the red wolves interstate for the purposes of study and the reintroduction programs, this is not sufficient to make the red wolf a "thing" in interstate commerce. *See, e.g., Lopez*, 514 U.S. at 559 (rejecting application of prong two to Gun-Free School Zones Act, despite the fact that the regulated guns likely traveled through interstate commerce); *National Assoc. of Home Builders v. Babbitt*, 130 F.3d 1041, 1046, 327 U.S. App. D.C. 248 (D.C. Cir. 1997) ("NAHB") (rejecting notion that Delhi Sands Flower-Loving Fly was a "thing" in interstate commerce). Therefore, if 50 C.F.R. § 17.84(c) is within the commerce power, it must be sustained under the third prong of *Lopez*.

Under the third *Lopez* test, regulations have been upheld when the regulated activities "arise out of or are connected with a commercial transaction, which viewed in the aggregate, substantially affects interstate commerce." *Lopez*, 514 U.S. at 561. In *Morrison*, the Supreme Court noted, "In every case where we have sustained federal regulation under *Wickard*'s aggregation principle, the regulated activity was of an apparent commercial character." *Morrison*, 2000 WL 574361, at 37 n.4. The Court in *Lopez* likewise placed great emphasis on the "commercial concerns that are central to the Commerce Clause." *Lopez*, 514 U.S. at 583 (Kennedy, J., concurring); *see also Hoffman v. Hunt*, 126 F.3d 575, 586–87 (4th Cir. 1997) (noting the importance of the distinction between "the regulation of, on the one hand, those activities that are commercial or economic in nature . . . and, on the other hand, those activities that are not").

Although the connection to economic or commercial activity plays a central role in whether a regulation will be upheld under the Commerce Clause, economic activity must be understood in broad terms. Indeed, a cramped view of commerce would cripple a foremost federal power and in so doing would eviscerate national authority. The *Lopez* Court's characterization of the regulation of home-grown wheat in *Wickard v. Filburn*, 317 U.S. 111, 63 S. Ct. 82, 87 L. Ed. 122 (1942), as a case involving economic activity makes clear the breadth of this concept. The Court explained that "even *Wickard*, which is perhaps the most far reaching example of Commerce Clause authority over intrastate activity, involved economic activity in a way that the possession of a gun in a school zone does not." *Lopez*, 514 U.S. at 560; *accord Morrison*, 2000 WL 574361, at 7. *See also Brzonkala*, 169 F.3d at 835 (explaining that the Court has a "relatively broad understanding of such [economic] activity"). In fact, our understanding of commerce may not be limited to its "18th-century" forms. *See Lopez*, 514 U.S. at 574 (Kennedy, J., concurring). While we must enforce meaningful limits on the commerce power, we must also be mindful of the "Court's relatively generous conception of economic activity." *Brzonkala*, 169 F.3d at 835.

Lopez and *Morrison* rest on the principle that where a federal statute has only a tenuous connection to commerce and infringes on areas of traditional state concern, the courts should not hesitate to exercise their constitutional obligation to hold that the statute exceeds an enumerated federal power. Respect for our federal system of government was integral to those decisions. *See Lopez*, 514 U.S. at 561 n.3; *Morrison*, 2000 WL 574361, at 11. Yet *Lopez* also counsels that "where economic activity substantially affects interstate commerce, legislation regulating that activity will be sustained." 514 U.S. at 560. In enforcing limits on the Congress, we must be careful not to overstep the judicial role. To strike down statutes that bear substantially upon commerce is to overstep our own authority even as we fault Congress for exceeding limits on its power. The irony of disregarding limits on ourselves in the course of enforcing limits upon others will assuredly not be lost on those who look to courts to respect restraints imposed by rules of law.

With these basic principles in mind, we consider appellants' challenge to § 17.84(c).

III.

Appellants argue that the federal government cannot limit the taking of red wolves on private land because this activity cannot be squared with any of the three categories that Congress may regulate under its commerce power. Appellants assert that 50 C.F.R. § 17.84(c) is therefore beyond the reach of congressional authority under the Commerce Clause.

We disagree. It was reasonable for Congress and the Fish and Wildlife Service to conclude that § 17.84(c) regulates economic activity. The taking of red wolves implicates a variety of commercial activities and is closely connected to several interstate markets. The regulation in question is also an integral part of the overall federal scheme to protect, preserve, and rehabilitate endangered species, thereby conserving valuable wildlife resources important to the welfare of our country. Invalidating this provision would call into question the historic power of the federal government to preserve scarce resources in one locality for the future benefit of all Americans.

A.

To fall within Congress' commerce power, this regulation must have a "substantial relation to interstate commerce" — it must "substantially affect interstate commerce." *Lopez*, 514 U.S. at 559. The Supreme Court recently emphasized that "in those cases where we have sustained federal regulation of intrastate activity based upon the activity's substantial effects on interstate commerce, the activity in question has been some sort of economic endeavor." *Morrison*, 2000 WL 574361, at 8. Intrastate activities may be subject to federal regulation if they have a "meaningful connection with a particular, identifiable economic enterprise or transaction." *Brzonkala*, 169 F.3d at 834. We therefore must consider whether the taking of red wolves on private land is "in any sense of the phrase, economic activity." *Morrison*, 2000 WL 574361, at 9.

Unlike the Violence Against Women Act (VAWA) in *Morrison* and the Gun-Free School Zones Act (GFSZA) in *Lopez*, § 17.84(c) regulates what is in a meaningful sense economic activity. The Court in Morrison explained that both the VAWA and the GFSZA involved activity that was noneconomic and only tenuously linked to interstate commerce. 2000 WL 574361, at 7–9. Yet the taking of a red wolf on private land is unlike gender-motivated violence or guns near schools. The protection of commercial and economic assets is a primary reason for taking the wolves. Farmers and ranchers take wolves mainly because they are concerned that the animals pose a risk to commercially valuable livestock and crops. Indeed, appellants' arguments focus quite explicitly on these economic concerns — they want freer rein to protect their property and investments in the land [citation omitted]; *id.* at 12.

The relationship between red wolf takings and interstate commerce is quite direct — with no red wolves, there will be no red wolf related tourism, no scientific research, and no commercial trade in pelts. We need not "pile inference upon inference," *Lopez*, 514 U.S. at 567, to reach this conclusion. While a beleaguered species may not presently have the economic impact of a large commercial enterprise, its eradication nonetheless would have a substantial effect on interstate commerce. And through preservation the impact of an endangered species on commerce will only increase.

Because the taking of red wolves can be seen as economic activity in the sense considered by *Lopez* and *Morrison*, the individual takings may be aggregated for the purpose of Commerce Clause analysis. *See Morrison*, 2000 WL 574361, at 37 n.4. While the taking of one red wolf on private land may not be "substantial," the takings of red wolves in the aggregate have a sufficient impact on interstate commerce to uphold this regulation. This is especially so where, as here, the regulation is but one part of the broader scheme of endangered species legislation.

Further, § 17.84(c) is closely connected to a variety of interstate economic activities. Whether the impact of red wolf takings on any one of these activities qualifies as a substantial effect on interstate commerce is something we need not address. We have no doubt that the effect of the takings on these varied activities in combination qualifies as a substantial one. The first nexus between the challenged regulation and interstate commerce is tourism. The red wolves are part of a $29.2 billion national wildlife-related recreational industry that involves tourism and interstate travel. *See Heart of Atlanta Motel*, 379 U.S. at 256 (finding it is well-established that "commerce among the States . . . consists of intercourse and traffic between their citizens" (internal quotation marks omitted)). Many tourists travel to North Carolina from throughout the country for "howling events" — evenings of listening to wolf howls accompanied by educational programs. These howlings are a regular occurrence at the Alligator River National Wildlife Refuge. According to a study conducted by Dr. William E. Rosen of Cornell University, the recovery of the red wolf and increased visitor activities could result in a significant regional economic impact. *See* William E. Rosen, Red Wolf Recovery in Northeastern North Carolina and the Great Smoky Mountains National Park: Public Attitudes and Economic Impacts (unpublished, Joint Appendix at 633). Rosen estimates that northeastern North Carolina could see an increase of between $39.61 and $183.65 million per year in tourism-related activities, and that the Great Smoky Mountains National Park could see an increase of between $132.09 and $354.50 million per year. This is hardly a trivial impact on interstate commerce. Appellants understandably seek to criticize the Rosen study, but concede that the howling events attract interstate tourism and that red wolf program volunteers come from all around the country. . . .

Tourism, however, is not the only interstate commercial activity affected by the taking of red wolves. The regulation of red wolf takings is also closely connected to a second interstate market — scientific research. Scientific research generates jobs. It also deepens our knowledge of the world in which we live. The red wolf reintroduction program has already generated numerous scientific studies. For example, the red wolf is used as a model for other carnivore reintroductions. *See* Donald E. Moore III & Roland Smith, *The Red Wolf as a Model for Carnivore Re-introductions*, 62 Symp. Zool. Soc. Lond. 263 (1990). Scientists have also studied how the red wolf affects small mammal populations and how the wolves interact with the ecosystem as a whole. *See, e.g.*, Bryan T. Kelly, Alligator River National Wildlife Refuge Red Wolf (Canis Rufus) Scat Analysis: Preliminary Analyses of Mammalian Prey Consumed by Year, Season, Pack, Sex, and Age (April 1994) (unpublished, Joint Appendix at 942). By studying the effects of red wolves on the ecosystem, scientists learn about the interdependence of plants and animals, as well as how other threatened species may be reintroduced in the future. Scientific research can also reveal other uses for animals — for instance, approximately 50 percent of all modern medicines are derived from wild plants or animals. *See* Norman Myers, A Wealth of Wild Species: Storehouse for Human Welfare 4 (1983). Protection of the red wolves on private land thus encourages further research that may have inestimable future value, both for scientific knowledge as well as for commercial development of the red wolf.

The anti-taking regulation is also connected to a third market — the possibility of a renewed trade in fur pelts. Wolves have historically been hunted for their pelts. *See* Stanley P. Young & Edward A. Goldman, The Wolves of North America I, 165–70 (1964). Congress had the renewal of trade in mind when it enacted the ESA. The Senate Report noted that the protection of an endangered species "may permit the regeneration of that species to a level where controlled exploitation of that species can be resumed. In such a case businessmen may profit from the trading and marketing of that species for an indefinite number of years, where otherwise it would have been completely eliminated from commercial channels." S. Rep. No.

91-526, at 3 (1969), *reprinted in* 1969 U.S.C.C.A.N. 1413, 1415. The American alligator is a case in point. In 1975, the American alligator was nearing extinction and listed as endangered, but by 1987 conservation efforts restored the species. Now there is a vigorous trade in alligator hides. *See* Catharine L. Krieps, *Sustainable Use of Endangered Species Under CITES: Is it a Sustainable Alternative?*, 17 U. Pa. J. Int'l Econ. L. 461, 479–80 (1996) (explaining that many environmentalists are now encouraging the purchase of alligator products to create an incentive for protecting alligators and their habitats). Although alligator hides have more recently been a part of interstate commercial trade and red wolves were sold for their pelts primarily in the nineteenth century, this temporal difference is beside the point. It is not for the judiciary to move from species to species, opining that species A possesses great commercial potential, but species B does not. Assessing the relative scientific value and commercial impact of alligators and red wolves is for Congress and the FWS, informed as they are by biologists, economists, and others whose expertise is best delivered to the political branches, not the courts.

Finally, the taking of red wolves is connected to interstate markets for agricultural products and livestock. For instance, appellant landowners find red wolves a menace because they threaten livestock and other animals of economic and commercial value. By restricting the taking of red wolves, § 17.84(c) is said to impede economic development and commercial activities such as ranching and farming. This effect on commerce, however, still qualifies as a legitimate subject for regulation. It is well-settled under Commerce Clause cases that a regulation can involve the promotion or the restriction of commercial enterprises and development. Indeed, "the motive and purpose of a regulation of interstate commerce are matters for the legislative judgment." *United States v. Darby*, 312 U.S. 100, 115, 61 S. Ct. 451, 85 L. Ed. 609 (1941). We recognize that "Congress can regulate interstate commerce for any lawful motive." *United States v. Soderna*, 82 F.3d 1370, 1374 (7th Cir. 1996). The regulation here targets takings that are economically motivated — farmers take wolves to protect valuable livestock and crops. It is for Congress, not the courts, to balance economic effects — namely whether the negative effects on interstate commerce from red wolf predation are outweighed by the benefits to commerce from a restoration of this species. To say that courts are ill-suited for this act of empirical and political judgment is an understatement.

It is anything but clear, for example, that red wolves harm farming enterprises. They may in fact help them, and in so doing confer additional benefits on commerce. For instance, red wolves prey on animals like raccoons, deer, and rabbits — helping farmers by killing the animals that destroy their crops. . . . Given the existing economic and commercial activity involving red wolves and wildlife generally, Congress could find that conservation of endangered species and economic growth are mutually reinforcing. It is simply not beyond the power of Congress to conclude that a healthy environment actually boosts industry by allowing commercial development of our natural resources.

Section 17.84(c) aims to reverse threatened extinction and conserve the red wolf for both current and future use in interstate commerce . . . The full payoff of conservation in the form of tourism, research, and trade may not be foreseeable. Yet it is reasonable for Congress to decide that conservation of species will one day produce a substantial commercial benefit to this country and that failure to preserve a species will result in permanent, though unascertainable, commercial loss.

Extinction, after all, is irreversible. If a species becomes extinct, we are left to speculate forever on what we might have learned or what we may have realized. If we conserve the species, it will be available for the study and benefit of future generations. In any event, it is for Congress to choose between inaction and preservation, not for the courts.

The protection of the red wolf on both federal and private land substantially affects interstate commerce through tourism, trade, scientific research, and other potential economic activities. To overturn this regulation would start courts down the road to second-guessing all kinds of legislative judgments. There is a "rational basis" as defined by *Lopez* for sustaining this regulation. We therefore hold that the anti-taking provision at issue here involves regulable economic and commercial activity as understood by current Commerce Clause jurisprudence.

B.

This regulation is also sustainable as "an essential part of a larger regulation of economic activity, in which the regulatory scheme could be undercut unless the intrastate activity were regulated." *Lopez*, 514 U.S. at 561. The Supreme Court in *Hodel v. Indiana* stated: "A complex regulatory program . . . can survive a Commerce Clause challenge without a showing that every single facet of the program is independently and directly related to a valid congressional goal. It is enough that the challenged provisions are an integral part of the regulatory program and that the regulatory scheme when considered as a whole satisfies this test." 452 U.S. 314, 329 n.17 (1981).

Appellants repeatedly argue that individual takings of red wolves have only an insubstantial effect on interstate commerce and therefore that the application of the regulation to private landowners is invalid. But we emphasize that the effect on commerce must be viewed not from the taking of one wolf, but from the potential commercial differential between an extinct and a recovered species. A single red wolf taking may be insubstantial by some measures, but that does not invalidate a regulation that is part of the ESA and that seeks conservation not only of any single animal, but also recovery of the species as a whole. The Supreme Court in *Lopez* was emphatic on this point: " 'where a general regulatory statute bears a substantial relation to commerce, the de minimis character of individual instances arising under that statute is of no consequence.' " 514 U.S. at 558 (alteration in original) (quoting *Maryland v. Wirtz*, 392 U.S. 183, 197 n.27, 88 S. Ct. 2017, 20 L. Ed. 2d 1020 (1968)); *see also Perez v. United States*, 402 U.S. 146, 154, 91 S. Ct. 1357, 28 L. Ed. 2d 686 (1971) ("Where the class of activities is regulated and that class is within the reach of federal power, the courts have no power to excise, as trivial, individual instances of the class." (internal quotation marks omitted)).

As the Supreme Court has stated, "if it is interstate commerce that feels the pinch, it does not matter how local the operation which applies the squeeze." *Heart of Atlanta Motel*, 379 U.S. at 258 (internal quotation marks omitted). . . . Yet under appellants' theory, the more endangered the species, the less authority Congress has to regulate the taking of it. According to this view, endangered species would lie beyond congressional protection because there are too few animals left to make a commercial difference. Such reasoning would eviscerate the comprehensive federal scheme for conserving endangered species and turn congressional judgment on its head.

Appellants protest they do not ask us to overturn the ESA. They simply want us to excise as unconstitutional a disfavored provision that places a strain on their agricultural activities. But given that Congress has the ability to enact a broad scheme for the conservation of endangered species, it is not for the courts to invalidate individual regulations. If appellants think this regulation unwise, they must make their plea to Congress.***

IV.

Upholding this regulation is consistent with the "first principles" of a Constitution that establishes a federal government of enumerated powers. *See Lopez,* 514 U.S. at 552. *Lopez* and *Morrison* properly emphasize that we must carefully evaluate legislation in light of our federal system of government. "The Constitution requires a distinction between what is truly national and what is truly local." *Morrison,* 2000 WL 574361, at 11. We must particularly scrutinize regulated activity that "falls within an area of the law where States historically have been sovereign and countenance of the asserted federal power would blur the boundaries between the spheres of federal and state authority." *Brzonkala,* 169 F.3d at 837 (internal quotation marks omitted).

A.

It is imperative to set forth at the outset the historic roles of federal and state authority in this area. The regulated activity at issue here does not involve an "area of traditional state concern," one to which "States lay claim by right of history and expertise." *Lopez,* 514 U.S. at 580, 583 (Kennedy, J., concurring).

[In the remainder of this portion of the opinion, the court argued, first, that control over wildlife historically was not a traditional area of state concern thereby insulated from the reach of federal power. It reached the same conclusion regarding state regulation of local land use, announcing that Congress certainly has power to regulate private land use for the purpose of protecting wildlife.]***

D.

. . . The rationale for this regulation thus stops far short of conferring upon Congress a broad police power. It is instead appellants' arguments for invalidating this regulation that go too far. If the federal government cannot regulate the taking of an endangered or threatened species on private land, its conservation and preservation efforts would be limited to only federal lands. A ruling to this effect would place in peril the entire federal regulatory scheme for wildlife and natural resource conservation.

[The remainder of this majority opinion responds to the dissent. This portion and the dissenting opinion are omitted].

Affirmed.

NOTES AND QUESTIONS

1. ***Gibbs Look-Alikes.*** *Accord National Association of Home Builders v. Babbitt*, 130 F.3d 1041 (D.C. Cir. 1997). In *Home Builders*, the Circuit Court for the District of Columbia reviewed the constitutionality of ESA applicability to the New Delhi Sands Fly, which was found to occupy a small area in California. Unlike the wolves in *Gibbs*, these flies did not wander from state to state or from habitat to habitat, nor did they attract tourists, nor was there any prospective market in them. Nonetheless, the court, in another 2-1 decision, found the regulation to satisfy both the first and third prongs of *Lopez*. The measure was held to qualify as a regulation of the channels of interstate commerce because the statute served:

> to prevent the eradication of an endangered species by a hospital that is presumably being constructed using materials and people from outside the state and which will attract employees, patients, and students from both inside and outside the state. Thus, like regulations preventing racial discrimination or labor exploitation, regulations preventing the taking of endangered species prohibit interstate actors from using the channels of interstate commerce to "promote or spread[] evil, whether of a physical, moral or economic nature." (citation omitted).

Home Builders, 130 F.3d at 1048.

In addition, the court found that the regulated activity substantially affected interstate commerce, for two reasons. First, the loss of the species would deprive interstate commerce of "an important natural resource — biodiversity." *Home Builders*, 130 F.3d at 1054. Second, "[t]he taking of the Fly and other endangered animals can also be regulated by Congress as an activity that substantially affects interstate commerce because it is the product of destructive interstate competition. It is a principle deeply rooted in Commerce Clause jurisprudence that Congress is empowered to act to prevent destructive interstate competition." *Home Builders*, 130 F.3d at 1054.

Judge Wald's majority opinion prompted a vigorous dissent by Judge Sentelle, the first analytical paragraph of which follows:

> The proposition that the federal government can, under the Interstate Commerce Clause, regulate an activity which is neither interstate nor commerce, reminds me of the old chestnut: If we had some ham, we could fix some ham and eggs, if we had some eggs. With neither ham nor eggs, the chances of fixing a recognizable meal requiring both amount to nil. Similarly, the chances of validly regulating something which is neither commerce nor interstate under the heading of the interstate commerce power must likewise be an empty recitation. I recognize that for some decades of jurisprudential development, the Commerce Clause has been used as the justification for the regulation of a plethora of activities not apparently within its text. *See, e.g., Wickard v. Filburn*, 317 U.S. 111, 63 S. Ct. 82, 87 L. Ed. 122 (1942) (regulating the consumption of home-grown wheat). So wide-ranging has been the application of the Clause as to

prompt one writer to "wonder why anyone would make the mistake of calling it the Commerce Clause instead of the 'hey-you-can-do whatever-you-feel-like clause.' " Judge Alex Kozinski, *Introduction to Volume 19*, 19 HARV. J.L. PUB. POL. 1, 5 (1995). However, in 1995, the Supreme Court brought an end to the galactic growth of the Clause's application and reminded Congress that the words of that Clause, like the rest of the Constitution, have content, in *United States v. Lopez*, 514 U.S. 549, 115 S. Ct. 1624, 131 L. Ed. 2d 626 (1995). While I would have found the present application of the ESA to be outside the enumerated powers of Congress under the Commerce Clause even in the world before *Lopez*, after that controlling decision, I think there can be no doubt.

Home Builders, 130 F.3d at 1061.

Judge Sentelle went on to argue that speculation about the potential value of specific species for medicinal purposes or otherwise is merely that, speculation, and is insufficient as a justification for Commerce Clause regulation. Moreover, he asserted, the Commerce Clause authorizes regulation of commerce, not the regulation of ecosystems.

For a more recent Endangered Species Act case of a similar ilk, holding that the Commerce Clause allows the federal government to protect a fish (the Alabama sturgeon) found only in one state and not used for any commercial purpose, on the theory that entirely intrastate activities are regulable so long as the activity in the aggregate substantially affects interstate commerce, see *Alabama-Tombigbee Rivers Coalition v. Kempthorne*, 477 F.3d 1250 (11th Cir. 2007), *cert. denied*, 552 U.S. 1097, 128 S. Ct. 877 (2008).

2. *The Migratory Bird Rule.* Commerce Clause issues arise frequently with respect to regulation of wetlands. Loosely defined, wetlands are saturated areas that support water-dependent vegetation. Wetlands can be large (consider the Everglades) or small. The dredging and filling of wetlands is regulated by § 404 of the Clean Water Act. *See* Chapter 10, *infra*. In one noteworthy case, EPA brought an action against a developer for filling in a soybean field. *Hoffman Homes v. U.S. Environmental Protection Agency* ("*Hoffman Homes II*"), 999 F.2d 256 (7th Cir. 1993). The developer defended on Commerce Clause grounds because the soybean field, while falling under the definition of "wetland," was only one acre in size, was isolated, had no interstate commercial significance, and was not even used by migratory birds. In EPA's view, regulation was constitutionally warranted because there existed a theoretical possibility that migratory birds would use the wetland (the "migratory bird rule"). In the agency's view, so long as the wetland constituted a suitable habitat for migratory birds before it was filled in, even if migratory birds had not actually used it, Clean Water Act regulation of it was constitutional. The Seventh Circuit ruled against EPA on evidentiary grounds: as no migratory birds had, in fact, used the wetland, the court was unconvinced the wetland was a suitable habitat for migratory birds. *Accord Leslie Salt Co. v. United States*, 896 F.2d 354 (9th Cir. 1990); *Utah v. Marsh*, 740 F.2d 799 (10th Cir. 1984).

The Seventh Circuit considered EPA's migratory bird rule again six years later in a case presenting slightly different facts. In *Solid Waste Agency v. U.S. Army Corps of Engineers*, 191 F.3d 845 (7th Cir. 1999), *rev'd on other grounds*, 531 U.S.

159, 121 S. Ct. 675 (2001) (*see* Chapter 10, *infra*), the site regulated under the auspices of the Clean Water Act had actually been used by migratory birds. Relying on the "cumulative impact doctrine" of *Wickard v. Filburn*, 317 U.S. 111, 63 S. Ct. 82, 87 L. Ed. 122 (1942), the court found the Commerce Clause authorized the regulation: "The effect may not be observable as each isolated pond used by the birds for feeding, nesting, and breeding is filled, but the aggregate effect is clear, and that is all the Commerce Clause requires." *Solid Waste Agency*, 191 F.3d at 849–50.

C. CONSIDERATIONS OF FEDERALISM

"The federal system rests on what might at first seem a counterintuitive insight, that 'freedom is enhanced by the creation of two governments, not one.' *Alden v. Maine*, 527 U.S. 706, 758, 119 S. Ct. 2240, 144 L. Ed. 2d 636 (1999). The Framers concluded that allocation of powers between the National Government and the States enhances freedom, first by protecting the integrity of the governments themselves, and second by protecting the people, from whom all governmental powers are derived." *Bond v. United States*, __ U.S. __, 131 S. Ct. 2355, 2364 (2011).

In the preceding section, we discussed federal and state empowerment. Now we turn to a discussion of the allocation of powers in our federalist system and limitations on their exercise.

1. The Tenth Amendment

The Tenth Amendment is a brief epistle of enormous significance. Stating merely that "the powers not delegated to the United States by the Constitution, nor prohibited by it to the States, are reserved to the States respectively, or to the people[,]" the measure has provoked quarrels in the Supreme Court and an inconsistent jurisprudence from it. A core question is whether the Tenth Amendment is merely a sum-up provision that states the obvious, or whether it affirmatively designs the relationship of the federal government with the states.

NEW YORK v. UNITED STATES
505 U.S. 144, 112 S. Ct. 2408 (1992)

O'CONNOR, J., delivered the opinion of the Court, in which REHNQUIST, C.J., and SCALIA, KENNEDY, SOUTER, and THOMAS, JJ., joined, and in Parts III-A and III-B of which WHITE, BLACKMUN, AND STEVENS, JJ., joined. WHITE, J., filed an opinion concurring in part and dissenting in part, in which BLACKMUN and STEVENS, JJ., joined. STEVENS, J., filed an opinion concurring in part and dissenting in part.

JUSTICE O'CONNOR delivered the opinion of the Court.

This case implicates one of our Nation's newest problems of public policy and perhaps our oldest question of constitutional law. The public policy issue involves the disposal of radioactive waste: In this case, we address the constitutionality of three provisions of the Low-Level Radioactive Waste Policy Amendments Act of

1985, Pub. L. 99-240, 99 Stat. 1842, 42 U.S.C. § 2021b et seq. The constitutional question is as old as the Constitution: It consists of discerning the proper division of authority between the Federal Government and the States. We conclude that while Congress has substantial power under the Constitution to encourage the States to provide for the disposal of the radioactive waste generated within their borders, the Constitution does not confer upon Congress the ability simply to compel the States to do so. We therefore find that only two of the Act's three provisions at issue are consistent with the Constitution's allocation of power to the Federal Government.

I

We live in a world full of low level radioactive waste. Radioactive material is present in luminous watch dials, smoke alarms, measurement devices, medical fluids, research materials, and the protective gear and construction materials used by workers at nuclear power plants. Low level radioactive waste is generated by the Government, by hospitals, by research institutions, and by various industries. The waste must be isolated from humans for long periods of time, often for hundreds of years. Millions of cubic feet of low level radioactive waste must be disposed of each year.

Our Nation's first site for the land disposal of commercial low level radioactive waste opened in 1962 in Beatty, Nevada. Five more sites opened in the following decade: Maxey Flats, Kentucky (1963), West Valley, New York (1963), Hanford, Washington (1965), Sheffield, Illinois (1967), and Barnwell, South Carolina (1971). Between 1975 and 1978, the Illinois site closed because it was full, and water management problems caused the closure of the sites in Kentucky and New York. As a result, since 1979 only three disposal sites — those in Nevada, Washington, and South Carolina — have been in operation. Waste generated in the rest of the country must be shipped to one of these three sites for disposal. *See* Low-Level Radioactive Waste Regulation 39–40 (M. Burns ed. 1988).

In 1979, both the Washington and Nevada sites were forced to shut down temporarily, leaving South Carolina to shoulder the responsibility of storing low level radioactive waste produced in every part of the country. The Governor of South Carolina, understandably perturbed, ordered a 50% reduction in the quantity of waste accepted at the Barnwell site. The Governors of Washington and Nevada announced plans to shut their sites permanently. . . .

Faced with the possibility that the Nation would be left with no disposal sites for low level radioactive waste, Congress responded by enacting the Low-Level Radioactive Waste Policy Act, Pub. L. 96-573, 94 Stat. 3347. Relying largely on a report submitted by the National Governors' Association, . . . Congress declared a federal policy of holding each State "responsible for providing for the availability of capacity either within or outside the State for the disposal of low-level radioactive waste generated within its borders," and found that such waste could be disposed of "most safely and efficiently . . . on a regional basis." § 4(a)(1), 94 Stat. 3348. The 1980 Act authorized States to enter into regional compacts that, once ratified by Congress, would have the authority beginning in 1986 to restrict the use of their disposal facilities to waste generated within member States. § 4(a)(2)(B), 94 Stat.

3348. The 1980 Act included no penalties for States that failed to participate in this plan.

By 1985, only three approved regional compacts had operational disposal facilities; not surprisingly, these were the compacts formed around South Carolina, Nevada, and Washington, the three sited States. The following year, the 1980 Act would have given these three compacts the ability to exclude waste from nonmembers, and the remaining 31 States would have had no assured outlet for their low level radioactive waste. With this prospect looming, Congress once again took up the issue of waste disposal. The result was the legislation challenged here, the Low-Level Radioactive Waste Policy Amendments Act of 1985.

The 1985 Act was again based largely on a proposal submitted by the National Governors' Association. In broad outline, the Act embodies a compromise among the sited and unsited States. The sited States agreed to extend for seven years the period in which they would accept low level radioactive waste from other States. In exchange, the unsited States agreed to end their reliance on the sited States by 1992.

The mechanics of this compromise are intricate. . . .

The Act provides three types of incentives to encourage the States to comply with their statutory obligation to provide for the disposal of waste generated within their borders.

1. Monetary incentives. One quarter of the surcharges collected by the sited States must be transferred to an escrow account held by the Secretary of Energy. § 2021e(d)(2)(A). The Secretary then makes payments from this account to each State that has complied with a series of deadlines. . . .

2. Access incentives. The second type of incentive involves the denial of access to disposal sites. States that fail to meet the July 1986 deadline may be charged twice the ordinary surcharge for the remainder of 1986 and may be denied access to disposal facilities thereafter. § 2021e(e)(2)(A). States that fail to meet the 1988 deadline may be charged double surcharges for the first half of 1988 and quadruple surcharges for the second half of 1988, and may be denied access thereafter. § 2021e(e)(2)(B). States that fail to meet the 1990 deadline may be denied access. § 2021e(e)(2)(C). Finally, States that have not filed complete applications by January 1, 1992, for a license to operate a disposal facility, or States belonging to compacts that have not filed such applications, may be charged triple surcharges. §§ 2021e(e)(1)(D), 2021e(e)(2)(D).

3. The take title provision. The third type of incentive is the most severe. The Act provides: "If a State (or, where applicable, a compact region) in which low-level radioactive waste is generated is unable to provide for the disposal of all such waste generated within such State or compact region by January 1, 1996, each State in which such waste is generated, upon the request of the generator or owner of the waste, shall take title to the waste, be obligated to take possession of the waste, and shall be liable for all damages directly or indirectly incurred by such generator or owner as a consequence of the failure of the State to take possession of the waste as soon after January 1, 1996, as the generator or owner notifies the State that the waste is available for shipment." § 2021e(d)(2)(C).

These three incentives are the focus of petitioners' constitutional challenge.

In the seven years since the Act took effect, Congress has approved nine regional compacts, encompassing 42 of the States. All six unsited compacts and four of the unaffiliated States have met the first three statutory milestones.

New York, a State whose residents generate a relatively large share of the Nation's low level radioactive waste, did not join a regional compact. Instead, the State complied with the Act's requirements by enacting legislation providing for the siting and financing of a disposal facility in New York. The State has identified five potential sites, three in Allegany County and two in Cortland County. Residents of the two counties oppose the State's choice of location.

Petitioners — the State of New York and the two counties — filed this suit against the United States in 1990. They sought a declaratory judgment that the Act is inconsistent with the Tenth and Eleventh Amendments to the Constitution, with the Due Process Clause of the Fifth Amendment, and with the Guarantee Clause of Article IV of the Constitution. The States of Washington, Nevada, and South Carolina intervened as defendants. The District Court dismissed the complaint. 757 F. Supp. 10 (NDNY 1990). The Court of Appeals affirmed. 942 F.2d 114 (CA2 1991). Petitioners have abandoned their Due Process and Eleventh Amendment claims on their way up the appellate ladder; as the case stands before us, petitioners claim only that the Act is inconsistent with the Tenth Amendment and the Guarantee Clause.

II

A

In 1788, in the course of explaining to the citizens of New York why the recently drafted Constitution provided for federal courts, Alexander Hamilton observed: "The erection of a new government, whatever care or wisdom may distinguish the work, cannot fail to originate questions of intricacy and nicety; and these may, in a particular manner, be expected to flow from the establishment of a constitution founded upon the total or partial incorporation of a number of distinct sovereignties." The Federalist No. 82, p. 491 (C. Rossiter ed. 1961). Hamilton's prediction has proved quite accurate. While no one disputes the proposition that "the Constitution created a Federal Government of limited powers," *Gregory v. Ashcroft*, 501 U.S. 452, 457 (1991); and while the Tenth Amendment makes explicit that "the powers not delegated to the United States by the Constitution, nor prohibited by it to the States, are reserved to the States respectively, or to the people"; the task of ascertaining the constitutional line between federal and state power has given rise to many of the Court's most difficult and celebrated cases. At least as far back as *Martin v. Hunter's Lessee*, 1 Wheat. 304, 324 (1816), the Court has resolved questions "of great importance and delicacy" in determining whether particular sovereign powers have been granted by the Constitution to the Federal Government or have been retained by the States.

These questions can be viewed in either of two ways. In some cases the Court has inquired whether an Act of Congress is authorized by one of the powers delegated to Congress in Article I of the Constitution. *See, e.g., Perez v. United States,* 402 U.S. 146 (1971); *McCulloch v. Maryland,* 4 Wheat. 316 (1819). In other cases the Court has sought to determine whether an Act of Congress invades the province of state sovereignty reserved by the Tenth Amendment. *See, e.g., Garcia v. San Antonio Metropolitan Transit Authority,* 469 U.S. 528 (1985); *Lane County v. Oregon,* 7 Wall. 71 (1869). In a case like this one, involving the division of authority between federal and state governments, the two inquiries are mirror images of each other. If a power is delegated to Congress in the Constitution, the Tenth Amendment expressly disclaims any reservation of that power to the States; if a power is an attribute of state sovereignty reserved by the Tenth Amendment, it is necessarily a power the Constitution has not conferred on Congress. *See United States v. Oregon,* 366 U.S. 643, 649 (1961); *Case v. Bowles,* 327 U.S. 92, 102 (1946); *Oklahoma ex rel. Phillips v. Guy F. Atkinson Co.,* 313 U.S. 508, 534 (1941).

It is in this sense that the Tenth Amendment "states but a truism that all is retained which has not been surrendered." *United States v. Darby,* 312 U.S. 100, 124 (1941). As Justice Story put it, "this amendment is a mere affirmation of what, upon any just reasoning, is a necessary rule of interpreting the constitution. Being an instrument of limited and enumerated powers, it follows irresistibly, that what is not conferred, is withheld, and belongs to the state authorities." 3 J. Story, Commentaries on the Constitution of the United States 752 (1833). This has been the Court's consistent understanding: "The States unquestionably do retain a significant measure of sovereign authority . . . to the extent that the Constitution has not divested them of their original powers and transferred those powers to the Federal Government." *Garcia v. San Antonio Metropolitan Transit Authority, supra,* at 549 (internal quotation marks omitted).

Congress exercises its conferred powers subject to the limitations contained in the Constitution. Thus, for example, under the Commerce Clause Congress may regulate publishers engaged in interstate commerce, but Congress is constrained in the exercise of that power by the First Amendment. The Tenth Amendment likewise restrains the power of Congress, but this limit is not derived from the text of the Tenth Amendment itself, which, as we have discussed, is essentially a tautology. Instead, the Tenth Amendment confirms that the power of the Federal Government is subject to limits that may, in a given instance, reserve power to the States. The Tenth Amendment thus directs us to determine, as in this case, whether an incident of state sovereignty is protected by a limitation on an Article I power.

The benefits of this federal structure have been extensively catalogued elsewhere, *see, e.g., Gregory v. Ashcroft,* 501 U.S. at 457–460; Merritt, *The Guarantee Clause and State Autonomy: Federalism for a Third Century,* 88 COLUM. L. REV. 1, 3–10 (1988); McConnell, *Federalism: Evaluating the Founders' Design,* 54 U. CHI. L. REV. 1484, 1491–1511 (1987), but they need not concern us here. Our task would be the same even if one could prove that federalism secured no advantages to anyone. It consists not of devising our preferred system of government, but of understanding and applying the framework set forth in the Constitution. "The question is not what power the Federal Government ought to have but what powers in fact have been given by the people." *United States v. Butler,* 297 U.S. 1, 63 (1936).

This framework has been sufficiently flexible over the past two centuries to allow for enormous changes in the nature of government. The Federal Government undertakes activities today that would have been unimaginable to the Framers in two senses; first, because the Framers would not have conceived that any government would conduct such activities; and second, because the Framers would not have believed that the Federal Government, rather than the States, would assume such responsibilities. Yet the powers conferred upon the Federal Government by the Constitution were phrased in language broad enough to allow for the expansion of the Federal Government's role. . . . [The Court then discussed several instances where it has chosen to read the scope of federal enumerated powers more broadly because of underlying changes in society.]

The actual scope of the Federal Government's authority with respect to the States has changed over the years, therefore, but the constitutional structure underlying and limiting that authority has not. In the end, just as a cup may be half empty or half full, it makes no difference whether one views the question at issue in this case as one of ascertaining the limits of the power delegated to the Federal Government under the affirmative provisions of the Constitution or one of discerning the core of sovereignty retained by the States under the Tenth Amendment. Either way, we must determine whether any of the three challenged provisions of the Low-Level Radioactive Waste Policy Amendments Act of 1985 oversteps the boundary between federal and state authority.

B

Petitioners do not contend that Congress lacks the power to regulate the disposal of low level radioactive waste. Space in radioactive waste disposal sites is frequently sold by residents of one State to residents of another. Regulation of the resulting interstate market in waste disposal is therefore well within Congress' authority under the Commerce Clause. Cf. *Philadelphia v. New Jersey*, 437 U.S. 617, 621–623 (1978); *Fort Gratiot Sanitary Landfill, Inc. v. Michigan Dept. of Natural Resources*, 504 U.S. 353, 359 (1992). Petitioners likewise do not dispute that under the Supremacy Clause Congress could, if it wished, pre-empt state radioactive waste regulation. Petitioners contend only that the Tenth Amendment limits the power of Congress to regulate in the way it has chosen. Rather than addressing the problem of waste disposal by directly regulating the generators and disposers of waste, petitioners argue, Congress has impermissibly directed the States to regulate in this field.

Most of our recent cases interpreting the Tenth Amendment have concerned the authority of Congress to subject state governments to generally applicable laws. The Court's jurisprudence in this area has traveled an unsteady path. *See Maryland v. Wirtz*, 392 U.S. 183 (1968) (state schools and hospitals are subject to Fair Labor Standards Act); *National League of Cities v. Usery*, 426 U.S. 833 (1976) (overruling *Wirtz*) (state employers are not subject to Fair Labor Standards Act); *Garcia v. San Antonio Metropolitan Transit Authority*, 469 U.S. 528 (1985) (overruling *National League of Cities*) (state employers are once again subject to Fair Labor Standards Act). *See also New York v. United States*, 326 U.S. 572 (1946); *Fry v. United States*, 421 U.S. 542 (1975); *Transportation Union v. Long Island R. Co.*, 455 U.S. 678 (1982); *EEOC v. Wyoming*, 460 U.S. 226 (1983); *South Carolina v.*

Baker, 485 U.S. 505 (1988); *Gregory v. Ashcroft, supra.* This case presents no occasion to apply or revisit the holdings of any of these cases, as this is not a case in which Congress has subjected a State to the same legislation applicable to private parties. *Cf. FERC v. Mississippi*, 456 U.S. 742, 758–759 (1982).

This case instead concerns the circumstances under which Congress may use the States as implements of regulation; that is, whether Congress may direct or otherwise motivate the States to regulate in a particular field or a particular way. Our cases have established a few principles that guide our resolution of the issue.

1

As an initial matter, Congress may not simply "commandeer the legislative processes of the States by directly compelling them to enact and enforce a federal regulatory program." *Hodel v. Virginia Surface Mining & Reclamation Assn., Inc.*, 452 U.S. 264, 288 (1981). . . .

. . . While Congress has substantial powers to govern the Nation directly, including in areas of intimate concern to the States, the Constitution has never been understood to confer upon Congress the ability to require the States to govern according to Congress' instructions. *See Coyle v. Oklahoma*, 221 U.S. 559, 565 (1911). The Court has been explicit about this distinction. "Both the States and the United States existed before the Constitution. The people, through that instrument, established a more perfect union by substituting a national government, acting, with ample power, *directly upon the citizens*, instead of the Confederate government, which acted with powers, greatly restricted, only upon the States." *Lane County v. Oregon*, 7 Wall., at 76 (emphasis added). The Court has made the same point with more rhetorical flourish, although perhaps with less precision, on a number of occasions. In Chief Justice Chase's much-quoted words, "the preservation of the States, and the maintenance of their governments, are as much within the design and care of the Constitution as the preservation of the Union and the maintenance of the National government. The Constitution, in all its provisions, looks to an indestructible Union, composed of indestructible States." *Texas v. White*, 7 Wall. 700, 725 (1869). *See also Metcalf & Eddy v. Mitchell*, 269 U.S. 514, 523 (1926) ("neither government may destroy the other nor curtail in any substantial manner the exercise of its powers"); *Tafflin v. Levitt*, 493 U.S. 455, 458 (1990) ("under our federal system, the States possess sovereignty concurrent with that of the Federal Government"); *Gregory v. Ashcroft*, 501 U.S. at 461 ("the States retain substantial sovereign powers under our constitutional scheme, powers with which Congress does not readily interfere").

Indeed, the question whether the Constitution should permit Congress to employ state governments as regulatory agencies was a topic of lively debate among the Framers. [At this juncture, the Court undertook a discussion of constitutional history]. . . .

In the end, the Convention opted for a Constitution in which Congress would exercise its legislative authority directly over individuals rather than over States. . . .

In providing for a stronger central government, therefore, the Framers explicitly chose a Constitution that confers upon Congress the power to regulate individuals, not States. As we have seen, the Court has consistently respected this choice. We have always understood that even where Congress has the authority under the Constitution to pass laws requiring or prohibiting certain acts, it lacks the power directly to compel the States to require or prohibit those acts. *E.g., FERC v. Mississippi*, 456 U.S., at 762–766; *Hodel v. Virginia Surface Mining & Reclamation Assn.*, Inc., 452 U.S., at 288–289; *Lane County v. Oregon*, 7 Wall., at 76. The allocation of power contained in the Commerce Clause, for example, authorizes Congress to regulate interstate commerce directly; it does not authorize Congress to regulate state governments' regulation of interstate commerce.

2

This is not to say that Congress lacks the ability to encourage a State to regulate in a particular way, or that Congress may not hold out incentives to the States as a method of influencing a State's policy choices. Our cases have identified a variety of methods, short of outright coercion, by which Congress may urge a State to adopt a legislative program consistent with federal interests. Two of these methods are of particular relevance here.

First, under Congress' spending power, "Congress may attach conditions on the receipt of federal funds." *South Dakota v. Dole*, 483 U.S. at 206. Such conditions must (among other requirements) bear some relationship to the purpose of the federal spending, *id.*, at 207–208, and n. 3; otherwise, of course, the spending power could render academic the Constitution's other grants and limits of federal authority. Where the recipient of federal funds is a State, as is not unusual today, the conditions attached to the funds by Congress may influence a State's legislative choices. *See Kaden, Politics, Money, and State Sovereignty: The Judicial Role*, 79 COLUM. L. REV. 847, 874–881 (1979). *Dole* was one such case: The Court found no constitutional flaw in a federal statute directing the Secretary of Transportation to withhold federal highway funds from States failing to adopt Congress' choice of a minimum drinking age. Similar examples abound. *See, e.g., Fullilove v. Klutznick*, 448 U.S. 448, 478–480 (1980); *Massachusetts v. United States*, 435 U.S. 444, 461–462 (1978); *Lau v. Nichols*, 414 U.S. 563, 568–569 (1974); *Oklahoma v. Civil Service Comm'n*, 330 U.S. 127, 142–144 (1947).

Second, where Congress has the authority to regulate private activity under the Commerce Clause, we have recognized Congress' power to offer States the choice of regulating that activity according to federal standards or having state law pre-empted by federal regulation. *Hodel v. Virginia Surface Mining & Reclamation Assn., Inc.*, 456 U.S. at 288. *See also FERC v. Mississippi*, 452 U.S. at 764–765. This arrangement, which has been termed "a program of cooperative federalism," *Hodel*, 456 U.S. at 289, is replicated in numerous federal statutory schemes. These include the Clean Water Act, 86 Stat. 816, as amended, 33 U.S.C. § 1251 et seq., *see Arkansas v. Oklahoma*, 503 U.S. 91, 101 (1992) (Clean Water Act "anticipates a partnership between the States and the Federal Government, animated by a shared objective"); the Occupational Safety and Health Act of 1970, 84 Stat. 1590, 29 U.S.C. § 651 et seq., see *Gade v. National Solid Wastes Management Assn.*, 505 U.S. at 97 (1992); the Resource Conservation and Recovery Act of 1976, 90 Stat. 2796, as amended, 42 U.S.C. § 6901 et seq., *see United States Dept. of Energy v. Ohio*, 503 U.S. 607, 611–612 (1992); and the Alaska National Interest Lands Conservation Act, 94 Stat. 2374, 16 U.S.C. § 3101 et seq., *see Kenaitze Indian Tribe v. Alaska*, 860 F. 2d 312, 314 (CA9 1988), *cert. denied*, 491 U.S. 905 (1989).

By either of these two methods, as by any other permissible method of encouraging a State to conform to federal policy choices, the residents of the State retain the ultimate decision as to whether or not the State will comply. If a State's citizens view federal policy as sufficiently contrary to local interests, they may elect to decline a federal grant. If state residents would prefer their government to devote its attention and resources to problems other than those deemed important by Congress, they may choose to have the Federal Government rather than the State bear the expense of a federally mandated regulatory program, and they may continue to supplement that program to the extent state law is not preempted. Where Congress encourages state regulation rather than compelling it, state governments remain responsive to the local electorate's preferences; state officials remain accountable to the people.

By contrast, where the Federal Government compels States to regulate, the accountability of both state and federal officials is diminished. If the citizens of New York, for example, do not consider that making provision for the disposal of radioactive waste is in their best interest, they may elect state officials who share their view. That view can always be preempted under the Supremacy Clause if is contrary to the national view, but in such a case it is the Federal Government that makes the decision in full view of the public, and it will be federal officials that suffer the consequences if the decision turns out to be detrimental or unpopular. But where the Federal Government directs the States to regulate, it may be state officials who will bear the brunt of public disapproval, while the federal officials who devised the regulatory program may remain insulated from the electoral ramifications of their decision. Accountability is thus diminished when, due to federal coercion, elected state officials cannot regulate in accordance with the views of the local electorate in matters not preempted by federal regulation. *See* Merritt, 88 COLUM. L. REV., at 61–62; La Pierre, *Political Accountability in the National Political Process — The Alternative to Judicial Review of Federalism Issues*, 80 NW. U. L. REV. 577, 639–665 (1985).

With these principles in mind, we turn to the three challenged provisions of the Low-Level Radioactive Waste Policy Amendments Act of 1985.

III

The parties in this case advance two quite different views of the Act. As petitioners see it, the Act imposes a requirement directly upon the States that they regulate in the field of radioactive waste disposal in order to meet Congress' mandate that "each State shall be responsible for providing . . . for the disposal of . . . low-level radioactive waste." 42 U.S.C. § 2021c(a)(1)(A). Petitioners understand this provision as a direct command from Congress, enforceable independent of the three sets of incentives provided by the Act. Respondents, on the other hand, read this provision together with the incentives, and see the Act as affording the States three sets of choices. According to respondents, the Act permits a State to choose first between regulating pursuant to federal standards and losing the right to a share of the Secretary of Energy's escrow account; to choose second between regulating pursuant to federal standards and progressively losing access to disposal sites in other States; and to choose third between regulating pursuant to federal standards and taking title to the waste generated within the State. Respondents thus interpret § 2021c(a)(1)(A), despite the statute's use of the word "shall," to provide no more than an option which a State may elect or eschew.

The Act could plausibly be understood either as a mandate to regulate or as a series of incentives. Under petitioners' view, however, § 2021c(a)(1)(A) of the Act would clearly "commandeer the legislative processes of the States by directly compelling them to enact and enforce a federal regulatory program." *Hodel v. Virginia Surface Mining & Reclamation Assn., Inc.*, 452 U.S. at 288. We must reject this interpretation of the provision for two reasons. First, such an outcome would, to say the least, "upset the usual constitutional balance of federal and state powers." *Gregory v. Ashcroft*, 501 U.S. at 460. "It is incumbent upon the federal courts to be certain of Congress' intent before finding that federal law overrides this balance," *ibid.* (internal quotation marks omitted), but the Act's amenability to an equally plausible alternative construction prevents us from possessing such certainty. Second, "where an otherwise acceptable construction of a statute would raise serious constitutional problems, the Court will construe the statute to avoid such problems unless such construction is plainly contrary to the intent of Congress." *Edward J. DeBartolo Corp. v. Florida Gulf Coast Building & Construction Trades Council*, 485 U.S. 568, 575 (1988). This rule of statutory construction pushes us away from petitioners' understanding of § 2021c(a)(1)(A) of the Act, under which it compels the States to regulate according to Congress' instructions.

We therefore decline petitioners' invitation to construe § 2021c(a)(1)(A), alone and in isolation, as a command to the States independent of the remainder of the Act. Construed as a whole, the Act comprises three sets of "incentives" for the States to provide for the disposal of low level radioactive waste generated within their borders. We consider each in turn.

[In the next several sections of the opinion, the Court finds the monetary incentives and the access incentives to be constitutional under the Tenth Amendment. It then discusses the "take title" provision]:

The take title provision is of a different character. This third so-called "incentive" offers States, as an alternative to regulating pursuant to Congress' direction, the option of taking title to and possession of the low level radioactive waste generated within their borders and becoming liable for all damages waste generators suffer as a result of the States' failure to do so promptly. In this provision, Congress has crossed the line distinguishing encouragement from coercion . . . .

The take title provision offers state governments a "choice" of either accepting ownership of waste or regulating according to the instructions of Congress. Respondents do not claim that the Constitution would authorize Congress to impose either option as a freestanding requirement. On one hand, the Constitution would not permit Congress simply to transfer radioactive waste from generators to state governments. Such a forced transfer, standing alone, would in principle be no different than a congressionally compelled subsidy from state governments to radioactive waste producers. The same is true of the provision requiring the States to become liable for the generators' damages. Standing alone, this provision would be indistinguishable from an Act of Congress directing the States to assume the liabilities of certain state residents. Either type of federal action would "commandeer" state governments into the service of federal regulatory purposes, and would for this reason be inconsistent with the Constitution's division of authority between federal and state governments. On the other hand, the second alternative held out to state governments — regulating pursuant to Congress' direction — would, standing alone, present a simple command to state governments to implement legislation enacted by Congress. As we have seen, the Constitution does not empower Congress to subject state governments to this type of instruction.

Because an instruction to state governments to take title to waste, standing alone, would be beyond the authority of Congress, and because a direct order to regulate, standing alone, would also be beyond the authority of Congress, it follows that Congress lacks the power to offer the States a choice between the two. Unlike the first two sets of incentives, the take title incentive does not represent the conditional exercise of any congressional power enumerated in the Constitution. In this provision, Congress has not held out the threat of exercising its spending power or its commerce power; it has instead held out the threat, should the States not regulate according to one federal instruction, of simply forcing the States to submit to another federal instruction. A choice between two unconstitutionally coercive regulatory techniques is no choice at all. Either way, "the Act commandeers the legislative processes of the States by directly compelling them to enact and enforce a federal regulatory program," *Hodel v. Virginia Surface Mining & Reclamation Assn., Inc., supra,* at 288, an outcome that has never been understood to lie within the authority conferred upon Congress by the Constitution. . . .

VII

Some truths are so basic that, like the air around us, they are easily overlooked. Much of the Constitution is concerned with setting forth the form of our government, and the courts have traditionally invalidated measures deviating from that form. The result may appear "formalistic" in a given case to partisans of the measure at issue, because such measures are typically the product of the era's perceived necessity. But the Constitution protects us from our own best intentions: It divides power among sovereigns and among branches of government precisely so that we may resist the temptation to concentrate power in one location as an expedient solution to the crisis of the day. The shortage of disposal sites for radioactive waste is a pressing national problem, but a judiciary that licensed extra-constitutional government with each issue of comparable gravity would, in the long run, be far worse.

States are not mere political subdivisions of the United States. State governments are neither regional offices nor administrative agencies of the Federal Government. The positions occupied by state officials appear nowhere on the Federal Government's most detailed organizational chart. The Constitution instead "leaves to the several States a residuary and inviolable sovereignty," The Federalist

No. 39, p. 245 (C. Rossiter ed. 1961), reserved explicitly to the States by the Tenth Amendment.

Whatever the outer limits of that sovereignty may be, one thing is clear: The Federal Government may not compel the States to enact or administer a federal regulatory program. The Constitution permits both the Federal Government and the States to enact legislation regarding the disposal of low level radioactive waste. The Constitution enables the Federal Government to pre-empt state regulation contrary to federal interests, and it permits the Federal Government to hold out incentives to the States as a means of encouraging them to adopt suggested regulatory schemes. It does not, however, authorize Congress simply to direct the States to provide for the disposal of the radioactive waste generated within their borders. While there may be many constitutional methods of achieving regional self-sufficiency in radioactive waste disposal, the method Congress has chosen is not one of them. The judgment of the Court of Appeals is accordingly

Affirmed in part and reversed in part.

[Concurring and Dissenting opinions omitted.]

NOTES AND QUESTIONS

1. ***Cooperative Federalism.*** *New York* explains the constitutional basis for "cooperative federalism," a central feature of many federal pollution control statutes. Those statutes provide for state enforcement of federal standards, but they take care not to coerce states. If a state fails to abide by a federal statutory directive, it suffers no penalty for that failure, save the fact that the federal government will implement those standards on its own and thereafter maintain a more robust presence in the state. In many instances, states would rather take the lead in environmental enforcement than endure the federal presence. *See* Chapters 9–11, *infra.*

States are more inclined to take on the responsibility of enforcing federal standards when the federal government helps with the costs. That is what the federal government does.

2. ***Related Issues.*** Suppose a federal statute imposed requirements not upon a state or a state agency but upon state employees. Would such a requirement implicate the Tenth Amendment? May the federal government act to entirely displace and render null and void a state regulatory program of longstanding duration, one fully authorized by the state's sovereign police power and qualifying as a traditional area of state regulatory activity?

3. ***Executive Order No. 12,612.*** On October 26, 1987, President Ronald Reagan issued an Executive Order, entitled "Federalism," to formally establish the position of the executive branch on matters of federal and state power. Exec. Order No. 12,612, 52 Fed. Reg. 41,685 (Oct. 30, 1987). The Order provided, in relevant part, that "[i]n the absence of clear constitutional or statutory authority, the presumption of sovereignty should rest with the individual States. Uncertainties should be resolved against regulation at the national level." *Id.* at § 2(i). The Order further directed that "[f]ederal action limiting the policymaking discretion of the States

should be taken only where constitutional authority for the action is clear and certain and the national activity is necessitated by the presence of a problem of national scope." *Id.* at § 3(b).

4. ***Low Level Radioactive Waste Regulation.*** *New York* describes low level radioactive waste ("LLRW") as "present in luminous watch dials, smoke alarms, measurement devices, medical fluids, research materials, and the protective gear and construction materials used by workers at nuclear power plants." *See New York*, 505 U.S. 144, *supra*. Such wastes can also include wiping rags, mops, filters, reactor water treatment residues, parts from inside reactor vessels of nuclear power plants, and laboratory animal carcasses and tissues. Major generators of LLRWs include utilities, medical facilities, agricultural and scientific research institutions, and providers of consumer products and services. The federal Nuclear Regulatory Commission has classified LLRWs as Class A (least radioactivity), Class B (relatively more radioactivity), and Class C (containing the highest relative concentrations of radioactivity). For disposal purposes, regulated LLRWs are packaged in containers suitable for the level of hazard they present; in some cases, encasement in lead is necessary. Supposedly, the best method of disposing of these "radwastes" is in above-ground concrete vaults designed to resist erosion, cracking, and even tornadoes and earthquakes. The vaults can be large: one such vault is 30 feet tall, 650 feet long, 25 feet wide, and contains 12 cells. When filled, vaults can be sealed with additional concrete and capped. The more usual disposal method is in trenches. There are currently three LLRW disposal sites in the nation. They are located in Barnwell, North Carolina (Class A–C wastes), Richland, Washington (Class A–C wastes), and Clive, Utah (Class A wastes only). Approximately 4 million cubic feet of LLRWs were disposed of in 2005, over 3.9 million cubic feet of which were transferred to the Utah site. The South Carolina site, on the other hand, took in the lion's share of LLRWs as measured by curies.

2. Preemption

"This Constitution, and the Laws of the United States which shall be made in Pursuance thereof; and all Treaties made, or which shall be made, under the authority of the United States, shall be the Supreme Law of the Land; and the Judges in every State shall be bound thereby, any Thing in the Constitution or Laws of any State to the Contrary notwithstanding." U.S. CONST., art. VI, cl. 2.

FEIKEMA v. TEXACO, INC.
16 F.3d 1408 (4th Cir. 1994)

JUDGES: MURNAGHAN and NIEMEYER, CIRCUIT JUDGES, and YOUNG, SENIOR UNITED STATES DISTRICT JUDGE for the District of Maryland, sitting by designation.

NIEMEYER, CIRCUIT JUDGE:

The question of first impression presented on this appeal is whether the Resource Conservation and Recovery Act, 42 U.S.C. § 6901 et seq., or an administrative order entered pursuant to it, preempts state common law causes of action for nuisance and trespass. Several homeowners in Fairfax, Virginia, filed a complaint in March 1993 against Texaco, Inc. and Star Enterprises (collectively "Texaco"), alleging that a plume of oil which leaked from a nearby petroleum distribution terminal owned by Texaco damaged and continues to damage their properties. The complaint requested injunctive relief and demanded damages in an unspecified amount. The district court dismissed the complaint on preemption grounds, and the homeowners appealed. Concluding that the claims for injunctive relief are pre-empted but that claims for state law damages are not, we vacate the judgment and remand the case for further proceedings consistent with this opinion.

I

Texaco owns and operates a petroleum distribution terminal located at 3800 Pickett Road in Fairfax, Virginia. The terminal, also known as the Tank Farm, consists of office and warehouse facilities, a truck loading rack, nine aboveground storage tanks with a total storage capacity of over 17 million gallons, and eleven underground storage tanks with a total capacity of 40,000 gallons. The Tank Farm is located above a "recharge" area of an aquifer, which is a major underground water source for nearby creeks and streams. It is also near residential properties owned by the homeowners in this case and by others.

Beginning sometime in 1988, petroleum products, consisting of diesel fuel, aviation fuel and gasoline, leaked into the soil and groundwater at the Tank Farm and the surrounding land, and an oil plume began moving toward the properties of the homeowners. Some constituent parts of these petroleum products are toxic and, under certain conditions, constitute a health hazard. Sometime in September 1990, visible petroleum products appeared in Crook Branch Creek which flows near and along the homeowners' properties. The Virginia State Water Control Board ("the State Board") investigated the leak. Pursuant to the direction of the State Board, Texaco conducted tests on the tanks and the lines, installed on-site and off-site monitoring wells, and installed an oil recovery trench along a portion of the Tank Farm. Although almost 7,000 gallons of oil were recovered by these means, the State Board concluded that leaking was continuing and that the appropriate control or elimination of such release had not been implemented. In May 1991, the State Board requested that the United States Environmental Protection Agency (the "EPA") assume responsibility for investigating the oil leak and recovering the released products. In response, the EPA created an interagency task force to take further steps.

Proceeding under the authority granted by section 311(c) of the Clean Water Act, 33 U.S.C. § 1321(c), section 1431 of the Safe Drinking Water Act, 42 U.S.C. § 300i, and section 7003 of the Resource Conservation and Recovery Act ("RCRA"), 42 U.S.C. § 6973, the EPA conducted an investigation, held a hearing, and negotiated an administrative consent order (the "Consent Order") with Texaco, which was entered on September 23, 1991. The EPA found, as a basis for the Consent Order, that if proper measures were not implemented, petroleum would continue to move under the Tank Farm with the natural ground water flow and would migrate to and enter sanitary and storm sewer pipes, eventually entering the basements of residences in the immediate vicinity of the Tank Farm. The EPA also determined that the plume might present an imminent and substantial endangerment to health or the environment within the meaning of section 7003(a) of the RCRA, 42 U.S.C. § 6973(a).

The Consent Order required Texaco to place booms on Crook Branch Creek to contain the oily sheen on the surface, and to use sorbent to collect and clean up the oil. The EPA also ordered Texaco to excavate and remove soils contaminated with oil, to operate an emergency measures pumping system, and to monitor weekly wells and storm sewers for the presence of oil. In addition, the EPA put forth an "Emergency Measures Plan," requiring Texaco, inter alia, to develop an appropriate corrective actions plan to eliminate the leaks; to submit this plan to EPA for review and approval; and to implement EPA-approved corrective actions under an EPA-approved schedule. While the order addressed measures to eliminate the causes of the leaking and to neutralize the adverse effects of the oil plume, it recognized that the response action might not address all contamination and that additional long-term measures might be required. The order was scheduled to terminate when its directives were met to the EPA's satisfaction. Since the entry of the order, Texaco has undertaken the corrective steps as required, and there is no evidence in the record that it is not complying with the terms of the order, which still remains in effect.

In March 1993, the homeowners filed a complaint against Texaco under the district court's diversity jurisdiction, alleging claims for nuisance and trespass under Virginia common law. In their complaint, the homeowners alleged that "even under a Consent Order with and under the direction of the Environmental Protection Agency," Texaco has failed to remedy the leaking, and that they "have had, and continue to be threatened with actual petroleum pollution from the Tank Farm in the soils of the creeks on or near their property." The complaint further alleged that the pollution confronts them with a nuisance that "threatens the destruction of their property and danger to their health," and that "direct and actual pollution of the creek beds and the flow of globules of free phase hydrocarbons under their property constitute a trespass" upon their properties. The homeowners requested permanent injunctive relief for greater remedial measures than those included in the Consent Order, and they demanded "such damages, interest and costs to which the Plaintiffs may be justly entitled."

On Texaco's motion to dismiss the complaint under Federal Rule of Civil Procedure 12(b)(6), the district court dismissed the action on preemption grounds. The court stated:

> I think the injunctive relief of the type the plaintiffs seek here would conflict with and frustrate probably the purpose of Congress in its EPA remediation efforts under the RCRA. Even though the plaintiffs do not purport to bring their action under that, I think that Act and the action taken here with the remediation effort and order preempts this field, and I think that any injunction I would issue would conflict with that.

This appeal followed.***

III

We now turn to the principal question presented on appeal, whether the RCRA, or the administrative order entered pursuant to it, preempts state common law causes of action. A review of the applicable preemption principles is useful.

The Supremacy Clause of the United States Constitution mandates that "the Laws of the United States . . . shall be the supreme Law of the Land; and the Judges in every State shall be bound thereby, any Thing in the Constitution or Laws of any State to the Contrary notwithstanding." U.S. CONST. art. VI, § 2. Thus, federal legislation, if enacted pursuant to Congress' lawful authority, can nullify conflicting state or local actions. *See McCulloch v. Maryland*, 17 U.S. (4 Wheat.) 316, 427, 4 L. Ed. 579 (1819); *Worm v. American Cyanamid Co.*, 970 F.2d 1301, 1304–05 (4th Cir. 1992).

There are two ways for preemption to occur. First, Congress may expressly provide that federal law supplants state authority in a particular field, or its intent to preempt may be implicit in regulating so pervasively in the field as not to leave any room within which a state may act. *See Rice v. Santa Fe Elevator Corp.*, 331 U.S. 218, 230, 67 S. Ct. 1146, 91 L. Ed. 1447 (1947); *Worm*, 970 F.2d at 1304. And second, even absent an express or implied congressional intent to preempt state authority in a field, state law is preempted to the extent that it actually conflicts with federal law. *See Pacific Gas & Elec. Co. v. State Energy Resources Conservation & Dev. Com.*, 461 U.S. 190, 204, 103 S. Ct. 1713, 75 L. Ed. 2d 752 (1983).

As the Supreme Court recently instructed, "consideration of issues arising under the Supremacy Clause 'starts with the assumption that the historic police powers of the States are not to be superseded by . . . Federal Act unless that [is] the clear and manifest purpose of Congress.'" *Cipollone v. Liggett Group, Inc.*, 112 S. Ct. 2608, 2617, 120 L. Ed. 2d 407 (1992) (quoting *Rice v. Santa Fe Elevator Corp.*, 331 U.S. 218, 230, 67 S. Ct. 1146, 91 L. Ed. 1447 (1947)). Moreover, in deciphering congressional intent, we are guided by principles of federalism. Where "the regulated conduct touched interests so deeply rooted in local feeling and responsibility, . . . in the absence of compelling congressional direction, [the court] could not infer that Congress had deprived the States of the power to act." *San Diego Bldg. Trades Council v. Garmon*, 359 U.S. 236, 244, 79 S. Ct. 773, 3 L. Ed. 2d 775 (1959). Particularly with respect to the potential preemption of common law actions, the Supreme Court has instructed,

> A common-law right, even absent a saving clause, is not to be abrogated "unless it be found that the preexisting right is so repugnant to the statute that the survival of such right would in effect deprive the subsequent statute of its efficacy; in other words, render its provisions nugatory."

Nader v. Allegheny Airlines, Inc., 426 U.S. 290, 298, 96 S. Ct. 1978, 48 L. Ed. 2d 643 (1976) (quoting *Texas & Pacific R. Co. v. Abilene Cotton Oil Co.*, 204 U.S. 426, 437, 27 S. Ct. 350, 51 L. Ed. 553 (1907)). The ultimate touchstone of preemption analysis is the purpose of Congress. *See Malone v. White Motor Corp.*, 435 U.S. 497, 504, 98 S. Ct. 1185, 55 L. Ed. 2d 443 (1978). When Congress' intent regarding preemption is unclear, state law must nevertheless yield when it conflicts with federal law. In making the determination of whether state law conflicts with federal law, the test to apply is whether "it is impossible to comply with both state and federal law" or whether "the state law stands as an obstacle to the accomplishment of the full purposes and objectives" of federal law. *Silkwood v. Kerr-McGee Corp.*, 464 U.S. 238, 248, 104 S. Ct. 615, 78 L. Ed. 2d 443 (1984); *see also Worm*, 970 F.2d at 1305.

With such principles at hand, we now turn to the facts to see whether the RCRA, or the administrative consent order entered in this case under section 7003 of the RCRA, preempts state law trespass or nuisance actions.

A

The RCRA contains no provision which mandates comprehensive preemption of all state laws in the field of hazardous waste removal being regulated by the Act. The task, therefore, is to determine whether the regulatory scheme is so comprehensive in that field as to leave no room within which the states may act, or whether any provisions in the Act actually conflict with the state causes of action.

Although the RCRA is national in scope and universal in coverage, we believe that its provisions do not regulate so pervasively as to occupy the field completely. Any doubt on this point is removed by the explicit provisions in the Act which reveal a contrary intent. First, even though the RCRA declares that it is a "national policy of the United States that, wherever feasible, the generation of hazardous waste is to be reduced or eliminated as expeditiously as possible," 42 U.S.C. § 6902(b), a separate provision also states that it is the will of Congress that the RCRA guide "a cooperative effort among the Federal, State, and local governments and private enterprises." 42 U.S.C. § 6902(a)(11). In addition, provisions in the RCRA allow states to run their own waste management programs, although the Act does require federal approval of such state plans. *See* 42 U.S.C. § 6943. Thus, the legislation seems to contemplate state law action, rather than preempt it in its entirety.

The homeowners argue that the general savings clause found in the RCRA is conclusive of Congress' intent to preserve state common law actions. That clause states:

> (f) Other Rights Preserved:
>
> Nothing in this section shall restrict any right which any person (or class of persons) may have under any statute or common law to seek enforcement of any standard or requirement relating to the management of solid waste or hazardous waste, or to seek any other relief (including relief against the Administrator or a State agency).

42 U.S.C. § 6972(f). Although the Supreme Court has acknowledged that a savings clause such as § 6972(f) does "negate[] the inference that Congress 'left no room' for state causes of action," *International Paper Co. v. Ouellette*, 479 U.S. 481, 492, 107 S. Ct. 805, 93 L. Ed. 2d 883 (1987), that negation, standing alone, is not determinative of the preemption analysis. In *Ouellette*, the Supreme Court found that a similar savings clause found in the Clean Water Act did not compel the finding that there was no preemption, stating, "[the savings clause] merely says that 'nothing in this section,' i.e., the citizen-suit provisions, shall affect an injured party's

right to seek relief under state law; it does not purport to preclude preemption of state law by other provisions of the Act." 479 U.S. at 493. The same conclusion is therefore reached under the RCRA, because 42 U.S.C. § 6972(f) also is found in a general citizen-suit provision of the RCRA. The natural reading of the phrase, "nothing in this section shall restrict" does not preclude preemption by other sections of the RCRA. The Supreme Court in Ouellette also cautioned against giving too much meaning to such savings clauses:

> The fact that the language of [the saving clause] is repeated in haec verba in the citizen-suit provisions of a vast array of environmental legislation . . . indicates that it does not reflect any considered judgment about what other remedies were previously available or continue to be available under any particular statute.

479 U.S. at 494 n.14 (citation omitted). Notwithstanding these admonitions, when we consider the entire legislative scheme of the RCRA together with the language of 42 U.S.C. § 6972(f), we are led to conclude that the RCRA does not preempt by implication the field staked out by the Act's regulation. Nevertheless, it remains to be determined whether state common law actions are preempted by an actual conflict with some provision of the Act.

B

Texaco contends that the relief requested by the homeowners in their common law claims would conflict with the EPA's authority under section 7003 of the RCRA to act on "imminent hazards," or with the Consent Order entered pursuant to section 7003. Texaco maintains that it was the intent of Congress that once the EPA acts under the imminent hazard provision, it has the exclusive authority to remedy the hazard.

Section 7003 of the RCRA, as amended in 1984, states:

Imminent Hazard:

(a) Authority of Administrator

> Notwithstanding any other provision of this chapter, upon receipt of evidence that the past or present handling, storage, treatment, transportation or disposal of any solid waste or hazardous waste may present an imminent and substantial endangerment to health or the environment, the Administrator may bring suit on behalf of the United States in the appropriate district court against any person . . . who has contributed or who is contributing to such handling, storage, treatment, transportation or disposal to restrain such person. . . . The Administrator may also, after notice to the affected State, take other action under this section including, but not limited to, issuing such orders as may be necessary to protect public health and the environment.

42 U.S.C. § 6973(a).

We find nothing in section 7003 that gives the EPA exclusive authority to act, nor do we find anything to suggest such a conclusion in the legislative history. . . .

. . . On the contrary, the legislative history recited indicates that while Congress intended for the EPA to have broad authority to act in an imminent hazard situation, it also intended such action to complement other efforts and remedies. Finding nothing in the language of the Act or in its legislative history which confers on the EPA the exclusive authority to act in such situations, we conclude that section 7003, which authorizes the EPA to act, does not, in the absence of some EPA action, conflict with the state law causes of action asserted by the homeowners.

Our conclusion does not end our preemption analysis, however. We must still examine whether the Consent Order, entered pursuant to the EPA's authority under § 7003, preempts the homeowners' state law claims on the ground that any state law remedy would conflict with the Consent Order.

C

Texaco argues that homeowners are, through their state law actions for nuisance and trespass, seeking injunctive relief that would conflict with the existing Consent Order between Texaco and the EPA. Texaco argues further that complying with any court order based on state law would force Texaco to violate the Consent Order's requirement that any corrective action be submitted to and approved by the EPA. Thus, Texaco maintains that any such state law remedies are preempted by the Consent Order.

Article VI of the Constitution provides for the supremacy of federal laws over "anything" in the constitution or laws of the states that conflict. Although the issue is not explicitly raised by the homeowners in this case, we must first establish that the EPA's Consent Order may derive rights of supremacy from the clause that elevates federal laws.

The Supreme Court has held that federal regulations issued by agencies have "no less preemptive effect than federal statutes." *Capital Cities Cable, Inc. v. Crisp*, 467 U.S. 691, 699, 104 S. Ct. 2694, 81 L. Ed. 2d 580 (1984) (quoting *Fidelity Federal Savings & Loan Assn. v. De la Cuesta*, 458 U.S. 141, 153, 73 L. Ed. 2d 664, 102 S. Ct. 3014 (1982)). Indeed, even if an agency, rather than Congress, resolves to preempt an area, its determination will be enforced to preempt conflicting state regulations so long as the determination represents "a reasonable accommodation of conflicting policies that are within the agency's domain." *Capital Cities*, 467 U.S. at 700. The court's role in that case is to determine only whether the agency exceeded its statutory authority or acted arbitrarily. *See Fidelity Federal*, 458 U.S. at 153.

Accordingly, we hold that when the EPA, acting within valid statutory authority of the RCRA and not arbitrarily, enters into a consent order, that order will also preempt conflicting state regulation, including a federal court order based on state common law. *See United States v. Akzo Coatings of America, Inc.*, 949 F.2d 1409, 1454–57 (6th Cir. 1991) (holding that consent decree entered into between the EPA and defendants to engage in remedial cleanup of hazardous waste pursuant to CERCLA preempted further state law actions seeking injunctive and declaratory relief that would conflict with the consent decree); *cf. Colorado v. Idarado Mining Co.*, 916 F.2d 1486 (10th Cir. 1990) (holding that states may not obtain an order under CERCLA apart from the terms of a valid administrative consent order obtained by the EPA under CERCLA), *cert. denied*, 499 U.S. 960, 113 L. Ed. 2d 648, 111 S. Ct. 1584 (1991).

We have previously held that the test for determining whether state law conflicts with federal law is whether "it is impossible to comply with both state and federal law" or whether "the state law stands as an obstacle to the accomplishment of the full purposes and objectives" of federal law. *Worm*, 970 F.2d at 1305 (quoting *Silkwood*, 464 U.S. at 248). The same test applies in determining whether a state-ordered injunction would conflict with the EPA's Consent Order.

The Consent Order entered on September 23, 1991, required Texaco to implement certain immediate remedial measures, to submit to the EPA emergency measures plans for EPA review and selection, and once a plan is selected, to implement the plan under an EPA-approved schedule. While the immediate requirements have been satisfied, the record does not reveal the status of the plan because the complaint in this case was dismissed at an early stage. There is, however, no evidence that the EPA is, to date, in any way dissatisfied with Texaco's progress.

In these circumstances, the injunctive relief requested by the homeowners from the court would conflict with the remedial measures selected and supervised by the EPA. The homeowners, in their complaint, have asked the district court to order excavation, treatment and replacement of contaminated soil to a specified depth and over a specified area; they have requested that the court direct "enhanced ground water extraction and bio-remediation to reduce the off-site contamination"; and they have requested the construction of a "free phase hydrocarbon trench removal system across the water table." The EPA order addresses the same site and conditions covered by the homeowners' suit and provides its mandatory response, as authorized by § 7003 of the RCRA. Not only would the court, if it granted the relief, be substituting its judgment for the authorized judgment of the EPA, the court also would be usurping the review role given by statute to the EPA. *See* 42 U.S.C. § 6973.

Accordingly, we hold that the homeowners' claims with respect to the contamination described in the complaint, to the extent they seek injunctive relief before the EPA's Consent Order is fulfilled and terminated, are preempted by the EPA's Consent Order. . . .

IV

. . . .

Texaco conceded at oral argument that if the complaint were construed as one for damages as well as for injunctive relief, they would agree that the RCRA does not preempt the damages claims. We think the law confirms its position.

The Supreme Court has held repeatedly that state law damages claims are not necessarily preempted by federal statutes that regulate the same field. For instance, in *Cipollone [v. Liggett Group, Inc.*, 112 S. Ct. 2608 (1992)], the Supreme Court held that a federal warning label requirement on cigarette packages does not preempt state common law damage actions. In *Silkwood [v. Kerr-McGee. supra]*, the Supreme Court also held that federal statute regulating nuclear safety did not preempt state law tort suits seeking damages. Similarly, we held in *Worm v. American Cyanamid Co.* [*supra*] that the Federal Insecticide, Fungicide and Rodenticide Act did not preempt state tort actions seeking damages for breach of federally-imposed standards.

Moreover, state law damages claims would not conflict with the Consent Order, which makes no provision for the payment of damages to the homeowners. Indeed, section 7003, the provision under which the order was entered, gives the EPA authority to seek injunctive relief but no authority to seek damages on behalf of private parties.

V

[Remainder of majority opinion, and the concurring opinion, are omitted].

NOTES AND QUESTIONS

1. ***Problems.*** Assume that both the federal and state governments establish legal controls on the discharge of pollutants by persons into waters such as rivers, lakes, and streams. Using the principles of conflict preemption, what is the preemptive effect of federal legislation in the following examples:

(A)   federal law prohibits any discharge of Pollutant A into the nation's waters at a concentration in excess of ten parts of Pollutant A for each one million parts of water in the waste stream (a 10 ppm standard); state law requires a concentration of no more than 5 ppm (a more stringent standard);

(B)   federal law imposes a 10 ppm standard on Pollutant A; state law imposes a 15 ppm standard (a less stringent standard);

(C)   federal law imposes a 10 ppm standard; state law imposes a 10 ppm standard (an equally stringent standard);

(D)   federal law imposes a 10 ppm standard for Pollutant A; state law imposes 10 ppm standard for Pollutant A and a 5 ppm standard for Pollutant B. Pollutant B is unregulated by federal law;

(E)   federal law imposes a 10 ppm standard for Pollutant A. State law requires Pollutant A to be discharged at no less than 15 ppm;

(F)   federal law imposes a 10 ppm standard; state law requires the installation a particular piece of pollution control technology that will allow for compliance with the federal standard but which increases the cost of compliance with that federal standard by a factor of ten;

(G)   Please answer (A) to (F) above, but assume that federal law has occupied the field.

2. ***Savings Clauses.*** When Congress enacted its fleet of pollution control statutes, it did not seek to supplant state law-based pollution control statutes. On the contrary, it wanted to preserve state law, at least to some extent. Accordingly,

these federal statutes have "savings clause" provisions in them. *See, e.g.*, § 510 of the Clean Water Act:

> *State authority.* Except as expressly provided in this chapter, nothing in this chapter shall (1) preclude or deny the right of any State or political subdivision thereof or interstate agency to adopt or enforce (A) any standard or limitation respecting discharges of pollutants, or (B) any requirement respecting control or abatement of pollution; except that if [a federal water pollution restriction] is in effect . . . , such State or political subdivision or interstate agency may not adopt or enforce any [state law-based water pollution restriction] which is less stringent than the [counterpart federal restriction].

33 U.S.C. § 1370. *See also* 16 U.S.C. § 1535(f) (Endangered Species Act); 42 U.S.C. § 6991g (Resource Conservation and Recovery Act (relating to regulation of underground storage tanks)); 42 U.S.C. § 9658 (Comprehensive Environmental Response, Compensation, and Liability Act).

By expressly preempting less stringent state pollution control standards, these savings clauses establish the federal standard as the legal floor below which no pollution control measure may fall.

3. *Two Masters.* Since both federal and state law operate in this area of regulation, a single action by a person may contravene both federal and state law and expose the violator to litigation and penalties in both federal and state court. Would dual litigation of this sort violate any constitutional rights of the defendant? (no)

4. *Citizen Suits.* The plaintiff in a cause of action in federal court which alleges a violation of a federal pollution control program requirement will typically be the federal agency which administers the program. On numerous occasions, however, the plaintiff can be a member of the public. This is because federal pollution control statutes often contain "citizen suit" provisions that authorize private individuals to file lawsuits to enforce provisions of federal law. *See, e.g.*, 33 U.S.C. § 1365 (Clean Water Act); 42 U.S.C. § 7604 (Clean Air Act); 42 U.S.C. § 6972 (Resource Conservation and Recovery Act); 16 U.S.C. § 1540 (Endangered Species Act); 42 U.S.C. § 9659 (Comprehensive Environmental Response, Compensation, and Liability Act). Under typical citizen suit provisions, an individual may file a cause of action against a polluter if the relevant federal agency has failed to do so, but only upon notice to the agency of the individual's intention to take up the matter.

Citizen suit provisions in federal statutes may expressly preserve the rights of citizen suit plaintiffs to proceed under state or common law. *See, e.g.*, 33 U.S.C. § 1365(e) (Clean Water Act); 42 U.S.C. § 7604(e) (Clean Air Act); 42 U.S.C. § 6972(f) (Resource Conservation and Recovery Act); 42 U.S.C. § 9659(h) (Comprehensive Environmental Response, Compensation, and Liability Act). *See also Feikema*, 16 F.3d 1408, *supra*. These are savings clauses of a sort because, while they may not negate the preemptive effects of *other* provisions of the federal statutes in which they appear, they "negate the inference" that state law has been preempted entirely.

5. ***Displacement of Federal Common Law.*** The above material examines how federal law can preempt state law. Indeed, both federal statutory and common law can preempt state law. The reader should be aware as well that federal statutory law can displace *federal* common law. This is not preemption in the classic sense; thus, the term "displacement." *See, e.g., American Electric Power v. Connecticut*, 131 S. Ct. 2527 (2011): "Legislative displacement of federal common law does not require the "same sort of evidence of a clear and manifest [congressional] purpose" demanded for preemption of state law . . . (*citation omitted*). . . . '[D]ue regard for the presuppositions of our embracing federal system . . . as a promoter of democracy,' . . . (*citations omitted*) . . . does not enter the calculus, for it is primarily the office of Congress, not the federal courts, to prescribe national policy in areas of special federal interest . . . (*citation omitted*). . . . The test for whether congressional legislation excludes the declaration of federal common law is simply whether the statute 'speak[s] directly to [the] question' at issue . . . (*citations omitted*)." (The *AEP* decision is set forth in Chapter 9, *infra*).

3. Dormant Commerce Clause

"The Congress shall have Power . . . to regulate Commerce with foreign Nations, and among the several States, and with the Indian Tribes." U.S. Const., art. I, § 8, cl. 3. "Although the Commerce Clause is by its text an affirmative grant of power to Congress to regulate interstate and foreign commerce, the Clause has long been recognized as containing a self-executing negative command prohibiting states from taking certain actions respecting interstate commerce even in the absence of federal action." *CTS Corp. v. Dynamics Corp. of Am.*, 481 U.S. 69, 87, 107 S. Ct. 1637 (1987); *see also Oregon Waste Sys. v. Department of Envtl. Quality*, 511 U.S. 93, 97, 114 S. Ct. 1345, 1349 (1994). One of the "great silences of the Constitution," *H. P. Hood & Sons, Inc. v. Du Mond*, 336 U.S. 525, 535, 69 S. Ct. 657, 663 (1949), this limitation is known as the dormant Commerce Clause.

UNITED HAULERS ASSOCIATION, INC. v. ONEIDA-HERKIMER SOLID WASTE MANAGEMENT AUTHORITY
550 U.S. 330, 127 S. Ct. 1786 (2007)

Roberts, C. J., delivered the opinion of the Court, except as to Part II-D. Souter, Ginsburg, and Breyer, JJ., joined that opinion in full. Scalia, J., filed an opinion concurring as to Parts I and II-A through II-C. Thomas, J., filed an opinion concurring in the judgment. Alito, J., filed a dissenting opinion, in which Stevens and Kennedy, JJ., joined.

Chief Justice Roberts delivered the opinion of the Court, except as to Part II-D.

"Flow control" ordinances require trash haulers to deliver solid waste to a particular waste processing facility. In *C & A Carbone, Inc. v. Clarkstown*, 511 U.S. 383, 114 S. Ct. 1677, 128 L. Ed. 2d 399 (1994), this Court struck down under the Commerce Clause a flow control ordinance that forced haulers to deliver waste to a particular *private* processing facility. In this case, we face flow control ordinances quite similar to the one invalidated in *Carbone*. The only salient difference is that the laws at issue here require haulers to bring waste to facilities owned and operated by a state-created public benefit corporation. We find this difference constitutionally significant. Disposing of trash has been a traditional government activity for years, and laws that favor the government in such areas — but treat every private business, whether in-state or out-of-state, exactly the same — do not discriminate against interstate commerce for purposes of the Commerce Clause. Applying the Commerce Clause test reserved for regulations that do not discriminate against interstate commerce, we uphold these ordinances because any incidental burden they may have on interstate commerce does not outweigh the benefits they confer on the citizens of Oneida and Herkimer Counties.

I

Located in central New York, Oneida and Herkimer Counties span over 2,600 square miles and are home to about 306,000 residents. Traditionally, each city, town, or village within the Counties has been responsible for disposing of its own waste. Many had relied on local landfills, some in a more environmentally responsible fashion than others.

By the 1980s, the Counties confronted what they could credibly call a solid waste " 'crisis.' " Brief for Respondents 4. Many local landfills were operating without permits and in violation of state regulations. Sixteen were ordered to close and remediate the surrounding environment, costing the public tens of millions of dollars. These environmental problems culminated in a federal clean-up action against a landfill in Oneida County; the defendants in that case named over 600 local businesses and several municipalities and school districts as third-party defendants.

The "crisis" extended beyond health and safety concerns. The Counties had an uneasy relationship with local waste management companies, enduring price fixing, pervasive overcharging, and the influence of organized crime. Dramatic price hikes were not uncommon: In 1986, for example, a county contractor doubled its waste disposal rate on six weeks' notice.

Responding to these problems, the Counties requested and New York's Legislature and Governor created the Oneida-Herkimer Solid Waste Management Authority (Authority), a public benefit corporation. See N. Y. Pub. Auth. Law Ann. § 2049-aa et seq. (West 1995). The Authority is empowered to collect, process, and dispose of solid waste generated in the Counties. § 2049-ee(4). To further the Authority's governmental and public purposes, the Counties may impose "appropriate and reasonable limitations on competition" by, for instance, adopting "local laws requiring that all solid waste . . . be delivered to a specified solid waste management-resource recovery facility." § 2049-tt(3).

In 1989, the Authority and the Counties entered into a Solid Waste Management Agreement, under which the Authority agreed to manage all solid waste within the Counties. Private haulers would remain free to pick up citizens' trash from the curb, but the Authority would take over the job of processing the trash, sorting it, and sending it off for disposal. To fulfill its part of the bargain, the Authority agreed to purchase and develop facilities for the processing and disposal of solid waste and recyclables generated in the Counties.

The Authority collected "tipping fees"[1] to cover its operating and maintenance costs for these facilities. The tipping fees significantly exceeded those charged for waste removal on the open market, but they allowed the Authority to do more than the average private waste disposer. In addition to landfill transportation and solid waste disposal, the fees enabled the Authority to provide recycling of 33 kinds of materials, as well as composting, household hazardous waste disposal, and a number of other services. If the Authority's operating costs and debt service were not recouped through tipping fees and other charges, the agreement provided that the Counties would make up the difference.

As described, the agreement had a flaw: Citizens might opt to have their waste hauled to facilities with lower tipping fees. To avoid being stuck with the bill for facilities that citizens voted for but then chose not to use, the Counties enacted "flow control" ordinances requiring that all solid waste generated within the Counties be delivered to the Authority's processing sites. Private haulers must obtain a permit from the Authority to collect waste in the Counties. Penalties for noncompliance with the ordinances include permit revocation, fines, and imprisonment.

Petitioners are United Haulers Association, Inc., a trade association made up of solid waste management companies, and six haulers that operated in Oneida and Herkimer Counties when this action was filed. In 1995, they sued the Counties and the Authority under Rev. Stat. § 1979, 42 U.S.C. § 1983, alleging that the flow control laws violate the Commerce Clause by discriminating against interstate commerce. They submitted evidence that without the flow control laws and the associated $86-per-ton tipping fees, they could dispose of solid waste at out-of-state facilities for between $37 and $55 per ton, including transportation.

The District Court read our decision in *Carbone*, 511 U.S. 383, 114 S. Ct. 1677, 128 L. Ed. 2d 399, as categorically rejecting nearly all flow control laws. The court ruled in the haulers' favor, enjoining enforcement of the Counties' laws. The Second Circuit reversed, reasoning that *Carbone* and our other dormant Commerce Clause precedents allow for a distinction between laws that benefit public as opposed to private facilities. 261 F.3d 245, 263 (2001). Accordingly, it held that a statute does not discriminate against interstate commerce when it favors local government at the expense of all private industry. The court remanded to let the District Court decide whether the Counties' ordinances nevertheless placed an incidental burden on interstate commerce, and if so, whether the ordinances' benefits outweighed that burden.

On remand and after protracted discovery, a Magistrate Judge and the District Court found that the haulers did not show that the ordinances imposed *any* cognizable burden on interstate commerce. The Second Circuit affirmed, assuming that the laws exacted some toll on interstate commerce, but finding any possible burden "modest" compared to the "clear and substantial" benefits of the ordinances. 438 F.3d 150, 160 (2006). Because the Sixth Circuit had recently issued a conflicting decision holding that a flow control ordinance favoring a public entity *does* facially

---

[1] Tipping fees are disposal charges levied against collectors who drop off waste at a processing facility. They are called "tipping" fees because garbage trucks literally tip their back end to dump out the carried waste. As of 1995, haulers in the Counties had to pay tipping fees of at least $86 per ton, a price that ballooned to as much as $172 per ton if a particular load contained more than 25% recyclables.

discriminate against interstate commerce, see *Nat'l Solid Wastes Mgmt. Ass'n v. Daviess County*, 434 F.3d 898 (2006), we granted certiorari, 548 U.S. ___, 127 S. Ct. 35, 165 L. Ed. 2d 1013 (2006).

II

A

The Commerce Clause provides that "Congress shall have Power . . . to regulate Commerce with foreign Nations, and among the several States." U.S. CONST., Art. I, § 8, cl. 3. Although the Constitution does not in terms limit the power of States to regulate commerce, we have long interpreted the Commerce Clause as an implicit restraint on state authority, even in the absence of a conflicting federal statute. See *Case of the State Freight Tax*, 82 U.S. 232, 21 L. Ed. 146, 15 Wall. 232, 279, 4 Brewster's Reports 202 (1873); *Cooley v. Board of Wardens of Port of Philadelphia ex rel. Soc. for Relief of Distressed Pilots*, 53 U.S. 299, 13 L. Ed. 996, 12 How. 299, 318 (1852).

To determine whether a law violates this so-called "dormant" aspect of the Commerce Clause, we first ask whether it discriminates on its face against interstate commerce. *Am. Trucking Ass'ns v. Mich. PSC*, 545 U.S. 429, 433, 125 S. Ct. 2419, 162 L. Ed. 2d 407 (2005); *Fort Gratiot Sanitary Landfill, Inc. v. Michigan Dep't. of Natural Resources*, 504 U.S. 353, 359, 112 S. Ct. 2019, 119 L. Ed. 2d 139 (1992). In this context, " 'discrimination' simply means differential treatment of in-state and out-of-state economic interests that benefits the former and burdens the latter." *Oregon Waste Sys. v. Department of Envtl. Quality*, 511 U.S. 93, 99, 114 S. Ct. 1345, 128 L. Ed. 2d 13 (1994); *New Energy Co. of Ind. v. Limbach*, 486 U.S. 269, 273, 108 S. Ct. 1803, 100 L. Ed. 2d 302 (1988). Discriminatory laws motivated by "simple economic protectionism" are subject to a "virtually *per se* rule of invalidity," *Philadelphia v. New Jersey*, 437 U.S. 617, 624, 98 S. Ct. 2531, 57 L. Ed. 2d 475 (1978), which can only be overcome by a showing that the State has no other means to advance a legitimate local purpose, *Maine v. Taylor*, 477 U.S. 131, 138, 106 S. Ct. 2440, 91 L. Ed. 2d 110 (1986).

B

Following the lead of the Sixth Circuit in *Daviess County*, the haulers argue vigorously that the Counties' ordinances discriminate against interstate commerce under *Carbone*. In *Carbone*, the town of Clarkstown, New York, hired a private contractor to build a waste transfer station. According to the terms of the deal, the contractor would operate the facility for five years, charging an above-market tipping fee of $81 per ton; after five years, the town would buy the facility for one dollar. The town guaranteed that the facility would receive a certain volume of trash per year. To make good on its promise, Clarkstown passed a flow control ordinance requiring that all nonhazardous solid waste within the town be deposited at the transfer facility. *See* 511 U.S., at 387, 114 S. Ct. 1677, 128 L. Ed. 2d 399.

This Court struck down the ordinance, holding that it discriminated against interstate commerce by "hoarding solid waste, and the demand to get rid of it, for the benefit of the preferred processing facility." *Id.*, at 392, 114 S. Ct. 1677, 128 L. Ed. 2d 399. The dissent pointed out that all of this Court's local processing cases involved laws that discriminated in favor of *private* entities, not public ones. *Id.*, at 411 (opinion of Souter, J.). According to the dissent, Clarkstown's ostensibly private transfer station was "essentially a municipal facility," *id.*, at 419, 114 S. Ct. 1677, 128 L. Ed. 2d 399, and this distinction should have saved Clarkstown's ordinance because favoring local government is by its nature different from favoring a particular private company. The majority did not comment on the dissent's public-private distinction. . . .

. . . *Carbone* cannot be regarded as having decided the public-private question.

C

The flow control ordinances in this case benefit a clearly public facility, while treating all private companies exactly the same. Because the question is now squarely presented on the facts of the case before us, we decide that such flow control ordinances do not discriminate against interstate commerce for purposes of the dormant Commerce Clause.

Compelling reasons justify treating these laws differently from laws favoring particular private businesses over their competitors. "Conceptually, of course, any notion of discrimination assumes a comparison of substantially similar entities." *General Motors Corp. v. Tracy*, 519 U.S. 278, 298, 117 S. Ct. 811, 136 L. Ed. 2d 76 (1997) (footnote omitted). But States and municipalities are not private businesses — far from it. Unlike private enterprise, government is vested with the responsibility of protecting the health, safety, and welfare of its citizens. See *Metropolitan Life Ins. Co. v. Massachusetts*, 471 U.S. 724, 756, 105 S. Ct. 2380, 85 L. Ed. 2d 728 (1985) ("The States traditionally have had great latitude under their police powers to legislate as to the protection of the lives, limbs, health, comfort, and quiet of all persons" (internal quotation marks omitted)). These important responsibilities set state and local government apart from a typical private business. Cf. *Tracy, supra,* at 313, 117 S. Ct. 136 L. Ed. 2d 76 (Scalia, J., concurring) ("Nothing in this Court's negative Commerce Clause jurisprudence" compels the conclusion "that private marketers engaged in the sale of natural gas are similarly situated to public utility companies").

Given these differences, it does not make sense to regard laws favoring local government and laws favoring private industry with equal skepticism. As our local processing cases demonstrate, when a law favors in-state business over out-of-state competition, rigorous scrutiny is appropriate because the law is often the product of "simple economic protectionism." *Wyoming v. Oklahoma*, 502 U.S. 437, 454, 112 S. Ct. 789, 117 L. Ed. 2d 1 (1992); *Philadelphia v. New Jersey*, 437 U.S., at 626–627. Laws favoring local government, by contrast, may be directed toward any number of legitimate goals unrelated to protectionism. Here the flow control ordinances enable the Counties to pursue particular policies with respect to the handling and treatment of waste generated in the Counties, while allocating the costs of those policies on citizens and businesses according to the volume of waste they generate.

The contrary approach of treating public and private entities the same under the dormant Commerce Clause would lead to unprecedented and unbounded interference by the courts with state and local government. The dormant Commerce Clause is not a roving license for federal courts to decide what activities are appropriate for state and local government to undertake, and what activities must be the province of private market competition. In this case, the citizens of Oneida and Herkimer Counties have chosen the government to provide waste management services, with a limited role for the private sector in arranging for transport of waste from the curb to the public facilities. The citizens could have left the entire matter for the private sector, in which case any regulation they undertook could not discriminate against interstate commerce. But it was also open to them to vest responsibility for the matter with their government, and to adopt flow control ordinances to support the government effort. It is not the office of the Commerce Clause to control the decision of the voters on whether government or the private sector should provide waste management services. "The Commerce Clause significantly limits the ability of States and localities to regulate or otherwise burden the flow of interstate commerce, but it does not elevate free trade above all other values." *Maine v. Taylor*, 477 U.S., at 151, 106 S. Ct. 2440, 91 L. Ed. 110. *See Exxon Corp. v. Governor of Maryland*, 437 U.S. 117, 127, 98 S. Ct. 2207, 57 L. Ed. 2d 91 (1978) (Commerce Clause does not protect "the particular structure or method of operation" of a market).

We should be particularly hesitant to interfere with the Counties' efforts under the guise of the Commerce Clause because "waste disposal is both typically and traditionally a local government function." 261 F.3d at 264 (case below) (Calabresi, J., concurring); see *USA Recycling, Inc. v. Town of Babylon*, 66 F.3d 1272, 1275 (CA2 1995) ("For ninety years, it has been settled law that garbage collection and disposal is a core function of local government in the United States"); M. Melosi, Garbage in the Cities: Refuse, Reform, and the Environment, 1880–1980, pp. 153–155 (1981). Congress itself has recognized local government's vital role in waste management, making clear that "collection and disposal of solid wastes should continue to be primarily the function of State, regional, and local agencies." Resource Conservation and Recovery Act of 1976, 90 Stat. 2797, 42 U.S.C. § 6901(a)(4). The policy of the State of New York favors "displacing competition with regulation or monopoly control" in this area. N. Y. Pub. Auth. Law Ann. § 2049-tt(3). We may or may not agree with that approach, but nothing in the Commerce Clause vests the responsibility for that policy judgment with the Federal Judiciary.

Finally, it bears mentioning that the most palpable harm imposed by the ordinances — more expensive trash removal — is likely to fall upon the very people who voted for the laws. Our dormant Commerce Clause cases often find discrimination when a State shifts the costs of regulation to other States, because when "the burden of state regulation falls on interests outside the state, it is unlikely to be alleviated by the operation of those political restraints normally exerted when interests within the state are affected." *Southern Pacific Co. v. Arizona ex rel. Sullivan*, 325 U.S. 761, 767–768, n. 2, 65 S. Ct. 1515, 89 L. Ed. 1915 (1945). Here, the citizens and businesses of the Counties bear the costs of the ordinances. There is no reason to step in and hand local businesses a victory they could not obtain through the political process.

We hold that the Counties' flow control ordinances, which treat in-state private business interests exactly the same as out-of-state ones, do not "discriminate against interstate commerce" for purposes of the dormant Commerce Clause.[2]

D

The Counties' flow control ordinances are properly analyzed under the test set forth in *Pike v. Bruce Church, Inc.*, 397 U.S. 137, 142, 90 S. Ct. 844, 25 L. Ed. 2d 174 (1970), which is reserved for laws "directed to legitimate local concerns, with effects upon interstate commerce that are only incidental." *Philadelphia v. New Jersey*, 437 U.S., at 624, 98 S. Ct. 2531, 57 L. Ed. 2d 475. Under the *Pike* test, we will uphold a nondiscriminatory statute like this one "unless the burden imposed on [interstate] commerce is clearly excessive in relation to the putative local benefits." 397 U.S., at 142, 90 S. Ct. 844, 25 L. Ed. 2d 174; *Northwest Central Pipeline Corp. v. State Corporation Comm'n of Kan.*, 489 U.S. 493, 525–526, 109 S. Ct. 1262, 103 L. Ed. 2d 509 (1989).

After years of discovery, both the Magistrate Judge and the District Court could not detect *any* disparate impact on out-of-state as opposed to in-state businesses. The Second Circuit alluded to, but did not endorse, a "rather abstract harm" that may exist because "the Counties' flow control ordinances have removed the waste generated in Oneida and Herkimer Counties from the national marketplace for waste processing services." 438 F.3d at 160. We find it unnecessary to decide whether the ordinances impose any incidental burden on interstate commerce because any arguable burden does not exceed the public benefits of the ordinances.

The ordinances give the Counties a convenient and effective way to finance their integrated package of waste-disposal services. While "revenue generation is not a local interest that can justify *discrimination* against interstate commerce," *Carbone*, 511 U.S., at 393, 114 S. Ct. 1677, 128 L. Ed. 2d 399 (emphasis added), we think it is a cognizable benefit for purposes of the *Pike* test.

At the same time, the ordinances are more than financing tools. They increase recycling in at least two ways, conferring significant health and environmental benefits upon the citizens of the Counties. First, they create enhanced incentives for recycling and proper disposal of other kinds of waste. Solid waste disposal is expensive in Oneida-Herkimer, but the Counties accept recyclables and many forms of hazardous waste for free, effectively encouraging their citizens to sort their own trash. Second, by requiring all waste to be deposited at Authority facilities, the Counties have markedly increased their ability to enforce recycling laws. If the

---

[2] The Counties and their *amicus* were asked at oral argument if affirmance would lead to the "Oneida-Herkimer Hamburger Stand," accompanied by a "flow control" law requiring citizens to purchase their burgers only from the state-owned producer. Tr. of Oral Arg. 33–34 (Counties), 45–46, 49–50 (*amicus* State of New York). We doubt it. "The existence of major in-state interests adversely affected by [a law] is a powerful safeguard against legislative abuse." *Minnesota v. Clover Leaf Creamery Co.*, 449 U.S. 456, 473, n. 17, 101 S. Ct. 715, 66 L. Ed. 2d 659 (1981). Recognizing that local government may facilitate a customary and traditional government function such as waste disposal, without running afoul of the Commerce Clause, is hardly a prescription for state control of the economy. In any event, Congress retains authority under the Commerce Clause as written to regulate interstate commerce, whether engaged in by private or public entities. It can use this power, as it has in the past, to limit state use of exclusive franchises. *See, e.g., Gibbons v. Ogden*, 22 U.S. 1, 6 L. Ed. 23, 9 Wheat. 1, 221 (1824).

haulers could take waste to any disposal site, achieving an equal level of enforcement would be much more costly, if not impossible. For these reasons, any arguable burden the ordinances impose on interstate commerce does not exceed their public benefits.

* * *

The Counties' ordinances are exercises of the police power in an effort to address waste disposal, a typical and traditional concern of local government. The haulers nevertheless ask us to hold that laws favoring public entities while treating all private businesses the same are subject to an almost *per se* rule of invalidity, because of asserted discrimination. In the alternative, they maintain that the Counties' laws cannot survive the more permissive *Pike* test, because of asserted burdens on commerce. There is a common thread to these arguments: They are invitations to rigorously scrutinize economic legislation passed under the auspices of the police power. There was a time when this Court presumed to make such binding judgments for society, under the guise of interpreting the Due Process Clause. See *Lochner v. New York*, 198 U.S. 45, 25 S. Ct. 539, 49 L. Ed. 937 (1905). We should not seek to reclaim that ground for judicial supremacy under the banner of the dormant Commerce Clause. The judgments of the United States Court of Appeals for the Second Circuit are affirmed.

It is so ordered.

JUSTICE SCALIA, concurring in part.

I join Part I and Parts II-A through II-C of the Court's opinion. I write separately to reaffirm my view that "the so-called 'negative' Commerce Clause is an unjustified judicial invention, not to be expanded beyond its existing domain." *GMC v. Tracy*, 519 U.S. 278, 312, 117 S. Ct. 811, 136 L. Ed. 2d 761 (1997) (Scalia, J., concurring). "The historical record provides no grounds for reading the Commerce Clause to be other than what it says — an authorization for Congress to regulate commerce." *Tyler Pipe Indus. v. Washington State Dep't of Revenue*, 483 U.S. 232, 263, 107 S. Ct. 2810, 97 L. Ed. 2d 199 (1987) (Scalia, J., concurring in part and dissenting in part).

I have been willing to enforce on *stare decisis* grounds a "negative" self-executing Commerce Clause in two situations: "(1) against a state law that facially discriminates against interstate commerce, and (2) against a state law that is indistinguishable from a type of law previously held unconstitutional by the Court." *West Lynn Creamery, Inc. v. Healy*, 512 U.S. 186, 210, 114 S. Ct. 2205, 129 L. Ed. 2d 157 (1994) (SCALIA, J., concurring in judgment). As today's opinion makes clear, the flow-control law at issue in this case meets neither condition. It benefits a *public entity* performing a traditional local-government function and treats *all private entities* precisely the same way. "Disparate treatment constitutes discrimination only if the objects of the disparate treatment are, for the relevant purposes, similarly situated." *Camps Newfound/Owatonna, Inc. v. Town of Harrison*, 520 U.S. 564, 601, 117 S. Ct. 1590, 137 L. Ed. 2d 852 (1997) (Scalia, J., dissenting). None of this Court's cases concludes that public entities and private entities are similarly situated for Commerce Clause purposes. To hold that they are "would broaden the negative Commerce Clause beyond its existing scope, and intrude on a regulatory sphere traditionally occupied by . . . the States." *Tracy, supra,* at 313, 117 S. Ct. 811, 136 L. Ed. 2d 761 (Scalia, J., concurring).

I am unable to join Part II-D of the principal opinion, in which the plurality performs so-called "*Pike* balancing." Generally speaking, the balancing of various values is left to Congress — which is precisely what the Commerce Clause (the *real* Commerce Clause) envisions.

JUSTICE THOMAS, concurring in the judgment.

I concur in the judgment. Although I joined *C & A Carbone, Inc. v. Clarkstown,* 511 U.S. 383, 114 S. Ct. 1677, 128 L. Ed. 2d 399 (1994), I no longer believe it was correctly decided. The negative Commerce Clause has no basis in the Constitution and has proved unworkable in practice. *See Camps Newfound/Owatonna, Inc. v. Town of Harrison,* 520 U.S. 564, 610–620, 117 S. Ct. 1590, 137 L. Ed. 2d 852 (1997) (Thomas, J., dissenting); *Tyler Pipe Indus. v. Washington State Dep't of Revenue,* 483 U.S. 232, 259–265, 107 S. Ct. 2810, 97 L. Ed. 2d 199 (1987) (Scalia, J., concurring in part and dissenting in part); *License Cases,* 5 How. 504, 578–586, 46 U.S. 504, 12 L. Ed. 256 (1847) (Taney, C. J.). As the debate between the majority and dissent shows, application of the negative Commerce Clause turns solely on policy considerations, not on the Constitution. Because this Court has no policy role in regulating interstate commerce, I would discard the Court's negative Commerce Clause jurisprudence. . . .

[In the balance of his opinion, JUSTICE THOMAS bemoaned the inconsistency of dormant commerce clause jurisprudence, and argued that *Lochner,* cited in the majority opinion, was cause for rejecting the jurisprudence rather than "tweak"(ing) it.]

JUSTICE ALITO, with whom JUSTICE STEVENS and JUSTICE KENNEDY join, dissenting.

In *C & A Carbone, Inc. v. Clarkstown,* 511 U.S. 383, 114 S. Ct. 1677, 128 L. Ed. 2d 399 (1994), we held that "a so-called flow control ordinance, which required all solid waste to be processed at a designated transfer station before leaving the municipality," discriminated against interstate commerce and was invalid under the Commerce Clause because it "deprived competitors, including out-of-state firms, of access to a local market." *Id.,* at 386, 114 S. Ct. 1677, 128 L. Ed. 2d 399. Because the provisions challenged in this case are essentially identical to the ordinance invalidated in *Carbone,* I respectfully dissent.

I

. . . .

This case cannot be meaningfully distinguished from *Carbone.* As the Court itself acknowledges, "the only salient difference" between the cases is that the ordinance invalidated in *Carbone* discriminated in favor of a privately owned facility, whereas the laws at issue here discriminate in favor of "facilities owned and operated by a state-created public benefit corporation." *Ante,* at 1. The Court relies on the distinction between public and private ownership to uphold the flow-control laws, even though a straightforward application of *Carbone* would lead to the opposite result. See *ante*, at 10–12. The public-private distinction drawn by the Court is both illusory and without precedent.

II

The fact that the flow control laws at issue discriminate in favor of a government-owned enterprise does not meaningfully distinguish this case from *Carbone*. The preferred facility in *Carbone* was, to be sure, nominally owned by a private contractor who had built the facility on the town's behalf, but it would be misleading to describe the facility as private. In exchange for the contractor's promise to build the facility for the town free of charge and then to sell it to the town five years later for $1, the town guaranteed that, during the first five years of the facility's existence, the contractor would receive "a minimum waste flow of 120,000 tons per year" and that the contractor could charge an above-market tipping fee. 511 U.S., at 387, 114 S. Ct. 1677, 128 L. Ed. 2d 399. If the facility "received less than 120,000 tons in a year, the town [would] make up the tipping fee deficit." *Ibid*. To prevent residents, businesses, and trash haulers from taking their waste elsewhere in pursuit of lower tipping fees (leaving the town responsible for covering any shortfall in the contractor's guaranteed revenue stream), the town enacted an ordinance "requiring all nonhazardous solid waste within the town to be deposited at" the preferred facility. *Ibid*.

This Court observed that "the object of this arrangement was to amortize the cost of the transfer station: The town would finance *its new facility* with the income generated by the tipping fees." *Ibid*. (emphasis added). "In other words" the Court explained, "the flow control ordinance was a financing measure," *id*., at 393, 114 S. Ct. 1677, 128 L. Ed. 2d 399, for what everyone — including the Court — regarded as *the town's* new transfer station.

The only real difference between the facility at issue in *Carbone* and its counterpart in this case is that title to the former had not yet formally passed to the municipality. The Court exalts form over substance in adopting a test that turns on this technical distinction, particularly since, barring any obstacle presented by state law, the transaction in *Carbone* could have been restructured to provide for the passage of title at the beginning, rather than the end, of the 5-year period.

[Remainder of opinion omitted.]

NOTES AND QUESTIONS

1. ***Subsequent Discrimination Cases.*** The Supreme Court has characterized "discrimination" for purposes of the dormant Commerce Clause as "differential treatment of in-state and out-of-state economic interests that benefits the former and burdens the latter." *Oregon Waste Systems, Inc. v. Dep't of Environmental Quality*, 511 U.S. 93, 99, 114 S. Ct. 1345, 1350 (1994). In *Maharg, Inc. v. Van Wert Solid Waste Mgm't Dist.*, 249 F.3d 544 (6th Cir. 2001), the Court of Appeals for the Sixth Circuit found no discrimination against interstate commerce where participation in a waste disposal plan was voluntary. In *U & I Sanitation v. City of*

Columbus, 205 F.3d 1063 (8th Cir. 2000), the Court of Appeals for the Eighth Circuit found no discrimination against interstate commerce where the local government effectively eliminated the entire market for waste disposal. The *U & I Sanitation* court, however, did find this arrangement to constitute an undue burden on interstate commerce.

Discriminations against interstate commerce by the exercise of state taxation authority, akin to those involving state police powers, have been held to be unconstitutional. *New Energy Company of Indiana v. Limbach*, 486 U.S. 269, 108 S. Ct. 1803 (1988). Accordingly, as a general matter (but see below), a state may not tax a transaction or incident more heavily when it crosses state lines than when it occurs entirely within the state. *Armco, Inc. v. Hardesty*, 467 U.S. 638, 104 S. Ct. 2620 (1984).

2. *Non-Facial Discrimination.* A statute or ordinance need not discriminate in an overt, facial way to violate the dormant Commerce Clause. It is enough if a non-facially discriminatory provision discriminates in practical effect. *See, e.g., Waste Management Holdings, Inc. v. Gilmore*, 252 F.3d 316 (4th Cir. 2001): when it was learned that New York City planned to send 14,000 tons of solid wastes per day to landfills in the State of Virginia, legislators from the Old Dominion State, fearing they would all "drown in a sea of garbage," enacted a statute capping the amount of garbage that landfills in the State could receive. *Waste Management*, 252 F.3d at 327. This statute did not discriminate by design against interstate commerce as compared with intrastate commerce, but the court nonetheless held it did so in practical effect.

Buttressing the court's decision was its finding that the statute was enacted for a discriminatory purpose. In reaching this conclusion, the court identified probative factors for determining discriminatory intent:

(1) evidence of a "consistent pattern" of actions by the decision-making body disparately impacting members of a particular class of persons;

(2) historical background of the decision, which may take into account any history of discrimination by the decision-making body or the jurisdiction it represents;

(3) the specific sequence of events leading up to the particular decision being challenged, including any significant departures from normal procedures; and

(4) contemporary statements by decision makers on the record or in minutes of their meetings.

Waste Management, 252 F.3d at 336.

Should discriminatory intent, without more, cause a statute to violate the dormant Commerce Clause?

3. *Market Participant Doctrine.* An interesting offshoot of dormant Commerce Clause jurisprudence is the "market participant doctrine." Under the doctrine, sometimes called the market participation "exception," when a state or municipality is participating as a private actor in a market, as distinct from regulating the market, the dormant Commerce Clause is inapplicable. Accordingly, when a state is merely spending its own funds or selling or purchasing a product, its actions are free from constitutional invalidation on dormant Commerce Clause grounds. *See, e.g., Reeves, Inc. v. Stake,* 447 U.S. 429, 100 S. Ct. 2271 (1980) (a state regulation which restricted cement sales to in-state residents when the cement was produced in a state-owned plant did not violate the dormant Commerce Clause because the state was acting as a market participant). As a market participant, a governmental entity may impose burdens on interstate commerce, so long as the imposition is incidental to its commercial activity.

Consequently, a state's refusal to sell an item in the marketplace would not trigger dormant Commerce Clause invalidation. *See, e.g., South-Central Timber Dev., Inc. v. Wunnicke,* 467 U.S. 82 (1984) ("[T]he limit of the market participant doctrine must be that it allows a State to impose burdens on commerce within the market in which it is a participant, but allows it to go no further.").

The market participation doctrine is especially apt in flow control cases because municipalities often structure waste disposal programs by employing contractual arrangements with solid waste haulers or processors. When municipalities do that, they are participating in the market. The core question is whether a governmental entity's use of a contract as the mechanism to accomplish a governmental duty, as distinct from using an ordinance or statute, should free the governmental entity from dormant Commerce Clause restraints. The Court of Appeals for the Second Circuit held that it did. *Incorporated Villages of Rockville Centre v. Town of Hempstead,* 196 F.3d 395 (2d Cir. 1999) (use of contracts held to constitute market participation, even if the contracts were formed because of municipalities' threats of regulation); *accord SSC Corp v. Town of Smithtown,* 66 F.3d 502 (2d Cir. 1995) (a municipality's contractual arrangement with private haulers to take all garbage to the municipal incinerator, the tipping fee from which would go to the haulers, is protected by the market participation exception).

Should the Oneida-Herkimer Solid Waste Management Authority in *United Haulers* have qualified as a market participant?

4. *Department of Revenue v. Davis.* A more recent case, *Department of Revenue v. Davis,* 553 U.S. 328, 128 S. Ct. 1801 (2008), offers additional context to the principles set forth above. At issue in *Davis* was Kentucky's practice of exempting from state taxation interest income produced by municipal bonds issued in-state, while taxing interest income produced by in-state non-municipal bonds and all out-of-state bonds. The Supreme Court found this taxation scheme did not violate the dormant Commerce Clause. First, noting that tax schemes of this sort have a "long pedigree," *Id.* at 335, 128 S. Ct. at 1806, the Court found no actionable discrimination against interstate commerce:

> the Kentucky tax scheme parallels the ordinance upheld in *United Haulers:* it "benefit[s] a clearly public [issuer, that is, Kentucky], while treating all private [issuers] exactly the same." . . . (internal citations omitted) . . . There is no forbidden discrimination because Kentucky, as a public entity, does not have to treat itself as being "substantially similar" to the other bond issuers in the market.

Thus, *United Haulers* provides a firm basis for reversal. Just like the ordinances upheld there, Kentucky's tax exemption favors a traditional government function without any differential treatment favoring local entities over substantially similar out-of-state interests. This type of law does "not 'discriminate against interstate commerce' for purposes of the dormant Commerce Clause." (citation omitted).

Id. at 343, 128 S. Ct. at 1811.

Second, the Court viewed the taxation scheme as governed by the market participant doctrine, and for that reason immune from dormant Commerce Clause scrutiny, despite the obvious fact that non-sovereign market participants cannot levy taxes. Indeed, the power to tax is seen by many as a quintessential governmental power. The Court was not impressed: "when Kentucky exempts its bond interest, it is competing in the market for limited investment dollars, alongside private bond issuers and its sister States, and its tax structure is one of the tools of competition." *Id.* at 345, 128 S. Ct. at 1812.

The short of it is that states may use regulatory power to secure for themselves competitive advantages in markets.

5. Undue Burden. As indicated in *United Haulers* and a legion of other cases, state statutes that discriminate against interstate commerce are not the only ones that can offend the dormant Commerce Clause. Also offensive are state statutes which impose an "undue burden" on interstate commerce. With respect to this second prong of dormant Commerce Clause jurisprudence: "the practical effect of [a] statute must be evaluated not only by considering the consequences of the statute itself, but also by considering how the challenged statute may interact with the legitimate regulatory regimes of other States and what effect would arise if not one, but many or every, State adopted similar legislation." *Healy v. The Beer Institute, Inc.*, 491 U.S. 324, 336, 109 S. Ct. 2491 (1989).

With respect to the undue burden prong of dormant Commerce Clause jurisprudence, however, state taxation cases receive a somewhat more relaxed scrutiny. In *Commonwealth Edison Company v. Montana*, 453 U.S. 609, 101 S. Ct. 2946 (1981), the Court allowed a coal severance tax to stand even though the burden of the state's taxation fell disproportionately on out-of-state entities. The burden was disproportionate because 90% of the coal mined in Montana was shipped for use outside Montana; thus, in real terms, the tax was paid overwhelmingly by out-of-state consumers. (The tax was the same for all coal mined in Montana, so there was no facial discrimination against interstate commerce.)

The Court upheld the provision, applying a four-part test. Under this test, a tax will pass dormant Commerce Clause scrutiny if (a) it is "applied to an activity with a substantial nexus to the taxing state," (b) it is "fairly apportioned," (c) it "does not discriminate against interstate commerce," and (d) it is "fairly related to the services provided by the state." *Complete Auto Transit, Inc. v. Brady*, 430 U.S. 274, 279, 97 S. Ct. 1076, 1079 (1977). The Court made clear that proceeds from such taxes may ordinarily be used for any purpose, not merely for purposes related to the taxable event. *Oklahoma Tax Comm'n v. Jefferson Lines, Inc.*, 514 U.S. 175, 115 S. Ct. 1331 (1995).

For a summary of cases applying the *Complete Auto Transit* test, see *Goldberg v. Sweet*, 488 U.S. 252, 260, n.12, 109 S. Ct. 582, 588, n.12 (1989).

6. *Effect of Congressional Authorization.* It has long been held that Congress may "[confer] upon the States an ability to restrict the flow of interstate commerce that they would not otherwise enjoy. If Congress ordains that the States may freely regulate an aspect of interstate commerce, any action taken by a State within the scope of the congressional authorization is rendered invulnerable to Commerce Clause challenge." *Western & Southern Life Ins. Co. v. State Bd. of Equalization of Cal.*, 451 U.S. 648, 652–53, 101 S. Ct. 2070 (1981) (internal citations omitted).

7. *Additional Reading.* There is vigorous debate about whether courts are capable of making these judgments coherently and, as suggested by the opinion of Justices Scalia and Thomas in *United Haulers*, whether they ought to engage in this enterprise at all. For an interesting argument maintaining the illegitimacy of the dormant Commerce Clause, see Redish and Nugent, *The Dormant Commerce Clause and the Constitutional Balance of Federalism*, 1987 DUKE L.J. 569 (1987).

D. RIGHTS OF INDIVIDUALS

1. Eminent Domain

Eminent domain is the power "to take private property for public use by the state, municipalities, and private persons authorized to exercise functions of public character." BLACK'S LAW DICTIONARY 523 (6th ed. 1990). The right is held by every "independent government," and, since it is a matter of sovereignty, it need not be affirmed by constitutional declaration. *Boom Co. v. Patterson*, 98 U.S. 403 (1879). Constitutions, rather, serve only to limit the power. *Id.* The Takings Clause of the Fifth Amendment to the U.S. Constitution, which provides that private property shall not "be taken for public use without just compensation," qualifies as both an acknowledgment of the existence of the eminent domain power in the federal arena and a major limitation on its exercise.

As the text of the Fifth Amendment suggests, the power may be exercised only for a "public use" and only if the deprived property owner receives "just compensation" for the property rights he or she loses. Our review does not examine what constitutes "just compensation" — there exists a host of cases on that subject — but focuses, rather, on the pivotal question of what is a "public use."

In most instances, what qualifies as a public use is not controversial. There is no dispute, for example, when eminent domain authority is used to enable the construction or expansion of a public highway or for other such routine purposes. But controversy may arise when government uses eminent domain authority to accomplish goals more political in nature. The following case is the most recent declaration of the United States Supreme Court on the Public Use Clause. The case has been severely edited.

KELO v. CITY OF NEW LONDON
545 U.S. 469; 125 S. Ct. 2655 (2005)

STEVENS J., delivered the opinion of the Court, in which KENNEDY, SOUTER, GINSBURG, and BREYER, JJ., joined. KENNEDY, J., filed a concurring opinion, *post*, p. 490. O'CONNOR, J., filed a dissenting opinion, in which REHNQUIST, C. J., and SCALIA and THOMAS, JJ., joined, *post*, p. 494. THOMAS, J., filed a dissenting opinion, *post*, p. 505.

In 2000, the city of New London approved a development plan that, in the words of the Supreme Court of Connecticut, was "projected to create in excess of 1,000 jobs, to increase tax and other revenues, and to revitalize an economically distressed city, including its downtown and waterfront areas." 268 Conn. 1, 5, 843 A.2d 500, 507 (2004). In assembling the land needed for this project, the city's development agent has purchased property from willing sellers and proposes to use the power of eminent domain to acquire the remainder of the property from unwilling owners in exchange for just compensation. The question presented is whether the city's proposed disposition of this property qualifies as a "public use" within the meaning of the Takings Clause of the Fifth Amendment to the Constitution.

I

The city of New London (hereinafter City) sits at the junction of the Thames River and the Long Island Sound in southeastern Connecticut. Decades of economic decline led a state agency in 1990 to designate the City a "distressed municipality." In 1996, the Federal Government closed the Naval Undersea Warfare Center, which had been located in the Fort Trumbull area of the City and had employed over 1,500 people. In 1998, the City's unemployment rate was nearly double that of the State, and its population of just under 24,000 residents was at its lowest since 1920.

These conditions prompted state and local officials to target New London, and particularly its Fort Trumbull area, for economic revitalization. To this end, respondent New London Development Corporation (NLDC), a private nonprofit entity established some years earlier to assist the City in planning economic development, was reactivated. In January 1998, the State authorized a $5.35 million bond issue to support the NLDC's planning activities and a $10 million bond issue toward the creation of a Fort Trumbull State Park. In February, the pharmaceutical company Pfizer Inc. announced that it would build a $300 million research facility on a site immediately adjacent to Fort Trumbull; local planners hoped that Pfizer would draw new business to the area, thereby serving as a catalyst to the area's rejuvenation. After receiving initial approval from the city council, the NLDC continued its planning activities and held a series of neighborhood meetings to educate the public about the process. In May, the city council authorized the NLDC to formally submit its plans to the relevant state agencies for review. Upon obtaining state-level approval, the NLDC finalized an integrated development plan focused on 90 acres of the Fort Trumbull area.

The Fort Trumbull area is situated on a peninsula that juts into the Thames River. The area comprises approximately 115 privately owned properties, as well as the 32 acres of land formerly occupied by the naval facility (Trumbull State Park now occupies 18 of those 32 acres). [The development plan, which divided the area into numerous affected "parcels," was far-reaching, calling for a waterfront hotel, new marinas, restaurants, and shopping facilities, a museum, commercial space, and other amenities. All of this was intended "to capitalize on the arrival of the Pfizer facility and the new commerce it was expected to attract."]

The city council approved the plan in January 2000, and designated the NLDC as its development agent in charge of implementation. See Conn. Gen. Stat. § 8-188 (2005). The city council also authorized the NLDC to purchase property or to acquire property by exercising eminent domain in the City's name. § 8-193. The NLDC successfully negotiated the purchase of most of the real estate in the 90-acre area, but its negotiations with petitioners failed. As a consequence, in November 2000, the NLDC initiated the condemnation proceedings that gave rise to this case. . . .

II

Petitioner Susette Kelo has lived in the Fort Trumbull area since 1997. She has made extensive improvements to her house, which she prizes for its water view. Petitioner Wilhelmina Dery was born in her Fort Trumbull house in 1918 and has lived there her entire life. Her husband Charles (also a petitioner) has lived in the house since they married some 60 years ago. In all, the nine petitioners own 15 properties in Fort Trumbull — 4 in parcel 3 of the development plan and 11 in parcel 4A. Ten of the parcels are occupied by the owner or a family member; the other five are held as investment properties. There is no allegation that any of these properties is blighted or otherwise in poor condition; rather, they were condemned only because they happen to be located in the development area.

In December 2000, petitioners brought this action in the New London Superior Court. They claimed, among other things, that the taking of their properties would violate the "public use" restriction in the Fifth Amendment. After a 7-day bench trial, the Superior Court granted a permanent restraining order prohibiting the taking of the properties located in parcel 4A (park or marina support). It, however, denied petitioners relief as to the properties located in parcel 3 (office space). App. to Pet. for Cert. 343–350.

After the Superior Court ruled, both sides took appeals to the Supreme Court of Connecticut. That court held, over a dissent, that all of the City's proposed takings were valid. It began by upholding the lower court's determination that the takings were authorized by chapter 132, the State's municipal development statute. See Conn. Gen. Stat. § 8-186 *et seq* (2005). That statute expresses a legislative determination that the taking of land, even developed land, as part of an economic development project is a "public use" and in the "public interest." 268 Conn., at 18–28, 843 A. 2d, at 515–521. Next, relying on cases such as *Hawaii Housing Authority v. Midkiff*, 467 U.S. 229, 104 S. Ct. 2321, 81 L. Ed. 2d 186 (1984), and *Berman v. Parker*, 348 U.S. 26, 75 S. Ct. 98, 99 L. Ed. 27 (1954), the court held that such economic development qualified as a valid public use under both the Federal and State Constitutions. 268 Conn., at 40, 843 A. 2d, at 527.

Finally, adhering to its precedents, the court went on to determine, first, whether the takings of the particular properties at issue were "reasonably necessary" to achieving the City's intended public use, *id.*, at 82–84, 843 A. 2d, at 552–553, and, second, whether the takings were for "reasonably foreseeable needs," *id.*, at 93–94, 843 A. 2d, at 558–559. The court upheld the trial court's factual findings as to parcel 3, but reversed the trial court as to parcel 4A, agreeing with the City that the intended use of this land was sufficiently definite and had been given "reasonable attention" during the planning process. *Id.*, at 120–121, 843 A. 2d, at 574.

The three dissenting justices would have imposed a "heightened" standard of judicial review for takings justified by economic development. Although they agreed that the plan was intended to serve a valid public use, they would have found all the takings unconstitutional because the City had failed to adduce "clear and convincing evidence" that the economic benefits of the plan would in fact come to pass. *Id.*, at 144, 146, 843 A. 2d, at 587, 588 (Zarella, J., joined by Sullivan, C. J., and Katz, J., concurring in part and dissenting in part).

We granted certiorari to determine whether a city's decision to take property for the purpose of economic development satisfies the "public use" requirement of the Fifth Amendment. 542 U.S. 965, 159 L. Ed. 2d 857, 125 S. Ct. 27 (2004).

III

Two polar propositions are perfectly clear. On the one hand, it has long been accepted that the sovereign may not take the property of *A* for the sole purpose of transferring it to another private party *B*, even though *A* is paid just compensation. On the other hand, it is equally clear that a State may transfer property from one private party to another if future "use by the public" is the purpose of the taking; the condemnation of land for a railroad with common-carrier duties is a familiar example. Neither of these propositions, however, determines the disposition of this case. . . .

The disposition of this case therefore turns on the question whether the City's development plan serves a "public purpose." Without exception, our cases have defined that concept broadly, reflecting our longstanding policy of deference to legislative judgments in this field.

[At this juncture, the Court discussed its past decisions in *Berman v. Parker*, 348 U.S. 26, 75 S. Ct. 98, 99 L. Ed. 27 (1954), *Hawaii Housing Authority v. Midkiff*, 467 U.S. 229, 104 S. Ct. 2321, 81 L. Ed. 2d 186 (1984), and *Ruckelshaus v. Monsanto Co.*, 467 U.S. 986, 104 S. Ct. 2862, 81 L. Ed. 2d 815 (1984), and noted its practice of respecting states on federalism grounds.]

IV

Those who govern the City were not confronted with the need to remove blight in the Fort Trumbull area, but their determination that the area was sufficiently distressed to justify a program of economic rejuvenation is entitled to our deference. The City has carefully formulated an economic development plan that it believes will provide appreciable benefits to the community, including — but by no means limited to — new jobs and increased tax revenue. As with other exercises in urban planning and development, the City is endeavoring to coordinate a variety of commercial, residential, and recreational uses of land, with the hope that they will form a whole greater than the sum of its parts. To effectuate this plan, the City has invoked a state statute that specifically authorizes the use of eminent domain to promote economic development. Given the comprehensive character of the plan, the thorough deliberation that preceded its adoption, and the limited scope of our review, it is appropriate for us, as it was in *Berman*, to resolve the challenges of the individual owners, not on a piecemeal basis, but rather in light of the entire plan. Because that plan unquestionably serves a public purpose, the takings challenged here satisfy the public use requirement of the Fifth Amendment.

To avoid this result, petitioners urge us to adopt a new bright-line rule that economic development does not qualify as a public use. Putting aside the unpersuasive suggestion that the City's plan will provide only purely economic benefits, neither precedent nor logic supports petitioners' proposal. Promoting economic development is a traditional and long accepted function of government. There is, moreover, no principled way of distinguishing economic development from the other public purposes that we have recognized. . . .

It is further argued that without a bright-line rule nothing would stop a city from transferring citizen *A*'s property to citizen *B* for the sole reason that citizen *B* will put the property to a more productive use and thus pay more taxes. Such a one-to-one transfer of property, executed outside the confines of an integrated development plan, is not presented in this case. While such an unusual exercise of government power would certainly raise a suspicion that a private purpose was afoot, the hypothetical cases posited by petitioners can be confronted if and when they arise. They do not warrant the crafting of an artificial restriction on the concept of public use. . . .

Alternatively, petitioners maintain that for takings of this kind we should require a "reasonable certainty" that the expected public benefits will actually accrue. Such a rule, however, would represent an even greater departure from our precedent. "When the legislature's purpose is legitimate and its means are not irrational, our cases make clear that empirical debates over the wisdom of takings — no less than debates over the wisdom of other kinds of socioeconomic legislation — are not to be carried out in the federal courts." *Midkiff*, 467 U.S., at 242, 81 L. Ed. 2d 186, 104 S. Ct. 2321. . . .

. . . We emphasize that nothing in our opinion precludes any State from placing further restrictions on its exercise of the takings power. Indeed, many States already impose "public use" requirements that are stricter than the federal baseline. Some of these requirements have been established as a matter of state constitutional law, while others are expressed in state eminent domain statutes that carefully limit the grounds upon which takings may be exercised. As the submissions of the parties and their *amici* make clear, the necessity and wisdom of using eminent domain to promote economic development are certainly matters of legitimate public debate. This Court's authority, however, extends only to determining whether the City's proposed condemnations are for a "public use" within the meaning of the Fifth Amendment to the Federal Constitution. Because over a century of our case law interpreting that provision dictates an affirmative answer to that question, we may not grant petitioners the relief that they seek.

The judgment of the Supreme Court of Connecticut is affirmed.

It is so ordered.

JUSTICE KENNEDY, concurring.

I join the opinion for the Court and add these further observations. . . .

The trial court concluded . . . that benefitting Pfizer was not "the primary motivation or effect of this development plan"; instead, "the primary motivation for [respondents] was to take advantage of Pfizer's presence." *Id.*, at 276. Likewise, the trial court concluded that "[t]here is nothing in the record to indicate that . . . [respondents] were motivated by a desire to aid [other] particular private entities." *Id.*, at 278. See also *ante*, at 478, 162 L. Ed. 2d, at 450–451. Even the dissenting justices on the Connecticut Supreme Court agreed that respondents' development plan was intended to revitalize the local economy, not to serve the interests of Pfizer, Corcoran Jennison, or any other private party. 268 Conn. 1, 159, 843 A.2d 500, 595 (2004) (ZARELLA, J., concurring in part and dissenting in part). This case, then, survives the meaningful rational basis review that in my view is required under the Public Use Clause.

. . . In sum, while there may be categories of cases in which the transfers are so suspicious, or the procedures employed so prone to abuse, or the purported benefits are so trivial or implausible, that courts should presume an impermissible private purpose, no such circumstances are present in this case.

For the foregoing reasons, I join in the Court's opinion.

JUSTICE O'CONNOR, with whom the Chief Justice, JUSTICE SCALIA, and JUSTICE THOMAS join, dissenting.

Over two centuries ago, just after the Bill of Rights was ratified, Justice Chase wrote:

> "An Act of the Legislature (for I cannot call it a law) contrary to the great first principles of the social compact, cannot be considered a rightful exercise of legislative authority. . . . A few instances will suffice to explain what I mean. . . . [A] law that takes property from A and gives it to B: It is against all reason and justice, for a people to entrust a Legislature with such powers; and, therefore, it cannot be presumed that they have done it." *Calder v. Bull*, 3 U.S. 386, 1 L. Ed. 648, 3 Dallas 386 (1798) (emphasis deleted).

Today the Court abandons this long-held, basic limitation on government power. Under the banner of economic development, all private property is now vulnerable to being taken and transferred to another private owner, so long as it might be upgraded — i.e., given to an owner who will use it in a way that the legislature deems more beneficial to the public — in the process. To reason, as the Court does, that the incidental public benefits resulting from the subsequent ordinary use of private property render economic development takings "for public use" is to wash out any distinction between private and public use of property — and thereby effectively to delete the words "for public use" from the Takings Clause of the Fifth Amendment. Accordingly I respectfully dissent. . . .

Where is the line between "public" and "private" property use? We give considerable deference to legislatures' determinations about what governmental activities will advantage the public. But were the political branches the sole arbiters of the public-private distinction, the Public Use Clause would amount to little more than hortatory fluff. An external, judicial check on how the public use requirement is interpreted, however limited, is necessary if this constraint on government power is to retain any meaning. See *Cincinnati v. Vester*, 281 U.S. 439, 446, 50 S. Ct. 360, 74 L. Ed. 950 (1930) ("It is well established that . . . the question [of] what is a public use is a judicial one").

Our cases have generally identified three categories of takings that comply with the public use requirement, though it is in the nature of things that the boundaries between these categories are not always firm. Two are relatively straightforward and uncontroversial. First, the sovereign may transfer private property to public ownership — such as for a road, a hospital, or a military base. See, *e.g., Old Dominion Land Co. v. United States*, 269 U.S. 55, 46 S. Ct. 39, 70 L. Ed. 162 (1925); *Rindge Co. v. County of Los Angeles*, 262 U.S. 700, 43 S. Ct. 689, 67 L. Ed. 1186 (1923). Second, the sovereign may transfer private property to private parties, often common carriers, who make the property available for the public's use — such as with a railroad, a public utility, or a stadium. See, *e.g., National Railroad Passenger Corporation v. Boston & Maine Corp.*, 503 U.S. 407, 112 S. Ct. 1394, 118 L. Ed. 2d 52 (1992); *Mt. Vernon-Woodberry Cotton Duck Co. v. Alabama Interstate Power Co.*, 240 U.S. 30, 36 S. Ct. 234, 60 L. Ed. 507 (1916). But "public ownership" and "use-by-the-public" are sometimes too constricting and impractical ways to define the scope of the Public Use Clause. Thus we have allowed that, in certain circumstances and to meet certain exigencies, takings that serve a public purpose also satisfy the Constitution even if the property is destined for subsequent private use. See, *e.g., Berman v. Parker*, 348 U.S. 26, 75 S. Ct. 98, 99 L. Ed. 27 (1954); *Hawaii Housing Authority v. Midkiff*, 467 U.S. 229, 104 S. Ct. 2321, 81 L. Ed. 2d 186 (1984).

This case returns us for the first time in over 20 years to the hard question of when a purportedly "public purpose" taking meets the public use requirement. It presents an issue of first impression: Are economic development takings constitutional? I would hold that they are not. . . .

In moving away from our decisions sanctioning the condemnation of harmful property use, the Court today significantly expands the meaning of public use. It holds that the sovereign may take private property currently put to ordinary private use, and give it over for new, ordinary private use, so long as the new use is predicted to generate some secondary benefit for the public — such as increased tax revenue, more jobs, maybe even esthetic pleasure. But nearly any lawful use of real private property can be said to generate some incidental benefit to the public. Thus, if predicted (or even guaranteed) positive side effects are enough to render transfer from one private party to another constitutional, then the words "for public use" do not realistically exclude *any* takings, and thus do not exert any constraint on the eminent domain power.

[Justice O'Connor went on to excoriate Justice Kennedy's proposal that "courts may divine illicit purpose by a careful review of the record" as unworkable, easily manipulated, and flawed in any event: "If it is true that incidental public benefits from new private use are enough to ensure the "public purpose" in a taking, why should it matter, as far as the Fifth Amendment is concerned, what inspired the taking in the first place?"]

Any property may now be taken for the benefit of another private party, but the fallout from this decision will not be random. The beneficiaries are likely to be those citizens with disproportionate influence and power in the political process, including large corporations and development firms. As for the victims, the government now has license to transfer property from those with fewer resources to those with more

. . . .

I would hold that the takings in both Parcel 3 and Parcel 4A are unconstitutional, reverse the judgment of the Supreme Court of Connecticut, and remand for further proceedings.

JUSTICE THOMAS, dissenting.

[In his opinion, Justice Thomas bemoaned how far afield the Court has gone from the original meaning of the Public Use Clause. He argued, *inter alia*, that the term "public use" as defined in the 18th century "means that either the government or its citizens as a whole must actually "employ" the taken property." He argued the current ill-advised path of the jurisprudence was due in part to errant decisions of the past and the Court adopting "its modern reading blindly. . . . " He also cautioned against conferring too much deference on these legislative judgments: "We would not defer to a legislature's determination of the various circumstances that establish, for example, when a search of a home would be reasonable, see, *e.g.*, *Payton v. New York*, 445 U.S. 573, 589–590, 100 S. Ct. 1371, 63 L. Ed. 2d 639 (1980), or when a convicted double-murderer may be shackled during a sentencing proceeding without on-the-record findings, see *Deck v. Missouri*, 544 U.S. 622, 125 S. Ct. 2007, 161 L. Ed. 2d 953 (2005), or when state law creates a property interest protected by the Due Process Clause, see, *e.g.*, *Castle Rock v. Gonzales, post*, at 756–758, 125 S. Ct. 2796, 162 L. Ed. 2d 658; *Board of Regents of State Colleges v. Roth*, 408 U.S. 564, 576, 92 S. Ct. 2701, 33 L. Ed. 2d 548 (1972); *Goldberg v. Kelly*, 397 U.S. 254, 262–263, 90 S. Ct. 1011, 25 L. Ed. 2d 287 (1970)."

For all these reasons, I would revisit our Public Use Clause cases and consider returning to the original meaning of the Public Use Clause: that the government may take property only if it actually uses or gives the public a legal right to use the property. . . .

[As a final point, Justice Thomas predicted that the future consequences of this decision would fall disproportionately on the weakest members of society and especially on minority groups.]

NOTES AND QUESTIONS

1. (A) *Kelo Past.* The decision in *Kelo* was foreseeable given two earlier Supreme Court decisions, both of which were discussed in *Kelo* itself. The cases were *Berman v. Parker*, 348 U.S. 26, 75 S. Ct. 98 (1954), and *Hawaii Housing Authority v. Midkiff*, 467 U.S. 229, 104 S. Ct. 2321 (1984). In a portion of Justice O'Connor's dissenting opinion not produced above, the impact of these cases was set forth:

> There is a sense in which this troubling result follows from errant language in *Berman* and *Midkiff*. In discussing whether takings within a blighted neighborhood were for a public use, *Berman* began by observing: "We deal, in other words, with what traditionally has been known as the police power." 348 U.S., at 32, 99 L. Ed. 27, 75 S. Ct. 98. From there it declared that "[o]nce the object is within the authority of Congress, the right to realize it through the exercise of eminent domain is clear." *Id.*, at 33, 99 L. Ed. 27, 75 S. Ct. 98. Following up, we said in *Midkiff* that "[t]he 'public use' requirement is coterminous with the scope of a sovereign's police powers." 467 U.S., at 240, 81 L. Ed. 2d 186, 104 S. Ct. 2321. This language was unnecessary to the specific holdings of those decisions. *Berman* and *Midkiff* simply did not put such language to the constitutional test, because the takings in those cases were within the police power but also for "public use" for the reasons I have described. The case before us now demonstrates why, when deciding if a taking's purpose is constitutional, the police power and "public use" cannot always be equated.

For his part, Justice Thomas flatly declared these earlier cases "erred by equating the eminent domain power with the police power of States."

(B) *Kelo Present.* *Kelo* has been hugely controversial, and most of the reaction has been negative. Since it was handed down, 43 states by one count have approved ballot measures or legislation to curtail the power to exercise eminent domain authority for purely economic development purposes. In addition, the Supreme Courts of Ohio, Oklahoma, and Michigan have issued rulings of the same ilk. The State of New Hampshire amended its constitution for these purposes as well. In November 2005, the United States House of Representatives adopted an anti-*Kelo* bill by a vote of 376–38; the bill has not become law.

Suzette Kelo's house was sold for one dollar and moved to another location by the purchaser. The house now stands as a stark pink symbol of the controversy. Pfizer announced plans in 2009 to leave New London.

In one interesting repercussion, an activist group in Weare, New Hampshire, the Committee for the Protection of Natural Rights, petitioned the local Board of Selectmen to use its eminent domain power to take title to property of then-Associate Justice David H. Souter of the U.S. Supreme Court. Justice Souter, who voted with the majority in *Kelo*, owns a home in Weare. The group wanted to build the "Lost Liberty Inn" on the site, which would come complete with the "Just Desserts Café" and a museum with a permanent exhibit on the loss of freedom in America. The Board, convening for a traditional New England town hall meeting, defeated the proposal, on the apparent theory Justice Souter was just doing his job.

An artist's representation of the proposed Lost Liberty Inn. The building at left, Justice Souter's home, would have become the Just Desserts Café. Courtesy of the Committee for Protection of Natural Rights.

(C) *Kelo Future.* As a 5-4 decision of recent vintage, *Kelo's stare decisis* value is less than firm. There are four new members of the Court since *Kelo* — Chief Justice Roberts and Associate Justices Alito, Sotomayor and Kagan. They replace four Justices, two of whom voted in the majority in *Kelo* and two of whom dissented.

2. *Preemptive Strikes.* Assume the ABC Corporation operated a manufacturing plant on Misty Creek, the main waterway in the Town of Just Desserts. The company has a bad reputation for polluting at its facilities in other states. Fearing the worst, the Town exercised its eminent domain power to take title to the property and make it into a restaurant/shopping mecca along the Creek. May it do so?

3. *Just Compensation.* Since it is extremely difficult to overturn an exercise of eminent domain authority on public use grounds, the bulk of litigation focuses on the issue of just compensation. The questions are (1) what harms qualify for compensation? and (2) how should "just compensation" be measured? As a general matter, courts have held that just compensation is fair market value, not replacement value, of the affected property. What is important is what the holder of property rights lost, not what the taker gained. *Boston Chamber of Commerce v. Boston*, 217 U.S. 189, 195, 30 S. Ct. 459 (1910).

2. The Takings Clause

As noted at the beginning of this section, the Takings Clause of the Fifth Amendment to the Federal Constitution provides that private property shall not "be taken for public use without just compensation." U.S. CONST., amend. V.

In its earliest deliberations, the United States Supreme Court held the Clause to be applicable in the classic circumstance, that is, when the federal government exercises eminent domain power. But the Court was soon called upon to consider whether the Clause might apply on occasions not implicating the eminent domain power. As the following non-exhaustive list of cases demonstrates, it wasted no time doing so:

• In *Pumpelly v. Green Bay Co.*, 80 U.S. 166 (1872), the Court found the Takings Clause to apply when government flooded private land, stating that:

. . . [i]t would be a very curious and unsatisfactory result . . . that if the government refrains from the absolute conversion of real property to the uses of the public it can destroy its value entirely, can inflict irreparable and permanent injury to any extent, can, in effect, subject it to total destruction without making any compensation, because, in the narrowest sense of that word, it is not taken for the public use.

Id. at 177–78.

• In *United States v. Lynah*, 188 U.S. 445, 23 S. Ct. 349 (1903), the Court extended the principle to cases where flooding involved only a portion of a parcel of land and even when the flooding was recurring rather than permanent.

• In *United States v. Cress*, 243 U.S. 316, 328, 37 S. Ct. 380, 385 (1917), the Court required compensation for the taking of a "partial" *de facto* easement interest over a portion of land.

• In *United States v. Causby*, 328 U.S. 256, 66 S. Ct. 1062 (1946), the Court required compensation in a case not involving a deprivation of possessory rights of the affected landowner. In *Causby*, the complained-of transgression was the federal government's practice of persistently flying bombers, transports, and fighter planes at low altitudes over the plaintiff's land. The aircraft noise and vibration were sufficient to destroy the landowner's chicken business and make normal residential use of the property impossible. Rejecting the federal government's argument that its aircraft operations caused "incidental" injuries only, *Id.* at 260, 66 S. Ct. at 1065, the Court found these invasions of airspace to be "in the same category" as permanent occupations of land. *Id.* at 265, 66 S. Ct. at 1068.

• In *Pennsylvania Coal v. Mahon*, 260 U.S. 393, 43 S. Ct. 158 (1922), a case called the "Everest" of takings decisions, Bruce A. Ackerman, Private Property and the Constitution 156 (1977), the Court extended takings protections in a case where the government's action was not invasive, but regulatory. *Pennyslvania Coal* examined the constitutionality of the Commonwealth of Pennsylvania's Kohler Act, which forbade mining of anthracite coal (with some exceptions) in such a way as to cause land subsidence and destruction of or harm to residential structures. The Pennys-lvania Coal Company argued it had both contract and property rights to mine such coal even if doing so caused subsidence. Justice Oliver Wendell Holmes, writing for the majority, began his analysis with one of the most quoted passages in the literature of the Supreme Court:

Government hardly could go on if to some extent values incident to property could not be diminished without paying for every such change in the general law. As long recognized, some values are enjoyed under an implied limitation and must yield to the police power. But obviously the implied limitation must have its limits, or the contract and due process clauses are gone. One fact for consideration in determining such limits is the extent of the diminution. When it reaches a certain magnitude, in most if not in all cases there must be an exercise of eminent domain and compensation to sustain the act.

Id. at 412, 43 S. Ct. at 159.

Justice Holmes's views in *Pennsylvania Coal* were vigorously opposed by another giant of the court, Justice Louis Brandeis. In dissent, Justice Brandeis argued that the Kohler Act was an appropriate regulation of personal behavior and should not be subject to Takings Clause invalidation. In his view, prohibiting one person from destroying the residence of another was fully within the reach of the police power:

> Every restriction upon the use of property imposed in the exercise of the police power deprives the owner of some right theretofore enjoyed, and is, in that sense, an abridgment by the State of rights in property without making compensation. But restriction imposed to protect the public health, safety or morals from dangers threatened is not a taking. The restriction here in question is merely the prohibition of a noxious use. The property so restricted remains in the possession of its owner. The State does not appropriate it or make any use of it. The State merely prevents the owner from making a use which interferes with paramount rights of the public. Whenever the use prohibited ceases to be noxious, — as it may because of further change in local or social conditions, — the restriction will have to be removed and the owner will again be free to enjoy his property as heretofore.

Id. at 417, 43 S. Ct. at 161.[3]

That is where takings law stood for about fifty years, as the Supreme Court entered into a period of inactivity on the issue. In the thirty years since it again has taken up the issue, the Court has changed takings doctrine in ways never envisioned a century ago. In many ways, the changes have created more confusion than they have shed light: as one commenter put it, even before the Court roiled the pot yet again, figuring out when a taking of private property has occurred is "the lawyer's equivalent of the physicist's hunt for the quark." CHARLES HAAR, LAND-USE PLANNING

---

[3] While most academicians take the view that *Pennsylvania Coal* is a giant step forward in takings law, it may be the case does not involve the Takings Clause at all. In the author's view, it is a substantive due process case finding invalidity with the Kohler Act itself as distinct from invalidating the Act's application to Penn Central's property. Consider the major components of the decision. As an initial matter, Justice Holmes specifically accepted the litigants' invitation to decide the case by assessing "the general validity of the act." *Id.* at 414, 43 S. Ct. at 159–60. Then he went on to lament the legal state of affairs if regulation could diminish property rights with abandon. Property rights still have some sum and substance, he argued, "or the contract and due process clauses are gone." *Id.* at 413, 43 S. Ct. at 159.

What Justice Holmes was saying in *Pennsylvania Coal* was that any statute that too seriously burdens property rights inadequately promotes the public welfare, and for that reason can be unconstitutional. In this case, Justice Holmes reasoned, the enormous detriment the statute visited on private property justified the conclusion that the statute was not a reasonable means to a legitimate end. Of course, a statute of this configuration might fail for Takings Clause purposes as well, but that was not the message of *Pennsylvania Coal*.

Justice Brandeis's dissent ratified this reading of the case. As the dissent put it, the Kohler Act easily survived substantive due process review because it was a "restriction imposed to protect the public health, safety or morals from dangers threatened." *Id.* at 417, 43 S. Ct. at 161. "[T]he state merely prevents the owner from making a use which interferes with paramount rights of the public." *Id.* at 417, 43 S. Ct. at 161. Both the Holmes's majority opinion and Brandeis's dissent relied for their respective conclusions on appraisals of the reasonableness of the Kohler Act. Nowhere in *Pennsylvania Coal* did Justice Holmes or Justice Brandeis mention the Takings Clause.

766 (3d ed. 1976), *quoted in Williamson County Regional Planning Comm'n v. Hamilton Bank*, 473 U.S. 172, 199, n.17, 105 S. Ct. 3108, 3123, n.17 (1985). In words of another commenter, takings law in the current day is simply a "mess." Daniel A. Farber, *Public Choice and Just Compensation*, 9 CONST. COMMENT. 279 (1992).

In this section, we are concerned with what are known as "regulatory takings," those takings caused, if at all, by government regulation restricting the use of land. As a general matter, regulatory takings doctrine is divided into two branches. One branch deals with so-called "total takings," the condition that exists when government regulation strips land of all use or value. The second branch deals with the much larger universe of cases in which regulations have diminished use rights in, or value of, land, but not entirely.

a. Total Takings

LUCAS v. SOUTH CAROLINA COASTAL COUNCIL
505 U.S. 1003, 112 S. Ct. 2886 (1992)

JUDGES: SCALIA, J., delivered the opinion of the Court, in which REHNQUIST, C.J., and WHITE, O'CONNOR, and THOMAS, JJ., joined. KENNEDY, J., filed an opinion concurring in the judgment. BLACKMUN, J., and STEVENS, J., filed dissenting opinions. SOUTER, J., filed a separate statement.

JUSTICE SCALIA delivered the opinion of the Court.

In 1986, petitioner David H. Lucas paid $975,000 for two residential lots on the Isle of Palms in Charleston County, South Carolina, on which he intended to build single-family homes. In 1988, however, the South Carolina Legislature enacted the Beachfront Management Act, S.C. Code § 48-39-250 *et seq.* (Supp. 1990) (Act), which had the direct effect of barring petitioner from erecting any permanent habitable structures on his two parcels. *See* § 48-39-290(A). A state trial court found that this prohibition rendered Lucas's parcels "valueless." Pet. for Cert. 37. This case requires us to decide whether the Act's dramatic effect on the economic value of Lucas's lots accomplished a taking of private property under the Fifth and Fourteenth Amendments requiring the payment of "just compensation." U.S. CONST., Amdt. 5.

I

A

South Carolina's expressed interest in intensively managing development activities in the so-called "coastal zone" dates from 1977 when, in the aftermath of Congress's passage of the federal Coastal Zone Management Act of 1972, 86 Stat. 1280, as amended, 16 U.S.C. § 1451 *et seq.*, the legislature enacted a Coastal Zone Management Act of its own. *See* S.C. Code § 48-39-10 *et seq.* (1987). In its original form, the South Carolina Act required owners of coastal zone land that qualified as a "critical area" (defined in the legislation to include beaches and immediately adjacent sand dunes, § 48-39-10(J)) to obtain a permit from the newly created South Carolina Coastal Council (respondent here) prior to committing the land to a "use other than the use the critical area was devoted to on [September 28, 1977]." § 48-39-130(A).

In the late 1970s, Lucas and others began extensive residential development of the Isle of Palms, a barrier island situated eastward of the City of Charleston. Toward the close of the development cycle for one residential subdivision known as "Beachwood East," Lucas in 1986 purchased the two lots at issue in this litigation for his own account. No portion of the lots, which were located approximately 300 feet from the beach, qualified as a "critical area" under the 1977 Act; accordingly, at the time Lucas acquired these parcels, he was not legally obliged to obtain a permit from the Council in advance of any development activity. His intention with respect to the lots was to do what the owners of the immediately adjacent parcels had already done: erect single-family residences. He commissioned architectural drawings for this purpose.

The Beachfront Management Act brought Lucas's plans to an abrupt end. Under that 1988 legislation, the Council was directed to establish a "baseline" connecting the landward-most "points of erosion . . . during the past forty years" in the region of the Isle of Palms that includes Lucas's lots. § 48-39-280(A)(2) (Supp. 1988). In action not challenged here, the Council fixed this baseline landward of Lucas's parcels. That was significant, for under the Act construction of occupable improvements was flatly prohibited seaward of a line drawn 20 feet landward of, and parallel to, the baseline, § 48-39-290(A) (Supp. 1988). The Act provided no exceptions.

B

Lucas promptly filed suit in the South Carolina Court of Common Pleas, contending that the Beachfront Management Act's construction bar effected a taking of his property without just compensation. Lucas did not take issue with the validity of the Act as a lawful exercise of South Carolina's police power, but contended that the Act's complete extinguishment of his property's value entitled him to compensation regardless of whether the legislature had acted in furtherance of legitimate police power objectives. Following a bench trial, the court agreed. Among its factual determinations was the finding that "at the time Lucas purchased the two lots, both were zoned for single-family residential construction and . . . there were no restrictions imposed upon such use of the property by either the State of South Carolina, the County of Charleston, or the Town of the Isle of Palms." . . . The trial court further found that the Beachfront Management Act decreed a permanent ban on construction insofar as Lucas's lots were concerned, and that this prohibition "deprived Lucas of any reasonable economic use of the lots, . . . eliminated the unrestricted right of use, and rendered them valueless." *Id.* at 37. The court thus concluded that Lucas's properties had been "taken" by operation of the Act, and it ordered respondent to pay "just compensation" in the amount of $1,232,387.50. *Id.* at 40.

The Supreme Court of South Carolina reversed. It found dispositive what it described as Lucas's concession "that the Beachfront Management Act [was] properly and validly designed to preserve . . . South Carolina's beaches." 304 S.C. 376, 379, 404 S.E.2d 895, 896 (1991). Failing an attack on the validity of the statute as such, the court believed itself bound to accept the "uncontested . . . findings" of the South Carolina legislature that new construction in the coastal zone — such as petitioner intended — threatened this public resource. *Id.* at 383, 404 S.E.2d, at 898. The Court ruled that when a regulation respecting the use of property is designed "to prevent serious public harm," *id.* at 383, 404 S.E.2d, at 899 (citing, inter alia, *Mugler v. Kansas*, 123 U.S. 623 (1887)), no compensation is owing under the Takings Clause regardless of the regulation's effect on the property's value.

Two justices dissented. They acknowledged that our *Mugler* line of cases recognizes governmental power to prohibit "noxious" uses of property — i.e., uses of property akin to "public nuisances" — without having to pay compensation. But they would not have characterized the Beachfront Management Act's "primary purpose [as] the prevention of a nuisance." 304 S. Ct. at 395 (Harwell, J., dissenting). To the dissenters, the chief purposes of the legislation, among them the promotion of tourism and the creation of a "habitat for indigenous flora and fauna," could not fairly be compared to nuisance abatement. *Id.* at 396, 404 S.E.2d, at 906. As a consequence, they would have affirmed the trial court's conclusion that the Act's obliteration of the value of petitioner's lots accomplished a taking.

We granted certiorari.

. . . .

III

A

Prior to Justice Holmes' exposition in *Pennsylvania Coal Co. v. Mahon*, 260 U.S. 393 (1922), it was generally thought that the Takings Clause reached only a "direct appropriation" of property, *Legal Tender Cases*, 12 Wall. 457, 551 (1871), or the functional equivalent of a "practical ouster of [the owner's] possession." *Transportation Co. v. Chicago*, 99 U.S. 635, 642 (1879). *See also Gibson v. United States*, 166 U.S. 269, 275–276 (1897). Justice Holmes recognized in *Mahon*, however, that if the protection against physical appropriations of private property was to be meaningfully enforced, the government's power to redefine the range of interests included in the ownership of property was necessarily constrained by constitutional limits. 260 U.S., at 414–415. If, instead, the uses of private property were subject to unbridled, uncompensated qualification under the police power, "the natural tendency of human nature [would be] to extend the qualification more and more until at last private property disappeared." *Id.* at 415. These considerations gave birth in that case to the oft-cited maxim that, "while property may be regulated to a certain extent, if regulation goes too far it will be recognized as a taking." *Ibid.*

Nevertheless, our decision in *Mahon* offered little insight into when, and under what circumstances, a given regulation would be seen as going "too far" for purposes of the Fifth Amendment. In 70-odd years of succeeding "regulatory takings" jurisprudence, we have generally eschewed any "'set formula'" for determining how far is too far, preferring to "engage in . . . essentially ad hoc, factual inquiries," *Penn Central Transportation Co. v. New York City*, 438 U.S. 104, 124 (1978) (quoting *Goldblatt v. Hempstead*, 369 U.S. 590, 594 (1962)). *See* Epstein, *Takings: Descent and Resurrection*, 1987 SUP. CT. REV. 1, 4. We have, however, described at least two discrete categories of regulatory action as compensable without case-specific inquiry into the public interest advanced in support of the restraint. The first encompasses regulations that compel the property owner to suffer a physical "invasion" of his property. In general (at least with regard to permanent invasions), no matter how minute the intrusion, and no matter how weighty the public purpose behind it, we have required compensation. For example, in *Loretto v. Teleprompter Manhattan CATV Corp.*, 458 U.S. 419 (1982), we determined that New York's law requiring landlords to allow television cable companies] to emplace cable facilities in their apartment buildings constituted a taking, *id.* at 435–440, even though the facilities occupied at most only 1 1/2 cubic feet of the landlords' property, *see id.* at 438, n. 16. *See also United States v. Causby*, 328 U.S. 256, 265, and n. 10 (1946) (physical invasions of airspace); cf. *Kaiser Aetna v. United States*, 444 U.S. 164 (1979) (imposition of navigational servitude upon private marina).

The second situation in which we have found categorical treatment appropriate is where regulation denies all economically beneficial or productive use of land. *See Agins*, 447 U.S., at 260; see also *Nollan v. California Coastal Comm'n*, 483 U.S. 825, 834 (1987); *Keystone Bituminous Coal Assn. v. DeBenedictis*, 480 U.S. 470, 495 (1987); *Hodel v. Virginia Surface Mining & Reclamation Assn., Inc.*, 452 U.S. 264, 295–296 (1981). As we have said on numerous occasions, the Fifth Amendment is violated when land-use regulation "does not substantially advance legitimate state interests or *denies an owner economically viable use of his land.*" *Agins, supra*, at 260 (citations omitted) (emphasis added).

We have never set forth the justification for this rule. Perhaps it is simply, as Justice Brennan suggested, that total deprivation of beneficial use is, from the landowner's point of view, the equivalent of a physical appropriation. See *San Diego Gas & Electric Co. v. San Diego*, 450 U.S., at 652 (Brennan, J., dissenting). "For what is the land but the profits thereof?" 1 E. Coke, Institutes ch. 1, § 1 (1st Am. ed. 1812). Surely, at least, in the extraordinary circumstance when no productive or economically beneficial use of land is permitted, it is less realistic to indulge our usual assumption that the legislature is simply "adjusting the benefits and burdens of economic life," *Penn Central Transportation Co.*, 438 U.S., at 124, in a manner that secures an "average reciprocity of advantage" to everyone concerned. *Pennsylvania Coal Co. v. Mahon*, 260 U.S., at 415. And the *functional* basis for permitting the government, by regulation, to affect property values without compensation — that "Government hardly could go on if to some extent values incident to property could not be diminished without paying for every such change in the general law," *id.* at 413 — does not apply to the relatively rare situations where the government has deprived a landowner of all economically beneficial uses.

On the other side of the balance, affirmatively supporting a compensation requirement, is the fact that regulations that leave the owner of land without economically beneficial or productive options for its use — typically, as here, by requiring land to be left substantially in its natural state — carry with them a heightened risk that private property is being pressed into some form of public service under the guise of mitigating serious public harm. *See, e.g., Annicelli v. South Kingstown*, 463 A.2d 133, 140–141 (R.I. 1983) (prohibition on construction adjacent to beach justified on twin grounds of safety and "conservation of open space"); *Morris County Land Improvement Co. v. Parsippany-Troy Hills Township*, 40 N.J. 539, 552–553, 193 A.2d 232, 240 (1963) (prohibition on filling marshlands imposed in order to preserve region as water detention basin and create wildlife refuge). . . . We think, in short, that there are good reasons for our frequently expressed belief that when the owner of real property has been called upon to sacrifice *all* economically beneficial uses in the name of the common good, that is, to leave his property economically idle, he has suffered a taking.

B

The trial court found Lucas's two beachfront lots to have been rendered valueless by respondent's enforcement of the coastal-zone construction ban. Under Lucas's theory of the case, which rested upon our "no economically viable use" statements, that finding entitled him to compensation. Lucas believed it unnecessary to take issue with either the purposes behind the Beachfront Management Act, or the means chosen by the South Carolina Legislature to effectuate those purposes. The South Carolina Supreme Court, however, thought otherwise. In its view, the Beachfront Management Act was no ordinary enactment, but involved an exercise of South Carolina's "police powers" to mitigate the harm to the public interest that petitioner's use of his land might occasion. 304 S.C. at 384, 404 S.E.2d at 899. By neglecting to dispute the findings enumerated in the Act or otherwise to challenge the legislature's purposes, petitioner "conceded that the beach/dune area of South Carolina's shores is an extremely valuable public resource; that the erection of new construction, *inter alia*, contributes to the erosion and destruction of this public resource; and that discouraging new construction in close proximity to the beach/dune area is necessary to prevent a great public harm." *Id.* at 382–383, 404 S.E.2d at 898. In the court's view, these concessions brought petitioner's challenge within a long line of this Court's cases sustaining against Due Process and Takings Clause challenges the State's use of its "police powers" to enjoin a property owner from activities akin to public nuisances. *See Mugler v. Kansas*, 123 U.S. 623 (1887) (law prohibiting manufacture of alcoholic beverages); *Hadachek v. Sebastian*, 239 U.S. 394 (1915) (law barring operation of brick mill in residential area); *Miller v. Schoene*, 276 U.S. 272 (1928) (order to destroy diseased cedar trees to prevent infection of nearby orchards); *Goldblatt v. Hempstead*, 369 U.S. 590 (1962) (law effectively preventing continued operation of quarry in residential area).

It is correct that many of our prior opinions have suggested that "harmful or noxious uses" of property may be proscribed by government regulation without the requirement of compensation. For a number of reasons, however, we think the South Carolina Supreme Court was too quick to conclude that that principle decides the present case. The "harmful or noxious uses" principle was the Court's early attempt to describe in theoretical terms why government may, consistent with the Takings Clause, affect property values by regulation without incurring an obligation to compensate — a reality we nowadays acknowledge explicitly with respect to the full scope of the State's police power.

"Harmful or noxious use" analysis was . . . simply the progenitor of our more contemporary statements that "land-use regulation does not effect a taking if it 'substantially advances legitimate state interests. . . . ' " *Nollan, supra*, at 834 (quoting *Agins v. Tiburon*, 447 U.S., at 260); *see also Penn Central Transportation Co., supra*, at 127; *Euclid v. Ambler Realty Co.*, 272 U.S. 365, 387–388 (1926).

The transition from our early focus on control of "noxious" uses to our contemporary understanding of the broad realm within which government may regulate without compensation was an easy one, since the distinction between "harm-preventing" and "benefit-conferring" regulation is often in the eye of the beholder. It is quite possible, for example, to describe in *either* fashion the ecological, economic, and aesthetic concerns that inspired the South Carolina legislature in the present case. One could say that imposing a servitude on Lucas's land is necessary in order to prevent his use of it from "harming" South Carolina's ecological resources; or, instead, in order to achieve the "benefits" of an ecological preserve. . . . Whether one or the other of the competing characterizations will come to one's lips in a particular case depends primarily upon one's evaluation of the worth of competing uses of real estate. . . . A given restraint will be seen as mitigating "harm" to the adjacent parcels or securing a "benefit" for them, depending upon the observer's evaluation of the relative importance of the use that the restraint favors. When it is understood that "prevention of harmful use" was merely our early formulation of the police power justification necessary to sustain (without compensation) any regulatory diminution in value; and that the distinction between regulation that "prevents harmful use" and that which "confers benefits" is difficult, if not impossible, to discern on an objective, value-free basis; it becomes self-evident that noxious-use logic cannot serve as a touchstone to distinguish regulatory "takings" — which require compensation — from regulatory deprivations that do not require compensation.

A fortiori the legislature's recitation of a noxious-use justification cannot be the basis for departing from our categorical rule that total regulatory takings must be compensated. If it were, departure would virtually always be allowed. The South Carolina Supreme Court's approach would essentially nullify *Mahon*'s affirmation of limits to the noncompensable exercise of the police power. Our cases provide no support for this: None of them that employed the logic of "harmful use" prevention to sustain a regulation involved an allegation that the regulation wholly eliminated the value of the claimant's land. . . .

Where the State seeks to sustain regulation that deprives land of all economically beneficial use, we think it may resist compensation only if the logically antecedent inquiry into the nature of the owner's estate shows that the proscribed use interests were not part of his title to begin with. This accords, we think, with our "takings" jurisprudence, which has traditionally been guided by the understandings of our citizens regarding the content of, and the State's power over, the "bundle of rights" that they acquire when they obtain title to property. It seems to us that the property owner necessarily expects the uses of his property to be restricted, from time to time, by various measures newly enacted by the State in legitimate exercise of its police powers; "as long recognized, some values are enjoyed under an implied limitation and must yield to the police power." *Pennsylvania Coal Co. v. Mahon*, 260 U.S., at 413. And in the case of personal property, by reason of the State's traditionally high degree of control over commercial dealings, he ought to be aware of the possibility that new regulation might even render his property economically worthless (at least if the property's only economically productive use is sale or manufacture for sale), *see Andrus v. Allard*, 444 U.S. 51, 66–67 (1979) (prohibition on sale of eagle feathers). In the case of land, however, we think the notion pressed by the Council that title is somehow held subject to the "implied limitation" that the State may subsequently eliminate all economically valuable use is inconsistent with the historical compact recorded in the Takings Clause that has become part of our constitutional culture.

Where "permanent physical occupation" of land is concerned, we have refused to allow the government to decree it anew (without compensation), no matter how weighty the asserted "public interests" involved, *Loretto v. Teleprompter Manhattan CATV Corp.*, 458 U.S., at 426 — though we assuredly *would* permit the government to assert a permanent easement that was a pre-existing limitation upon the landowner's title. *Compare Scranton v. Wheeler*, 179 U.S. 141, 163 (1900) (interests of "riparian owner in the submerged lands . . . bordering on a public navigable water" held subject to Government's navigational servitude), *with Kaiser Aetna v. United States*, 444 U.S., at 178–180 (imposition of navigational servitude on marina created and rendered navigable at private expense held to constitute a taking). We believe similar treatment must be accorded confiscatory regulations, i.e., regulations that prohibit all economically beneficial use of land: Any limitation so severe cannot be newly legislated or decreed (without compensation), but must inhere in the title itself, in the restrictions that background principles of the State's law of property and nuisance already place upon land ownership. A law or decree with such an effect must, in other words, do no more than duplicate the result that could have been achieved in the courts — by adjacent landowners (or other uniquely affected persons) under the State's law of private nuisance, or by the State under its complementary power to abate nuisances that affect the public generally, or otherwise.

On this analysis, the owner of a lake bed, for example, would not be entitled to compensation when he is denied the requisite permit to engage in a landfilling operation that would have the effect of flooding others' land. Nor the corporate owner of a nuclear generating plant, when it is directed to remove all improvements from its land upon discovery that the plant sits astride an earthquake fault. Such regulatory action may well have the effect of eliminating the land's only economically productive use, but it does not proscribe a productive use that was previously permissible under relevant property and nuisance principles. The use of these properties for what are now expressly prohibited purposes was always unlawful, and (subject to other constitutional limitations) it was open to the State at any point to make the implication of those background principles of nuisance and property law explicit. *See* Michelman, *Property, Utility, and Fairness, Comments on the Ethical Foundations of "Just Compensation" Law*, 80 HARV. L. REV. 1165, 1239–1241 (1967). In light of our traditional resort to "existing rules or understandings that stem from an independent source such as state law" to define the range of interests that qualify for protection as "property" under the Fifth (and Fourteenth) Amendments, *Board of Regents of State Colleges v. Roth*, 408 U.S. 564, 577 (1972); *see, e.g., Ruckelshaus v. Monsanto Co.*, 467 U.S. 986, 1011–1012 (1984); *Hughes v.*

Washington, 389 U.S. 290, 295 (1967) (Stewart, J., concurring), this recognition that the Takings Clause does not require compensation when an owner is barred from putting land to a use that is proscribed by those "existing rules or understandings" is surely unexceptional. When, however, a regulation that declares "off-limits" all economically productive or beneficial uses of land goes beyond what the relevant background principles would dictate, compensation must be paid to sustain it.

The "total taking" inquiry we require today will ordinarily entail (as the application of state nuisance law ordinarily entails) analysis of, among other things, the degree of harm to public lands and resources, or adjacent private property, posed by the claimant's proposed activities, *see, e.g.*, Restatement (Second) of Torts §§ 826, 827, the social value of the claimant's activities and their suitability to the locality in question, *see, e.g., id.* §§ 828(a) and (b), 831, and the relative ease with which the alleged harm can be avoided through measures taken by the claimant and the government (or adjacent private landowners) alike, *see, e.g., id.* §§ 827(e), 828(c), 830. The fact that a particular use has long been engaged in by similarly situated owners ordinarily imports a lack of any common-law prohibition (though changed circumstances or new knowledge may make what was previously permissible no longer so, see Restatement (Second) of Torts, *supra*, § 827, comment G). So also does the fact that other landowners, similarly situated, are permitted to continue the use denied to the claimant.

It seems unlikely that common-law principles would have prevented the erection of any habitable or productive improvements on petitioner's land; they rarely support prohibition of the "essential use" of land, *Curtin v. Benson*, 222 U.S. 78, 86 (1911). The question, however, is one of state law to be dealt with on remand. We emphasize that to win its case South Carolina must do more than proffer the legislature's declaration that the uses Lucas desires are inconsistent with the public interest, or the conclusory assertion that they violate a common-law maxim such as sic utere tuo ut alienum non laedas. As we have said, a "State, by ipse dixit, may not transform private property into public property without compensation. . . . " *Webb's Fabulous Pharmacies, Inc. v. Beckwith*, 449 U.S. 155, 164, 101 S.Ct. 446, 452 (1980). Instead, as it would be required to do if it sought to restrain Lucas in a common-law action for public nuisance, South Carolina must identify background principles of nuisance and property law that prohibit the uses he now intends in the circumstances in which the property is presently found. Only on this showing can the State fairly claim that, in proscribing all such beneficial uses, the Beachfront Management Act is taking nothing.

The judgment is reversed and the cause remanded for proceedings not inconsistent with this opinion.

So ordered.

[Additional opinions are omitted. In a separate statement, Justice Souter argued that the Court should not have heard this case because it became apparent subsequently that the effect of the statutory ban was less than a total deprivation of the plaintiff's property rights. In a concurrence, Justice Kennedy argued that the common law of nuisance is "too narrow a confine for the exercise of regulatory power in a complex and interdependent society." Justice Blackmun's dissent relied on the presumption of constitutionality ("the State has the power to prevent any use of property it finds to be harmful to its citizens, and . . . a state statute is entitled to a presumption of constitutionality") and on the "noxious use" principle set forth in *Pennsylvania Coal*'s dissenting opinion. Justice Stevens objected to the proclamation of a categorical rule for takings law, on the theory that the majority ruling essentially "freezes" state's abilities to revise land use law.]

NOTES AND QUESTIONS

1. ***Postscript.*** After this decision, the state settled with *Lucas* for a reported $1.5 million. The Coastal Council then offered the lands for sale, saying that "with a house to either side and in between the lots, it is reasonable and prudent to allow houses to be built." *See* H. Jane Lehman, *Accord Ends Fight Over Use of Land*, WASH. POST., July 17, 1993, at E1.

2. ***The Categorical Rules.*** Lucas declares two categorical, or *per se*, rules (i.e., rules calling for a finding of a taking "without case-specific inquiry"). The first situation is where the regulation accomplishes a permanent physical occupation of the burdened land. Does the physical occupation test prohibit the government from placing pollution monitoring equipment on the land of a polluter?

Lucas's other *per se* rule declares a categorical taking "where regulation denies all economically beneficial or productive use of land." Does this categorical takings rule apply if the denial of all economically beneficial use of property is temporary, not permanent? In *Tahoe-Sierra Preservation Council, Inc. v. Tahoe Regional Planning Agency*, 535 U.S. 302, 122 S. Ct. 1465 (2002), the question was whether moratoria on property development lasting for nineteen years, in place pending the adoption of a regional land use plan, caused an unconditional taking on its face. Refusing to find a *per se* taking, the Supreme Court held these should be decided on a case-by-case basis.

3. ***The Nuisance Exception.*** Justice Scalia declared in *Lucas* that "[W]here the State seeks to sustain regulation that deprives land of all economically beneficial use, we think it may resist compensation only if the logically antecedent inquiry into the nature of the owner's estate shows that the proscribed use interests were not part of his title to begin with." This is the so-called nuisance exception. Why is there a nuisance exception? Justice Scalia explained in *Lucas* that regulations so severe as to prohibit all economically beneficial use of land "cannot be newly legislated or decreed (without compensation), but must inhere in the title itself, in the restrictions that background principles of the State's law of property and nuisance already place upon land ownership. A law or decree with such an effect must, in other words, do no more than duplicate the result that could have been achieved in the courts — by adjacent landowners (or other uniquely affected persons) under the State's law of private nuisance, or by the State under its complementary power to abate nuisances that affect the public generally, or otherwise." *See supra.* What are your thoughts on the legal efficacy of this exception? Does it make sense to have an exception to a categorical rule?

4. ***Takings and Personal Property.*** *Lucas* implies in dicta that personal property should receive less Takings Clause protection than real property because of the "historical compact recorded in the Takings Clause that has become part of

our constitutional culture." Do you agree with this reading of the Constitution?

Part of the reason personal property receives reduced protection was explained in *Lucas* as follows:

> it seems to us that the property owner necessarily expects the uses of his property to be restricted, from time to time, by various measures newly enacted by the State in its legitimate exercise of its police powers. . . . [I]n the case of personal property, by reason of the State's traditionally high degree of control over commercial dealings, [the owner of personal property] ought to be aware of the possibility that new regulation might even render his property economically worthless (at least if the property's only economically productive use is sale or manufacture for sale).

Do you agree it should be relevant in this context that persons "ought to be aware of the possibility" that onerous regulation might be coming their way? Should rights under the Takings Clause be dependent on a person's state of mind?

5. *The Denominator Problem.* How does one know if a taking is total? Assume a parcel of land, 100 acres in size, contains a 10-acre wetland, which by federal regulation must be left in its pristine, undeveloped condition. Does such a use prohibition constitute a total taking of the 10-acre parcel or a "less than total" taking of the 100-acre parcel? How should such a determination be made?

b.   Less Than Total Takings

PENN CENTRAL TRANSPORTATION CO. v. NEW YORK CITY
438 U.S. 104, 98 S. Ct. 1646 (1978)

[New York City enacted the Landmark Preservation Law, which precluded plaintiff from constructing office space above the Grand Central Terminal in Manhattan. Plaintiff argued this regulation worked a taking in violation of the Federal Constitution. The lower court found for the City.]

Mr. Justice Brennan delivered the opinion of the Court.

The question presented is whether a city may, as part of a comprehensive program to preserve historic landmarks and historic districts, place restrictions on the development of individual historic landmarks — in addition to those imposed by applicable zoning ordinances — without effecting a "taking" requiring the payment of "just compensation." Specifically, we must decide whether the application of New York City's Landmarks Preservation Law to the parcel of land occupied by Grand Central Terminal has "taken" its owners' property in violation of the Fifth and Fourteenth Amendments.

I

A

Over the past 50 years, all 50 States and over 500 municipalities have enacted laws to encourage or require the preservation of buildings and areas with historic or aesthetic importance. These nationwide legislative efforts have been precipitated by two concerns. The first is recognition that, in recent years, large numbers of historic structures, landmarks, and areas have been destroyed without adequate consideration of either the values represented therein or the possibility of preserving the destroyed properties for use in economically productive ways. The second is a widely shared belief that structures with special historic, cultural, or architectural significance enhance the quality of life for all. Not only do these buildings and their workmanship represent the lessons of the past and embody precious features of our heritage, they serve as examples of quality for today. "[Historic] conservation is but one aspect of the much larger problem, basically an environmental one, of enhancing — or perhaps developing for the first time — the quality of life for people."

New York City, responding to similar concerns and acting pursuant to a New York State enabling Act, adopted its Landmarks Preservation Law in 1965. *See* N.Y.C. Admin. Code, ch. 8-A, § 205-1.0 *et seq.* (1976). The city acted from the conviction that "the standing of [New York City] as a world-wide tourist center and world capital of business, culture and government" would be threatened if legislation were not enacted to protect historic landmarks and neighborhoods from precipitate decisions to destroy or fundamentally alter their character. § 205-1.0(a). The city believed that comprehensive measures to safeguard desirable features of the existing urban fabric would benefit its citizens in a variety of ways: e.g., fostering "civic pride in the beauty and noble accomplishments of the past"; protecting and enhancing "the city's attractions to tourists and visitors"; "[supporting] and [stimulating] business and industry"; "[strengthening] the economy of the city"; and promoting "the use of historic districts, landmarks, interior landmarks and scenic landmarks for the education, pleasure and welfare of the people of the city." § 205-1.0(b).

The New York City law is typical of many urban landmark laws in that its primary method of achieving its goals is not by acquisitions of historic properties, but rather by involving public entities in land-use decisions affecting these properties and providing services, standards, controls, and incentives that will encourage preservation by private owners and users. While the law does place special restrictions on landmark properties as a necessary feature to the attainment of its larger objectives, the major theme of the law is to ensure the owners of any such properties both a "reasonable return" on their investments and maximum latitude to use their parcels for purposes not inconsistent with the preservation goals. . . .

Final designation as a landmark results in restrictions upon the property owner's options concerning use of the landmark site. First, the law imposes a duty upon the owner to keep the exterior features of the building "in good repair" to assure that the law's objectives not be defeated by the landmark's falling into a state of irremediable disrepair. *See* § 207-10.0(a). Second, the Commission must approve in advance any proposal to alter the exterior architectural features of the landmark or to construct any exterior improvement on the landmark site, thus ensuring that decisions concerning construction on the landmark site are made with due consideration of both the public interest in the maintenance of the structure and the landowner's interest in use of the property. *See* §§ 207-4.0 to 207-9.0. . . .

B

This case involves the application of New York City's Landmarks Preservation Law to Grand Central Terminal (Terminal). The Terminal, which is owned by the Penn Central Transportation Co. and its affiliates (Penn Central), is one of New York City's most famous buildings. Opened in 1913, it is regarded not only as providing an ingenious engineering solution to the problems presented by urban railroad stations, but also as a magnificent example of the French beaux-arts style.

The Terminal is located in midtown Manhattan. Its south facade faces 42d Street and that street's intersection with Park Avenue. At street level, the Terminal is bounded on the west by Vanderbilt Avenue, on the east by the Commodore Hotel, and on the north by the Pan-American Building. Although a 20-story office tower, to have been located above the Terminal, was part of the original design, the planned tower was never constructed. The Terminal itself is an eight-story structure which Penn Central uses as a railroad station and in which it rents space not needed for railroad purposes to a variety of commercial interests. The Terminal is one of a number of properties owned by appellant Penn Central in this area of midtown Manhattan. The others include the Barclay, Biltmore, Commodore, Roosevelt, and Waldorf-Astoria Hotels, the Pan-American Building and other office buildings along Park Avenue, and the Yale Club. At least eight of these are eligible to be recipients of development rights afforded the Terminal by virtue of landmark designation. . . .

On January 22, 1968, appellant Penn Central, to increase its income, entered into a renewable 50-year lease and sublease agreement with appellant UGP Properties, Inc. (UGP), a wholly owned subsidiary of Union General Properties, Ltd., a United Kingdom corporation. Under the terms of the agreement, UGP was to construct a multistory office building above the Terminal. UGP promised to pay Penn Central $1 million annually during construction and at least $3 million annually thereafter. The rentals would be offset in part by a loss of some $700,000 to $1 million in net rentals presently received from concessionaires displaced by the new building. . . .

[Applicants were denied development rights.]

II

The issues presented by appellants are (1) whether the restrictions imposed by New York City's law upon appellants' exploitation of the Terminal site effect a "taking" of appellants' property for a public use within the meaning of the Fifth Amendment, which of course is made applicable to the States through the Fourteenth Amendment, see *Chicago, B. & Q. R. Co. v. Chicago*, 166 U.S. 226, 239 (1897), and, (2), if so, whether the transferable development rights afforded appellants constitute "just compensation" within the meaning of the Fifth Amendment. We need only address the question whether a "taking" has occurred. . . .

Before considering appellants' specific contentions, it will be useful to review the factors that have shaped the jurisprudence of the Fifth Amendment injunction "nor shall private property be taken for public use, without just compensation." The question of what constitutes a "taking" for purposes of the Fifth Amendment has proved to be a problem of considerable difficulty. While this Court has recognized that the " Fifth Amendment's guarantee . . . [is] designed to bar Government from forcing some people alone to bear public burdens which, in all fairness and justice, should be borne by the public as a whole," *Armstrong v. U.S.*, 364 U.S. 40, 49 (1960), this Court, quite simply, has been unable to develop any "set formula" for determining when "justice and fairness" require that economic injuries caused by public action be compensated by the government, rather than remain disproportionately concentrated on a few persons. *See Goldblatt v. Hempstead*, 369 U.S. 590, 594 (1962). Indeed, we have frequently observed that whether a particular restriction will be rendered invalid by the government's failure to pay for any losses proximately caused by it depends largely "upon the particular circumstances [in that] case." *United States v. Central Eureka Mining Co.*, 357 U.S. 155, 168 (1958); *see United States v. Caltex, Inc.*, 344 U.S. 149, 156 (1952).

In engaging in these essentially ad hoc, factual inquiries, the Court's decisions have identified several factors that have particular significance. The economic impact of the regulation on the claimant and, particularly, the extent to which the regulation has interfered with distinct investment-backed expectations are, of course, relevant considerations. *See Goldblatt v. Hempstead, supra*, at 594. So, too, is the character of the governmental action. A "taking" may more readily be found when the interference with property can be characterized as a physical invasion by government, *see, e.g., United States v. Causby*, 328 U.S. 256 (1946), than when interference arises from some public program adjusting the benefits and burdens of economic life to promote the common good.

"Government hardly could go on if to some extent values incident to property could not be diminished without paying for every such change in the general law," *Pennsylvania Coal Co. v. Mahon*, 260 U.S. 393, 413 (1922), and this Court has accordingly recognized, in a wide variety of contexts, that government may execute laws or programs that adversely affect recognized economic values. Exercises of the taxing power are one obvious example. A second are the decisions in which this Court has dismissed "taking" challenges on the ground that, while the challenged government action caused economic harm, it did not interfere with interests that were sufficiently bound up with the reasonable expectations of the claimant to constitute "property" for Fifth Amendment purposes. . . .

More importantly for the present case, in instances in which a state tribunal reasonably concluded that "the health, safety, morals, or general welfare" would be promoted by prohibiting particular contemplated uses of land, this Court has upheld land-use regulations that destroyed or adversely affected recognized real property interests. *See Nectow v. Cambridge*, 277 U.S. 183, 188 (1928). Zoning laws are, of course, the classic example, *see Euclid v. Ambler Realty Co.*, 272 U.S. 365 (1926) (prohibition of industrial use); *Gorieb v. Fox*, 274 U.S. 603, 608 (1927) (requirement that portions of parcels be left unbuilt); *Welch v. Swasey*, 214 U.S. 91 (1909) (height restriction). . . .

[The Court also addressed plaintiffs' argument that the Landmark Law abrogated the "air rights" above the Terminal]:

"Taking" jurisprudence does not divide a single parcel into discrete segments and attempt to determine whether rights in a particular segment have been entirely abrogated. In deciding whether a particular governmental action has effected a taking, this Court focuses rather both on the character of the action and on the nature and extent of the interference with rights in the parcel as a whole — here, the city tax block designated as the "landmark site." . . .

[The Court found, in any event, that the New York law might well have permitted the construction of some smaller structure above the Terminal. Moreover, reasoned the Court] . . . to the extent appellants have been denied the right to build above the Terminal, it is not literally accurate to say that they have been denied *all* use of even those pre-existing air rights. Their ability to use these rights has not been abrogated; they are made transferable to at least eight parcels in the vicinity of the Terminal, one or two of which have been found suitable for the construction of new office buildings. Although appellants and others have argued that New York City's transferable development-rights program is far from ideal, the New York courts here supportably found that, at least in the case of the Terminal, the rights afforded are valuable. While these rights may well not have constituted "just compensation" if a "taking" had occurred, the rights nevertheless undoubtedly mitigate whatever financial burdens the law has imposed on appellants and, for that reason, are to be taken into account in considering the impact of regulation. . . . (emphasis in original).

Affirmed.

JUSTICE REHNQUIST, joined by CHIEF JUSTICE BURGER and JUSTICE STEVENS, dissented:

. . . Appellees are not prohibiting a nuisance. . . . Penn Central is . . . [denied rights] . . . because it did *too good* a job in designing and building [the Terminal]." (emphasis in original.)

NOTES AND QUESTIONS

1. *Striking the Balance.* While the test established in *Penn Central* remains the most widely used legal test in regulatory takings cases, it fails to produce predictable results, for several reasons. First, the decision characterizes takings cases as "essentially ad hoc inquiries," an assertion drawn from *Goldblatt v. Town of Hempstead*, 369 U.S. 590, 82 S. Ct. 987 (1962), which stated that "[T]here is no set formula to determine where regulation ends and taking begins[.]" 369 U.S. 590, 594, 82 S. Ct. 987, 990 (1962). Declaring takings cases to be "ad hoc inquiries" is a virtual invitation to judges to resolve disputes by their own lights, rather than by honoring Supreme Court precedents. Second, *Penn Central* elevates considerations of "justice and fairness" into a central position in takings analysis, giving judges

even more leeway to fashion results to their liking. With respect to decisional mechanics, *Penn Central* fails to instruct judges how to strike a balance among the three designated factors, nor does the case explain what the factors mean. On this latter point, however, other cases have shed some light:

(A) *Economic Impact of the Regulation. Lucas* states that a total devaluation of property or a denial of all economically beneficial or productive use of land is *per se* a taking. *See supra.* But how far can legislation fall short of totally denying such economically beneficial and productive use and still survive constitutional scrutiny? The short answer is very far. So long as a regulation falls short of leaving land "economically idle" or dooming it to only token use, it is unlikely it will be disqualified on economic impact grounds. *See, e.g., Goldblatt v. Hempstead,* 369 U.S. 590, 594, 82 S. Ct. 987, 990 (1962) (holding that the deprivation of the most beneficial use of land is not an indication, without more, of a taking); *Hadachek v. Sebastian,* 239 U.S. 394, 36 S. Ct. 143 (1915) (an 87-1/2% diminution in value not a taking); *Palazzolo v. Rhode Island,* 533 U.S. 606, 121 S. Ct. 2448 (2001) (no taking when a regulation allows construction of a single dwelling only on an 18-acre parcel, thereby devaluing property from $3.2 million to $200,000); *Concrete Pipe and Products of California v. Construction Laborers Pension Trust for Southern California,* 508 U.S. 602, 645, 113 S. Ct. 2264, 2291 (1993) ("mere diminution in the value of property, however serious, is insufficient to demonstrate a taking").

See also Andrus v. Allard, 444 U.S. 51, 65–66, 100 S. Ct. 318, 327 (1979) ("[A]t least where an owner possesses a full 'bundle' of property rights, the destruction of one 'strand' of the bundle is not a taking, because the aggregate must be viewed in its entirety."). *But see Kaiser Aetna v. United States,* 444 U.S. 164, 178–79, 100 S. Ct. 383, 392–93 (1979) (holding, under the "logic" of *Pennsylvania Coal,* that a "fundamental element" of property, the right to exclude, "fall[s] within [the] category of interests that the government cannot take without compensation").

Would a state's use of its police power to take title to all of a person's property at death run afoul of the Takings Clause? *See Hodel v. Irving,* 481 U.S. 704, 107 S. Ct. 2076 (1987) (yes). Whose property rights are taken in this instance? Those of the deceased? Those of the recipients under the decedent's will or intestacy laws?

(B) *Interference with Investment-Backed Expectations ("IBEs").* As announced in *Penn Central,* this factor is a subunit of the "economic impact" factor. The origin of the IBE factor is said to be a law review article which maintained the validity of regulations that deprive only "desires or goals of property owners which are not 'distinctly crystalized.' " *See* Craig A. Peterson, *Land Use Regulatory "Takings" Revisited: The New Supreme Court Approaches,* 39 HASTINGS L.J. 335, 346 (1988) (indicating the concept came from Michelman, *Property, Utility, and Fairness: Comments on the Ethical Foundations of "Just Compensation" Law,* 80 HARV. L. REV. 1165, 1230–34 (1967)). In a sense, IBEs elevate to constitutional status what is known as "prospect theory," the idea that people perceive a greater loss when deprived of a right already exercised and realized than they do when deprived of a right still in the opportunity stage. In a sense, IBEs affirm "a bird in the hand is worth two in the bush."

The "investment-backed" part of this test brings to constitutional relevance the idea that property rights that have been made the subject of expenditures or other detrimental action by landowners warrant greater protection than what might be thought of as gratuitous property rights. The "expectations" part of IBEs promotes the idea that property rights can be burdened more significantly if the holder of the rights knew or should have known that regulation was in place or on its way. The Court had confirmed this latter point in the context of personal property in *Lucas, supra,* and in *Concrete Pipe, supra,* when it held that a requirement for additional financial contributions by employers to employee pension plans did not upset investment-backed expectations because employers, well aware of the longstanding federal regulation of pension plans, "could have had no reasonable expectation that [they] would not be faced with liability." *Concrete Pipe,* 508 U.S. at 646, 113 S. Ct. at 2292.

A later United States Supreme Court decision, however, was less accepting of the potentially disqualifying impact of the expectations component of IBEs. *Palazzolo v. Rhode Island,* 533 U.S. 606, 121 S. Ct. 2448 (2001), examined the plight of persons who acquired property rights after the enactment of a burdensome land use regulation. The issue was whether such persons were categorically excluded from relief because they knew or should have known of the regulatory prohibition coming in. If so, the argument goes, the regulation could not have interfered with expectations, investment-backed or otherwise. The Supreme Court rejected this "coming to the taking" argument unequivocally, declining to accept a rule that *de facto* would absolve a state of takings liability regardless of any other considerations and, additionally, would strip landowners of much of the capacity to transfer property in the future. In the Court's words, "[t]he State may not put so potent a Hobbesian stick into the Lockean bundle." *Palazzolo,* 533 U.S. at 627, 121 S. Ct. at 2462. Unreasonable statutes "do not become less so through passage of time or title. Were we to accept the State's rule, the post-enactment transfer of title would absolve the State of its obligation to defend any action restricting land use, no matter how extreme or unreasonable. A State would be allowed, in effect, to put an expiration date on the Takings Clause. This ought not to be the rule. Future generations, too, have a right to challenge unreasonable limitations on the use and value of land." *Palazzolo,* 533 U.S. at 627, 121 S. Ct. at 2463.

(C) *Character of the Government Action.* This factor makes relevant for takings purposes the inherent worthiness of a government regulation. For an historical argument that this factor is appropriate, despite sparse constitutional history on the question, see, for example, Joseph L. Sax, *Takings and the Police Power,* 74 YALE L.J. 36 (1964). Under this "character factor," a regulation deemed more worthwhile or necessary may impose a greater burden on property rights than one deemed to be less worthwhile or necessary. *See, e.g., Keystone Bituminous Coal Ass'n v. De Benedictis,* 480 U.S. 470, 107 S. Ct. 1232 (1987). *Keystone* involved a statutory restriction on coal mining much like the Kohler Act examined in *Pennsylvania Coal.* The Supreme Court declined to find a taking in *Keystone,* in part because it viewed the statute under examination to be a justifiable protection against land subsidence. In its words, "the character of the government action involved here leans heavily against a taking; the Commonwealth of Pennsylvania has acted to arrest what it perceives to be a significant threat to the common welfare." *Keystone,* 480 U.S. at 485, 107 S. Ct. at 1242.

In the same vein, governmental regulatory actions seem to fare better for takings purposes than government direct actions. In *Penn Central*, Justice Brennan identified tax laws, zoning laws, and (curiously) laws interfering with interests insufficient to qualify as "property" as among the group of relatively more worthy measures. *Penn Central*, 438 U.S. at 124–25, 98 S. Ct. at 2659. Governmental actions which "promote the health, safety, morals or general welfare" are in this group as well. *Penn Central*, 438 U.S. at 125, 98 S. Ct. at 2659.

While the character factor can help a statute survive takings scrutiny on many occasions, it can reduce a statute's chances on others. As *Lucas* affirms, for example, any regulation that implements a permanent physical invasion on property must fail. For this holding, *Lucas* drew upon *Loretto v. Teleprompter Manhattan CATV Corp.*, 458 U.S. 419, 102 S. Ct. 3164 (1982), which examined a requirement obligating property owners to accede to installation of cable television transmission lines on the exteriors of their buildings. In *Loretto*, the Court found this to be a permanent physical invasion, and, hence, a taking, even though the estimated damages to plaintiff were valued at one dollar. Another case, *Kaiser Aetna v. United States*, 444 U.S. 164, 100 S. Ct. 383 (1979), which held unconstitutional a statute that deprived a landowner of a fundamental property right, also can be read as a judicial objection based on character grounds.

The Court also has objected on takings grounds to statutes that single out individuals. *See, e.g., Yee v. City of Escondido*, 503 U.S. 519, 522–23, 112 S. Ct. 1522, 1526 (1992) ("where the government merely regulates the use of property, compensation is required only if considerations such as the purpose of the regulation or the extent to which it deprives the owner of the economic use of the property suggest that the regulation has unfairly singled out the property owner to bear a burden that should be borne by the public"). *See also Pennell v. Tri-County Apartment House Owners Ass'n*, 485 U.S. 1, 108 S. Ct. 849 (1988). In *Pennell*, lessors of residential properties contested a law that limited the amount of rentals they could charge tenants whose incomes fell below a floor level. The lessors argued that such a provision placed a financial burden on a few (rent-controlled lessors) to help effect a remedy for a problem societal in scope (poverty) and, for that reason, a taking was accomplished. Although the majority, per Justice Rehnquist, found no taking under these circumstances, Justice Scalia, in dissent, argued the statute worked a "facial taking." *Pennell*, 485 U.S. 1. He wrote:

> [The poverty] is no more caused or exploited by landlords than it is by the grocers who sell needy renters their food, or the department stores that sell them their clothes, or the employers who pay them their wages, or the citizens of San Jose holding the higher-paying jobs from which they are excluded. . . . Here the City is not "regulating" rents in the relevant sense of preventing rents that are excessive; rather, it is using the occasion of rent regulation . . . to establish a welfare program privately funded by those landlords who happen to have "hardship" tenants.

Pennell, 485 U.S. at 22, 108 S. Ct. at 863.

Recently, however, the character factor suffered a setback of sorts when the Court overruled its 1980 decision in *Agins v. Tiburon*, 447 U.S. 255, 100 S. Ct. 2138 (1980). *Agins* had held, on classic character grounds, that any regulation that fails to "substantially advance legitimate state interests" is a taking for that reason. *Lingle v. Chevron, USA, Inc.*, 544 U.S. 528, 125 S. Ct. 2074 (2005), unanimously rejected that holding: "[W]e conclude that this formula prescribes an inquiry in the nature of a due process, not a takings, test, and that it has no proper place in our takings jurisprudence." *Lingle*, 544 U.S. at 540, 125 S. Ct. at 2083.

2. *Right-to-Farm Laws.* Recall the decision of *Weinhold v. Wolf*, in Chapter 2, *supra*, in which the defendant attempted (unsuccessfully) to invoke a statutory defense (the "right-to-farm" law) to secure an immunity from common law nuisance liability (in *Weinhold*, the dispute involved odors released from a hog operation). Suppose the defense had been available to the defendant in *Weinhold* and had precluded plaintiff's lawsuit. Could the plaintiff have argued that the right-to-farm law worked an unconstitutional taking of plaintiff's property rights? The Iowa Supreme Court decided this question in *Bormann v. Board of Supervisors in and for Kossuth County, Iowa*, 584 N.W.2d 309 (Iowa 1998), *cert. denied*, 119 S. Ct. 1096 (1999) (held: a taking).

3. *The "Nexus" Test.* In *Nollan v. California Coastal Commission*, 483 U.S. 825, 107 S. Ct. 3141 (1987), a local governmental entity granted a permit to a landowner to allow her to replace a bungalow on oceanfront property with a larger house. It conditioned the permit, however, by requiring the plaintiff to grant to the public an easement across its private beach, which was situated between two public beaches. *Held*, per Justice Scalia, the condition caused a taking because it did not relate to the underlying purpose for which the permit itself was issued. If the condition were related, that is, if it somehow removed the adverse effects the construction of a larger house would produce, it could be legitimate as an exercise of land use authority and not be a taking. But here the absence of any such nexus doomed the provision. If what a state really wants is access for members of the public across a private beach, it must use its eminent domain power, not its police power, to get it.

Any such nexus must manifest a "rough proportionality." *Dolan v. City of Tigard*, 512 U.S. 374, 114 S. Ct. 2309 (1994). In other words, the exaction demanded by a governmental entity must bear a "reasonable relationship" to the expected impact of the permission the entity intends to give. *Dolan*, 512 U.S. 374. The Supreme Court has restricted the use of the rough proportionality standard to takings cases involving exactions. *City of Monterey v. Del Monte Dunes*, 526 U.S. 687, 119 S. Ct. 1624 (1998).

4. *Deprivation Issues.* A necessary prerequisite to a successful takings claim is a showing that a government regulation has actually deprived a person of property rights. In some cases, this can be a problem. Consider the following cases:

(A) *Palmyra Pac. Seafoods, L.L.C. v. United States*, 561 F.3d 1361 (Fed. Cir. 2009). *Palmyra* examined the question when contract rights qualify as "property" for purposes of the Takings Clause. Contract rights, as a general matter, do so qualify. *See, e.g., Lynch v. United States*, 292 U.S. 571, 579, 54 S. Ct. 840, 843 (1934) ("The Fifth Amendment commands that property be not taken without making just compensation. Valid contracts are property, whether the obligor be a private individual, a municipality, a State or the United States."); *United States v. Petty Motor Co.*, 327 U.S. 372, 66 S. Ct. 596 (1946) (holding the destruction of a right to renew a lease to be a compensable taking). But *Palmyra* advises caution. Mere government regulation of behavior authorized by private contract, as a general matter, does *not* implicate the Takings Clause because the regulation is not seen as a taking of the contract itself, but is seen rather as a taking of the subject matter of the contract. In other words, in the absence of government actually assuming a contract, no taking is deemed to have occurred if and when government regulation does no more than render a contract right worthless. In *Palmyra*, the court held that a government prohibition of commercial fishing activity worked no taking, even though it adversely affected the value of plaintiff's privately issued license rights.

(B) ***Mugler v. Kansas***, **123 U.S. 623, 8 S. Ct. 273 (1887).** The State of Kansas had prohibited by statute the manufacture of intoxicants for other than medical, scientific, or mechanical purposes. *Mugler*, 123 U.S. at 623, 8 S. Ct. at 295. The plaintiff, who brewed and sold beer before the statute was enacted, argued the measure, as applied to him, caused a taking. The Court disagreed:

> A prohibition simply upon the use of property for purposes that are declared, by valid legislation, to be injurious to the health, morals, or safety of the community, cannot, in any just sense, be deemed a taking or an appropriation of property for the public benefit. Such legislation does not disturb the owner in the control or use of his property for lawful purposes, nor restrict his right to dispose of it, but is only a declaration by the State that its use by any one, for certain forbidden purposes, is prejudicial to the public interests.

Mugler, 123 U.S. at 668–69, 8 S. Ct. at 273.

For other cases announcing the same principle in different contexts, see *Powell v. Pennsylvania*, 127 U.S. 678, 8 S. Ct. 992 (1888) (regulating the manufacture of margarine not a taking); *Hadachek v. Sebastian*, 239 U.S. 394, 36 S. Ct. 143 (1915) (prohibiting the operation of a brickyard in a residential neighborhood not a taking); *Miller v. Schoene*, 276 U.S. 272, 48 S. Ct. 246 (1928) (requiring the destruction of disease-carrying cedar trees not a taking); and *Goldblatt v. Hempstead*, 369 U.S. 590, 82 S. Ct. 987 (1962) (prohibiting the operation of a gravel pit not a taking).

The idea here, first introduced in Justice Brandeis's discussion of noxious uses in his dissent in *Pennsylvania Coal* and elaborated by Justice Scalia in *Lucas*, is a straightforward one: since no one has a property right to use land in a noxious way, that is, in a way that wrongly harms others, a government regulation that does nothing more than prohibit such behavior cannot implicate the Takings Clause. A regulation of this sort, *per force*, cannot be an interference with property rights. Thus, even if the regulation reduced property value to zero, there can be no cognizable takings claim.

The difficulty is determining which uses of land implicate property rights and which do not. In *Lucas*, the reader will recall, Justice Scalia went so far as to disparage courts' ability to even make these determinations: "[T]he distinction between 'harm-preventing' and 'benefit-conferring' regulation is often in the eye of the beholder."

(C) ***Just v. Marinette County***, **56 Wis. 2d 7, 201 N.W.2d 761 (1972).** *Just* dealt with an ordinance in place to protect shore land areas from erosion and other pollution problems. The ordinance prohibited the placement of fill material too close to shorelines of lakes and rivers:

> This case causes us to re-examine the concepts of public benefit in contrast to public harm and the scope of an owner's right to use of his property. In the instant case, we have a restriction on the use of a citizens' property, not to secure a benefit for the public, but to prevent a harm from the change in the natural character of the citizens' property. We start with the premise that lakes and rivers in their natural state are unpolluted and the pollution which now exists is man made. The state of Wisconsin . . . has a duty to eradicate the present pollution and to prevent further pollution in its navigable waters. This is not, in a legal sense, a gain or a securing of a benefit by the maintaining of the natural status quo of the environment. What makes this case different from most condemnation or police power zoning cases is the interrelationship of the wetlands, the swamps and the natural environment of shore lands to the purity of the water and to such natural resources as navigation, fishing, and scenic beauty. Swamps and wetlands were once considered wasteland, undesirable, and not picturesque. . . .
>
> Is the ownership of a parcel of land so absolute that man can change its nature to suit any of his purposes? The great forests of our state were stripped on the theory man's ownership was unlimited. But in forestry, the land at least was used naturally, only the natural fruit of the land (the trees) were taken. The despoilage was in the failure to look to the future and provide for the reforestation of the land. An owner of land has no absolute and unlimited right to change the essential natural character of his land so as to use it for a purpose for which it was unsuited in its natural state and which injures the rights of others. The exercise of the police power in zoning must be reasonable and we think it is not an unreasonable exercise of that power to prevent harm to public rights by limiting the use of private property to its natural uses.

Id. at 15–16, 201 N.W.2d at 767–68. *See, e.g.*, Richard Ausness, *Regulatory Takings & Wetland Protection in the Post-*Lucas *Era*, 30 LAND & WATER L. REV. 349, 403–04 (1995) ("*Lucas* is inconsistent with the reasoning of *Just v. Marinette County* and other cases that concluded that property owners have no inherent right to change the 'natural' character of their land.").

(D) *Stevens v. City of Cannon Beach*, **317 Or. 131, 854 P.2d 449 (1993), cert. denied, 510 U.S. 1207, 114 S. Ct. 1332 (1994).** *Stevens* was a beachfront property case akin to *Lucas*. The Oregon court held plaintiffs "were on notice that exclusive use of the dry sand areas was not a part of the 'bundle of rights' that they acquired, because public use of dry sand areas 'is so notorious that notice of the custom on the part of persons buying land along the shore must be presumed.' " *Stevens*, 317 Or. at 139, 854 P.2d at 454.

(E) *Broughton Lumber Co. v. United States*, **30 Fed. Cl. 239 (1994).** A logging company with a state water right to transport logs down a stream wanted to convert its right for use in hydropower generation. It secured a preliminary permit from the Federal Energy Regulatory Commission to do so, but intervening legislation creating a national scenic area ended that possibility. The plaintiffs claimed a taking under these facts, but the court found the plaintiff's interest in the water for electricity generation purposes was too speculative. Apparently, only seven percent of applications for such permits ever result in a completed project. "A compensable interest in property based on an expected future use must be grounded on much larger certainties than opinion testimony about the likelihood of gaining future regulatory approval." *Broughton*, 30 Fed. Cl. at 243.

5. *Judicial Takings.* In the classic circumstance, government action that "takes" private property in violation of the Federal Constitution is action of the executive branch. But a recent United States Supreme Court decision suggests that courts, too, "take" property unconstitutionally if and when they recharacterize property rights so to deprive landowners of fundamental property rights. In *Stop the Beach Renourishment, Inc. v. Florida Department of Environmental Protection et al.*, 130 S. Ct. 2592 (2010), four Justices (Chief Justice Roberts and Associate Justices Alito, Scalia, and Thomas) so ruled. The other Justices viewed resolution of the issue to be unnecessary to the decision in the case.

Notably, if the Supreme Court ultimately decides as a matter of law that judicial takings are possible, it will have necessarily, if perhaps quietly, answered a significant jurisprudential question, whether courts make new law or merely interpret existing law. It would seem impossible for a court to affirmatively "take" property if all it does is interpret existing law.

Chapter 4

THE NATIONAL ENVIRONMENTAL POLICY ACT

"I believe, Mr. President, when historians look back to the years 1969 and 1970, they will say those were watershed years in terms of the U.S. environmental movement. Congress, concerned that the environment needed greater protection, took the lead and enacted major environmental statutes. . . . Of all these and other significant actions that took place in those 2 years, few can rival in importance the creation of the National Environmental Policy Act. Signed into law on January 1, 1970, it is a short and simple law with dramatic purpose. To declare a national policy which will encourage productive and enjoyable harmony between man and his environment. . . . NEPA has been a tremendous success and has changed forever the way our Government makes decisions affecting the environment." *Statement of Sen. John Chafee*, from TWENTY YEARS OF ENVIRONMENTAL PROGRESS, Senate proceedings, Mar. 24, 1992, Cong. Rec. S4141.

SYNOPSIS

A. **INTRODUCTION**

B. **EXCEPTIONS TO APPLICABILITY**

C. **WHETHER TO PREPARE AN ENVIRONMENTAL IMPACT STATEMENT**

D. **ENVIRONMENTAL IMPACT STATEMENTS**
    1. **The Role of EISs in Decisionmaking**
    2. **EIS Content and Availability Requirements**

A. INTRODUCTION

We begin with a brief historical recitation of the genesis of the National Environmental Policy Act.

TWENTIETH ANNUAL REPORT OF THE COUNCIL ON ENVIRONMENTAL QUALITY
18–20 (1990)[1]

* * *

HISTORICAL PERSPECTIVE

In the early 1960s when several committees of Congress began seriously looking into pollution problems, the nature and extent of such problems were not fully understood. In hearings and seminars that spanned several Congresses, legislators learned that pollution was part of a multifaceted problem, having its roots in technologically induced change and "involving natural and social sciences, economics, and governmental and private institutions." Even more vexing was the revelation that no single environmental problem could be considered separately, "that apparently isolated changes interact in unanticipated ways and that the eventual restoration of environmental quality will depend upon the solution of a series of interrelated problems, none of which can be understood in isolation from its fellows." Indeed, the problem appeared so overwhelming that one observer, summarizing the views offered by several experts in the field during a joint committee hearing, was "left with a vaguely uneasy feeling that if we see the continuous complex here as one set of interconnecting realities that have to be understood as a total system, we may be broadening our interests so much that it is impossible to act on it all."

The complexities and interrelatedness of the "pollution problem" caused Congress to reevaluate its practice of passing laws in response to specific episodes of environmental degradation, a practice that had led to passage of the Federal Water Pollution Control Act of 1948 and the Air Pollution Control Act of 1955. The single-solution approach typified in those statutes was unworkable, and environmental laws in general were "floundering due to inadequate information, and misinterpretation of existing facts." Many in Congress began to see the need for a comprehensive approach to the environment, one that was capable of anticipating environmentally disruptive activities and avoiding them, rather than just reacting to episodes of pollution with abatement laws.

With a greater sense of purpose and perhaps some frustration, Congress began to look more closely at the federal establishment. The federal government in the 1960s was seen to be both a major cause of environmental degradation and a major source of regulatory authority. Consequently, the federal government itself became the principal focus of further efforts to fashion a comprehensive approach to the environment.

An area where improvements had long been thought necessary, and for which legislation had been introduced as far back as the early 1960s, was the organization of the federal government. In the 1960s environmental responsibilities were divided among 15 to 20 federal departments and agencies receiving direction and funding

---

[1] Copyright © 1990. Reprinted with permission.

from two dozen different Congressional committees. Reorganization of the government on a large scale, however, was not desired; nor did it "seem practical to remedy the situation by any superimposed 'czar' of environmental quality. . . . " Existing institutions were thought to be up to the task, but there was no "coordinating group capable of systems analysis and broad management of federal projects." The concept of an advisory council that "would exert a preemptive coordinating role and strive to prevent, rather than correct environmental degradation," although not new, took firm hold in Congress in the late 1960s.

A Council on Environmental Quality was the centerpiece of H.R. 12549, introduced by Representative John Dingle of Michigan and others in February 1969. The purpose of the bill was to create "a council which can provide a consistent and expert source of review of national policies, environmental problems and trends, both long-term and short-term. Such a council would act entirely independently of the executive, mission-oriented agencies." The council envisioned in H.R. 12549 would have been composed of five members and located in the Executive Office of the President. With few changes, notably the number of members, the centerpiece of H.R. 12549 became a constituent element of NEPA.

Many in Congress believed that no amount of coordination would be able to overcome the tendency for agencies to pursue their primary missions, few of which at that time included environmental quality. Further, it was apparent that great potential existed for "conflicts when environmental quality is managed by different policies, originating in conservation, agriculture, esthetics, recreation, economic development, human health, and so forth." For this reason, federal agencies needed an overall policy for the environment . . . which integrates these purposes and objectives and which provides for choice when they are incompatible . . . [mindful that] [c]hoices are not always quantitative and tradeoffs are not systematic."

Given the intricacies and interrelatedness of the human environment, a policy oriented toward very specific goals or objectives was seen as impractical. Thus, it was believed that "a comprehensive policy toward the environment cannot help but be philosophical rather than specific."

What was to become the national environmental policy was prepared at the direction of Senator Henry Jackson of Washington, who considered the policy a means of establishing priorities and giving expression to "our national goals and aspirations- . . . [serving] a constitutional function in that people may refer to it for guidance in making decisions where environmental values are found to be in conflict with other values." According to Senator Jackson:

> A properly drafted Congressional statement of national environmental policy, along with a requirement for official statements of environmental findings in federal decisions and legislative proposals, will effectively make the quality of the environment everyone's responsibility. No agency will then be able to maintain that it has no mandate or no requirement to consider the environmental consequences of its actions.

The need for a comprehensive environmental policy was never seriously disputed. It was recognized, however, that the mere declaration of a national environmental policy would not assure pursuit of its objectives. Agencies could very well ignore a statement of policy if not compelled somehow to do otherwise. The concept of self-policing by federal agencies that pollute or license pollution was flatly rejected. A mechanism to implement the policy was needed, an " 'action-forcing' process that could be put into operation."

NEPA would be that mechanism. The statute is divisible into two functional parts, one substantive and one procedural. The substantive part, § 101, announces the nation's environmental policy: "it is the continuing policy of the Federal Government [in cooperation with other public and private entities] to use all practicable means and measures, including financial and technical assistance, in a manner calculated to foster and promote the general welfare, to create and maintain conditions under which man and nature can exist in productive harmony, and fulfill the social, economic, and other requirements of present and future generations of Americans." § 101(a), 42 U.S.C. § 4331(a). Section 101(b) specifies the government's responsibility to act in ways so that "the Nation may—

(1) fulfill the responsibilities of each generation as trustee of the environment for succeeding generations;

(2) assure for all Americans safe, healthful, productive, and esthetically and culturally pleasing surroundings;

(3) attain the widest range of beneficial uses of the environment without degradation, risk to health or safety, or other undesirable and unintended consequences;

(4) preserve important historic, cultural, and natural aspects of our national heritage, and maintain, wherever possible, an environment which supports diversity and variety of individual choice;

(5) achieve a balance between population and resource use which will permit high standards of living and a wide sharing of life's amenities; and

(6) enhance the quality of renewable resources and approach the maximum attainable recycling of depletable resources.

§ 101(b), 42 U.S.C. 4331(b).

The procedural part of NEPA is found in § 102. That provision identifies the steps to be taken to implement the substantive goals of § 101. First, it declares, "the policies, regulations and public laws of the United States shall be interpreted in accordance with the policies set forth in this chapter. . . ." § 102(1), 42 U.S.C. § 4332(1). For more information on this provision, see A NOTE ON NEPA § 102(1) at the conclusion of this Chapter. Second, § 102 requires federal agencies to undertake several responsibilities, see § 102(2), 42 U.S.C. 4332(2), the most important of which is to prepare environmental impact statements ("EISs") to accompany major initiatives.

Importantly, as indicated in the reading above, NEPA also created a governmental unit to orchestrate compliance with the statute. The Council on Environmental Quality ("CEQ"), located within the Executive Office of the President, has the job of coordinating the whole of the federal environmental effort to implement

NEPA. Its assignment is to oversee agency implementation of the EIS process and to referee disagreements among agencies. CEQ also works to develop environmental policies and initiatives. The Chair of CEQ, appointed by the President with the advice and consent of the Senate, serves as the principal environmental policy adviser to the President. CEQ reports annually to the President on the state of the environment.

How NEPA should operate in the real world was the subject of the *Calvert Cliffs* decision of the D.C. Circuit. *Calvert Cliffs* was the first comprehensive interpretation of the new statute.

CALVERT CLIFFS' COORDINATING COMMITTEE, INC. v. U.S. ATOMIC ENERGY COMMISSION
449 F.2d 1109 (D.C. Cir. 1971)

J. Skelly Wright, Circuit Judge:

These cases are only the beginning of what promises to become a flood of new litigation — litigation seeking judicial assistance in protecting our natural environment. Several recently enacted statutes attest to the commitment of the Government to control, at long last, the destructive engine of material "progress." But it remains to be seen whether the promise of this legislation will become a reality. Therein lies the judicial role. In these cases, we must for the first time interpret the broadest and perhaps most important of the recent statutes: the National Environmental Policy Act of 1969 (NEPA). We must assess claims that one of the agencies charged with its administration has failed to live up to the congressional mandate. Our duty, in short, is to see that important legislative purposes, heralded in the halls of Congress, are not lost or misdirected in the vast hallways of the federal bureaucracy.

NEPA, like so much other reform legislation of the last 40 years, is cast in terms of a general mandate and broad delegation of authority to new and old administrative agencies. It takes the major step of requiring all federal agencies to consider values of environmental preservation in their spheres of activity, and it prescribes certain procedural measures to ensure that those values are in fact fully respected. Petitioners argue that rules recently adopted by the Atomic Energy Commission to govern consideration of environmental matters fail to satisfy the rigor demanded by NEPA. The Commission, on the other hand, contends that the vagueness of the NEPA mandate and delegation leaves much room for discretion and that the rules challenged by petitioners fall well within the broad scope of the Act. We find the policies embodied in NEPA to be a good deal clearer and more demanding than does the Commission. We conclude that the Commission's procedural rules do not comply with the congressional policy. Hence we remand these cases for further rule making.

I

We begin our analysis with an examination of NEPA's structure and approach and of the Atomic Energy Commission rules which are said to conflict with the requirements of the Act. The relevant portion of NEPA is Title I, consisting of five sections. Section 101 sets forth the Act's basic substantive policy: that the federal government "use all practicable means and measures" to protect environmental values. Congress did not establish environmental protection as an exclusive goal; rather, it desired a reordering of priorities, so that environmental costs and benefits will assume their proper place along with other considerations. In Section 101(b), imposing an explicit duty on federal officials, the Act provides that "it is the continuing responsibility of the Federal Government to use all practicable means, consistent with other essential considerations of national policy," to avoid environmental degradation, preserve "historic, cultural, and natural" resources, and promote "the widest range of beneficial uses of the environment without . . . undesirable and unintended consequences."

Thus the general substantive policy of the Act is a flexible one. It leaves room for a responsible exercise of discretion and may not require particular substantive results in particular problematic instances. However, the Act also contains very important "procedural" provisions — provisions which are designed to see that all federal agencies do in fact exercise the substantive discretion given them. These provisions are not highly flexible. Indeed, they establish a strict standard of compliance.

NEPA, first of all, makes environmental protection a part of the mandate of every federal agency and department. The Atomic Energy Commission, for example, had continually asserted, prior to NEPA, that it had no statutory authority to concern itself with the adverse environmental effects of its actions. Now, however, its hands are no longer tied. It is not only permitted, but compelled, to take environmental values into account. Perhaps the greatest importance of NEPA is to require the Atomic Energy Commission and other agencies to consider environmental issues just as they consider other matters within their mandates. This compulsion is most plainly stated in Section 102. There, "Congress authorizes and directs that, to the fullest extent possible: (1) the policies, regulations, and public laws of the United States shall be interpreted and administered in accordance with the policies set forth in this Act. . . . " Congress also "authorizes and directs" that "(2) all agencies of the Federal Government shall" follow certain rigorous procedures in considering environmental values. Senator Jackson, NEPA's principal sponsor, stated that "no agency will [now] be able to maintain that it has no mandate or no requirement to consider the environmental consequences of its actions." He characterized the requirements of Section 102 as "action-forcing" and stated that "otherwise, these lofty declarations [in Section 101] are nothing more than that."

The sort of consideration of environmental values which NEPA compels is clarified in Section 102(2)(A) and (B). In general, all agencies must use a "systematic, interdisciplinary approach" to environmental planning and evaluation "in decision-making which may have an impact on man's environment." In order to include all possible environmental factors in the decisional equation, agencies must "identify and develop methods and procedures . . . which will insure that presently unquantified environmental amenities and values may be given appropriate consideration in decisionmaking along with economic and technical considerations." "Environmental amenities" will often be in conflict with "economic and technical considerations." To "consider" the former "along with" the latter must involve a balancing process. In some instances environmental costs may outweigh economic and technical benefits and in other instances they may not. But NEPA mandates a rather finely tuned and "systematic" balancing analysis in each instance.

To ensure that the balancing analysis is carried out and given full effect, Section 102(2)(C) requires that responsible officials of all agencies prepare a "detailed statement" covering the impact of particular actions on the environment, the environmental costs which might be avoided, and alternative measures which might alter the cost-benefit equation. The apparent purpose of the "detailed statement" is to aid in the agencies' own decision making process and to advise other interested agencies and the public of the environmental consequences of planned federal action. Beyond the "detailed statement," Section 102(2)(D) requires all agencies specifically to "study, develop, and describe appropriate alternatives to recommended courses of action in any proposal which involves unresolved conflicts concerning alternative uses of available resources." This requirement, like the "detailed statement" requirement, seeks to ensure that each agency decision maker has before him and takes into proper account all possible approaches to a particular project (including total abandonment of the project) which would alter the environmental impact and the cost-benefit balance. Only in that fashion is it likely that the most intelligent, optimally beneficial decision will ultimately be made. Moreover, by compelling a formal "detailed statement" and a description of alternatives, NEPA provides evidence that the mandated decision making process has in fact taken place and, most importantly, allows those removed from the initial process to evaluate and balance the factors on their own.

Of course, all of these Section 102 duties are qualified by the phrase "to the fullest extent possible." We must stress as forcefully as possible that this language does not provide an escape hatch for footdragging agencies; it does not make NEPA's procedural requirements somehow "discretionary." Congress did not intend the Act to be such a paper tiger. Indeed, the requirement of environmental consideration "to the fullest extent possible" sets a high standard for the agencies, a standard which must be rigorously enforced by the reviewing courts.

Unlike the substantive duties of Section 101(b), which require agencies to "use all practicable means consistent with other essential considerations," the procedural duties of Section 102 must be fulfilled to the "fullest extent possible." This contrast, in itself, is revealing. But the dispositive factor in our interpretation is the expressed views of the Senate and House conferees who wrote the "fullest extent possible" language into NEPA. They stated:

> . . . The purpose of the new language is to make it clear that each agency of the Federal Government shall comply with the directives set out in . . . [Section 102(2)] unless the existing law applicable to such agency's operations expressly prohibits or makes full compliance with one of the directives impossible. . . . Thus, it is the intent of the conferees that the provision 'to the fullest extent possible' shall not be used by any Federal agency as a

means of avoiding compliance with the directives set out in section 102. Rather, the language in section 102 is intended to assure that all agencies of the Federal Government shall comply with the directives set out in said section 'to the fullest extent possible' under their statutory authorizations and that no agency shall utilize an excessively narrow construction of its existing statutory authorizations to avoid compliance.

Thus the Section 102 duties are not inherently flexible. They must be complied with to the fullest extent, unless there is a clear conflict of statutory authority. Considerations of administrative difficulty, delay or economic cost will not suffice to strip the section of its fundamental importance.

We conclude, then, that Section 102 of NEPA mandates a particular sort of careful and informed decisionmaking process and creates judicially enforceable duties. The reviewing courts probably cannot reverse a substantive decision on its merits, under Section 101, unless it be shown that the actual balance of costs and benefits that was struck was arbitrary or clearly gave insufficient weight to environmental values. But if the decision was reached procedurally without individualized consideration and balancing of environmental factors — conducted fully and in good faith — it is the responsibility of the courts to reverse. As one District Court has said of Section 102 requirements: "It is hard to imagine a clearer or stronger mandate to the Courts."

In the cases before us now, we do not have to review a particular decision by the Atomic Energy Commission granting a construction permit or an operating license. Rather, we must review the Commission's recently promulgated rules which govern consideration of environmental values in all such individual decisions. The rules were devised strictly in order to comply with the NEPA procedural requirements — but petitioners argue that they fall far short of the congressional mandate.

The period of the rules' gestation does not indicate overenthusiasm on the Commission's part. NEPA went into effect on January 1, 1970. On April 2, 1970 — three months later — the Commission issued its first, short policy statement on implementation of the Act's procedural provisions. After another span of two months, the Commission published a notice of proposed rule making in the Federal Register. Petitioners submitted substantial comments critical of the proposed rules. Finally, on December 3, 1970, the Commission terminated its long rule making proceeding by issuing a formal amendment, labeled. Appendix D, to its governing regulations. Appendix D is a somewhat revised version of the earlier proposal and, at last, commits the Commission to consider environmental impact in its decision making process.

The procedure for environmental study and consideration set up by the Appendix D rules is as follows: Each applicant for an initial construction permit must submit to the Commission his own "environmental report," presenting his assessment of the environmental impact of the planned facility and possible alternatives which would alter the impact. When construction is completed and the applicant applies for a license to operate the new facility, he must again submit an "environmental report" noting any factors which have changed since the original report. At each stage, the Commission's regulatory staff must take the applicant's report and prepare its own "detailed statement" of environmental costs, benefits and alternatives. The statement will then be circulated to other interested and responsible agencies and made available to the public. After comments are received from those sources, the staff must prepare a final "detailed statement" and make a final recommendation on the application for a construction permit or operating license.

Up to this point in the Appendix D rules petitioners have raised no challenge. However, they do attack four other, specific parts of the rules which, they say, violate the requirements of Section 102 of NEPA. Each of these parts in some way limits full consideration and individualized balancing of environmental values in the Commission's decision making process. (1) Although environmental factors must be considered by the agency's regulatory staff under the rules, such factors need not be considered by the hearing board conducting an independent review of staff recommendations, unless affirmatively raised by outside parties or staff members. (2) Another part of the procedural rules prohibits any such party from raising nonradiological environmental issues at any hearing if the notice for that hearing appeared in the Federal Register before March 4, 1971. (3) Moreover, the hearing board is prohibited from conducting an independent evaluation and balancing of certain environmental factors if other responsible agencies have already certified that their own environmental standards are satisfied by the proposed federal action. (4) Finally, the Commission's rules provide that when a construction permit for a facility has been issued before NEPA compliance was required and when an operating license has yet to be issued, the agency will not formally consider environmental factors or require modifications in the proposed facility until the time of the issuance of the operating license. Each of these parts of the Commission's rules will be described at greater length and evaluated under NEPA in the following sections of this opinion.

II

NEPA makes only one specific reference to consideration of environmental values in agency review processes. Section 102(2)(C) provides that copies of the staff's "detailed statement" and comments thereon "shall accompany the proposal through the existing agency review processes." The Atomic Energy Commission's rules may seem in technical compliance with the letter of that provision. They state:

12. If party to a proceeding . . . raises any [environmental] issue . . . the Applicant's Environmental Report and the Detailed Statement will be offered in evidence. The atomic safety and licensing board will make findings of fact on, and resolve, the matters in controversy among the parties with regard to those issues. Depending on the resolution of those issues, the permit or license may be granted, denied, or appropriately conditioned to protect environmental values.

13. When no party to a proceeding . . . raises any [environmental] issue . . . such issues will not be considered by the atomic safety and licensing board. Under such circumstances, although the Applicant's Environmental Report, comments thereon, and the Detailed Statement will accompany the application through the Commission's review processes, they will not be received in evidence, and the Commission's responsibilities under the

National Environmental Policy Act of 1969 will be carried out in toto outside the hearing process.

The question here is whether the Commission is correct in thinking that its NEPA responsibilities may "be carried out in toto outside the hearing process" — whether it is enough that environmental data and evaluations merely "accompany" an application through the review process, but receive no consideration whatever from the hearing board.

We believe that the Commission's crabbed interpretation of NEPA makes a mockery of the Act. What possible purpose could there be in the Section 102(2)(C) requirement (that the "detailed statement" accompany proposals through agency review processes) if "accompany" means no more than physical proximity — mandating no more than the physical act of passing certain folders and papers, unopened, to reviewing officials along with other folders and papers? What possible purpose could there be in requiring the "detailed statement" to be before hearing boards, if the boards are free to ignore entirely the contents of the statement? NEPA was meant to do more than regulate the flow of papers in the federal bureaucracy. The word "accompany" in Section 102(2)(C) must not be read so narrowly as to make the Act ludicrous. It must, rather, be read to indicate a congressional intent that environmental factors, as compiled in the "detailed statement," be considered through agency review processes.

Beyond Section 102(2)(C), NEPA requires that agencies consider the environmental impact of their actions "to the fullest extent possible." The Act is addressed to agencies as a whole, not only to their professional staffs. Compliance to the "fullest" possible extent would seem to demand that environmental issues be considered at every important stage in the decision making process concerning a particular action — at every stage where an overall balancing of environmental and nonenvironmental factors is appropriate and where alterations might be made in the proposed action to minimize environmental costs. Of course, consideration which is entirely duplicative is not necessarily required. But independent review of staff proposals by hearing boards is hardly a duplicative function. A truly independent review provides a crucial check on the staff's recommendations. The Commission's hearing boards automatically consider nonenvironmental factors, even though they have been previously studied by the staff. Clearly, the review process is an appropriate stage at which to balance conflicting factors against one another. And, just as clearly, it provides an important opportunity to reject or significantly modify the staff's recommended action. Environmental factors, therefore, should not be singled out and excluded, at this stage, from the proper balance of values envisioned by NEPA.

The Commission's regulations provide that in an uncontested proceeding the hearing board shall on its own "determine whether the application and the record of the proceeding contain sufficient information, and the review of the application by the Commission's regulatory staff has been adequate, to support affirmative findings on" various nonenvironmental factors. NEPA requires at least as much automatic consideration of environmental factors. In uncontested hearings, the board need not necessarily go over the same ground covered in the "detailed statement." But it must at least examine the statement carefully to determine whether "the review . . . by the Commission's regulatory staff has been adequate." And it must independently consider the final balance among conflicting factors that is struck in the staff's recommendation.

The rationale of the Commission's limitation of environmental issues to hearings in which parties affirmatively raise those issues may have been one of economy. It may have been supposed that, whenever there are serious environmental costs overlooked or uncorrected by the staff, some party will intervene to bring those costs to the hearing board's attention. Of course, independent review of the "detailed statement" and independent balancing of factors in an uncontested hearing will take some time. If it is done properly, it will take a significant amount of time. But all of the NEPA procedures take time. Such administrative costs are not enough to undercut the Act's requirement that environmental protection be considered "to the fullest extent possible." . . . It is, moreover, unrealistic to assume that there will always be an intervenor with the information, energy and money required to challenge a staff recommendation which ignores environmental costs. NEPA establishes environmental protection as an integral part of the Atomic Energy Commission's basic mandate. The primary responsibility for fulfilling that mandate lies with the Commission. Its responsibility is not simply to sit back, like an umpire, and resolve adversary contentions at the hearing stage. Rather, it must itself take the initiative of considering environmental values at every distinctive and comprehensive stage of the process beyond the staff's evaluation and recommendation. . . .

IV

The sweep of NEPA is extraordinarily broad, compelling consideration of any and all types of environmental impact of federal action. However, the Atomic Energy Commission's rules specifically exclude from full consideration a wide variety of environmental issues. First, they provide that no party may raise and the Commission may not independently examine any problem of water quality — perhaps the most significant impact of nuclear power plants. Rather, the Commission indicates that it will defer totally to water quality standards devised and administered by state agencies and approved by the federal government under the Federal Water Pollution Control Act. Secondly, the rules provide for similar abdication of NEPA authority to the standards of other agencies:

> With respect to those aspects of environmental quality for which environmental quality standards and requirements have been established by authorized Federal, State, and regional agencies, proof that the applicant is equipped to observe and agrees to observe such standards and requirements will be considered a satisfactory showing that there will not be a significant, adverse effect on the environment. Certification by the appropriate agency that there is reasonable assurance that the applicant for the permit or license will observe such standards and requirements will be considered dispositive for this purpose.

10 C.F.R. § 50, App. D, at 249.

The most the Commission will do is include a condition in all construction permits and operating licenses requiring compliance with the water quality or other standards set by such agencies. The upshot is that the NEPA procedures, viewed by the Commission as superfluous, will wither away in disuse, applied only to those environmental issues wholly unregulated by any other federal, state or regional body.

We believe the Commission's rule is in fundamental conflict with the basic purpose of the Act. NEPA mandates a case-by-case balancing judgment on the part of federal agencies. In each individual case, the particular economic and technical benefits of planned action must be assessed and then weighed against the environmental costs; alternatives must be considered which would affect the balance of values. . . . The magnitude of possible benefits and possible costs may lie anywhere on a broad spectrum. Much will depend on the particular magnitudes involved in particular cases. In some cases, the benefits will be great enough to justify a certain quantum of environmental costs; in other cases, they will not be so great and the proposed action may have to be abandoned or significantly altered so as to bring the benefits and costs into a proper balance. The point of the individualized balancing analysis is to ensure that, with possible alterations, the optimally beneficial action is finally taken.

Certification by another agency that its own environmental standards are satisfied involves an entirely different kind of judgment. Such agencies, without overall responsibility for the particular federal action in question, attend only to one aspect of the problem: the magnitude of certain environmental costs. They simply determine whether those costs exceed an allowable amount. Their certification does not mean that they found no environmental damage whatever. In fact, there may be significant environmental damage (e.g., water pollution), but not quite enough to violate applicable (e.g., water quality) standards. Certifying agencies do not attempt to weigh that damage against the opposing benefits. Thus the balancing analysis remains to be done. It may be that the environmental costs, though passing prescribed standards, are nonetheless great enough to outweigh the particular economic and technical benefits involved in the planned action. The only agency in a position to make such a judgment is the agency with overall responsibility for the proposed federal action — the agency to which NEPA is specifically directed.

The Atomic Energy Commission, abdicating entirely to other agencies' certifications, neglects the mandated balancing analysis. Concerned members of the public are thereby precluded from raising a wide range of environmental issues in order to affect particular Commission decisions. And the special purpose of NEPA is subverted.

Arguing before this court, the Commission has made much of the special environmental expertise of the agencies which set environmental standards. NEPA did not overlook this consideration. Indeed, the Act is quite explicit in describing the attention which is to be given to the views and standards of other agencies. Section 102 (2)(C) provides:

> Prior to making any detailed statement, the responsible Federal official shall consult with and obtain the comments of any Federal agency which has jurisdiction by law or special expertise with respect to any environmental impact involved. Copies of such statement and the comments and

views of the appropriate Federal, State, and local agencies, which are authorized to develop and enforce environmental standards, shall be made available to the President, the Council on Environmental Quality and to the public. . . .

Thus the Congress was surely cognizant of federal, state and local agencies "authorized to develop and enforce environmental standards." But it provided, in Section 102(2)(C), only for full consultation. It most certainly did not authorize a total abdication to those agencies. Nor did it grant a license to disregard the main body of NEPA obligations. . . .

The Commission relies upon the flexible NEPA mandate to "use all practicable means consistent with other essential considerations of national policy." As we have previously pointed out, however, that mandate applies only to the substantive guidelines set forth in Section 101 of the Act. . . . The procedural duties, the duties to give full consideration to environmental protection, are subject to a much more strict standard of compliance. By now, the applicable principle should be absolutely clear. NEPA requires that an agency must — to the fullest extent possible under its other statutory obligations — consider alternatives to its actions which would reduce environmental damage. That principle establishes that consideration of environmental matters must be more than a pro forma ritual. Clearly, it is pointless to "consider" environmental costs without also seriously considering action to avoid them. Such a full exercise of substantive discretion is required at every important, appropriate and nonduplicative stage of an agency's proceedings. . . .

A full NEPA consideration of alterations in the original plans of a facility, then, is both important and appropriate well before the operating license proceedings. It is not duplicative if environmental issues were not considered in granting the construction permit. And it need not be duplicated, absent new information or new developments, at the operating license stage. In order that the preoperating license review be as effective as possible, the Commission should consider very seriously the requirement of a temporary halt in construction pending its review and the "backfitting" of technological innovations. For no action which might minimize environmental damage may be dismissed out of hand. Of course, final operation of the facility may be delayed thereby. But some delay is inherent whenever the NEPA consideration is conducted — whether before or at the license proceedings. It is far more consistent with the purposes of the Act to delay operation at a stage where real environmental protection may come about than at a stage where corrective action may be so costly as to be impossible.

Thus we conclude that the Commission must go farther than it has in its present rules. It must consider action, as well as file reports and papers, at the preoperating license stage. As the Commission candidly admits, such consideration does not amount to a retroactive application of NEPA. Although the projects in question may have been commenced and initially approved before January 1, 1970, the Act clearly applies to them since they must still pass muster before going into full operation. All we demand is that the environmental review be as full and fruitful as possible.

VI

We hold that, in the four respects detailed above, the Commission must revise its rules governing consideration of environmental issues. We do not impose a harsh burden on the Commission. For we require only an exercise of substantive discretion which will protect the environment "to the fullest extent possible." No less is required if the grand congressional purposes underlying NEPA are to become a reality.

Remanded for proceedings consistent with this opinion.

NOTES AND QUESTIONS

1. *Calvert Cliffs and Statutory Interpretation. Calvert Cliffs* is a landmark decision in environmental and natural resources law mainly because it held that the National Environmental Policy Act really means something. In particular, the case breathed life into § 102(2) of the statute, which was found to impose significant and enforceable obligations on federal agencies. The result has been the elevation of NEPA to prominent stature in environmental and natural resources law. An indicator of that stature is the frequency of judicial consideration of the measure. A recent LEXIS search in the federal courts library, using the search terms "National Environmental Policy Act," yielded well over 3000 citations. *See also* WILLIAM H. RODGERS, JR., ENVIRONMENTAL LAW § 9.1.C.3, at 817–18 (2d ed. 1994) (attesting to NEPA's production of "hundreds of injunctions, thousands of cases, tens of thousands of impact statements, hundreds of thousands of environmental assessments.").

Calvert Cliffs' reading of NEPA was by no means assured. NEPA, by its terms, only requires agencies to take the procedural steps of § 102 "to the fullest extent possible." Judge Wright eschewed the notion that this modifying phrase might serve as "an escape hatch for footdragging agencies," but he easily could have found the phrase to be just that. Judicial reporters are replete with decisions that dilute the impact of legal obligations because the statute imposing the obligation required the task be done only to the extent "appropriate" or "reasonable," or "as much as possible."

Why did Judge Wright choose to give a full measure of rigor to the obligations of § 102? He offered two reasons. First, he noted the distinction between the phrasing of § 101, which requires compliance by use of "all practicable means consistent with other essential considerations" with that of § 102, which requires compliance "to the fullest extent possible." Judge Wright found this contrast to be "revealing" although not dispositive.

What was dispositive for Judge Wright was NEPA's legislative history. In particular, he cited the report of Senate and House conferees which specified that the "fullest extent possible" language should not serve to excuse agency nonchalance. Thus was raised the longstanding issue of the role legislative history should play in the search for statutory meaning. Proponents of using legislative history assert it sheds important light on the meaning of often ambiguous legislative text. Associate Justice Stephen Breyer of the U.S. Supreme Court, an advocate for use of legislative history, has stated that "using legislative history to help interpret unclear statutory language seems natural. Legislative history helps a court understand the context and purpose of a statute." Stephen Breyer, *On the Uses of Legislative History in Interpreting Statutes*, 65 S. CAL. L. REV. 845, 848 (1992).

Opponents maintain that legislative history is irrelevant to statutory meaning. Associate Justice Antonin Scalia of the U.S. Supreme Court, a leader in this camp, has commented that "it is simply incompatible with democratic government, or indeed, even with fair government, to have the meaning of a law determined by what the lawgiver meant, rather than by what the lawgiver promulgated. . . . It is the *law* that governs, not the intent of the lawgiver." ANTONIN SCALIA, A MATTER OF INTERPRETATION: FEDERAL COURTS AND THE LAW 17 (1997). Scalia and others maintain as well that legislative history is unreliable in any event. Lastly, they bemoan the ease with which legislative history can be manipulated by persons who prefer one interpretation of an ambiguous statute over another. As Judge Sentelle noted, reviewing legislative history is like "looking over a crowd and picking out your friends." *Citizens Coal Council v. Norton*, 330 F.3d 478, 484 (D.C. Cir. 2003).

If his opinion in *Calvert Cliffs* is a gauge, Judge Skelly Wright counted himself among those who view legislative history as a helpful analytical tool. Might there be other reasons he opted for such a strong proenvironment reading of NEPA? One possibility is a convergence of factors external to the case but possibly influential on the Judge. First, it is clear that Judge Wright did not seem to hold federal agencies in high regard: witness his fear, expressed in *Calvert Cliffs*, that "important legislative purposes" could be "lost or misdirected in the vast hallways of the federal bureaucracy." Second, because he presided over numerous environmental law cases, Judge Wright assuredly came to look upon himself as an expert on environmental law and regulation in his own right. Third, he viewed himself unabashedly as a judicial activist, and a liberal one at that. For an interesting analysis of Judge Wright in this regard, drawn from his own comments about himself and others on the D.C. Circuit, see GARY LAWSON, FEDERAL ADMINISTRATIVE LAW 246 n.31 (4th ed. 2007).[2]

2. *Executive Orders No. 11514 and 11991*. Shortly after NEPA was enacted, President Richard Nixon issued Executive Order 11514, which directed the Council on Environmental Quality to issue guidelines on how NEPA should be implemented across the federal government. Despite these guidelines, agencies complained during the 1970s that NEPA imposed too heavy a work burden and caused too much delay. These concerns prompted President Jimmy Carter to issue Executive Order 11991, which instructed CEQ to issue regulations to make NEPA compliance less burdensome. These regulations, as amended, may be found at 40 C.F.R. Parts 1500–17.

---

[2] The United States Supreme Court later trimmed the activist wings of the D.C. Circuit, at least with respect to the judicial imposition of procedures on executive agencies, in *Vermont Yankee Nuclear Power Corp. v. Natural Resources Defense Council, Inc.*, 435 U.S. 519, 98 S. Ct. 1197 (1978).

NEPA AT 19: A PRIMER ON AN "OLD" LAW WITH SOLUTIONS TO "NEW" PROBLEMS
19 ENVTL. L. RPTR. 10060 (1989)[3]

. . . .

Regulatory Structure

The CEQ regulations implementing the procedural provisions of NEPA apply to all federal agencies of the government, excluding Congress and any of its institutions, the judiciary, and the President, including the performance of staff functions for the President. The CEQ regulations are generic in nature, and do not address the applicability of the various procedural requirements to specific agency actions. Instead, each federal department and agency is required to prepare its own NEPA procedures that address that agency's compliance in relation to its particular mission. CEQ reviews and approves all agency procedures and amendments to those procedures.

The agency procedures are required to establish specific criteria for and identification of three classes of actions: those that require preparation of an environmental impact statement; those that require preparation of an environmental assessment; and those that are categorically excluded from further NEPA review. Additionally, agencies are required to address NEPA compliance for actions initiated outside of the federal government that require federal approval, the introduction of supplemental EISs into the administrative record, the integration of NEPA analysis into the agency decisionmaking process, and to name a contact office for further information or documents prepared under NEPA.

Categorical Exclusions

"Categorical exclusions" refer to acts falling within a predesignated category of actions that do not individually or cumulatively have a significant effect on the human environment. Thus, no documentation of environmental analysis is required. Agencies may list either very specific actions, or a broader class of actions with criteria and examples for guidance. However, federal officials must be alert to extraordinary circumstances in which a normally excluded action may have a significant environmental effect. A categorical exclusion is not an exemption from compliance with NEPA, but merely an administrative tool to avoid paperwork for those actions without significant environmental effects.

Environmental Assessments

An environmental assessment ("EA") is supposed to be a concise public document that may be prepared to achieve any of the following purposes: to provide sufficient evidence and analysis for determining whether to prepare an EIS; to aid an agency's compliance with NEPA when no EIS is necessary; and to facilitate

---

[3] Copyright © 1989 Environmental Law Institute, Washington, D.C. Reprinted with permission from ELR — The Environmental Law Reporter. All rights reserved.

preparation of an EIS if one is necessary. An EA should include a brief discussion of the need for the proposal, of alternatives as required by NEPA § 102(2)(E), and of the environmental impacts of the proposed action and alternatives. It should list agencies and persons consulted. An EA is followed by one of two conclusions: either a Finding of No Significant Impact ("FONSI") or a decision to prepare an EIS. A FONSI briefly presents the reasons why an action, not otherwise categorically excluded, will not have a significant effect on the human environment. It may include a summary of the EA, or simply be attached to the EA. Neither EAs nor FONSIs are filed in a central location (unlike EISs, which are filed with the Office of Federal Activities in the Environmental Protection Agency). However, they are public documents, and the agency responsible for their preparation must involve the public in an appropriate manner.

Agencies have discretion in selecting the appropriate level of public circulation of EAs and FONSIs, but there are two circumstances in which an agency is required to make a FONSI available for public review for thirty days. The first situation is when the proposed action is, or is closely similar to, an action which normally requires an EIS; the second case arises if the nature of the proposed action is without precedent in the agency's experience.

While the EA and FONSI process is a valuable and even essential tool, it has been subjected, far too often, to two types of abuse. On the one hand, some compliance has reduced the EA analysis to a one-page form that is so cursory that it is questionable whether the underlying decision about whether to prepare an EIS is sound. On the other hand, an EA all too frequently takes on the look, feel, and form of an EIS, complete with the same qualitative contents and volume and weight. There can be several reasons for this, but certainly one unfortunate rationale has been to avoid as much public involvement as an EIS would stimulate, while being prepared to turn the EA into an EIS rapidly if a court would so order. Agency officials thinking of that approach would be far better advised to simply proceed with circulation of the document as an EIS.

Environmental Impact Statements

The primary purpose of an EIS is to serve as an action-forcing device to ensure that the policies and goals defined in NEPA are infused into the ongoing programs and actions of the federal government. It must provide full and fair discussion of significant environmental impacts and shall inform decisionmakers and the public of the reasonable alternatives that would avoid or minimize adverse impacts or enhance the quality of the human environment. In preparing EISs, agencies should focus on significant environmental issues and alternatives and reduce paperwork and the accumulation of extraneous background data. Texts should be concise, clear, and to the point, and should be supported by evidence that the agency has made the necessary environmental analyses. An EIS is more than a disclosure document; it should be used by federal officials to plan actions and make decisions. . . .

Two types of EISs that have received less attention than the typical project-specific EIS are the programmatic EIS and the legislative EIS. Programmatic EISs must be prepared prior to an agency's decision regarding a major program, plan, or policy with significant environmental impacts. It may be broad in scope, followed by site-specific EISs or EAs prepared at subsequent stages. The process of preparing a broad statement and subsequent, more narrowly focused NEPA documents is referred to as tiering. Legislative EISs meet the statutory requirement for a "detailed statement on proposals for legislation which would significantly affect the quality of the human environment." Although there are some modifications, the procedures for preparation of legislative EISs are similar to EISs prepared for proposals for executive branch action.

Once the decision is made to prepare an EIS of any type, the proponent federal agency publishes a Notice of Intent ("NOI") in the Federal Register. The NOI should describe the proposed action and possible alternatives, the agency's intent to prepare an EIS, the agency's proposed scoping process, and any planned scoping meetings, and the name and address of a contact person in the agency.

The agency must then engage in the "scoping process," a process to determine the scope of issues to be addressed in the EIS and for identifying the significant issues related to a proposed action. Scoping may or may not include meetings, but the process should involve interested parties at all levels of government, and all interested private citizens and organizations. Scoping is also the appropriate point to allocate responsibilities among lead and cooperating agencies, identify other environmental requirements that are applicable to the proposal, set any time and page limits, and, in general, structure the process in such a way that all identifiable participants are informed and involved at appropriate points. A well designed scoping process can have an extremely positive ripple effect throughout the rest of the NEPA process.

The next step is preparation of a draft EIS. The EIS may be prepared either by the lead agency, with assistance from any cooperating agencies, or by a contractor. However, if a contractor prepares the EIS, the contractor should be chosen by the agency and must execute a disclosure statement prepared by the lead agency, specifying that the contractor has no financial or other interest in the outcome of the project. The agency may accept information from any party, including the applicant, but it always has the duty to independently evaluate such information.

The content requirements of an EIS, from cover sheet to appendices, are set out in the CEQ regulations. The "heart" of the EIS is the alternatives analysis, which inevitably leads to the question of which alternatives must be analyzed. The answer to that, like the answer to the question of what is "significant," is addressed on a case-by-case basis, with the key judicial standard being that of reasonableness.

If the proposed action is the subject of a request for a federal permit or regulatory approval for a proposed action, the federal agency must consider both public and private purpose and need. Courts have stressed the need to consider the objectives of the permit applicant, but they have also emphasized the requirement for the agency to exercise independent judgment as to the appropriate articulation of objective purpose and need. Thus, NEPA requires the agency to consider both public and private purpose and need in formulating the alternatives to be examined in an EIS.

Once the draft EIS is prepared, it must be circulated for at least 45 days for public comment and review. Federal agencies with jurisdiction by law or special expertise with respect to any of the relevant environmental impacts are expected to comment, although this may take the form of a "no comment" letter. At the conclusion of the comment period, the agency must evaluate the comment letters and respond to th e substantive comments in the final EIS. The final EIS is sent to all parties who commented on the draft EIS. No decision may be made concerning the proposed action until at least 30 days after the Notice of Availability of the final EIS or 90 days after the publication of the Notice of Availability of the draft EIS, whichever is later.

At the time of decision, the decisionmaker must sign a Record of Decision ("ROD"). The ROD states what the decision is, identifies which alternatives were considered by the agency in making the decision, specifies which alternatives were considered by the agency in making the decision, specifies which alternatives were considered to be environmentally preferable, and discusses factors that were balanced by the decisionmaker. Further, the ROD states whether all practical methods to avoid or minimize environmental harm are being adopted, and if not, why not. The ROD also includes a description of any applicable enforcement and monitoring programs.

B. EXCEPTIONS TO APPLICABILITY

The National Environmental Policy Act does not always apply according to its terms. In some circumstances it has been ruled to be inapplicable by courts, and in others by the Council on Environmental Quality, in its regulations at 40 C.F.R. Parts 1500–07. (Note that CEQ's regulations are binding on all federal agencies except where compliance with them would be "inconsistent with other statutory requirements." 40 C.F.R. § 1500.3.) In the following circumstances, the statute, or at least the requirements of § 102(2) thereof, has been found not to apply:

(1) *Statutory conflicts*: The NEPA EIS requirement does not apply to government action where the statute authorizing the government action makes NEPA inapplicable. Sometimes a statute expressly makes NEPA inapplicable. *See, e.g.,* Clean Water Act, § 511(c)(1), 33 U.S.C.A. § 1371(c)(1). In other cases, a statute might impliedly make NEPA inapplicable. In this regard, *see, e.g., Alabama v. EPA,* 911 F.2d 499, 504 (11th Cir. 1990) (holding that NEPA does not apply to EPA's permit decisions under § 3005 of the federal Resource Conservation and Recovery Act because RCRA, enacted after NEPA and specifically directing the EPA permitting process, represents an implied exception to NEPA applicability).

(2) *Nondiscretionary actions:* NEPA does not apply to agency actions compelled by statute and regarding which the agency has no discretion. *Flint Ridge Development Co. v. Scenic Rivers Ass'n,* 426 U.S. 776, 96 S. Ct. 2430 (1976).

(3) *Functionally equivalent actions:* By judicial fiat, NEPA does not apply when the action of the agency is itself the "functional equivalent" of an EIS. *See, e.g., Environmental Defense Fund, Inc. v. United States Environmental Protection Agency,* 489 F.2d 1247 (D.C. Cir. 1973) (NEPA does not apply to the "environmentally protective regulatory activities of the Administrator conducted under the registration cancellation provision of the [Federal Insecticide, Fungicide, and Rodenticide Act].") While declining to endorse a broader exemption for EPA, the

court stated: "we see little need in requiring a NEPA statement from an agency whose raison d'etre is the protection of the environment and whose decision on suspension is necessarily infused with the environmental considerations so pertinent to Congress in designing the statutory framework." *Id.* at 1256; *Portland Cement Ass'n v. Ruckelshaus*, 486 F.2d 375 (D.C. Cir. 1973) (EPA's promulgation of stationary source standards for cement plants under the Clean Air Act does not fall under NEPA as the Clean Air Act is the "functional equivalent" of an environmental impact statement). The idea is a logical one: if an agency decision by its very nature implicates a careful consideration of environmental issues, there is no need for an EIS. As long as the statutory and regulatory framework under [the statute] "provides for orderly consideration of diverse environmental factors and . . . [strikes] a workable balance between some of the advantages and disadvantages of full application of NEPA," the "functional equivalent" doctrine applies. *Alabamians for a Clean Env't v. Thomas*, 26 Env't Rep. Cas. 2116, 2122 (N.D. Ala. 1987).

(4) *Emergencies*: Emergency actions may not be subject to NEPA. CEQ's regulations provide:

> Where emergency circumstances make it necessary to take an action with significant environmental impact without observing the provisions of these regulations, the Federal agency taking the action should consult with the Council about alternative arrangements. Agencies and the Council will limit such arrangements to actions necessary to control the immediate impacts of the emergency. Other actions remain subject to NEPA review.

40 C.F.R. § 1506.11.

(5) *Categorical exclusions*: As noted in the preceding article, federal agencies, in accordance with rules established by the Council on Environmental Quality, may identify categories of actions which shall be exempt from NEPA. 40 C.F.R. § 1501 et seq.; *see, e.g., Jones v. Gordon*, 792 F.2d 821 (9th Cir. 1986). Under CEQ's regulations, however, each categorical exclusion must "provide for extraordinary circumstances in which a normally excluded action may have a significant environmental effect." 40 C.F.R. § 1508.4. Some courts require agencies, if an extraordinary circumstance might exist, to engage in a particularized examination before making a decision regarding its presence, *see, e.g., Rhodes v. Johnson*, 153 F.3d 785 (7th Cir. 1998), while others tend to defer to agencies' interpretations of their own regulations when, for example, the agency identifies a particular action as falling within its categorical exclusions. *Southwest Center for Biological Diversity v. U.S. Forest Service*, 100 F.3d 1443 (9th Cir. 1996); *City of Alexandria, Va. v. Federal Highway Administration*, 756 F.2d 1014 (4th Cir. 1985).

CEQ is encouraging the expanded use of categorical exclusions as part of its efforts to streamline the NEPA process. On September 19, 2007, the EPA published new rules establishing 15 additional categorical exclusions. 72 Fed. Reg. 53,651 (Sept. 19, 2007).

(6) *Appropriation requests:* While section 102(2)(C) applies to "proposals for legislation," it does not apply to requests for Congressional appropriations. *Andrus v. Sierra Club*, 442 U.S. 347, 99 S. Ct. 2335 (1979) (since appropriations do not involve "planning and decisionmaking" such as that which accompanies the forma-

tion of underlying legislation, but rather serve only to implement authorized programs, the CEQ regulation which distinguishes requests for appropriations for purposes of NEPA applicability is valid).

(7) *Extraterritorial actions:* NEPA does not have international application. *Greenpeace USA v. Stone*, 748 F. Supp. 749 (D. Haw. 1990), *appeal dismissed as moot*, 924 F.2d. 175 (9th Cir. 1991) (a federal statute should be construed as applying only within the territorial jurisdiction of the United States unless Congress has explicitly provided for extraterritorial application. NEPA contains no such explicit provision). *See also Environmental Defense Fund v. Massey*, 986 F.2d 528, 533 (D.C. Circuit 1993) ("NEPA is designed to regulate conduct occurring within the territory of the United States, and imposes no substantive requirements which could be interpreted to govern conduct abroad.").

(8) *Moving targets*: No EIS is necessary for "moving targets." For example, the federal courts have held that the Office of the U.S. Trade Representative need not prepare an EIS on the North American Free Trade Agreement. *See Public Citizen v. U.S. Trade Representative*, 5 F.3d 549 (D.C. Cir. 1993). The reason is that NAFTA is not a "final agency action" unless and until the President submits the agreement to Congress for approval. In addition, the President could intervene and renegotiate provisions at his election. Would an EIS be required at the time of presidential submission? No, because the President is not an agency.

C.   WHETHER TO PREPARE AN ENVIRONMENTAL IMPACT STATEMENT

Once it is clear that NEPA applies, the issue becomes how. Typically, attention shifts to § 102(2)(C), which, as noted above, requires agencies to prepare an EIS to accompany any agency recommendation or report on proposals for legislation as well as for any "major federal action significantly affecting the quality of the human environment."

Since the vast majority of disputes involving NEPA involves the latter category of actions, the question becomes what is a "major federal action significantly affecting the quality of the human environment." Answering that requires a parsing of terms:

"Federal": What makes an action "federal"? Actions taken by federal agencies qualify as federal. Thus, if the federal government builds a dam, issues a grant, runs a prison, or tests a nuclear explosive device, it has taken a "federal" action. What if it takes a regulatory action, such as denying a permit? Certainly this action is "federal" as well. Would the provision of federal funding to support an otherwise private endeavor also qualify? *See, e.g., Friends of the Earth, Inc. v. Coleman*, 518 F.2d 323 (9th Cir. 1975). *Coleman* held that NEPA's EIS requirements apply to federally funded portions of an airport expansion project. The court, however, declined to apply the requirements of NEPA to locally funded portions of the same expansion project because those portions did not exhibit the requisite "functional interdependence" with the federally funded portions. *Id.* at 329. The locally funded portions, rather, were "distinct projects with separate functions and independent justifications." *Id.* at 328. Hence, they were not deemed to be "federal actions."

Is an action "federal" simply because there is a significant possibility at the outset of activities that federal funding will be available at some point later on? *See Atlanta Coalition on Transp. Crisis, Inc. v. Atlanta Regional Comm'n.*, 599 F.2d 1333 (5th Cir. 1979) (no).

Does a state project become "federal" for NEPA purposes because federal officials are involved? *See Almond Hill School v. United States Department of Agriculture*, 768 F.2d 1030 (9th Cir. 1985):

> There are no clear standards for defining the point at which federal participation transforms a state or local project into major federal action. The matter is simply one of degree. . . . "Marginal" federal action will not render otherwise local action federal. "Where federal funding is not present, this court has generally been unwilling to impose the NEPA requirement." . . . The employment of federal officials in a state project, however, may be a factor in making the determination of whether the action is sufficiently federal to require an EIS when the officials are significantly involved in the state project.
>
> Here, no federal funds have been sought by the state or spent on the state's . . . project. The appellants attempt to base their federal characterization of the project on the presence of three federal officials on the state's eight-member . . . advisory board. . . . [These officials, however] did not possess the authority to implement those aspects of the . . . program challenged here. This is primarily a state project that is neither controlled nor funded by the federal government to any significant degree.

Id. at 1031.

"Major" and *"significantly affecting the quality of the human environment"*: Here lies the more contentious issue. Every federal action that is "major" and that "significantly affects the quality of the human environment" must be accompanied by an EIS. What do these terms mean? CEQ has declared that "major" has "no meaning independent of 'significantly.'" 40 C.F.R. § 1508.18. Therefore, the search is for effects that are significant. What are effects? "Effects" and "impacts" are "synonymous" terms, 40 C.F.R. § 1508.8(b), and include "ecological (such as the effects on natural resources and on the components, structures and functioning of affected ecosystems), aesthetic, historic, cultural, economic, social, or health, whether direct, indirect, or cumulative." *Id.* Effects can be adverse or beneficial.

To prevail on a claim that a federal agency should have prepared an EIS, a claimant need not demonstrate that significant effects will occur. A "showing that there are substantial questions whether a project may have a significant effect on the environment is sufficient." *Anderson v. Evans*, 350 F.3d 815, 831 (9th Cir. 2003).

There are limits on what effects are important for NEPA purposes. First, effects that are essentially unrelated to the physical environment are not relevant. Thus, purely economic effects of a federal action do not trigger a requirement to prepare an EIS. *See, e.g., Central South Dakota Cooperative Grazing Dist. v. Dep't of Agriculture*, 266 F.3d 889 (8th Cir. 2001) (since the effects of the agency's decision to limit grazing on federal lands were economic only, no EIS is necessary); *Churchill Truck Lines, Inc. v. United States*, 533 F.2d 411, 416 (8th Cir. 1976) (economic interests are "clearly not within the zone of interests to be protected by [NEPA]"). Nor are certain psychological effects relevant to NEPA. *Metropolitan Edison Co. v. People Against Nuclear Energy*, 460 U.S. 766, 103 S. Ct. 1556 (1983), involved the licensing of a nuclear power plant at Three Mile Island in Pennsylvania. Residents maintained that bringing the plant back into operation, after its sister unit had suffered a serious accident, would increase their levels of anxiety, tension, and fear. The Court found these psychological impacts to be too "remote" and too insufficiently causally related to a change in the physical environment to be reviewable in an EIS. The same is true of effects predominantly aesthetic. In *Olmstead Citizens for a Better Community v. United States*, 793 F.2d. 201 (8th Cir. 1986), plaintiffs feared the proposed conversion of part of a mental hospital campus into a federal prison hospital would cause a proliferation of drugs, weapons, and crime in the neighborhood. The court, however, declined to expand NEPA applicability beyond physical effects:

> While there is no "bright-line" between the "physical" and the "socioeconomic" in the urban context, an impact statement generally should be necessary only when the federal action poses a threat to the physical resources of the area because of anticipated traffic, population-concentration, or water-supply problems or involves the irreversible alteration of a rare site. . . . [Here, the physical changes] . . . are the additions of harsh lighting, a double perimeter security fence with barbed wire, and a one-lane perimeter security road to be traversed by an armed mobile patrol. The main impact alleged from these changes, however, is apparently aesthetic, and the Seventh Circuit has suggested that aesthetic concerns alone should rarely be sufficient to compel preparation of an environmental impact statement.

Id. at 205–06.

Even when effects do implicate the physical environment, "where an agency has no ability to prevent a certain effect due to its limited statutory authority over the relevant actions, the agency cannot be considered a legally relevant 'cause' of the effect." Hence, under NEPA and the implementing CEQ regulations, the agency need not consider these effects in its EA when determining whether its action is a major federal action. *Department of Transportation v. Public Citizen*, 541 U.S. 752, 124 S. Ct. 2204 (2004). Plaintiffs in *Public Citizen* were concerned with adverse effects on air quality that would accompany a decision to lift a trade moratorium on Mexican motor carriers. The decision to lift or not lift the moratorium, however, was not the agency's to make." Such matters aside, whether an effect is "significant" depends generally upon its context and intensity.

CITY OF DALLAS, TEXAS v. HALL
562 F.3d 712 (5th Cir. 2009), *cert. denied*, 130 S. Ct. 1500 (2010)

JUDGES: Before SMITH and SOUTHWICK, CIRCUIT JUDGES, and ENGELHARDT, DISTRICT JUDGE.[4]

KURT D. ENGELHARDT, DISTRICT JUDGE:

After preparing an Environmental Assessment ("EA") of the proposed Neches Wildlife Refuge in East Texas, the U.S. Fish & Wildlife Service ("FWS") announced its Finding of No Significant Impact ("FONSI"), obviating the need to prepare an Environmental Impact Statement ("EIS"). FWS then set an acquisition boundary for the refuge and accepted a conservation easement within that boundary. These actions precluded a reservoir the City of Dallas ("City") and the Texas Water Development Board ("TWDB") had proposed for the same site. The City and TWDB sued in federal district court claiming that the EA that FWS prepared was flawed, that under the National Environmental Policy Act ("NEPA") the agency was required to prepare an EIS, and that the establishment of the refuge violated the Tenth Amendment. The district court dismissed several of the Appellants' claims and granted FWS' motion for summary judgment on others. We AFFIRM.

I. BACKGROUND

In 1961, the State of Texas first identified a site along the Upper Neches River in Anderson and Cherokee Counties as a potential reservoir to serve the growing Dallas/Ft. Worth Metroplex. Dubbed the Fastrill Reservoir, the site was again included in a state water agency resources plan in 1984, and in the 1997 and 2001 regional water plans issued by TWDB. The City and TWDB's plan envisioned constructing the reservoir in 2050 and tapping it in 2060. There is nothing in the record prior to 2005 that indicates that the City or TWDB took any steps to develop the site beyond including it — among other possible reservoir sites — in regularly updated planning documents.

In 1985, FWS identified the same site as a possible wildlife refuge, since its native bottomland hardwood forest and wetlands provide an important wintering habitat for migrating waterfowl. That year, FWS listed the site as high-priority for protection. FWS approved a preliminary refuge proposal in 1988 and prepared a draft EA, but put the project aside for lack of funding. The project was revived in 2003 and the agency initiated public comment in June 2004. Public workshops were held in July 2004 and FWS made a presentation to the regional water planning group in October of that year. Another EA was prepared, which listed three alternatives: no action, the recommended 25,281-acre configuration, and a narrower 15,294-acre configuration. The EA referenced the reservoir proposal and noted that both the larger and smaller refuge configurations would prevent the reservoir from being built. The EA was distributed to public officials and interested groups, open meetings were held in May 2005, and it was open for public review and comment for

---

[4] District Judge of the Eastern District of Louisiana, sitting by designation.

two weeks that same month. More than 1,600 comments were received, but the EA was not revised, and a "final" EA was not issued. On July 28, 2005, FWS concluded that an EIS was unnecessary and prepared a FONSI.

By early 2005, the City was aware that FWS had revived the refuge proposal. On March 9, 2005, the Dallas City Council passed a resolution expressing a desire to work with FWS on a plan that would allow the reservoir and the refuge to coexist and authorizing a feasibility study. On August 16th, the Texas legislature designated the Fastrill Reservoir as a "critical resource," and the January 2006 regional water plan recommended building the reservoir as part of its water management strategy. Meetings were also held between the director of FWS and City representatives to discuss alternative sites for the refuge, and state and FWS representatives continued to communicate through the first half of 2006 about alternative plans that would allow a refuge and a reservoir to coexist. The City and TWDB scheduled — though did not actually begin — a series of engineering and environmental studies. By June 11, 2006, the day FWS designated an "acquisition boundary" for the refuge encompassing the larger 25,281-acre site, the feasibility study was not completed nor had Appellants taken any concrete steps toward planning the reservoir, such as applying for permits. Accompanying the designation was a Conceptual Management Plan outlining how land within the boundary would be acquired. The Neches Wildlife Refuge was set to come into existence when FWS, by purchase or donation, took title to or an interest in property within the acquisition boundary. On August 23, 2006, FWS accepted a one-acre conservation easement from a landowner within the acquisition boundary.

TWDB and the City filed the instant suits on January 10, 2007, arguing *inter alia* that the EA was flawed, that FWS should have prepared an EIS, and that the refuge violated the Tenth Amendment. On October 24, 2007, the district court dismissed five of the City's claims, including the constitutional claim, and two of TWDB's claims, under Rule 12(b)(6). The parties filed cross-motions for partial summary judgment on the NEPA claims, and on June 30, 2008, the district court denied the Appellants' motions and granted FWS's motion. Relying heavily on *Sabine River Auth. v. U.S. Dep't of the Interior*, 951 F.2d 669 (5th Cir. 1992), the district court held that an EIS was not required because the establishment of the acquisition boundary did not cause any change in the physical environment. The court concluded that the refuge's effect on the City's water supply was speculative and not within the scope of NEPA. The court also found that the EA considered a reasonable range of alternatives and evaluated the necessary information. The City and TWDB moved for an injunction pending appeal and for entry of final judgment, which were granted on July 28, 2008. The parties subsequently filed a joint motion to amend the judgment, which was granted on September 4, 2008. Notice of appeal was filed on September 8, 2008, and the appeal was expedited on September 22, 2008.

II. DISCUSSION

A. *Standard of Review*

We review the district court's grant of summary judgment *de novo. Terrebonne Parish Sch. Bd. v. Mobil Oil Corp.*, 310 F.3d 870, 877 (5th Cir. 2002). The court may only set aside an agency's decision not to prepare an EIS where a plaintiff establishes that the decision was "arbitrary, capricious, an abuse of discretion, or otherwise not in accordance with law." 5 U.S.C. § 706(2)(A); *see also Marsh v. Or. Natural Res. Council*, 490 U.S. 360, 375–76, 109 S. Ct. 1851, 104 L. Ed. 2d 377 (1989); *Kleppe v. Sierra Club*, 427 U.S. 390, 412, 96 S. Ct. 2718, 49 L. Ed. 2d 576 (1976). Under this highly deferential standard of review, a reviewing court has the least latitude in finding grounds for reversal. *Sabine River*, 951 F.2d at 678. Courts may not use review of an agency's environmental analysis as a guise for second-guessing substantive decisions committed to the discretion of the agency. But "[i]n conducting our NEPA inquiry, we must 'make a searching and careful inquiry into the facts and review whether the decision . . . was based on consideration of the relevant factors and whether there has been a clear error of judgment.' " *Marsh*, 490 U.S. at 378 (citation omitted).

We review *de novo* a district court's dismissal pursuant to Rule 12(b)(6). *Ballard v. Wall*, 413 F.3d 510, 514 (5th Cir. 2005). "All of the plaintiff's allegations must be accepted as true, and the dismissal will be affirmed only if it appears that no relief could be granted under any set of facts that could be proven consistent with the allegations." *Id.* at 514–15 (internal quotation omitted). However, "conclusory allegations or legal conclusions masquerading as factual conclusions will not suffice to prevent a motion to dismiss." *Taylor v. Books A Million, Inc.*, 296 F.3d 376, 378 (5th Cir. 2002) (quotation omitted).

B. *Sufficiency of the Environmental Assessment*

NEPA does not require federal agencies to favor an environmentally preferable course of action, but rather requires that they take a "hard look at environmental consequences." *Robertson v. Methow Valley Citizens Council*, 490 U.S. 332, 350, 109 S. Ct. 1835, 104 L. Ed. 2d 351 (1989) (quoting *Kleppe*, 427 U.S. at 410 n.21). The statute requires "all agencies of the Federal Government . . . [to] include [an EIS] in every recommendation or report on proposals for . . . major Federal actions significantly affecting the quality of the human environment." 42 U.S.C. § 4332(2). An EIS is not necessary when the federal action is not major or does not have a "significant impact on the environment." *Sabine River*, 951 F.2d at 677. To determine whether an EIS is necessary, an agency will perform an EA. *Sierra Club v. Espy*, 38 F.3d 792, 802 (5th Cir. 1994); 40 C.F.R. § 1508.9(a)(1) (defining an EA as a "concise public document" that "[b]riefly provide[s] sufficient evidence and analysis for determining whether to prepare an environmental impact statement or a finding of no significant impact"). An EA is "a rough cut, low-budget environmental impact statement designed to show whether a full-fledged environmental impact statement — which is very costly and time-consuming to prepare and has been the kiss of death to many a federal project — is necessary." *Sabine River*, 951 F.2d at 677 (citing *Cronin v. U.S. Dep't. of Agriculture*, 919 F.2d 439, 443 (7th Cir. 1990)).

An EA will result in a finding that an EIS is necessary or in a FONSI, indicating that no further study of environmental impacts is warranted. *La. Crawfish Producers Ass'n-West v. Rowan*, 463 F.3d 352, 356 (5th Cir. 2006).

1. Failure to Consider Alternatives

An EA must discuss alternatives to the planned action, but need not discuss all proposed alternatives. *See* 40 C.F.R. § 1508.9(b) (assessment "[s]hall include brief discussions of the need for the proposal, of alternatives . . . of the environmental impacts of the proposed action and alternatives, and a listing of agencies and persons consulted"); *see also La. Crawfish Ass'n*, 463 F.3d at 355 (NEPA "does not require that all proposed alternatives, no matter their merit, be discussed in the EA."). "[T]he range of alternatives that the [agency] must consider decreases as the environmental impact of the proposed action becomes less and less substantial." *Sierra Club*, 38 F.3d at 803; *see also Highway J Citizens Group v. Mineta*, 349 F.3d 938, 960 (7th Cir. 2003) ("When . . . an agency makes an informed decision that the environmental impact will be small . . . a less extensive search [for alternatives] is required."). The rejection of even viable and reasonable alternatives, after an appropriate evaluation, is not arbitrary and capricious. *See Miss. River Basin Alliance v. Westphal*, 230 F.3d 170, 177 (5th Cir. 2000).

The EA in this case noted that "the area under consideration was identified in a preliminary study by the Texas Water Plan as an area with the potential for development as a reservoir. . . . " It also noted that the City was considering a feasibility study of the reservoir. It analyzed the effects of three different alternatives (no action, a larger refuge, and a smaller refuge) along multiple lines such as climate and air quality, water resources, vegetation, land use, and cultural resources. In each instance, the EA acknowledged and attempted to analyze the effect the alternative would have on the reservoir proposal. The EA also analyzed the cumulative impact of the refuge in conjunction with other "past, present, and reasonably foreseeable future actions," including the reservoir.

Appellants argue that FWS was required to consider an alternative that would allow the refuge and the reservoir to coexist. In the EA, however, FWS noted that it was unable to evaluate fully any such dual proposal, since plans for the reservoir were "speculative in the short-term, . . . not definitive in scope or purpose, and . . . far beyond the planning horizon for the refuge proposal (i.e., 20 years)." Additionally, after several weeks of consultation between staff at FWS, the City, and TWDB, a TWDB biologist admitted to the director of TWDB that "an alternative site that is equal to or bigger and/or better than the North Neches site has not yet been identified." The director echoed this assessment in a letter to FWS. Only after the closure of the public comment period and the drafting of the FONSI did FWS receive a proposal for alternative refuge sites. The alternatives included four other sites that Appellants claimed were of greater environmental value, since there was more bottomland hardwood extant at these sites. Each of these alternatives, however, envisioned building the Fastrill Reservoir and the resulting inundation of the Upper Neches area, with destruction of vegetation in that region. The record reveals no alternative that allowed construction of the reservoir *and* served FWS' goal of preserving the bottomlands and wetlands of the Upper Neches. Under the circumstances, and especially given that FWS concluded that the project had no significant environmental impact, *see Sierra Club*, 38 F.3d at 803, this range of alternatives was reasonable.

2. Failure to Consider Impacts

An EA must analyze both the direct and indirect effects of the proposed action that are "reasonably foreseeable," 42 U.S.C. § 4332(C)(ii); 40 C.F.R. §§ 1502.16(a) & (b); 40 C.F.R. § 1508.7, which we have defined as effects that are "sufficiently likely to occur that a person of ordinary prudence would take [them] into account in reaching a decision." *City of Shoreacres v. Waterworth*, 420 F.3d 440, 453 (5th Cir. 2005). "Reasonable foreseeability" does not include "highly speculative harms" that "distort[ ] the decisionmaking process" by emphasizing consequences beyond those of "greatest concern to the public and of greatest relevance to the agency's decision." *Robertson*, 490 U.S. at 355–56 (internal quotation marks and citations omitted). "[A] 'but for' causal relationship is insufficient to make an agency responsible for a particular effect under NEPA and the relevant regulations. Rather, a plaintiff mounting a NEPA challenge must establish that an alleged effect will ensue as a 'proximate cause,' in the sense meant by tort law, of the proposed agency action." *City of Shoreacres*, 420 F.3d at 452.

Appellants argue that FWS was required to analyze the effect of establishing the refuge on the City's water supply and urban planning process, given projected population growth. The cases cited by Appellants are inapposite, however, since they concern the effect of federal actions on *existing* water sources, not proposed water sources. *See Sierra Club v. Marsh*, 769 F.2d 868 (1st Cir. 1985) (effect of port development runoff); *City of Davis v. Coleman*, 521 F.2d 661 (9th Cir. 1975) (effect of industrial development runoff); *California v. Dep't of Transp.*, 260 F. Supp. 2d 969 (N.D. Cal. 2003) (effect of airport construction); *Simmans v. Grant*, 370 F. Supp. 5 (S.D. Tex. 1974) (effect of eliminating water source). Plaintiffs do not cite to any authority for the proposition that an agency must account for the effects on a municipal water supply of precluding a proposed but as-yet-nonexistent water source.

Further, the effects of establishing the refuge, and thus precluding the reservoir, are highly speculative and cannot be shown to be the proximate cause of future water shortages in Dallas. The City and TWDB never committed to constructing the reservoir and may never have done so, or may have constructed a reservoir at another site. Besides including it in periodically updated planning documents, the City and TWDB have never taken any concrete steps toward constructing the reservoir, such as seeking permits, acquiring property, or commencing any of the hydrological, fiscal, or environmental studies necessary to a major public works project. In fact, the City and TWDB have never even settled upon the exact position of the dam or footprint of the reservoir. Thus, the City and TWDB have never identified the precise role the reservoir — even if constructed and tapped in 2060 — will play in supplying the region's future water needs. Further, the City argues that water shortages in the region will begin as early as 2010, yet the reservoir would not be tapped earlier than 2060. Given the uncertainty over whether the reservoir will be constructed and its impact on water supplies, and the long time frame for the project, the effects of establishing the refuge on water supplies are not concrete enough, nor closely enough related to the federal action, to require that they be included in the EA.

3. Reliance on Old Data

Appellants argue that FWS relied upon old data in its EA. Properly analyzing the risks of an action requires an agency to use updated information or data; reliance on out-of-date or incomplete information may render the analysis of effects speculative and uncertain, warranting the preparation of an EIS. *See Klamath-Siskiyou Wildlands Ctr. v. U.S. Forest Service*, 373 F. Supp. 2d 1069, 1081 (E.D. Cal. 2004). In this case much of the data in the EA was lifted from the earlier EA prepared in 1988. The City and TWDB note that there has been degradation of the site and that a significant portion of the Upper Neches bottomland hardwoods have been cleared. However, the City and TWDB have not shown that this information was so flawed that it precluded assessment of reasonably foreseeable impacts. Nor is it clear how, in this case, additional information as to environmental degradation of the Upper Neches would cause FWS to conclude it should leave the site unprotected. In this sense, the instant case differs from those cited by Appellants, where additional or updated information was needed before a reasoned decision could be made as to whether to intrude on a site. *See, e.g., The Lands Council v. Powell*, 395 F.3d 1019, 1031 (9th Cir. 2005) (additional information on animal habitat needed before timber harvest could commence); *Idaho Sporting Congress v. Thomas*, 137 F.3d 1146, 1150 (9th Cir. 1998) (additional information on trout habitat needed before logging could commence), *overruled on different grounds, The Lands Council v. McNair*, 537 F.3d 981, 997 (9th Cir. 2008); *Klamath-Siskiyou Wildlands Ctr.*, 373 F. Supp. 2d at 1081 (additional information on owl population needed before logging could commence).

Undoubtedly, were a plaintiff to show that a site had become so degraded — for example, by substantial clearcutting of the bottomland hardwoods such that it would not support migrating waterfowl even if protected — such a showing may well render the decision to rely on older data arbitrary within the meaning of NEPA. No such showing has been made in this instance. Here, the use of older data in an EA — by definition a "rough cut, low-budget" assessment of environmental impacts on the way to determining whether an EIS is necessary, *see Sabine River*, 951 F.2d at 677 — cannot be said to be unreasonable. Nor does the use of this data in this instance support forcing the agency to engage in a process likely, because of its lengthy timeline, to permit further environmental degradation of the site before a decision is reached.

4. The FWS Decision Making Process

Finally, the City and TWDB also argue that the decision making process FWS engaged in was a sham. Appellants point to several flaws: FWS's choice of a 20-year project horizon for analysis of impacts, its failure to coordinate with local and state planning agencies in violation of CEQ regulations, and its failure to publish a "final" EA. The record reveals that FWS engaged in an extensive process of public education and public comment and even worked with officials from the City and

TWDB to identify an alternative site that would allow the refuge and the reservoir to coexist. Emails between various FWS officials reveal nothing more than an appropriate advocacy for a favored agency alternative. In arguing that FWS was required to publish a "final" EA, Appellants cite only to non-binding internal policy memos and not to any binding regulation or statute. Appellants' assertion that FWS abused its discretion by failing to "coordinate" with the local, regional, and state water planning process falls short, since neither NEPA nor any of the other statutes the City or TWDB cite require an agency to insinuate itself into state planning processes in the manner suggested. Finally, Appellants fail to show that FWS's 20-year planning horizon was arbitrary and capricious under the circumstances. As the district court noted, "FWS must set some kind of time frame for its evaluations; it cannot have an interminable planning period." *City of Dallas, Tex. v. Hall*, 2008 U.S. Dist. LEXIS 49944, (N.D. Tex. June 30, 2008).2008 WL 2622809, at 14 n.10

B. *Requirement of an EIS*

In arguing that an EIS was required, Appellants attempt to distinguish this case from *Sabine River*. In that case, strikingly similar to the present one, FWS set an acquisition boundary for a wildlife refuge on 3,800 acres in East Texas, and accepted a negative, no-development easement from a landowner inside the acquisition boundary. *See Sabine River*, 951 F.2d at 674–76. The designation precluded the construction of a proposed reservoir. *Id.* at 673. The reservoir was in the preliminary planning stage, and the state agency with jurisdiction over it had "obtained none of the necessary federal and state permits, had secured no funding, and had not yet entered into any firm contracts for the 300 thousand plus acre feet of water that the reservoir would generate each year." *Id.* We concluded that "the acquisition of a negative easement which by its terms prohibits any change in the *status quo* does not amount to 'major Federal action[ ] significantly affecting the quality of the human environment.' . . . The acquisition of a negative easement which prohibits development does not result in the requisite 'change' to the physical environment." *Id.* at 679–80 (citations omitted). The acceptance of such an easement is "tantamount to inaction," and thus the acceptance "did not effectuate any change to the environment which would otherwise trigger the need to prepare an EIS." *Id.* at 680. In the instant case, the district court properly set forth the factors to consider in applying *Sabine River*: whether the agency action (1) precludes any development of the land, (2) changes the character or function of the land, and (3) prohibits any change in the *status quo* of the land. *City of Dallas, Tex.*, 2008 U.S. Dist. LEXIS 49944, 2008 WL 2622809 at 5.

The City argues that three independent authorities dictate that an EIS was required in this instance: FWS's own NEPA guidelines, the NEPA implementing regulations issued by the U.S. Department of the Interior ("DOI"), and the NEPA implementing regulations issued by the Council on Environmental Quality ("CEQ"). The FWS guidelines include a number of criteria to assist the agency in determining whether an EIS is needed. Among these are "increased safety or health hazards," 550 FW 3.3(B)(2)(e), and "[a]dverse effects on municipal, industrial, or agricultural water supply or quality . . . ," *id.* at 3.3(B)(2)(i). The City points to these guidelines and argues that an EIS is required to weigh adequately the health and water supply effects of not building the reservoir. But these guidelines have no binding force. *See Coliseum Square Ass'n, Inc. v. Jackson*, 465 F.3d 215, 229 (5th Cir. 2005) ("Generally, to be legally binding on an agency, its own publications must have been 'promulgated pursuant to a specific statutory grant of authority and in conformance with the procedural requirements imposed by Congress.' ") (citation omitted). When agency publications have not been promulgated pursuant to a specific grant of statutory authority, an agency's decision to analyze impacts by other methods is not automatically arbitrary and capricious. *Id.* at 230. These guidelines were not promulgated pursuant to law. Further, by their own terms, they are meant to *assist* in determining whether an EIS is necessary, not *dictate* when an EIS is necessary, and carefully note that whether any of the criteria triggers the need for an EIS depends in each instance on "the severity and duration of effects." FW550 3.3(B)(2).

The DOI regulations the City points to are binding on the agency, but they do not mandate the preparation of an EIS in this case. In the regulations, among the "Major Actions Normally Requiring an EIS" are "major new refuge system units . . . which involve substantive conflicts over existing State and local land use [or] significant controversy over the environmental effects of the proposal." 62 Fed. Reg. 2375, 2382. The City argues that the refuge meets both these criteria. But by their own terms, the regulations "normally" require preparation of an EIS but do not dictate preparation in each case. Further, the regulations clearly envision that when, pursuant to an EA, the agency determines that an action will have no major environmental impacts, an EIS is not required even when the action otherwise meets the criteria. *Id.* In this case, after preparing an EA the agency made a reasoned decision that there were no significant environmental effects.

More importantly, by their own terms the regulations only envision preparation of an EIS when there is a conflict with "existing" State and local land use or where there is "significant" controversy over environmental effects. In this case, while a feasibility study has been completed, the City and TWDB have taken no concrete steps to develop the reservoir (such as applying for permits), much less put any land to use. The development of an acquisition boundary does not conflict with existing State and local use, but merely with a potential future use. Further, the City and TWDB have been unable to show with any specificity the effects of setting the acquisition boundary. A controversy such as this one — over the highly speculative, uncertain effects of not building a particular reservoir — cannot be "significant" within the meaning of both the regulations and NEPA.

Similarly, while the CEQ regulations that the City points to are binding on federal agencies, *see Fritiofson v. Alexander*, 772 F.2d 1225, 1236 (5th Cir. 1985), they do not mandate the preparation of an EIS in this case. The regulations merely require an agency to determine whether an action is one that normally requires an EIS. *See* 40 C.F.R. § 1501.4(a). If the agency determines that the action does not normally require an EIS, it then prepares an EA and makes a finding as to whether the proposed action has significant environmental impacts. *Id.* at 1501.4(b). In this case, as described above, FWS properly prepared an EA and made a FONSI, as envisioned by the CEQ regulations.

TWDB also argues that the instant case is distinguishable from *Sabine River* because the refuge designation in this case will cause changes in the physical environment. As noted in the EA, FWS envisions removing non-native tree species in the refuge and reintroducing native hardwood and evergreen species. TWDB argues that this distinguishes the case from *Sabine River*, where there was no evidence that the refuge site would be changed in any way by the acceptance of an easement. *See Sabine River Auth. v. U.S. Dep't of the Interior*, 745 F. Supp. 388, 394 (E.D. Tex. 1990). However, as the district court noted in its order denying Appellants' motion for partial summary judgment, the action at issue here is the establishment of an acquisition boundary for the refuge. The establishment of that boundary does not effect any change in the physical environment, but merely authorizes the purchase of property from willing buyers or the acceptance of conservation easements. Once sufficient land is acquired, FWS will be required to comply with NEPA in formulating a Comprehensive Conservation Plan to guide refuge forest management. If changes in the physical environment are proposed in that plan, an EIS may be required. But the present federal action will have no significant physical effects such that an EIS is required.

As in *Sabine River*, where the acceptance of a negative, non-development easement was "tantamount to inaction," *Sabine River*, 951 F.2d at 680, setting an acquisition boundary for the refuge does not effect a change in the use or character of land or in the physical environment. Thus, it is not a "major Federal action[] significantly affecting the quality of the human environment," 42 U.S.C. § 4332(2), and no EIS is necessary under the requirements of NEPA.

C. *Tenth Amendment Claims* (discussion omitted)

III. CONCLUSION

For the foregoing reasons, we AFFIRM the decisions of the district court.

NOTES AND QUESTIONS

1. ***The Structure of Environmental Litigation.*** There are several foundational points concerning NEPA that are worthy of some emphasis at this early stage in the course. First, judicial contests involving governmental regulatory actions often involve any of three challenges, either separately or in combination. The first is an assertion that the agency exceeded its organic authority, that it either lacked the power to do what it did on an absolute basis or it lacked the power to do what it did in the particular way it did it. This issue was not implicated in *Dallas*. The second challenge is that the agency violated some generally applicable environmental legislation. In this case, that legislation was NEPA; often the Endangered Species Act comes into play as well. *See* Chapter 7, *infra*. The third challenge is usually procedural in nature. In federal law, challenges of this sort often find their root in the Administrative Procedure Act, 5 U.S.C. § 551 et seq.

A second matter, more specific to NEPA: please observe the bifurcated nature of FONSI challenges. In these cases, two distinct disputes will always arise. The first is whether the EA is adequate in its *content*. If a court finds the EA to be inadequate in this regard, it will require a repair of the inadequacies. The second, entirely independent, dispute questions whether the agency FONSI *decision*, a decision that should be based on the EA itself, was proper. In some cases, a decision might be ruled legally indefensible even in the presence of an adequate EA.

A third matter worthy of your observations is the interplay of statutes and rules. Agencies typically have what is known as rulemaking authority, the power to enact rules and regulations of an interstitial sort. Rulemaking allows an agency to "flesh out" and make more particular the commands of the statute the agency administers. Rulemaking can be a lengthy and convoluted process, sometimes taking years to complete. In the usual circumstance, agencies are not required to engage in rulemaking. If they like, they can choose to let the agency's statute, in effect, fend for itself. But agencies have found the rulemaking option to be virtually irresistible. Why? Rulemaking allows agencies to craft the content of the law more to their liking. You will note that part of the contest in *Dallas* dealt with these matters. In *Dallas*, plaintiffs challenged the FWS for direct violations of NEPA, for violations of the Department of the Interior's rules (in place to implement NEPA and binding on the FWS, a subunit of DOI), and for violations of CEQ's rules, which are binding generally on federal agencies. Had the plaintiffs prevailed in any of these challenges, they would have won the case.

For more about rulemaking, see the *Note on Administrative Law #1*, which immediately follows this note material.

2. **FONSIs.** The D.C. Circuit has established four criteria to assess the validity of an agency FONSI decision: (a) whether the agency accurately identified the critical environmental concerns; (b) whether it took a "hard look" at those environmental concerns; (c) whether it made a convincing case for its FONSI decision; and (d) if there are significant impacts, whether it found that changes in the action or project sufficiently reduced the impacts. *Sierra Club v. U.S. Dep't of Transportation*, 753 F.2d 120 (D.C. Cir. 1985).

As criterion (d), above, implies, EAs will often recommend specific actions that might be taken to mitigate environmental harms otherwise to be caused by a project. Is this a sensible procedure, or does this effectively transform the EA into an EIS? The D.C. Circuit says it is sensible, at least where adoption of the EA mitigation measures would completely remove adverse environmental impacts. In such a case, the threshold of "significant" effects would not be crossed. Requiring an EIS in this circumstance, commented the court, would trivialize NEPA and would "diminish its utility in providing useful environmental analysis for major federal actions that truly affect the environment." *Cabinet Mountains Wilderness/ Scotchman's Peak Grizzly Bears v. Peterson*, 685 F.2d 678, 682 (D.C. Cir. 1982).

3. **Affirmative Declarations and Injunctions.** In *Dallas*, the end product of the EA process was a FONSI. On other occasions, the end product is a determination to go forward with an EIS, a decision sometimes referred to as an affirmative declaration. When an agency issues an affirmative declaration, the question arises what can be done by the agency during the time the EIS is under preparation. In the past, the answer was usually nothing, as courts would grant injunctive relief. Such a prohibition could disable the agency for years. The Supreme Court, however, recently clarified that courts should not presume that injunctive relief is automatically justified in these circumstances. In the Court's words, "[N]o such thumb on the scale is warranted." *Monsanto Co. v. Geertson Seed Farms*, 130 S. Ct. 2743, 2757

(2010). Terming an injunction a "drastic" remedy, *id.* at 2761, the Court allowed that injunctions should issue only if the requisite four-part test is satisfied: (1) there must be an irreparable injury; (2) remedies at law are inadequate to cure the injury; (3) considering the balance of hardship between plaintiff and defendant, an equitable remedy is warranted; and (4) the public interest would not be disserved by the issuance of a permanent injunction. *Id.* at 2756.

Buttressing this holding were CEQ's regulations, which by negative implication contemplate some agency action during this interim period, even if qualified. Section 1506.1(a) thereof provides that "no action concerning the proposal shall be taken which would (1) Have an adverse environmental impact; or (2) Limit the choice of reasonable alternatives." 40 C.F.R. § 1506.1(a). Adding to that message is 1506.1(c), which states that "While work on a required program environmental impact statement is in progress and the action is not covered by an existing program statement, agencies shall not undertake in the interim any major Federal actions covered by the program which may significantly affect the quality of the human environment unless such action" meets specified requirements. 40 C.F.R. § 1506.1(c).

As one might expect, injunctive relief is also inadvisable when U.S. foreign policy considerations outweigh the desirability of the relief. *Winter v. Natural Resources Defense Council*, 555 U.S. 7, 129 S. Ct. 365 (2008); *Environmental Defense Fund v. Massey*, 986 F.2d 528, 535 (D.C. Cir. 1993).

4. *SEISs.* Suppose an agency determines an EIS is necessary because a proposed action is a major federal action significantly affecting the quality of the human environment. Does this mean that only one EIS needs to be done? The answer is usually yes — one EIS is plenty. Not infrequently, however, the issue arises whether a supplemental EIS ("SEIS") should be prepared. When might an agency be required to initiate the EIS process a second (or third) time? NEPA does not comment on this matter, and one would think that at some juncture agency actions reach a point of no return. CEQ regulations, however, call for supplemental EISs in two situations. First, an SEIS is required if "(1) [t]he agency makes substantial changes in the proposed action that are relevant to environmental concerns[.]" 40 C.F.R. § 1509(c)(1)(i); *New Mexico ex rel. Richardson v. Bureau of Land Management*, 565 F.3d 683 (10th Cir. 2009). Second, and more interestingly, the regulations call for an SEIS if "(ii) [t]here are significant circumstances or information relevant to environmental concerns and bearing on the proposed action or its impacts." 40 C.F.R. § 1509(c)(1)(ii). Does this regulation mean that every time significant new information comes along an SEIS must be prepared? The Supreme Court has made clear the answer is no:

> [a]n agency need not supplement an EIS every time new information comes
> to light after the EIS is finalized. To require otherwise would render agency
> decisionmaking intractable, always awaiting updated information only to
> find the new information outdated by the time a decision is made.

Marsh v. Oregon Natural Resources Council, 490 U.S. 360, 373, 109 S. Ct. 1851, 1859 (1989) (footnotes omitted). Still, the Court noted, an agency may not blithely ignore significant new information. Rather, it must take a "hard look" at new information to determine whether to prepare an SEIS. *Marsh*, 490 U.S. at 385, 109

S. Ct. at 1865. The *Marsh* Court cautioned that agency decisions whether to supplement EISs should not be overruled by the judiciary unless those decisions are arbitrary or capricious. *Marsh*, 490 U.S. at 385. There must be a "clear error of judgment" to justify a reversal. *See also Headwaters, Inc. v. Bureau of Land Management*, 914 F.2d 1174 (9th Cir. 1990).

More particularly, the Supreme Court has held that no SEIS is contemplated by NEPA unless there is some ongoing "major federal action" yet to occur. In *Norton v. Southwest Utah Wilderness Alliance*, 542 U.S. 55, 124 S. Ct. 2373 (2004), plaintiffs argued the federal Bureau of Land Management should prepare an SEIS because of a substantial increase in off-road vehicle use on federal wilderness lands. The BLM was managing these lands under the auspices of a land use plan prepared in accordance with the Federal Land Policy and Management Act (*see* Chapter 5, *infra*). A unanimous Supreme Court denied the claim because the land use plan was already completed and had already been approved. As this was a *fait accompli*, there remained no ongoing major federal action and, *per force*, no legal basis for requiring an SEIS. Had the BLM taken some affirmative action, such as amending the plan, additional analysis under NEPA would have been necessary.

NOTE ON ADMINISTRATIVE LAW #1[5]

Even at this early stage of the course, it is surely apparent to the reader that environmental and natural resources law is resplendent with statutes and administrative "rules and regulations" (the two quoted terms are used together or separately, and interchangeably). *Dallas* is apt testimony to this reality.

Where do these regulations come from? In the main, they are the handiwork of administrative agencies, such as the Environmental Protection Agency, the Department of Interior, and the Council on Environmental Quality. Agencies may enact rules only if the statutes they administer supply them the substantive authority to do so. The CEQ, for example, enjoys rulemaking power by virtue of several statutory authorizations, including NEPA itself, the Environmental Quality Act of 1970, as amended, 42 U.S.C. § 4371 et seq., § 309 of the Clean Water Act (*see* Chapter 10, *infra*), 42 U.S.C. § 7609, and Executive Order 11514, as amended. 40 C.F.R. § 1500.3. EPA, for its part, has rulemaking authority courtesy of the several organic acts, including the Clean Air Act, the Clean Water Act, and the Resource Conservation and Recovery Act. *See, e.g.,* Chapters 9–11, *infra*.

Rules are, in effect, little statutes. They are used by agencies to define statutory terms, establish regulatory programs, and otherwise fill in the programmatic details Congress routinely and understandably omits. A rule can create rights and impose obligations beyond what the rule's enabling statute itself provides. Any such rights and obligations, however, must be contemplated by the rule's authorizing legislation. If a rule "goes too far" in this regard, it will be considered

---

[5] This is the first of four "Notes on Administrative Law" that appear at various points in this book. The material is inserted to assist students who have not learned administrative law. If you have already taken a course in this subject area, or have learned administrative law by some other mechanism, you should feel free to skip this Note. If you have not done so, however, you should both read this Note and resolve to master this important subject area at some future time.

to be *ultra vires* and will be found by a court of law to be of no force and effect.

When agencies establish rules, they must do so in conformance with an established set of procedures. The procedures agencies must follow derive generally from two sources. The first is the agency's "organic law," the statute that instructs the agency to construct a regulatory program in the first place (and, in the typical case, authorizes the agency to do so by use of rulemaking). The second source is a statute of general applicability, enacted specifically to establish procedural prerequisites for rulemaking. In the federal arena, this statute is the Administrative Procedure Act, 5 U.S.C. §§ 551, 553–559, 701–706. Note that states have their own "APAs" as well.

As a general matter, the procedural format followed by agencies when they engage in rulemaking is a process known as *"informal rulemaking." See* 5 U.S.C. § 553. This involves, first, the formal act of proposing to the public its suggested rule. An agency does this by placing a comprehensive announcement of its intentions and ideas, as well as a copy of the text of the proposed rule, in the Federal Register, which can be thought of as the executive branch's "newspaper" of sorts. Subsequent to this *"proposal"* stage comes the *comment period*. During this time, the agency learns of the public's reactions to its proposal. Often, thousands of comments are received. The agency must then consider the comments. The hope is the agency can learn something by considering these comments and might thereby produce a better final product. After considering the comments, the agency enacts its rule in final form. This is known as *"promulgation"* of the rule. A promulgated rule has the same force and effect as does the statute that authorized it. After rules are promulgated, they are virtually always challenged in legal proceedings. A fair number of the cases you will read in this course are challenges to such rules. The issues in these cases are substantive (Did the agency have the power to do what it did? Did the agency act with sufficient wisdom in making the regulatory choices it made?) and procedural (Did the agency comply with the various procedural obligations incumbent upon it?). In our casebook, we do not explore issues of procedural irregularity.

In the *Dallas* case, however, the major challenge was to the FWS's FONSI. A decision to forego the preparation of an EIS is not rulemaking. Rather, when an agency issues a FONSI, or for that matter, when it files a lawsuit or assesses a penalty against a polluter, or otherwise issues an "order," it is undertaking what is known in the Administrative Procedure Act as an "adjudication." As with rulemaking, agencies can undertake adjudicative actions only if authorized to do so by enabling legislation. Also as with rulemaking, when adjudicating, agencies must follow an authorized set of procedures. On many occasions, the procedures an agency must follow in these circumstances are quite minimal (in situations known as *"informal adjudication"*) but in others, the adjudication must be more procedurally elaborate. On these latter occasions, persons may enjoy an array of process rights, including the right to present evidence in oral or documentary form, the right to a decision based on the record of the proceeding, the right to a decision made by a dispassionate "administrative law judge," the right to rebut adverse evidence, and so forth. These *"formal adjudications,"* however, will rarely provide the full array of process rights routinely available in Article III or state courts. In many agency adjudications, for example, hearsay rules are not in play, and cross-examination of witnesses may be disallowed.

D.   ENVIRONMENTAL IMPACT STATEMENTS

1.   The Role of EISs in Decisionmaking

Assuming an EIS is required, what role should it play in framing or influencing an agency's final decision to go forward with a project as proposed, or as modified, or not at all?

The role of EISs in agency decisionmaking has been a matter of debate. Without doubt, Congress intended EISs to be informational documents. Their mere presence would make agencies aware of the environmental consequences of proposed actions. That awareness, in turn, would encourage agencies to be more solicitous of environmental protection and conservation. Given these facts, it seems obvious that EISs were intended by Congress to play some sort of substantive role in agency decisionmaking.

But how? Is the role of an EIS advisory only? Does it merely stand on the sidelines cajoling agencies into environmentally benign courses of action? If that were the case, agencies would be free to completely disregard an EIS's recommendations. Alternatively, does an EIS have some force and effect? Can it be read as amending an agency's organic law to require the implementation of more environmentally friendly courses of action?

The courts were split during the 1970s on this issue. The United States Supreme Court addressed the matter in 1978 in its decision in *Vermont Yankee Nuclear Power Corp. v. Natural Resources Defense Council*, 435 U.S. 519, 98 S. Ct. 1197 (1978). In that case, it declared NEPA to have "altered slightly the statutory balance." *Id.* at 551, 98 S. Ct. at 1215. But the Court clarified that "NEPA does not set forth substantive goals for the Nation . . . its mandate to the agencies is essentially procedural. . . . It is to insure a fully informed and well-considered decision, not necessarily a decision the judges of the Court of Appeals or of this Court would have reached had they been members of the decisionmaking unit of the agency." *Id.* at 558, 98 S. Ct. at 1219. Two years later, the Court reiterated the point in *Strycker's Bay Neighborhood Council v. Karlen*, 444 U.S. 223, 100 S. Ct. 497 (1980): in "a decision subject to NEPA's procedural requirements, the only role for a court is to insure that the agency has considered the environmental consequences; it cannot 'interject itself within the area of discretion of the executive as to the choice of the action to be taken.' " *Id.* at 227–28, 100 S. Ct. at 500 (*citing Kleppe v. Sierra Club*, 427 U.S. 390, 410, n.21 (1976)).

A close reading of these comments reveals a lurking ambiguity. *Vermont Yankee*, by indicating that agency decisions must be "well-considered" and noting that NEPA had "altered slightly the statutory balance," intimated the possibility that § 102(2)(C) might impose some substantive obligations on agencies. And *Strycker's Bay* could be read as merely a judicial statement in favor of deferential review of agency decisions.

The ambiguity is no longer.

ROBERTSON v. METHOW VALLEY CITIZENS COUNCIL
490 U.S. 332, 109 S. Ct. 1835 (1989)

JUSTICE STEVENS delivered the opinion of the Court.

We granted certiorari to decide two questions of law. As framed by petitioners, they are:

1. Whether the National Environmental Policy Act requires federal agencies to include in each environmental impact statement: (a) a fully developed plan to mitigate environmental harm; and (b) a "worst case" analysis of potential environmental harm if relevant information concerning significant environmental effects is unavailable or too costly to obtain.

2. Whether the Forest Service may issue a special use permit for recreational use of national forest land in the absence of a fully developed plan to mitigate environmental harm.'

Concluding that the Court of Appeals for the Ninth Circuit misapplied the National Environmental Policy Act of 1969 (NEPA), 83 Stat. 852, 42 U.S.C. § 4321 et seq., and gave inadequate deference to the Forest Service's interpretation of its own regulations, we reverse and remand for further proceedings.

The Forest Service is authorized by statute to manage the national forests for "outdoor recreation, range, timber, watershed, and wildlife and fish purposes." 74 Stat. 215, 16 U.S.C. § 528. *See also* 90 Stat. 2949, 16 U.S.C. § 1600 et seq. Pursuant to that authorization, the Forest Service has issued "special use" permits for the operation of approximately 170 alpine and nordic ski areas on federal lands. *See* H. R. Rep. No. 99709, pt. 1, p. 2 (1986).

The Forest Service permit process involves three separate stages. The Forest Service first examines the general environmental and financial feasibility of a proposed project and decides whether to issue a special use permit. *See* 36 C.F.R. § 251.54(f) (1988). Because that decision is a "major Federal action" within the meaning of NEPA, it must be preceded by the preparation of an Environmental Impact Statement (EIS). 42 U.S.C. § 4332. If the Service decides to issue a permit, it then proceeds to select a developer, formulate the basic terms of the arrangement with the selected party, and issue the permit. The special use permit does not, however, give the developer the right to begin construction. *See* 36 C.F.R. § 251.56(c) (1988). In a final stage of review, the Service evaluates the permittee's "master plan" for development, construction, and operation of the project. Construction may begin only after an additional environmental analysis (although it is not clear that a second EIS need always be prepared) and final approval of the developer's master plan. This case arises out of the Forest Service's decision to issue a special use permit authorizing the development of a major destination alpine ski resort at Sandy Butte in the North Cascades mountains.

Sandy Butte is a 6,000 foot mountain located in the Okanogan National Forest in Okanogan County, Washington. At present Sandy Butte, like the Methow Valley it overlooks, is an unspoiled, sparsely populated area that the district court characterized as "pristine." In 1968, Congress established the North Cascades National

Park and directed the Secretaries of Interior and Agriculture to agree on the designation of areas within and adjacent to the park for public uses, including ski areas. 82 Stat. 926, 930, 16 U.S.C. §§ 90, 90d3. A 1970 study conducted by the Forest Service pursuant to this congressional directive identified Sandy Butte as having the highest potential of any site in the State of Washington for development as a major downhill ski resort.

In 1978, Methow Recreation, Inc. (MRI) applied for a special use permit to develop and operate its proposed "Early Winters Ski Resort" on Sandy Butte and an 1,165 acre parcel of land it had acquired adjacent to the National Forest. The proposed development would make use of approximately 3,900 acres of Sandy Butte; would entice visitors to travel long distances to stay at the resort for several days at a time; and would stimulate extensive commercial and residential growth in the vicinity to accommodate both vacationers and staff.

In response to MRI's application, the Forest Service, in cooperation with state and county officials, prepared an EIS known as the Early Winters Alpine Winter Sports Study (Early Winters Study or Study). The stated purpose of the EIS was "to provide the information required to evaluate the potential for skiing at Early Winters" and "to assist in making a decision whether to issue a Special Use Permit for downhill skiing on all or a portion of approximately 3900 acres of National Forest System land." A draft of the Study was completed and circulated in 1982, but release of the final EIS was delayed as Congress considered including Sandy Butte in a proposed wilderness area. When the Washington State Wilderness Act of 1984 was passed, however, Sandy Butte was excluded from the wilderness designation, and the EIS was released.

The Early Winters Study is a printed document containing almost 150 pages of text and 12 appendices. It evaluated five alternative levels of development of Sandy Butte that might be authorized, the lowest being a "no action" alternative and the highest being development of a 16lift ski area able to accommodate 10,500 skiers at one time. The Study considered the effect of each level of development on water resources, soil, wildlife, air quality, vegetation and visual quality, as well as land use and transportation in the Methow Valley, probable demographic shifts, the economic market for skiing and other summer and winter recreational activities in the Valley, and the energy requirements for the ski area and related developments. The Study's discussion of possible impacts was not limited to onsite effects, but also, as required by Council on Environmental Quality (CEQ) regulations, see 40 C.F.R. § 1502.16(b) (1987), addressed "offsite impacts that each alternative might have on community facilities, socioeconomic and other environmental conditions in the Upper Methow Valley." As to offsite effects, the Study explained that "due to the uncertainty of where other public and private lands may become developed," it is difficult to evaluate offsite impacts, id., at 76, and thus the document's analysis is necessarily "not site-specific," id., at 1. Finally, the Study outlined certain steps that might be taken to mitigate adverse effects, both on Sandy Butte and in the neighboring Methow Valley, but indicated that these proposed steps are merely conceptual and "will be made more specific as part of the design and implementation stages of the planning process." Id., at 14.

The effects of the proposed development on air quality and wildlife received particular attention in the Study. In the chapter on "Environmental Consequences," the first subject discussed is air quality. As is true of other subjects, the discussion included an analysis of cumulative impacts over several years resulting from actions on other lands as well as from the development of Sandy Butte itself. The Study concluded that although the construction, maintenance, and operation of the proposed ski area "will not have a measurable effect on existing or future air quality," the offsite development of private land under all five alternatives — including the "no action" alternative — "will have a significant effect on air quality during severe meteorological inversion periods." *Id.*, at 65. The burning of wood for space heat, the Study explained, would constitute the primary cause of diminished air quality and the damage would increase incrementally with each of the successive levels of proposed development. *Ibid.* The Study cautioned that without efforts to mitigate these effects, even under the "no action" alternative, the increase in automobile, fireplace, and wood stove use would reduce air quality below state standards, but added that "[t]he numerous mitigation measures discussed" in the Study "will greatly reduce the impacts presented by the model." *Id.*, at 67.

In its discussion of air quality mitigation measures, the EIS identified actions that could be taken by the county government to mitigate the adverse effects of development, as well as those the Forest Service itself could implement at the construction stage of the project. The Study suggested that Okanogan County develop an air quality management plan, requiring weatherization of new buildings, limiting the number of wood stoves and fireplaces, and adopting monitoring and enforcement measures. In addition, the Study suggested that the Forest Service require that the master plan include procedures to control dust and to comply with smoke management practices.

In its discussion of adverse effects on area wildlife, the EIS concluded that no endangered or threatened species would be affected by the proposed development and that the only impact on sensitive species was the probable loss of a pair of spotted owls and their progeny. *Id.*, at 75. With regard to other wildlife, the Study considered the impact on 75 different indigenous species and predicted that within a decade after development vegetational change and increased human activity would lead to a decrease in population for 31 species, while causing an increase in population for another 24 species on Sandy Butte. *Ibid.* Two species, the pine marten and nesting goshawk, would be eliminated altogether from the area of development. *Ibid.*

In a comment in response to the draft EIS, the Washington Department of Game voiced a special concern about potential losses to the State's largest migratory deer herd, which uses the Methow Valley as a critical winter range and as its migration route. The state agency estimated that the total population of mule deer in the area most likely to be affected was "better than 30,000 animals" and that "the ultimate impact on the Methow deer herd could exceed a 50 percent reduction in numbers." The agency asserted that "Okanogan County residents place of great deal of importance on the area's deer herd." In addition, it explained that hunters had "harvested" 3,247 deer in the Methow Valley area in 1981, and that in 1980 hunters on average spent $1,980 for each deer killed in Washington, they had contributed over $6 million to the State's economy. Because the deer harvest is apparently proportional to the size of the herd, the state agency predicted that "Washington business can expect to lose over $3 million annually from reduced recreational opportunity." The Forest Service's own analysis of the impact on the deer herd was more modest. It first concluded that the actual operation of the ski hill would have only a "minor" direct impact on the herd, but then recognized that the offsite effect of the development "would noticeably reduce numbers of deer in the Methow [Valley] with any alternative." *Id.*, at 76. Although its estimate indicated a possible 15 percent decrease in the size of the herd, it summarized the State's contrary view in the text of the EIS, and stressed that offsite effects are difficult to estimate due to uncertainty concerning private development.

As was true of its discussion of air quality, the EIS also described both onsite and offsite mitigation measures. Among possible onsite mitigation possibilities, the Study recommended locating runs, ski lifts, and roads so as to minimize interference with wildlife, restricting access to selected roads during fawning season, and further examination of the effect of the development on mule deer migration routes. Offsite options discussed in the Study included the use of zoning and tax incentives to limit development on deer winter range and migration routes, encouragement of conservation easements, and acquisition and management by local government of critical tracts of land. As with the measures suggested for mitigating the offsite effects on air quality, the proposed options were primarily directed to steps that might be taken by state and local government.

Ultimately, the Early Winters Study recommended the issuance of a permit for development at the second highest level considered — a 16lift ski area able to accommodate 8,200 skiers at one time. On July 5, 1984, the Regional Forester decided to issue a special use permit as recommended by the Study. In his decision, the Regional Forester found that no major adverse effects would result directly from the federal action, but that secondary effects could include a degradation of existing air quality and a reduction of mule deer winter range. He therefore directed the supervisor of the Okanogan National Forest, both independently and in cooperation with local officials, to identify and implement certain mitigating measures.

Four organizations (respondents) opposing the decision to issue a permit appealed the Regional Forester's decision to the Chief of the Forest Service. After a hearing, he affirmed the Regional Forester's decision. Stressing that the decision, which simply approved the general concept of issuing a 30year special use permit for development of Sandy Butte, did not authorize construction of a particular ski area and, in fact, did not even act on MRI's specific permit application, he concluded that the EIS's discussion of mitigation was "adequate for this stage in the review process."

Thereafter, respondents brought this action under the Administrative Procedure Act, 5 U.S.C. §§ 701–706, to obtain judicial review of the Forest Service's decision. Their principal claim was that the Early Winters Study did not satisfy the requirements of NEPA, 42 U.S.C. § 4332. With the consent of the parties, the case was assigned to a United States Magistrate. *See* 28 U.S.C. § 636(c). After a trial, the Magistrate filed a comprehensive written opinion and concluded that the EIS was adequate. Specifically, he found that the EIS had adequately disclosed the adverse impacts on the mule deer herd and on air quality and that there was no duty to prepare a "worst case analysis" because the relevant information essential to a reasoned decision was available. In concluding that the discussion of offsite, or secondary, impacts was adequate, the Magistrate stressed that courts apply a "rule of reason" in evaluating the adequacy of an EIS and "take the uncertainty and speculation involved with secondary impacts into account in passing on the adequacy of the discussion of secondary impacts." On the subject of mitigation, he explained that "[m]ere listing . . . is generally inadequate to satisfy the CEQ regulations," but found that "in this EIS there is more — not much more — but more than a mere listing of mitigation measures." Moreover, emphasizing the tiered nature of the Forest Service's decisional process, the Magistrate noted that additional mitigation strategies would be included in the master plan, that the Forest Service continues to develop mitigation plans as further information becomes available, and that the Regional Forester's decision conditioned issuance of the special use permit on execution of an agreement between the Forest Service, the State of Washington, and Okanogan County concerning mitigation.

Concluding that the Early Winters Study was inadequate as a matter of law, the Court of Appeals reversed. *Methow Valley Citizens Council v. Regional Forester*, 833 F.2d 810 (CA9 1987). The court held that the Forest Service could not rely on " 'the implementation of mitigation measures' " to support its conclusion that the impact on the mule deer would be minor "since not only has the effectiveness of these mitigati on measures not yet been assessed, but the mitigation measures themselves have yet to be developed." It then added that if the agency had difficulty obtaining adequate information to make a reasoned assessment of the environmental impact on the herd, it had a duty to make a so-called "worst case analysis." Such an analysis is " 'formulated on the basis of available information, using reasonable projections of the worst possible consequences of a proposed action.' " *Save our Ecosystems*, 747 F.2d, at 1244–45 (quoting 46 Fed. Reg. 18032 (1981).

The court found a similar defect in the EIS's treatment of air quality. Since the EIS made it clear that commercial development in the Methow Valley will result in violations of state air quality standards unless effective mitigation measures are put in place by the local governments and the private developer, the Court of Appeals concluded that the Forest Service had an affirmative duty to "develop the necessary mitigation measures before the permit is granted." (emphasis in original) (footnote omitted). The court held that this duty was imposed by both the Forest Service's own regulations and § 102 of NEPA *Ibid.* It read the statute as imposing a substantive requirement that "action be taken to mitigate the adverse effects of major federal actions." For this reason, it concluded that "an EIS must include a fair discussion of measures to mitigate the adverse environmental impacts of a proposed action." The Court of Appeals concluded by quoting this paragraph from an opinion it had just announced:

> "The importance of the mitigation plan cannot be overestimated. It is a determinative factor in evaluating the adequacy of an environmental impact statement. Without a complete mitigation plan, the decisionmaker is unable to make an informed judgment as to the environmental impact of the project — one of the main purposes of an environmental impact statement." (quoting *Oregon Natural Resources Council v. Marsh*, 832 F.2d 1489, 1493 (CA9 1987), *rev'd, post,* p. 360)).

II

. . . .

The statutory requirement that a federal agency contemplating a major action prepare . . . an environmental impact statement serves NEPA's "action-forcing" purpose in two important respects. It ensures that the agency, in reaching its decision, will have available and will carefully consider detailed information concerning significant environmental impacts; it also guarantees that the relevant information will be made available to the larger audience that may also play a role in both the decisionmaking process and the implementation of that decision.

Simply by focusing the agency's attention on the environmental consequences of a proposed project, NEPA ensures that important effects will not be overlooked or underestimated only to be discovered after resources have been committed or the die otherwise cast. Moreover, the strong precatory language of § 101 of the Act and the requirement that agencies prepare detailed impact statements inevitably bring pressure to bear on agencies "to respond to the needs of environmental quality."

Publication of an EIS, both in draft and final form, also serves a larger informational role. It gives the public the assurance that the agency "has indeed considered environmental concerns in its decisionmaking process," and, perhaps more significantly, provides a springboard for public comment. Thus, in this case the final draft of the Early Winters Study reflects not only the work of the Forest Service itself, but also the critical views of the Washington State Department of Game, the Methow Valley Citizens Council, and Friends of the Earth, as well as many others, to whom copies of the draft Study were circulated. Moreover, with respect to a development such as Sandy Butte, where the adverse effects on air quality and the mule deer herd are primarily attributable to predicate offsite development that will be subject to regulation by other governmental bodies, the EIS serves the function of offering those bodies adequate notice of the expected consequences and the opportunity to plan and implement corrective measures in a timely manner.

The sweeping policy goals announced in § 101 of NEPA are thus realized through a set of "action-forcing" procedures that require that agencies take a " 'hard look' at environmental consequences," and that provide for broad dissemination of relevant environmental information. Although these procedures are almost certain to affect the agency's substantive decision, it is now well settled that NEPA itself does not mandate particular results, but simply prescribes the necessary process. *See Strycker's Bay Neighborhood Council, Inc. v. Karlen,* 444 U. S. 223, 227–228 (1980) (per curiam); *Vermont Yankee Nuclear Power Corp. v. Natural Resources Defense Council, Inc.,* 435 U. S. 519, 558 (1978). If the adverse environmental effects of the proposed action are adequately identified and evaluated, the agency is not constrained by NEPA from deciding that other values outweigh the environmental costs. In this case, for example, it would not have violated NEPA if the Forest Service, after complying with the Act's procedural prerequisites, had decided that the benefits to be derived from downhill skiing at Sandy Butte justified the issuance of a special use permit, notwithstanding the loss of 15 percent, 50 percent, or even 100 percent of the mule deer herd. Other statutes may impose substantive environmental obligations on federal agencies, but NEPA merely prohibits uninformed — rather than unwise — agency action.

To be sure, one important ingredient of an EIS is the discussion of steps that can be taken to mitigate adverse environmental consequences. The requirement that an EIS contain a detailed discussion of possible mitigation measures flows from both the language of the Act and, more expressly, from CEQ's implementing regulations. Implicit in NEPA's demand that an agency prepare a detailed statement on "any adverse environmental effects which cannot be avoided should the proposal be implemented," 42 U.S.C. § 4332(C)(ii), is an understanding that the EIS will discuss the extent to which adverse effects can be avoided. More generally, omission of a reasonably complete discussion of possible mitigation measures would undermine the "action-forcing" function of NEPA. Without such a discussion, neither the agency nor other interested groups and individuals can properly evaluate the severity of the adverse effects. An adverse effect that can be fully remedied by, for example, an inconsequential public expenditure is certainly not as serious as a similar effect that can only be modestly ameliorated through the commitment of vast public and private resources. Recognizing the importance of such a discussion in guaranteeing that the agency has taken a "hard look" at the environmental consequences of proposed federal action, CEQ regulations require that the agency discuss possible mitigation measures in defining the scope of the EIS, 40 C.F.R. § 1508.25(b) (1987), in discussing alternatives to the proposed action, § 1502.14(f), and consequences of that action, § 1502.16(h), and in explaining its ultimate decision, § 1505.2(c).

There is a fundamental distinction, however, between a requirement that mitigation be discussed in sufficient detail to ensure that environmental consequences have been fairly evaluated, on the one hand, and a substantive requirement that a complete mitigation plan be actually formulated and adopted, on the other. In this case, the offsite effects on air quality and on the mule deer herd cannot be mitigated unless nonfederal government agencies take appropriate action. Since it is those state and local governmental bodies that have jurisdiction over the area in which the adverse effects need be addressed and since they have the authority to mitigate them, it would be incongruous to conclude that the Forest Service has no power to act until the local agencies have reached a final conclusion on what mitigating measures they consider necessary. Even more significantly, it would be inconsistent with NEPA's reliance on procedural mechanisms — as opposed to substantive, result-based standards — to demand the presence of a fully developed plan that will mitigate environmental harm before an agency can act. *Cf. Baltimore Gas & Electric Co.*, 462 U.S., at 100 ("NEPA does not require agencies to adopt any particular internal decisionmaking structure").

Because NEPA imposes no substantive requirement that mitigations measures actually be taken, it should not be read to require agencies to obtain an assurance that third parties will implement particular measures.

We thus conclude that the Court of Appeals erred, first, in assuming that "NEPA requires that 'action be taken to mitigate the adverse effects of major federal actions,'" and, second, in finding that this substantive requirement entails the further duty to include in every EIS "a detailed explanation of specific measures which will be employed to mitigate the adverse impacts of a proposed action," 833 F.2d, at 819 (emphasis supplied).

III

The Court of Appeals also concluded that the Forest Service had an obligation to make a "worst case analysis" if it could not make a reasoned assessment of the impact of the Early Winters project on the mule deer herd. Such a "worst case analysis" was required at one time by CEQ regulations, but those regulations have since been amended. Moreover, although the prior regulations may well have expressed a permissible application of NEPA, the Act itself does not mandate that uncertainty in predicting environmental harms be addressed exclusively in this manner. Accordingly, we conclude that the Court of Appeals also erred in requiring the "worst case" study.

In 1977, President Carter directed the CEQ promulgate binding regulations implementing the procedural provisions of NEPA. Exec. Order No. 11991, 3 C.F.R. 123 (1977 Comp.). Pursuant to this presidential order, CEQ promulgated implementing regulations. Under § 1502.22 of these regulations — a provision which became known as the "worst case requirement" — CEQ provided that if certain information relevant to the agency's evaluation of the proposed action is either unavailable or too costly to obtain, the agency must include in the EIS a "worst case analysis and an indication of the probability or improbability of its occurrence." 40 C.F.R. § 1502.22 (1985). In 1986, however, CEQ replaced the "worst case" requirement with a requirement that federal agencies, in the face of unavailable information concerning a reasonably foreseeable significant environmental consequence, prepare "a summary of existing credible scientific evidence which is relevant to evaluating the . . . adverse impacts" and prepare an "evaluation of such impacts based upon theoretical approaches or research methods generally accepted in the scientific community." 40 C.F.R. § 1502.22(b) (1987). The amended regulation thus "retains the duty to describe the consequences of a remote, but potentially severe impact, but grounds the duty in evaluation of scientific opinion rather than in the framework of a conjectural 'worst case analysis.' " 50 Fed. Reg. 32237 (1985).

The Court of Appeals recognized that the "worst case analysis" regulation has been superseded, yet held that "[t]his rescission . . . does not nullify the requirement . . . since the regulations was merely a codification of prior NEPA case law." This conclusion, however, is erroneous in a number of respects. Most notably, review of NEPA case law reveals that the regulation, in fact, was not a codification of prior judicial decisions. The cases cited by the Court of Appeals ultimately rely on the Fifth Circuit's decision in *Sierra Club v. Sigler*, 695 F.2d 957 (1983). *Sigler*, however, simply recognized that the "worst case analysis" regulation codified the "judicially created principl[e]" that an EIS must "consider the probabilities of the occurrence of any environmental effects it discusses." *Id.*, at 970–971. As CEQ recognized at the time it superseded the regulation, case law prior to the adoption of the "worst case analysis" provision did require agencies to describe environmental impacts even in the face of substantial uncertainty, but did not require that this obligation necessarily be met through the mechanism of a "worst case analysis." *See* 51 Fed. Reg. 15625 (1986). CEQ's abandonment of the "worst case analysis" provision, therefore, is not inconsistent with any previously established judicial interpretation of the statute.

Nor are we convinced that the new CEQ regulation is not controlling simply because it was preceded by a rule that was in some respects more demanding. In *Andrus v. Sierra Club*, 442 U.S., at 358, we held that CEQ regulations are entitled to substantial deference. In that case we recognized that although less deference may be in order in some cases in which the " 'administrative guidelines' " conflict " 'with earlier pronouncements of the agency,' " *ibid.* (quoting *General Electric Co. v. Gilbert*, 429 U. S. 125, 143 (1976)), substantial deference is nonetheless appropriate if there appears to have been good reason for the change, 442 U.S., at 358. Here, the amendment only came after the prior regulation had been subjected to considerable criticism. Moreover, the amendment was designed to better serve the twin functions of an EIS — requiring agencies to take a "hard look" at the consequences of the proposed action and providing important information to other groups and individuals. CEQ explained that by requiring that an EIS focus on reasonably foreseeable impacts, the new regulation "will generate information and discussion on those consequences of greatest concern to the public and of greatest relevance to the agency's decision," 50 Fed. Reg. 32237 (1985), rather than distorting the decision making process by overemphasizing highly speculative harms, 51 Fed. Reg. 15624–15625 (1986); 50 Fed. Reg. 32236 (1985). In light of this well-considered basis for the change, the new regulation is entitled to substantial deference.

IV

The Court of Appeals also held that the Forest Service's failure to develop a complete mitigation plan violated the agency's own regulations. [The Court found no such violation of the Forest Service's regulations.]

V

In sum, we conclude that NEPA does not require a fully developed plan detailing what steps will be taken to mitigate adverse environmental impacts and does not require a "worst case analysis." In addition, we hold that the Forest Service has adopted a permissible interpretation of its own regulations. The judgment of the Court of Appeals is accordingly reversed and the case is remanded for further proccedings consistent with this opinion.

It is so ordered.

JUSTICE BRENNAN, concurring.

I write separately to highlight the Court's observation that "one important ingredient of an EIS is the discussion of steps that can be taken to mitigate adverse environmental consequences."

NOTE

NEPA after Methow Valley. Thus, we see that there is no cause of action available under NEPA to protest an agency's failure to adopt the recommendations of an EIS. NEPA requires preparation of an EIS, but not compliance with that document's recommendations. *See Methow Valley, supra; see also Noe v. MARTA*, 485 F. Supp. 501 (N.D. Ga. 1980), *aff'd*, 644 F.2d 434 (5th Cir.), *cert. denied*, 454 U.S. 1126, 102 S. Ct. 977 (1981). *Cf. Calvert Cliffs*, 449 F.2d at 1117 ("What possible purpose could there be in requiring the 'detailed statement' to be before hearing boards, if the boards are free to ignore entirely the contents of the statement? NEPA was meant to do more than regulate the flow of papers in the federal bureaucracy.").

Might there be a cause of action elsewhere? Theoretically, a cause of action could be framed under the Administrative Procedure Act ("APA"), 5 U.S.C. § 551 et seq. As the reader has seen, § 706(2) of the APA authorizes courts, *inter alia*, to "hold unlawful and set aside agency action, findings and conclusions found to be . . . arbitrary, capricious, an abuse of discretion, or otherwise not in accordance with law." 5 U.S.C. § 706(2)(A). Agency decisions are deemed to violate this provision if they are not "based on relevant factors" or if they manifest a "clear error of judgment." *Citizens to Preserve Overton Park v. Volpe*, 401 U.S. 402, 91 S. Ct. 814 (1971). There seem to be no cases, however, where such a cause of action has succeeded. *See, e.g.,* WILLIAM H. RODGERS, JR., ENVIRONMENTAL LAW 861 (2d ed. 1994) ("[D]iligent researchers are still looking for the project that could not be built under NEPA because the environmental costs exceeded the economic benefits.").

If agencies are free to ignore the recommendations of EISs, has NEPA become the "paper tiger" Judge Wright wrote of in *Calvert Cliffs*? The CEQ certainly does not think so. In 1997, it issued a report detailing the performance of the Act in its first 25 years. Council on Environmental Quality, *The National Environmental Policy Act: A Study of Its Effectiveness After Twenty-five Years* (Jan. 1997) ("CEQ Report"). CEQ concluded that NEPA is a "success" because it made agencies take a hard look at the potential environmental consequences of their actions and brought the public into the decision-making arena. Still, CEQ observed, agencies are sometimes prone to engage in consultation only after their decisions, at least for all practical purposes, have been made. This leads the public to feel excluded from the decision-making process, which in turn produces unnecessary public opposition to what may well be worthy agency action. CEQ also conceded that NEPA can present agencies with significant administrative burdens. *Id.* at iii. Beyond that, agencies sometimes think of EISs as an end in themselves, rather than as an aid to decision making.

Perhaps most significantly, the CEQ Report bemoaned the practice of agencies to use NEPA on a "once and for all" basis. As characterized by CEQ, "results from intensive research, modeling, and other computations or expert opinions are analyzed, the analysis of potential environmental impacts is prepared, mitigation measure are identified, and a document is released for public review. Unfortunately, most often the process ends there." *Id.* at 31. In CEQ's view, this practice of using NEPA on a "snapshot" basis is undesirable. NEPA, rather, should play a role not only at the outset of a project, but during construction and operation phases as well. The heart and soul of NEPA would no longer be "predict, mitigate, and implement"; it would become "predict, mitigate, implement, monitor, and adapt." *Id.* at 32.

CEQ's name for this pro-mid-course corrections approach is "adaptive environmental management." CEQ elaborates: "Instead of investing extensive resources into the initial analysis, the adaptive management approach would allow agencies to develop objective criteria for 'significant' environmental change in the status of the resource or ecosystem of concern (be it rangelands, wetlands, or forests). An agency can then analyze and approve a plan or project with an uncertain outcome, monitoring the status of the resource to make corrective changes to the project or mitigation plan to ensure that significant degradation does not occur. By incorporating adaptive management into their NEPA analyses, agencies can move beyond simple compliance and better target environmental improvement." *Id.* at 33. Projects could remain assuredly benign to the environment for the entirety of their useful lives.

A NOTE ON ENVIRONMENTAL JUSTICE

Suppose that a manufacturing facility, Plant D, is scheduled for construction in Lowlands, a residential area that already serves as a home to Plants A, B, and C, which are polluters. Plant D needs a federal permit as a prerequisite to construction. The issue is whether the permitting of Plant D constitutes a "major federal action significantly affecting the quality of the human environment." As we have seen, this determination requires an assessment of direct, indirect, and cumulative effects. The EA, therefore, must examine the character of the proposed site, i.e., "the incremental impact of the [construction of Plant D] when added to other past, present, and reasonably foreseeable future actions[.]" 40 C.F.R. § 1508.7.

In addition to these considerations, should the EA consider the state of affairs in other locales? Specifically, should it assess whether nearby locales are free, or relatively free, of polluting facilities, while Lowlands seems to be getting more than its share? And if that is the case, should that fact bear on the determination whether to proceed with an EIS? Expressed otherwise, should an EA contain a *comparative* impacts analysis? The text of NEPA announces no such obligation. Currently, however, a comparative analysis of this sort is necessary if Lowlands happens to be populated predominantly by persons of color or low income.

The reason is found in the Environmental Justice ("EJ") movement. Prompted in large part by a 1987 study prepared by the United Church of Christ, entitled *Toxic Waste and Race in the United States: A National Report on the Racial and Socio-Economic Characteristics of Communities with Hazardous Waste Sites*, the EJ movement maintains that a disproportionate number of polluting facilities, especially hazardous waste disposal sites, have been constructed in areas populated predominantly by persons of color and low income. The movement asserts this proliferation is racist in origin. In response to this initiative, President Bill Clinton issued an Executive Order 12,898 on February 11, 1994, which provides in relevant part:

§ 1101. Agency Responsibilities. To the greatest extent practicable and permitted by law, and consistent with the principles set forth in the report on the National Performance Review, each Federal agency shall make achieving environmental justice part of its mission by identifying and addressing, as appropriate, disproportionately high and adverse human health or environmental effects of its programs, policies, and activities on minority populations and low-income populations in the United States and its territories and possessions, the District of Columbia, the Commonwealth of Puerto Rico, and the Commonwealth of the Mariana Islands.

For the full text of the Order, see 59 Fed. Reg. 7629 (Feb. 11, 1994).

This order has changed the way federal agencies comply with NEPA. EPA, for example, released "draft guidance" on July 12, 1996, which proposed that its EIS evaluations should consider environmental justice factors such as demographics, economic conditions, human health and risk issues, and cultural differences. Accordingly, early in the NEPA process, the agency "should identify the presence of minority or low-income communities and whether such communities are likely to experience adverse environmental health effects as a result of proposed federal actions." The inclusion of such considerations, the draft commented, would allow for a "more focused analysis that identifies significant effects that might otherwise have been diluted by an examination of a larger population or area [.]" "[E]nvironmental justice concerns," it added, "should always trigger the serious evaluation of alternatives as mitigation options." In September 2011, the agency announced a plan to incorporate EJ concerns across rulemaking, permitting, and enforcement activities. It plans to assess the success of this plan over the preceding three years in 2014, the 20th anniversary of the Executive Order, and at that point determine its next steps.

As EPA's new plan demonstrates, the EJ movement is not confined to situations involving NEPA. Indeed, since the movement implicates core concepts of equality under the law, it also has called upon the Equal Protection Clauses of the Federal Constitution and Title VI of the Civil Rights Act of 1964 for legal support. Indeed, these provisions can serve as substantive bases to contest an agency decision to locate a sewage treatment plant, a cement plant, a hazardous waste treatment or disposal plant, or any other polluting facility. Title VI, for example, expressly provides that no person shall "on the grounds of race, color, or national origin, be denied the benefits of, or be subjected to discrimination under any program or activity" covered by that legislation. 42 U.S.C. § 2000d.

However, the Equal Protection Clauses and Title VI have proven to be of limited value to EJ plaintiffs because they prohibit only hard-to-prove *intentionally* discriminatory actions. *See, e.g., Regents of University of California v. Bakke*, 438 U.S. 265, 98 S. Ct. 2733 (1978); *Alexander v. Choate*, 469 U.S. 287, 105 S. Ct. 712 (1985). Thus, if the motivation behind a siting decision is entirely for reasons of economics or politics, no cause of action lies regardless of whether the targeted locale is already overburdened with polluting facilities.

What EJ plaintiffs prefer is a disparate impact standard. For a *prima facie* case under this standard, plaintiffs need to demonstrate a statistically significant disproportionate and adverse impact on minorities, and beyond that, a causal connection between the agency action or policy and that disproportionate and adverse impact. *See, e.g., New York Environmental Justice Alliance v. Giuliani*, 214 F.3d 65 (2d Cir. 2000). This burden of proof presents its own level of difficulty: proving a causal connection can be difficult, especially when an agency policy, as distinct from an agency permit issuance, is at issue. Moreover, figuring out who is a member of a minority group, and which minorities are affected by which actions, can be difficult. This difficulty, if anything, was exacerbated by the 2000 census, which introduced a new classification system allowing persons to designate themselves as members of more than one minority group. Still, with a disparate impact standard, plaintiffs at least do not need to prove the defendant's mental state, i.e., that defendant intended to discriminate.

Thanks to the United States Department of Justice ("DOJ"), plaintiffs have been using the disparate impact standard. This is because the DOJ promulgated rules that forbid recipients of federal funding, including state governments and private persons, to "utilize criteria or methods of administration which have the *effect* of subjecting individuals to discrimination because of their race, color, or national origin." 28 C.F.R. § 42.104(b)(2) (emphasis added). Thus did DOJ attempt to restore the disparate impact standard to Title VI cases.

The disparate impact standard, however, is no longer available for nongovernment EJ plaintiffs. In *Alexander v. Sandoval*, 532 U.S. 275, 121 S. Ct. 1511 (2001), a case involving the State of Alabama's practice of administering driving license examinations in the English language only, the Supreme Court, assuming the DOJ's regulations calling for a disparate impact standard were valid, concluded that no private right of action exists to enforce those regulations. (There remains a private right of action to enforce DOJ regulations prohibiting intentional discrimination.) The decision was 5-4, with Associate Justice Antonin Scalia writing for the majority. *Sandoval* means that agencies are still obligated to follow the DOJ regulations, but the public may not bring an action in the event an agency fails to meet its obligation.

Even though this was described as a devastating blow to EJ proponents, indeed as a "dagger in the middle of the forehead," *BNA Daily Environmental Report*, Apr. 25, 2001, still, from the point of view of EJ plaintiffs, all may not be lost. While *Sandoval* rules out disparate impact causes of action under Title VI, there still remains a cause of action to enforce Title VI regulations under 42 U.S.C. § 1983. Justice Stevens, in his dissent in *Sandoval*, allowed for that possibility, and at least one subsequent decision has determined this alternative avenue is available, at least when the enforceable interest is implicit within the statute authorizing the regulation. *South Camden Citizens in Action v. New Jersey Department of Environmental Protection*, 274 F. 3d 771 (3d Cir. 2001), *cert. denied*, 536 U.S. 939, 122 S. Ct. 2621 (2002). So the disparate impact standard lives.

The hotly debated question underlying all of this is whether it actually is a common practice to site plants for racist reasons. One view on the issue was well stated by Richard Samp, Chief Counsel of the Washington Legal Foundation: "I've never known a company to purposely choose a site that was more expensive than an alternative site simply because they wanted to stick it to some racial minority. They go to a particular site because they think it is the best one available to them at the cheapest cost." *All Things Considered* (National Public Radio, May 7, 2001).

Unsurprisingly, residents of burdened localities often tend to view the matter differently. Empirical data one way or the other has been in short supply. But data has come in. Using census information, an environmental group, Environmental Defense, assembled a database to shed light on the magnitude of the EJ problem. The group compared four environmental risks — toxic chemical releases, cancer risks from hazardous air pollutants, hazardous materials sites under the Comprehensive Environmental Response, Compensation and Liability Act (*see* Chapter 12, *infra*), and so-called "criteria" air pollutants (*see* Chapter 9, *infra*) — with seven demographic factors: race and ethnicity; income; poverty; childhood poverty; education; job classification; and home ownership. Environmental Defense concluded its data, while informative, falls short of providing a clear picture of national trends with respect to environmental justice. This information, managed by an organization called Green Media Toolshed, is available at www.scorecard.org. While informative, the data has not been updated for at least five years.

A final note: in October 2003, the U.S. Commission on Civil Rights issued a report entitled *Not In My Backyard*. One hundred ninety-four pages in length, this report found that the Environmental Protection Agency, the Department of Housing and Urban Development, the Department of Transportation, and the Department of the Interior have failed to fully implement the 1994 Executive Order. *See* www.usccr.gov/pubs/pubsndx.htm. For a fifty-state survey of legislation, policies, and initiatives relating to environmental justice, see *Environmental Justice For All*, a publication of the American Bar Association and Hastings College of the Law, 2004.

CEQ's Guidance to agencies regarding complying with the Executive Order on environmental justice may be found at http://ceq.hss.doe.gov/nepa/regs/ej/justice.pdf.

2. EIS Content and Availability Requirements

We have now seen that the role of an EIS in agency decision making is procedural. This section discusses the procedural requirements of § 102(2)(C). Specifically, it assesses the who, what, when, and how of the provision. Note that CEQ's regulations play an important part in determining the mechanics of agency compliance with NEPA's requirements. Those regulations, however, require each federal agency to adopt its own procedures "as necessary" for NEPA compliance. 40 C.F.R. § 1507, 3(a).

(A) Who?: Who must prepare an EIS? The federal agency responsible for the action under review has the responsibility to prepare the EIS. That responsibility does not mean that the agency must, in every case, actually write the document. It does mean, however, that the agency is ultimately responsible for it. Accordingly, if an agency contracts with an outside entity to write the document, the agency must nonetheless adopt the EIS as its own and take on full legal responsibility for it.

In many instances, more than one agency is involved in a proposed action. In such a case, the common practice is to choose one of the group to act as lead agency; if they cannot agree, the determination is left to the CEQ. 40 C.F.R. § 1501.5. The lead agency can designate cooperating agencies, and conversely, nonlead agencies can request to be cooperating agencies. 40 C.F.R. § 1501.6. EISs should contain a list of the names and qualifications of the persons primarily responsible for document preparation. 40 C.F.R. § 1502.17.

(B) What?: The information an EIS should contain is specified by § 102(2)(C) itself. The section lists five matters that must be covered. They are:

(i)   the environmental impact of the proposed action,

(ii)   any adverse environmental effects which cannot be avoided should the proposal be implemented,

(iii)   alternatives to the proposed action,

(iv)   the relationship between local short-term uses of man's environment and the maintenance and enhancement of long-term productivity, and

(v)   any irreversible and irretrievable commitments of resources which would be involved in the proposed action should it be implemented.

§ 102(2)(C), 42 U.S.C. § 4332(2)(C).

Of these five components, the most important are the first and the third.

The first requirement, calling for review of environmental impacts, obligates agencies to examine *direct, indirect, and cumulative effects* of those proposed actions. "Direct" effects are those which are "caused by the action and occur at the same time and place." 40 C.F.R. § 1508.8(a). "Indirect" effects are also caused by the action but "are later in time or farther removed in distance, but are still reasonably foreseeable." 40 C.F.R. § 1508.8(b). To understand indirect effects, think of a proposal to build a new federal office building in a rural area. Indirect impacts of such a project would include construction of access roads to serve the soon-to-arrive workforce, increases in air pollution from additional automobiles, and other urbanization changes.

The Ninth Circuit Court of Appeals has taken the idea of "foreseeable" indirect effects to a new level. In *San Luis Obispo Mothers for Peace v. Nuclear Regulatory Commission*, 449 F.3d 1016 (9th Cir. 2006), *cert. denied, PG&E v. San Luis Obispo Mothers for Peace*, 127 S. Ct. 1124 (2007), the court held that EISs prepared by the NRC must consider the potential environmental impacts of sabotage and terrorism. The idea apparently is that issuance of permits and licenses authorizing construction and operation of nuclear facilities leads to the presence of such facilities, which in turn increases the risk of a terrorist attack because, *inter alia*, such facilities are ideal targets for terrorists. Furthermore, the court commented, omitting examination of this potential impact was inconsistent with post-9/11 governmental policies and efforts to deter terrorism. (Query the legal *gravitas* of this objection.) The court was unpersuaded by the fact that the probability of such attacks is unquantifiable and highly speculative: "The numeric probability of a specific attack is not required in order to assess likely modes of attack, weapons, and vulnerabilities of a facility, and the possible impact of each of these on the physical environment, including the assessment of various release scenarios." *Id.* at 1031. For a contrary view, see *New Jersey Department of Environmental Protection v. Nuclear Regulatory Commission*, 561 F.3d 132 (3d Cir. 2009), In *New Jersey*, the Third Circuit Court of Appeals concluded that an EIS need not consider the potential impacts of a terrorist attack because of the lack of any reasonably close causal relationship between the presence of a nuclear facility and the environmental effects of a hypothetical aircraft attack. The court was influenced by the fact that any such attack would require the occurrence of two events external to the NRC, the independent act of a criminal and the failure of other government agencies to protect the public. The Third Circuit's analysis would seem to reject the "but for" approach to causation embodied in *Mothers for Peace.*

Finally, in addition to considering direct and indirect effects, EISs must study cumulative effects. Cumulative effects are impacts on the environment "which result[s] from the incremental impact of the action when added to other past, present, and reasonably foreseeable future actions regardless of what agency (Federal or nonFederal) or person undertakes such other actions. Cumulative impacts can result from individually minor but collectively significant actions taking place over a period of time." 40 C.F.R. § 1508.7. In other words, EISs must take into account the location at which a proposed action would take place. In addition, they must also examine *other* projects slated for construction in the same area. *See, e.g., Kleppe v. Sierra Club*, 427 U.S. 390, 410, 96 S. Ct. 2718 (1976) (stating that "when several proposals for actions that will have cumulative or synergistic environmental impact upon a region are pending concurrently before an agency, their environmental consequences must be considered together"). *See also Earth Island Institute v. U.S. Forest Service*, 351 F.3d 1291, 1304 (9th Cir. 2003) ("[a] single NEPA review document is required for distinct projects when there is a single proposal governing the projects or when the projects are connected, cumulative, or similar actions under the regulations implementing NEPA." (quoting *Native Ecosystems Council v. Dombeck*, 304 F.3d 886, 893–94 (9th Cir. 2002)).

However, courts have been unwilling to take this principle too far. Said the D.C. Circuit: "an EIS need not delve into the possible effects of a hypothetical project, but need only focus on the impact of the particular proposal at issue and other pending or recently approved proposals that might be connected to or act cumulatively with the proposal at issue." *National Wildlife Federation v. Federal Energy Regulatory Comm'n*, 912 F.2d 1471, 1478 (D.C. Cir. 1990). And the Fourth Circuit has added: "[g]enerally, an administrative agency need consider the impact of other proposed projects when developing an EIS for a pending project only if the projects are so interdependent that it would be unwise or irrational to complete one without the others." *Webb v. Gorsuch*, 699 F.2d 157, 161 (4th Cir. 1983).

Ever in the vanguard, the Ninth Circuit Court of Appeals stirred up some controversy when it ruled that the agency setting corporate average fuel economy ("CAFÉ") standards must analyze the cumulative impacts the standard would cause with respect to climate change:

> The impact of greenhouse gas emissions on climate change is precisely the kind of cumulative impacts analysis that NEPA requires agencies to conduct. Any given rule setting a CAFE standard might have an "individually minor" effect on the environment, but these rules are "collectively significant actions taking place over a period of time." 40 C.F.R. § 1508.7; . . . Thus, NHTSA must provide the necessary contextual information

about the cumulative and incremental environmental impacts of the Final
Rule in light of other CAFE rulemakings and other past, present, and
reasonably foreseeable future actions, regardless of what agency or person
undertakes such other actions.

Center for Biological Diversity v. National Highway Traffic Safety Administration, 538 F.3d 1172, 1215–16 (9th Cir. 2008).

Tough duty, to be sure. Query whether the NHTSA has the institutional capacity
to competently undertake an examination of this scope and complexity.

The third requirement of § 102(2)(C) of NEPA stipulates that EISs must
examine *alternatives* to proposed courses of action. How broad is this requirement?
The statute does not require consideration of alternatives "whose effect cannot be
reasonably ascertained, and whose implementation is deemed remote and speculative." *Life of the Land v. Brinegar*, 485 F.2d 460, 472 (9th Cir. 1973), *cert. denied*, 416
U.S. 961, 94 S. Ct. 1979 (1974). Nor need an agency consider alternatives which are
infeasible or ineffective. *California v. Block*, 690 F.2d 753 (9th Cir. 1982); *see also*
Kilroy v. Ruckelshaus, 738 F.2d 1448, 1454 (9th Cir. 1984) (agency need not examine
alternatives that are "remote from reality"). Last, agencies do not have to
undertake separate analyses of alternatives which are not significantly distinguishable from other alternatives already considered, or which have substantially similar
consequences. *Northern Plains Resource Council v. Lujan*, 874 F.2d 661 (9th Cir.
1989). Thus, an agency's consideration of alternatives "is sufficient if it considers an
appropriate range of alternatives, even if it does not consider every available
alternative." *Headwaters, Inc. v. Bureau of Land Management*, 914 F.2d 1174, 1181
(9th Cir. 1990). "[C]ommon sense . . . teaches us that . . . [an EIS] . . . cannot be
found wanting simply because the agency failed to include every alternative device
and thought conceivable by the mind of man." *Vermont Yankee Nuclear Power Corp.
v. Natural Resources Defense Council*, 435 U.S. 519, 551, 98 S. Ct. 1197, 1215
(1978).[6]

Note, however, that NEPA's requirement for examination of alternatives requires agencies to consider how things might be if the agency abandoned its

---

[6] The consideration of alternatives is so important that it must be done even when an agency is not
preparing an EIS. Section 102(2)(E) of NEPA, 42 U.S.C. § 4332(2)(E), requires agencies to "study,
develop, and describe appropriate alternatives to recommended courses of action in any proposal which
involves unresolved conflicts concerning alternative uses of available resources." *See, e.g., Bob Marshall
Alliance v. Hodel*, 852 F.2d 1223, 1228–29 (1988):

> [C]onsideration of alternatives is critical to the goals of NEPA even where a proposed action
> does not trigger the EIS process. This is reflected in the structure of the statute: while an EIS
> must also include alternatives to the proposed action, 42 U.S.C. § 4332(2)(C)(iii) (1982), the
> consideration of alternatives requirement is contained in a separate subsection of the statute
> and therefore constitutes an independent requirement. *See id.* § 4332(2)(E). The language and
> effect of the two subsections also indicate that the consideration of alternatives requirement
> is of wider scope than the EIS requirement. The former applies whenever an action involves
> conflicts, while the latter does not come into play unless the action will have significant
> environmental effects. An EIS is required where there has been an irretrievable commitment
> of resources; but unresolved conflicts as to the proper use of available resources may exist well
> before that point. Thus the consideration of alternatives requirement is both independent of,
> and broader than, the EIS requirement. . . . [citations omitted] In short, any proposed
> federal action involving unresolved conflicts as to the proper use of resources triggers NEPA's
> consideration of alternatives requirement, whether or not an EIS is also required.

proposed action entirely. EISs, in other words, must address the "no-action" alternative.

(C) When?:

The statute clearly states when an impact statement is required[.] Under the first sentence of § 102(2)(C) the moment at which an agency must have a final statement ready 'is the time at which it makes a recommendation or report on a proposal for federal action. The procedural duty imposed upon agencies by this section is quite precise, and the role of the courts in enforcing that duty is similarly precise. A court has no authority to depart from the statutory language and, by a balancing of court-devised factors, determine a point during the germination process of a potential proposal at which an impact statement should be prepared. . . . The contemplation of a project and the accompanying study thereof do not necessarily result in a proposal for major federal action.

Kleppe v. Sierra Club, 427 U.S. 390, 405–06, 96 S. Ct. 2718, 2728 (1976).

The EIS must be incorporated into the agency's decisional processes "at the earliest possible time." *Thomas v. Peterson*, 753 F.2d 754, 760 (9th Cir. 1985).

(D) How?: The governing standard regarding contents of an EIS is reasonableness. Courts have stated that evaluations in an EIS should be of a quality sufficient to enable decision makers to fairly weigh environmental considerations, and to enable the public to meaningfully comprehend those same considerations. *See, e.g., Town of Huntington v. Marsh*, 859 F.2d 1134 (2d Cir. 1988). EISs, moreover, must be well organized and clearly written. *Oregon Environmental Council v. Kunzman*, 817 F.2d 484 (9th Cir. 1987).

NOTES

1. *NEPA and the Supreme Court.* There have been fourteen NEPA cases decided on the merits by the United States Supreme Court. In each of these cases, the Court reversed a court of appeals judgment that favored environmental plaintiffs. In reverse chronological order, the cases are:

Norton v. Southwest Utah Wilderness Alliance, 542 U.S. 55, 124 S. Ct. 2373 (2004) (supplementation of an EIS is necessary only if there remains some "major federal action" yet to occur);

Department of Transportation v. Public Citizen, 541 U.S. 752, 124 S. Ct. 2204 (2004) (an EA need not consider environmental effects which the agency is powerless to prevent. *(Cf. Mothers for Peace, supra)*;

Robertson v. Methow Valley Citizens Council, 490 U.S. 332, 109 S. Ct. 1835 (1989) (NEPA does not impose a substantive duty on agencies to mitigate adverse environmental effects or a duty to include a fully developed mitigation plan in an EIS; NEPA does not require "worst case" analysis);

Marsh v. Oregon Natural Resources Council, 490 U.S. 360, 109 S. Ct. 1851 (1989) (agency decision not to prepare supplemental EIS is reviewed under "arbitrary and capricious" standard of APA; courts must defer to informed discretion of agency on issues requiring high degree of technical expertise, but should independently review the record to assure that agency took the required "hard look");

Baltimore Gas & Electric Co. v. Natural Resources Defense Council, 462 U.S. 87, 103 S. Ct. 2246 (1983) (while an agency must allow all significant environmental risks to be factored into a decision whether to undertake a proposed action, it may determine in a generic proceeding that a particular risk is insufficient to affect any individual decision, so long as that determination is not arbitrary and capricious);

Metropolitan Edison Co. v. People Against Nuclear Energy, 460 U.S. 766, 103 S. Ct. 1556 (1983) (contentions of psychological health damage caused by risk of accident at nuclear reactor are not cognizable under NEPA — for an effect to be cognizable there must be a reasonably close causal relationship between the effect and a change in the physical environment);

Weinberger v. Catholic Action of Hawaii, 454 U.S. 139, 102 S. Ct. 197 (1981) (since information relating to the storage of nuclear weapons is exempt from disclosure under the Freedom of Information Act, courts cannot require an EIS on the possible storage of nuclear weapons at a facility; Ninth Circuit's requirement of a "hypothetical EIS" in this situation is unsupported by the language of the statute);

Strycker's Bay Neighborhood Council v. Karlen, 444 U.S. 223, 100 S. Ct. 497 (1980) (per curiam) ("once an agency has made a decision subject to NEPA's procedural requirements, the only role for a court is to insure that the agency has considered the environmental consequences; it cannot interject itself within the area of discretion of the executive as to the choice of the action to be taken");

Andrus v. Sierra Club, 442 U.S. 347, 99 S. Ct. 2335 (1979) (no EIS required for agencies' appropriation requests, since they are not proposals for legislation or proposals for major federal actions; CEQ regulations are entitled to substantial deference);

Vermont Yankee Nuclear Power Corp. v. Natural Resources Defense Council, 435 U.S. 519, 98 S. Ct. 1197 (1978) (where agency addresses environmental issue in a rulemaking, NEPA cannot be used by reviewing court to impose procedures beyond those specified in the APA);

Consumers Power Co. v. Aeschliman, 435 U.S. 519, 98 S. Ct. 1197 (1978) (decided in conjunction with *Vermont Yankee*) (challengers must meaningfully alert the agency of their contentions; agency may require a threshold showing of materiality before having to respond to comments; duty to consider alternatives "must be bounded by some notion of feasibility");

Kleppe v. Sierra Club, 427 U.S. 390, 96 S. Ct. 2718 (1976) (agency need not prepare an EIS on activities in entire region unless there has been an actual "proposal" for a regional plan of development; a comprehensive EIS may be required when several proposals for action will have cumulative or synergistic environmental impacts, but agency decision not to prepare such an EIS will be upheld unless arbitrary and capricious);

Flint Ridge Development Co. v. Scenic Rivers Ass'n, 426 U.S. 776, 96 S. Ct. 2430 (1976) (duty to prepare an EIS must yield before "a clear and unavoidable conflict in statutory authority");

Aberdeen & Rockfish R.R. v. SCRAP, 422 U.S. 289, 95 S. Ct. 2336 (1975) (EIS not required until the agency makes a recommendation or report on a proposal for action).

See David C. Shelton, *Is the Supreme Court Hostile to NEPA? Some Possible Explanations for a 120 Record*, prepared for presentation at the conference on *NEPA at Twenty: The Past, Present, and Future of the National Environmental Policy Act*, Portland, Oregon, Oct. 27, 1989.

2.   *SEPAs.* At least sixteen states and the District of Columbia and Puerto Rico have enacted their own NEPA-like statutes. These statutes, commonly referred to as "SEPAs," vary. Some, unlike NEPA, directly govern the substance of agency decision making. Most SEPAs, like NEPA, require consideration of environmental impacts if proposed state actions may produce significant environmental effects, although the threshold considerations triggering the state law-based EIS process may differ from those of the federal legislation. SEPAs typically apply to all categories of state actions, including government-undertaken projects, permitting, and subsidies.

"Where State laws or local ordinances have environmental impact statement requirements in addition to but not in conflict with those in NEPA, federal agencies shall cooperate in fulfilling these requirements as well as those of federal laws so that one document will comply with all applicable laws." 40 C.F.R. § 1506.2(c).

A NOTE ON NEPA § 102(1)

Section 102(1) of NEPA requires that "the policies, regulations and public laws of the United States shall be interpreted in accordance with the policies set forth in this chapter." § 102(1), 42 U.S.C. § 4332(1). This duty is to be accomplished "to the fullest extent possible." § 102. Despite thousands of opportunities, this subsection has rarely been used and has never been determinative of the resolution of a disputed case. The Supreme Court, in fact, has never discussed § 102(1), and lower federal courts only rarely. Virtually all we know from the courts is that the provision does not authorize the disregard of a clear nondiscretionary duty established by organic law. *See, e.g., NRDC, Inc. v. Berklund*, 609 F.2d 553 (D.C. Cir. 1979) (holding NEPA did not authorize the U.S. Department of Interior to reject lease applications on independent NEPA grounds contrary to the governing organic statute, the Mineral Lands Leasing Act). In the Court's words: "the plain meaning of the [MLLA] as well as an undisturbed administrative practice for nearly 60 years leaves the Secretary no discretion to deny a . . . lease . . . to a qualified applicant." *NRDC*, 609 F.2d at 558. *Accord Cape May Greene, Inc. v. Warren*, 698 F.2d 179 (3d Cir. 1982). *Cf. Environmental Defense Fund v. Mathews*, 410 F. Supp. 336, 338 (D.D.C. 1976) ("[W]e find that NEPA [§ 102(1)] provides [the Food and Drug Administration] with supplementary authority to base its substantive decisions on all environmental considerations including those not expressly identified in the [Food, Drug, and Cosmetic Act] and FDA's other statutes.").

Yet there are many instances in which § 102(1) could play a role. One such instance was *Calvert Cliffs*. The D.C. Circuit in that case, the reader will recall, examined the adequacy of the Atomic Energy Commission's interpretation of its regulations under the Atomic Energy Act. The *Calvert Cliffs* court could have held that the agency's diluted view of its statutory obligations, as expressed in its regulations, violated § 102(1) because it promoted NEPA's goals not at all, and certainly not "to the fullest extent possible."

Methow Valley was another opportunity. In that case (and, for that matter, in *Vermont Yankee* and *Strycker's Bay*), the Supreme Court could have used § 102(1) to read life into § 102(2), to justify a holding that a complete and unwarranted disregard of EIS recommendations is reversible error. The *Methow Valley* Court could have called upon § 102(1) as well to assess whether the Forest Service had violated its own regulations. Those regulations required that applications for special use permits include "measures and plans for the protection and rehabilitation of the environment during construction, operation, maintenance, and termination of the project," 36 C.F.R. § 251.54(e)(4) (1988), and that "[e]ach special use authorization . . . contain[s] . . . [t]erms and conditions which will . . . minimize damage to scenic and esthetic values and fish and wildlife habitat and otherwise protect the environment." 36 C.F.R. § 251.56(a)(1)(ii). The Court found "no basis for concluding that the Forest Service's own regulations must . . . be read in all cases to condition issuance of a special use permit on consideration (and implementation) of offsite mitigation measures." *Id.* at 357, 109 S. Ct. at 1849. Could not § 102(1) have served as a basis to find just such a general requirement, or at least to find one in this case? In an informal discussion, your author was told by a highly placed CEQ official that § 102(1) has no legal validity, that any attempt to use it to influence the exercise of agency discretion would be "a long shot." In this official's view, the Supreme Court's declaration that NEPA is procedural stripped § 102(1) of any vitality it might have had. This view, however, overlooks both the clear text of § 102(1) and the fact that the Supreme Court's NEPA decisions examine § 102(2), not § 102(1).

Chapter 5

FEDERAL LANDS

"[The public lands represent] in a sense, the breathing space of the nation." *Richard M. Nixon*, February 8, 1971

SYNOPSIS

A. INTRODUCTION

The public lands of the United States extend from the northern reaches of Alaska to the most distant southeast points of Florida. They encompass frozen tundras, lush agricultural lands, breathtaking vistas, wildlife habitat, urban parks, deltas, forests, mineral lands, and just about every other natural setting you can imagine. They include Mount McKinley, North America's highest point, and Death Valley, its lowest. The public lands span about 740 million acres or about one-third of the nation's approximately 2.3 billion-acre total land area. This acreage is titled in the United States in fee simple absolute. In addition to these properties, the federal government holds less-than-fee interests, such as waterfowl easements and reserved mineral interests, in more than 60 million additional acres. Federal lands can be found in every state, but particularly in the eleven western states and in Alaska. Alaska itself, in fact, contains about one-half of all the public lands. Beyond these holdings, the federal government controls the resources of the outer continental shelf ("OCS"). The OCS is comprised of offshore submerged lands underlying the oceans extending out from the coastal states, measuring from a point three miles off the nation's dryland border seaward to the edge of the high seas, and comprising about 860,000 square miles. (The individual coastal states hold the rights to natural resources in the territorial sea, the submerged lands extending seaward for three miles from the states' respective coastlines. *See infra*.) Finally, the federal government controls fishing rights out to 200 miles.

How the government manages federal lands significantly affects the environmental health of the nation, to say nothing of its economic welfare. In this chapter, we survey federal lands and their management. We begin our inquiry with an historical overview of the assembly of the public lands. An historical understanding is helpful to better appreciate current federal land management policies. After this review, coverage shifts to an examination of the constitutional and statutory authorities available to the Congress and the president to manage public lands. These authorities allow public lands to be dedicated to specific uses, to be distributed to individuals under several allocation schemes, and to be withdrawn as circumstances warrant. Last, the chapter introduces the federal agencies responsible for federal land management and surveys the specific legal regimes governing the extraction of minerals, harvesting of timber, consumption of forage, and the use for recreation of the public lands.

B. HISTORICAL BACKGROUND

1. Acquisition of the Public Lands

The story of federal lands begins with their assembly. Federal land acquisition can be said to have begun in 1781, the year in which the Articles of Confederation were ratified by the original states. The national government created by the Articles was weak, but it at least had enough power to begin the process of acquiring lands to expand the borders of the nation. The process would ultimately lead to the federal government assuming the rank of the nation's chief landowner and landlord.

How the federal government took on this status is a story of politics, graft, and opportunity. At the time the Articles of Confederation were adopted, seven states (Connecticut, Georgia, Massachusetts, New York, North Carolina, South Carolina, and Vermont) held claims to land between the Appalachian Mountains and the Mississippi River.[1] This became a matter of immediate concern to unlanded states. Led by Maryland, unlanded states maintained that territorial possessions ought to be held in common by all so that no states would be subordinate. The unlanded states wanted also to be able to reward their soldiers for Revolutionary War service in the same way that landed states could. To resolve the controversy, the landed states ceded their claims to the federal government during the 1780s. And so it happened that by 1790, the federal government, now reformed by the ratification of the United States Constitution in 1789, was already holding title to approximately 10% of the nation's land.

The next seventy-five years brought additional acquisitions. Foreign nations with claims to land on the North American continent, specifically England, France, Russia, Spain, and Mexico, one by one yielded their lands to the new nation. The single most significant land transfer during these years was the Louisiana Purchase of 1803, which in one fell swoop doubled the size of the United States, at the cost of three cents per acre. But there were many others as well:

- In 1818, by treaty with England, the United States secured the lands south of the 49th parallel from Lake Superior to the Rocky Mountains, lands that determine the modern border with Canada (no cost).

- In 1819, by treaty with Spain, the United States secured what is now Florida (no cost).

- In 1846, the Oregon Compromise with England set the Canadian boundary at a single latitude west to the Pacific Ocean, adding 180 million acres to the federal storehouse (no cost).[2]

- In 1848, the Treaty of Guadaloupe Hidalgo with Spain brought into federal title what is now the nation's southwest, including California, from Mexico (cost: $15 million).

- In 1850, the United States purchased from Texas, itself annexed five years earlier, lands comprising what are now New Mexico, Colorado, and Oklahoma (cost: assumption of $10 million debt).

- In 1853, the Gadsen Purchase brought to the nation the southern strip of what is now New Mexico and Arizona to establish a southern transcontinental railroad service (cost: $10 million).

---

[1] Of the seven, New York based its claims on concessions from the Iroquois Indians, while the others traced their claims back to colonial charters from England.

[2] The national expansion into the Pacific Northwest was the origin of the famous election slogan, "Fifty four forty or fight." As American settlers migrated into the Pacific Northwest, and demands for annexation of the area from England grew, supporters of soon-to-be-elected President James Polk used the slogan in demanding land up to the parallel of 54 degrees and 40 minutes. After Polk's election, the compromise allowed for the United States to have land up to the 49th parallel. MARION CLAWSON, UNCLE SAM'S ACRES 28–29 (1951).

- In 1867, in what was popularly known as "Seward's Folly," named after the government official spearheading the acquisition, the federal government purchased Alaska from Russia (cost: $7.2 million). As a result, the federal government held title to almost 80% of the total land area of the United States by the middle of the 19th century. This 365 million acres would comprise the last addition to the public domain.

2. Phases of Federal Land Policy

Even during the period of acquisition of the public lands, it was settled wisdom that the best ultimate use of those public lands would be to transfer ownership of them to individuals and business entities. It was agreed such transfers would both accelerate human settlement of the expansive west and assure the development of natural resources, all to the betterment of the nation as a whole. Disposing of the lands, even at bargain prices, would provide a much-needed shot of revenue to boot. Not unexpectedly, the government was quite successful in its efforts to transfer its lands into private title: in the roughly two centuries from 1780 to the present, it depleted land holdings by more than one billion acres.

This era in federal land management is aptly known as the disposition phase. It was, in actuality, more a fervor than a phase, and, over time it gave rise to serious concerns that too much land was being lost. Why should the government give away natural resources, especially if it might be faced with the prospect of buying them back later? Under prevailing statutes, moreover, the dispositions were often accomplished by the unilateral actions of the acquiring parties, a process the government could not control. This growing apprehension signaled the beginning of a second phase of federal land policy, known as the withdrawal or retrenchment phase. This second phase was more a reassessment than a repudiation of the first.

In this second phase, the government slowed the pace of disposition and commensurately acted to protect much of the storehouse of federal land from private acquisition. To that end, national parks were created for the recreational use of the public at large. Similarly, natural resources on public "disposition lands" were made subject to leasing mechanisms that the government could control. And some disposition lands, ownership of which was about to be wrested from the government, were simply reclassified.

In the current day, federal policy has matured into a third phase, often referred to as the management or stewardship phase. An amalgam of its predecessors, this phase places the emphasis on land retention. Dispositions are still authorized, but only if doing so inures to the "maximum benefit for the general public." *See* 43 U.S.C. § 1391. Federal lands, moreover, are managed for long-term benefit. In some instances the lands serve a single dominant use; in others they are managed for several (often conflicting) uses.

It is impossible to declare with any certainty the beginning and end dates of these phases. If put to the task, however, one could select 1780, the date of the first land transfers away from the federal government, as the beginning of the disposition phase. The year 1872, at which time Yellowstone National Park was set aside for wilderness and recreational use, can suffice as the beginning of the withdrawal phase. Finally, 1960, the year of enactment of the federal Multiple Use-Sustained Yield Act, might be an appropriate starting point for the stewardship period. Note that the start of one phase did not signal the end of its predecessor. On the contrary, federal land policy has been more a matter of drift than sharp turns. For detailed reading on this saga of United States history, see PAUL W. GATES, HISTORY OF PUBLIC LAND LAW DEVELOPMENT (1967).

a.   Alienation of the Public Lands

There are many mechanisms by which the federal government has transferred lands to the private sector:

(i) Grants to Settlers

A significant land disposal mechanism has been grants to settlers. These grants were preceded and facilitated by a good deal of federal groundwork. In accordance with the Land Ordinance of 1785, the government undertook the daunting task of surveying the vast west. The survey divided the west into square townships. Each township in turn was divided into 36 sections of 640 acres each. Survey in hand, the government was positioned to alienate lands on the grand scale. It proceeded to grant "patents" to land to thousands of persons, to reward military service, to make fertile the "Great American Desert," and for other purposes. The most significant legislative enactment to this end was the Homestead Act of 1862 (Act of May 20, 1862, 12 Stat. 392 (1862)). Under the terms of the Homestead Act, a settler could secure title to a parcel of land, not greater than a quarter-section in size, or 160 acres, if she or he agreed to live on the land and improve it with due diligence. About 287 million acres of federal land, mostly fertile lands in what is now the midwestern "breadbasket" of the nation, transferred into private hands under the terms of this legislation. In the more arid western states, where larger acreages were needed to entice settlers, the Desert Lands Act of 1877, 43 U.S.C. §§ 321, 339, worked to the same end. The Desert Lands Act applied to the eleven western states, awarding settlers 640-acre parcels.

(ii) Grants to Railroads

With the vast reaches of the west and midwest becoming evermore populated, the government concluded there was a need for a continental rail transportation system. Accordingly, it made lands available for this purpose as well. Land grants to railroads were made between 1862 and 1871. The first such grant was made by President Abraham Lincoln in a measure that also established the grantee, the Union Pacific Railroad. Act of July 1, 1862, 12 Stat. 489. Railroad companies typically received not only rights of way, but also alternating sections of land on either side of each right of way. (In 1975, the Railroad Right of Way Act, 43 U.S.C. § 934 et seq. (1975), expanded these existing rights of way laterally to 100 feet on either side of the central rail line, and extended rights to "take from the public lands adjacent to the line of said road, material, earth, stone, and timber necessary for the construction of said railroad." *Id.* at 934). By these grant mechanisms, railroads secured title to over 130 million acres of public land. *See, e.g.,* Thomas E. Root, *Railroad Land Grants from Canals to Transcontinentals,* ABA 17-36 & Appendix C (1987). Interestingly, the amount of railroad trackage on federal land has decreased in this century. In 1920, railroads had 272,000 miles of track on federal land; by 1990, the trackage was reduced to 141,000 miles. Lawrence S. Lim, *Walking the Line: Rails-to-Trails Conversions and Preseault v. Interstate Commerce Comm'n*, 53 OHIO ST. L.J. 337 (1992).

(iii) Grants to States

(A) *Charter Grants*: Lands were made available to states as well. Following the model state charter by which Ohio entered the Union in 1803, the government granted to incoming states, themselves carved out of federal lands, at least one section, specifically Section 16, in each township for educational purposes (after 1848, this allocation would double, and would double again with the admissions of Arizona, Utah, and New Mexico). These grants facilitated the establishment of land grant universities and primary and secondary schools. Grants to states for these purposes transferred almost 80 million acres out of federal title, or an expanse roughly equivalent in size to New England, plus New York and New Jersey.

(B) *Offshore Submerged Lands:* The story of federal disposition of lands to states did not end with charter grants. There remained the matter of offshore submerged lands. By international law, the United States government holds title to submerged lands reaching out under the Atlantic and Pacific Oceans and the Gulf of Mexico to at least a distance of three miles.[3]

In the United States, however, the federal government no longer holds title to these often resource-rich submerged lands. It transferred these title interests to the coastal states via the Submerged Lands Act of 1953, 43 U.S.C. § 1301 et seq. This means that coastal states own the submerged lands for a seaward distance of three miles from their shores. From the three-mile demarcation line seaward out to the edge of the continental shelf, the lands remain titled in the federal government. (No nation owns land beneath the high seas.)

(C) *Equal Footing Doctrine*: Federal lands also have come into state title by means of the equal footing doctrine. Strongly associated with the sovereign status of states, this doctrine transfers title as a matter of constitutional law rather than by express federal legislative choice. *See, e.g., Montana v. United States*, 450 U.S. 544, 552 (1981). The doctrine traces back to 1842 when, in accordance with the common law of England, the United States Supreme Court declared that the original thirteen states held title to submerged lands underlying navigable streams. *Martin v. Waddell*, 41 U.S. (16 Pet.) 367 (1842). Streams were deemed navigable if they were navigable in fact, susceptible to navigation if modified, or affected by the ebb and flow of tides (in some instances, different segments of the same stream could be navigable and nonnavigable). *See generally* Johnson & Austin, *Recreational Rights and Titles to Beds on Western Lakes and Streams*, 7 NAT. RESOURCES J. 1, 7 (1967). When additional states were carved out of federal lands, the argument arose that they, like the original thirteen, should have title to submerged lands underlying navigable waters. The Supreme Court agreed. *Pollard's Lessee v. Hagan*, 44 U.S. (3 How.) 212 (1845). In the Court's view, because the Federal

---

[3] The United States has declared its territorial sea to extend to twelve miles. *See* Proclamation No. 5928 of Dec. 27, 1988, 54 Fed. Reg. 777.

Constitution was premised on the notion that all states should be on an equal footing, title to submerged lands underlying navigable waterways transferred automatically to each new state upon its admission to the Union. *Id.* at 230. If two states happen to share a navigable waterway as a common border, whether the waterway be a minor navigable stream or a Great Lake, each is deemed to hold title to the middle thread, or thalweg, of that waterway.

The equal footing doctrine creates a strong presumption in favor of the state when claims are made to lands titled in the federal government at the time of that state's admission into the Union. "A court deciding a question of title to the bed of navigable water must . . . begin with a strong presumption against defeat of a State's title." *United States v. Alaska*, 521 U.S. 1, 34, 117 S. Ct. 1888, 1906 (1997). But the presumption is not irrebuttable. In a 2001 decision, the United States Supreme Court ruled, 5-4, that certain submerged lands underlying Lake Coeur d'Alene in Idaho remained in federal title, to be devoted to the use and benefit of the Coeur d'Alene Indian Tribe, and did not transfer to the State of Idaho at its admission into the Union, because Congress intended to reserve the title. *Idaho v. United States*, 533 U.S. 262, 121 S. Ct. 2135 (2001). Expressions of congressional intent to defeat a state's title should be "definitely declared or otherwise made very plain." *Montana, supra*, 450 U.S. at 552.

Notably, the equal footing doctrine has been limited in its scope: it has not prevailed to secure to the states title to the whole of the federal public domain. *See, e.g., United States v. Clifford Gardner*, 107 F.3d 1314 (9th Cir. 1997).

One recent case has propelled the equal footing doctrine into a renewed high relief. *PPL Montana v. State of Montana*, 355 Mont. 402, 229 P.3d 421 (2010), involved three rivers in Montana the beds of which are titled in the State because the streams were "navigable" in 1889, the year Montana joined the Union. The State decided it deserved compensation from PPL, a wholesale electricity generator, for the latter's use of the riverbeds as sites for its hydropower dams from 2000 through 2007. The Montana Supreme Court agreed, to the tune of damages in the amount of nearly $40 million! (To determine the damages amount, the lower court used a "profitability" approach: it determined net profits secured by PPL during the period and allocated 50% of that amount to the State. The Montana Supreme Court found no error in the use of this methodology.) Thereafter, the U.S. Supreme Court granted certiorari, but only in part. 131 S. Ct. 3019 (2011). Later in the year, the Court reversed on the ground that Montana had improperly determined that the affected portions of the riverbed were navigable. *PPL Montana LLC v. Montana*, 132 S. Ct. 1215 (2011).

(iv) Land Sales

Another mechanism of disposition is land sales. Unlike the mechanisms previously discussed, this one retains viability. Land sales, at least for lands under the control of the Bureau of Land Management ("BLM") of the U.S. Department of Interior, are governed by § 203 of the Federal Land Policy and Management Act ("FLPMA"), 43 U.S.C. § 1713. Under that section, the government must receive at least fair market value for any parcel it sells. Section 203(d), 43 U.S.C. § 1713(d). FLPMA also calls for use of competitive bidding procedures to secure the best price. Section 203(f), 43 U.S.C. § 1713(f). Sales may go forward only for tracts that are "difficult and uneconomic to manage" as part of the public lands; are not "suitable" for management by any other federal agency; no longer serve the purposes for which the lands were acquired; or if the disposal will "serve important public objectives." Section 203(a), 43 U.S.C. § 1713(a). As a general matter, conveyances of land by the federal government, excepting land exchanges, *infra*, may not include transfers of mineral rights. Section 209, 43 U.S.C. § 1719. Monies paid by purchasers go to the federal treasury. Sales of parcels greater than 2,500 acres in size require congressional approval. Section 203(c), 43 U.S.C. § 1713(c).

(v) Land Exchanges

The federal government also can alienate title to public lands through land exchanges. The land exchange mechanism has been useful to satisfy outstanding charter-based claims of states to lands, to minimize patchwork patterns of land ownership, and to facilitate management of federal lands. It also helps to stop persons from using private land "inholdings" in ways deleterious to nearby or surrounding federal land. Entirely discretionary with the government, exchanges are governed by § 206 of the Federal Land Policy and Management Act, which provides that "[a] tract of public land or interests therein may be disposed of by exchange by the Secretary under this Act . . . where the Secretary . . . determines that the public interest will be well served by making that exchange." Section 206, 43 U.S.C. § 1716. Regulations implementing this provision may be found at 43 C.F.R. Part 2200 (Bureau of Land Management) and 36 C.F.R. Part 254, Subpart A (Forest Service).

While the era of land grants is largely over, land exchanges still take place frequently. (A great many exchanges have taken place in Utah, for example, as a result of the Grand Staircase-Escalante national monument designation.) Exchanges can take years to complete. The government is most interested in a land exchange if the privately owned parcel is valuable for wildlife or recreation, or is contiguous to federal land, or if the acquisition would facilitate access to federal lands. Since exchanges are only permissible for parcels of approximately equal value, properties under consideration must be appraised for market value. Appraising value can be difficult, especially for lands that are diverse and undeveloped. Supervised by federal land agencies such as the Bureau of Land Management or the Forest Service, land exchanges often require accompanying environmental impact statements, prepared under the auspices of the National Environmental Policy Act (*see* Chapter 4, *supra*). *See, e.g., Muckleshoot Indian Tribe v. U.S. Forest Service*, 177 F.3d 800 (9th Cir. 1999). Interstate exchanges are impermissible, and in the case of the Forest Service, interforest exchanges are impermissible as well. For more complete information on land exchanges, including an explanation of the principles governing the process and a step-by-step flowchart on how the process works, see www.blm.gov/nhp/what/lands/realty.

The final result of all of this is that federal holdings have shrunk from over 1.8 billion acres to nearly 740 million acres today. Of these federal holdings, 92.7% are in the West (in fact, almost 54% of all the land in the West is federal land), 4% in the Midwest, 3% in the south, and a scant 0.03% in the East. About 56.6 million acres are tribal or Native-"owned" lands. To see the federal lands configuration in any particular state, visit the map site of the United States Geological Service at www.nationalatlas.gov. For percentages of federal land within specific states, see the following figure entitled "Federal Land as a Percentage of Total State Land Area."

Federal Land as a Percentage of Total State Land Area

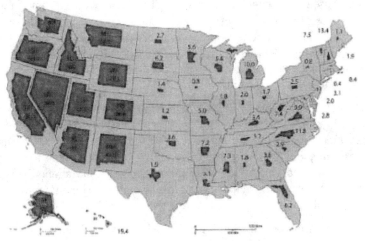

Data source: U.S. General Services Administration, *Federal Real Property Profile 2004*, excludes trust properties.

b.   Retention and Management

As noted earlier, the federal government no longer freely alienates title to public lands. Instead, it now keeps lands in federal title, preferring to manage them for maximum public long-term benefit. What this means in many cases is that lands are managed to serve a multitude of uses. The term "uses" is defined broadly, to include not just commercially valuable pursuits, but also recreation, conservation, and even preservation. The following article encapsulates the thinking behind this retention and management policy. (We will survey the particulars of federal land management in the current day in Part D of this Chapter, *infra*.)

MARION CLAWSON, UNCLE SAM'S ACRES[4]
(1951 (reprint 1970))[5]

WHY FEDERAL LAND OWNERSHIP?

What are the reasons why federal ownership of some classes of land is believed by some to be more satisfactory than private ownership? Very little farm land is federally owned. Federal lands are generally forested or covered with grasses and shrubs usable only for grazing. Federal ownership of such land owes much of its

---

[4] Mr. Clawson was Director of the Bureau of Land Management, United States Department of Interior, at the time of publication of the article.

[5] Every effort has been made to find the holder of the original copyright, if any, to this article. Should anyone have information, please contact the author of this casebook.

existence and strength to the following arguments:

1. Land management for multiple uses or benefits is more likely and is more satisfactory under federal than under private ownership. Much of the remaining federal land can be and is used at the same time for several purposes — timber production, recreation, grazing, mineral production, watersheds, and others. Within some limits, these uses do not compete seriously. But a private owner is more likely to be interested in but one of these uses or values, rather than in several or in all of them. Thus, if he is a lumberman, he is likely not to want to be bothered with grazing and almost surely won't want to give special consideration to recreation. A federal land administering agency is more likely to be able to balance one potential use against another, and to secure a substantial amount of each.

2. The development of land uses which produce nonmonetary benefits or satisfactions is particularly likely to be stressed and be more successful under public than under private land ownership. As our standard of living rises, as we have more leisure time, and as we become more mobile, our use of land for recreational, wildlife, and other non-monetary uses increases. A public agency can afford to encourage such uses, and perhaps make some investments for them, when a private landowner cannot.

3. The conservation of some land, particularly forest and watershed land, has in general been more successful under federal than under private ownership. We have not yet proven on a large scale that private land ownership can produce trees; it can cut them, but its record in growing them is still meager. The values created by good watershed management do not accrue to the landowner, in most cases, but to someone else further down the stream. While conceivably the landowner might sell watershed management to a down-stream landowner, in practice we have handled the problem by keeping and even putting much watershed land into public ownership.

4. Experience has shown that private ownership of some types of land is unsatisfactory, either because of damage to the land itself or because it is impossible to support an economic enterprise on it. While much of this land might be capable of private ownership under different uses, in practice it may be easier to deal with the problem by having the land in public ownership. . . .

. . . .

A mere recitation of the areas and uses of the federally owned lands minimize their importance to the communities in which they lie. The federally owned lands are not an empire separate and apart from the economy and life of the community; rather, they are an integral part of it.

Federally owned land has special significance for another reason. For nearly 100 years, the Federal Government and its leaders have sought to obtain better and more enduring use of land and its resources in this country. This effort, feeble at first, has become intensified in recent decades. With approximately one-fourth of the total area of the United States in its ownership and under its direct control, the Federal Government is in a position where its example as a landowner is probably far more important than its preaching. If it really seeks wise and enduring land use as a national policy, then let the Government practice it on its own lands.

C. POWER OVER FEDERAL LAND

1. Constitutional Authority

The federal government enjoys a paramount authority over federal lands by virtue of the Federal Constitution. While there are several identifiable constitutional powers available to the federal government for public land management purposes, including the Commerce Clause and the General Welfare Clause, the most important constitutional provisions for these purposes are the following:

Article I, § 8, cl. 17 (the "Jurisdiction Clause"): Congress shall have power to exercise exclusive Legislation in all Cases whatsoever over such District (not exceeding ten Miles square) as may, by Cession of particular States, and the Acceptance of Congress, become the Seat of the Government of the United States, and to exercise like Authority over all Places purchased by the Consent of the Legislature of the State in which the Same shall be, for the Erection of Forts, Magazines, Arsenals, dock-Yards, and other needful Buildings.

Article IV, § 3, cl. 2 (the " Property Clause"): The Congress shall have Power to dispose of and make all needful Rules and Regulations respecting the Territory or other Property belonging to the United States.

Lands subject to the Jurisdiction Clause (so-called because the phrase "exclusive Legislation" has been interpreted to mean "exclusive jurisdiction") are those which have been acquired (often reacquired) from private owners or from states. These lands are called "federal enclaves," and include federal lands within the District of Columbia, some military bases, post offices, and the like. Even some national parks fall within this category.

The governing legal structure for an enclave can take one of three forms:

— *exclusive:* the federal government possesses all authority of the state, except that the state can serve process in the area for activities that occur outside the area;

— *concurrent:* the federal government has powers, but the states have those same powers and can exercise them concurrently;

— *partial:* the federal government has powers normally possessed by the state, but the state has some other powers beyond rights to serve process.

Far more important than the Jurisdiction Clause, however, is the Property Clause. The Property Clause applies to all non-enclave federal lands, i.e., the public domain lands, which make up the overwhelming percentage of federal land holdings. It is the Property Clause, therefore, that applies to all federal lands secured by the federal government before states were carved out of those lands.

Federal power supplied by the Property Clause was described by the Public Land Law Review Commission as "proprietorial," expressing a sense of a limited managerial authority in the United States over these lands, with a significant residuum of authority vested in the respective states. This description is much too modest in the present day.

KLEPPE v. NEW MEXICO
426 U.S. 529, 96 S. Ct. 2285 (1976)

MR. JUSTICE MARSHALL delivered the opinion of the Court.

At issue in this case is whether Congress exceeded its powers under the Constitution in enacting the Wild Free-roaming Horses and Burros Act.

I

The Wild Free-roaming Horses and Burros Act, 85 Stat. 649, 16 U.S.C. §§ 1331-1340 (1970 ed., Supp. IV), was enacted in 1971 to protect "all unbranded and unclaimed horses and burros on public lands of the United States," § 2 (b) of the Act, 16 U.S.C. § 1332(b) (1970 ed., Supp. IV), from "capture, branding, harassment, or death." § 1, 16 U.S.C. § 1331 (1970 ed., Supp. IV). The Act provides that all such horses and burros on the public lands administered by the Secretary of the Interior through the Bureau of Land Management (BLM) or by the Secretary of Agriculture through the Forest Service are committed to the jurisdiction of the respective Secretaries, who are "directed to protect and manage [the animals] as components of the public lands . . . in a manner that is designed to achieve and maintain a thriving natural ecological balance on the public lands." § 3(a), 16 U.S.C. § 1333(a) (1970 ed., Supp. IV). If protected horses or burros "stray from public lands onto privately owned land, the owners of such land may inform the nearest federal marshal or agent of the Secretary, who shall arrange to have the animals removed." § 4, 16 U.S.C. § 1334 (1970 ed., Supp. IV).

Section 6, 16 U.S.C. § 1336 (1970 ed., Supp. IV), authorizes the Secretaries to promulgate regulations, *see* 36 C.F.R. § 231.11 (1975) (Agriculture); 43 C.F.R. pt. 4710 (1975) (Interior), and to enter into cooperative agreements with other landowners and with state and local governmental agencies in furtherance of the Act's purposes. On August 7, 1973, the Secretaries executed such an agreement with the New Mexico Livestock Board, the agency charged with enforcing the New Mexico Estray Law, N.M. Stat. Ann. § 47-14-1 et seq. (1966). The agreement acknowledged the authority of the Secretaries to manage and protect the wild free-roaming horses and burros on the public lands of the United States within the State and established a procedure for evaluating the claims of private parties to ownership of such animals.

The Livestock Board terminated the agreement three months later. Asserting that the Federal Government lacked power to control wild horses and burros on the public lands of the United States unless the animals were moving in interstate commerce or damaging the public lands and that neither of these bases of regulation was available here, the Board notified the Secretaries of its intent

to exercise all regulatory, impoundment and sale powers which it derives from the New Mexico Estray Law, over all estray horses, mules or asses found running at large upon public or private lands within New Mexico. . . . This includes the right to go upon Federal or State lands to take possession of said horses or burros, should the Livestock Board so desire. App. 67, 72.

The differences between the Livestock Board and the Secretaries came to a head in February 1974. On February 1, 1974, a New Mexico rancher, Kelley Stephenson, was informed by the BLM that several unbranded burros had been seen near Taylor Well, where Stephenson watered his cattle. Taylor Well is on federal property, and Stephenson had access to it and some 8,000 surrounding acres only through a grazing permit issued pursuant to § 3 of the Taylor Grazing Act, 48 Stat. 1270, as amended, 43 U.S.C. § 315b. After the BLM made it clear to Stephenson that it would not remove the burros and after he personally inspected the Taylor Well area, Stephenson complained to the Livestock Board that the burros were interfering with his livestock operation by molesting his cattle and eating their feed.

Thereupon the Board rounded up and removed 19 unbranded and unclaimed burros pursuant to the New Mexico Estray Law. Each burro was seized on the public lands of the United States and, as the director of the Board conceded, each burro fit the definition of a wild free-roaming burro under § 2(b) of the Act. App. 43. On February 18, 1974, the Livestock Board, pursuant to its usual practice, sold the burros at a public auction. After the sale, the BLM asserted jurisdiction under the Act and demanded that the Board recover the animals and return them to the public lands.

On March 4, 1974, appellees filed a complaint in the United States District Court for the District of New Mexico seeking a declaratory judgment that the Wild Free-roaming Horses and Burros Act is unconstitutional and an injunction against its enforcement. A three-judge court was convened pursuant to 28 U.S.C. § 2282.

Following an evidentiary hearing, the District Court held the Act unconstitutional and permanently enjoined the Secretary of the Interior (Secretary) from enforcing its provisions. The court found that the Act "conflicts with . . . the traditional doctrines concerning wild animals," *New Mexico v. Morton*, 406 F. Supp. 1237, 1238 (1975), and is in excess of Congress' power under the Property Clause of the Constitution, Art. IV, § 3, cl. 2. That Clause, the court found, enables Congress to regulate wild animals found on the public land only for the "protection of the public lands from damage of some kind." 406 F. Supp., at 1239 (emphasis in original). Accordingly, this power was exceeded in this case because "[t]he statute is aimed at protecting the wild horses and burros, not at protecting the land they live on." *Ibid.* We noted probable jurisdiction, 423 U.S. 818 (1975), and we now reverse.

II

The Property Clause of the Constitution provides that "Congress shall have Power to dispose of and make all needful Rules and Regulations respecting the Territory or other Property belonging to the United States." U.S. Const., Art. IV, § 3, cl. 2. In passing the Wild Free-roaming Horses and Burros Act, Congress deemed the regulated animals "an integral part of the natural system of the public lands" of the United States, § 1, 16 U.S.C. § 1331 (1970 ed., Supp. IV), and found that their management was necessary "for achievement of an ecological balance on the public lands." H.R. Conf. Rep. No. 92-681, p. 5 (1971). According to Congress, these animals, if preserved in their native habitats, "contribute to the diversity of life forms within the Nation and enrich the lives of the American people." § 1, 16 U.S.C. § 1331 (1970 ed., Supp. IV). *See* Hearing on Protection of Wild Horses and Burros on Public Lands before the Subcommittee on Public Lands of the Senate Committee on Interior and Insular Affairs, 92d Cong., 1st Sess., 69, 122, 128, 138, 169, 183 (1971). Indeed, Congress concluded, the wild free-roaming horses and burros "are living symbols of the historic and pioneer spirit of the West." § 1, 16 U.S.C. § 1331 (1970 ed., Supp. IV). Despite their importance, the Senate committee found:

> [These animals] have been cruelly captured and slain and their carcasses used in the production of pet food and fertilizer. They have been used for target practice and harassed for 'sport' and profit. In spite of public outrage, this bloody traffic continues unabated, and it is the firm belief of the committee that this senseless slaughter must be brought to an end. S. Rep. No. 92-242, pp. 1 2 (1971).

For these reasons, Congress determined to preserve and protect the wild free-roaming horses and burros on the public lands of the United States. The question under the Property Clause is whether this determination can be sustained as a "needful" regulation "respecting" the public lands. In answering this question, we must remain mindful that, while courts must eventually pass upon them, determinations under the Property Clause are entrusted primarily to the judgment of Congress. *United States v. San Francisco*, 310 U.S. 16, 29 30 (1940); *Light v. United States*, 220 U.S. 523, 537 (1911); *United States v. Gratiot*, 14 Pet. 526, 537 538 (1840).

Appellees argue that the Act cannot be supported by the Property Clause. They contend that the Clause grants Congress essentially two kinds of power: (1) the power to dispose of and make incidental rules regarding the use of federal property; and (2) the power to protect federal property. According to appellees, the first power is not broad enough to support legislation protecting wild animals that live on federal property; and the second power is not implicated since the Act is designed to protect the animals, which are not themselves federal property, and not the public lands. As an initial matter, it is far from clear that the Act was not passed in part to protect the public lands of the United States or that Congress cannot assert a property interest in the regulated horses and burros superior to that of the State. But we need not consider whether the Act can be upheld on either of these grounds, for we reject appellees' narrow reading of the Property Clause.

Appellees ground their argument on a number of cases that, upon analysis, provide no support for their position. . . .

In brief, . . . appellees have presented no support for their position that the Clause grants Congress only the power to dispose of, to make incidental rules regarding the use of, and to protect federal property. This failure is hardly surprising, for the Clause, in broad terms, gives Congress the power to determine what are "needful" rules "respecting" the public lands. *United States v. San*

Francisco, 310 U.S., at 29 30; *Light v. United States*, 220 U.S., at 537; *United States v. Gratiot*, 14 Pet., at 537 538. And while the furthest reaches of the power granted by the Property Clause have not yet been definitively resolved, we have repeatedly observed that "[the] power over the public land thus entrusted to Congress is without limitations." *United States v. San Francisco, supra*, at 29. *See Ivanhoe Irrig. Dist. v. McCracken*, 357 U.S. 275, 294 295 (1958); *Alabama v. Texas*, 347 U.S. 272, 273 (1954); *FPC v. Idaho Power Co.*, 344 U.S. 17, 21 (1952); *United States v. California*, 332 U.S. 19, 27 (1947); *Gibson v. Chouteau*, 13 Wall. 92, 99 (1872); *United States v. Gratiot, supra*, at 537.

The decided cases have supported this expansive reading. It is the Property Clause, for instance, that provides the basis for governing the Territories of the United States. *Hooven & Allison Co. v. Evatt*, 324 U.S. 652, 673 674 (1945); *Balzac v. Porta Rico*, 258 U.S. 298, 305 (1922); *Dorr v. United States*, 195 U.S. 138, 149 (1904); *United States v. Gratiot, supra*, at 537; *Sere v. Pitot*, 6 Cranch 332, 336 337 (1810). *See also Vermilya-Brown Co. v. Connell*, 335 U.S. 377, 381 (1948). And even over public land within the States, "[t]he general Government doubtless has a power over its own property analogous to the police power of the several States, and the extent to which it may go in the exercise of such power is measured by the exigencies of the particular case." *Camfield v. United States, supra*, at 525. We have noted, for example, that the Property Clause gives Congress the power over the public lands "to control their occupancy and use, to protect them from trespass and injury and to prescribe the conditions upon which others may obtain rights in them. . . ." *Utah Power & Light Co. v. United States*, 243 U.S. 389, 405 (1917). And we have approved legislation respecting the public lands "[i]f it be found to be necessary for the protection of the public, or of intending settlers [on the public lands]." *Camfield v. United States, supra*, at 525. In short, Congress exercises the powers both of a proprietor and of a legislature over the public domain. *Alabama v. Texas*, supra, at 273; *Sinclair v. United States*, 279 U.S. 263, 297 (1929); *United States v. Midwest Oil Co.*, 236 U.S. 459, 474 (1915). Although the Property Clause does not authorize "an exercise of a general control over public policy in a State," it does permit "an exercise of the complete power which Congress has over particular public property entrusted to it." *United States v. San Francisco, supra*, at 30 (footnote omitted). In our view, the "complete power" that Congress has over public lands necessarily includes the power to regulate and protect the wildlife living there.

III

Appellees argue that if we approve the Wild Free-roaming Horses and Burros Act as a valid exercise of Congress' power under the Property Clause, then we have sanctioned an impermissible intrusion on the sovereignty, legislative authority, and police power of the State and have wrongly infringed upon the State's traditional trustee powers over wild animals. The argument appears to be that Congress could obtain exclusive legislative jurisdiction over the public lands in the State only by state consent, and that in the absence of such consent Congress lacks the power to act contrary to state law. This argument is without merit.

Appellees' claim confuses Congress' derivative legislative powers, which are not involved in this case, with its powers under the Property Clause. Congress may acquire derivative legislative power from a State pursuant to Art. I, § 8, cl. 17, of the Constitution by consensual acquisition of land, or by nonconsensual acquisition followed by the State's subsequent cession of legislative authority over the land. *Paul v. United States*, 371 U.S., at 264; *Fort Leavenworth R. Co. v. Lowe*, 114 U.S., at 541 542. In either case, the legislative jurisdiction acquired may range from exclusive federal jurisdiction with no residual state police power, *e.g.*, *Pacific Coast Dairy v. Dept. of Agriculture of Cal.*, 318 U.S. 285 (1943), to concurrent, or partial, federal legislative jurisdiction, which may allow the State to exercise certain authority. *E.g.*, *Paul v. United States, supra*, at 265; *Collins v. Yosemite Park Co.*, 304 U.S. 518, 528 530 (1938); *James v. Dravo Contracting Co.*, 302 U.S. 134, 147 149 (1937).

But while Congress can acquire exclusive or partial jurisdiction over lands within a State by the State's consent or cession, the presence or absence of such jurisdiction has nothing to do with Congress' powers under the Property Clause. Absent consent or cession a State undoubtedly retains jurisdiction over federal lands within its territory, but Congress equally surely retains the power to enact legislation respecting those lands pursuant to the Property Clause. *Mason Co. v. Tax Comm'n of Washington*, 302 U.S. 186, 197 (1937); *Utah Power & Light Co. v. United States*, 243 U.S., at 403 405; *Ohio v. Thomas*, 173 U.S. 276, 283 (1899). And when Congress so acts, the federal legislation necessarily overrides conflicting state laws under the Supremacy Clause. U.S. Const., Art. VI, cl. 2. *See Hunt v. United States*, 278 U.S., at 100; *McKelvey v. United States*, 260 U.S. 353, 359 (1922). As we said in *Camfield v. United States*, 167 U.S., at 526, in response to a somewhat different claim: "A different rule would place the public domain of the United States completely at the mercy of state legislation."

Thus, appellees' assertion that "[a]bsent state consent by complete cession of jurisdiction of lands to the United States, exclusive jurisdiction does not accrue to the federal landowner with regard to federal lands within the borders of the State," Brief for Appellees 24, is completely beside the point; and appellees' fear that the Secretary's position is that "the Property Clause totally exempts federal lands within state borders from state legislative powers, state police powers, and all rights and powers of local sovereignty and jurisdiction of the states," *id.*, at 16, is totally unfounded. The Federal Government does not assert exclusive jurisdiction over the public lands in New Mexico, and the State is free to enforce its criminal and civil laws on those lands. But where those state laws conflict with the Wild Free-roaming Horses and Burros Act, or with other legislation passed pursuant to the Property Clause, the law is clear. The state laws must recede. *McKelvey v. United States, supra*, at 359.

Again, none of the cases relied upon by appellees are to the contrary. . . .

Appellees' contention that the Act violates traditional state power over wild animals stands on no different footing. Unquestionably the States have broad trustee and police powers over wild animals within their jurisdictions. *Toomer v. Witsell*, 334 U.S. 385, 402 (1948); *Lacoste v. Department of Conservation*, 263 U.S. 545, 549 (1924); *Geer v. Connecticut*, 161 U.S. 519, 528 (1896). But, as *Geer v. Connecticut* cautions, those powers exist only "in so far as [their] exercise may be not incompatible with, or restrained by, the rights conveyed to the Federal government by the Constitution." *Ibid.* "No doubt it is true that as between a State and its inhabitants the State may regulate the killing and sale of [wildlife], but it does not follow that its authority is exclusive of paramount powers." *Missouri v. Holland*, 252 U.S. 416, 434 (1920). Thus, the Privileges and Immunities Clause, U.S. Const., Art. IV, § 2, cl. 1, precludes a State from imposing prohibitory licensing fees on nonresidents shrimping in its waters, *Toomer v. Witsell, supra*; the Treaty Clause, U.S. Const., Art. II, § 2, permits Congress to enter into and enforce a treaty to protect migratory birds despite state objections, *Missouri v. Holland, supra*; and the Property Clause gives Congress the power to thin overpopulated herds of deer on federal lands contrary to state law. *Hunt v. United States*, 278 U.S. 96 (1928). We hold today that the Property Clause also gives Congress the power to protect wildlife on the public lands, state law notwithstanding.

IV

In this case, the New Mexico Livestock Board entered upon the public lands of the United States and removed wild burros. These actions were contrary to the provisions of the Wild Free-roaming Horses and Burros Act. We find that, as applied to this case, the Act is a constitutional exercise of congressional power under the Property Clause. We need not, and do not, decide whether the Property Clause would sustain the Act in all of its conceivable applications.

Appellees are concerned that the Act's extension of protection to wild free-roaming horses and burros that stray from public land onto private land, § 4, 16 U.S.C. § 1334 (1970 ed., Supp. IV), will be read to provide federal jurisdiction over every wild horse or burro that at any time sets foot upon federal land. While it is clear that regulations under the Property Clause may have some effect on private lands not otherwise under federal control, *Camfield v. United States*, 167 U.S. 518 (1897), we do not think it appropriate in this declaratory judgment proceeding to determine the extent, if any, to which the Property Clause empowers Congress to protect animals on private lands or the extent to which such regulation is attempted by the Act. We have often declined to decide important questions regarding "the scope and constitutionality of legislation in advance of its immediate adverse effect in the context of a concrete case," *Longshoremen v. Boyd*, 347 U.S. 222, 224 (1954), or in the absence of "an adequate and full-bodied record." *Public Affairs Press v. Rickover*, 369 U.S. 111, 113 (1962). *Cf. Eccles v. Peoples Bank*, 333 U.S. 426 (1948). We follow that course in this case and leave open the question of the permissible reach of the Act over private lands under the Property Clause.

For the reasons stated, the judgment of the District Court is reversed, and the case is remanded for further proceedings consistent with this opinion.

It is so ordered.

NOTES AND QUESTIONS

1. *Legislative and Proprietary. Kleppe* states that the Property Clause gives the federal government a power over federal property "analogous to the police power of the several states," allowing the government to exercise "the powers both

of a proprietor and of a legislature over the public domain." Would it make any difference if a federal regulation was an expression of proprietary authority only? *See, e.g.*, Engdahl, *State and Federal Power over Federal Property*, 18 ARIZ. L. REV. 283 (1976).

2. ***Applicability.*** Do you think the Property Clause gives the federal government power to control activities on private land that are near to public lands? If so, when? *See, e.g., Camfield v. United States*, 167 U.S. 518, 17 S. Ct. 864 (1897). *See also* Sax, *Helpless Giants: The National Parks and the Regulation of Private Lands*, 75 MICH. L. REV. 239 (1976).

3. ***Delegation of the Power.*** By statute, the plenary authority of administration of public lands, including mineral lands, has been delegated to the Department of Interior, which has broad authority to issue rules and regulations for those purposes. *Best v. Humboldt Placer Mining Co.*, 371 U.S. 334, 83 S. Ct. 379 (1963). The Department has authority to:

> (a) perform all duties relating to the sale of public lands, "or in anywise respecting such public lands, and also, such as relate to private claims of land, and the issuing of patents for all grants and of land under the authority of the Government." 43 U.S.C. § 2 (1994);

> (b) enforce the provisions of Title 43 of the U.S. Code. 43 U.S.C. § 1201 (1994);

> (c) supervise the public business relating to the Bureau of Land Management. 43 U.S.C. § 1457 (1994);

> (d) administer the exploration and purchase of valuable mineral rights under the General Mining Law. 30 U.S.C. § 22 (1994); and

> (e) prevent unnecessary or undue degradation of the public lands. 43 U.S.C. § 1732(b) (1994).

2. Power to Withdraw and Reserve Federal Lands

During the disposition phase of federal land management, it became clear to many persons in government and elsewhere that the pendulum had swung too far, that the federal government's hellbent rush to dispose of lands was destructive to the public interest. The government was losing title interests to lands and natural resources even though it would surely need those lands and resources in the future. When the time came, the government would be in the embarrassing and costly position of having to buy back those property rights. The obvious remedy would have been to amend the disposition statutes. But, as students of government know, legislative relief can be hard to come by, especially when the relief involves terminating an entitlement. Perhaps for these reasons, Congress was conspicuously unresponsive as federal lands were transferring rapidly into private control. For that reason, the executive branch moved into the breach by denying access to public lands on its own. It did this by simply declaring select lands to be off limits from the operation of the disposition statutes. This practice of executive withdrawal and reservation became commonplace, and, predictably, encountered a major constitutional challenge.

UNITED STATES v. MIDWEST OIL CO.
236 U.S. 459, 35 S. Ct. 309 (1915)

MR. JUSTICE LAMAR delivered the opinion of the court.

All public lands containing petroleum or other mineral oils and chiefly valuable therefor, have been declared by Congress to be "free and open to occupation, exploration and purchase by citizens of the United States . . . under regulations prescribed by law." Act of February 11, 1897, c. 216, 29 Stat. 526; R. S. 2319, 2329.

As these regulations permitted exploration and location without the payment of any sum, and as title could be obtained for a merely nominal amount, many persons availed themselves of the provisions of the statute. Large areas in California were explored; and petroleum having been found, locations were made, not only by the discoverer but by others on adjoining land. And, as the flow through the well on one lot might exhaust the oil under the adjacent land, the interest of each operator was to extract the oil as soon as possible so as to share what would otherwise be taken by the owners of nearby wells.

The result was that oil was so rapidly extracted that on September 17, 1909, the Director of the Geological Survey made a report to the Secretary of the Interior which, with enclosures, called attention to the fact that, while there was a limited supply of coal on the Pacific coast and the value of oil as a fuel had been fully demonstrated, yet at the rate at which oil lands in California were being patented by private parties it would "be impossible for the people of the United States to continue ownership of oil lands for more than a few months. After that the Government will be obliged to repurchase the very oil that it has practically given away. . . . " "In view of the increasing use of fuel by the American Navy there would appear to be an immediate necessity for assuring t he conservation of a proper supply of petroleum for the Government's own use . . . " and "pending the enactment of adequate legislation on this subject, the filing of claims to oil lands in the State of California should be suspended."

This recommendation was approved by the Secretary of the Interior. Shortly afterwards he brought the matter to the attention of the President who, on September 27, 1909, issued the following Proclamation:

Temporary Petroleum Withdrawal No. 5.

In aid of proposed legislation affecting the use and disposition of the petroleum deposits on the public domain, all public lands in the accompanying lists are hereby temporarily withdrawn from all forms of location, settlement, selection, filing, entry, or disposal under the mineral or nonmineral public-land laws. All locations or claims existing and valid on this date may proceed to entry in the usual manner after field investigation and examination.

The list attached described an area aggregating 3,041,000 acres in California and Wyoming — though, of course, the order only applied to the public lands therein, the acreage of which is not shown.

On March 27, 1910, six months after the publication of the Proclamation, William T. Henshaw and others entered upon a quarter section of this public land in Wyoming so withdrawn. They made explorations, bored a well, discovered oil and thereafter assigned their interest to the Appellees, who took possession and extracted large quantities of oil. On May 4, 1910, they filed a location certificate.

As the explorations by the original claimants, and the subsequent operation of the well, were both long after the date of the President's Proclamation, the Government filed, in the District Court of the United States for the District of Wyoming, a Bill in Equity against the Midwest Oil Company and the other Appellees, seeking to recover the land and to obtain an accounting for 50,000 barrels of oil alleged to have been illegally extracted. The court sustained the defendant's demurrer and dismissed the bill. Thereupon the Government took the case to the Circuit Court of Appeals of the Eighth Circuit which rendered no decision but certified certain questions to this court, where an order was subsequently passed directing the entire record to be sent up for consideration.

The case has twice been fully argued. Both parties, as well as other persons interested in oil lands similarly affected, have submitted lengthy and elaborate briefs on the single and controlling question as to the validity of the Withdrawal Order. On the part of the Government it is urged that the President, as Commander-in-Chief of the Army and Navy, had power to make the order for the purpose of retaining and preserving a source of supply of fuel for the Navy, instead of allowing the oil land to be taken up for a nominal sum, the Government being then obliged to purchase at a great cost what it had previously owned. It is argued that the President, charged with the care of the public domain, could, by virtue of the executive power vested in him by the Constitution (Art. 2, § 1), and also in conformity with the tacit consent of Congress, withdraw, in the public interest, any public land from entry or location by private parties.

The Appellees, on the other hand, insist that there is no dispensing power in the Executive and that he could not suspend a statute or withdraw from entry or location any land which Congress had affirmatively declared should be free and open to acquisition by citizens of the United States. They further insist that the withdrawal order is absolutely void since it appears on its face to be a mere attempt to suspend a statute supposed to be unwise, in order to allow Congress to pass another more in accordance with what the Executive thought to be in the public interest.

1. We need not consider whether, as an original question, the President could have withdrawn from private acquisition what Congress had made free and open to occupation and purchase. The case can be determined on other grounds and in the light of the legal consequences owing from a long continued practice to make orders like the one here involved. For the President's proclamation of September 27, 1909, is by no means the first instance in which the Executive, by a special order, has withdrawn land which Congress, by general statute, had thrown open to acquisition by citizens. And while it is not known when the first of these orders was made, it is certain that "the practice dates from an early period in the history of the government." *Grisar v. McDowell*, 6 Wall. 381. Scores and hundreds of these orders have been made; and treating them as they must be (*Wolsey v. Chapman*, 101 U.S.

769), as the act of the President, an examination of official publications will show that (excluding those made by virtue of special congressional action, *Donnelly v. United States*, 228 U.S. 255) he has during the past 80 years, without express statutory authority — but under the claim of power so to do — made a multitude of Executive Orders which operated to withdraw public land that would otherwise have been open to private acquisition. They affected every kind of land — mineral and nonmineral. The size of the tracts varied from a few square rods to many square miles and the amount withdrawn has aggregated millions of acres. The number of such instances cannot, of course, be accurately given, but the extent of the practice can best be appreciated by a consideration of what is believed to be a correct enumeration of such Executive Orders mentioned in public documents.

They show that prior to the year 1910 there had been issued

> 99 Executive Orders establishing or enlarging Indian Reservations; 109 Executive Orders establishing or enlarging Military Reservations and setting apart land for water, timber, fuel, hay, signal stations, target ranges and rights of way for use in connection with Military Reservations; 44 Executive Orders establishing Bird Reserves.

In the sense that these lands may have been intended for public use, they were reserved for a public purpose. But they were not reserved in pursuance of law or by virtue of any general or special statutory authority. For, it is to be specially noted that there was no act of Congress providing for Bird Reserves or for these Indian Reservations. There was no law for the establishment of these Military Reservations or defining their size or location. There was no statute empowering the President to withdraw any of these lands from settlement or to reserve them for any of the purposes indicated.

But when it appeared that the public interest would be served by withdrawing or reserving parts of the public domain, nothing was more natural than to retain what the Government already owned. And in making such orders, which were thus useful to the public, no private interest was injured. For prior to the initiation of some right given by law the citizen had no enforceable interest in the public statute and no private right in land which was the property of the people. The President was in a position to know when the public interest required particular portions of the people's lands to be withdrawn from entry or location; his action inflicted no wrong upon any private citizen, and being subject to disaffirmance by Congress, could occasion no harm to the interest of the public at large. Congress did not repudiate the power claimed or the withdrawal orders made. On the contrary it uniformly and repeatedly acquiesced in the practice and, as shown by these records, there had been, prior to 1910, at least 252 Executive Orders making reservation for useful, though non-statutory purposes.

This right of the President to make reservations, and thus withdraw land from private acquisition, was expressly recognized in *Grisar v. McDowell*, 6 Wall. 364 (9), 381 (1867), where it was said that "from an early period in the history of the Government it has been the practice of the President to order, from time to time, as the exigencies of the public service required, parcels of land belonging to the United States to be reserved from sale and set apart for public uses." . . .

2. It may be argued that while these facts and rulings prove a usage they do not establish its validity. But government is a practical affair intended for practical men. Both officers, law-makers and citizens naturally adjust themselves to any long-continued action of the Executive Department — on the presumption that unauthorized acts would not have been allowed to be so often repeated as to crystallize into a regular practice. That presumption is not reasoning in a circle but the basis of a wise and quieting rule that in determining the meaning of a statute or the existence of a power, weight shall be given to the usage itself — even when the validity of the practice is the subject of investigation . . .

3. These decisions do not, of course, mean that private rights could be created by an officer withdrawing for a Rail Road more than had been authorized by Congress in the land grant act. *Southern Pacific v. Bell*, 183 U.S. 685; *Brandon v. Ard*, 211 U.S. 21. Nor do these decisions mean that the Executive can by his course of action create a power. But they do clearly indicate that the long-continued practice, known to and acquiesced in by Congress, would raise a presumption that the withdrawals had been made in pursuance of its consent or of a recognized administrative power of the Executive in the management of the public lands. This is particularly true in view of the fact that the land is property of the United States and that the land laws are not of a legislative character in the highest sense of the term (Art. 4, § 3) "but savor somewhat of mere rules prescribed by an owner of property for its disposal." *Butte City Water Co. v. Baker*, 196 U.S. 126.

These rules or laws for the disposal of public land are necessarily general in their nature. Emergencies may occur, or conditions may so change as to require that the agent in charge should, in the public interest, withhold the land from sale; and while no such express authority has been granted, there is nothing in the nature of the power exercised which prevents Congress from granting it by implication just as could be done by any other owner of property under similar conditions. The power of the Executive, as agent in charge, to retain that property from sale need not necessarily be expressed in writing. *Lockhart v. Johnson*, 181 U.S. 520; *Bronson v. Chappell*, 12 Wall. 686; *Campbell v. City of Kenosha*, 5 Wall. 194.

For it must be borne in mind that Congress not only has a legislative power over the public domain, but it also exercises the powers of the proprietor therein. Congress "may deal with such lands precisely as a private individual may deal with his farming property. It may sell or withhold them from sale." *Camfield v. United States*, 167 U.S. 524; *Light v. United States*, 220 U.S. 536. Like any other owner it may provide when, how and to whom its land can be sold. It can permit it to be withdrawn from sale. Like any other owner, it can waive its strict rights, as it did when the valuable privilege of grazing cattle on this public land was held to be based upon an "implied license growing out of the custom of nearly a hundred years." *Buford v. Houtz*, 133 U.S. 326. So too, in the early days the "Government, by its silent acquiescence, assented to the general occupation of the public lands for mining." *Atchison v. Peterson*, 20 Wall. 512. If private persons could acquire a privilege in public land by virtue of an implied congressional consent, then for a much stronger reason, an implied grant of power to preserve the public interest would arise out of like congressional acquiescence.

The Executive, as agent, was in charge of the public domain; by a multitude of orders extending over a long period of time and affecting vast bodies of land, in many States and Territories, he withdrew large areas in the public interest. These orders were known to Congress, as principal, and in not a single instance was the act of the agent disapproved. Its acquiescence all the more readily operated as an implied grant of power in view of the fact that its exercise was not only useful to the public but did not interfere with any vested right of the citizen.

4. The appellees, however, argue that the practice thus approved, related to Reservations — to cases where the land had been reserved for military or other special public purposes — and they contend that even if the President could reserve land for a public purpose or for naval uses, it does not follow that he can withdraw land in aid of legislation.

When analyzed, this proposition, in effect, seeks to make a distinction between a Reservation and a Withdrawal — between a Reservation for a purpose, not provided for by existing legislation, and a Withdrawal made in aid of future legislation. It would mean that a Permanent Reservation for a purpose designated by the President, but not provided for by a statute, would be valid, while a merely Temporary Withdrawal to enable Congress to legislate in the public interest would be invalid. It is only necessary to point out that, as the greater includes the less, the power to make permanent reservations includes power to make temporary withdrawals. For there is no distinction in principle between the two. The character of the power exerted is the same in both cases. In both, the order is made to serve the public interest and in both the effect on the intending settler or miner is the same.

But the question need not be left solely to inference, since the validity of withdrawal orders, in aid of legislation, has been expressly recognized in a series of cases involving a number of such orders, made between 1850 and 1862. [citations omitted]

. . . .

But that the existence of this power was recognized and its exercise by the Executive assented to by Congress, is emphasized by the fact that the above-mentioned withdrawals were issued after the Report which the Secretary of the Interior made in 1902, in response to a resolution of the Senate calling for information "as to what, if any, of the public lands have been withdrawn from disposition under the settlement or other laws by order of the Commissioner of the General Land Office and *what, if any, authority of law exists for such order of withdrawal.*"

The answer to this specific inquiry was returned March 3, 1902, (Senate Doc. 232, 57th Cong., 1st Sess., Vol. 17). On that date the Secretary transmitted to the Senate the elaborate and detailed report of the Commissioner of the Land Office, who in response to the inquiry as to the authority by which withdrawals had been made, answered that

> the power of the Executive Department of the Government to make reservations of land for public use, and to temporarily withdraw lands from appropriation by individuals as exigencies might demand, to prevent fraud, to aid in proper administration and in aid of pending legislation is one that has been long recognized both in the acts of Congress and the decisions of

the court; . . . that this power has been long exercised by the Commissioner of the General Land Office is shown by reference to the date of some of the withdrawals enumerated. . . . The attached list embraces only such lands as were withdrawn by this office, acting on its own motion, in cases where the emergencies appeared to demand such action in furtherance of public interest and does not include lands withdrawn under express statutes so directed.

The list, which is attached, refers to withdrawal orders about 100 in number, issued between 1870 and 1902. Many of them were in aid of the administration of the land laws to correct boundaries; to prevent fraud; to make a classification of the land, and like good — but non-statutory — reasons. Some were made to prevent settlements while the question was being considered as to whether the lands might not be included in a forest reservation to be thereafter established. One in 1889 (referred to also in 28 L. D. 358) was made in order to afford the State of Nebraska an opportunity to procure legislative relief, as in the *Iowa* cases above cited.

This report refers to Withdrawals and not to *Reservations*. It is most important in connection with the present inquiry as to whether Congress knew of the practice to make temporary withdrawals and knowingly assented thereto. It will be noted that the Resolution called on the Department to state the extent of such withdrawals and the authority by which they were made. The officer of the Land Department in his answer shows that there have been a large number of withdrawals made for good but for non-statutory reasons. He shows that these 92 orders had been made by virtue of a long-continued practice and under claim of a right to take such action in the public interest "as exigencies might demand. . . ." Congress with notice of this practice and of this claim of authority, received the Report. Neither at that session nor afterwards did it ever repudiate the action taken or the power claimed. Its silence was acquiescence. Its acquiescence was equivalent to consent to continue the practice until the power was revoked by some subsequent action by Congress.

Reversed.

MR. JUSTICE MCREYNOLDS took no part in the decision of this case.

DISSENT: MR. JUSTICE DAY with whom concurred MR. JUSTICE MCKENNA and MR. JUSTICE VANDEVANTER, dissenting [omitted].

NOTES AND QUESTIONS

1. *Withdrawals and Reservations.* A withdrawal can be accomplished by executive order, by statute, or by administrative order. It can be permanent or temporary in duration, in order to maintain the status quo until new legislation can be enacted, or for other purposes. It can be made in conjunction with other land management initiatives and it can be complete or partial in its injunctive effect.

A "reservation" of federal land also makes land unavailable to the public. A reservation is different from a withdrawal in that the former dedicates land for an affirmative purpose. For example, land can be "reserved" for use as a wildlife refuge or as a national park, for military use, or for any other designated purpose. Legally, there is little difference between a withdrawal and a reservation. There is no question that Congress has the constitutional authority to withdraw or reserve federal land. The Property Clause expressly grants the authority, and the Supreme Court in *Kleppe* embraced the substantial breadth of that power. Not unexpectedly, Congress has exercised this authority frequently. One major exercise was in the form of the Taylor Grazing Act of 1934, 43 U.S.C.A. § 315 et seq., which withdrew millions of acres from the operation of the homesteading laws. Similarly, the Alaska Native Claims Settlement Act of 1971, 43 U.S.C.A. §§ 1601 et seq., accomplished the withdrawal of much of Alaska.

Congress can delegate its withdrawal and reservation powers to the executive, and has done so on numerous occasions. Perhaps the most notable example of Congressional delegation was the Pickett Act of 1910, 43 U.S.C. § 141 2. The Act, noted in *Midwest Oil* (in a portion of the opinion not reproduced in this text), provided that "[t]he President may, at any time, in his discretion, temporarily withdraw from the United States, including Alaska, and reserve the same for water power sites, irrigation, classification of lands, or other public purposes to be specified in the orders of withdrawals, and such withdrawals or reservations shall remain in force by him or by an Act of Congress." (Enacted on June 25, 1910, the Pickett Act did not apply retroactively to affect the September 27, 1909 withdrawal implicated in *Midwest Oil*.)

Every president, however, has steadfastly argued that, in addition to whatever powers the Congress might have delegated, the executive also has "inherent" authority under Article II of the Constitution to accomplish these ends. Presidents have withdrawn lands on this basis as well, especially for military purposes and for establishment of Indian reservations. What does *Midwest Oil* tell us of the president's constitutional authorities to withdraw federal lands?

2. *FLPMA and Withdrawals.* In 1976, the Federal Land Policy and Management Act ("FLPMA"), 43 U.S.C. § 1701 et seq., expressly repealed the executive authority acknowledged by *Midwest Oil:*

> Effective on and after the date of approval of this Act, the implied authority of the President to make withdrawals and reservations resulting from the acquiescence of the Congress (*U.S. v. Midwest Oil Co.*, 236 U.S. 459) . . . [is] repealed.

Section 704(a), Pub. Law 94-576, 90 Stat. 2792.

FLPMA went on to specify new executive withdrawal authority. First, the statute redefined the term "withdrawal," giving it a meaning broad enough to encompass "reservations" as that term has been used:

> The term "withdrawal" means withholding an area of Federal land from settlement, sale, location, or entry, under some or all of the general land laws, for the purpose of limiting activities under those laws in order to maintain other public values in the area or reserving the area for a particular public purpose or program; or transferring jurisdiction over an area of Federal land, other than "property" governed by the Federal

Property and Administrative Services Act, as amended (40 U.S.C. 472) from one department, bureau or agency to another department, bureau or agency.

FLPMA § 103(j), 43 U.S.C. § 1702(j).

Second, in § 204, FLPMA reestablished the withdrawal power in the executive branch, "but only in accordance with the provisions and limitations of this section." Section 204(a), 43 U.S.C. § 1714(a). The limitations imposed by the section are largely procedural. For withdrawals of lands comprising less than 5,000 acres, the procedural burdens are relatively light. *See* § 204(d), 43 U.S.C. § 1714(d). For withdrawals of lands of 5000 or more acres, congressional approval is required. Section 204(c), 43 U.S.C. § 1714(c). Much of the procedural burden, therefore, is thrust upon Congress, rather than the executive branch. *Id.* The major substantive restriction on executive withdrawal authorities is a prohibition on modifying or revoking withdrawals made by Congress itself, and those made for national monuments or wildlife refuges. *See* § 204(j). Notably, some withdrawals, for example, the reservation of land for use as a national park, can only be made by Congress. Section 204(e) of the statute is directed specifically to emergency withdrawals, the type implicated in *Midwest Oil*. It gives the president essentially an unfettered authority.

3.   *Withdrawals and Reservations in the Current Day.* The need to withdraw or reserve federal land to protect against private claims is less urgent in the current day. Only one law, the General Mining Law of 1872, presently allows individuals by their own initiative to secure title to federal lands. *See infra.* Other such disposition statutes, such as the Homestead Act of 1862, have been repealed. Moreover, Congress codified the national policy of retaining public lands in federal title in the Federal Land Policy and Management Act of 1976. 43 U.S.C. § 1701(a)(1). But presidents still continue to withdraw lands, especially pursuant to the delegated authority of the American Antiquities Preservation Act, 34 Stat. 225, 16 U.S.C. § 431 ("Antiquities Act"). For more on the Antiquities Act, see the discussion of "national monuments," *infra.*

3.   Federal Reserved Water Rights

The power to withdraw and reserve federal lands and minerals has been extended to water. In this context, however, the legal issues can be somewhat more complex because state law generally controls water rights allocations among individuals. States control water rights because the federal government has acquiesced to this result. *See, e.g., California v. United States*, 438 U.S. 645, 98 S. Ct. 2985 (1978):

> The history of the relationship between the Federal Government and the States in the reclamation of the arid lands of the Western States is both long and involved, but through it runs the consistent thread of purposeful and continued deference to state water law by Congress.

Id. at 653, 98 S. Ct. at 2990. *See also* Chapter 8, *infra.* Accordingly, it is states, not the federal government, that determine to whom water is allocated. The effect of allocation is to create property rights in water in individuals.

Any attempt by the federal government to withdraw or reserve water already appropriated to individuals under state law would run afoul of the Takings Clause of the Fifth Amendment of the Federal Constitution. Thus, if the federal government wants property rights to appropriated water, it must secure those rights by purchase, eminent domain, or some other legal mechanism. But what of waters that are unappropriated under state law? May the federal government secure rights to these waters, free of obligations to pay compensation, by the same withdrawal or reservation mechanisms used to curtail public access to public lands? The answer to this question is yes: the federal government may do so, and it has. *See, e.g.*, The Wild and Scenic Rivers Act, 16 U.S.C. §§ 1271, 1284(c) (in which Congress expressly reserved the amount of water "necessary to fulfill the purposes of the Act."). The next question is whether federal withdrawals and reservations of water rights can occur in the absence of an express statutory declaration.

CAPPAERT v. UNITED STATES
426 U.S. 128, 96 S. Ct. 2062 (1976)

MR. CHIEF JUSTICE BURGER delivered the opinion of the Court.

The question presented in this litigation is whether the reservation of Devil's Hole as a national monument reserved federal water rights in unappropriated water.

Devil's Hole is a deep limestone cavern in Nevada. Approximately 50 feet below the opening of the cavern is a pool 65 feet long, 10 feet wide, and at least 200 feet deep, although its actual depth is unknown. The pool is a remnant of the prehistoric Death Valley Lake System and is situated on land owned by the United States since the Treaty of Guadalupe Hidalgo in 1848, 9 Stat. 922. By the Proclamation of January 17, 1952, President Truman withdrew from the public domain a 40-acre tract of land surrounding Devil's Hole, making it a detached component of the Death Valley National Monument. Proclamation No. 2961, 3 C.F.R. 147 (1949 1953 Comp.). The Proclamation was issued under the American Antiquities Preservation Act, 34 Stat. 225, 16 U.S.C. § 431, which authorizes the President to declare as national monuments "objects of historic or scientific interest that are situated upon the lands owned or controlled by the Government of the United States . . . "

Devil's Hole. Photo by Terry Fisk. National Park Service.
(Photo not part of Supreme Court opinion.)

The 1952 Proclamation notes that Death Valley was set aside as a national monument "for the preservation of the unusual features of scenic, scientific, and educational interest therein contained." The Proclamation also notes that Devil's Hole is near Death Valley and contains a "remarkable underground pool." Additional preambulary statements in the Proclamation explain why Devil's Hole was being added to the Death Valley National Monument:

> Whereas the said pool is a unique subsurface remnant of the prehistoric chain of lakes which in Pleistocene times formed the Death Valley Lake System, and is unusual among caverns in that it is a solution area in distinctly striated limestone, while also owing its formation in part to fault action; and

> Whereas the geologic evidence that this subterranean pool is an integral part of the hydrographic history of the Death Valley region is further confirmed by the presence in this pool of a peculiar race of desert fish, and zoologists have demonstrated that this race of fish, which is found nowhere else in the world, evolved only after the gradual drying up of the Death Valley Lake System isolated this fish population from the original ancestral stock that in Pleistocene times was common to the entire region; and

> Whereas the said pool is of such outstanding scientific importance that it should be given special protection, and such protection can be best afforded by making the said forty-acre tract containing the pool a part of the said monument. . . .

The Proclamation provides that Devil's Hole should be supervised, managed, and directed by the National Park Service, Department of the Interior. Devil's Hole is fenced off, and only limited access is allowed by the Park Service.

The Cappaert petitioners own a 12,000-acre ranch near Devil's Hole, 4,000 acres of which are used for growing Bermuda grass, alfalfa, wheat, and barley; 1,700 to 1,800 head of cattle are grazed. The ranch represents an investment of more than $7 million; it employs more than 80 people with an annual payroll of more than $340,000.

In 1968 the Cappaerts began pumping groundwater on their ranch on land 2 ½ miles from Devil's Hole; they were the first to appropriate groundwater. The groundwater comes from an underground basin or aquifer which is also the source of the water in Devil's Hole. After the Cappaerts began pumping from the wells near Devil's Hole, which they do from March to October, the summer water level of the pool in Devil's Hole began to decrease. Since 1962 the level of water in Devil's Hole has been measured with reference to a copper washer installed on one of the walls of the hole by the United States Geological Survey. Until 1968, the water level, with seasonable variations, had been stable at 1.2 feet below the copper marker. In 1969 the water level in Devil's Hole was 2.3 feet below the copper washer; in 1970, 3.17 feet; in 1971, 3.48 feet; and, in 1972, 3.93 feet.

When the water is at the lowest levels, a large portion of a rock shelf in Devil's Hole is above water. However, when the water level is at 3.0 feet below the marker or higher, most of the rock shelf is below water, enabling algae to grow on it. This in turn enables the desert fish (cyprinodon diabolis, commonly known as Devil's Hole pup sh), referred to in President Truman's Proclamation, to spawn in the spring. As the rock shelf becomes exposed, the spawning area is decreased, reducing the ability of the fish to spawn in sufficient quantities to prevent extinction.

In April 1970 the Cappaerts, pursuant to Nevada law, Nev. Rev. Stat. § 533.325 (1973), applied to the State Engineer, Roland D. Westergard, for permits to change the use of water from several of their wells. Although the United States was not a party to that proceeding and was never served, employees of the National Park Service learned of the Cappaerts' application through a public notice published pursuant to Nevada law. § 533.360. An official of the National Park Service filed a protest as did a private firm. Nevada law permits interested persons to protest an application for a permit; the protest may be considered by the State Engineer at a hearing. § 533.365. A hearing was conducted on December 16, 1970, and a field solicitor of the Department of the Interior appeared on behalf of the National Park Service. He presented documentary and testimonial evidence, informing the State Engineer that because of the declining water level of Devil's Hole the United States had commissioned a study to determine whether the wells on the Cappaerts' land were hydrologically connected to Devil's Hole and, if so, which of those wells could be pumped safely and which should be limited to prevent lowering of the water level in Devil's Hole. The Park Service field solicitor requested either that the Cappaerts' application be denied or that decision on the application be postponed until the studies were completed.

The State Engineer declined to postpone decision. At the conclusion of the hearing he stated that there was no recorded federal water right with respect to Devil's Hole, that the testimony indicated that the Cappaerts' pumping would not unreasonably lower the water table or adversely affect existing water rights, and that the permit would be granted since further economic development of the

Cappaerts' land would be in the public interest. In his oral ruling the State Engineer stated in part that "the protest to the applications that are the subject of this hearing are overruled and the applications will be issued subject to existing rights." The National Park Service did not appeal. See Nev. Rev. Stat. § 533.450 (1973).

In August 1971 the United States, invoking 28 U.S.C. § 1345, sought an injunction in the United States District Court for the District of Nevada to limit, except for domestic purposes, the Cappaerts' pumping from six specific wells and from specific locations near Devil's Hole. The complaint alleged that the United States, in establishing Devil's Hole as part of Death Valley National Monument, reserved the unappropriated waters appurtenant to the land to the extent necessary for the requirements and purposes of the reservation. The complaint further alleged that the Cappaerts had no perfected water rights as of the date of the reservation. The United States asserted that pumping from certain of the Cappaerts' wells had lowered the water level in Devil's Hole, that the lower water level was threatening the survival of a unique species of fish, and that irreparable harm would follow if the pumping were not enjoined. On June 2, 1972, the United States filed an amended complaint, adding two other specified wells to the list of those to be enjoined.

The Cappaerts answered, admitting that their wells draw water from the same underlying sources supplying Devil's Hole, but denying that the reservation of Devil's Hole reserved any water rights for the United States. The Cappaerts alleged that the United States was estopped from enjoining use of water under land which it had exchanged with the Cappaerts. The State of Nevada intervened on behalf of the State Engineer as a party defendant but raised no affirmative defenses.

On June 5, 1973, the District Court, by Chief Judge Roger D. Foley, entered a preliminary injunction limiting pumping from designated wells so as to return the level of Devil's Hole to not more than 3.0 feet below the marker. Detailed findings of fact were made and the District Judge then appointed a Special Master to establish specific pumping limits for the wells and to monitor the level of the water at Devil's Hole. The District Court found that the water from certain of the wells was hydrologically connected to Devil's Hole, that the Cappaerts were pumping heavily from those wells, and that pumping had lowered the water level in Devil's Hole. The court also found that the pumping could be regulated to stabilize the water level at Devil's Hole and that neither establishing an artificial shelf nor transplanting the fish was a feasible alternative that would preserve the species. The District Court further found that if the injunction did not issue "there is grave danger that the Devil's Hole pup fish may be destroyed, resulting in irreparable injury to the United States." 375 F. Supp. 456, 460 (1974).

The District Court then held that in establishing Devil's Hole as a national monument, the President reserved appurtenant, unappropriated waters necessary to the purpose of the reservation; the purpose included preservation of the pool and the pup fish in it. The District Court also held that the federal water rights antedated those of the Cappaerts, that the United States was not estopped, and that the public interest required granting the injunction. On April 9, 1974, the District Court entered its findings of fact and conclusions of law substantially unchanged in a final decree permanently enjoining pumping that lowers the level of the water below the 3.0-foot level. 375 F. Supp. 456 (1974).

The Court of Appeals for the Ninth Circuit affirmed, 508 F.2d 313 (1974), in a thorough opinion by Senior District Judge Gus J. Solomon, sitting by designation, holding that the implied-reservation-of-water doctrine applied to groundwater as well as to surface water. The Court of Appeals held that "[t]he fundamental purpose of the reservation of the Devil's Hole pool was to assure that the pool would not suffer changes from its condition at the time the Proclamation was issued in 1952 . . . ." *Id.*, at 318. The Court of Appeals further held that neither the Cappaerts nor their successors in interest had any water rights in 1952, nor was the United States estopped from asserting its water rights by exchanging land with the Cappaerts. In answer to contentions raised by the intervenor Nevada, the Court of Appeals held that "the United States is not bound by state water laws when it reserves land from the public domain," *id.*, at 320, and does not need to take steps to perfect its rights with the State; that the District Court had concurrent jurisdiction with the state courts to resolve this claim; and, that the state administrative procedures granting the Cappaerts' permit did not bar resolution of the United States' suit in Federal District Court.

We granted certiorari to consider the scope of the implied-reservation-of-water-rights doctrine. 422 U.S. 1041 (1975). We affirm.

I

Reserved-Water-Rights Doctrine

This Court has long held that when the Federal Government withdraws its land from the public domain and reserves it for a federal purpose, the Government, by implication, reserves appurtenant water then unappropriated to the extent needed to accomplish the purpose of the reservation. In so doing the United States acquires a reserved right in unappropriated water which vests on the date of the reservation and is superior to the rights of future appropriators. Reservation of water rights is empowered by the Commerce Clause, Art. I, § 8, which permits federal regulation of navigable streams, and the Property Clause, Art. IV,§ 3, which permits federal regulation of federal lands. The doctrine applies to Indian reservations and other federal enclaves, encompassing water rights in navigable and nonnavigable streams. *Colorado River Water Cons. Dist. v. United States*, 424 U.S. 800, 805 (1976); *United States v. District Court for Eagle County*, 401 U.S. 520, 522 523 (1971); *Arizona v. California*, 373 U.S. 546, 601 (1963); *FPC v. Oregon*, 349 U.S. 435 (1955); *United States v. Powers*, 305 U.S. 527 (1939); *Winters v. United States*, 207 U.S. 564 (1908).

Nevada argues that the cases establishing the doctrine of federally reserved water rights articulate an equitable doctrine calling for a balancing of competing interests. However, an examination of those cases shows they do not analyze the doctrine in terms of a balancing test. For example, in *Winters v. United States, supra*, the Court did not mention the use made of the water by the upstream landowners in sustaining an injunction barring their diversions of the water. The "Statement of the Case" in *Winters* notes that the upstream users were homesteaders who had invested heavily in dams to divert the water to irrigate their land, not an unimportant interest. The Court held that when the Federal Government reserves land, by implication it reserves water rights sufficient to accomplish the purposes of the reservation.

In determining whether there is a federally reserved water right implicit in a federal reservation of public land, the issue is whether the Government intended to reserve unappropriated and thus available water. Intent is inferred if the previously unappropriated waters are necessary to accomplish the purposes for which the reservation was created. . . . Both the District Court and the Court of Appeals held that the 1952 Proclamation expressed an intention to reserve unappropriated water, and we agree. The Proclamation discussed the pool in Devil's Hole in four of the five preambles and recited that the "pool . . . should be given special protection." Since a pool is a body of water, the protection contemplated is meaningful only if the water remains; the water right reserved by the 1952 Proclamation was thus explicit, not implied.

Also explicit in the 1952 Proclamation is the authority of the Director of the Park Service to manage the lands of Devil's Hole Monument "as provided in the act of Congress entitled 'An Act to establish a National Park Service, and for other purposes,' approved August 25, 1916 (39 Stat. 535; 16 U.S.C. 1 3). . . . " The National Park Service Act provides that the "fundamental purpose of the said parks, monuments, and reservations" is "to conserve the scenery and the natural and historic objects and the wild life therein and to provide for the enjoyment of the same in such manner and by such means as will leave them unimpaired for the enjoyment of future generations." 39 Stat. 535, 16 U.S.C. § 1.

The implied-reservation-of-water-doctrine, however, reserves only that amount of water necessary to ful ll the purpose of the reservation, no more. *Arizona v. California, supra,* at 600 601. Here the purpose of reserving Devil's Hole Monument is preservation of the pool. Devil's Hole was reserved "for the preservation of the unusual features of scenic, scientific, and educational interest." The Proclamation notes that the pool contains "a peculiar race of desert fish . . . which is found nowhere else in the world" and that the "pool is of . . . outstanding scientific importance. . . . " The pool need only be preserved, consistent with the intention expressed in the Proclamation, to the extent necessary to preserve its scientific interest. The fish are one of the features of scientific interest. The preamble noting the scientific interest of the pool follows the preamble describing the fish as unique; the Proclamation must be read in its entirety. Thus, as the District Court has correctly determined, the level of the pool may be permitted to drop to the extent that the drop does not impair the scientific value of the pool as the natural habitat of the species sought to be preserved. The District Court thus tailored its injunction, very appropriately, to minimal need, curtailing pumping only to the extent necessary to preserve an adequate water level at Devil's Hole, thus implementing the stated objectives of the Proclamation.

Petitioners in both cases argue that even if the intent of the 1952 Proclamation were to maintain the pool, the American Antiquities Preservation Act did not give the President authority to reserve a pool. Under that Act, according to the Cappaert petitioners, the President may reserve federal lands only to protect archaeologic sites. However, the language of the Act which authorizes the President to proclaim as national monuments "historic landmarks, historic and prehistoric structures, and other objects of historic or scientific interest that are situated upon the lands owned or controlled by the Government" is not so limited. The pool in Devil's Hole and its rare inhabitants are "objects of historic or scientific interest." *See generally Cameron v. United States*, 252 U.S. 450, 451 456 (1920).

II

Groundwater

No cases of this Court have applied the doctrine of implied reservation of water rights to groundwater. Nevada argues that the implied-reservation doctrine is limited to surface water. Here, however, the water in the pool is surface water. The federal water rights were being depleted because, as the evidence showed, the "[g]roundwater and surface water are physically interrelated as integral parts of the hydrologic cycle." Here the Cappaerts are causing the water level in Devil's Hole to drop by their heavy pumping. It appears that Nevada itself may recognize the potential interrelationship between surface and groundwater since Nevada applies the law of prior appropriation to both. Nev. Rev. Stat. §§ 533.010 et seq., 534.020, 534.080, 534.090 (1973). Thus, since the implied-reservation-of-water-rights doctrine is based on the necessity of water for the purpose of the federal reservation, we hold that the United States can protect its water from subsequent diversion, whether the diversion is of surface or groundwater.

III

State Law

Petitioners in both cases argue that the Federal Government must perfect its implied water rights according to state law. They contend that the Desert Land Act of 1877, 19 Stat. 377, 43 U.S.C. § 321, and its predecessors severed nonnavigable water from public land, subjecting it to state law. That Act, however, provides that patentees of public land acquire only title to land through the patent and must acquire water rights in nonnavigable water in accordance with state law. This Court held in *FPC v. Oregon*, 349 U.S. 435, 448 (1955), that the Desert Land Act does not apply to water rights on federally reserved land. . . .

The Cappaert petitioners argue that *FPC v. Oregon, supra*, must be overruled since, inter alia, the Court was unaware at the time that case was decided that there was no longer any public land available for homesteading. However, whether or not there was public land available for homesteading in 1955 is irrelevant to the meaning of the 1877 Act. The Desert Land Act still provides that the water rights of those who received their land from federal patents are to be governed by state law. That there may be no more federal land available for homesteading does not mean the Desert Land Act now applies to all federal land. Since the Act is inapplicable, determination of reserved water rights is not governed by state law but derives from the federal purpose of the reservation; the fact that the water rights here reserved apply to nonnavigable rather than navigable waters is thus irrelevant.

Since *FPC v. Oregon, supra,* was decided, several bills have been introduced in Congress to subject at least some federal water uses to state appropriation doctrines, but none has been enacted into law. . . .

Federal water rights are not dependent upon state law or state procedures and they need not be adjudicated only in state courts; federal courts have jurisdiction under 28 U.S.C. § 1345 to adjudicate the water rights claims of the United States. . . . The McCarran Amendment, 66 Stat. 560, 43 U.S.C. § 666, did not repeal § 1345 jurisdiction as applied to water rights. 424 U.S., at 808 809. Nor, as Nevada suggests, is the McCarran Amendment a substantive statute, requiring the United States to "perfect its water rights in the state forum like all other land owners." The McCarran Amendment waives United States sovereign immunity should the United States be joined as a party in a state-court general water rights' adjudication, and the policy evinced by the Amendment may, in the appropriate case, require the United States to adjudicate its water rights in state forums.

[The portion of the opinion dealing with res judicata and collateral estoppel is omitted.]

We hold, therefore, that as of 1952 when the United States reserved Devil's Hole, it acquired by reservation water rights in unappropriated appurtenant water sufficient to maintain the level of the pool to preserve its scientific value and thereby implement Proclamation No. 2961. Accordingly, the judgment of the Court of Appeals is

Affirmed.

NOTES AND QUESTIONS

1. *Devil's Hole.* Devil's Hole was left behind when lakes during the Pleistocene Age receded 50,000 to 500,000 years ago. Other than the tiny pupfish, the only creatures residing in its 90–100 degree waters are snails and flatworms. The pupfish are about 250–500 in number, and live near the ten-foot mouth of the pool down to a depth of about ninety feet. The pupfish have been in residence at this location for over 20,000 years. Below the mouth of the pool is a dark network of caverns so vast that it has never been fully explored. At the mouth of the pool stands a monument which reads, "In the small pool at the bottom of this limestone cavern lives the entire population of Cyprinodon diabolis, one type of desert pupfish. These fish live in what is probably the most restricted environment of any animal in the world." Devil's Hole was made part of the Death Valley National Monument in 1952.

Monitoring the fluctuating water levels of the pool had been a continuing challenge. Because the entrance to the pool is located about forty miles from the main part of Death Valley National Monument, National Park Service rangers had to drive to and from Devil's Hole to check water levels several times daily. In later times, however, a wireless remote monitoring system, using satellite technology, was installed.

While the *Cappaert* decision saved the pupfish, Devil's Hole is not yet free of jeopardy. Nearby Las Vegas, the fastest growing metropolitan area in the nation, is competing for the pool's waters.

2. *Effect of Reservation.* Once federal water rights are reserved, state law cannot extinguish them. Supremacy Clause, U.S. CONST., art. VI, cl. 2.

3. *Congressional Intent.* *Cappaert* tells us that the legal test for federal withdrawal or reservation of water rights is congressional intent. Ideally, Congress should announce that intention, or lack thereof, in statutory text. Sometimes it will do so. *See, e.g.*, § 102(d), 100 P.L. 696; 102 Stat. 4571 (1988) (reserving water rights for the San Pedro National Riparian Conservation Area in Arizona); *see also* text preceding *Cappaert, supra.* On other occasions, Congress may clearly state its intention not to reserve water. *See, e.g.*, § 304, 100 P.L. 696, 102 Stat. 4576 (1988) (expressly declining to reserve water rights for the Hagerman Fossils Bed National Monument in Idaho, due to "unique circumstances").

Of course, *Cappaert* presented the question whether a statutory reservation of land might impliedly reserve water rights as well. In such a circumstance, discerning congressional intent is all the more difficult. Would you conjecture that the mere passage of a federal land management statute, an enactment unrelated to any formal withdrawal or reservation of specific public lands, might effect a reservation of water rights? Notably, one district court held that the enactment of the Wilderness Act of 1964 effected a reservation of federal water rights on the twenty-four wilderness areas administered by the Forest Service. *Sierra Club v. Lyng*, 661 F. Supp. 1490 (D. Colo. 1987). On review, the Tenth Circuit declined to examine the issue on ripeness grounds. *Sierra Club v. Yeutter*, 911 F.2d 1405 (10th Cir. 1990).

In *United States v. New Mexico*, 438 U.S. 696, 98 S. Ct. 3012 (1978), the Supreme Court decided the same issue with respect to the Multiple-Use Sustained-Yield Act of 1960, the legislation that empowers the U.S. Forest Service, part of the Department of Agriculture, to administer national forest lands. This statute expanded the permissible purposes for which lands in the national forest system are to be managed to include, in addition to timber production, recreation, grazing, watershed management, and fish and wildlife promotion. Did this legislation accomplish an implied reservation of water rights for these newly designated forest uses? In a 5-4 opinion, the Court said no: "Congress did not intend . . . [by its enactment of the Act] . . . to expand the reserved rights of the United States." *Accord United States v. Denver*, 656 P.2d 1, 26 (Colo. 1982) ("When Congress passed the [Multiple Use Sustained Yield Act], it was aware of the reserved rights doctrine. [citations omitted]. Congress, however, chose not to reserve additional water explicitly. In the face of its silence, we must assume that Congress intended the federal government to proceed like any other appropriator and to apply for or purchase water rights when there was a need for water."); *In re Snake River Adjudication*, 133 Idaho 525, 532, 988 P.2d 1199, 1206 (1999) ("[The Multiple-Use Sustained-Yield Act] was intended to broaden the purposes for which the national forests had been administered, but did not create a reservation of land and moreover, did not establish an express or implied reservation of water because the expanded purposes created . . . are merely supplemental and secondary.").

In dissent, Justice Powell, joined by Justices Brennan, White, and Marshall, disagreed:

> I do not agree . . . that the forests which Congress intended to "improve and protect" are the still, lifeless places envisioned by the Court. In my view, the forests consist of the birds, animals, and fish — the wildlife — that inhabit them, as well as the trees, flowers, shrubs and grasses. I therefore would hold that the United States is entitled to so much water as is necessary to sustain the wildlife of the forests, as well as the plants.

Id. at 719, 98 S. Ct. at 3023–24.

New Mexico is the most recent decision from the United States Supreme Court on these matters.

4.   *De facto Reservations.* A federal statute can reserve water rights *de facto* by limiting the use of federal lands. The Wilderness Act, *infra*, and the Endangered Species Act, *see* Chapter 7, *infra*, are apt examples of this.

5.   *Indian Reserved Water Rights.* In the landmark case of *Winters v. United States*, 207 U.S. 564, 28 S. Ct. 207 (1908), the question arose whether the federal government impliedly reserves water rights for American Indians when it reserves land for their occupancy. In *Winters*, a tribe of Indians living on the Ft. Belknap Reservation in Montana, and using the waters of the Milk River, objected when upstream defendants diverted the river's stream flow for their own purposes. Defendants claimed a right to divert the water under state law; the tribe claimed a prior right by virtue of an implied water rights reservation made on the tribe's behalf by the federal government when it set aside Ft. Belknap in 1888 for the tribe's use. To resolve the dispute, the Supreme Court examined the agreement that resulted in the creation of Ft. Belknap, and ruled for the tribe, largely on the theory that ambiguities in agreements and treaties with Indians should be resolved in their favor.

6.   *McCarran Amendment.* Federal reserved water rights questions make it to federal courts less frequently in the current day due to the McCarran Amendment, which consents to joinder of the United States in state court proceedings in "any suit (1) for the adjudication of rights to the use of water of a river system or other source, or (2) for the administration of such rights, where it appears the United States is the owner of or is in the process of acquiring water rights by appropriation under State law, by purchase, by exchange, or otherwise, and the United States is a necessary party to such suit." 43 U.S.C. § 666(a).

4.   The Wilderness Act of 1964

At the turn of the twentieth century, it became apparent to people like Theodore Roosevelt, Gifford Pinchot, and John Muir that certain of the federal lands should be reserved for the recreational use of members of the public. This recognition was the genesis of a new "conservation ethic" which eventually culminated in the establishment of national parks, monuments, and other recreational lands. But the new ethic did not stop there. Fifty years later, this heightened respect for nature qua nature produced the wilderness movement. The idea behind wilderness is definitely not recreation. The idea behind wilderness, rather, is the simple — some would say elegant — notion that the best use of some lands is to not use them at all, that to render land commercially worthless is to secure its highest value. That the wilderness movement could take root in a nation dedicated to productivity and individuality is one of the truly remarkable political stories of our national history.

President Theodore Roosevelt and John Muir, founder of the Sierra Club, at Glacier Point, Yosemite Valley, California, 1903. Library of Congress.

The culmination of this far-reaching movement is the Wilderness Act of 1964, 16 U.S.C. §§ 113–1136. The Act is the legal tool by which federal lands can be preserved, as distinct from conserved. The Act has a tone and feel rarely found in legislative products:

> A wilderness, in contrast with those areas where man and his own works dominate the landscape, is hereby recognized as an area where the earth and its community of life are untrammeled by man, where man himself is a visitor who does not remain. An area of wilderness is further defined to mean in this chapter an area of undeveloped Federal land retaining its primeval character and influence, without permanent improvements or human habitation, which is protected and managed so as to preserve its

natural conditions and which (1) generally appears to have been affected primarily by the forces of nature, with the imprint of man's work substantially unnoticeable; (2) has outstanding opportunities for solitude or a primitive and unconfined type of recreation; (3) has at least five thousand acres of land or is of sufficient size as to make practicable its preservation and use in an unimpaired condition; and (4) may also contain ecological, geological, or other features of scientific, educational, scenic, or historical value.

16 U.S.C. § 1131(c).

What is the story of the Wilderness Act? Prior to 1960, the authority of federal agencies (as distinct from the President) to withdraw lands was somewhat in doubt. That ambiguity had not deterred the Secretary of Agriculture, however, from engaging in the practice of withdrawing forest lands for wilderness purposes. Predictably, the legality of these "administrative wilderness areas" was tested in the courts. The litigation produced a victory for the Secretary. *McMichael v. United States*, 355 F.2d 283 (9th Cir. 1965). For devotees of wilderness, though, administrative wilderness areas were not good enough. For one thing, they lacked permanence: they could be undesignated as easily as they were designated. Beyond that, there were no assurances federal land management agencies would be pro-wilderness in any event, namely because public lands can be commercially valuable. Administrative wilderness areas, moreover, could be made subject to a variety of restrictions that would dilute the impact of wilderness designation.

As such, wilderness proponents wanted *statutory* wilderness protection. The first inroad in this direction came in the form of the Multiple-Use Sustained Yield Act of 1960, 16 U.S.C.A. § 528 et seq., which ratified the Secretary of Agriculture's administrative wilderness areas. The zenith would come four years later, with passage of the Wilderness Act.

The Wilderness Act began by making previously designated wilderness areas, 54 in number and 9.1 million acres in area, the first components of what is called the National Wilderness Preservation System. At the same time, it reserved the power to designate new wilderness areas exclusively for Congress. 16 U.S.C. § 1131(a). The statute went on to require the Forest Service to study another 5.4 million acres to see if those lands warranted inclusion in the System. It required the Department of Interior to undertake similar studies respecting park and refuge lands under its control. Reports on the suitability of these "wilderness study areas" were to be sent to the president 10 years thereafter.[6]

---

[6] Resource lands controlled by the Bureau of Land Management were not included, perhaps because these lands were thought to be the least valuable of the federal holdings. Notably, the Boundary Waters Canoe Area of Superior National Forest in Minnesota was excepted from coverage as well. The BWCA was left to be managed by administrative regulations "in accordance with the general purpose of maintaining, without unnecessary restrictions on other uses, including that of timber, the primitive character of the area." 16 U.S.C. § 1133(d)(5). Motorboat usage in the BWCA was expressly ratified. *Id.* In short, the Act maintained the tradition of multiple use in the BWCA. Minnesota Public Interest Research Group v. Butz, 541 F.2d 1292 (8th Cir. 1976). A separate Boundary Waters Canoe Area Wilderness Act was passed in 1978, repealing former Section 1133(d)(5) and terminating timber contracts one year after enactment.

Under the terms of the Act, any federal lands can be designated as wilderness. Once designated, wilderness lands continue to be managed by the same agency with management responsibility before designation. 16 U.S.C. § 1131(b). But management of wilderness lands is decidedly in pursuit of a much different goal. The goal is preservation. Section 1133(c) of the Act makes the point unambiguously: "there shall be no commercial enterprise and no permanent road within any wilderness area designated by this chapter and, except as necessary to meet minimum requirements for the administration of the area for the purpose of this chapter (including measures required in emergencies involving the health and safety of persons within the area), there shall be no temporary road, no use of motor vehicles, motorized equipment or motorboats, no landing of aircraft, no other form of mechanical transport, and no structure or installation within any such area."[7] The Act grandfathers in any uses in place at the time of designation. 16 U.S.C. § 1133(d).

Lands are added to the wilderness system in either of two ways. Sometimes Congress simply adds the new addition to the list of sites directly governed by the Wilderness Act. The list may be found at 16 U.S.C.A. § 1132 and the "Note" that follows it. On many occasions, Congress creates new wilderness areas by separate federal legislation. These separate bills may refer to the Wilderness Act but may add differing requirements to govern the new addition.

There are relatively few judicial decisions on this subject, mainly because flat prohibitions leave little room for litigation. But cases come along still, especially when wilderness management conflicts with recreational or other uses on contiguous or nearby non-wilderness land.

STUPAK-THRALL v. UNITED STATES
70 F.3d 881 (6th Cir. 1995)

[The United States Forest Service of the Department of Agriculture imposed surface use restrictions for Crooked Lake, located in Michigan's Upper Peninsula near the Wisconsin border. The vast majority of the Lake's shoreline, about 95%, lies within the Sylvania Wilderness Area. The Forest Service adopted "Amendment No. 1" which prohibited, among other things, the use of "sail-powered watercraft," "watercraft designed for or used as floating living quarters," and "nonburnable disposable food and beverage containers."]

KAREN NELSON MOORE, CIRCUIT JUDGE:

Plaintiffs own a small piece of land abutting the lake's northern shore, and, therefore, like the federal government itself, are riparian to the lake. They argue

---

[7] Not that humans are entirely banned. The Act also provided that "[n]othing in this chapter shall prevent within national forest wilderness areas any activity, including prospecting, for the purpose of gathering information about mineral or other resources, information about mineral or other resources, if such activity is carried on in a manner compatible with the preservation of the wilderness environment." 16 U.S.C. § 1133(d)(2). The Act also authorized continued mining on forest lands designated as wilderness until midnight, December 31, 1983. 16 U.S.C. § 1133(d)(3). Finally, the protective provisions of the Act were made "subject to existing private rights." 16 U.S.C. § 1133(c).

More than 12 million people visit wilderness areas annually.

that, in their capacity as riparians, they have rights to use the surface of the Lake in the ways prohibited by the Forest Service. Specifically, they argue that the Forest Service's actions, taken under authority of the federal Wilderness Act, cannot stand, because the Wilderness Act itself requires the protection of valid existing rights:

> Except as specifically provided for in this chapter, and *subject to existing private rights*, there shall be no commercial enterprise and no permanent road within any wilderness area designated by this chapter and, except as necessary to meet minimum requirements for the administration of the area for purposes of this chapter, . . . there shall be no temporary road, no use of motor vehicles, motorized equipment or motorboats, no landing of aircraft, no other form of mechanical transport, and no structure or installation within any such area.

Wilderness Act, Sec. 1133(c) (emphasis added).

Plaintiffs argue as well that the federal act which specifically created the wilderness area, the Michigan Wilderness Act, contains the same kind of provision, its terms being made "subject to valid existing rights." Pub. Law 100-184, Sec. 5; 101 Stat. 1274, 1275 76 (1987). As their riparian rights include the right to boating and other recreational uses of riparian waters, plaintiffs contend the regulatory restrictions must fail.

There can be little question that Congress has the power to regulate Crooked Lake in the manner described by Amendment No. 1's management prescriptions. The Property Clause gives Congress broad authority to decide what are "needful" regulations "respecting" federal property. *Kleppe* instructs: "We must remain mindful that, while courts must eventually pass upon them, determinations under the Property Clause are entrusted primarily to the judgment of Congress." 426 U.S. at 536. In this case, the management prescriptions at issue are clearly tailored toward protecting federal property. The avowed purpose of the prohibition against sailboats, houseboats, and "nonburnable" food containers is "to protect and perpetuate wilderness character and values." Wilderness Management Amendment No. 1, IV 5.1-1. There is no doubt that the restrictions assist in protecting the wilderness character of the area. The Wilderness Act itself states that "wilderness" is defined as "an area where the earth and its community of life are untrammeled by man . . . retaining its primeval character and influence, without permanent improvements or human habitation." 16 U.S.C. Sec. 1131(c). Certainly, Congress could rationally conclude that certain forms of mechanical transport, including sailboats and houseboats, should be excluded from the Sylvania Wilderness in order to preserve the "wilderness character" of the property. The protection of wilderness character is a valid objective under the Property Clause to the same extent that Congress's objectives in enacting the Wild Free-Roaming Horses and Burros Act in *Kleppe*, "for achievement of an ecological balance on the public lands," were valid. 426 U.S. at 535. Just as Congress's authority may sometimes extend to purely private property in order to provide adequate protection of public property, so in this instance may federal regulations encompass shared property rights between the United States and private owners, at least to the extent that the regulations are designed to govern the portion of the water surface contained completely within the borders of government-owned land. This at a minimum is what the Property Clause allows — regulation to protect not only the government's own riparian interest in the lake, but also its interest in the surrounding national wilderness.

. . . .

III [omitted]

. . . .

IV

What distinguishes this case from others applying the Property Clause is that the statutory scheme for the federal wilderness areas appears to make explicit room for state law. Therefore, although the Forest Service might otherwise have the delegated authority to regulate in line with the Property Clause, Congress in the Wilderness Act and MWA expressly made such regulation "subject to existing private rights" or "subject to valid existing rights." In order to determine how much of a limitation this might be on the Forest Service, we must examine the scope of such "existing" rights under state law.

As indicated earlier, riparian rights are not absolute. [The court at this point discounted the idea that federal power might be found in the common law riparian "reasonable use" doctrine, which allows riparian owners certain recreational rights. In the court's language, "the 'reasonable use' doctrine itself only makes sense when one riparian owner challenges another's use as unreasonable and the court makes a subsequent determination of reasonableness. It is inapplicable when one riparian proprietor unilaterally decides to ban certain uses of others, whether or not the uses themselves are unreasonable, and whether or not the banning proprietor actually has the power to do so. Indeed, the federal government's ability to impose restrictions does not stem from its status as a fellow riparian proprietor; it stems from its status as a sovereign."]***

Instead, we find that Amendment No. 1's management prescriptions are permissible because they constitute a legitimate exercise of the sovereign's police power. The Michigan Supreme Court has explicitly held that local governments may regulate their citizens' riparian rights pursuant to their inherent police powers. In *Miller v. Fabius Township Board*, 366 Mich. 250, 114 N.W.2d 205 (Mich. 1962), the court allowed time restrictions on waterskiing. In *Square Lake Hills Condo. Assn. v. Bloomfield Township*, 437 Mich. 310, 471 N.W.2d 321 (Mich. 1991), the court allowed regulation of boat docking and launching. In *Square Lake Hills*, especially, the court made it clear that plaintiffs' recreational riparian rights were subject to regulation for the protection of "health, safety, and welfare" of the general public. *Id.* at 322. The federal government's actions here are similar to those of the townships in *Miller* and *Square Lake Hills*, except that the "general public" in this case is the nation at large instead of the local community, and the power now comes from a highly particularized source, the Property Clause, rather than from the state's inherent powers. *Kleppe* in fact makes the comparison explicit: "The general Government doubtless has a power over its own property analogous to the police power of the several States, and the extent to which it may go in the exercise of such power is measured by the exigencies of the particular case." 426 U.S. at 540, *citing Camfield*, 167 U.S. at 525. *Kleppe* continues by stating that "Congress exercises the powers both of a proprietor and of a legislature over the public domain." 426 U.S. at 540.

Thus, the Forest Service possesses a power delegated to it by Congress that is "analogous to the police power," and its exercise of this federal power does not violate Congress's express limitation deferring to "existing" state law rights in the wilderness acts, so long as it does not exceed the bounds of permissible police power regulation under state law. The management prescriptions of Amendment No. 1 are clearly valid restrictions within the state law police power. According to *Square Lake Hills*, validity depends upon reasonableness, which in turn "depends upon the particular facts of each case." 471 N.W.2d at 324. "The test for determining whether an ordinance is reasonable requires us to assess the existence of a rational relationship between the exercise of police power and the public health, safety, morals, or general welfare in a particular manner in a given case." Id. (citations omitted). *See also People v. McKendrick*, 188 Mich. App. 128, 468 N.W.2d 903, 908 (Mich. Ct. App. 1991). As has already been noted, Amendment No. 1's purpose of preserving wilderness character is undoubtedly a proper aim under the Property Clause's police power and under Congress's delegation to the Forest Service, and the prohibition of certain forms of mechanical transport and certain types of food containers on Crooked Lake is certainly rationally related to achieving this goal. The prohibitions are also a reasonable means of doing so. They do not affect plaintiffs' rights to "natural" riparian uses, only plaintiffs' "artificial" uses — in this case (as in *Miller* and *Square Lake Hills*), for "commercial profit and recreation." *Thompson*, 154 N.W.2d at 484. Plaintiffs do not argue that they need to use sailboats or houseboats in order to subsist, or even that they need them for transportation. In fact, as the district court found, "there is no evidence that sailboats or houseboats, which are now banned, have ever been used on the lake." 843 F. Supp. at 334. Moreover, the determination that regulations should only apply to the area of the lake lying within the wilderness shoreline provides another reasonable limit on the scope of Amendment No.1's prescriptions. Given the "minimal impact on plaintiffs' riparian uses of Crooked Lake," 843 F. Supp. at 334, we conclude that the Forest Service's restrictions here are a valid exercise of the police power under state law, and they are therefore a valid exercise of the police power conferred on the Forest Service by the Property Clause and limited by Congress's express reservation for state law rights in the wilderness acts. We reiterate that we do not refer to state law for the sake of determining the scope of Congress's regulatory power under the Property Clause. State law only affects the Forest Service's authority here, and it does so only because Congress has placed a specific constraint on the Forest Service's regulatory authority, requiring that it be exercised "subject to" plaintiffs' "existing" state law property rights.

If sailboats and houseboats have indeed never been used on Crooked Lake, one could justifiably ask why this action was even brought in the first place. The answer, it appears, is that plaintiffs are going after a bigger fish Amendment No. 5, which regulates motorboat use on wilderness lakes. The Forest Service had not issued Amendment No. 5 when this case was originally filed, and the amendment does not go into effect until April 1996. Nevertheless, at various points in their brief, plaintiffs intertwine the Amendment No. 5 issue with their discussion of Amendment No. 1, and they use a significant amount of space to attack the merits of the motorboat restrictions. We decline plaintiffs' invitation to decide the motorboat issue, as it has not been properly presented in this court. Plaintiffs cannot short-circuit the administrative process by challenging Forest Service regulations here, before they have been decided upon in the appropriate agency proceedings. *See Lavapies v. Bowen*, 883 F.2d 465, 468 (6th Cir. 1989) (*citing Weinberger v. Sal*, 422 U.S. 749, 95 S. Ct. 2457, 45 L. Ed. 2d 522 (1975)). The Secretary of Agriculture has set forth specific appeals procedures for land and resource management plans in 36 C.F.R. Sec. 217, and plaintiffs' appeal of Amendment No. 5 is currently making its way through this administrative pipeline. As plaintiffs have failed to exhaust their administrative remedies, we will not address their arguments regarding the motorboat restrictions.

[Remainder of opinion omitted.]

NOTES

1. ***The National Wilderness Preservation System.*** According to the National Wilderness Preservation System Database, the National Wilderness Preservation System contains 757 units comprising more than 109 million acres. *See* http://www.wilderness.net/index.cfm?fuse=NWPS&sec=fastfacts. Almost five percent of federal land is wilderness. The smallest wilderness is a six-acre site at Pelican Island, Florida. The largest single wilderness area is the Wrangell-St. Elias wilderness in Alaska, which exceeds nine million acres in size. States with the most wildernesses by number are California, Arizona, Colorado, and Nevada. By acreage, Alaska leads the pack, with 53% all wilderness located there. States with no wilderness areas are Connecticut, Delaware, Iowa, Kansas, Maryland, and Rhode Island.

A significant addition to the ranks of federal wilderness, accomplished by use of independent legislation, occurred on October 31, 1994, when President Bill Clinton signed the California Desert Protection Act. The Act designated as wilderness about 7.7 million acres land managed by the Bureau of Land Management and Forest Service in that state. It added about three million acres to the national park system as well, including the Death Valley and Joshua Tree National Parks and the Mojave National Preserve. In its specific provisions, the Act permits hunting and grazing on the wilderness lands. Then-Secretary of Interior Bruce Babbitt called the legislation "America's most significant environmental victory in more than a decade."

2. ***The Archeological Resources Protection Act.*** A federal statute analogous to the Wilderness Act, in that it operates to insulate public lands from human intrusion, is the Archeological Resources Protection Act of 1979, 16 U.S.C. §§ 470aa–470ll. The statute prohibits unauthorized "removal, damage, alteration, or defacement" of archeological resources on public lands. 16 U.S.C. § 470ee(a). Archeological resources include pottery, basketry, bottles, tools, graves, rock paintings, human skeletal remains, and other items of interest. 16 U.S.C. § 470bb(1). The Act provides that "no person may sell, purchase, exchange, transport, receive, or offer to sell, purchase or exchange" any such artifact. 16

U.S.C. § 470ee(b). Violators may face criminal fines in amounts not exceeding $10,000, or incarceration for not more than one year, or both, 16 U.S.C. § 470ee(d), as well as civil penalties. 16 U.S.C. § 470ff. Interestingly, ignorance of the law can be a defense in a criminal prosecution under the statute. *See, e.g., United States v. Lynch*, 233 F.3d 1139, 1142 (9th Cir. 2000) (quoting Representative Stewart Udall: "Certainly, no sponsor of this legislation and probably no reasonable person would want some overzealous bureaucrat to arrest a Boy Scout who finds an arrowhead along a trail or a purple bottle out in the desert. . . . The thrust of this act is not to harass the casual visitor who happens to find some exposed artifact, but to stop the needless, careless, and intentional destruction of archeological sites and organized and intentional theft of the valuable remains of previous civilizations.").

D. FEDERAL LAND MANAGEMENT

Our review thus far has surveyed the source of federal power over public lands and the exercise of those powers both to dispose of federal lands and, in a reactive mode, to arrest that disposition. Let us now take a look at federal land management in the current day. At present, federal lands are pledged to a variety of uses. In some cases, such as with national parks, a single, aka "dominant" use (recreation) is all that is allowed by law. (In the case of wilderness, no permanent use is allowed at all.) But for the vast majority of federal lands, the management regime is not "dominant use," but "multiple use." As the name suggests, the idea is to allow lands to serve the variety of uses for which they are suited. This idea may sound good in theory, but it can be exceedingly difficult to pull off in practice. Recreation and mining, for example, do not easily mix.

In this final part of Chapter 5, we look to the management regimes that govern the public lands. This review entails, first, an introduction to the four federal agencies with land management responsibilities, and second, a review of the legal principles that govern: (a) mineral lands, managed chiefly by the Bureau of Land Management of the Department of Interior; (b) forest lands, managed chiefly by the Forest Service of the Department of Agriculture; (c) grazing lands, managed chiefly by the Bureau of Land Management; and (d) recreation and wildlife lands, managed by the National Park Service and the Fish and Wildlife Service of the Department of Interior.

1. Managing Agencies

As mentioned above, the federal agencies with significant management authority over the public lands are four in number:

a. The Forest Service of the U.S. Department of Agriculture

b. The Bureau of Land Management (BLM) of the U.S. Department of the Interior

c. The Fish and Wildlife Service of the U.S. Department of the Interior

d. The National Park Service of the U.S. Department of the Interior.

The Forest Service

As its name indicates, the Forest Service is the executive entity with management authority over the national forests, which comprise approximately one-fourth of all public lands. National forest land is located in overwhelming proportion in the western states, and especially Alaska.

The Forest Service operates under the authority of three major statutory enactments. They are the Organic Act of 1897, 16 U.S.C. § 475 et seq., which was the agency's first organic authority, the Multiple Use-Sustained Yield Act of 1960, 16 U.S.C. § 528 et seq., and the Forest and Rangeland Renewable Resources Planning Act of 1974, 16 U.S.C. § 1600 et seq., better known in its expanded form as the National Forest Management Act. Under the Organic Act, national forests were managed largely for purposes of timber production. The Multiple Use-Sustained Yield Act enlarged the universe of uses of national forests to include outdoor recreation, range use, watershed management, and fish and wildlife maintenance. The 1960 legislation also declared a "sustained yield" management regime which was described as "the achievement and maintenance in perpetuity of a high-level annual or regular periodic output of the various renewable resources of the national forests without impairment of the productivity of the land." Overall, the MUSYA called for management of all "the various renewable surface resources of the national forests" to best serve the needs of the American people. Section 4(b), 16 U.S.C. § 531(b).

The Multiple Use-Sustained Yield Act also required the Forest Service to prepare a multiple use plan for each forest. Completed plans serve as a guide for future agency management decisions. The National Forest Management Act enlarged the Forest Service's planning responsibility by requiring more long-term planning. Under the NFMA, the Forest Service is obligated to prepare detailed plans spanning a decade in length. *See infra.*

The Bureau of Land Management

The BLM manages approximately 60 percent of onshore federal lands, or about 470 million acres. Almost two-thirds of the BLM lands are located in Alaska, and virtually the entirety of the remainder is found in the eleven western states. A good deal of this land is open for public use and resource exploitation, including grazing.

The BLM also takes a dominant role in managing oil resources, mainly oil reserves, in offshore federal lands.

The BLM does not have cohesive organic legislation governing its management operations. Thus, for varying purposes at varying locations, the BLM will take action as authorized by the Stock Raising Homestead Act, Act of Dec. 29, 1916, 39 Stat. 862 (1916), the General Mining Law of 1872, 30 U.S.C. § 22 et seq., the Mineral Leasing Act of 1920, 30 U.S.C. § 181 et seq., the Taylor Grazing Act of 1934, Act of June 28, 1934, 43 U.S.C. § 315 et seq., and other measures. A single enactment that best qualifies for the status of organic authority, however, is the Federal Land Policy and Management Act, 43 U.S.C. §§ 1701 1782. Enacted in 1976, FLPMA represents a congressional attempt to bring some consistency and coherence to BLM public lands management. Like the NFMA, FLPMA is premised on management of federal lands for multiple uses. *See infra.*

The Fish and Wildlife Service

A subunit of the Department of Interior, the Fish and Wildlife Service is in charge of the National Wildlife Refuge System, an array of refuges totaling more than 30 million acres. As their name indicates, wildlife refuges are land areas set aside for the protection and conservation of fish and wildlife. Since its inception, the FWS has managed wildlife refuges under authority of the National Wildlife Refuge System Administration Act of 1966, 16 U.S.C. § 668dd et seq. Since 1997, however, its major organic authority has been the National Wildlife Refuge System Improvement Act ("NWRSIA"). The NWRSIA was enacted to resolve controversies regarding conflicting multiple uses of refuges. *See infra.*

The National Park Service

The National Park Service administers the National Park System, which spans more than 23 million acres of land. Park lands are in place for recreational purposes. The NPS manages national parks under authority of the National Park Service Act of 1916, 16 U.S.C. § 1 et seq., which stipulated the governing purposes as follows:

> To conserve the scenery and the natural and historic objects and the wildlife therein and to provide for the enjoyment of the same in such manner and by such means as will leave them unimpaired for the enjoyment of future generations.

16 U.S.C. § 1.

The pieces that make up the national park system include natural, historic, and recreational areas. The natural areas are the national parks and monuments. National monuments are designated for their scientific significance under authority of a 1906 statute, the American Antiquities Preservation Act, 16 U.S.C. § 431. Historic areas are diverse lands having historical or archeological significance. And recreation areas encompass an array of lands, including national seashores, lakeshores, scenic parkways, wild and scenic rivers, and other such parcels. *See infra.*

2. Management Regimes

a. Mineral Lands

i. The General Mining Act of 1872

Early legislation allowed for miners, by their own independent actions, to secure rights to minerals on the public lands. The major statute creating this self-initiation method of mineral rights acquisition was the General Mining Act of 1872, 30 U.S.C. §§ 22–39, commonly referred to as the "General Mining Law" or "GML." In this subsection, we will examine how this statute operates. Note that "operates" is in the present tense: the GML is still good law.

The General Mining Act of 1872 is the major statutory provision governing the rights of individuals to secure so-called hard rock minerals from the public lands. The GML provides that, with some exceptions, "all valuable mineral deposits in lands belonging to the United States shall be free and open to exploration and purchase, and the lands in which the minerals are found shall be open to occupation and purchase, by U.S. citizens." 30 U.S.C. § 22. This provision allows for mineral extraction on federal lands "held for disposal under the land laws." Not all federal lands fall into this category. "Only where the United States has indicated that the lands are held for disposal under the land laws does the section apply; and it never applies where the United States directs that the disposal be only under other laws." *Oklahoma v. Texas*, 258 U.S. 574, 600, 42 S. Ct. 406, 416 (1922). *See also Federal Power Comm'n v. Oregon*, 349 U.S. 435, 448, 75 S. Ct. 832, 840 (1955) (*quoting United States v. O'Donnell*, 303 U.S. 501, 510, 58 S. Ct. 708, 714 (1938) ("it is a familiar principle of public land law that statutes providing generally for disposal of the public domain are inapplicable to lands which are not unqualifiedly subject to sale and disposition because they have been appropriated to some other purpose")).

Beyond that, not all "minerals" are subject to the GML. What are minerals? Neither the Act nor the BLM tells us. The term, moreover, is maddeningly imprecise: the *Oxford Dictionary* defines it, first, as "any substance which is obtained by mining," and second, as "any natural substance that is neither animal or vegetable." THE SHORTER OXFORD ENGLISH DICTIONARY 1327 (1973). *See also* Braunstein, *All That Glitters: Discovering the Meaning of Mineral in the Mining Law of 1872*, 21 LAND & WATER L. REV. 297 (1986). What is a mineral for purposes of the GML remains a question even to this day. In one relatively recent case, the United States Supreme Court decided that *water* is not a mineral for purposes of the GML, not because water could not be, but because Congress did not intend to include water under the statute. *Andrus v. Charlestone Stone Products Co.*, 436 U.S. 604, 98 S. Ct. 2002 (1978) (Congress intended to protect the pre-existing water rights regime; to conclude otherwise would "def[y] common sense") *Andrus*, 436 U.S. at 614, 98 S. Ct. at 2008. For more on water rights, see Chapter 8.

Such matters aside, at its enactment the GML applied to all "minerals" except for coal, which was already the subject of disposition under the Coal Lands Act of 1864, 13 Stat. 205, as amended by the Coal Lands Act of 1873, 17 Stat. 607. (In succeeding years, Congress by legislative action has withdrawn an array of specific minerals from the ambit of the statute. These later statutes alter the reach of the GML, but not its design. *See infra*.)

How does one go about securing property rights to minerals on federal land under the GML? The first step is to "locate" a claim. Mineral claims can be lode (relating to embedded minerals) or placer (relating to minerals found in loose sediments). (Non-mineral claims can be for millsites (for acreages, not to exceed five acres, necessary to facilitate mineral extraction and related activities) and tunnel sites (to facilitate discoveries and extractions of minerals).) To "locate" a claim, miners physically enter federal land in search of minerals and stake out the find. They need not identify the minerals they seek at this time; identification is required, however, at a later stage. Location must be made in accordance with rules of the applicable mining district, which rules govern "the location, manner of recording, [and the] amount of work necessary to hold possession of a mining claim." 30 U.S.C. § 28. Each location must be distinctly marked. *Id.* State law, to the extent it does not conflict with federal law, may also impose restrictions on the location process.

The GML gives protection to miners engaged in locating and prospecting by the doctrine of *pedis possessio*, which stipulates that the party making the first good faith entrance onto federal land for purposes of making a discovery shall be given priority over those arriving subsequently. When a "junior locator" contests the right of a "senior locator" to prospect, the latter can prevail by showing either a first-in-time right to possession or by demonstrating the junior locator's entry was not undertaken in good faith. Good faith has been described as "honesty of purpose and absence of intent to defraud." *Goldfield Mines, Inc. v. Hand*, 147 Ariz. 498, 505, 711 P.2d 637, 644 (Ct. App. 1985). It has been held that good faith is lacking where a junior seeks possession solely on the basis of defects in a senior's claims. *See, e.g., Columbia Standard Corp. v. Ranchers Exploration & Dev't., Inc.*, 468 F.2d 547 (10th Cir. 1972). To successfully invoke the protections of the doctrine of *pedis possessio*, the senior must be in actual occupancy of the land. *Id.* The senior must be working toward a discovery of "valuable mineral deposits" as well. 30 U.S.C. § 22. A relaxation in occupancy opens the door for a peaceful entry by another. *Goldfield Mines*, 147 Ariz. 498, *supra*. Rights secured by this mechanism have been held to be transferrable. *United Western Minerals Co. v. Hannsen*, 147 Colo. 272, 363 P.2d 677 (1961).

Minerals, once discovered, may only be secured under the GML if they are "valuable." Whether they are valuable has been the subject of a fair measure of litigation. The major case on the issue is *United States v. Coleman*, 390 U.S. 599, 88 S. Ct. 1327 (1968). The case examined a determination of the Secretary of Interior to the effect that, for mineral to be "valuable," they must able to be "extracted, removed, and marketed at a profit.' " *Coleman*, 390 U.S. at 601, 88 S. Ct at 1330. This so-called "marketability test" was viewed by petitioners in the case as a departure from the earlier test, known as the "prudent man" test. Held the Court:

> . . . The Secretary's determination that the quartzite deposits did not qualify as valuable mineral deposits because the stone could not be marketed at a profit does no violence to the statute. Indeed, the marketability test is an admirable effort to identify with greater precision and objectivity the factors relevant to a determination that a mineral deposit is "valuable." It is a logical complement to the "prudent-man test" which the Secretary has been using to interpret the mining laws since 1894. Under this "prudent-man test" in order to qualify as "valuable mineral deposits," the discovered deposits must be of such a character that "a person of ordinary prudence would be justified in the further expenditure of his labor and means, with a reasonable prospect of success, in developing a valuable mine. . . . " *Castle v. Womble*, 19 L.D. 455, 457 (1894). This Court has approved the prudent-man formulation and interpretation on numerous occasions. See, for example, *Chrisman v. Miller*, 197 U.S. 313, 322; *Cameron v. United States*, 252 U.S. 450, 459; *Best v. Humboldt Placer Mining Co.*, 371 U.S. 334, 335 336. Under the mining laws Congress has made public lands available to people for the purpose of mining valuable mineral deposits and not for other purposes. The obvious intent was to reward and encourage the discovery of minerals that are valuable in an economic sense. Minerals which no prudent man will extract because there is no demand for them at a price higher than the cost of extraction and transportation are hardly economically valuable. Thus, profitability is an important consideration in applying the prudent-man test, and the marketability test which the Secretary has used here merely recognizes this fact.

The marketability test also has the advantage of throwing light on a claimant's intention, a matter which is inextricably bound together with valuableness. For evidence that a mineral deposit is not of economic value and cannot in all likelihood be operated at a pro t may well suggest that a claimant seeks the land for other purposes. Indeed, as the Government points out, the facts of this case — the thousands of dollars and hours spent building a home on 720 acres in a highly scenic national forest located two hours from Los Angeles, the lack of an economically feasible market for the stone, and the immense quantities of identical stone found in the area outside the claims — might well be thought to raise a substantial question as to respondent Coleman's real intention.

Coleman, 390 U.S. at 602–03, 88 S. Ct. at 1330–31.

Accordingly, in the Court's view, the marketability test is merely a "refinement" of the prudent man test. *Coleman*, 390 U.S. at 603, 88 S. Ct. at 1330.

Upon making a valuable discovery, locators must post a notice at the site, and file a mining claim at the proper government office. The filing must contain the name of the locator, the date of the location, and a description of the claim. Locators must invest at least $100 per year in labor or improvements on each claim. 30 U.S.C. § 26.

Once a claim is recorded, the claimant has an "unpatented mining right." Having an unpatented mining right means the miner has exclusive possession of (a) surface rights, (b) intraliminal rights (veins and lodes lying inside of the surface lines as those lines extend downward vertically), and (c) extralateral rights (rights to follow a vein or lode downward even as it extends beyond the subterranean dimensions of the overlying parcel). *See, e.g., The Wilderness Society v. Dombeck*, 168 F.3d 367 (9th Cir. 1999). The right is "property" in a real sense, and accordingly, may be sold, mortgaged, taxed, inherited, and otherwise used by the holder of the interest. It also enjoys the protections of the Takings Clause. *See, e.g., United States v. Shumway*, 199 F.3d 1093, 1103 (9th Cir. 1999) ("The owner of a mining claim owns property, and is not a mere social guest of the Department of the Interior to be shooed out the door when the Department chooses."). There are no requirements for payment of royalties to the government for hardrock minerals produced from the land. There are no requirements in the GML for the reclaiming of sites when mining activity is completed.

But the unpatented mining right is not unlimited. The holder of the mining right possesses the land only for mining-related purposes: the "right of enjoyment which Congress intended to grant extends only to mining uses." *United States v. Rizzinelli*, 182 F. 675 (D. Idaho 1910). Beyond that, the right of possession does not include the right to exclude the public from pursuit of normal recreational activities. *See e.g., United States v. Curtis-Nevada Mines, Inc.*, 611 F.2d. 1277 (9th Cir. 1980).

Miners need not stop with the unpatented mining right. While not required, and not necessary in many cases, locators may obtain patents to located lands. 30 U.S.C. § 29. Once a patent application is received, the right to a patent accrues, so long as the application itself comports with all applicable legal requirements and is accompanied by the appropriate fee. *See, e.g., United States v. Shumway*, 199 F.3d 1093 (9th Cir. 1999). The patent review process involves two stages. First is the mineral examination stage, during which the applicant's compliance with the mining laws is verified. The second stage is "secretarial review." Instituted in 1993, this stage assures that patent issuances come personally from the Secretary of the Interior. The Department has a duty under the "rule of reason" to issue patents without undue delay. In this regard "reasonable means expeditious." *Independence Mining Co. v. Babbitt*, 885 F. Supp. 1356, 1361 (D. Nev. 1995). Yet, even a five-year wait may not be sufficient to compel issuance of the "truly extraordinary measure of a writ of mandamus." *Babbitt*, 885 F. Supp. at 1364. Once a patent is received, the recipient must file annually and show evidence of assessment work or at least of intention to hold the claim. Issuance of a patent typically creates in the patentholder a fee simple absolute interest in the parcel for which the patent is issued. Because of that, some patented sites are no longer used for mining, having been transformed into ski resorts or other recreational facilities. Patented lands are subject to state taxation, land use controls, and other such restrictions, to the same extent as other interests in property.

NOTES AND QUESTIONS

1. *GML and NEPA.* Does the issuance of a patent under the GML require the preparation of an EIS under NEPA? *See, e.g., State of South Dakota v. Andrus,* 614 F.2d 1190 (8th Cir.), *cert. denied,* 449 U.S. 822 (1980) (no EIS is necessary, since the issuance of a patent is a nondiscretionary act).

2. *GML Today.* Despite the restrictions on mining, it is widely agreed that the General Mining Law has been, and remains, a boon for miners. Any private citizen or corporation can patent land for bargain basement prices, historically not more than $5 an acre. A particularly illustrative example: on March 16, 1994, under the provisions of the GML, then-Secretary of Interior Bruce Babbitt signed over 1,793 acres of federal land in Nevada, estimated to contain $10 billion in gold, to a domestic subsidiary of a foreign company. The government expected to receive less than $10,000 in fees from the recipient company. Babbitt called the transaction "the biggest ripoff since the Yankees stole Babe Ruth from the Red Sox for pocket change." The Director of the Office of Management and Budget lamented the loss of such valuable public resources "for less money than they charge NBA players for fighting during a game."

Still, as a general matter, the mining of hardrock minerals on federal land is in decline. There has been a serious downturn in production due to market forces. A precipitous decline occurred in 1992 as well, when an annual fee of $100 per claim was legislated. Pub. L. No. 102-381, 106 Stat. 374, 1378 79 (1992). By operation of law, over 400,000 claims were voided after the fees were imposed. Since that time, the number of mining claims in force has remained at about 300,000.

3. *Environmental Protection on Federal Mining Lands.* Mining rights are subject to independent government regulation, like any other property interest. The government, therefore, can regulate mining activity to protect the environment and for other legitimate purposes. Is regulation of mining on public land needed? Note that federal lands are strewn with abandoned mining sites which have never been cleaned up: by one estimate, there are more than 557,000 of these. These sites cause significant contamination of surface and ground water. Abandoned mining sites release vast amounts of toxic chemicals, including mercury, hydrogen, cyanide gas, heavy metals, and arsenic. The cost of cleaning these sites has been estimated to range between $32 billion and $71 billion. One study identified mining, along with grazing, as the most destructive federally subsidized use of federal land. *See Taking from the Taxpayer: Public Subsidies for Natural Resource Development,* House Natural Resources Committee, Aug. 8, 1994.

The BLM acted to regulate mining for environmental purposes in 1980. 43 C.F.R. Part 3809 ("surface management regulations" or "3809 regulations"). Its primary authority for the 3809 regulations was the Federal Land Policy and Management Act of 1976, 43 U.S.C. § 1701 et seq. FLPMA obligates the Secretary of Interior to "take any action necessary to prevent unnecessary or undue degradation of the [public] lands." Section 302(b), 43 U.S.C. § 1732(b). (The BLM also relied on the General Mining Law itself, which provides that the process of securing rights to minerals shall be done "under regulations prescribed by law." 30 U.S.C. § 22.)

These regulations have proven to be contentious. The dispute has centered on the meaning of "unnecessary or undue degradation" ("UUD"). In the 1980 regulations, BLM viewed this phrase to mean essentially any degradation more severe than would be expected if a mining site were operated prudently, in accordance with generally applicable environmental protection statutes, assuming mitigation of harms caused. 45 Fed. Reg. 78,910 (Nov. 26, 1980). In the 1990s, however, the BLM commenced a rulemaking to review and amend the 1980 regulations. It undertook the review in part to address a new mining technique known as "heap-leach" mining, which involves the use of cyanide to extract trace amounts of minerals from massive amounts of low-grade ore. The BLM's efforts culminated in a new rulemaking. 65 Fed. Reg. 69,997, Nov. 21, 2000. (The regulations were designated to take effect on January 10, 2001, during the final hours of the Clinton Administration.) The 2000 regulations tossed aside the so-called "prudent man" standard of the 1980 regulations in favor of a "substantial irreparable harm" ("SIH") standard. The SIH standard was significantly tougher than its predecessor. Under the SIH standard, BLM would be empowered to deny a mining permit if the proposed mining site was environmentally sensitive or culturally significant. *Id.* at 70,016. In other words, the BLM could stop a mining activity in its tracks based on environmental considerations.

The Bush Administration amended the 2000 regulations. 66 Fed. Reg. 54,834 (Oct. 30, 2001). The new regulations eliminated the SIH standard for reasons of unworkability, expense, and a projected 10–30% decline in mineral production the 2000 regulations supposedly would have caused. In the 2001 regulations, BLM concluded that FLPMA's reference to "unnecessary or undue degradation" precluded BLM from disapproving any activity "necessary to mining" — regardless of the environmental harm that activity might cause.

The 2001 regulations were challenged in *Mineral Policy Center v. Norton*, 292 F. Supp. 2d 30 (D.D.C. 2003). The District Court in that case flatly rejected the BLM's legal interpretation: "FLPMA, by its plain terms, vests the Secretary of the Interior with the authority — and indeed the obligation — to disapprove of an otherwise permissible mining operation because the operation, though necessary for mining, would unduly harm or degrade the public land." *Mineral Policy Center*, 292 F. Supp. 2d 30. Still, the court found no indication the 2001 regulations were inadequate as written to prevent UUD as required by FLPMA. The court remanded the regulations on other grounds.

Note that FLPMA § 302(b), in addition to the much-debated UUD requirement, contains the following language, which went undiscussed in the *Mineral Policy Center* decision: "no provision of this Act shall in any way amend the Mining Law of 1872 or impair the rights of any locators or claims under that Act."

4. *More on FLPMA.* Enacted largely due to the efforts of Senator Henry (Scoop) Jackson of Washington, the Federal Land Policy and Management Act, 43 U.S.C. §§ 1701–1785 (1976), is the most important public land management statute of the twentieth century. While it serves as the organic law for the Bureau of Land

Management, it also does much more. First, FLPMA cleaned up unwieldy records regarding claims to mineral rights on public lands. It did this by requiring that all claimants file with BLM within three years, or forfeit their claims. Section 314, 43 U.S.C. § 1744. It followed this up with an ongoing requirement for an inventory of public lands, lest the problem arise again. Section 201(a), 43 U.S.C. § 1711(a). Second, FLPMA established generally applicable land management principles, for example, by placing new constraints on land exchanges, § 206, 43 U.S.C. § 1716, and sales, § 203, 43 U.S.C. § 1713, and by specifying the executive's extra-constitutional withdrawal authority, § 204, 43 U.S.C. § 1714. *See supra.* Last, it modified predecessor legislation with respect to BLM lands, and to a lesser extent, to lands managed by the Forest Service, by imposing a multiple use regime on those lands as well as by calling for the preparation and use of plans to coordinate management efforts. Section 102(8), 43 U.S.C. § 1701(8); § 202, 43 U.S.C. § 1712.

5. *Legislative Enactments.* As noted above, Congress has moved in the last century to limit the reach of the GML, largely by withdrawing from its ambit a variety of minerals and assigning those minerals to other statutes which in turn, allocate them to individuals, if at all, by a leasing mechanism. For a snapshot of these legislative enactments and the current arrangement of statutes governing the extraction of minerals from federal land, see the chart below.

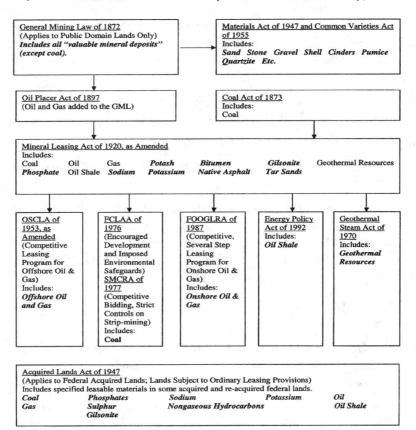

MINERAL RIGHTS ALLOCATIONS ON FEDERAL LANDS
(Does not include Native American Lands. Bold italics print indicates current allocation authority.)

*Key to acronyms: OCSLA — Outer Continental Shelf Lands Act; FCLAA —
Federal Coal Leasing Amendments Act; SMCRA — Surface Mining Control and
Reclamation Act; FOOGLRA — Federal Onshore Oil and Gas Leasing Reform
Act.*

Minerals that remain under the governance of the GML are the "hardrock"
minerals, including gold, silver, platinum, uranium, molybdenum, and some others.

ii.   The Mineral Leasing Act of 1920

The most significant of the statutes that accomplished a withdrawal of minerals
from the ambit of the GML, and the statute upon which we next focus our
attention, is the Mineral Leasing Act ("MLA") of 1920, 30 U.S.C.A. § 181 et seq.
The MLA withdrew fossil fuels such as oil, gas, oil shale, native asphalt, and
bitumen, and chemical minerals such as phosphate, potash, and sodium from the
GML and brought them under the MLA itself. (Recall that post-MLA legislation
has resulted in the withdrawal of some of these minerals from its — the MLA's —
reach. *See* chart, *supra*.) The MLA allows leasing of these minerals by U.S.
citizens, corporations, states, territories, and (for certain minerals) municipalities.
As with the other post-GML mineral allocation statutes, the MLA relies upon
competitive bidding. With competitive bidding, a party requests the Bureau of
Land Management to offer certain lands for leasing; alternatively, the BLM can
decide to do so on its own. Once the offer is publicized, eligible persons submit bids
in line with very particularized and exhaustive requirements. The United States
may reject all bids if it chooses, and indeed it should do so if all bids are
inadequate.

As exemplified by the MLA, the generic differences between these leasing
mechanisms and the self-initiation system of the GML are the following:

(1)   leasing systems grant no right of self-initiation to individuals;

(2)   leasing systems secure to the United States royalties, rents, or other
       payments for leased resources;

(3)   leases contain provisions designed to protect other public resources, and
       to comply with requirements for environmental protection. Accordingly,
       lessees must submit operation and reclamation plans and have them
       approved by the BLM before beginning extraction activities;

(4)   the United States has discretion in choosing the lessee;

(5)   the United States can force lessees to diligently develop the leased
       resource; and

(6)   the United States has greater authority under leasing mechanisms to
       manage extraction activities for environmental, land use, or other
       purposes.

Leases vary in duration. Coal leases typically have an initial term of 20 years;
competitive oil and gas leases generally have terms of 10 years (up from 5), and
noncompetitive leases usually have terms of 10 years as well. In most cases, leases

can be extended if the leasehold is producing minerals in commercial quantities. Leases can be cancelled for violations.

Acreage limitations also vary. Oil and gas leases, and geothermal leases, are typically limited to 2,560 acres. Oil shale leases may cover up to 5120 acres. No person may secure coal leases so to aggregate a "logical mining unit" greater than 25,000 acres.

Bids normally offer royalties for the federal government, in the range of 12½% to 25% for oil and gas, and perhaps 10% for geothermal steam. Lease bids typically also offer some bonus; it is this bonus that makes for a winning accepted bid, for the royalty percentage is usually fixed in advance of the bidding itself.

While competitive bidding is required at all times under some statutes, the Mineral Leasing Act established a different procedure when minerals to be leased are (if at all) in an area not known to contain such resources. In such cases, a prospecting permit would be issued to the first qualified applicant, who was required to pay a minimal filing fee and the first year's rental (25 cents per acre but not less than $20). The holder of a prospecting permit had to diligently explore for minerals, for the permit was set to expire two years after its issuance (although it could be extended in some circumstances). Moreover, failure to explore constituted grounds for cancellation of the permit. A valuable discovery, however, entitled the permit holder to a "preference-right" on a non-competitive basis, as a reward for the expense and time consumed in the discovery process. These noncompetitive leases returned royalties to the United States at rates established in advance of issuance of the leases, and no bonuses were received from lessees. The noncompetitive leasing system was so rapt with fraud that it was suspended in 1980. The system is no longer available for oil, gas, and coal.

Unlike the case with hardrock minerals, the extraction of fossil fuels on federal lands has climbed in recent years. In 1991, federal coal production stood at 285 million tons; in 1998, it was at 371 million tons. Production of oil and gas on federal lands has increased also, largely due to offshore leasing.

iii.   The Outer Continental Shelf Lands Acts

The last allocation statute we will review is the federal law that controls availability of minerals on offshore federal land, the Outer Continental Shelf Lands Act of 1953 ("OCSLA"), as amended in 1978, 43 U.S.C.A. § 1331 et seq. There has been fervent interest in securing rights to oil under OCSLA because offshore oil reserves, especially in the Gulf of Mexico and the Pacific Ocean, are substantial. It has been estimated that about 20 percent of United States production of domestic oil and gas comes from federal lands comprising the Outer Continental Shelf.

Managed by the Bureau of Ocean Energy Management, Regulation and Enforcement (BOEMRE), formerly the Mineral Management Service of the U.S. Department of Interior, rights are secured by leasing, and leases are awarded by a process of competitive bidding. OCSLA, however, allows the Secretary of the Interior to try other bidding systems. *See Watt v. Energy Action Educational Foundation*, 454 U.S. 151, 102 S. Ct. 205 (1981).

Securing a lease for offshore oil and gas involves several stages. First, the DOI prepares a five-year leasing plan, which is submitted to Congress and the president for review. Once the plan is in place, DOI holds a lease sale, for which bids are solicited. Affected states may submit recommendations at this stage, and the DOI is constrained to accept them if they strike a reasonable balance between the national interest and the well-being of the state. 43 U.S.C. § 1345(a) (1976 ed., Supp. V). (Local governments are also permitted to submit recommendations, and the Secretary "may" accept these. 43 U.S.C. § 1345(a), (c) (1976 ed., Supp. V).) Lessees must take care to prevent pollution during all stages of exploration, development, production and transportation of oil and gas materials. 30 C.F.R. § 250.300(a).

Working in conjunction with OCSLA is the Coastal Zone Management Act ("CZMA") of 1972, 16 U.S.C. § 1451 et seq. An attempt at cooperative federalism, the CZMA incorporates states into the federal decision-making process of OCSLA. Under the CZMA, states, helped by federal funding, may fashion management plans for their coastal areas. These plans are then submitted for federal approval to two agencies. The federal Department of Commerce is directed to approve any plan that sufficiently takes into account the national interest in the siting and operation of energy facilities, and the Department of Interior, in its so-called "consistency review" function, must approve state plans if they are compatible with federal land management.

Potential lessees under OCSLA must submit exploration plans to the DOI and have them approved before large-scale exploration is warranted. Exploration plans must certify that proposed extraction activities comport with state management programs prepared under the CZMA. The DOI will disapprove plans that are inconsistent or that would likely result in serious harm to the environment unless the Secretary of Commerce determines to the contrary or finds the exploration plan to be in the interest of national security. 43 U.S.C. § 1340(c)(1) (2) (1976 ed., Supp. V).

Only after all of this may development and production begin. At this stage yet another plan, and the additional review by affected states and localities that comes with it, is necessary. 43 U.S.C. §§ 1345(a), 1351(a)(3) (1976 ed., Supp. V). *See generally Secretary of the Interior v. California*, 464 U.S. 312, 104 S. Ct. 656 (1984); 43 U.S.C. § 1345(c) (1976 ed., Supp. V).

NOTES

1. ***Federal Revenues.*** Revenues to the federal government for oil extracted from federal lands are based on the value of the oil. Regulations governing valuation of crude oil produced from onshore and offshore federal leases were amended in 2004. 69 Fed. Reg. 24,959 (May 5, 2004).

As a general matter, mineral leasing revenues are substantial: for fiscal years 1991–2000, they totaled almost $50 billion. In accordance with federal statutes, the federal government shares these revenues with states. In fiscal year 2000, for example, states received over $840 million out of a total revenue of almost $8 billion, American Indian tribes and allottees received about $235 million, and special funds, including the Historic Preservation Fund and the Land and Water Conservation

Fund (which funds most federal land acquisitions in the current day), received almost $1.6 billion.

2. *ANILCA.* OCS leases on federal lands within Alaska must comply with the Alaska National Interest Lands Conservation Act ("ANILCA") to protect native subsistence rights. Under this statute, the government must show that any restriction on subsistence uses is necessary and that reasonable steps are being taken to minimize adverse impacts. Courts have been instructed to balance competing interests in reaching these decisions; the public interest in preserving subsistence resources is one factor in the decision-making mix. *See Amoco Production Co. v. Village of Gambell*, 480 U.S. 531, 107 S. Ct. 1396 (1987).

3. *Other Statutes.* There are other federal statutes which affect oceanic resource acquisition and protection. The first is the so-called "Ocean Dumping Act," formally known as the Marine Protection, Research and Sanctuaries Act of 1972 ("MPRSA"). It controls routine dumping of materials into the ocean (as distinct from accidental spills) by means of a permit system administered by the United States Environmental Protection Agency. Second, § 311 of the Clean Water Act penalizes and requires clean-up of accidental or intentional spills. Third is the Oil Pollution Act of 1990, enacted after the Exxon Valdez spill in Alaskan waters.

Federal statutes that protect living species will be covered later in these materials.

4. NEPA. The predominant legal authority used to challenge federal mineral leasing is the National Environmental Policy Act. *See* Chapter 4, *supra.* (As sarcastically stated by some persons in the energy business, NEPA stands for "no energy project anywhere.")

b. Timber Lands

The national forests comprise approximately one-fourth of all public lands or about 187 million acres. The overwhelming percentage of this land, about 85% or 160 million acres, is found in the western states, including Alaska. Overall, there are 155 national forests in 40 states. The vast majority of federal forest lands are managed by the Forest Service, established in the Department of Agriculture in 1905. (Some of the federal forest lands, particularly in the Pacific Northwest, are managed by the Bureau of Land Management under authority of Federal Land Management and Policy Act of 1976.)

In its early years, the Service managed forest lands under the authority of the 1897 Forest Service Organic Act, 16 U.S.C. § 471 et seq., which expressed a threefold purpose for forest management: timber, water, and forest protection. In the first half of the twentieth century, timbering on the public lands was a minor enterprise most lumber came from private lands.

The years following World War II, however, saw a surge in consumer demand for timber, due in large part to housing needs of returning troops and the post-war baby boom.[8] This demand brought pressure to bear on the national forests unlike

---

[8] For an interesting account of the transformation of America in the middle of the twentieth century,

anything before. Whereas annual timber production from the national forests in the 1920s was less than one billion board feet, by the 1960s it had spiked to more than twelve times that amount. Bureau of Census, *Historical Statistics of the United States*, Series L 15–23, p. 534 (1970). Subject to this pressure, the Forest Service became a timber production agency. This transformation, in turn, provoked a cascade of objection from the then-forming environmental movement.

A focal point of the national debate was the logging practice known as "even-aged management." Even-aged management involves any of three harvesting methods. The first is clearcutting. Clearcutting is the removal of virtually all trees in a target area, followed by the planting of a replacement stand. It is, in other words, a "clean sweep" method of timber production. The second type, seedtree cutting, is a diluted version of clearcutting. By this method, about ten trees are left in place on each acre of land to produce seeds to regenerate a new stand. Last is shelterwood cutting, which calls for leaving about 20 trees per acre, both for reseeding purposes and to give some protection to new growth. Because even-aged management involves neither the process of selecting each tree to be harvested nor any significant expertise in the logger, it is remarkably less expensive than traditional "uneven-aged" or "selection" management.

The controversy over even-aged management centers on the environmental consequences of the practice. The pro-conservation community objects strenuously to all forms of even-aged management, and especially clearcutting, in large part for aesthetic reasons — these practices can leave a scarred and torn landscape — but also for classic environmental reasons: even-aged management reduces habitat for certain wildlife species, diminishes soil quality, adds to erosion and sediment pollution, especially when severe slopes are cut, and can lead to uniform replacement forests, made up of trees identical in type and age. The forest industry promotes a kinder view of even-aged management. It argues the practice helps much wildlife, including deer, ruffed grouse, bobwhite, and songbirds, by increasing the amount of open space these species need. Beyond that, the industry contends, these practices can rid a forest of infected stands of trees and can help shade intolerant plants, such as Douglas fir trees, pine trees, aspen, and others. Finally, it asserts, when natural seeding is combined with artificial reforestation, a replacement forest can be diverse, and even genetically superior, to its predecessor. *See, e.g., Clearcutting — The Position of the Society of American Foresters, available at* www.safnet.org/. *See also* G. Tyler Miller, Jr., Living in the Environment 641 (10th ed. 1998).

The battle over even-aged management, coupled with the heightened demand for forest products, inevitably found its way to the hallways of Congress. A result was the 1960 Multiple Use-Sustained Yield Act ("MUSYA"), 16 U.S.C. §§ 528–531. While not repealing the Organic Act, the MUSYA established new goals for forest management. The Act designated forests for the multiple uses of recreation, range, timber, watershed, and fish and wildlife.[9] The Act stipulated further that forests

---

including a discussion on the proliferation of tract housing, as typified by "Levittown," a 17,000 cookie-cutter house construction project in Hempstead, Long Island, New York, see David Halberstam, The Fifties Ch. 9 (1993).

[9] The Act defined "multiple use" as "the management of all the various renewable surface resources

should be managed for the long term, that is, on a sustained yield basis.[10]

However, announcing multiple use goals and realizing them are two different things, and eliminating even-aged management is another matter entirely. In the view of many observers, the MUSYA did not change forest management in any appreciable way. Even in a multiple use era, the Forest Service was able to designate timber production as the single most important use for the great majority of forest lands.

As it turned out, it was neither MUSYA, nor NEPA, nor the Endangered Species Act (*see* Chapter 7, *infra*) that produced the environmentalists' ringing victory over even-aged management. Instead, it was the original Organic Act. In *West Virginia Div. of Izaak Walton League of America, Inc. v. Butz*, 522 F.2d 945 (4th Cir. 1975), the so-called "Monongahela case" (named after the forest in West Virginia implicated in the facts), plaintiffs charged that clearcutting violated the Organic Act because that legislation called for the culling of "dead, matured, and large growth" trees, as distinct from all trees in a forest, and required, furthermore, that trees be "marked and designated" before cutting. 16 U.S.C. § 476. The Forest Service conceded it was not enforcing these requirements, but argued essentially that the requirements should be ignored as inappropriate and unworkable. The court rejected the contention:

> Economic exigencies . . . do not grant the courts a license to rewrite a statute no matter how desirable the purpose or result might be. "If the words of the statute are clear, the court should not add to or alter them to accomplish a purpose that does not appear on the face of the statute or from its legislative history." [Citation omitted.]

We are not insensitive to the fact that our reading of the Organic Act will have serious and far-reaching consequences, and it may well be that this legislation enacted over seventy-five years ago is an anachronism which no longer serves the public interest. However, the appropriate forum to resolve this complex and controversial issue is not the courts but the Congress. The controlling principle was stated in *United States v. City and County of San Francisco*, 310 U.S. 16, 29–30, 60 S. Ct. 749, 84 L. Ed. 1050 (1940):

> Article 4, § 3, Cl. 2 of the Constitution provides that "The Congress shall have Power to dispose of and make all needful Rules and

---

of the national forests so that they are utilized in the combination that will best meet the needs of the American people; making the most judicious use of the land for some or all of these resources or related services over areas large enough to provide sufficient latitude for periodic adjustments in use to conform to changing needs and conditions; that some land will be used for less than all of the resources; and harmonious and coordinated management of the various resources, each with the other, without impairment of the productivity of the land, with consideration being given to the relative value of the various resources, and not necessarily the combination of uses that will give the greatest dollar return or the greatest unit output." MUSYA § 4(a), 16 U.S.C. § 531 (a).

[10] The Act defined "sustained yield of the several products and services" as "the achievement and maintenance in perpetuity of a high-level annual or regular periodic output of the various renewable resources of the national forests without impairment of the productivity of the land." MUSYA § 4(b), 16 U.S.C. § 531(b).

Regulations respecting the Territory and other Property belonging to the United States." The power over the public land thus entrusted to Congress is without limitations. "And it is not for the courts to say how that trust shall be administered. That is for Congress." (footnotes omitted).

Id. at 954–55.

The Forest Service chose not to appeal the decision to the Supreme Court.

In 1976, Congress repealed the Organic Act and replaced it with the National Forest Management Act ("NFMA") of 1976, 16 U.S.C. § 1604 et seq. The NFMA imposed a tighter management regime on the Forest Service, but it still authorized a limited use of even-aged management practices. No longer may even-aged management be undertaken in disregard of habitat requirements of fish and wildlife. *See, e.g., Sierra Club v. Peterson*, 185 F.3d 349 (5th Cir. 1999).

The NFMA was part of a triple whammy imposed on the timber industry in the early 1970s. In 1970, Congress had passed the National Environmental Policy Act ("NEPA"). NEPA required federal agencies, including the Forest Service, to examine and explain proposed actions in environmental impact statements, and provided an independent ground for challenging Forest Service decisions. *See* Chapter 4, *supra*. In 1976, Congress enacted the Endangered Species Act ("ESA"), the substantive requirements of which have independently restricted and, in many circumstances, eliminated logging operations in order to protect species of animals or plants falling under its umbrella of protection. *See* Chapter 7, *infra*. Together, and with the assistance of the Wilderness Act of 1964, these statutory tools have reduced timber production on federal lands enormously. Timber production on federal lands in the 1980s approximated 10–12 billion board feet per year, but the yield as of 2000 was 3–4 billion board feet.

The most significant political development involving national forests involves the designation of much of it for wilderness uses. Recall the preceding discussion of the requirement imposed on the Forest Service by the Wilderness Act to determine which forest areas, if any, should be included in the National Wilderness Preservation System. The Service undertook the task by examining "roadless areas" within the forests, specifically those larger than 5,000 acres in size or adjacent to areas already designated as wilderness. Roadless areas were selected for this purpose because, at least on a categorical basis, they offer the greatest potential for future membership in the wilderness system. As described by the Forest Service, roadless areas:

> provide clean drinking water and function as biological strongholds for populations of threatened and endangered species. They provide large, relatively undisturbed landscapes that are important to biological diversity and the long-term survival of many at-risk species. Inventoried roadless areas provide opportunities for dispersed outdoor recreation, opportunities that diminish as open space and natural settings are developed elsewhere. They also serve as bulwarks against the spread of non-native invasive plant species and provide reference areas for study and research.

66 Fed. Reg. 3445 (Jan. 12, 2001).

The Service's efforts in this regard, known as "RARE II" ("roadless area review and evaluation"), produced significant results. Whereas the Wilderness Act itself declared 9.1 million acres of forest land to be wilderness effective upon enactment, the RARE II process resulted in the addition of about 26 million more acres, so that as of 2000 about 18% of the national forest system is wilderness. *Remarks of Prof. Joseph Feller*, ALI-ABA Conference on Environmental Law, Bethesda, Md. (Feb. 8, 2001.)

Thus, the breakdown is fundamentally as follows: 51% of inventoried forest lands is designated as roaded areas (roughly 93 million acres); 18% is wilderness (roughly 35 million acres); and the remaining 31% is roadless non-wilderness (roughly 58.5 million acres). *Id.*

This last 31% has been the focus of intense controversy. The following (severely edited) judicial decision recites this history and offers a sense of the intractability, complexity, and durability of many of these controversies.

STATE OF WYOMING v. U.S. DEPARTMENT OF AGRICULTURE
661 F.3d 1209 (10th Cir. 2011)

JUDGES: Before MURPHY, ANDERSON, and HOLMES, CIRCUIT JUDGES.

HOLMES, CIRCUIT JUDGE.

Defendants Forest Service[1] and Defendants-Intervenors-Appellants Environmental Groups[2] appeal the district court's order setting aside and permanently enjoining the Roadless Area Conservation Rule ("Roadless Rule"), which the Forest Service promulgated in 2001. In setting aside the Roadless Rule, the district court held that the rule violated the Wilderness Act of 1964 ("Wilderness Act"), 16 U.S.C. §§ 1131-36, and the National Environmental Policy Act of 1969 ("NEPA"), 42 U.S.C. §§ 4321-70. *See Wyoming v. U.S. Dep't of Agric.*, 570 F. Supp. 2d 1309 (D. Wyo. 2008). . . .

I. BACKGROUND. . . .

B. *History of the Roadless Rule*

The RARE II undertaking, completed in 1979, produced a nationwide inventory of roadless areas that the Forest Service found worthy of some level of protection. Over the next two decades, however, the Forest Service began permitting road construction to occur in some of those inventoried roadless areas ("IRAs") on a site-specific basis. 66 Fed. Reg. 3244, 3246 (Jan. 12, 2001); *see also Kootenai Tribe of Idaho v. Veneman*, 313 F.3d 1094, 1105 (9th Cir. 2002) . . . During that time, roads were constructed, and other development occurred, on 2.8 million acres of those IRAs. 66 Fed. Reg. at 3246; *Kootenai Tribe*, 313 F.3d at 1105.

In the late 1990s, the Forest Service began to reevaluate its road-management policy in response to changes in public opinion, shifts in resource demands, budget constraints regarding the management of the NFS road system, and an increase in scientific knowledge regarding the effects that roads have on NFS lands. *See* 63 Fed. Reg. 4350, 4350 (Jan. 28, 1998). The agency published an advance notice of proposed rulemaking in January of 1998, which solicited public comment on future regulation and protection of IRAs. *Id.* The Forest Service thereafter adopted an eighteen-month moratorium on road construction in most IRAs — the "Interim Roadless Rule" — which ran from March 1999 through August 2000. 64 Fed. Reg. 7290, 7290 (Feb. 12, 1999). The Interim Roadless Rule "temporarily suspend[ed] decisionmaking regarding road construction and reconstruction in many unroaded areas within the National Forest System," in order to "retain resource management options in those unroaded areas subject to suspension from the potentially adverse effects associated with road construction, while the Forest Service develop[ed] a revised road management policy." *Id.*

While the Interim Roadless Rule was in effect, in October of 1999, President William J. Clinton "direct[ed] the Forest Service to develop . . . regulations to provide appropriate long-term protection for most or all of these currently inventoried 'roadless' areas" in the NFS. Aplt. App. at 1524 (Memorandum from President William Clinton to the Secretary of Agriculture (Oct. 13, 1999)). On October 13, 1999, in response to President Clinton's directive, as well as public comments received on the 1998 advanced notice of proposed rulemaking and the Interim Roadless Rule, the Forest Service published a notice of intent ("NOI") to prepare an environmental impact statement ("EIS") in accordance with NEPA, and to "initiat[e] a public rulemaking process to propose the protection of remaining roadless areas within the National Forest System." 64 Fed. Reg. 56,306, 56,306 (Oct. 19, 1999). The NOI announced the agency's intent to promulgate a two-part rule for protection of roadless areas: (1) "[P]art one would immediately restrict certain activities, such as road construction, in unroaded portions of inventoried roadless areas, as previously identified in RARE II and existing forest plan inventories"; and (2) "[p]art two would establish national direction for managing [IRAs], and for determining whether and to what extent similar protections should be extended to uninventoried roadless areas," a process that "would be implemented at the forest plan level through the plan amendment and NEPA process." *Id.* at 56,307.

The NOI also initiated a sixty-day "scoping period," during which the agency sought public comment on the nature and scope of the issues and alternatives to be analyzed during the NEPA process. *Id.* During the sixty-day scoping period, the Forest Service received more than 517,000 comments in response to the NOI, held 187 meetings around the nation (including several in Wyoming) attended by approximately 16,000 citizens, and launched a Roadless Area Conservation website (roadless.fs.fed.us) to provide information about the rulemaking. 66 Fed. Reg. at 3248; 64 Fed. Reg. 67,822, 67,825-29 (Dec. 3, 1999). Despite several requests, the Forest Service declined to extend the scoping period beyond the initial sixty days.

On May 10, 2000, the Forest Service issued a draft EIS ("DEIS") and proposed Roadless Rule. *See generally* 65 Fed. Reg. 30,276 (May 10, 2000); Aplt. App. at 425 (Draft Environmental Impact Statement, dated May 2000) [hereinafter DEIS]. The DEIS identified 54.3 million acres of IRAs that were subject to the proposed rule. 65 Fed. Reg. at 30,276. The stated purposes of the proposed rule were "to immediately stop activities that have the greatest likelihood of degrading desirable characteristics of inventoried roadless areas," and "to ensure that ecological and social characteristics of inventoried roadless and other unroaded areas are identified and considered through local forest planning efforts." DEIS at S-4; *see also id.* at 1-12 (stating that the first objective of the rule was to "[p]revent activities that can most directly threaten [IRAs] by implementing national prohibitions against road construction and reconstruction").

The proposed rule was two-fold, composed of (1) a "Prohibition Rule," which banned road construction and reconstructions in IRAs, and (2) a "Procedural Rule," which required forest managers to identify additional roadless areas during the forest planning process and determine whether such areas warranted protection under individual forest plans. *See* 65 Fed. Reg. at 30,288 (to be codified at 36 C.F.R. §§ 294.12, 294.13). The Forest Service considered four alternatives to the Prohibition Rule in detail in the DEIS — a "no-action" alternative and three alternatives prohibiting road building and timber harvest to varying degrees. *See id.* at 2–3 to 2–6. Specifically, the four prohibition alternatives analyzed were: (1) Alternative 1 — the "no action" alternative, *id.* at 2-4; (2) Alternative 2 — a prohibition on "road construction and reconstruction within unroaded portions of [IRAs]," *id.* at 2-4 to 2-5; (3) Alternative 3 — a prohibition on "road construction, reconstruction, and timber harvest except for stewardship purposes within unroaded portions of [IRAs]," *id.* at 2-5; and (4) Alternative 4 — a prohibition on "road construction, reconstruction[,] and all timber harvest within unroaded portions of [IRAs]," *id.* at 2-6. In the DEIS, the Forest Service designated Alternative 2 as the preferred alternative for the prohibition rule.

Other alternatives to the Prohibition Rule were addressed by the Forest Service, such as allowing more (rather than less) road building and development, but those alternatives were eliminated from detailed environmental analysis because they were inconsistent with the purpose of protecting IRAs or for other reasons. *Id.* at 2-15 to 2-20. The Forest Service provided sixty-nine days for public comment on the DEIS and proposed rule, 65 Fed. Reg. at 30,276, during which it received more than a million responses and held more that 430 public meetings drawing at least 23,000 people nationwide. 66 Fed. Reg. at 3248.

In November 2000, the Forest Service issued a final EIS ("FEIS"). 65 Fed. Reg. 69,512 (Nov. 17, 2000); Aplt. App. at 520 (Final Environmental Impact Statement, dated Nov. 9, 2009) [hereinafter FEIS]. The FEIS included several changes to the proposed action that were not included in the DEIS. First, it increased the total acreage of IRAs subject to the Prohibition Rule from 54.3 million acres to 58.5 million acres. FEIS at 2-23. The revised figure included 4.2 million acres of IRAs not identified in the DEIS or proposed rule. *Id.* Second, it made the rule applicable to both the "unroaded" and "roaded" portions of IRAs; that is, the Roadless Rule would "now apply to the entire area within the boundaries of an [IRA]," whereas the 2.8 million acres of "roaded" IRAs were not subject to the prohibitions in the proposed rule as it was described in the DEIS. *Id.*[7] Third, the FEIS changed the preferred alternative — previously identified as Alternative 2, which prohibited road construction and reconstruction in IRAs — to Alternative 3, which, as described in the FEIS, prohibited "[r]oad construction, reconstruction (including temporary construction) *and* timber harvest except for stewardship purposes" in

IRAs, subject to a few limited exceptions. FEIS at 2-13 to 2-14 (emphasis added). Fourth, the FEIS eliminated the procedural aspect of the rule, leaving only the Prohibition Rule, due to the Forest Service's decision to incorporate such procedures into a separate and distinct set of forest planning regulations. *See* FEIS at 1-16 (stating that "the Forest Service determined that the procedures contemplated in the [proposed] Roadless Rule should be an explicit part of the plan revision process, and addressed them at 36 CFR 219.9(b)(8) of the final Planning Regulations").

Following the issuance of the FEIS, the Forest Service received additional public comments on the FEIS and the modified preferred alternative. 66 Fed. Reg. at 3248. The comments submitted in response to the FEIS "were considered by the agency in the development of the final rule" and were admitted into the administrative record. *Id.*

On January 12, 2001, the Forest Service issued the final Roadless Rule and the Record of Decision on the rule. 66 Fed. Reg. at 3244-72. The final Roadless Rule — which mirrors the preferred alternative from the FEIS (Alternative 3) — prohibits road construction and reconstruction in IRAs, and prohibits the cutting, sale, or removal of timber from IRAs, subject to limited exceptions. *Id.* at 3272–73 (to be codified at 36 C.F.R. §§ 294.10-.14).

The final Roadless Rule was applicable to the 58.5 million acres of IRAs identified in the FEIS, which amounts to approximately one-third of all NFS lands and approximately 2% of the land base of the continental United States. 66 Fed. Reg. at 3245. As specific to Wyoming, "[t]he Roadless Rule affects 3.25 million acres (or 35%) of the 9.2 million acres of National Forest System land in [the state]." *Wyoming*, 570 F. Supp. 2d at 1326; *see also* FEIS at 3-4 tbl.3-1, 3-61 tbl.3-9, A-4. The Roadless Rule was to take effect on March 12, 2001. 66 Fed. Reg. at 3244. Under the Roadless Rule, as promulgated, "this vast national forest acreage, for better or worse, was more committed to pristine wilderness, and less amenable to road development for purposes permitted by the Forest Service." *Kootenai Tribe*, 313 F.3d at 1106.

C. *Procedural History*

This is not the first instance in which this court has considered a challenge to the Roadless Rule brought by Wyoming.[11] On May 18, 2001, shortly after the Roadless Rule was promulgated, Wyoming filed its first complaint in the United States District Court for the District of Wyoming challenging the legality of the Roadless Rule under several federal environmental statutes, including NEPA, the Wilderness

---

[11] Since 2001, the Roadless Rule has been the subject of at least nine lawsuits, including suits filed in federal district court in Idaho, Utah, North Dakota, Wyoming, Alaska, and the District of Columbia.

Of particular importance, on May 10, 2001, the United States District Court for the District of Idaho found that the plaintiffs had demonstrated likely success on the merits of their claims . . . Based on this ruling, the district court subsequently issued a preliminary injunction prohibiting the implementation of the Roadless Rule. *Kootenai Tribe of Idaho v. Veneman*, 142 F. Supp. 2d 1231 (D. Idaho 2001). On appeal, the Ninth Circuit reversed the district court's judgment and remanded the case. *Kootenai Tribe*, 313 F.3d at 1094.

Act, the Wyoming Wilderness Act of 1984, NFMA, and MUSYA. A number of environmental organizations intervened on behalf of the Forest Service, in defense of the rule. On July 14, 2003, the Wyoming district court ruled that the Roadless Rule was promulgated in violation of NEPA and the Wilderness Act, and therefore permanently enjoined enforcement of the rule. *Wyoming v. U.S. Dep't of Agric.*, 277 F. Supp. 2d 1197, 1239 (D. Wyo. 2003). The Forest Service chose not to appeal the district court's decision to this court; however, the Defendant-Intervenors did file an appeal with the Tenth Circuit.

During the pendency of that appeal — in May of 2005 — the Forest Service adopted the State Petitions Rule, which superseded the Roadless Rule. *See* State Petitions for Inventoried Roadless Area Management, 70 Fed. Reg. 25,654 (May 13, 2005) (to be codified at 36 C.F.R. pt. 294). Because the Roadless Rule had been superseded, this court dismissed the appeal as moot, vacated the district court's July 14, 2003, decision, and remanded the case to the district court to dismiss without prejudice. *Wyoming v. U.S. Dep't of Agric.*, 414 F.3d 1207, 1213 (10th Cir. 2005).

Subsequently, several states and environmental groups challenged the Forest Service's State Petitions Rule in the United States District Court for the Northern District of California. On October 11, 2006, a district court judge of that court set aside the State Petitions Rule for violating NEPA and the Endangered Species Act of 1973, 16 U.S.C. §§ 1531-44, and reinstated the Roadless Rule, despite the fact that the Wyoming district court had already found that the rule violated federal law. *California ex rel. Lockyer v. U.S. Dep't of Agric.*, 459 F. Supp. 2d 874 (N.D. Cal. 2006).[12]

After the Roadless Rule was reinstated by the California district court, Wyoming brought a renewed challenge to the rule in the District of Wyoming, asserting violations of the Wilderness Act, NEPA, MUSYA, and NFMA. On August 12, 2008, the Wyoming district court ruled — for the second time — that the Roadless Rule was promulgated in violation of the Wilderness Act and NEPA, and issued a permanent, nationwide injunction. *Wyoming v. U.S. Dep't of Agric.*, 570 F. Supp. 2d 1309, 1355 (D. Wyo. 2008). The Environmental Groups filed a timely appeal with this court.

II. DISCUSSION

A. *Standard of Review* [omitted]

B. *Wilderness Act Claim*

Wyoming's Wilderness Act claim asserts that the Roadless Rule constitutes a *de facto* designation of "wilderness" in contravention of the process established by Congress in the Wilderness Act of 1964. The district court agreed, holding that the "Forest Service, through the promulgation of the Roadless Rule, designated 58.5

---

[12] On appeal, the Ninth Circuit affirmed the district court's reinstatement of the Roadless Rule. *California ex rel. Lockyer v. U.S. Dep't of Agric.*, 575 F.3d 999 (9th Cir. 2009).

million acres of National Forest land as a *de facto* wilderness area in violation of the Wilderness Act," and therefore the rule was "promulgated in excess of [the] Forest Service's statutory jurisdiction and authority." *Wyoming*, 570 F. Supp. 2d at 1349–50. We conclude that the district court erred in finding that the Forest Service promulgated the rule in violation of the Wilderness Act. [discussion omitted].

b. Roadless Rule Was Promulgated Pursuant to Broad Authority Granted in Organic Act and MUSYA [The court concluded the broad discretion afforded the Forest Service by these statutes authorized the Roadless Rule]. . . .

C. *NEPA Claims*

Wyoming asserts that the Forest Service, in promulgating the Roadless Rule, violated NEPA in seven ways. Specifically, it argues that the Forest Service failed to comply with the NEPA requirements regarding: (1) scoping, (2) cooperating-agency status, (3) consideration of a reasonable range of alternatives in the EIS, (4) consideration of the cumulative impacts of the proposed action in the EIS, (5) preparation of a supplemental impact statement, (6) inclusion of site-specific analysis in the EIS, and (7) an objective "hard look" at the environmental consequences of agency action, by instead predetermining the outcome of the NEPA process. The district court ruled in favor of Wyoming on all its NEPA claims except for two — the site-specific analysis claim, on which it found in favor of the Forest Service, *Wyoming*, 570 F. Supp. 2d at 1340–41, and the predetermination claim, which it did not specifically rule on. On appeal, we consider all seven of Wyoming's NEPA claims. [The court rejected each of these claims] . . . [Discussion of MUSYA and NFMA claims omitted]

III. CONCLUSION

For the foregoing reasons, we REVERSE the district court's order granting Plaintiff declaratory relief and issuing a permanent injunction, and REMAND the case for the district court to VACATE the permanent injunction.

NOTE

The Healthy Forest Restoration Act. In December 2003, Congress passed and President Bush signed into law the Healthy Forest Restoration Act ("HFRA"), 16 U.S.C. § 6501 et seq. Inspired by the massive fire in Yellowstone National Park in 1988, and by serious fire problems in 2000 and 2002, the HFRA attempts to reduce the risk of such catastrophic events. It does so in part by authorizing "fuel reduction projects," which in the main refer to removal of trees and brush that increase fire risk. The Act has been controversial. Environmentalists worry that logging companies will take large trees for commercial purposes under the pretense of reducing fire hazard.

c. Grazing Lands

Approximately three-fourths of federal land, a land area well over twice the size of California, has been used for grazing of livestock. About 18,000 persons, largely ranchers and hobbyists, hold permits for grazing. *See infra.* While the federal land acreage allocated for grazing activity is enormous, the beef production from federal lands comprises a small percentage of national production, likely less than five percent.

Often inadequately monitored, grazing has resulted in a good deal of environmental degradation, in the form of erosion, ecosystem destruction, and water pollution.

An assertion often made is that these harms are due to overgrazing. *See, e.g., The Tragedy of the Commons*, Chapter 1, *supra.* Overgrazing would seem to result from the formula used to compute grazing fees, which, in a common view, systematically keeps those fees at below market value. The cost to graze one cow and a calf for a month approximates $1.35, while, according to the General Accounting Office, the fee BLM would need to charge to recoup grazing costs is roughly five times greater. Efforts of the Clinton administration to increase grazing fees were no match for the opposition of western United States Senators.

Even though artificially low fees would tend to encourage overgrazing, the use of public lands for grazing, as measured in "animal unit months" ("AUMs"), has been in decline for many years. In 1953, the number of AUMs was 18.2 million. By 2010, it had dropped to 12.4 million AUMs. Beef production from federal lands is less than three percent of the national total.

Grazing on federal land was a customary practice long before the enactment of federal legislation specifically regulating it. In *Buford v. Houtz*, 133 U.S. 320, 10 S. Ct. 305 (1890), the Supreme Court ratified the practice:

> We are of opinion that there is an implied license, growing out of the custom of nearly a hundred years, that the public lands of the United States, especially those in which the native grasses are adapted to the growth and fattening of domestic animals, shall be free to the people who seek to use them where they are left open and unenclosed, and no act of government forbids this use.*** The government of the United States, in all its branches, has known of this use, has never forbidden it, nor taken any steps to arrest it. No doubt it may be safely stated that this has been done with the consent of all branches of the government, and, as we shall attempt to show, with its direct encouragement.
>
> The whole system of the control of the public lands of the United States as it had been conducted by the government, under acts of Congress, shows a liberality in regard to their use which has been uniform and remarkable. They have always been open to sale at very cheap prices. Laws have been enacted authorizing persons to settle upon them, and to cultivate them, before they acquire any title to them. While in the incipiency of the settlement of these lands, by persons entering upon them, the permission to do so was a tacit one, the exercise of this permission became so important that Congress, by a system of laws, called the preemption laws, recognized

this right so far as to confer a priority of the right of purchase on the persons who settled upon and cultivated any part of this public domain. During the time that the settler was perfecting his title, by making the improvements which that statute required and paying, by installments or otherwise, the money necessary to purchase it, both he and all other persons who desired to do so had full liberty to graze their stock upon the grasses of the prairies and upon other nutritious [sic] substances found upon the soil.

The value of this privilege grew as the population increased, and it became a custom for persons to make a business or pursuit of gathering herds of cattle or sheep, and raising them and fattening them for market upon these unenclosed lands of the government of the United States. Of course the instances became numerous in which persons purchasing land from the United States put only a small part of it in cultivation, and permitted the balance to remain unenclosed and in no way separated from the lands owned by the United States. All the neighbors who had settled near one of these prairies or on it, and all the people who had cattle that they wished to graze upon the public lands, permitted them to run at large over the whole region, fattening upon the public lands of the United States, and upon the unenclosed lands of the private individual, without let or hindrance. The owner of a piece of land, who had built a house or enclosed twenty or forty acres of it, had the bene t of this universal custom, as well as the party who owned no land. Everybody used the open unenclosed country, which produced nutritious grasses, as a public common on which their horses, cattle, hogs and sheep could run and graze.

Buford, 133 U.S. at 326–28, 10 S. Ct. at 307–08.

Federal regulation of grazing on public lands did not come in any cohesive form until enactment of the Taylor Grazing Act ("TGA") of 1934, 43 U.S.C. § 315 et seq. (named after Rep. Edward Taylor of Colorado). Characterized as an act "to stop injury to the public grazing lands by preventing overgrazing and soil deterioration, to provide for their orderly use, improvement and development, to stabilize the livestock industry dependent upon the public range, and for other purposes," the Act was by design a multiple-use statute. 48 Stat. 1269.

The TGA was enacted in large part to curtail the deterioration of range conditions, but in the view of many, it has been implemented more for the benefit of ranchers than for environmental quality.

The TGA remains the governing legislation to this day. The Act calls for the establishment of grazing districts and gives preference rights for grazing on districted lands to landowners, settlers, and water rights holders on or near the districts themselves. Grazing permits last for a maximum of ten years, but notably, in contrast with the mineral laws, "the issuance of a permit . . . shall not create any right, title, interest, or estate in or to the lands." Section 3, 48 Stat. 1271.

Grazing is now subject to latter-enacted statutes as well. The National Environmental Policy Act (*see* Chapter 4, *supra*), of course, is one. The Endangered Species Act is another (*see* Chapter 7, *infra*). In addition, certain provisions of the Federal

Land Policy and Management Act of 1976 apply to grazing. FLPMA, however, is respectful of grazing rights secured pursuant to the TGA. Section 1752(h) of FLPMA provides that "[n]othing in this Act shall be construed as modifying in any way law existing on [FLPMA's enactment date] with respect to the creation of right, title, interest, or estate in or to the public lands or lands in National Forests by issuance of grazing permits and leases." If anything, FLPMA enhances grazing rights by allowing compensation for ranchers who have installed "permanent improvements" on the public land when their grazing rights are cancelled. *Id.* at § 43 U.S.C. § 1752(g).

For an interesting review of the history of grazing and of some current issues, see *Public Lands Council v. Babbitt*, 529 U.S. 728, 120 S. Ct. 1815 (2000). *Public Lands Council* was the first federal lands/grazing decision from the United States Supreme Court in more than twenty-five years.

See also Joseph M. Feller, *Back to the Present: The Supreme Court Refuses to Move Public Range Law Backward, But Will the BLM Move Public Range Management Forward?*, 31 ENVTL. L. REP. 10021 (2001). In December 2003, the Department of the Interior proposed new regulations to govern grazing on public lands. 68 Fed. Reg. 68,452 (Dec. 8, 2003). Final rules were promulgated in 2006. Because of court decrees, those rules have been modified in several particulars. To review the rules as modified, go to BLM's website, www.blm.gov.

NOTE

Public Rights to Water. In addition to forage, livestock need water. There was considerable concern in early years that a relatively few stockraisers might secure rights to water under state law, and thereby *de facto* secure for themselves the exclusive benefit of public lands. Recognizing this possibility, the government acted to keep water available to all stockraisers. In § 10 of the Stock Raising Homestead Act, Congress provided:

> That lands containing water holes or other bodies of water needed or used by the public for watering purposes shall not be designated under this Act [for entry] but may be reserved under the provisions of the [Pickett] Act . . . , and such land heretofore or hereafter reserved shall, while so reserved, be kept and held open to the public use for such purposes under such general rules and regulations as the Secretary of the Interior may prescribe.

Pub. L. No. 64-290, § 10, 30 Stat. 862, 865 (1917).

Ten years later, President Calvin Coolidge issued an executive order accomplishing the withdrawal:

> Under and pursuant to the provisions of the [Pickett] Act . . . it is hereby ordered that every smallest legal subdivision of the public-land surveys which is vacant unappropriated unreserved public land and contains a spring or water hole, and all land within one quarter of a mile of every spring or water hole located on unsurveyed public land be, and the same is hereby, withdrawn from settlement, location, sale, or entry, and

reserved for public use in accordance with the provisions of Section 10 of [the Stock Raising Homestead Act], and in aid of pending legislation.

Selections, 51 Land Dec. at 457 (quoting Exec. Or. Pub. Water Reserve No. 107 (Apr. 17, 1926)). *See generally* James Muhn, *Public Water Reserves: The Metamorphosis of a Public Land Policy*, 21 J.Land, Resources & Envtl L. 67 (2001).

d. Recreation and Wildlife Lands

The last category of federal lands we examine are recreation and wildlife lands. The recreation lands of the United States are the national parks and monuments (and sundry other parcels — *see infra*). The wildlife lands are the national wildlife refuges. Note that multiple use lands, such as mineral and timber lands, can serve recreation and wildlife interests. Multiple use lands, however, are not limited to those uses.

i. National Park System

By recent tally, there are 384 national park units comprising more than 80 million acres. The National Park System has been assembled by congressional action and by use of revenues from the Land and Water Conservation Fund, 16 U.S.C. §§ 4601-4 to 4601-11, established in 1965 and itself funded largely by royalties from offshore oil and gas leasing.

(1) National Parks

The national parks are often referred to as the jewels of the federal lands. The first national park, Yellowstone Park in northwest Wyoming, is stunning for its geysers and thermal pools. Glacier National Park of Montana offers breathtaking views of the untamed Rocky Mountains. Yosemite National Park represents the best California has to offer. The largest national park is the Wrangell-St. Elias National Park and Preserve in Alaska. Encompassing more than 13,200,000 acres, this single park accounts for more than 16% of the entire National Park System.

Glacier National Park. National Park Service

The national parks are managed by the National Park Service of the U.S. Department of Interior under its organic legislation, the National Park Service Organic Act, 16 U.S.C. § 1 et seq. The Act calls for management of the parks, as well as of national monuments, *see infra*, and other recreation lands, "to conserve the scenery and the natural and historic objects and the wild life therein and to provide for the enjoyment of the same in such manner and by such means as will leave them unimpaired for the enjoyment of future generations." *Id.* The Act characterizes the parks as "distinct in character" but still forming one system of public lands "as cumulative expressions of a single national heritage." 16 U.S.C. § 1a-1. The Act prohibits hunting as a general matter, but allows fishing, with the proviso that fish be released back into the waters. 16 U.S.C. § 3201; 36 C.F.R. §§ 2.2, 2.3. Mining is prohibited in the parks, although mining rights that predate park designations are honored. 36 C.F.R. Part 9. While the Organic Act is the organizing principle for the parks, still each park is subject to its own set of particularized directives.[13] The NPS regulations governing the parks are located at 36 C.F.R. § 1.1 et seq.

The Park Service has managed its lands by using general management plans. The plans must include, but not be limited to:

(1)   measures for the preservation of the area's resources;

(2)   indications of the types and general intensities of development (including visitor circulation and transportation patterns, systems and modes) associated with public enjoyment and use of the area, including general locations, timing of implementation, and anticipated costs;

(3)   identification of and implementation commitments for visitor carrying capacities for all areas of the unit; and

(4)   indications of potential modifications to the external boundaries of the unit, and the reasons therefor.

16 U.S.C. § 1a-7(b).

Managing the parks can be difficult, largely because the Organic Act obligates the NPS to pursue contradictory ends. The Service must protect the parks from impairment while contemporaneously facilitating what has become an intense level of public use. The consensus is that parks and other federal recreational lands have suffered impairment in real terms in recent years. As part of the effort to reverse this slide, a demonstration project was established to allow the NPS to retain visitor fees collected at various units of the park system, rather than lose those revenues to the federal treasury. Under the program, 80% of collected fees were made available to improve the site at which the fees were collected. This new revenue stream resulted in access and infrastructure improvements without markedly affecting the numbers of visitors.

---

[13] The index to the Organic Act, which gives citations to these specific authorities for the many subunits of the park system, runs almost 60 pages.

(2)   **National Monuments**

National monuments are *de facto* national parks. They are created by action of the president in accordance with the American Antiquities Preservation Act, 34 Stat. 225, 16 U.S.C. § 431 ("Antiquities Act"). Enacted in 1906, this statute proclaims that:

> The President of the United States is authorized, in his discretion, to declare by public proclamation historic landmarks, historic and prehistoric structures, and other objects of historic or scientific interest that are situated upon the lands owned or controlled by the Government of the United States to be national monuments, and may reserve as a part thereof parcels of land, the limits of which in all cases shall be confined to the smallest area compatible with the proper care and management of the objects to be protected.

16 U.S.C. § 431.

The discretion available to the president under the Antiquities Act is broad. *See, e.g., Tulare County v. Bush*, 306 F.3d 1138 (D.C. Cir. 2002), *cert. denied*, 540 U.S. 813, 124 S. Ct. 63 (2003).

Various presidents have used this authority to establish, in the aggregate, more than 100 monuments in 24 states and the Virgin Islands, covering some 70 million acres or about 10% of all federal lands. National monuments can be on a small scale — President Bill Clinton, for example, designated Abraham Lincoln's summer retreat as a monument. They can be large as well: the Grand Canyon started out as a national monument. Also designated under the Act: Death Valley and Muir Woods in California; Glacier Bay, Misty Fjords, and Admiralty Island in Alaska; the Grand Tetons in Wyoming; portions of Washington's Olympic Peninsula; and Utah's Bryce and Zion canyons. Like the Grand Canyon, some of these have since been designated as national parks. In 1978, President Jimmy Carter used the Antiquities Act to set aside more than 50 million acres of federal land in Alaska, lands which later received statutory protection by virtue of the Alaska National Interest Lands Conservation Act. Presidents Ronald Reagan and George H.W. Bush were the only presidents in the history of the statute *not* to create a national monument.[14]

President Bill Clinton was singularly active in using the Antiquities Act. He designated more land as national monuments in the lower 48 states than any president preceding him. His most significant reservation occurred on September 18, 1996, when he created the Grand Staircase-Escalante National Monument, an expanse of 1.7 million acres of federal lands in southern Utah, second only in size in the lower 48 states to Death Valley. The reservation was particularly controversial, not only because it came during the heat of a presidential election campaign, but also because it was done without consultation with state officials or the public.

---

[14] An interesting aside: since 1950, because of the flap caused by President Franklin Roosevelt's reservation of the Grand Tetons, no additional monuments can be created in Wyoming under the Antiquities Act without congressional authorization. 16 U.S.C. § 431a. This provision is the only amendment to the Act in its history.

(Fearing adverse political reaction in Utah, President Clinton announced the new monument while in Colorado.)

In 2006, President George W. Bush established the largest national monument ever — the Northwest Hawaiian Islands Marine National Monument. Comprising almost 140,000 square miles, the monument's extensive reefs are home to literally thousands of marine species, many of which are exclusive to the area. The monument is managed by the National Oceanic and Atmospheric Administration.

Several legal questions remain almost 100 years after the enactment of the Antiquities Act. First is whether the statute was repealed with the enactment of FLPMA in 1976. There has been no judicial ruling to this effect, and with designations continuing apace since 1976, there is little indication that Congress finds merit in the idea. Second is the question of the size of designated parcels. The Antiquities Act stipulates that monument boundaries "shall be confined to the smallest area compatible with the proper care and management of the objects to be protected." 16 U.S.C. § 431. Yet, as we have seen, national monuments can be anything but confined. A third question goes to management. The National Park Service Organic Act, 16 U.S.C. § 1 et seq., designates the National Park Service as the managing agency for national monuments, yet several Clinton directives have purported to leave management authority with the BLM or FS, the agencies in charge before designation. A last issue is revocability. May a monument established by presidential proclamation be de-designated by subsequent proclamation? This issue received some attention during the Bush Administration. *See, e.g.*, BNA Daily Environment Report, Jan. 5, 2001. The judiciary has never ruled on the question, although an early opinion of the U.S. Department of Justice indicated the president lacks revocation authority. *Proposed Abolishment of Castle Pinckney National Monument*, 39 U.S. Opp. Atty. Gen. 185 (1938) ("[T]he Executive can no more destroy his own authorized work, without some other legislative sanction, than any other person can. To assert such a principle is to claim for the Executive the power to repeal or alter an act of Congress at will."). *Cf. Midwest Oil, supra.*

(3) Other Federal Lands

Lands in the National Park System are not limited to parks and monuments. The System includes other lands as well, lands that go by a variety of names and are difficult to categorize. Diverse in character and size (the smallest unit of these is the Thaddeus Kosciuszko National Memorial in Pennsylvania, comprising about 1/50 of an acre), these lands may fall, at least in a formal sense, under one of the land categories we have already encountered.

The following material, largely taken from the website of the Department of Interior, lists these diverse areas and gives a short explanation of each:

ALTERNATIVE LAND DESIGNATIONS IN THE NATIONAL PARK SYSTEM

National Preserve: National preserves are areas having characteristics associated with national parks, but in which Congress has permitted continued public hunting, trapping, oil/gas exploration and extraction. Many existing national preserves, without sport hunting, would qualify for national park designation.

National Historic Site: Usually, a national historic site contains a single historical feature that was directly associated with its subject. Derived from the Historic Sites Act of 1935, a number of historic sites were established by secretaries of the Interior, but most have been authorized by acts of Congress.

National Historical Park: This designation generally applies to historic parks that extend beyond single properties or buildings.

National Memorial: A national memorial is commemorative of an historic person or episode; it need not occupy a site historically connected with its subject.

National Battlefield: This general title includes national battlefield, national battlefield park, national battlefield site, and national military park. In 1958, an NPS committee recommended "national battlefield" as the single title for all such park lands.

National Cemetery: There are presently 14 national cemeteries in the National Park System, all of which are administered in conjunction with an associated unit and are not accounted for separately.

National Recreation Area: Twelve NRAs in the system are centered on large reservoirs and emphasize water-based recreation. Five other NRAs are located near major population centers. Such urban parks combine scarce open spaces with the preservation of significant historic resources and important natural areas in locations that can provide outdoor recreation for large numbers of people.

National Seashore: Ten national seashores have been established on the Atlantic, Gulf and Pacific coasts; some are developed and some are relatively primitive. Hunting is allowed at many of these sites.

National Lakeshore: National lakeshores, all on the Great Lakes, closely parallel the seashores in character and use.

National River: There are several variations to this category: national river and recreation area, national scenic river, wild river, etc. The first was authorized in 1964 and others were established following passage of the Wild and Scenic Rivers Act of 1968, 16 U.S.C. § 1271 et seq.

National Parkway: The title parkway refers to a roadway and the parkland paralleling the roadway. All were intended for scenic motoring along a protected corridor and often connect cultural sites.

National Trail: National scenic trails and national historic trails are the titles given to these linear parklands (over 3,600 miles) authorized under the National Trails System Act of 1968.

National Fish Hatchery: There are 66 of these. They produce 160 million fish valued at $5 billion. *Affiliated Area:* In an Act of August 18, 1970, the National Park System was defined in law as, "any area of land and water now or hereafter administered by the Secretary of the Interior through the National Park Service for park, monument, historic, parkway, recreational or other purposes." The Affiliated Areas comprise a variety of locations in the United States and Canada that preserve significant properties outside the National Park System. Some of these have been recognized by Acts of Congress, others have been designated national historic sites by the Secretary of the Interior under authority of the

Historic Sites Act of 1935. All draw on technical or financial aid from the National Park Service.

ii.   National Wildlife Refuges

The National Wildlife Refuge System is a collection of federal lands designated as havens for wildlife. President Theodore Roosevelt established the first refuge in 1903 on Pelican Island in Florida. Congress approved the president's action, and Roosevelt went on to designate fifty more refuges. The refuge system grew again in the 1930s as hunters became increasingly concerned about waterfowl losses caused by wetlands reductions and drought. As of 2000, there were 509 wildlife refuges comprising approximately 92 million acres in all fifty states and territories of the nation. They came into being largely by the mechanisms of executive withdrawal and congressional enactments.

Some refuges are tiny; the largest is the Arctic National Wildlife Refuge, which covers 19.6 million acres of northeast Alaska. Hunting is allowed in 283 refuges and fishing in 276. About 29 million people visit refuges each year. Refuges are managed by the United States Fish and Wildlife Service of the Department of Interior. It was not until the enactment of the National Wildlife Refuge System Administration Act of 1966 that the refuges were consolidated into a system, with a somewhat uniform management regime. The NWRSAA directs the Fish and Wildlife Service to "administer a national network of lands and waters for the conservation, management, and where appropriate, restoration of the fish, wildlife, and plant resources and their habitats within the United States." Section 4(a)(2), 16 U.S.C. § 668dd(a)(2).

The major difficulty for refuge managers is determining which uses to allow. The NWRSAA expressly permits hunting, fishing, and other recreational uses on refuge lands but only if they are "compatible with" the overarching conservation purpose. Section 4(d)(1), 16 U.S.C. § 688dd(d)(1). The issue is what uses are compatible. In fact, the agency's compatibility determinations have come under fire. One legal challenge brought by the National Audubon Society resulted in a settlement requiring an end to all secondary refuge uses unless and until a determination was made, in writing, that the uses were, in fact, compatible. Settlement in hand, the Service proceeded to inventory over 500 refuges and over 50 uses, and found a wide array of permitted secondary pursuits: walking, hiking, and backpacking were allowed on more than 130 refuges; hunting was allowed on more than 220; wildlife observation, photography, environmental education, and interpretation were undertaken on more than 300 refuges; and power boating, jet-skiing, horseback riding, and camping were allowed on more than 100. *See* 1997 U.S. Code and Administrative News 1798-7 to 1798-8.

This litigation and the resultant inventory prompted the Congress to enact the National Wildlife Refuge System Improvement Act ("NWRSIA") of 1997. Thus did the Fish and Wildlife Service finally receive an "organic law" to call its own, joining the ranks of the Forest Service and the National Park Service, *inter alia*. The NWRSIA attempts to impose some uniformity onto refuge management by shoring up defects of the 1966 legislation. The NWRSIA begins by reemphasizing conservation of wildlife and plants as the primary use for all refuges, and in that regard calls for refuge-by-refuge comprehensive conservation plans. The Act addresses the matter of compatible uses as well. It defines "compatible use" as "a wildlife-dependent recreational use or any other use of a refuge that, in the sound professional judgment of the Director, will not materially interfere with or detract from the fulfillment of the mission of the System or the purposes of the refuge." Section 5(1), 16 U.S.C. § 668ee(1). A "wildlife-dependent recreational use" is, in turn, defined as "use of a refuge involving hunting, fishing, wildlife observation and photography, or environmental education and preservation." Section 5(2), 16 U.S.C. § 688ee(2). Among compatible uses, wildlife-dependent uses are slated to receive priority over all other compatible uses. Section 4(a)(3)(C), 16 U.S.C. § 688dd(a)(3)(C). Thus, to the extent that mineral or timber production, grazing, power boating, horseback riding, and other pursuits might be compatible at all, they are relatively disfavored. Rights to undertake compatible uses on wildlife refuges are secured by permit. The Fish and Wildlife Service's regulations implementing the NWRSIA are located at 50 C.F.R. Part 25.

The refuges are financially supported by revenues from sale of Duck Stamps and by user fees.

Chapter 6

THE PUBLIC TRUST DOCTRINE

"The people have a right to clean air, pure water, and to the preservation of the natural, scenic, historic and esthetic values of the environment. Pennsylvania's public natural resources are the common property of all the people, including generations yet to come. As trustee of these resources, the commonwealth shall conserve and maintain them for the benefit of all the people." *Article I, section 27, of the Pennsylvania Constitution.*

SYNOPSIS

A. **INTRODUCTION**

B. *ILLINOIS CENTRAL*

C. **THE PUBLIC TRUST DOCTRINE IN STATE LAW**

A. INTRODUCTION

In its classic form, the public trust doctrine is a restraint on government power both narrow in scope and dramatic in effect. It provides that title in lands submerged by navigable waters may not be alienated to private ownership if doing so would frustrate public use of the lands and, more importantly, of the waters that overlie those lands. *See Illinois Central Railroad v. Illinois*, 146 U.S. 387, 13 S. Ct. 110 (1892), *infra*. Any such purported transfer is revocable if not invalid *ab initio*.

The public trust doctrine derives its historical roots from ancient Roman law, which categorized natural resources by function. Roman property law divided real property into categories, which in turn determined the rights of individuals and the public at large to use the lands. *See, e.g.*, Richard Ausness, *Water Rights, The Public Trust Doctrine, and the Protection of Instream Uses*, 1986 U. ILL. L. REV. 407, 407–09. In Rome, property other than conventional private property (held by persons in their individual capacities), fell into three major classifications. Some properties were *res nullius*, viewed as belonging to no one. Other properties were *res publicae*, belonging to the state. Still other property was *res communes*, belonging to everyone. *See, e.g.*, Frank J. Trelease, *Government Ownership and Trusteeship of Water*, 45 CAL. L. REV. 638, 640 (1957). The so-called *res communes* lands were so highly valued in the Roman system that individual members of the public, despite lack of formal title, could bring legal proceedings to protect them from destructive private action. Jan S. Stevens, *The Public Trust: A Sovereign's Ancient Prerogative Becomes the People's Environmental Right*, 14 U.C. DAVIS L.

REV. 195, n.3 (1980).[1]

These principles of Roman law migrated to England. In England, *res communes* resources could include land, seas, seashores, air, and running water. Title to these resources (excepting, perhaps, air), however, lay in the powerful royalty, which had secured these property interests during feudal times. Thus was created a problem: the crown could royally squander these resources. To avert such indiscretions, an arrangement was finally worked out, by which ascendants to the throne were compelled to manage these especially valued resources in trust for the public. Thus was the protection of public resources molded into a "trust" form, a form which substantially circumscribed, in this specific context, the common law-based land use and disposal powers normally enjoyed by holders of fee interests in property. To the extent that private property rights were limited, public rights were enhanced.

With the passage of time, the public trust doctrine waned in England. Nonetheless, it traveled quietly with the early settlers to America. The doctrine's presence on these shores became known when state courts invoked it to adjudicate private disputes over riverbeds. The first decision announcing a common law-based public trust doctrine was *Arnold v. Mundy*, 6 N.J.L. 1 (1821), a New Jersey Supreme Court decision involving claims to oysters planted in a riverbed. The plaintiff in *Arnold* claimed property rights to the streambed and to the oysters he had planted there, based on an unbroken chain of title running from the time of admission of the state. The court, however, held that title to the streambed, and hence to the oysters, lay in the state because the public trust doctrine nullified the initial transfer upon which plaintiff's chain of title depended. *Id.* at 14. As the court termed it, a transfer of these property rights away from the state "would be contrary to the great principles of our constitution, and never could be borne by a free people." *Id.* at 13. (The New Jersey court later overruled *Arnold*, in *Gough v. Bell*, 22 N.J.L. 441 (1850), *aff'd* 23 N.J.L. 624 (1852)).

B. *ILLINOIS CENTRAL*

The public trust doctrine received its greatest boost when the United States Supreme Court weighed in.

---

[1] Additional minor classifications existed also. Some property was *res universitatis*, belonging to a corporate body rather than to any one individual. *See* T. SANDARS, THE INSTITUTES OF JUSTINIAN 160 (1876). *See also* Coquillette, *Mosses from an Old Manse: Another Look at Some Historic Property Cases About the Environment*, 12 LAND USE & ENV'T L. REV. 67 (1981). Other properties in Roman law were *res sacrae* or *res religiosae*, properties devoted to service of God, and *res sanctae*, properties such as city gates and walls which needed special protection. *Id.* at 82. *See also* Richard J. Lazarus, *Changing Conceptions of Property and Sovereignty in Natural Resources: Questioning the Public Trust Doctrine*, 71 IOWA L. REV. 631, 633–35 (1986).

ILLINOIS CENTRAL RAILROAD v. ILLINOIS
146 U.S. 387, 13 S. Ct. 110 (1892)

Mr. Justice Field delivered the opinion of the court.

This suit was commenced on the 1st of March, 1883, in a Circuit Court of Illinois, by an information or bill in equity, led by the Attorney General of the State, in the name of its people against the Illinois Central Railroad Company, a corporation created under its laws, and against the city of Chicago. The United States were also named as a party defendant, but they never appeared in the suit, and it was impossible to bring them in as a party without their consent. The alleged grievances arose solely from the acts and claims of the railroad company, but the city of Chicago was made a defendant because of its interest in the subject of the litigation.

The object of the suit is to obtain a judicial determination of the title of certain lands on the east or lake front of the city of Chicago, situated between the Chicago River and Sixteenth street, which have been reclaimed from the waters of the lake, and are occupied by the tracks, depots, warehouses, piers and other structures used by the railroad company in its business; and also of the title claimed by the company to the submerged lands, constituting the bed of the lake, lying east of its tracks, within the corporate limits of the city, for the distance of a mile, and between the south line of the south pier near Chicago River extended eastwardly, and a line extended, in the same direction, from the south line of lot 21 near the company's round-house and machine shops. The determination of the title of the company will involve a consideration of its right to construct, for its own business, as well as for public convenience, wharves, piers and docks in the harbor.

We agree with the court below that, to a clear understanding of the numerous questions presented in this case, it was necessary to trace the history of the title to the several parcels of land claimed by the company. And the court, in its elaborate opinion, (33 Fed. Rep. 730) for that purpose referred to the legislation of the United States and of the State, and to ordinances of the city and proceedings thereunder, and stated, with great minuteness of detail, every material provision of law and every step taken. We have with great care gone over the history detailed and are satisfied with its entire accuracy. It would, therefore, serve no useful purpose to repeat what is, clearly and fully narrated. In what we may say of the rights of the railroad company, of the State, and of the city, remaining after the legislation and proceedings taken, we shall assume the correctness of that history.

The State of Illinois was admitted into the Union in 1818 on an equal footing with the original States in all respects. Such was one of the conditions of the cession from Virginia of the territory northwest of the Ohio River, out of which the State was formed. But the equality prescribed would have existed if it had not been thus stipulated. There can be no distinction between the several States of the Union in the character of the jurisdiction, sovereignty and dominion which they may possess and exercise over persons and subjects within their respective limits. The boundaries of the State were prescribed by Congress and accepted by the State in its original Constitution. They are given in the bill. It is sufficient for our purpose to observe that they include within their eastern line all that portion of Lake Michigan lying east of the main land of the State and the middle of the lake south of latitude forty-two degrees and thirty minutes. . . .

. . . .

The case proceeds upon the theory and allegation that the defendant, the Illinois Central Railroad Company, has, without lawful authority, encroached, and continues to encroach, upon the domain of the State, and its original ownership and control of the waters of the harbor and of the lands thereunder, upon a claim of rights acquired under a grant from the State and ordinance of the city to enter the city and appropriate land and water two hundred feet wide in order to construct a track for a railway, and to erect thereon warehouses, piers and other structures in front of the city, and upon a claim of riparian rights acquired by virtue of ownership of lands originally bordering on the lake in front of the city. It also proceeds against the claim asserted by the railroad company of a grant by the State, in 1869, of its right and title to the submerged lands, constituting the bed of Lake Michigan lying east of the tracks and breakwater of the company, for the distance of one mile, and between the south line of the south pier extended eastwardly and a line extended in the same direction from the south line of lot twenty-one south of and near the machine shops and round-house of the company; and of a right thereby to construct at its pleasure, in the harbor, wharves, piers and other works for its use.

The State prays a decree establishing and confirming its title to the bed of Lake Michigan and exclusive right to develop and improve the harbor of Chicago by the construction of docks, wharves, piers and other improvements, against the claim of the railroad company, that it has an absolute title to such submerged lands by the act of 1869, and the right, subject only to the paramount authority of the United States in the regulation of commerce, to fill all the bed of the lake within the limits above stated, for the purpose of its business; and the right, by the construction and maintenance of wharves, docks and piers, to improve the shore of the lake for the promotion generally of commerce and navigation. And the State, insisting that the company has, without right, erected and proposes to continue to erect wharves and piers upon its domain, asks that such alleged unlawful structures may be ordered to be removed, and the company be enjoined from erecting further structures of any kind.

. . . .

We do not deem it material, for the determination of any questions presented in this case, to describe in detail the extensive works of the railroad company under the permission given to locate its road within the city by the ordinance. It is sufficient to say that when this suit was commenced it had reclaimed from the waters of the lake a tract, two hundred feet in width, for the whole distance allowed for its entry within the city, and constructed thereon the tracks needed for its railway, with all the guards against danger in its approach and crossings as specified in the ordinance, and erected the designated breakwater beyond its tracks on the east, and the necessary works for the protection of the shore on the west. Its works in no respect interfered with any useful freedom in the use of the waters of the lake for commerce, foreign, interstate or domestic. They were constructed under the authority of the law by the requirement of the city as a condition of its consent that the company might locate its road within its limits, and cannot be regarded as such an encroachment upon the domain of the State as to require the interposition of the court for their removal or for any restraint in their use.

. . . .

We proceed to consider the claim of the railroad company to the ownership of submerged lands in the harbor, and the right to construct such wharves, piers, docks and other works therein as it may deem proper for its interest and business. The claim is founded upon the third section of the act of the legislature of the State passed on the 16th of April, 1869, the material part of which is as follows:

SEC. 3. The right of the Illinois Central Railroad Company under the grant from the State in its charter, which said grant constitutes a part of the consideration for which the said company pays to the State at least seven per cent of its gross earnings, . . . is hereby confirmed; and all the right and title of the State of Illinois in and to the submerged lands constituting the bed of Lake Michigan, and lying east of the tracks and breakwater of the Illinois Central Railroad Company, for the distance of one mile, . . . are hereby granted in fee to the said Illinois Central Railroad Company, its successors and assigns: provided, however, that the fee to said lands shall be held by said company in perpetuity, and that the said company shall not have power to grant, sell or convey the fee to the same; and that all gross receipts from use, profits, leases or otherwise of said lands, or the improvements thereon, or that may hereafter be made thereon, shall form a part of the gross proceeds, receipts and income of the said Illinois Central Railroad Company, . . . and provided also, that nothing herein contained shall authorize obstructions to the Chicago harbor, or impair the public right of navigation. . . .

The act, of which this section is a part, was accepted by a resolution of the board of directors of the company. . . . On the 15th of April, 1873, the legislature of Illinois repealed the act. The questions presented relate to the validity of the section cited of the act and the effect of the repeal upon its operation.

The section in question has two objects in view: one was to confirm certain alleged rights of the railroad company under the grant from the State in its charter and under and "by virtue of its appropriation, occupancy, use and control, and the riparian ownership incident" thereto, in and to the lands submerged or otherwise lying east of a line parallel with and four hundred feet east of the west line of Michigan Avenue, in fractional sections ten and fifteen. The other object was to grant to the railroad company submerged lands in the harbor.

. . . .

This clause is treated by the counsel of the company as an absolute conveyance to it of title to the submerged lands. . . .

. . . .

The question, therefore, to be considered is whether the legislature was competent to thus deprive the State of its ownership of the submerged lands in the harbor of Chicago, and of the consequent control of its waters; or, in other words, whether the railroad corporation can hold the lands and control the waters by the grant, against any future exercise of power over them by the State.

That the State holds the title to the lands under the navigable waters of Lake Michigan, within its limits, in the same manner that the State holds title to soils under tide water, by the common law, we have already shown, and that title necessarily carries with it control over the waters above them whenever the lands are subjected to use. But it is a title different in character from that which the State holds in lands intended for sale. It is different from the title which the United States hold in the public lands which are open to preemption and sale. It is a title held in trust for the people of the State that they may enjoy the navigation of the waters, carry on commerce over them, and have liberty of fishing therein freed from the obstruction or interference of private parties. The interest of the people in the navigation of the waters and in commerce over them may be improved in many instances by the erection of wharves, docks and piers therein, for which purpose the State may grant parcels of the submerged lands; and, so long as their disposition is made for such purpose, no valid objections can be made to the grants. It is grants of parcels of lands under navigable waters, that may afford foundation for wharves, piers, docks and other structures in aid of commerce, and grants of parcels which, being occupied, do not substantially impair the public interest in the lands and waters remaining, that are chiefly considered and sustained in the adjudged cases as a valid exercise of legislative power consistently with the trust to the public upon which such lands are held by the State. But that is a very different doctrine from the one which would sanction the abdication of the general control of the State over lands under the navigable waters of an entire harbor or bay, or of a sea or lake. Such abdication is not consistent with the exercise of that trust which requires the government of the State to preserve such waters for the use of the public. The trust devolving upon the State for the public, and which can only be discharged by the management and control of property in which the public has an interest, cannot be relinquished by a transfer of the property. The control of the State for the purposes of the trust can never be lost, except as to such parcels as are used in promoting the interests of the public therein, or can be disposed of without any substantial impairment of the public interest in the lands and waters remaining. It is only by observing the distinction between a grant of such parcels for the improvement of the public interest, or which when occupied do not substantially impair the public interest in the lands and waters remaining, and a grant of the whole property in which the public is interested, that the language of the adjudged cases can be reconciled. General language sometimes found in opinions of the courts, expressive of absolute ownership and control by the State of lands under navigable waters, irrespective of any trust as to their use and disposition, must be read and construed with reference to the special facts of the particular cases. A grant of all the lands under the navigable waters of a State has never been adjudged to be within the legislative power; and any attempted grant of the kind would be held, if not absolutely void on its face, as subject to revocation. The State can no more abdicate its trust over property in which the whole people are interested, like navigable waters and soils under them, so as to leave them entirely under the use and control of private parties, except in the instance of parcels mentioned for the improvement of the navigation and use of the waters, or when parcels can be disposed of without impairment of the public interest in what remains, than it can abdicate its police powers in the administration of government and the preservation of the peace. In the administration of government the use of such powers may for a limited period be delegated to a municipality or other body, but there always remains with the State the right to revoke those powers and exercise them in a more direct manner, and one more conformable to its wishes. So with trusts connected with public property, or property of a special character, like lands under navigable waters, they cannot be placed entirely beyond the direction and control of the State.

The harbor of Chicago is of immense value to the people of the State of Illinois in the facilities it affords to its vast and constantly increasing commerce; and the idea that its legislature can deprive the State of control over its bed and waters and place the same in the hands of a private corporation created for a different purpose, one limited to transportation of passengers and freight between distant points and the city, is a proposition that cannot be defended.

The area of the submerged lands proposed to be ceded by the act in question to the railroad company embraces something more than a thousand acres, being, as stated by counsel, more than three times the area of the outer harbor, and not only including all of that harbor but embracing adjoining submerged lands which will, in all probability, be hereafter included in the harbor. It is as large as that embraced by all the merchandise docks along the Thames at London; is much larger than that included in the famous docks and basins at Liverpool; is twice that of the port of Marseilles, and nearly if not quite equal to the pier area along the water front of the city of New York. And the arrivals and clearings of vessels at the port exceed in number those of New York, and are equal to those of New York and Boston combined. Chicago has nearly twenty-five per cent of the lake carrying trade as compared with the arrivals and clearings of all the leading ports of our great inland seas. In the year ending June 30, 1886, the joint arrivals and clearances of vessels at that port amounted to twenty-two thousand and ninety-six, with a tonnage of over seven millions; and in 1890 the tonnage of the vessels reached nearly nine millions. As stated by counsel, since the passage of the Lake Front Act, in 1869, the population of the city has increased nearly a million souls, and the increase of commerce has kept pace with it. It is hardly conceivable that the legislature can divest the State of the control and management of this harbor and vest it absolutely in a private corporation. Surely an act of the legislature transferring the title to its submerged lands and the power claimed by the railroad company, to a foreign State or nation would be repudiated, without hesitation, as a gross perversion of the trust over the property under which it is held. So would a similar transfer to a corporation of another State. It would not be listened to that the control and management of the harbor of that great — city a subject of concern to the whole people of the State — should thus be placed elsewhere than in the State itself. All the objections which can be urged to such attempted transfer may be urged to a transfer to a private corporation like the railroad company in this case. Any grant of the kind is necessarily revocable, and the exercise of the trust by which the property was held by the State can be resumed at any time. Undoubtedly there may be expenses incurred in improvements made under such a grant which the State ought to pay; but, be that as it may, the power to resume the trust whenever the State judges best is, we think, incontrovertible. The position advanced by the railroad company in support of its claim to the ownership of the submerged lands and the right to the erection of wharves, piers and docks at its pleasure, or for its business in the harbor of Chicago, would place every harbor in the country at the mercy of a majority of the legislature of the State in which the harbor is situated.

We cannot, it is true, cite any authority where a grant of this kind has been held invalid, for we believe that no instance exists where the harbor of a great city and its commerce have been allowed to pass into the control of any private corporation. But the decisions are numerous which declare that such property is held by the State, by virtue of its sovereignty, in trust for the public. The ownership of the navigable waters of the harbor and of the lands under them is a subject of public concern to the whole people of the State. The trust with which they are held, therefore, is governmental and cannot be alienated, except in those instances mentioned of parcels used in the improvement of the interest thus held, or when parcels can be disposed of without detriment to the public interest in the lands and waters remaining.

This follows necessarily from the public character of the property, being held by the whole people for purposes in which the whole people are interested.

. . . .

. . . We hold, therefore, that any attempted cession of the ownership and control of the State in and over the submerged lands in Lake Michigan, by the act of April 16, 1869, was inoperative to affect, modify or in any respect to control the sovereignty and dominion of the State over the lands, or its ownership thereof, and that any such attempted operation of the act was annulled by the repealing act of April 15, 1873, which to that extent was valid and effective. There can be no irrepealable contract in a conveyance of property by a grantor in disregard of a public trust, under which he was bound to hold and manage it.

DISSENT: MR. JUSTICE SHIRAS, with whom concurred MR. JUSTICE GRAY and MR. JUSTICE BROWN, dissenting.

That the ownership of a State in the lands underlying its navigable waters is as complete, and its power to make them the subject of conveyance and grant is as full, as such ownership and power to grant in the case of the other public lands of the State, I have supposed to be well settled.

. . . .

The opinion of the majority, if I rightly apprehend it, ... concedes that a State does possess the power to grant the rights of property and possession in such lands to private parties, but the power is stated to be, in some way restricted to "small parcels, or where such parcels can be disposed of without detriment to the public interests in the lands and waters remaining." But it is difficult to see how the validity of the exercise of the power, if the power exists, can depend upon the size of the parcel granted. . . .

. . . .

Doubtless there are limitations, both expressed and implied, on the title to and control over these lands by the company. As we have seen, the company is expressly forbidden to obstruct Chicago harbor, or to impair the public right of navigation. So, from the nature of the railroad corporation and of its relation to the State and the public, the improvements put upon these lands by the company must be consistent with their duties as common carriers, and must be calculated to promote the efficiency of the railroad in the receipt and shipment of freight from and by the lake. But these are incidents of the grant and do not operate to defeat it.

. . . .

Should the State of Illinois see, in the great and unforeseen growth of the city of Chicago and of the lake commerce, reason to doubt the prudence of her legislature in entering into the contract created by the passage and acceptance of the act of 1869, she can take the rights and property of the railroad company in these lands by a constitutional condemnation of them.

NOTES AND QUESTIONS

1. *A Closer Look.* *Illinois Central* remains the major judicial decision in support of the public trust doctrine. It has been cited repeatedly by state courts as a source of authority for the doctrine and is a staple in casebooks on natural resources law. In large part because of *Illinois Central*, all states now have public trust doctrines. But what is the decision's legal foundation? Unfortunately, the case is silent on this seminal question. One commentator has suggested the doctrine to be a corollary to the navigational servitude, *see* Chapter 8, *infra*, and having its roots in the Commerce Clause. Charles F. Wilkinson *The Headwaters of the Public Trust: Some Thoughts on the Source and Scope of the Traditional Doctrine*, 19 ENVTL L. 425, 458 59 (1989). Professor Wilkinson argues states may expand the doctrine but may not abrogate it. *Id.* at 461–62.

Could *Illinois Central* be justified as an expression of federal common law? *See, e.g., Oregon ex rel. State Land Board v. Corvallis Sand and Gravel Company*, 429 U.S. 363, 379 80, 97 S. Ct. 582, 591 (1977):

> [U]nder our federal system, property ownership is not governed by a general federal law, but rather by the laws of the several States. "The great body of law in this country which controls acquisition, transmission, and transfer of property, and defines the rights of its owners in relation to the state or to private parties, is found in the statutes and decisions of the state." Davies Warehouse Co. v. Bowles, 321 U.S. 144, 155, 64 S. Ct. 474, 480, 88 L. Ed. 635 (1944). This is particularly true with respect to real property, for even when federal common law was in its heyday under the teachings of Swift v. Tyson, 10 L.Ed. 865, 16 Pet. 1 (1842), an exception was carved out for the local law of real property. *Id.* at 18.

See also Board of Regents of State Colleges v. Roth, 408 U.S. 564, 577, 92 S. Ct. 2701, 2709 (1972) ("[P]roperty interests . . . are not created by the Constitution. Rather, they are created and their dimensions are defined by existing rules or understandings that stem from an independent source such as state law — rules or understandings that secure certain benefits and that support claims of entitlement to those benefits.")

Alternatively, is the doctrine merely a manifestation of traditional property theory? Consider: (a) under English law, title in important public resources was burdened by trust obligations; (b) English law was imported into state law; (c) thus, title to public resources held by states carries the same trust obligations. Good reasoning?

2. *Good Law?* The Supreme Court has never specifically affirmed *Illinois Central* and may currently disfavor it. *See, e.g., Phillips Petroleum Co. v. Mississippi*, 484 U.S. 469, 483, 108 S. Ct. 791, 799 (1988) (a state's management of lands underlying navigable waters should accord with each state's views "of justice and policy."); *Montana v. United States*, 450 U.S. 544, 551, 101 S. Ct. 1245, 1251 (1981) ("[a] State's power over the beds of navigable waters remains subject to only one limitation: the paramount power of the United States to ensure that such waters remain free to interstate and foreign commerce"); *United States v. Oregon*, 295 U.S. 1, 14, 55 S. Ct. 610, 615 (1935) ("upon the admission of a State to the Union, the title of the United States to lands underlying navigable waters within the States passes to it, as incident to the transfer to the State of local sovereignty, and is subject only to the paramount power of the United States to control such waters for purposes of navigation in interstate and foreign commerce"). *See also Appleby v. City of New York*, 271 U.S. 364 (1926), in which the Supreme Court declared that the conclusion in *Illinois Central* "was necessarily a statement of Illinois law." *Appleby*, 271 U.S. at 395. *See generally* Eric Pearson, *Illinois Central and the Public Trust Doctrine in State Law*, 15 VA. ENVTL. L.J. 713 (1996).

3. *Praise and Criticism.* The academic community has welcomed the public trust doctrine with open arms. The major article that revived the doctrine in the current day is Joseph L. Sax, *The Public Trust Doctrine in Natural Resources Law: Effective Judicial Intervention*, 68 MICH. L. REV. 471 (1970). Professor Sax's support for the doctrine was rooted in his healthy disgust for government squandering of valuable natural resources. *Id.* at 474. In his view, the doctrine has a singular ability to work into the law a logical and necessary ethic of environmental protection as well as a respect for "certain interests . . . so intrinsically important to every citizen that their free availability tends to mark the society as one of citizens rather than of serfs." *Id.* Professor Sax followed up on these themes ten years later in *Liberating the Public Trust Doctrine from Its Historical Shackles*, 14 U.C. DAVIS L. REV. 185 (1980). Other articles praising the doctrine include Harrison C. Dunning, *The Public Trust: A Fundamental Doctrine of American Property Law*, 19 ENVTL. L. 515 (1989), and Charles F. Wilkinson, *The Public Trust Doctrine in Public Land Law*, 14 U.C. DAVIS L. REV. 269 (1980).

However, the doctrine is not universally applauded. In the view of some commentators, it is counter-majoritarian, at least when it originates by judicial fiat. By this view, when courts invoke the public trust doctrine to reverse a decision of a legislature, they usurp the legislature's policymaking function. *See, e.g.,* Huffman, *Trusting the Public Interest to Judges: A Comment on the Public Trust Writings of Professor Sax, Wilkinson, Dunning and Johnson*, 63 DENV. U. L. REV. 565 (1986); Steven Jawetz, *The Public Trust Totem in Public Land Law: Ineffective and Undesirable Judicial Intervention*, 14 U.C. DAVIS L. REV. 455 (1982).

C.   THE PUBLIC TRUST DOCTRINE IN STATE LAW

The public trust doctrine varies from state to state. It can vary by origin. As we have seen, it can arise from judicial decision. But it can arise also by constitution (see, for example, the quote that introduces this chapter, *supra; see also Lawrence v. Clark County*, 254 P.3d 606 (Nev. 2011) (locating the public trust doctrine in the "gift clause" of the state's constitution)), or by statute. The doctrine can vary in physical reach as well. When applicable to submerged lands, its landward limit may be the low water mark, the ordinary low water mark, the winter tide, the neap tide, the highest tide, the vegetation line, or the mean high water mark. The doctrine can also vary in applicability. Originally reaching only submerged lands, the doctrine has since been held to apply to resources such as marine life, wildlife, sand and gravel, rural park lands, battlefields, archeological remains, and a downtown area. *See* Richard J. Lazarus, *Changing Conceptions of Property and Sovereignty in Natural Resources: Questioning the Public Trust Doctrine*, 71 IOWA L. REV. 631, 649 n.1 (1986). And it can vary in function. The doctrine has served to promote public pursuits such as hunting, fishing, boating, swimming, ecological preservation, and scientific study, *see, e.g., Marks v. Whitney*, 491 P.2d 374, 380 (Cal. 1971), and public rights to use navigable and nonnavigable waterways, *see, e.g., Montana Coalition for Stream Access v. Curran*, 682 P.2d 163, 171 (Mont. 1984). The doctrine has forced government agencies to plan for long-term conservation and development of natural resources as a prerequisite to issuing water rights permits. *United Plainsmen Association v. North Dakota State Water Conservation Commission*, 247 N.W.2d 457 (N.D. 1976). The public trust doctrine has even been used as an interpretive device, which in one case converted "the rocks" of a private entity's arguments into "no more than shifting sands." *State ex rel Rohrer v. Credle*, 369 S.E.2d 825, 832 (N.C. 1988).

NATIONAL AUDUBON SOCIETY v. SUPERIOR COURT OF ALPINE COUNTY
33 Cal. 3d 419, 189 Cal. Rptr. 346, 658 P.2d 709 (1983)

OPINION: BROUSSARD, J.

Mono Lake, the second largest lake in California, sits at the base of the Sierra Nevada escarpment near theeastern entrance to Yosemite National Park. The lake is saline; it contains no fish but supports a large population of brine shrimp which feed vast numbers of nesting and migratory birds. Islands in the lake protect a large breeding colony of California gulls, and the lake itself serves as a haven on the migration route for thousands of Northern Phalarope, Wilson's Phalarope, and Eared Grebe. Towers and spires of tufa on the north and south shores are matters of geological interest and a tourist attraction.

Although Mono Lake receives some water from rain and snow on the lake surface, historically most of itssupply came from snowmelt in the Sierra Nevada. Five freshwater streams — Mill, Lee Vining, Walker, Parker and Rush Creeks — arise near the crest of the range and carry the annual runoff to the west shore of the lake. In 1940, however, the Division of Water Resources, the predecessor to the present California Water Resources Board, granted the Department of Water and

Power of the City of Los Angeles (hereafter DWP) a permit to appropriate virtually the entire flow of four of the five streams owing into the lake. DWP promptly constructed facilities to divert about half the flow of these streams into DWP's Owens Valley aqueduct. In 1970 DWP completed a second diversion tunnel, and since that time has taken virtually the entire flow of these streams.

Mono Lake
Photograph courtesy of the Mono Lake Committee

As a result of these diversions, the level of the lake has dropped; the surface area has diminished by one-third; one of the two principal islands in the lake has become a peninsula, exposing the gull rookery there to coyotes and other predators and causing the gulls to abandon the former island. The ultimate effect of continued diversions is a matter of intense dispute, but there seems little doubt that both the scenic beauty and the ecological values of Mono Lake are imperiled.

Plaintiffs led suit in superior court to enjoin the DWP diversions on the theory that the shores, bed and waters of Mono Lake are protected by a public trust. Plaintiffs' suit was transferred to the federal district court, which requested that the state courts determine the relationship between the public trust doctrine and the water rights system, and decide whether plaintiffs must exhaust administrative remedies before the Water Board prior to filing suit. The superior court then entered summary judgments against plaintiffs on both matters, ruling that the public trust doctrine offered no independent basis for challenging the DWP diversions, and that plaintiffs had failed to exhaust administrative remedies. Plaintiffs petitioned us directly for writ of mandate to review that decision; in view of the importance of the issues presented, we issued an alternative writ.

This case brings together for the first time two systems of legal thought: the appropriative water rights system which since the days of the gold rush has dominated California water law, and the public trust doctrine which, after evolving as a shield for the protection of tidelands, now extends its protective scope to navigable lakes. Ever since we first recognized that the public trust protects environmental and recreational values (Marks v. Whitney (1971) 6 Cal.3d 251 [98 Cal.Rptr. 790, 491 P.2d 374]), the two systems of legal thought have been on a collision course. They meet in a unique and dramatic setting which highlights the clash of values. Mono Lake is a scenic and ecological treasure of national signi cance, imperiled by continued diversions of water; yet, the need of Los Angeles for water is apparent, its reliance on rights granted by the board evident, the cost of curtailing diversions substantial.

Attempting to integrate the teachings and values of both the public trust and the appropriative water rights system, we have arrived at certain conclusions which we brie y summarize here. In our opinion, the core of the public trust doctrine is the state's authority as sovereign to exercise a continuous supervision and control over the navigable waters of the state and the lands underlying those waters. This authority applies to the waters tributary to Mono Lake and bars DWP or any other party from claiming a vested right to divert waters once it becomes clear that such diversions harm the interests protected by the public trust. The corollary rule which evolved in tideland and lakeshore cases barring conveyance of rights free of the trust except to serve trust purposes cannot, however, apply without modification to flowing waters. The prosperity and habitability of most of this state requires the diversion of great quantities of water from its streams for purposes unconnected to any navigation, commerce, fishing, recreation, or ecological use relating to the source stream. The state must have the power to grant nonvested usufructuary rights to appropriate water even if diversions harm public trust uses. Approval of such diversion without considering public trust values, however, may result in needless destruction of those values. Accordingly, we believe that before state courts and agencies approve water diversions they should consider the effect of such diversions upon interests protected by the public trust, and attempt, so far as feasible, to avoid or minimize any harm to those interests.

The water rights enjoyed by DWP were granted, the diversion was commenced, and has continued to the present without any consideration of the impact upon the public trust. An objective study and reconsideration of the water rights in the Mono Basin is long overdue. The water law of California which we conceive to be an integration including both the public trust doctrine and the board-administered appropriative rights system permits such a reconsideration; the values underlying that integration require it.

With regard to the secondary issue of exhaustion of administrative remedies, the powers, experience, and expertise of the Water Board all argue in favor of granting that agency primary jurisdiction. Long-established precedent, however, declares that courts have concurrent jurisdiction in water right controversies. The Legislature, instead of overturning that precedent, has implicitly acknowledged its vitality by providing a procedure under which the courts can refer water rights disputes to the water board as referee. We therefore conclude that the courts may continue to exercise concurrent jurisdiction, but note that in cases where the board's experience or expert knowledge may be useful the courts should not hesitate to seek such aid. . . .

        . . . .

DWP expects that its future diversions of about 100,000 acre-feet per year will lower the lake's surface level another 43 feet and reduce its surface area by about 22 square miles over the next 80 to 100 years, at which point the lake will gradually approach environmental equilibrium (the point at which in ow from precipitation, groundwater and nondiverted tributaries equals out ow by evaporation and other means). At this point, according to DWP, the lake will stabilize at a level 6,330 feet above the sea's, with a surface area of approximately 38 square miles. Thus, by DWP's own estimates, unabated diversions will ultimately produce a lake that is about 56 percent smaller on the surface and 42 percent shallower than its natural size.

Plaintiffs consider these projections unrealistically optimistic. They allege that, 50 years hence, the lake will be at least 50 feet shallower than it now is, and hold less than 20 percent of its natural volume. Further, plaintiffs fear that "the lake will not stabilize at this level," but "may continue to reduce in size until it is dried up." Moreover, unlike DWP, plaintiffs believe that the lake's gradual recession indirectly causes a host of adverse environmental impacts. Many of these alleged impacts are related to an increase in the lake's salinity, caused by the decrease in its water volume.

As noted above, Mono Lake has no outlets. The lake loses water only by evaporation and seepage. Natural salts do not evaporate with water, but are left behind. Prior to commencement of the DWP diversions, this naturally rising salinity was balanced by a constant and substantial supply of fresh water from the tributaries. Now, however, DWP diverts most of the fresh water in ow. The resultant imbalance between inflow and outflow not only diminishes the lake's size, but also drastically increases its salinity.

Plaintiffs predict that the lake's steadily increasing salinity, if unchecked, will wreck havoc throughout the local food chain. They contend that the lake's algae, and the brine shrimp and brine flies that feed on it, cannot survive the projected salinity increase. To support this assertion, plaintiffs point to a 50 percent reduction in the shrimp hatch for the spring of 1980 and a startling 95 percent reduction for the spring of 1981. These reductions affirm experimental evidence indicating that brine shrimp populations diminish as the salinity of the water surrounding them increases. (See Task Force Report at pp. 20 21.) DWP admits these substantial reductions, but blames them on factors other than salinity.

[The court then discusses other potential environmental problems, such as danger to wildlife, and then disposes of preliminary issues.]

2. The Public Trust Doctrine in California.

"By the law of nature these things are common to mankind the air, running water, the sea and consequently the shores of the sea." (Institutes of Justinian 2.1.1.) From this origin in Roman law, the English common law evolved the concept of the public trust, under which the sovereign owns "all of its navigable waterways and the lands lying beneath them 'as trustee of a public trust for the bene t of the people.'" (*Colberg, Inc. v. State of California ex rel. Dept. Pub. Wks.* (1967) 67 Cal.2d 408, 416 [62 Cal.Rptr. 401, 432 P.2d 3].) The State of California acquired title as trustee to such lands and waterways upon its admission to the union; from the earliest days its judicial decisions have recognized and enforced the trust obligation.

Three aspects of the public trust doctrine require consideration in this opinion: the purpose of the trust; the scope of the trust, particularly as it applies to the nonnavigable tributaries of a navigable lake; and the powers and duties of the state as trustee of the public trust. We discuss these questions in the order listed.

(a) The purpose of the public trust.

The objective of the public trust has evolved in tandem with the changing public perception of the values and uses of waterways. As we observed in *Marks v. Whitney*, supra, 6 Cal.3d 251, "[p]ublic trust easements [were] traditionally defined in terms of navigation, commerce and fisheries. They have been held to include the right to fish, hunt, bathe, swim, to use for boating and general recreation purposes the navigable waters of the state, and to use the bottom of the navigable waters for anchoring, standing, or other purposes." (P. 259.) We went on, however, to hold that the traditional triad of uses — navigation, commerce and fishing — did not limit the public interest in the trust res. In language of special importance to the present setting, we stated that "[t]he public use to which tidelands are subject are sufficiently flexible to encompass changing public needs. In administering the trust the state is not burdened with an outmoded classi cation favoring one mode of utilization over another. [Citation.] There is a growing public recognition that one of the most important public uses of the tidelands — a use encompassed within the tidelands trust — is the preservation of those lands in their natural state, so that they may serve as ecological units for scienti c study, as open space, and as environments which provide food and habitat for birds and marine life, and which favorably affect the scenery and climate of the area." (Pp. 259 260.)

Mono Lake is a navigable waterway. (*City of Los Angeles v. Aitken, supra*, 10 Cal. App.2d 460, 466.) It supports a small local industry which harvests brine shrimp for sale as fish food, which endeavor probably quali es the lake as a "fishery" under the traditional public trust cases. The principal values plaintiffs seek to protect, however, are recreational and ecological — the scenic views of the lake and its shore, the purity of the air, and the use of the lake for nesting and feeding by birds. Under *Marks v. Whitney, supra*, 6 Cal.3d 251, it is clear that protection of these values is among the purposes of the public trust.

(b) The scope of the public trust.

. . . .

It is, however, well settled in the United States generally and in California that the public trust is not limited by the reach of the tides, but encompasses all navigable lakes and streams.

. . . .

Mono Lake is, as we have said, a navigable waterway. The beds, shores and waters of the lake are without question protected by the public trust. The streams diverted by DWP, however, are not themselves navigable. Accordingly, we must address in this case a question not discussed in any recent public trust case — whether the public trust limits conduct affecting nonnavigable tributaries to navigable waterways.

. . . .

We conclude that the public trust doctrine, as recognized and developed in California decisions, protects navigable waters from harm caused by diversion of nonnavigable tributaries.

(c) Duties and powers of the state as trustee.

In the following review of the authority and obligations of the state as administrator of the public trust, the dominant theme is the state's sovereign power and duty to exercise continued supervision over the trust. One consequence, of importance to this and many other cases, is that parties acquiring rights in trust property generally hold those rights subject to the trust, and can assert no vested right to use those rights in a manner harmful to the trust.

As we noted recently in *City of Berkeley v. Superior Court, supra*, 26 Cal.3d 515, the decision of the United States Supreme Court in *Illinois Central Railroad Company v. Illinois, supra*, 146 U.S. 387, "remains the primary authority even today, almost nine decades after it was decided." . . .

. . . .

In *State of California v. Superior Court (Fogerty), supra*, 29 Cal.3d 240, 249, we stated that owners of shoreline property in Lake Tahoe would be entitled to compen-sation if enforcement of the public trust required them to remove improvements. By implication, however, the determination that the property was subject to the trust, despite its implication as to future uses and improvements, was not considered a taking requiring compensation.

In summary, the foregoing cases amply demonstrate the continuing power of the state as administrator of the public trust, a power which extends to the revocation of previously granted rights or to the enforcement of the trust against lands long thought free of the trust.

Except for those rare instances in which a grantee may acquire a right to use former trust property free of trust restrictions, the grantee holds subject to the trust, and while he may assert a vested right to the servient estate (the right of use subject to the trust) and to any improvements he erects, he can claim no vested right to bar recognition of the trust or state action to carry out its purposes.

Since the public trust doctrine does not prevent the state from choosing between trust uses, . . . [case citations omitted]. . . . the Attorney General of California, seeking to maximize state power under the trust, argues for a broad concept of trust uses. In his view, "trust uses" encompass all public uses, so that in practical effect the doctrine would impose no restrictions on the state's ability to allocate trust property. We know of no authority which supports this view of the public trust. . . .

. . . .

3. The California Water Rights System.

. . . .

4. The relationship between the Public Trust Doctrine and the California Water Rights System.

. . . .

. . . In our opinion, both the public trust doctrine and the water rights system embody important precepts which make the law more responsive to the diverse needs and interests involved in the planning and allocation of water resources. To embrace one system of thought and reject the other would lead to an unbalanced structure, one which would either decry as a breach of trust appropriations essential to the economic development of this state, or deny any duty to protect or even consider the values promoted by the public trust. Therefore, seeking an accommodation which will make use of the pertinent principles of both the public trust doctrine and the appropriative water rights system, and drawing upon the history of the public trust and the water rights system, the body of judicial precedent, and the views of expert commentators, we reach the following conclusions:

a. The state as sovereign retains continuing supervisory control over its navigable waters and the lands beneath those waters. This principle, fundamental to the concept of the public trust, applies to rights in flowing waters as well as to rights in tidelands and lakeshores; it prevents any party from acquiring a vested right to appropriate water in a manner harmful to the interests protected by the public trust.

b. As a matter of current and historical necessity, the Legislature, acting directly or through an authorized agency such as the Water Board, has the power to grant usufructuary licenses that will permit an appropriator to take water from flowing streams and use that water in a distant part of the state, even though this taking does not promote, and may unavoidably harm, the trust uses at the source stream. The population and economy of this state depend upon the appropriation of vast quantities of water for uses unrelated to in-stream trust values. California's Constitution (*see* art. X, 2), its statutes (*see* Wat. Code, 100, 104), decisions (*see, e.g., Waterford I. Dist. v. Turlock I. Dist.*(1920) 50 Cal. App. 213, 220 [194 P. 757]), and commentators (e.g., Hutchins, *The Cal. Law of Water Rights, op. cit. supra*, p. 11) all emphasize the need to make efficient use of California's limited water resources: all recognize, at least implicitly, that efficient use requires diverting water from in-stream uses. Now that the economy and population centers of this state have developed in reliance upon appropriated water, it would be disingenuous to hold that such appropriations are and have always been improper to the extent that they harm public trust uses, and can be justi ed only upon theories of reliance or estoppel.

c. The state has an af rmative duty to take the public trust into account in the planning and allocation of water resources, and to protect public trust uses whenever feasible. Just as the history of this state shows that appropriation may be necessary for efficient use of water despite unavoidable harm to public trust values, it demonstrates that an appropriative water rights system administered without consideration of the public trust may cause unnecessary and unjusti ed harm to trust interests. As a matter of practical necessity the state may have to approve appropriations despite foreseeable harm to public trust uses. In so doing, however, the state must bear in mind its duty as trustee to consider the effect of the taking on the public trust, and to preserve, so far as consistent with the public interest, the uses protected by the trust.

. . . .

Once the state has approved an appropriation, the public trust imposes a duty of continuing supervision over the taking and use of the appropriated water. In exercising its sovereign power to allocate water resources in the public interest, the state is not con ned by past allocation decisions which may be incorrect in light of current knowledge or inconsistent with current needs.

The state accordingly has the power to reconsider allocation decisions even though those decisions were made after due consideration of their effect on the public trust. The case for reconsidering a particular decision, however, is even stronger when that decision failed to weigh and consider public trust uses. In the case before us, the salient fact is that no responsible body has ever determined the impact of diverting the entire flow of the Mono Lake tributaries into the Los Angeles Aqueduct. This is not a case in which the Legislature, the Water Board, or any judicial body has determined that the needs of Los Angeles outweigh the needs of the Mono Basin, that the bene t gained is worth the price. Neither has any responsible body determined whether some lesser taking would better balance the diverse interests. Instead, DWP acquired rights to the entire flow in 1940 from a water board which believed it lacked both the power and the duty to protect the Mono Lake environment, and continues to exercise those rights in apparent disregard for the resulting damage to the scenery, ecology, and human uses of Mono Lake.

It is clear that some responsible body ought to reconsider the allocation of the waters of the Mono Basin. No vested rights bar such reconsideration.

. . . .

6. Conclusion

. . . .

This opinion is but one step in the eventual resolution of the Mono Lake controversy. We do not dictate any particular allocation of water. Our objective is to resolve a legal conundrum in which two competing systems of thought the public trust doctrine and the appropriative water rights system existed independently of each other, espousing principles which seemingly suggested opposite results. We hope by integrating these two doctrines to clear away the legal barriers which have so far prevented either the Water Board or the courts from taking a new and objective look at the water resources of the Mono Basin. The human and environmental uses of Mono Lake uses protected by the public trust doctrine deserve to be taken into account. Such uses should not be destroyed because the state mistakenly thought itself powerless to protect them.

[Concurring opinion and dissenting opinion omitted.]

NOTES AND QUESTIONS

1. ***Postscript.*** In settlement of the *Audubon* litigation, the parties signed an agreement requiring Los Angeles to reduce lake levels to no lower than 6,391 feet above sea level. At this level, most of the "spires of tufa" would again be submerged. Los Angeles is replacing Mono Lake water with water from the Colorado River and other sources. Los Angeles has also undertaken water conservation initiatives.

2. ***Form and Function.*** Is the public trust doctrine value-neutral? Could it be used, for example, to require resource development on public lands? Or is it restricted to promoting "pro-environment" or "pro-conservation" ends?

After *Audubon*, does the public trust doctrine still find its moorings in concepts of property law? If not, how does this bear on its relationship with takings principles?

3. ***The Public Trust Doctrine in Federal Law.*** Because of its historical origins, one could speculate the public trust doctrine might reside in federal law as well as in state law. Just as the doctrine cabins the exercise of the police power at the state level, so also could it cabin the exercise of, say, the Property Clause power at the federal level. In fact, the United States Supreme Court has found the public trust doctrine to exist in federal law, but in that context it seems to expand government power, not reduce it. In *Light v. United States*, 220 U.S. 523, 31 S. Ct. 485 (1911), for example, a defendant, who had pastured cattle on federal land in violation of federal regulations, argued that the government could not withdraw large bodies of public land from public access. The Supreme Court's opinion had none of the ring of *Illinois Central* about it:

> [I]t is not for the courts to say how th[e public] trust shall be administered. That is for Congress to determine. The courts cannot compel it to set aside the lands for settlement; or to suffer them to be used for agricultural or grazing purposes, nor interfere when, in the exercise of its discretion, Congress establishes a forest reserve for what it decides to be national and public purposes. In the same way and in the exercise of the same trust it may disestablish a reserve, and devote the property to some other national and public purpose. These are rights incident to proprietorship, to say nothing of the power of the United States as a sovereign over the property belonging to it.

Light, 220 U.S. at 537, 31 S. Ct. at 488. *See also United States v. San Francisco*, 310 U.S. 16, 60 S. Ct. 749 (1940) (decisions under the Property Clause are primarily for Congress); *United States v. Trinidad Coal Co.*, 137 U.S. 160, 11 S. Ct. 57 (1890) (public trust doctrine found to justify a land disposal statute); Eric Pearson, *The Public Trust Doctrine in Federal Law*, 24 J. Land Resources & Envtl L. 173 (2004).

Do you think the federal public trust doctrine should have been applied in *Midwest Oil*?

Chapter 7

ENDANGERED SPECIES ACT

"The first rule of intelligent tinkering is to save all the pieces." *Aldo Leopold*

SYNOPSIS

A. INTRODUCTION
B. SECTION 4
　　1. The Listing Process
　　2. Designation of Critical Habitat
C. SECTION 7
D. SECTION 9
E. STATUTORY FLEXIBILITY INITIATIVES
F. ADMINISTRATIVE FLEXIBILITY INITIATIVES

A. INTRODUCTION

The Nature Conservancy has calculated that one-third of all U.S. plants and animals are at risk of extinction. Since the European discovery of North America, 110 "irreplaceable" flora and fauna have disappeared, and another 416 are "missing." Approximately 7,000 U.S. species are threatened, and, according to an estimate of the U.S. Public Interest Research Group, 50,000 plants and animals become extinct worldwide each year. One quarter of the world's species might be gone within 50 years. At risk among the "charismatic megafauna" are the Giant Panda, the Asian Tiger, the Kemp's Ridley Sea Turtle, the Black-Footed Ferret, the Karner Blue Butterfly, the Northern Right Whale, the Orangutan, the Roseate Tern, the Florida Panther, and the Black Rhinoceros.

The extinction of species is of international concern. A massive and persistent demand for wildlife products, especially in the United States, the Far East, and western Europe, is threatening "thousands of species of flora and fauna," according to a report prepared for the United Nations Convention on International Trade in Endangered Species of Wild Fauna and Flora ("CITES").[1] Many species are at risk of extinction; exemplifying the problem are rhinos (about 25,000 left in the wild by one estimate), tigers (about 3,000 remaining), and giant pandas (about 2,000 remaining). The CITES report has estimated global illegal trade in wildlife at $5

---

[1] CITES has 172 member nations and controls trade in about 5,000 species of animals and 28,000 species of plants.

279

billion. One example of this illegal trade: by one estimate, 100,000 wild birds are smuggled into the United States from Mexico each year. Illegal trade is not the sole reason for species jeopardy. The plight of elephants in Mozambique is emblematic of the larger problem. Their numbers have declined from approximately 60,000 in 1974 to about 12,000 in 2002 (the last population estimate available). This drop prompted the United States government to ban imports of elephant products to this nation. *See, e.g., Franks v. Salazar*, No. 09-0942 (D.C. Cir. Oct. 6, 2011). Habitat loss, toxic chemicals, and other such factors are significant contributors as well. Beyond that, it is not abnormal for species to become extinct. It has been estimated that 99% of all species ever in existence have already passed on. GREGG EASTERBROOK, A MOMENT ON THE EARTH, THE COMING AGE OF ENVIRONMENTAL OPTIMISM 552 (1995).

In this chapter, we will review the legal framework in place to protect these non-human living creatures. We begin with a brief historical recitation.

KAREN P. SHELDON, OVERVIEW OF WILDLIFE LAW
in ENVIRONMENTAL LAW — FROM RESOURCES TO RECOVERY § 6.1(B)(2), at 203–09 (1993)[2]

. . . .

Milestones in the History of Wildlife

The critical milestones for wildlife in the United States relate to its terrible decline in the early years of the Republic, to the efforts to secure its continued existence and protection, and to increases in understanding about the effects of human actions on populations and habitat. Because much of the understanding of wildlife and effort to protect it are expressed in law, these milestones are guides to the discussion of the evolution of wildlife law.

(a) The Era of Free Taking — 1600s-1850s

The early history of European exploration and occupation of North America is one of virtually unrestrained slaughter of animals — for food, for fashion, and later to aid the settlement of the West by subduing Indians through the extermination of the buffalo. Wildlife species that today exist only in remnant populations on federal lands in the West once covered the continent. Wolves were so prevalent in Massachusetts in the early1700s that local citizens seriously considered building a fence across Cape Cod to protect livestock from predation. Bison ranged through New York and Pennsylvania and as far south as Georgia. The last bison east of the Mississippi River was killed in 1801. Woodland caribou and other large and small mammals and hundreds of species of birds and fish existed in the forests and waters of the East Coast.

From the 1700s to the 1850s, many of these species, particularly those that could be eaten, were subjected to hunting pressures no population could withstand. Most of this hunting was carried out by market or "pot" hunters who sold venison, wild

---

[2] Reprinted from CAMPBELL-MOHN, BREEN & FUTRELL, ENVIRONMENTAL LAW — FROM RESOURCES TO RECOVERY, Copyright © 1993, with permission of Thomson Reuters.

fowl, fish, and shellfish to a public with limited domestic sources of meat. Passenger pigeons, once the largest number of birds of one species ever known on one continent, were clubbed, netted, shot, and trapped for food and sport. So were the heath hen, wild turkey, ruffed grouse, and quail. In 200years, the immense wealth of wildlife all but disappeared from the East.

Expansion westward in the 1800s was accompanied by wildlife losses as well. In 1806, the demand for beaver hats sent mountain men into the Oregon Territory and the Rocky Mountains, where they virtually trapped out the beaver in less than 40 years. When the market for beaver fell in the late 1830s, it was replaced by the demand for buffalo skins and meat. In 1840, one fur company alone sent 67,000 buffalo skins down the Missouri River to St. Louis.

Once the Great Plains fell to the plow and the advance of the railroads in the 1860s and 1870s, the buffalo and the Indian culture that depended on it were doomed. By 1900, nearly 60 million buffalo had been destroyed to make way for settlers and agriculture.

(b) Gestures of Regret — 1850s-1900

By the second half of the 19th century, the decimation of wildlife had taken its toll. Americans began to realize that the vast natural resources of their nation were not inexhaustible. The conservation of wildlife was acknowledged as an important goal, one that required public involvement. Private citizens created organizations dedicated to the welfare of wildlife. Among the earliest of these were groups of recreational hunters who believed in the "sport" of taking wildlife according to rules designed to avoid waste and prevent extinction. These groups supported enactment of state laws to protect wildlife and to restrain its exploitation. In the 1850s, many states passed game laws setting seasons and bag limits to stem the terrible decline of wildlife. Unfortunately, these laws were "largely gestures of regret," too late to save what had existed and without effective means of enforcement.

(c) The Rise of Conservation — 1900-20

By the 1880s, it was clear that the states were unable to enforce their wildlife laws and that the alarming drop in wildlife populations was a national problem requiring federal action. In 1884, George Grinnell, a prominent sportsman and editor of *Forest and Stream*, began to advocate the establishment of interest groups to lobby Congress on behalf of wildlife. Grinnell founded the National Audubon Society (1886) and the Boone and Crockett Club (1888), both of which were instrumental in achieving passage of the Lacey Act of 1900, the first federal wildlife statute.

The Lacey Act, which prohibits the interstate shipment of wildlife taken in violation of state law, is one of the most important pieces of wildlife legislation ever passed. It not only put the market hunters out of business and prohibited the importation of foreign wildlife, except by permit, it gave real authority to the U.S. Biological Survey, predecessor to the U.S. Fish and Wildlife Service. The Survey, founded in 1885 to carry out a national biological survey and various bird studies, was charged with the administration and implementation of the Lacey Act. This signaled the beginning of active federal involvement in wildlife management and protection.

In the years following the enactment of the Lacey Act, Congress vested increasing authority over wildlife in federal agencies, thereby fostering the development of effective federal institutions for wildlife management and protection. Between 1900 and 1913, for example, Congress concluded the Fur Seal Treaty, regulating the harvest of the Northern fur seal; enacted the Federal Tariff Act, which prohibited the importation of feathers and other parts of certain birds used in millinery; and enacted the Migratory Bird Act of 1913, which gave control over migratory birds to the federal government.

The federal statutes expressed a new theme in wildlife law: conservation. The recognition of the importance of conserving wildlife corresponded to the growing federal interest in the retention and conservation of other resources of the federal lands. In the late 1800s and early 1900s, the active disposition of federal lands into private hands pursuant to statutes like the Mining Law of 1872 and the Homestead Act was arrested by the recognition of the importance of retaining lands with special values in the public domain. Yellowstone Park was set aside in 1872 to protect its stunning natural resources, including its wildlife, and other park designations followed. Forest lands were reserved, initially by Presidents McKinley and Theodore Roosevelt, and then by Congress under the Forest Reserve Act of1891 and other statutes. A few years later, in 1911, Congress enacted the Weeks Act, which called for the reacquisition of private lands to provide for federal forests in the East. Although these forests were not reserved explicitly for wildlife conservation, the protection of habitat that was accomplished was beneficial.

The conservation movement of the early 1900s reflected two strands of thought about conserving wildlife and other natural resources: a utilitarian view and a preservation view. The utilitarian view, represented by people like Gifford Pinchot, the creator of the Forest Service and head of Roosevelt's National Conservation Committee, regarded conservation as "the use of natural resources for the greatest good of the greatest number for the longest time." Implicit in this outlook is the idea that natural resources should be managed in a sustainable way to assure continued human use.

The preservation view was not utilitarian. Taking its antecedents from H.D. Thoreau, and listening hard to the words of John Muir, it called for a realization of the intrinsic value of wildlife and wild places not measured by human use.

Neither the utilitarian nor the preservation view, however, regarded conservation of predators, "pests," and "vermin" with the same benevolent attitude extended to other wildlife. These species were systematically and ruthlessly attacked.

(d) Lessons of Failure — 1920-40

Early conservation efforts focused on reintroduction of species and the elimination of predators. These efforts, along with controls on hunting and trapping, were thought to be appropriate to recover diminished wildlife populations. While the restrictions on hunting and trapping did halt the precipitous decline of target species, reintroduction and predator control were spectacularly unsuccessful wildlife management tools.

Efforts to introduce or reintroduce wildlife began in colonial times, but reached a fever pitch in the early 1900s. Hundreds of attempts were made to restore or stock species in areas where wildlife was diminished or extirpated. European variants of American species were released across the United States. Game farms were established to raise animals for transfer to the wild. Animals were transported from one part of the country to another, regardless of whether the new area was appropriate range or habitat.

Most of these efforts failed. Where they succeeded, the results were often harmful or fatal to native species. Rarely did the introduced species function as intended in its new ecosystem. The English sparrow, for example, which was imported to eat cankerworms, turned out to be a voracious eater of agricultural seeds. The carp, brought in as a food source after the Civil War, so muddies a stream in its foraging for food that the waters are uninhabitable by other fish.

One of the most disastrous wildlife management efforts, and one that has been repeated across the West, was the elimination of the natural predators of the mule deer on the Kaibab Plateau in the 1920s. Following destruction of the wolves, bobcats, cougars, and coyotes that had kept the herd in balance, the Kaibab deer population exploded. Thousands died of starvation after over grazing ruined the habitat.

By the 1920s it was apparent that other wildlife management techniques were required. The failures of reintroduction and predator contributed to the development of the science of wildlife management and to an expanded role for the federal government in all aspects of wildlife regulation and protection.

Aldo Leopold, whose field experience later included the Kaibab deer situation, was the first person to work out the fundamental principles of wildlife management. In 1920, he began a study of the relationships among animal and plant species that altered the previously held assumptions about how wild animal populations function. Leopold articulated the principle of carrying capacity — the idea that an ecosystem can support only a certain number of a single species — which is now a central premise of wildlife biology. Leopold's book, *Game Management*, published in 1929, remains a basic text in the field.

Leopold's new approach to wildlife management fostered much scientific research and the recognition of wildlife management as a profession. In 1935, the Biological Survey established a network of wildlife research units at land grant universities. This Cooperative Wildlife Research Unit Program began training thousands of wildlife professionals. In 1936, the first North American Wildlife Conference was held, assembling biologists, agency administrators, hunters, and other persons interested in wildlife to discuss wildlife issues. In 1940, the Biological Survey and the Bureau of Fisheries were merged into the Fish and Wildlife Service and located in the Department of the Interior (DOI). It was an encouraging time for wildlife.

(e) A Corner Is Turned — 1940-70

By 1940, a corner had been turned for many significant wildlife species. There was no longer danger of widespread extinctions of once common animals like the passenger pigeon. Game species, particularly elk and deer, were increasing in numbers and distribution. Waterfowl habitat was being set aside in federal wildlife refuges, although the low numbers of waterfowl were still a concern. Other wildlife habitat became available, serendipitously, as Americans left the farm and moved to the city. In the late 1930s the rate of conversion of forest land to agriculture slowed and then reversed. In addition, the federal government was funding wildlife projects across the country through the Federal Aid to Wildlife Restoration Act.

This good news masked the plight of species dependent on water as development continued to encroach on wetlands and polluted habitat. It also masked the plight of species of no value to hunters and fishers, and those that continued to be the target of predator and pest control programs.

Perhaps the most significant factor in achieving wildlife protection during this period was the change in public attitude. By World War II, wildlife was used less for commercial production of furs and food than for consumptive and nonconsumptive recreation. The utilitarian view of wildlife that had prevailed through most of U.S. history, even during the conservation movement, gave way further to the idea that wildlife should be preserved for its own intrinsic value. The regard for wildlife extended to all species, with the exception of predators and pests, not just to those that could be hunted, trapped, and hooked.

The attitude change is seen most clearly in the efforts to protect species in danger of extinction. In North America, more than 500 species are known to have become extinct since 1600. In 1945, the Smithsonian Institute published the first endangered species list of 40 animals, including several that are recognizable today: the black footed ferret, the California condor, and the whooping crane. The list was part of the Smithsonian's program to identify and aid species in trouble.

Until 1966, endangered species' protection, such as it was, was carried out in state and federal wildlife programs geared to other purposes, principally game management. The first federal law designed to protect endangered species was the Endangered Species Act (ESA) of 1966, which directed the Secretary of the Interior to conduct a program of endangered species protection and authorized the expenditure of $15 million from the Land and Water Conservation Fund for acquisition of endangered species habitat. The act did not prohibit or limit the taking of endangered species, and, therefore, was regarded as weak.

The 1966 ESA was superseded by the Endangered Species Act of 1973, which made a significant change in the federal approach to endangered species protection. The 1973 ESA declared it unlawful to take any member of an endangered species, regardless of where the species was found. Thus, the killing of endangered species was prohibited on private and state, as well as federal, lands. Critical habitat protection and a process for intergovernmental consultation to prevent federal actions from jeopardizing the continued existence of endangered species were also added.

(f) Awake After Silent Spring — 1970-present

Concern for endangered species carried forward to the 1970s, joining with the flowering of the environmental movement. Wildlife benefitted from the host of statutes passed during the beginning of the decade: the Clean Air Act, the Clean Water Act, the National Environmental Policy Act, the Marine Mammal Protection Act, the National Forest Management Act, the Federal Land Policy and Management Act, and so on. These laws reflect a new understanding of the impact of human activities on the environment and direct significant federal resources to environmental clean-up and to a change in industrial practices that cause pollution.

For wildlife, the single most important event of the period may well be the publication in 1962 of Rachel Carson's *Silent Spring*, which described the terrible threat posed by DDT (dichloro-diphenyl-trichloro-ethane)and other pesticides to the osprey, brown pelican, peregrine falcon, and other birds, animals, and fish. Once again, common animals were at the brink of disappearing. Although it took 10 years from publication of the book, the Environmental Protection Agency (EPA) banned the use of DDT and related pesticides in 1972. In the years since then, the affected bird species, particularly the brown pelican, have made a remarkable comeback.

At the present time, the future for many species of American wildlife is uncertain. Understanding of wildlife needs has grown tremendously, but so has the human impact on wildlife habitat and water resources. More is known about the causes of species decline and extinction, but a corresponding understanding of how to solve these problems is lacking. Wildlife law will continue to be an important vehicle for grappling with these issues.

The preceding historical piece demonstrates that, while conservation of wildlife became a national goal early in the last century, efforts to accomplish the goal lagged seriously behind. Hampering pro-conservation efforts were a severely deficient understanding of the operation of natural ecosystems and a propensity to favor some species while ignoring, if not affirmatively demolishing, others. The result was a virtual parade of species-specific federal statutes,[3] which in the aggregate failed to sustain wildlife populations. What was sought, therefore, was a statute that would protect the whole of threatened wildlife rather than designated subgroups, and would do so by mandatory, not voluntary, controls. The first statute to do that was the Endangered Species Act of 1973, 16 U.S.C. §§ 1531–1543 ("ESA").[4]

---

[3] In addition to the Lacey Act, 16 U.S.C. § 701 and 18 U.S.C. §§ 42–44, and the other measures noted in the Sheldon piece, other federal enactments specifically aimed at protecting wildlife include: the Migratory Bird Treaty Act of 1918, 16 U.S.C. § 703 et seq.; the Black Bass Act of 1926, 44 Stat. 576, as amended, 16 U.S.C. § 851 et seq. (1976 ed.); the Migratory Bird Conservation Act of 1929, 16 U.S.C. § 715 et seq.; the Fish and Wildlife Coordination Act of 1934, 16 U.S.C. § 661 et seq.; the Bald Eagle Protection Act of 1940, 16 U.S.C. § 668 et seq.; the Wild Free-Roaming Horses and Burros Act of 1971, 16 U.S.C. §§ 1331–1340; the Marine Mammal Protection Act of 1972, 16 U.S.C. § 1361 et seq.; and the Magnuson Fishery Conservation and Management Act of 1976, 16 U.S.C. § 1801 et seq.

[4] As noted in the Sheldon excerpt, *see supra*, the Endangered Species Act of 1966 was "weak," largely because compliance with its provisions was voluntary. In 1969, Congress followed it up with the Endangered Species Conservation Act, 83 Stat. 275, repealed, 87 Stat. 903, which limited the import and

The ESA simply towers over all other wildlife protection measures. Not long after its enactment, the United States Supreme Court described it as "the most comprehensive legislation for the preservation of endangered species ever enacted by any nation." *Tennessee Valley Authority v. Hill*, 437 U.S. 153, 180, 98 S. Ct. 2279, 2294 (1978); *see infra*. Former Secretary of Interior Bruce Babbitt characterized the statute as "undeniably the most innovative, wide-reaching, and successful environmental law which has been enacted in the last quarter century." Bruce Babbitt, *The Endangered Species Act and "Takings": A Call for Innovation Within the Terms of the Act*, 24 ENVTL. L. 355, 356 (1994).

One would speculate that a far-reaching legislative initiative of this sort would have generated a great deal of controversy in the Congress, but, as a political matter, enacting the ESA turned out to be easy. For one thing, Congress was distracted by more compelling problems, namely the Middle East oil embargo and the looming prospect of a presidential impeachment. For another, the Congress was suffering from a serious lack of appreciation for what it was doing. The conventional wisdom was that there would be perhaps 100 species that might warrant protection. Congress did not foresee the legislation it was about to enact would go far beyond protecting the grand statements of natural evolution, like the bald eagle, wolf, and grizzly, all the way to furbish louseworts, kangaroo rats, mollusks, and a wide array of plants. As one congressman put it, "The fact is that if Congress knew in 1974 how the Act would have turned out, it never would have passed the legislation in the first place — at least not in this form." Congressman Bill Thomas, *Externalization of Federal Public Policy Costs: The Endangered Species Act*, 8 FORDHAM ENVTL. L.J. 171, 175 (1996).

But Congress did not know. Its debate on the bill was cursory, focusing on the arguably insignificant issue whether the federal government should supplant traditional state wildlife regulation. In the end, the Senate enacted the statute 92-0, and the House followed suit by 355-4. President Richard Nixon signed the bill into law on December 28, 1973.

In the years since its enactment, the ESA has become precisely what Congress did not envision. It is broadly protective of hundreds of species of plants and animals. Protection comes at a significant cost — the Act has discomfitted the plans and expectations of thousands of people at a cost in the many millions of dollars.

In the remainder of this chapter, we examine this prodigious statute. Our coverage will center on the ESA's major regulatory provisions, §§ 4, 7, and 9. Section 4, 16 U.S.C. § 1533, is the ESA's triggering mechanism. It establishes the process by which species are listed as endangered or threatened, and thereby warrant the protective shield of the statute. Section 4 also calls for designations of "critical habitat" for each protected species. Once the trigger is pulled, § 7, 16 U.S.C. § 1536, and § 9, 16 U.S.C. § 1538, bring the force of the statute into play. Section 7 is a broad prohibition on any action by the federal government that might jeopardize an endangered or threatened species or destroy or adversely modify its critical habitat. Section 9, applicable to all persons, including the federal govern-

---

sale of species in danger of "worldwide extinction." Neither of these statutes decelerated the increasingly rapid rate of species extinction.

ment, prohibits a variety of independent actions that could injure, directly or indirectly, those same species. The chapter concludes with a look at statutory and administrative initiatives undertaken to work some flexibility into the regulatory system.

B. SECTION 4

1. The Listing Process

NORTHWEST ECOSYSTEM ALLIANCE v. U.S. FISH AND WILDLIFE SERVICE
475 F.3d 1136 (9th Cir. 2007)

GOODWIN, CIRCUIT JUDGE:

The United States Fish and Wildlife Service (the "Service") denied a petition to classify western gray squirrels in Washington state as an endangered "distinct population segment" ("DPS") under the Endangered Species Act ("ESA"), 16 U.S.C. § 1531 et seq. Plaintiff-appellants Northwest Ecosystem Alliance, Center for Biological Diversity, and Tahoma Audubon Society (collectively, the "Alliance") sought review of the Service's decision in the district court, which entered summary judgment upholding the Service's determination. The Alliance led a timely notice of appeal. We affirm.

I. BACKGROUND

A. *The Endangered Species Act* Congress enacted the ESA to "provide a means whereby ecosystems upon which endangered species and threatened species depend may be conserved, [and] to provide a program for the conservation of such endangered species and threatened species." 16 U.S.C. § 1531(b). The ESA requires the Service to identify and list species that are "endangered" or "threatened."[5] 16 U.S.C. § 1533. The Service may list a species, on its own initiative, through notice-and-comment rulemaking. 16 U.S.C. § 1533(b)(5). Alternatively, a species may become listed through the petition process provided by the Administrative Procedure Act ("APA"), 5 U.S.C. § 553(e). Any interested person may petition the Service to add or remove a species from the list. *Id.*; 16 U.S.C. § 1533(b)(3)(A). Upon receiving such a petition, the Service must promptly determine whether the petition is supported by "substantial scientific or commercial information." 16 U.S.C. § 1533(b)(3)(A). If so, the Service is to "commence a review of status of the species concerned." *Id.* The Service is required to make a finding on the status of the species

---

[5] [Ed. note: If terrestrial species are involved, the subunit with listing authority is the Fish and Wildlife Service ("FWS"), by virtue of a delegation of power by the United States Department of Interior, the larger agency of which the FWS is a part. If ocean species or anadromous fish are involved, the subunit with listing authority is the National Marine Fisheries Service ("NMFS"), by virtue of a similar delegation of power by the United States Department of Commerce, the larger agency of which the NMFS is a part.]

within twelve months and publish its finding in the Federal Register. 16 U.S.C. § 1533(b)(3)(B). The Service must make its decision "solely on the basis of the best scientific and commercial data available." 16 U.S.C. § 1533(b)(1)(A). If the Service finds that a petitioned action is warranted, it must promptly publish a proposed regulation to implement its finding. 16 U.S.C. § 1533(b)(3)(B)(ii). A decision by the Service to deny a petitioned action is subject to judicial review. 16 U.S.C. § 1533(b)(3)(C)(ii).[6]

The definition of the term "species" is at the heart of the instant appeal. The ESA defines "species" to include "any subspecies of fish or wildlife or plants, and any *distinct population segment* of any species of vertebrate fish or wildlife which interbreeds when mature." 16 U.S.C. § 1532(16) (emphasis added). Thus, a population of wildlife that does not constitute a taxonomic species may nevertheless qualify for listing as a DPS. The statute does not expressly define the term "distinct population segment." The Service and the National Marine Fisheries Service ("NMFS") have jointly adopted a policy statement to guide their evaluation of whether a population group should be treated as a DPS. Policy Regarding the Recognition of Distinct Vertebrate Population Segments Under the Endangered Species Act, 61 Fed. Reg. 4722 (Feb. 7, 1996) ("DPS Policy"). The DPS Policy sets forth two factors for consideration: the "[d]iscreteness of the population segment in relation to the remainder of the species to which it belongs," and the "significance of the population segment to the species to which it belongs." *Id.* at 4725. Discreteness is satisfied if a population segment is "separated from other populations of the same taxon as a consequence of physical, physiological, ecological, or behavioral factors," or if a population's boundaries are marked by international borders. *Id.* Significance, in turn, is analyzed under four nonexclusive factors: (1) whether the population persists in a unique or unusual ecological setting; (2) whether the loss of the population would cause a "significant gap" in the taxon's range; (3) whether the population is the only surviving natural occurrence of a taxon; and (4) whether the population's genetic characteristics are "markedly" different from the rest of the taxon. *Id.* A population qualifies as a DPS if it is both discrete and significant. *Id.* If a population is deemed to be a DPS, the inquiry then proceeds to whether it is endangered or threatened. *Id.*

B. *Western Gray Squirrels in Washington*

Sciurus griseus griseus, a subspecies of the western gray squirrel, is the largest native tree squirrel in the Pacific Northwest. Status Review and 12-Month Finding for a Petition To List the Washington Population of the Western Gray Squirrel, 68 Fed. Reg. 34,628, 34,629 (June 10, 2003) ("Final Finding"). Members of the subspecies are "silvery-gray with dark flanks and creamy white underneath." *Id.* They live in trees, rarely venture into open spaces, and subsist principally on acorn and nuts. Historically, the western gray squirrel was widespread throughout Washington, Oregon, California, and western Nevada. *Id.* at 34,630. Today, the western gray squirrel is fairly common in California, where it is a regulated game species, with an estimated population of eighteen million. *Id.* at 34,631. In Oregon, the subspecies is not rare and is legally hunted, but its distribution appears to be much reduced from historical levels. *Id.* at 34,632. In Nevada, the western gray

---

[6] [Ed. note: the process that governs listing decisions also governs delisting decisions.]

squirrel is rare and has been classified as a "protected species" under state law. *Id.* at 34,631.

In Washington, the western gray squirrel once ranged from the Puget Sound to the Columbia River, and from the Cascade Mountains to Lake Chela. *Id.* at 34,632. The population has long been separated from the rest of the subspecies by the Columbia River. During the last century, its distribution has been reduced to three geographically isolated populations: the Puget Trough population, the North Cascades population, and the South Cascades population. . . .

C. *Procedural History*

On January 4, 2001, the Service received a petition led by the Alliance requesting an emergency rule to list the Washington population of the western gray squirrel as an endangered or threatened species. On October 29, 2002, the Service published its initial finding that the petition presented substantial information to indicate that one or more distinct population segments of western gray squirrels may exist in Washington. 90 day Finding for a Petition To List the Washington Population of the Western Gray Squirrel as Endangered or Threatened, 67 Fed. Reg. 65,931. The Service proceeded with a twelve-month status review. An early draft decision prepared by the Service's staff scientists recommended listing the Washington population as an endangered DPS. However, the Service ultimately denied the petition in a June 2003 decision published in the Federal Register. Final Finding, 68 Fed. Reg. at 34,628. The Service determined that the Washington population was not significant, under the DPS Policy, to the taxon to which it belonged.

On November 3, 2003, the Alliance filed a complaint in the District of Oregon seeking declaratory and injunctive relief against the Service and its officials. The Alliance contended that the Service's decision was arbitrary and capricious. On August 2, 2004, the district court granted summary judgment for the Service.

This appeal presents two issues: (1) whether the Service's construction of the term "distinct population segment" is entitled to Chevron deference, and if so, whether the Service's construction is reasonable; and (2) whether the Service's denial of the petition was arbitrary and capricious.

II. JURISDICTION AND STANDARD OF REVIEW

The district court had subject matter jurisdiction under 28 U.S.C. § 1331 and 16 U.S.C. § 1540(c) & (g). We have appellate jurisdiction pursuant to 28 U.S.C. § 1291.

We review de novo the district court's grant of summary judgment. *United States v. City of Tacoma*, 332 F.3d 574, 578 (9th Cir.2003). As discussed below, we review the Service's interpretation of the ESA, as expressed in the DPS Policy, under the analytic framework laid out in *Chevron U.S.A., Inc. v. Natural Res. Def. Council, Inc.*, 467 U.S. 837, 104 S. Ct. 2778, 81 L. Ed. 2d 694 (1984). We review the Service's decision on the Washington gray squirrel under the APA, which provides that an agency action may be set aside only if it is "arbitrary, capricious, an abuse of discretion, or otherwise not in accordance with law." 5 U.S.C. § 706(2)(A). This standard of review is "highly deferential, presuming agency action to be valid and affirming the agency action if a reasonable basis exists for its decision." *Indepen-*

dent Acceptance Co. v. California, 204 F.3d 1247, 1251 (9th Cir. 2000) (citations omitted). We may not consider information outside of the administrative record, *Love v. Thomas*, 858 F.2d1347, 1356 (9th Cir. 1988), and may not "substitute [our] judgment for that of the agency." *Citizens To Preserve Overton Park v. Volpe*, 401 U.S. 402, 416, 91 S. Ct. 814, 28 L. Ed. 2d 136 (1971), *abrogated on other grounds by Califano v. Sanders*, 430 U.S. 99, 105, 97 S. Ct. 980, 51 L. Ed. 2d 192 (1977). Our task is simply to ensure that the agency "considered the relevant factors and articulated a rational connection between the facts found and the choices made." *Nat'l Ass'n of Home Builders v. Norton*, 340 F.3d 835, 841 (9th Cir. 2003) (quoting *Baltimore Gas & Elec. Co. v. Natural Res. Def. Council, Inc.*, 462 U.S. 87, 105, 103 S. Ct. 2246, 76 L. Ed. 2d 437 (1983)); *see also Blue Mountain Biodiversity Project v. Blackwood*, 161 F.3d 1208, 1211 (9th Cir.1998) (court must determine whether the agency decision was "based on a consideration of the relevant factors") (citation omitted).

III. DISCUSSION

A. *Whether the DPS Policy Is Entitled to Chevron Deference*

The Alliance contends that the DPS Policy's requirement that a population be significant to its taxon is unlawfully restrictive. The Alliance does not seek to invalidate the DPS Policy on its face, but only as applied here.

A court reviewing an administrative interpretation of a statute must first ascertain whether Congress has spoken clearly on the issue. *Chevron*, 467 U.S. at 842 44. If the statute is clear, we "must give effect to the unambiguously expressed intent of Congress" regardless of the agency's view. *Id.* at 843. If the statute is ambiguous, however, we do not simply impose our own independent interpretation. *Id.* Rather, we must determine how much deference to give to the administrative interpretation. *Id.; United States v. Mead Corp.*, 533U.S. 218, 227 31, 121 S. Ct. 2164, 150 L. Ed. 2d 292 (2001). The precise degree of deference warranted depends on the statute and agency action at issue. *Mead*, 533 U.S. at 227 31. Under *Chevron's* classic formulation,

> [i]f Congress has explicitly left a gap for an agency to fill, there is an express delegation of authority to the agency to elucidate a specific provision of the statute by regulation. Such legislative regulations are given controlling weight unless they are arbitrary, capricious, or manifestly contrary to the statute.

467 U.S. at 844. If *Chevron* deference is inapplicable because Congress has not delegated interpretative authority to the agency, the agency's views still "constitute a body of experience and informed judgment to which courts and litigants may properly resort for guidance." *Skidmore v. Swift & Co.*, 323 U.S. 134, 140, 65 S. Ct. 161, 89 L.Ed. 124 (1944). The "fair measure of deference" may then range from "great respect" to "near indifference," depending on "the degree of the agency's care, its consistency, formality, and relative expertness, and . . . the persuasiveness of the agency's position." *Mead*, 533 U.S. at 228.

The ESA does not expressly define "distinct population segment," and the parties agree that the term has no generally accepted scientific meaning. Because the statutory term is elastic, we must decide whether the DPS Policy is entitled to deference under the *Chevron* standard, or under the less deferential *Skidmore* standard.

Chevron deference applies "when it appears that Congress delegated authority to the agency generally to make rules carrying the force of law, and that the agency interpretation claiming deference was promulgated in the exercise of that authority." *Mead*, 533 U.S. at 226 27. "[D]elegation of such authority may be shown in a variety of ways, as by an agency's power to engage in adjudication or notice-and-comment rulemaking, or by some other indication of a comparable congressional intent." *Id.* at 227. "It is fair to assume generally that Congress contemplates administrative action with the effect of law when it provides for a relatively formal administrative procedure tending to foster the fairness and deliberation that should underlie a pronouncement of such force." *Id.* at 230. In the ESA, Congress expressly delegated authority to the Service to develop criteria for evaluating petitions to list endangered species. Under 16 U.S.C. § 1533(h)(2), the Service is required to publish, in the Federal Register, guidelines on "criteria for making findings . . . with respect to petitions." The Service must also "provide to the public notice of, and opportunity to submit written comments on, any guideline (including amendment thereto) proposed to be established under this subsection." 16 U.S.C. § 1533(h). In substance, the formality § 1533(h) requires for policy statements is indistinguishable from notice-and-comment rulemaking under the APA. *Compare* 16 U.S.C. § 1533(h) with 5 U.S.C. § 553. This fact weighs in favor of affording *Chevron* deference.

The Alliance contends that the DPS Policy is an informal policy statement that lies "beyond the *Chevron* pale." *Mead*, 533 U.S. at 234; *see Christensen v. Harris County*, 529 U.S. 576, 587, 120 S. Ct. 1655, 146 L. Ed. 2d 621 (2000) ("[I]nterpretations contained in policy statements, agency manuals, and enforcement guidelines, all of which lack the force of law[,] do not warrant *Chevron*-style deference."). However, one important reason for denying *Chevron* deference to policy statements is that they are generally exempt from the public notice-and-comment procedures required by § 553 of the APA. 5 U.S.C. § 553(b)(3)(A); *cf. Mead*, 533 U.S. at 232–234 (denying *Chevron* deference to letter rulings adopted without public notice and comment); *Christensen*, 529 U.S. at 587 (advisory opinion letter adopted without notice and comment); *Reno v. Koray*, 515 U.S. 50, 61, 115 S. Ct. 2021, 132 L. Ed. 2d 46 (1995) (internal agency guideline adopted without notice and comment). In contrast, § 1533(h) of the ESA expressly requires public notice and comment for both the creation and the modi cation of the DPS Policy. These procedural rigors, combined with the express congressional command to the Service to develop guidelines, distinguish the DPS Policy from garden-variety policy statements that do not enjoy *Chevron* status.

Notwithstanding the robust process through which the DPS Policy emerged, the Alliance submits that *Chevron* deference is inappropriate because the DPS Policy does not have the "force of law." *Mead*, 533 U.S. at 227. The Alliance emphasizes that the Service had considered adopting the DPS Policy as a rule, but ultimately decided to adopt it as a policy statement instead. This argument is unpersuasive. The DPS Policy was not formulated in response to any party's petition but rather as a definitive statement of how the Service would conduct all future "evaluation[s] of distinct vertebrate population segments for the purposes of listing, delisting, and reclassifying under the Act." 61 Fed. Reg. at 4725. The Alliance has presented no evidence that the DPS Policy has ever been treated (by the Service or parties presenting petitions to list species) as anything other than legally binding. We therefore hold that the DPS Policy is entitled to *Chevron* deference.

B. *Whether the DPS Policy Is a Reasonable Construction of the ESA*

An agency interpretation that enjoys *Chevron* status must be upheld if it is based on a reasonable construction of the statute. *Chevron*, 467 U.S. at 843–45. The Alliance argues that the DPS Policy cannot withstand scrutiny even under the deferential *Chevron* standard.

First, the Alliance challenges the DPS Policy's requirement that a population be both discrete and significant in order to qualify as a "distinct population segment." The Alliance asserts that the words "distinct" and "discrete" are synonyms. *Webster's Third New International Dictionary* 659 (2002). Thus, they contend, any requirement that a population be significant in addition to being discrete is an additional hurdle not contemplated by the statute. However, the term "distinct" is not as limited in meaning as the Alliance suggests. "Distinct" can mean "notable" or "unusual." *Id.* It is not inconsistent with common usage, nor is it unreasonable, for the Service to construe "distinct" to mean both "discrete," in the sense of being separate from others, and "significant," in the sense of being notable.

Second, the Alliance claims that the significance requirement conflates separate statutory definitions. The term "significant" appears in the ESA's definition of "endangered species," which is defined as "any species which is in danger of extinction throughout all or a significant portion of its range. . . ." 16 U.S.C. § 1532(6). The DPS Policy incorporates a separate significance requirement into the definition of "distinct population segment," which is in turn part of the statutory definition of "species," 16 U.S.C. § 1532(16). The Alliance argues that the DPS Policy conflates the statutory definitions of "species" and "endangered species," reducing the latter to mere surplusage. Actually, the two significance requirements serve different functions. The significance requirement in the DPS Policy pertains to whether a population qualifies as a species, while significance in § 1532(6) relates to whether a species is endangered. The two terms overlap to some extent in application, but they are not identical. For example, a population may be significant under the DPS Policy if it has distinctive ecological or biological traits, but that has no bearing on whether the population is actually in danger of extinction for purposes of § 1532(6).

Third, the Alliance argues that the DPS Policy reflects an impermissibly narrow understanding of the ESA's purpose and focuses excessively on conserving genetic resources. In the Alliance's view, the Service's attention to genetic resources is inappropriate in light of Congress's finding, expressed in the ESA's preamble, that wildlife have "esthetic, ecological, educational, historical, recreational, and scientific value." 16 U.S.C. § 1531(a)(3). The DPS Policy actually describes the ESA's purposes as follows: "The Services understand the Act to support interrelated goals of conserving genetic resources and maintaining natural systems and biodiversity over a representative portion of their historic occurrence. The draft policy was intended to recognize both these intentions, but without focusing on either to the exclusion of the other." 61 Fed. Reg. at 4723. That statement is not inconsistent with the ESA's expressly stated goal of providing "a means whereby the ecosystems upon which endangered species and threatened species depend may be conserved." 16 U.S.C. § 1531(b). In addition, the significance requirement (which is the only portion of the DPS Policy to which the Alliance objects) may be satisfied not only by evidence of genetic differences but also by a population's persistence in unusual ecological settings, its status as the only natural surviving occurrence of a taxon, or evidence that its loss would result in a significant gap in its taxon's range. These are not the hallmarks of a policy that focuses on the conservation of genetic resources at the expense of all the other goals of the ESA.

Fourth, the Alliance argues that the Service, in formulating the DPS Policy, improperly considered congressional policy preferences expressed after the enactment of the ESA. After the ESA was amended to encompass distinct population segments, the General Accounting Office proposed that Congress repeal the amendment to prevent a proliferation of endangered species listings. Although Congress declined to adopt the proposal, a Senate committee report cautioned that it was "aware of the great potential for abuse" of the Service's DPS authority. S. Rep. No. 96-151, at 7 (1979). The report further stated an expectation that the Service would "use the ability to list populations *sparingly* and only when the biological evidence indicates that such action is warranted." *Id.* (emphasis added). The DPS Policy expressed an intent to follow that instruction. 61 Fed. Reg. at 4722. The Alliance contends that the policy views of a subsequent Congress should not be considered in interpreting a statutory term. The Alliance's position might be more persuasive if we were construing the statutory term on a blank slate, but that is not the situation here. We are reviewing an agency determination under the deferential *Chevron* standard. So long as the agency action is not manifestly contrary to the statute, it is not improper for the agency to consider the views of the elected branches in interpreting an ambiguous statutory term. *See Chevron*, 467 U.S. at 866 ("[F]ederal judges who have no constituency have a duty to respect the legitimate policy choices made by those who do."). Here the committee report's language was not in obvious tension with the statutory text and the Service did not err by relying on it in part.

Fifth, the Alliance contends that the DPS Policy has been applied inconsistently, pointing to *National Association of Home Builders* as support for its claim. However, the western pygmy-owl's preliminary listing in that case took place before the DPS Policy was issued in 1996 and thus cannot be used to show inconsistency in the policy's application. 340 F.3d at 839. Similarly, the bald eagle, grizzly bear, and gray wolf listings that the Alliance cites all took place well before 1996 (the last of the three was in 1978) and hence shed no light on the faithfulness of the Service's adherence to the DPS Policy. The Alliance also offers recent examples of discrete, endangered populations that were not granted protection by the Service (because they failed the significance requirement) — but, crucially, offers no examples of populations that were granted protection under the DPS Policy despite being found insignificant to their taxon.

For all these reasons, the DPS Policy is a reasonable construction of "distinct population segment."

C. *Whether the Service's Denial of the Petition Was Arbitrary and Capricious*

Applying the DPS Policy, the Service found that western gray squirrels in Washington constitute a discrete population, but are not significant to the taxon. It therefore denied the petition. The Alliance vigorously challenges the Service's determination on the "significance" prong.

We note that the Service's internal draft finding of May 16, 2003 recommended granting the petitioned action. The Alliance complains that the Service's final finding reached the opposite conclusion without citing any new data. However, the Service may change its mind after internal deliberation. *See Southwestern Ctr. for Biological Diversity v. Bureau of Reclamation*, 143 F.3d 515, 523 (9th Cir. 1998). The only question before us is whether the Service, in reaching its ultimate finding, "considered the relevant factors and articulated a rational connection between the facts found and the choices made." *Nat'l Ass'n of Home Builders*, 340 F.3d at 841.

The DPS Policy sets forth the following four factors to be used to determine a population's significance to its taxon:

1. Persistence of the discrete population segment in an ecological setting unusual or unique for the taxon,

2. Evidence that loss of the discrete population segment would result in a significant gap in the range of a taxon,

3. Evidence that the discrete population represents the only surviving natural occurrence of a taxon that may be more abundant elsewhere as an introduced population outside its historic range, or

4. Evidence that the discrete population segment differs markedly from other populations of the species in its genetic characteristics.

61 Fed. Reg. at 4725. The Service found that the first, second, and fourth factors warranted analysis and that none of those factors established the Washington gray squirrels' significance to their taxon. The Alliance argues that the Service's findings on those factors were arbitrary and capricious, and not supported by the scientific evidence in the record.

[In the balance of the opinion, the court discussed the first, second, and fourth factors and found the findings of the FWS to be not arbitrary and capricious.]

IV. CONCLUSION

As set forth above, the DPS Policy is entitled to *Chevron* deference. Under the *Chevron* standard, the DPS Policy was a reasonable construction of the ESA. The Service's decision denying the petition was not arbitrary or capricious.

Affirmed.

NOTE

Better Late Than Never. *Alliance* is the first circuit court of appeals decision to examine the validity of the Service's interpretation of the meaning of "distinct population segment."

NOTE ON ADMINISTRATIVE LAW #2[7]

The *Alliance* decision depended almost entirely upon principles of administrative law. The government won the case because the court opted to review the legitimacy of the agency's action deferentially. This Note discusses briefly how courts go about the important task of reviewing agency actions.

Section 706(2) of the Administrative Procedure Act ("APA"), *see supra*, instructs federal courts how to go about the task of judicial review. As would be expected, the provision requires courts to set aside rules and adjudications that are *ultra vires*, procedurally defective, or unconstitutional. Importantly, § 706(2) also instructs courts to overturn agency actions that lack "substantial evidence" or that are "arbitrary, capricious, an abuse of discretion, or otherwise not in accordance with law." Courts follow these latter statutory directives closely on some occasions, cursorily on others, and sometimes not at all.

As a general matter, the standard of review a court uses depends on what the court is reviewing. If a court is reviewing the content of an agency rule that establishes a regulatory program, or a decision that constitutes an exercise of agency discretionary authority (such as when an agency decides where to allow the construction of a nuclear power plant or how to balance and give weight to a list of decision-making factors), the court will routinely use the "arbitrary and capricious test." Using this standard of review, the court will find the agency action to be "arbitrary, capricious, an abuse of discretion, or otherwise not in accordance with law" if any of several conditions are manifest: if the agency failed to base its decision on a consideration of all relevant factors, if there was a clear error of judgment, or if the agency's inquiry was not searching and careful. Under this standard of review, the court does not substitute its judgment for that of the agency. Rather, a court should overturn an agency action on this basis only if the choice made by the agency was inexcusably erroneous. A major case discussing this standard of review is *Citizens to Preserve Overton Park v. Volpe*, 401 U.S. 402, 91 S. Ct. 814 (1971).

If, on the other hand, a court is reviewing the propriety of an agency's factual findings — for example, the agency determined a nuclear power plant is "unsafe" in violation of a requirement that it be "safe" — the mandated standard of review typically is the "substantial evidence" test. This test, as a general matter, requires a reviewing court to see if there exists "such relevant evidence as a reasonable mind might accept as adequate to support [the] conclusion." *Universal Camera Corp. v. National Labor Relations Board*, 340 U.S. 474, 477, 71 S. Ct. 456, 459 (1951). As with the arbitrary and capricious test, it is not for a court in these circumstances to substitute its factual finding for that of an agency. Rather, the agency determination should be overturned only if the evidence is undeniably unsupportive of it.

---

[7] This is the second of four "Notes on Administrative Law" that appear at various points in this book. The material is inserted to assist students who have not learned administrative law. If you have already taken a course in this subject area, or have learned administrative law by some other mechanism, you should feel free to skip this Note. If you have not done so, however, you should both read this Note and resolve to master this important subject area at some future time.

Most controversial is the standard of review used by federal courts when they evaluate an agency's interpretation of the meaning of a statute the agency administers. In these instances, the United States Supreme Court declared a review standard without referring to the APA. The review standard it declared is twofold. When a court reviews an agency's interpretation of the meaning of what is perceived by the court to be an *unambiguous* statutory term or phrase, the court may disregard the agency's interpretation entirely. On such occasions, courts should reach their own independent determinations of statutory meaning. Unlike the arbitrary and capricious and substantial evidence tests, this review standard is entirely non-deferential to agencies: a court will give no weight to the agency's interpretation. On the other hand, when a court reviews an agency's interpretation of the meaning of what is perceived by the court to be an *ambiguous* statutory term or phrase, a court will affirm the agency interpretation if it is "permissible." This review standard, obviously, is quite deferential to agencies. This twofold standard of review was announced in a tremendously important decision entitled *Chevron U.S.A. v. Natural Resources Defense Council*, 467 U.S. 837, 104 S. Ct. 2778 (1984) (discussed at some length in *Alliance, supra*. The non-deferential review standard is known as *Chevron* Step One review, and the deferential standard (as you surely just now intuited) is known as *Chevron* Step Two review. (Collectively, this standard is known as the "Chevron Two Step.") Step One is uncontroversial: courts are in place to declare the meaning of law, right? But Step Two has been quite controversial. Many legal commenters maintain Step Two is nothing less than a willful abdication of review authority by the judiciary.

Expect to see *Chevron* play an exceedingly important role as we proceed through this text.

SOUTHWEST CENTER FOR BIOLOGICAL DIVERSITY v. BABBITT
215 F.3d 58 (D.C. Cir. 2000)

JUDGES: Before: EDWARDS, CHIEF JUDGE, RANDOLPH and ROGERS, CIRCUIT JUDGES.

EDWARDS, CHIEF JUDGE: The only issue raised on appeal in this case is whether the Endangered Species Act ("Act") requires the Fish and Wildlife Service to conduct an on-site population count of birds when the currently available data are sparse and calculations of a bird species population must of necessity be based on estimates. The Act provides that the Secretary of the Interior must make decisions whether to list a species as endangered or threatened "solely on the basis of the best scientific and commercial data available to him." 16 U.S.C. § 1533(b)(1)(A)(1994). Appellees, the Southwest Center for Biological Diversity, et al., ("Center"), argued below that the best available evidence demonstrates that the Fish and Wildlife Service should list the Queen Charlotte goshawk as a threatened or endangered species under 16 U.S.C. § 1533. Appellants, Bruce Babbitt, et al., ("Government") countered that the data did not compel such a listing. The principal dispute between the parties before the District Court was over what to make of the best available data, not whether such data existed. The District Court, however, sidestepped the parties' real dispute and concluded instead that the best available data simply was not good enough.

Indeed, instead of resolving the parties' dispute on the basis of the best available data in the record, the District Court issued an order remanding the case back to the Fish and Wildlife Service with instructions to count the goshawk population. *See Southwest Ctr. for Biological Diversity v. Babbitt, Civ. No.* 98-934, Order (D.D.C. July 20, 1999) ("Order"), reprinted in Joint Appendix ("J.A.") 1973. Appellants now challenge this order, claiming that the District Court's decision is completely at odds with the statute. We agree. The statute provides that the Secretary's decision must be made "solely on the basis of the best scientific and commercial data available to him." Therefore, on the record at hand, the District Court was without authority to order the Secretary to conduct an independent population count of the birds. Accordingly, we reverse the District Court's order, and we remand the case to the District Court for proper consideration of the parties' positions in light of the Act and an assessment of the available evidence.

I. FACTS

On May 9, 1994, the Southwest Center for Biological Diversity filed a petition requesting that the Queen Charlotte goshawks, which are a "large, but rarely-seen" subspecies of hawks, be listed as threatened or endangered under the Act. *Southwest Ctr. for Biological Diversity v. Babbitt,* 939 F. Supp. 49, 50 (D.D.C. 1996); *see* 16 U.S.C. § 1533(b)(3)(A) (1994).[8] On May 19, 1995, the Fish and Wildlife Service found that, based on the best available scientific and commercial evidence, no listing was warranted. *See Babbitt,* 939 F. Supp. at 51. This initial decision was based on the Fish and Wildlife Service's conclusion that the Forest Service would address land management options to ensure goshawk habitat conservation. The Center challenged this decision, and, on September 25, 1996, the District Court granted a summary judgment in favor of the Center, finding that the Secretary could not rely on the Forest Service's possible future actions "as an excuse for not making a determination based on the existing record." *Id.* at 52.

On remand, the Fish and Wildlife Service once again declined to list the Queen Charlotte goshawk as a threatened or endangered species, and the Center once again challenged the agency's determination. In a July 9, 1999 hearing before the District Court, the Government argued that its sole obligation under the Endangered Species Act is to consider and act on the best available data, which the Government claimed it had done. The District Court persisted, however, in suggesting that a population count was necessary. *See, e.g.,*Trial Tr. at 2-3, reprinted in J.A. 1913–14. The trial judge could not be moved from this position, not even by plaintiffs' acknowledgment that the District Court was required to assess the parties' positions in light of the best available evidence, not a population count. Following argument by the parties, the District Court issued an opinion on July 20, 1999, remanding the case to the Fish and Wildlife Service "for a more reliable determination of the Queen Charlotte goshawk population. . . ." Order at 3,

---

[8] [Ed. note: the listing petition was granted in August 1994, triggering the 12-month period within which the agency was to decide whether a listing was warranted. *Southwest Center for Biological Diversity v. Babbitt,* 939 F. Supp. 49, 50–51 (D.D.C. 1996).]

reprinted in J.A. 1975. This appeal followed.

II. Analysis

On the record before us, it is clear that the District Court exceeded its authority in ordering the Government to conduct a population count of the goshawk species. 16 U.S.C. § 1533(a)(1) instructs the Secretary to

> determine whether any species is an endangered species or a threatened species because of any of the following factors:
>
> (A) the present or threatened destruction, modi cation, or curtailment of its habitat or range;
>
> (B) overutilization for commercial, recreational, scientific or educational purposes;
>
> (C) disease or predation;
>
> (D) the inadequacy of existing regulatory mechanisms; or
>
> (E) other natural or manmade factors affecting its continued existence.

16 U.S.C. § 1533(a)(1) (1994). The Secretary is to make such a determination "solely on the basis of the best scientific and commercial data available to him. . . ." 16 U.S.C. § 1533(b)(1)(A). Read together, the two statutory provisions require the Secretary to list a species as endangered or threatened if, based solely on the best available data, any of § 1533(a)(1)'s five factors are sufficiently implicated. The "best available data" requirement makes it clear that the Secretary has no obligation to conduct independent studies. As we noted in *City of Las Vegas v. Lujan*, 891 F.2d 927, 933, 282 U.S. App. D.C. 57 (D.C. Cir. 1989), in the context of emergency listings under 16 U.S.C. § 1533(b)(7), 16 U.S.C. § 1533(b)(1)(A) "merely prohibits the Secretary from disregarding available scientific evidence that is in some way better than the evidence he relies on. Even if the available scientific and commercial data were quite inconclusive, he may — indeed must — still rely on it at that stage."

Appellees do not claim — for good reason, we think — that the statute's reference to "best scientific data available" requires the Secretary to find and consider any information that is arguably susceptible to discovery. In other words, appellees never have contended in this case that the Government is obliged to conduct an on-site population count of the goshawk. And appellees never have contended that the Secretary acted on the basis of no data. Rather, appellees have argued that the best available scientific data in this record demonstrate that the goshawk is already on the verge of extinction due to low population estimates and "some 'natural or manmade factors affecting its continued existence.' " Appellees Br. at 20 (quoting 16 U.S.C. § 1533(a)(1)(E)). This is the issue that properly was before the District Court, and this is the issue that should have been decided below.

The trial judge, however, ignored the statute, disregarded the parties' arguments, and determined instead that, because he found the available evidence inconclusive, the Secretary was obligated to find better data. The Government forthrightly concedes that "the district court's view has a superficial appeal — certainly the [Fish and Wildlife Service] would like to know how many [Queen

Charlotte] goshawks there are . . . ." Reply Br. at 3. But, as the Government contends (with no real contest from appellees), this superficial appeal cannot circumvent the statute's clear wording: The Secretary must make his decision as to whether to list a species as threatened or endangered "solely on the basis of the best scientific and commercial data available to him. . . ." 16 U.S.C. § 1533(b)(1)(A); Reply Br. at 3 ("The court's view is at odds with both the practical realities of endangered species work and the governing legal regime."). The Secretary argued below that the best available evidence supports the Government's decision not to list the goshawk, while the Center argued that the available evidence supports the opposite view. The District Court's responsibility was to assess the evidence and resolve the parties' dispute. The court's decision to sidestep this responsibility by imposing an obligation upon the Secretary to find better data was error.

III. Conclusion

For the foregoing reasons, we reverse the District Court's decision to remand the case to the Fish and Wildlife Service, and we remand the case to the District Court for consideration of the parties' positions in light of the Endangered Species Act and an assessment of the available evidence.

NOTES

1. *"Available."* *Southwest Center* stands for the proposition that only "available" data needs to be considered in a listing decision, and, of that, only the "best scientific and commercial" data. What constitutes "available" information is unrevealed in the statute. However, the opinion sheds some light on the matter: "available" information is not the universe of information "arguably susceptible to discovery." But would "available" encompass information *reasonably* susceptible to discovery? One would think, for example, that the Secretary should have a legal obligation to review current scientific literature. For what purpose is 12 months allotted for species status review if not at least for that? The question then becomes, if current scientific literature is "available," why is information collectable by an on-site population count not also "available"? Instead of grappling with these matters, *Southwest Center* merely cited *City of Las Vegas v. Lujan*, 891 F.2d 927 (D.C. Cir. 1989), to support its ruling. But *City of Las Vegas* assumed the availability of information. *City of Las Vegas*, moreover, involved an *emergency* listing of a species, which is an entirely different matter than the "routine" listing considered in *Southwest Center*. Section 4(b)(7), 16 U.S.C. § 1533(b)(7).

An unanswered question is whether weak information should ever produce an affirmative decision to list a species. Note that § 4(b)(3) of the ESA, 16 U.S.C. § 1533(b)(3), requires petitioners to present "substantial . . . information indicating that the petitioned action may be warranted" and calls for listing only where the "listing is warranted." The Administrative Procedure Act, moreover, expressly places the burden of proof on the "proponent" of a rule, at least when formal proceedings are called for. APA § 556(d), 5 U.S.C. § 556(d).

Cf. Blue Water Fisherman's Ass'n. v. National Marine Fisheries Service, 226 F. Supp. 2d 330, 338 (D. Mass. 2002) ("The agency's conclusion need not be airtight and indisputable. When an agency relies on the analysis and opinion of experts and employs the best evidence available, the fact that the evidence is 'weak,' and thus not dispositive, does not render the agency's determination 'arbitrary and capricious.' ") (citing *Greenpeace Action v. Franklin*, 14 F.3d 1324, 1336 (9th Cir. 1992)).

2. *"Best."* The ESA requires, as we have seen, that listing determinations be based solely upon the best scientific and commercial data available. How should an agency determine which of the evidence arrayed before it is "best" and therefore worthy of its consideration? In this regard, see, for example, *W. Watershed Projects v. Kempthorne*, 2008 U.S. Dist. LEXIS 84017 (D. Idaho Oct. 17, 2008):

> An agency has a fair degree of latitude in deciding what rational approach should be used to comply with the statutory mandate that its decision be based on the "best" scientific evidence then available. In some cases the agency may rely on its own in-house biologists as experts to gather and analyze scientific information relating to a particular species. *See, e.g.*, Northern Spotted Owl, et al. v. Hodel, 716 F. Supp. 479 (W.D. Wash. 1988). In other cases, such as here, an agency may turn to outside experts to constitute the necessary scientific forum to develop and analyze the best available science. Once these experts have opined on matters such as whether a species is in danger of being threatened or endangered based on the best available scientific evidence, it can then be left to the agency managers to make the final decision of whether the listing requirements set forth in 16 U.S.C. § 1533(a)(1) have been met.

> When deciding on a particular methodology to obtain and review the scientific information, it is proper for the courts to defer to the agencies in such areas. "The rationale for deference is particularly strong when the [agency] is evaluating scientific data within its technical expertise. '[I]n an area characterized by scientific and technological uncertainty[,] . . . this court must proceed with particular caution, avoiding all temptations to direct the agency in a choice between rational alternatives." (citations omitted).

3. *Other Conservation Efforts.* How should the presence of conservation efforts by other governmental entities bear on a listing decision? The answer may depend on the status of the effort. There would seem to be three possibilities: (a) an effort not yet in place but projected; (b) one "newly implemented" but not yet "operational"; and (c) one both implemented and in operation. Clearly, conservation efforts that fall into category (c) should be considered in listing decisions. *See, e.g., Defenders of Wildlife v. Babbitt*, 1999 U.S. Dist. LEXIS 10366 (S.D. Cal. June 14, 1999). But, as the *Defenders* court notes, there is disagreement among federal courts with respect to categories (a) and (b). Your view? Note that ESA § 4(a)(1)(D) directs decision makers to examine the "inadequacy of existing regulatory mechanisms."

4. *Affirmative Commerce Clause.* Is the Endangered Species Act a constitutional exercise of the Congress's affirmative Commerce Clause authorities, even when it is applied to protect a subspecies of no known economic value and located solely on a discrete intrastate parcel of land? *See, e.g., Gibbs v. Babbitt*, 214 F.3d 483

(4th Cir. 2000), *cert. denied*, 531 U.S. 1145, 121 S. Ct. 1081 (2001). *See also* Chapter 3, *supra*.

5. *Update.* As of September 2011, there were 795 species of plants and 585 species of animals listed as endangered or threatened in the United States. The number of species designated as candidates for listing was 252. The number delisted stood at 49. Of those, 21 were delisted because the species recovered and 10 were delisted because the species became extinct. The remainder were delisted largely because of data errors. The list of endangered and threatened species may be found at 50 C.F.R. Part 17.

2. Designation of Critical Habitat

In addition to listing endangered and threatened species, the ESA requires the appropriate Secretary to designate a "critical habitat" for all listed species. Section 4(a)(3), 16 U.S.C. § 1533(a)(3); *Bennett v. Spear*, 520 U.S. 154, 117 S. Ct. 1154 (1997). Critical habitats can span enormous areas. In 2010, the FWS designated a critical habitat for the Mexican Spotted Owl that spans 8.6 million acres across federal lands in Arizona, Colorado, New Mexico, and Utah. The Ninth Circuit Court of Appeals affirmed the designation. *Arizona Cattle Growers' Ass'n v. Salazar*, 606 F.3d 1160 (9th Cir. 2009), *cert. denied*, 131 S. Ct. 1471 (2011). The critical habitat for the bull trout covers almost 19,000 miles of streams, almost 500,000 acres of lakes and reservoirs, and over 750 miles of marine shoreline in five states. USFWS, *Endangered and Threatened Wildlife and Plants; Revised Designation of Critical Habitat for Bull Trout in the Coterminous United States; Final Rule*, 75 Fed. Reg. 63898 (Oct. 18, 2010) (Bull trout habitat rule).

The ESA contemplates designation of both "occupied" and "unoccupied" critical habitat. Occupied critical habitat is defined as "the specific areas within the geographic area occupied by the species, at the time it is listed . . . on which are found those physical or biological features (I) essential to the conservation of the species and (II) which may require special management considerations or protection." Section 3(5)(A)(i), 16 U.S.C. § 1532(5)(A)(i). Except in special circumstances determined by the Secretary, critical habitat "shall not include the entire geographic area which can be occupied" by the species. Section 3(5)(C), 16 U.S.C. § 1532(5)(C). "Occupied" critical habitat has been interpreted to mean areas within which a species is "likely to be present," as distinct from the relatively fewer areas within which a species "resides." *Arizona Cattle Growers Ass'n. v. Salazar*, 606 F.3d 1160, 1165 (9th Cir. 2010), *cert. denied*, 131 S.Ct. 1471 (2011). "Unoccupied" critical habitat consists of "specific areas outside the geographical area occupied by the species at the time it is listed . . . upon a determination by the Secretary that such areas are essential for the conservation of the species." Section 3(5)(A)(ii), 16 U.S.C. § 1532(5)(A)(ii).

The ESA requires a designation of critical habitat concurrent with the listing of a species "to the maximum extent prudent or determinable." Section 4(a)(3), 16 U.S.C. § 1533(a)(3). The designation should be made "on the basis of the best scientific data available and after taking into consideration the economic impact, and any other relevant impact, of specifying any particular area as critical habitat." Section 4(b)(2), 16 U.S.C. § 1533(b)(2). Congress speculated that a "not prudent" finding would be rare. *See. e.g., Natural Resources Defense Council v. U.S. Department of Interior, infra.* Still, the FWS has declined on many occasions to designate critical habitat contemporaneous with its decisions to list endangered and threatened species. As of February 2001, for example, despite having listed 736 plants and 511 animals, the agency had designated critical habitat on only 142 occasions. As of September 2011, CHDs are in place for 608 species.

The following judicial decision represents the first time a federal court of appeals reversed a FWS determination to forego designating a critical habitat. There have since been others: *see, e.g., Sierra Club v. U.S. Fish and Wildlife Service,* 245 F.3d 434 (5th Cir. 2001) (decision to not designate a critical habitat for the threatened Gulf sturgeon was arbitrary and capricious); *Conservation Council for Hawaii v. Babbitt,* 2 F. Supp. 2d 1280 (D. Haw. 1998) (decision to not designate critical habitat for 245 endangered plants in Hawaii was arbitrary and capricious).

NATURAL RESOURCES DEFENSE COUNCIL v. UNITED STATES DEPARTMENT OF INTERIOR
113 F.3d 1121 (9th Cir. 1997)

JUDGES: Before: HARRY PREGERSON, DOROTHY W. NELSON, and DIARMUID F. O'SCANNLAIN, CIRCUIT JUDGES.

PREGERSON, CIRCUIT JUDGE:

This case presents the question whether the defendants violated the Endangered Species Act by failing to designate critical habitat for the coastal California gnatcatcher. Upon cross-motions for summary judgment, the district court denied the plaintiffs' motion and granted summary judgment for the defendants. We have jurisdiction pursuant to 28 U.S.C. § 1291. We reverse.

FACTS

The coastal California gnatcatcher is a songbird unique to coastal southern California and northern Baja California. The gnatcatcher's survival depends upon certain subassociations of coastal sage scrub, a type of habitat that has been severely depleted by agricultural and urban development. Approximately 2500 pairs of gnatcatchers survive in southern California today.

On March 30, 1993, the U.S. Fish and Wildlife Service (the "Service") listed the gnatcatcher under the Endangered Species Act (the "Act") as a "threatened species." 58 Fed. Reg. 16742 (1993). Under section 4 of the Act, the listing of a threatened species must be accompanied by the concurrent designation of critical habitat for that species "to the maximum extent prudent and determinable." 16 U.S.C. § 1533(a)(3). The designation of critical habitat in turn triggers the protections of section 7 of the Act. Section 7 requires that federal agencies consult with the Secretary of the Interior (the "Secretary") to ensure that actions authorized, funded, or carried out by federal agencies do not harm critical habitat. *Id.* § 1536(a)(2).

At the time of the gnatcatcher's listing as a threatened species, the Service found that coastal sage scrub habitat loss posed "a significant threat to the continued existence of the coastal California gnatcatcher." 58 Fed. Reg. at 16748. Nevertheless, the Service concluded that critical habitat designation would not be "prudent" within the meaning of section 4 for two reasons. *Id.* at 16756. First, the Service claimed that the public identification of critical habitat would increase the risk that landowners might deliberately destroy gnatcatcher habitat. Second, the Service claimed that critical habitat designation "would not appreciably benefit" the gnatcatcher because most gnatcatcher habitat is found on private lands to which section 7's consultation requirement does not apply.

The Natural Resources Defense Council, the National Audubon Society, and biologist Elisabeth Brown (collectively, the "plaintiffs") challenged the Service's failure to designate critical habitat in this suit against the Service, various Service officials, the Secretary, and the U.S. Department of the Interior (collectively, the "defendants"). Each side moved for summary judgment. The district court denied the plaintiffs' motion and granted summary judgment to the defendants.

On this appeal, the plaintiffs contend that the district court erred in granting summary judgment to the defendants rather than the plaintiffs. In response, the defendants contend that the case is moot and must therefore be dismissed for lack of jurisdiction; or, in the alternative, that the district court's grant of summary judgment for the defendants should be affirmed. . . .

[Discussion of standard of review and justiciability omitted.]

II. The Service's Failure to Designate Critical Habitat

Section 4 of the Act requires that the gnatcatcher's listing as a threatened species be accompanied by concurrent designation of critical habitat "to the maximum extent prudent and determinable":

> The Secretary, by regulation promulgated in accordance with subsection (b) of this section and *to the maximum extent prudent* and determinable —
>
> (A) shall, concurrently with making a determination under paragraph (1) that a species is an endangered species or a threatened species, designate any habitat of such species which is then considered to be critical habitat; and
>
> (B) may, from time-to-time thereafter as appropriate, revise such designation.

16 U.S.C. § 1533(a)(3) (emphasis added).

The Act itself does not define the term "prudent." The Service has defined what would not be prudent, however, in the regulations promulgated under the Act. According to the regulations, critical habitat designation is not prudent "when one or both of the following situations exist":

> (i) The species is threatened by taking or other human activity, and identification of critical habitat can be expected to *increase the degree of such threat to the species*, or

(ii) Such designation of critical habitat *would not be beneficial to the species.*

50 C.F.R. § 424.12(a)(1)(I) (ii) (1996) (emphasis added).

When the Service published the gnatcatcher's final listing as a threatened species, the Service stated that critical habitat designation would not be prudent under either prong of the regulatory definition. 58 Fed. Reg. at 16756. The final listing fails to show, however, that the Service adequately "considered the relevant factors and articulated a rational connection between the facts found and the choice made" as required under *Resources Ltd.*, 35 F.3d at 1304 (*quoting Pyramid Lake Paiute Tribe*, 898 F.2d at 1414).

A. *Increased Threat to the Species*

The Service's first reason for declining to designate critical habitat was that designation would increase the degree of threat to the gnatcatcher. 58 Fed. Reg. at 16756. The final listing referred to eleven cases in which landowners or developers had destroyed gnatcatcher sites; in two of these cases, habitat was destroyed after the Service notified local authorities that gnatcatchers were present at a proposed development site. *Id.* at 16753,16756. On the basis of this history, the Service concluded that because the publication of critical habitat descriptions and maps would enable more landowners to identify gnatcatcher sites, designating critical habitat "would likely make the species more vulnerable to [prohibited takings] activities." *Id.* at 16756.

This "increased threat" rationale fails to balance the pros and cons of designation as Congress expressly required under section 4 of the Act. Section 4(b)(2) states that the Secretary may only exclude portions of habitat from critical habitat designation "if he determines that the benefits of such exclusion outweigh the benefits of specifying such area as part of the critical habitat." 16 U.S.C. § 1533(b)(2) (emphasis added). In addition, the Service itself has said that it will forgo habitat designation as a matter of prudence only "in those cases in which the possible adverse consequences would outweigh the benefits of designation." 49 Fed. Reg. 38900, 38903 (1984) (emphasis added).

In this case, the Service never weighed the benefits of designation against the risks of designation. The final listing decision cited only eleven cases of habitat destruction, out of 400,000 acres of gnatcatcher habitat. The listing did not explain how such evidence shows that designation would cause more landowners to destroy, rather than protect, gnatcatcher sites. The absence of such an explanation is particularly troubling given that the record shows these areas had already been surveyed extensively in other gnatcatcher or coastal sage scrub studies published prior to the date of final listing.

By failing to balance the relative threat of coastal sage scrub takings both with and without critical habitat designation, the Service failed to consider all relevant factors as required under *Resources Ltd.*, 35 F.3d at 1304. The Service's reliance on the "increased threat" exception to section 4 designation was therefore improper.

B. *No Benefit to the Species*

The Service's second reason for declining to designate habitat was that designation "would not appreciably benefit the species." 58 Fed. Reg. at 16756. According to the Service's final listing decision, most populations of gnatcatchers are found on private lands to which section 7's consultation requirement would not apply. *Id.* The final listing decision suggests that designation may only be deemed "beneficial to the species" and therefore "prudent" if it would result in the application of section 7 to "the *majority* of land-use activities occurring within critical habitat." *Id.* (emphasis added).

By rewriting its "beneficial to the species" test for prudence into a "beneficial to most of the species" requirement, the Service expands the narrow statutory exception for imprudent designations into a broad exemption for imperfect designations. This expansive construction of the "no benefit" prong to the imprudence exception is inconsistent with clear congressional intent.

The fact that Congress intended the imprudence exception to be a narrow one is clear from the legislative history, which reads in part:

> The committee intends that in most situations the Secretary will . . . designate critical habitat at the same time that a species is listed as either endangered or threatened. *It is only in rare circumstances where the specification of critical habitat concurrently with the listing would not be beneficial to the species.*

H.R. Rep. No. 95-1625 at 17 (1978), reprinted in 1978 U.S.C.C.A.N. 9453, 9467 (emphasis added). *See also Enos v. Marsh*, 769 F.2d 1363, 1371 (9th Cir. 1985) (holding that the Secretary "may only fail to designate a critical habitat under *rare* circumstances") (emphasis added); *Northern Spotted Owl v. Lujan*, 758 F. Supp. 621, 626(W.D. Wash. 1991) ("This legislative history leaves little room for doubt regarding the intent of Congress: The designation of critical habitat is to coincide with the final listing decision absent *extraordinary* circumstances.") (emphasis added).

By expanding the imprudence exception to encompass all cases in which designation would fail to control "the *majority* of land-use activities occurring within critical habitat," 58 Fed. Reg. at 16756 (emphasis added), the Service contravenes the clear congressional intent that the imprudence exception be a rare exception. Since "the court, as well as the agency, must give effect to the unambiguously expressed intent of Congress," *Chevron*, 467U.S. at 842–43, we reject the Service's suggestion that designation is only necessary where it would protect the majority of species habitat.

In the present case, the Service found that of approximately 400,000 acres of gnatcatcher habitat, over 80,000 acres were publicly-owned and therefore subject to section 7 requirements. 58 Fed. Reg. at 16743. Other privately-owned lands would also be subject to section 7 requirements if their use involved any form of federal agency authorization or action. *See* 16 U.S.C. § 1536(a)(2).

The Service does not explain why a designation that would benefit such a large portion of critical habitat is not "beneficial to the species" within the plain meaning of the regulations and "prudent" within the clear meaning of the statute. Accordingly, we conclude that the Service's "no benefit" argument fails to "articulate [ ] a rational connection between the facts found and the choice made" as required under *Resources Ltd.*, 35 F.3d at 1304. The Service's reliance on the "no benefit" exception to section 4 designation was therefore improper.

C. Less Benefit to the Species

In addition to the above two rationales which were stated in the final listing, the defendants now offer a third argument in defense of the Service's failure to designate critical habitat. The defendants contend that a "far superior" means of protecting gnatcatcher habitat is provided by the state-run "comprehensive habitat management program" created under California's Natural Communities Conservation Program ("NCCP"). The Service has endorsed the NCCP as a "special rule" for gnatcatcher protection under section 4(d) of the Act, 16 U.S.C. § 1533(d).

Regulations under the Act provide that "the reasons for not designating critical habitat will be stated in the publication of proposed and final rules listing a species." 50 C.F.R. § 424.12(a). The NCCP alternative was not identified in the Service's proposed or final listings as a reason not to designate critical habitat. Therefore, this argument is not properly before us for consideration. *See Olin Corp. v. FTC*, 986 F.2d 1295, 1305 n.9 (9th Cir.1993) (declining to review potential justification for FTC ruling because "the Commission did not explicitly consider this argument in its opinion").

Even if we were to consider the NCCP alternative, however, the existence of such an alternative would not justify the Service's failure to designate critical habitat. The Act provides that designation of critical habitat is necessary except when designation would not be "prudent" or "determinable." 16 U.S.C. § 1533(a)(3). The Service's regulations de ne "not prudent" as "increasing the degree of [takings] threat to the species" or "not . . . beneficial to the species." 50 C.F.R. § 424.12(a)(1)(I) (ii) (emphasis added). Neither the Act nor the implementing regulations sanctions nondesignation of habitat when designation would be merely less beneficial to the species than another type of protection.

In any event, the NCCP alternative cannot be viewed as a functional substitute for critical habitat designation. Critical habitat designation triggers mandatory consultation requirements for federal agency actions involving critical habitat. The NCCP alternative, in contrast, is a purely voluntary program that applies only to non-federal land-use activities. The Service itself recognized at the time of its final listing decision that "no substantive protection of the coastal California gnatcatcher is currently provided by city/county enrollments [in the NCCP]." 58 Fed. Reg. at 16754. Accordingly, we reject the defendants' post hoc invocation of the NCCP to justify the Service's failure to designate critical habitat.

Conclusion

The Service failed to discharge its statutory obligation to designate critical habitat when it listed the gnatcatcher as a threatened species, or to articulate a rational basis for invoking the rare imprudence exception. We therefore reverse the district court's finding that the Service's actions were not "arbitrary, capricious, an abuse of discretion or otherwise not in accordance with law."

Accordingly, we reverse the district court's grant of summary judgment to the defendants; reverse the denial of summary judgment to the plaintiffs; and remand to the district court with directions to remand to the Service so that the Service may issue a new decision consistent with this opinion.

Reversed and Remanded

DISSENT: O'SCANNLAIN, CIRCUIT JUDGE, dissenting:

[The dissent argued first, that determinations of prudence need not include a weighing of benefits and risks of designation (all that is required is a "rational decision-making process"). Still, the dissent noted, the Service did conduct a balancing test, and the conclusion it reached based on that balancing effort was both "rational" and "defensible."

Second, the dissent argued that "the majority takes too narrow a view of the phrase 'beneficial to the species.' The question should not be whether any member of the species would be better off by a slender margin, but whether the species as a whole would benefit from the designation. Even though the gnatcatchers in most of the habitat would not benefit, reasons the majority, some of the gnatcatchers would benefit, and hence designation would be beneficial for the species. The problem with this argument is that it overlooks the Service's expert opinion, to which we are required to defer, that designation may harm the gnatcatchers when landowners intentionally destroy the habitat. Even though individual pockets of gnatcatchers may benefit, the species as a whole may not."]

NOTE

The FWS is no fan of CHDs: "the critical habitat designation usually affords little extra protection to most species, and in some cases it can result in harm to the species. This harm may be due to negative public sentiment to the designation, to inaccuracies in the initial area designated, and to the fact that there is often a misconception among other Federal agencies that if an area is outside of the designated critical habitat area, then it is of no value to the species." http://www.fws.gov/endangered/what-we-do/critical-habitats-faq.html (site visited September 2011).

NEW MEXICO CATTLE GROWERS v. UNITED STATES FISH AND WILDLIFE SERVICE
248 F.3d 1277 (10th Cir. 2001)

JUDGES: Before TACHA, CHIEF JUDGE, KELLY, CIRCUIT JUDGE, and LUNGSTRUM,[9] DISTRICT JUDGE.

TACHA, CHIEF CIRCUIT JUDGE.

The New Mexico Cattle Growers Association, New Mexico Farm & Livestock Bureau, New Mexico Wool Growers, Inc., New Mexico Wheat Growers Association, New Mexico Public Lands Council, Albuquerque Production Credit Association, Coalition of Arizona/New Mexico Counties for Stable Economic Growth, and Hidalgo County Cattle Growers Association (collectively "Appellants") all represent, in some fashion, elements of New Mexico's agricultural industry. Appellants appeal an order of the district court dismissing their suit against Appellee U.S. Fish & Wildlife Service ("FWS"). We exercise jurisdiction pursuant to the Administration Procedures Act ("APA"), 28 U.S.C. §§ 701-06, and reverse.

I.

The Southwestern Willow Flycatcher ("flycatcher"), empidonax traillii extimus, is one of four sub-species of the willow flycatcher, a small bird that nests in riparian areas along river beds. On July 23, 1993, the FWS published its "Proposed Rule to List the Southwestern Willow Flycatcher as Endangered With Critical Habitat." 58 Fed. Reg. 39495. On February 27, 1995, the FWS issued its "Final Rule Determining Endangered Status for the Southwestern Willow Flycatcher." 60 Fed. Reg. 10694. The Final Rule listed the flycatcher as endangered, but deferred the critical habitat designation ("CHD") in order to gather more information. However, the FWS did not, on its own initiative, move forward with the CHD for the flycatcher.

On March 20, 1997, the U.S. District Court for the District of Arizona, in the case *Southwest Ctr. for Biological Diversity v. Babbitt*, Civ. No. 96-1874-PHX-RGS (D. Ariz. March 20, 1997), ordered the FWS to complete the CHD for the flycatcher within 120 days. Pursuant to the court order, the FWS issued its CHD for the flycatcher on July 22, 1997. At that time, the known population of the flycatcher was between 300 and 500 nesting pairs spread across seven states and parts of Mexico. The CHD designated eighteen critical habitat units, including four in New Mexico, totaling 599 miles of stream and river beds.

The Endangered Species Act ("ESA"), which controls CHDs, requires the FWS to perform an economic analysis of the effects of the CHD before making a final designation. 16 U.S.C. § 1533(b)(2). In order to determine what the "economic impact" of a CHD will be, the FWS has adopted an incremental baseline approach (the "baseline approach"). The baseline approach utilized by the FWS is premised

---

[9] HONORABLE JOHN W. LUNGSTRUM, CHIEF DISTRICT JUDGE for the District of Kansas, sitting by designation.

on the idea that the listing of the species (which will occur prior to or simultaneously with the CHD) will have economic impacts that are not to be considered. The primary statutory rationale for this position comes from 16 U.S.C. § 1533(b)(1)(A), which states that listing determinations be made "solely on the basis of the best scientific and commercial data available." Thus, the baseline approach moves any economic impact that can be attributed to listing below the baseline and, when making the CHD, takes into account only those economic impacts rising above the baseline. Using the baseline approach, the FWS determined that the flycatcher CHD resulted in no economic impact, stating that "critical habitat designation will . . . result in no additional protection for the Flycatcher nor have any additional economic effects beyond those that may have been caused by listing and by other statutes." Division of Economics, U.S. Fish and Wildlife Service, Economic Analysis of Critical Habitat Designation for the Southwestern Flycatcher, S3 (1997).

The appellants filed suit in district court in March 1998, challenging the flycatcher designation and alleging that the FWS had violated various provisions of both the ESA and the National Environmental Protection Act("NEPA"). . . .

Specifically, the appellants make the following arguments on appeal: (1) that the FWS's adoption of the baseline approach to measuring the economic impact of the flycatcher CHD is an erroneous construction and, thus, a violation of the ESA; (2) that the district court erred in ruling the declaration and its attachments admissible; (3) that the FWS misapplied the critical habitat definition set forth in the ESA; (4) that the FWS violated NEPA by applying the baseline approach to the environmental impact analysis undertaken in the EA; (5) that the FWS failed to address adequate alternatives to the CHD pursuant to NEPA; and (6) that the FWS, in making the flycatcher CHD, failed to properly cooperate with state and local agencies as required by NEPA. Because we rule in favor of the appellants on the first issue raised by holding that the baseline approach to economic impact analysis is not permitted by the ESA, thus setting aside the flycatcher CHD, we need not address any of the other issues raised.

II.

[In this section, the court decided to review the decision of the FWS without deference because the agency's determinations were made informally, rather than by rule in accordance with procedures of the APA. The FWS conceded that no deference was due].

III.

Our primary task in construing statutes is to "determine congressional intent, using 'traditional tools of statutory interpretation.'" *NLRB v. United Food & Commercial Workers Union*, 484 U.S. 112, 123, 98 L. Ed. 2d429, 108 S. Ct. 413 (1987) (quoting *INS v. Cardoza-Fonseca*, 480 U.S. 421, 446, 107 S. Ct. 1207, 94 L. Ed. 2d 434 (1987)). "As in all cases requiring statutory construction, 'we begin with the plain language of the law.'" *St. Charles Inv. Co. v. CIR*, 232 F.3d 773, 776 (10th Cir. 2000) (quoting *United States v. Morgan*, 922 F.2d 1495, 1496 (10th Cir. 1991)). "In so doing, we will assume that Congress's intent is expressed correctly in the ordinary meaning of the words it employs. . . . Where the language of the statute is plain, it is improper for this Court to consult legislative history in determining congressional intent." *Id.* However, "if the statutory language is ambiguous, a court can then resort to legislative history as an aid to interpretation." *United States v. Simmonds*, 111 F.3d 737, 742 (10th Cir. 1997).

Enacted in 1973, the ESA, 16 U.S.C. § 1531 et seq., was the congressional response to increasing concern about the extent to which "various species of fish, wildlife, and plants in the United States have been rendered extinct as a consequence of economic growth and development untempered by adequate concern and conservation." 16 U.S.C. § 1531(a)(1). The stated purpose of the ESA is, in part, "to provide a means whereby the ecosystems upon which endangered species and threatened species depend may be conserved, [and] to provide a program for the conservation of such endangered species and threatened species." *Id.* § 1531(b).

The process set forth in the ESA for the protection of endangered and threatened species and the conservation of their ecosystem begins by granting the Secretary of the Interior, through the FWS, authority to list species in need of protection as either endangered or threatened. *Id.* § 1533(a). The ESA enumerates the factors to be considered by the agency when making a listing decision, including "the present or threatened destruction, modification, or curtailment of its habitat or range." *Id.* § 1533(a)(1). Further, the ESA specifically requires that the listing determination be based "solely on the basis of the best scientific and commercial data available." *Id.* § 1533(b)(1)(A). Thus, economic analysis is not a factor in the listing determination. Once a species is listed, all federal agencies are required to consult with the FWS to "insure that any action authorized, funded, or carried out by such agency . . . is not likely to jeopardize the continued existence of any endangered species or threatened species." *Id.* § 1536(a)(2).

In addition to the protections afforded listed species by the ESA, the Act requires the agency to designate "critical habitat" for all listed species, to the extent determinable. *Id.* § 1533(a)(3). Critical habitat is defined as:

> (i) the specific areas within the geographic area occupied by the species, at the time it is listed . . . on which are found those physical or biological features (I) essential to the conservation of the species and (II) which may require special management considerations or protection; and (ii) specific areas outside the geographic area occupied by the species at the time it is listed . . . upon a determination by the Secretary that such areas are essential for the conservation of the species.

Id. § 1532(5)(A). Thus, the CHD may include specific areas found both inside of and outside of the geographic area occupied by the species.

The CHD is required to be based on "the best scientific data available" considering "the economic impact, and any other relevant impact, of specifying any particular area as critical habitat." *Id.* § 1533(b)(2). The agency "may exclude" a particular area from the CHD if the agency determines that "the benefits of such exclusion outweigh the benefits of specifying such area as part of the critical habitat, unless . . . the failure to designate such area . . . will result in the extinction of the species concerned." *Id.* § 1533(b)(2). Once critical habitat is designated, federal agencies must consult with the FWS to "insure that any action authorized, funded, or carried out by such agency . . . is not likely to . . . result in the destruction or adverse modification of [designated critical] habitat." *Id.* § 1536(a)(2). Thus, agency action that is prohibited is both (1) action that is likely to jeopardize the existence of a listed species and (2) action that is likely to result in the adverse modification of any area within a CHD.

The crux of the statutory dispute is in determining the meaning of "economic impact" in 16 U.S.C. § 1533(b)(2).The baseline approach adopted by the FWS utilizes a "but for" method for determining what economic impacts flow from the CHD. Thus, unless an economic impact would not result but for the CHD, that impact is attributable to a different cause (typically listing) and is not an "economic impact . . . of specifying any particular area as critical habitat." Conversely, the approach advocated by the appellants would take into account all of the economic impact of the CHD, regardless of whether those impacts are caused co-extensively by any other agency action (such as listing) and even if those impacts would remain in the absence of the CHD. The issue presented is a question of first impression in this circuit and, to our knowledge, has not been decided by any of our sister circuits.

The root of the problem lies in the FWS's long held policy position that CHDs are unhelpful, duplicative, and unnecessary. Between April 1996 and July 1999, more than 250 species had been listed pursuant to the ESA, yet CHDs had been made for only two. S. Rep. No. 106-126, at 2 (1999). Further, while we have held that making a CHD is mandatory once a species is listed, *Forest Guardians v. Babbitt*, 174 F.3d 1178, 1186 (10th Cir. 1999), the FWS has typically put off doing so until forced to do so by court order. S. Rep. No. 106-126, at 2 (1999).

In turn, the policy position of the FWS finds its root in the regulations promulgated by the FWS in 1986 defining the meaning of both the "jeopardy standard" (applied in the context of listing) and the "adverse modification standard" (applied in the context of designated critical habitat). Action violating the jeopardy standard is action reasonably expected "to reduce appreciably the likelihood of both the survival and recovery of a listed species." 50 C.F.R. 402.02. Action violating the adverse modification standard is action "that appreciably diminishes the value of critical habitat for both the survival and recovery of a listed species." *Id.* Thus, the standards are defined as virtually identical, or, if not identical, one (adverse modification) is subsumed by the other (jeopardy). *See Am. Rivers v. Nat'l Marine Fisheries Serv.*, 1999 U.S. App. LEXIS 3860 (9th Cir. Jan. 11,1999) (agreeing with the agency that " 'jeopardy' and 'critical habitat' . . . are 'closely related,' and [thus] the jeopardy discussion properly 'encompasses' the critical habitat analysis"). While these regulatory definitions are not before us today, they have been the cause of much confusion in that they inform the FWS's interpretation of the ESA's economic impact language.

Consistent with its long standing position, the FWS argues in the instant case that the impacts of the flycatcher listing and the flycatcher CHD are co-extensive. The FWS stated in its economic analysis that, because all actions "that result in adverse modification of critical habitat will also result in a jeopardy decision, designation of critical habitat for the flycatcher is not expected to result in any incremental restrictions on agency activities." Division of Economics, U.S. Fish and Wildlife Service, Economic Analysis of Critical Habitat Designation for the Southwestern Flycatcher, S3 (1997). The CHD itself states that "common to both [the jeopardy standard and the adverse modification standard] is an appreciable detrimental effect on both survival and recovery of a listed species," and thus "actions satisfying the standard for adverse modification are nearly always found to also jeopardize the species concerned, and the existence of a critical habitat designation does not materially affect the outcome of consultation." 60 Fed. Reg. 39,131 (July 22, 1997). Moreover, the FWS continues to assert that agency action that is "likely to adversely modify critical habitat but not to jeopardize the species for which it is designated are extremely rare historically, and none have been issued in recent years." Appellee's Brief at 31.

However, as we have previously said, the fact that the FWS says that no real impact flows from the CHD does not make it so. *Catron County Bd. of Comm'rs v. United States Fish & Wildlife Serv.*, 75 F.3d 1429, 1436 (10thCir. 1996) ("We disagree with the [Ninth Circuit] that no actual impact flows from the critical habitat designation. Merely because the Secretary says it does not make it so. The record in this case suggests that the impact will be immediate and the consequences could be disastrous."). Because *Catron County* dealt with whether an environmental impact statement had to be prepared pursuant to NEPA when the FWS made a CHD, the court was dealing specifically with the environmental impacts of the CHD rather than its economic impacts. However, our holding in that case casts doubt on the FWS's position in this case.

In fact, the district court in this case, by granting the appellants standing to challenge the CHD, implicitly acknowledged that they have been impacted by the flycatcher CHD. *N.M. Cattle Growers Ass'n v. United States Fish & Wildlife Serv.*, 81 F. Supp. 2d 1141, 1153 (D.N.M. 1999) (holding that the appellants had alleged an injury in fact owing from the flycatcher CHD). If none of the impacts of the CHD are actually attributable to the CHD, the district court's standing decision is rendered incoherent. If the injury alleged is attributable wholly to listing, then the appellants suffer no injury from the CHD, and cannot establish standing to challenge it. The district court's standing determination further points to the inconsistency between the policy position of the FWS and the language of the ESA itself. But the question of whether the impacts of listing and a CHD are co-extensive is not the precise question before us. Rather, the question is whether the FWS must analyze all of the economic impacts of critical habitat designation (regardless of whether the impacts are co-extensive with other causes), or only those impacts that are a "but for" result of the CHD.

It is true that the ESA clearly bars economic considerations from having a seat at the table when the listing determination is being made. "The addition of the word 'solely' is intended to remove from the process of the listing or delisting of species any factor not related to the biological status of the species. . . . Economic considerations have no relevance to determinations regarding the status of species." H.R. Rep. No. 97-567, pt. 1, at 29 (1982), reprinted in 1982 U.S.C.C.A.N. 2807. However, Congress clearly intended that economic factors were to be considered in connection with the CHD. 16 U.S.C. § 1533(b)(2).

The statutory language is plain in requiring some kind of consideration of economic impact in the CHD phase. Although 50 C.F.R. 402.02 is not at issue here, the regulation's definition of the jeopardy standard as fully encompassing the adverse modification standard renders any purported economic analysis done utilizing the baseline approach virtually meaningless. We are compelled by the canons of statutory interpretation to give some effect to the congressional directive that economic impacts be considered at the time of critical habitat designation. *Bridger Coal Co./Pac. Minerals, Inc. v. Dir., Office of Workers' Compensation Programs*, 927 F.2d 1150, 1153 (10th Cir. 1991) ("We will not construe a statute in a way that renders words or phrases meaningless, redundant, or superfluous."). Because economic analysis done using the FWS's baseline model is rendered essentially without meaning by 50 C.F.R. § 402.02, we conclude Congress intended that the FWS conduct a full analysis of all of the economic impacts of a critical habitat designation, regardless of whether those impacts are attributable co-extensively to other causes. Thus, we hold the baseline approach to economic analysis is not in accord with the language or intent of the ESA.

The FWS contends that should they be forced to abandon the baseline approach and consider all of the economic impact of a CHD, even if that impact is attributable co-extensively to another cause, they will be injecting economic analysis improperly into the listing process. The only two federal courts to consider this question come to essentially the same conclusion. *N. M. Cattle Growers Ass'n*, 81 F. Supp. 2d at 1158; *Trinity County Concerned Citizens v. Babbitt*, 1993 WL 650393 (D.D.C. Sept. 20, 1993) (holding that absent the baseline approach, "the Secretary would be required to include . . . certain costs that might have already been incurred as a result of the listing of the species, for example, through the ESA's jeopardy and take provisions," even though "the Secretary is expressly forbidden from considering such economic costs in making the decision to list species"). We cannot agree.

Requiring that the FWS comply with the intent of the legislative body by considering economic impacts at a point subsequent to listing does not inject economic considerations into the listing process, but rather, situates those considerations in precisely the spot intended by Congress. Moreover, should this ruling result in certain areas being excluded from future CHDs, it will not undermine congressional intent that economic factors be excluded from the listing decision. The listing of the species will remain in effect and the significant protections afforded a species by listing will not be undermined. Indeed, if the FWS's position that the protections afforded by a CHD are subsumed by the protections of listing is accepted, this ruling will result in no decreased protection for endangered species or their habitat.

IV.

As set forth above, the baseline approach to economic analysis pursuant the 16 U.S.C. § 1533(b)(2) is expressly rejected. The flycatcher CHD is thus set aside and the FWS is instructed to issue a new flycatcher CHD in compliance with this opinion as required by the ESA. Accordingly, the decision of the district court is REVERSED and the case is REMANDED to the district court for proceedings not inconsistent with this decision.

NOTES

1. ***More on Economic Impact.*** *New Mexico Cattle Growers* holds that agencies must conduct "a full analysis of all of the economic impacts of a critical habitat designation, regardless of whether those impacts are attributable co-extensively to other causes." *See supra*. Does this mean that agencies must consider cumulative impacts akin to the requirements of the National Environmental Policy Act (*see* Chapter 4, *supra*)? The answer is no:

> While NEPA's regulations expressly require consideration of cumulative impacts, 40 C.F.R. § 1508.25(a)(2), 1508.7, neither ESA nor its implementing regulations do so. Rather, the plain language of ESA directs the agency to consider only those impacts caused by the critical habitat designation itself. ESA § 4(b)(2), 16 U.S.C. 1533(b)(2) (requiring the agency to consider "the economic impact . . . of specifying any particular area as critical habitat"). It is sensible to require a more thorough analysis under NEPA than under ESA. NEPA imposes requirements before the government takes action that might have negative consequences for the environment; ESA imposes requirements before the government takes action that will *protect* the environment.

Home Builders Ass'n of Northern California v. U.S. Fish and Wildlife Service, 616 F.3d 983, 992 (9th Cir. 2010).

2. ***ESA and NEPA.*** Do the requirements of the National Environmental Policy Act apply to decisions taken under the Endangered Species Act? It has been held that NEPA process, *see* Chapter 4, *supra*, does not apply to species listing decisions, *Pacific Legal Foundation v. Andrus*, 657 F.2d 829 (6th Cir. 1981), but there is a split of authority regarding NEPA's applicability to designations of critical habitat of those listed species. The Ninth Circuit has held that NEPA is inapplicable to such decisions, *Douglas County v. Babbitt*, 48 F.3d. 1495 (9th Cir. 1995), *cert. denied*, 116 S. Ct. 1292 (1996) (holding that listing has "displaced" the provisions of NEPA), but the Tenth Circuit has held the opposite. *Catron County Board of Comm'rs., New Mexico v. United States Fish and Wildlife Serv.*, 75 F.3d 1429 (10th Cir. 1996). In the latter case, consistent with *Cattle Growers*, the court disagreed that no impacts flow from the habitat designation decision. It stipulated as well that ESA procedures did not supplant those of NEPA, and argued that compliance with NEPA would further the goals of the ESA, not the opposite, as suggested by the *Douglas* court. At this writing, the United States Supreme Court has not resolved this split in the circuits, and no decision is pending. For a discussion of the applicability of NEPA to agency implementation of the Endangered Species Act, see Lori Hackleman Patterson, *NEPA's Stronghold: A Noose for the Endangered Species Act?*, 27 CUMB. L. REV. 753 (1996–97) (arguing in favor of exemption).

C. SECTION 7

The listing of a species triggers the applicability of the major regulatory provisions of the ESA, §§ 7 and 9 respectively. We begin with a look at § 7. Euphemistically entitled "Inter-agency Cooperation," the section provides in salient part:

> Each federal agency shall, in consultation with and with the assistance of the Secretary, insure that any action authorized, funded, or carried out by such agency . . . is not likely to jeopardize the continued existence of any endangered species or threatened species or result in the destruction or adverse modification of habitat of such species which is determined by the Secretary . . . to be critical.

Section 7(a)(2), 16 U.S.C. § 1536(a)(2) (1976 ed.)

Compliance with this directive is accomplished via a three-step process. First, a federal agency proposing to take an action must inquire of the FWS or the NMFS whether any threatened or endangered species "may be present" in the area of the proposed action. Section 7(c)(1), 16 U.S.C. § 1536(c)(1). Second, if such a species may be present, the agency must prepare a "biological assessment" examining whether the species "is likely to be affected" by the proposed action. *Id.* The biological assessment may be prepared in conjunction with and be a part of an environmental impact statement or environmental assessment under the National Environmental Policy Act. *Id.* Failure to prepare a biological assessment is a significant procedural violation of the ESA and constitutes grounds for issuance of an injunction to halt the federal action. *Thomas v. Peterson*, 753 F.2d 754 (9th Cir. 1985). Third, if the assessment concludes the species is "likely to be affected," the agency must formally "consult" with the FWS or NMFS. Section 7(a)(3), 16 U.S.C. § 1536(a)(3) ("jeopardy consultation"). Consultation is also required if an agency action might result in destruction of any designated critical habitat. Section 7(a)(2), 16 U.S.C. § 1536(a)(2) ("habitat consultation"). *See, e.g., Pacific Coast Federation of Fisherman's Assn's v. U.S. Bureau of Reclamation*, 138 F. Supp. 2d 1228 (N.D. Cal. 2001). The formal consultation process results in a "biological opinion" ("BiOp" (often referred to as a "B.O.")) issued by the FWS or NMFS. Section 7(b), 16 U.S.C. § 1536(b). The BiOp is the vehicle used to determine whether the proposed federal action would jeopardize a species or destroy or adversely modify its critical habitat.

The first task is to understand what § 7(a)(2) means.

TENNESSEE VALLEY AUTHORITY v. HILL
437 U.S. 153, 98 S. Ct. 2279 (1978)

MR. CHIEF JUSTICE BURGER delivered the opinion of the Court.

The questions presented in this case are (a) whether the Endangered Species Act of 1973 requires a court to enjoin the operation of a virtually completed federal dam — which had been authorized prior to 1973 — when, pursuant to authority vested in him by Congress, the Secretary of the Interior has determined that operation of the dam would eradicate an endangered species; and (b) whether continued congressional appropriations for the dam after 1973 constituted an implied repeal of the Endangered Species Act, at least as to the particular dam.

The Little Tennessee River originates in the mountains of northern Georgia and flows through the national forest lands of North Carolina into Tennessee, where it converges with the Big Tennessee River near Knoxville. The lower 33 miles of the Little Tennessee takes the river's clear, free-flowing waters through an area of great natural beauty. Among other environmental amenities, this stretch of river is said to contain abundant trout. Considerable historical importance attaches to the areas immediately adjacent to this portion of the Little Tennessee's banks. To the south of the river's edge lies Fort Loudon, established in 1756 as England's southwestern outpost in the French and Indian War. Nearby are also the ancient sites of several native American villages, the archeological stores of which are to a large extent unexplored. These include the Cherokee towns of Echota and Tennase, the former being the sacred capital of the Cherokee Nation as early as the 16th century and the latter providing the linguistic basis from which the State of Tennessee derives its name.

In this area of the Little Tennessee River the Tennessee Valley Authority, a wholly owned public corporation of the United States, began constructing the Tellico Dam and Reservoir Project in 1967, shortly after Congress appropriated initial funds for its development. Tellico is a multipurpose regional development project designed principally to stimulate shoreline development, generate sufficient electric current to heat 20,000 homes, and provide flat water recreation and flood control, as well as improve economic conditions in "an area characterized by underutilization of human resources and out migration of young people." Hearings on Public Works for Power and Energy Research Appropriation Bill, 1977, before a Subcommittee of the House Committee on Appropriations, 94th Cong., 2d Sess., pt. 5, p. 261 (1976). Of particular relevance to this case is one aspect of the project, a dam which TVA determined to place on the Little Tennessee, a short distance from where the river's waters meet with the Big Tennessee. When fully operational, the dam would impound water covering some 16,500 acres — much of which represents valuable and productive farmland — thereby converting the river's shallow, fast-flowing waters into a deep reservoir over 30 miles in length.

The Tellico Dam has never opened, however, despite the fact that construction has been virtually completed and the dam is essentially ready for operation. Although Congress has appropriated monies for Tellico every year since 1967, progress was delayed, and ultimately stopped, by a tangle of lawsuits and administrative proceedings. After unsuccessfully urging TVA to consider alternatives to damming the Little Tennessee, local citizens and national conservation groups brought suit in the District Court, claiming that the project did not conform to the requirements of the National Environmental Policy Act of 1969 (NEPA), 83 Stat. 852, 42 U.S.C. § 4321 *et seq.* After finding TVA to be in violation of NEPA, the District Court enjoined the dam's completion pending the filing of an appropriate environmental impact statement. *Environmental Defense Fund v. TVA*, 339F. Supp. 806 (ED Tenn.), *aff'd*, 468 F.2d 1164 (CA6 1972). The injunction remained in effect until late 1973, when the District Court concluded that TVA's final environmental impact statement for Tellico was in compliance with the law. *Environmental Defense Fund v. TVA*, 371 F. Supp. 1004 (ED Tenn. 1973), *aff'd*, 492 F.2d 466 (CA6 1974).

A few months prior to the District Court's decision dissolving the NEPA injunction, a discovery was made in the waters of the Little Tennessee which would profoundly affect the Tellico Project. Exploring the area around Coytee Springs, which is about seven miles from the mouth of the river, a University of Tennessee ichthyologist, Dr. David A. Etnier, found a previously unknown species of perch, the snail darter, or *Percina (Imostoma) tanasi.* This three-inch, tannish-colored fish, whose numbers are estimated to be in the range of 10,000 to 15,000, would soon engage the attention of environmentalists, the TVA, the Department of the Interior, the Congress of the United States, and ultimately the federal courts, as a new and additional basis to halt construction of the dam.

Snail Darter

Percina tanasi, breeding male
(Image not to scale; image not part of Supreme Court opinion)

Until recently the finding of a new species of animal life would hardly generate a cause célèbre. This is particularly so in the case of darters, of which there are approximately 130 known species, 8 to 10 of these having been identified only in the last five years.[10] The moving force behind the snail darter's sudden fame came some four months after its discovery, when the Congress passed the Endangered Species Act of 1973 (Act), 87 Stat. 884, 16U.S.C. § 1531 et seq. (1976 ed.). This legislation, among other things, authorizes the Secretary of the Interior to declare species of animal life "endangered" and to identify the "critical habitat" of these creatures. When a species or its habitat is so listed, the following portion of the Act relevant here becomes effective:

> The Secretary [of the Interior] shall review other programs administered by him and utilize such programs in furtherance of the purposes of this chapter. All other Federal departments and agencies shall, in consultation with and with the assistance of the Secretary, utilize their authorities in furtherance of the purposes of this chapter by carrying out programs for the conservation of endangered species and threatened species listed pursuant to section 1533 of this title and by taking such action necessary to insure that actions authorized, funded, or carried out *by them do not jeopardize the continued existence of such endangered species and threatened species* or result in the destruction or modification of habitat of such species which is determined by the Secretary, after consultation as appropriate with the affected States, to be critical. 16 U.S.C. § 1536 (1976 ed.) (emphasis added).

In January 1975, the respondents in this case and others petitioned the Secretary of the Interior to list the snail darter as an endangered species. After receiving comments from various interested parties, including TVA and the State of

---

[10] In Tennessee alone there are 85 to 90 species of darters, *id.*, at 131, of which upward to 45 live in the Tennessee River system. *Id.*, at 130.New species of darters are being constantly discovered and classified — at the rate of about one per year. *Id.*, at 131. This is a difficult task for even trained ichthyologists since species of darters are often hard to differentiate from one another. *Ibid.*

Tennessee, the Secretary formally listed the snail darter as an endangered species on October 8, 1975. 40 Fed. Reg. 47505-47506; *see* 50 C.F.R. 17.11(I) (1976). In so acting, it was noted that "the snail darter is a living entity which is genetically distinct and reproductively isolated from other fishes." 40 Fed. Reg. 47505. More important for the purposes of this case, the Secretary determined that the snail darter apparently lives only in that portion of the Little Tennessee River which would be completely inundated by the reservoir created as a consequence of the Tellico Dam's completion. *Id.*, at 47506.[11] The Secretary went on to explain the significance of the dam to the habitat of the snail darter:

> [The] snail darter occurs only in the swifter portions of shoals over clean gravel substrate in cool, low-turbidity water. Food of the snail darter is almost exclusively snails which require a clean gravel substrate for their survival. *The proposed impoundment of water behind the proposed Tellico Dam would result in total destruction of the snail darter's habitat. Ibid.* (emphasis added).

Subsequent to this determination, the Secretary declared the area of the Little Tennessee which would be affected by the Tellico Dam to be the "critical habitat" of the snail darter. 41 Fed. Reg. 13926-13928 (1976) (to be codified as 50 C.F.R. § 17.81). Using these determinations as a predicate, and notwithstanding the near completion of the dam, the Secretary declared that pursuant to § 7 of the Act, "all Federal agencies must take such action as is necessary to insure that actions authorized, funded, or carried out by them do not result in the destruction or modification of this critical habitat area." 41 Fed. Reg. 13928 (1976) (to be codified as 50 C.F.R. § 17.81 (b)). This notice, of course, was pointedly directed at TVA and clearly aimed at halting completion or operation of the dam.

During the pendency of these administrative actions, other developments of relevance to the snail darter issue were transpiring. Communication was occurring between the Department of the Interior's Fish and Wildlife Service and TVA with a view toward settling the issue informally. These negotiations were to no avail, however, since TVA consistently took the position that the only available alternative was to attempt relocating the snail darter population to another suitable location. To this end, TVA conducted a search of alternative sites which might sustain the fish, culminating in the experimental transplantation of a number of snail darters to the nearby Hiwassee River. However, the Secretary of the Interior was not satisfied with the results of these efforts, finding that TVA had presented "little evidence that they have carefully studied the Hiwassee to determine whether or not" there were

---

[11] Searches by TVA in more than 60 watercourses have failed to find other populations of snail darters. App. 36, 410 412. The Secretary has noted that "more than 1,000 collections in recent years and additional earlier collections from central and east Tennessee have not revealed the presence of the snail darter outside the Little Tennessee River." 40 Fed. Reg. 47505 (1975). It is estimated, however, that the snail darter's range once extended throughout the upper main Tennessee River and the lower portions of its major tributaries above Chattanooga — all of which are now the sites of dam impoundments. *See* Hearings on Public Works for Water and Power Development and Energy Research Appropriation Bill, 1978, before a Subcommittee of the House Committee on Appropriations, 95th Cong., 1st Sess., pt. 4, pp. 240 241 (1977) (statement of witness for TVA); Hearings on Endangered Species Act Oversight, before the Subcommittee on Resource Protection of the Senate Committee on Environment and Public Works, 95th Cong., 1st Sess., 291 (1977); App. 139.

"biological and other factors in this river that [would] negate a successful transplant."[12] 40 Fed. Reg. 47506 (1975).

Meanwhile, Congress had also become involved in the fate of the snail darter. Appearing before a Subcommittee of the House Committee on Appropriations in April 1975 — some seven months before the snail darter was listed as endangered — TVA representatives described the discovery of the fish and the relevance of the Endangered Species Act to the Tellico Project. Hearings on Public Works for Water and Power Development and Energy Research Appropriation Bill, 1976, before a Subcommittee of the House Committee on Appropriations, 94th Cong., 1st Sess., pt. 7, pp. 466–467 (1975); Hearings on H.R. 8122, Public Works for Waterand Power Development and Energy Research Appropriations for Fiscal Year 1976, before a Subcommittee of the Senate Committee on Appropriations, 94th Cong., 1st Sess., pt. 4, pp. 3775–3777 (1975). At that time TVA presented a position which it would advance in successive forums thereafter, namely, that the Act did not prohibit the completion of a project authorized, funded, and substantially constructed before the Act was passed. TVA also described its efforts to transplant the snail darter, but contended that the dam should be finished regardless of the experiment's success. Thereafter, the House Committee on Appropriations, in its June 20, 1975, Report, stated the following in the course of recommending that an additional $29 million be appropriated for Tellico:

> The *Committee* directs that the project, for which an environmental impact statement has been completed and provided the Committee, should be completed as promptly as possible. . . . H.R. Rep. No. 94-319, p. 76 (1975). (Emphasis added.)

Congress then approved the TVA general budget, which contained funds for continued construction of the Tellico Project. In December 1975, one month after the snail darter was declared an endangered species, the President signed the bill into law. Public Works for Water and Power Development and Energy Research Appropriation Act, 1976, 89 Stat. 1035, 1047.

In February 1976, pursuant to § 11(g) of the Endangered Species Act, 87 Stat. 900, 16 U.S.C. § 1540(g) (1976ed.), respondents filed the case now under review, seeking to enjoin completion of the dam and impoundment of the reservoir on the ground that those actions would violate the Act by directly causing the extinction of the species *Percina (Imostoma) tanasi.* The District Court denied respondents' request for a preliminary injunction and set the matter for trial. Shortly thereafter the House and Senate held appropriations hearings which would include discussions of the Tellico budget.

At these hearings, TVA Chairman Wagner reiterated the agency's position that

---

[12] The Fish and Wildlife Service and Dr. Etnier have stated that it may take from 5 to 15 years for scientists to determine whether the snail darter can successfully survive and reproduce in this new environment. See General Accounting Office, The Tennessee Valley Authority's Tellico Dam Project Costs, Alternatives, and Benefits 4 (Oct. 14, 1977). In expressing doubt over the long-term future of the Hiwassee transplant, the Secretary noted: "That the snail darter does not already inhabit the Hiwassee River, despite the fact that the fish has had access to it in the past, is a strong indication that there may be biological and other factors in this river that negate a successful transplant." 40 Fed. Reg. 47506 (1975).

the Act did not apply to a project which was over 50% finished by the time the Act became effective and some 70% to 80% complete when the snail darter was officially listed as endangered. It also notified the Committees of the recently filed lawsuit's status and reported that TVA's efforts to transplant the snail darter had "been very encouraging." Hearings on Public Works for Water and Power Development and Energy Research Appropriation Bill, 1977, before a Subcommittee of the House Committee on Appropriations, 94th Cong., 2d Sess., pt. 5, pp. 261–262 (1976); Hearings on Public Works for Water and Power Development and Energy Research Appropriations forFiscal Year 1977, before a Subcommittee of the Senate Committee on Appropriations, 94th Cong., 2d Sess., pt. 4, pp. 3096-3099 (1976).

Trial was held in the District Court on April 29 and 30, 1976, and on May 25, 1976, the court entered its memorandum opinion and order denying respondents their requested relief and dismissing the complaint. The District Court found that closure of the dam and the consequent impoundment of the reservoir would "result in the adverse modification, if not complete destruction, of the snail darter's critical habitat," making it "highly probable" that "the continued existence of the snail darter" would be "[jeopardized]." 419 F. Supp. 753, 757 (EDTenn.). Despite these findings, the District Court declined to embrace the plaintiffs' position on the merits: that once a federal project was shown to jeopardize an endangered species, a court of equity is compelled to issue aninjunction restraining violation of the Endangered Species Act.

In reaching this result, the District Court stressed that the entire project was then about 80% complete and, based on available evidence, "there [were] no alternatives to impoundment of the reservoir, short of scrapping the entire project." *Id.*, at 758. The District Court also found that if the Tellico Project was permanently enjoined, "some $53 million would be lost in nonrecoverable obligations," *id.*, at 759, meaning that a large portion of the $78 million already expended would be wasted. The court also noted that the Endangered Species Act of 1973 was passed some seven years after construction on the dam commenced and that Congress had continued appropriations for Tellico, with full awareness of the snail darter problem. Assessing these various factors, the District Court concluded:

> "At some point in time a federal project becomes so near completion and so incapable of modification that a court of equity should not apply a statute enacted long after inception of the project to produce an unreasonable result . . . . Where there has been an irreversible and irretrievable commitment of resources by Congress to a project over a span of almost a decade, the Court should proceed with a great deal of circumspection."

Id., at 760. To accept the plaintiffs' position, the District Court argued, would inexorably lead to what it characterized as the absurd result of requiring "a court to halt impoundment of water behind a fully completed dam if an endangered species were discovered in the river on the day before such impoundment was scheduled to take place. We cannot conceive that Congress intended such a result." *Id.*, at 763.

Less than a month after the District Court decision, the Senate and House Appropriations Committees recommended the full budget request of $9 million for continued work on Tellico. See S. Rep. No. 94-960, p. 96(1976); H.R. Rep. No.

94-1223, p. 83 (1976). In its Report accompanying the appropriations bill, the Senate Committee stated:

> "During subcommittee hearings, TVA was questioned about the relationship between the Tellico project's completion and the November 1975 listing of the snail darter (a small 3-inch fishwhich was discovered in 1973) as an endangered species under the Endangered Species Act. TVA informed the Committee that it was continuing its efforts to preserve the darter, while working towards the scheduled 1977 completion date. TVA repeated its view that the Endangered Species Act did not prevent the completion of the Tellico project, which has been under construction for nearly a decade. The subcommittee brought this matter, as well as the recent U.S. District Court's decision upholding TVA's decision to complete the project, to the attention of the full Committee. *The Committee does not view* the Endangered Species Act as prohibiting the completion of the Tellico project at its advanced stage and directs that this project be completed as promptly as possible in the public interest." S. Rep. No. 94-960, *supra*, at 96. (Emphasis added.)

On June 29, 1976, both Houses of Congress passed TVA's general budget, which included funds for Tellico; the President signed the bill on July 12, 1976. Public Works for Water and Power Development and Energy Research Appropriation Act, 1977, 90 Stat. 889, 899.

Thereafter, in the Court of Appeals, respondents argued that the District Court had abused its discretion by not issuing an injunction in the face of "a blatant statutory violation." 549 F.2d 1064, 1069 (CA6 1977). The Court of Appeals agreed, and on January 31, 1977, it reversed, remanding "with instructions that a permanent injunction issue halting all activities incident to the Tellico Project which may destroy or modify the critical habitat of the snail darter." *Id.*, at 1075. The Court of Appeals directed that the injunction "remain in effect until Congress, by appropriate legislation, exempts Tellico from compliance with the Act or the snail darter has been deleted from the list of endangered species or its critical habitat materially redefined." *Ibid.* The Court of Appeals accepted the District Court's finding that closure of the dam would result in the known population of snail darters being "significantly reduced if not completely extirpated." *Id.*, at 1069. TVA, in fact, had conceded as much in the Court of Appeals, but argued that "closure of the Tellico Dam, as the last stage of a ten-year project, falls outside the legitimate purview of the Act if it is rationally construed." *Id.*, at 1070. Disagreeing, the Court of Appeals held that the record revealed a prima facie violation of § 7 of the Act, namely that TVA had failed to take "such action . . . necessary to insure" that its "actions" did not jeopardize the snail darter or its critical habitat.

The reviewing court thus rejected TVA's contention that the word "actions" in § 7 of the Act was not intended by Congress to encompass the terminal phases of ongoing projects. Not only could the court find no "positive reinforcement" for TVA's argument in the Act's legislative history, but also such an interpretation was seen as being "inimical to . . . its objectives." 549 F.2d, at 1070. By way of illustration, that court pointed out that "the detrimental impact of a project upon an endangered species may not always be clearly perceived before construction is well underway."

Id., at 1071. Given such a likelihood, the Court of Appeals was of the opinion that TVA's position would require the District Court, sitting as a chancellor, to balance the worth of an endangered species against the value of an ongoing public works measure, a result which the appellate court was not willing to accept. Emphasizing the limits on judicial power in this setting, the court stated:

> "Current project status cannot be translated into a workable standard of judicial review. Whether a dam is 50% or 90% completed is irrelevant in calculating the social and scientific costs attributable to the disappearance of a unique form of life. Courts are ill-equipped to calculate how many dollars must be invested before the value of a dam exceeds that of the endangered species. Our responsibility under 1540(g)(1)(A) is merely to preserve the status quo where endangered species are threatened, thereby guaranteeing the legislative or executive branches sufficient opportunity to grapple with the alternatives." *Ibid.*

As far as the Court of Appeals was concerned, it made no difference that Congress had repeatedly approved appropriations for Tellico, referring to such legislative approval as an "advisory [opinion]" concerning the proper application of an existing statute. In that court's view, the only relevant legislation was the Act itself, "[the] meaning and spirit" of which was "clear on its face." *Id.*, at 1072.

Turning to the question of an appropriate remedy, the Court of Appeals ruled that the District Court had erred by not issuing an injunction. While recognizing the irretrievable loss of millions of dollars of public funds which would accompany injunctive relief, the court nonetheless decided that the Act explicitly commanded precisely that result:

"It is conceivable that the welfare of an endangered species may weigh more heavily upon the public conscience, as expressed by the final will of Congress, than the writeoff of those millions of dollars already expended for Tellico in excess of its present salvageable value."

Id., at 1074.

Following the issuance of the permanent injunction, members of TVA's Board of Directors appeared before Subcommittees of the House and Senate Appropriations Committees to testify in support of continued appropriations for Tellico. The Subcommittees were apprised of all aspects of Tellico's status, including the Court of Appeals' decision. TVA reported that the dam stood "ready for the gates to be closed and the reservoir filled, "Hearings on Public Works for Water and Power Development and Energy Research Appropriation Bill, 1978, before a Subcommittee of the House Committee on Appropriations, 95th Cong., 1st Sess., pt. 4, p. 234 (1977), and requested funds for completion of certain ancillary parts of the project, such as public use areas, roads, and bridges. As to the snail darter itself, TVA commented optimistically on its transplantation efforts, expressing the opinion that the relocated fish were "doing well and [had] reproduced." *Id.*, at 235, 261–262.

Both Appropriations Committees subsequently recommended the full amount requested for completion of the Tellico Project. In its June 2, 1977, Report, the House Appropriations Committee stated:

"It is *the Committee's view* that the Endangered Species Act was not intended to halt projects such as these in their advanced stage of completion, and [the Committee] strongly recommends that these projects not be stopped because of misuse of the Act." H.R. Rep. No. 95-379, p. 104. (Emphasis added).

As a solution to the problem, the House Committee advised that TVA should cooperate with the Department of the Interior "to relocate the endangered species to another suitable habitat so as to permit the project to proceed as rapidly as possible." *Id.*, at 11. Toward this end, the Committee recommended a special appropriation of $2 million to facilitate relocation of the snail darter and other endangered species which threatened to delay or stop TVA projects. Much the same occurred on the Senate side, with its Appropriations Committee recommending both the amount requested to complete Tellico and the special appropriation for transplantation of endangered species. Reporting to the Senate on these measures, the Appropriations Committee took a particularly strong stand on the snail darter issue:

> "*This committee has not viewed* the Endangered Species Act as preventing the completion and use of these projects which were well under way at the time the affected species were listed as endangered. If the act has such an effect, which is contrary to *the Committee's understanding* of the intent of Congress in enacting the Endangered Species Act, funds should be appropriated to allow these projects to be completed and their benefits realized in the public interest, the Endangered Species Act notwithstanding." S. Rep. No. 95-301, p. 99 (1977). (Emphasis added).

TVA's budget, including funds for completion of Tellico and relocation of the snail darter, passed both Houses of Congress and was signed into law on August 7, 1977. Public Works for Water and Power Development and Energy Research Appropriation Act, 1978, 91 Stat. 797.

We granted certiorari, 434 U.S. 954 (1977), to review the judgment of the Court of Appeals.

II

We begin with the premise that operation of the Tellico Dam will either eradicate the known population of snail darters or destroy their critical habitat. Petitioner does not now seriously dispute this fact. In any event, under § 4(a)(1) of the Act, 87 Stat. 886, 16 U.S.C. § 1533(a)(1) (1976 ed.), the Secretary of the Interior is vested with exclusive authority to determine whether a species such as the snail darter is "endangered" or "threatened" and to ascertain the factors which have led to such a precarious existence. By § 4(d) Congress has authorized — indeed commanded — the Secretary to "issue such regulations as he deems necessary and advisable to provide for the conservation of such species." 16 U.S.C. § 1533(d) (1976 ed.). As we have seen, the Secretary promulgated regulations which declared the snail darter an endangered species whose critical habitat would be destroyed by creation of the Tellico Reservoir. Doubtless petitioner would prefer not to have these regulations on the books, but there is no suggestion that the Secretary exceeded his authority or abused his discretion in issuing the regulations. Indeed, no judicial review of the Secretary's determinations has ever been sought and hence the validity of his actions are not open to review in this Court.

Starting from the above premise, two questions are presented: (a) would TVA be in violation of the Act if it completed and operated the Tellico Dam as planned? (b) if TVA's actions would offend the Act, is an injunction the appropriate remedy for the violation? For the reasons stated hereinafter, we hold that both questions must be answered in the affirmative.

(A)

It may seem curious to some that the survival of a relatively small number of three-inch fish among all the countless millions of species extant would require the permanent halting of a virtually completed dam for which Congress has expended more than $100 million. The paradox is not minimized by the fact that Congress continued to appropriate large sums of public money for the project, even after congressional Appropriations Committees were apprised of its apparent impact upon the survival of the snail darter. We conclude, however, that the explicit provisions of the Endangered Species Act require precisely that result.

One would be hard pressed to find a statutory provision whose terms were any plainer than those in § 7 of the Endangered Species Act. Its very words affirmatively command all federal agencies "to *insure* that actions *authorized, funded,* or *carried out* by them do not *jeopardize* the continued existence" of an endangered species or "*result* in the destruction or modification of habitat of such species. . . ." 16 U.S.C. § 1536 (1976 ed.). (Emphasis added.) This language admits of no exception. Nonetheless, petitioner urges, as do the dissenters, that the Act cannot reasonably be interpreted as applying to a federal project which was well under way when Congress passed the Endangered Species Act of 1973. To sustain that position, however, we would be forced to ignore the ordinary meaning of plain language. It has not been shown, for example, how TVA can close the gates of the Tellico Dam without "carrying out" an action that has been "authorized" and "funded" by a federal agency. Nor can we understand how such action will "i *nsure*" that the snail darter's habitat is not disrupted.[13] Accepting the Secretary's determinations, as we must, it is clear that TVA's proposed operation of the dam will have precisely the opposite effect, namely the *eradication* of an endangered species.

Concededly, this view of the Act will produce results requiring the sacrifice of the anticipated benefits of the project and of many millions of dollars in public funds. But examination of the language, history, and structure of the legislation under review here indicates beyond doubt that Congress intended endangered species to

---

[13] In dissent, Mr. Justice Powell argues that the meaning of "actions" in § 7 is "far from 'plain,'" and that "it seems evident that the 'actions' referred to are not all actions that an agency can ever take, but rather actions that the agency is deciding whether to authorize, to fund, or to carry out." Aside from this bare assertion, however, no explanation is given to support the proffered interpretation. This recalls Lewis Carroll's classic advice on the construction of language:

"'When *I* use a word,' Humpty Dumpty said, in rather a scornful tone, 'it means just what I choose it to mean, neither more nor less.'" Through the Looking Glass, in The Complete Works of Lewis Carroll 196 (1939).

be afforded the highest of priorities. . . .

[The Court then discussed legislation preceding the ESA and factual findings underlying the enactment of the ESA.]

As it was finally passed, the Endangered Species Act of 1973 represented the most comprehensive legislation for the preservation of endangered species ever enacted by any nation. Its stated purposes were "to provide a means whereby the ecosystems upon which endangered species and threatened species depend may be conserved," and "to provide a program for the conservation of such . . . species. . . ." 16 U.S.C. § 1531(b) (1976 ed.). In furtherance of these goals, Congress expressly stated in § 2 (c) that "all Federal departments and agencies *shall seek to conserve endangered species* and threatened species . . ." 16 U.S.C. § 1531(c) (1976 ed.). (Emphasis added.) Lest there be any ambiguity as to the meaning of this statutory directive, the Act specifically defined "conserve" as meaning "to use and the use of *all methods and procedures which are necessary* to bring *any endangeredspecies* or threatened species to the point at which the measures provided pursuant to this chapter are no longer necessary." § 1532(2). (Emphasis added.) Aside from § 7, other provisions indicated the seriousness with which Congress viewed this issue: Virtually all dealings with endangered species, including taking, possession, transportation, and sale, were prohibited, 16 U.S.C. § 1538 (1976 ed.), except in extremely narrow circumstances, see § 1539(b). The Secretary was also given extensive power to develop regulations and programs for the preservation of endangered and threatened species. § 1533(d). Citizen involvement was encouraged by the Act, with provisions allowing interested persons to petition the Secretary to list a species as endangered or threatened, § 1533(c)(2) . . . and bring civil suits in United States district courts to force compliance with any provision of the Act, §§ 1540(c) and (g). . . .

[The Court next discussed the path of the ESA through Congress and quotes statements of significant legislators during the Congressional consideration of the measure.]

It is against this legislative background[14] that we must measure TVA's claim that the Act was not intended to stop operation of a project which, like Tellico Dam, was near completion when an endangered species was discovered in its path. While there is no discussion in the legislative history of precisely this problem, the totality of congressional action makes it abundantly clear that the result we reach today is wholly in accord with both the words of the statute and the intent of Congress. The plain intent of Congress in enacting this statute was to halt and reverse the trend toward species extinction, whatever the cost. This is reflected not only in the stated policies of the Act, but in literally every section of the statute. All persons, including federal agencies, are specifically instructed not to "take" endangered species, meaning that no one is "to harass, harm, pursue, hunt, shoot, wound, kill, trap, capture, or collect" such life forms. 16 U.S.C. §§ 1532(14), 1538(a)(1)(B) (1976 ed.).

---

[14] When confronted with a statute which is plain and unambiguous on its face, we ordinarily do not look to legislative history as a guide to its meaning. *Ex parte Collett*, 337 U.S. 55, 61 (1949), and cases cited therein. Here it is not necessary to look beyond the words of the statute. We have undertaken such an analysis only to meet Mr. Justice Powell's suggestion that the "absurd" result reached in this case, is not in accord with congressional intent.

Agencies in particular are directed by §§ 2 (c) and 3(2) of the Act to "use . . . *all methods* and procedures which are necessary" to preserve endangered species. 16 U.S.C. §§ 1531(c), 1532(2) (1976 ed.) (emphasis added). In addition, the legislative history undergirding § 7 reveals an explicit congressional decision to require agencies to afford first priority to the declared national policy of saving endangered species. The pointed omission of the type of qualifying language previously included in endangered species legislation reveals a conscious decision by Congress to give endangered species priority over the "primary missions" of federal agencies.

It is not for us to speculate, much less act, on whether Congress would have altered its stance had the specific events of this case been anticipated. In any event, we discern no hint in the deliberations of Congress relating to the 1973 Act that would compel a different result than we reach here. Indeed, the repeated expressions of congressional concern over what it saw as the potentially enormous danger presented by the eradication of *any* endangered species suggest how the balance would have been struck had the issue been presented to Congress in 1973. . . .

. . . [N]either the Endangered Species Act nor Art. III of the Constitution provides federal courts with authority to make such fine utilitarian calculations. On the contrary, the plain language of the Act, buttressed by its legislative history, shows clearly that Congress viewed the value of endangered species as "incalculable." Quite obviously, it would be difficult for a court to balance the loss of a sum certain — even $100 million — against a congressionally declared "incalculable" value, even assuming we had the power to engage in such a weighing process, which we emphatically do not.

In passing the Endangered Species Act of 1973, Congress was also aware of certain instances in which exceptions to the statute's broad sweep would be necessary. Thus, § 10, 16 U.S.C. § 1539 (1976 ed.), creates a number of limited "hardship exemptions," none of which would even remotely apply to the Tellico Project. In fact, there are no exemptions in the Endangered Species Act for federal agencies, meaning that under the maxim *expressio unius est exclusio alterius*, we must presume that these were the only "hardship cases" Congress intended to exempt. *Cf. National Railroad Passenger Corp. v. National Assn. of Railroad Passengers*, 414 U.S. 453, 458 (1974).

Notwithstanding Congress' expression of intent in 1973, we are urged to find that the continuing appropriations for Tellico Dam constitute an implied repeal of the 1973 Act, at least insofar as it applies to the Tellico Project. . . .

There is nothing in the appropriations measures, as passed, which states that the Tellico Project was to be completed irrespective of the requirements of the Endangered Species Act. These appropriations, in fact, represented relatively minor components of the lump-sum amounts for the *entire* TVA budget. To find a repeal of the Endangered Species Act under these circumstances would surely do violence to the " 'cardinal rule . . . that repeals by implication are not favored.' " *Morton v. Mancari*, 417 U.S. 535, 549 (1974), quoting *Posadas v. National City Bank*, 296 U.S. 497, 503 (1936). In *Posadas* this Court held, in no uncertain terms, that "the intention of the legislature to repeal must be clear and manifest." *Ibid. See Georgia v. Pennsylvania R. Co.*, 324 U.S. 439, 456 457 (1945) ("Only a clear

repugnancy between the old . . . and the new [law] results in the former giving way
. . ."); *United States v. Borden Co.*, 308 U.S. 188, 198–199 (1939) ("[Intention] of the
legislature to repeal 'must be clear and manifest.' . . . '[A] positive repugnancy
[between the old and the new laws]' "); *Wood v. United States*, 16 Pet. 342,363 (1842),
must be a positive repugnancy . . ."). In practical terms, this "cardinal rule" means
that "[in] the absence of some affirmative showing of an intention to repeal, the only
permissible justification for a repeal by implication is when the earlier and later
statutes are irreconcilable." *Mancari, supra*, at 550.

The doctrine disfavoring repeals by implication "applies with full vigor when . . .
the subsequent legislation is an appropriations measure." *Committee for Nuclear
Responsibility v. Seaborg*, 149 U.S. App. D.C. 380, 382, 463F.2d 783, 785 (1971)
(emphasis added); *Environmental Defense Fund v. Froehlke*, 473 F.2d 346, 355
(CA8, 1972). This is perhaps an understatement since it would be more accurate to
say that the policy applies with even *greater* force when the claimed repeal rests
solely on an Appropriations Act. We recognize that both substantive enactments and
appropriations measures are "Acts of Congress," but the latter have the limited and
specific purpose of providing funds for authorized programs. When voting on
appropriations measures, legislators are entitled to operate under the assumption
that the funds will be devoted to purposes which are lawful and not for any purpose
forbidden. Without such an assurance, every appropriations measure would be
pregnant with prospects of altering substantive legislation, repealing by implication
any prior statute which might prohibit the expenditure. . . .

(B)

Having determined that there is an irreconcilable conflict between operation of
the Tellico Dam and the explicit provisions of § 7 of the Endangered Species Act, we
must now consider what remedy, if any, is appropriate. It is correct, of course, that
a federal judge sitting as a chancellor is not mechanically obligated to grant an
injunction for every violation of law. This Court made plain in *Hecht Co. v. Bowles*,
321 U.S. 321, 329(1944), that "[a] grant of *jurisdiction* to issue compliance orders
hardly suggests an absolute duty to do so under any and all circumstances." As a
general matter it may be said that "[since] all or almost all equitable remedies are
discretionary, the balancing of equities and hardships is appropriate in almost any
case as a guide to the chancellor's discretion." D. Dobbs, Remedies 52 (1973). Thus,
in *Hecht Co.* the Court refused to grant an injunction when it appeared from the
District Court findings that "the issuance of an injunction would have 'no effect by
way of insuring better compliance in the future' and would [have been] 'unjust' to
[the] petitioner and not 'in the public interest.' " 321 U.S., at 326.

But these principles take a court only so far. Our system of government is, after
all, a tripartite one, with each branch having certain defined functions delegated to
it by the Constitution. While "[it] is emphatically the province and duty of the
judicial department to say what the law is," *Marbury v. Madison*, 1 Cranch 137,
177(1803), it is equally — and emphatically — the exclusive province of the
Congress not only to formulate legislative policies and mandate programs and
projects, but also to establish their relative priority for the Nation. Once Congress,
exercising its delegated powers, has decided the order of priorities in a given area,

it is for the Executive to administer the laws and for the courts to enforce them when enforcement is sought.

Here we are urged to view the Endangered Species Act "reasonably," and hence shape a remedy "that accords with some modicum of common sense and the public weal." But is that our function? We have no expert knowledge on the subject of endangered species, much less do we have a mandate from the people to strike a balance of equities on the side of the Tellico Dam. Congress has spoken in the plainest of words, making it abundantly clear that the balance has been struck in favor of affording endangered species the highest of priorities, thereby adopting a policy which it described as "institutionalized caution."

Our individual appraisal of the wisdom or unwisdom of a particular course consciously selected by the Congress is to be put aside in the process of interpreting a statute. Once the meaning of an enactment is discerned and its constitutionality determined, the judicial process comes to an end. We do not sit as a committee of review, nor are we vested with the power of veto. The lines ascribed to Sir Thomas More by Robert Bolt are not without relevance here:

> "The law, Roper, the law. I know what's legal, not what's right. And I'll stick to what's legal. . . . I'm *not* God. The currents and eddies of right and wrong, which you find such plain-sailing, I can't navigate, I'm no voyager. But in the thickets of the law, oh there I'm a forester. . . . What would you do? Cut a great road through the law to get after the Devil? . . . And when the last law was down, and the Devil turned round on you — where would you hide, Roper, the laws all being flat? . . . This country's planted thick with laws from coast to coast — Man's laws, not God's — and if you cut them down . . . d'you really think you could stand upright in the winds that would blow then? . . . Yes, I'd give the Devil benefit of law, for my own safety's sake." R. Bolt, A Man for All Seasons, Act I, p. 147 (Three Plays, Heinemann ed. 1967).

We agree with the Court of Appeals that in our constitutional system the commitment to the separation of powers is too fundamental for us to pre-empt congressional action by judicially decreeing what accords with "common sense and the public weal." Our Constitution vests such responsibilities in the political branches.

Affirmed.

MR. JUSTICE POWELL, with whom MR. JUSTICE BLACKMUN joins, dissenting.

[The dissent argued the ESA and its legislative history need not be read to apply to all "actions." Specifically, It should not apply to projects either completed or substantially completed. Instead of offering up "an extreme example of a literalist construction, not required by the language of the Act and adopted without regard to its manifest purpose[,]" argued Powell, the Court should "adopt a permissible construction that accords with some modicum of common sense and the public weal."]:

"[Frequently] words of general meaning are used in a statute, words broad enough to include an act in question, and yet a consideration of the whole legislation, or of the circumstances surrounding its enactment, or of the absurd results which follow from giving such broad meaning to the words, makes it unreasonable to believe that the legislator intended to include the particular act." *Church of the Holy Trinity v. United States*, 143 U.S. 457, 459 (1892). The result that will follow in this case by virtue of the Court's reading of § 7 makes it unreasonable to believe that Congress intended that reading. Moreover, § 7 may be construed in a way that avoids an "absurd result" without doing violence to its language. . . .

[Justice Powell concluded the statute should apply to prospective actions only, i.e., "actions with respect to which the agency has reasonable decisionmaking alternatives still available, actions not yet carried out."]

MR. JUSTICE REHNQUIST, dissenting.

[CHIEF JUSTICE REHNQUIST contended the ESA does not compel the issuance of an injunction, and the refusal of the District Court to issue one in this case was not abusive.]

NOTES AND QUESTIONS

1. *Section 7 after TVA v. Hill. Tennessee Valley Authority v. Hill* is to the ESA what *Calvert Cliffs* (*see* Chapter 4, *supra*) was to NEPA except for the significant distinction that *TVA v. Hill* cannot be overruled by a higher court. The decision alerted the world that the ESA would be understood according to its text. "[I]nsure no jeopardy" would mean *make absolutely certain not even a little bit of jeopardy* takes place. And more: it has been held subsequently that the Secretary must "do far more than merely avoid elimination of the protected species; he must bring such species back from the brink so that they may be removed from the protected class, and he must use all necessary methods to do so." *Carson-Truckee Water Conservancy Dist. v. Watt*, 549 F. Supp. 704 (D. Nev. 1982), *aff'd*, 741 F.2d 257 (9th Cir. 1984). Do you read § 7 as requiring the Secretary to undertake affirmative restoration efforts?

2. *BiOps and EISs.* Does a BiOp play the same role in agency decision making as an EIS does? *See, e.g., Bennett v. Spear*, 520 U.S. 154, 169–70, 117 S. Ct. 1154, 1164–65 (1997):

By the Government's own account, while the Service's Biological Opinion theoretically serves an "advisory function," 51 Fed. Reg. 19928 (1986), in reality it has a powerful coercive effect on the action agency:

The statutory scheme . . . presupposes that the biological opinion will play a central role in the action agency's decisionmaking process, and that it will typically be based on an administrative record that is fully adequate for the action agency's decision insofar as ESA issues are concerned. . . . [A] federal agency that chooses to deviate from the recommendations contained in a biological opinion bears the burden of "articulating in its administrative record its reasons for disagreeing with the conclusions of a biological opinion," 51 Fed. Reg. 19,956 (1986). In the government's experience, action agencies very rarely choose to engage in conduct that the Service has concluded is likely to jeopardize the continued existence of a listed species." Brief for Respondents 20-21.

What this concession omits to say, moreover, is that the action agency must not only articulate its reasons for disagreement (which ordinarily requires species and habitat investigations that are not within the action agency's expertise), but that it runs a substantial risk if its (inexpert) reasons turn out to be wrong. A Biological Opinion of the sort rendered here alters the legal regime to which the action agency is subject. . . . The action agency is technically free to disregard the Biological Opinion and proceed with its proposed action, but it does so at its own peril (and that of its employees), for "any person" who knowingly "takes" an endangered or threatened species is subject to substantial civil and criminal penalties, including imprisonment. See §§ 1540(a) and (b) (authorizing civil fines of up to $25,000 per violation and criminal penalties of up to $50,000 and imprisonment for one year).

3. **Postscript.** The Supreme Court's decision in *TVA v. Hill*, handed down on June 15, 1978, was less than warmly received in high places. Particularly troubled by the decision was then-Republican Minority Leader of the United States Senate, Senator Howard H. Baker of Tellico's home state of Tennessee. A devotee of the water project, Senator Baker took on the completion of the Tellico project as his personal mission.

As a first volley, Senator Baker engineered an important amendment to the ESA. At his behest, on November 10, 1978, less than five months after the decision in *TVA v. Hill*, the Congress created the Endangered Species Committee ("ESC"). *See* § 7(e), 16 U.S.C. § 1536(e). One of the bluest of blue-ribbon panels, the Committee has seven designated members: the Secretaries of Agriculture, Army, and Interior, the Chairman of the Council of Economic Advisors, the Administrators of the Environmental Protection Agency and the National Oceanic and Atmospheric Administration, and one individual from the affected state. Section 7(e)(3), 16 U.S.C. § 1536(e)(3). Aptly nicknamed the "God Squad," the Committee is authorized to issue wholesale exemptions from the provisions of § 7. Senator Baker provided in the legislation that Tellico would be the ESC's first order of business.

The ESC promptly took up the matter, but, on January 23, 1979, voted against exempting Tellico. Notably, all six federal members of the panel voted to deny. The major motivation for the negative vote, however, was not the snail darter, but Tellico itself. As the Chairman of the Council of Economic Advisors, Charles Schultze, put it, "[The project] does not pay. The costs clearly outweigh the benefits. It would have cost $35 million to complete it and we would be inundating $40 million worth of land. You would lose important Indian archeological sites, scenic values and the river in its natural state." Margot Hornblower, *Panel Junks TVA Dam; Cites Cost, Not Snail Darter*, WASH. POST, Jan. 24, 1979, at A12.

At this point, Senator Baker settled on a more blunt approach, to simply have Congress authorize the project. Working with Rep. John J. Duncan, a Tennessee colleague in the House of Representatives, amendments were offered to that effect. The authorization passed the House in the summer of 1979. The story is that the amendment was hidden in a larger bill and that the House had no idea it was voting to construct the Tellico Dam. The Senate followed suit on September 19, 1979, after a good bit of blatant arm-twisting by the Minority Leader. The measure arrived at President Jimmy Carter's desk as part of a $10.8 billion energy and water resources spending bill. Despite his on-the-record opposition to Tellico, President Carter signed the measure into law, reportedly to avoid congressional reprisals on other important pending legislation. On November 29, 1979, the dam was completed and waters impounded. The result was Lake Tellico, a 15,860-acre lake with miles of shoreline. Dotting the shores are an estimated 2,000 residential homes known as Tellico Village.

In 1980, additional snail darters were discovered 80 miles south of the damsite, and more were found later in Alabama and Georgia. Dr. Etnier, who made the original discovery that triggered the *TVA v. Hill* saga, explained the other colonies of snail darters were not found sooner because scientists misunderstood the species' tolerance for pollution. Apparently, snail darters can withstand a great deal more contamination than was earlier believed. On July 5, 1984, nine years after it was listed as endangered, the snail darter was downgraded to "threatened." 49 Fed Reg. 27,510, 27,514.

4. *Northern Spotted Owl.* A longstanding ESA controversy involves the northern spotted owl, which populates timberlands in the Pacific Northwest. In 1987, litigation had begun to protect the spotted owl on timberlands managed by BLM, which comprise the bulk of the owl habitat. The theory was that logging operations were threatening the continued existence of the species. At this time, though, the spotted owl had not been designated under the ESA, so plaintiffs were relying on NEPA arguments to effect an end to logging activities. The case resulted in the entry of an injunction against the loggers.

Congress became involved in the controversy as well. It enacted § 318 of the Interior and Related Agencies Appropriations Act for FY 1990, Pub. L. No. 101-121, 103 Stat. 701, 745–50 (1990), which expressly allowed resumption of timber operations in these old growth forests in Oregon and Washington in FY 1992. The Ninth Circuit, however, ruled § 318 to be unconstitutional as violating separation of powers principles because it interfered with ongoing litigation. As the court termed it, § 318 was an instruction to the court "to reach a particular result in pending cases identified by caption and case number." *Seattle Audubon Society et al. v. Robertson*, 914 F.2d 1311, 1314 (9th Cir. 1990).

At about this same time, the Fish and Wildlife Service designated the spotted owl as "threatened" throughout its entire range, a designation that remains in place at this writing. *See* 55 Fed. Reg. 26,114 (June 26, 1990). After designation, the Bureau of Land Management, which manages federally owned owl habitat lands, took steps to stop timber harvesting in the range until further notice. That effort was deterred, at least in part, when the Endangered Species Committee exempted 13 timber sales from the ESA, thereby allowing injury to the owls. 57 Fed. Reg. 23,405 (1992). On

June 6, 1994, the court-ordered injunction was lifted on the theory that the Forest Service's new forest management plan made the ban unnecessary. That plan was again revised in subsequent years.

The controversy continues on. In June 2011, the FWS announced yet another revised forest management plan. The new plan affects about 22,000 acres of federal land, is projected to reduce logging in those areas, and is viewed as a step toward an experimental new approach to protecting northern spotted owls: a program to kill up to a few hundred barred owls because they "out-compete" the northern spotted owls. (Good idea?) According to the FWS, the population of the northern spotted owl is declining at about three per cent each year.

For more information about the spotted owl controversy, see Andrea L. Hungerford, *Changing the Management of Public Forest Lands: The Role of the Spotted Owl Injunctions*, 24 ENVTL. L. 1396 (1994); Victor M. Sher, *Travels with Strix: The Spotted Owl's Journey Through the Federal Courts*, 14 PUB. LAND L. REV. 41 (1993).The spotted owl recovery plan may be found at http://www.fws.gov/ oregonfwo/Species/Data/NorthernSpottedOwl/Recovery/Library/Documents/ RevisedNSORecPlan2011.pdf.

5. ***Survival and Recovery.*** In *Sierra Club v. U.S. Fish and Wildlife Service*, 245 F.3d 434 (5th Cir. 2001), a regulation implementing § 7 was found to violate the ESA. Section 7, the reader will recall, requires "habitat consultation" (as distinct from "jeopardy consultation") whenever an agency action might "result in the destruction or adverse modification of [designated] habitat." Section 7(a)(2), 16 U.S.C. § 1536(a)(2). The regulation defined "destruction or adverse modification" as "a direct or indirect alteration that appreciably diminishes the value of critical habitat for *both the survival and recovery* of a listed species." 50 C.F.R. § 402.02 (emphasis added). The court found this regulation to violate the ESA because it does not require habitat consultation where an agency action affects survival alone. The gravamen of the court's reasoning was that critical habitat is "essential to conservation" and conservation speaks to recovery, not just survival. Thus, there should be habitat consultation on both counts.

D. SECTION 9

BABBITT v. SWEET HOME CHAPTER OF COMMUNITIES FOR A GREAT OREGON
515 U.S. 687, 115 S. Ct. 2407 (1995)

JUDGES: STEVENS, J., delivered the opinion of the Court, in which O'CONNOR, KENNEDY, SOUTER, GINSBURG, and BREYER, JJ., joined. O'CONNOR, J., filed a concurring opinion. SCALIA, J., filed a dissenting opinion, in which REHNQUIST, C. J., and THOMAS, J., joined.

The Endangered Species Act of 1973, 87 Stat. 884, 16 U.S.C. § 1531 (1988 ed. and Supp. V) (ESA or Act), contains a variety of protections designed to save from extinction species that the Secretary of the Interior designates as endangered or threatened. Section 9 of the Act makes it unlawful for any person to "take" any endangered or threatened species. The Secretary has promulgated a regulation that defines the statute's prohibition on takings to include "significant habitat modification or degradation where it actually kills or injures wildlife." This case presents the question whether the Secretary exceeded his authority under the Act by promulgating that regulation.

I

Section 9(a)(1) of the Endangered Species Act provides the following protection for endangered species:

> "Except as provided in sections 1535(g)(2) and 1539 of this title, with respect to any endangered species of fish or wildlife listed pursuant to section 1533 of this title it is unlawful for any person subject to the jurisdiction of the United States to —. . . .

> "(B) take any such species within the United States or the territorial sea of the United States[.]" 16 U.S.C. § 1538(a)(1).

Section 3(19) of the Act defines the statutory term "take":

> "The term 'take' means to harass, harm, pursue, hunt, shoot, wound, kill, trap, capture, or collect, or to attempt to engage in any such conduct." 16 U.S.C. § 1532(19).

The Act does not further define the terms it uses to define "take." The Interior Department regulations that implement the statute, however, define the statutory term "harm":

> "*Harm* in the definition of 'take' in the Act means an act which actually kills or injures wildlife. Such act may include significant habitat modification or degradation where it actually kills or injures wildlife by significantly impairing essential behavioral patterns, including breeding, feeding, or sheltering." 50 C.F.R. § 17.3 (1994).

This regulation has been in place since 1975.

. . . .

Respondents in this action are small landowners, logging companies, and families dependent on the forest products industries in the Pacific Northwest and in the Southeast, and organizations that represent their interests. They brought this declaratory judgment action against petitioners, the Secretary of the Interior and the Director of the Fish and Wildlife Service, in the United States District Court for the District of Columbia to challenge the statutory validity of the Secretary's regulation defining "harm," particularly the inclusion of habitat modification and degradation in the definition. Respondents challenged the regulation on its face. Their complaint alleged that application of the "harm" regulation to the red-cockaded woodpecker, an endangered species, and the northern spotted owl, a threatened species, had injured them economically. App.17-23.

. . . .

II

. . . .

The text of the Act provides three reasons for concluding that the Secretary's interpretation is reasonable. First, an ordinary understanding of the word "harm" supports it. The dictionary definition of the verb form of "harm" is "to cause hurt or damage; to injure." Webster's Third New International Dictionary 1034 (1966). In the context of the ESA, that definition naturally encompasses habitat modification that results in actual injury or death to members of an endangered or threatened species.

Respondents argue that the Secretary should have limited the purview of "harm" to direct applications of force against protected species, but the dictionary definition does not include the word "directly" or suggest in any way that only direct or willful action that leads to injury constitutes "harm." Moreover, unless the statutory term "harm" encompasses indirect as well as direct injuries, the word has no meaning that does not duplicate the meaning of other words that § 3 uses to define "take." A reluctance to treat statutory terms as surplusage supports the reasonableness of the Secretary's interpretation. [citation omitted.]

Second, the broad purpose of the ESA supports the Secretary's decision to extend protection against activities that cause the precise harms Congress enacted the statute to avoid. In *TVA v. Hill*, 437 U.S. 153, 98 S. Ct. 2279, 57 L. Ed. 2d 117 (1978), we described the Act as "the most comprehensive legislation for the preservation of endangered species ever enacted by any nation." *Id.*, at 180. Whereas predecessor statutes enacted in 1966 and 1969 had not contained any sweeping prohibition against the taking of endangered species except on federal lands, *see id.*, at 175, the 1973 Act applied to all land in the United States and to the Nation's territorial seas. As stated in § 2 of the Act, among its central purposes is "to provide a means whereby the ecosystems upon which endangered species and threatened species depend may be conserved. . . ." 16 U.S.C. § 1531(b).

In *Hill*, we construed § 7 as precluding the completion of the Tellico Dam because of its predicted impact on the survival of the snail darter. *See* 437 U.S. at 193. Both our holding and the language in our opinion stressed the importance of the statutory policy. "The plain intent of Congress in enacting this statute," we recognized, "was to halt and reverse the trend toward species extinction, whatever the cost. This is reflected not only in the stated policies of the Act, but in literally every section of the statute." *Id.*, at 184. Although the § 9 "take" prohibition was not at issue in *Hill*, we took note of that prohibition, placing particular emphasis on the Secretary's inclusion of habitat modification in his definition of "harm." In light of that provision for habitat protection, we could "not understand how TVA intends to operate Tellico Dam without 'harming' the snaildarter." *Id.*, at 184, n. 30. Congress' intent to provide comprehensive protection for endangered and threatened species supports the permissibility of the Secretary's "harm" regulation.

Respondents advance strong arguments that activities that cause minimal or unforeseeable harm will not violate the Act as construed in the "harm" regulation. Respondents, however, present a facial challenge to the regulation. *Cf. Anderson v. Edwards*, 514 U.S. 143, 155-153, n. 6 (1995) . . . ; *INS v. National Center for*

Immigrants'Rights, Inc., 502 U.S. 183, 188, 112 S. Ct. 551, 116 L. Ed. 2d 546 (1991). Thus, they ask us to invalidate the Secretary's understanding of "harm" in every circumstance, even when an actor knows that an activity, such as draining a pond, would actually result in the extinction of a listed species by destroying its habitat. Given Congress' clear expression of the ESA's broad purpose to protect endangered and threatened wildlife, the Secretary's definition of "harm" is reasonable.

Third, the fact that Congress in 1982 authorized the Secretary to issue permits for takings that § 9(a)(1)(B) would otherwise prohibit, "if such taking is incidental to, and not the purpose of, the carrying out of an otherwise lawful activity," 16 U.S.C. § 1539(a)(1)(B), strongly suggests that Congress understood § 9(a)(1)(B) to prohibit indirect as well as deliberate takings. *Cf. NLRB v. Bell Aerospace Co. of Textron, Inc.*, 416 U.S. 267, 274–275, 40L. Ed. 2d 134, 94 S. Ct. 1757 (1974). The permit process requires the applicant to prepare a "conservation plan" that specifies how he intends to "minimize and mitigate" the "impact" of his activity on endangered and threatened species, 16 U.S.C. § 1539(a)(2)(A), making clear that Congress had in mind foreseeable rather than merely accidental effects on listed species. No one could seriously request an "incidental" take permit to avert § 9 liability for direct, deliberate action against a member of an endangered or threatened species, but respondents would read "harm" so narrowly that the permit procedure would have little more than that absurd purpose. "When Congress acts to amend a statute, we presume it intends its amendment to have real and substantial effect." *Stone v. INS*, 514 U.S. 386, 397, 115 S. Ct. 1537, 131 L. Ed. 2d 465 (1995). . . . Congress' addition of the § 10 permit provision supports the Secretary's conclusion that activities not intended to harm an endangered species, such as habitat modification, may constitute unlawful takings under the ESA unless the Secretary permits them.

. . . .

We need not decide whether the statutory definition of "take" compels the Secretary's interpretation of "harm," because our conclusions that Congress did not unambiguously manifest its intent to adopt respondents' view and that the Secretary's interpretation is reasonable suffice to decide this case. *See generally Chevron U.S.A. Inc. v. Natural Resources Defense Council, Inc.*, 467 U.S. 837, 81 L. Ed. 2d 694, 104 S. Ct. 2778 (1984). The latitude the ESA gives the Secretary in enforcing the statute, together with the degree of regulatory expertise necessary to its enforcement, establishes that we owe some degree of deference to the Secretary's reasonable interpretation. *See* Breyer, *Judicial Review of Questions of Law and Policy*, 38 ADMIN. L. REV. 363, 373 (1986).

III

[Herein a discussion of the legislative history of the Endangered Species Act.]

IV

When it enacted the ESA, Congress delegated broad administrative and interpretive power to the Secretary. *See* 16 U.S.C. §§ 1533, 1540(f). The task of defining and listing endangered and threatened species requires an expertise and attention to detail that exceeds the normal province of Congress. Fashioning appropriate standards for issuing permits under § 10 for takings that would otherwise violate § 9 necessarily requires the exercise of broad discretion. The proper interpretation of a term such as "harm" involves a complex policy choice. When Congress has entrusted the Secretary with broad discretion, we are especially reluctant to substitute our views of wise policy for his. *See Chevron*, 467 U.S. at 865–866. In this case, that reluctance accords with our conclusion, based on the text, structure, and legislative history of the ESA, that the Secretary reasonably construed the intent of Congress when he defined "harm" to include "significant habitat modification or degradation that actually kills or injures wildlife."

In the elaboration and enforcement of the ESA, the Secretary and all persons who must comply with the law will confront difficult questions of proximity and degree; for, as all recognize, the Act encompasses a vast range of economic and social enterprises and endeavors. These questions must be addressed in the usual course of the law, through case-by-case resolution and adjudication.

The judgment of the Court of Appeals is reversed.

It is so ordered.

JUSTICE O'CONNOR, concurring.

My agreement with the Court is founded on two understandings. First, the challenged regulation is limited to significant habitat modification that causes actual, as opposed to hypothetical or speculative, death or injury to identifiable protected animals. Second, even setting aside difficult questions of scienter, the regulation's application is limited by ordinary principles of proximate causation, which introduce notions of foreseeability. . . .

In my view, the regulation is limited by its terms to actions that actually kill or injure individual animals. Justice Scalia disagrees, arguing that the harm regulation "encompasses injury inflicted, not only upon individual animals, but upon populations of the protected species." At one level, I could not reasonably quarrel with this observation: death to an individual animal always reduces the size of the population in which it lives, and in that sense, "injures" that population. But by its insight, the dissent means something else. Building upon the regulation's use of the word "breeding," Justice Scalia suggests that the regulation facially bars significant habitat modification that actually kills or injures *hypothetical* animals (or, perhaps more aptly, causes potential additions to the population not to come into being). Because "impairment of breeding does not 'injure' living creatures," Justice Scalia reasons, the regulation *must* contemplate application to "a population of animals which would otherwise have maintained or increased its numbers."

I disagree. As an initial matter, I do not find it as easy as Justice Scalia does to dismiss the notion that significant impairment of breeding injures living creatures. To raze the last remaining ground on which the piping plover currently breeds, thereby making it impossible for any piping plovers to reproduce, would obviously injure the population (causing the species' extinction in a generation). But by completely preventing breeding, it would also injure the individual living bird, in the same way that sterilizing the creature injures the individual living bird. To "injure" is, among other things, "to impair." Webster's Ninth New Collegiate Dictionary 623(1983). One need not subscribe to theories of "psychic harm," to recognize that to make it impossible for an animal to reproduce is to impair its most essential physical functions and to render that animal, and its genetic material, biologically obsolete. This, in my view, is actual injury.

In any event, even if impairing an animal's ability to breed were not, *in and of itself*, an injury to that animal, interference with breeding can cause an animal to suffer other, perhaps more obvious, kinds of injury. The regulation has clear application, for example, to significant habitat modification that kills or physically injures animals which, because they are in a vulnerable breeding state, do not or cannot flee or defend themselves, or to environmental pollutants that cause an animal to suffer physical complications during gestation. Breeding, feeding, and sheltering are what animals do. If significant habitat modification, by interfering with these essential behaviors, actually kills or injures an animal protected by the Act, it causes "harm" within the meaning of the regulation. In contrast to Justice Scalia, I do not read the regulation's "breeding" reference to vitiate or somehow to qualify the clear actual death or injury requirement, or to suggest that the regulation contemplates extension to nonexistent animals. . . .

By the dissent's reckoning, the regulation at issue here, in conjunction with 16 U.S.C. § 1540(1), imposes liability for any habitat-modifying conduct that ultimately results in the death of a protected animal, "regardless of whether that result is intended or even foreseeable, and no matter how long the chain of causality between modification and injury." Even if § 1540(1) does create a strict liability regime (a question we need not decide at this juncture), I see no indication that Congress, in enacting that section, intended to dispense with ordinary principles of proximate causation. Strict liability means liability without regard to fault; it does not normally mean liability for every consequence, however remote, of one's conduct. . . . I would not lightly assume that Congress, in enacting a strict liability statute that is silent on the causation question, has dispensed with this well-entrenched principle. In the absence of congressional abrogation of traditional principles of causation, then, private parties should be held liable under § 1540(1) only if their habitat-modifying actions proximately cause death or injury to protected animals. . . .

JUSTICE SCALIA, with whom THE CHIEF JUSTICE and JUSTICE THOMAS join, dissenting.

I think it unmistakably clear that the legislation at issue here (1) forbade the hunting and killing of endangered animals, and (2) provided federal lands and federal funds *for the acquisition of private lands*, to preserve the habitat of endangered animals. The Court's holding that the hunting and killing prohibition incidentally preserves habitat on private lands imposes unfairness to the point of financial ruin — not just upon the rich, but upon the simplest farmer who finds his land conscripted to national zoological use. I respectfully dissent. . . .

[Remainder of opinion omitted.]

NOTES AND QUESTIONS

1. *The "Take" Prohibition.* Thus, the ESA elevates a subset of wildlife and plant life to a virtual state of invulnerability, at least insofar as the human threat is concerned. Should there be any limits on the principle? Should one be entitled to kill a protected animal if one paid for it and owns it? (Under state law, one surely can own a member of a protected species. *See, e.g., Pierson v. Post*, 3 Cai. R. 175, 2 Am. Dec. 264 (N.Y. Sup. Ct. 1805).) Cannot one kill what one owns? If federal law precludes this, does the law cause an unconstitutional taking? Assume that a person owned an animal before its species was listed. If the animal were old and suffering, might the owner "put it to sleep"? Would that act violate § 9? Alternatively, might a person kill a protected animal in self-defense? *See* § 11(a)(3), 16 U.S.C. § 1540(a)(3) (providing that civil penalties not be imposed if the actor was motivated by "a good faith belief that he was acting to protect himself or herself, a member of his or her family or any other individual from bodily harm"). *See also Christy v. Hodel*, 857 F.2d 1324 (9th Cir. 1988), *cert. denied*, 490 U.S. 1114 (1989). In *Christy*, a rancher killed one of a group of marauding grizzly bears that was attacking the rancher's herd of sheep. For this action, he was assessed a civil penalty of $3,000 for violating the ESA and its regulations. The court upheld the penalty, finding no statutory right to kill the grizzly in defense of property. The court declined to imply such a right as a matter of constitutional law: "In light of the Supreme Court's admonition that we exercise restraint in creating new definitions of substantive due process, we decline plaintiffs' invitation to construe the fifth amendment as guaranteeing the right to kill federally protected wildlife in defense of property." *Christy*, 857 F.2d at 1330.

2. *Land Transfers.* The government is legally able to transfer land that serves as habitat for endangered species, because the transfer of land, without more, does not *per se* jeopardize a listed species. But both §§ 7 and 9 play a role. Section 7 applies to the act of negotiating and executing a contract for sale; accordingly, a proposed sale would trigger a re-initiation of consultation with the FWS. If the land were ultimately transferred to private control, § 9 would come into play, prohibiting the private owner from harming the species.

The practical problem with such a transaction is finding a purchaser. One way to do that is by changing the legal framework governing the sale. *See, e.g., Tinoqui-Chalola Council v. Department of Interior*, 232 F.3d 1300 (9th Cir. 2000). In that case, the Department of Energy needed to sell an oil field south of Bakersfield, California. The seventh largest oil field in the United States at 47,000 acres, the parcel was home to several endangered species. The DOE needed to sell the field because the National Defense Authorization Act of 1996, Pub. L. No. 104-106, 3412(a), 110 Stat. 631, 631 32 (1997) ("DAA"), instructed it to do so within two years of the statute's effective date. The court held under these facts that the DOE did not need to re-initiate consultation with F&W: "Bypassing the DAA, Congress waived the DOE's duty to re-initiate consultation under section 7 as to the . . . sale." *Tinoqui-Chalola*, 232 F.3d at 1309. The Act, actually, did more than that. It also made the incidental take statement governing the government's activities on the oil field transferrable to the purchaser. *See* § E, *infra*. So long as the purchaser's activities on the parcel remain identical to the activities evaluated in the biological opinion, no new incidental take permit was necessary. *Tinoqui-Chalola*, 232 F.3d at 1309.

E. STATUTORY FLEXIBILITY INITIATIVES

As interpreted in both *TVA v. Hill* and *Sweet Home*, the ESA epitomizes inflexibility. The statute applies according to its terms, regardless of the press of competing considerations. This uncompromising rigor engendered a flood of objection over the course of many years. The call for reform was so incessant that amending the Act became necessary if only to avoid an outright repeal. Both Congress and the Executive were moved to make significant changes.[15]

The first significant change of this sort was the creation of the Endangered Species Committee ("ESC"). See Notes following *TVA v. Hill*. The ESC, by a vote of five of the seven designated Committee members, can exempt a project from the strictures of § 7. Section 7(h)(1), 16 U.S.C. § 1536(h)(1). To warrant an exemption, there must be "no reasonable and prudent alternatives" to the agency action, the benefits of the action must "clearly outweigh" the benefits of alternative actions that are more "consistent" with wildlife protection, the action must be of "regional or national significance," and there must be no "irreversible or irretrievable commitment of resources" that would foreclose alternative actions. In addition, exempted actions must be accompanied by reasonable mitigation measures. Section 7(h)(1)(A) (B), 16 U.S.C. § 1536(h)(1)(A), (B).

The ESC has convened only rarely. Contemporaneous with the exemption denial in the Tellico Dam case, the ESC granted an exemption to the Grayrocks water project on the Laramie River in Wyoming. This project was at issue because the Laramie feeds the North Platte River, which in turn feeds the Platte River, which serves as habitat for endangered whooping cranes during their semiannual migrations to Nebraska. Grayrocks prevailed before the ESC because project sponsors agreed to manage water releases to avoid harming the cranes and to establish and fund a crane protection organization, The Crane Trust, Inc. (formerly known as the Platte River Whooping Crane Habitat Maintenance Trust). Head-quartered in Wood River, Nebraska, the Trust is still in place working to preserve habitat for whoopers. The ESC was called into action again in 1992, when it exempted 13 BLM timber sales in the Pacific Northwest. See Notes and Questions following *TVA v. Hill*. Exemption decisions are themselves exempt from the requirements of NEPA. Section 7(k), 16 U.S.C. § 1536(k).

Much more important than the ESC in the scheme of things are the amendatory provisions regarding incidental takings. In the first decade after enactment of the ESA, the complaint was made that even if a government agency fully complied with § 7, it might still cause an incidental or unintentional injury to a member of a

---

[15] Many attempts to amend the legislation have not been successful. In 1998, for example, one bill offered tax incentives to landowners for voluntary habitat preservation, and another bill proposed a heightened evidentiary showing before a species might be listed and an increase in requirements for recovery plans for species. Both bills failed. In the preceding year, another bill promoted an increase in use of cost-benefit analysis and comparative risk assessment in environmental regulation, a proposal that would have affected the ESA. That bill failed as well.

protected species and thereby be exposed to liability. A private actor acting on private land, moreover, could do the same and face § 9 liability. To remedy the potential for inflexible application of the ESA, in 1982 the Congress amended §§ 7 and 9 by creating a mechanism to exempt from the prohibitions of the ESA takings of species that were merely incidental to actions otherwise allowable. "Incidental takes" are "takings that result from, but are not the purpose of, carrying out an otherwise lawful activity conducted by the Federal agency or applicant." 50 C.F.R. § 402.02 (1996).

(a) *Incidental take statements ("ITSs"):* Section 7 was amended to incorporate "incidental take statements." Section 7, as now constructed, instructs the Secretary to identify in ITSs "those reasonable and prudent alternatives which he believes would not violate [§ 7(a)(2)] and can be taken by the Federal agency or applicant in implementing the agency action." Section 7(b)(3)(A), 16 U.S.C. § 1536(b)(3)(A). "Reasonable and prudent alternatives" ("RPAs") are defined as:

> alternative actions identified during formal consultation that can be imple-
> mented in a manner consistent with the intended purpose of the action, that
> can be implemented consistent with the scope of the Federal agency's
> authority and jurisdiction, that is economically and technologically feasible,
> and that the [Service] believes will avoid the likelihood of jeopardizing the
> continued existence of listed species.

50 C.F.R. § 2.02 (1996). Where the Service concludes that a federal action or the implementation of any RPA and the resultant incidental take of a listed species will not violate § 7(a)(2), the Secretary must provide an ITS with the biological opinion. Section 7(b)(4), 16 U.S.C. § 1536(b)(4); 50 C.F.R. § 402.14(I) (1996). An ITS must specify the impact of the incidental taking on the species, specify the "reasonable and prudent measures that the Secretary considers necessary or appropriate to minimize such impact," and set forth "terms and conditions" that must be complied with by the federal agency to implement the reasonable and prudent measures. *Id.* Thereafter, so long as there is compliance with the terms and conditions of the statement, any incidental takings are exempted from liability. Section 7(o), 16 U.S.C. § 1536(o).

This process has been somewhat troublesome from the point of view of environmentalists. As it turns out, action agencies frequently fail to implement the conditions of an ITS in timely fashion. To compound the problem, the FWS often has simply adjusted the time line to allow the failure, a practice that belies the overarching message of *TVA v. Hill.*

The day for breezily extending deadlines would seem to have come to an end, however. In *Southwest Center for Biological Diversity v. Babbitt,* 170 F. Supp. 2d 931 (D. Ariz., 2000), *aff'd,* 314 F.3d 1060 (9th Cir. 2002), the court held that, since the original deadlines in the BiOp were mandatory, revisions of them were only justified upon a scientific determination that the extension would not jeopardize the species.

(b) *Incidental take permits ("ITPs"):* Section 9 was amended, *de facto,* by the addition of § 10. Section 10(a)(1)(B) of the ESA now authorizes the Secretary to permit "any taking otherwise prohibited by [§ 9] if such taking is incidental to, and not the purpose of, the carrying out of an otherwise lawful activity." Section

10(a)(1)(B), 16 U.S.C. § 1538(a)(1)(B). If the Secretary finds that any such taking would be incidental, would be mitigated appropriately, and would not "appreciably reduce the likelihood of the survival and recovery of the species in the wild," he or she is instructed to issue the permit. Section 10(a)(2)(B), 16 U.S.C. § 1538(a)(2)(B). No ITP, however, may be issued unless the applicant has submitted to the Secretary a conservation plan, typically known as a "habitat conservation plan" or an "HCP." HCPs are legally binding agreements in which a landowner adopts conservation measures in exchange for permission from the federal government to develop property. HCPs must be adequately funded. They often are designed to be in force for more than fifty years.

In the more than 25 years since § 10 came into being, there have been several hundred incidental take permits issued. Only a relative few of these have been challenged in the courts. For a case finding an HCP to be insufficient, see *National Wildlife Federation v. Babbitt*, 128 F. Supp. 2d 1274 (E.D. Cal. 2000) (holding the HCP failed to meet the substantive standards of the ESA and lacked an EIS under NEPA). For some information on ITPs, see *Volusia County, infra*, and the Notes and Questions that follow.

LOGGERHEAD TURTLE v. COUNTY COUNCIL OF VOLUSIA COUNTY, FLORIDA
148 F.3d 1231 (11th Cir. 1998), *cert. denied*, 526 U.S. 1081, 119 S. Ct. 1488 (1999)

JUDGES: Before HATCHETT, CHIEF JUDGE, and RONEY and CLARK, SENIOR CIRCUIT JUDGES. RONEY, SENIOR CIRCUIT JUDGE, dissenting.

OPINION: HATCHETT, CHIEF JUDGE:

[The loggerhead sea turtle and the green sea turtle ("turtles") were designated as threatened and endangered respectively in 1978. 50 C.F.R. § 1711. These species of turtles, which live in the Gulf of Mexico and in the South Atlantic, are known to come ashore on to the beaches of Volusia County, which sports about forty miles of Atlantic Ocean coastline in northeast Florida. The turtles come ashore from May to October, during their nesting season, to lay eggs. After laying their eggs, mother turtles return to the sea.

After an incubation period of about two months, turtle hatchlings break out of their shells and emerge from the sand. Emerging at nighttime when sands are cooling, they instinctively attempt to reach the sea. In normal circumstances, they can do so in a matter of minutes. Because of risks of dehydration, predators, and exhaustion, it is essential that they do so. The hatchlings are guided in this trek to safety by the light of the night sky reflecting on the waters of the sea.

Turtles on the beaches of Volusia County, however, have faced two significant barriers to this age-old natural process. First is "urban glow." The inland ambient light caused by the proliferation of private residences near the beaches has been shown to confuse turtles. Instead of making their way to the sea, hatchlings have been observed moving inland toward city lights. The mistake spells certain doom.

The second problem is vehicular traffic. Vehicles driven on the beaches: can crush eggs or recently emerged hatchlings; cause ruts in the sand, which trap turtles and cause them to migrate not to the sea but in the rut itself; disorient turtles with their headlights; compact sand, reducing the supply of oxygen to underlying eggs and thereby interfering with incubation; and shift sand off incubating eggs, making them vulnerable to predators and weather.

In 1994, the U.S. Fish and Wildlife Service ("FWS"), the agency with jurisdiction over nesting turtles (the National Marine Fisheries Service has jurisdiction over turtles in the sea), warned the County of the problem of vehicular access. The County set to work to develop a conservation plan. As developed, the plan attempted to restrict vehicular beach access, create a conservation zone, assure beach raking to remove ruts, and enforce a "turtle-friendly" lighting ordinance. The County also hired an environmental consultant and pledged to work with a volunteer "turtle patrol." It applied on July 17, 1995, to the FWS for an "incidental take permit" ("ITP") under § 10 of the Endangered Species Act.

However, on June 8, 1995, a month before it applied for an ITP, Volusia County was sued in federal court under the Endangered Species Act's citizen suit provision, 16 U.S.C. § 1540(g)(1)(A), to enjoin all beach vehicular access to the beach during the turtles' nesting season, and to require the County to enforce a "Model Lighting Ordinance for Sea Turtle Protection."

On August 1, 1995, the District Court for the Middle District of Florida denied the requested injunctive relief on the beach lighting issue because it was unable to conclude that specific lights for which the County was responsible was disorienting turtles. 896 F. Supp 1181. Moreover, the court viewed itself as lacking authority to require enactment of any particular piece of legislation. *Id.* at 1181. On the beach access issue, the court foundVolusia County responsible for ensuring the well-being of protected turtles because of its regulatory authority. It determined also that the County's practice of permitting nighttime vehicular use of the beaches was causing a "taking" of listed turtles. Consequently, it enjoined the nighttime use. *Id.* at 1192.

On November 21, 1996, the FWS issued an ITP to the County. "As part of the permit process, Volusia County agreed to adopt extensive mitigatory measures, including the development of a 'Beach Lighting ManagementPlan' " under which the County was required, inter alia, to survey every lighting sources, study their impacts and implement methods to correct light sources that misorient sea turtles." *Loggerhead Turtles v. Babbitt*, 92 F.Supp. 1296, 1299 1300. The District Court then dismissed the cause of action before it as to all issues. *Id.*

Plaintiffs appealed at this point to the 11th Circuit Court of Appeals, where the issue was the legal effect of the ITP.] . . .

The loggerhead sea turtle (*Caretta caretta*) and green sea turtle (*Chelonia mydas*) with appellants Shirley Reynolds and Rita Alexander (collectively the Turtles) challenge the district court's dismissal of their case brought pursuant to the Endangered Species Act (ESA), 16 U.S.C. §§ 1531 1544 (1994). They present: (1) anissue of first impression, whether the incidental take permit exception to the ESA's "take" prohibition applies to an activity performed as a purely mitigatory measure upon which the issuing agency conditions the permit; (2)an issue of standing, whether a governmental entity's regulatory control of minimum wildlife protection standards can cause redressable injury to protected wildlife in locations where non-party governmental entities possess supplemental authority to regulate and/or exclusively control enforcement; and (3) an issue of pleading amendment, whether another federally protected sea turtle should have been allowed to join the Turtles as a party. We reverse on all issues and remand for further proceedings.

[The following text covers only the first of these issues.]. . . .

II. Issues

We address . . . : (1) whether the district court erred in concluding that Volusia County's incidental take permit excepted it from liability for taking protected sea turtles through artificial beachfront lighting[.]

III. Contentions

As to [this] issue, the Turtles contend that Volusia County's incidental take permit authorizes only incidental takes of sea turtles from beach driving, not from artificial beachfront lighting. The Turtles argue that to fall within the incidental take permit exception to the "take" prohibition, the Service's permission must be express and activity-specific. The Turtles also assert that the district court could not infer such permission from the Service's conditioning the permit on lighting-related mitigatory measures.

Volusia County responds that under the permit, it must survey every light source, study their impacts and implement methods to correct light sources that misorient sea turtles. Volusia County argues that given those extensive mitigatory requirements, the Service clearly contemplated that it be excepted from liability for any incidental takes that artificial beachfront lighting causes during the life of the permit. . . .

IV. Discussion

Under the ESA, it is unlawful to "take" endangered or threatened wildlife unless a statutory exception applies. 16 U.S.C. § 1538(a)(1)(B) (1994) (the "take" prohibition); *see* 50 C.F.R. § 17.31(a) (1997) (the "take" prohibition applies to threatened as well as endangered wildlife). Defined broadly, "take" means "to harass, harm, pursue, hunt, shoot, wound, kill, trap, capture, or collect[.]" 16 U.S.C. § 1532(19); *see Babbitt v. Sweet Home Chapter of Communities for a Great Or.*, 515 U.S. 687, 115 S. Ct. 2407, 2416, 132 L. Ed. 2d 597 (1995) ("Congress intended 'take' to apply broadly to cover indirect as well as purposeful actions."). It is equally unlawful "to attempt to commit, solicit another to commit, or cause to be committed" a "take." 16 U.S.C. § 1538(g).

"Harass" and "harm," within the meaning of "take," are defined through regulation. The Secretary of the Interior, through the Service, has construed "harass" as "an intentional or negligent act or omission which creates the likelihood of injury to wildlife by annoying it to such an extent as to significantly disrupt normal behavioral patterns which include, but are not limited to, breeding, feeding or sheltering." 50 C.F.R. § 17.3; *see* 16 U.S.C. § 1533(d) (delegating regulatory authority to the "Secretary"); *Sweet Home*, 515 U.S. 687, 115 S. Ct. at 2410 & n. 2 (noting that the Secretary of the Interior, through the Director of the Service, promulgated 50 C.F.R. § 17.3).

The crux of the Turtles' artificial beachfront lighting allegations centered on "harm," "an act which actually kills or injures wildlife" that may include "significant habitat modification or degradation where it actually kills or injures wildlife by significantly impairing essential behavioral patterns, including breeding, feeding or sheltering." 50 C.F.R. § 17.3 (the "harm" regulation). At the preliminary injunction stage, the district court found "overwhelming" evidence that artificial beachfront lighting "harms" sea turtles on Volusia County's beaches. 896 F. Supp. at 1180–81. Similarly, at the summary judgment stage, the district court found a genuine factual dispute "as to whether the artificial beachfront lighting controlled by Volusia County is responsible for "taking' sea turtles."

A.

The incidental take permit exception to the "take" prohibition and its regulatory constructions, including the "harm" regulation, can be found in 16 U.S.C. § 1539(a). As relevant to this case, the Service "may permit, under such terms and conditions as [it] shall prescribe . . . any taking otherwise prohibited by section § 1538(a)(1)(B) of [the ESA] if such taking is incidental to, and not the purpose of, the carrying out of an otherwise lawful activity." 16 U.S.C. § 1539(a)(1)(B). As a prerequisite to receiving an incidental take permit, the applicant must submit a habitat conservation plan that specifies: "(I) the impact which will likely result from such taking; (ii) what steps the applicant will take to minimize and mitigate such impacts, and the funding that will be available to implement such steps; (iii) what alternative actions to such taking the applicant considered and the reasons why such alternatives are not being utilized; and (iv) such other measures that the [issuing agency] may require as being necessary or appropriate for purposes of the plan." 16 U.S.C. § 1539(a)(2)(A). Service regulations further instruct the applicant to include a "complete description of the activity sought to be authorized" and "the common and scientific names of the species sought to be covered by the permit, as well as the number, age, and sex of such species, if known[.]" 50 C.F.R. § 17.22(b)(1)(I) (ii) (endangered wildlife); 50 C.F.R. § 17.32(b)(1)(iii)(A) (B) (threatened wildlife).

We turn first to the Turtles' contention that Volusia County's incidental take permit does not expressly authorize takings through artificial beachfront lighting. Such express authority, if it exists, can be found only within the four corners of the permit. *See generally* 16 U.S.C. § 1539(a) (issuing official must "prescribe" the permit's "terms and conditions"). In its introductory headline, Volusia County's incidental take permit states that the Service "authorizes incidental take within the Defined Area or County Beaches, associated with the activities described in Condition F below, of [appellant loggerhead sea turtle, appellant green sea turtle, leatherback sea turtle, hawksbill sea turtle (*Eretmochelys imbricata*) and Kemp's ridley sea turtle (*Lepidochelys kempii*)]conditioned upon implementation of the terms and conditions of this Permit." Condition F, in turn, lists eleven "authorized" types of incidental take: . . .

Indisputably, these eleven types of incidental takes relate only to vehicular access on Volusia County's beaches. None of the eleven authorized activities listed in Condition F concerns artificial beachfront lighting. The only form of lighting mentioned in Condition F is vehicular headlights.

Although the majority of its conditions concern beach driving, the incidental take permit does address artificial beachfront lighting [in] Condition G of the permit, entitled "Mitigation/Minimization Measures."

The mitigation measures relative to artificial beachfront lighting occupy less than two out of twenty-five pagesof Volusia County's incidental take permit: . . .

In light of the foregoing, it is readily apparent that the incidental take permit exhaustively lists all authorized activities within Condition F and all mitigation measures within Condition G. Activities relative to driving on the beach are mentioned in both conditions. Activities relative to artificial beachfront lighting, however, are mentioned only in Condition G. Given the permit's structure, the express authority to take sea turtles through artificial beachfront lighting — if the Service had so intended — would be memorialized in Condition F. This absence is dispositive. Accordingly, Volusia County lacks the Service's express permission to take sea turtles incidentally through artificial beachfront lighting.

Volusia County argues that even if it lacks the Service's express permission, it has the Service's implied permission to take sea turtles incidentally through artificial beachfront lighting because the Service expressly conditioned the permit on Volusia County's implementation of detailed lighting-related mitigatory measures. This argument presents an issue of first impression in this and other circuits, whether the incidental take permit exception (16 U.S.C. § 1539(a)) to the "take" prohibition (16 U.S.C. § 1538(a)(1)(B)) applies to, and thus excepts from liability, an activity performed as a purely mitigatory measure upon which the Service conditions the permit. We hold that it does not.

The ESA's text and the Service's regulations provide every indication that incidental take permission must be express and activity-specific. To be excepted from liability, the ESA mandates that the "take" be "incidental to . . . the carrying out of an . . . *activity*." 16 U.S.C. § 1539(a)(1)(B) (emphasis added). Moreover, in addressing the requirements of the habitat conservation plan, the ESA semantically separates the "action[]" at issue from the applicant's intentions to "mitigate" the taking. *Compare* 16 U.S.C. § 1539(a)(2)(A)(iii) ("what alternative *actions* to such taking the applicant considered") (emphasis added) *with* 16 U.S.C. § 1539(a)(2)(A)(ii) ("what steps the applicant will take to minimize and mitigate such impacts") (emphasis added). *See generally Friends of Endangered Species, Inc. v. Jantzen*, 760 F.2d 976, 984 (9th Cir. 1985) (separating semantically the activity for which the applicants sought an incidental take permit — a development "project" — from the mitigatory measures — "restrictions" on the development). Furthermore, before the Service issues an incidental take permit, the fact-finding official must resolve at least two statutorily distinct questions: (1) whether the *activity* will be free of purposeful takes; and (2) whether the applicant will *mitigate* the authorized takes' effect. *Compare* 16 U.S.C. § 1539(a)(2)(B)(I) ("the *taking* will be incidental") (emphasis added) *with* 16 U.S.C. § 1539(a)(2)(B)(ii) ("the applicant will . . . minimize and mitigate the impacts of such taking") (emphasis added).

The statutory dividing line between activities sought to be permitted and mitigatory measures is further reinforced in the Service's regulations. The Service requires applicants to describe completely "the *activity* sought to be authorized." 50 C.F.R. §§ 17.22(b)(1)(I), 17.32(b)(1)(iii)(A) (emphasis added); *see also* 50 C.F.R. § 222.22(b)(4) (incidental take permit applications to the National Marine Fisheries Service must include a "detailed description of the proposed *activity*") (emphasis added). The incidental take permit, in turn, "may authorize a single transaction, a series of transactions, or a number of *activities* [.]" 50 C.F.R. §§ 17.22, 17.32 (emphasis added).

Finally, the Service emphasizes that the "authorizations on the face of a permit which set forth specific . . . *methods* of taking . . . are to be strictly construed and shall not be interpreted to permit similar or related matters outside the scope of strict construction." 50 C.F.R. § 13.42 (emphasis added); *see also* 50 C.F.R. § 222.22(d) (incidental take permits that the National Marine Fisheries Service issues must "contain such terms and conditions as the Assistant Administrator deems necessary and appropriate, including . . . the authorized *method of taking*") (emphasis added).

Even the Service's informal publication advises applicants to describe specifically "all *actions* . . . that . . . are likely to result in incidental take" so that the permit holder "can determine the applicability of the incidental take authorization to the *activities* they undertake." United States Fish & Wildlife Serv., Dep't of the Interior; Nat'l Marine Fisheries Serv., Dep't of Commerce, Habitat Conservation Planning Handbook (Nov.1996), at 3-12 to 3-13 (emphasis added). Otherwise, the Service warns, "broadly defined types of *activities* . . . generally would not be authorized." Habitat Handbook, at 3-13 (emphasis added).

The content of Volusia County's application and correspondence with the Service reflects the statutory and regulatory dividing line between authorized activities and mitigatory measures. In its initial application to the Service, Volusia County "completely described . . . the activity sought to be authorized" as "vehicular access toVolusia County beaches[.]" (Citing 50 C.F.R. §§ 17.22(b)(1)(I).) A follow-up letter from a Service official acknowledging receipt of the application summarized that Volusia County sought "a permit to cover any incidental take of sea turtles that may occur on Volusia County beaches . . . as a result of *vehicular access* to countybeaches." (Emphasis added.) Another follow-up letter from the Service pointedly expressed that it is important to state for the record that the County of Volusia is not seeking incidental take authority for marine sea turtles resulting from lights owned or operated by the County. The purpose of any such discussion in the habitat conservation plan . . . is to provide mitigation for impacts to marine sea turtles resulting from *permitted activities*. The [incidental take permit] application you submitted requests incidental take authority for sea turtle species from *beach-driving* and associated activities only. (Emphasis added.)

Finally, in a responsive letter to the Service, an assistant county attorney reiterated that "Volusia County is seeking an Incidental Take Permit for vehicles

[sic] access to the beaches. However, Volusia County has addressed lighting throughout its permit application as a mitigating factor." (Emphasis added.)

Contrary to Volusia County's position, no published case law even purports to suggest that purely mitigatory measures fall within the scope of the incidental take permit exception, 16 U.S.C. § 1539(a) . . . .

Volusia County argues that the Service "clearly anticipated" takes resulting from artificial beachfront lighting in the incidental take permit . . . . We are not convinced. . . .

In any event, the law governing incidental take statements issued under 16 U.S.C. § 1536(b), . . . differs from the law governing incidental take permits issued under 16 U.S.C. § 1539(a), the statutory source in this case. *See generally Ramsey [v. Kantor]*, 96 F.3d [434], at 439 [(9th Cir. 1996)]. First, the issuing agency's prerequisite findings are not the same. To permit an incidental taking under 16 U.S.C. § 1536(b), the issuing agency must conclude, in pertinent part, that:

> [1] the agency action will not [likely jeopardize the continued existence of any protected species or result in the destruction or adverse modification of its critical habitat ("likely jeopardize protected species")], or [the agency] offers reasonable and prudent alternatives which the Secretary believes would not [jeopardize protected species]; [and]
>
> [2] the taking of an endangered species or a threatened species incidental to the agency action will not [likely jeopardize protected species][.]

16 U.S.C. § 1536(b)(4) (incorporating by reference 16 U.S.C. § 1536(a)(2)). To permit an incidental taking under 16 U.S.C. § 1539(a), however, the issuing agency must find, in pertinent part, that:

[1]   the taking will be incidental;

[2]   the applicant will . . . minimize and mitigate the impacts of such taking;

[3]   the applicant will ensure that adequate funding for the [habitat conservation] plan will be provided;

[4]   the taking will not appreciably reduce the likelihood of the survival and recovery of the species in the wild; and

[5]   the [other measures that the issuing agency may require] will be met[.]

16 U.S.C. § 1539(a)(2)(B) (incorporating by reference 16 U.S.C. § 1539(a)(2)(A)(iv)). Both, of course, require a finding that the take sought to be authorized will be "incidental." Both also focus on the ultimate effect of the incidental take on the species. *See* 16 U.S.C. § 1539(a)(2)(B)(iv) ("the taking will not appreciably reduce the likelihood of the survival and recovery of the species in the wild"); 50 C.F.R. § 402.02 (proposed action "jeopardizes" the species at issue if it can "reasonably . . . be expected, directly or indirectly, to reduce appreciably the likelihood of both the survival and recovery of a listed species in the wild by reducing the reproduction, numbers, or distribution of that species"). Only 16 U.S.C. § 1539, however, expressly requires a finding of future mitigation. . . .

A second important difference between an incidental take statement 16 U.S.C. § 1536(b)) and an incidental take permit (16 U.S.C. § 1539(a)) lies in the broad language of 16 U.S.C. § 1536(o), which applies only to holders or beneficiaries of the former. Under section 1536(o), "any taking that is in compliance with the terms and conditions specified in [an incidental take statement issued under 16 U.S.C. § 1536(b)] shall not be considered tobe a prohibited taking of the species concerned." 16 U.S.C. § 1536(o)(2). No similar provision applies to "any" taking in compliance with an incidental take permit's terms and conditions, including mitigatory measures. The closest analogous provision in section 1539 appears only in the converse: the issuing official "shall revoke [an incidental take permit] if he finds that the permittee is not complying with the terms and conditions of the permit." 16 U.S.C. § 1539(a)(2)(C).

Finally, the prohibitions that underlie the incidental take exceptions are unique. The prohibition that underlies the incidental take statement exception applies only to federal agencies, and imposes upon them a duty to consult with the statement-issuing agency and ensure that their proposed action will not likely "jeopardize the continued existence of any endangered species or threatened species or result in the destruction or adverse modification of [critical] habitat[.]" 16 U.S.C. § 1536(a)(2) (the "jeopardy" clause). The prohibition that underlies the incidental take permit exception applies to federal, state, local and private actors, and creates no similar duty to consult. *See* 16 U.S.C. §§ 1532(13), 1538(a)(1)(B) (the "take" prohibition). Additionally, the "jeopardy" clause applies to protected fish, wildlife and plants, whereas the "take" prohibition applies only to protected fish and wildlife. *See* 16 U.S.C. §§ 1532(16), 1536(a)(2), 1538(a)(1). Consequently, some activities — especially those relating to land use — are more likely to result in "jeopardy" than a "take." *See Sweet Home*, 115 S. Ct. at 2415 ("Section 7 [16 U.S.C. § 1536] imposes a broad, affirmative duty to avoid adverse habitat modifications that § 9 [16 U.S.C. § 1539] does not replicate, and § 7 does not limit its admonition to habitat modification that actually kills or injures wildlife.") (internal quotation marks and citations omitted); Andrew J. Doyle, Note, *Sharing Home Sweet Homewith Federally Protected Wildlife*, 25 STETSON L. REV. 889, 911 n. 174 (1996) ("It is easier to 'jeopardize' than it is to 'harm.' "). These differences further militate against broadening the scope of the incidental take permit exception (16 U.S.C. § 1539(a)) even if some courts have suggested that section 1536(o) serves to broaden the scope of the incidental take statement exception (16 U.S.C. 1536(b)). *See Ramsey*, 96 F.3d at 441 ("Any taking . . . that complies with the conditions set forth in the incidental take statement is permitted."). *See generally Mount Graham Red Squirrel v. Espy*, 986 F.2d 1568, 1580 (9th Cir.1993) ("Under [16 U.S.C. § 1536], . . . limited takings may be permitted if they are incorporated into the 'terms and conditions' of a Reasonable and Prudent Alternative drawn up in connection with the issuance of a Biological Opinion.").

The fact remains that no court has been presented with the issue facing us today. To be sure, protecting troubled wildlife is serious business. *See Tennessee Valley Auth. v. Hill*, 437 U.S. 153, 174, 98 S. Ct. 2279, 57 L. Ed. 2d 117 (1978) ("The language, history, and structure of the [Endangered Species Act] indicates beyond doubt that Congress intended endangered species to be afforded the highest of priorities."); *Strahan v. Linnon*, 967 F.Supp. 581, 618 (D. Mass. 1997) ("The

Endangered Species Act is a powerful and substantially unequivocal statute."). Consequently, permits that purport to excuse takes of wildlife must be clear on their face. *See* 50C.F.R. § 13.42 ("The authorizations on the face of a permit which . . . permit a specifically limited matter [ ] are to be strictly construed [.]"); *see also* 50 C.F.R. § 220.42. In this case, "the Secretary . . . permitted" only takes of sea turtles incidental to driving on the beach. 16 U.S.C. § 1539(a)(1). Accordingly, the district court erred in dismissing the Turtles' claim that artificial beachfront lighting takes sea turtles.

[Remainder of opinion omitted.]

Reversed and Remanded.

DISSENT: RONEY, SENIOR CIRCUIT JUDGE, dissenting:

[Dissent omitted.]

NOTES AND QUESTIONS

1. ***Update.*** In September 2011, NOAA and the Fish and Wildlife Service issued a final rule changing the listing of loggerhead sea turtles under the Endangered Species Act from a single threatened species to nine distinct population segments, five listed as endangered and four as threatened. The agencies did so to better protect the turtles on regional bases.

2. ***Liability Issues.*** With a moment's reflection, it becomes obvious why plaintiffs selected Volusia County to be its defendant. It is far more efficient from a plaintiff's point of view to sue a single defendant who can mandate an array of species-protective actions than it is to locate, serve, and proceed in court against an undefined and indeterminate group of occasional beach users and residents. The County, for its part, did not view itself as an appropriate defendant. On remand, the District Court considered the question:

> Congress imposed upon federal agencies the responsibility for implementing and enforcing the Act. The Act authorizes the Secretary of the Interior to enter into management and cooperation agreements with the States, whose participation in conservation programs the Act encourages. The Act requires no affirmative conservation action by states or local governments. The Act neither compels nor precludes local regulation; it preempts that which is in conflict. Volusia County cannot be made to assume liability for the act of its private citizens merely because it has chosen to adopt regulations to ameliorate sea turtle takings. Such an anomalous result would frustrate the intent and purpose of the Act's cooperative agreement provisions. Accordingly, the Court finds that Volusia County has not violated the Endangered Species Act by enacting and enforcing its Minimum Standards for Sea Turtle Protection.

Loggerhead Turtle v. County Council of Volusia County, 92 F. Supp. 2d 1296, 1308 (M.D. Fla. 2000). The court noted that a possible remedy would be the adoption of federal beach lighting regulations.

So, after all the wrangling, Volusia County was found to be free of liability! Do you think the District Court was correct in finding no liability? For another view, see *Strahan v. Coxe*, 127 F.3d 155 (1st Cir. 1997). *Strahan* held the ESA "not only prohibits the acts of those parties that directly exact the taking, but also bans those acts of a third party that bring about the acts exacting a taking." *Strahan*, 127 F.3d at 163. In *Strahan*, plaintiffs contended the State of Massachusetts was liable for the taking of endangered whales by fishing vessels because it had licensed the fishing activity:

> The defendants argue that the statute was not intended to prohibit state licensure activity because such activity cannot be a "proximate cause" of the taking. The defendants direct our attention to long-standing principles of common law tort in arguing that the district court improperly found that its regulatory scheme "indirectly causes" these takings. Specifically, the defendants contend that to construe the proper meaning of "cause" under the ESA, this court should look to common law principles of causation and further contend that proximate cause is lacking here. The defendants are correct that when interpreting a term in a statute which is, like "cause" here, well-known to the common law, the court is to presume that Congress intended the meaning to be interpreted as in the common law. . . . We do not believe, however, that an interpretation of "cause" that includes the "indirect causation" of a taking by the Commonwealth through its licensing scheme falls without the normal boundaries.

> . . . [W]hereas it is possible for a person licensed by Massachusetts to use a car in a manner that does not risk the violations of federal law suggested by the defendants, it is not possible for a licensed commercial fishing operation to use its gillnets or lobster pots in the manner permitted by the Commonwealth without risk of violating the ESA by exacting a taking. Thus, the state's licensure of gillnet and lobster pot fishing does not involve the intervening independent actor that is a necessary component of . . . other licensure schemes. . . . Where the state has licensed an automobile driver to use thatautomobile and her license in a manner consistent with both state and federal law, the violation of federal [law] is caused only by the actor's conscious and independent decision to disregard or go beyond the licensed purposes of her automobile use and instead to violate federal, and possibly state, law.

Strahan, 127 F.3d at 163–64.

Do you view *Volusia County* and *Strahan* as inconsistent with each other, or merely distinguishable on the facts? What would your advice be to a municipality about to enact a zoning ordinance permitting the residential development of land occupied by members of an endangered species? What advice would you have for the EPA which, in its administration of the Federal Insecticide, Fungicide and Rodenticide Act ("FIFRA," 7 U.S.C. §§ 136–136y), is proposing to approve "registration" of a pesticide known to kill both target and non-target species? (Registration of a pesticide under FIFRA constitutes approval for its sale and distribution. FIFRA allows the registration of any pesticide which will "perform its intended function without unreasonable adverse effects on the environment.")

3.   *HCPs.* As mentioned in the notes preceding *Volusia,* HCPs are voluntary binding agreements between the government and the permittee. Since Volusia County has been determined not to be liable under the ESA, is it free to disregard its HCP? Or, having entered into the agreement, is the County bound to honor it, despite the erroneous premise? There is relatively little case law to answer questions involving HCPs.

4.   *ITPs, § 7, and NEPA.* Must the FWS or the NMFS, when it issues an ITP, comply with § 7 of the ESA? If so, with whom must it consult? Do you suppose ITP decisions and ITS preparations fall under § 102(2)(C) of NEPA?

F.   ADMINISTRATIVE FLEXIBILITY INITIATIVES

The FWS and the NMFS are not empowered to revise statutes; they are constrained, rather, to operate within the parameters of statutes they administer. Still, these agencies have done what they can administratively to make the ESA operate more flexibly. Information on these flexibility initiatives follows:

(a) Candidate Conservation Agreements: CCAs are formal agreements between the FWS and independent parties, primarily other federal agencies, state and local agencies, and conservation organizations, designed to make listing unnecessary by meeting the conservation needs of candidate or proposed species. Signatories agree to implement specific actions to stabilize or restore species.

(b) Candidate Conservation Agreements with Assurances: CCAAs are FWS agreements with private landowners who face land use restrictions if a species is listed. Under a CCAA, a landowner agrees to manage private land in a way that protects and restores populations of species or their habitats on that land. In return, the FWS agrees to issue to the landowner an ITP under § 10(a)(1)(A) of the statute, authorizing any "takes" that might accompany habitat modification or other CCAA-authorized actions. Moreover, should a species covered by the CCAA be listed subsequently, the landowner will be free from the otherwise applicable new land use restrictions — so long as the landowner abides by the CCAA.

(c) Safe Harbor Agreements: SHAs afford to listed species essentially the same protections that CCAAs afford to candidate and proposed species. SHAs allow landowners who voluntarily take steps to attract endangered species onto private land or attempt to increase the numbers or distribution of such species to avoid prosecution for takings.

(d) Exemptions from Prosecution for Incidental Takes of Threatened Species: In 1994, the FWS and NMFS announced an exemption policy for certain incidental takes of threatened species. Under the policy, certain persons, specifically occupiers of single residential households, persons involved in one-time activities affecting five or fewer acres of contiguous property acquired before an affected species was listed, and persons undertaking "negligible" activities, are exempt from prosecution. (The policy extends solely to threatened species on the belief that exemptions for endangered species could only be granted if the ESA itself were rewritten.)

(e) The "No Surprises" and Permit Revocation Rules. Perhaps the most significant of the flexibility initiatives are the No Surprises and Permit Revocation

Rules. See the following case.

SPIRIT OF THE SAGE COUNCIL v. KEMPTHORNE
511 F. Supp. 2d 31 (D.D.C. 2007)

EMMET G. SULLIVAN, UNITED STATES DISTRICT JUDGE.

MEMORANDUM OPINION

Native American and environmental organizations and their members have brought this action challenging the validity of two federal rules under the Endangered Species Act ("ESA"), the No Surprises Rule and Permit Revocation Rule ("PRR", collectively "the Rules"), which were promulgated by the Fish and Wildlife Service ("FWS") and National Marine Fisheries Service ("NMFS", collectively "the Services"). In 2003 and 2004, the Court ruled that the PRR had been promulgated without providing adequate opportunity for public comment, remanded the Rules to the agencies, ordered the Services to complete the proceedings upon remand within one year, and enjoined use of the Rules in the interim. The Services have now complied with the required procedures and repromulgated the PRR. Pending before the Court are the parties' cross-motions for summary judgment, which dispute both this Court's jurisdiction as well as the merits of plaintiffs' claims under the Administrative Procedures Act ("APA"). Upon consideration of the motions and supporting memoranda, the responses and replies thereto, the applicable law, the arguments made at the motions hearing on May 30, 2007, and the entire record, the Court determines that the it has jurisdiction and that the Rules are lawful under the APA. Therefore, for the reasons stated herein, plaintiffs' motion for summary judgment is DENIED, and defendants' motion for summary judgment is GRANTED.

BACKGROUND

A. Factual and Regulatory Background

The background of the parties and the statutory framework was discussed in detail in the Court's 2003 opinion, *Spirit of the Sage Council v. Norton*, 294 F. Supp. 2d 67, 73-80 (D.D.C. 2003) (hereinafter "Spirit I"), and need only be summarized here. Plaintiffs are a number of organizations who allege that their members regularly photograph, observe, study and otherwise enjoy endangered and threatened species and their habitats. *Id.* at 73-74. FWS and NMFS are agencies within the Department of the Interior and Department of Commerce respectively, which have been delegated the responsibilities under the ESA. *Id.* at 75. . . .

Section 9 of the ESA, with certain statutory exceptions, makes it unlawful for any person to "take" a member of any species listed as endangered or threatened. *Id.* at 75–76. In 1982, Congress amended the ESA to authorize the Services to permit otherwise prohibited takings of endangered or threatened species, if they are "incidental to, and not the purpose of, the carrying out of an otherwise lawful activity." *Id.* at 76 (quoting 16 U.S.C. § 1539(a)(1)(B)). Incidental take permits

("ITP") are available to landowners and developers who agree to mitigate impacts to listed species through a Habitat Conservation Plan ("HCP"), which must satisfy both ESA statutory criteria and further requirements in the Services' regulations. *Id.*

Under Section 10 of the ESA, an applicant seeking an ITP authorizing it to "take" endangered or threatened species in the course of its activities on private land must prepare a HCP specifying, *inter alia*, the impact of the taking, measures to minimize the impact, and any other measures required by the Services. 16 U.S.C. § 1539(a)(2)(A). In order to issue an ITP, the Services "must find that the taking will be incidental; the applicant will, to the maximum extent practicable, minimize and mitigate the impacts of such taking; the applicant will ensure that adequate funding for the plan will be provided; [and] the taking will not appreciably reduce the likelihood of the survival and recovery of the species in the wild." 16 U.S.C. § 1539(a)(2)(B).

In 1994, the government announced the "No Surprises" policy, which required Services approving ITPs to provide landowners with "assurances" that once an ITP was approved, even if circumstances subsequently changed in such a way as to render the HCP inadequate to conserve listed species, the Services would not impose additional conservation and mitigation requirements that would increase costs or further restrict the use of natural resources beyond the original plan. *Spirit I*, 294 F. Supp. 2d at 77. Despite numerous objections, the Services promulgated a final No Surprises Rule, which essentially codified the No Surprises policy. *Id.* at 78. The new rule provides that "no additional land use restrictions or financial compensation will be required of the permit holder with respect to species covered by the permit, even if unforeseen circumstances arise after a permit is issued indicating that additional mitigation is needed for a given species covered by a permit." *Id.* (quoting No Surprises Rule, 63 Fed. Reg. 8859, 8863 (Feb. 23, 1998), codified at 50 C.F.R. §§ 17.22, 17.32). In the first decade following the enactment of Section 10 of the ESA, only 14 ITPs were issued, but between 1994 and 2002, 379 ITPs with No Surprises assurances have been issued, covering approximately 30 million acres and affecting more than 200 endangered or threatened species. *Id.* at 79.

While this Court was considering the original motions for summary judgment in this case, the FWS promulgated the Permit Revocation Rule ("PRR"). *Id.* The PRR amends the regulations specifically applicable to ITPs, which now include the No Surprises Rule, and provides, in pertinent part, that an ITP "may not be revoked . . . unless continuation of the permitted activity would be inconsistent with the criterion set forth in 16 U.S.C. § 1539(a)(2)(B)(iv) and the inconsistency has not been remedied [by the Services] in a timely fashion." *Id.* (quoting Safe Harbor Agreements and Candidate Conservation Agreements With Assurances, 64 Fed. Reg. 32,706, 32,712-14 (Jun. 17, 1999), codified at 50 C.F.R. §§ 17.22(b), 17.32(b)). 16 U.S.C. § 1539(a)(2)(B)(iv) sets forth, as one of the conditions for issuance of an ITP, that "the taking will not appreciably reduce the likelihood of the survival and recovery of the species in the wild." *Id.* at 79 n.2. In effect, the PRR specifies that the Services will not revoke an ITP unless continuation of the permit puts a listed species in jeopardy of extinction. *See id.* at 86.

B. Procedural History

Before the Court in 2003 were plaintiffs' arguments that the No Surprises Rule and PRR violated the ESA and APA. *Id.* at 80. [The Court then reviewed the three findings of the 2003 decision: plaintiffs had standing, the matter was ripe for review, and the PRR rule was promulgated in violation of the requirements of the Administrative Procedure Act. The court remanded the PRR rule for agency reconsideration. Since the NPR was "sufficiently intertwined" with the PRR, the court remanded that rule as well. After some haggling, the Services repromulgated the PRR "without substantial change." The matter then made its way again to the District Court.]

. . . Plaintiffs contend that the PRR and No Surprises Rule contravene the ESA and are arbitrary and capricious under the APA. In their motion, defendants initially contend that plaintiffs lack standing and that their claims are not ripe for review. On the merits, defendants argue that the PRR and No Surprises Rule are reasonable constructions of the ESA, and that the Services' explanations of the rules comply with the APA. . . .

[Discussions of standard of review omitted]

ANALYSIS

[Discussion of ripeness and standing omitted]

III. Whether the Rules are Contrary to the ESA

Plaintiffs' primary argument is that the PRR contravenes the ESA, and therefore is not "in accordance with law" under the APA. *See* 5 U.S.C. § 706(2)(A). In determining whether an action is "in accordance with law" within the meaning of that provision, the court must apply the familiar framework established by *Chevron U.S.A. Inc. v. Natural Res. Defense Council, Inc.*, 467 U.S. 837, 842–43, 104 S. Ct. 2778, 81 L. Ed. 2d 694 (1984). Under "step one" of *Chevron* analysis, the court must ascertain whether Congress had a specific intent on the issue before the Court. *Natural Res. Def. Council v. EPA*, 194 F.3d 130, 135, 338 U.S. App. D.C. 340 (D.C. Cir. 1999). In doing so, the Court must consider " 'the particular statutory language at issue, as well as the language and design of the statute as a whole.' " *Halverson v. Slater*, 129 F.3d 180, 184, 327 U.S. App. D.C. 97 (D.C. Cir. 1997) (quoting *K Mart Corp. v. Cartier, Inc.*, 486 U.S. 281, 291, 108 S. Ct. 1811, 100 L. Ed. 2d 313 (1988)). Only if the Court determines that Congress "has not spoken to the question at issue, does *Chevron* step two" ordinarily "come into play, requiring the court to defer to the agency's reasonable interpretation of the statute." *South. Cal. Edison Co. v. FERC*, 195 F.3d 17, 23, 338 U.S. App. D.C. 402 (D.C. Cir. 1999).

The PRR significantly narrows the circumstances under which the Services may revoke ITPs. The court previously analyzed the change effected by the PRR:

> Prior to promulgation of the PRR, the Services could revoke an ITP once "the population(s) of the wildlife or plant that is the subject of the permit declines to the extent that continuation of the permitted activity would be detrimental to maintenance *or* recovery of the affected *popula-*

tion." See 50 C.F.R. § 13.28(a)(5) (emphasis added). It appears beyond dispute that, following promulgation of the PRR, the Services can no longer revoke an ITP under these circumstances. 50 C.F.R. § 17.22 (An ITP "may not be revoked for any reason except those set forth in § 13.28(a)(1) through (4) or unless continuation of the permitted activity would be inconsistent with the criterion set forth in 16 U.S.C. 1539(a)(2)(B)(iv) and the inconsistency has not been remedied in a timely fashion."). Instead, so long as "the taking will not appreciably reduce the likelihood of the survival and recovery of the species in the wild," the permittee commits no procedural violations, and the law does not change, the PRR precludes the Services from revoking an ITP.

Spirit I, 294 F. Supp. 2d at 86. Plaintiffs focus on the difference that the original revocation standard refers to maintenance and recovery in the disjunctive, whereas the PRR requires a showing that both survival and recovery of a species must be threatened before an ITP can be revoked. *See id.* Thus, if activity under an ITP hinders the recovery of a species, but not its survival, then the Services are foreclosed from revoking the permit under the PRR.

Plaintiffs argue that the PRR is contrary to the ESA under *Chevron* step one because the ESA as a whole and Section 10 in particular require measures that insure the survival and recovery of listed species. Plaintiffs' argument is based on the definition of "conservation" under the ESA. The ESA defines "conservation" as all methods that can be employed to "bring any endangered species or threatened species to the point at which the measures provided pursuant to this [Act] are no longer necessary." 16 U.S.C. § 1532(3). Conservation is thus "a much broader concept than mere survival," and encompasses "recovery of a threatened or endangered species." *Sierra Club v. FWS*, 245 F.3d 434, 441–42 (5th Cir. 2001). "Indeed, in a different section of the ESA, the statute distinguishes between 'conservation' and 'survival.' " *Id.* at 442 (citing 16 U.S.C. § 1533(f)(1)); *see Gifford Pinchot Task Force v. FWS*, 378 F.3d 1059, 1070 (9th Cir. 2004) ("By these definitions, it is clear that Congress intended that conservation and survival be two different (though complementary) goals of the ESA.").

Under ESA Section 10, parties seeking an ITP must submit a "habitat conservation plan" ("HCP") specifying the impact of the taking, measures to minimize the impact, and any other measures required by the Services. 16 U.S.C. § 1539(a)(2)(A). Plaintiffs argue that because this document is called a "conservation" plan, ITP holders must necessarily be required to "conserve" species, *i.e.* use all measures to promote species' recovery. *See* 16 U.S.C. § 1532(3). It would follow then that ITPs should be revoked when the recovery of a species is imperiled. In addition, plaintiffs contend that the overall purpose of the ESA is to "halt *and reverse the trend* towards species extinction, whatever the cost." *TVA v. Hill*, 437 U.S. 153, 184, 98 S. Ct. 2279, 57 L. Ed. 2d 117 (1978) (emphasis added). Thus, the issuance and revocation of ITPs arguably should utilize a recovery-based standard.

If ESA Section 10 did not further define the components of an HCP and requirements for granting an ITP, plaintiffs may have had a strong claim. The more specific provisions of Section 10, however, fatally undermine plaintiffs' arguments. Section 10 requires that an ITP applicant's conservation plan must specify, *inter alia,* "the impact which will likely result from such taking" and "what steps the applicant will take to minimize and mitigate such impacts, and the funding that will be available to implement such steps." 16 U.S.C. § 1539(a)(2)(A)(i), (ii). These requirements speak to minimizing impact upon species, but do not address at all the recovery of species.

Section 10 also includes specific findings that the Services must make in order to grant an ITP:

(i) the taking will be incidental;

(ii) the applicant will, to the maximum extent practicable, minimize and mitigate the impacts of such taking;

(iii) the applicant will ensure that adequate funding for the plan will be provided;

(iv) the taking will not appreciably reduce the likelihood of the survival and recovery of the species in the wild.

16 U.S.C. § 1539(a)(2)(B). These statutory criteria directly undercut plaintiffs' arguments that ITPs must promote the recovery of listed species. To the contrary, applicants are only required to minimize and mitigate the impact on species "to the maximum extent possible." *Id.*[16] More importantly, applicants are only required not to reduce "the likelihood of the survival *and* recovery of the species." *Id.* (emphasis added). Therefore, ITPs may be granted if the likelihood of recovery, but not survival, is appreciably reduced. *See* 50 C.F.R. § 402.02 (defining an act to "jeopardize the continued existence of" a species if it "reasonably would be expected . . . to reduce appreciably the likelihood of both the survival and recovery" of the species). Thus, while applicants must submit a "conservation" plan, the statutory text makes clear that ITPs can be granted even if doing so threatens the recovery of a listed species. To the extent that there is a conflict between the general definition of "conservation" and the specific criteria in 16 U.S.C. § 1539(a)(2)(B), the "specific statutory language should control more general language when there is a conflict between the two." *Nat'l Cable & Telecomm. Ass'n, Inc. v. Gulf Power Co.,* 534 U.S. 327, 335, 122 S. Ct. 782, 151 L. Ed. 2d 794 (2002).[17]

Finally, Section 10 contains a specific provision regarding the revocation of permits. "The Secretary shall revoke a permit issued under this paragraph if he

---

[16] "The words 'maximum extent possible' signify that the applicant may do something less than fully minimize and mitigate the impacts of the take where to do more would not be practicable." *Nat'l Wildlife Fed'n v. Norton,* 306 F. Supp. 2d 920, 928 (E.D. Cal. 2004).

[17] One district court has reached the opposite conclusion, but did so without closely scrutinizing the statutory text of ESA Section 10. *Sw. Ctr. For Biological Diversity v. Bartel,* 470 F. Supp. 2d 1118, 1129 (S.D. Cal. 2006) (An ITP "permit application must satisfy the ESA goal of conservation, which will allow the species to recover in order to reverse the trend to extinction." (internal quotation marks omitted)). Another district court also summarily reached the opposition conclusion, in dicta, without analysis. *Sierra Club v. Babbit,* 15 F. Supp. 2d, 1274, 1278 n.3 (S.D. Ala. 1998) ("Pursuant to section 10, the FWS may issue a permit for the 'incidental take' of some members of the species, if the applicant for the permit submits a 'conservation plan' that will — as its name plainly connotes — help 'conserve' the entire species by facilitating its survival and recovery."). Given the lack of statutory analysis, neither opinion is persuasive.

finds that the permittee is not complying with the terms and conditions of the permit." 16 U.S.C. § 1539(a)(2)(C). This provision mandates revocation for failing to abide by an ITP's conditions, but does not require revocation due to a threat to a species' recovery. Therefore, when ESA section 10 is analyzed closely, it becomes clear that the specific provisions of the ESA do not require ITPs to promote or even maintain the recovery of listed species. Thus, the PRR does not fail under *Chevron* step one.

Plaintiffs nonetheless argue that a recovery-based standard must be applied to ITPs following a recent Ninth Circuit decision, *Gifford Pinchot Task Force v. FWS*, 378 F.3d 1059 (9th Cir. 2004). That case, however, concerned an entirely different section of the ESA. At issue was the FWS's interpretation of "destruction or adverse modification" of a designated "critical habitat" of a listed species in 16 U.S.C. § 1536(a)(2). *Id.* at 1069. The court found the FWS regulation in question to be invalid under *Chevron* step one because it protected only the survival of listed species, but not their recovery. *See id.* at 1069–70. The court based its conclusion on the definition of "critical habitat," which includes areas "essential to the conservation of the species." *Id.* at 1070 (citing 16 U.S.C. § 1532(5)(A)). The same logic cannot be applied to ITPs. While the recovery-based definition of conservation was central to defining critical habitats, the same cannot be said for ITPs. Instead, as described above, the specific statutory provisions in ESA Section 10 demonstrate the Congress did not intend ITPs to have to promote or maintain the recovery of listed species. Accordingly, the Court rejects plaintiffs' argument that the PRR is invalid under *Chevron* step one.

At *Chevron* step two, when "the statute is silent or ambiguous with respect to the specific issue, the question . . . is whether the agency's answer is based on a permissible construction of the statute." *Ranbaxy Laboratories Ltd. v. Leavitt*, 469 F.3d 120, 124, 373 U.S. App. D.C. 377 (D.C. Cir. 2006) (quoting *Chevron*, 467 U.S. at 843). Plaintiffs argue that the PRR is invalid under *Chevron* step two because it contradicts the ESA's general purpose of protecting the recovery of listed species. For the reasons already discussed, however, the statutory text of ESA section 10 demonstrates Congressional intent to allow the Services to grant ITPs even if they do not protect the recovery of listed species.

Moreover, the PRR adopts a facially reasonable policy for revocation. Under the PRR, ITPs may be revoked if continuation of the permitted activity would be inconsistent with the statutory criteria for issuing the permit initially, and the inconsistency has not been remedied by the Services in a timely fashion. *See* 50 C.F.R. §§ 17.22(b), 17.32(b). Because the ESA only sets forth specific criteria for the issuance of ITPs, it is a perfectly logical policy to trigger revocation of ITPs when those criteria can no longer be met. Accordingly, the Court concludes that the PRR is a permissible and reasonable construction of the ESA. *See Chevron*, 467 U.S. at 843.

Plaintiffs contend that the No Surprises Rule is also contrary to the law, especially in light of its close relation to the PRR. Specifically, they argue that it is contrary to law "for the Services to extend unprecedented regulatory assurances to all ITP holders without even requiring that their ITPs/HCPs be compatible with species recovery and, indeed, even where the ITPs/HCPs may be detrimental to such recovery." Thus, plaintiffs' argument is that the No Surprises Rule is contrary to the ESA because it makes more permanent conditions in an ITP that may not promote or maintain the recovery of listed species. As discussed, the ESA does not require ITPs to promote or maintain the recovery of species. Therefore, the Court concludes that the No Surprises Rule is not contrary to the ESA.

IV. Whether the Rules are Arbitrary and Capricious

Plaintiffs argue that the Rules are arbitrary and capricious because the Services have failed to articulate a reasoned basis for the rules. "The scope of review under the 'arbitrary and capricious' standard is narrow and a court is not to substitute its judgment for that of the agency. Nevertheless, the agency must examine the relevant data and articulate a satisfactory explanation for its action." *AT&T Corp. v. FCC*, 236 F.3d 729, 734, 344 U.S. App. D.C. 362 (D.C. Cir. 2001) (quoting *Motor Vehicle Mfs. Ass'n v. State Farm Mut. Auto. Ins. Co.*, 463 U.S. 29, 43, 103 S. Ct. 2856, 77 L. Ed. 2d 443 (1983) ("State Farm")). In addition, "when an agency determines to change an existing regulatory regime it must do so on the basis of 'reasoned analysis.' " *Id.* at 735 (quoting *State Farm*, 463 U.S. at 42).

Plaintiffs have challenged several alleged defects in the Services' justifications for the new Rules. Each will be considered in turn. First, plaintiffs argue that the Services have failed to explain how allowing ITPs that impede recovery of listed species, under the PRR, is consistent with the ESA. The Services, however, have clearly explained that they believe that matching the ITP revocation criteria to the statutory ITP issuance criteria more accurately reflected Congressional intent. ITP Revocation Regulations-Final Rule, 69 Fed. Reg. at 71727. As discussed in Section III, *supra*, this was a reasonable policy choice given the underlying statutory provisions.

Second, plaintiffs argue that the Services have failed to explain why the PRR's standard for revocation of ITPs is drafted in discretionary rather than mandatory terms. The Services, however, explained that permit revocation decisions are always fact-intensive and require the exercise of agency discretion, so it is more appropriate to describe permit revocation standards in discretionary rather than mandatory terms. *Id.* at 71728. The statutory revocation standard, 16 U.S.C. § 1539(a)(2)(C), implies that agencies have discretion in revoking permits because some discretionary investigation is necessary before the agencies can "find" that permit-holders are not complying with the terms of the ITP. *See Envtl. Prot. Info. Ctr. v. FWS*, No. 04-4647, 2005 U.S. Dist. LEXIS 30843, 2005 WL 3021939, at *9–10 (N.D. Cal. 2005) (holding that agencies have discretion in investigating and revoking ITPs). Therefore, it is rational for the Services to phrase the PRR in discretionary terms.

Third, plaintiffs argue that the Services have failed to explain why the PRR's standard for revocation is triggered by jeopardy to a species, but not impairment of a species' critical habitat. Again, the Services rationally explained that since the statutory ITP issuance criteria only refer to jeopardy of a species, that same standard should be used for the revocation of ITPs. *See* ITP Revocation Regulations-Final Rule, 69 Fed. Reg. at 71728; Section III, *supra*.

Fourth, plaintiffs argue that the Services' justification for the No Surprises Rule

— that it was necessary to create greater incentives for landowners to engage in conservation under ESA Section 10 — is inconsistent with the ESA. The ITP framework is an alternative to regulation through the enforcement against illegal "takings" of listed species under ESA Section 9. *See* Daniel J. Rohlf, *Jeopardy Under the Endangered Species Act: Playing a Game*, 41 Washburn L.J. 114, 123–25 (Fall 2001). While strict in theory, enforcement-based regulation may be flawed because illegal take prosecutions are difficult, expensive, and therefore rare. *See id.* at 123 ("in a five year period from 1988 to 1993, the General Accounting Office identified only eight successful prosecutions nationwide against habitat destruction that resulted in take of protected species"). Thus, Section 10 permitting creates an alternate, private/public method of habitat conservation. *See id.* at 124. In order to encourage the use of ITPs, Congress directed the Services to provide "adequate assurances . . . to the financial and development communities that a section 10(a) permit can be made available for the life of the project." H.R. Conf. Rep. No. 97-835 at 30–31, 1982 U.S.C.C.A.N. 2871–72. Thus, it is rational for the Services to follow Congressional intent, and create incentives for private landowners to apply for and utilize ITPs.

Fifth, plaintiffs argue that the Services have failed to explain why the No Surprises Rule grants assurances that ITP conditions will not be modified even though ITPs can still be revoked under the PRR. The Services explained, however, that revoking an ITP is a "last resort," and thus that the PRR only slightly reduces the permittees' interest in a secure ITP, and does not significantly impair the desired incentive to provide landowners who assist listed species with cost certainty. *See* ITP Revocation Regulations-Final Rule, 69 Fed. Reg. at 71,729–30.

Sixth, plaintiffs argue that the Services have failed to explain how the No Surprises Rule is tenable given the government's duty under the ESA to insure that any government action "is not likely to jeopardize the continued existence" of a listed species. As the Services concede, the issuance of an ITP constitutes a federal action that must be reviewed in an intra-agency consultation under ESA Section 7. *Spirit I*, 294 F. Supp. 2d at 76. Therefore, before issuing an ITP, the Services must find that doing so "is not likely to jeopardize the continued existence of any [listed] species or result in the destruction or adverse modification of habitat of such species." 16 U.S.C. § 1536(a)(2); *see Sw. Ctr. For Biological Diversity v. Bartel*, 470 F. Supp. 2d 1118, 1129 (S.D. Cal. 2006). Depending on the conditions imposed by the ITP, it is certainly possible that issuing an ITP with No Surprises assurances may satisfy the no-jeopardy standard. Since this is a facial challenge, and the No Surprises Rule is not logically inconsistent with the no-jeopardy standard, it is appropriate for the Court to presume that the Services will faithfully execute their duties under Section 7 and reasonably determine whether an ITP complies with the no-jeopardy standard at the time of issuance.

Finally, plaintiffs argue that the Services have failed to explain why the No Surprises Rule does not require an ITP holder to address foreseeable changed circumstances if those circumstances were not addressed at the time of the ITP's issuance. Plaintiffs argue that this policy gives ITP applicants an incentive not to discuss foreseeable changed circumstances when they apply for an ITP. The Services have explained, however, that "[a]ll reasonably foreseeable circumstances, including natural catastrophes that normally occur in the area, should be addressed in the HCP." No Surprises Rule, 63 Fed. Reg. 8859, 8863 (Feb. 23, 1998). If ITP applicants fail to address foreseeable circumstances, the Services can deny the ITP application. Therefore, the Services can handle plaintiffs' concern under the Rules. Finding none of plaintiffs' arguments persuasive, the Court concludes that the Rules are not arbitrary and capricious under the APA.

CONCLUSION

For the foregoing reasons, plaintiffs' motion for summary judgment is DENIED, and defendants' motion for summary judgment is GRANTED.

NOTES AND QUESTIONS

1. *Ecosystem Management.* How would you modify the Endangered Species Act if given the opportunity? One suggested approach is "ecosystem management." The idea is to change the statutory focus from protecting discrete species, and only some of them at that, to protecting entire ecosystems. Ecosystem management would allow for earlier intervention, without the legal necessity of awaiting a species' near-extinction, and would reach beyond a select organism or two to protecting all plants and animals in a habitat. By necessity, it would call for a combined effort by federal and state governmental agencies, and presumably would be multidisciplinary in approach. Some efforts of this sort are underway at present. Do you think this approach holds promise?

2. *State ESAs.* Many states have their own state-law endangered species acts. *See, e.g.,* The Nebraska Endangered Species and Conservation Act ("NESCA"), Neb. Rev. Stat. §§ 37-430 to 37-438 (Reissue 1984). Modeled after the federal ESA, the NESCA varies from the ESA in several important particulars. For example, while the federal ESA requires federal agencies to insure their actions are "not likely to jeopardize" endangered species, the Nebraska counterpart demands that agencies "do not jeopardize" endangered species. *Id.* at § 37-435(3).

A NOTE ON THE ANIMAL WELFARE AND ANIMAL RIGHTS MOVEMENTS

Well before the federal government moved to protect endangered species by statute, individual efforts to do so were underway. In the nineteenth century, with the creation of the American Society for the Prevention of Cruelty to Animals ("ASPCA"), the Animal Welfare Movement rose to prominence. Utilitarian in philosophy, Animal Welfarists have sought greater protection and care for animals essentially by balancing their interests with those of humans. By one approach, the human interest should receive some greater weight in the balancing; other Welfarists would weigh human and animal interests equally. Accordingly, Welfarists may disagree on the propriety of animal experimentation. But, however the balance is struck, the idea is to maximize the interests of both communities. Significantly, Welfarists operate within the current legal system. They accept the traditional view of animals as property. They do not propose formal legal rights for non-humans.

Relatively more recent in origin, the Animal Rights Movement does not accept the current legal regime as justified. On the contrary, Animal Rights adherents maintain that all living things have legal and political rights. Phrased in another way, animals are not mere property, subject to the free will of humans. Because they are living, they have rights co-equal with those of humans. Rightists insist, moreover, that these rights are non-negotiable, and, *per force*, should be honored in the human legal system. Given this approach, it is not surprising that Rightists strenuously object to animal experimentation for the same reasons they would discourage a policy of human experimentation. In the opinion of an adherent of this view, the law should be modified in the short term to recognize highly cognitive animals, and, in the long term, to include other animals. STEVEN M. WISE, RATTLING THE CAGE: TOWARD LEGAL RIGHTS FOR ANIMALS, at xvi, 362 (2000). *See also* Robert Verchick, *A New Species of Rights Rattling the Cage: Toward Legal Rights for Animals*, 89 CAL. L. REV. 207 (2001).

There are a number of organizations involved in these matters. A non-exhaustive list includes the American Society for the Prevention of Cruelty to Animals (*see* www.aspca.org); the Animal Legal Defense Fund (*see* www.aldf.org); the Humane Society of the United States (*see* www.hsus.org); and People for the Ethical Treatment of Animals (*see* www.peta.org).

Chapter 8

WATER RIGHTS

"Water is the lifeblood of peoples and economies. Water entitlements establish and sustain a social order." *Public Land Review*, Spring 1990.

"We'll never know the worth of water 'till the well goes dry." *Scottish Proverb*.

SYNOPSIS

A. INTRODUCTION

B. SURFACE WATERS
   1. Riparianism
   2. Prior Appropriation

C. GROUNDWATER

D. FEDERAL WATER RIGHTS
   1. Federal Legislation and Water Projects
   2. The Navigational Servitude

A. INTRODUCTION

An increasingly important area of natural resource law involves rights to water. As population increases and water distribution systems deteriorate, the contest for water among competing interests has intensified, and the stakes have grown. The concern about future water availability extends to entire regions of the nation, to municipalities, and down to family farmers as well.

In this section, we take a brief look at the law governing water rights. Our goal is not to teach a three-credit course in the span of a single chapter, but rather to introduce the structure of the legal system of water rights allocation. This chapter first reviews how state law allocates rights to water, and then examines the effect of federal law on that legal condition.

Legal systems controlling water are usually divided into two distinct and often independent parts. One controls allocation of rights to surface water, namely, running streams, lakes, ponds, and the like. The other controls allocation of rights to groundwater. Groundwater is found in formations called aquifers, which are saturated soils (not free-flowing bodies of subsurface water). Groundwater can migrate through soils, but it ordinarily does so quite slowly.

It is hydrologic nonsense to allocate legal rights in surface water and groundwater independently in all circumstances, because groundwater can become surface water, and vice-versa. In many cases, for example, extracting groundwater can lower flow levels of surface streams; similarly, diverting surface waters can lower the "water table" — the upper level of groundwater. These two hydrologic regimes, however, have been treated independently by law, as if they never interrelate. The reason is timing — the law developed before there was a fuller understanding of hydrology.

The law allocates water, as one would expect, for uses. Uses can be categorized as either "consumptive" or "non-consumptive." A consumptive use is one that removes the water from its source and precludes its return; a non-consumptive use is one which does not result in permanent loss of the water from the source. Many uses are both consumptive and non-consumptive. Irrigation is one. Much irrigation water is consumed by plants or expired into the atmosphere. To that extent, irrigation is a consumptive use. Some irrigation water, however, can make its way back to its original source, i.e., its "stream of origin" (when dealing with surface waters), in the form of "irrigation return flows." To this extent, the use is non-consumptive.

When water taken from one waterway is transported to another, the use is deemed to be consumptive insofar as the stream of origin is concerned. An example on the grand scale, known as an "interbasin transfer," would be the removal of water from the Missouri River "basin" or "watershed" (the land area which drains into the Missouri River), and the transport of that water into the Ohio River basin. (On this notion of "basin" or "watershed," you might note that both the Missouri River and the Ohio River, for example, are "subbasins" of the Mississippi. Thus, the above-noted transfer would not be consumptive insofar as the main stem of the Mississippi is concerned.) Likewise, a transfer of water from the Platte River basin in Nebraska to the Little Blue River basin in Nebraska would be a consumptive use insofar as the Platte River is concerned.

Uses can also be categorized by location. Some are "out-of-stream" uses (water diverted from a source for use on land near or far from the source), and others are "instream" uses (water serving a use while remaining in its natural location). Irrigation is an example of an out-of-stream use while hydropower generation is an example of instream use.

Uses of water by type include domestic use, irrigation (the most massive use by quantity), industrial or manufacturing use (which can be consumptive or non-consumptive), waste disposal, recreation, aesthetics, wildlife and aquatic life maintenance, hydropower generation, and aquifer recharge.

Two legal systems allocate surface water rights among individuals. The first system is riparianism, the water rights allocation system used in most eastern states, where water is relatively abundant. The second is the prior appropriation system, which is found in most western states, where water is relatively scarce. (The 100th longitudinal meridian is considered to be the divider between eastern and western states; that median runs from North Dakota to Texas.) As you read these materials, give some thought on why riparianism is found in states with abundant water, and why prior appropriation is in place in arid states.

You might also give some thought to the overall role legal constraints should play in the matter of water allocation. Why should the law get involved at all (other than to provide a market, that is)? Should not the market system, that (sometimes) great unregulated barter-and-sale mechanism that allocates resources and commodities generally, be allowed to allocate water as well? Under a market system, persons who most highly value water presumably would get it, because they would be willing to pay the highest price for it. Under this scenario, water would be used for its most highly valued purposes. If this is an appropriate national goal for a water rights allocation system, why intervene with law? Why not let market forces allocate the water?

One of the great water law scholars, the late Frank Trelease, has commented on this question: "Water law should provide for maximum benefits from the use of the resource, and this end should be reached by means of granting private property rights in water, secure enough to encourage development and flexible enough for economic forces to change them to better uses, and subject to public regulation only when private economic action does not protect the public interests." FRANK TRELEASE, POLICIES FOR WATER LAW: PROPERTY, ECONOMIC FORCES, AND PUBLIC REGULATION (1965).

B. SURFACE WATERS

1. Riparianism

The riparian system of water law arrived in this nation from England. England is a country with abundant water supplies. Under English law, persons who own land that abuts a waterway enjoy rights to take water for personal use. These persons are known as "riparians" and the abutting land they own is "riparian land." (Beachfront land abutting lakes or tidal areas is often referred to as "littoral" rather than riparian). A parcel of land can be riparian to one stream and "nonriparian" to another.

Thus, under the riparian system, one who owns a defined parcel of land bordering a stream, or through which a stream runs, is a riparian and has rights to water in the stream. Water can be taken out of the stream for use on the riparian land. The right to the water is secured by virtue of land ownership, and is lost upon transfer of the title interest to the riparian land (at which time the new landowner gets that right).

This system has its virtues. First, by limiting water rights to landowners, the demand on the water resource (i.e., the potential for a "tragedy of the commons") is reduced. Second, the system obviates any need for a system of recording or otherwise certifying water rights. Third, water rights have a decent measure of security — they cannot be taken away easily. This allows water rights holders to plan and rely on the continued availability of the right. And (a virtue to some) the system inures to the benefit of the landed set.

Critics of riparianism stipulate that it prevents maximum use of water, and therefore, from an economic perspective, is anti-growth.

The basic features of the riparian water rights system are:

- the system applies only to canalized surface waters. This includes rivers, lakes, and some ponds;

- the right to water depends on land ownership. It makes no difference how much land fronts the waterway to which the land is riparian. Nonuse of the right does not result in loss of it; loss occurs upon land transfer. If a stream shifts out of its channel, land once riparian may become nonriparian, and the water right may be lost;

- water must be used (in most jurisdictions) on the riparian land itself, or not at all. Additionally, water must be used within the watershed of the stream of origin;

- there are no gallonage limitations on the right. Rather, water must be dedicated to a "reasonable use." If the use is reasonable, all the water necessary for that use may be taken as a matter of right;

- in times of shortage, riparians must share the burden of reducing water use. In this way, riparian rights are "correlative."

NOTES

1. **Natural Law Doctrine.** This outline of riparian law describes the so-called "reasonable use" theory of riparianism. In olden times, in England especially, the so-called "natural flow doctrine" governed riparianism. Under this form of riparianism, one could not justify use of water based on considerations of reasonableness. Rather, a use was justified only if it in no way impaired the natural flow of a stream. As stated traditionally, under the natural flow doctrine, "[e]very proprietor of lands on the banks of a river has naturally an equal right to the use of the water which flows in the stream adjacent to his lands, as it was wont to run (*currere solebat*) without diminution or alteration." (*Chancellor Kent*). This doctrine has fallen into disuse because it effectively prohibits out-of-stream water uses, a condition unworkable in an industrialized society. (This system did make an exception: water used for domestic purposes could be removed from the stream.)

2. **Riparian Land.** The determination of what land is "riparian" depends on the legal configuration of title. The entirety of a contiguous parcel of riparian land is riparian. If, however, that parcel is divided into two or more subparcels, one of which does not abut the waterway, the new non-abutting subparcel, no longer riparian, may lose its water right. If these subparcels are later reunited, the water right may or may not be regained, depending on the jurisdiction.

3. **Nonriparian Uses.** In "reasonable use" jurisdictions (and all jurisdictions are of this type these days), nonriparian uses typically have been entirely prohibited as *per se* unreasonable. Over time, some states have lifted this restriction either partially (allowing some nonriparian uses) or entirely (treating nonriparian uses on the same par as riparian uses).

4. **Use Rights.** Water rights are use rights, unlike rights in land. Downstream riparians have a great interest in how upstream riparians use water, especially

regarding the consumptive nature of upstream use. Thus water rights do not supply the water right holder with exclusive possession; the right holder has exclusive right to use but must return the unused portion to the stream.

Because of this condition, the doctrine of adverse possession is inapplicable to water rights. In its place, however, is the doctrine of adverse use, which operates on essentially the same principles as the doctrine of adverse possession. One with such rights is called an "adverse user"; once the adverse use right has matured, the holder is said to have "prescriptive rights" in the water.

Give some thought on how the adverse use doctrine would, or should, operate in the field of riparian water law.

5. *Accretion, Avulsion, Reliction, Access, and Contact.* Riparian landowners not only enjoy rights to remove water from streams. They may also enjoy property rights related to accretion, avulsion, reliction, access, and contact. Following is a severely edited decision from the United States Supreme Court concerning these matters. Omitted in this recitation are the Court's lengthy discussions of the intriguing issue of judicial takings, i.e., whether it is possible for the judicial branch of government, as distinct from the executive branch, to violate the Takings Clause.

STOP THE BEACH RENOURISHMENT, INC., v. FLORIDA DEPARTMENT OF ENVIRONMENTAL PROTECTION
130 S. Ct. 2592 (2010)

JUSTICE SCALIA announced the judgment of the Court and delivered the opinion of the Court with respect to Parts I, IV, and V, and an opinion with respect to Parts II and III, in which THE CHIEF JUSTICE, JUSTICE THOMAS, and JUSTICE ALITO join.

We consider a claim that the decision of a State's court of last resort took property without just compensation in violation of the Takings Clause of the Fifth Amendment, as applied against the States through the Fourteenth, see *Dolan* v. *City of Tigard*, 512 U.S. 374, 383–384, 114 S. Ct. 2309, 129 L. Ed. 2d 304 (1994).

I

A

Generally speaking, state law defines property interests, *Phillips* v. *Washington Legal Foundation*, 524 U.S. 156, 164, 118 S. Ct. 1925, 141 L. Ed. 2d 174 (1998), including property rights in navigable waters and the lands underneath them, see *United States* v. *Cress*, 243 U.S. 316, 319–320, 37 S. Ct. 380, 61 L. Ed. 746 (1917); *St. Anthony Falls Water Power Co.* v. *St. Paul Water Comm'rs*, 168 U.S. 349, 358–359, 18 S. Ct. 157, 42 L. Ed. 497 (1897). In Florida, the State owns in trust for the public the land permanently submerged beneath navigable waters and the foreshore (the land between the low-tide line and the mean high-water line). a. Const., Art. X, § 11; *Broward* v. *Mabry*, 58 a. 398, 407–409, 50 So. 826, 829–830 (1909). Thus, the mean high-water line (the average reach of high tide over the preceding 19 years) is the ordinary boundary between private beachfront, or littoral property, and state-owned land. See *Miller* v. *Bay-To-Gulf, Inc.*, 141 a. 452, 458–460, 193 So. 425, 427–428 (1940) *(per curiam);* a. Stat. §§ 177.27(14)-(15), 177.28(1) (2007).

Littoral owners have, in addition to the rights of the public, certain "special rights" with regard to the water and the foreshore, *Broward*, 58 a., at 410, 50 So., at 830, rights which Florida considers to be property, generally akin to easements, see ibid.; *Thiesen* v. *Gulf, Florida & Alabama R. Co.*, 75 a. 28, 57, 78, 78 So. 491, 500, 507 (1918) (on rehearing). These include the right of access to the water, the right to use the water for certain purposes, the right to an unobstructed view of the water, and the right to receive accretions and relictions to the littoral property. *Id.*, at 58–59, 78 So., at 501; *Board of Trustees of Internal Improvement Trust Fund* v. *Sand Key Assoc., Ltd.*, 512 So. 2d 934, 936 (a. 1987). This is generally in accord with well-established common law, although the precise property rights vary among jurisdictions. Compare *Broward, supra*, at 409–410, 50 So., at 830, with 1 J. Lewis, Law of Eminent Domain § 100 (3d ed. 1909); 1 H. Farnham, Law of Waters and Water Rights § 62, pp. 278–280 (1904) (hereinafter Farnham).

At the center of this case is the right to accretions and relictions. Accretions are additions of alluvion (sand, sediment, or other deposits) to waterfront land; relictions are lands once covered by water that become dry when the water recedes. F. Maloney, S. Plager, & F. Baldwin, Water Law and Administration: The Florida Experience § 126, pp. 385–386 (1968) (hereinafter Maloney); 1 Farnham § 69, at 320. (For simplicity's sake, we shall refer to accretions and relictions collectively as accretions, and the process whereby they occur as accretion.) In order for an addition to dry land to qualify as an accretion, it must have occurred gradually and imperceptibly — that is, so slowly that one could not see the change occurring, though over time the difference became apparent. *Sand Key, supra*, at 936; *County of St. Clair* v. *Lovingston*, 90 U.S. 46, 23 L. Ed. 59, 23 Wall. 46, 66–67 (1874). When, on the other hand, there is a "sudden or perceptible loss of or addition to land by the action of the water or a sudden change in the bed of a lake or the course of a stream," the change is called an avulsion. *Sand Key, supra*, at 936; see also 1 Farnham § 69, at 320.

In Florida, as at common law, the littoral owner automatically takes title to dry land added to his property by accretion; but formerly submerged land that has become dry land by avulsion continues to belong to the owner of the seabed (usually the State). See, *e.g., Sand Key, supra*, at 937; Maloney § 126.6, at 392; 2 W. Blackstone, Commentaries on the Laws of England 261-262 (1766) (hereinafter Blackstone). Thus, regardless of whether an avulsive event exposes land previously submerged or submerges land previously exposed, the boundary between littoral property and sovereign land does not change; it remains (ordinarily) what was the mean high-water line before the event. See *Bryant* v. *Peppe*, 238 So. 2d 836, 838–839 (a. 1970); J. Gould, Law of Waters § 158, p. 290 (1883). It follows from this that, when a new strip of land has been added to the shore by avulsion, the littoral owner has no right to subsequent accretions. Those accretions no longer add to *his* property, since the property abutting the water belongs not to him but to the State. See Maloney § 126.6, at 393; 1 Farnham § 71a, at 328.

B

In 1961, Florida's Legislature passed the Beach and Shore Preservation Act, 1961 a. Laws ch. 61-246, as amended, a. Stat. §§ 161.011-161.45 (2007). The Act establishes procedures for "beach restoration and nourishment projects," § 161.088, designed to deposit sand on eroded beaches (restoration) and to maintain the deposited sand (nourishment). §§ 161.021(3), (4). A local government may apply to the Department of Environmental Protection for the funds and the necessary permits to restore a beach, see §§ 161.101(1), 161.041(1). When the project involves placing fill on the State's submerged lands, authorization is required from the Board of Trustees of the Internal Improvement Trust Fund, see § 253.77(1), which holds title to those lands, § 253.12(1).

Once a beach restoration "is determined to be undertaken," the Board sets what is called "an erosion control line." §§ 161.161(3)-(5). It must be set by reference to the existing mean high-water line, though in theory it can be located seaward or landward of that. See § 161.161(5). Much of the project work occurs seaward of the erosion-control line, as sand is dumped on what was once submerged land. See App. 87–88. The fixed erosion-control line replaces the fluctuating mean high-water line as the boundary between privately owned littoral property and state property. § 161.191(1). Once the erosion-control line is recorded, the common law ceases to increase upland property by accretion (or decrease it by erosion). § 161.191(2). Thus, when accretion to the shore moves the mean high-water line seaward, the property of beachfront landowners is not extended to that line (as the prior law provided), but remains bounded by the permanent erosion-control line. Those landowners "continue to be entitled," however, "to all common-law riparian rights" other than the right to accretions. § 161.201. If the beach erodes back landward of the erosion-control line over a substantial portion of the shoreline covered by the project, the Board may, on its own initiative, or must, if asked by the owners or lessees of a majority of the property affected, direct the agency responsible for maintaining the beach to return the beach to the condition contemplated by the project. If that is not done within a year, the project is canceled and the erosion-control line is null and void. § 161.211(2), (3). Finally, by regulation, if the use of submerged land would "unreasonably infringe on riparian rights," the project cannot proceed unless the local governments show that they own or have a property interest in the upland property adjacent to the project site. a. Admin. Code Rule 18-21.004(3)(b) (2009).

C

In 2003, the city of Destin and Walton County applied for the necessary permits to restore 6.9 miles of beach within their jurisdictions that had been eroded by several hurricanes. The project envisioned depositing along that shore sand dredged from further out. See *Walton Cty.* v. *Stop the Beach Renourishment, Inc.*, 998 So. 2d 1102, 1106 (a. 2008). It would add about 75 feet of dry sand seaward of the mean high-water line (to be denominated the erosion-control line). The Department issued a notice of intent to award the permits, App. 27-41, and the Board approved the erosion-control line, *id.*, at 49–50.

The petitioner here, Stop the Beach Renourishment, Inc., is a nonprofit corporation formed by people who own beachfront property bordering the project area (we shall refer to them as the Members). It brought an administrative challenge to the proposed project, see *id.*, at 10-26, which was unsuccessful; the Department approved the permits. Petitioner then challenged that action in state court under the Florida Administrative Procedure Act, a. Stat. § 120.68 (2007). The District Court of Appeal for the First District concluded that, contrary to the Act's preservation of "all common-law riparian rights," the order had eliminated two of the Members' littoral rights: (1) the right to receive accretions to their property; and (2) the right to have the contact of their property with the water remain intact. *Save Our Beaches, Inc.* v. *Florida Dept. of Environmental Protection*, 27 So. 3d 48, 57 (2006). This, it believed, would be an unconstitutional taking, which would "unreasonably infringe on riparian rights," and therefore require the showing under a. Admin. Code Rule 18-21.004(3)(b) that the local governments owned or had a property interest in the upland property. It set aside the Department's final order approving the permits and remanded for that showing to be made. 27 So. 3d, at 60. It also certified to the Florida Supreme Court the following question (as rephrased by the latter court):

"On its face, does the Beach and Shore Preservation Act unconstitutionally deprive upland owners of littoral rights without just compensation?" 998 So. 2d, at 1105 (footnotes omitted).

The Florida Supreme Court answered the certified question in the negative, and quashed the First District's remand. *Id.*, at 1121. It faulted the Court of Appeal for not considering the doctrine of avulsion, which it concluded permitted the State to reclaim the restored beach on behalf of the public. *Id.*, at 1116–1118. It described the right to accretions as a future contingent interest, not a vested property right, and held that there is no littoral right to contact with the water independent of the littoral right of access, which the Act does not infringe. *Id.*, at 1112, 1119–1120. Petitioner sought rehearing on the ground that the Florida Supreme Court's decision itself effected a taking of the Members' littoral rights contrary to the Fifth and Fourteenth Amendments to the Federal Constitution. The request for rehearing was denied. We granted certiorari, 557 U.S. ___, 129 S. Ct. 2792; 174 L. Ed. 2d 290 (2009).

. . . .

IV

We come at last to petitioner's takings attack on the decision below. . . .

Petitioner argues that the Florida Supreme Court took two of the property rights of the Members by declaring that those rights did not exist: the right to accretions, and the right to have littoral property touch the water (which petitioner distinguishes from the mere right of access to the water). Under petitioner's theory, because no prior Florida decision had said that the State's filling of submerged tidal lands could have the effect of depriving a littoral owner of contact with the water and denying him future accretions, the Florida Supreme Court's judgment in the present case abolished those two easements to which littoral property owners had been entitled. This puts the burden on the wrong party. There is no taking unless petitioner can show that, before the Florida Supreme Court's decision, littoral-property owners had rights to future accretions and contact with the water superior to the State's right to fill in its submerged land. Though some may think the question close, in our view the showing cannot be made.

Two core principles of Florida property law intersect in this case. First, the State as owner of the submerged land adjacent to littoral property has the right to fill that land, so long as it does not interfere with the rights of the public and the rights of littoral landowners. See *Hayes* v. *Bowman*, 91 So. 2d 795, 799–800 (a. 1957) (right to fill conveyed by State to private party); *State ex rel. Buford* v. *Tampa*, 88 a. 196, 210–211, 102 So. 336, 341 (1924) (same). Second, as we described *supra*, at 3–4, if an avulsion exposes land seaward of littoral property that had previously been submerged, that land belongs to the State even if it interrupts the littoral owner's contact with the water. See *Bryant*, 238 So. 2d, at 837, 838–839. The issue here is whether there is an exception to this rule when the State is the cause of the avulsion. Prior law suggests there is not. In *Martin* v. *Busch*, 93 a. 535, 112 So. 274 (1927), the Florida Supreme Court held that when the State drained water from a lakebed belonging to the State, causing land that was formerly below the mean high-water line to become dry land, that land continued to belong to the State. *Id.*, at 574, 112 So., at 287; see also *Bryant*, *supra*, at 838–839 (analogizing the situation in *Martin* to an avulsion). " 'The riparian rights doctrine of accretion and reliction,' " the Florida Supreme Court later explained, " 'does not apply to such lands.' " *Bryant*, *supra*, at 839 (quoting *Martin*, *supra*, at 578, 112 So., at 288 (Brown, J., concurring)). This is not surprising, as there can be no accretions to land that no longer abuts the water.

Thus, Florida law as it stood before the decision below allowed the State to fill in its own seabed, and the resulting sudden exposure of previously submerged land was treated like an avulsion for purposes of ownership. The right to accretions was therefore subordinate to the State's right to fill. *Thiesen* v. *Gulf, Florida & Alabama R. Co.* suggests the same result. That case involved a claim by a riparian landowner that a railroad's state-authorized filling of submerged land and construction of tracks upon it interfered with the riparian landowners' rights to access and to wharf out to a shipping channel. The Florida Supreme Court determined that the claimed right to wharf out did not exist in Florida, and that therefore only the right of access was compensable. 75 a., at 58–65, 78 So., at 501–503. Significantly, although the court recognized that the riparian-property owners had rights to accretion, see *id.*, at 64–65, 78 So., at 502–503, the only rights it even suggested would be infringed by the railroad were the right of access (which the plaintiff had claimed) and the rights of view and use of the water (which it seems the plaintiff had not claimed), see *id.*, at 58–59, 78, 78 So., at 501, 507.

The Florida Supreme Court decision before us is consistent with these background principles of state property law. Cf. *Lucas*, 505 U.S., at 1028-1029, 112 S. Ct. 2886, 120 L. Ed. 2d 798; *Scranton* v. *Wheeler*, 179 U.S. 141, 163, 21 S. Ct. 48, 45 L. Ed. 126 (1900). It did not abolish the Members' right to future accretions, but merely held that the right was not implicated by the beach-restoration project, because the doctrine of avulsion applied. See 998 So. 2d, at 1117, 1120–1121. The Florida Supreme Court's opinion describes beach restoration as the reclamation by the State of the public's land, just as *Martin* had described the lake drainage in that case. Although the opinion does not cite *Martin* and is not always clear on this point, it suffices that its characterization of the littoral right to accretion is consistent with *Martin* and the other relevant principles of Florida law we have discussed.

What we have said shows that the rule of *Sand Key*, which petitioner repeatedly invokes, is inapposite. There the Florida Supreme Court held that an artificial accretion does not change the right of a littoral-property owner to claim the accreted land as his own (as long as the owner did not cause the accretion himself). 512 So. 2d, at 937–938. The reason *Martin* did not apply, *Sand Key* explained, is that the drainage that had occurred in *Martin* did not lower the water level by " 'imperceptible degrees,' " and so did not qualify as an accretion. 512 So. 2d, at 940–941.

The result under Florida law may seem counter-intuitive. After all, the Members' property has been deprived of its character (and value) as oceanfront property by the State's artificial creation of an avulsion. Perhaps state-created avulsions ought to be treated differently from other avulsions insofar as the property right to accretion is concerned. But nothing in prior Florida law makes such a distinction, and *Martin* suggests, if it does not indeed hold, the contrary. Even if there might be different interpretations of *Martin* and other Florida property-law cases that would prevent this arguably odd result, we are not free to adopt them. The Takings Clause only protects property rights as they are established under state law, not as they might have been established or ought to have been established. We cannot say that the Florida Supreme Court's decision eliminated a right of accretion established under Florida law.

Petitioner also contends that the State took the Members' littoral right to have their property continually maintain contact with the water. To be clear, petitioner does not allege that the State relocated the property line, as would have happened if the erosion-control line were *landward* of the old mean high-water line (instead of identical to it). Petitioner argues instead that the Members have a separate right for the boundary of their property to be always the mean high-water line. Petitioner points to dicta in *Sand Key* that refers to "the right to have the property's contact with the water remain intact," 512 So. 2d, at 936. Even there, the right was included in the definition of the right to access, *ibid.*, which is consistent with the Florida Supreme Court's later description that "there is no independent right of contact with the water" but it "exists to preserve the upland owner's core littoral right of access to the water," 998 So. 2d, at 1119. Petitioner's expansive interpretation of the dictum in *Sand Key* would cause it to contradict the clear Florida law governing avulsion. One cannot say that the Florida Supreme Court contravened established property law by rejecting it.

Because the Florida Supreme Court's decision did not contravene the established property rights of petitioner's Members, Florida has not violated the Fifth and Fourteenth Amendments. The judgment of the Florida Supreme Court is therefore affirmed.

It is so ordered.

JUSTICE STEVENS took no part in the decision of this case.

[Concurring opinions by JUSTICES KENNEDY and BREYER omitted.]

2. Prior Appropriation

In the eastern United States, where precipitation usually exceeds evaporation, there is relatively little need for irrigation. And when irrigation is necessary, there is usually a stream nearby from which to take water. That, however, is not the case in the expansive western United States. In these vast reaches, evaporation exceeds precipitation. In the west, irrigation is the rule, not the exception. To irrigate, moreover, water must be transported over long distances. The Supreme Court commented on this phenomenon in the major decision of *California v. United States*, 438 U.S. 645, 648–49, 98 S. Ct. 2985, 2987–88 (1978):

> Those who first set foot in North America from ships sailing the tidal estuaries of Virginia did not confront the same problems as those who sailed at boats down the Ohio River in search of new sites to farm. Those who cleared the forests in the old Northwest Territory faced totally different physiographic problems from those who built sod huts on the Great Plains. The final expansion of our Nation in the 19th century into the arid lands beyond the hundredth meridian of longitude, which had been shown on early maps as the "Great American Desert," brought the participants in that expansion face to face with the necessity for irrigation in a way that no previous territorial expansion had.
>
>   . . . .
>
> [The] afternoon of July 23, 1847, was the true date of the beginning of modern irrigation. It was on that afternoon that the first band of Mormon pioneers built a small dam across City Creek near the present site of the Mormon Temple and diverted sufficient water to saturate some 5 acres of exceedingly dry land. Before the day was over they had planted potatoes to preserve the seed." During the subsequent half century, irrigation expanded throughout the arid States of the West, supported usually by private enterprise or the local community.

For reasons that became apparent upon reflection, settlers in the west found the riparian rights system unsuitable. Accordingly, a different system of water rights developed. The prior appropriation system was either engrafted on to the riparian system (in so-called "California doctrine" states) or it arose as the initial water rights allocation system (in so-called "Colorado doctrine" states). The following case is regarded as the one that "created" the prior appropriation system.

IRWIN v. PHILLIPS
5 Cal. 140 (1855)

HEYDENFELDT, J., delivered the opinion of the Court. MURRAY, C.J., concurred.

The several assignments of error will not be separately considered, because the whole merits of the case depend really on a single question, and upon that question the case must be decided. The proposition to be settled is whether the owner of a canal in the mineral region of this State, constructed for the purpose of supplying water to miners, has the right to divert the water of a stream from its natural channel, as against the claims of those who, subsequent to the diversion, take up lands along the banks of the stream, for the purpose of mining. It must be premised that it is admitted on all sides that the mining claims in controversy, and the lands through which the stream runs and through which the canal passes, are a part of the public domain, to which there is no claim of private proprietorship; and that the miners have the right to dig for gold on the public lands was settled by this Court in the case of *Hicks et al. v. Bell et al.*, 3 Cal. 219.

It is insisted by the appellants that in this case the common law doctrine must be invoked, which prescribes that a water course must be allowed to flow in its natural channel. But upon an examination of the authorities which support that doctrine, it will be found to rest upon the fact of the individual rights of landed proprietors upon the stream, the principle being both at the civil and common law that the owner of lands on the banks of a water course owns to the middle of the stream, and has the right in virtue of his proprietorship to the use of the water in its pure and natural condition. In this case the lands are the property either of the State or of the United States, and it is not necessary to decide to which they belong for the purposes of this case. It is certain that at the common law the diversion of water courses could only be complained of by riparian owners, who were deprived of the use, or those claiming directly under them. Can the appellants assert their present claim as tenants at will? To solve this question it must be kept in mind that their tenancy is of their own creation, their tenements of their own selection, and subsequent, in point of time, to the diversion of the stream. They had the right to mine where they pleased throughout an extensive region, and they selected the bank of a stream from which the water had been already turned, for the purpose of supplying the mines at another point.

Courts are bound to take notice of the political and social condition of the country which they judicially rule. In this State the larger part of the territory consists of mineral lands, nearly the whole of which are the property of the public. No right or intent of disposition of these lands has been shown either by the United States or the State governments, and with the exception of certain State regulations, very limited in their character, a system has been permitted to grow up by the voluntary action and assent of the population, whose free and unrestrained occupation of the mineral region has been tacitly assented to by the one government, and heartily encouraged by the expressed legislative policy of the other. If there are, as must be admitted, many things connected with this system, which are crude and undigested, and subject to fluctuation and dispute, there are still some which a universal sense of necessity and property have so firmly fixed as that they have come to be looked upon as having the force and effect of res judicata. Among these the most important are the rights of miners to be protected in the possession of their selected localities, and the rights of those who, by prior appropriation, have taken the waters from their natural beds, and by costly artificial works have conducted them for miles over mountains and ravines, to supply the necessities of gold diggers, and without which the most important interests of the mineral region would remain without development. So fully recognized have become these rights, that without any specific legislation conferring or confirming them, they are alluded to and spoken of in various acts of the Legislature in the same manner as if they were rights which had been vested by the most distinct expression of the will of the law makers; as for instance, in the Revenue Act "canals and water races" are declared to be property subject to taxation, and this when there was none other in the State than such as were devoted to the use of mining. Section 2 of Article IX. of the same Act, providing for the assessment of the property of companies and associations, among others mentions "dam or dams, canal or canals, or other works for mining purposes." This simply goes to prove what is the purpose of the argument, that however much the policy of the State, as indicated by her legislation, has conferred the privilege to work the mines, it has equally conferred the right to divert the streams from their natural channels, and as these two rights stand upon an equal footing, when they conflict, they must be decided by the fact of priority, upon the maxim of equity, qui prior est in tempore, potior est in jure. The miner who selects a piece of ground to work, must take it as he finds it, subject to prior rights, which have an equal equity, on account of an equal recognition from the sovereign power. If it is upon a stream, the waters of which have not been taken from their bed, they cannot be taken to his prejudice; but if they have been already diverted, and for as high and legitimate a purpose as the one he seeks to accomplish, he has no right to complain, no right to interfere with the prior occupation of his neighbor, and must abide the disadvantages of his own selection.

It follows from this opinion that the judgement of the Court below was substantially correct, upon the merits of the case presented by the evidence, and it is therefore *affirmed*.

The prior appropriation system is far different from the riparian system. The operative features of the prior appropriation system are:

- the right to water inures upon the act of taking water (and applying it to a beneficial use). Land ownership is irrelevant to water right acquisition, and the water may be used on other than riparian land. Usually, taking water means diverting it out of its stream of origin. The requirement of a diversion as an element in securing a prior appropriation right has been dropped in some states, however, so as to allow "instream" rights to water;

- a right to water is superior (i.e., "senior") or inferior (i.e., "junior") to another's right based on the time at which the right is secured. The operative principle is "first in time, first in right." Senior rights are said to have "priority" over juniors;

- rights to water are quantified;

- cessation of use (i.e., abandonment) extinguishes the right. Rights can also be forfeited for violations of governing statutes or regulations;

- the use to which water is applied must be "beneficial";

- in times of shortage, the rights are clearly not correlative. Juniors must yield to seniors in such times. In other words, a junior appropriator may have to cease diverting water entirely so that enough water will remain in the stream to satisfy the entirety of the right of the senior appropriator;

- unlike the riparian system, which is largely common law-based, the prior appropriation system is managed by state regulatory agencies, and its requirements are specified by statute and agency regulation.

NOTES AND QUESTIONS

1. ***Efficiency Considerations.*** Water taken for use on land typically is transported by ditches or pipes. When ditches, especially earthen ditches, serve as water conduits, water can be lost both to ground infiltration and to evaporation. Losses can be substantial in arid regions. Do you think an inordinately wasteful use of water should be viewed as non-beneficial so as to strip one of a prior appropriation water right? Or should these "efficiency" considerations be irrelevant?

On a related note, since prior appropriation rights are quantified, at what location should the amount of water diverted from a stream be measured? At the point of diversion? At the point of application to its ultimate use?

2. ***Regulation.*** In the current day, an appropriator must comply with administrative rules and regulations to secure a water right. For example, instead of physically diverting water, the appropriator must apply for a permit to do so. Issuance of a permit constitutes award of the right. Compliance with permit terms is necessary to retain the right. For their part, agencies keep track of available stream flows. Notably, agencies may grant water rights to persons even when all of the water in a stream is already appropriated. Why would an agency "overappropriate" a stream?

3. ***Changing Uses.*** As noted above, uses must be "beneficial." Should persons be allowed to switch from one use to another freely? Or should a switch in use be deemed a request for a new prior appropriation right (with a new, and later, priority date)?

4. ***Takings.*** A prior appropriation right is a property right. Assume that a government agency passed a regulation indicating that all ditches had to be lined to reduce water loss. Could that regulation cause an unconstitutional taking? What if the agency took measures to reduce the quantity or change the priority date of a water right to the detriment of the right holder? Taking?

5. ***Salvaged and Imported Waters.*** Persons sometimes effectively add to the available water in a stream. They can do so, for example, by eliminating foliage that itself removes water and transpires it into the atmosphere. This foliage, collectively known as "phreatophytes," can take away a surprisingly large amount of water otherwise available for beneficial use. Should an appropriator be given "credit" for

such "salvaged" waters? In the parlance of water lawyers, should such water be "free from the call of the river"?

Another way to increase flow in a stream is by "importing" water from another watershed. Should an appropriator be given credit for imported waters?

6. *Adverse Use.* Should the doctrine of adverse use have more or less applicability to the prior appropriation system than to the riparian system? Why?

A NOTE ON DIFFUSE WATERS

The riparian and prior appropriation systems of water allocation deal with rights to water found in discrete channels. These systems do not control rights to water found in a diffuse state, that is, water which is not in a channel or other discrete "conveyance" but which instead is washing over the land. For diffuse waters, a separate rights regime exists. Normally, one who captures diffuse water owns it, in a complete sense (akin to ownership of land). Capture and containment give rise to the right.

Controversy over diffuse waters often arises in a different context, however. Persons often do not want the diffuse water on their land. So they push it off on to nearby land titled in another. May a person do that? As a general matter, the answer is yes. Disputes of this sort frequently are decided by use of the "common enemy rule." As the name indicates, this common law doctrine stipulates that diffuse water is the common enemy of all and therefore may be removed by any person from her land, without liability. *Jorgenson v. Stephens*, 10 N.W.2d 337 (Neb. 1943). *See also Bulldog Battery Corp. v. Pica Investments, Inc.*, 736 N.E.2d 333 (Ind. Ct. App. 2000). An exception to the common enemy rule, in place in some jurisdictions, requires that diffuse waters be removed in some reasonable fashion. *Currens v. Sleek*, 983 P.2d 626 (Wash. 1999); *Hall v. Wood*, 443 So. 2d 834 (Miss. 1983). Removal should not cause unnecessary damage or injury to the land of another. *Snyder v. Platte Valley Public Power and Irrigation District*, 13 N.W.2d 160 (Neb. 1944); *Zollinger v. Carter*, 837 S.W.2d 613 (Tenn. Ct. App. 1992). The mere fact of damage to another's property, however, is not *per se* proof of unreasonableness or negligence. *See, e.g., Erickson v. Tyler*, 186 N.W.2d 123 (Neb. 1971); *Sheehan v. Flynn*, 61 N.W. 462 (Minn. 1894); *Ambrosio v. Perl-Mack Const. Co.*, 351 P.2d 803 (Colo. 1960).

C. GROUNDWATER

Groundwater is water which "occurs or moves, seeps, filters, or percolates through the ground under the surface of the land." *Metropolitan Utilities District v. Merritt Beach Co.*, 140 N.W.2d 626 (Neb. 1966). It is an extremely important natural resource in this country: not only is it the source of drinking water for about one-half of the nation's population, it also supplies agriculture with irrigation at a clip of over 50 billion gallons a day. Groundwater is also a stressed natural resource. Excessive pumping of groundwater has brought about a variety of adverse consequences. Groundwater depletions, *inter alia*, render water wells either obsolete or more costly to use; in coastal areas, they enable saltwater to intrude, often to the ruination of the groundwater resource itself; they lower surface water levels in lakes and rivers; and they stimulate land subsidence. The problem of groundwater depletion is national: see, for example, the United States Geological Service map, below.

Areas where subsidence has been attributed to ground-water pumpage (Land Subsidence in the United States, USGS Circular 1182)

The problem is also global. By one estimate, the rate of shrinkage of groundwater reserves internationally has doubled between 1960 and 2000. American Geophysical Union, Release 10-30, September 2010. The highest rates of depletion can be found in places like northwest India, northeast China, northeast Pakistan, California's central valley and America's midwest. *Id.*

How are property rights to groundwater secured in the United States? In some states, the right to use groundwater arises by virtue of land ownership: the owner of overlying land has rights to extract water for use on that overlying land. In many "overlying rights" jurisdictions, water use is permissible only on the overlying land itself; transfer of water for use on other parcels is prohibited. Other jurisdictions may allow use on non-overlying land.

While there are no specific quantitative limitations in place in overlying rights jurisdictions, use of more than a reasonable amount, however determined, is disallowed. But this requirement of reasonableness is not an injunction against harming other users. A water user may extract water, for example, in such large quantities that little or none is left for others to extract, and still qualify as reasonable. The mere fact of harm to another, standing alone, is insufficient to demonstrate unreasonableness.

Overlying rights to groundwater are essentially correlative. Consequently, in times of shortage, all users must reduce their amounts of use for the benefit of all other users.

In other states, groundwater rights are not determined by title to overlying land. In these jurisdictions, allocations of groundwater may be accomplished by use of a prior appropriation system, the features of which are essentially identical to those of the surface water prior appropriation system. In prior appropriation jurisdictions, groundwater rights are separate from interests in land, are quantified, are subject to a beneficial use requirement, and so on.

A NOTE ON INTERSTATE ALLOCATION

Streams often cross state borders, and when they do, states need to determine how to divvy up the waters. Such interstate allocation of water among states can be accomplished in any of three ways. The first is equitable apportionment. This method calls upon the Supreme Court to make the call, using equitable principles to guide it. *See, e.g., Kansas v. Colorado*, 206 U.S. 46, 27 S. Ct. 655 (1907). This rationale for allocating water is perhaps most appropriately used when competing states have different intrastate allocation systems (i.e., one uses riparian principles and the other prior appropriation). When both states are prior appropriation jurisdictions, the Court may simply allow the existing intrastate-vested rights to remain, and thereby *de facto* determine the interstate allocation. However, this is not always the case. In *Colorado v. New Mexico*, 459 U.S. 176, 103 S. Ct. 539 (1982), the Court did not simply rely on existing intrastate appropriations to undergird the equitable apportionment, as to do so would have sanctioned waste and inefficient use of water.

The second allocation method is by "interstate compact." As the name indicates, interstate compacts are state agreements on the allocation of waters in an interstate stream. Such compacts are permitted by the U.S. Constitution (art. I, § 10, cl. 3) but must be ratified by Congress. Interstate compacts are binding on water users within states, regardless of their participation, or lack thereof, in proceedings producing the compact.

The third method is federal legislation. Congress has the power to allocate water among states, and has done so (a major example: The Boulder Canyon Project Act of 1928). Congress can allocate by legislation even if its allocation would contravene an interstate compact already in place.

D.   FEDERAL WATER RIGHTS

1.   Federal Legislation and Water Projects

We have already observed the prominence of state law in the legal world of water rights allocations. State law controls by default because the federal government has acquiesced to the operation of state law in this arena. Of course, the federal government could do so. It has ample constitutional authority to take over the field. Its authorities include the General Welfare Clause, art. I, §§ 8 and 9; the Treaties Clause, art. II, § 2, which can authorize projects on international waters; the Property Clause, art. IV, § 3; the Common Defense Clause, art. I, §§ 8 and 9, and, of course, the staple of federal constitutional power, the Commerce Clause, art. I, § 8. But, excepting the creation of federal reserved water rights, *see* Chapter 5, *supra*, the federal government has chosen not to use its authorities to supplant the states.

When the federal government has acted in this area, it has not been to reorder water rights allocations, but to enable the construction of water projects. We now look briefly at federal actions to effect the construction or regulation of water projects, for irrigation, electricity production, flood control, or other purposes. What impact have these actions had on the state water rights allocation schemes? The following case explores the impact of state law.

CALIFORNIA v. FEDERAL ENERGY REGULATORY COMMISSION[1]
495 U.S. 490, 110 S. Ct. 2024 (1990)

O'CONNOR, J.

This case concerns overlapping federal and state regulation of a hydroelectric project located near a California stream. California seeks to ensure that the project's operators maintain water flowing in the stream sufficient, in the State's judgment, to protect the stream's fish. The Federal Government claims the exclusive authority to set the minimum stream flows that the federally licensed power plant must maintain. Each side argues that its position is consistent with the Federal Power Act, 16 U.S.C. § 791a et seq. (1982 ed.), and, in particular, with § 27 of that Act. We granted certiorari to resolve these competing claims.

I

The Rock Creek hydroelectric project lies near the confluence of the South Fork American River and one of the river's tributaries, Rock Creek. Rock Creek runs through federally managed land located within California. The project draws water from Rock Creek to drive its generators and then releases the water near the confluence of the stream and river, slightly less than one mile from where it is drawn. The state and federal requirements at issue govern the "minimum flow rate" of water that must remain in the bypassed section of the stream and that thus remains unavailable to drive the generators.

In 1983, pursuant to the Federal Power Act (FPA), the Federal Energy Regulatory Commission (FERC) issued a license authorizing the operation of the Rock Creek project. Section 4(e) of the FPA empowers FERC to issue licenses for projects "necessary or convenient . . . for the development, transmission, and utilization of power across, along, from, or in any of the streams . . . over which Congress has jurisdiction." 16 U.S.C. § 797(e) (1982 ed.). Section 10(a) of the Act also authorizes FERC to issue licenses subject to the conditions that FERC deems best suited for power development and other public uses of the waters. 16 U.S.C. § 802(b) (1982 ed.). Congress' subsequent amendments to those provisions expressly direct that FERC consider a project's effect on fish and wildlife as well as "power and development purposes." Electric Consumers Projection Act of 1986, Pub. L. 99-495, 100 Stat. 1243, 16 U.S.C. § 797(e), 803(a). FERC issued the 1983 license and set minimum flow rates after considering the project's economic feasibility and

---

[1] [Ed. Note: This case is also referred to as "*Rock Creek*."]

environmental consequences. In part to protect trout in the stream, the license required that the project maintain interim minimum flow rates of 11 cubic feet per second (cfs) during May through September and 15 cfs during the remainder of the year. The license also required the licensee to submit studies recommending a permanent minimum flow rate, after consulting with federal and state fish and wildlife protection agencies. The licensee submitted a report recommending that FERC adopt the interim flow rates as permanent rates. The California Department of Fish and Game (CDFG) recommended that FERC require significantly higher minimum flow rates.

The licensee had also applied for state water permits, and in 1984 the State Water Resources Control Board (WRCB) issued a permit that conformed to FERC's interim minimum flow requirements but reserved the right to set different permanent minimum flow rates. When the WRCB in 1987 considered a draft order requiring permanent minimum flow rates of 60 cfs from March through June and 30 cfs during the remainder of the year, the licensee petitioned FERC for a declaration that FERC possessed exclusive jurisdiction to determine the project's minimum flow requirements. The licensee, by then respondent Rock Creek Limited Partnership, also claimed that the higher minimum flow rates sought by the WRCB would render the project economically infeasible.

In March 1987, FERC issued an order directing the licensee to comply with the minimum flow requirements of the federal permit. In that order, FERC concluded that the task of setting minimum flows rested within its exclusive jurisdiction. The Commission reasoned that setting minimum flow requirements was integral to its planning and licensing process under FPA § 10(a); giving effect to competing state requirements "would interfere with the Commission's balancing of competing considerations in licensing" and would vest in States a veto power over federal projects inconsistent with the FPA, as interpreted in *First Iowa Hydro-Electric Cooperative v. FPC*, 328 U.S. 152 (1946). FERC also directed an administrative law judge to hold a hearing to determine the appropriate permanent minimum flow rates for the project. After considering proposals and arguments of the licensee, the CDFG, and FERC staff, the administrative law judge set the minimum flow rate for the project at 20 cfs during the entire year. Four days after FERC's declaratory order, the WRCB issued an order directing the licensee to comply with the higher minimum flow requirements contained in its draft order. . . . [The Court of Appeals for the Ninth Circuit affirmed. . . .]

We granted certiorari and we now affirm.

II

In the Federal Power Act of 1935, 49 Stat. 863, Congress clearly intended a broad federal rule in the development and licensing of hydroelectric power. That broad delegation of power to the predecessor of FERC, however, hardly determines the extent to which Congress intended to have the Federal Government exercise exclusive powers, or intended to pre-empt concurrent state regulation of matters affecting federally licensed hydroelectric projects. The parties' dispute regarding the latter issue turns principally on the meaning of 27 of the FPA, which provides the clearest indication of how Congress intended to allocate the regulatory authority of the States and the Federal Government. That section provides:

> "Nothing contained in this chapter shall be construed as affecting or intending to affect or in any way to interfere with the laws of the respective States relating to the control, appropriation, use, or distribution of water used in irrigation or for municipal or other uses, or any vested right acquired therein." 16 U.S.C. § 821 (1982 ed.).

Were this a case of first impression, petitioner's argument based on the statute's language could be said to present a close question. As petitioner argues, California's minimum stream flow requirement might plausibly be thought to "relat[e] to the control, appropriation, use, or distribution of water used . . . for . . . other uses," namely the generation of power or the protection of fish. This interpretation would accord with the "presumption against finding preemption of state law in areas traditionally regulated by the States" and " 'with the assumption that the historic police powers of the States were not to be superseded by the Federal Act unless that was the clear and manifest purpose of Congress.' " *California v. ARC America Corp.*, 490 U.S. (1989) (slip op., at 5), *quoting Rice v. Santa Fe Elevator Corp.*, 331 U.S. 218, 230 (1947); *see California v. United States*, 438 U.S. 645, 653 663 (1978) (tracing States' traditional powers over exploitation of water). Just as courts may not find state measures pre-empted in the absence of clear evidence that Congress so intended, so must they give full effect to evidence that Congress considered and sought to preserve the States' coordinate regulatory role in our federal scheme.

But the meaning of § 27 and the pre-emptive effect of the FPA are not matters of first impression. Forty-four years ago, this Court in First Iowa construed the section and provided the understanding of the FPA that has since guided the allocation of state and federal regulatory authority over hydroelectric projects. The Court interpreted § 27 as follows:"

> "The effect of § 27, in protecting state laws from supersedure, is limited to laws as to the control, appropriation, use or distribution of water in irrigation or for municipal or other uses of the same nature. It therefore has primary, if not exclusive, reference to such proprietary rights. The phrase 'any vested right acquired therein' further emphasizes the application of the section to property rights. There is nothing in the paragraph to suggest a broader scope unless it be the words 'other uses.' Those words, however, are confined to rights of the same nature as those relating to the use of water in irrigation or for municipal purposes." *First Iowa*, 328 U.S., at 175 176 (emphasis added)."

The Court interpreted § 27's reservation of limited powers to the States as part of the congressional scheme to divide state from federal jurisdiction over hydroelectric projects and, "in those fields where rights are not thus 'saved' to the States . . . to let the supersedure of the state laws by federal legislation take its natural course." Id., at 176.

We decline at this late date to revisit and disturb the understanding of § 27 set forth in First Iowa.

. . . .

Petitioner asks this Court fundamentally to restructure a highly complex and long-enduring regulatory regime, implicating considerable reliance interests of licensees and other participants in the regulatory process. That departure would be inconsistent with the measured and considered change that marks appropriate adjudication of such statutory issues. . . .

Adhering to *First Iowa's* interpretation of § 27, we conclude that the California requirements for minimum instream flows cannot be given effect and allowed to supplement the federal flow requirements. A state measure is "pre-empted to the extent it actually conflicts with federal law, that is, when it is impossible to comply with both state and federal law, or where the state law stands as an obstacle to the accomplishment of the full purposes and objectives of Congress." *Silkwood v. Kerr-McGee Corp.*, 464 U.S. 238, 248 (1984) (citations omitted). As Congress directed in FPA § 10(a), FERC set the conditions of the license, including the minimum stream flow, after considering which requirements would best protect wildlife and ensure that the project would be economically feasible, and thus further power development. Allowing California to impose significantly higher minimum stream flow requirements would disturb and conflict with the balance embodied in that considered federal agency determination. FERC has indicated that the California requirements interfere with its comprehensive planning authority, and we agree that allowing California to impose the challenged requirements would be contrary to congressional intent regarding the Commission's licensing authority and would "constitute a veto of the project that was approved and licensed by FERC."

For the foregoing reasons, the decision of the Court of Appeals for the Ninth Circuit is *Affirmed.*

NOTES

1. *Reclamation Act.* Because many hydropower projects are governed by the Federal Power Act, this determination of the statute's preemptive effect is significant. Another important federal statute is the Reclamation Act of 1902, as amended, 43 U.S.C. § 371 *et seq.* This statute is applicable to many irrigation projects. The section of the Reclamation Act which establishes its preemptive effect is § 8, 43 U.S.C. § 383, which provides in part:

> [N]othing in this Act shall be construed as affecting or intended to affect or in any way interfere with the laws of any State or Territory relating to the control, appropriation, use, or distribution of water used in irrigation, or any vested right acquired thereunder, and the Secretary of the Interior, in carrying out the provisions of this Act, shall proceed in conformity with such laws, and nothing herein shall in any way affect any right of any State or of the Federal Government or of any landowner, appropriator, or user of water in, to, or from any interstate stream or the waters thereof.

Rock Creek, in a portion of the opinion not provided above, discussed the preemptive effect of § 8 of the Reclamation Act and distinguished it from § 27 of the Federal Power Act:

[T]he FPA envisioned a considerably broader and more active federal oversight role in hydropower development than did the Reclamation Act. Section 8, after referring to State water laws relating to water used in irrigation and preserved by the Act, contains an explicit direction that "the Secretary of the Interior, in carrying out the provisions of this Act, shall proceed in conformity with such [state] laws." This language has no counterpart in § 27 and was crucial to the Court's interpretation of § 8. *See California v. United States*, 438 U.S., at 650, 664 665, 674 675. . . . The Secretary in executing a particular reclamation project is in a position analogous to a licensee under the FPA, and need not comply with state laws conflicting with congressional directives respecting particular reclamation projects; similarly, a federal licensee under the FPA need not comply with state requirements that conflict with the federal license provisions established pursuant to the FPA's directives. An additional textual difference is that § 8 refers only to "water used in irrigation" and contains no counterpart to § 27's reference to "other uses." . . . Laws controlling water used in irrigation relate to proprietary rights . . . and § 8 does not indicate the appropriate treatment of laws relating to other water uses that do not implicate proprietary rights. . . .

2. ***Federal-State Relations.*** As you can see, while these federal statutes have preemptive effect, they have not been enacted to accomplish a complete preemption of state law. Accordingly, as mentioned above, when the federal government seeks to construct an irrigation project under the Reclamation Act, it must endeavor to secure water rights under state law. Once it has done so, it can enter into contractual or other arrangements with irrigators for the provision of water from the stored accumulation. *See, e.g.*, A Note on the Klamath River Controversy, *infra*. The federal government cannot by legal fiat secure rights to waters already appropriated under state law without contravening constitutional takings principles.

3. ***Bureau of Reclamation.*** Federal involvement has been central to virtually the entirety of large-scale water resource development in the United States, and the major federal actor for these purposes has been the Bureau of Reclamation. The Bureau has been described as the largest purveyor of water in the West. Indeed, the agency diverts between 40 percent and 85 percent of the annual flow of major western river systems such as the Colorado, Rio Grande, Snake, Sacramento, and San Joaquin.

Still, the era of big government water projects is all but over — economic and environmental considerations, and especially the dearth of feasible sites, have seen to that. Consequently, the role of the Bureau, which was originally to develop water supplies to facilitate settlement of the arid West, is changing. The Bureau has become less a water resources development agency and more a water resources management and protection agency. In addition to irrigation, the Bureau's responsibilities now include water conservation, hydroelectric power generation, municipal and industrial water supplies, flood control, outdoor recreation, enhancement of fish and wildlife habitats, and research.

In the current day, if more water is required for urban areas, endangered species preservation, or for other purposes, it must come from some other use. The prime target is agriculture. *See generally Water Use Conflicts in the West: Implications of Reforming the Bureau of Reclamation's Water Supply Policies*, § 3 (Aug. 1997).

4. *Removals of Water Projects.* The Bureau has been called upon of late to handle a new problem, the removal of water projects. FERC licenses for water projects are in the process of expiring, and many more will expire during the next couple of decades. When that happens, the question arises whether the Bureau has authority to order removal of the water projects themselves. It may be the Bureau has such authority, but, on the other hand, once a license is no longer in force, it may be the Bureau's regulatory participation is at an end.

Dam removals present more than legal problems. Removals can be difficult to accomplish as a matter of ecosystem management. A particular problem is what to do with pollution-laden sediment that may have piled up over many years behind an impoundment structure. Changes in flow patterns produced by a dam removal, moreover, can disturb investment-backed riparian uses as well as jeopardize fish and fauna.

A NOTE ON THE KLAMATH RIVER CONTROVERSY

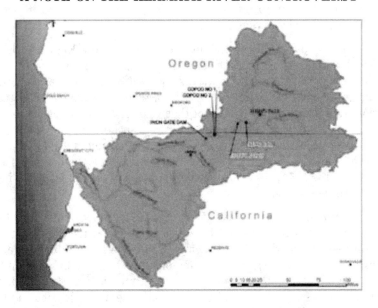

The Klamath River is a stream 250 miles in length originating in southern Oregon, meandering southwest through the Cascade Mountains into northern California and ultimately flowing into the Pacific Ocean. The Klamath River Basin, approximately 16,000 square miles in size, is the drainage basin for the Klamath River, the Lost River, and the Link River, as well as various other waterways (see map, above). The Klamath River Basin is home to a longstanding agricultural community which has relied on the River for irrigation for well over one hundred years. For more than ten years, the Basin has been the focus of a fierce political and legal dispute, one that implicates a host of matters central to our study of environmental law.

The bedrock issue in the controversy, but surely not the sole issue, is who owns property rights to water in the River. Here are the salient facts. Klamath River water has for many years been delivered to irrigators courtesy of the Klamath River Project, a Reclamation Act water impoundment and system of channels, dikes, and reservoirs authorized by Congress in 1905. The Project supplies water for about 240,000 acres of cropland and to several national wildlife refuges. To facilitate the Project, Oregon enacted a statute in 1905 to allow the federal government to secure water rights to the Klamath River — as you are aware, the federal government has elected to proceed under state law to secure water rights — so that it might then enter into contracts with water districts desirous of a steady supply of waters to irrigators they serve (who thereby become third-party beneficiaries to the contracts). Under the terms of the contracts, the managing federal agency, the Bureau of Reclamation of the Department of Interior, took on the obligation of supplying agreed-upon quantities of waters to the districts.

In connection with these events, Oregon and California entered into their own contractual relationship, the Klamath Basin Compact. The Compact, which received the consent of the Congress, as it must, provides, *inter alia*, that "the United States shall not, without payment of just compensation, impair any rights to the use of water for [domestic or irrigation purposes]."

There was peace in the valley until the year 2001 when the Klamath River Basin area suffered a serious drought. Despite the drought, it seems there remained sufficient water for the Bureau to honor its contract obligations, if not in whole at least in part, but the Bureau chose not to do so. Instead, it ceased all distributions of irrigation waters from April to July of that year. It did so because the Klamath River is home to the coho salmon, the shortnose suckerfish, and the Lost River suckerfish, all of which have been listed as endangered under the federal Endangered Species Act (*see* Chapter 7, *supra*). According to biological opinions issued in compliance with the ESA, cessation of water releases was necessary to "insure no jeopardy" to those species.

This elimination of water distributions triggered an as yet unfinished tangle of legal proceedings in both state and federal courts. Plaintiffs water districts and irrigators argued, *inter alia*, the following: (1) the decision to cease delivery of water constituted an unconstitutional taking of water rights held by plaintiff water districts and irrigators; (2) that same action constituted actionable breaches of the numerous contracts between the United States and the water districts; and (3) that same action impaired water rights secured to plaintiffs by virtue of the Klamath Basin Compact.

After a series of shuffles back and forth between federal and state courts, the matter reached the Circuit Court of Appeals for the Federal Circuit in February 2011. The Circuit Court answered some of the questions and then, you guessed it, remanded for further consideration. Held the court:

(1) There may or may not be an unconstitutional taking here. Despite the incontrovertible fact that the federal government holds legal title to the water under Oregon law, still plaintiffs may have acquired a "beneficial or equitable" interest in

the water by virtue of the 1905 Oregon statute or, perhaps, by virtue of the Compact or the issuance of water permits. The court decided to remand to the Federal Court of Claims to determine, based on a three-factor Oregon law test (the specific factors of which are not recited here) precisely what the interests of the plaintiffs might be. Interestingly, the Circuit Court suggested that, if the state law test were satisfied, plaintiffs could secure relief under the Takings Clause (but for one additional uncertainty — whether later events, the details of which we need not explore, might have "altered" the situation so to dissipate the otherwise cognizable takings claim).

The interesting aspect of this reasoning is its implied premise that a deprivation of a "beneficial and equitable" interest under Oregon law, as distinct from the deprivation of a "legal" or title interest under Oregon law, could qualify for Takings Clause relief. Apparently influenced by the idea that property interests are created not by the Federal Constitution but by independent sources such as state law, the Circuit Court supposed the question should be resolved by state law. If so, the court is on fragile ground, for the meaning of "property" for Takings Clause purposes may vary from that term's meaning in the variable common law of states. *See, e.g., Webb's Fabulous Pharmacies, Inc. v. Beckwith*, 449 U.S. 155, 101 S. Ct. 446 (1980) (noted in Chapter 3, *supra*). It may be that a "beneficial or equitable" interest in water under state law is simply not a property interest for Takings Clause purposes. It is not for the courts of Oregon, moreover, to have the final word on the issue of applicability of the Takings Clause. Allowing such a curiosity would represent an abdication by the federal courts to states of the power and duty to interpret the Constitution.

(2) There may be an actionable breach of contract action implicated in these facts. It is certain under the facts, of course, that the Bureau failed to deliver waters as contemplated by the contracts, and that might well on its face constitute a breach. But, still, it may not be a breach of contract given the Bureau's predicament: the Bureau could not honor its contractual obligations without violating the ESA. Because of this predicament, the government invoked the so-called "sovereign act doctrine," which bars actions against the government from violating contracts to which it is a party if the breach was caused by the government's "public and general acts as a sovereign." The Circuit Court found virtue in that argument, but remanded to determine if the breach occurred because compliance with the contract was "impossible." "Impossible" has been defined as "commercially impracticable."

In this regard, query whether the Court could have ruled that compliance with the contracts by an executive agency of the federal government was made illegal by the ESA? And would that not have been reason enough to excuse performance?

By one estimate, damages could come to $20 million if the government loses. Stay tuned.

2. The Navigational Servitude

The United States Supreme Court has found a "navigational servitude" to exist in situations where the federal government exercises Commerce Clause authority to regulate navigation on a stream or other waterway. This servitude interest is distinctly different from the authorities secured to the federal government through the Constitution's enumerated powers.

UNITED STATES v. CHEROKEE NATION OF OKLAHOMA
480 U.S. 700, 107 S. Ct. 1487 (1987)

CHIEF JUSTICE REHNQUIST delivered the opinion of the Court.

In *Choctaw Nation v. Oklahoma*, 397 U.S. 620 (1970), the Court determined that certain treaties between the Cherokee, Chickasaw, and Choctaw Tribes and the United States granted to the Tribes fee simple title to the riverbed underlying speci ed portions of the Arkansas River in Oklahoma. The Court found the circumstances sufficient to overcome the "strong presumption against conveyance by the United States" of title to the bed of a navigable water. *Montana v. United States*, 450 U.S. 544, 552 (1981). *See United States v. Holt State Bank*, 270 U.S. 49 (1926). The question presented in this case is whether the United States must pay the Cherokee Nation compensation for damage to these riverbed interests caused by navigational improvements which it has made on the Arkansas River. The damage to sand and gravel deposits resulted from the McClellan-Kerr Project, approved by Congress in 1946, Act of July 24, 1946, ch. 595, 60 Stat. 634, 635 636, and designed to improve navigation by construction of a channel in the Arkansas River from its mouth at the Mississippi to Catoosa, Oklahoma. The project was completed in 1971.

After our decision in *Choctaw Nation*, the Cherokee Nation sought compensation from the Government. Congress refused to fund the claim after the Department of the Interior and the Army Corps of Engineers concluded that the United States' navigational servitude rendered it meritless. *See* Department of the Interior and Related Agencies Appropriations for 1980: Hearings Before a Subcommittee of the House Committee on Appropriations, 96th Cong., 1st Sess., pt. 7, pp. 379 392 (1979). Congress did, however, provide respondent with the opportunity to seek judicial relief, conferring jurisdiction on the United States District Court for the Eastern District of Oklahoma to determine "any claim which the Cherokee Nation of Oklahoma may have against the United States for any and all damages to Cherokee tribal assets related to and arising from the construction of the [McClellan-Kerr Project]." H. R. 2329, 97th Cong., 1st Sess. (1981).

The Cherokee Nation filed a complaint contending that the construction of the McClellan-Kerr Project resulted in a taking under the Fifth Amendment of the Tribe's riverbed interests without just compensation. The United States in response claimed that its navigational servitude precluded liability for the alleged taking. The District Court granted the Tribe's motion for summary judgment, finding that the decision in Choctaw Nation created a "unique situation by which a portion of the navigable Arkansas River is, essentially, a private waterway belonging exclusively to the Cherokee Nation." App. to Pet. for Cert. 26a. Because the United States did not reserve its navigational servitude in the relevant treaties, the court held, it owed the Tribe just compensation.

A divided panel of the Court of Appeals for the Tenth Circuit affirmed, adopting a different analysis. 782 F.2d 871 (1986). The court rejected the District Court's conclusion that the United States' failure to reserve its navigational servitude defeated that interest. It found it "certain [that] the United States retained a navigational servitude in the Arkansas River." *Id.*, at 876. Nevertheless, the court held that the servitude was insufficient to protect the United States from liability. Finding that "the assertion of a navigational servitude on particular waters acknowledges *only* that the property owner's right to *use* these waters is shared with the public at large," *id.*, at 877, the court believed that the effect of the navigational servitude varied with the owner's intended use:" When the exercise of that public power affects private ownership rights not connected to a navigational use, the court must balance the public and private interests to decide whether just compensation is due." *Ibid.* Applying this test, the court concluded that though the Cherokee Nation could not interfere with the United States' exercise of the navigational servitude, it had a right to compensation for any consequent loss of property or diminution in value.

We think the Court of Appeals erred in formulating a balancing test to evaluate this assertion of the navigational servitude. No such "balancing" is required where, as here, the interference with in-stream interests results from an exercise of the Government's power to regulate navigational uses of "the deep streams which penetrate our country in every direction." *Gibbons v. Ogden*, 9 Wheat. 1, 195 (1824). Though "this Court has never held that the navigational servitude creates a blanket exception to the Takings Clause whenever Congress exercises its Commerce Clause authority to promote navigation," *Kaiser Aetna v. United States*, 444 U.S. 164, 172 (1979), there can be no doubt that "[the] Commerce Clause confers a unique position upon the Government in connection with navigable waters." *United States v. Rands*, 389 U.S. 121, 122 (1967). It gives to the Federal Government "a 'dominant servitude,' *FPC v. Niagara Mohawk Power Corp.*, 347 U.S. 239, 249 (1954), which extends to the entire stream and the stream bed below ordinary high-water mark. The proper exercise of this power is not an invasion of any private property rights in the stream or the lands underlying it, for the damage sustained does not result from taking property from riparian owners within the meaning of the Fifth Amendment but from the lawful exercise of a power to which the interests of riparian owners have always been subject." *Rands, supra*, at 123.[2] *See also United States v. Kansas City Life Ins. Co.*, 339 U.S. 799, 808 (1950); *Scranton v. Wheeler*, 179 U.S. 141, 163 (1900).

The application of these principles to interference with streambed interests has not depended on balancing this valid public purpose in light of the intended use of those interests by the owner. Thus, in *Lewis Blue Point Oyster Cultivation Co. v. Briggs*, 229 U.S. 82 (1913), the Court held that no taking occurred where dredging carried out under the direction of the United States destroyed oysters that had been cultivated on privately held lands under the waters of the Great South Bay in New York. The decision rested on the view that the dominant right of navigation

---

[2] Though Rands spoke in terms of riparian owners, rather than those holding fee simple title to riverbed interests, our cases make clear that the navigational servitude is dominant to riverbed interests no matter how acquired. *See, e.g., United States v. Chicago, M., St. P. & P. R. Co.*, 312 U.S. 592, 596 (1941) ("Whether, under local law, the title to the bed of the stream is retained by the State or the title of the riparian owner extends to the thread of the stream, or . . . to low-water mark, the rights of the title holder are subject to the dominant power of the federal Government in respect of navigation.") (footnotes omitted).

"must include the right to use the bed of the water for every purpose which is in aid of navigation." *Id.*, at 87. The Court did not rely on the particular use to which the private owners put the bed, but rather observed that their very title to the submerged lands "is acquired and held subject to the power of Congress to deepen the water over such lands or to use them for any structure which the interest of navigation, in its judgment, may require." Id., at 88. See also *United States v. Commodore Park*, 324 U.S. 386, 390 (1945); *United States v. Chicago, M., St. P. & P. R. Co.*, 312 U.S. 592, 596 597 (1941).

These well-established principles concerning the exercise of the United States' dominant servitude would, in the usual case, dictate that we reject respondent's "takings" claim. We do not understand respondent to argue otherwise. [citations omitted]. Instead, the Cherokee Nation asserts that its title to the Arkansas River bed is unique in scope and that interference with that interest requires just compensation. Respondent does not rely explicitly on any language of the relevant treaties, but rather on its reading of *Choctaw Nation v. Oklahoma*, 397 U.S. 620 (1970). We have noted that *Choctaw Nation* involved "very peculiar circumstances," *Montana v. United States*, 450 U.S., at 555, n. 5, in that "the Indians were promised virtually complete sovereignty over their new lands." *Choctaw Nation, supra*, at 635. These circumstances allowed the claimants to overcome the strong presumption against conveyance of riverbed interests by the United States, designed to protect the interests of the States under the equal-footing doctrine. *See Montana v. United States, supra*, at 551 553; *Shively v. Bowlby*, 152 U.S. 1, 48 50 (1894). Respondent urges that these circumstances further indicate that the United States abandoned its navigational servitude in the area. Thus, in respondent's view, the treaties by which it gained fee simple title to the bed of the Arkansas River were such as to make the Arkansas River a "private stream," Brief for Respondent 28, "not intended as a public highway or artery of commerce." *Id.*, at 23.

We think that the decision in *Choctaw Nation* was quite generous to respondent, and we refuse to give a still more expansive and novel reading of respondent's property interests. There is certainly nothing in *Choctaw Nation* itself that suggests such a broad reading of the conveyance. To the contrary, the Court expressly noted that the United States had no interest in retaining title to the submerged lands because "it had all it was concerned with in its *navigational easement* via the constitutional power over commerce." *Choctaw Nation*, supra, at 635 (emphasis added). The parties, including respondent here, clearly understood that the navigational servitude was dominant no matter how the question of riverbed ownership was resolved. *See, e.g.*, Brief for Petitioner in *Cherokee Nation v. Oklahoma*, O.T. 1969, No. 59, p. 19 ("[There] is nothing in the conveyance of title to the land beneath the navigable waters which conflicts with the power of the Government to hold such lands for navigation").

Any other conclusion would be wholly extraordinary, for we have repeatedly held that the navigational servitude applies to *all* holders of riparian and riverbed interests. *See Montana v. United States, supra*, at 555; *United States v. Grand River Dam Authority*, 363 U.S. 229, 233 (1960); *United States v. Chandler- Dunbar Water Power Co.*, 229 U.S. 53, 63 (1913), citing *Gibson v. United States*, 166 U.S. 269, 271 (1897). Indeed, even when the sovereign States gain "the absolute right to all their navigable waters and the soils under them for their own common use" by operation of the equal-footing doctrine, *Martin v. Waddell*, 16 Pet. 367, 410 (1842), this "absolute right" is unquestionably subject to "the paramount power of the United States to ensure that such waters remain free to interstate and foreign commerce." *Montana v. United States, supra*, at 551. If the States themselves are subject to this servitude, we cannot conclude that respondent — though granted a degree of sovereignty over tribal lands — gained an exemption from the servitude simply because it received title to the riverbed interests. Such a waiver of sovereign authority will not be implied, but instead must be " 'surrendered in unmistakable terms.' " *Bowen v. Public Agencies Opposed to Social Security Entrapment*, 477 U.S. 41, 52 (1986), quoting *Merrion v. Jicarilla Apache Tribe*, 455 U.S. 130, 148 (1982). Respondent can point to no such terms.

We also reject respondent's suggestion that the fiduciary obligations of the United States elevate the Government's actions into a taking. It is, of course, well established that the Government in its dealings with Indian tribal property acts in a fiduciary capacity. *See Seminole Nation v. United States*, 316 U.S. 286, 296 297 (1942). When it holds lands in trust on behalf of the tribes, the United States may not "give the tribal lands to others, or . . . appropriate them to its own purposes, without rendering, or assuming an obligation to render, just compensation for them." *United States v. Creek Nation*, 295 U.S. 103, 110 (1935). These principles, however, do little to aid respondent's cause, for they do not create property rights where none would otherwise exist but rather presuppose that the United States has interfered with existing tribal property interests. As we have explained, the tribal interests at issue here simply do not include the right to be free from the navigational servitude, for exercise of the servitude is "not an invasion of any private property rights in the stream or the lands underlying it. . . . " *United States v. Rands*, 389 U.S. at 123.

The judgment of the Court of Appeals is reversed, and the case is remanded for further proceedings consistent with this opinion. It is so ordered.

NOTES AND QUESTIONS

1.   *United States v. Rands,* **389 U.S. 121, 88 S. Ct. 265(1967).** Cited in the main text, *Rands* is a major statement on the navigational servitude:

> The Commerce Clause confers a unique position upon the Government in connection with navigable waters. 'The power to regulate commerce comprehends the control for that purpose, and to the extent necessary, of all the navigable waters of the United States. . . . For this purpose, they are the public property of the nation, and subject to all the requisite legislation by Congress. . . . This power to regulate navigation confers upon the United States a "dominant servitude" . . . which extends to the entire stream and the stream bed below ordinary high-water mark. The proper exercise of this power is not an invasion of any private property rights in the stream or the lands underlying it, for the damage sustained does not result from taking property from riparian owners within the meaning of the Fifth Amendment but from the lawful exercise of a power to which the interests of riparian owners have always been subject. . . . Thus, without being constitutionally obligated to pay compensation, the

United States may change the course of a navigable stream . . . or otherwise impair or destroy a riparian owner's access to navigable waters, . . . even though the market value of the riparian owner's land is substantially diminished.

The navigational servitude of the United States does not extend beyond the high-water mark. Consequently, when fast lands are taken by the Government, just compensation must be paid. But "just as the navigational privilege permits the Government to reduce the value of riparian lands by denying the riparian owner access to the stream without compensation for his loss . . . it also permits the Government to disregard the value arising from this same fact of riparian location in compensating the owner when fast lands are appropriated."

Rands, 389 U.S. at 123–24.

The constitutional principle established in the last-supplied sentence of *Rands* evoked sufficient controversy to prompt its statutory reversal in § 111 of the Rivers and Harbors and Flood Control Act of 1970. Congress can waive the servitude if it wishes and elect to pay compensation.

2. *Legal Origin.* What is the source of the navigational servitude? *Cherokee Nation* states it is a property right finding its source in the affirmative Commerce Clause. Since when does an enumerated power in the federal government create a property right in it? Perhaps the navigational servitude finds its source elsewhere. Justice Blackmun has given one view: "what is at issue is a matter of power, not of property. The servitude, in order to safeguard the Federal Government's paramount control over waters used in interstate commerce, limits the power of the States to create conflicting interests based on local law. That control does not depend on the form of the water body or the manner in which it was created, but on the fact of navigability and the corresponding commercial significance the waterway attains." *Kaiser Aetna v. United States*, 444 U.S. 164, 185 89, 100 S. Ct. 383, 396–97 (1979) (Blackmun, J., dissenting).

Why is there not a "dominant servitude" created when the government exercises Commerce Clause authorities in contexts other than navigation on waterways? Why does the Takings Clause not operate here but continue to operate with respect to other Commerce Clause applications? You might compare the federal navigational servitude to the public trust doctrine, at least as it was invoked by California in the Mono Lake case.

3. *The Navigational Servitude and the Submerged Lands Act.* The Submerged Lands Act transferred certain submerged lands underlying the Atlantic and Pacific Oceans and the Gulf of Mexico to coastal states. *See* Chapter 5, *supra*. In § 6(a) thereof, 43 U.S.C. § 1314(a), the statute speaks to the matter of the navigational servitude as it relates to those transferred lands: "The United States retains all its navigational servitude and rights in and powers of regulation and control of said lands and navigable waters for the constitutional purposes of commerce, navigation, national defense, and international affairs, all of which shall be paramount to, but shall not be deemed to include, proprietary rights of ownership, or the rights of management, administration, leasing, use, and development of the lands and natural resources which are specifically recognized, confirmed, established, and vested in and assigned to the respective States and others by section 3 of this Act." *See also United States v. Alaska*, 503 U.S. 569, 586, 112 S. Ct. 1606, 1616 (1992).

4. *State Navigational Servitudes.* Some states now have their own navigational servitudes, based on state law and presumably tied to *intra*-state commerce regulation.

Chapter 9

THE CLEAN AIR ACT

"There is no choice but to breathe the air, whether it is clean or polluted. Air is inhaled regardless of its quality. This is a national resource that should be protected as our parks and national monuments are protected." *Senate Report No. 101-228*, accompanying the 1990 Amendments to the Clean Air Act, P.L. 101-549 (Nov. 15, 1990), U.S. Code Congressional and Administrative News, 101st Cong., 2d Sess.(1990), at 3389.

SYNOPSIS

A. INTRODUCTION

The American Lung Association, in a study conducted at the University of California School of Medicine, has reported that lung function among persons living in chronically polluted areas can decline to a degree comparable to that of persons who smoke more than a pack of cigarettes a day. *American Journal of Respiratory and Critical Care Medicine,* May 1994. The study was done in and near Los Angeles, then considered to be the most polluted air basin in the United States, at least with respect to ozone and year-round particle pollution. (In the arena of short-term particle pollution, Pittsburgh has now risen to the top of the charts; Bakersfield, California, is a challenger for the title of most polluted urban area.) In its State of the Air 2011 report, the American Lung Association has reported that over half the nation suffers air pollution levels that are "dangerous." A study published in August 2007 in the *American Journal of Respiratory and Critical Care Medicine,* established for the first time a significant link between air pollution and cardiovascular risk in young adults. Young adults suffer as well from even low exposures to ozone, according to a study undertaken by the U.S. Environmental Protection Agency and the University of North Carolina. *Lung Function and Inflammatory Responses in Healthy Young Adults Exposed to 0.06 ppm Ozone for 6.6 Hours,* published in the American Journal of Respiratory and Critical Care Medicine, January 2011.

These are but several of a legion of studies and reports that have demonstrated the serious adverse health effects of unclean air. Since people breathe about 300 gallons of air a day, this public health concern was sure to find its way into the federal legislative arena, and it did so, as early as 1955. In that year, Congress authorized a limited federal involvement, merely instructing the Surgeon General of the United States to study the problem. 69 Stat. 322. While modest, this legislative intervention was at least a federal foot in the door. In 1960, Congress acted again, this time authorizing the Surgeon General to study health risks from emissions from motor vehicles. 74 Stat. 162. In 1963 and 1967, it expanded federal research efforts. 77 Stat. 392; Air Quality Act of 1967, 81 Stat. 485.

These early initiatives reflected the prevailing view of that time that pollution control should be primarily the purview of states. This view changed as the 1970s neared and it became appallingly clear that relying on states to clean the nation's air was a failed strategy. For one thing, air pollution had become a problem of national dimension, beyond the capacity of states, acting singly, to solve. If a state cleaned up, it might still be polluted by its upwind neighbors. State regulatory efforts were hampered also by political realities. Major polluting industries often exerted substantial political sway in the halls of state legislatures. In many cases, industries were able to entirely frustrate state air pollution regulatory initiatives by bandying the prospect of massive worker layoffs. Since the public had come to view pollution as an unavoidable cost of economic prosperity, it was tough, if not impossible, to assemble the political will to clamp down on large industrial sources of air pollution.

Given this political impasse, and bolstered by the staunch leadership of a true champion of environmental protection, Senator Edmund Muskie of Maine, among others, Congress finally took decisive action. Abandoning its earlier respectful deference, this time it "took a stick to the States." The result was the Clean Air Act ("CAA") Amendments of 1970, Pub. L. 91-604. The CAA did not remove states from the game, to be sure, but it unambiguously supplanted them: in the new federal-state partnership to regulate air pollution, the senior partner would be Uncle Sam.

Senator Edmund Muskie of Maine.
Used by permission. Copyright © Stephen O. Muskie

The Clean Air Act of 1970, as amended, 42 U.S.C. § 7401 et seq., remains the all-important statute regulating air pollution emissions in this nation. In this chapter, we will take an historical approach in our examination of it. Our inquiry begins with a review of the statute's original design, for upon that all else is built. The original Act relied on three major initiatives. First, it attempted to limit emissions of the most common pollutants by a regulatory system involving states. Under the plan, the federal government determines how clean the air should be, using "national ambient air quality standards" ("NAAQSs") for that purpose, and states then endeavor to accomplish the actual cleaning, typically by using "source emission limitations" or "source standards." Second, the CAA instituted a separate set of standards for so-called "new sources." The idea behind "new source performance standards" was that industrial facilities not yet constructed should be designed and built to operate in as clean a manner as possible. Last, the Act made specific provision for hazardous air pollutants, sometimes known as "air toxics."

After a review of the original statute, we will examine the amendments to the statute enacted in 1977. These amendments were borne of congressional frustration at the uneven success achieved by the original enactment. The 1977 amendments imposed new restrictions on emissions of air pollutants in both "dirty air" and "clean air" areas.

Following that, we review the Clean Air Act Amendments of 1990, Congress's most comprehensive revision to the statute. The 1990 amendments added several entirely new regulatory provisions, including an innovative market-based regulatory approach to reduce acid deposition. Concluding the Chapter is a discussion of the issue of climate change.

The Clean Air Act is divisible into two halves. The half upon which we will focus is regulation of so-called "stationary sources" of air pollution, including factories, incinerators, and other such facilities. The other half imposes regulation upon "mobile sources" of air pollution, i.e., cars, trucks, railroad engines and the like. We do not cover mobile source regulation in these materials.

B. THE 1970 ACT

1. Regulation of Criteria Pollutants

a. National Ambient Air Quality Standards

The primary concern of the drafters of the Clean Air Act of 1970 was to rid the air of the most commonly found air pollutants. "Air pollutant" is defined by the Act as:

> any air pollution agent or combination of such agents, including any physical, chemical, biological, radioactive (including source material, special nuclear material, and byproduct material) substance or matter which is emitted into or otherwise enters the ambient air. Such term includes any precursors to the formation of any air pollutant, to the extent the Administrator has identified such precursor or precursors for the particular purpose for which the term "air pollutant" is used.

Section 302(g), 42 U.S.C. § 7602(g).

Commonly found air pollutants include:

- *Carbon Monoxide* (CO): this colorless and odorless gas enters the atmosphere primarily from tailpipes of gasoline-powered vehicles. Inhalation adversely affects the body's capacity to carry oxygen in the bloodstream, which in turn can cause various cardiovascular and other problems.

- *Hydrocarbons* (HC): emitted into the air when fuels are incompletely combusted, these pollutants can combine with nitrogen oxides to form photochemical oxidants, or smog, a complicated and hazy mixture of gases, including ozone. Hydrocarbons can irritate eyes and lungs, harm vegetation, and produce odors.

- *Lead* (Pb): ingestion of this heavy metal is shown to cause brain damage, especially in children. For more information, see the text accompanying the *Lead Industries* case, *infra*.

- *Nitrogen Dioxide* (NO_2): produced by combustion of fossil fuels, these pollutants react in the atmosphere with volatile organic compounds (VOCs) to form ozone. They contribute to lung damage and respiration problems.

- *Ozone* (O_3): commonly known as smog, ozone is found in the stratosphere, where it works to shield the Earth from ultraviolet radiation, and in the troposphere, where it is a component of photochemical smog. In that latter capacity, ozone adversely affects respiration, damages the lungs, and contributes to asthma, nasal congestion, and the like. Ninety percent of ozone inhaled into the lungs is never exhaled. Instead, ozone reacts rapidly with cells and tissues that line the respiratory tract.

- *Particulate Matter* (PM_{10} and $PM_{2.5}$): this pollutant includes materials which are normally liquid or solid in form but have become airborne. Fine particulates, those of 10 microns or less in diameter ("PM_{10}"), can invade the body, causing a variety of health problems. Very fine particulates, those of 2.5 microns or less in diameter ($PM_{2.5}$), have also been linked to cardiovascular problems among the elderly.

- *Sulfur Dioxide* (SO_2): emitted largely during combustion of fossil fuels, this pollutant contributes to acid deposition, aggravates respiratory activity, and contributes to lung disability.

The Clean Air Act first called for the division of the nation into air quality control regions ("AQCRs"). Section 107, 42 U.S.C. § 7407. AQCRs are the geographic units within which pollution controls apply. There have been 247 AQCRs designated under the Act.

To bring about a reduction in emissions of air pollutants, the Act directed EPA to establish national ambient air quality standards ("NAAQSs") for commonly found air pollutants, and set time frames within which they should be attained in each AQCR. NAAQSs are minimal standards for cleanliness of air, set on a pollutant-by-pollutant basis. Pollutants for which NAAQSs are in place are known as "criteria" air pollutants, for reasons that will become clear upon your reading of the case which follows. The Clean Air Act calls for primary and secondary NAAQSs. Section 109, 42 U.S.C. § 7409. Primary NAAQSs are to be set at levels that are "requisite to protect the public health, while 'allowing an adequate margin of safety.'" Section 109(b)(1), 42 U.S.C. 7409(b)(1). Secondary NAAQSs are to be set at levels "requisite to protect the public welfare from any known or anticipated adverse effects associated with the presence of such air pollutant in the ambient air." Section 109(b)(2), 42 U.S.C. § 7409(b)(2).

Even though the term "public" is undefined in the statute, the *Lead Industries* case, *infra*, makes clear that the term includes discrete subunits of the general population. This means that EPA is not limited to creating ambient standards designed to protect the healthy adult only. On the contrary, the agency is legally authorized to fashion more stringent NAAQSs to protect more vulnerable population subgroups such as children and the elderly. *See, e.g.*, Senate Report No. 91-1196, at 10 (specifying that "sensitive citizens" — children, for example, or people with asthma, emphysema, or other respiratory conditions rendering them particularly vulnerable to air pollution — "should be protected").[1]

---

[1] General considerations do not always control specific cases. In one instance, EPA declined to revise the NAAQS for sulfur dioxide to protect one population subgroup, asthmatics, from "high level short-term SO_2 bursts," that is, temporary severe exposures to sulfur dioxide, on the theory that there was no public health problem. In EPA's view, these so-called bursts were "localized," "site-specific," and "infrequent," and not the type of "ubiquitous" health problem for which an NAAQS was appropriate. *American Lung Ass'n v. U.S. Environmental Protection Agency*, 134 F.3d 388, 391 92 (D.C. Cir. 1998), *cert. denied*, 528 U.S. 818, 120 S. Ct. 58 (1999). Reviewing the agency refusal, the D.C. Circuit Court of Appeals conceded that EPA might be right to decide that excessive exposures to sulfur dioxide to be suffered by 41,500 asthmatics do not rise to the level of "a public health problem warranting national protective regulation, or that three or six or twelve annual exposures present no cause for annual concern[.]" The court nonetheless remanded the case because EPA failed to plausibly explain why the "local" nature of this pollution precluded regulation. *Id.* at 392.

The EPA' has promulgated NAAQSs for each of the above-listed pollutants (the NAAQS for hydrocarbons was repealed in 1983). These standards are set forth in the chart that immediately follows.

National Ambient Air Quality Standards

Pollutant	Primary Standards		Secondary Standards	
	Level	Averaging Time	Level	Averaging Time
Carbon Monoxide	9 ppm (10 mg/m^3)	8-hour	None	
	35 ppm (40 mg/m^3)	1-hour		
Lead	0.15 μg/m^3	Rolling 3-Month Average	Same as Primary	
Nitrogen Dioxide	53 ppb	Annual (Arithmetic Average)	Same as Primary	
	100 ppb	1-hour	None	
Particulate Matter (PM$_{10}$)	150 μg/m^3	24-hour	Same as Primary	
Particulate Matter (PM$_{2.5}$)	15.0 μg/m3	Annual (Arithmetic Average)	Same as Primary	
	μg/m^3	24-hour	Same as Primary	
Ozone	0.075 ppm (2008 std)	8-hour	Same as Primary	
	.08 ppm (1997 std)	8-hour	Same as Primary	
	0.12 ppm	1-hour	Same as Primary	
Sulfur Dioxide	0.03 ppm (1971 std)	Annual (Arithmetic Average)	0.5 ppm	3-hour
	0.14 ppm (1971 std)	24-hour		
	75 ppb	1-hour	None	

Legend: ppm - parts per million; ppb - parts per billion: μg/m^3 - micrograms per cubic meter. Source: 40 C.F.R. §§ 50.4–50.13; http://www.epa.gov/air/criteria.html. Current as of September 2011. Methodology of measurement can vary dramatically among the pollutants. The 1997 8-hour standard for ozone remains in place as EPA undertakes rulemaking to transition to the 2008 standard.

At this point, you should read §§ 107–109 of the Clean Air Act and the *Lead Industries* case, which follows this introductory material. *Lead Industries* examines the validity of national ambient air quality standard established for the pollutant,

---

From all of this, one may rightly conclude the Clean Air Act is in reality more a public health and welfare measure than a classic "environmental law" in place to improve environmental quality for its own sake.

lead. Air pollution from lead is not a new problem. The ambient air in the ancient Roman Empire was apparently heavily contaminated with lead from open-air furnaces, so much so that the entire northern hemisphere was fouled for centuries. Airborne lead particles made it as far north as the Arctic as early as 500 B.C. to 300 B.C. A major cause was the introduction of silver coinage. Silver was extracted from lead in smelters, a process that apparently resulted in enormous pollutant loadings. *See, e.g.*, Curt Suplee, *Environment: Roman Air was Full of Lead*, WASH. POST, Sept. 26, 1994, at A2.

In the current day, lead remains a problem. While lead exposure levels have declined dramatically in the last twenty years, in large part because of reduced use of lead in gasoline, soldered cans, and paint, the public is still exposed to this material from house dust, soils, and water delivery pipes. Exposure to lead can cause numerous health problems, including interferences with the nervous and immune systems and with kidney function. It can also disrupt reproductive, developmental, and cardiovascular systems. In children especially, it can interfere with cognitive functions as well. *See, e.g.*, http://www.epa.gov/oaqps001/lead/health.html. More than 900,000 children younger than six years of age, largely those of low-income families living in older homes, have elevated levels of lead in their bloodstreams. *See, e.g.*, M.J. Friedrich, *Poor Children Subject to "Environmental Injustice"*, 283 JAMA 23 (June 2000); Thomas D. Matte, *Reducing Blood Lead Levels: Benefits and Strategies*, 281 JAMA 24 (June 1999). A draft risk assessment released by the Environmental Protection Agency in July 2007 declared that persons with high exposures to lead can lose ten IQ points. At the *mean* level of exposure in the United States, losses of one to three points are commonplace.

LEAD INDUSTRIES ASS'N, INC. v. U.S. ENVIRONMENTAL PROTECTION AGENCY
647 F.2d 1130 (D.C. Cir. 1980)

WRIGHT, CHIEF JUDGE:

This is the third occasion on which this court has been asked to review Environmental Protection Agency (EPA or Agency) regulations promulgated under authority of the Clean Air Act, as amended, 42 U.S.C. § 7401 et seq. (Supp. I 1977) (the Act), and specifically designed to deal with the health problems associated with lead in the ambient air. . . .

II. THE STATUTORY SCHEME

The first step toward establishing national ambient air quality standards for a particular pollutant is its addition to a list, compiled by EPA's Administrator, of pollutants that cause of contribute to air pollution "which may reasonably be anticipated to endanger public health or [welfare.]" Section 108(a)(1), 42 U.S.C. § 7408(a)(1).Within twelve months of the listing of a pollutant under Section 108(a) the Administrator must issue "air quality criteria" for the pollutant. Section 108 makes it clear that the term "air quality criteria" means something different from the conventional meaning of "criterion"; such "criteria" do not constitute "standards" or "guidelines," but rather refer to a document to be prepared by EPA which is to provide the scientific basis for promulgation of air quality standards for the pollutant. This criteria document must "accurately reflect the latest scientific knowledge useful in indicating the kind and extent of all identifiable effects on public health or welfare which may be expected from the presence of such pollutant in the ambient air, in varying quantities." Section108(a)(2), 42 U.S.C. § 7408(a)(2).

At the same time as he issues air quality criteria for a pollutant, the Administrator must also publish proposed national primary and secondary air quality standards for the pollutant. Section 109(a)(2), 42 U.S.C. § 7409(a)(2). National primary ambient air quality standards are standards "the attainment and maintenance of which in the judgment of the Administrator, based on such criteria and allowing an adequate margin of safety, are requisite to protect the public health." Section 109(b)(1), 42 U.S.C. § 7409(b)(1). Secondary air quality standards "specify a level of air quality the attainment and maintenance of which in the judgment of the Administrator, based on such criteria, is requisite to protect the public welfare from any known or anticipated adverse effects associated with the presence of such air pollutant in the ambient air." Section 109(b)(2), 42 U.S.C. § 7409(b)(2). Effects on "the public welfare" include "effects on soils, water, crops, vegetation, manmade materials, animals, wildlife, weather, visibility, and climate, damage to and deterioration of property, and hazards to transportation, as well as effects on economic values and on personal comfort and well being." Section 302(h), 42 U.S.C. § 7602(h). The Administrator is required to submit the proposed air quality standards for public comment in a rulemaking proceeding, the procedure for which is prescribed by Section307(d) of the Act, 42 U.S.C. § 7607(d).

Within six months of publication of the proposed standards the Administrator must promulgate final primary and secondary ambient air quality standards for the pollutant. Section 307(d)(10), 42 U.S.C. § 7607(d)(10). Once EPA has promulgated national ambient air quality standards, responsibility under the Act shifts from the federal government to the states. Within nine months of promulgation of the standards each state must prepare and submit to EPA for approval a state implementation plan. Section 110(a)(1), 42 U.S.C. § 7410(a)(1). These state implementation plans must contain emission limitations and all other measures necessary to attain the primary standards "as expeditiously as practicable," but no later than three years after EPA approval of the plan, and to attain the secondary standards within a reasonable period of time. Section 110(a)(2)(A) & (B), 42 U.S.C. § 7410(a)(2)(A) & (B). The Administrator is authorized to extend the deadline for attainment of the primary air quality standards by two years, but thereafter it must be met. Section 110(e), 42 U.S.C. § 7410(e). . . .

[The court then discusses at length the rulemaking proceedings leading up to the establishment of the primary ambient air quality standard for lead, the criteria document used by the agency, and the scope of review to be used by the court. Thereafter, it discusses the arguments put forth in the case]:

V. Statutory Authority

The petitioners' first claim is that the Administrator exceeded his authority under the statute by promulgating a primary air quality standard for lead which is more stringent than is necessary to protect the public health because it is designed to protect the public against "subclinical" effects which are not harmful to health. According to petitioners, Congress only authorized the Administrator to set primary air quality standards that are aimed at protecting the public against health effects which are known to be clearly harmful. They argue that Congress so limited the Administrator's authority because it was concerned that excessively stringent air quality standards could cause massive economic dislocation. . . .

This argument is totally without merit. [Plaintiff] is unable to point to anything in either the language of the Act or its legislative history that offers any support for its claim that Congress, by specifying that the Administrator is to allow an "adequate margin of safety" in setting primary air quality standards, thereby required the Administrator to consider economic or technological feasibility. . . .

The legislative history of the Act [also] shows the Administrator may not consider economic and technological feasibility in setting air quality standards; the absence of any provision requiring consideration of these factors was no accident; it was the result of a deliberate decision by Congress to subordinate such concerns to the achievement of health goals. Exasperated by the lack of significant progress toward dealing with the problem of air pollution under the Air Quality Act of 1967, 81 STAT. 485, and prior legislation, Congress abandoned the approach of offering suggestions and setting goals in favor of "taking a stick to the States in the form of the Clean Air Amendments of 1970. . . ." *Train v. Natural Resources Defense Council, Inc.,* supra, 421 U.S. at 64; see *Union Electric Co. v. EPA,* 427 U.S. 246, 256 257 (1976). Congress was well aware that, together with Sections 108 and110, Section 109 imposes requirements of a "technology-forcing" character. . . .

It may well be that underlying [plaintiff's] argument is its feeling that Congress could not or should not have intended this result, and that this court should supply relief by grafting a requirement of economic or technological feasibility onto the statute. The Supreme Court confronted a similar suggestion in the Tellico Damcase. *TVA v. Hill,* 437 U.S. 153 (1978). There TVA argued that the Endangered Species Act should not be construed to prevent operation of the dam since it had already been completed at a cost of approximately $100million, Congress had appropriated funds for the dam even after the Act was passed, and the species at risk — the snail darter — was relatively unimportant and ways might ultimately be found to save it. The Court rejected the invitation to "view the . . . Act ' reasonably,' and hence shape a remedy that ' accords with some modicum of common sense and the public weal.' " *Id.* at 194. . . .

[The court then discussed LIA's arguments that the Clean Air Act only allows regulation to remove health threats that are clearly determined]:

LIA's argument appears to touch on two issues. The first concerns the type of health effects on which the Administrator may base air quality standards, i.e., the point at which the Administrator's regulatory authority may be exercised. This issue, as LIA suggests, does concern the limits that the Act, and its legislative history, may place on the Administrator's authority. The second issue appears to be more in the nature of an evidentiary question: whether or not the evidence in the record substantiates the Administrator's claim that the health effects on which the standards were based do in fact satisfy the requirements of the Act. Although these two issues are closely related, they are conceptually distinct, and they are best examined separately.

Section 109(b) does not specify precisely what Congress had in mind when it directed the Administrator to prescribe air quality standards that are "requisite to protect the public health." The legislative history of the Act does, however, provide some guidance. The Senate Report explains that the goal of the air quality standards must be to ensure that the public is protected from "adverse health effects." S. Rep. No. 91-1196, *supra*, at 10. And the report is particularly careful to note that especially sensitive persons such as asthmatics and emphysematics are included within the group that must be protected. . . .

The Administrator begins by pointing out that the Act's stated goal is "to protect and enhance the quality of the Nation's air resources so as to promote the public health and welfare and the productive capacity of its [population.]" Section 101(b)(1), 42 U.S.C. § 7401(b)(1). This goal was reaffirmed in the 1977 Amendments. . . .

We agree that LIA's interpretation of the statute is at odds with Congress' directives to the Administrator. . . . It may be that it reflects LIA's view that the Administrator must show that there is a "medical consensus that [the effects on which the standards were based] are harmful. . . . " If so, LIA is seriously mistaken. This court has previously noted that some uncertainty about the health effects of air pollution is inevitable. And we pointed out that "[awaiting] certainty will often allow for only reactive, not preventive [regulatory action]." *Ethyl Corp. v. EPA, supra*, 541 F.2d at 25. Congress apparently shares this view; it specifically directed the Administrator to allow an adequate margin of safety to protect against effects which have not yet been uncovered by research and effects whose medical significance is a matter of disagreement . . .

Questions involving the environment are particularly prone to uncertainty. Technological man has altered his world in ways never before experienced or anticipated. The health effects of such alterations are often unknown, sometimes unknowable. While a concerned Congress has passed legislation providing for protection of the public health against gross environmental modi cations, the regulators entrusted with the enforcement of such laws have not thereby been endowed with a prescience that removes all doubt from their decisionmaking. Rather, speculation, conflicts in evidence, and theoretical extrapolation typify their every action. How else can they act, given a mandate to protect the public health but only a slight or non-existent data base from which to draw? . . . Sometimes, of course, relatively certain proof of danger or harm from such modi cations can readily be found. But, more commonly, "reasonable medical concerns" and theory long precede certainty. Yet the statutes — and common sense — demand regulatory action to prevent harm, even if the regulator is less than certain that harm is otherwise inevitable.

Undoubtedly, certainty is the scientific ideal — to the extent that even science can be certain of its truth. But certainty in the complexities of environmental medicine may be achievable only after the fact, when scientists have the opportunity for leisurely and isolated scrutiny of an entire mechanism. . . .

[The court then undertakes an extensive examination of the EPA's decisionmaking on this particular standard, both substantively and procedurally, and dismisses the contentions of petitioners.]

We have accorded these cases the most careful consideration, combining as we must careful scrutiny of the evidence in the record with deference to the Administrator's judgments. We conclude that in this rulemaking proceeding the Administrator complied with the substantive and procedural requirements of the Act, and that his decisions are both adequately explained and amply supported by evidence in the record. Accordingly, we reject petitioners' claims of error. The regulations under review herein are

Affirmed.

NOTES AND QUESTIONS

1. *NAAQs and Emissions Controls.* As we will see in the upcoming section, NAAQSs drive the stringency of emissions controls. Accordingly (but subject to exceptions; *see infra*), if the ambient air is loaded with, say, sulfur dioxide, polluters will have to cut back emissions of that pollutant so that the ambient air will exhibit the mandated level of cleanliness. If the ambient air is relatively free of that pollutant, on the other hand, polluters enjoy a free, or freer, ride.

2. *Technology Forcing.* *Lead Industries* comments that NAAQSs are "technology forcing." What does this mean? Assume you are a member of a regulated industry in a polluted AQCR and are under orders to reduce your emissions of sulfur dioxide by 85% from present levels. The vexing problem for you is plain: it cannot be done. There is no pollution control technology in existence that can reduce emissions of SO_2 from your plant by the requisite percentage. The Clean Air Act, in short, is requiring you to do what is technologically impossible. Of course, it is not actually *impossible*; you could always just shut down the plant entirely. And, in fact, if you fail to clean up your emissions by the requisite 85% in the three or however many years you are granted, you will have to do just that. So, if you want to stay in business, you had better get about the task of inventing a pollution control technology. *That* is what technology-forcing means. Why did Congress do such a thing? The answer is twofold: the job had to be done and Congress believed industry would be able to advance the state of technology to get the job done. After all, the nation had just placed a man on the moon, so cleaning up air emissions should be a piece of cake.

Right?

Still, is there a constitutional question here? Are there grounds on which to challenge this scheme? If a plant actually had to shut down, would this be an unconstitutional taking?

3. *Costs; Nondelegation Doctrine.* The holding in *Lead Industries* that NAAQSs should be fashioned without regard to considerations of the unavoidable costs of implementation of that standard. Despite the decision, however, the issue remained a matter of lingering dispute for over twenty years. It is no longer. In *Whitman v. American Trucking Ass'n*, 531 U.S. 457, 121 S. Ct. 903 (2001), the

Court firmly rejected the idea that costs should play a role in NAAQS formulations. Writing for the majority, Justice Scalia relied on the normal meaning of the statute's text. A "clear" "textual commitment of authority" was necessary, and was not to be found in the text of the statute. Justice Scalia commented further that a contrary interpretation of that text would run afoul of canons of statutory interpretation, especially the whole act rule and the canon known as *noscitur a sociis* (for a recitation of these rules and canons, *see, e.g.*, Appendix Two, *infra*).

Note that, while *American Trucking* dealt specifically with primary NAAQSs, its holding applies to secondary NAAQSs as well. *American Trucking* is additionally significant for its resolution of a major separation of powers issue, whether the CAA's delegation of authority to EPA to set NAAQSs violates the nondelegation doctrine. The Court found no violation. Loosely described, the nondelegation doctrine maintains that legislative power (the type of power exercised when health-based standards are established) should be exercised by the Congress, not by the executive branch (of which EPA is a card-carrying member). The nondelegation doctrine is no longer a serious player in federal law, especially after *American Trucking*. American Trucking also resolved another issue involving implementation of the revised ozone NAAQS.

4. ***Judicial Review.*** National ambient air quality standards are effective and enforceable upon promulgation. They may be challenged in court by filing a petition with the Circuit Court of Appeals of the District of Columbia. *See* § 307(b)(1), 42 U.S.C. § 7607(b)(1). Routinely, promulgations of NAAQSs are challenged. As a general matter, once an NAAQS has survived judicial review, it may not be challenged in subsequent enforcement proceedings. *See* § 307(b)(2), 42 U.S.C. § 7607(b)(2).

5. ***NAAQSs and NEPA.*** Is the promulgation of an NAAQS a "major federal action significantly affecting the quality of the human environment" for purposes of the National Environmental Policy Act? *See* 15 U.S.C. § 793(c)(1) ("No action taken under the Clean Air Act shall be deemed a major Federal action significantly affecting the quality of the human environment within the meaning of the [NEPA]").

b. Emissions Limitations

Once ambient standards are in place under §§ 108–109 of the Clean Air Act, the task becomes to affix specific emissions limits on pollution sources. Compliance with these "source standards," in turn, should result in improvement of overall air quality to levels stipulated by the NAAQSs.

In an arrangement known as "cooperative federalism," the Clean Air Act allocates to states the task of fashioning emissions limitations and requiring compliance with them, subject to EPA's approval. Section 110 of the Act explains how this is accomplished. The section calls for states to prepare plans for meeting the NAAQSs, which plans are known as state implementation plans, or "SIPs." SIPs are submitted to EPA. Upon receipt of a SIP, EPA must ultimately approve or disapprove it, in whole or in part. Section 110(a)(3), 42 U.S.C. § 7410(a)(3); § 110(k), 42 U.S.C. § 7410(k); 40 C.F.R. Part 52. Once approved, a SIP becomes the framework for achieving the NAAQS for which it was prepared. SIPs have elaborate content requirements. *See* § 110(a)(2) 42 U.S.C. § 7410(a)(2); 40 C.F.R. Part 51.

The United States Supreme Court declared early on that states enjoy substantial discretion in fashioning source standards within their SIPs:

> The [Environmental Protection] Agency is plainly charged by the Act with the responsibility for setting the national ambient air standards. Just as plainly, however, it is relegated by the Act to a secondary role in the process of determining and enforcing the specific, source-by-source emission limitations which are necessary if the national standards it has set are to be met. Under § 110(a)(2), the Agency is required to approve a state plan which provides for the timely attainment and subsequent maintenance of ambient air standards, and which also satisfies that section's other general requirements. The Act gives the Agency no authority to question the wisdom of a State's choices of emission limitations if they are part of a plan which satisfies the standards of § 110(a)(2), and the Agency may devise and promulgate a specific plan of its own only if a State fails to submit an implementation plan which satisfies those standards. § 110(c). Thus, so long as the ultimate effect of a State's choice of emission limitations is compliance with the national standards for ambient air, the State is at liberty to adopt whatever mix of emission limitations it deems best suited to its particular situation.

Train v. Natural Resources Defense Council, Inc., 421 U.S. 60, 78, 95 S. Ct. 1470, 1481 (1975).

Not only are states authorized to choose the most suitable "mix of emission limitations," but the EPA is constrained to approve SIPs even if it believes the selected emission limitations are economically or technologically infeasible. *See Union Electric Co. v. EPA*, 427 U.S. 246, 256, 96 S. Ct. 2518, 2525 (1976) ("Congress intended claims of economic and technological infeasibility to be wholly foreign to the Administrator's consideration of a state implementation plan."). The same broad discretion afforded to states with respect to initial SIPs extends to subsequent SIP revisions as well. States may revise SIPs as they wish. EPA must approve SIP revisions for them to be effective. So long as a proposed revision will not interfere with the attainment of the relevant NAAQS, EPA must approve it.

On some occasions, SIP revisions are prompted by individual polluters seeking variances or exceptions from the state. When a polluter seeks a variance, it does so on its own time:

> [A] polluter is subject to existing requirements [in a SIP] until such time as he obtains a variance, and variances are not available under the revision authority until they have been approved by both the State and the Environmental Protection Agency. Should either entity determine that granting the variance would prevent attainment or maintenance of national air standards, the polluter is presumably within his rights in seeking judicial review. This litigation, however, is carried out on the polluter's time, not the public's, for during its pendency the original regulations remain in

effect, and the polluter's failure to comply may subject him to a variety of enforcement procedures.

Train v. NRDC, 421 U.S. 60, 92, 95 S. Ct. 1470, 1488 (1975).

On other occasions, however, it is EPA that wants SIPs to be revised. Typically, EPA requires SIP revisions when an NAAQS for which a SIP is in place has itself been revised. In such instances, EPA will issue what is known as a "SIP call," in effect telling states that changes in their SIPs are necessary. *See, e.g., Michigan v. EPA*, 213 F.3d 663 (D.C. Cir. 2000) (evaluating an EPA SIP Call to 22 northeastern states to reduce NOx emissions). Sometimes EPA will issue a SIP call to upwind states because their air emissions are contributing to air quality problems in downwind states, a condition known as "transboundary air pollution." The EPA has express authority to do this under § 110(a)(2)(D)(i)(I), 42 U.S.C. § 7410(a)(2)(D)(i)(I). When EPA exercises this authority, states are bound to make the necessary changes in their SIPs for the benefit of downwind states.

In addition to the SIP call mechanism, downwind states may petition EPA to *directly* regulate stationary sources to stop transboundary air pollution. Section 126, 42 U.S.C. § 7426. After granting a § 126 petition, EPA will promulgate a rule to provide the requisite relief for downwind states. *See, e.g., Appalachian Power Co. v. U.S. Environmental Protection Agency*, 249 F.3d 1032 (D.C. Cir. 2001) (upholding an EPA rule setting limits on Nox emissions for nearly 400 electric power plants in twelve midwestern and southern states and the District of Columbia for the benefit of eight downwind states).

Failure to comply with SIP requirements exposes sources to potentially serious state-law-based penalties and injunctive actions. Industry remains unhappy with this latter fact. It has long maintained that perfect compliance with emission limitations is impossible because of numerous variables, human and technological, that inevitably bear on the industrial process. Even the best run plants, industry asserts, will experience malfunctions on occasion, especially during startup and shutdown operations. Since these malfunctions are unavoidable, the argument continues, the regulatory regime should accommodate by forgiving penalties otherwise to be assessed. And the accommodation should be in the form of a formal exoneration from prosecution.

EPA disagrees with these contentions. First, it claims a lack of legal authority to approve any SIP that features a formal exemption from liability because doing so might interfere with attainment of NAAQSs. Beyond that, as a general matter at least, EPA views industrial malfunction events as foreseeable. As such, malfunctions "may be addressed in the underlying standards themselves through narrowly tailored SIP revisions that take into account the potential impacts on ambient air quality caused by the inclusion of these allowances." Better yet, in EPA's view, the matter should be left to the prudent exercise of enforcement discretion. *See* Memorandum of U.S. Environmental Protection Agency, *State Implementation Plans (SIPs): Policy Regarding Excess Emission During Malfunctions, Startup, and Shutdown* (1999).

Despite these views, EPA has agreed that states may place in SIPs a provision affording industry an affirmative defense in limited circumstances. The restrictions are three: first, no affirmative defense can undermine attainment (thus, there can be no defense made available to an industry that can single-handedly cause a NAAQS exceedance; this is often the case with lead and SO_2 emitters); second, no affirmative defense can preclude injunctive relief; and third, no affirmative defense can impede either EPA or citizen enforcement (as distinct from state enforcement). *Id.*

What recourse exists if a state refuses to prepare a SIP? As a matter of federal constitutional law, is the federal government empowered to compel states to prepare an acceptable SIP? *See, e.g., New York v. United States*, in Chapter 3, *supra*. If the federal government cannot compel states to comply, what can it do? *See* CAA § 110(c), 42 U.S.C. § 7410(c) (welcome to the world of "FIPs"). Does EPA have any role to play if a person violates a state SIP, or if a state refuses to enforce its own SIP provisions? *See* CAA § 113(a)(1)–(2), 42 U.S.C. § 7413(a)(1)–(2).

Are states the only entities with responsibilities under § 110? What of Indian tribes? (Welcome to the world of "TIPs.") Section 301(d) of the Act, 42 U.S.C. § 7601(d), authorizes the EPA to treat Indian tribes as states. Section 110(o), 42 U.S.C. § 7410(o), in turn, allows for the submission of tribal implementation plans, which upon EPA approval apply to all areas "located within the exterior boundaries of the reservation." EPA regulations allow for these plans to govern emission limitations on tribal reservations, including fee interests held by nonmembers of the governing tribe. The regulations also allow the plans to regulate beyond the boundaries of reservation lands, to include Indian trust lands and pueblos. *See* 63 Fed. Reg. 7254 (1998), *codified* at 40 C.F.R. Parts 9, 35, 49, 50, and 81 (Tribal Authority Rule). EPA's regulations produced this latter result by defining "reservation" to include "trust lands that have been validly set apart for the use of a tribe even though the land has not been formally designated as a reservation." 63 Fed. Reg. at 7258. EPA's regulations were upheld on judicial review. *Arizona Public Service Co. v. Environmental Protection Agency*, 211 F.3d 1280 (D.C. Cir. 2000).

NOTES AND QUESTIONS

1. **Dispersion "Controls."** One way to clean the ambient air is to disperse air pollutants over a greater area. Dispersal of this sort can be accomplished by building extremely tall smokestacks. Pollutants released at higher elevations typically spread out and travel farther before settling to the ground and, therefore, tend to contribute less heavily to local pollution loadings. Is dilution the solution to pollution? *See* CAA § 123, 42 U.S.C. § 7423.

2. **Intermittent Controls.** Another way to clean ambient air is by using intermittent controls. Intermittent controls reduce air pollution concentrations by restricting emissions during times when pollution levels are high, and allowing more loading during times when air quality is better. Such intermittent controls are most easily accomplished by switching to less polluting fuels during bad times, and to other fuels in good times. Are these methods of pollution control consonant with the Clean Air Act? *See, e.g., Kennecott Copper v. Train*, 526 F.2d 1149 (9th Cir. 1975). *See also* § 123, 42 U.S.C. § 7423.

3. **Federal Facilities.** Using SIPs, can states regulate air emissions from federally owned and operated facilities? *See* CAA § 118, 42 U.S.C. § 7418.

2. New Source Performance Standards

a. Applicability

We have now reviewed the regulatory centerpiece of the Clean Air Act, the control of criteria pollutants by health-based NAAQSs, themselves primarily implemented through emissions limitations set forth in SIPs. We now turn to the second pollution control mechanism established in the 1970 Clean Air Act Amendments. Entitled "New Source Performance Standards" and found at § 111, 42 U.S.C. § 7411, the provision (as revised in some particulars in 1990) establishes performance requirements primarily for "new" sources. To understand how § 111 does this, it is best to begin by looking at the statutory text. As you do so, be sure to resolve the following questions: (a) to which entities and facilities does § 111 apply? (b) what are "new sources"? and (c) does § 111 apply to existing as well as new sources, and if so, how?

POTOMAC ELECTRIC POWER CO. v. U.S. ENVIRONMENTAL PROTECTION AGENCY
650 F.2d 509 (4th Cir. 1981)

PHILLIPS, CIRCUIT JUDGE:

The Potomac Electric Power Company (PEPCO) has petitioned this court, pursuant to § 307(b)(1) of the Clean Air Act, 42 U.S.C. § 7607(b)(1), for review of a decision of the Environmental Protection Agency (EPA), through one of its regional administrators, finding that the boiler at PEPCO's Chalk Point Unit #4 electric generating station is subject to the new source performance standard (NSPS), *see* 40 C.F.R. § 60.40 et seq., promulgated by the EPA for fossil fuel-fired steam generating units under the Clean Air Act, 42 U.S.C. § 7401 et seq. The regional administrator's decision was based on his determination that PEPCO had not "commenced construction" of the Chalk Point Unit #4 boiler prior to EPA's publication of the relevant NSPS on August 17, 1971.

Two questions are presented by PEPCO's petition for review of the regional administrator's decision. First, is the EPA's interpretation of the regulations it has promulgated for determining whether an NSPS is to be applied to a particular facility "plainly erroneous"? Second, was the regional administrator's decision, on application of the EPA's regulations and interpretation of those regulations to the facts of this case, arbitrary, capricious or an abuse of discretion? Answering both questions in the negative, we affirm the decision of the regional administrator that PEPCO's Chalk Point Unit #4 must comply with the NSPS promulgated for fossil fuel- red steam generators. . . .

[The court began by denying PEPCO's request for an injunction. PEPCO argued EPA had wrongfully withheld action in denying PEPCO's NSPS exemption request. The court found PEPCO lacked clean hands]:

. . . [E]ven if this court were to recognize PEPCO's potential right to relief, we believe PEPCO would be estopped from asserting any prejudice resulting from the EPA's delay in acting on its request for an NSPS exemption by its own lengthy delay in requesting that exemption. Although PEPCO began construction on its Chalk Point Unit #4 facility in late 1971, it did not ask for a ruling on the applicability of the NSPS to that facility, which PEPCO admittedly had the burden of requesting, 40 C.F.R. § 60.5(a), until 1977. PEPCO suggests that it only discovered the possibility of the NSPS' applicability to this facility two months prior to its request for a ruling. In view of the fact that several other utilities had long before requested rulings in this precise matter, we think that this major utility must be charged with at least constructive notice at a much earlier time, saving any question of actual notice.

I

Because the decision of the EPA concerning the applicability of an NSPS to a particular facility turns largely upon the facts of each case, a brief review of the facts underlying PEPCO's present petition for review is essential for an understanding of our disposition of this appeal. Chalk Point Units #3 and #4 are two of the four electric generating facilities that collectively comprise PEPCO's Chalk Point Generating Station south of Aguasco, Maryland. At the core of each unit is an oil-red boiler designed to generate steam to power a turbine that produces electricity. The two units share several ancillary facilities, including a common water treatment system, fuel oil tank farm and control room, and a single building houses the boilers and turbines for both units. Units #3 and #4 were planned in the late 1960s as a single procurement and were to be placed in service "back to back" in 1974 and 1975. A sudden and unprecedented decline in electricity use following the Arab Oil Embargo of 1973, however, caused construction of both units to be slowed after their commencement. Unit #3 was placed in service in 1975; Unit #4 is scheduled to go into operation in the fall of 1981.

The information that PEPCO later submitted to the EPA indicates that negotiations for the construction of Unit #4 were commenced in 1970 and that PEPCO was dealing primarily with General Electric (GE), United Engineers & Constructors (UE&C) and Combustion Engineering (CE). PEPCO's negotiations with GE were for the main turbine-generator and boiler feed pump turbines. On March 12, 1971, PEPCO awarded the order to GE subject to the final approval of PEPCO's board of directors and mutually agreeable contract terms. On March 25, 1971, GE confirmed the order but stipulated that PEPCO could cancel the order without charge up to the earlier of the 30-month period prior to shipment or the release of the units for engineering and manufacturing. On June 30, 1971, PEPCO notified GE of approval of the order by its board of directors. On August 2, 1971, the units were released by GE for design and manufacture. A formal contract for the units, however, was not signed until April 23, 1973.

PEPCO's negotiations with UE&C were for engineering and construction services at the Chalk Point site. The contract for these services was signed on November 12, 1974 but had an "effective date" of April 12, 1971. This contract covered services for both Units #3 and #4. Prior to August 17, 1971, UE&C had developed drawings that indicated the planned construction of Unit #4. Site preparation for Unit #4, however, did not begin until late 1971.

PEPCO's negotiations with CE were for fabrication of the boiler to be used in Unit #4. On August 17, 1970,PEPCO received a price quotation from CE on a boiler unit for an undetermined facility; that boiler was eventually used in Unit #4. A CE "Parts Shipment Forecast" dated February 18, 1971 listed this unit for initial parts shipment during the first quarter of 1973. The unit was listed as a "Forecast Unit" that was identified by an internal control number as contrasted to listing as a "Booked Unit" identified by a domestic contract number.

On March 11, 1971, CE stated in a letter to PEPCO that it had committed space in its production schedule for the Unit #4 boiler pending a final decision by PEPCO. Also included in the letter were a price quotation and a projected delivery date. On July 12, 1971, PEPCO sent a letter to CE stating that "we are now considering a design for proposed Chalk Point No. 4." This letter concluded with the statement that, "[s]ubject to a mutually satisfactory contract, it is our intent to award the No. 4 boiler unit to you." This letter also referred to a meeting between PEPCO and CE to be held on August 3, 1971 to review a design proposal for Unit #4.

Although a CE engineering and production team began to design the Unit #4 boiler after CE's August 3meeting with PEPCO, no subcontracts were let or materials acquired prior to August 17, 1971. On October 26, 1971, CE prepared a "Contract Abstract" for Unit #4 that included descriptions of the major boiler components, the total price, shipping and payment conditions, and an "award date" of July 12, 1971.

A formal contract for the Unit #4 boiler was not executed until April 18, 1973, at which time fabrication of the boiler was 75% complete. Affidavits later sworn to by PEPCO's Vice President for Nuclear Engineering and Environmental Affairs and CE's principal representative in the boiler negotiations, however, indicate that the parties felt that they had a binding agreement based on PEPCO's letter of July 12, 1971.

Construction of Chalk Point Unit #4, although slowed or "deferred" as a result of the 1973 oil embargo, has continued substantially uninterrupted to the present day. It was not until May 20, 1977, however, that PEPCO, pursuant to 40 C.F.R. § 60.5(a), requested a ruling from the EPA on whether Unit #4 would be subject to the NSPS for fossil fuel-fired steam generating units published by the EPA on August 17, 1971. Appended to this request were 156 pages of pertinent documents.

Fifteen months after receiving PEPCO's request, EPA communicated its first response to PEPCO a request for further information. This request, dated August 17, 1978, stated that the EPA had "preliminarily determined" that Unit #4 was subject to the 1971 NSPS for steam electric plants but requested additional information to determine the "exact status" of the unit. The reasons given for the EPA's preliminary determination were that construction of Unit #4 had been neither continuous nor of reasonable length, as required by 40 C.F.R. § 60.2(i). PEPCO supplied the requested information and urged that the EPA make its decision "just as quickly as possible."

At a meeting requested by PEPCO that took place on July 3, 1979, the EPA informed PEPCO for the first time that its ruling would turn on the question whether a "contractual obligation" to construct the Unit #4 boiler existed before August 17, 1971. Following PEPCO's compliance with two more EPA requests for information, the EPA staff briefed the regional administrator in October 1979 and again in March 1980. His final ruling on PEPCO's Chalk Point Unit #4 request was published on March 27, 1980. 45 Fed. Reg. 20,155 (1980). In this ruling the regional administrator determined that, because PEPCO had not entered into a "contractual obligation" on the Unit #4 boiler — the "affected facility" in the present case — PEPCO had not "commenced construction" at its Chalk Point Unit #4 prior to the EPA's publication of the NSPS for steam electric plants on August 17, 1971. He therefore concluded that the NSPS for steam electric plants was applicable to Unit #4.

II

Before addressing the specific issues raised by this appeal, a brief discussion of the regulatory scheme out of which they arise is essential. Section 111 of the Clean Air Act, 42 U.S.C. § 7411, requires that the EPA promulgate new source performance standards (NSPS), reflecting the best demonstrated pollution control technology, for application to any new stationary source, "the construction or modi cation of which is commenced after the publication of [the NSPS] applicable to such source." The only statutory guidance that the EPA is given in promulgating the NSPS, however, is the definition of "stationary source" in § 111(a)(3) of the Clean Air Act, 42U.S.C. § 7411(a)(3), as "any building, structure, facility, or installation which emits or may emit any air pollutant."

Based on this loosely defined statutory authorization, the EPA has promulgated a detailed regulatory scheme establishing and implementing the NSPS. *See* 40 C.F.R. Part 60. Included in this regulatory scheme is a subpart dealing with the procedural applications of the NSPS that are established in other subparts, see id. Subpart A, which is applicable "to the owner or operator of any stationary source which contains an affected facility, the construction or modification of which is commenced after the date of publication in this part of any standard applicable to that facility." *Id.* § 60.1. The term "affected facility" is defined as "any apparatus to which a standard is applicable." *Id.* § 60.2(e). The word "construction" is defined as the "fabrication, erection, or installation of an affected facility." *Id.* § 60.2(g). The word "commenced" is defined to require a showing "that an owner or operator has entered into a contractual obligation to undertake and complete, within a reasonable time, a continuous program of construction or modification." *Id.* § 60.2(I).[2]

Based on its interpretation of the regulations it has promulgated pursuant to the authorization of § 111 of the Clean Air Act, 42 U.S.C. § 7411, the EPA has contended that PEPCO's Chalk Point Unit #4 is subject to the NSPS for steam electric plants because PEPCO was unable to establish that, prior to the EPA's publication of the applicable NSPS on August 17, 1971, it had entered into a "contractual obligation"

---

[2] [Ed. note: The full definition of "commenced" in EPA's regulations is "that an owner or operator has undertaken a continuous program of construction or modifi cation or that an owner or operator has entered into a contractual obligation to undertake and complete, within a reasonable time, a continuous program of construction or modifi cation." 40 C.F.R. § 60.2.]

for "construction" of its Unit #4 boiler — which the EPA contends is the "affected facility" — so that PEPCO could not cancel that obligation without incurring "significant liability," either because an agreed upon cancellation fee had come into operation or because the manufacturer of the facility had made expenditures in reliance upon an agreement for construction of the facility. PEPCO, on the other hand, has contended that, under well-settled principles of contract law, it had entered into a "contractual obligation" for the construction of Chalk Point Unit #4 generating station, based either on its contract with UE&C to construct the entire Unit #4 generating station — which PEPCO contends is the "affected facility" — or on its contract with CE to construct the boiler that is to be used in that generating station.

We note at the outset that some of PEPCO's contentions may be read as challenging not only the EPA's interpretation of its regulations but also the regulations themselves. To the extent that the regulations themselves are challenged, the challenge is untimely and in the wrong court; section 307(b) of the Clean Air Act, 42 U.S.C. § 7607(b), requires that challenges to EPA regulations of nationwide applicability be brought within 60days of promulgation in the United States Court of Appeals for the District of Columbia Circuit. Since the procedural regulations governing application of the NSPS that are now under consideration were promulgated by the EPA on December 23, 1971, *see* 36 Fed. Reg. 24,876 (1971), any challenge to those regulations could only have been brought in the District of Columbia Circuit on or before February 23, 1972. This court therefore has jurisdiction to review only the EPA's interpretation of those regulations, and the scope of that review is limited to whether the EPA's interpretation is plainly erroneous. *See Udall v. Tallman*, 380 U.S. 1, 16 17 (1965); *Talley v. Mathews*, 550 F.2d 911, 919 (4th Cir. 1977).

A.

With respect to whether a "contractual obligation" was entered into for Unit #4 prior to publication of the applicable NSPS, PEPCO has argued persuasively that it had entered binding contracts with UE&C and CE prior to August 17, 1971 or, at the very least, it was liable to those companies on a theory of promissory estoppel. However, while principles of contract law undoubtedly would have been reasonable standards by which to determine the existence of a "contractual obligation" for purposes of 40 C.F.R. § 60.2(i), the fact remains that contract law principles are not the standards that were chosen by the EPA for that purpose. Therefore, we must restrict our analysis in the present case to whether the "significant liability" test contended for by EPA is a plainly erroneous interpretation of "contractual obligation."

The EPA has presented two cogent policy reasons for the use of its "significant liability" standard. The first policy argument is based on the congressional goal in § 111 of the Clean Air Act, 42 U.S.C. § 7401, of ensuring the best demonstrated system of pollution control in new sources of air pollution without requiring costly retrofitting of existing sources of pollution. *See* H.R. Rep. No. 95-294, 95th Cong., 1st Sess. 184 86 (1977). The EPA interpretation of "contractual obligation" effectuates this goal by requiring a commitment to construction of a polluting facility that cannot be entered into simply for purposes of avoiding the NSPS requirements while leaving the polluting company the option of cancelling or postponing the commitment with the incursion of little or no liability. Stated another way, the EPA's interpretation effectively requires the incorporation of new pollution control technology by all those who can do so without incurring "significant liability" as a result of the cancellation of a previous commitment.

The second policy reason asserted by EPA is essentially one of administrative convenience. The requirement of significant liability, based on either a cancellation fee or expenditures made in reliance on a construction contract by the contractor for a polluting facility, provides bright-line documentation by which the EPA may quickly and easily determine whether an applicant for exemption from NSPS has incurred a "contractual obligation" meriting that exemption. This interpretation thus avoids the often convoluted application of contract principles to masses of business correspondence that would be the result under PEPCO's interpretation.

Support for this argument is amply supplied by PEPCO's contention in the present case that it is "common practice" in the utility industry for a utility to use a "letter of intent" to signify the award of a "binding contract" to a contractor for the construction of an electric generating facility and that PEPCO's "award letter" of July 12, 1971 to CE was such a letter of intent. For the EPA to find a "contractual obligation" on the basis of this contention, however, would require the EPA to gather evidence of the purported usage of trade in the utility industry and to then determine whether the "award letter" of July 12, 1971, or possibly some other piece of documentation submitted by PEPCO, comported with this "common practice." When this type of inquiry is multiplied by the number of different industries in which the NSPS regulations must be applied, the EPA's argument of administrative convenience is transformed into one bordering on administrative necessity.

PEPCO has argued that these policy considerations should be rejected as post hoc reasoning. This argument, however, is undercut by the EPA's consistent determination in three earlier decisions that utilities that fail to meet the requirements of the "significant liability" test will not be exempted from NSPS. . . .

Based on the persuasive policy justifications presented by the EPA and that agency's consistent application of the "significant liability" standard, which has been upheld by other courts, we conclude that the EPA's requirement of "significant liability" to demonstrate a "contractual obligation" sufficient to exempt a pollution source from compliance with the relevant NSPS is not a plainly erroneous interpretation of 40 C.F.R. § 60.2(i).

B.

A similar analysis can be applied to the EPA's conclusion that a power plant's boiler is the "affected facility" for which a "contractual obligation" had to exist for exemption in the present case. PEPCO contends that this interpretation is unreasonable and that the only reasonable interpretation is that "affected facility" refers to an entire electric generating facility and not just its boiler. The EPA's interpretation, however, is supported by a number of considerations.

First, EPA's interpretation comports with a tracing of the relevant regulations.

"Affected facility" is equated in 40 C.F.R. § 60.2(e) with "any apparatus to which a standard is applicable." With respect to a steam electric plant, the "affected facility" to which the NSPS is applicable is "each fossil fuel-fired steam electric generating unit." *Id.* 60.40(a)(1). "Fossil fuel-fired steam generating unit" is in turn defined as a "furnace or boiler." *Id.* § 60.41(a).Thus, the definition of "affected facility" as a "boiler" seems compelled by a reading of the pertinent regulations. . . .

. . . [P]erhaps most persuasively, the EPA's requirement for exemption of a "contractual obligation" for construction of the "boiler" as the "affected facility" is supported by common sense. PEPCO contends that the EPA can base its exemption determination only on construction of a "functional entity" and that, therefore, the EPA should find an exemption if there was a "contractual obligation" for any portion of PEPCO's Chalk Point Unit #4, including its turbine generator and the equipment and buildings it shares with Unit #3, that is essential to its ultimate operation as a power plant. Such a construction, however, would create a means of avoidance of the NSPS that we do not believe Congress possibly could have intended. Through the simple expedient of planning generating units in tandem and providing for their use of some common equipment or facilities — a practice that utility companies seem to follow often — a utility could obtain exemption of both units from the NSPS even though it actually "commenced construction" of only one unit prior to publication of the relevant NSPS and the best demonstrated technology could be incorporated into the second unit at little or no retrofitting cost. Such a two-for-one exemption is obviously absurd, but it is the logical result of PEPCO's interpretation of the unit for which a "contractual obligation" must be incurred in order to qualify for an exemption.

We therefore conclude that it is not plainly erroneous for the EPA, in making its exemption determination, to focus on a power plant's boiler as the "affected facility" for which a "contractual obligation" had to exist prior to publication of the relevant NSPS.

C.

[In this section of the opinion, the court commented on the relevance of § 111 to "construction" of equipment in place to support an "affected facility." The court held that construction of support facilities essential to the erection and installation of the affected facility is "construction" for purposes of the section. The opinion concluded with a discussion of whether the EPA's refusal to exempt PEPCO from § 111 applicability was arbitrary, capricious, or an abuse of discretion. The court upheld EPA's action.]

Affirmed As Modified.

NOTE

Modifications. Observe that the standards of § 111 apply not only to new sources but to existing sources that have been modified. *See* § 111(a)(2), 42 U.S.C. § 7411(a)(2) (defining "new source" to include "any stationary source, the construction or *modification* of which is commenced after the publication of regulations." (emphasis added)); *see also* § 111(a)(4), 42 U.S.C. § 7411(a)(4) (defining "modification"). As you might expect, there has been substantial litigation about what changes in a source constitute "modification" so to bring the source under § 111. Our discussion of this critical issue is postponed until coverage of the Prevention of Significant Deterioration program, *infra*.

NOTE ON ADMINISTRATIVE LAW #3[3]

In the second Note on Administrative Law, we discussed how courts review agency actions. The Note concluded with a discussion of *Chevron, supra,* wherein the Supreme Court established the "*Chevron* Two Step" review standard. That standard, the reader will recall, governs how courts should pass on the propriety of agency interpretations of the statutes they administer. Of the two steps in *Chevron,* Step Two is clearly the more important, and not just for the controversy it engenders. It is more important because it applies when statutes are ambiguous, and the vast majority of statutes are ambiguous.

Notably, in *PEPCO,* the court was not reviewing an agency's interpretation of the meaning of a statute the agency administered. Rather, the court in *PEPCO* was called upon to assess the propriety of the agency's interpretation of its own regulation. (The statute in *PEPCO* spoke of "construction" being "commenced," the regulation in turn defined "commenced" as occurring when parties enter into a "contractual obligation," and, last, the agency interpreted "contractual obligation" as arising when parties incur "significant liability.") The question: how should courts review the propriety of an agency's interpretation of the meaning of its own regulation?

The law in this circumstance is not entirely settled. Some courts have used the *Chevron* Two Step standard on the theory that the same principles that control judicial review of an agency's interpretation of a statute ought to control review of an agency's interpretation of a regulation. Other courts, though, have accorded even greater deference, on the theory that agencies should know, better than anyone else, what a regulation actually means. Why? Because the agency wrote the regulation.

On this theory, an agency's interpretation of its own regulation "becomes of controlling weight unless it is plainly erroneous or inconsistent with the regulation." This standard of review is often referred to as *Seminole Rock* deference, after the case in which the standard was originally announced, or *Auer* deference, after a later case affirming the same principle. *Bowles v. Seminole Rock & Sand Co.,* 325 U.S. 410, 414, 65 S. Ct. 1215 (1945); *Auer v. Robbins,* 519 U.S. 452, 461 63, 117 S. Ct. 905 (1997).

---

[3] This is the third of four "Notes on Administrative Law" that appear at various points in this book. The material is inserted to assist students who have not learned administrative law. If you have already taken a course in this subject area, or have learned administrative law by some other mechanism, you should feel free to skip this Note. If you have not done so, however, you should both read this Note and resolve to master this important subject area at some future time.

b. Operation

Once issues of applicability are resolved, issues of operation arise. How does § 111 affect new sources? In particular, who must fashion emission standards under this section and upon what basis? How does this process compare with that of §§ 107–110 of the Act?

LIGNITE ENERGY COUNCIL v. U.S. ENVIRONMENTAL PROTECTION AGENCY
198 F.3d 930 (D.C. Cir. 1999)

JUDGES: Before: EDWARDS, CHIEF JUDGE, SILBERMAN AND HENDERSON, CIRCUIT JUDGES.

OPINION: PER CURIAM:

Petitioners challenge EPA's new source performance standards for nitrogen oxides emissions from utility and industrial boilers. We conclude that EPA did not exceed its discretion under section 111 of the Clean Air Act in promulgating these standards, and therefore deny the petitions.

Fossil-fuel fired steam generating units ("boilers") emit nitrogen oxides (NOx), air pollutants that can cause deleterious health effects and contribute to the formation of acid rain. Section 111 of the Clean Air Act requires EPA to establish performance standards for the emission of NOx from newly constructed boilers; these "new source performance standards" are to be set at a level that reflects the degree of emission limitation achievable through the application of the best system of emission reduction which (taking into account the cost of achieving such reduction and any nonair quality health and environmental impact and energy requirements) the Administrator determines has been adequately demonstrated. 42 U.S.C. § 7411(a)(1). In its 1990 Clean Air Act Amendments Congress specifically directed EPA to exercise its section 111 authority and establish new Nox standards that incorporate "improvements in methods for the reduction of emissions of oxides of nitrogen." 42U.S.C. § 7651f(c)(1).

In response to these statutory mandates, EPA promulgated a rule lowering its NOx new source performance standards to.15 lb/MMBtu (pounds of NOx emitted per million BTU burned) for utility boilers and.20 lb/MMBtu for industrial boilers. *See* 63 Fed. Reg. 49,442, 49,443 (1998) (to be codified at 40 C.F.R. pt. 60). These standards reflect the level of NOx emissions achievable by what EPA considers to be the "best demonstrated system" of emissions reduction: the use of selective catalytic reduction (SCR) in combination with combustion control technologies. Petitioners' central claim is that EPA selected SCR as the basis for its NOx standards without properly balancing the factors that section 111 requires it to "take into account." Because section 111 does not set forth the weight that be should assigned to each of these factors, we have granted the agency a great degree of discretion in balancing them, *see, e.g.*, *New York v. Reilly*, 969 F.2d 1147, 1150, 297 U.S. App. D.C. 147 (D.C. Cir. 1992); EPA's choice will be sustained unless the environmental or economic costs of using the technology are exorbitant. *See*

National Asphalt Pavement Ass'n v. Train, 539 F.2d 775, 786, 176 U.S. App. D.C. 296 (D.C. Cir. 1976).

Petitioners argue that SCR is not the "best demonstrated system" under section 111 because the incremental cost of reducing NOx emissions is considerably higher with SCR than with combustion controls. Recent improvements in combustion controls will enable many boilers to attain emissions levels close to EPA's SCR-based standards; accordingly, petitioners assert that EPA should have based its standards on these less expensive technologies. However, in light of EPA's unchallenged findings showing that the new standards will only modestly increase the cost of producing electricity in newly constructed boilers, *see* 62 Fed. Reg. 36,948,36,958 (1997) (proposed NOx revisions), we do not think that EPA exceeded its considerable discretion under section 111. Moreover, petitioners' argument stressing the comparable environmental merits of advanced combustion controls is to a certain extent self-defeating, since the new source performance standards set by EPA are not technology-forcing, and continuing advances in combustion control technologies will reduce the amount of NOx reduction that must be captured by the more expensive SCR technology.

It was also within EPA's discretion to issue uniform standards for all utility boilers, rather than adhering to its past practice of setting a range of standards based on boiler and fuel type. *See, e.g.*, 44 Fed. Reg. 33,580 (1979) (establishing varying NOx emissions standards for utility boilers). Petitioners recognize that EPA is not required by law to subcategorize — section 111 merely states that "the Administrator may distinguish among classes, types, and sizes within categories of new sources," 42 U.S.C. § 7411(b)(2) (emphasis added) — but argue that it was arbitrary and capricious for EPA to decline to do so. EPA explains that its change to uniform standards is justified by SCR's performance characteristics: Unlike the technologies on which past new source performance standards were based, flue gas treatment technologies like SCR limit NOx emissions after combustion, and the effectiveness of SCR is thus far less dependent upon boiler design or fuel type. Petitioners respond that there are reasons to expect SCR to perform less adequately on boilers burning high-sulfur coals, but EPA collected continuous emissions monitoring data on two high-sulfur coal-fired utility boilers that showed that the.15lb/MMBtu standard was achievable, and supplemented this study with similar evidence from foreign utility boilers. EPA also considered petitioners' concerns about the impact of alkaline metals on the performance of the catalyst used in the SCR process, and concluded that such "catalyst poisoning" is not a significant problem in coal-fired boilers. *See* 63 Fed. Reg. at 49,445. Mindful of the high degree of deference we must show to EPA's scientific judgment, *see, e.g.*, *Appalachian Power Co. v. EPA*, 135 F.3d 791, 801-02, 328 U.S. App. D.C. 379 (D.C. Cir. 1998), we accept these determinations and sustain EPA's uniform standard for utility boilers.

Petitioners offer a broader challenge to EPA's.20 lb/ MMBtu standard for industrial boilers, claiming that SCR is not "adequately demonstrated" for any coal-fired industrial boilers. EPA was unable to collect emissions data for the application of SCR to these boilers, but this absence of data is not surprising for a new technology like SCR, nor does it in and of itself defeat EPA's standard. Because it applies only to new sources, we have recognized that section 111 "looks toward what may fairly be projected for the regulated future, rather than the state of the art at present." *Portland Cement Ass'n v. Ruckelshaus*, 486 F.2d 375, 391, 158 U.S. App. D.C. 308(D.C. Cir. 1973). Of course, where data are unavailable, EPA may not base its determination that a technology is adequately demonstrated or that a standard is achievable on mere speculation or conjecture, *see, e.g., National Asphalt Pavement Ass'n*, 539 F.2d at 787, but EPA may compensate for a shortage of data through the use of other qualitative methods, including the reasonable extrapolation of a technology's performance in other industries. *See, e.g., Weyerhaeuser Co. v. Costle*, 590 F.2d 1011, 1054, 191 U.S. App. D.C. 309 n.70 (D.C. Cir.1978).

EPA has done precisely that here, concluding from its study of utility boilers that SCR is "adequately demonstrated" and the.20 lb/MMBtu standard is "achievable" for coal-fired industrial boilers as well. Utility and industrial boilers are similar in design and both categories of boilers can attain similar levels of NOx emissions reduction through combustion controls, which means that SCR will be required to capture comparable quantities of NOx for both boiler types. While petitioners argue that SCR is less likely to be effective on industrial boilers because they have widely fluctuating load cycles, EPA has shown that SCR can be successfully applied to coal-fired utility boilers under a "wide range of operating conditions" including those analogous to the load cycles of industrial boilers. 63 Fed. Reg. at 49,444. We think that it was reasonable for EPA to extrapolate from its studies of utility boilers in setting an SCR-based new source performance standard for coal-fired industrial boilers.

We also sustain EPA's application of the.20 lb/MMBtu standard to combination boilers, which simultaneously combust a mixture of fuels. The preexisting NOx emissions standards established a range of values for combustion boilers that varied by fuel type: while combination boilers burning natural gas with non-coal solid fuels (e.g., wood) were subject to a.30 lb/MMBtu standard, the performance standards for combination boilers combusting coal with oil or natural gas were determined based upon the proportion of the boiler's total heat input provided by each fuel. *See* 51 Fed. Reg. 42,768, 42,790 (1986). It is difficult to understand petitioners' objection to the application of the industrial boiler standard to boilers burning natural gas and wood. A reduction of that standard from.30 to.20 lb/MMBtu is perfectly reasonable in light of the significant advances in Nox emissions technology since 1986; indeed, EPA studies show that wood-red boilers can reach emissions levels far lower than.20 lb/MMBtu through the application of flue gas treatment technologies. And our conclusion that the.20 lb/MMBtu standard is achievable for boilers burning only coal necessarily defeats petitioners' objection that the industrial boiler standard is unreasonable as applied to combination boilers burning coal simultaneously with other fuels with lower NOx emissions characteristics.

Petitioners' final objection is to EPA's valuation of steam energy produced by "cogeneration facilities." EPA's adoption of an output-based standard for utility boilers raised the question of how to calculate the energy produced by these units, which generate thermal steam energy in addition to electrical energy. Steam energy produced by cogeneration facilities is exported for several different industrial uses; however, because of inefficiencies in transporting and converting steam, only a fraction of steam energy produced by cogeneration facilities is actually used in the industrial process. EPA resolved this problem by assigning a 50% credit for steam energy when determining a cogeneration unit's output. *See* 63 Fed. Reg. at 49,447. Petitioners describe this credit as an arbitrary and capricious "discounting" of steam energy's value, but it just as easily could be called a subsidy: The maximum efficiency for the conversion of steam to electrical energy is only 38%, and EPA's final rule justifies the 50% credit on the ground that it will encourage cogeneration. *Id.* In light of the difficulties that would attend calculating the useful energy of steam heat produced by cogeneration facilities on a unit-by-unit basis, we conclude that EPA's resolution of this issue was acceptable.

The petitions for review are denied.

So ordered.

NOTES AND QUESTIONS

1. ***Tech-based Regulation.*** Section 111 stipulates that new sources shall meet emission limitations reflecting "the degree of emission reduction achievable through the application of the best system of continuous emission reduction which (taking into consideration the cost of achieving such emissions reduction, any nonair quality health and environmental impact and energy requirements) the Administrator determines has been adequately demonstrated [for the category of sources subject to the limitation]." Section 111(a)(1), 42 U.S.C. § 7411(a)(1). For short, this standard has been referred as the "best demonstrated technology" or "BDT" standard, *New York v. Reilly*, 969 F.2d 1147 (D.C. Cir. 1992). BDT, it should be clear, is not a health-based standard like those governing establishment of NAAQSs. It is, rather, technology-based. You might give some thought to the use of "tech-based" standards generically. Are tech-based standards a better approach to pollution control than health-based standards? What are their advantages and disadvantages? If you were administering a pollution control program, would you prefer a tech-based or a health-based regulatory system?

2. ***Unintended Consequences.*** In the view of some observers, the NSPS program is proof of the adage, attributed to Fred Emery, that "regulation is the substitution of error for chance." The obvious goal underlying § 111 was to ensure that plants coming on line be state-of-the-art with respect to pollution controls. It was thought § 111 would usher in a shiny new generation of efficient and clean industrial facilities. But in significant measure, that has not happened. Instead, many industrial entities, in order to avoid the high costs of compliance with § 111 (and with other CAA programs such as Nonattainment and Prevention of Significant Deterioration — *see infra*), have chosen to string out the operating lives of their old, leaky plants.

3. Hazardous Air Pollutants

Commonly referred to as air toxics or toxic air pollutants, hazardous air pollutants are substances known or suspected to cause cancer or other serious adverse health effects. Air toxics are emitted from thousands of sources, including major stationary sources, mobile sources, and smaller "area sources," such as dry cleaners. Section 112 of the Clean Air Act, 42 U.S.C. § 7412, addresses hazardous air pollutants. As originally enacted in 1970, its purpose was to provide emission standards for pollutants "which in trace quantities in the ambient air contribute to a high risk of serious irreversible or incapacitating effects on health." Continuing Senate Debate on S. 4358, 93rd Cong. (1970) (statement of Senator Jennings Randolph, Chairman, Committee on Public Works). The provision defined a hazardous pollutant as any "air pollutant to which no ambient air quality standard is applicable and which in the judgment of the Administrator causes, or contributes to, air pollution which may be reasonably be anticipated to result in an increase in mortality or an increase in serious irreversible, or incapacitating reversible, illness." Section 112(a)(1), 42 U.S.C. § 7412(a)(1) (1982). It called upon EPA to designate a list of pollutants meeting the statutory definition, and to develop "national emission standards for hazardous air pollutants" ("NESHAPS") on a pollutant-by-pollutant basis. Congress directed that each such standard be set at a level assuring "an ample margin of safety to protect the public health." Section 112(b)(1)(B), 42 U.S.C. § 7412(b)(1)(B) (1982).

For two decades following § 112's enactment, EPA dragged its feet in implementing the provision. The reasons were several. One was EPA's belief that much of the hazardous air pollution problem would be solved by the new source performance standards of § 111.Another, more important, reason was § 112 itself. For one thing, Congress gave EPA little guidance on the meaning of "ample margin of safety." Thus the agency was forced to face the vexing problem of so-called "nonthreshold" pollutants. As distinguished from "threshold" pollutants, nonthreshold pollutants are those for which science has determined no safe minimal level of exposure. EPA reasoned that only a zero emissions standard for nonthreshold pollutants would satisfy § 112.[4]

Congress contemplated this severe standard because it thought the number of hazardous pollutants would be small. (By latest count, the number of hazardous pollutants designated for purposes of § 112 is 188. *See infra.*) Understandably, EPA was extremely hesitant to set air toxics standards certain to cause catastrophic effects in major sectors of the domestic economy. Simply put, it wanted to take costs into account.[5]

Industry agreed with that sentiment: one industry trade group, the Chemical Manufacturers Association, for example, characterized zero-emission standards as

---

[4] There was some legislative history supporting this result. Senator Edmund Muskie, for example, had characterized the health-based standard of § 112 as meaning "that a plant would be required to close because of the absence of control techniques. It could include emission standards which allowed for no measurable emissions." Summary of Conference Report presented to the U.S. Senate, *reprinted in* A Legislative History of the Clean Air Act of 1970, Ser. No. 93-18, 93d Cong. 2d. Sess., at 133 (1974).

[5] On some occasions it did precisely that. For the nonthreshold hazardous pollutant, asbestos, for example, EPA refused to establish a zero emissions standard, because, in its view, such a standard "would result in the prohibition of many activities which are extremely important; moreover, the available evidence relating the health hazards of asbestos does not suggest that such prohibition is necessary to protect public health." 38 Fed. Reg. 8820 (4/6/73). In the case of vinyl chloride, the agency hit the issue head-on, stating it did not believe Congress wanted the agency to close major industries. Accordingly, the agency set a NESHAP for vinyl chloride based on best available control technology, unless costs would be "grossly disproportionate" to benefits derived therefrom. 40 Fed. Reg. 59534 (Dec. 24, 1975).

arbitrary, unenforceable, and inequitable, as well as impossible to meet or measure.

In any event, by 1990, EPA had designated as hazardous air pollutants only eight substances. These were asbestos, benzene, beryllium, coke oven emissions, inorganic arsenic, mercury, radionuclides, and vinyl chloride. 40 C.F.R. § 61.01(a). (It had, however, considered others for potential listing. *See* 40 C.F.R. § 61.01(b).)

Due to § 112's unworkability and EPA's poor record of implementation, Congress rewrote the provision in the 1990 Clean Air Act Amendments. The new legislation was designed to lighten the agency's burdens, in part by setting aside the health-based regulatory approach in favor of a rigorous technology-based approach. We take up § 112 in its revised form later in the chapter.

C. THE 1977 AMENDMENTS

Congress understood as it engaged the enterprise of air pollution regulation that it was embarking on a grand experiment. It was obvious the Clean Air Act would work revolutionary changes in the way industry does business, would transform the way the public viewed the environment, and, most importantly, would demand an extensive national commitment by government, the scientific community, the regulated community, and the public at large. Therefore, Congress committed itself to review its handiwork five years hence, to see what had gone right or wrong. When the time came to do so, the august body was displeased with what it saw. In many places, especially in urban areas, air quality still remained unhealthful, and in some areas had even worsened. In addition, in another manifestation of the law of unintended consequences, the Act was having a deleterious effect on historically clean air basins. Some of these areas were being degraded down to the level of the ambient standards because industries, acting in their economic self-interest, were moving operations out of dirty air areas into clean air areas. In not insignificant measure, pollution was being diffused rather than removed, a phenomenon known as the "greying of America."

Congress, still imbued with a sense of mission but mindful of weakness in the domestic economy at the time, moved to correct these problems. After a couple of years of wrangling and debate, the result was the 1977 Amendments. The 1977 Amendments added two major parts to the statute. Part D, entitled "Nonattainment," was installed for the purpose of cleaning "nonattainment areas," those air basins not in compliance with NAAQSs. Part C, entitled "Prevention of Significant Deterioration" ("PSD"), was installed for the purpose of arresting the deterioration of air basins having air quality already in compliance with, or better than, the NAAQSs. These new Parts, as we shall see, have changed the structure and reality of air quality regulation, most significantly by affixing rigorous emissions controls on major new sources. For that reason, regulatory efforts under both Parts C and D are referred to collectively as "new source review" ("NSR") (even though the provisions of these Parts apply to major *modified* sources as well). NSR has been the major regulatory focus under the Clean Air Act since its inception in 1977, and there is every indication it will remain EPA's main emphasis. We look at each of these statutory subparts in the next sections.

1. Nonattainment

Sections 171–179B, 42 U.S.C. §§ 7501–09B, of the Act are the major operative provisions governing the nonattainment program. A very careful reading of these provisions is in order, for it is the only way to appreciate the complexity and the mechanics of this program. As you examine the new provisions, you will come to understand how significant the new legislation really was. The amendments largely recast the focus of the federal air pollution control effort. First, with NSR, the regulatory emphasis shifted to "major" polluters. The brunt of air pollution control was made to fall on these entities because of Congress's belief that large polluters cause the most damage to air resources and are financially best able to clean up emissions.

Second, the amendments represented a significant movement toward tech-based controls.

The amendments also altered the relationship between the federal government and the states. Since the amendments became law, states have enjoyed less of a free hand in determining the contents of their SIPs. If the 1970 Act "took a stick to the states," the 1977 amendments took a two-by-four.

The first task under Part D is to determine which areas are nonattainment for a criteria pollutant. Assuming an area is designated as a nonattainment area, the second task is to determine its appropriate classification within the nonattainment regulatory regime (a determination made necessary by the 1990 amendments; *see* Part D [1], *infra*). After that, the states must submit to EPA revised SIPs that demonstrate how the host of new emission restrictions that come with nonattainment designation will be implemented.

Once EPA has approved the SIPs, the often difficult task of administering the program begins.

IN THE MATTER OF NJPDES PERMIT NO. NJ 0055247
216 N.J. Super. 1; 522 A.2d 1002 (N.J. Super. Ct. 1987)

JUDGES: PRESSLER, BAIME AND ASHBEY.

BAIME, J:

These are consolidated appeals by the Ironbound Committee Against Toxic Waste and seven named individuals from the issuance of four permits by the Department of Environmental Protection (DEP) authorizing respondent American Ref-Fuel Company (Ref-Fuel) to construct a resource recovery facility in the City of Newark. Although appellants purport to appeal from the issuance of four permits, only two are actually challenged. More specifically, appellants attack the action of the DEP in issuing an Air Pollution Control Permit and a Solid Waste Permit. Our thorough review of appellants' brief reveals no specific challenge to the DEP's issuance of a NJPDES Permit or a Water Supply Allocation Permit.

Although ambiguously phrased, appellants advance one substantive and four procedural arguments in support of their claim that the permits were issued unlawfully. Substantively, appellants challenge the Air Pollution Control Permit on the basis that the emission limitation for particulate matter is not sufficiently stringent and that the applicable regulatory provisions obliged the DEP to require the use of more advanced anti-pollutant equipment. Procedurally, appellants argue that the DEP acted improperly by prematurely issuing the Solid Waste Permit. They claim that prior to issuance of the permit the DEP should have required Ref-Fuel to submit a full disclosure statement and background review check of all the company's principals. Appellants also assert that the permit was issued improperly because Ref-Fuel failed to designate a back-up residual land ll. They further contend that before issuing the permit the DEP was required to comply with the legislative directive set forth in *N.J.S.A.* 13:1E-168a(2) which mandates the promulgation of rules and regulations providing for state-of-the-art air emission technology for resource recovery facilities. Finally, appellants argue that the DEP improperly obtained and used technical information not available at the time of the public hearings thereby precluding meaningful comment and review by interested citizens and groups.

We have carefully reviewed the record and find no merit in any of the contentions advanced. We are thoroughly convinced that the DEP complied meticulously with all federal and state statutory and regulatory provisions. We are also entirely satisfied that the factual findings and conclusions reached by the DEP are amply supported by substantial evidence present in the record and that the agency did not act in an arbitrary or capricious manner. We affirm.

The salient facts are not in dispute and are essentially a matter of public record. In July 1979, the Essex County Board of Freeholders adopted a solid waste management plan which provided for the development of are source recovery facility. The plan was subsequently amended to reflect an agreement between the Essex County Division of Solid Waste Management and the Industrial Development Department of the Port Authority which, among other things, designated Blanchard Street in Newark as the site for the proposed facility. Both the original plan and the modi cations were approved by the DEP and Ref-Fuel was ultimately selected through the competitive bidding process to construct the facility.

On December 14, 1983, Ref-Fuel submitted to the Division of Waste Management a "solid waste facility application package" including a comprehensive engineering design and environmental impact statement. Following its review of the documents submitted, the Division issued draft permits for operation of the proposed facility and scheduled a public hearing. The DEP gave notice that public comments would be accepted between November 17, 1984 and January 18, 1985 and that a hearing would be conducted on December 17, 1984. The notice stated that the DEP would consider all comments presented and would issue responses to all significant issues raised. The notice also apprised the public of the locations where copies of the draft permits and supporting applications could be obtained. So too, the DEP promised to furnish additional information upon request.

We need not recount specifically what transpired at the public hearings. Suffice it to say, the hearings took place over the course of several days. Seventy individuals testified and approximately one thousand people attended.

After the conclusion of the hearings and the public comment period, the DEP forwarded all materials to three consultants it had retained for their review and response. Among the factors to be reviewed were the combustion system design especially with regard to dioxin emissions, risk assessments for selected air contaminants which the proposed facility would emit and the advantages and disadvantages of alternative air pollution control systems.

Following receipt of the reports submitted by the consultants, the DEP's hearing officer issued his final recommendations. The hearing officer's findings and conclusions are set forth in an extremely comprehensive report. The hearing officer recommended that the DEP approve the permits contingent upon Ref-Fuel's acceptance of several revisions, modi cations and additions. These changes included (1) increased monitoring of emission data and periodic transmission of such information to the DEP, (2) reduction of the "allowable emission concentration of particulate matter from 0.02 to 0.015 grains per dry standard cubic foot of stack gas and (3) reduction of the duration of the registration from ten to five years. These conditions were ultimately incorporated in the DEP's final permit approvals which became effective on December 30, 1985. These appeals followed.

I

We first address appellants' argument that the emission limitations set forth in the DEP's approval is not sufficiently stringent. Appellants contend that anti-pollutant equipment utilized in other states and municipalities has resulted in lower emission rates than that allowed by the permit issued by the DEP. Appellants assert that the DEP acted in an arbitrary and capricious manner in not requiring Ref-Fuel to employ advanced technology and in allowing a higher emission rate than that which can otherwise be achieved.

A brief description of the federal and state statutory and regulatory provisions is necessary for a full understanding of the issues presented. The federal Clean Air Act, 42 U.S.C. § 7401 *et seq.*, divides regions into attainment and nonattainment areas. 42 1 U.S.C. § 7407. Those areas with pollutant levels at or below national air quality standards as defined by the federal Act constitute "attainment areas." 42 U.S.C. § 7407. Those with pollutant levels above the maximum air quality standards are "nonattainment areas." 42 U.S.C. § 7407 and § 7501(2).

A facility which is located in an attainment area must employ an emission limitation which reflects the "best available control technology." (BACT). BACT is defined in the federal Act as:

> [a]n emission limitation based on the maximum degree of reduction of each pollutant . . . which the permitting authority, on a case-by-case basis, taking into account energy, environmental, and economic impacts and other costs, determines is achievable for such facility through application of production processes and available methods, systems, and techniques. . . . [42 U.S.C. § 7479(3)].

BACT does not require any particular engineering design. Rather, it mandates an achievable limitation taking into account certain factors enumerated in the regulations. Significantly, BACT involves a balancing of economic and technological considerations.

If, on the other hand, the facility is located in a nonattainment area, far more stringent standards are applied. Specifically, the applicant must use technology capable of achieving the "lowest available emission rate" (LAER).Under the Act, LAER is defined as:

[t]hat rate of emissions which reflects

(A) the most stringent emission limitation which is contained in the implementation [plan] of any State for such class or category of source, unless the owner or operator of the proposed source demonstrates that such limitations are not achievable, or

(B) the most stringent emission limitation which is achieved and practice by such class or category of source, which ever is more stringent. [42 U.S.C. § 7501(3)].

Obviously, LAER is a more stringent emissions limitation because it bars consideration of cost and other factors enumerated in the definition of BACT.

The federal Act contains one further refinement designed to insure effective regulation of emissions. When it adopted the federal Act, Congress conferred upon the states the primary authority for enforcing proper air quality in their respective geographic areas. 42 U.S.C. § 7407(a). If a state has a program that is essentially equivalent or more stringent than the federal regulatory scheme, it can seek authorization from the Environmental Protection Agency to administer its standards in lieu of its federal counterparts. New Jersey has received full authorization to apply its standards in both attainment and nonattainment areas. *See* 40 C.F.R. § 52.157; 46 *Fed. Reg.* 21996 (April 15, 1981); 48 *Fed. Reg.* 16738 (April 19, 1983).

Essex County is a nonattainment area for particulates and the entire state is a nonattainment area for ozone. Under New Jersey regulations, "[e]ach new or altered equipment and facility is controlled to the degree which represents the lowest available emission rate (LAER) for the relevant criteria pollutant." *N.J.A.C.* 7:27-18.2(c)(1). LAER is defined by the New Jersey regulation as:

the rate of emission from any equipment, facility, or control apparatus which incorporates advances in the art of air pollution control developed for the kind and amount of air contaminant emitted by the equipment or facility. For the purposes of this subject, advances in the art of air pollution control shall result in an emission limitation at least as stringent as:

(1) The most stringent emission limitation which is contained in the implementation plan of any state for such class or category of equipment or facility, unless the owner or operator of the proposed equipment or facility demonstrates that such limitations are not achievable; or

(2) The most stringent emission limitation which is achieved in practice by such class or category of equipment of facility; whichever is more stringent. In no event shall the application of this term permit proposed new or altered equipment or facilities to emit any pollutant in

excess of the amount allowable under applicable federal new source standards of performance. [*N.J.A.C.* 7:27-18.1].

In addition, New Jersey regulations impose a requirement that the equipment used "incorporates advances in the art of air pollution control developed for the kind and amount of air contaminant emitted by the applicant's equipment." *N.J.A.C.* 7:27-8.4(b).

It is against this statutory and regulatory backdrop that we consider appellants' contentions. Appellants argue that the permits issued by the DEP do not require the use of the best available control technology(BACT). As accepted by the DEP, the proposed facility's air pollution control technology would include oil- red burners, dry scrubbers and an electrostatic precipitator.[6] Appellants assert that the DEP should have required a fabric filter rather than an electrostatic precipitator.[7] They contend that a fabric filter is required by the BACT standard. Appellants also claim that the DEP's approval of 0.015 grains per dry standard cubic foot does not comport with LAER.

We reject these contentions. Initially, we note that appellants' citation of the BACT standard is clearly incorrect. As we have noted, Essex County is a nonattainment area for particulates and the entire state is a nonattainment area for ozone. Hence, BACT is inapplicable. Rather, it was incumbent upon the DEP to apply the LAER standard. Because New Jersey has been authorized to enforce its own program which, as we have observed, is more stringent than its federal counterpart, the DEP was required to apply the LAER standard set forth in *N.J.A.C.* 7:27-18.2(c)(1) and the "advances in the art" standard set forth in *N.J.A.C.* 7:27-8.4(b).

Based upon those standards, we are entirely satisfied that the findings and conclusions of the DEP are fully supported by substantial credible evidence present in the record. *Mayflower Securities v. Bureau of Securities*, 64 N.J. 85, 92 93 (1973); *Close v. Kordulak*, 44 N.J. 589, 599 (1965). We are equally convinced that the determinations of the DEP were not arbitrary or capricious. The fact that one of the consultants retained by the DEP reached a conclusion different from that ultimately adopted by the agency does not compel a different result. We are to review the action of the DEP, not that of the consultant. Where as here, the Legislature has entrusted an administrative agency with the responsibility of selecting the means of achieving an articulated statutory policy, the relation or nexus between the remedy and the goal sought to be accomplished is peculiarly a matter for administrative competence. *In re Marvin Gastman*, 147 *N.J. Super.* 101, 110 (App. Div.1977). It is a basic tenet of judicial review that the courts are not free to substitute their judgment for that of the administrative agency charged with the responsibility of executing a policy enunciated by the Legislature. *See Barry v. Arrow Pontiac, Inc.*, 100 *N.J.* 57, 70 71 (1985); *Bergen Pines Hosp. v. Dept. of Human Services*, 96 N.J. 456, 477 (1984); *Dougherty v. Human Services Dep't*, 91 *N.J.* 1, 12 (1982); *New*

---

[6] An electrostatic precipitator collects dust particles by drawing them to collection plates using a powerful electric field.

[7] A fabric filter, also known as a bag house, separates particles by either gravity settling, direct sieving, impingement, diffusion and/or electrostatic attraction.

Jersey Guild of Hearing Aid Dispensers v. Long, 75 *N.J.* 544,561 (1978). In sum, we are fully convinced that the DEP's resolution of the issues presented was entirely reasonable and that its findings and conclusions are amply supported by the record.

[Parts II through V of the opinion, which deal with ancillary issues, are omitted.]

VI

Our thorough review of the record in light of the arguments advanced by appellants convinces us that the permits were properly granted. Accordingly, the action of the DEP in issuing all four permits is affirmed in all respects.

NORTH BATON ROUGE ENVIRONMENTAL ASSOCIATION ET AL. v. LOUISIANA DEPARTMENT OF ENVIRONMENTAL QUALITY
805 So. 2d 255 (La. Ct. App. 2001)

JUDGES: FOIL AND PETTIGREW, JJ., AND KLINE, J. Pro Tem.

PETTIGREW, J:

North Baton Rouge Environmental Association ("NBREA") and the Louisiana Environmental Action Network("LEAN") sought judicial review of a decision by the Louisiana Department of Environmental Quality ("DEQ")that granted a permit to Exxon Chemical Americas ("Exxon") for the construction of a new polypropylene plant adjacent to its existing facility in East Baton Rouge Parish. The Nineteenth Judicial District Court upheld the permit grant and NBREA and LEAN appealed to this court.

We affirm.

FACTS

On December 23, 1997, Paxon Polymer Company (subsequently acquired by Exxon) submitted to DEQ an application for a Part 70 Operating Permit for the construction and operation of a new polypropylene production unit adjacent to its existing Baton Rouge Polyolefins Plant ("BRPO"). Polypropylene is a non-hazardous food-grade plastic material used in the manufacture of many commonly used household products. The plant is located in East Baton Rouge Parish, which, for the past several years, has been designated part of a five-parish non-attainment area for ozone pollution.

Non-attainment status signifies that an area has failed to meet the National Ambient Air Quality Standard for specific pollutants. For this reason, facilities in the area have undertaken mandatory and voluntary changes aimed at reducing the proportion of ozone that is related to industrial activities. In return, the participating facilities receive economic benefits and security for future business operations.

To accommodate industrial growth in non-attainment areas, state and federal agencies responsible for controlling ozone have developed incentive-based regulations aimed at reducing the proportion of ozone emissions related to industrial activities. See LAC 33:III.601(B)(1). These regulations allow new permits to be issued where new emissions are "offset" by past emission reductions and the Lowest Achievable Emissions Rate ("LAER") is achieved by the new or modified emission source. These offsets or emission reduction credits ("ERCs")encourage voluntary over-compliance and are set at a higher figure than the emissions that the offsets cover; e.g., in this instance, a ratio of 1.2 to 1. Over time, air emissions will decrease, and a net air quality benefit will occur in the non-attainment area.

These ERCs are calculated in tons per year ("TPY") and are evidenced by, and registered in, the ERC bank established by DEQ pursuant to La. R.S. 30:2054(B)(3). The ERC bank only allows deposits of ERCs when the applicant voluntarily reduces volatile organic compounds ("VOC") emissions by more than is required by law (i.e., they are surplus) and only when said applicant agrees to permanently reduce such emissions through accepting enforceable permits or orders. 42 U.S.C. § 7503 and LAC 33:III.607(F) and 605. Reductions cannot be creditable as offsets if they are required by law; they must be voluntary and in excess of legal requirements. 42 U.S.C. § 7503(c)(2). Once created, banked ERCs are protected and can be used by the certificate owner, whether the original owner or the owner by transfer. LAC 33:III.623. If a company desires to make improvements or additions to its facility that would result in an emissions increase, it must acquire credits from the bank (either on its own, or by contract from someone else) and "cash" them out at a ratio of 1.2 banked TPY of emissions for every proposed 1 TPY of new emissions. 42 U.S.C. 7511(c)(1). These ERCs can, within ten years, be utilized by the same facility, between different facilities of the same company, or transferred between companies for the construction of new projects. This emissions trading market allows companies seeking to build new plants or to expand existing plants to purchase pollution reductions. Pursuant to DEQ regulations, a Non-attainment New Source Review ("NNSR") is required for any modification to an existing stationary source that will cause an increase of 25 tons per year or more of VOCs. LAC 33:III.504(D)(4).

The net increase in VOC emissions associated with the Exxon BRPO polypropylene project is 32.54 TPY. Therefore, offsets were required at a ratio of 1.2 to 1, totaling 39.05 TPY. Accordingly, on January 20, 1998, BRPO received a transfer of 40 tons of VOC emissions credits from the account of Exxon's Baton Rouge Chemical Plant. DEQ notified Exxon on January 23, 1998, that its permit application was administratively complete. An ERC bank certificate was issued by DEQ on February 18, 1998, reflecting that 40 tons were transferred and applied to offset emissions for the BRPO Title V Permit.

Copies of a draft permit were forwarded to Exxon, the East Baton Rouge Parish Library and the EPA on June 25, 1998. On July 7, 1998, DEQ published a public notice in the Baton Rouge daily newspaper The Advocate, asking for public comments on the proposed facility. On July 23, 1998, the EPA sent a letter to DEQ expressing concerns over the draft permit for Exxon's polypropylene plant, particularly regarding Exxon's proposed offsetting, alternative site analysis, and compliance with other new source requirements under state and federal law. DEQ responded to and addressed each question posed by the EPA and provided back-up documentation where necessary. On August 7, 1998, DEQ received a letter from the North Baton Rouge Environmental Association (NBREA) requesting a public hearing in the nearby Alsen community and a ninety-day extension of the public comment period.

After addressing the concerns raised by the EPA, DEQ received oral approval from EPA for [the] proposed air permit. Notice of the public hearing was published in The Advocate in an enlarged format on September 15, 1998; however, prior to the announcement in the newspaper, Exxon notified NBREA of the date and location of the public hearing. A copy of the public notice was also hand-delivered to NBREA's president, Ms. Juanita Stewart. Pursuant to a request from Ms. Florence Robinson of NBREA, DEQ forwarded a copy of the draft permit and application to the Southern University Library.

On October 12, 1998, Ms. Mary Lee Orr, executive director of LEAN, also sent a letter to DEQ requesting a thirty-day extension of the public comment period. DEQ held a public hearing at the Alsen Community Center on October 14, 1998, at which time the public comment period was extended until 4:30 p.m. on October 30, 1998. Air permit No. 2581-VO was ultimately issued by DEQ on November 24, 1998. Since that date, the BRPO plant has been constructed and commenced operation in May 2000.

ACTION OF THE TRIAL COURT

Following DEQ's decision to grant a permit to Exxon for construction of the polypropylene facility, NBREA and LEAN led the instant action seeking judicial review pursuant to La. R.S. 30:2050.21, in the Nineteenth Judicial District Court on December 23, 1998. Exxon, as the permittee in this matter, was permitted to intervene in the case on January 26, 1999.

In a motion led November 23, 1999, DEQ moved to supplement the administrative record pursuant to La.R.S. 30:2050.21(D), for the purpose of adding two documents and two exhibits that were before the agency when it made its decision, but were inadvertently omitted from the record. Said motion was granted by the trial court on November 29, 1999.

A hearing was held on January 31, 2000, at which time oral arguments were presented by all parties. The district court, *ex proprio motu*, raised the issue of whether Louisiana's ERC banking program was constitutional, and requested additional briefs from the parties on this issue.

Oral argument was rescheduled for March 15, 2000. Prior to the March hearing, a number of interested parties led amicus curiae briefs in this matter; namely, the Louisiana Mid-Continent Oil & Gas Association, the City of Baton Rouge/Parish of East Baton Rouge, the Baton Rouge Chamber of Commerce and the Louisiana Chemical Association.

The district court ruled in favor of DEQ at the March hearing and held that DEQ did not abuse its discretion in granting the permit to Exxon. Following the signing of the judgment on April 5, 2000, the district court denied NBREA and LEAN's application for rehearing. This appeal followed.

Assignments of Error

In connection with their appeal in this matter, NBREA and LEAN have set forth the following assignments of error:

1. The Court below erred in upholding the permit despite evidence in the record that clearly demonstrates DEQ and Exxon's failure to comply with Nonattainment New Source Review requirements.

2. The Court below erred in allowing Exxon to supplement the record after the fact and without following the proper procedure for supplementation of an administrative record.

3. The Court below failed to rule on DEQ's noncompliance with this Court's ruling in Rubicon, which requires DEQ to respond to all reasonable public comments.

4. The Court below erred in finding that DEQ complied with its constitutional duty as public trustee of the environment.

Standard of Review
(omitted)

Discussion

In their initial assignment of error, NBREA and LEAN contend that the district court erred in upholding the issuance of the permit in light of evidence that DEQ and Exxon failed to comply with Non-attainment New Source Review requirements. Specifically, NBREA and LEAN argue that despite the fact that the record did not demonstrate compliance with federal law and state air regulations, DEQ granted a permit to Exxon, and the district court affirmed this decision. NBREA and LEAN now ask this court to reverse that decision. . . . [The court found no merit to this contention.]

The second error assigned by NBREA and LEAN is that the district court erred in allowing Exxon to supplement the record with evidence of Exxon's compliance without following the proper procedure for supplementation of an administrative record. . . . [The court found no error.]

In their third assignment of error, NBREA and LEAN contend that the district court failed to rule on DEQ's noncompliance with this court's ruling in In the Matter of Rubicon, Inc., 95-0108 (La. App. 1 Cir. 2/14/96), 670 So.2d 475, 483, which requires DEQ to respond to all reasonable public comments. Specifically, NBREA and LEAN argue that DEQ failed to respond to their charge that the permitting of this facility is tantamount to environmental racism.

At the public hearing held regarding the permitting of the Exxon facility on October 14, 1998, Ms. Florence Robinson, a member of NBREA, charged:

Alsen is probably one of the best examples of environmental racism in the nation. The problem here goes far beyond mere environmental justice concerns. It is a case of outright discrimination. Many do not like to hear the term racism brought up today, claiming that that is all in the past. Unfortunately, Alsen has been forced to continue to endure the racist actions of the past. The decision to industrialize Alsen was not made by the people of Alsen. In fact, because of their race, the people of Alsen were deliberately and systematically denied the right to participate in government and shape their own destinies. Now, Alsen is told it must live with these racist decisions. This is clearly an injustice, and is unamerican [sic].

In a letter addressed to DEQ and dated October 30, 1998, Exxon responded to the environmental justice concerns expressed by Ms. Robinson. Exxon cited a history of voluntary emissions reductions and stated that it did not feel that the allegations of environmental discrimination were valid. Additionally, DEQ, in its Public Comment Response Summary, responded to Ms. Robinson's comments and stated:

> The property owned by Exxon Chemical Americas upon which the polypropylene unit will be constructed is within the industrial areas designated by The Plan of Government of the Parish of East Baton Rouge and the City of Baton Rouge for industrial development. The new Polypropylene Plant will be constructed in Industrial Area 3 located in north Baton Rouge, west of U.S. Highway No. 61 (Old Bayou Sara Road). By letter dated July 26, 1995, from the Office of the Planning Commission and signed by Richard E. Barker (Planner IV), the property was confirmed to be zoned M-2 Heavy Industrial.

The district court, in its reasons for judgment, stated:

> The environmental justice review issue. It is unfortunate that the original zoning placed this industrial complex next to [the community of] Alsen. The fact that it was done a long time ago, doesn't make any difference in considering environmental justice because a lot of things were done a long time ago that were not right . . . Placing this industrial area in the neighborhood of the Alsen community does not appear to be intentionally racist. It's between a railroad and a river in a relatively rural area. Exxon has used a plant facility that was already in existence. They're actually putting out less pollution than the plant that was there previously. Considering the other policy considerations, should Exxon locate this some place where there is an area where there is no pollution? That's not a particularly good idea. Should they locate it in another industrial area? Well, that only moves the problem to somebody else's city. Overall, in the balance, I cannot find that DEQ abused its discretion in putting [the Exxon plant] in an industrial area at the site of a prior plant that actually probably produced more pollution than the system that's been proposed.

Upon review of the record, we cannot say that DEQ failed to respond to the charges leveled by NBREA and LEAN. The Exxon facility at issue is situated in an industrially zoned area adjacent to a state highway, a railroad, and the Mississippi River. We conclude, as did the district court, that it is unfortunate that the Alsen community is also situated in this general area; however, this fact alone does not constitute environmental racism. This assignment of error is without merit.

The final assignment of error raised by NBREA and LEAN is that the district court erred in holding that DEQ complied with its constitutional duty as public trustee of the environment.

The district court, in it reasons for judgment, opined:

> The next question is, weighing all those factors, is permitting a thirty-four or so ton ozone release in the East Baton Rouge area when we're not in attainment a violation of the constitutional standards [as set forth] in Save Ourselves Inc. v. Louisiana Environmental Control Commission, 452 So. 2d 1152 (La. 1984). That requires a balancing effect. Exxon itself has been one of those industries which has significantly reduced emissions. It has done little things, like paid people to be on jury duty, which we always appreciate. They've put money back in the community. The question is, even though I don't like the fact that we're putting thirty-four tons of ozone back in the air when we're not in attainment, should Exxon, which has done a lot to reduce emissions, be the one that suffers the consequences of our not being in attainment?

In balancing the pros and cons required by the constitution in Save Ourselves, the court finds that this small amount, which seemed to me when we took over this case to be a large amount, . . . that thirty-two tons is a small amount compared to a couple of days of automobile pollution, [and] does not outweigh other consideration.

Therefore, we find that DEQ did not abuse its discretion, and their decision is supported by a preponderance of the evidence.

In their brief to this court, NBREA and LEAN contend that DEQ is constitutionally mandated to protect the quality of the environment in the state. NBREA and LEAN further cite La. R.S. 30:2014, which provides that the secretary of DEQ acts as the primary trustee of the environment and must consider and follow the will and intent of the Constitution and statutory law in making any determination about the granting or denial of permits.

In its brief, Exxon responds with the argument that:

> DEQ is not obligated to deny a permit simply because this is a nonattainment area. In this case, DEQ recognized that permitting Exxon's expansion would not have any significant impact on public health or the environment, and that these 32 TPY will not prevent the attainment or maintenance of the ozone [National Ambient Air Quality Standard].

Upon consideration of the arguments put forth by the parties, and careful review of the record in this matter, this court declines to substitute its judgment for that of DEQ, EPA, and the legislature. It is the opinion of this court that DEQ did not violate its constitutional duty to act as trustee of the environment.

CONCLUSION

For the above and foregoing reasons, the judgment of the district court that upheld DEQ's issuance of a Part70 Operating Permit to Exxon for the construction and operation of a new polypropylene production facility is hereby affirmed. All costs associated with this appeal shall be borne equally by appellants, NBREA and LEAN.

Affirmed.

NOTES AND QUESTIONS

1. *Monitoring.* EPA tracks air quality by using monitors. Monitors are getting better, but they do not tell a perfect story. For example, one monitor might be in a particularly dusty, urban location, while another might be placed in a spot relatively unaffected by dust. If monitors record inaccurate data about ambient air concentrations, the whole regulatory system becomes skewed.

Well aware of this problem, EPA has engaged in alternative methods of calibrating monitoring data. One method is "spatial monitoring." By this approach, the agency averages the results from air quality monitors across a given region. Critics argue that spatial monitoring can result in the agency ignoring pollution "hot spots," thereby shortchanging persons most in need of air quality improvement. Another approach is to give greater weight to results from monitors located in areas of higher population density. Such "population-weighted monitoring" is often criticized for making health protection dependent upon how many neighbors one has.

2. *State of the Air.* Air quality in this country is improving. According to EPA: "between 1980 and 2009, gross domestic product increased 122 percent, vehicle miles traveled increased 95 percent, energy consumption increased 22 percent, and U.S. population grew by 35 percent. During the same time period, total emissions of the six principal air pollutants dropped by 57 percent." In addition, between 1990 and 2009, emissions of air toxics decreased by 35 percent. www.epa.gov/air/airtrends/index.html (visited Oct. 2011). EPA maintains, moreover, that the CAA will provide $2 trillion in benefits while preventing over 230,000 early deaths in 2020 alone, mostly due to decreases in concentrations of fine particulates and ground level ozone. A worst case assessment by the agency estimates health benefits produced by the CAA by 2020 to be three times greater than the costs imposed by the statute; the agency's best case scenario projects these benefits to be 90 times greater than the associated costs. http://www.epa.gov/air/sect812/prospective2.html.

To see air quality monitoring information on an air pollutant near you, see www.epa.gov/airdata.

2. Prevention of Significant Deterioration

Since the 1970 Clean Air Act contained no explicit provision designed to protect air resources that were cleaner than required by the NAAQSs, the EPA thought it had no authority to enact regulations to that end. It believed it could act to clean up the "dirty air areas," but could not maintain the "clean air areas." These latter areas, it believed, could be degraded down to the level of the ambient standards. This meant that manufacturers, faced with costly SIP obligations, could simply relocate to other locales with clean skies and easy SIPs. Environmentalists, however, thought the 1970 CAA authorized EPA to prevent the "significant deterioration" of air quality in parts of the country where ambient standards were being met. To test the theory, the Sierra Club filed a lawsuit against EPA in 1972, and, surprisingly, it won. *Sierra Club v. Ruckelshaus*, 344 F. Supp. 253 (D.D.C. 1972), *aff'd*, 2 ENVTL. L. REP. 20656 (D.C. Cir. 1972), *aff'd sub nom. Fri v. Environmental Protection Agency*, 412 U.S. 541, 93 S. Ct. 2770 (1973). According to the District Court for the District of Columbia, EPA's authority to protect clean air areas lay in the "purposes" clause of the Act, § 101(b), 42 1 U.S.C. § 7401(b). In that section, Congress had declared a purpose of the Act to be *"to protect and enhance* the quality of the Nation's air resources so as to promote the public health and welfare and the productive capacity of its population." Section 101(b)(1), 42 U.S.C. § 7401(b)(1) (emphasis added). This language, coupled with legislative history and past administrative interpretations of the statute, convinced the court that EPA could move in this direction.

Armed with this newfound authority, EPA enacted regulations in 1974 to maintain clean air areas. Thereafter, when it amended the CAA in 1977, Congress incorporated much of the EPA regulations in new Part C. Congress's concerns were both environmental and economic. On the one hand, it wanted clean air areas to stay that way, at least as much as possible. On the other, it wanted to forestall any single industry from consuming the entire "increment" of clean air in an AQCR (that is, polluting it all the way down to the NAAQS), thus foreclosing future industrial growth. *See, e.g.*, Senate Debate on S. 252, 95th Cong. (1977) (statement of Edmund Muskie, Committee on Environment and Public Works).

ENVIRONMENTAL DEFENSE v. ENVIRONMENTAL PROTECTION AGENCY
489 F.3d 1320 (D.C. Cir. 2007)

KAREN LECRAFT HENDERSON, CIRCUIT JUDGE:

As part of the Clean Air Act (CAA), the Congress created a program entitled "Prevention of Significant Deterioration of Air Quality" (PSD), which is designed to protect air quality in national parks and similar scenic and recreational areas. 42 U.S.C. ch. 85, subch. I, pt. C (CAA §§ 160–169b, 42 U.S.C. §§ 7470-92). In 1988 the Environmental Protection Agency (EPA) promulgated regulations to implement the PSD program for nitrogen oxides (NO[x]. Prevention of Significant Deterioration for Nitrogen Oxides, 53 Fed. Reg. 40,656 (October 17,1988) (1988 Rule). In 1990, the court reviewed the 1988 Rule and remanded the regulations to EPA. Envtl. Def. Fund, Inc. v. EPA, 283 U.S. App. D.C. 169, 898 F.2d 183 (D.C. Cir. 1990). EPA issued a new final rule in 2005. Prevention of Significant Deterioration for Nitrogen Oxides, 70 Fed. Reg. 59,582 (Oct. 12, 2005) (codified at 40 C.F.R. §§ 51.166, 52.21) (2005 Rule). Petitioner Environmental Defense seeks review of the 2005 Rule. Because EPA followed our directives in *Environmental Defense Fund* and its regulations reflect a reasonable interpretation of the applicable CAA PSD provisions, we deny the petition for review.

I.

The CAA requires that EPA promulgate a primary and a secondary National Ambient Air Quality Standard(NAAQS) for each air pollutant for which EPA has issued "air quality criteria" pursuant to CAA section 108, 42 U.S.C. § 7408. 42 U.S.C. § 7409(a); *see generally Whitman v. Am. Trucking Ass'ns*, 531 U.S. 457, 462, 121 S. Ct.903, 149 L. Ed. 2d 1 (2001). After the NAAQS is established for a particular pollutant, each state must submit to EPA a list of all areas in the state, designating each area as "attainment" (i.e., it meets the NAAQS); "nonattainment" (i.e., it does not meet the NAAQS) or "unclassifiable" (i.e., it "cannot be classified on the basis of available information as meeting or not meeting the [NAAQS]"). 42 U.S.C. § 7407. The state must then develop and submit to EPA a "State Implementation Plan" (SIP) which "provides for implementation, maintenance, and enforcement of [the NAAQs]." *Id.* § 7410(a)(1).

In 1977, the Congress amended the CAA to add the PSD provisions in order to "protect the air quality in national parks and similar areas of special scenic or recreational value, and in areas where pollution was within the national ambient standards, while assuring economic growth consistent with such protection." *Envtl. Def. Fund*, 898 F.2d at 184 (citing CAA § 160, 42 U.S.C. § 7470). The PSD provisions require that each applicable SIP "shall contain emission limitations and such other measures as may be necessary, as determined under regulations promulgated under this part, to prevent significant deterioration of air quality in each region (or portion thereof) designated pursuant to section 7407 of [title 42] as attainment or unclassifiable." 42 U.S.C. § 7471. The PSD establishes three classes of subject attainment or unclassifiable areas:

Class I — comprising mainly large national parks and national wilderness areas;

Class II — regions where the ambient air quality levels more than meet the national standards; and

Class III — regions meeting the definition of Class I or Class II areas but redesignated at the behest of a state for higher levels of industrial development.

Envtl. Def. Fund, 898 F.2d at 185 (citing CAA §§ 162, 164, 42 U.S.C. §§ 7472, 7474). For each of the three Classes, the Congress required that EPA establish numerical emission limits for specific pollutants.

For "Set I" pollutants — i.e., sulfur oxide and particulate matter — CAA § 163 establishes for each Class "maximum allowable increases" — called "increments" and expressed in micrograms per cubic meter ([mu] g/m — "over baseline concentrations." 42 U.S.C. § 7473. The "baseline concentration" is defined as "the ambient concentration levels which exist at the time of the first application for a permit" by a major emitting facility. *Id.* § 7479(4).

For "Set II" pollutants — namely, hydrocarbons, carbon monoxide, photochemical oxidants and, at issue here, NO[x], the Congress declined to set specific incremental or other limits, leaving the task to EPA. Subsection166(a) directs that for these pollutants EPA "shall conduct a study and not later than two years after

August 7, 1977, promulgate regulations to prevent the significant deterioration of air quality which would result from the emissions of such pollutants." *Id.* § 7476(a). Subsection 166(c) further directs that the regulations "shall provide specific numerical measures against which permit applications may be evaluated, a framework for stimulating improved control technology, protection of air quality values, and fulfill the goals and purposes set forth in section 7401 and section 7470 of [title 42]." *Id.* § 7476(c). More specifically, subsection 166(d) instructs that the regulations "shall provide specific measures at least as effective as the increments established in section 7473 of [title 42] to fulfill such goals and purposes, and may contain air quality increments, emission density requirements, or other measures." *Id.* § 7476(d).

A. 1988 PSD Rule

EPA issued a proposed rule for PSD of NO[x] on February 8, 1988. Prevention of Significant Deterioration for Nitrogen Oxides, 53 Fed. Reg. 3698 (Feb. 8, 1988). On October 17, 1988, EPA issued the final rule, in which it decided to adopt an increment limitation system for NO [x] similar to the increment scheme the Congress had prescribed for Set I pollutants — and had contemplated that EPA might adopt for Set II pollutants, *see* 42 U.S.C. § 7476(d) (Set II regulations "may contain air quality increments"). Accordingly, EPA established increment limits "by reference to" — that is, as a percentage of — the NAAQS it had promulgated for NO [x] pursuant to 42 U.S.C. § 7409 because the "Congress used the NAAQS for [Set I] pollutants as the benchmark for determining what constitutes 'significant deterioration' " and "because the NAAQS constitute the basic measure of air quality under the Act." 53 Fed. Reg. at 3700. EPA also chose the same percentages for Set II that the Congress had for Set I: 2.5% for Class I areas, 25% for Class II areas and 50% for Class III areas. *Id.* at 3704–05.In addition, EPA promulgated NO [x] increments for only one nitrogen oxide compound, nitrogen dioxide (NO[2]), based on the NO [2] NAAQS — notwithstanding the statute calls for regulating "nitrogen oxides" generally — because NO [2] was "the pollutant on which the national ambient air quality standards (NAAQS) for nitrogenoxides were based," 53 Fed. Reg. at 40,656, and thus was "the only compound for which it had established an ambient standard" on which to base an increment, *Envtl. Def. Fund*, 898 F.2d at 185.

B. Environmental Defense Fund, Inc. v. EPA

In *Environmental Defense Fund*, the court reviewed the 1988 Rule and found it failed to comply with the Congress's directives in two respects. . . . [First, the court held that EPA lacked complete discretion to establish Set II increments at Set I levels (the so-called absolute safe harbor), as EPA had seemingly assumed. Instead, the CAA provides a so-called contingent safe harbor for EPA, which means it can promulgate Set II increments to mimic the Set I standards only if the statute warrants such a mimicry. Second, the court rejected EPA's establishment of an increment based solely on the relevant NAAQS, since the NAAQSs are in the statute for general health protection purposes, while PSD emphasizes specific areas and natural settings.]

C. 2005 PSD Rule

On February 23, 2005, EPA issued a proposed rule, Prevention of Significant Deterioration for Nitrogen Oxides, 70 Fed. Reg. 8880 (Feb. 23, 2005), in which it "responded to the court's opinion" in *Environmental Defense Fund* and proposed to adopt the contingent safe harbor interpretation of subsections 166(c) and (d) endorsed by the court and, based thereon, NO[x] increments as in the 1988 Rule. Final Rule, 70 Fed. Reg. at 59,586. On October 12, 2005, EPA issued its final rule, which followed the same path. EPA there set out "five central elements" as the basis for its regulations. *Id.* [The elements were: (a) preference for a "holistic analysis," by which EPA endeavored to study the whole of the regulation, rather than focus on constituent parts; (b) ratification of the contingent safe harbor approach; (c) identification of eight "statutory factors," compliance with which EPA considered mandatory; (d) use of a balancing analysis when competing objectives of environmental protection and economic development presented themselves; and (e) a determination to allow states to implement alternatives to increments in their SIPs, assuming statutory goals are met.]

Based on these five elements, EPA announced it was "retaining the existing NO increments without change" and "amending the text of [its] PSD regulations at 40 CFR 51.166 to clarify that any State may employ an alternative approach to the NO [2] increments if the State's approach meets certain requirements." *Id.* at 59,595–96 (footnote omitted). *See* 40 C.F.R. § 51.166(c)(2) (new subsection allowing State to "demonstrate that it has alternative measures in its plan other than maximum allowable increases that satisfy the requirements in sections 166(c) and 166(d) of the Clean Air Act for nitrogenoxides"). EPA then set out in detail the balancing analysis it had conducted, explaining how six components of its NO[x] PSD regulations advance the eight statutory factors it had identified. *See* 70 Fed. Reg. at 59,596–99. . . .

Finally, EPA justified its decision to prescribe increments for NO [2] only and based on the NAAQS on the ground that the NO [2] increment, in conjunction with EPA's impending fine particulate matter increment rule, will limit emissions of other nitrogen oxide compounds as well.

The petitioner filed its petition for review on December 12, 2005.

II.

Because "we read the ambiguities and perplexities of the statute as delegating to the agency a broad interpretive authority, as we must under *Chevron U.S.A. Inc. v. NRDC*, 467 U.S. 837, 843 44, 104 S. Ct. 2778, 81L. Ed. 2d 694 (1984)," *Envtl. Def. Fund*, 898 F.2d at 189 (parallel citation omitted), we defer to EPA's "permissible construction of the statute," *Chevron*, 467 U.S. at 843. . . . Applying this deferential standard, we uphold EPA's 2005 PSD Rule as reflecting a reasonable statutory interpretation.

As our summary of EPA's 2005 PSD Rule demonstrates, on remand EPA scrupulously followed the court's instructions in *Environmental Defense Fund*. EPA expressly adopted the court's contingent safe harbor approach (in lieu of EPA's earlier absolute safe harbor), explaining in detail how the NAAQS-based increments, along with other measures, fulfill the PSD's statutory goals (expressed as eight "factors"), as section 166(c) requires. EPA also explained why it did not promulgate standards, incremental or otherwise, for nitrogen oxide compounds other than NO [2]. Nonetheless, the petitioner challenges the 2005 PSD Rule on several grounds.

A. Duty to Preserve, Protect and Enhance Air Quality

The petitioner's primary objection is that EPA violated its duty under section 160(2), as incorporated into section 166, to make a finding that the NO [x] PSD regulations fulfill the statutory goal to "preserve, protect and enhance" the air quality in parks and other natural areas. *See* 42 U.S.C. § 7470(2); *see also id.* § 7401.Additionally, the petitioner argues, EPA could not reasonably have made such a finding because the increments as promulgated do not fulfill this goal. We find this double-barreled challenge unpersuasive.

First, EPA did expressly find that the PSD regulations fulfill the statutory goal to preserve, protect, and enhance air quality — among the several goals EPA is called upon to balance. *See Envtl. Def. Fund*, 898 F.2d at 189 ("subsection (c) commands a broad weighing of factors") . . . In particular EPA must, as it recognized in the 2005 Rule, *see* 70 Fed. Reg. at 59,588, balance the potentially conflicting goals in subsections160(2) and 160(3) to protect air quality and to promote economic growth. . . . And this is precisely what EPA did. The 2005 Rule includes an extensive explanation of how EPA balanced the eight statutory factors and how their promulgated regulations satisfy various of them. *See* 70 Fed. Reg. at 59,596 99. Of particular importance here, EPA expressly found that the statutory goal to preserve, protect and enhance air quality is fulfilled through the area classifications system, *id.* at 59,597, the AQRV review, *id.* at 59,597-98, the Additional Impacts Analysis, *id.* at 59,599, and the use of the BACT standard, *id.* at 59,599; *see supra* pp. 8, 13 14.

For the second part of its argument, the petitioner relies largely on the historical evidence that in the fifteen years since the Set II increments were first promulgated in 1988, air quality in parks and natural areas has deteriorated. We see two flaws in the petitioner's reasoning.

First, it overlooks the Congress's apparent intent when it expressly adopted an increment program for Set I pollutants in section 163 and authorized EPA to do so for Set II pollutants in section 166. By its nature, such an increment limitation system does not reduce existing concentration levels but rather limits increases. Thus, EPA reasonably viewed the statutory PSD program as "designed to be a growth management program that limits the deterioration of air quality beyond baseline levels that may be caused by the construction of major new and modified sources." *Id.* at 59,589. The petitioner's real beef is with EPA's determination that this goal is met by using the same increment methodology for Set II pollutants (and NO [x] in particular) that the Congress used for Set I and thereby setting the significant deterioration bar at the same level as the Congress did for Set I. Given EPA's adherence to the statute's requirements, as the court delineated them in *Environmental Defense Fund*, we do not believe that in doing so EPA abused the considerable discretion that section 166 grants it to establish Set II PSD measures.

Second, in the 2005 Rule, EPA noted that the deterioration that has occurred has not been nationwide but is limited to specific areas, "primarily in the West," *id.* at 59,603, a problem EPA did not believe could be directly alleviated through the PSD program because the Congress intended EPA to establish nationally uniform PSD measures (as the Congress itself established for Set II pollutants). EPA explained:

> We continue to believe that the PSD program is intended to allow the air quality in each area of the country attaining the NAAQS, and with the same area classification, to "deteriorate" by the same amount for each subject pollutant, regardless of the existing air quality when the increment is initially triggered in a particular area, as long as such growth allowed within the constraints of the increment does not cause adverse impacts on site-specific AQRVs or other important values. In this way, the PSD increments avoid having a disproportionate impact on growth that might disadvantage some communities, recognizing that the increments in themselves would not address existing negative impacts but cannot allow significant new adverse impacts. Congress established the foundation for uniform national increments when it created increments for SO 2 and PM under section 165 of the Act.

Id. at 59,601 (footnote omitted); *see also id.* at 59,602 ("[W]e do not believe it is permissible or appropriate for us to establish uniform increments at levels so stringent that they prevent any adverse impact on the most sensitive receptors in any part of the U.S."). EPA's construction of the statute is consistent with the path the Congress chose in mandating specific uniform national increments for Set I pollutants in section 163. It is also supported by the legislative history of section 163, which indicates that the Congress deliberately selected uniform increments because it deemed locally individualized increments to be inequitable. . . .

B. PSD Regulations for Ozone and Particulate Matter

Next, the petitioner contends EPA unlawfully "ignored the contribution of NO [x] to formation of ozone and fine particulate matter," Pet'r Br. at 31, which are secondary pollutants "formed in part by reactions of NO [x] emissions with other pollutants in the atmosphere," 70 Fed. Reg. at 59,590. We believe that EPA reasonably justified its decision not to address either fine particulate matter or ozone in the NO [x] PSD regulations on the ground that the statutory PSD provisions require EPA to establish regulations specific to both fine particulate matter, 42 U.S.C. §§ 7473, 7476(f), and ozone ("photochemical oxidants"), *id.* § 7476(a), and EPA intends to do just that in separate rulemakings. . . .

C. Promulgating Only NO [2] Increment

[The Court upheld EPA's determination to regulate NO2 exclusively as scientific and technical evidence was insufficient to regulate other compounds of nitrogen.]

In sum, the Congress expressly conferred on EPA broad discretion to establish PSD limitation measures and EPA did so in conformance with the statutory directives. Under our deferential standard of review, we therefore uphold the 2005 Rule for Prevention of Significant Deterioration for Nitrogen Oxides as a reasonable implementation of the Set II PSD statutory provisions and, accordingly, deny the petition for review.

So ordered.

ROGERS, CIRCUIT JUDGE, concurring: I join the court in denying the petition challenging the final rule implementing the program for the Prevention of Significant Deterioration of Air Quality ("PSD") for Nitrogen Oxides. 70 Fed. Reg. 59,582 (Oct. 12, 2005) (codified at 40 C.F.R. §§ 51.166, 52.21) ("2005 Rule"). I write separately because the rule sits at the outer boundary of reasonableness — the "holistic" approach adopted by EPA in the 2005 Rule is at present less than the sum of its parts.

In the fifteen years between this court's remand in *Environmental Defense Fund, Inc. v. EPA*, 898 F.2d 183, 283 U.S. App. D.C. 169 (D.C. Cir. 1990), and promulgation of the 2005 Rule, air quality has deteriorated seriously. *See* 70 Fed. Reg. at 59,593 95. One of the express purposes of the PSD program adopted by Congress in the Clean Air Act Amendments of 1977 was "to preserve, protect, and enhance the air quality" in national parks, wilderness areas, and similar scenic and recreational areas. 42 U.S.C. § 7470(2); *see Envtl. Def. Fund*, 898 F.2d at 184 (citing 42 U.S.C. § 7470); Op. at 1-2. Nonetheless, EPA has chosen "a growth management" approach designed to "limit[] the deterioration of air quality," Op. at 17 (quoting 70 Fed. Reg. at 59,589); *see* 70 Fed. Reg. at 59,588 89, 59,600, which is not quite the same as preserving, protecting, and enhancing.

In 1990, the court noted that if EPA had kept to the statutory two-year deadline for issuing Set II PSD limits and "piggybacked the PSD increments on the ambient [air quality] standards . . . , the increments would have been at risk of being rendered obsolete almost immediately after promulgation." *Envtl. Def. Fund*, 898 F.2d at 190. By waiting fifteen years, EPA has promulgated a rule with no change in the increments that may already be obsolete, especially because no other programs, such as reviews by the Federal Land Manager and State permitting authority, have prevented substantial environmental deterioration in the interim, *see* 70 Fed. Reg. at 59,593 95; *see also* Petitioner's Reply Br. at 8 & n.4.

EPA deflects petitioner's individual criticisms of its approach by responding that its holistic approach "satisf[ies]" the statutory requirements. *See* 70 Fed. Reg. at 59,596, 59,605. No doubt, a holistic approach is permissible. But the parts of a holistic rule must still comport with the statutory requirements, and EPA offers no opinion that its balancing approach will ameliorate the decline in air quality experienced in the last fifteen years much less enhance air quality, as the statute contemplates, *see* 42 U.S.C. § 7470(2). *See, e.g.*, 70 Fed. Reg. at 59,587 89, 59,610. The court struggles to find such an opinion. *See* Op. at 16–17. Despite the requirement to accommodate both the interests of environmental protection and economic growth, *see* 42 U.S.C. § 7470 (2)-(3), EPA has focused on "maximiz[ing] opportunities for economic growth," 70 Fed. Reg. at 59,588. Allowing the States to redesignate Class II areas as Class III, *see id.* at 59,597; Op. at 12, does not suggest an accommodation so much as a capitulation to economic growth at the expense of environmental concerns. Additionally, to demonstrate that it has met the statutory requirements, EPA relies on regulatory controls for ozone and fine particulate matter that it has yet to propose much less promulgate, *see* 70 Fed. Reg. at 59,590; Op. at 19. . . .

Nonetheless, as the court observes, EPA has adhered to the interpretation deemed permissible by the court in 1990, *see* Op. at 2, 15, 17, 21; *Envtl. Def. Fund*, 898 F.2d at 188–89, and considered the relevant statutory factors, *see* Op. at 22; 70 Fed. Reg. at 59,596 99. Additionally, there are expert judgments that underlie the 2005 Rule, *see* Op. at 21, and EPA has offered a minimally cogent explanation of its approach, *see id.* at 20-22.Accordingly, the petition for review fails to show that EPA's interpretation is not permissible under *Chevron U.S.A. Inc. v. NRDC*, 467 U.S. 837, 842–44, 104 S. Ct. 2778, 81 L. Ed. 2d 694 (1984).

NOTES

1. *Update.* In 2009, EPA adopted a new National Enforcement Initiative for fiscal years 2011–2013. The new Initiative focuses PSD enforcement efforts on four industrial sectors: coal-fired power plants, glass manufacturing plants, cement manufacturing plants, and sulfuric and nitric acid production plants. EPA estimates that the pollution reductions it will secure through this Initiative will produce between $6 billion and $15 billion in health benefits.

2. *BACT — Who Decides?* As indicated in *Environmental Defense*, states take the lead in implementing the PSD program in their respective SIPs. Under Part C of the statute, states must focus a good deal of their efforts on new or modified "major emitting facilities." Section 165, 42 U.S.C. § 7475. Among other requirements, these entities must secure permits and must meet emission standards based on best available control technology ("BACT"). Choices by states in this regard may not be reversed by EPA so long as the SIP meets the goals of the program itself. Given this operational construct, has EPA any redress if a state chooses emission standards for a new or modified major emitting facility based on a faulty BACT determination? This question has finally been answered definitively: "In notably capacious terms, Congress armed EPA with authority to issue orders stopping construction when "a State is not acting in compliance with any [CAA] requirement or prohibition . . . relating to the construction of new sources or the modification of existing sources," § 7413(a)(5), or when "construction or modification of a major emitting facility . . . does not conform to the requirements of [the PSD program], § 7477." *Alaska Dep't of Environmental Conservation v. Environmental Protection Agency*, 540 U.S. 461, 484, 124 S. Ct. 983, 999 (2004).

3. *"Potential to Emit."* A major early issue focused on determining which facilities qualify as "major." The statute declares a facility to be major if it emits or has the potential to emit, either 100 tons per year of any air pollutant for specified types of facilities or 250 tons per year for any other facility. Section 169(1), 42 U.S.C. § 7479(1). The question was how to determine whether a facility has the "potential to emit" more than the specified tonnages. EPA argued the determination should be made by looking at a facility's raw capacity to emit; industry, on the other hand, argued the determination should be made taking into account pollution control equipment slated for use at the facility. The United States Supreme Court ruled in favor of the industry position. *Alabama Power Co. v. Costle*, 636 F.2d 323 (D.C. Cir. 1979).

4. *"Area to Which this Part Applies."* Another early issue was whether the preconstruction requirements of § 165 applied only to new or modified major emitting facilities physically located within PSD areas, or whether these obligations might affix to such entities wherever they might be located, if their operations affected a downwind PSD area. Relying on the language of § 165(a), which makes the PSD program applicable to any major emitting facility "constructed in any area to which this part applies," the Supreme Court opted for the former interpretation. The Court held, however, that EPA could "promulgate rules to require the inclusion of such provisions in the SIP of the state whose clean air area is affected, of the state which is the source of the adverse impact, or of both." *Alabama Power, supra*, at 367.

A NOTE ON "MODIFICATION"

For many individuals and corporations, the best way to avoid the cost and hassle of NSR is by making sure existing major sources do not undergo a "modification." This is because the most burdensome NSR requirements, under both Parts C and D of the CAA, fall on new or "modified" major sources. Avoiding modification can be tricky, though, since all plants require alteration and equipment replacement during their useful lives. And each of these activities can easily qualify as a "modification." Section 111 of the CAA defines "modification" as follows: "any physical change [in], or change in the method of operation of, a stationary source which increases the amount of any air pollutant emitted by such source or which results in the emission of any air pollutant not previously emitted." Section 111(a)(4), 42 U.S.C. § 7411(a)(4). The § 111 definition applies to NSR.

Given this fact, it might be surprising to learn that EPA issues only 140–175 PSD permits each year to major sources, and most of these are for new, as distinct from modified, sources. Why so few? Manufacturers are not seeking PSD permits in large numbers mainly for three reasons. The first reason is the obvious one: on some occasions, manufacturers modify plants but fail to notify environmental agencies of their actions. They simply would rather stay under the radar. The second reason is perhaps predictable. Manufacturers may decline to alter their plants because doing so would expose them to NSR requirements. They simply do not wish to absorb the costs associated with "modified" status. A knowledgeable former EPA official argues the incentive to avoid plant upgrading has resulted in a fleet of large, leaky facilities remaining in service long beyond their expected useful lives. Comments of Bruce C. Buckheit, Director, Air Enforcement Division, U.S. Environmental Protection Agency, at the ALI-ABA Conference on Environmental Law (Bethesda, MD, Feb. 8, 2001).

The third reason for the relative paucity of permit issuances can be traced to EPA itself. EPA decided to allow many industrial entities to alter plants without taking on the dreaded "modified" status. It did so by promulgating a regulatory subdefinition of "modification" that excepted from the term actions qualifying as "maintenance, repair, and replacement which the Administrator determines to be routine." 40 C.F.R. § 60.14(e); 40 C.F.R. § 52.21(b)(2)(iii).

The issue has become what is "routine maintenance, repair, and replacement" ("RMRR"). EPA did not define this phrase in its regulations, opting instead to decide these questions on a case-by-case, "common sense," basis, taking into account the nature, scope, extent, and cost of each alleged RMRR project. But, predictably, EPA and the regulated community vigorously disagree on what RMRR is. EPA argued for years that substantial changes to plants nearing the end of their useful lives are about as close to RMRR as a heart transplant is to a flu shot. Industry has countered that even significant plant alterations can fall short of "modification." In industry's view, for example, even the replacement of primary and essential components of a manufacturing facility is "routine." This dispute has provoked a good deal of litigation. The leading case, which failed to definitively resolve the question, was *Wisconsin Electric Power Company v. Reilly*, 893 F.2d 901 (7th Cir. 1990) ("WEPCO"). For a case siding with EPA's position, see *United States v. Ohio Edison Co.*, 276 F. Supp. 2d 829 (S.D. Ohio 2003); for one siding with industry, see *United States v. Duke Energy Corp.*, 278 F. Supp. 2d 619 (M.D.N.C. 2003).

The controversy heated up with EPA's seeming change of heart, as evidenced by a new rule it promulgated after the change of administrations. 68 Fed. Reg. 61,247 (Oct. 27, 2003) ("2003 NSR rule"). The 2003 NSR rule primarily addressed the matter of equipment replacement projects ("ERPs"). It declared that ERPs qualify as RMRR if (a) the new equipment is identical or functionally equivalent to the replaced equipment; (b) the cost of the ERP does not exceed 20% of the replacement value of the process unit of which the replaced equipment is a part; and (c) the replacement does not change the process unit's basic design parameters. *Id. State of New York v. EPA*, No. 02-1387 (D.C. Cir. 2003). Environmentalists viewed the 2003 NSR rule as a complete cave-in by the Administration. In particular, they maintained the 20% cost factor was a gaping hole that would allow polluters to avoid a "modification" designation with virtual impunity. In other words, the rule as they saw it essentially gutted NSR. Industry, which reportedly suggested the 20% cost factor to the Administration and never expected to get it, pooh-poohed the whole affair as much ado about very little. As one industry lawyer (a former EPA general counsel) put it: "NSR benefits health only incidentally and indirectly in the way that anything that reduces pollution may also have ancillary health benefits, but that is not the program's purpose or focus." E. Donald Elliott, NSR, *An Industry Lawyer's Perspective on the Ongoing Battle Over Who Speaks for EPA*, EM, 27–29 (Jan. 2004). This argument, at bottom, asserts it is the NAAQS system that protects the public health, not NSR. EPA, for its part, maintained these regulatory changes inure to environmental quality by encouraging upgrades at plants that otherwise remain unimproved. The rule, contended the agency, should encourage a cleaner, more efficient fleet of manufacturing facilities.

The 2003 NSR rule was immediately challenged in court. On December 24, 2003, two days before the rule would have come into effect, the D.C. Circuit Court of Appeals issued an order to stay the rule pending review. In 2006, it vacated the rule, finding the statutory definition of "modification," which expressly encompasses "any physical change" that results in an increase of emitted pollutants or the "emission of any air pollutant not previously emitted," § 111, 42 U.S.C. § 7411, to mean what it says. *New York v. EPA*, 443 F.3d 880, 883 (D.C. Cir. 2006), *cert. denied*, 127 S. Ct. 2127 (2007).

A related issue that has been hotly contested centers on the word, "increase." For purposes of the NSPS program, EPA interpreted "increase" to mean any increase in the hourly rate of emissions. For PSD, the agency interpreted the very same term, taken from the very same statutory provision (§ 111), to mean any increase in total annual emissions. Can EPA give the same statutory term two different meanings? The Supreme Court said it could: "[A] given term in the same statute may take on distinct characters from association with distinct statutory objects calling for different implementation strategies." *Environmental Defense v. Duke Energy Corp.*, 549 U.S. 561, 574, 127 S. Ct. 1423, 1432 (2007). A ratification of EPA's longstanding policy, *Duke* is considered to be a substantial victory for the Agency, on the theory that measuring emissions increases on an annual basis is more restrictive for industry and results in a greater number of plants obligated to meet NSR requirements.

A NOTE ON EMISSIONS TRADING

The regulations we have seen thus far are known as "command-and-control" regulations. Regulations of this type operate as the name indicates: they require a set of responses, leaving few or no options available to the regulated community. Command-and-control regulations have been criticized for sweeping too broadly and inflexibly across industry. When not attuned to peculiarities of industrial operations, such regulations can be costly, inefficient, and unduly burdensome.

There are several alternatives to command-and-control regulations. One is taxation, which can work to encourage environment-friendly behavior. Another, more of which we shall see shortly, is market-based regulation. Market-based regulatory approaches include items such as marketable permits, emission fees, fees on sale of items the use of which contribute to pollution, incentives to reduce automobile emissions or automobile use, and many others. EPA has required market-based regulatory options in areas deemed to be in extreme nonattainment for ozone. (At this writing, only the Los Angeles, California, and portions of the San Joaquin Valley, California air basins fall in this category.) It has required as well economic incentive programs for serious carbon monoxide nonattainment areas failing to reach emission reduction milestones. These alternatives allow the regulated community more flexibility in choosing how to most cost-effectively meet regulatory goals.

But these alternatives to command-and-control regulations are often unavailable for use because federal legislation does not allow for them. That has been EPA's experience. Accordingly, since the early 1980s, EPA has been trying to work more flexibility into its command-and-control regulatory structure, and nowhere more concertedly than in its regulation of air quality. It has done so by a variety of emissions trading techniques:

(a) *Bubbles*: Bubbles are intra-source trade-offs. Bubbles allow existing plants, or groups of plants, to increase emissions at some sources so long as they compensate for the additional emissions by decreasing them at other sources. To be approved, each bubble must produce results equivalent to or better than the otherwise mandated baseline. Thus, use of the bubble in no way worsens air quality. A bubble may not be employed to avoid otherwise applicable technology-based emission standards, nor may it relieve an entity of the obligation of reasonable further progress in nonattainment areas. Bubbles are approved, if at all, through the SIP revision process. EPA has implemented the bubble concept at every opportunity. *See, e.g.*, 52 Fed. Reg. 28,946 (1987); *ASARCO v. EPA*, 578 F.2d 319 (D.C. Cir. 1978). EPA has instituted a bubble in the nonattainment program, *Chevron v. Natural Resources Defense Council*, 467 U.S. 837, 104 S. Ct. 2778 (1984), and in the PSD program, *Alabama Power, supra*, 636 F.2d at 402.

(b) *Netting*: Netting can be used to exempt "modifications" of existing major sources from certain preconstruction permit requirements of NSR, so long as the exemption produces no net emissions increase, or at a minimum, no increase deemed to be significant. The idea is that "netting out" makes the modification only minor and, therefore, free of certain preconstruction permit obligations. Netting is unavailable for use in avoiding new source performance standards, national emissions standards for hazardous air pollutants, or other such requirements.

(c) *Emissions Offsets*: Major new stationary sources in nonattainment areas may only come on line if there is secured sufficient additional emissions reductions at other sources to more than offset the emissions projected from the new source. As we have seen, these offsets are authorized by the Part D of the CAA, added in 1977. *See supra*.

(d) *Emissions Reduction Banking*: This tool allows sources to earn emission reduction credits ("ERCs") and save them for later use in bubble, netting, or emissions offset transactions. In some instances, ERCs may be sold or transferred to other entities seeking to meet CAA regulatory requirements.

Each of these emissions trading vehicles are voluntary with sources, and EPA does not require states to afford these options within their SIPs. If states choose to make these options available, they may do so by rule or on a case-by-case basis.

D.   THE 1990 AMENDMENTS

We complete our review of stationary source regulation under the Clean Air Act with a survey of the amendments brought into the Act in 1990. The 1990 amendments were divided into eight titles. Of these, we will decline review of three.[8]

The five we will review, albeit briefly, are:

- Title I: Provisions for Attainment and Maintenance of National Ambient Air Standards,

- Title III: Hazardous Air Pollutants,

- Title IV: Acid Deposition Control,

- Title V: Permits, and

- Title VI: Stratospheric Ozone Protection.

---

[8] Title II, dealing with regulation of mobile sources of air pollution, is beyond the scope of our course. Title VII, relating to enforcement, is better investigated in a course in Environmental Litigation. And Title VIII, containing miscellaneous provisions, is not essential to our survey.

1. National Ambient Air Quality Standards

As we have seen, the 1970 CAA called for attainment of primary ambient air quality standards by 1975. When that goal fell by the wayside, the Act was amended. The 1977 Clean Air Act Amendments posited a ten-year compliance framework, but, as the 1990s approached, the goal remained unmet. Despite impressive gains in many quarters, still more than half of the nation's population was breathing unhealthful air. The chief offenders were carbon monoxide, ozone, and particulate matter. These pollutants remained abundantly present in the ambient air for several reasons, including the propensity of states to understate emissions in inventories submitted to the EPA, the use of erroneous models to project air quality gains, the failure to adequately enforce existing regulatory standards, design flaws in the standards themselves, and the inertia of agencies in the face of circumstances calling for change.

Accordingly, in Title I of the 1990 amendments, Congress retooled the nonattainment provisions, mainly by subcategorizing nonattainment areas. The Amendments called for classifying nonattainment area for CO, O_3, and PM as one of five types: *marginal, moderate, serious, severe,* or *extreme*. The idea was to build into the Act a scheme for incremental progress in meeting the NAAQSs for these pollutants. Different requirements were established for each subcategorized area — the more polluted the area, the stiffer the requirements (for extreme areas, for example, construction moratoria may be in order). The Act went on to mandate remedial actions when areas fail to improve air quality over time, and added the additional deterrence of authorizing restrictions on the availability of federal highway funds. The Amendments called for attainment over five years, although EPA was authorized to extend the date by another five years.

Other features of Title I include a mandatory enlargement of ozone nonattainment areas, to better reflect this pollutant's pattern of travel over hundreds of miles after emission; new requirements for monitoring; additional funding to assist emissions inventory efforts; shifting of federal transportation expenditures in nonattainment areas to discourage single occupancy vehicle use; and payments of fees to EPA of no less than $15 per ton of VOC, NOx, CO, and PM_{10} emitted.

2. Hazardous Air Pollutants

Hazardous air pollutants, often referred to as "air toxics," are governed by § 112 of the Clean Air Act. *See supra.* As discussed earlier in this chapter, § 112 as originally enacted was unwieldy. The obligation of identifying which pollutants qualified as hazardous constituted one major difficulty for EPA, while fashioning health-based emissions standards furnishing an "ample" margin of safety was another. Frustrated, EPA found itself devoting its energies to other pursuits.

Observing the inertia of the program, Congress finally got to the task of revising § 112 in 1990. The result was a major rewrite, a reworking of § 112 from the ground up. Congress began by relieving EPA of its first burden, identifying which pollutants are hazardous. The new § 112 begins by listing the hazardous air pollutants subject to the provision. The rewritten provision specifies 187 pollutants or chemical groups to be regulated. Section 112(b)(1), 42 U.S.C. § 7412(b)(1). Notably, EPA is empowered to revise and modify the list. Section 112(b)(2), 42 U.S.C. § 7412(b)(2). Included in Congress's list are substances such as benzene, dioxin, mercury, chromium, and methylisocyanate, the pollutant that killed more than 2,000 people in the 1984 disaster at Bhopal, India. Commensurate with this change, "hazardous air pollutant" is now defined as "any air pollutant listed pursuant to subsection (b) of this section." Section 112(a)(6), 42 U.S.C. § 7412(a)(6).

That done, Congress required new emissions standards for hazardous air pollutant emissions based on "maximum achievable control technology" ("MACT") and "generally achievable control technology" ("GACT"). The MACT standard, applicable to categories and subcategories of "new," see § 112(a)(1), 42 U.S.C. § 7412(a)(1), or existing "major," see § 112(a)(4), 42 U.S.C. § 7412(a)(4), sources, requires "the maximum degree of reduction in emissions of the hazardous air pollutants subject to this section (including a prohibition on such emissions, where achievable) that the Administrator, taking into consideration the cost of achieving such emission reduction, and any non-air quality health and environmental impacts and energy requirements, determines is achievable," § 112(d)(2), 42 U.S.C. § 7412(d)(2). What constitutes MACT may vary depending upon whether a source is "new" or "existing." Section 112(d)(3), 42 U.S.C. § 7412(d)(3). The GACT standard, less stringent than MACT but undefined in the legislation, is applicable to new or existing "area" sources. See § 112(a)(2), 42 U.S.C. § 7412(a)(2); see also § 112(d)(5), 42 U.S.C. § 7412(d)(5). EPA is directed to list only those area sources that present "a threat of adverse effects to human health or the environment." Section 112(c)(3), 42 U.S.C. § 7412(c)(3). If the Administrator finds an emission limitation to be infeasible in a particular case, she may promulgate in its place a "design, equipment, work practice, or operational standard." Section 112(h)(1), 42 U.S.C. § 7412(h)(1). Where no applicable emissions limitations are in place, EPA can make a case-by-case determination. Section 112(g)(2)(A) (B), 42 U.S.C. § 7412(g)(2)(A)–(B).

In enacting this new regulatory scheme, Congress projected a 75% decrease in air toxics emissions. However, in the event the new controls failed to clean the air to healthful levels, it supplied EPA with authority to implement more stringent health-based standards to solve the problem. Thus did the Congress relegate the previously required "ample margin of safety" health-based standard to a backup role. Section 112(f), 42 U.S.C. § 7412(f).

The 1990 amendments also provided that no person may modify, construct, or reconstruct a major source of air toxics without implementing MACT. "Modification" is defined in terms of increased emissions of any hazardous air pollutant, § 112(a)(5), 42 U.S.C. § 7412(a)(5), but modifications are made expressly subject to a statutory offset policy. Section 112(g)(1)(A), 42 U.S.C. § 7412(g)(1)(A).

In July 1992, pursuant to § 112(c)(1), EPA published an initial list of categories of sources that emit hazardous air pollutants. 57 Fed. Reg. 31,576 (1992). About seventeen months later, it published a schedule for promulgation of emission standards for these listed source categories, as required by § 112(e). 58 Fed. Reg. 63,941 (1993). In March 1994, it promulgated final rules to implement the section. 59 Fed. Reg. 12,408 (1994).

How does EPA determine MACT? For "new" sources, those for which construction begins after EPA publishes emission standards, § 111(a)(2), 42 U.S.C. § 7411(a)(2), MACT requires a degree of reduction of emissions not "less stringent than the emission control that is achieved in practice by the best controlled similar source." Section 112(d)(3), 42 U.S.C. § 7412(d)(3). For existing sources, the degree of reduction of emissions "shall not be less stringent than the average emission limitation achieved by the best performing 12 percent of the existing sources (for which the Administrator has emissions information)." *Id.* EPA uses a two-step process to implement these requirements. First the Agency establishes minimum stringency requirements known as "emission floors," which "apply without regard to either costs or the other factors and methods listed in section7412(d)(2)." *National Lime Ass'n v. EPA*, 233 F.3d 625, 629 (D.C. Cir. 2000) ("*National Lime II*"). Then, for each pollutant and source category, it determines whether stricter standards, known as "beyond-the-floor" limits, are achievable in light of the factors listed in § 112(d)(2), 42 U.S.C. § 7412(d)(2). *National Lime II*, 233 F.3d at 629. *See generally Cement Kiln Recycling Coalition v. U.S. Environmental Protection Agency*, 255 F.3d 855 (D.C. Cir. 2001).

Since the enactment of the revisions to § 112, EPA has issued rules to control air toxics emissions from 96 categories of major industrial polluters, such as chemical plants, steel mills, oil refineries, and aerospace facilities, and has moved to regulate emissions from smaller sources as well. More recently, it has been busy issuing new MACT standards for Portland cement plants, 75 Fed. Reg. 54,970 (2010), and industrial boilers, 75 Fed. Reg, 32,006 (2010). The Agency also entered into a consent decree requiring the preparation of MACT standards for coal- and oil-fired electricity generating units ("EGUs"). *American Nurses Ass'n v. Jackson*, (decree filed Dec. 18, 2010). EPA had earlier taken these EGUs off the list of sources subject to MACT standards, but its delisting decision was overturned by judicial decree. *New Jersey v. EPA*, 517 F.3d 574 (D.C. Cir. 2008).

3. Acid Deposition Control

Sulfur and nitrogen oxides, emitted into the ambient air largely from combustion of fossil fuels, react in the upper atmosphere to form compounds. After transport over potentially long distances, these compounds fall to ground level in the form of pollutants such as particulate matter (sulfates and nitrates), SO_2, NO_2, nitric acid, and, when reacting with volatile organic compounds (VOCs), ozone. This process is known as acid deposition. Acid deposition takes both dry and wet forms (hence, the familiar term, "acid rain").

The national problem with acid deposition was explained by the Senate in its report accompanying the enactment of Title IV:

SENATE REPORT NO. 101-228
101st. Cong. 2d Sess., U.S. Code Congressional and Administrative News,
at 3645–47

Sources and acid rain. Acid rain is created when oxides of sulfur and nitrogen are emitted most often from electric utilities and then transformed in the atmosphere or on surfaces into sulfuric and nitric acids. The process is relatively straightforward.

Sulfur (S) is contained in almost all fossil fuels, but especially coal. When burned, the sulfur combines with the oxygen in the air to create sulfur dioxide (SO_2).

Sulfur dioxide (SO_2) is a colorless gas, so it cannot be seen with the naked eye. It is, nevertheless, a powerful lung irritant which can cause lung seizures in asthmatics and other sensitive groups. When SO_2 is transformed into sulfate, a process which begins almost immediately, it escapes regulation under the Clean Air Act. SO_2 emitted by powerplants and other industrial sources combines with oxygen in the atmosphere to form sulfate (SO_4).

Sulfate (SO_4) is an extremely fine particle, capable of reaching the deepest recesses of the lung. Coincidentally, the sulfate particle is also perfectly sized for reducing visibility. This is one reason that airport visibility measurements are sometimes used as a surrogate for sulfate concentrations. When sulfate settles out of the air onto leaves, buildings or other surfaces it attracts water, which converts it into sulfuric acid ($H_2 SO_4$). If inhaled, the lung's own moisture supports the conversion. And, if the SO_4 is washed out [of] the air by fog, clouds, mist or rain, it has become "acid" rain, as it is popularly called.

Sulfuric acid ($H_2 SO_4$) is powerfully corrosive and can therefore directly damage tissues and materials. But it can also start a chemical reaction of its own, with effects that ripple through an ecosystem. When common dirt is washed in acid, heavy metals that were tightly bound to the soil particles — aluminum, lead, and mercury are three examples — are dissolved, entering the water runoff in massive quantities. Aluminum, for example, increases 1000 percent for every 100 percent increase in rainfall acidity. Thus if the acidity of rain increases 10-fold — which almost all agree is a fair definition of how "acid" today's acid rain is — the aluminum content of rainwater runoff increases 10,000 percent.

Exactly what damages can be fairly attributed to aluminum and other heavy metals freed by acid rain has not been sorted out completely. It is well established that the aluminum is extremely toxic to fish if it reaches lakes and streams. Many scientist believe that it is aluminum which is primarily responsible for the losses of lakes throughout Scandinavia, Canada and New England, rather than the sulfuric acid itself. It is equally clear that some of the other heavy metals — especially lead, cadmium and mercury — can pose a serious threat to human health as drinking water contaminants. Whether they are reaching these dangerous levels because of acid rain and, if so, in how many cases, is unclear.

Nitric acid (HNO_3). Nitrogen undergoes a fairly similar process of conversion: nitrogen (N_2) combines with oxygen (O_2) to form several different oxides ($N_2 O_2$, $N_2 O$, NO_2, etc.). These, in turn, form nitrates which, when exposed to water convert to nitric acid. There are, however, some important differences.

Oxides of nitrogen ($N_2 O_2$, $N_2 O$, NO_2) can be created because nitrogen is found both in fuels and in the air. Roughly 80 percent of the air is nitrogen, and almost all fuels other than natural gas also contain it. But the oxides are not formed until the heat and pressure of the combustion process are brought to bear. The combustion may take place in the cylinder of a car or the furnace of a giant coal-fired powerplant. But in either case, the combustion temperature and pressure are determinants of how much nitrogen is converted to oxides of nitrogen.

These oxides, like SO_2, are irritants which are regulated under the Clean Air Act. And, again like SO_2, they escape its coverage when they combine with oxygen to form nitrates (NO_3).

Nitrates (NO_3), like sulfates, are fine particles which can reach the cellular levels of the lung. Unlike sulfates, nitrates and other nitrogen-based compounds are considered beneficial to vegetation because they are plant nutrients. For this reason, some scientists and policy makers have tended to minimize the role which oxides of nitrogen, nitrates and nitric acid have played in the damage caused by acid rain and plans for its control.

Within the past several years, however, as scientists have searched for plausible explanations for the forest damages found throughout much of Europe and Eastern North America, they have begun to question whether one answer might be an "over fertilizing" effect of nitrogen compounds. There have also been suggestions that nitric acid could free heavy metals before being taken up by vegetation.

Nitric acid (HNO_3) thus may or may not be the equal of sulfuric acid in terms of the damages caused by acid rain. But the bill, including this title, imposes additional controls on nitrogen for reasons in addition to concerns over acid rain; namely, the role which it plays in the formation of ozone.

Ozone (O_3), better known as an ingredient in "smog", is the indicator for a variety of chemicals which are formed when the combination of nitrogen and organic chemicals (e.g., gasoline) are exposed to sunlight. Ozone is a powerful bleach, so effective at destroying organic matter that it is used by some cities to disinfect their drinking water supplies.

Although the chain of chemical reactions which leads to the formation of ozone and other oxidants is not completely understood, there is no disagreement that there are three essential ingredients. Without all three, ozone is not formed in substantial quantities. These are hydrocarbons, oxides of nitrogen, and sunlight. Historically, the Federal government has relied on a strategy of controlling ozone by controlling hydrocarbons emissions. This has achieved mixed results, leading some States to begin implementing a strategy based on controlling oxides of nitrogen. California has been the leading advocate of this approach and, according to State officials, has enjoyed considerable success.

Both ozone and acid aerosols pervade the atmosphere of eastern North America. Any one of them may pose a potent threat standing alone. But in combination, their impacts are multiplicative. This has been established in laboratory studies, but the extent to which these experiments represent the real environment [is] unclear. Nitrogen and its compounds, however, play a substantial role whether the specific problem being examined is acid rain, ozone, or the synergistic effects of the two.

———————

New Title IV of the 1990 amendments added an entirely new program to control acid deposition. 42 U.S.C. §§ 7651–7651o. With respect to nitrogen oxide emissions, the Act sought a two million ton reduction from emissions levels of the year 2000. To do this, the Act employed a conventional regulatory approach, establishing emission limitations for some sources and directing EPA to fashion others based on "the degree of reduction achievable through the retrofit application of the best system of continuous emission reduction, taking into account available technology, costs and energy and environmental impacts." Section 407(b)(1) (2), 42 U.S.C. § 7651f(b)(1)–(2).

However, Title IV is more interesting for its market-based regulation of sulfur dioxide (SO_2) emissions. Rather than opt for traditional command-and-control, the Act established for these emissions an innovative cap-and-trade regulatory system. As described in President George H. W. Bush's signing statement, the idea was to "set tough standards, allow freedom of choice in how to meet them, and let the power of markets help us in allocating the costs most efficiently." *Statement by President George Bush upon Signing S. 1630*, 26 WEEKLY COMPILATION OF PRESIDENTIAL DOCUMENTS, 1824, Nov. 19, 1990, *reprinted at* U.S. Code Congressional and Administrative News, 101st Cong., 2d Sess., at 3887.

The SO_2 control provisions exemplified the approach. For SO_2 emissions, the legislation first imposed a national cap of 8.95 million tons of emissions per year on electric utilities, an amount representing a ten million ton reduction from 1980 emission levels, § 403(a)(1), 42 U.S.C. § 7651b(a)(1); § 405(a)(3), 42 U.S.C. § 7651d(a)(3).(Note: the text of the Act reads "8.90 million tons." § 403(a)(1), 42 U.S.C. § 7651b(a)(1).) The Act contemplated reaching this goal over two phases. Phase I represented an interim step toward the goal. In Phase I, effective from 1995–2000, 110 designated utilities with major coal-fired generating units were required to reduce emissions to 2.50 pounds of SO_2 per million British thermal units of fuel consumed, as measured against benchmark years 1985–1987. Section 404, 42 U.S.C. § 7651c. To start the game, each of these utility units was allocated, free of charge, a predetermined number of pollution allowances on an annual basis; each allowance authorized the emission of one ton of sulfur dioxide for one year. Beginning in 1995, the Act prohibited polluters from emitting SO_2 in excess of their total number of Phase I allowances.

Beginning in 2000, Phase II of the program kicked in. Phase II brought under regulation all fossil fuel-fired power plants and further restricted aggregate allowances to a number assuring attainment of the 8.95 million ton national goal. Section 405(3), 42 U.S.C. § 7651d(3). Beginning in 2000, polluters must have reduced SO_2 emissions to no more than authorized by their Phase II allowances.[9]

Thus, to comply with the law, a utility has two options, to be taken singly or in concert. First, the utility can reduce emissions by changing the fuel it uses, or by installing pollution control equipment (typically, "scrubbers"), or both. In addition, and here is the innovative part of the system, the utility can engage in allowance trading. With this option, a regulated utility can keep high its emissions and still solve its legal problem by securing a sufficient number of allowances to make up the difference. Entities may do this because the Act declares allowances to be fully

---

[9] In addition to these annual allocations, in accordance with the legislation, EPA established three reserves. The first two reserves supply additional pollution rights for persons who (a) install high performance technologies ("qualifying Phase I technologies") (§ 404(d), 42 U.S.C. § 7651c(d)), or (b) implement customer-oriented conservation measures or renewable energy generation. The third reserve supplies additional allowances to persons who buy them at EPA-sponsored auctions.

marketable — they can be bought, sold, traded, or banked for future use or sale. Section 402, 42 U.S.C. § 7651. These transactions may occur independently among contracting parties or at an EPA-sponsored auction. Auctions are held in March of each year at the Chicago Board of Trade.

It is up to each utility to determine how best to meet its legal obligation. One utility might decide to rely fully on emissions reductions, while another might aggressively enter the marketplace to buy allowances. A utility that can reduce emissions cheaply might pull back more than is required and sell the difference, or carry those "credits" over for use in subsequent years. Another utility might both reduce emissions and purchase allowances. And so it goes.

By all accounts, the cap-and-trade program has been a huge success. Beneficial results were immediate. EPA reported that sulfate precipitation after 1995 fell to levels 10–25% below what would have been expected otherwise, with major gains in regions that need it most, such as the Ohio Valley. EPA attributed this improvement directly to Phase I emission reductions. (Comparatively, nitrate concentrations did not change appreciably.) EPA, *National Air Quality and Emissions Trends Report* (1997). In meeting the 1995 levels, utilities used 5,302,081 allowances, or 61% of the total issued by EPA for that year; those not used were carried over for later use. By one estimate, total emissions reductions exceeded statutory goals by 39%. Emissions, moreover, declined in every state having a regulated utility unit. Not a single utility failed to meet its Phase I-required SO_2 emissions reductions obligation, according to an EPA report dated August 8, 1996. By 2009, SO_2 emissions from power plants fell to 5.7 million tons, a 67% reduction from 1980 levels. http://www.epa.gov/airmarkets/progress/ARP09_4.html#keyresultsso2 www.epa.gov/air/acidrain/index.html (visited September 2004). There has been no need for enforcement.

The program accomplished these positive environmental results at exceedingly low cost. When the 1990 amendments were under consideration by Congress, skeptical utilities warned that cleaning the air of SO_2 would cost as much as $1500 a ton. EPA itself countered with a $600 per ton cost estimate. Yet, in the first auction, held in 1994, allowances traded in the $150 range. In the following year, prices dipped to about $125–130. In 1999, allowances sold in the "spot auction" went for an average of $200 and seven-year-advance allowances traded at approximately $165. Some utilities purchased tens of thousands of allowances; others were sellers. And it is not only emitters who participate. Organizations as diverse as the Creighton University Environmental Law Society, the Clean Air Conservancy, and even elementary school classes have submitted bids in the auctions. Non-commercial entities typically "retire" the allowances they purchase.

The most recent results of the program, those for 2009, indicate progress has continued apace. For that year, EPA allocated 9.5 million SO_2 allowances. When added to the 8.5 million unused allowances carried over from prior years, there were a total of 18 million allowances available for use in 2009. Acid rain production sources emitted approximately 5.7 million tons of SO_2 in 2009, obviously far less than the allowances allocated for the year, and far less than the total allowances available. In 2010, the total number of Title IV allowances allocated annually dropped to 8.95 million and remains statutorily fixed at that level. Compliance remains at 100 percent.

4. Permits

Another significant alteration of the 1990 amendments is its installation of a comprehensive permit system to streamline stationary source regulation. The idea of using permits had been gaining credence for twenty years. For one thing, permits have proven to be facile regulatory tools under the Clean Water Act (*see* Chapter 10, *infra*), in large part because they assemble in one easily found location the universe of requirements imposed on a regulated entity. As such, permits assist sources wanting to comply, and they effectively rob those which would not comply of excuses based on mistake. SIPs, moreover, have been increasingly seen as unwieldy and better suited for planning than for enforcement and program implementation. *See, e.g.*, Stephen E. Roady, *Permitting and Enforcement Under the Clean Air Act Amendments of 1990*, 21 ENVTL. L. REV. 10,178 (News & Analysis) (Apr. 1991).

Congress imposed its new permit requirements in what is now Subchapter V of the Act. As a general matter, the new provisions prohibit sources from operating without a permit, and declare unlawful activities that contravene the terms of a permit. "Major" sources, "affected sources" under the acid deposition program, new sources under § 111, sources of hazardous pollutants subject to § 112, and sources already subject to permitting under Parts C (PSD) and D (Nonattainment) fall under the requirements. Section 502(a), 42 U.S.C. § 7661a(a).

Permits serve as a convenient location for a compendium of requirements and conditions. First and foremost, they announce the emission limitations applicable to permitted sources. In addition, they stipulate each source's schedule of compliance, its monitoring requirements, "and other such conditions as are necessary to assure compliance with applicable requirements of this chapter, including the requirements of the applicable implementation plan." Section 504(a), 42 U.S.C. § 7661c(a). As a general matter, compliance with a permit is deemed to be compliance with the Act. This latter principle is known as the "permit shield." Section 504(f), 42 U.S.C. § 7661c(f).

5. Stratospheric Ozone Protection

Finally, Title VI imposes controls for the purpose of protecting stratospheric ozone. These controls are in addition to those in place under the Clean Air Act's Section 108–110 SIP process, which are aimed primarily at reducing concentrations of ozone at ground level. (At ground level, ozone is a threat to life; at high levels, it saves lives.) Congress enacted Title VI for two independent reasons. First is global warming. Ozone-depleting substances in the atmosphere are seen as contributors to this perceived calamity in the making, although, as discussed in the Note that follows, the science is in conflict on this issue. The second, and more important reason, has to do with the penetration of harmful ultraviolet rays from the Sun through the Earth's atmosphere. Too much ultraviolet radiation can cause skin cancer, cataracts, and genetic aberrations in humans. Ozone in the upper atmosphere performs the helpful function of blocking ultraviolet rays.

The call for stratospheric ozone protection arose in 1974, when two scientists from the University of California published a paper demonstrating that chlorofluorocarbons, or "CFCs," destroy ozone. CFCs have been used primarily for refrigeration and as aerosols. CFCs and other ozone-depleting substances (for a list, see CAA § 602 et seq., 42 U.S.C. § 7671a et seq.) have been floating high into the atmosphere for many years. At high altitudes, they come into contact with the stratospheric ozone layer, and work to destroy it.

For reasons not entirely clear, the greatest destruction of upper-level ozone has taken place in skies over the Antarctic, where a "hole" in the ozone layer has appeared each September through December since the 1970s. The hole is characterized by reduced levels of ozone: ozone concentrations outside the hole are generally in the 7–7.5 ppm range, but inside the hole the concentrations fall to about 4 ppm. The hole measures at least 2,400 kilometers in diameter, encompassing literally *millions* of square miles. While ozone emissions have decreased over the past several decades, because of past emissions, the hole has continued to enlarge.

The international community has taken steps to address the ozone depletion problem. In the United States, use of ozone-depleting materials was more than halved in the 1990s, in part because of a federal tax increasing the cost of such materials from about fifty cents a pound to five dollars. Under the Montreal Protocol on Substances that Deplete the Ozone Layer, almost every country in the world, including the European Union and the United States, agreed to stop CFC production and importation. (The phase-out in developing countries was projected for 2010.)

Title VI constitutes the Congress's response to the "environmental crisis" of ozone depletion. Senate Report No. 101-228, accompanying the Clean Air Act Amendments of 1990, U.S. Code Congressional and Administrative News, 101st Cong. 2d Sess., at 3768. It calls for elimination of production of CFCs "as expeditiously as possible." Production of so-called "Class I substances," mostly CFCs, was made illegal as of January 1, 2000. Section 604(b), 42 U.S.C. § 7671c(b). Production of "Class II substances," mostly hydrochloroflurocarbons, or HCFCs (which are ozone-unfriendly, but not as much as CFCs), must begin phasing out in 2015 and cease as of January 1, 2030. Section 605, 42 U.S.C. § 7671d. Title VI also calls for recycling and emissions reductions in the interim. Section 608, 42 U.S.C. § 7671g.

E. CLIMATE CHANGE

The temperature of air near the surface of the Earth has increased by 0.74°C (plus or minus 0.18°C) since the late nineteenth century, and the warming trend may be accelerating. The year 1995, during which an iceberg the size of Rhode Island broke off Antarctica, was at one time ranked as the warmest year of the century, but 1998 was later thought to overtake it. Currently, according to EPA, the warmest years over the last century "have likely been" 2010, 2005 (tied with 2010, according to the National Oceanic and Atmospheric Administration (NOAA) but behind it according to the World Meteorological Organization), 1998, 2002, 2003, and 2006, presumably in that order. Each year since 2000 has ranked in the top 15, it is also claimed. *See, e.g.*, http://www.noaanews.noaa.gov.

An awakened scientific interest in climate change and a highly attentive media have brought this geological trend into prominence as a political issue. The public at large, not just in this nation but around the world, fears a warming pattern that, it is said, could produce an array of harrowing consequences. In the short term, those consequences might include flooding of low-lying regions, disruption of agriculture, and the wholesale disturbance, if not destruction, of natural ecosystems. In the long term, nothing less than human survival could be at risk. While this abiding concern is only now finding formal expression in the body of environmental or natural resources law, its high profile earns its coverage here.

Why is the planet warm at all? The Earth basks in a blanket of warmth because of the good services of the planet's atmosphere. Heat energy from the Sun enters the atmosphere in the form of light. After solar light has penetrated, it comes into contact with the surface of the planet, which reflects a good portion of it back into outer space. Indeed, this is the key to global warmth: not all of the heat that makes its way in escapes out again. Much is trapped by the atmosphere.

The reason for solar heat's poor escape record has to do with wavelengths. When light from the Sun arrives at its planetary target, it has a relatively short wavelength (the one observable to the human eye). The wavelength, in turn, is a product of the measure of heat: the more heat content, the shorter the wavelength. Solar light is able to penetrate to the Earth's surface because the gases in the atmosphere are transparent to visible light. Upon contact with the relatively cool surface of the planet, however, the light is changed to infrared radiation, which has a longer wavelength. Infrared radiation cannot exit the planet as readily as the light that entered it because the same atmospheric gases that are transparent to visible light are opaque to infrared radiation. Accordingly, upon exit, the atmosphere absorbs reflected infrared radiation. Some of this absorbed radiation ultimately radiates out into space, but a good deal of it re-radiates back to the planetary surface. Because this phenomenon resembles the function of a greenhouse, it has been called the "greenhouse effect." Atmospheric gases that provide this important heat-trapping service are known as "greenhouse gases" ("GHGs").

The greenhouse effect, by overall standards, is obviously a good thing. (By one estimate, if there were no GHGs, the planet would be 59 degrees Fahrenheit colder on average than it is now, too cold to support life.) The worry is not that the globe is warm, but that it might be getting too warm. In short, maybe we are getting too much of a good thing.

The purported cause of global warming is the increasing accumulation of greenhouse gases in the atmosphere. The most prominent GHGs are five. They are carbon dioxide (CO_2), methane (CH_4), nitrous oxide (NO_2), water vapor (H_2O), and chlorofluorocarbons (CFCs). These gases make their way into the stratosphere from a variety of sources, human and non-human. CO_2 is a product of natural processes such as respiration and photosynthesis, but also comes from combustion of waste materials and carbon-containing fossil fuels. And come it does: in 2010 alone, CO_2 emissions into the atmosphere increased by 5.8 % from 2009 levels, according to the Joint Research Center of the European Commission. It is estimated that levels of CO_2 in the atmosphere have increased by almost 30% since the industrial revolution. By some projections, by 2100, if nothing is done, concentrations will be yet again 30–150% higher. Methane finds its way to the atmosphere from landfills, natural gas and petroleum operations, agriculture, and mining. While not as prevalent in the atmosphere as CO_2, methane reputedly is 20–50 times more efficient in trapping heat than CO_2. Nitrous oxide, released from fertilizers and fuel combustion, is found in even lesser amounts than methane, but is about 300 times more effective in trapping heat than CO_2. Atmospheric concentrations of nitrous oxides are purported to have risen 13% over the past two centuries. Water vapor is virtually omnipresent, and may or may not be in the form of clouds. Finally, CFCs, also blamed for thinning the ozone layer, *see supra*, find their way into the atmosphere largely from spray cans and refrigeration.

EPA has asserted that humans account for 98% of U.S. CO_2 emissions, 24% of methane emissions, and 18% of NO_2 emissions. The United States is a major contributor, said by some to be responsible for about one-fifth of total global greenhouse gas emissions. Theoretically, as atmospheric greenhouse gases increase in quantity, more trapping of heat will occur, and temperatures will rise. There is hardly any disagreement on the plausibility of this theory: the United Nations Intergovernmental Panel on Climate Change ("IPCC") has announced it is 90% confident that humans are causing global warming. As recently as five years ago, scientists were exceedingly more uncertain regarding the state of the science. (The IPCC has issued global warming reports at five year intervals since 1966. Its most recent report, as of this writing, came out in May 2007.)

Nonetheless, there remain numerous outstanding scientific uncertainties. First are questions of the reliability of scientific data and the capacity of scientists to interpret that data. Data accumulation on the amount of ongoing warming has been imprecise in many instances, and collection methods non-uniform. This is of great concern because even slight errors in information can seriously skew the final projections. In addition, the amount of data that must be analyzed is monumental. It has been said that a computer would have to track and evaluate over five million data parameters to reach a scientifically viable analytical result.

Second, the data currently in place, even if it were unassailable on credibility grounds, may not demonstrate an unprecedented warming trend. Based on ice core data and other indirect indicators, current Earth temperatures are currently at about the planet's 3,000 year average. Atmospheric temperatures, moreover, as distinct from surface air temperatures, have not risen over the last two decades; they did rise, apparently, during the 1970s. Planetary temperatures, in any event, have been anything but constant. From 800–1200 A.D., the "Medieval Warm Period," the northern hemisphere was so hot that Vikings cultivated Greenland and Newfoundland. By 1300, the "Little Ice Age" had begun. This cooling trend persisted until the early twentieth century. However, from the 1890s to the 1940s, surface temperatures inched up again, only to fall from the 1940s to the 1970s. For reasons not understood, tropospheric air temperatures warmed during the 1970s more than did surface air temperatures. In the last thirty-five years, stratospheric air temperatures have cooled. In short, the current warming trend may not be out of the ordinary. It may be within geologic deviations.

Third is the vexing problem of causation. Are humans a major reason for the warming, or are natural forces the real culprit? Note that warming trends seem to correlate with solar activity. Heat emanations from the Sun can vary significantly over decades and centuries, and records going back a couple of centuries show a strong correlation between increases in temperature in the northern hemisphere and this variable energy output (apparently, there is no similar data available for the southern hemisphere). The drought in the Amazon in 2010 is blamed for releasing 1.8 billion tons of CO_2 into the atmosphere. Another variable is volcanic activity. When Mount Pinatubo in the Phillippines erupted in 1991, global temperatures actually declined for a time, and did so precipitously at stratospheric levels. Additionally, if CO_2 emissions by humans were a major cause of global warming, one might expect the bulk of warming to have taken place in the wake of the Industrial Revolution, when human CO_2 contributions dramatically increased. But most of the warming took place in the three centuries preceding the Industrial Revolution.

Another uncertainty is the Earth's absorptive capacity. In fact, there may be self-mitigating natural responses to warming. When fossil fuel combustion releases CO_2, for example, it also releases sulfate aerosols. In the atmosphere, these latter substances reflect away solar radiation, producing a cooling effect. How much? Who knows? In the same vein, increased evaporation resulting from warmer temperatures could cause increased cloud production and a concomitant blockage of solar radiation.

In the current day, an entirely new theory is now under serious consideration. It posits the notion that subatomic particles from outer space, so-called "cosmic rays," are a major player. It seems that these particles, when in the atmosphere, increase cloud formation. The more clouds in the sky, the cooler the Earth becomes, because clouds retard the quantum of penetrating light. The presence of these particles is in turn influenced by solar winds. Thus, it might be that "[h]eavenly bodies might be driving long-term weather trends." Anne Jolis, *"The Other Climate Theory"*, Wall Street Journal, online.wsj.com, Sept. 7, 2011.

In addition, temperature increases should invigorate the growth of plants. Plants, of course, function to remove CO_2 from the atmosphere.

Another debate centers on the effects global warming will produce. Media coverage would lead one to conclude the effects of warming will be both negative and cataclysmic. The media, for example, trumpeted former Vice President Al Gore's prediction that warming would raise sea levels by 20 feet, causing the inundation of entire countries. Some media elements have blamed global warming for hugely increased damage caused by hurricanes and other cataclysmic weather events.

But much of this doomsday scenario may be overstated. The IPCC, for example, now estimates that, should warming continue as projected, sea levels should rise only 17 inches by 2100. It seems true as well that recent hurricanes have caused greater injury and damage of late not because the storms are more fierce, but because a far greater number of people now live in areas vulnerable to hurricanes.

In addition, it defies logic to think the effects of global warming should be exclusively negative. Thus far, for example, the warming effect has more raised cold temperatures than warm ones. What this means is that colder parts of the planet have warmed up more than already hotter parts have warmed; i.e., Arctic and temperate regions have experienced more warming than the tropics. On balance, this might be good. Just as warming can risk life, so also can it save life. By one estimate, since 1970 higher temperatures have averted 620,000 deaths that would have resulted from cold temperatures, while increasing by 130,000 the number of heat-related deaths, for a net saving of 490,000 lives.

Such potential benefits are not reasons to embrace warming, to be sure, but they should be part of the discussion.

So, where does this all leave us? The two scientific conclusions central to the global warming debate seem to be fairly well demonstrated. They are: (1) the planet is in a warming phase; and (2) human activity would seem to be at least a partial cause. Assuming these facts to be true, and even if global warming might produce some ecological benefits rather than none whatsoever, it is nonetheless reasonable as a matter of policy to conclude that humans ought to do *something* about it. Under these circumstances, a policy discouraging GHG emissions is not demonstrably unwise. But what should be done? The Bush Administration took a cautious approach. On the one hand, the White House announced support for reductions in greenhouse gas emissions, primarily by implementing clean energy technologies and promoting conservation. It also increased research into the causes of global warming, pledged a joint venture with other nations to monitor climate change, and promoted international cooperative efforts on the issue. Significantly, however, it declined to endorse the Kyoto Protocol, the major international treaty directed at the problem. Under the terms of the Protocol, signatory nations pledged to reduce their GHG emissions to about 5% below 1990 emissions levels by the year 2012. (The Clinton Administration, however, agreed in the Protocol for the United States to reduce its emissions by 7%. Japan and Canada agreed to 6% reductions, and Australia signed on for 8%.)

Calling the treaty "fatally flawed," President George W. Bush objected to it on several grounds. First, of course, was the matter of scientific uncertainty. *See, e.g., supra.* Beyond that, the treaty exempts from its terms major emitting nations such as China, now the largest greenhouse gas emitter, and India. (In 2010, China emitted 9 billion metric tons of CO_2, compared to 5.2 billion metric tons from the United States and 4 billion metric tons from the European Union; India's emissions have been calculated to be about 1.75 billion metric tons.) In President Bush's view, efforts to reduce warming must be shared by all nations. Accordingly, the burden should not fall in disproportionate measure on the United States, which produces approximately 16% of global emissions. While not stating so directly, surely the President was mindful of economic considerations as well. Compliance with the treaty, according to the Department of Energy under President Clinton, would cost the United States millions of jobs, and somewhere in the range of $300 billion to $400 billion, or about 3–4% of the gross domestic product, per year.

The treaty took effect on February 16, 2005, following ratification of it by Russia in October 2004. Russia's ratification brought the number of ratifying nations to 125, but, more significantly, brought into the fold nations responsible for at least 55% of total global CO_2 emissions. By its terms, the treaty could not take effect until that latter benchmark was reached.

(A side note: Russia's decision to ratify was substantially eased by economic realities. Because of a general economic downturn, Russia's emissions as of 2004 stood at approximately 25% *below* 1990 levels. This means that, under the terms of the treaty, Russia can sell its excess emissions for profits potentially in the "billions" of dollars. For that reason, and because Russia lacks the capacity to monitor emissions, it will be years before any curtailments of emissions become necessary, if ever. Last, Russia is the beneficiary of economic concessions from Europe, supplied to it to encourage its Kyoto ratification. Morning Edition, *National Public Radio*, October 22, 2004.)

For its part, the United States Senate voted 95-0 in July 1997, to not ratify unless and until all nations were included under the terms of the treaty and only if the treaty would not seriously harm the domestic economy. Four months thereafter, despite that unanimous Senate vote, former Vice President Al Gore signed the Protocol on behalf of the United States. His signature did not bind the nation to the terms of the treaty.

The Bush Administration's decision to forego participation in Kyoto was assuredly the correct one. Even if every GHG-emitting country ratified Kyoto, and each complied with its terms, the benefit would be a reduction in global warming of only 0.3 degrees F in 2100 from what it otherwise would have been; the otherwise expected warming of 4.7 degrees F would be reached in 2105 rather than 2100. Similarly, the projected warming-caused rise in sea levels would be forestalled by a mere four years. Such small benefits arguably do not justify such exorbitant costs. Beyond that, Kyoto is *not* being complied with. Of the 41 nations monitored by the United Nations, 34 increased GHG emissions between 2000 and 2004. Between 2000 and 2007, for that matter, Europe has performed less well than the United States, at least in percentage terms. In that period, European emissions have jumped 3.8% while U.S. emissions are up 2.5%. In the most recent years, signatory nations have reduced their emissions, by about 5% compared to 1990 emission levels, but that progress is due to slumping economies traceable to the global economic downturn.

If Kyoto is not the solution, what is? Assuming the goal of reducing global warming is in large part to prevent human suffering, some persons contend the world should focus its finite resources on improving health and welfare across the planet, and especially in the Third World, rather than on reducing emissions of greenhouse gases. Currently, four million people die each year from malnutrition, three million from HIV/AIDS, and two million from lack of clean drinking water. From a cost-benefit perspective, focusing on solving these massive problems could be a more cost-efficient way to go about alleviating human suffering than reducing GHGs. In the estimate of some, the "bang for the buck" would be 50 to 100 times better. In addition, improving the human condition in these ways would mean nations would themselves become wealthier. Increased wealth, in turn, would enable nations to better deal with whatever adverse effects global warming might ultimately present. For an extensive discussion of these policy options, see BJØRN LOMBORG, COOL IT (2007).

Despite the foregoing, the push in this country has been to reduce emissions of GHGs, especially CO_2. In one development, ten states banded together to take action on their own to reduce GHG emissions from electricity generators within their borders. The states were Connecticut, Delaware, Maine, Maryland, Massachusetts, New Hampshire, New Jersey, New York, Rhode Island, and Vermont. (New Jersey dropped out in 2011). Participating in what is known as the Regional Greenhouse Gas Initiative ("RGGI"), they designed a cap-and-trade program in 2005 and have reported that, as of 2009, GHG emissions are down 33% from 2005 levels. The report concedes that, while the RGGI has had a positive impact, other factors, including a weak economy, also contributed to these reductions. http://www.rggi.org/docs/Retrospective_Analysis_Draft_White_Paper.pdf. Emissions trading authorized by the Initiative decreased dramatically in 2010 due to falling prices in the natural gas market and the economic downturn. Meanwhile, in October 2011, California adopted a mix of cap-and-trade controls and new state taxes intended to reduce GHG emissions by nearly 30% from power plants, manufacturers, and vehicles by 2020. The program is scheduled to kick off in 2013.

The Bush Administration, for its part, declined to take action of this sort based in part on its view that it lacked legal authority to do so. It argued CO_2, which is part of "air," could not qualify as well as a "pollutant" of that same air. That theory is no longer viable because of a 5-4 decision of the United States Supreme Court in *Massachusetts v. EPA*, 549 U.S. 497, 127 S. Ct. 1438 (2007). *Massachusetts* flatly declared CO_2 and other greenhouse gases to be pollutants under the Act. The decision did not mandate CAA regulation; it concluded only that such regulation was within the subject matter jurisdiction of the Act. After the decision was handed down, the Bush Administration directed EPA to set greenhouse gas emission standards for new motor vehicles by the end of 2008 — the Administration apparently restricted its directive to mobile sources because *Massachusetts* dealt only with that portion of the CAA.

Since then, much has transpired. First, EPA issued a reporting rule, requiring thousands of emitters to report to EPA what GHGs they are releasing, and in what quantities. In addition, in December 2009, it issued its long-awaited "endangerment" finding. In it, the agency concluded that greenhouse gas emissions from motor vehicles "cause, or contribute to, air pollution which may reasonably be anticipated to endanger public health or welfare." Section 202(a)(1), 42 U.S.C.A. Section 7521(a)(1); 74 Fed. Reg. 66496. The endangerment finding opens the door for designation of CO_2 as a criteria pollutant. More recently, EPA has initiated efforts to reduce GHG emissions from light-duty and heavy-duty vehicles, to impose GHG emission controls under § 111 for fossil-fuel fired power plants, and to affix BACT emissions controls on new or modified major GHG-emitting stationary sources. To facilitate the BACT initiative, the agency issued a SIP call requiring 13 states to modify their PSD programs to allow for issuance of permits to GHG-emitting facilities. EPA left states with the option of fashioning their own revisions or simply adopting a FIP already designed for these purposes. At this writing, all of the states except Texas have announced their intentions to adopt the FIP. Texas has flatly refused to modify its SIP for these purposes. Accordingly, EPA is managing the program in Texas; the Agency issued its first greenhouse gas emissions permit within that state in November 2011. At this writing, the endangerment finding and the vehicle emissions initiative are being challenged in the D.C. Circuit Court of Appeals. *Coalition for Responsible Regulation v. EPA*, Nos. 09-1322 and 10-1092.

In June 2010, EPA promulgated its GHG "tailoring rule." 75 Fed. Reg. 31,514. The rule limits application of these PSD BACT controls to the largest sources. According to EPA, without the rule, PSD requirements would apply to as many as six million GHG-emitting sources, a situation that would overwhelm permitting authorities. The rule was immediately challenged in the D.C. Circuit Court of Appeals. *Coalition for Responsible Regulation v. EPA*, D.C. Cir., No. 10-1073. Challengers contend that any refusal by the Agency to apply its rule to fewer than all sources governed by the CAA's PSD program would violate the statute. Invoking what it called the doctrines of "absurd results," "administrative necessity," and "one-step-at-a-time," EPA maintains that limiting the number of sources covered by the program in this context is a justifiable exercise of discretion. As stated in its brief filed with the court in September 2011: "when faced with overwhelming burdens in the administration of statutory requirements, or where application of the literal language of a statute would actually subvert congressional intent, the agency does not get to blow up the statute. Instead, the agency must still apply the statute, and it must do so in a manner that adheres as closely as possible to Congress' intent while assuring that implementation proceeds in a feasible manner." At this writing, no decision has issued.

For its part, the Obama Administration assembled the Interagency Climate Change Adaptation Task Force, in October 2009. The Executive Order mandating the Task Force directed more than 20 federal agencies and executive branch offices to undertake research and public outreach to enable the formation of a national climate change adaptation strategy. According to the "Progress Report of the Interagency Climate Change Adaptation Task Force: Recommended Actions in Support of a National Climate Change Adaptation Strategy," issued in October 2010, the time to act is now: "Adaptive actions should not be delayed to wait for a complete understanding of climate change impacts, as there will always be some uncertainty." The report is available online.

EPA's resolve to move forward, however, may be waning. At this writing, it appears EPA may be disinclined to remain assertive on this issue, presumably because of a fragile economy and potential adverse political repercussions. In fact, EPA's disinclination may well find its source in the White House. In March 2011, President Obama delivered the major address of his presidency on national energy policy. In the address, while the President spoke at length of prices at the pump and of the need to increase investments in renewable energy sources, he spoke not at all of the threat of climate change nor of the need to reduce GHG emissions (he did say the words, "carbon dioxide," once).

A federal statutory and regulatory lethargy on these matters brings into heightened relief the federal common law of nuisance. Might federal common law accomplish what federal statutory and regulatory law forsakes?

AMERICAN ELECTRIC POWER COMPANY, INC. v. CONNECTICUT
131 S. Ct. 2527 (2011)

GINSBURG, J., delivered the opinion of the Court, in which ROBERTS, C. J., and SCALIA, KENNEDY, BREYER, and KAGAN, JJ., joined. ALITO, J., filed an opinion concurring in part and concurring in the judgment, in which THOMAS, J., joined. SOTOMAYOR, J., took no part in the consideration or decision of the case.[10]

We address in this opinion the question whether the plaintiffs (several States, the city of New York, and three private land trusts) can maintain federal common law public nuisance claims against carbon-dioxide emitters (four private power companies and the federal Tennessee Valley Authority). As relief, the plaintiffs ask for a decree setting carbon-dioxide emissions for each defendant at an initial cap, to be further reduced annually. The Clean Air Act and the Environmental Protection Agency action the Act authorizes, we hold, displace the claims the plaintiffs seek to pursue. . . .

II

The lawsuits we consider here began well before EPA initiated the efforts to regulate greenhouse gases just described. In July 2004, two groups of plaintiffs filed separate complaints in the Southern District of New York against the same five major electric power companies. The first group of plaintiffs included eight States and New York City, the second joined three nonprofit land trusts; both groups are respondents here. The defendants, now petitioners, are four private companies and the Tennessee Valley Authority, a federally owned corporation that operates fossil-fuel fired power plants in several States. According to the complaints, the defendants "are the five largest emitters of carbon dioxide in the United States." App. 57, 118. Their collective annual emissions of 650 million tons constitute 25 percent of emissions from the domestic electric power sector, 10 percent of emissions from all domestic human activities, *ibid.*, and 2.5 percent of all anthropogenic emissions worldwide, App. to Pet. for Cert. 72a.

By contributing to global warming, the plaintiffs asserted, the defendants' carbon-dioxide emissions created a "substantial and unreasonable interference with public rights," in violation of the federal common law of interstate nuisance, or, in the alternative, of state tort law. The States and New York City alleged that public lands, infrastructure, and health were at risk from climate change. The trusts urged that climate change would destroy habitats for animals and rare species of trees and plants on land the trusts owned and conserved. All plaintiffs sought injunctive relief requiring each defendant "to cap its carbon dioxide emissions and then reduce them by a specified percentage each year for at least a decade."

---

[10] [Ed. note: Justice Sotomayor was originally a member of the Second Circuit panel that was considering this case, but was elevated to the United States Supreme Court before the matter was deliberated by at the circuit court level. Accordingly, the other two judges of the three-judge panel decided the case. They were in agreement on their decision.]

The District Court dismissed both suits as presenting non-justiciable political questions, citing *Baker* v. *Carr*, 369 U.S. 186, 82 S. Ct. 691, 7 L. Ed. 2d 663 (1962), but the Second Circuit reversed, 582 F.3d 309 (2009). On the threshold questions, the Court of Appeals held that the suits were not barred by the political question doctrine, *id.*, at 332, and that the plaintiffs had adequately alleged Article III standing, *id.*, at 349.

Turning to the merits, the Second Circuit held that all plaintiffs had stated a claim under the "federal common law of nuisance." *Id.*, at 358, 371. For this determination, the court relied dominantly on a series of this Court's decisions holding that States may maintain suits to abate air and water pollution produced by other States or by out-of-state industry. *Id.*, at 350–351; see, *e.g.*, *Illinois* v. *Milwaukee*, 406 U.S. 91, 93, 92 S. Ct. 1385, 31 L. Ed. 2d 712 (1972) (*Milwaukee I*) (recognizing right of Illinois to sue in federal district court to abate discharge of sewage into Lake Michigan).

The Court of Appeals further determined that the Clean Air Act did not "displace" federal common law. In *Milwaukee* v. *Illinois*, 451 U.S. 304, 316-319, 101 S. Ct. 1784, 68 L. Ed. 2d 114 (1981) (*Milwaukee II*), this Court held that Congress had displaced the federal common law right of action recognized in *Milwaukee I* by adopting amendments to the Clean Water Act, 33 U.S.C. § 1251 *et seq.* That legislation installed an all-encompassing regulatory program, supervised by an expert administrative agency, to deal comprehensively with interstate water pollution. The legislation itself prohibited the discharge of pollutants into the waters of the United States without a permit from a proper permitting authority. *Milwaukee II*, 451 U.S., at 310–311, 101 S. Ct. 1784, 68 L. Ed. 2d 114 (citing § 1311). At the time of the Second Circuit's decision, by contrast, EPA had not yet promulgated any rule regulating greenhouse gases, a fact the court thought dispositive. 582 F.3d at 379–381. "Until EPA completes the rulemaking process," the court reasoned, "we cannot speculate as to whether the hypothetical regulation of greenhouse gases under the Clean Air Act would in fact 'spea[k] directly' to the 'particular issue' raised here by Plaintiffs." *Id.*, at 380.

We granted certiorari. 562 U.S. ___, 131 S. Ct. 813, 178 L. Ed. 2d 530 (2010).

III

The petitioners contend that the federal courts lack authority to adjudicate this case. Four members of the Court would hold that at least some plaintiffs have Article III standing under *Massachusetts*, which permitted a State to challenge EPA's refusal to regulate greenhouse gas emissions, 549 U.S., at 520–526, 127 S. Ct. 1438, 167 L. Ed. 248; and, further, that no other threshold obstacle bars review. Four members of the Court, adhering to a dissenting opinion in *Massachusetts*, 549 U.S., at 535, 127 S. Ct. 1438, 167 L. Ed. 248, or regarding that decision as distinguishable, would hold that none of the plaintiffs have Article III standing. We therefore affirm, by an equally divided Court, the Second Circuit's exercise of jurisdiction and proceed to the merits. See *Nye* v. *United States*, 313 U.S. 33, 44, 61 S. Ct. 810, 85 L. Ed. 1172 (1941).

IV

A

"There is no federal general common law," *Erie R. Co.* v. *Tompkins*, 304 U.S. 64, 78, 58 S. Ct. 817, 82 L. Ed. 1188 (1938), famously recognized. In the wake of *Erie*, however, a keener understanding developed. See generally Friendly, In Praise of *Erie* — And of the New Federal Common Law, 39 N.Y. U. L. Rev. 383 (1964). *Erie* "le[ft] to the states what ought be left to them," *id.*, at 405, and thus required "federal courts [to] follow state decisions on matters of substantive law appropriately cognizable by the states," *id.*, at 422. *Erie* also sparked "the emergence of a federal decisional law in areas of national concern." *Id.*, at 405. The "new" federal common law addresses "subjects within national legislative power where Congress has so directed" or where the basic scheme of the Constitution so demands. *Id.*, at 408, n. 119, 421–422. Environmental protection is undoubtedly an area "within national legislative power," one in which federal courts may fill in "statutory interstices," and, if necessary, even "fashion federal law." *Id.*, at 421–422. As the Court stated in *Milwaukee I*: "When we deal with air and water in their ambient or interstate aspects, there is a federal common law." 406 U.S., at 103, 92 S. Ct. 1385, 31 L. Ed. 2d 712.

Decisions of this Court predating *Erie*, but compatible with the distinction emerging from that decision between "general common law" and "specialized federal common law," Friendly, *supra*, at 405, have approved federal common law suits brought by one State to abate pollution emanating from another State. See, *e.g.*, *Missouri* v. *Illinois*, 180 U.S. 208, 241–243, 21 S. Ct. 331, 45 L. Ed. 497 (1901) (permitting suit by Missouri to enjoin Chicago from discharging untreated sewage into interstate waters); *New Jersey v. City of New York*, 283 U.S. 473, 477, 481–483, 51 S. Ct. 519, 75 L. Ed. 1176 (1931) (ordering New York City to stop dumping garbage off New Jersey coast); *Georgia* v. *Tennessee Copper Co.*, 240 U.S. 650, 36 S. Ct. 465, 60 L. Ed. 846 (1916) (ordering private copper companies to curtail sulfur-dioxide discharges in Tennessee that caused harm in Georgia). See also *Milwaukee I*, 406 U.S., at 107, 92 S. Ct. 1385, 31 L. Ed. 2d 712 (post-*Erie* decision upholding suit by Illinois to abate sewage discharges into Lake Michigan). The plaintiffs contend that their right to maintain this suit follows inexorably from that line of decisions.

Recognition that a subject is meet for federal law governance, however, does not necessarily mean that federal courts should create the controlling law. Absent a demonstrated need for a federal rule of decision, the Court has taken "the prudent course" of "adopt[ing] the readymade body of state law as the federal rule of decision until Congress strikes a different accommodation." *United States* v. *Kimbell Foods, Inc.*, 440 U.S. 715, 740, 99 S. Ct. 1448, 59 L. Ed. 2d 711 (1979); see *Bank of America Nat'l Trust & Sav. Ass'n* v. *Parnell*, 352 U.S. 29, 32–34, 77 S. Ct. 119, 1 L. Ed. 2d 93 (1956). And where, as here, borrowing the law of a particular State would be inappropriate, the Court remains mindful that it does not have creative power akin to that vested in Congress. See *Missouri* v. *Illinois*, 200 U.S. 496, 519, 26 S. Ct. 268, 50 L. Ed. 572 (1906) ("fact that this court must decide does not mean, of course, that it takes the place of a legislature"); cf. *United States* v.

Standard Oil Co. of Cal., 332 U.S. 301, 308, 314, 67 S. Ct. 1604, 91 L. Ed. 2067 (1947) (holding that federal law determines whether Government could secure indemnity from a company whose truck injured a United States soldier, but declining to impose such an indemnity absent action by Congress, "the primary and most often the exclusive arbiter of federal fiscal affairs").

In the cases on which the plaintiffs heavily rely, States were permitted to sue to challenge activity harmful to their citizens' health and welfare. We have not yet decided whether private citizens (here, the land trusts) or political subdivisions (New York City) of a State may invoke the federal common law of nuisance to abate out-of-state pollution. Nor have we ever held that a State may sue to abate any and all manner of pollution originating outside its borders.

The defendants argue that considerations of scale and complexity distinguish global warming from the more bounded pollution giving rise to past federal nuisance suits. Greenhouse gases once emitted "become well mixed in the atmosphere," 74 Fed. Reg. 66514; emissions in New Jersey may contribute no more to flooding in New York than emissions in China. Cf. Brief for Petitioners 18-19. The plaintiffs, on the other hand, contend that an equitable remedy against the largest emitters of carbon dioxide in the United States is in order and not beyond judicial competence. See Brief for Respondents Open Space Institute et al. 32–35. And we have recognized that public nuisance law, like common law generally, adapts to changing scientific and factual circumstances. *Missouri*, 200 U.S., at 522, 26 S. Ct. 268, 50 L. Ed. 572 (adjudicating claim though it did not concern "nuisance of the simple kind that was known to the older common law"); see also *D'Oench, Duhme & Co.* v. *FDIC*, 315 U.S. 447, 472, 62 S. Ct. 676, 86 L. Ed. 956 (1942) (Jackson, J., concurring) ("federal courts are free to apply the traditional common-law technique of decision" when fashioning federal common law).

We need not address the parties' dispute in this regard. For it is an academic question whether, in the absence of the Clean Air Act and the EPA actions the Act authorizes, the plaintiffs could state a federal common law claim for curtailment of greenhouse gas emissions because of their contribution to global warming. Any such claim would be displaced by the federal legislation authorizing EPA to regulate carbon-dioxide emissions.

B

"[W]hen Congress addresses a question previously governed by a decision rested on federal common law," the Court has explained, "the need for such an unusual exercise of law-making by federal courts disappears." *Milwaukee II*, 451 U.S., at 314, 101 S. Ct. 1784, 68 L. Ed. 2d 114 (holding that amendments to the Clean Water Act displaced the nuisance claim recognized in *Milwaukee I*). Legislative displacement of federal common law does not require the "same sort of evidence of a clear and manifest [congressional] purpose" demanded for preemption of state law. *Id.*, at 317, 101 S. Ct. 1784, 68 L. Ed. 2d 114. " '[D]ue regard for the presuppositions of our embracing federal system . . . as a promoter of democracy,' " *id.*, at 316, 101 S. Ct. 1784, 68 L. Ed. 2d 114 (quoting *San Diego Building Trades Council* v. *Garmon*, 359 U.S. 236, 243, 79 S. Ct. 773, 3 L. Ed. 2d 775 (1959)), does not enter the calculus, for it is primarily the office of Congress, not the federal courts, to prescribe national policy in areas of special federal interest. *TVA* v. *Hill*, 437 U.S. 153, 194, 98 S. Ct. 2279, 57 L. Ed. 2d 117 (1978). The test for whether congressional legislation excludes the declaration of federal common law is simply whether the statute "speak[s] directly to [the] question" at issue. *Mobil Oil Corp.* v. *Higginbotham*, 436 U.S. 618, 625, 98 S. Ct. 2010, 56 L. Ed. 2d 581 (1978); see *Milwaukee II*, 451 U.S., at 315, 101 S. Ct. 1784, 68 L. Ed. 2d 114; *County of Oneida* v. *Oneida Indian Nation of N. Y.*, 470 U.S. 226, 236–237, 105 S. Ct. 1245, 84 L. Ed. 2d 169 (1985).

We hold that the Clean Air Act and the EPA actions it authorizes displace any federal common law right to seek abatement of carbon-dioxide emissions from fossil-fuel fired power plants. *Massachusetts* made plain that emissions of carbon dioxide qualify as air pollution subject to regulation under the Act. 549 U.S., at 528–529, 127 S. Ct. 1438, 167 L. Ed. 2d 248. And we think it equally plain that the Act "speaks directly" to emissions of carbon dioxide from the defendants' plants.

[The Court then discussed § 111 of the Clean Air Act, which in the Court's view addresses the matter of carbon dioxide emissions.] The Act itself thus provides a means to seek limits on emissions of carbon dioxide from domestic power plants — the same relief the plaintiffs seek by invoking federal common law. We see no room for a parallel track.

C

The plaintiffs argue, as the Second Circuit held, that federal common law is not displaced until EPA actually exercises its regulatory authority, *i.e.*, until it sets standards governing emissions from the defendants' plants. We disagree.

The sewage discharges at issue in *Milwaukee II*, we do not overlook, were subject to effluent limits set by EPA; under the displacing statute, "[e]very point source discharge" of water pollution was "prohibited unless covered by a permit." 451 U.S., at 318–320, 101 S. Ct. 1784, 68 L. Ed. 2d 114 (emphasis deleted). As *Milwaukee II* made clear, however, the relevant question for purposes of displacement is "whether the field has been occupied, not whether it has been occupied in a particular manner." *Id.*, at 324, 101 S. Ct. 1784, 68 L. Ed. 2d 114. Of necessity, Congress selects different regulatory regimes to address different problems. Congress could hardly preemptively prohibit every discharge of carbon dioxide unless covered by a permit. After all, we each emit carbon dioxide merely by breathing.

The Clean Air Act is no less an exercise of the legislature's "considered judgment" concerning the regulation of air pollution because it permits emissions *until* EPA acts. See *Middlesex County Sewerage Auth.* v. *National Sea Clammers Ass'n*, 453 U.S. 1, 22, n. 32, 101 S. Ct. 2615, 69 L. Ed. 2d 435 (1981) (finding displacement although Congress "allowed some continued dumping of sludge" prior to a certain date). The critical point is that Congress delegated to EPA the decision whether and how to regulate carbon-dioxide emissions from power plants; the delegation is what displaces federal common law. Indeed, were EPA to decline to regulate carbon-dioxide emissions altogether at the conclusion of its ongoing § [111] rulemaking, the federal courts would have no warrant to employ the federal common law of nuisance to upset the agency's expert determination.

EPA's judgment, we hasten to add, would not escape judicial review. . . . If the plaintiffs in this case are dissatisfied with the outcome of EPA's forthcoming rulemaking, their recourse under federal law is to seek Court of Appeals review, and, ultimately, to petition for certiorari in this Court.

Indeed, this prescribed order of decisionmaking — the first decider under the Act is the expert administrative agency, the second, federal judges — is yet another reason to resist setting emissions standards by judicial decree under federal tort law. The appropriate amount of regulation in any particular greenhouse gas-producing sector cannot be prescribed in a vacuum: as with other questions of national or international policy, informed assessment of competing interests is required. Along with the environmental benefit potentially achievable, our Nation's energy needs and the possibility of economic disruption must weigh in the balance.

The Clean Air Act entrusts such complex balancing to EPA in the first instance, in combination with state regulators. . . .

It is altogether fitting that Congress designated an expert agency, here, EPA, as best suited to serve as primary regulator of greenhouse gas emissions. The expert agency is surely better equipped to do the job than individual district judges issuing ad hoc, case-by-case injunctions. Federal judges lack the scientific, economic, and technological resources an agency can utilize in coping with issues of this order. See generally *Chevron U. S. A. Inc.* v. *NRDC*, 467 U.S. 837, 865–866, 104 S. Ct. 2778, 81 L. Ed. 2d 694 (1984). Judges may not commission scientific studies or convene groups of experts for advice, or issue rules under notice-and-comment procedures inviting input by any interested person, or seek the counsel of regulators in the States where the defendants are located. Rather, judges are confined by a record comprising the evidence the parties present. Moreover, federal district judges, sitting as sole adjudicators, lack authority to render precedential decisions binding other judges, even members of the same court.

Notwithstanding these disabilities, the plaintiffs propose that individual federal judges determine, in the first instance, what amount of carbon-dioxide emissions is "unreasonable," and then decide what level of reduction is "practical, feasible and economically viable," These determinations would be made for the defendants named in the two lawsuits launched by the plaintiffs. Similar suits could be mounted, counsel for the States and New York City estimated, against "thousands or hundreds or tens" of other defendants fitting the description "large contributors" to carbon-dioxide emissions.

The judgments the plaintiffs would commit to federal judges, in suits that could be filed in any federal district, cannot be reconciled with the decisionmaking scheme Congress enacted. The Second Circuit erred, we hold, in ruling that federal judges may set limits on greenhouse gas emissions in face of a law empowering EPA to set the same limits, subject to judicial review only to ensure against action "arbitrary, capricious, . . . or otherwise not in accordance with law." § 7607(d)(9).

V

The plaintiffs also sought relief under state law, in particular, the law of each State where the defendants operate power plants. See App. 105, 147. The Second Circuit did not reach the state law claims because it held that federal common law governed. 582 F.3d at 392; see *International Paper Co.* v. *Ouellette*, 479 U.S. 481, 488, 107 S. Ct. 805, 93 L. Ed. 2d 883 (1987) (if a case "should be resolved by reference to federal common law[,] . . . state common law [is] preempted"). In light of our holding that the Clean Air Act displaces federal common law, the availability *vel non* of a state lawsuit depends, *inter alia*, on the preemptive effect of the federal Act. *Id.*, at 489, 491, 497, 107 S. Ct. 805, 93 L. Ed. 883 (holding that the Clean Water Act does not preclude aggrieved individuals from bringing a "nuisance claim pursuant to the law of the *source* State"). None of the parties have briefed preemption or otherwise addressed the availability of a claim under state nuisance law. We therefore leave the matter open for consideration on remand.

For the reasons stated, we reverse the judgment of the Second Circuit and remand the case for further proceedings consistent with this opinion.

It is so ordered.

JUSTICE ALITO, with whom JUSTICE THOMAS joins, concurring in part and concurring in the judgment.

I concur in the judgment, and I agree with the Court's displacement analysis on the assumption (which I make for the sake of argument because no party contends otherwise) that the interpretation of the Clean Air Act, 42 U.S.C. § 7401 *et seq.*, adopted by the majority in *Massachusetts* v. *EPA*, 549 U.S. 497, 127 S. Ct. 1438, 167 L. Ed. 2d 248 (2007), is correct.

NOTES

1. ***Effect of AEP.*** Some lawyers are remarking that *AEP* may not be the end of federal common law nuisance suits in the GHG world. According to this line of argument, causes of action for damages or declaratory judgments, as distinct from those seeking regulatory modifications, may survive the decision. In addition, it is observed, *AEP* did not stipulate *when* the CAA displaced federal common law. Was it at initial enactment of the statute in 1970, or perhaps when CO_2 was declared to be a pollutant in 2007? GHG emissions predating the preemption might be subject to actions for damages. If causes of action for damages are allowed, a looming possibility is major litigation by foreign nations (China?) for past harms. At this writing, the Ninth Circuit Court of Appeals is set to decide a case that might bear upon these matters. The district court decision before the Ninth Circuit is *Kivalina* v. *Exxon Mobil Corp.*, 663 F. Supp. 2d 863 (N.D. Cal. 2009).

2. ***Emissions Data.*** EPA announced in February 2011, that GHG emissions in the United States decreased by 2.9% between 2007 and 2008, and another 6% the following year, primarily due to the nation's economic slump and to switches by industry from coal to natural gas. GHG emissions remain 7.4% above 1990 emissions levels. The report is available at www.epa.gov.

3. ***Carbon Capture.*** Carbon capture and storage projects are those which, as the name indicates, capture GHG emissions before their escape into the environment and typically redirect them underground where, presumably, they can do no

harm. At this writing, there are eight large-scale carbon capture and storage projects in operation around the globe at this writing. Six more are under construction and 10 more await a final investment decision in the next 12 months. Report of the Global Carbon Capture and Storage Institute, released October 4, 2011, http://cdn.globalccsinstitute.com. The challenge regarding carbon capture is to develop a technology available on a large scale at an affordable price. If such a technology would appear, the GHG regulatory status quo would undergo an avulsive change. The Obama Administration is financially subsidizing the development of such a technology.

4. *Global Warming and the Endangered Species Act.* In addition to finding expression in the CAA, concerns about global warming are getting attention in the world of endangered species protection. The reader will recall that § 9 of the Endangered Species Act prohibits adverse modification of the critical habitat areas of protected species by private persons. *See, e.g., Sweet Home,* in Chapter 7, *supra.* A contention made with increasing frequency is that CO_2 emissions by polluters, by causing global warming, are doing just that. If this can be shown to be true, the massive injunctive power of the ESA could come to bear on CO_2 polluters. But all may not be so simple. Recall that a necessary proof under § 9 is to find an injury to an identifiable member of the protected species proximately caused by the implicated CO_2 emissions. *Id.* That would be a difficult standard to satisfy in this context.

The issue has arisen with respect to polar bears, which are designated as threatened under the ESA. In 2008, the Fish and Wildlife Service issued a special rule establishing protective standards for the polar bear. While the agency was required to analyze the environmental impacts of its rule under NEPA, it did not need to consider the impact of GHG emissions on polar bears in its rulemaking. *In re Polar Bear Endangered Species Act Listing and 4(d) Rule Litigation,* D.D.C., No. 08-764, Oct. 17, 2011. ("The Service concluded based on the evidence before it that Section 4(d) of the ESA is not a useful or appropriate tool to alleviate the particular threat to the polar bear from climate change caused by global greenhouse gas emissions, and plaintiffs have offered no compelling evidence to the contrary.")

Chapter 10

THE CLEAN WATER ACT

"Water is the most critical resource issue of our lifetime and our children's lifetime. The health of our waters is the principal measure of how we live on the land." *Statement of Luna Leopold*, quoted in Clean Water Action Plan: Restoring and Protecting America's Waters, U.S. EPA and U.S. DOA (1998), at 1.

SYNOPSIS

A. INTRODUCTION

Just as the nation's air resources have been in need of a good cleaning, so also have the nation's waters. Before the onset of federal regulation, water pollution problems were addressed at the state and local level chiefly by resort to the common law of nuisance and negligence, and by attempts to balance competing water uses. Only after World War II did the federal government take a seat at the table. Wanting states to maintain the lead, it chose for itself a decidedly subordinate role. Consequently, the announced policy of the Water Pollution Control Act of 1948 was not to clean water, but was, rather, "to recognize, preserve, and protect the primary responsibilities of the States in controlling water pollution[.]" Water Pollution Control Act of 1948, § 1, 62 Stat. 1155. The federal government intended to assist states by funding their water pollution control efforts and by coordinating interstate pollution abatement efforts.[1]

---

[1] The legislation did propound a diluted brand of federal enforcement. If the Surgeon General found

The Federal Water Pollution Control Act of 1956 built on this structure by instructing the Surgeon General to prepare "comprehensive programs for eliminating or reducing" pollution. FWPCA, 2, 70 Stat. 498.

These cautious federal interventions produced little improvement in water quality. In 1965, Congress acted again, this time requiring states to establish water quality standards for streams and to fashion implementation plans. (Sound familiar?) This legislation did not work either. A major reason was the legislation's ambivalence. The legislation attempted to facilitate a multiplicity of stream uses, but some of these uses, such as recreation, protection of aquatic life, and drinking water protection, required cleaner water, while others, such as agricultural and industrial use, depended on reduced water quality. States compounded this problem of ambivalence with ineffectual enforcement. Many states left implementation plans unfinished, and others relied on education initiatives and cajolery as their enforcement methodologies. The predictable result was slow progress to protect water quality, and even less water quality improvement.

Repeated tinkering by the Congress notwithstanding, effective federal intervention did not take place until eye-openers such as the combustion of urban rivers[2] elevated the issue to national prominence. The Federal Water Pollution Control Act of 1972, later renamed the Clean Water Act, was the result. Opposed by states, industry, and President Nixon (it was enacted over his veto), the legislation came into being primarily because of strong Senate leadership. Despite several amendments in succeeding years, the 1972 Act remains to this day the core of the federal water pollution control program.

As you read through these materials, you will recognize concepts similar to those already seen in Chapter 9's coverage of the Clean Air Act. Terminology varies, however. Instead of stationary and mobile sources, the CWA speaks of *point* and *nonpoint sources*. Instead of emission limitations or standards, here we see *effluent limitations* or *standards*. Instead of criteria pollutants, we see *conventional pollutants*. Hazardous pollutants are *toxic pollutants* or, simply, *toxics*. *National ambient air quality standards* (NAAQSs) give way to *water quality standards* ("WQSs"). Water pollutants are not emitted; they are *discharged*. No FIPs or SIPs here, either. Look instead for *National Pollutant Discharge Elimination System* ("NPDES") permits as the vehicle to implement regulatory standards. In both the Clean Air and Clean Water Acts you will find new source performance standards, citizen suit provisions, saving clauses, provisions for judicial review, definitional

---

an unhealthful condition, he could give notice to the polluter. If nothing resulted from this, he could give notice to the polluter and the state. If still nothing happened, the Federal Security Administrator was authorized to hold a hearing. If the hearing produced no progress, he could then request the U.S. Attorney General to file a lawsuit. If a lawsuit was filed, the federal court was authorized to render "such judgment . . . as the public interest and the equities of the case may require." WQA of 1948, § 2(d), 62 Stat. 1156–57.

[2] A major event in national environmental history was the spontaneous combustion of the Cuyahoga River in Cleveland, Ohio, on June 29, 1969. A small amount of oil and chemical-soaked floating debris caught fire, drifted downstream, and in turn, ignited two wooden railroad trestles. The fire was extinguished in a scant 25 minutes, and received only sparse local media coverage, but the event took on national significance as a symbol of the nation's water pollution crisis. Randy Newman even wrote a song about it (representative lyrics: "Burn on, big river, burn on").

sections, regulation of federal facilities, and a host of other like provisions.

But the Clean Water Act ("CWA") was not merely a retooled Clean Air Act ("CAA") applied to water. On the contrary, the CWA adopts an approach to pollution control fundamentally distinct from that of its counterpart (at least as the CAA was originally designed). On a basic level, the CWA has at its core a hard-edged resolve noticeably absent in the 1970 CAA. A comparison of the goal statements of the two statutes is illustrative. The 1970 Clean Air Act called for "protect[ing] and enhanc[ing] the quality of the Nation's air resources so to promote the public health and welfare and the productive capacity of its population." CAA § 101(b)(1), 42 U.S.C. § 7401(b)(1). The 1972 CWA, however, while calling for a restoration of the integrity of the nation's waters, § 101(a), 33 U.S.C. § 1251(a), went on to pronounce as its specific goal, inter alia, the zero discharge of pollutants by 1985, and, as an interim measure, the attainment of "fishable and swimmable" waters by 1983.[3] The CWA, in short, abhors the concept of "good enough."

The statutes are divergent in regulatory approach as well. Signaling a decisive rejection of the regulatory philosophy embraced only two years earlier, the 1972 CWA declined to construct for water the health-based standards/implementation plan regulatory model used in the CAA. Instead, the CWA's frontline soldier is technology-based standards. Effluent limitations imposed on dischargers, accordingly, spring in the main from considerations of technological feasibility, not from calculations of how clean receiving waters should be. See generally § 301, 33 U.S.C. § 1311. The CWA moves health-based effluent standards to a backup position. See §§ 302 & 303, 33 U.S.C. § 1312 & 1313.

The Senate Report accompanying the 1972 Act explained the reasoning behind this significant change:

> Under the 1965 Act, water quality standards were to be set as the control mechanism. States were to decide the uses of water to be protected, the kinds and amounts of pollutants to be permitted, the degree of pollution abatement to be required, the time to be allowed a polluter for abatement.
>
> The water quality standards program is limited in its success. After five years, many States do not have approved standards. Officials are still

---

[3] The complete text of the 1972 Clean Water Act's goal statements is as follows:

(1) it is the national goal that the discharge of pollutants into the navigable waters be eliminated by 1985;

(2) it is the national goal that wherever attainable, an interim goal of water quality which provides for the protection and propagation of fish, shellfish, and wildlife and provides for recreation in and on the water be achieved by July 1, 1983;

(3) it is the national policy that the discharge of toxic pollutants in toxic amounts be prohibited;

(4) it is the national policy that federal financial assistance be provided to construct publicly owned waste treatment works;

(5) it is the national policy that areawide waste treatment management planning processes be developed and implemented to assure adequate control of sources of pollutants in each state; and

(6) it is the national policy that a major research and demonstration effort be made to develop technology necessary to eliminate the discharge of pollutants into the navigable waters, waters of the contiguous zone, and the oceans. Section 101(a)(1)–(6).

working to establish relationships between pollutants and water uses. Time schedules for abatement are slipping away because of failure to enforce, lack of effluent controls, and disputes over Federal-State standards.

The Committee adopted this substantial change because of the great difficulty associated with establishing reliable and enforceable precise effluent limitations on the basis of a given stream quality. Water quality standards, in addition to their deficiencies in relying on the assimilative capacity of receiving waters, often cannot be translated into effluent limitations defendable in court tests, because of the imprecision of models for water quality and the effects of effluents in most waters.

Under this Act the basis of pollution prevention and elimination will be the application of effluent limitations. Water quality will be a measure of program effectiveness and performance, not a means of elimination and enforcement.

The Committee recommends the change to effluent limits as the best available mechanism to control water pollution. With effluent limits, the Administrator can require the best control technology; he need not search for a precise link between pollution and water quality.

Senate Report No. 92-414, U.S. Code Congressional and Administrative News, 92d Cong. 2d Sess. at 3675.

The water pollution world, as structured by the 1972 Clean Water Act, is divided into two distinct regulatory regimes. One deals with point sources and the other with nonpoint. Point sources, generally speaking, are pipes, outfalls and other such confined channels that physically discharge pollutants; nonpoint sources of pollution are all sources not point sources. Point sources, we will see, are governed chiefly by the aforementioned technology-based effluent standards. The CWA focuses predominantly upon point sources, an emphasis consistent with Congress's understanding in 1972 that industry was the major cause of water pollution.

The CWA was amended in 1977 and again in 1987. Because these amendments refined the legislation more so than revised it, this chapter is organized differently than Chapter 9. Here, we consider point and nonpoint source regulation in distinct sections, and review changes in legislation internally within those sections.

The particulars of the Clean Water Act can be found by reviewing the legislation itself, which is in your statutory supplement. Please take notice of the various subchapters of the enactment, but pay most attention to Subchapters III, IV, and V.

After reviewing the overall organization of the Act, the best place to start a particularized inquiry is § 301(a). This section is the statute's triggering mechanism, for it largely determines the subject matter reach of the legislation. This section is considered by some knowledgeable observers to be the most important single statutory provision in the entirety of pollution control law. Can you see why?

It is important to understand what the specific words and phrases within § 301(a) mean. In this regard, please consult the CWA's definitional section, § 502, 33 U.S.C. § 1362.

B. ISSUES OF APPLICABILITY

SOUTH FLORIDA WATER MANAGEMENT DISTRICT v. MICCOSUKEE TRIBE OF INDIANS
541 U.S. 95, 124 S. Ct 1537 (2004)

Justice O'Connor delivered the opinion of the Court.

Petitioner South Florida Water Management District operates a pumping facility that transfers water from a canal into a reservoir a short distance away. Respondents Miccosukee Tribe of Indians and the Friends of the Everglades brought a citizen suit under the Clean Water Act contending that the pumping facility is required to obtain a discharge permit under the National Pollutant Discharge Elimination System. The District Court agreed and granted summary judgment to respondents. A panel of the United States Court of Appeals for the Eleventh Circuit affirmed. Both the District Court and the Eleventh Circuit rested their holdings on the predicate determination that the canal and reservoir are two distinct water bodies. For the reasons explained below, we vacate and remand for further development of the factual record as to the accuracy of that determination.

I

A

The Central and South Florida Flood Control Project (Project) consists of a vast array of levees, canals, pumps, and water impoundment areas in the land between south Florida's coastal hills and the Everglades. Historically, that land was itself part of the Everglades, and its surface and groundwater flowed south in a uniform and unchanneled sheet. Starting in the early 1900's, however, the State began to build canals to drain the wetlands and make them suitable for cultivation. These canals proved to be a source of trouble; they lowered the water table, allowing salt water to intrude upon coastal wells, and they proved incapable of controlling flooding. Congress established the Project in 1948 to address these problems. It gave the United States Army Corps of Engineers the task of constructing a comprehensive network of levees, water storage areas, pumps, and canal improvements that would serve several simultaneous purposes, including flood protection, water conservation, and drainage. These improvements fundamentally altered the hydrology of the Everglades, changing the natural sheet flow of ground and surface water. The local sponsor and day-to-day operator of the Project is the South Florida Water Management District (District).

Five discrete elements of the Project are at issue in this case. One is a canal called "C-11." C-11 collects groundwater and rainwater from a 104 square-mile area in south central Broward County. App. 110. The area drained by C-11 includes urban, agricultural, and residential development, and is home to 136,000 people. At the western terminus of C-11 is the second Project element at issue here: a large pump station known as "S-9." When the water level in C-11 rises above a set level, S-9 begins operating and pumps water out of the canal. The water does not travel far. Sixty feet away, the pump station empties the water into a large undeveloped wetland area called "WCA-3," the third element of the Project we consider here. WCA-3 is the largest of several "water conservation areas" that are remnants of the original South Florida Everglades. The District impounds water in these areas to conserve fresh water that might otherwise flow directly to the ocean, and to preserve wetlands habitat. *Id.*, at 112.

Using pump stations like S-9, the District maintains the water table in WCA-3 at a level significantly higher than that in the developed lands drained by the C-11 canal to the east. Absent human intervention, that water would simply flow back east, where it would rejoin the waters of the canal and flood the populated areas of the C-11 basin. That return flow is prevented, or, more accurately, slowed, by levees that hold back the surface waters of WCA-3. Two of those levees, L-33 and L-37, are the final two elements of the Project at issue here. The combined effect of L-33 and L-37, C-11, and S-9 is artificially to separate the C-11 basin from WCA-3; left to nature, the two areas would be a single wetland covered in an undifferentiated body of surface and ground water flowing slowly southward.

B

As the above description illustrates, the Project has wrought large-scale hydrologic and environmental change in South Florida, some deliberate and some accidental. Its most obvious environmental impact has been the conversion of what were once wetlands into areas suitable for human use. But the Project also has affected those areas that remain wetland ecosystems.

Rain on the western side of the L-33 and L-37 levees falls into the wetland ecosystem of WCA-3. Rain on the eastern side of the levees, on the other hand, falls on agricultural, urban, and residential land. Before it enters the C-11 canal, whether directly as surface runoff or indirectly as groundwater, that rainwater absorbs contaminants produced by human activities. The water in C-11 therefore differs chemically from that in WCA-3. Of particular interest here, C-11 water contains elevated levels of phosphorous, which is found in fertilizers used by farmers in the C-11 basin. When water from C-11 is pumped across the levees, the phosphorous it contains alters the balance of WCA-3's ecosystem (which is naturally low in phosphorous) and stimulates the growth of algae and plants foreign to the Everglades ecosystem.

The phosphorous-related impacts of the Project are well known and have received a great deal of attention from state and federal authorities for more than 20 years. A number of initiatives are currently under way to reduce these impacts and thereby restore the ecological integrity of the Everglades. Respondents Miccosukee Tribe of Indians and the Friends of the Everglades (hereinafter simply Tribe), impatient with the pace of this progress, brought this Clean Water Act suit in the United States District Court for the Southern District of Florida. They sought, among other things, to enjoin the operation of S-9 and, in turn, the conveyance of water from C-11 into WCA-3.

C

Congress enacted the Clean Water Act (Act) in 1972. Its stated objective was "to restore and maintain the chemical, physical, and biological integrity of the Nation's waters." 86 Stat 816, 33 U.S.C. § 1251. To serve those ends, the Act prohibits "the discharge of any pollutant by any person" unless done in compliance with some provision of the Act. § 1311(a). The provision relevant to this case, § 1342, establishes the National Pollutant Discharge Elimination System, or "NPDES." Gene rally speaking, the NPDES requires dischargers to obtain permits that place limits on the type and quantity of pollutants that can be released into the Nation's waters. The Act defines the phrase " 'discharge of a pollutant' " to mean "any addition of any pollutant to navigable waters from any point source." § 1362(12). A " 'point source,' " in turn, is defined as "any discernible, confined and discrete conveyance," such as a pipe, ditch, channel, or tunnel, "from which pollutants are or may be discharged." § 1362(14).

According to the Tribe, the District cannot operate S-9 without an NPDES permit because the pump station moves phosphorous-laden water from C-11 into WCA-3. The District does not dispute that phosphorous is a pollutant, or that C-11 and WCA-3 are "navigable waters" within the meaning of the Act. The question, it contends, is whether the operation of the S-9 pump constitutes the "discharge of [a] pollutant" within the meaning of the Act. . . .

II

The District and the Federal Government, as amicus, advance three separate arguments, any of which would, if accepted, lead to the conclusion that the S-9 pump station does not require a point source discharge permit under the NPDES program. Two of these arguments involve the application of disputed contentions of law to agreed-upon facts, while the third involves the application of agreed-upon law to disputed facts. For reasons explained below, we decline at this time to resolve all of the parties' legal disagreements, and instead remand for further proceedings regarding their factual dispute.

A

In its opening brief on the merits, the District argued that the NPDES program applies to a point source "only when a pollutant originates from the point source," and not when pollutants originating elsewhere merely pass through the point source. Brief for Petitioner 20. This argument mirrors the question presented in the District's petition for: "Whether the pumping of water by a state water management agency that adds nothing to the water being pumped constitutes an 'addition' of a pollutant 'from' a point source triggering the need for a National Pollutant Discharge Elimination System permit under the Clean Water Act." Pet. for Certificate. Although the Government rejects the District's legal position, Brief for United States as Amicus Curiae 21, it and the Tribe agree with the factual proposition that S-9 does not itself add any pollutants to the water it conveys into WCA-3.

This initial argument is untenable, and even the District appears to have abandoned it in its reply brief. Reply Brief for Petitioner 2. A point source is, by definition, a "discernible, confined, and discrete *conveyance*." § 1362(14) (emphasis added). That definition makes plain that a point source need not be the original source of the pollutant; it need only convey the pollutant to "navigable waters," which are, in turn, defined as "the waters of the United States." § 1362(7). Tellingly, the examples of "point sources" listed by the Act include pipes, ditches, tunnels, and conduits, objects that do not themselves generate pollutants but merely transport them. § 1362(14). In addition, one of the Act's primary goals was to impose NPDES permitting requirements on municipal wastewater treatment plants. *See, e.g.*, § 1311(b)(1)(B) (establishing a compliance schedule for publicly owned treatment works). But under the District's interpretation of the Act, the NPDES program would not cover such plants, because they treat and discharge pollutants added to water by others. We therefore reject the District's proposed reading of the definition of " 'discharge of a pollutant' " contained in § 1362(12). That definition includes within its reach point sources that do not themselves generate pollutants.

B

Having answered the precise question on which we granted certiorari, we turn to a second argument, advanced primarily by the Government as *amicus curiae* in merits briefing and at oral argument. For purposes of determining whether there has been "any addition of any pollutant to navigable waters from any point source," *ibid.*, the Government contends that all the water bodies that fall within the Act's definition of " 'navigable waters' " (that is, all "the waters of the United States, including the territorial seas," § 1362(7)) should be viewed unitarily for purposes of NPDES permitting requirements. Because the Act requires NPDES permits only when there is an addition of a pollutant "to navigable waters," the Government's approach would lead to the conclusion that such permits are not required when water from one navigable water body is discharged, unaltered, into another navigable water body. That would be true even if one water body were polluted and the other pristine, and the two would not otherwise mix. *See Catskill Mountains Chapter of Trout Unlimited, Inc. v. New York*, 273 F.3d 481, 492 (2nd Cir. 2001); *Dubois v. United States Dep't of Agric.*, 102 F.3d 1273 (1st Cir. 1996). Under this "unitary waters" approach, the S-9 pump station would not need an NPDES permit.

1

The "unitary waters" argument focuses on the Act's definition of a pollutant discharge as "any addition of any pollutant to navigable waters from any point source." § 1362(12). The Government contends that the absence of the word "any" prior to the phrase "navigable waters" in § 1362(12) signals Congress' understanding that NPDES permits would not be required for pollution caused by the engineered transfer of one "navigable water" into another. It argues that Congress intended that such pollution instead would be addressed through local nonpoint source pollution programs. Section 1314(f)(2)(F), which concerns nonpoint sources, directs the Environmental Protection Agency (EPA) to give States information on the evaluation and control of "pollution resulting from . . . changes in the movement, flow, or circulation of any navigable waters or ground waters, including changes caused by the construction of dams, levees, channels, causeways, or flow diversion facilities."

We note, however, that § 1314(f)(2)(F) does not explicitly exempt nonpoint pollution sources from the NPDES program if they *also* fall within the "point source" definition. And several NPDES provisions might be read to suggest a view contrary to the unitary waters approach. For example, under the Act, a State may set individualized ambient water quality standards by taking into consideration "the designated uses of the navigable waters involved." 33 U.S.C. § 1313(c)(2)(A). Those water quality standards, in turn, directly affect local NPDES permits; if standard permit conditions fail to achieve the water quality goals for a given water body, the State must determine the total pollutant load that the water body can sustain and then allocate that load among the permit-holders who discharge to the water body. § 1313(d). This approach suggests that the Act protects individual water bodies as well as the waters of the United States as a whole.

The Government also suggests that we adopt the "unitary waters" approach out of deference to a longstanding EPA view that the process of "transporting, impounding, and releasing navigable waters" cannot constitute an " 'addition' " of pollutants to " 'the waters of the United States.' " Brief for United States as *Amicus Curiae* 16. But the Government does not identify any administrative documents in which EPA has espoused that position. Indeed, an *amicus* brief filed by several former EPA officials argues that the agency once reached the opposite conclusion. See Brief for Former Administrator Carol M. Browner et al. as *Amici Curiae* 17 (citing In re *Riverside Irrigation Dist., 1975 WL 23864* (Off. Gen. Couns., June 27, 1975) (irrigation ditches that discharge to navigable waters require NPDES permits even if they themselves qualify as navigable waters)). The "unitary waters" approach could also conflict with current NPDES regulations. For example, 40 CFR § 122.45(g)(4) (2003) allows an industrial water user to obtain "intake credit" for pollutants present in water that it withdraws from navigable waters. When the permit holder discharges the water after use, it does not have to remove pollutants that were in the water before it was withdrawn. There is a caveat, however: EPA extends such credit "only if the discharger demonstrates that the intake water is drawn from the same body of water into which the discharge is made." The NPDES program thus appears to address the movement of pollutants among water bodies, at least at times.

Finally, the Government and numerous *amici* warn that affirming the Court of Appeals in this case would have significant practical consequences. If we read the Clean Water Act to require an NPDES permit for every engineered diversion of one navigable water into another, thousands of new permits might have to be issued, particularly by western States, whose water supply networks often rely on engineered transfers among various natural water bodies. *See* Brief for Colorado et al. as *Amici Curiae* 2-4. Many of those diversions might also require expensive treatment to meet water quality criteria. It may be that construing the NPDES program to cover such transfers would therefore raise the costs of water distribution prohibitively, and violate Congress' specific instruction that "the authority of each State to allocate quantities of water within its jurisdiction shall not be superseded, abrogated or otherwise impaired" by the Act. § 1251(g). On the other hand, it may be that such permitting authority is necessary to protect water quality, and that the States or EPA could control regulatory costs by issuing general permits to point sources associated with water distribution programs. *See* 40 CFR §§ 122.28, 123.25 (2003).[4] Indeed, that is the position of the one State that has interpreted the Act to cover interbasin water transfers. See Brief for Pennsylvania Department of Environmental Protection as *Amicus Curiae* 11-18.

2

Because WCA-3 and C-11 are both "navigable waters," adopting the "unitary waters" approach would lead to the conclusion that the District may operate S-9 without an NPDES permit. But despite its relevance here, neither the District nor the Government raised the unitary waters approach before the Court of Appeals or in their briefs respecting the petition for certiorari. (The District adopted the position as its own in its reply brief on the merits.) Indeed, we are not aware of any reported case that examines the unitary waters argument in precisely the form that the Government now presents it. As a result, we decline to resolve it here. Because we find it necessary to vacate the judgment of the Court of Appeals with respect to a third argument presented by the District, the unitary waters argument will be open to the parties on remand.

C

In the courts below, as here, the District contended that the C-11 canal and WCA-3 impoundment area are not distinct water bodies at all, but instead are two hydrologically indistinguishable parts of a single water body. The Government agrees with the District on this point, claiming that because the C-11 canal and WCA-3 "share a unique, intimately related, hydrological association," they "can appropriately be viewed, for purposes of Section 402 of the Clean Water Act, as parts of a single body of water." Brief for United States in Opposition 13. The Tribe does not dispute that if C-11 and WCA-3 are simply two parts of the same water body, pumping water from one into the other cannot constitute an "addition" of pollutants. As the Second Circuit put it in *Trout Unlimited*, "[i]f one takes a ladle of soup from a pot, lifts it above the pot, and pours it back into the pot, one has not 'added' soup or anything else to the pot." 273 F.3d at 492. What the Tribe disputes is the accuracy of the District's factual premise; according to the Tribe, C-11 and WCA-3 are two pots of soup, not one.

The record does contain information supporting the District's view of the facts. [The Court then discussed the varying factual contentions of the parties.] . . .

We do not decide here whether the District Court's test is adequate for determining whether C-11 and WCA-3 are distinct. Instead, we hold only that the

---

[4] [Ed. Note: An applicant for an individual NPDES permit must provide information about, among other things, the point source itself, the nature of the pollutants to be discharged, and any water treatment system that will be used. General permits greatly reduce that administrative burden by authorizing discharges from a category of point sources within a specified geographic area. Once EPA or a state agency issues such a permit, covered entities, in some cases, need take no further action to achieve compliance with the NPDES besides adhering to the permit conditions. See 40 C.F.R. § 122.28(b)(2)(v) (2003).]

District Court applied its test prematurely. Summary judgment is appropriate only where there is no genuine issue of material fact. *See Celotex Corp. v. Catrett*, 477 U.S. 317, 106 S. Ct. 2548, 91 L. Ed. 2d 265 (1986). The record before us leads us to believe that some factual issues remain unresolved. . . .

We find that further development of the record is necessary to resolve the dispute over the validity of the distinction between C-11 and WCA-3. After reviewing the full record, it is possible that the District Court will conclude that C-11 and WCA-3 are not meaningfully distinct water bodies. If it does so, then the S-9 pump station will not need an NPDES permit. In addition, the Government's broader "unitary waters" argument is open to the District on remand. Accordingly, the judgment of the United States Court of Appeals for the Eleventh Circuit is vacated, and the case is remanded for further proceedings consistent with this opinion.

It is so ordered.

[JUSTICE SCALIA's partial concurrence and dissent is omitted.]

NOTES

1. *Unitary Waters.* While the Supreme Court in *Miccosukee* declined to resolve the unitary waters debate, due to an insufficient record, lower courts largely rejected EPA's view. *See, e.g., Catskill Mountains Ch. of Trout Unlimited, Inc. v. City of New York*, 273 F.3d 481, 491 (2d Cir. 2001) ("[T]he transfer of water containing pollutants from one body of water to another, distinct body of water is plainly an addition and thus a 'discharge' that demands an NPDES permit."); *Dague v. City of Burlington*, 935 F.2d 1343, 1354–55 (2d Cir. 1991) (holding that pollutants are not "added" only when first deposited into a navigable water); *Dubois v. U.S. Dep't of Agriculture.*, 102 F.3d 1273, 1296 (1st Cir. 1996) ("[T]here is no basis in law or fact for the . . . 'singular entity' [unitary waters] theory.").

Not to be deterred, EPA took the matter into its own hands by enacting a regulation adding to the list of "discharges" excluded from CWA regulation the following:

> (i) Discharges from a water transfer. Water transfer means an activity that conveys or connects waters of the United States without subjecting the transferred water to intervening industrial, municipal, or commercial use. This exclusion does not apply to pollutants introduced by the water transfer activity itself to the water being transferred.

40 C.F.R. § 122.3(I) (2008).

Thus did EPA enshrine its unitary waters position as regulatory law. Upon review, the Eleventh Circuit Court of Appeals, relying upon *Chevron* Step Two, *see supra*, offered the following reasoning and holding:

> Sometimes it is helpful to strip a legal question of the contentious policy interests attached to it and think about it in the abstract using a hypothetical. Consider the issue this way: Two buckets sit side by side, one

with four marbles in it and the other with none. There is a rule prohibiting "any addition of any marbles to buckets by any person." A person comes along, picks up two marbles from the first bucket, and drops them into the second bucket. Has the marble-mover "add[ed] any marbles to buckets"? On one hand, as the Friends of the Everglades might argue, there are now two marbles in a bucket where there were none before, so an addition of marbles has occurred. On the other hand, as the Water District might argue and as the EPA would decide, there were four marbles in buckets before, and there are still four marbles in buckets, so no addition of marbles has occurred. Whatever position we might take if we had to pick one side or the other of the issue, we cannot say that either side is unreasonable.

Like the marbles rule, the Clean Water Act's language about "any addition of any pollutant to navigable waters from any point source," 33 U.S.C. § 1362(12), is ambiguous. The EPA's regulation adopting the unitary waters theory is a reasonable, and therefore permissible, construction of the language. Unless and until the EPA rescinds or Congress overrides the regulation, we must give effect to it.

Friends of the Everglades v. South Florida Water Mgmt. Dist., 570 F.3d 1210, 1228 (11th Cir. 2009), *cert. denied*, 131 S. Ct. 643 (2010).

2.   *CWA and Groundwater.* Does the CWA authorize EPA to protect groundwater? Does groundwater fall under the definition of "waters of the United States," or does that phrase relate solely to surface waters? EPA believes the CWA allows it to regulate discharges to groundwater if that groundwater is hydrologically connected to surface water, even if the former is not itself a "water of the United States" because "such discharges are effectively discharges to the directly connected surface waters." *See, e.g.*, 56 Fed. Reg. 64,876. EPA thus has adopted a "purposive" reading of the statute, using the CWA's underlying purpose of restoring and maintaining the nation's water quality and integrity as its interpretive guidepost.

The federal courts remain split on the question. The Seventh Circuit has ruled the CWA does not apply in this situation. *Village of Oconomowoc Lake v. Dayton Hudson Corp.*, 24 F.3d 962 (7th Cir. 1994). Likewise, the First and Fifth Circuits have also held the CWA to be inapplicable. *Rice v. Harken Exploration Company*, 250 F.3d 264 (5th Cir. 2001) (holding that the possibility that groundwater might contaminate surface waters was insufficient to establish liability); *Town of Norfolk v. U.S. Army Corps of Engineers*, 968 F.2d 1438 (1st Cir. 1992) (deferring to the Army Corps' definition of "groundwaters" as not "waters of the United States" under the CWA).

For its part, in *Quivira Mining Co. v. E.P.A.*, 765 F.2d 126, 129 (10th Cir. 1985), the Tenth Circuit Court of Appeals determined the CWA applied when polluted water "soak[ed] into the earth's surface, bec[a]me part of the underground aquifers, and after a lengthy period, perhaps centuries, the underground water move[d] toward eventual discharge" in surface waters. *See also Friends of Santa Fe County v. LAC Minerals*, 892 F. Supp. 1333, 1358 (D.N.M. 1995) (the Tenth Circuit's construction of the CWA's jurisdictional reach forecloses "any argument that the CWA does not protect groundwater with some connection to surface waters");

Sierra Club v. Colorado Refining Co., 838 F. Supp. 1428, 1434 (D. Colo. 1993) ("discharge of any pollutant into 'navigable waters' includes such discharge which reaches 'navigable waters' through groundwater").

There is disagreement on the issue even within circuits. In the Ninth Circuit, for example, *compare Idaho Rural Council v. Bosma*, 143 F. Supp. 2d 1169 (D. Idaho 2001) (the "the CWA extends federal jurisdiction over groundwater that is hydrologically connected to surface waters), *with Umatilla Waterquality Protective Association, Inc. v. Smith Frozen Foods, Inc.*, 962 F. Supp. 1312 (D. Or. 1997) (the CWA does not extend to hydrologically connected groundwater). In the Eighth Circuit, *compare Williams Pipeline Co. v. Bayer Corp.*, 964 F. Supp. 1300 (S.D. Iowa 1997) ("the unpermitted discharges of pollutants through spills, leaks, and other releases into the groundwater and into [a] wetland area . . . violated the CWA"), *with Patterson Farm, Inc. v. City of Britton*, 22 F. Supp. 2d 1085 (D.S.D. 1998) (under the *Hecla* rationale, the court lacks subject-matter jurisdiction even if the plaintiff alleged that discharges into groundwater were migrating to surface water).

We will further engage the question of what are "waters of the United States" in our coverage of Section 404. *See* Part E, *infra*.

THE NATIONAL COTTON COUNCIL OF AMERICA v. UNITED STATES ENVIRONMENTAL PROTECTION AGENCY
553 F.3d 927 (6th Cir. 2009), *cert. denied*, 130 S. Ct. 1505 (2010)

JUDGES: Before: GUY, SUHRHEINRICH, and COLE, CIRCUIT JUDGES.

COLE, CIRCUIT JUDGE. These proceedings involve a final regulation issued by the Environmental Protection Agency (the "EPA") under the Clean Water Act, 33 U.S.C. § 1251 et seq. The Clean Water Act regulates the discharge of "pollutants" into the nation's waters by, among other things, requiring entities that emit "pollutants" to obtain a National Pollutant Discharge Elimination System ("NPDES") permit. *Id.* §§ 1311(a), 1342. On November 27, 2007, the EPA issued a Final Rule concluding that pesticides applied in accordance with the Federal Insecticide, Fungicide, and Rodenticide Act (the "FIFRA") are exempt from the Clean Water Act's permitting requirements. See 71 Fed. Reg. 68,483 (Nov. 27, 2006) (the "Final Rule"). Two different groups of Petitioners — one representing environmental interest groups and the other representing industry interest groups — oppose the EPA's Final Rule as exceeding the EPA's interpretive authority. The EPA defends the Final Rule by arguing that the terms of the Clean Water Act are ambiguous and that the Final Rule is a reasonable construction of the Clean Water Act entitled to deference from this Court. We cannot agree. The Clean Water Act is not ambiguous. Further, it is a fundamental precept of this Court that we interpret unambiguous expressions of Congressional will as written. Chevron U.S.A., Inc. v. Natural Res. Def. Council, Inc., 467 U.S. 837, 842–43, 104 S. Ct. 2778, 81 L. Ed. 2d 694 (1984). Therefore, we hold that the EPA's Final Rule is not a reasonable interpretation of the Act and VACATE the Final Rule.

I. BACKGROUND

A. *The Regulatory Background*

Congress enacted the Clean Water Act "to restore and maintain the chemical, physical and biological integrity of the Nation's waters." Nat'l Wildlife Fed'n v. Consumers Power Co., 862 F.2d 580, 582 (6th Cir. 1988) (quoting 33 U.S.C. § 1251(a)). The goal of the Clean Water Act is to achieve "water quality which provides for the protection and propagation of fish, shellfish, and wildlife and provides for recreation in and on the water." 33 U.S.C. § 1251(a)(2). Thus, the Act provides that "the discharge of any pollutant by any person shall be unlawful." *Id.* § 1311(a). "Pollutant" is a statutorily defined term that includes, at least, "dredged spoil, solid waste, incinerator residue, sewage, garbage, sewage sludge, munitions, chemical wastes, biological materials, radioactive materials, heat, wrecked or discarded equipment, rock, sand, cellar dirt and industrial, municipal, and agricultural waste discharged into water." *Id.* § 1362(6). The Supreme Court has held that this list is not exhaustive and that "pollutant" should be interpreted broadly. Rapanos v. United States, 547 U.S. 715, 724, 126 S. Ct. 2208, 165 L. Ed. 2d 159 (2006).

The Clean Water Act prohibits the discharge of any "pollutant" into navigable waters from any "point source" unless the EPA issues a permit under the NPDES permitting program, 33 U.S.C. §§ 1311(a), 1342, where a "point source" is "any discernible, confined, and discrete conveyance . . . from which pollutants are or may be discharged." *Id.* § 1362(14). The permitting program constitutes an exception to the Clean Water Act's prohibition on pollutant discharges into the Nation's waters. *Id.* §§ 1311(a), 1342; 40 C.F.R. § 122.3. Thus, if a party obtains a permit, the discharge of pollutants in accordance with that permit is not unlawful. *Id.*

Before a permit is issued, the EPA, or a state agency that has been approved by the EPA, evaluates the permit application to ensure that the discharge of a pollutant under the proposed circumstances will not cause undue harm to the quality of the water. See 33 U.S.C. § 1342. In addition to granting permits for specific discharges, the EPA and state authorities may also grant general permits that allow for the discharge of a specific pollutant or type of pollutant across an entire region. *Id.* For example, prior to the EPA's adoption of the Final Rule, the State of Washington had issued a general permit to allow for the application of all aquatic pesticides in the State. *See* Aquatechnex v. Washington Dep't of Ecology, PCHB No. 02-090, 2002 WA ENV LEXIS 87, *2-5 (Pollution Control Hr'gs Bd. Dec. 24, 2002). As a result, users of aquatic pesticides in Washington could discharge those pesticides covered by the rule without obtaining a permit. These general permits "greatly reduce [the] administrative burden by authorizing discharges from a category of point sources within a specified geographic area." S. Florida Water Mgmt. Dist. v. Miccosukee Tribe of Indians, 541 U.S. 95, 108, 124 S. Ct. 1537, 158 L. Ed. 2d 264 n.* (2004) (citing 40 C.F.R. § 122.28(b)(2)(v)). "Once [the] EPA or a state agency issues such a [general] permit, covered entities, in some cases, need take no further action to achieve compliance with the NPDES besides adhering to the permit conditions." *Id.*

2. The Federal Insecticide, Fungicide, and Rodenticide Act

The EPA also regulates the labeling and sale of pesticides under the Federal Insecticide, Fungicide, and Rodenticide Act. Under the FIFRA, all pesticides sold in the United States must be registered with the EPA. See 7 U.S.C. § 136 et seq. The EPA approves an insecticide for registration only when it finds that the chemical, "when used in accordance with widespread and commonly recognized practice . . . [,] will not generally cause unreasonably adverse effects on the environment." No Spray Coalition v. City of New York, 351 F.3d 602, 604–05 (2d Cir. 2003) (quoting 7 U.S.C. § 136a(c)(5)(D)). Under the FIFRA, the EPA issues a "label" for each registered pesticide, indicating the manner in which it may be used; the statute makes it unlawful "to use any pesticide in a manner inconsistent with its labeling." Id. (quoting 7 U.S.C. § 136j(a)(2)(G)).

For nearly thirty years prior to the adoption of the Final Rule, pesticide labels issued under the FIFRA were required to contain a notice stating that the pesticide could not be "discharge[d] into lakes, streams, ponds, or public waters unless in accordance with an NPDES permit." EPA's Policy and Criteria Notice 2180.1 (1977). Despite amendments made to the FIFRA's labeling requirements over the years, pesticide labels have always included a notice about the necessity of obtaining an NPDES permit. . . .

3. The Regulatory Framework Under the Final Rule

Under the Clean Water Act, pollutants may only be discharged according to a permit unless they fit into one of the exceptions listed in the federal regulations at 40 C.F.R. § 122.3. The Final Rule revises the regulations by adding pesticides to these exceptions as long as they are used in accordance with the FIFRA's requirements. 71 Fed. Reg. at 68,485, 68,492. Specifically, the Final Rule states that pesticides applied consistently with the FIFRA do not require an NPDES permit in the following two circumstances:

(1) The application of pesticides directly to waters of the United States in order to control pests. Examples of such applications include applications to control mosquito larvae, aquatic weeds, or other pests that are present in waters of the United States.

(2) The application of pesticides to control pests that are present over waters of the United States, including near such waters, where a portion of the pesticides will unavoidably be deposited to waters of the United States in order to target the pests effectively; for example, when insecticides are aerially applied to a forest canopy where waters of the United States may be present below the canopy or where pesticides are applied over or near water for control of adult mosquitoes or other pests. 40 C.F.R. § 122.3(h).

Although the EPA, through its Final Rule, takes the position that pesticides are not generally pollutants, it makes an exception for "pesticide residuals," which "include[] excess amounts of pesticide." 71 Fed. Reg. at 68,487. "Pesticide residuals" are those portions of the pesticide that "remain in the water after the application and its intended purpose (elimination of targeted pests) have been completed. . . . " Id. The EPA concedes that pesticide residue (unlike pesticides generally) is a pollutant under the Clean Water Act because it is "waste[] of the pesticide application." *Id.* Nonetheless, the EPA contends that pesticide residue is not subject to the NPDES permitting program because "at the time of discharge to a water of the United States, the material in the discharge must be both a pollutant, and from a point source." *Id.* According to the EPA, the residue cannot be subject to the permitting program because by the time it becomes a pollutant it is no longer from a "point source." Since no "point source" is at play, the EPA reasons, pesticide residue is a "nonpoint source pollutant" and therefore not subject to the permitting requirements. *Id.*

B. *Procedural Background*

Timely petitions for review of the Final Rule were filed in the First, Second, Third, Fourth, Fifth, Sixth, Seventh, Eighth, Ninth, Tenth, and D.C. Circuits by either the "Industry Petitioners" or the "Environmental Petitioners." The petitions for review were consolidated in this circuit by an order of the Judicial Panel on Multidistrict Litigation, under 28 U.S.C. §§ 1407 and 2112(a)(3). The self-titled "Industry Intervenors" filed a motion to intervene in support of the Final Rule.

Environmental Petitioners filed a timely motion to dismiss the petitions because of lack of subject matter jurisdiction or, alternatively, to transfer the cases to the Ninth Circuit. Industry Petitioners, the EPA, and Industry Intervenors opposed this motion. The Environmental Petitioners have also filed a complaint challenging the Final Rule in the Northern District of California in order to preserve review of the Final Rule in the event this Court grants their motion to dismiss. On July 24, 2007, we denied the motion to transfer and deferred the decision on the question of subject matter jurisdiction. . . .

III. Discussion

. . . .

B. *The Parties' Positions*

1. The Petitioners

Environmental Petitioners argue: (1) that the EPA exceeded its authority under the Clean Water Act in issuing a rule that excludes pesticides from the definition of "pollutant" under 33 U.S.C. § 1362(6); (2) that the EPA exceeded its authority under the Clean Water Act when it determined that, while pesticides are discharged by point sources, the residue of these pesticides is nonetheless a "nonpoint source pollutant"; and (3) that the EPA may not exempt FIFRA compliant applications of pesticides from the requirements of the Clean Water Act. Industry Petitioners, on the other hand, argue that the Final Rule is arbitrary and capricious because it treats pesticides applied in violation of the FIFRA as pollutants, while it treats the very same pesticides used in compliance with the FIFRA as non-pollutants. In other words, the Industry Petitioners complain that whether something constitutes a pollutant should not hinge upon compliance with the FIFRA.

2. The EPA

As described above, the EPA's Final Rule exempts from the NPDES permitting program pesticides that are applied directly to the Nation's waters, or near such waters, in order to control pests. 40 C.F.R. § 122.3(h). The EPA says that its Final Rule exempts both pesticides generally and "pesticide residue," which includes "excess pesticide." 71 Fed. Reg. at 68,487.

The EPA provides two reasons that its Final Rule is reasonable. First, the EPA argues that the Clean Water Act as it applies to pesticides is ambiguous. The EPA contends that it reasonably determined that pesticides applied according to the FIFRA requirements are not pollutants and therefore are not subject to the NPDES permitting program. The EPA reasons that "Congress defined the term 'pollutant' in the Clean Water Act to mean one of 16 specific items." (EPA Br. at 22.) Of these sixteen, the EPA states that pesticides, which are either chemical or biological in nature, may only be considered to be "chemical wastes" or "biological materials." 71 Fed. Reg. at 68,486. The EPA argues that pesticides are not "chemical wastes" in the ordinary dictionary definition of the word "waste," because waste is that which is "eliminated or discarded as no longer useful or required after the completion of a process." *Id.* (quoting The New Oxford American Dictionary 1905 (Elizabeth J. Jewell & Frank Abate eds., 2001)). Rather than being wastes, the EPA reasons that pesticides applied according to the FIFRA's labeling requirements "are products that the EPA has evaluated and registered for the purpose of controlling target organisms, and are designed, purchased, and applied to perform that purpose." *Id.* The EPA next concludes that pesticides applied in accordance with the FIFRA are not "biological materials" because to find otherwise would lead to the anomalous result "that biological pesticides are pollutants, while chemical pesticides used in the same circumstances are not." *Id.*

The EPA's second argument attempts to justify its Final Rule as applied to pesticide residue. In contrast to pesticides generally, which the EPA contends are not pollutants, the EPA concedes that pesticide residue and excess pesticide are pollutants within the meaning of the Clean Water Act because "they are wastes of the pesticide application." 71 Fed. Reg. at 68,487. The EPA also concedes that pesticides are discharged from a point source. *Id.* at 68,487-88. Nonetheless, the EPA concludes that no permit is required for pesticide applications that result in excess or residue pesticide because it interprets the Clean Water Act as requiring permits only for discharges that are "both a pollutant, and from a point source" at the time of discharge. *Id.* at 68,487.

C. *Analysis*

1. Are Pesticides Unambiguously "Pollutants" Within the Meaning of the Act

The first question under Chevron is whether the Clean Water Act unambiguously includes pesticides within its definition of "pollutant." Under this first step, this Court determines "whether Congress has directly spoken to the precise question at issue." 467 U.S. at 842. This is determined by "employing traditional tools of statutory construction." *Id.* The meaning of a statute "is determined by reference to the language itself, the specific context in which that language is used, and the broader context of the statute as a whole." Robinson v. Shell Oil Co., 519 U.S. 337, 341, 117 S. Ct. 843, 136 L. Ed. 2d 808 (1997); *see also* Dole v. United Steelworkers of Am., 494 U.S. 26, 35, 110 S. Ct. 929, 108 L. Ed. 2d 23 (1990) ("Our 'starting point is the language of the statute,' . . . but 'in expounding a statute, we are not guided by a single sentence or member of a sentence, but look to the provisions of the whole law, and to its object and policy.' ") (citations omitted). If Congress's intent is clear from the statutory language, then "that intent must be given effect." Chevron, 467 U.S. at 842–43.

As noted above, the Clean Water Act defines "pollutant" as "dredged spoil, solid waste, incinerator residue, sewage, garbage, sewage sludge, munitions, chemical wastes, biological materials, radioactive materials, heat, wrecked or discarded equipment, rock, sand, cellar dirt and industrial, municipal, and agricultural waste discharged into water." 33 U.S.C. § 1362(6). This Court has previously concluded that the "broad generic terms" included in the definition of "pollutant" demonstrate Congress's intent to capture more than just the items expressly enumerated. United States v. Hamel, 551 F.2d 107, 110 (6th Cir. 1977) (concluding that the Clean Water Act covers, at a minimum, those pollutants covered under the Refuse Act, which applies to "all foreign substances" not explicitly exempted from coverage); see also, e.g., Cedar Point Oil Co., 73 F.3d at 565 ("[T]he breadth of many of the items in the list of 'pollutants' tends to eviscerate any restrictive effect."); No Spray Coalition, Inc., 2005 U.S. Dist. LEXIS 11097, at *17 (citing S. Rep. No. 92-414 at 76 (1972), reprinted in 1972 U.S.C.C.A.N. 3668, 3742). However, we need not consider the term's breadth today. Rather, we find the plain language of "chemical waste" and "biological materials" in § 1362(6) to be unambiguous as to pesticides. This Court must, therefore, give effect to the Congress's expressed intent. See Chevron, 467 U.S. at 842–43.

a. Chemical Waste

Generally, a court should give a word in a statute its "ordinary, contemporary, common meaning, absent an indication Congress intended [it] to bear some different import." Grand Traverse Band of Ottawa & Chippewa Indians v. Office of U.S. Attorney, 369 F.3d 960, 967 (6th Cir. 2004) (quoting Williams v. Taylor, 529 U.S. 420, 431–32, 120 S. Ct. 1479, 146 L. Ed. 2d 435 (2000)). The EPA refers the Court to The New Oxford American Dictionary (Jewell & Abate eds. 2001), which defines waste as "eliminated or discarded as no longer useful or required after the completion of a process." *Id.* at 1905. Industry Petitioners point the Court to Black's Law Dictionary (8th ed. 2004), which defines waste as "[r]efuse or superfluous material, esp. that after a manufacturing or chemical process." *Id.* at 1621. Similarly, the Ninth Circuit has accepted the American Heritage Dictionary's definition of waste as "any useless or worthless byproduct of a process or the like; refuse or excess material." N. Plains Res. Council v. Fidelity Exploration & Dev. Co., 325 F.3d 1155, 1161 (9th Cir. 2003); Fairhurst v. Hagener, 422 F.3d 1146, 1149 (2005).

Under any of these definitions of "waste," "chemical waste" for the purposes of the Clean Water Act would include "discarded" chemicals, "superfluous" chemicals, or "refuse or excess" chemicals. As such, under a plain-meaning analysis of the term, we cannot conclude that all chemical pesticides require NPDES permits. Rather, like our sister circuit in Fairhurst, we conclude that: so long as the chemical pesticide "is intentionally applied to the water [to perform a particular useful purpose] and leaves no excess portions after performing its intended purpose[] it is not a 'chemical waste,' " 422 F.3d at 1149, and does not require an NPDES permit. *Id.*

On the other hand, as Environmental Petitioners argue and the EPA concedes, excess pesticide and pesticide residue meet the common definition of waste. To this extent, the EPA's Final Rule is in line with the expressed intent of Congress, as the Rule defines these pesticide residues as pollutants "because they are wastes of the pesticide application." 71 Fed. Reg. at 68,487. The EPA aptly states: [P]esticides applied to land but later contained in a waste stream, including storm water regulated under the Clean Water Act, could trigger the requirement of obtaining an NPDES permit. . . . In addition, if there are residual materials resulting from pesticides that remain in the water after the application and its intended purpose has been completed, the residual materials are pollutants because they are substances that are no longer useful or required after the completion of a process.(EPA Br. 29–30.) This Court agrees.

Therefore, at least two easily defined sets of circumstances arise whereby chemical pesticides qualify as pollutants under the Clean Water Act. In the first circumstance, a chemical pesticide is initially applied to land or dispersed in the air — these pesticides are sometimes referred to as either "terrestrial pesticides" or "aerial pesticides" and include applications "above" or "near" waterways. At some point following application, excess pesticide or residual pesticide finds its way into the navigable waters of the United States. Pesticides applied in this way and later affecting the water are necessarily "discarded," "superfluous," or "excess" chemical. Such chemical pesticide residuals meet the Clean Water Act's definition of "chemical waste."

In the second circumstance, a chemical pesticide is applied directly and purposefully to navigable waters to serve a beneficial purpose — such pesticides are often referred to as "aqueous" or "aquatic" pesticides. As contemplated by the EPA, if residual aquatic pesticide "remain[s] in the water after the application and [the pesticide's] intended purpose has been completed," then the residue would likewise qualify as a "chemical waste." (EPA Br. 29–30.) As such, these chemical wastes would unambiguously fall within the ambit of the Clean Water Act.

This second scenario, of course, leads to the inevitable quandary that both non-waste aqueous pesticide and pesticide residual are applied to water at the same moment, which then gives rise to the question of how the EPA can regulate and permit the residual. However, this problem is more theoretical than practical. In reality, whether or not a particular chemical pesticide needs to be regulated can be easily answered by both the EPA's and industry's experience with that pesticide. If, as was the case in Fairhurst, a chemical such as antimycin leaves no excess portions after performing its intended purpose, then that chemical's use need not be regulated. See Fairhurst, 422 F.3d at 1149. If, on the other hand, a chemical pesticide is known to have lasting effects beyond the pesticide's intended object, then its use must be regulated under the Clean Water Act. *See also* Headwaters, Inc. v. Talent Irrigation Dist., 243 F.3d 526, 532–33 (9th Cir. 2001).

b. Biological Materials

Continuing our review under Chevron, we must examine the "ordinary, contemporary, [and] common meaning" of "biological materials." Grand Traverse Band, 369 F.3d at 967. Environmental Petitioners point out that Webster's Third New International Dictionary (Gove ed. 1993) defines "material" as "of, relating to, or consisting of matter" and "the basic matter from which the whole or the great part of something is made." *Id.* at 1392. The Oxford English Dictionary provides that "material" is "that which constitutes the substance of a thing (physical or nonphysical); a physical substance; a material thing." . . . The plain, unambiguous nature of this language compels this Court to find that matter of a biological nature, such as biological pesticides, qualifies as a biological material and falls under the Clean Water Act if it is "discharged into water." 33 U.S.C. § 1362(6).

The EPA points to Ninth Circuit case law that holds that "mussel shells and mussel byproduct are not pollutants" under the Clean Water Act. Ass'n to Protect Hammersley, Eld & Totten Inlets v. Taylor, 299 F.3d 1007, 1016 (9th Cir. 2002). The Hammersley court found the Clean Water Act to be "ambiguous on whether 'biological materials' means all biological matter regardless of quantum and nature." *Id.* While that case is distinguishable, we choose a more limited analysis.[5] We see our obligation not as defining the outermost bounds of "biological materials," but rather simply as deciding whether biological pesticides fit into the ordinary meaning of "biological materials."

The term "biological materials" cannot be read to exclude biological pesticides or their residuals. The EPA's Final Rule treats biological pesticides no differently from chemical pesticides, exempting both from NPDES permitting requirements in certain circumstances. *See* 71 Fed. Reg. at 68,492. We find this interpretation to be contrary to the plain meaning of the Clean Water Act. In 33 U.S.C. § 1362, Congress purposefully included the term "biological materials," rather than a more limited term such as "biological wastes." Congress could easily have drafted the list of pollutants in the Clean Water Act to include "chemical wastes" and "biological wastes." But, here, the word "waste" does not accompany "biological materials." Thus, if we are to give meaning to the word "waste" in "chemical waste," we must recognize Congress's intent to treat biological and chemical pesticides differently.

This interpretation is consistent with the precedent of this Court and others. In National Wildlife Federation v. Consumers Power Co., 862 F.2d 580 (6th Cir. 1988), we determined that "[m]illions of pounds of live fish, dead fish and fish remains annually discharged in Lake Michigan by [a] facility are pollutants within the meaning of the [Clean Water Act], since they are "biological materials." Likewise, the District Court of Maine determined that "salmon feces and urine that exit the net pens and enter the waters are pollutants as they constitute 'biological materials'

---

[5] The Hammersley court based its conclusion on the fact that shells and shell byproduct of shellfish-farming facilities are the result of natural biological processes, not the result of a transforming human process. *See* Hammersley, 299 F.3d at 1016–17.

or 'agricultural wastes.' " United States Pub. Interest Research Group v. Atl. Salmon of Maine, 215 F. Supp. 2d 239, 247 (D. Me. 2002) (citing Higbee v. Starr, 598 F. Supp. 323, 330–31 (D. Ark. 1984) aff'd, 782 F.2d 1048 (8th Cir. 1985)). Biological pesticides similarly must be considered "biological materials." Biological pesticides consist of artificial concentrations of viruses, bacteria, fungi, plant materials, and/or other biological materials. *See* Pesticides: Glossary, U.S. EPA, available at http:// www.epa.gov/pesticides/glossary. Congress defined "pollution" as "the man-made or man-induced alteration of the chemical, physical, biological, and radiological integrity of water." 33 U.S.C. § 1362(19). Adding biological pesticides to water undeniably alters its biological integrity. Therefore, we find biological pesticides to be "biological materials" under the Clean Water Act.

2. *Are Chemical Pesticide Residuals Added to the Water by "Point Sources?"*

The EPA further defends its Final Rule by arguing that excess pesticide and residue pesticide are not discharged from a "point source." In other words, though excess and residue pesticides have exactly the same chemical composition and are discharged from the same point source at exactly the same time as the original pesticide, and though excess and residue pesticides would not enter the Nation's waterways but for the discharge of the original pesticide, the EPA concludes that excess and residue pesticides are not discharged from a "point source" because at the moment of discharge there is only pesticide. This is so, according to the EPA, because excess and residue pesticides do not exist until after the discharge is complete, and therefore "should be treated as a nonpoint source pollutant." 71 Fed. Reg. at 65,847.

The Clean Water Act defines "point source" as "any discernible, confined, and discrete conveyance," including a variety of mechanisms such as "container," "rolling stock," or "vessel or other floating craft." 33 U.S.C. § 1362(14). The EPA and the courts agree that pesticides are applied by point sources. See 71 Fed. Reg. at 65,847; League of Wilderness Defenders v. Forsgren, 309 F.3d 1181, 1185 (9th Cir. 2002); Headwaters, 243 F.3d at 528. The EPA argues that, at the time of discharge, the pesticide is a nonpollutant, and the excess pesticide and pesticide residues are not created until later, presumably after they are already in the water. Therefore, according to the EPA, pesticides at the time of discharge do not require permits because they are not yet excess pesticides or residue pesticides. But there is no requirement that the discharged chemical, or other substance, immediately cause harm to be considered as coming from a "point source." Rather, the requirement is that the discharge come from a "discernible, confined, and discrete conveyance," 33 U.S.C. § 1362(14), which is the case for pesticide applications.

The EPA offers no direct support for its assertion that a pesticide must be "excess" or "residue" at the time of discharge if it is to be considered as discharged from a "point source." This omission of authority is understandable, as none exists. The Clean Water Act does not create such a requirement. Instead, it defines "discharge of a pollutant" as "any addition of any pollutant to navigable waters from any point source." 33 U.S.C. § 1362(12). The EPA's attempt at temporally tying the "addition" (or "discharge") of the pollutant to the "point source" does not follow the plain language of the Clean Water Act. Injecting a temporal requirement to the "discharge of a pollutant" is not only unsupported by the Act, but it is also contrary to the purpose of the permitting program, which is "to prevent harmful discharges into the Nation's waters." Defenders of Wildlife, 127 S. Ct. at 2525. If the EPA's interpretation were allowed to stand, discharges that are innocuous at the time they are made but extremely harmful at a later point would not be subject to the permitting program. Further, the EPA's interpretation ignores the directive given to it by Congress in the Clean Water Act, which is to protect water quality. As the EPA itself recognizes, "Congress generally intended that pollutants be controlled at the source whenever possible." 73 Fed. Reg. at 33,702 (citing S. Rep. No. 92-414, p. 77 (1972)). Here, it is certainly possible for pesticide residue to be controlled at its source because the discharge of the pesticide introduces such residue into the water.

The EPA's newly asserted temporal element also runs contrary to its own recent interpretation of the Clean Water Act's term "addition." See 73 Fed Reg. 33,697 (June 13, 2008). The EPA determined that transfers of water from one body of water to another do not constitute the "addition" of a pollutant to the new body of water, and in doing so clarified its understanding of the term "addition." 73 Fed Reg. 33,697. The EPA explained: Given the broad definition of "pollutant," transferred (and receiving) water will always contain intrinsic pollutants, but the pollutants in transferred water are already in "the waters of the United States" before, during, and after the water transfer. Thus, there is no "addition"; nothing is being added "to" "the waters of the United States" by virtue of the water transfer, because the pollutant at issue is already part of "the waters of the United States" to begin with.

. . . .

As noted above, EPA's longstanding position is that an NPDES pollutant is "added" when it is introduced into a water from the "outside world" by a point source. Gorsuch, 693 F.2d at 174–75. Id. at 33,701. Given the EPA's understanding of "addition" of a pollutant as stated above, it is clear that under the meaning of the Clean Water Act, pesticide residue or excess pesticide — even if treated as distinct from pesticide — is a pollutant discharged from a point source because the pollutant is "introduced into a water from the 'outside world' by" the pesticide applicator from a "point source." See id. This interpretation coincides with the method of determining whether a discharge is from a "point source" that the Supreme Court recently cited with approval: "For an addition of pollutants to be from a point source, the relevant inquiry is whether — but for the point source — the pollutants would have been added to the receiving body of water." Miccosukee, 541 U.S. at 103 (quoting Florida Water Mgmt. Dist. v. Miccosukee Tribe of Indians, 280 F.3d 1364, 1368 (11th Cir. 2002)). It is clear that but for the application of the pesticide, the pesticide residue and excess pesticide would not be added to the water; therefore, the pesticide residue and excess pesticide are from a "point source."

3. May the Final Rule Stand?

For all of these reasons, we conclude that the statutory text of the Clean Water Act forecloses the EPA's Final Rule. The EPA properly argues that excess chemical pesticides and chemical pesticide residues, rather than all chemical pesticides, are pollutants. However, the Final Rule does not account for the differences between chemical and biological pesticides under the language of the Clean Water Act. Further, because the Act provides that residual and excess chemical pesticides are added to the water by a "point source" there is no room for the EPA's argument that residual and excess pesticides do not require an NPDES permit. The "point source" from which the residue originates is easily discernable and necessarily must "be controlled at the source." *See* 73 Fed. Reg. at 33,702. Given all of the above in combination with the EPA's interpretation that "[p]oint sources need only convey pollutants into navigable waters to be subject to the Act," *id.* at 33,703, dischargers of pesticide pollutants are subject to the NDPES permitting program in the Clean Water Act. As such, the EPA's Final Rule cannot stand. Because the Clean Water Act's text bars the Final Rule we make no determination regarding the validity of the issuance of the Final Rule under the APA, nor do we analyze the relationship between the Clean Water Act and the FIFRA.

CONCLUSION

For the foregoing reasons, Environmental Petitioners' petitions are GRANTED in part and DENIED in part, and Industry Petitioners' petitions are DENIED in whole. We VACATE the Final Rule.

NOTES AND QUESTIONS

1. ***Update.*** Effective October 31, 2011, releases of pesticides into navigable waters are governed by a general permit established on that date by EPA. The permit has effect in states in which EPA has operational authority — Alaska, Idaho, Massachusetts, New Mexico, Oklahoma, and Washington, D.C., as well as in most U.S. territories and Indian country. BNA Daily Environmental Report, November 2, 2011. For more on permitting under the Clean Water Act, see *infra*.

2. ***"Pollutant."*** *Cf. Waste Action Project v. Dawn Mining Corp.*, 137 F.3d 1426 (9th Cir. 1998) ("[A]lthough the CWA defines 'pollutant' to include radioactive materials, the CWA's legislative history makes clear that Congress did not intend for the CWA to regulate any materials that the [Atomic Energy Commission (now the Nuclear Regulatory Commission)] was already regulating under the [Atomic Energy Act].").

3. ***The Enemy Is Not Us.*** Can a human being be a "point source" under the Clean Water Act? In *United States v. Plaza Health Laboratories*, 3 F.3d 643 (2d Cir. 1993), *cert. denied*, 512 U.S. 1245 (1994), an individual appealed his criminal conviction under §§ 301 and 309(c)(2) for knowingly discharging pollution "from a point source" into the Hudson River. He had on at least two occasions emptied vials of human blood into the river. The District Court had ruled that a human could be a point source for purposes of the statute.

The Court of Appeals reversed, holding that the statutory term is used "invariably" in the context of pollution from municipal and industrial discharges. *Plaza Health*, 3 F.3d at 646. The Court also found the Act would be unintelligible if read this way:

. . . we assume that Congress did not intend the awkward meaning that would result if we were to read "human being" into the definition of "point source." Section 1362(12)(A) defines "discharge of a pollutant" as "any addition of any pollutant to navigable waters from any point source." Enhanced by this definition, § 1311(a) reads in effect "the addition of any pollutant to navigable waters from any point source by any person shall be unlawful" (emphasis added). But were a human being to be included within the definition of "point source," the prohibition would then read: "the addition of any pollutant to navigable waters from any person by any person shall be unlawful," and this simply makes no sense. As the statute stands today, the term "point source" is comprehensible only if it is held to the context of industrial and municipal discharges.

Plaza Health, 3 F.3d at 647.

C. POINT SOURCE REGULATION

1. Effluent Limitations

In the 1972 Act, the Congress established a system of effluent limitations to control discharges of pollutants from point sources into navigable waters:

(A) *Effluent limitations based on "best practicable control technology currently available"* ("BPT" or "BPCTCA"): Section 301(b)(1)(A), 33 U.S.C. § 1311(b)(1)(A). These are interim standards for point sources.

(B) *Effluent limitations based on "best available technology economically achievable"* ("BAT" or BATEA"): Section 301(b)(2)(A), 33 U.S.C. § 1311(b)(2)(A). These are more stringent, permanent standards to be implemented after BPT.

(C) *Effluent limitations for new sources*: (new source performance standards ("NSPS")): Section 306, 33 U.S.C. § 1316. These are the CWA's analog to the new source performance standards of § 111 of the CAA.

(D) *Effluent limitations based on secondary treatment*: Sections 301(b)(1)(B), 304(d), 33 U.S.C. §§ 1311(b)(1)(B), 1314(d). These are standards for treatment of municipal wastewaters from sewage treatment plants. Primary treatment is a physical sedimentation process for removal of "settleable solids" from a waste stream. Secondary treatment refers to a physical/biological process for removing solids and pollutants characterized by biological oxygen demand ("BOD") and pH. It relies largely on chlorination of wastewater. Tertiary treatment is more elaborate pollution removal involving elimination of additional pollutants such as non-biodegradable toxics.

(E) *Effluent limitations for pretreatment*: Section 307(b), 33 U.S.C. § 1317(b). In the water pollution world, in addition to direct dischargers — those who deposit pollutants directly into "navigable waters" — there are also indirect dischargers. These entities discharge pollutants into sewer systems that then convey the materials into navigable waters. To bring these entities under the regulatory umbrella, Congress took two steps. First, it declared discharges into sewer systems to be the legal equivalent of direct discharges into navigable waters.

Second, it established pretreatment standards. These technology-based effluent limitations are designed to ensure that indirect dischargers neither upset sewage treatment plants nor cause those plants to exceed their own secondary treatment effluent limitations.

This array of standards remains in place to the present. In 1977, however, Congress amended the CWA to refine these standards and in the process created an additional standard. Why it did so warrants some attention. As EPA assumed its massive regulatory obligations under the original legislation, it took what appears to be the path of least resistance. It concentrated its BAT regulation development efforts to limit discharges of "conventional" pollutants, such as BOD, total suspended solids, oil and grease, fecal coliform, and pH. Conversely, it did not focus its efforts on restraining discharges of toxic pollutants. Why? Like criteria pollutants governed by the NAAQSs of the Clean Air Act, the commonly found conventional pollutants were easier to regulate because they were made regulable under the above-recited technology-based standards. Toxic pollutants, on the other hand, fell under a more cumbersome health-based regulatory system. Section 307(a), 33 U.S.C. § 1317(a). Under § 307(a), the agency had to undertake a process not unlike the one imposed for hazardous air pollutants under § 112 of the pre-1990 CAA. *See* Chapter 9, *supra*. First, it had to identify toxic pollutants within ninety days of enactment of the statute, taking into account each substance's toxicity, persistence, degradability, presence in water, and effects it caused on important organisms, and thereafter establish for each an effluent standard deemed sufficient to protect human health and the environment, with an "ample margin of safety." Section 307(a)(1), (4), 86 Stat. at 856, 857. Faced with the prospect of unsure science, inadequate administrative resources and funding, and too much other work to do, this task was one EPA preferred to avoid.

Predictably, the environmental community objected, filing a wave of lawsuits. One such case, led by the Natural Resources Defense Council in the District Court for the District of Columbia, resulted in the now-famous (in narrow circles) "Flannery Decree," a consent decree named for Judge Thomas A. Flannery, who approved the decree. The decree contained a list of 65 classes of toxic pollutants — the list was later refined to designate 129 "priority" pollutants from 34 industrial categories. In the decree, EPA agreed to refocus its regulatory efforts on these pollutants. The list became EPA's game plan governing virtually all of its BAT work for a ten-year period.[6]

These developments prompted Congress to enter the affray. Like the environmental community, Congress also wanted EPA to focus on toxic pollutants. Accordingly, it amended § 301(b)(2)(C) in 1977 to make BAT applicable to a broad list of toxic substances and to command EPA to regulate those substances on an expedited basis. Congress derived its list from the Flannery Decree. (Because of continuing problems with toxic water pollutants, the Congress revisited the

---

[6] The decree was upheld by a divided panel of the District of Columbia Circuit. *Citizens for a Better Environment v. Gorsuch*, 718 F.2d 1117 (D.C. Cir. 1983). In 1992, because of EPA's violations of the aforementioned consent decree, the NRDC and EPA entered into another consent decree. This later decree required EPA to promulgate about eighteen new or revised standards for several industrial categories.

problem again in 1987, when it added § 304(m), 33 U.S.C. § 1314(m), to force development of regulations in the BAT toxic and nonconventional pollutants programs. As of October, 2011, EPA had designated 65 toxic pollutants. 40 C.F.R. § 401.15.) For the conventional pollutants, Congress devised a new technology-based standard, best conventional pollution control technology ("BCT"), a tech-based standard less stringent than BAT but more stringent than BPT. Section 301(b)(2)(E), 33 U.S.C. § 1311(b)(2)(E). (The list of designated conventional pollutants may be found at 40 C.F.R. § 401.16 (1987).) Thus, the post-1977 lineup remained essentially the same, except that BCT substituted for BAT with respect to conventional pollutants. BAT, was, accordingly, reserved for toxic pollutants. Section 301(b)(2)(A) & (C), 33 U.S.C. § 1311(b)(2)(A) & (C). For the remaining universe of pollutants, the "non-conventional non-toxics," BAT is the standard. Section 301(b)(2)(F), 33 U.S.C. § 1311(b)(2)(F).

When EPA engages in CWA regulation, it prefers to do so in an administratively expedient way. Accordingly, it often will regulate an entire category of industry in one fell swoop by establishing numerical effluent limitations representing BPT, BAT, BCT, and pretreatment in a single rulemaking. Whether the CWA authorized EPA to manage its workload in these efficient ways was the subject of early, and crucial, litigation. One early landmark Supreme Court decision, *E. I. Du Pont de Nemours & Co. v. Train*, 430 U.S. 112, 97 S. Ct. 965 (1977), resolved the major question whether EPA could regulate point sources on an industry-wide basis, establishing effluent limitations for classes of plants at one time (which EPA preferred) or, alternatively, whether it could only regulate dischargers on a case-by-case basis (which industry preferred). The dispute involved the interplay of § 301, 33 U.S.C. § 1311, which identifies the standards to be used, and § 304, 33 U.S.C. § 1314, which describes how the agency should determine effluent limitations in specific cases. The *Du Pont* decision saved the EPA from an administrative nightmare:

> The broad outlines of the parties' respective theories may be stated briefly. EPA contends that § 301(b) authorizes it to issue regulations establishing effluent limitations for classes of plants. The permits granted under § 402, in EPA's view, simply incorporate these across-the-board limitations, except for the limited variances allowed by the regulations themselves and by § 301(c). The § 304(b) guidelines, according to EPA, were intended to guide it in later establishing § 301 effluent-limitation regulations. Because the process proved more time consuming than Congress assumed when it established this two-stage process, EPA condensed the two stages into a single regulation.

> In contrast, petitioners contend that § 301 is not an independent source of authority for setting effluent limitations by regulation. Instead, § 301 is seen as merely a description of the effluent limitations which are set for each plant on an individual basis during the permit-issuance process. Under the industry view, the § 304 guidelines serve the function of guiding the permit issuer in setting the effluent limitations.

> The jurisdictional issue is subsidiary to the critical question whether EPA has the power to issue effluent limitations by regulation. Section

509(b)(1), 86 Stat. 892, 33 U.S.C. 1369(b)(1), provides that "[r]eview of the Administrator's action . . . (E) in approving or promulgating any effluent limitation . . . under section 301" may be had in the courts of appeals. On the other hand, the Act does not provide for judicial review of § 304 guidelines. If EPA is correct that its regulations are "effluent limitation[s] under section 301," the regulations are directly reviewable in the Court of Appeals. If industry is correct that the regulations can only be considered § 304 guidelines, suit to review the regulations could probably be brought only in the District Court, if anywhere. Thus, the issue of jurisdiction to review the regulations is intertwined with the issue of EPA's power to issue the regulations.

The statutory language concerning the 1983 limitations, in particular, leaves no doubt that these limitations are to be set by regulation. Subsection (b)(2)(A) of § 301 states that by 1983 "effluent limitations for categories and classes of point sources" are to be achieved which will require "application of the best available technology economically achievable for such category or class[.]" These effluent limitations are to require elimination of all discharges if "such elimination is technologically and economically achievable for a category or class of point sources[.]" This is "language difficult to reconcile with the view that individual effluent limitations are to be set when each permit is issued." *American Meat Institute v. EPA*, 526 F.2d 442, 450 (CA7 1975). The statute thus focuses expressly on the characteristics of the "category or class" rather than the characteristics of individual point sources. Normally, such class-wide determinations would be made by regulation, not in the course of issuing a permit to one member of the class.

Thus, we find that § 301 unambiguously provides for the use of regulations to establish the 1983 effluent limitations. Different language is used in § 301 with respect to the 1977 limitations. Here, the statute speaks of effluent limitations for point sources," rather than "effluent limitations for categories and classes of point sources." Nothing elsewhere in the Act, however, suggests any radical difference in the mechanism used to impose limitations for the 1977 and 1983 deadlines. *See American Iron & Steel Institute v. EPA*, 526 F. 2d 1027, 1042 n. 32 (CA3 1975). . . .

In sum, the language of the statute supports the view that § 301 limitations are to be adopted by the Administrator, that they are to be based primarily on classes and categories, and that they are to take the form of regulations.

Du Pont, 430 U.S. at 124–28, 97 S. Ct. at 973–75.

Twenty years later, EPA was challenged for establishing secondary treatment effluent limitations for wastewater treatment plants on a case-by-case basis. The Tenth Circuit Court of Appeals, deferring to EPA's reading of the statute, upheld the practice. *Maier v. U.S. Environmental Protection Agency*, 114 F.3d 1032 (10th Cir. 1997).

Another issue noted in *Du Pont*, and resolved at the Circuit Court level, was whether effluent limitations could be expressed as a single number. The Fourth Circuit had ruled that single number limitations were permitted by the statute:

> The regulations impose limitations in terms of single numbers rather than in a range of numbers. Industry attacks this method saying in effect that EPA promulgated guidelines and that guidelines are not absolutes. Nothing in the Act prohibits the Administrator from using single numbers in establishing effluent limitations. The use of a single number limitation for discharge, permits any discharge from zero up to the allowed amount, subject always to the principle of presumptive validity which we have stated.

> We are aware that the Third Circuit, *American Iron and Steel Institute v. EPA, supra*, has held that the regulations there considered are invalid because "they failed to provide meaningful ranges or guidance in considering individual factors." 526 F.2d [1027] at 1046 [(1975)]. On the facts presented to us, we cannot accept that conclusion. The EPA has promulgated zero discharge limitations with regard to many of the discharge sources which are before us. If a range is required, a zero discharge provision violates the Act. An objective of the Act is the elimination of all pollutant discharges by 1985. § 101(a)(1). The expertise of the Administrator is persuasive as to whether the limitations be fixed in single numbers or ranges. A claim of arbitrary action in this regard may be considered in court review under § 509(b)(1)(E) of the issuance or denial of a permit. Then specific facts may be presented and the problem will be actual rather than hypothetical. It may be that with some categories ranges are desirable and with others single numbers are appropriate. We are dealing with the general problem and decline to make advisory statements covering specific applicability. For the purposes of the suit before us relating to "inorganic chemicals manufacturing," we accept the Administrator's use of single numbers.

E. I. Du Pont de Nemours & Company v. Train, 541 F.2d 1018, 1029–30 (4th Cir. 1976).

Given the holding of the United States Supreme Court in *Du Pont* in favor of mandatory effluent limitations that could be installed into permits, the Third Circuit Court of Appeals abandoned its position on the "single-number v. range" issue, bringing itself into line with the other federal circuits. *American Iron and Steel Institute v. EPA*, 568 F.2d 284, 296 (3d Cir. 1977).

––––––––––

The process of preparing regulations is a laborious one. Before proposing new effluent limitations, EPA must engage in a good deal of data gathering. To this end, the agency will survey scientific studies, published literature, and information from trade associations and manufacturers. It also will hold meetings with industry representatives and will send them data collection portfolios and questionnaires to secure operations information. EPA is interested particularly in information on the chemical composition of industries' influent and effluent. To this end, it often conducts its own waste stream sampling. All collected samples are subjected to rigorous laboratory analysis.

Simultaneous with this data collection effort, the agency also surveys the available pollution control technologies that might be useful in reducing the pollutant loadings of discharges (*see infra*). The end result is the proposal of effluent limitations representing BPT, BAT, BCT, pretreatment, and secondary treatment, as applicable. When subsequently promulgated, these standards take on the force and effect of law.

Note that EPA need not establish an effluent limitation for every pollutant found in an industry's waste stream. On many occasions, only one or several may be regulated. The agency knows that installing pollution control equipment to remove a regulated pollutant will result in the removal of other, unregulated, pollutants as well.

In the next sections, we examine how EPA establishes BPT, BAT, and BCT effluent limitations.

a. Best Practicable Technology (BPT)

As noted above, BPT represented the interim technology-based standards that point sources were required to meet during the time EPA was fashioning BAT and other permanent standards. As was forecast, it has declined in significance over the 40 years of the CWA's lifetime. Accordingly, we cover the issue of BPT regulation sparingly in these materials.

The CWA section establishing the BPT program is § 304(b)(1)(B) of the Act, 33 U.S.C. § 1314(b)(1)(B). This provision identifies the factors bearing on BPT in two groups. First, the EPA is instructed to

> include consideration of the total cost of application of technology in relation to the effluent reduction benefits to be achieved from such application, and second, they shall also take into account the age of equipment and facilities involved, the process employed, the engineering aspects of the application of various types of control techniques, process changes, non-water quality environmental impact (including energy requirements), and such other factors as the Administrator deems [appropriate].

These factors are known as the comparison and consideration factors, respectively. In an early decision, the District of Columbia Court of Appeals specified how these factors should be used by EPA when choosing a BPT technology:

> Based on our examination of the statutory language and the legislative history, we conclude that Congress mandated a particular structure and weight for the 1977 comparison factors, that is to say, a "limited" balancing test. In contrast, Congress did not mandate any particular structure or weight for the many consideration factors. Rather, it left EPA with discretion to decide how to account for the consideration factors, and how much weight to give each factor. In response to these divergent congressional approaches, we conclude that, on the one hand, we should examine

EPA's treatment of cost and benefit under the 1977 standard to assure that the Agency complied with Congress' "limited" balancing directive. On the other hand, our scrutiny of the Agency's treatment of the several consideration factors seeks to assure that the Agency informed itself as to their magnitude, and reached its own express and considered conclusion about their bearing. More particularly, we do not believe that EPA is required to use any specific structure such as a balancing test in assessing the consideration factors, nor do we believe that EPA is required to give each consideration factor any specific weight.

Weyerhaeuser Co. v. Costle, 590 F.2d 1011, 1045 (D.C. Cir 1978).

The court then discussed the meaning of a "limited" balancing test for comparison factors. It began by noting the legislative history of the CWA. That history stipulates that "the balancing test between total cost and effluent reduction benefits is intended to limit the application of technology only where the additional degree of effluent reduction is wholly out of proportion to the costs of achieving such marginal level of reduction for any class or category of sources." A legislative History of the Water Pollution Control Act Amendments of 1972, at 170 (statement of Senator Muskie), *Weyerhauser* at 1045, n.52. With that in mind, the court considered plaintiffs' arguments that EPA was required to do an overall cost-benefit analysis as well as another cost-benefit analysis for each "additional increment of waste treatment control, from bare minimum to complete pollution removal."

[Held the Court: EPA must perform a cost-benefit analysis but it has "some" discretion on how to do it. Costs need not be balanced against benefits]:

> . . . with pinpoint precision. A requirement that EPA perform the elaborate task of calculating incremental balances would bog the Agency down in burdensome proceedings on a relatively subsidiary task. Hence, the Agency need not on its own undertake more than a net cost-benefit balancing to fulfill its obligation under Section 304.

Id. at 1048.

NOTE

BPT Variances. Section 301(c) of the 1972 CWA expressly provided for variances from BAT standards, but no provision of the Act did so for BPT. Undeterred, EPA created a variance for BPT by regulation. As expected, EPA's regulation was challenged, but surprisingly, the regulation was upheld. *See E. I. Du Pont de Nemours v. Train*, 430 U.S. 112, 97 S. Ct. 965 (1977) (variances from BPT standards are appropriate as necessary to the regulatory scheme despite the lack of any language to that effect in the Clean Water Act). *See also Chemical Manufacturers Association v. Natural Resources Defense Council*, 470 U.S. 116 (1985). In *EPA v. National Crushed Stone Association*, 449 U.S. 64, 101 S. Ct. 295 (1980), the Court held that, to secure a BPT variance, the discharger must demonstrate that the "factors relating to the equipment or facilities involved, the process applied, or other such factors relating to such discharger are fundamentally different from the factors considered in the establishment of the guidelines." *Id.* BPT variances, however, are not available to a discharger upon a showing of financial hardship. "FDF" ("fundamentally different factors") variances are now made available in § 301(n) of the Act. To better understand what is "fundamental," see *Georgia-Pacific Co. v. U.S. Environmental Protection Agency*, 671 F.2d 1235 (9th Cir. 1982).

For more information on variances, see the notes following American Paper Institute, *infra.*

b.   Best Available Technology (BAT)

KENNECOTT v. U.S. ENVIRONMENTAL PROTECTION AGENCY
780 F.2d 445 (4th Cir. 1985)

WILKINSON, CIRCUIT JUDGE:

Petitioners challenge the effluent limitations set by the Environmental Protection Agency for the non-ferrous metals manufacturing industry. EPA established the limitations in a rulemaking pursuant to the Clean Water Act of 1977, 33 U.S.C. § 1251 1376 (1982). Congress passed the Clean Water Act as an amendment to the Federal Water Pollution Control Act of 1972. The amendment preserves the fundamental purpose of the 1972 Act: "to restore and maintain the chemical, physical, and biological integrity of the Nation's waters." 33 U.S.C. § 1251. In setting effluent limitations for the nonferrous metals industry, EPA acted to implement this congressional mandate to clean up the nations' navigable waterways. We have reviewed with care petitioners' challenges to these regulations. We conclude, however, the EPA has properly discharged the task it is required by Congress to perform.

I.

The instant action re flects the tensions recurrent in every case of environmental regulation. The first group of petitioners here produce substantial amounts of the country's primary copper, lead, and zinc. Others recycle discarded lead batteries for a variety of uses, and still another produces columbium-tantalum, of importance to the aerospace, energy, and transportation industries. The industries contend that the effluent limitations adopted by EPA in the name of the Act are unachievable and will impose widespread costs upon the industries themselves and upon those who depend for their economic livelihood upon non-ferrous metals use.

EPA in turn states that petitioners discharge massive amounts of pollutants, over 3 million pounds annually, including "some of the most toxic metals found in industrial waste streams . . . lead, cadmium, arsenic, antimony, and zinc." It contends these pollutants create "a variety of serious adverse health and environmental effects, including cancer, brain damage, and kidney failure." The effluent limits are, in EPA's view, based upon achievable technologies and must be met promptly to fulfill the basic purposes of the Clean Water Act.

The record in this case is voluminous. The rulemaking itself is highly technical.

Petitioners have challenged EPA's choice of data, its statistical methods, and its economic analysis. It is something of an understatement to say that the expertise of the parties with regard to the non-ferrous metals industry exceeds that of this court. Without suspending our critical faculties, we nonetheless believe that the benefit of the doubt in the battle of the data belongs to the agency in which Congress has reposed responsibility for administration of the Act, *see* 33 U.S.C. § 1251(d). In addition, this court is bound by the general rules of deference that run throughout administrative law. We may not overturn the agency's judgment simply because we might have drafted different regulations; remand is limited to those cases in which the agency has acted without reasonable basis. *American Meat Inst. v. EPA*, 526 F.2d 442, 450 (7th Cir. 1975).

We begin with the philosophy of the Clean Water Act. . . .

For the purposes of this case, the non-ferrous metals industry was generally subject to BAT requirements. Defining Best Available Technology requires substantial technical expertise in evaluating both the efficiency of advanced technologies and the adaptability of those technologies to the production processes of the companies in this case. Our review of the EPA rulemaking is appropriately cautious. As this court has previously noted, "The scope of our review is further colored by the policy of the Clean Water Act and the sophisticated data evaluations mandated by that lengthy and complicated statute. . . . Further, technological and scientific issues, such as those presented in this case, are by their very nature difficult to resolve by traditional principles of judicial decisionmaking." *Reynolds Metals Co. v. EPA*, 760 F.2d 549, 558 59 (4th Cir. 1985).

We proceed, however, on the understanding that Best Available Technology was the means chosen by Congress to achieve "the national goal that the discharge of pollutants into the navigable waters be eliminated by 1985," 33 U.S.C. § 1251(a)(1), a goal that implies some urgency to the environmental task that Congress set. While Congress was careful to require agency consideration of such factors as the cost to industry of achieving appropriate effluent reductions, it left EPA some latitude in defining BAT, permitting in addition to enumerated criteria, the consideration of "such other factors as the Administrator deems appropriate." See 33 U.S.C. 1314(b)(2)(B).

To achieve a reasoned result in a dispute over technologies, EPA is bound to consider industry data, but it is not bound to accept it. Any other resolution would undermine the integrity of agency decision-making. For obvious reasons, this court should be loathe to compel an agency to accept data submitted by a regulated industry. That does not imply we are blind to the capacities of agencies to enthrone their own agendas and dismiss contending views. In considering petitioners' challenges to the non-ferrous metals rulemaking, we ask whether EPA's technical judgments find support in the record and whether they re flect the rule of reason, not the imposition of flat.

The deference to the technical expertise of the Administrator supplements the deference generally required of courts reviewing administrative actions. [At this juncture, the court discusses the appropriate judicial scope of review standards applicable to administrative decisionmaking]. . . .

EPA did not approach casually the task of non-ferrous metals rulemaking. In 1977, the agency began gathering data for the proposed rules which it published on February 17, 1983. 48 Fed. Reg. 7032 7126. Data was obtained from plant visits, plant samplings, studies of scientific journals, and consultations with industry. Three hundred and nineteen firms, operating 416 facilities, received questionnaires from EPA asking for information on flow rates, production rates, wastewater treatment, and cost. *Id.* at 7044. Each plant visited by EPA also received an opportunity to comment on the trip report prepared by the agency. Various of the petitioners met with EPA both before and after publication of the proposed rules.

The resulting record ran 24,000 pages. EPA solicited public comment on all aspects of the regulations, highlighting points on which the agency wanted additional information. Id. at 7073. The initial comment period lasted eleven weeks. EPA reopened the comment period twice and accepted late-filed comments from one of the petitioners. 48 Fed. Reg. 50906 (Nov. 4, 1983); 48 Fed. Reg. 52604 (Nov. 21, 1983).

The agency considered the comments and contacted each petitioner with follow-up inquiries. The comments led EPA to re-examine its selections of model technologies and data bases. EPA likewise considered additional data on the treatment of lead and ammonia, as well as continuing to request and evaluate data from plants that had not previously submitted data. The long process of gathering data and the ongoing dialogue with the industry culminated in the final rule promulgated March 8, 1984.

We do not imply, in detailing this lengthy consideration, that a matter of the magnitude and complexity of non-ferrous metals rulemaking deserved anything less. We note only that an appellate court cannot be oblivious to the expenditure of effort that preceded its consideration and that, if the process has been a fair one, a time does come when rulemaking may cease and compliance must commence.

II.

For the purposes of this appeal, petitioners have been grouped according to industry. The first group of petitioners are Choanocyte, American Mining Congress, AJAX, Inc., OZARK Incorporated, St. Joe Minerals corporation, and GET Products Corporation (hereinafter "Kennecott"). Together these companies are responsible for much of the United States production of primary copper, primary lead and primary zinc. . . .

Kennecott objects to the non-ferrous metals rulemaking, arguing that the agency's data base was flawed, that petitioners were not given the opportunity to comment on part of the model technology, sulfide precipitation, and that EPA incorrectly calculated flow allowances. After carefully considering petitioners' numerous and specific objections, we have concluded that EPA acted within the bounds of its discretion when it set effluent limits for the primary metals industry.

A.

When it set effluent limits for the primary metals industry, EPA used as its model technology a waste treatment process called lime, settle and filtration (L,S&F). Briefly, this treatment technique works in the following way: adding lime to wastewater increased the pH; it makes the wastewater more alkaline. At different pHs, different metals precipitate, that is, emerge from solution and become suspended as solids in the wastewater. Eventually, most solids settle at the bottom of the tank. The precipitate can then be disposed of separately from the wastewater. The wastewater is often subsequently filtered through coal or sand in order to remove additional suspended solids.

A number of industries use lime and settle. Beginning in the late 1970's, EPA collected data from six such industries (aluminum forming, battery manufacturing, secondary lead, coil coating, copper forming, and porcelain enameling). After deleting unreliable data, EPA compiled the Combined Metals Data Base (CMDB). The agency then used the CMDB to calculate achievable effluent limitations for several related industries, including the primary base metals industry.

Kennecott objects to EPA's use of the CMDB. It argues that the CMDB data was limited, that the wastewaters of CMDB plants differed significantly from those of the primary metals plants, and that EPA should not have rejected data submitted by the primary metals industry.

Kennecott's basic objection is that EPA used data from the waste treatment systems of other industries (the CMDB) rather than using data submitted by the primary metals industry. Specifically, Kennecott makes the following argument: EPA's data base was limited, containing only 300 raw and treated data points from nineteen plants. EPA did not obtain samples from any given plants over a long term; therefore, the data cannot accurately reflect long-term performance. Kennecott contends that long-term data is necessary because fluctuations in pollutant concentrations occur even in properly operated treatment facilities due to "seasonal changes in temperature and precipitation, production surges or slow downs" and other variables. Because EPA did not collect enough samples, over a long enough period of time, Kennecott contends that the data does not accurately reflect achievable concentrations. Therefore, Kennecott says, petitioners will not be able to meet the effluent limitations.

In response, EPA notes that courts customarily defer to an agency's choice of data, and that in any case, EPA could use the CMDB to predict long-term performance accurately. On the first point, the agency is indisputably correct. This court has consistently given EPA a reasonable leeway in its selection of data and statistical methods. *FMC Corp. v. Train*, 539 F.2d 973, 986 (4th Cir. 1976). "[W]e note that an agency's data selection and choice of statistical methods are entitled to great deference . . . and its conclusions with respect to data and analysis need only fall within a 'zone of reasonableness.' " Reynolds Metals, 760 F.2d at 559 (citations omitted). The question is thus whether EPA acted reasonably in basing effluent limitations for the primary base metals industry on the CMDB.

EPA contends that it does not necessarily need long-term data to predict long-term performance. It notes that the data base at issue here has been used in regulations in a number of other metals industries. By using well-established statistical methods, EPA could factor in the variability one would expect in an optimally operating plant. It is true that prediction of long-term performance would not account for fluctuations resulting from operational failures. However, the agency argues that plants with operating problems do not represent the Act's goal of Best Available Technology. *FMC Corp. v. Train*, 539 F.2d at 986. ("The purpose of these variability factors is to account for the routine fluctuations that occur in plant operation, not to allow for poor performances.") Moreover, the agency contends that the addition of second-step sulfide precipitation to the model technology further reduces the variability of lime and settle treatment. *See* subsection IIB, *infra*. Courts have traditionally respected the agency's selection of a data base in the fact of challenges that the data failed to account for variable pollution loads, *Ass'n of Pac. Fisheries v. EPA*, 615 F.2d 694, 812–13 (9th Cir. 1980); *American Petroleum Inst. v. EPA*, 540 F.2d 1023, 1035–36 (10th Cir. 1976). The number of data points here is not in significant, and there must exist some reasonable termination point in the process of data collection.

Kennecott responds that even if EPA collected a sufficient number of data points, the CMDB remains flawed. It argues that the CMDB wastewater is so different from the wastewater in the primary metals industries that EPA cannot use the CMDB to set effluent limits that would apply to Kennecott. Without quantifying its claim, Kennecott says that the base metals industry has "huge amounts of wastewater," "tremendously high concentrations of metals," and a "very large variety of different metals" in the wastewater. EPA's similarly unquantified response is that the wastewaters in the CMDB industries and those of the primary base metals industry are indeed comparable. The agency agrees that the differences in concentration of metals may be statistically significant. However, there is evidence to show that the treatability of wastewater depends on the solubility of the pollutants, not on their concentrations. A difference in concentration of influents would thus not affect the concentration of effluents. See Proposed Rules, 48 Fed. Reg. 7050 (Feb. 17, 1983). This judgment constitutes a reasonable basis for EPA's belief that the wastewaters are comparable. We cannot say that EPA has acted arbitrarily or capriciously in using the CMDB to set effluent limitations for the primary metals industries.

Finally, we do not believe that EPA acted arbitrarily in rejecting the data submitted by the industry. EPA examined the data from petitioners' plants and concluded that six of the plants were not operating properly, and the seventh was unrepresentative. EPA determined that three plants were improperly operating one or more steps of the lime and settle process; they had ineffective pH adjustment, inadequate wastewater settling time, or lacked wastewater equalization. Plants use equalization to send more uniform loads of pollutants to the treatment system, ensuring that the system is not overloaded. In three other plants, patterns of extreme variability in treated effluents suggested to EPA that the plants were not equalizing their wastewaters properly. Finally, EPA considered that the seventh plant was unrepresentative because nearly all of its wastewater came from sources not related to the manufacturing processes covered by these regulations. We cannot say, therefore, that EPA abused its discretion by rejecting the industry data.

B.

EPA had originally proposed lime, settle and filtration as the BAT for treating wastewater in the primary base metals industry. Commentators objected that they would not be able to meet the proposed effluent limitations. In the Final Rules, EPA responded that any plant unable to meet the effluent limitations by using the model lime, settle and filtration technology could add an additional step: sulfide precipitation. While the APA requires the opportunity for public participation in rulemaking, "there is no question that an agency may promulgate a final rule that differs in some particulars from its proposal." Chocolate Manufacturers, 755 F.2d at 1103-04. . . .

[In the next portion of this section of the opinion, the court finds that EPA complied with the requisite rulemaking procedural requirements.] . . .

There remains the question of whether EPA acted arbitrarily in selecting sulfide precipitation as part of the Best Available Technology. Kennecott argues that sulfide precipitation will not reduce effluent concentrations to the required levels. Specifically, Kennecott charges that data from the model plants which currently use sulfide precipitation (Ashio, Japan; Boliden, Sweden; AMAX Ft. Madison) cannot be used to predict achievable concentrations at Kennecott's plants, because conditions at the two groups of plants are so different. Kennecott notes that the plant in Ashio, Japan, for example, uses sulfde precipitation to produce arsenic trioxide as an end-product, rather than to treat wastewater. EPA replies that the ultimate disposition of the solid precipitate is irrelevant, as long as the concentration levels of pollutants in the wastewater are acceptable.

The model technology may exist at a plant not within the primary base metals industry. Congress contemplated that EPA might use technology from other industries to establish the Best Available Technology. Reynolds Metals, 760 F.2d at 562. Progress would be slowed if EPA were invariably limited to treatment schemes already in force at the plants which are the subject of the rulemaking. Congress envisioned the scanning of broader horizons and asked EPA to survey related industries and current research to find technologies which might be used to decrease the discharge of pollutants. leg. Hist. at 170.

To determine that technology from one industry can be applied to another, the agency must:

(1) show that the transfer technology is available outside the industry;

(2) determine that the technology is transferable to the industry;

(3) make a reasonable prediction that the technology if used in the industry will be capable of removing the increment required by the effluent standards.

[citations omitted].

EPA has demonstrated that sulfide precipitation — a process it terms "familiar" and "well established" — is available outside the primary base metals industry and that the technology is transferable to that industry. The agency notes that "the low solubility of metal sulfides" has made sulfide precipitation a more effective treatment than the conventional lime and settle process. We do not think it disqualifying that the Ashio plant, for example, uses sulfide precipitation to produce an end-product rather than to clean its wastewater, so long as the process adequately reduces pollutant concentrations in wastewater. Again, granting the agency a proper measure of deference in technical judgments, it was not arbitrary for EPA to decide that sulfide precipitation would remove pollutants to the degree required by the effluent limitations.

Kennecott discusses two other differences between the sulfide precipitation process at the model plants and the process at the primary base metals plants. Kennecott points out that the Ashio plant treats wastewater in batches, while the primary base metals plants treat wastewater continuously. EPA answers that the choice of the batch or continuous processes affects only cost, not effectiveness, and that study demonstrates the installation and operation of sulfide precipitation is economically achievable.

Kennecott also notes that all three model plants use sulfide pretreatment, rather than sulfide polishing. Again, EPA believes that the difference is irrelevant; whether sulfide precipitation is the step before or after L,S&F will not affect the achievability of the desire effluent limitations. The critical matter, in the agency's judgment, is the application of the proper amount of precipitant and the maintenance of proper levels of pH, factors entirely independent of the timing of wastewater treatment.

We hold that EPA had a reasonable basis for deciding that the sulfide precipitation technology is transferable. We are unable to conclude the agency acted arbitrarily or capriciously in selecting sulfide precipitation as part of the Best Available Technology for the primary base metals industry.

C.

EPA expresses its effluent limitations as "mass limits." EPA derives the mass limit by multiplying the maximum concentration level of a pollutant times water flow. The agency sets flow allowances as well as concentration limits in order to prevent plants from avoiding "the regulatory impact by diluting their effluent." *Weyerhaeuser Co. v. Costle*, 590 F.2d 1011, 1059 (D.C. Cir. 1978). In setting flow allowances, the agency uses a "building block approach." That is, EPA sets a flow allowance for each individual process step; the state or regional permit writer then calculates the total flow allowance for each individual plant by summing the allowances for each process step used at that plant.

Kennecott contends that EPA improperly denied a flow allowance for a step on the process of manufacturing primary lead called blast furnace slag granulation. In the final rules, the BAT standard for blast furnace slag granulation is zero discharge. The New Source Performance Standard (NSPS), which governs new plants, is also zero discharge. Because Congress thought that new plants have the opportunity to install the best and most efficient production processes, NSPS is normally at least as stringent as, if not more stringent than, BAT. *American Iron and Steel Inst. v. EPA*, 526 F.2d 1027, 1058 59 (3d Cir. 1975). Obviously, nothing can be more stringent than zero discharge.

The blast furnace slag granulation step can be either a wet or a dry process. Kennecott contends that dry slag is not an option because it produces uncontrollable dust. Therefore, plants use wet slag, which produces wastewater. Kennecott requests a flow allowance for this wastewater. EPA responds that zero discharge for blast furnace slag granulation is appropriate because three of four existing plants recycle 100 percent of their wastewater and thus achieve zero discharge for reasons which are not site-specific. The agency did not abuse its discretion in concluding that no flow allowance need be set for the blast furnace slag granulation process step.

With regard to the NSPS, Kennecott lodges one additional objection. It says that the NSPS is based on pyrometallurgical plants, but that new primary lead smelters are likely to be hydrometallurgical. Kennecott admits that no hydrometallurgical plant is in the process of being built or even contemplated. When such a plant is built, it can be designed according to EPA specifications. If zero discharge is indeed impossible for a hydrometallurgical plant, EPA has said that at that time, it will receive a petition for a new rulemaking. 48 Fed. Reg. 8764 (Mar. 8, 1984).

D.

On occasion, EPA sets catastrophic storm allowances. These allowances permit a plant to discharge additional wastewater under emergency circumstances. Some plants hold liquid waste in "surface impoundments," which are simply natural or man-made depressions. A catastrophic storm allowance permits a plant to discharge untreated wastewater when a storm of a certain size strikes and causes the surface impoundment to overflow. EPA has set no catastrophic storm allowances for primary lead and zinc plants. Copper smelters are permitted to discharge untreated wastewater if a "twenty-five year storm" occurs. A twenty-five year storm is a storm of such magnitude that it is likely to occur only once per quarter century.

Kennecott can no longer challenge the catastrophic storm allowances for zinc and copper. EPA denied the catastrophic storm allowance for zinc and copper. EPA denied the catastrophic storm allowance for zinc in a 1975 rulemaking; the BAT and BPT allowances for copper were set in 1975 and 1980. See 40 Fed. Reg. 528 (Feb. 27, 1975); 40 Fed. Reg. 8524 (Feb. 27, 1975); 45 Fed. Reg. 44929 (July 2, 1980). Petitioners failed to raise their objections within the ninety days specified by the Clean Water Act. 33 U.S.C. § 1369(b)(1).

Kennecott is free to challenge the denial of a storm allowance for the primary lead industry, but we do not find its arguments persuasive. EPA did not set a catastrophic storm allowance for primary lead plants because surface impoundments are not part of the model technology. 48 Fed. Reg. 7048 49 (Feb. 17, 1983). EPA made a conscious decision to discourage impoundments because of associated problems: the risk of groundwater contamination and the danger that heavy pollutants will be discharged all at once. Given EPA's reservations about impoundments and the fact that impoundments are not part of the model technology, EPA did not act arbitrarily in refusing to grant an allowance for catastrophic storms.

EPA also did not set allowances for non-scope flows, that is, wastewater which is not generated by the manufacturing process but comes from other sources like employee showers or handwashing. The preamble to the Final Rules asks permit writers to consider non-scope flows when they write permits for individual plants. 47 Fed. Reg. 8778 (March 8, 1984). Kennecott is concerned that because EPA does not specifically authorize allowances for non-scope flows in the body of the regulations, permit writers will erroneously deny allowances. However, EPA did not set allowances for non-scope flows because these flows are so idiosyncratic. We do not believe that EPA was required to list site-specific sources as a separate subpart of the final regulations. Individual plants will, of course, be able to challenge the flow allowances set by permit writers.

[The remainder of the opinion deals with procedural issues and the legal arguments of the other industry group, the secondary lead industry. It is omitted on the assumption that the foregoing gives you a sense of the game.]

NOTES AND QUESTIONS

1. ***BAT and BMPs.*** What does *Kennecott* tell us about the potential stringency of effluent limitations based on BAT? About the source of data upon which to base such effluent limitations?

In this regard, note that EPA has authority to establish discharge limitations for toxic pollutants which might be discharged "associated with or ancillary to" industrial processes otherwise regulated by BAT standards. Such ancillary discharges are "plant site runoff, spillage or leaks, sludge or waste disposal, and drainage from raw material storage" which "may contribute significant amounts of such pollutants to navigable waters." Requirements to control these discharges are to be based upon "best management practices" or "BMPs." *See* § 304(e), 33 U.S.C. § 1314.

2. ***BAT and BPT.*** Section 304 (b)(2)(B) of the CWA, 33 U.S.C. § 1314(b)(2)(B), provides that factors such as costs of achieving effluent reduction shall be "take[n] into account" by the agency in fashioning BAT standards. *See also Natural Resources Defense Council v. EPA*, 863 F.2d 1420 (9th Cir. 1988):

> Technology-based limitations under BAT must be both technologically available and economically achievable. *See* 33 U.S.C. § 1314(b)(2)(B). To be technologically available, it is sufficient that the best operating facilities are able achieve the limitation. *Association of Pac. Fisheries v. EPA*, 615 F.2d 794, 816 17 (9th Cir. 1980). To demonstrate economic achievability, no formal balancing of costs and benefits is required. *See id.* at 817 18. *Reynolds Metals Co. v. EPA*, 760 F.2d. 549, 565 (4th Cir. 1985); BAT should represent "a commitment of the maximum resources economically possible to the ultimate goal of eliminating all pollutant discharges." *See EPA v. National Crushed Stone Assn.*, 449 U.S. 64, 74, 101 S. Ct. 295, 302, 66 L.Ed. 2d 268 (1980). EPA has considerable discretion in weighing the costs of BAT. *American Iron and Steel. Inst. v. EPA*, 526 F.2d 589 (3d Cir. 1977). *Id.* at 1426.

What this means is that BAT standards cannot be less stringent than BPT, and in many instances should be more stringent. The differences between the two standards are basically three: (a) BAT is based on the best performer in an industry;

BPT is based on the average of exemplary performers; (b) BAT is based on end-of-pipe technologies and in-process changes, or both, and EPA may look beyond the regulated industry itself to find BAT; BPT is based primarily (but not exclusively) on end-of-pipe technologies from the regulated industry itself; and (c) BAT standards may only be established upon a consideration of the costs the chosen technology would impose; BPT standards may be established only upon a comparison of costs and benefits.

c. Best Conventional Technology (BCT)

AMERICAN PAPER INSTITUTE v. ENVIRONMENTAL PROTECTION AGENCY
660 F.2d 954 (4th Cir. 1981)

ERVIN, CIRCUIT JUDGE:

The petitioners in these consolidated cases seek judicial review of the actions of the Administrator of the Environmental Protection Agency (EPA) in issuing regulations pursuant to section 304(b)(4)(B) of the Clean Water Act ("the Act") promulgating effluent water limitations controlling conventional pollutants from private industrial sources in accordance with section 301(b)(2)(E) of the Act. This court is vested with the responsibility and authority for making a pre-enforcement examination of the EPA guidelines by section 509(b)(1)(e) of the Act.

Although the petitioners challenge the best conventional technology (BCT) regulations issued pursuant to section 304(b)(4)(B), their primary objection is to the methodology used by the Administrator in promulgating the regulations. In particular, the petitioners contend that Congress in section 304(b)(4)(B) mandated that EPA incorporate two main factors in its methodology for determining BCT: an industry cost-effectiveness test and a test that compares the cost for private industry to reduce its effluent levels with that incurred by publicly owned treatment works (POTWs) for a similar purpose. The petitioners assert that EPA considered only the latter factor and that EPA's benchmark for this latter factor was arbitrary and capricious. Some of the other challenges that the petitioners raise are that EPA used statistically unreliable and internally inconsistent data, and that deprived petitioners of their right to comment. We hold that all the regulations promulgated pursuant to section 301(b)(2)(E) must be invalidated on the ground that EPA did not consider all the factors mandated by section 304(b)(4)(B). The only other contention that has merit is that the data on which EPA relied in formulating its POTW benchmark are statistically unreliable.

I. BACKGROUND

In 1972, Congress amended the Federal Water Pollution Control Act to establish a timetable for achieving certain water pollution control objectives. Congress declared as its policy that the discharge of pollutants in our nation's navigable waters be eliminated by 1985. 33 U.S.C. § 1251(a)(1). With respect to private industrial sources, such as these petitioners, this achievement was to be accomplished in two stages: an interim level of control effective in 1977, and a final level effective in 1983. The 1977 standard was designated "best practicable technology" (BPT) and the more stringent 1983 standard was "best available technology" (BAT).

Five years later Congress undertook to re-examine these standards. Ultimately, the Federal Water Pollution Control Act was amended again, and the Act as amended became known as the Clean Water Act. Under the Clean Water Act, the 1977 requirements (BPT) were left intact, but changes were made in the 1983 requirements (BAT). As part of these changes, Congress established various standards and schedules for three classifications of pollutants: (1) conventional pollutants; (2) toxic substances; and (3) non-conventional non-toxic pollutants not otherwise classified. 33 U.S.C. § 1311. The strict BAT standards were retained for toxic pollutants known to be dangerous and for non-conventional non-toxic pollutants, the effects of which are uncertain, but the effective date for both categories was delayed.

While the parties disagree over precisely what Congress intended to do when it enacted the 1977 amendments to the Act and draw markedly different conclusions from the language of the amendments and the legislative history, it is clear that Congress felt that the results produced by the BPT had provided a high degree of water quality improvement, and that in some instances, BAT for conventional pollutants about which much was known might require treatment not deemed necessary to meet the 1983 water quality goals of the Act. Concern was expressed about requiring "treatment for treatment's sake," and there was much discussion about comparing the cost of treatment with the benefits obtained from the reductions achieved.

Out of this came the development of a new standard, best conventional pollutant control technology (BCT). The new requirement was described by one Senate-House conferee as "the equivalent of best practical technology or something a little BPT better, even as far as best available technology in some circumstances."

In directing EPA to promulgate regulations concerning BCT standards, Congress passed section 304(b)(4)(B) of the Act, which provides in part:

> Factors relating to the assessment of best conventional pollutant control technology (including measures and practices) shall include consideration of the reasonableness of the relationship between the costs of attaining a reduction in effluents and the effluent reduction benefits derived, and the comparison of the cost and level of reduction of such pollutants from the discharge from publicly owned treatment works to the cost and level of reduction of such pollutants from a class or category of industrial sources, and shall take into account the age of equipment and facilities involved, the process employed, the engineering aspects of the application of various types of control techniques, process changes, non-water quality environment impact (including energy requirements), and such other factors as the Administrator deems appropriate.

33 U.S.C. § 1314(b)(4)(B).

. . . .

Pursuant to this Congressional directive, EPA proceeded to carry out its duties. On August 23, 1978, proposed rules were published relating to 13 secondary industry categories. These rules also contained a methodology for determining the reasonableness of any proposed effluent limitation under the BCT criteria. Critical comments were received, and on April 2, 1979, a notice was published indicating that the use of two additional documents was being considered for the data contained therein and that such data might be used in the future for computing the costs and levels of pollutants from POTW. EPA published its final BCT determinations on August 29, 1979, and the petitioners led these petitions on May 9, 1980, thus presenting these final regulations for our review. . . .

II. ANALYSIS

A. Cost Effectiveness Test

EPA's position is that Congress did not require it to utilize an industry cost-effectiveness test, but instead only mandated a POTW cost comparison standard in arriving at BCT regulations for industry. In interpreting section 304(b)(4)(B), EPA concludes that the proposed effluent guidelines are not required to pass two reasonableness tests. In support of its position, EPA reads the seemingly dual requirements of section 304(b)(4)(B) as one, commanding only a consideration of reasonableness. It contends that the second clause in the relevant portion of section 304(b)(4)(B) sets forth the benchmark of reasonableness a comparison of the proposed BCT cost and level of effluent reduction for industry to the cost and level of reduction from the discharge of POTW.

We are unable to accept this suggested statutory interpretation. When faced with such a question, our starting point for discerning congressional intent is the words of the statute itself. *See American Textile Manufacturers Institute, Inc. v. Donovan*, 49 U.S.L.W. 4720, 4725 (U.S. June 16, 1981); *State Water Control Board v. Train*, 559 F.2d 921, 924 25 n.20 (4th Cir. 1977). The law which empowers EPA to act directs that EPA's effluent regulations "shall . . . specify factors to be taken into account in determining the best conventional pollutant control technology measures and practices to comply with section 1311(b)(2)(E) of this title to be applicable to any point source (other than publicly owned treatment works) within such categories or classes." 33 U.S.C. § 1314(b)(4)(B). Congress did not leave EPA free to select these factors. The statute continues:

> Factors relating to the assessment of best conventional pollutant control technology . . . shall include consideration of the reasonableness of the relationship between the costs of attaining a reduction in effluents and the effluent reduction benefits derived, and the comparison of the cost and level of reduction of such pollutants from the discharge from publicly owned treatment works to the cost and level of reduction of such pollutants from a class or category of industrial sources. Id. (emphasis added).

We find the language of this statute to be clear and straight-forward. We thus find no reason to resort to additional rules of statutory construction or to rely on the legislative history, which has minimum probative value because of the numerous conflicts contained therein.

EPA's construction of section 304(b)(4)(B) is contrary to the plain meaning of the words contained therein. EPA ignores the mandatory language of the law ("shall"), disregards the conjunctive ("and"), and completely eliminates the first factor. By its own admission, the agency made no effort to determine what it would cost an affected industry to remove a pound of pollutant past the BPT level nor did it compare the cost of such removal with the benefits derived from the removal, as specifically required by statute. *See American Textile Manufacturers Institute, Inc. v. Donovan*, 49 U.S.L.W. 4720, 4725 & n.30 (U.S. June 16, 1981).

This court has made it clear that EPA must be held to a standard of at least literal compliance with the language of a statute which it is authorized to implement. *Appalachian Power Co. v. Train*, 545 F.2d 1351, 1357 (4th Cir. 1976). Where, as here, the language of the Act is unambiguous and EPA has failed to comply with its directives, we must grant the petitions to set aside the regulations involved and remand the regulations to EPA for reconsideration. On remand EPA is to develop an industry cost-effectiveness test in accordance with the provisions of section 304(b)(4)(B), employ that test in a manner consistent with the statute, and re-examine all existing BCT regulations to ensure that they are not inconsistent with the proper employment or this industry cost-effectiveness test.

B. POTW Comparison Test

The petitioners also challenge the action of EPA in the formation and application of the POTW comparison test. They argue that EPA erred in using an incremental approach, i.e., one going beyond the cost of normal secondary treatment for POTWs, in arriving at a POTW benchmark. They also contend that even if EPA were permitted to use an incremental POTW comparison, it acted arbitrarily and capriciously because the increment was too large to comply with congressional intent. The petitioners also object to the POTW cost data as being inadequate and statistically unreliable. We reject each of these challenges, except the one directed to the errors in the cost data. . . .

1.

The petitioners specifically argue that EPA erred in concluding that it was appropriate to consider the cost of upgrading POTW beyond secondary treatment. The petitioners object to the POTW benchmark for several reasons because: (1) secondary treatment is the only specifically defined treatment level that POTW are required by law to meet; (2) advanced secondary treatment (AST), the increment which EPA chose, was not in existence when Congress enacted section 304 of the Act; and (3) the legislative history indicates that the POTW benchmark should be based on the average cost of normal secondary treatment.

We reject the petitioners' contentions. Section 304(b)(4)(B) explicitly authorizes EPA in establishing BCT limitations to compare "the cost and level of reduction of such pollutants from, the discharge from publicly owned treatment works to the cost and level of reduction of such pollutants from a class or category of industrial sources." This controlling statute unequivocally directs EPA to employ a POTW comparison test. Contrary to the suggestions, we find nothing on the face of the statute or in the legislative history to suggest that Congress intended for EPA to use a specific POTW benchmark. Although Congress specifically directed the use of this comparison test, it did not issue any instructions as to how EPA was to structure or administer the test.

EPA considered a number of ways in which a POTW test could be formulated. 43 Fed. Reg. 37,572 (1978). One of the suggestions was that the POTW benchmark be based on the average pollutant removal costs for secondary treatment at POTWs, i.e., the increment from no treatment to secondary treatment. 43 Fed. Reg. 37,572 (1978). In addition to looking at average POTW costs for secondary treatment, EPA considered various incremental approaches below secondary treatment. EPA rejected these proposals primarily because it felt that a proper POTW benchmark should be one roughly paralleling that with which it is to be compared — the industrial increment from BPT to BAT. Whereas industry was required to be at a BPT level in 1977, POTW were required to have met effluent limitations based upon secondary treatment by 1977. EPA believed that a relevant basis of comparison for POTWs would be at an incremental level beyond secondary treatment since BCT would be at a level at least equal to BPT and in many cases beyond BPT. EPA considered several such increments. After a careful consideration of various alternatives, EPA adopted a test employing a comparison of the cost of upgrading POTW from secondary treatment levels. The selection of this upgrade comparison does not do violence to the language of the statute, and we do not find it to be arbitrary or capricious.

Not only do the petitioners object to an incremental POTW benchmark, but they also object specifically to the use of the increment from secondary to AST as being too costly. In essence, the petitioners contend that even if EPA were permitted to use an incremental POTW benchmark, it should have used a narrower increment, one that more closely straddles the marginal cost of secondary treatment.

We reject this contention. We cannot substitute our judgment for that of EPA and condemn EPA for not choosing what we may consider to be the best increment. See *Ethyl Corp. v. EPA*, 541 F.2d 1, 36 (D.C. Cir.), *cert. denied*, 426 U.S. 941 (1976). While we are obligated to scrutinize the record, particularly in a complex technical case such as this one, "we must look at the [agency's] decision not as the chemist, biologist or statistician that we are qualified neither by training nor experience to be, but as a reviewing court exercising our narrowly defined duty of holding agencies to certain minimal standards of rationality." *Id.*

EPA based its proposal on separate and distinct technologies for small and large POTWs and arrived at POTW cost-effectiveness ratios at an increment progressing from normal secondary treatment at 30 mg/l each of BOD and TSS to better secondary treatment de ned as 12 mg/l each of BOD and TSS. 43 Fed. Reg. 37, 571 72 (1978).

. . . [T]here may be any number of increments based on slightly different technology or slightly different sizes of a given technology that EPA could have used. . . . Instead of using POTW cost reasonableness figures based on specific separate and distinct technologies employed by small and large POTWs, as it had proposed initially, in its final rules, EPA used a single POTW cost reasonableness figure based on the average of all cost-effective technologies used by POTWs operating beyond secondary treatment, but employing basic secondary treatment technology.

We cannot conclude that EPA acted arbitrarily and capriciously in choosing AST as the increment beyond secondary treatment for the POTW benchmark. While EPA sought to use an increment that narrowly straddled secondary treatment, i.e., one that closely approximated marginal cost, and although it admitted its failure to find the narrowest increment that would have more closely approximated marginal cost, there is no statutory mandate requiring EPA to use an increment that equals marginal cost.

EPA has rationally justified its use of the AST increment. AST is the "knee-of-the-curve" point, the maximum cost-effective level of control for POTWs. The increment from secondary treatment to AST for POTW was also determined by EPA to be roughly analogous to the industrial increment from BPT to BAT. While comments received by EPA have suggested that there may have been a narrower increment that EPA could have used, the suggestions by the commentors imply that EPA would have had to limit itself to a specific POTW technology to arrive at a smaller increment.

We are unwilling to place a straitjacket on EPA to so limit its decision making process. We find that EPA made its decision on its POTW comparison after it fully considered various alternatives, and that its decision is rationally based. We thus conclude that EPA's choice of an increment for POTW from secondary treatment to AST was neither arbitrary nor capricious.

3.

The petitioners also challenge the POTW benchmark on the grounds that the POTW cost data upon which it was based are inadequate, statistically unreliable, and internally inconsistent. Recently, we have been apprised that EPA confesses error in the data in the two documents on which it relied in formulating its POTW benchmark. EPA has moved this court for a voluntary remand, and the petitioners do not contest the propriety of a remand solely to allow EPA to correct its data errors. Under these circumstances, therefore, we find it proper to remand this aspect of the case to EPA, but only for the purpose of allowing it to correct its data errors and to revise its BCT figures accordingly.

III. Conclusion

We find no merit to the petitioners other challenges. Accordingly, we vacate the regulations promulgated pursuant to section 304 of the Act. We remand this action to the agency with instructions to devise a cost-effectiveness test in accordance with the guidelines of this opinion and to correct its data errors.

Affirmed in Part, Reversed in Part and Remanded.

DISSENT: PHILLIPS, CIRCUIT JUDGE, concurring and dissenting: [omitted.]

NOTES

1. ***Variances.*** In some cases, point sources might be spared, at least temporarily, the burden of meeting effluent limitations based on regulations establishing effluent limitations for BAT, BCT, BPT, or secondary treatment. They can be spared if they qualify for a variance. A variance protects a point source from failure to meet otherwise governing effluent limitations. Instead, the point source receives a less stringent limitation or is given a greater time within which to meet the governing standards, or both. On some occasions, variances may be granted because a plant is fundamentally different from those which formed the basis of the effluent limitations for that industrial category or subcategory (these are "FDF" or "fundamentally different factors" variances; see, for example, discussion of BPT, *supra*). Sometimes a variance may be granted if a point source will install a particularly innovative technology for its pollution control. In limited circumstances, variances are available based on receiving water quality or economic hardship.

Following is a list of variances allowed under the Clean Water Act.

BPT	FDF variance (nonstatutory)
BAT Toxics	301(c): economic hardship (*but see* § 301(1))
	301(k): innovative technology
	301(n): FDF
BAT Nonconventionals	301(c): economic hardship
	301(g): water quality variance for certain pollutants
	301(n): FDF
BCT Conventionals	301(k): innovative technology
	301(n): FDF (no variances)
NSPS	
POTW	301(h): water quality variance (for discharges into marine waters)

2. ***CWA Programmatic Data.*** The total number of point sources required to meet tech-based standards, and consequently to have NPDES permits, is about 400,000. There is some consensus that technology-based controls are the best command-and-control mechanisms to control pollution yet devised. Since the Clean Water Act was enacted in 1970, industrial discharges have declined precipitously. From 1987 to 1990 alone, the time during which "Phase II" BAT standards for toxic discharges came on line, industrial discharges of toxics fell from 412 million to 197 million pounds per year. Whereas thirty years ago, two-thirds of the nation's waters were considered to be "unhealthy," at present the percentage more closely approximates one-third.

This is true despite the fact that much of industry remains free of BAT regulation. In a 1989 report to Congress (the last time EPA apparently has made such a report), EPA indicated that fully four-fifths of the approximately 75,000 facilities discharging toxic or nonconventional pollutants were not subject to federal

BAT standards. EPA, *Report to Congress: Water Quality Improvement Study* 17 (1989). Moreover, many of the BAT standards that are in place are aging and no longer reflect what is currently the "best available technology."

Municipal discharges are deemed to have declined since 1972, from about 7 million to 4.3 million tons per day, while populations served by municipal facilities have increased from 90 million to 160 million people. This progress is largely due to the expenditure of $66 billion in federal funds for public treatment facilities.

2. Water Quality Standards

Water quality standards (WQSs) are the CWA's analog to the national ambient air quality standards of the Clean Air Act. Before 1972, the task of setting water quality standards was for states. Congress had not taken it on, fearing that assumption of this authority would be akin to federal zoning. H. Rep. 215, 89th Cong., 1st Sess., *reprinted in* U.S.C.C.A.N. 3313, 3320–23 (1965). In those days, state standards were submitted to the "federal administrator," who reviewed them for consistency with federal requirements. If a state did not adopt standards consistent with federal requirements, the administrator promulgated water quality uses and criteria. This arrangement, while awkward and fraught with administrative and enforcement problems, S. Rep. 92-414, 92d Cong., 2d Sess., *reprinted in* U.S.C.C.A.N., pp. 3668, 3669–77 (1972), remains in place by virtue of § 303 of the CWA. Under § 303, a state is required to promulgate a WQS and submit it to EPA for approval. Upon EPA approval, the state standard takes on force and effect. Section 303(c)(3), 33 U.S.C. § 1313(c)(3). EPA can establish a new standard if it finds the state did not adopt a WQS consistent with the Act or if it determines that another standard "is necessary to meet the requirements of [the Act]." Section 303(c)(4), 33 U.S.C. § 1313(c)(4).

NATURAL RESOURCES DEFENSE COUNCIL v. UNITED STATES ENVIRONMENTAL PROTECTION AGENCY
16 F.3d 1395 (4th Cir. 1993)

BRITT, DISTRICT JUDGE:

I. FACTS

[The Maryland Department of the Environment ("ME") and the Virginia State Water Control Board ("VSWCB") revised their water quality standards for dioxin, a "highly probable" potent carcinogen that originates primarily as a by-product of chlorine bleaching of pulp by the paper manufacturing industry, for a body of water used as a source of drinking water and edible fish. These water quality standards were intended to reduce risks of exposures that cause harm to humans.

The ME and VSWCB revised their standard to 1.2 parts per quadrillion ("ppq"), a concentration less stringent than EPA's guidance criterion of.0013 ppq. EPA had reached its guidance criterion of.0013 ppq by reference to its "1984 dioxin criteria document," a publication in which the agency summarized specific scientific information regarding dioxin toxicity. The criteria document's recommended.0013 ppq level represented EPA's judgment of the level of dioxin sufficient to present an excess risk of cancer to one out of every ten million persons.[7] The state's 1.2 ppq standard, on the other hand, was thought to present that same risk to one out of every ten thousand persons. The MDE (and presumably the VSWCB) chose the less stringent standard based on information from the U.S. Food and Drug Administration, which viewed dioxin as a less potent carcinogen.

EPA conceded to the court that its view of dioxin's cancer potency was among the conservative in the world. All parties conceded that the choice of a risk level is essentially a matter of policy preference. EPA approved the states' 1.2 ppq water quality standard for dioxin, prompting the lawsuit.]

II. STATUTORY SCHEME

The main purpose of the CWA is to "restore and maintain the chemical, physical, and biological integrity of the Nation's waters" by reducing, and eventually eliminating, the discharge of pollutants into these waters. 33 U.S.C. § 1251(a) (Supp. 1993). While the states and EPA share duties in achieving this goal, primary responsibility for establishing appropriate water quality standards is left to the states. *See id.* §§ 1251(b) (1982); [citations omitted]. EPA sits in a reviewing capacity of the state-implemented standards, with approval and rejection powers only. 33 U.S.C. § 1313(c) (1982 & Supp. 1993). Water quality standards are a critical component of the CWA regulatory scheme because such standards serve as a guideline for setting applicable limitations in individual discharge permits.

In an effort to meet the CWA's primary goal, section 402 of the Act (33 U.S.C. § 1342) establishes the National Pollutant Discharge Elimination System ("NPDES") permit program. Under this program, permits are issued by either the EPA or by states that have been allocated NPDES permitting authority. *Id.* § 1342 (1982 & Supp. 1993). However, a state's exercise of NPDES permitting authority is subject to EPA approval. *Id.* §§ 1342(c), (d) (1982 & Supp. 1993). All NPDES permits must take into account technology-based effluent limitations that reflect the pollution reduction achievable based on specific equipment or process changes, without reference to the effect on the receiving water, and, where necessary, more stringent limitations representing the level of control necessary to ensure that the receiving waters attain and maintain state water quality standards. *Id.* §§ 1311(b) (1982), 1313(c) (1982 & Supp. 1993).

Additionally, the CWA requires each state to adopt water quality standards for all waters of that state and to review them at least every three years. *Id.* §§ 1313(a), (b), (c)(1) (1982 & Supp. 1993). To adopt these standards, states must first classify the uses for which the water is to be protected, such as fishing and swimming, and

---

[7] EPA considered six factors in choosing numeric dioxin criteria: (1) cancer potency; (2) risk level; (3) fish consumption (the projected consumption levels of persons in the general population); (4) bioconcentration ("BC Factor" or "BCF"), which is a prediction of how concentrated a pollutant such as dioxin will be in the tissues of living organisms, such as fish, as compared to the concentration of that pollutant in the ambient water in which the fish lives. EPA calculated the dioxin BCF as 5000; (5) water intake; and (6) body weight. The first four of these factors were at issue in this case. *See infra.*

then each state must determine the level of water quality necessary to protect those uses. Thus, the following three factors are considered when adopting or evaluating a water quality standard: (1) one or more designated uses of the state waters involved; (2) certain water quality criteria, expressed as numeric pollutant concentration levels or narrative statements representing a quality of water that supports a particular designated use; and (3) an antidegradation policy to protect existing uses and high quality waters. *Id.* § 1313(c)(2)(A) (Supp. 1993); 40 C.F.R. § 131. [Ed. note: for an example of a such a regulation, see Note 1 following the case.]

States are directed to adopt numerical water quality criteria for specific toxic pollutants, such as dioxin, for which EPA has published numerical criteria guidance under 33 U.S.C. § 1314(a), if that pollutant can reasonably be expected to interfere with the designated uses of the states' waters. *Id.* § 1313(c)(2)(B) (Supp. 1993). As mentioned previously, states must submit their new or revised water quality standards to EPA for review. *Id.* § 1313(c)(2)(A) (Supp. 1993). On review, each submission must contain at least six elements: (1) use designations consistent with the CWA; (2) a description of methods used and analyses conducted to support revisions of water quality standards; (3) water quality criteria sufficient to protect the designated uses; (4) an antidegradation policy; (5) certification of compliance with state law; and (6) general information to assist EPA in determining the adequacy of the scientific basis for standards that do not include the "fishable/swimmable" uses as set forth in 33 U.S.C. 1251(a)(2). 40 C.F.R. § 131.6.

EPA regulations also provide that states should develop numerical criteria based on EPA's criteria guidance under § 304(a) of the CWA, EPA's criteria guidance modified to reflect site-specific conditions, or other scientifically defensible methods. 40 C.F.R. § 131.11(b)(1). Alternatively, states should establish narrative criteria or criteria based on biomonitoring methods if numerical criteria cannot be ascertained, or to supplement numerical criteria. Id. § 131.11(b)(2).

III. Discussion

. . . .

C. The District Court's Affirmance of EPA's Approval of
the Maryland and Virginia Dioxin Standards

Appellants argue that the district court's affirmance of EPA's approval of the Maryland and Virginia water standards should be reversed primarily for two reasons. First, they assert that EPA's approval was arbitrary and capricious because it was not based on all relevant factors, ignored key aspects of the record before it, and failed to show a rational connection between the facts found and the choices made. Second, they maintain that EPA's action was contrary to law because it did not ensure, as required by § 303(c) of the CWA (33 U.S.C. § 1313(c)), that state standards were consistent with the CWA; that is, that the standard protected all designated water uses.

Specifically, NRDC attacks EPA's assessment of the Maryland and Virginia standards regarding the first four factors used in the numeric dioxin criteria determination, namely: (1) cancer potency, (2) risk level, (3) fish consumption, and

(4) bioconcentration factor ("BCF"). Of these four, NRDC emphasizes its challenge with respect to the latter two factors, fish consumption and BCF. NRDC contends that these two factors, when considered together, are important because they determine the ultimate "exposure" of an individual to dioxin, while the remaining factors only involve choices about risk or toxicity.

1. Fish Consumption

EPA estimates, on a national average, that an individual eats 6.5 grams of fish per day. Maryland and Virginia used this estimate, inter alia, in calculating the 1.2 ppq water quality standard. Appellants argue that by affirming EPA's approval of the states' use of this estimate, the district court failed to require EPA to protect subpopulations with higher than average fish consumption, particularly recreational and subsistence fishers. Specifically, appellants contend that EPA's 6.5 grams per day fish consumption factor underestimates the actual fish consumption of subpopulations in Maryland and Virginia, and therefore is not protective of a designated use. Appellants further contend that EPA's use of the 6.5 grams per day fish consumption factor is unsupported by the record and violates EPA's own policy and regulations. They emphasize that Maryland and Virginia are coastal states and, as such, are entitled — according to EPA recommendations — to higher than average values for fish consumption.

Appellants argue that the risk is especially high for the Mattaponi and Native American peoples who live near a major paper mill in Virginia and who, it is argued, consume higher-than-average amounts of fish. EPA counters that the fish consumption of these subpopulations is speculative at best, that it is based on anecdotal evidence, and that there is no evidence that the fish that actually are consumed are maximum residue fish. In fact, EPA argues that the Native Americans fish in the streams primarily for shad and herring, both of which are anadromous fish that spend a large part of their lives in the oceans and migrate to the rivers only at certain stages during their lives.

The District Court concluded that the EPA, in exercising its judgment, "relied on scientifically defensible means to reach reasoned judgments regarding fish consumption levels." NRDC II, at 1276. We agree.

2. Bioconcentration Factor (BCF)

Based on EPA laboratory studies, dioxin is more soluble in fat tissues than it is in water. As a result, it tends to accumulate in fish fat tissues at concentrations higher than those present in the water. By averaging the fat content of fish likely to be eaten by an exposed population, a generic BCF can be calculated that reflects dioxin's presence in fish as some multiple of its concentration in ambient water. In its 1984 dioxin criteria document, EPA calculates a dioxin BCF of 5000 for fish of average (3%) lipid content. Maryland and Virginia used this BCF figure, inter alia, to derive their numeric water quality criteria.

Appellants challenge EPA's use and approval of a 5000 BCF. They essentially contend that the 5000 BCF figure is outdated because the latest scientific research suggests that a higher BCF should be used. Citing the administrative record, appellants emphasize that: (1) EPA admits that scientific literature and research has changed significantly since preparation of the 1984 dioxin criteria document; (2) EPA further admits that BCF factors now range from 26,000 to 150,000, depending on test species; (3) Virginia conducted a state-specific study which revealed a BCF calculation of 22,000; and (4) Maryland refused to conduct such a study. Appellants contend that, taking all of these factors into account, EPA ignored all the current scientific data and simply "defaulted" to its old BCF assumption. Appellants argue that EPA acted arbitrarily and improperly in not requiring a higher BCF, especially when Virginia and Maryland chose less stringent factors for cancer potency and risk. We disagree.

Once again, we are confronted with an area dominated by complex scientific inquiry and judgment. Although EPA is aware that some recent BCF studies suggested a higher BCF than 5000, EPA maintains that such results are inconclusive and that no compelling scientific evidence indicates that a 5000 BCF is no longer within the range of scientific defensibility. We simply are not in a position to second guess this technical decision by administrative experts. A review of the record does indicate that several more recent BCF studies have been conducted and that some have suggested a higher BCF; however, the court concludes that the best course of action is to leave this debate to the world of science to ultimately be resolved by those with specialized training in this field. Upon a careful review of the administrative record, we find no clear evidence showing that the 5000 BCF figure is not supported by sound scientific rationale. Accordingly, we hold that EPA did not act arbitrarily in approving the BCF figure used by Maryland and Virginia, and that EPA has made a rational connection between the facts found in the administrative record and its choice to approve the BCF figure. EPA's approval of the 5000 BCF will not be disturbed.

3. Protection of All Stream Uses

Appellants next contend that the district court ratified EPA's approval of the state dioxin standards without ensuring protection of all stream uses. Appellants suggest that when EPA adopted the 1.2 ppq standard, it was required to demonstrate that other stream uses were protected. They maintain that EPA ignored record evidence revealing that the 1.2 ppq standard could cause serious, direct, toxic effects to aquatic life and other wildlife that consume fish tainted with dioxin. Appellants thus argue that EPA did not follow the CWA, its regulations, or its own guidelines by asserting that the water quality criteria were intended to address only one of the minimum statutory uses, human health protection. Essentially, appellants claim that states must adopt a single criterion for dioxin that protects against all identifiable effects on human health, aquatic life, and wildlife. We disagree.

Section 303(c)(2)(A) of the CWA (33 U.S.C. § 1313(c)(2)(A) (Supp. 1993)) requires that new or revised water quality standards "consist of designated uses of the navigable waters involved and the water quality criteria for such waters based upon such uses." That section also provides: Such standards shall be such as to protect the public health or welfare, enhance the quality of water and serve the purposes of this chapter.

Such standards shall be established taking into consideration their use and value for public water supplies, propagation of fish and wildlife, recreational purposes, and agricultural, industrial, and other purposes, and also taking into consideration their use and value for navigation.

Id.

Reference to the regulations also is instructive: "A water quality standard . . . defines the water quality goals of a water body, or portion thereof, by designating the use or uses to be made of the water and by setting criteria necessary to protect the uses." 40 C.F.R. §§ 130.3, 131.2. The regulations define "criteria" as "elements of State water quality standards, expressed as constituent concentrations, levels, or narrative statements, representing a quality of water that supports a particular use. When criteria are met, water quality will generally protect the designated use." *Id.* § 131.3(b). Section 131.11(a) further provides that "states must adopt those water quality criteria that protect the designated use. Such criteria must be based on sound scientific rationale and must contain sufficient parameters or constituents to protect the designated use. For waters with multiple use designations, the criteria shall support the most sensitive use." *Id.* § 131.11(a).

As previously indicated, states should develop either numerical criteria based upon CWA guidance (or other scientific methods), or narrative criteria, if numerical criteria cannot be established. Narrative criteria might also be developed to supplement numerical criteria. *Id.* § 131.11(b). Clearly, the form of a particular state's water criteria may be either numeric or narrative, depending upon the designated use, as the district court correctly recognized. NRDC II, 806 F.2d at 1277.

In view of the above, we find that use of the term "criteria" in CWA § 303(c)(2)(A) and the regulations means that states may adopt multiple criteria for the same pollutant. Thus, where multiple uses are designated for a body of water, there may be multiple criteria applicable to it, as long as the criteria support the most sensitive use of that particular body of water. States have exclusive responsibility to designate water uses. *See* 40 C.F.R. § 131.10. However, in determining these use designations, states must take into account whether the body of water serves as a public water supply, its role in the protection and propagation of fish, shellfish and wildlife, recreation in and on the water, and agricultural, industrial, and other uses, including navigation. *Id.*

EPA avers that its review of the Maryland and Virginia standards was limited exclusively to protection of human health against any potential adverse effects (both cancerous and non-cancerous) caused by dioxin. The TSDs reflect this position. In reviewing the Virginia water quality standard, EPA stated:

The Virginia criterion for [dioxin] is designed to protect human health. Accordingly, EPA has limited its review to assessing the adequacy of the numeric criterion for that purpose. Virginia did not submit a criterion for [dioxin] for the protection of aquatic life. Depending on the circumstances, greater protection than is afforded by Virginia's 1.2 ppq criterion may be required for this purpose. In the absence of a numeric criterion for [dioxin] to protect aquatic life, Virginia's narrative criterion must, consistent with 40

C.F.R. § 122.44(d), be interpreted in individual permitting actions to prevent harm to aquatic life. §

J.A. at 280 81 (footnote omitted). EPA's comments in the Maryland TSD are similar:

The Maryland criterion for [dioxin] is designed to protect human health. §Accordingly, EPA's review is limited to assessing the adequacy of the numeric criterion for that purpose. In the absence of a numeric criterion for dioxin to protect aquatic life, Maryland's narrative criteria must be interpreted in individual permitting actions to prevent harm to aquatic life. See COMAR § 26.10.01.03.B(5)(b). Depending on the circumstances, greater protection than is afforded by Maryland's 1.2 ppq criterion may be required for this purpose.

Id. at 314 (footnote omitted). Thus, EPA duly acknowledged that dioxin may have adverse effects on aquatic life. However, EPA also noted that application of existing, separate narrative criteria protecting such aquatic life and wildlife could require more stringent controls in some cases than would be required through use of the human health criteria alone.

EPA conducted an extensive review of the adequacy of the states' criteria to protect human health, aquatic life and wildlife. Appellants have failed to cite any convincing authority showing that states have an obligation under the CWA or its accompanying regulations to adopt a single numeric criterion for dioxin that protects against all identifiable effects to human health, aquatic life, and wildlife.

D. Summary

We find that EPA's review of the Maryland and Virginia water quality standards was neither arbitrary nor capricious. Each review conducted by EPA was supported by lengthy, highly scientific, technical support documents explaining in detail EPA's rationale in approving the 1.2 ppq standards. EPA has satisfied this court that substantial evidence exists in the administrative record to support its decision, and that it acted rationally and in accordance with the CWA and its regulations. We therefore refuse to upset either EPA's decision to approve Maryland's and Virginia's adoption of the 1.2 ppq standard or the district court decision affirming the same.

[Remainder of opinion omitted]

For the foregoing reasons, the judgment of the district court is

Affirmed.

NOTE

WAC 173-201-045(1). Following is an example of a water quality standards regulation promulgated by the State of Washington. The regulation establishes uses and criteria for extraordinary, or Class AA, streams. The portion of the regulation announcing the State's antidegradation policy is omitted. (This is the regulatory provision implicated in the *Jefferson County* decision of the United States Supreme Court, discussed in note material later in this section. *See infra.*)

(1) Class AA (extraordinary).

(a) General characteristic. Water quality of this class shall markedly and uniformly exceed the requirements for all or substantially all uses.

(b) Characteristic uses. Characteristic uses shall include, but not be limited to, the following:

(i) Water supply (domestic, industrial, agricultural).

(ii) Stock watering.

(iii) Fish and shell fish: Salmonid migration, rearing, spawning, and harvesting. . . . Other fish migration, rearing, spawning, and harvesting. . . .

(iv) Wildlife habitat.

(v) Recreation (primary contact recreation, sport fishing, boating, and aesthetic enjoyment).

(vi) Commerce and navigation.

(c) Water quality criteria

(i) Fecal cominform organisms.

(A) Freshwater — fecal coliform organisms shall not exceed a geometric mean value of 50 organisms/100 mL, with not more than 10 percent of samples exceeding 100 organisms/100 mL.

(B) Marine water — fecal coliform organisms shall not exceed a geometric mean value of 14 organisms/100 mL, with not more than 10 percent of samples exceeding 43 organisms/100 mL.

(ii) Dissolved oxygen [shall exceed specific amounts].

(iii) Total dissolved gas shall not exceed 110 percent of saturation at any point of sample collection.

(iv) Temperature shall not exceed [certain levels].

(v) pH shall be within [a specified range].

(vi) Turbidity shall not exceed [specific levels].

(vii) Toxic, radioactive, or deleterious material concentrations shall be less than those which may affect public health, the natural aquatic environment, or the desirability of the water for any use.

(viii) Aesthetic values shall not be impaired by the presence of materials or their effects, excluding those of natural origin, which offend the senses of sight, smell, touch, or taste.

WAC 173-201-045(1).

AMERICAN WILDLANDS v. BROWNER
260 F.3d 1192 (10th Cir. 2001)

Judges: Before Tacha, Chief Judge, Reavley[8], and Lucero, Circuit Judges:

Tacha, Chief Circuit Judge.

This appeal presents a challenge by Appellant American Wildlands to the Environmental Protection Agency's ("the EPA") approval pursuant to the Clean Water Act of certain of Montana's water quality standards. Specifically, two questions are presented to this court for review: (1) whether the EPA properly approved Montana's statutory exemption from antidegradation review of nonpoint sources of pollution; and (2) whether the EPA properly approved Montana's mixing zone policies and procedures. The district court held in favor of the EPA. We exercise jurisdiction pursuant to 28 U.S.C. § 1291 and affirm.

I. Statutory and Regulatory Scheme

1. Point and Nonpoint Source Discharges

The Clean Water Act ("the Act") was adopted "to restore and maintain the chemical, physical, and biological integrity of the Nation's waters." 33 U.S.C. § 1251(a). To achieve this goal, Congress prohibited the discharge from a point source of any pollutant into the waters of the United States unless that discharge met specific requirements set forth in the Act. 33 U.S.C. § 1311(a). . . .

In order for point source discharges to be in compliance with the Act, such discharges must adhere to the terms of a National Pollutant Discharge Elimination System ("NPDES") permit issued pursuant to the Act. 33 U.S.C. § 1342. NPDES permits are issued by the EPA or, in certain jurisdictions, by state agencies authorized to do so by the EPA. 33 U.S.C. § 1342(a)-(d). Unlike point source discharges, nonpoint source discharges are not defined by the Act. One court has described nonpoint source pollution as "nothing more that [sic] a [water] pollution problem not involving a discharge from a point source." *Nat'l Wildlife Found. v. Gorsuch*, 224 U.S. App. D.C. 41, 693 F.2d 156, 166 n.28 (D.C. Cir. 1982) (internal quotation marks omitted).

Rather than vest the EPA with authority to control nonpoint source discharges through a permitting process, Congress required states to develop water quality standards for intrastate waters. 33 U.S.C. § 1313. Water quality standards consist of three elements: first, each water body must be given a "designated use," such as recreation or the protection of aquatic life; second, the standards must specify for each body of water the amounts of various pollutants or pollutant parameters that may be present without impairing the designated use; and finally, each state must adopt an antidegradation review policy which will allow the state to assess activities

---

[8] Honorable Thomas M. Reavley, Senior Circuit Judge, United States Court of Appeals for the Fifth Circuit, sitting by designation.

that may lower the water quality of the water body. 33 U.S.C. § 1313(c)(2)(A); 40 C.F.R. §§ 130.3, 130.10(d)(4), 131.6, 131.10, 131.11. Further, each state is required to identify all of the waters within its borders not meeting water quality standards and establish "total maximum daily loads" ("TMDL") for those waters. 33 U.S.C. § 1313(d). A TMDL defines the specified maximum amount of a pollutant which can be discharged into a body of water from all sources combined. Dioxin/ Organochlorine Ctr. v. Clarke, 57 F.3d 1517, 1520 (9th Cir. 1995). . . .

3. Antidegradation

The antidegradation review policies adopted by the states as a part of their water quality standards must be consistent with the federal antidegradation policy. 40 C.F.R. § 131.12. The EPA's regulations establish three levels of water quality protection: Tier I, Tier II, and Tier III. Tier I protection establishes the minimum water quality standard for all waters and requires that "existing instream water uses and the level of water quality necessary to protect the existing uses shall be maintained and protected." 40 C.F.R. § 131.12(a)(1). Tier II protection provides that, where the water quality of a water body exceeds that necessary to support aquatic life and recreation, that level of water quality shall be maintained unless the state determines that "allowing lower water quality is necessary to accommodate important economic or social development in the area in which the waters are located." 40 C.F.R. § 131.12(a)(2). Tier III protection provides that, where a water body "constitutes an outstanding National resource, such as waters of National and State parks and wildlife refuges and waters of exceptional recreational or ecological signi cance, that water quality shall be maintained and protected." 40 C.F.R. § 131.12(a)(3).

4. Mixing Zones

Pursuant to the EPA's regulations, a state may, at its discretion, include within its water quality standards "policies generally affecting . . . mixing zones." 40 C.F.R. § 131.13. Mixing zones are "areas where an effluent discharge undergoes initial dilution and are extended to cover the secondary mixing in the ambient water body. A mixing zone is an allocated impact zone where acute and chronic water quality criteria can be exceeded as long as a number of protections are maintained." Environmental Protection Agency, Water Quality Standards Handbook § 5.1.1, at 5-5 (2d ed.1994) (hereinafter Handbook). The protections that must be maintained include the absence of "toxic conditions to aquatic life," "objectionable deposits," "floating debris," "objectionable color, odor, taste, or turbidity," and substances resulting in "a dominance of nuisance species." Id. at 5-5 to 5-6. Mixing zones are allowable as a practical necessity because "it is not always necessary to meet all water quality criteria within the discharge pipe to protect the integrity of the water body as a whole. Sometimes it is appropriate to allow for ambient concentrations above the criteria in small areas near outfalls." Id. § 5.1, at 5-1. Should a state decide to include "policies generally affecting . . . mixing zones" within their water quality standards, those policies are subject to review and approval by the EPA. 40 C.F.R. § 131.13.

5. Montana's Policies

1. Montana's Exemption of Nonpoint Source Pollution from Antidegradation Review

In drafting its water quality standards, the Montana legislature exempted "existing activities that are nonpoint sources of pollution as of April 29, 1993" from antidegradation review with respect to Tier II waters. Mont. Code Ann. § 75-5317(2)(a). Further, nonpoint sources initiated after April 29, 1993 are exempted from antidegradation review with respect to Tier II waters "when reasonable land, soil, and water conservation practices are applied and existing and anticipated beneficial uses will be fully protected." Mont. Code Ann. §§ 75-5-317(2)(b).

2. Montana's Mixing Zone Policies and Procedures

Montana's antidegradation rules provide that, where degradation to a water body at the edge of a mixing zone is not significant, no antidegradation review of the mixing zone itself is required. Mont. Admin. R. § 17.30.715(1)(c), 17.30.505(1)(b). Montana does, however, impose a number of other requirements on mixing zones designed to limit their impact on the receiving water body. Montana requires that mixing zones have "(a) the smallest practicable size, (b) a minimum practicable effect on water uses, and (c) definable boundaries." Mont. Code Ann. § 75-5-301(4). A mixing zone may not "threaten or impair existing beneficial uses." Mont. Admin. R. § 17.30.506(1). A discharge permit may not be renewed if "there is evidence that the previously allowed mixing zone will impair existing or anticipated uses." Mont. Admin. R. § 17.30.505(1)(c). The Montana Department of Environmental Quality is required to consider various factors in deciding whether or not to grant a mixing zone, such as the toxicity and persistence of the substance being discharged and the cumulative effects of multiple mixing zones. Mont. Admin. R. § 17.30.506(2). Finally, the water quality within the mixing *zone* itself is regulated to prohibit discharge from blocking passage of aquatic organisms or from causing the death of organisms passing through the mixing zone. Mont. Admin. R. § 17.30.602(14).

II. PROCEEDINGS BELOW

American Wildlands filed this lawsuit in 1998, alleging that the EPA had failed to take timely action under section 303(c) of the Act to approve or disapprove Montana's new and revised water quality standards. The original complaint alleged that the EPA violated the Act by: (1) failing to approve or disapprove Montana's new and revised water quality standards; and (2) by failing to promptly prepare and promulgate replacement standards for those Montana standards that failed to meet the requirements of the Act. In October 1998, American Wildlands moved for summary judgment. The parties stayed briefing of that motion, however, when the EPA stipulated that it would complete its review of Montana's water quality standards by January 15, 1999.

On December 24, 1998, the EPA disapproved some of Montana's revised standards and approved others. The EPA addressed the remaining standards on January 26, 1999, again disapproving some and approving others. On March 31,

1999, American Wildlands amended its complaint to challenge the EPA's approval of several of Montana's standards. The district court affirmed each of the EPA's actions. *Am. Wildlands v. Browner*, 94 F. Supp. 2d 1150 (D. Colo. 2000). This appeal followed. Specifically, American Wildlands appeals the district court's conclusion that: (1) the EPA properly approved Montana water quality standards that exempt nonpoint source pollution from antidegradation review; and (2) the EPA properly approved Montana mixing zone policies and procedures exempting the areas within the mixing zone from antidegradation review. . . .

IV. THE EPA's APPROVAL OF MONTANA's WATER QUALITY STANDARDS

1. Montana's Standard Exempting Nonpoint Source Pollution from Antidegradation Review

It is the position of American Wildlands in this case that Montana's Tier II antidegradation policy, which does not consider nonpoint source pollution, is not consistent with the Act and must be disapproved by the EPA. The EPA maintains that the Act does not grant it authority to regulate nonpoint sources of pollution, and therefore, it is powerless to disapprove state antidegradation review policies on the basis of how those policies deal with nonpoint source pollution.

The district court, ruling in favor of the EPA, held that "nothing in the CWA demands that a state adopt a regulatory system for nonpoint sources." *Am. Wildlands*, 94 F. Supp. 2d at 1161. We agree. In the Act, Congress has chosen not to give the EPA the authority to regulate nonpoint source pollution. *See Kennecott Copper Corp. v. EPA*, 612 F.2d 1232, 1243 (10th Cir. 1979) (holding that the EPA lacks authority to regulate nonpoint sources of pollution); *Appalachian Power Co. v. Train*, 545 F.2d 1351, 1373 (4th Cir. 1976) ("Congress consciously distinguished between point source and nonpoint source discharges, giving EPA authority under the [Clean Water] Act to regulate only the former.").

Because the Act nowhere gives the EPA the authority to regulate nonpoint source discharges, the EPA's determination — that Montana's water quality standards exempting nonpoint source discharges from antidegradation review are consistent with the Act — is a permissible construction of the Act. It is true that states are required to "assure that there shall be achieved . . . cost-effective and reasonable best management practices for nonpoint source control." 40 C.F.R. § 131.12(a)(2). It is also true that the standard-setting process in 33 U.S.C. § 313 applies generally to waters polluted by both point source and nonpoint source pollution. 33 U.S.C. § 1313 (making no distinction between pollution from point and nonpoint sources). However, this does not mean, as American Wildlands argues, that states are required to regulate nonpoint sources at the antidegradation stage. Rather, the effect of nonpoint source discharges on water bodies will be diminished by state adoption of TMDLs for water bodies not meeting state water quality standards. Consequently, we find that the EPA did not act arbitrarily or misinterpret the Act when it approved Montana's antidegradation review rules.

B. Montana's Mixing Zone Policies and Procedures

American Wildlands argues that Montana's mixing zone policy allowing point source discharges to degrade water quality within the mixing zone so long as the discharge does not degrade the water quality outside the zone is inconsistent with the Act because it allows point source pollution to escape antidegradation review within certain areas of Montana's water bodies. The EPA maintains that the Act's antidegradation requirements apply to the waterbody as a whole, not specifically to the mixing zone. We find the EPA's interpretation of the Act to be permissible.

The use of mixing zones is widespread. Indeed, the water quality regulations specifically allow for their use. 40 C.F.R. § 131.13. "Practically every state and Puerto Rico have adopted mixing zone criteria. . . . " *P.R. Sun Oil Co. v. EPA*, 8 F.3d 73, 75 (1st Cir. 1993). As noted above, mixing zones are allowable as a practical necessity because "it is not always necessary to meet all water quality criteria within the discharge pipe to protect the integrity of the water body as a whole. Sometimes it is appropriate to allow for ambient concentrations above the criteria in small areas near outfalls." Handbook § 5.1, at 5-1. While "the entire extent of the water body is not required to be given full existing use protection," all effects "on the existing use must be limited to the area of the regulatory mixing zone." *Id.* § 4.4.4, at 4-6.

Moreover, courts have previously recognized that the reality of mixing zones makes measuring water quality standards at the edge of the zone a necessity. *P.R. Sun Oil Co.*, 8 F.3d at 75 ("Measuring pollutants at the edge of the mixing zone is widespread in the application of the Clean Water Act."); *Marathon Oil Co. v. EPA*, 830 F.2d 1346, 1349 (5th Cir. 1987) ("By definition, the effluent itself [within the mixing zone] does not meet water quality standards. . . . It necessarily follows, then, that the edge or outer circumference of the mixing zone is defined as the boundary at which water quality standards are first met."). Finally, as mentioned above, Montana has provided a number of safeguards to ensure that mixing zones do not damage the water quality of the entire water body. Consequently, we find that the EPA did not act arbitrarily or misinterpret the Act when it approved Montana's mixing zone policies.

V. CONCLUSION

In sum, we hold that the EPA's approval of Montana's water quality standards was not done arbitrarily or capriciously. Furthermore, the EPA's interpretation of the Clean Water Act implicit in its decision to approve those standards is permissible. Therefore, we *Affirm*.

NOTE

State of the Water. According to the 2000 Clean Water Act § 305 analysis of the nation's waterways, 39% of assessed rivers and streams, 51% of estuaries square miles, and 46% of assessed lake, pond, and reservoir acres (not including the Great Lakes) fail to meet all applicable water quality standards. In 2004, states reported that about 44 percent of stream miles, 64 percent of lake acres, and 33 percent of bay and estuarine square miles were not sufficiently clean to support fishing and swimming. The causes behind the impairment of these water bodies include pathogens, mercury, nutrients, and organic enrichment/low dissolved oxygen. Sources of pollution included agriculture, hydrologic modifications, and atmospheric deposition. EPA, The National Water Quality Inventory, Report to Congress (2004) (this Report is the last such document posted on EPA's website).

We have now surveyed the regime of standards governing point source water pollution control. Next, we look to the two mechanisms by which those standards are affixed to persons. The first is the broadly applicable certification program of § 401, 33 U.S.C. § 1341. The certification provision bars the issuance of any federal license or permit to authorize an activity that may result in a discharge, unless the applicant for that permit or license has secured from the appropriate state a certification that the activity will not violate state laws relating to water quality. Section 401(a)(1), 33 U.S.C. § 1341(a)(1).

The second implementation mechanism is the National Pollutant Discharge Elimination System, established in § 402 of the CWA, 33 U.S.C. § 1342. The NPDES is the CWA's permit system. Unlike the CAA, the CWA has always relied on permits as its implementation vehicle. Under § 402, no person may discharge pollutants into navigable waters except in accordance with an NPDES permit.

3.   Section 401: Certification

AMERICAN RIVERS, INC. v. FEDERAL ENERGY REGULATORY COMM'N
129 F.3d 99 (2d Cir. 1997)

[The Federal Energy Regulatory Commission ("FERC") issued hydropower licenses under the Federal Power Act to several projects, refusing to incorporate several conditions imposed by the State of Vermont pursuant to its authority under § 401 of the Clean Water Act. According to FERC, the rejected conditions were beyond the scope of the State's authority under § 401. Petitioners contend FERC must incorporate all state-imposed certification conditions; challenges to such conditions, it contends, may only be brought in court proceedings by licensees. The Court discussed that issue as well as the interrelationship of the certification requirement with the FPA.]

WALKER, CIRCUIT JUDGE:

. . . .

II. DISCUSSION

The principal dispute between petitioners and the Commission in this case surrounds the relative scope of authority of the states and the Commission under the CWA and the [Federal Power Act]. Petitioners' contention is straightforward, resting on statutory language. In their view, the plain language of § 401(d) indicates that FERC has no authority to review and reject the substance of a state certification or the conditions contained therein and must incorporate into its licenses the conditions as they appear in state certifications. FERC disagrees, arguing that the language of § 401(d) is not as clear as petitioners would have it. Rather, FERC contends, it is bound to accede only to those conditions that are within a state's authority under § 401, that is, conditions that are reasonably related to water quality and that otherwise conform to the dictates of § 401. *See Tunbridge Mill*, 68 Fed. Energy Reg. Comm'n Rep. (CCH) § 61,078 at 61,387. The Commission also argues that without the authority to reject state-imposed § 401 conditions its Congressionally mandated role under the FPA of ensuring comprehensive planning and development of hydropower would be undermined.

A. The Clean Water Act

Before considering the Commission's contentions regarding the CWA, we note that FERC's interpretation of § 401, or any other provision of the CWA, receives no judicial deference under the doctrine of *Chevron USA, Inc. v. Natural Resources Defense Council*, 467 U.S. 837, 104 S. Ct. 2778, 81 L. Ed. 2d 694 (1984), because the Commission is not Congressionally authorized to administer the CWA. *See* 33 U.S.C. § 1251(d) ("Except as otherwise expressly provided in this chapter, the Administrator of the Environmental Protection Agency . . . shall administer this chapter."); *see also West v. Bowen*, 879 F.2d 1122, 1137 (3d Cir. 1989) (holding that "no deference is owed an agency's interpretation of another agency's statute"); *Oregon Natural Desert Assoc. v. Thomas*, 940 F. Supp. 1534, 1540 (D. Or. 1996) (holding that United States Forest Service's interpretation of § 401 of the CWA is not entitled to deference because Congress delegated administration of the CWA to the EPA alone). Thus, we review de novo the Commission's construction of the CWA.

We begin, as we must, with the statute itself. In this case, the statutory language is clear. Section 401(a), which is directed both to prospective licensees and to the federal licensing agency (in this case, the Commission), provides, in relevant part:

> Any applicant for a Federal license or permit to conduct any activity . . . which may result in any discharge into the navigable waters, shall provide the licensing or permitting agency a certification from the State in which the discharge originates or will originate. . . . No license or permit shall be granted until the certification required by this section has been obtained or has been waived. . . . No license or permit shall be granted if certification has been denied by the State. . . .

33 U.S.C. § 1341(a). More important, § 401(d), reads, in pertinent part:

> Any certification provided under this section . . . shall become a condition on any Federal license or permit subject to the provisions of this section.

33 U.S.C. § 1341(d) (emphasis added). This language is unequivocal, leaving little room for FERC to argue that it has authority to reject state conditions it finds to be ultra vires. Rather, in this case, to the extent that the Commission contends that Congress intended to vest it with authority to reject "unlawful" state conditions, the

Commission faces a difficult task since it is generally assumed — absent a clearly expressed §legislative intention to the contrary — "that Congress expresses its purposes through the ordinary meaning of the words it uses. . . ." *Escondido Mut. Water Co. v. La Jolla Band of Mission Indians*, 466 U.S. 765, 772, 104 S. Ct. 2105, 80 L. Ed. 2d 753 (1984).

The Commission argues that, notwithstanding the mandatory language of the provision, § 401(d) itself restricts the substantive authority of states to impose conditions: "Section 401 authorizes states to impose only conditions that relate to water quality." Tunbridge Mill, 68 Fed. Energy Reg. Comm'n (CCH) ¶ 61,078 at 61,387. This is plainly true. Section 401(d), reasonably read in light of its purpose, restricts conditions that states can impose to those affecting water quality in one manner or another. *See* P.U.D. No. 1 of Jefferson County, 114 S. Ct. at 1909 (holding that a state's authority to impose conditions under § 401(d) "is not unbounded"). However, this is not tantamount to a delegation to FERC of the authority to decide which conditions are within the confines of § 401(d) and which are not. And this is the crux of the dispute in this case.

In addition to § 401(d), the Commission relies on several other provisions of the CWA in arguing that it has the authority to review and reject state-imposed conditions that are deemed by the Commission to exceed a state's power under § 401 of the CWA. In particular, the Commission invokes § 401(a)(3) and § 401(a)(5) of the CWA.

Section 401(a)(3) establishes a presumption that a state's § 401 certification obtained in order to procure a federal construction permit — for instance, a dredge-and-fill permit issued by the Army Corps of Engineers pursuant to § 404 of the CWA, 33 U.S.C. § 1344(a) — will fulfill the requirements for a subsequent federal permit governing the operation of the facility constructed pursuant to that certification. The presumption, however, may be overcome if certain conditions arise and the state then takes the procedural steps set forth by § 401(a)(3). However, even assuming the applicability of § 401(a)(3) to the facts of this case (a matter that is far from certain), the Commission has not established that it has been vested by Congress with the authority to determine whether state-imposed conditions are consistent with this provision. Nor has the Commission done so with respect to § 401(a)(5) of the CWA, 33 U.S.C. § 1341(a)(5), which provides the licensing agency (in this case FERC) with authority to enforce the terms of a license — which pursuant to § 401(d) include a state's § 401 certification conditions — once such a federal license has issued. Thus, the Commission's arguments relying on these provisions suffer from the same infirmity as does its argument relying on § 401(d). The Commission assumes the very question to be decided: whether FERC — and not a court of appropriate jurisdiction on appeal by an applicant — has the authority to review the legality of state-imposed § 401 conditions in the first instance. . . .

. . . While the Commission may determine whether the proper state has issued the certification or whether a state has issued a certification within the prescribed period, the Commission does not possess a roving mandate to decide that substantive aspects of state-imposed conditions are inconsistent with the terms of § 401.

B. The Federal Power Act

Independent of FERC's concerns that Vermont's § 401 conditions violate the terms of the CWA, the Commission contends that the § 401 conditions run afoul of the FPA. The Commission primarily fears that "to accept the conditions proposed would give the state the kind of governance and enforcement authority that is critical and exclusive to the Commission's responsibility to administer a license under the Federal Power Act, a power the Courts have repeatedly concluded belongs exclusively to the Commission." Brief of the Fed. Energy Regulatory Comm'n at 16. In particular, FERC argues (1) that the conditions that impose deadlines on construction conflict with § 13 of the FPA, 16 U.S.C. § 806, which places construction deadlines largely within the discretion of the Commission and generally contemplates that construction will be commenced within two years of the date of the license, *see First Iowa Hydro-Elec. Coop. v. Federal Power Comm'n*, 328 U.S. 152, 168 n.13, 66 S. Ct. 906, 90 L. Ed. 1143 (1946); (2) that the reopener conditions and pre-approval conditions violate § 6 of the FPA, 16 U.S.C. § 799, which provides that a license, once issued, "may be revoked only for the reasons and in the manner prescribed under the provisions of this chapter, and may be altered or surrendered only upon mutual agreement between the licensee and the Commission," as well as other provisions of the FPA, *see* 16 U.S.C. §§ 803(b), 820, 823b; and, (3) more generally, that the conditions "eviscerate the carefully balanced approach" to environmental concerns expressed in the Electric Consumers Protection Act ("ECPA"), Pub.L. No. 99-495, 100 Stat. 1243 (1986), amending the FPA, *see, e.g.*, 16 U.S.C. §§ 797(e), 803(a), 803(j).

We have no quarrel with the Commission's assertion that the FPA represents a congressional intention to establish "a broad federal role in the development and licensing of hydroelectric power." *California v. Federal Energy Regulatory Comm'n*, 495 U.S. 490, 496, 110 S. Ct. 2024, 109 L. Ed. 2d 474 (1990). Nor do we dispute that the FPA has a wide preemptive reach. *Id.* The CWA, however, has diminished this preemptive reach by expressly requiring the Commission to incorporate into its licenses state-imposed water-quality conditions. *See* 33 U.S.C. § 1341(a)(1). Although we are sympathetic to the Commission's suggestion that without the authority to reject states' conditions that are beyond the scope of § 401, the preemptive reach of the FPA may be narrowed at the will of the states, *see, e.g.*, Brief of Amici Curiae Edison Elec. Inst. at 14, the Commission's concerns are overblown.

The Commission fails to acknowledge appropriately its ability to protect its mandate from incursion by exercising the authority to refuse to issue a hydropower license altogether if the Commission concludes that a license, as conditioned, sufficiently impairs its authority under the FPA. *See, e.g. Escondido*, 466 U.S. at 778 n.20. If the Commission is concerned that the conditions imposed by a state "intrude upon the Commission's exclusive authority under the FPA," Brief of the Fed. Energy Regulatory Comm'n at 44, nothing in the CWA prevents it from protecting its field of authority by simply refusing to issue the license as so conditioned.

The Commission, however, has chosen to forgo this route, arguing that refusing to issue a license is not a "practical option" in relicensing cases, such as CVPS. *Id.* at 20 n.10. Although we understand that refusing to relicense a hydroelectric project would result in the disassembly of the project, presenting "serious practical and economic problems" and affecting all manner of local interests, *id.*, the Commission's dissatisfaction with the remedy of license denial is not reason enough to turn a blind eye to FERC's assumption of authority to review and reject a state's § 401 conditions. Rather, the Commission must establish that the authority it proposes is rooted in a Congressional mandate. And this they have failed to do.

Finally, with respect to the ECPA amendments to the FPA, the Commission is mistaken. Under these provisions, the Commission must "give equal consideration to . . . the protection, mitigation of damage to, and enhancement of, fish and wildlife . . . and the preservation of other aspects of environmental quality," 16 U.S.C. § 797(e), and must impose conditions, based on recommendations of relevant federal agencies and affected states, to "protect, mitigate damages to, and enhance, fish and wildlife . . . affected by the development, operation, and management of the project . . . .," 16 U.S.C. § 803(j)(1). *See United States Dep't of Interior v. Federal Energy Regulatory Comm'n*, 952 F.2d 538, 543 (D.C. Cir. 1992) (describing environmental aspects of the ECPA amendments). The Commission argues that absent the authority to reject state-imposed conditions beyond the scope of § 401 of the CWA, the carefully balanced approach of the ECPA amendments, in general, and § 10(j), 16 U.S.C. § 803(j), in particular, would be "eviscerated . . . through the simple expedient of [states'] labeling . . . recommendations 'conditions' to the Section 401 certification." Brief of the Fed. Energy Regulatory Comm'n at 39. In short, the Commission is concerned that it would be "held hostage" to every state imposed condition, compromising its role under the ECPA amendments of reconciling competing interests. *Id.* Such a result, the Commission contends, is impermissible under § 511(a) of the CWA, 33 U.S.C. § 1371(a), which provides, in part, that the Act "shall not be construed as . . . limiting the authority or functions of any officer or agency of the United States under any other law or regulation not inconsistent with this chapter. . . ."

The Commission's claim that the CWA — as we construe it — and the ECPA amendments are incompatible must be rejected. The Commission's concern that states will hold the Commission hostage through the § 401 process is misplaced because states' authority under § 401 is circumscribed in notable respects. First, applicants for state certification may challenge in courts of appropriate jurisdiction any state-imposed condition that exceeds a state's authority under § 401. In so doing, licensees will surely protect themselves against state-imposed ultra vires conditions. Second, even assuming that certification applicants will not always challenge ultra vires state conditions, the Commission may protect its mandate by refusing to issue a license which, as conditioned, conflicts with the FPA. In so doing, the Commission will not only protect its mandate but also signal to states and licensees the limits of its tolerance. Third, and most important, to the extent that the existence of states' authority to impose § 401 conditions may otherwise conflict with the ECPA amendments, the ECPA is inconsistent with the terms of the CWA, thus, making inapplicable § 511(a) of the CWA. *See* 33 § U.S.C. 1371(a) (the Act "shall not be construed as . . . limiting the authority or functions of any officer or agency of the United States under any other law or regulation not inconsistent with this chapter . . . ").

III. CONCLUSION

We have considered the Commission's remaining arguments and find them to be without merit. For the foregoing reasons, we grant the petition for review, vacate the orders of the Commission, and remand for proceedings consistent with this opinion.

NOTES AND QUESTIONS

1. **EPA Regulations.** EPA has promulgated regulations to govern the certification process. 40 C.F.R. Part 121. Under the rules, every certification must include a statement "that there is a reasonable assurance that the activity will be conducted in a manner which will not violate applicable water quality standards" and a statement of conditions deemed "necessary or desirable with respect to the discharge of the activity." 40 C.F.R. §§ 121.2(3), 121.2(4). It is EPA's role to determine whether a certified discharge will affect other states' water quality standards. 40 C.F.R. § 121.13. If a state is potentially affected, the information is forwarded to it for a hearing.

2. **Jefferson County.** The United States Supreme Court elevated § 401 in significance in its 1994 decision in *P.U.D. No. 1 of Jefferson County and City of Tacoma v. Washington Department of Ecology*, 511 U.S. 700, 114 S. Ct. 1900 (1994) ("*Jefferson County*"). The decision involved the proposed construction of a hydroelectric project on the Dosewallips River in Washington State. The project would have diverted water from a 1.2-mile reach of the River (the bypass reach), run the water through turbines to generate electricity, and then returned the water to the River below the bypass reach. Under the Federal Power Act (FPA), 41 Stat. 1063, as amended, 16 U.S.C. § 791 et seq., the petitioners were obligated to secure a license from the Federal Energy Regulatory Commission ("FERC") to build the project. Petitioners also needed to obtain the State's certification pursuant to § 401 of the Clean Water Act.

Relying on § 401, the State conditioned its certification upon compliance with the State's minimum stream flow requirements in place to protect salmon and steelhead runs. The State wanted the stream flow in the bypass reach to be no less than 100 to 200 cubic feet per second ("cfs") depending on the season. The problem was that such a flow requirement would mean the project could divert less water for electricity production purposes than it otherwise might, and this in turn would rob the project of much of its economic feasibility. The issue was whether conditions of this sort are permissible under § 401. The Court ruled in the affirmative. In the reasoning of the Court, § 401(d) expanded the State's authority to impose conditions on the certification of projects. The section provides that any certification shall set forth "any effluent limitations and other limitations . . . necessary to assure that any applicant "will comply with various provisions of the Act and with *any other appropriate requirement of state law.*" 33 U.S.C. § 1341(d) (emphasis added). Thus, held the Court, states are not limited to imposing only water quality limitations specifically tied to a "discharge."

In reaching this conclusion, the Court flatly rejected what it called the "artificial distinction" between water quantity and water quality, commenting that " 'pollution' may result from 'changes in the movement, flow, or circulation of any navigable waters . . . including changes caused by the construction of dams.' 33 U.S.C. §§ 1314(f). This concern with the flowage effects of dams and other diversions is also embodied in the EPA regulations, which expressly require existing dams to be operated to attain designated uses. 40 C.F.R. § 131.10(g)(4) (1992)." *Jefferson County*, 511 U.S. at 719, 114 S. Ct. at 1913.

The Court also agreed "that the State's minimum stream flow condition is a proper application of the state and federal antidegradation regulations, as it ensures that an 'existing instream water use' will be 'maintained and protected', 40 C.F.R. § 131.12(a)(1) (1993)." *Jefferson County*, 511 U.S. at 719, 114 S. Ct. at 1912.

Jefferson County is viewed by many persons as the most important case in years on the subject of certification under the Clean Water Act. (Do you see why?) Its underlying message has not been lost on the environmental community. Environmentalists, for example, sought to apply the § 401 certification process to federal grazing permits. Their argument was that grazing livestock destroy banks of streams and their vegetative cover, thereby causing rises in water temperature which can in turn be deadly to coldwater salmon, trout, and other fish. Grazing activities also can increase stream sedimentation and fecal coliform and fecal streptococci levels. However, in a test case before the Ninth Circuit, the argument that federal grazing permits may only be issued if accompanied by a CWA certification was rejected on the ground that the certification requirement was meant to apply only to point source releases. *Oregon Natural Desert Ass'n v. Dombeck*, 172 F.3d 1092 (9th Cir. 1998), *cert. denied*, 528 U.S. 964, 120 S. Ct. 397 (1999). *See also* Rosenhouse, *Construction and Application of § 401 Certification Requirement Under Federal Clean Water Act, 33 U.S.C.A. § 1341*, 17 A.L.R. Fed. 2d 309 (2011).

4.   The National Pollutant Discharge Elimination System

Section 402 of the Clean Water Act, 33 U.S.C. § 1342, establishes the primary regulatory tool by which effluent limitations are made applicable to specific point sources. That tool is the National Pollutant Discharge Elimination System ("NPDES"), which requires point sources to obtain permits. With the NPDES system in place, persons may discharge pollutants into waters of the United States only if they meet applicable effluent limitations and have a permit in hand confirming that right.

Permitting authority under § 402 may be transferred to states. State permitting programs go by the acronym, SPDES. As of 2011, the large majority of states had authority to issue SPDES permits in lieu of EPA's issuance of NPDES permits. The states where EPA retains permitting authority are Alaska, the District of Columbia, Massachusetts, New Hampshire, New Mexico, and Oklahoma. EPA also holds authority to issue NPDES permits in most U.S. territories and for many federal facilities.

AMERICAN FOREST AND PAPER ASSOCIATION v. U.S. ENVIRONMENTAL PROTECTION AGENCY
137 F.3d 291 (5th Cir. 1998)

JUDGES: Before JONES and SMITH, CIRCUIT JUDGES, and FITZWATER,[9] DISTRICT JUDGE.

OPINION: JERRY E. SMITH, CIRCUIT JUDGE:

Pursuant to the Clean Water Act ("CWA"), 33 U.S.C. § 1251 et seq., the Environmental Protection Agency ("EPA") delegated to Louisiana the responsibility for administering the Louisiana Pollutant Discharge Elimination System ("LPDES"). In exchange for its approval, EPA required Louisiana to consult with the Fish and Wildlife Service ("FWS") and the National Marine Fisheries Service ("NMFS") before issuing permits. If FWS or NMFS determines that the proposed permit threatens endangered species — and if Louisiana refuses to modify the permit — EPA will veto the permit under its continuing oversight authority. American Forest and Paper Association ("AFPA") challenges this rule as exceeding EPA's authority under the CWA. Because we agree that EPA lacked statutory authority, we grant the petition for review and vacate and remand the portion of the rule that imposes the consultation requirement and declares that EPA will veto any permit to which FWS or NMFS objects.

I.

Under the CWA, one needs a permit to discharge a pollutant. At least as an initial matter, permitting authority is vested in EPA through the National Pollutant Discharge Elimination System ("NPDES"). EPA may, however, delegate permitting authority to a state if the state demonstrates that it will comply with a list of enumerated requirements and that it will monitor and enforce the terms of the permits. See CWA§§ 402(b)(1) (9), 33 U.S.C. § 1342(b)(1)–(9). EPA does not enjoy wide latitude in deciding whether to approve or reject a state's proposed permit program. "Unless the Administrator of EPA determines that the proposed state program does not meet [the specified] requirements, he must approve the proposal." Save the Bay, Inc. v. EPA, 556 F.2d 1282, 1285 (5th Cir. 1977).

EPA retains oversight authority even when it delegates permitting authority to a state. Should the agency determine that a state is not complying with the CWA, it may withdraw its approval of the state program. EPA also retains oversight authority over individual permits issued under approved state programs. States are required to submit permit applications and proposed permits to EPA; the agency may veto a proposed permit if it concludes that the permit violates the CWA. See CWA § 402(d), 33 U.S.C. § 1342(d).

Until recently, EPA administered the permitting program in Louisiana through the NPDES. Before issuing a permit, EPA chose to consult with FWS and NMFS to ensure that endangered species would not be threatened by the discharges

---

[9] District Judge of the Northern District of Texas, sitting by designation.

contemplated in the permit. When EPA announced plans to delegate the permitting program to Louisiana, environmental groups cried foul, pointing out that because the Endangered Species Act ("ESA") does not apply to the states, nothing would prevent the issuance of permits that might harm endangered species.

EPA then devised the following scheme: In exchange for approving Louisiana's program, EPA directed the Louisiana Department of Environmental Quality ("LDEQ") to submit proposed permits to FWS and NMFS for review. If the federal agencies agree that the proposed permit does not threaten endangered species, the permit may be issued. But if the federal agencies conclude that the permit does threaten endangered species — and if LDEQ refuses to modify the permit to the agencies' satisfaction — EPA will exercise its veto power and formally object to the permit. Louisiana consented to this arrangement, and EPA issued its final rule. See Approval of Application by Louisiana To Administer the National Pollutant Discharge Elimination System Program, 61 Fed. Reg. 47,932 (1996).

EPA invoked CWA§§ 304(I), 33 U.S.C. § 1314(I), as authority for attaching this condition to its approval of Louisiana's program. That section allows EPA to promulgate guidelines "establishing the minimum procedural and other elements" for state permitting programs. The agency also pointed to ESA § 7(a)(2) as justifying its action. That section provides:

> Each Federal agency shall, in consultation with and with the assistance of the Secretary [of the Interior, Commerce, or Agriculture], insure that any action authorized, funded, or carried out by such agency . . . is not likely to jeopardize the continued existence of any endangered species or threatened species or result in the destruction or adverse modification of habitat of such species. . . .

16 U.S.C. § 1536(a)(2). The spirit of this general mandate is echoed in the statement of congressional purpose underlying the ESA, 16 U.S.C. § 1531(c)(1), which declares it "the policy of Congress that all Federal departments and agencies shall seek to conserve endangered species and threatened species and shall utilize their authorities in furtherance of the purposes of this chapter." . . .

[The following portions of the opinion, dealing with availability of review and issues of standing, are omitted.]

V.

EPA contends that its rule is authorized by CWA § 304(i), 33 U.S.C. § 1314(i), which directs EPA to promulgate guidelines governing state permitting programs under CWA § 402(b), 33 U.S.C. § 1342(b). EPA also suggests that its decision is not only authorized but compelled by ESA § 7(a)(2), 16 U.S.C. § 1536(a)(2). That section directs federal agencies to consult with FWS and NMFS before undertaking any "agency action," to ensure that the action will not threaten an endangered species. . . .

B.

Specifically, CWA § 402(b), 33 U.S.C. § 1342(b), provides that the EPA Administrator "shall approve" proposed state permitting programs that meet nine specified requirements. The key question is whether EPA may deny a state's proposed program based on a criterion — the protection of endangered species — that is not enumerated in § 402(b).

EPA calls our attention to CWA § 304(I), 33 U.S.C. § 1314(I), construing that section as authorizing the agency to regard the nine requirements of § 402(b) as minimum, not exhaustive, criteria. EPA further contends that because nothing in § 402(b) prohibits EPA from adding additional criteria, its interpretation of the statute is reasonable and worthy of deference. . . .

We cannot agree. The language of § 402(b) is firm: It provides that EPA "shall" approve submitted programs unless they fail to meet one of the nine listed requirements. We interpreted this language as non-discretionary in *Save the Bay, Inc. v. EPA*, 556 F.2d 1282 (5th Cir. 1977), noting that "the Amendments [to the CWA] set out the full list of requirements a state program must meet. . . . Unless the Administrator of EPA determines that the proposed state program does not meet these requirements, he must approve the proposal." Id. at 1285 & n.3. *See also Natural Resources Defense Council v. EPA*, 859 F.2d 156, 174 (D.C. Cir. 1988); *Citizens for a Better Env't v. EPA*, 596 F.2d 720, 722 (7th Cir. 1979).

EPA's claim is further weakened by CWA § 402(b)(6), 33 U.S.C. § 1342(b)(6), which grants EPA veto power over a proposed permit if the Secretary of the Army concludes that the discharges contemplated by the permit would substantially impair anchorage and navigation. Congress could have, but did not, grant EPA an analogous veto power to protect endangered species.

Nothing in § 304(I) undermines this conclusion. That subsection simply directs EPA to issue regulations governing the approval process for state programs. There is no hint that Congress intended to grant EPA authority to erect additional hurdles to the permitting process beyond those expressly noted in § 402(b). Moreover, neither section even mentions endangered species or the ESA. The statute's plain language directs EPA to approve proposed state programs that meet the enumerated criteria; particularly in light of the command "shall approve," § 304(I) cannot be construed to allow EPA to expand the list of permitting requirements. Applying *Chevron*, we conclude that Congress has spoken directly to the precise question at issue: EPA's discretion lies not in modifying the list of enumerated criteria, but simply in ensuring that those criteria are met. . . .

D.

Finally, EPA argues that ESA § 7(a)(2), when construed alongside the Court's broad reading of the statute in *Tennessee Valley Auth. v. Hill*, 437 U.S. 153, 173, 98 S. Ct. 2279, 57 L. Ed. 2d 117 (1978), compels EPA to do everything reasonably within its power to protect endangered species. The flaw in this argument is that if EPA lacks the power to add additional criteria to CWA § 402(b), nothing in the ESA grants the agency the authority to do so. Section 7 of the ESA merely requires EPA to consult with FWS or NMFS before undertaking agency action; it confers no substantive powers.

The District of Columbia Circuit construed ESA § 7(a)(2) in *Platte River Whooping Crane Critical Habitat Maintenance Trust v. FERC*, 962 F.2d 27, 295 U.S. App. D.C. 218 (D.C. Cir. 1992), holding that the statute "does not expand the powers conferred on an agency by its enabling act," but rather directs the agencies to "utilize" their existing powers to protect endangered species. 962 F.2d at 34. In that case, the petitioner, Whooping Crane Trust, pressed virtually the same argument EPA advances here. The court observed:

> The Trust reads section 7 essentially to oblige the [Federal Energy Regulatory Commission] to do "whatever it takes" to protect the threatened and endangered species that inhabit the Platte River basin; any limitations on FERC's authority contained in the [Federal Power Act] are implicitly superseded by this general command. . . . We think the Trust's interpretation of the ESA is far-fetched.

Id. We agree that the ESA serves not as a font of new authority, but as something far more modest: a directive to agencies to channel their existing authority in a particular direction. The upshot is that EPA cannot invoke the ESA as a means of creating and imposing requirements that are not authorized by the CWA.

Accordingly, we GRANT the petition for review and VACATE the portion of the rule that imposes the consultation requirement and declares that EPA will reject any proposed permit to which FWS or NMFS objects. This matter is REMANDED to the EPA for further appropriate proceedings.

NOTE

Additional Authority. Accord National Ass'n of Homebuilders v. Defenders of Wildlife, 551 U.S. 644, 127 S. Ct. 2518, 2536 (2007) ("§ 7 (a)(2)'s no-jeopardy duty covers only discretionary agency actions and does not attach to actions (like the NPDES permitting transfer authorization) that an agency is *required* by statute to undertake once certain specified triggering events have occurred") (emphasis in original).

ATLANTIC STATES LEGAL FOUNDATION v. EASTMAN KODAK CO.
12 F.3d 353 (2d Cir. 1993)

WINTER, CIRCUIT JUDGE:

This appeal raises the issue of whether private groups may bring a citizen suit pursuant to Section 505 of the Federal Water Pollution Control Act (commonly known as the Clean Water Act), 33 U.S.C. § 1365, to stop the discharge of pollutants not listed in a valid permit issued pursuant to the Clean Water Act ("CWA" or "the Act"), 33 U.S.C. § 1342 (1988). We hold that the discharge of unlisted pollutants is not unlawful under the CWA. We also hold that private groups may not bring such a suit to enforce New York State environmental regulations.

BACKGROUND

Appellee Eastman Kodak Company ("Kodak") operates an industrial facility in Rochester, New York that discharges wastewater into the Genesee River and Paddy Hill Creek under a State Pollutant Discharge Elimination System ("SPDES") permit issued pursuant to 33 U.S.C. § 1342. Appellant Atlantic States legal Foundation, Inc. ("Atlantic States") is a not-for-profit environmental group based in Syracuse, New York.

Kodak operates a wastewater treatment plant at its Rochester facility to purify waste produced in the manufacture of photographic supplies and other laboratory chemicals. The purification plant employs a variety of technical processes to filter harmful pollutants before discharge into the Genesee River at the King's Landing discharge point (designated Outfall 001) pursuant to its SPDES permit.

Kodak first received a federal permit in 1975. At that time, the pertinent regulatory scheme was the National Pollutant Discharge Elimination System ("NPDES") that was administered directly by the federal Environmental Protection Agency ("EPA"). Subsequently, 33 U.S.C. § 1342(b), (c) delegated authority to the states to establish their own programs in place of the EPA's. As a result, Kodak applied in July 1979 to renew its permit to the New York State Department of Environmental Conservation ("DEC"). The DEC declined to act on Kodak's renewal application, and Kodak's NPDES permit remained in effect. As part of the pending application for a SPDES permit, in April 1982 Kodak provided the DEC with a Form 2C describing estimated discharges of 164 substances from each of its outfalls. Kodak also submitted an Industrial Chemical Survey ("ICS") disclosing the amounts of certain chemicals used in Kodak's facility and whether they might appear in the plant's wastewater. Although the ICS originally requested information on 144 substances, including some broad classes such as "unspecified metals," the DEC restricted the inquiry to chemicals used in excess of specified minimum levels.

On the basis of these disclosures, DEC issued Kodak a SPDES permit, number 0001643, effective November 1, 1984, establishing specific effluent limitations for approximately 25 pollutants. The permit also included "action levels" for five other pollutants as well as for three of the pollutants for which it had established effluent limits. DEC further required Kodak to conduct a semi-annual scan of "EPA Volatile, Acid and Base/Neutral Fractions and PCB's priority pollutants on a 24-hr. composite sample." In May 1989, Kodak applied to renew the SPDES permit submitting a new Form 2C and ICS, but the 1984 permit will continue to remain in effect until DEC issues a final determination.

Kodak's SPDES permit contains both "general provisions" and "special reporting requirements" pursuant to EPA policy directives devised to implement the Clean Water Act and to DEC policy directives devised to implement both the Clean Water Act and New York law, N.Y. Envtl. Conserv. Law § 17-0815 (McKinney 1984).

The present action arises out of an ongoing dispute between Atlantic States and Kodak during which Atlantic States has claimed that Kodak both exceeded the effluent limits imposed by its SPDES permit and discharged pollutants for which Kodak had no discharge authorization. The procedural history of this dispute is set out in full in our previous decision, *Atlantic States Legal Found., Inc. v. Eastman Kodak Co.*, 933 F.2d 124 (2d Cir. 1991) ("*Atlantic States I*"). . . .

Atlantic States brought the present action under the citizen suit provision of Section 505, which permits private suits to enforce a CWA "effluent standard or limitation." 33 U.S.C. § 1365(a)(1)(A). Section 505 defines such an enforceable standard or limitation as, inter alia, "an unlawful act under . . . section 1311," and "a permit or condition thereof issued under section 1342 of this title, which is in effect under this chapter." 33 U.S.C. § 1365(f)(1), (6). The question then is whether Atlantic States' action seeks to enforce an "effluent standard or limitation" imposed by the Act or by Kodak's SPDES permit issued by the DEC.

A. *"Standards and Limitations" of the Clean Water Act*

Atlantic States argues first that the plain language of Section 301 of the CWA, 33 U.S.C. § 1311, prohibits the discharge of any pollutants not expressly permitted. With regard to this claim, therefore, Atlantic States' standing to bring this action turns on the merits of the action itself.

Section 301(a) reads: "Except as in compliance with this section and sections 1312, 1316, 1317, 1328, 1342, and 1344 of this title, the discharge of any pollutant by any person shall be unlawful." This prohibition is tempered, however, by a self-referential host of exceptions that allow the discharge of many pollutants once a polluter has complied with the regulatory program of the CWA. The exception relevant to the instant matter is contained in Section 402, which outlines the NPDES, 33 U.S.C. § 1342(a), and specifies the requirements for suspending the national system with the submission of an approved state program, 33 U.S.C. § 1342(b), (c). Section 402(k) contains the so-called "shield provision," 33 U.S.C. § 1342(k), which defines compliance with a NPDES or SPDES permit as compliance with Section 301 for the purposes of the CWA's enforcement provisions. The Supreme Court has noted that "The purpose of [Section 402(k)] seems to be . . . to relieve [permit holders] of having to litigate in an enforcement action the question whether their permits are sufficiently strict." *E.I. du Pont de Nemours & Co. v. Train*, 430 U.S. 112, 138 n.28, 97 S. Ct. 965, 51 L. Ed. 2d 204 (1977).

Atlantic States' view of the regulatory framework stands that scheme on its head. Atlantic States treats permits as establishing limited permission for the discharge of identified pollutants and a prohibition on the discharge of unidentified pollutants. Viewing the regulatory scheme as a whole, however, it is clear that the permit is intended to identify and limit the most harmful pollutants while leaving the control of the vast number of other pollutants to disclosure requirements. Once within the NPDES or SPDES scheme, therefore, polluters may discharge pollutants not specifically listed in their permits so long as they comply with the appropriate reporting requirements and abide by any new limitations when imposed on such pollutants.

The EPA lists tens of thousands of different chemical substances in the Toxic Substances Control Act Chemical Substance Inventory pursuant to 15 U.S.C. § 2607(b) (1988). However, the EPA does not demand even information regarding each of the many thousand chemical substances potentially present in a manufacturer's wastewater because "it is impossible to identify and rationally limit every chemical or compound present in a discharge of pollutants." Memorandum from EPA Deputy Assistant Administrator for Water Enforcement Jeffrey G. Miller to Regional Enforcement Director, Region V, at 2 (Apr. 28, 1976). "Compliance with such a permit would be impossible and anybody seeking to harass a permittee need only analyze that permittee's discharge until determining the presence of a substance not identified in the permit." *Id.* Indeed, Atlantic States conceded at oral argument that even plain water might be considered a "pollutant" under its view of the Act.

The EPA has never acted in any way to suggest that Atlantic States' absolutist and wholly impractical view of the legal effect of a permit is valid. In fact, the EPA's actions and policy statements have frequently contemplated discharges of pollutants not listed under a NPDES or SPDES permit. It has addressed such discharges by amending the permit to list and limit a pollutant when necessary to safeguard the environment without considering pre-amendment discharges to be violations calling for enforcement under the CWA. 33 U.S.C. §§ 1319, 1365. The EPA thus stated in its comments on proposed 40 C.F.R. § 122.68(a), which applied the "application-based" limits approach to implementation of the CWA reporting scheme,

> There is still some possibility . . . that a [NPDES or SPDES] permittee may discharge a large amount of a pollutant not limited in its permit, and EPA will not be able to take enforcement action against the permittee as long as the permittee complies with the notification requirements [pursuant to the CWA].

45 Fed. Reg. 33516, 33523 (1980). The EPA's statement went on to note that this possibility constituted a "regulatory gap," and that, "the final regulations control discharges only of the pollutants listed in the [NPDES or SPDES] permit application, which consist primarily of the listed toxic pollutants and designated hazardous substances." *Id.* . . .

The EPA is the federal agency entrusted with administration and enforcement of the CWA. 33 U.S.C. § 1251(d). As such, EPA's reasonable interpretations of the Act are due deferential treatment in the court. . . . Because the EPA's implementation of the CWA is entirely reasonable, we defer to it.

B. New York Environmental "Standards and Limitations"

Atlantic States argues alternatively that the permit itself provides grounds for enforcement of New York State's regulations. States may enact stricter standards for wastewater effluents than mandated by the CWA and federal EPA regulations. 33 U.S.C. § 1342(b). These states' standards may be enforced under the CWA by the states or the EPA, 33 U.S.C. § 1342(h), but private citizens have no standing to do so. New York chose to implement its own environmental policies through its DEC's issuance of SPDES permits pursuant to N.Y. Envtl. Conserv. Law § 17-0815 (McKinney 1984).

However, state regulations, including the provisions of SPDES permits, which mandate "a greater scope of coverage than that required" by the federal CWA and its implementing regulations are not enforceable through a citizen suit under 33 U.S.C. § 1365. 40 C.F.R. § 123.1(i)(2). *Cf. United States Dep't of Energy v. Ohio*, 118 L. Ed. 2d 255, 112 S. Ct. 1627, 1638 (1992) (holding that "penalties prescribed by state statutes approved by EPA and supplanting the CWA" did not "arise under federal law" and thus could not be enforced under 33 U.S.C. § 1319). . . .

. . . [E]ven if Atlantic States is right about New York law, the action would fail because New York would be implementing a regulatory scheme broader than the CWA, . . . and such broader state schemes are unenforceable through Section 505 citizen suits. A citizen's suit under Section 505 is thus barred either because Section 17-0815(3) and the final clause of General Provision 1(b) implement a program with broader scope than that promulgated under the CWA and EPA regulations or because the permit more narrowly interpreted shields Kodak from such an action.

Conclusion

For the reasons stated above, we affirm the order of the district court granting summary judgment to Kodak.

NOTES

1. ***Duty to Apply.*** Under the CWA, a point source can be liable not only for discharging without a permit, but also for failing to apply for a permit. When is there a duty to apply? By rule, EPA fastened such a duty upon operators of concentrated animal feeding operations ("CAFOs") if their facilities were designed, constructed, or operated "such that a discharge would occur." 73 Fed. Reg. 70,418 (Nov. 20, 2008). The duty applied even if the entity had no plans to discharge, nor was presently discharging. The rule did not survive judicial review. *National Pork Producers Council v. U. S. Environmental Protection Agency*, 635 F.3d 738 (5th Cir. 2011) (duty triggered by actual discharge).

2. ***Permits and Permitting.*** To secure an NPDES permit, applicants must submit effluent characteristics to EPA. Doing so may require collection of discharge samples. "Grab samples" are permissible for specified pollutants, including pH, temperature, cyanide, total phenols, residual chlorine, oil and grease, fecal coliform, and fecal streptococcus. For others, a 24-hour composite sample is required. Samples must be analyzed in accordance with specified testing methods. These sampling and analysis requirements do not apply if the pollutant is solely the result of intake. 40 C.F.R. § 122.21(g)(7)(I).

Except for toxic effluent standards and prohibitions in place under §§ 307 and 405 (relating to sewage sludge use or disposal), EPA's regulations implementing the NPDES program provide that compliance with a permit constitutes compliance with the CWA itself. "However, a permit may be modified, revoked and reissued, or terminated during its term for cause[.]" 40 C.F.R. § 122.5(a)(1). Permits are not property rights in respective permittees. 40 C.F.R. § 122.5(b). All permits expressly require applicants, *inter alia*, to comply with permit terms, to reapply for a new permit when necessary, to mitigate any discharges causing adverse effects to human health or the environment, to properly operate and maintain equipment, to monitor discharges and keep records, and to report a wide variety of information to the regulating agency. 40 C.F.R. § 122.41.

In the absence of established effluent limitations for a point source, EPA can set its performance standards in its NPDES permit on a case-by-case basis. CWA § 402(a)(1), 33 U.S.C. § 1342(a)(1). In some cases, the standard might be framed in terms of "best management practices." 40 C.F.R. § 122.2. EPA does not have authority to exempt point sources entirely from the NPDES program. *National Cotton, supra; Natural Resources Defense Council v. Costle*, 568 F.2d 1369 (D.C. Cir. 1977).

3. ***Bypasses, Upsets, and Excursions.*** Permits may contain provisions addressing bypasses and upsets. A *bypass* occurs when a waste stream is diverted away from pollution control equipment. The resulting "raw" discharge is permissible if it does not cause an exceedance of effluent limitations, "but only if it also is for essential maintenance to assure efficient operation." 40 C.F.R. § 122.41(m)(2). Bypasses are otherwise prohibited unless they are "unavoidable to prevent loss of life, personal injury, or severe property damage," there are "no feasible alternatives," and regulatory authorities are notified. 40 C.F.R. § 122.41(m)(4).

An *upset* is defined as "an exceptional incident in which there is unintentional and temporary noncompliance with technology-based effluent limitations because of factors beyond the reasonable control of permittee. An upset does not include noncompliance to the extent caused by operational error, improperly designed treatment facilities, inadequate treatment facilities, lack of preventative maintenance, or careless or improper operation." 40 C.F.R. § 122.41(n)(1). EPA's regulations allow the occurrence of an upset to serve as an affirmative defense to a cause of action for violation of the CWA. *Id.* at 122.41(n)(2). The burden of proof is on the permittee. *Id.* at 122.41(n)(2) (3).

An *excursion* is an exceedance of an effluent limitation not because of any act or omission on the part of a point source, but because pollution control equipment, for reasons unrelated to fault, simply failed to remove as much of a regulated pollutant as it should have. EPA's regulations do not address "excursions."

4. ***Antibacksliding.*** In 1987, the Congress added current § 402(o), 33 U.S.C. § 1342(o), the "antibacksliding" provision. Subject to exceptions listed in § 402(o)(2), the provision prohibits any renewal, reissuance, or modification of an existing permit so as "to contain effluent limitations which are less stringent than the comparable effluent limitations in the previous permit." Section 402(o)(1), 33 U.S.C. § 1342(o)(1). If effluent limitations have become more stringent during the effective period of a permit, the renewed, reissued, or modified permit must reflect those new, more stringent effluent limitations. Section 402(o)(3), 33 U.S.C. § 1342(o)(3).

5. ***General Permits.*** In addition to individual permits, the EPA can issue "general permits." Such permits typically cover all similar facilities in a given area. The EPA can issue a general permit if point sources in the covered area discharge the same types of wastes, require the same effluent limitations and operating restrictions, and require the same or similar monitoring. Use of general permits can vastly reduce EPA's administrative workload and that of permittees as well. One such example: in December 1994, the EPA issued a notice in the Federal Register to the effect that more than one thousand wastewater treatment facilities in Maine,

Massachusetts, and New Hampshire were eligible for inclusion under one of three general discharge permits.

A more recent example relates to the decision in *National Cotton* set forth earlier in this chapter. Recall that the Sixth Circuit Court of Appeals in *National Cotton* held that pesticide discharges were not exempt from NPDES permit requirements. In response to that decision, EPA has moved toward implementing a general permit system for pesticide dischargers. The general permit would set conditions applicable to all pesticide dischargers and would apply in states where EPA holds permitting authority. As of the end of 2011, EPA had not finished the task, despite court orders to do so. At this writing, the agency still must complete consultation as required by the Endangered Species Act. *See* Chapter 7, *supra*. Beyond that, once it has finalized its general permit, states administering their respective SPDES programs will need time to issue conforming general permits within their jurisdictions. Finally, EPA wishes to establish an electronic communications system to allow the "regulated community" to share information with the agency, so as to ensure an effective implementation regime and oversight capacity.

D. NONPOINT SOURCE REGULATION

As we have seen, the EPA has dedicated its best efforts to the abatement of pollution from point sources. And with good reason. Point sources were viewed by the Congress in 1972 as the major cause of water pollution, and, with the CWA riveting its attention upon them, EPA had good cause to make the valiant effort. This emphasis has yielded substantial benefits in the form of healthier and more aesthetically pleasing waterways. In recent times, however, the continued, virtually exclusive focus on point sources has come under attack. It has become clear that many waterways, despite the regulation of point sources discharging into them, remain foul. *See, e.g.*, Note, *State of the Water, supra*.

The reason is nonpoint source pollution. Nonpoint sources are the universe of sources that are not point sources. In other words, they are sources that discharge pollutants to waters of the United States other than through conduits, pipes, and other discrete conveyance mechanisms. Examples of nonpoint pollution include runoff from agricultural, ranch, and forest lands. Nonpoint pollution dwarfs point source pollution (one relevant statistic: a single cow gives off as much waste as 14.5 human beings). One dramatic indicator of the severity of nonpoint source pollution is the 6,800 square mile hypoxic, or oxygen-depleted, "dead zone" in the Gulf of Mexico at the mouth of the Mississippi River. The hypoxic condition of the Gulf is caused by excessive amounts of nutrients, primarily nitrogen and phosphorus, that have leached into the Mississippi River from upstream agricultural operations and then made their way downstream. For current information on the Gulf of Mexico, see www.gulfhypoxia.net. For current information on the "environmental profile" of a watershed near you, see www.epa.gov/surf.

Farms are a particularly significant source of nonpoint pollution. In fact, agriculture is the leading source of all water pollution. (Reputedly in second place is hydromodification, which reduces stream flows, and third is urban runoff.) Polluted runoff from agricultural lands harms surface and groundwater on a nationally significant scale. Unchecked soil erosion, furthermore, increases sedimentation of rivers and lakes, causing severe reductions in the availability of forage for aquatic life. (Farms also overtake wildlife habitat, but that is another matter.)

The CWA did not address in any effective way the significant pollution contribution from agriculture, in large part because Congress wrote farms out of a good deal of the Clean Water Act.[10] However, this is not to say that the 1972 CWA overlooked nonpoint source pollution entirely. Actually, the Act went to some length to address the problem. Sections 102 and 104 of the 1972 legislation, for example, called for EPA and state cooperation in comprehensive planning to protect fish and wildlife. Section 102, 33 U.S.C. § 1252, and § 104, 33 U.S.C. § 1254. Section 201 of the CWA authorized grants for "waste treatment management" on an "areawide" basis to "provide control or treatment of all point and nonpoint sources of pollution." Sections 201(c), 33 U.S.C. § 1281(c). And § 208 called for "areawide waste treatment management" planning by the states, expressly including plans for "nonpoint source" pollution. The legislation called on states to identify these areas, § 208(a)(2), 33 U.S.C. § 1281(a)(2), and thereafter "have in operation a continuing areawide waste treatment management planning process." Section 208(b)(1), 33 U.S.C. § 1281(b)(1). Section 208 plans were to include a variety of measures, the most germane of which were explicitly directed at "nonpoint source" pollution. And in 1987, Congress added another provision, § 319, to help address the problem.

But these statutory provisions produced no meaningful results. States blithely ignored them and EPA, busy with point sources, did, too. Looking around for some way to force EPA's hand, the environmental community decided to make its stand by relying on a provision we have already seen, § 303, 33 U.S.C. § 1313, the water quality standards provision of the original legislation. *See supra.* Specifically, it turned its attention to § 303(d), 33 U.S.C. § 1313(d).

Section 303(d) begins by calling on states to identify their "impaired waters," those water bodies or segments thereof in need of more cleaning even after BAT has done its work, and then to rank them, "taking into account the severity of the pollution and the uses to be made of such waters." Section 303(d)(1)(A), 33 U.S.C. § 1313(d)(1)(A). Having done that, states must determine the amounts of contamination, on a pollutant by pollutant basis, that can be added to the stream on a daily basis without causing a WQS exceedance. Section 303(d)(1)(C), 33 U.S.C. § 1313(d)(1)(C). It is up to EPA to identify the pollutants that are "suitable for such calculation." *Id.* The specific amounts that may be added are known as "total maximum daily loads," or "TMDLs." Section 303(d)(2), 33 U.S.C. § 1313(d)(2), then directs states to submit their lists of impaired waters (or their "water quality-limited segments," or "WQLSs") and the TMDLs established for them, to EPA for approval or disapproval. If EPA approves a state's submission, the state must then

---

[10] As we have seen, while the CWA prohibits the "discharge of any pollutant by any person," § 301(a), 33 U.S.C. § 1311(a), it focuses regulation on discharges from "point sources" and then excludes from the definition of "point source" "return flows from irrigated agriculture." Section 502(14), 33 U.S.C. § 1362(14). The CWA describes return flows as "nonpoint sources of pollution." Section 208(b)(2)(F), 33 U.S.C. § 1288(b)(2)(F). In 1987, in the CWA amendments addressing pollution by stormwater, Congress moved again to exempt agriculture, redefining "point source" to exclude "agricultural stormwater discharges." Section 502(14), 33 U.S.C. § 1362(14). And the § 404 wetlands program, *see infra*, was also written to exempt discharges from typical farming activities such as plowing, seeding, and cultivating. Section 404(f)(A), 33 U.S.C. § 1344(f)(A).

"incorporate" the lists and TMDLs into the "continuing planning process" required by § 303(e), 33 U.S.C. § 1313(e). If EPA disapproves a state's submission, however, EPA itself must do the work of identifying impaired waters in the affected state and establishing the requisite TMDLs. Section 303(d)(2), 33 U.S.C. § 1313(d)(2). Once the system is in place, limits on pollutant contributions from specific nonpoint sources should be quantified and regulated.

All of this would seem to have given the teeth to nonpoint source control back in 1972, but, as noted above, history has proven otherwise. EPA believed that BAT standards on point sources, coupled with "basin planning" under §§ 208 and 303(e) (without TMDLs), would clean streams fully and promptly, so it was not about to devote precious time and resources to what it viewed as an unnecessary safety net. Beyond that, the agency found the business of nonpoint regulation to be vexing: it can be extraordinarily difficult, for example, to calculate the precise pollutant loading traceable to each nonpoint source on a waterway. Consequently, EPA never did get around to designating the pollutants for which TMDLs were suitable, and, without such designations in place, the TMDL ball never started rolling. That was only one roadblock. Even after pollutants were finally designated (EPA now says all pollutants are suitable for TMDL development), EPA claimed it had no authority to do more than approve or disapprove submissions sent in by the states. Under this reading, if a state failed to submit anything, there being nothing to approve or disapprove, EPA's hands were tied.

After a time, the environmental community took severe exception to this willing impotence. A wave of judicial challenges ensued, and the environmentalists won. In *Scott v. City of Hammond*, 741 F.2d 992 (7th Cir. 1984), and in several other judicial challenges, environmentalists convinced the court that EPA had a good deal more power than it was letting on. In *Scott*, the court held that a state's failure to make a submission under § 303(d) should be viewed by EPA as a constructive and insufficient submission, which in turn sparks EPA's duty to act. (For a vivid recount of this history of the TMDL program, see Oliver A. Houck, *The Clean Water Act TMDL Program: Law, Policy and Implementation*, Environmental Law Institute (1999).)

In August 1999, EPA finally took up the TMDL banner on its own, albeit grudgingly, by proposing regulations for a national TMDL program. 64 Fed. Reg. 46,012 (1999). Things have not gone smoothly since then. Congress, it turned out, was quite unhappy with EPA's regulatory initiative, so, in June 2000, it added a rider to a military construction appropriation bill which prohibited the expenditure of any monies to effect a promulgation of the TMDL rule. This placed former President Clinton in an obvious bind. He solved the problem by having the EPA rush the TMDL proposal to promulgation while he delayed signing the appropriation bill. EPA promulgated the TMDL rule on July 13, 2000. 65 Fed. Reg. 43,586 (2000).

The rule remained controversial, in large part because of considerations of cost: on August 3, 2001, EPA projected the rule's national cost at somewhere between $900 million and $4.3 billion annually. As expected, the regulations were challenged by several lawsuits filed in the federal Court of Appeals for the District of Columbia. Upon taking office in January 2001, the Bush Administration asked the court to stay the litigation. It also delayed the effective date of the regulations pending additional administrative review. On December 27, 2002, EPA proposed to withdraw the rule entirely, and it did so on March 19, 2003.

Accordingly, more than 40 years after the enactment of § 303(d), at this writing there still remains relatively little in the way of nonpoint source regulation. With some states having done TMDL work, the program limps along, but vigorous it is not. For an update on the program, see www.epa.gov/owow/tmdl.

Since the withdrawal of the TMDL rule, attention has shifted to what EPA calls "watershed-based NPDES permitting," an approach favored by agriculture, some industries, states, and municipalities, as well as the United States Department of Agriculture, because it would return the focus to point source regulation, and, relatively speaking, take the heat off nonpoint sources. As EPA described it, watershed-based NPDES permitting is "an approach that produces NPDES permits that are issued to point sources on geographic or watershed bases to meet watershed goals." *See* EPA's Watershed-Based NPDES Permitting Policy Statement, Jan. 7, 2003, *available at* http://nepis.epa.gov/EPA/html/pubindex.html (specifying, *inter alia*, EPA's suggested six step process for watershed permitting). The idea is to issue permits to point sources affecting a single watershed instead of regulating each source in isolation. Such permits would contain performance standards that reflect the needs of the basin and the presence of other point sources within the basin rather than merely the technological capacities of the individual permittee. Determining the needs of a basin would require a "detailed, integrative, and inclusive watershed planning process." That process, in turn, would embody "monitoring and assessment activities that generate the data necessary for clear watershed goals to be established and permits to be designed to specifically address the goals." *Id.* EPA intends to do what it can in this regard on a case-by-case basis within the legal constraints of the CWA and NPDES regulations. As of the date of this writing, there has been no promulgation of a watershed rule or of a replacement TMDL rule.

A larger issue raised by all of this is whether watershed permitting, and TMDL development for that matter, would represent for water pollution control a step forward or backward. EPA views these approaches as innovative and cost-effective, but critics argue that environmental quality-based regulation has already been shown to be foolhardy.

NOTE

Water Quality Trading. In large part because of the success of the air emissions trading program, *see* Chapter 9, *supra*, EPA has endeavored to institute a cap-and-trade program for point and nonpoint source control. Its efforts culminated in EPA's "Water Quality Trading Policy" in January 2003 ("*Policy*"). As the Policy put it, "[M]arket-based approaches can . . . create economic incentives for innovation, emerging technology, voluntary pollution reductions and greater efficiency in improving the quality of the nation's waters." *Policy* at 2. Trading, moreover, "capitalizes on economies of scale and the control cost differentials among and between sources." *Policy* at 1.

As the agency views it, water trading would allow sources to meet regulatory obligations by using pollutant reductions created by other sources that can accomplish those reductions less expensively. Trading would be voluntary, subject to EPA approval on a case-by-case basis, and could not be done in lieu of mandatory CWA or regulatory requirements.

EPA envisions the establishment of trading areas, typically within a single watershed, and actively supports trading of specific pollutants, especially nutrients and sediments, both of which are nonpoint pollutants. In this regard, the Policy would allow for trading of nutrients and sediments pre-TMDL, to meet an established TMDL, or to maintain unimpaired waters. Not all trading could be "pound for pound." A ten-pound reduction of a pollutant, for example, might be weighted for trading purposes as something less than ten because only a lesser amount would find its way into the watershed area to be protected.

The regulatory authority, be it EPA or a state, would need to be mindful of the major potential pitfall of "hot spots," areas of high pollutant concentration. To avoid causing hot spots, it might be necessary to limit trading at stressed locations.

EPA implemented a trading mechanism for the western Long Island Sound. That water body, like the Gulf of Mexico, experiences a "dead zone" in summers, the result of excessive nutrient loadings. To eliminate this hypoxic condition, the Connecticut TMDL called for a 64% reduction of nitrogen discharges by 79 Connecticut POTW by the year 2014. The trading solution for this problem included the establishment of a Nitrogen Exchange that gave each POTW several options: each POTW may reduce nitrogen to the required regulatory level, or keep nitrogen discharges higher and buy offsetting nitrogen reductions from the Exchange, or reduce nitrogen discharges beyond the required regulatory level and sell the difference. As an administrative vehicle, in January 2002, EPA issued a single permit to all 79 POTWs. The permit established an aggregate cap for nitrogen discharges that declines every two years until 2014 as well as individual water quality standards-based nitrogen discharge limits for each POTW.

As of September 2003, 39 municipalities had purchased credits at a cost of over $1.3 million, 39 had sold credits for a total value of over $2.7 million, and the State of Connecticut had purchased all the excess credits at a cost of more than $1.4 million. EPA, which as part of this effort has helped POTWs fund upgrades in facilities, expected the 64% reduction goal to be reached five to six years early. As of 2007, water quality in the Sound was described as "poor," if perhaps improving.

As of 2011, EPA had 54 water trading programs or "frameworks" for such programs in place across 25 states. *See* http://water.epa.gov/type/watersheds/trading.

E. SECTION 404

A century ago, the Congress enacted a statute called the Rivers and Harbors Act of 1899, commonly known as the "Refuse Act." Brandishing civil and criminal penalties, the measure prohibited the discharge of any "refuse" unless authorized by a permit issued by the Secretary of the Army. The statute was promptly ignored. Not until 1971, after the emergence of the environmental movement, did the Refuse

Act stir from its long sleep, when, pursuant to an Executive Order, the U.S. Army Corps of Engineers promulgated regulations to implement it.

Contemporaneous with this development, Congress was considering the soon-to-be-enacted 1972 CWA. The Refuse Act having been discovered, Congress endeavored to fold it into the new legislation. Early on, it was included in § 402 (NPDES permits), but by the time the bill was ready for enactment, Congress had decided to enshrine the provisions of the Refuse Act in an independent location, the new CWA § 404, 33 U.S.C. § 1344.

Some alterations of the original legislation were in order, however, in large part because the newly created EPA was poised to become the central federal player in all things environmental. Thus, Congress needed to accommodate both the Corps and the new environmental agency. The Senate chose to give all regulatory responsibility to EPA, but the House proposed to continue authority in the Corps. The Conference substitute, as it turned out, split the difference. As enacted, § 404 keeps permitting authority in the Corps, (although states can take over this permitting function, see § 404(g), 33 U.S.C. § 1344(g)) but gives the EPA a veto power whenever it finds that a permitted § 404 discharge "will have an unacceptable adverse effect on municipal water supplies, shellfish beds and fishery areas (including spawning and breeding areas), wildlife, or recreational areas." Section 404(c), 33 U.S.C. § 1344(c). As of 2011, EPA has issued "Final § 404(c) Veto Determinations" only thirteen times, despite the filing of approximately 60,000 applications for § 404 permits annually. http://water.epa.gov/type/wetlands/outreach/upload/404c.pdf.

Section 404, in conjunction with § 301, prohibits disposal of "dredged and fill" materials into the navigable waters of the United States except in accordance with a permit. Section 404(a), 33 U.S.C. § 1344(a). Dredged material is "material dredged or excavated from the waters of the United States." 40 C.F.R. § 232.2. (EPA definition); 33 C.F.R § 323.2(c) (Corps definition). The term does not include trash or garbage. Fill material is any material placed into the waters of the United States which replaces portions of those waters with dry land or changes the bottom elevation of a water body. 40 C.F.R. § 232.2 (EPA definition); 33 C.F.R. § 323(e)(1) (Corps definition). Section 404 exempts from its reach "normal farming, silviculture, and ranching activities such as plowing, seeding, cultivating, minor drainage, harvesting for the production of food, fiber and forest products, or upland soil and water conservation practices." Section 404(f), 33 U.S.C. § 1344(f); 40 C.F.R. § 232.3 (EPA regulation); 33 C.F.R. § 323.4 (Corps regulation).

To the extent § 404 prohibits deposits of dredged and fill materials into lakes, rivers, and ponds, it serves as a natural companion to the NPDES permit system of § 402. But § 404 took on heightened controversy and significance after a crucial administrative decision on the matter of regulatory scope: the Secretary interpreted § 404 as prohibiting disposal of dredged and fill materials into (or onto) "wetlands." Wetlands, commonly held in either public or private title, are, as their name indicates, lands. That activities involving lands would fall under the regulatory ambit of a statute in place to protect waters was nothing short of an epiphany to many people. The debate became a battle for the future of the § 404 program, and its resolution awaited review by the highest court of the land.

UNITED STATES v. RIVERSIDE BAYVIEW HOMES, INC.
474 U.S. 121, 106 S. Ct. 455 (1985)

WHITE, J., delivered the opinion for a unanimous Court.

This case presents the question whether the Clean Water Act (CWA), 33 U.S.C. § 1251 et seq., together with certain regulations promulgated under its authority by the Army Corps of Engineers, authorizes the Corps to require landowners to obtain permits from the Corps before discharging fill material into wetlands adjacent to navigable bodies of water and their tributaries.

. . . .

The relevant provisions of the Clean Water Act originated in the Federal Water Pollution Control Act Amendments of 1972, 86 Stat. 816, and have remained essentially unchanged since that time. Under §§ 301 and 502 of the Act, 33 U.S.C. §§ 1311 and 1362, any discharge of dredged or fill materials into "navigable waters" — defined as the "waters of the United States" — is forbidden unless authorized by a permit issued by the Corps of Engineers pursuant to § 404, 33 U.S.C. § 1344. After initially construing the Act to cover only waters navigable in fact, in 1975 the Corps issued interim final regulations redefining "the waters of the United States" to include not only actually navigable waters but also tributaries of such waters, interstate waters and their tributaries, and nonnavigable intrastate waters whose use or misuse could affect interstate commerce. 40 Fed. Reg. 31320 (1975). More importantly for present purposes, the Corps construed the Act to cover all "freshwater wetlands" that were adjacent to other covered waters. A "freshwater wetland" was defined as an area that is "periodically inundated" and is "normally characterized by the prevalence offivegetation that requires saturated soil conditions for growth and reproduction." 33 C.F.R. § 209.120(d)(2)(h) (1976). In 1977, the Corps refined its definition of wetlands by eliminating the reference to periodic inundation and making other minor changes. The 1977 definition reads as follows:
"

> The term 'wetlands' means those areas that are inundated or saturated by surface or ground water at a frequency and duration sufficient to support, and that under normal circumstances do support, a prevalence of vegetation typically adapted for life in saturated soil conditions. Wetlands generally include swamps, marshes, bogs and similar areas."

33 C.F.R. § 323.2(c)(1978).[11]

. . . .

On a purely linguistic level, it may appear unreasonable to classify "lands," wet or otherwise, as "waters." Such a simplistic response, however, does justice neither to the problem faced by the Corps in defining the scope of its authority under § 404(a) nor to the realities of the problem of water pollution that the Clean Water Act was intended to combat. In determining the limits of its power to regulate

---

[11] [Ed. note: this definition, which is the same as that of the EPA (see 40 C.F.R. § 232.2) remains in place at this writing.]

discharges under the Act, the Corps must necessarily choose some point at which water ends and land begins. Our common experience tells us that this is often no easy task: the transition from water to solid ground is not necessarily or even typically an abrupt one. Rather, between open waters and dry land may lie shallows, marshes, mudflats, swamps, bogs — in short, a huge array of areas that are not wholly aquatic but nevertheless fall far short of being dry land. Where on this continuum to find the limit of "waters" is far from obvious.

Faced with such a problem of defining the bounds of its regulatory authority, an agency may appropriately look to the legislative history and underlying policies of its statutory grants of authority. Neither of these sources provides unambiguous guidance for the Corps in this case, but together they do support the reasonableness of the Corps' approach of defining adjacent wetlands as "waters" within the meaning of § 404(a). Section 404 originated as part of the Federal Water Pollution Control Act Amendments of 1972, which constituted a comprehensive legislative attempt "to restore and maintain the chemical, physical, and biological integrity of the Nation's waters." CWA § 101, 33 U.S.C. § 1251. This objective incorporated a broad, systemic view of the goal of maintaining and improving water quality: as the House Report on the legislation put it, "the word 'integrity'. . . refers to a condition in which the natural structure and function of ecosystems [are] maintained." H. R. Rep. No. 92-911, p.76 (1972). Protection of aquatic ecosystems, Congress recognized, demanded broad federal authority to control pollution, for "[water] moves in hydrologic cycles and it is essential that discharge of pollutants be controlled at the source." S. Rep. No.92-414, p. 77 (1972).

In keeping with these views, Congress chose to define the waters covered by the Act broadly. Although the Act prohibits discharges into "navigable waters," *see* CWA § 301(a), 404(a), 502(12), 33 U.S.C. §§ 1311(a), 1344(a), 1362(12), the Act's definition of "navigable waters" as "the waters of the United States" makes it clear that the term "navigable" as used in the Act is of limited import. In adopting this definition of "navigable waters," Congress evidently intended to repudiate limits that had been placed on federal regulation by earlier water pollution control statutes and to exercise its powers under the Commerce Clause to regulate at least some waters that would not be deemed "navigable" under the classical understanding of that term. *See* S. Conf. Rep. No. 92-1236, p. 144 (1972); 118 Cong. Rec. 33756 33757 (1972) (statement of Rep. Dingell).

Of course, it is one thing to recognize that Congress intended to allow regulation of waters that might not satisfy traditional tests of navigability; it is another to assert that Congress intended to abandon traditional notions of "waters" and include in that term "wetlands" as well. Nonetheless, the evident breadth of congressional concern for protection of water quality and aquatic ecosystems suggests that it is reasonable for the Corps to interpret the term "waters" to encompass wetlands adjacent to waters as more conventionally defined. Following the lead of the Environmental Protection Agency, see 38 Fed. Reg. 10834 (1973), the Corps has determined that wetlands adjacent to navigable waters do as a general matter play a key role in protecting and enhancing water quality:

> "The regulation of activities that cause water pollution cannot rely on
> . . . artificial lines . . . but must focus on all waters that together form the

entire aquatic system. Water moves in hydrologic cycles, and the pollution of this part of the aquatic system, regardless of whether it is above or below an ordinary high water mark, or mean high tide line, will affect the water quality of the other waters within that aquatic system. "For this reason, the landward limit of Federal jurisdiction under Section 404 must include any adjacent wetlands that form the border of or are in reasonable proximity to other waters of the United States, as these wetlands are part of this aquatic system." 42 Fed. Reg. 37128 (1977).

We cannot say that the Corps' conclusion that adjacent wetlands are inseparably bound up with the "waters" of the United States — based as it is on the Corps' and EPA's technical expertise is — unreasonable. In view of the breadth of federal regulatory authority contemplated by the Act itself and the inherent difficulties of defining precise bounds to regulable waters, the Corps' ecological judgment about the relationship between waters and their adjacent wetlands provides an adequate basis for a legal judgment that adjacent wetlands may be defined as waters under the Act.

This holds true even for wetlands that are not the result of flooding or permeation by water having its source in adjacent bodies of open water. The Corps has concluded that wetlands may affect the water quality of adjacent lakes, rivers, and streams even when the waters of those bodies do not actually inundate the wetlands. For example, wetlands that are not flooded by adjacent waters may still tend to drain into those waters. In such circumstances, the Corps has concluded that wetlands may serve to filter and purify water draining into adjacent bodies of water, see 33 C.F.R. § 320.4(b)(2)(vii) (1985), and to slow the flow of surface runoff into lakes, rivers, and streams and thus prevent flooding and erosion, see §§ 320.4(b)(2)(iv) and (v). In addition, adjacent wetlands may "serve significant natural biological functions, including food chain production, general habitat, and nesting, spawning, rearing and resting sites for aquatic . . . species." §§ 320.4(b)(2)(I). In short, the Corps has concluded that wetlands adjacent to lakes, rivers, streams, and other bodies of water may function as integral parts of the aquatic environment even when the moisture creating the wetlands does not find its source in the adjacent bodies of water. Again, we cannot say that the Corps' judgment on these matters is unreasonable, and we therefore conclude that a definition of "waters of the United States" encompassing all wetlands adjacent to other bodies of water over which the Corps has jurisdiction is a permissible interpretation of the Act. Because respondent's property is part of a wetland that actually abuts on a navigable waterway, respondent was required to have a permit in this case.

[Remainder of opinion omitted.]

NOTE

Why Protect Wetlands? EPA has given its views:

The discharge of dredged or fill material in wetlands is likely to damage or destroy habitat and adversely affect the biological productivity of wetlands ecosystems by smothering, by dewatering, by permanently

flooding, or by altering substrate elevation or periodicity of water movement. The addition of dredged or fill material may destroy wetland
vegetation or result in advancement of succession to dry land species. It
may reduce or eliminate nutrient exchange by a reduction of the system's
productivity, or by afiltering current patterns and velocities. Disruption or
elimination of the wetland system can degrade water quality by obstructing
circulation patterns that flush large expanses of wetland systems, by
interfering with the filtration function of wetlands, or by changing the
aquifer recharge capability of a wetland. Discharges can also change the
wetland habitat value for fish and wildlife. . . . When disruptions in flow
and circulation patterns occur, apparently minor loss of wetland acreage
may result in major losses through secondary impacts. Discharging fill
material in wetlands as part of municipal, industrial or recreational
development may modify the capacity of wetlands to retain and store
floodwaters and to serve as a buffer zone shielding upland areas from wave
actions, storm damage and erosion.

40 C.F.R. § 230.41(b).

SOLID WASTE AGENCY v. U.S. ARMY CORPS OF ENGINEERS ("*SWANCC*")
531 U.S. 159, 121 S. Ct. 675 (2001)

JUDGES: REHNQUIST, C.J., delivered the opinion of the Court, in which O'CONNOR,
SCALIA, KENNEDY, and THOMAS, JJ., joined. STEVENS, J., filed a dissenting opinion,
in which SOUTER, GINSBERG, and BREYER, JJ., joined.

Section 404(a) of the Clean Water Act (CWA or Act), 86 Stat. 884, as amended, 33
U.S.C. § 1344(a), regulates the discharge of dredged or fill material into "navigable
waters." The United States Army Corps of Engineers (Corps), has interpreted
§ 404(a) to confer federal authority over an abandoned sand and gravel pit in
northern Illinois which provides habitat for migratory birds. We are asked to decide
whether the provisions of § 404(a) may be fairly extended to these waters, and, if so,
whether Congress could exercise such authority consistent with the Commerce
Clause, U.S. Const., Art. I, § 8, cl. 3. We answer the first question in the negative and
therefore do not reach the second.

Petitioner, the Solid Waste Agency of Northern Cook County ("SWANCC"), is a
consortium of 23 suburban Chicago cities and villages that united in an effort to
locate and develop a disposal site for baled nonhazardous solid waste. The Chicago
Gravel Company informed the municipalities of the availability of a 533-acre parcel,
bestriding the Illinois counties Cook and Kane, which had been the site of a sand
and gravel pit mining operation for three decades up until about 1960. Long since
abandoned, the old mining site eventually gave way to a successional stage forest,
with its remnant excavation trenches evolving into a scattering of permanent and
seasonal ponds of varying size (from under one-tenth of an acre to several acres)
and depth (from several inches to several feet).

The municipalities decided to purchase the site for disposal of their baled nonhazardous solid waste. By law, SWANCC was required to file for various permits from Cook County and the State of Illinois before it could begin operation of its balefill project. In addition, because the operation called for the filling of some of the permanent and seasonal ponds, SWANCC contacted federal respondents (hereinafter respondents), including the Corps, to determine if a federal landfill permit was required under § 404(a) of the CWA, 33 U.S.C. § 1344(a).

Section 404(a) grants the Corps authority to issue permits "for the discharge of dredged or fill material into the navigable waters at specified disposal sites." *Ibid.* The term "navigable waters" is defined under the Act as "the waters of the United States, including the territorial seas." § 1362(7). The Corps has issued regulations defining the term "waters of the United States" to include

> "waters such as intrastate lakes, rivers, streams (including intermittent streams), mudflats, sandflats, wetlands, sloughs, prairie potholes, wet meadows, playa lakes, or natural ponds, the use, degradation or destruction of which could affect interstate or foreign commerce. . . . "

33 C.F.R. § 328.3(a)(3) (1999).

In 1986, in an attempt to "clarify" the reach of its jurisdiction, the Corps stated that § 404(a) extends to intrastate waters:

> "a. Which are or would be used as habitat by birds protected by Migratory Bird Treaties; or

> "b. Which are or would be used as habitat by other migratory birds which cross state lines; or

> "c. Which are or would be used as habitat for endangered species; or

> "d. Used to irrigate crops sold in interstate commerce."

51 Fed. Reg. 41217.

This last promulgation has been dubbed the "Migratory Bird Rule."

The Corps initially concluded that it had no jurisdiction over the site because it contained no "wetlands," or areas which support "vegetation typically adapted for life in saturated soil conditions," 33 C.F.R. §§ 328.3(b) (1999). However, after the Illinois Nature Preserves Commission informed the Corps that a number of migratory bird species had been observed at the site, the Corps reconsidered and ultimately asserted jurisdiction over the balefill site pursuant to subpart (b) of the "Migratory Bird Rule." The Corps found that approximately 121 bird species had been observed at the site, including several known to depend upon aquatic environments for a significant portion of their life requirements. Thus, on November 16, 1987, the Corps formally "determined that the seasonally ponded, abandoned gravel mining depressions located on the project site, while not wetlands, did qualify as 'waters of the United States'. . . based upon the following criteria: (1) the proposed site had been abandoned as a gravel mining operation; (2) the water areas and spoil piles had developed a natural character; and (3) the water areas are used as habitat by migratory bird [sic] which cross state lines." U.S. Army Corps of Engineers, Chicago District, Dept. of Army Permit Evaluation and Decision Document, Lodging of Petitioner, Tab No. 1, p. 6. . . .

This is not the first time we have been called upon to evaluate the meaning of § 404(a). In *United States v. Riverside Bayview Homes, Inc.*, 474 U.S. 121, 106 S. Ct. 455, 88 L. Ed. 2d 419 (1985), we held that the Corps had § 404(a) jurisdiction over wetlands that actually abutted on a navigable waterway. In so doing, we noted that the term "navigable" is of "limited import" and that Congress evidenced its intent to "regulate at least some waters that would not be deemed 'navigable' under the classical understanding of that term." *Id.* at 133. But our holding was based in large measure upon Congress' unequivocal acquiescence to, and approval of, the Corps' regulations interpreting the CWA to cover wetlands adjacent to navigable waters. *See* 474 U.S. at 135–139. We found that Congress' concern for the protection of water quality and aquatic ecosystems indicated its intent to regulate wetlands "inseparably bound up with the 'waters' of the United States." 474 U.S. at 134.

It was the significant nexus between the wetlands and "navigable waters" that informed our reading of the CWA in *Riverside Bayview Homes*. Indeed, we did not "express any opinion" on the "question of the authority of the Corps to regulate discharges of fill material into wetlands that are not adjacent to bodies of open water. . . . " 474 U.S. at 131 132, n. 8. In order to rule for respondents here, we would have to hold that the jurisdiction of the Corps extends to ponds that are not adjacent to open water. But we conclude that the text of the statute will not allow this.

. . . .

We thus decline respondents' invitation to take what they see as the next ineluctable step after *Riverside Bayview Homes*: holding that isolated ponds, some only seasonal, wholly located within two Illinois counties, fall under § 404(a)'s definition of "navigable waters" because they serve as habitat for migratory birds. As counsel for respondents conceded at oral argument, such a ruling would assume that "the use of the word navigable in the statute . . . does not have any independent significance." Tr. of Oral Arg. 28. We cannot agree that Congress' separate definitional use of the phrase "waters of the United States" constitutes a basis for reading the term "navigable waters" out of the statute. We said in *Riverside Bayview Homes* that the word "navigable" in the statute was of "limited effect" and went on to hold that § 404(a) extended to nonnavigable wetlands adjacent to open waters. But it is one thing to give a word limited effect and quite another to give it no effect whatever. The term "navigable" has at least the import of showing us what Congress had in mind as its authority for enacting the CWA: its traditional jurisdiction over waters that were or had been navigable in fact or which could reasonably be so made. *See, e.g., United States v. Appalachian Elec. Power Co.*, 311 U.S. 377, 407 408, 61 S. Ct. 291, 85 L. Ed. 243 (1940).

[The Court next explained why it declined to defer to the agency decision under the rule of *Chevron U.S.A. Inc. v. Natural Resources Defense Council, Inc.*, 467 U.S. 837, 104 S. Ct. 2778 (1984)]:

Where an administrative interpretation of a statute invokes the outer limits of Congress' power, we expect a clear indication that Congress intended that result. *See Edward J. DeBartolo Corp. v. Florida Gulf Coast Building & Constr. Trades Council*, 485 U.S. 568, 575, 108 S. Ct. 1392, 99 L. Ed. 2d 645 (1988). This requirement stems from our prudential desire not to needlessly reach constitutional issues and our assumption that Congress does not casually authorize administrative agencies to interpret a statute to push the limit of congressional authority. *See ibid.* This concern is heightened where the administrative interpretation alters the federal-state framework by permitting federal encroachment upon a traditional state power. See United States v. Bass, 404 U.S. 336, 349, 92 S. Ct. 515, 30 L. Ed. 2d 488 (1971) ("Unless Congress conveys its purpose clearly, it will not be deemed to have significantly changed the federal-state balance"). Thus, "where an otherwise acceptable construction of a statute would raise serious constitutional problems, the Court will construe the statute to avoid such problems unless such construction is plainly contrary to the intent of Congress." *DeBartolo*, 485 U.S. at 575.

These are significant constitutional questions raised by respondents' application of their regulations, and yet we find nothing approaching a clear statement from Congress that it intended § 404(a) to reach an abandoned sand and gravel pit such as we have here. Permitting respondents to claim federal jurisdiction over ponds and mudflats falling within the "Migratory Bird Rule" would result in a significant impingement of the States' traditional and primary power over land and water use. *See, e.g., Hess v. Port Authority Trans-Hudson Corporation*, 513 U.S. 30, 44, 115 S. Ct. 394, 130 L. Ed. 2d 245 (1994) ("Regulation of land use [is] a function traditionally performed by local governments"). Rather than expressing a desire to readjust the federal-state balance in this manner, Congress chose to "recognize, preserve, and protect the primary responsibilities and rights of States . . . to plan the development and use . . . of land and water resources. . . . " 33 U.S.C. § 1251(b). We thus read the statute as written to avoid the significant constitutional and federalism questions raised by respondents' interpretation, and therefore reject the request for administrative deference.

We hold that 33 C.F.R. § 328.3(a)(3) (1999), as clarified and applied to petitioner's balefill site pursuant to the "Migratory Bird Rule," 51 Fed. Reg. 41217 (1986), exceeds the authority granted to respondents under § 404(a) of the CWA. The judgment of the Court of Appeals for the Seventh Circuit is therefore

Reversed.

Justice Stevens, with whom Justice Souter, Justice Ginsburg, and Justice Breyer join, dissenting (omitted).

NOTE

Postscript. After *SWANCC*, the regulatory definition of "wetlands" was changed to remove isolated, solely intrastate water bodies. 69 U.S.L.W. 2561, March 20, 2001.

According to one estimate, even though *SWANCC* dealt with an isolated pond and not a wetland, the case eliminated CWA protection for 30 to 79% of the nation's wetlands. John Kusler, Attorney, Memorandum, *The SWANCC Decision and State Regulation of Wetlands*, Association of State Wetland Managers (Feb. 8, 2001). And that was before the decision in *Rapanos*.

RAPANOS v. UNITED STATES
547 U.S. 715; 126 S. Ct. 2208; 165 L. Ed. 2d 159 (2006)

SCALIA, J., announced the judgment of the Court, and delivered an opinion, in which ROBERTS, C.J., and THOMAS and ALITO, JJ., joined. ROBERTS, C.J., filed a concurring opinion. KENNEDY, J., filed an opinion concurring in the judgment. STEVENS, J., filed a dissenting opinion, in which SOUTER, GINSBERG, and BREYER, JJ., joined. BREYER, J., filed a dissenting opinion.

JUSTICE SCALIA announced the judgment of the Court, and delivered an opinion, in which the CHIEF JUSTICE, JUSTICE THOMAS, and JUSTICE ALITO join.

In April 1989, petitioner John A. Rapanos backfilled wetlands on a parcel of land in Michigan that he owned and sought to develop. This parcel included 54 acres of land with sometimes-saturated soil conditions. The nearest body of navigable water was 11 to 20 miles away. 339 F.3d 447, 449 (CA6 2003) (*Rapanos I*). Regulators had informed Mr. Rapanos that his saturated fields were "waters of the United States," 33 U.S.C. § 1362(7), that could not be filled without a permit. Twelve years of criminal and civil litigation ensued.

The burden of federal regulation on those who would deposit fill material in locations denominated "waters of the United States" is not trivial. In deciding whether to grant or deny a permit, the U.S. Army Corps of Engineers (Corps) exercises the discretion of an enlightened despot, relying on such factors as "economics," "aesthetics," "recreation," and "in general, the needs and welfare of the people," 33 CFR § 320.4(a) (2004). The average applicant for an individual permit spends 788 days and $271,596 in completing the process, and the average applicant for a nationwide permit spends 313 days and $28,915 not counting costs of mitigation or design changes. Sunding & Zilberman, The Economics of Environmental Regulation by Licensing: An Assessment of Recent Changes to the Wetland Permitting Process, 42 Natural Resources J. 59, 74–76 (2002). "Over $1.7 billion is spent each year by the private and public sectors obtaining wetlands permits." Id., at 81. These costs cannot be avoided, because the Clean Water Act "imposes criminal liability," as well as steep civil fines, "on a broad range of ordinary industrial and commercial activities." *Hanousek v. United States*, 528 U.S. 1102, 1103, 120 S. Ct. 860, 145 L. Ed. 2d 710 (2000) (Thomas, J., dissenting from denial of certiorari). In this litigation, for example, for backfilling his own wet fields, Mr. Rapanos faced 63 months in prison and hundreds of thousands of dollars in criminal and civil fines. See United States v. Rapanos, 235 F.3d 256, 260 (CA6 2000).

The enforcement proceedings against Mr. Rapanos are a small part of the immense expansion of federal regulation of land use that has occurred under the Clean Water Act — without any change in the governing statute — during the past five Presidential administrations. In the last three decades, the Corps and the Environmental Protection Agency (EPA) have interpreted their jurisdiction over "the waters of the United States" to cover 270-to-300 million acres of swampy lands in the United States including half of Alaska and an area the size of California in the lower 48 States. And that was just the beginning. The Corps has also asserted jurisdiction over virtually any parcel of land containing a channel or conduit —

whether man-made or natural, broad or narrow, permanent or ephemeral — through which rainwater or drainage may occasionally or intermittently flow. On this view, the federally regulated "waters of the United States" include storm drains, roadside ditches, ripples of sand in the desert that may contain water once a year, and lands that are covered by floodwaters once every 100 years. Because they include the land containing storm sewers and desert washes, the statutory "waters of the United States" engulf entire cities and immense arid wastelands. In fact, the entire land area of the United States lies in some drainage basin, and an endless network of visible channels furrows the entire surface, containing water ephemerally wherever the rain falls. Any plot of land containing such a channel may potentially be regulated as a "water of the United States."

I

. . . .

For a century prior to the CWA, we had interpreted the phrase "navigable waters of the United States" in the Act's predecessor statutes to refer to interstate waters that are "navigable in fact" or readily susceptible of being rendered so. *The Daniel Ball*, 77 U.S. 557, 19 L. Ed. 999, 10 Wall. 557, 563 (1871); *see also United States v. Appalachian Elec. Power Co.*, 311 U.S. 377, 406, 61 S. Ct. 291, 85 L. Ed. 243 (1940). After passage of the CWA, the Corps initially adopted this traditional judicial definition for the Act's term "navigable waters." See 39 Fed. Reg. 12119, codified at 33 CFR 209.120(d)(1) (1974); see also *Solid Waste Agency v. United States Army Corps of Eng'rs*, 531 U.S. 159, 168, 121 S. Ct. 675, 148 L. Ed. 2d 576 (2001) (*SWANCC*). After a District Court enjoined these regulations as too narrow, *Natural Resources Defense Council, Inc. v. Callaway*, 392 F. Supp. 685, 686 (D.C. D.C. 1975), the Corps adopted a far broader definition. See 40 Fed. Reg. 31324 31325 (1975); 42 Fed. Reg. 37144 (1977). The Corps' new regulations deliberately sought to extend the definition of "the waters of the United States" to the outer limits of Congress's commerce power. See id., at 37144, n. 2.

The Corps' current regulations interpret "the waters of the United States" to include, in addition to traditional interstate navigable waters, 33 CFR § 328.3(a)(1) (2004), "all interstate waters including interstate wetlands," § 328.3(a)(2); "all other waters such as intrastate lakes, rivers, streams (including intermittent streams), mudflats, sandflats, wetlands, sloughs, prairie potholes, wet meadows, playa lakes, or natural ponds, the use, degradation or destruction of which could affect interstate or foreign commerce," §§ 328.3(a)(3); "tributaries of [such] waters," § 328.3(a)(5); and "wetlands adjacent to [such] waters [and tributaries] (other than waters that are themselves wetlands)," § 328.3(a)(7). The regulation defines "adjacent" wetlands as those "bordering, contiguous [to], or neighboring" waters of the United States. § 328.3(c). It specifically provides that "wetlands separated from other waters of the United States by man-made dikes or barriers, natural river berms, beach dunes and the like are 'adjacent wetlands.'" *Ibid.* . . .

[The Court then reviewed its earlier decisions in *Riverside Bayview* and *SWANCC*.]

Even after *SWANCC*, the lower courts have continued to uphold the Corps' sweeping assertions of jurisdiction over ephemeral channels and drains as "tributaries." For example, courts have held that jurisdictional "tributaries" include the "intermittent flow of surface water through approximately 2.4 miles of natural streams and manmade ditches (paralleling and crossing under I-64)," *Treacy v. Newdunn Assocs., LLP*, 344 F.3d 407, 410 (CA4 2003); a "roadside ditch" whose water took "a winding, thirty-two mile path to the Chesapeake Bay," *United States v. Deaton*, 332 F.3d 698, 702 (CA4 2003); irrigation ditches and drains that intermittently connect to covered waters, *Community Assn. for Restoration of Environment v. Henry Bosma Dairy*, 305 F.3d 943, 954 955 (CA9 2002); *Headwaters, Inc. v. Talent Irrigation Dist.*, 243 F.3d 526, 534 (CA9 2001); and (most implausibly of all) the "washes and arroyos" of an "arid development site," located in the middle of the desert, through which "water courses . . . during periods of heavy rain," *Save Our Sonoran, Inc. v. Flowers*, 408 F.3d 1113, 1118 (CA9 2005).

These judicial constructions of "tributaries" are not outliers. Rather, they reflect the breadth of the Corps' determinations in the field. The Corps' enforcement practices vary somewhat from district to district because "the definitions used to make jurisdictional determinations" are deliberately left "vague." GAO Report 26; see also *id.*, at 22. But district offices of the Corps have treated, as "waters of the United States," such typically dry land features as "arroyos, coulees, and washes," as well as other "channels that might have little water flow in a given year." Id., at 20 21. They have also applied that definition to such manmade, intermittently flowing features as "drain tiles, storm drains systems, and culverts." *Id.*, at 24 (footnote omitted).

In addition to "tributaries," the Corps and the lower courts have also continued to defined "adjacent" wetlands broadly after SWANCC. For example, some of the Corps' district offices have concluded that wetlands are "adjacent" to covered waters if they are hydroponically connected "through directional sheet flow during storm events," GAO Report 18, or if they lie within the "100-year floodplain" of a body of water — that is, they are connected to the navigable water by flooding, on average, once every 100 years, *id.*, at 17, and n. 16. Others have concluded that presence within 200 feet of a tributary automatically renders a wetland "adjacent" and jurisdictional. *Id.*, at 19. And the Corps has successfully defended such theories of "adjacency" in the courts, even after SWANCC's excision of "isolated" waters and wetlands from the Act's coverage. One court has held since SWANCC that wetlands separated from flood control channels by 70-foot-wide berms, atop which ran maintenance roads, had a "significant nexus" to covered waters because, *inter alia*, they lay "within the 100 year floodplain of tidal waters." *Baccarat Fremont Developers,fillC v. United States Army Corps of Eng'rs*, 425 F.3d 1150, 1152, 1157 (CA9 2005). In one of the cases before us today, the Sixth Circuit held, in agreement with "the majority of courts," that "while a hydrological connection between the non-navigable and navigable waters is required, there is no 'direct abutment' requirement" under *SWANCC* for " 'adjacency.' " 376 F.3d 629, 639 (2004) *(Rapanos II)*. And even the most insubstantial hydrologic connection may be held to constitute a "significant nexus." One court distinguished *SWANCC* on the ground that "a molecule of water residing in one of these pits or ponds [in *SWANCC*] could not mix with molecules from other bodies of water" — whereas, in the case before it, "water molecules currently present in the wetlands will inevitably flow towards and mix with water from connecting bodies," and "[a] drop of rainwater landing in the Site is certain to intermingle with water from the [nearby river]." *United States v. Rueth Development Co.*, 189 F. Supp. 2d 874, 877 878 (ND Ind. 2002).

II

In these consolidated cases, we consider whether four Michigan wetlands, which lie near ditches or man-made drains that eventually empty into traditional navigable waters, constitute "waters of the United States" within the meaning of the Act. . . .

III

The Rapanos petitioners contend that the terms "navigable waters" and "waters of the United States" in the Act must be limited to the traditional definition of *The Daniel Ball*, which required that the "waters" be navigable in fact, or susceptible of being rendered so. See 77 U.S. 557, 10 Wall., at 563, 19 L. Ed. 999. But this definition cannot be applied wholesale to the CWA. The Act uses the phrase "navigable waters" as a *defined* term, and the definition is simply "the waters of the United States." 33 U.S.C. § 1362(7). Moreover, the Act provides, in certain circumstances, for the substitution of state for federal jurisdiction over "navigable waters . . . *other than* those waters which are presently used, or are susceptible to use in their natural condition or by reasonable improvement as a means to transport interstate or foreign commerce . . . including wetlands adjacent thereto." § 1344(g)(1) (emphasis added). This provision shows that the Act's term "navigable waters" includes something more than traditional navigable waters. We have twice stated that the meaning of "navigable waters" in the Act is broader than the traditional understanding of that term, *SWANCC*, 531 U.S., at 167, 121 S. Ct. 675, 148 L. Ed. 2d 576; *Riverside Bayview*, 474 U.S., at 133, 106 S. Ct. 455, 88 L. Ed. 2d 419. We have also emphasized, however, that the qualifier "navigable" is not devoid of significance, *SWANCC, supra,* at 172, 121 S. Ct. 675, 148 L. Ed. 2d 576.

We need not decide the precise extent to which the qualifiers "navigable" and "of the United States" restrict the coverage of the Act. Whatever the scope of these qualifiers, the CWA authorizes federal jurisdiction only over "waters." 33 U.S.C. § 1362(7). The only natural definition of the term "waters," our prior and subsequent judicial constructions of it, clear evidence from other provisions of the statute, and this Court's canons of construction all confirm that "the waters of the United States" in § 1362(7) cannot bear the expansive meaning that the Corps would give it.

The Corps' expansive approach might be arguable if the CWA defined "navigable waters" as "water of the United States." But "the waters of the United States" is something else. The use of the definite article ("the") and the plural number ("waters") show plainly that § 1362(7) does not refer to water in general. In this form, "the waters" refers more narrowly to water "as found in streams and bodies forming geographical features such as oceans, rivers, [and] lakes," or "the flowing or moving masses, as of waves or floods, making up such streams or bodies." Webster's New International Dictionary 2882 (2d ed. 1954) (hereinafter Webster's Second). On this definition, "the waters of the United States" include only relatively permanent, standing or flowing bodies of water.[12] The definition refers to water as found in "streams," "oceans," "rivers," "lakes," and "bodies" of water "forming geographical features." *Ibid.* All of these terms connote continuously present, fixed bodies of water, as opposed to ordinarily dry channels through which water occasionally or intermittently flows. Even the least substantial of the definition's terms, namely "streams," connotes a continuous flow of water in a permanent channel — especially when used in company with other terms such as "rivers," "lakes," and "oceans."[13] None of these terms encompasses transitory puddles or ephemeral flows of water.

The restriction of "the waters of the United States" to exclude channels containing merely intermittent or ephemeral flow also accords with the common-sense understanding of the term. In applying the definition to "ephemeral streams," "wet meadows," storm sewers and culverts, "directional sheet flow during storm events," drain tiles, man-made drainage ditches, and dry arroyos in the middle of the desert, the Corps has stretched the term "waters of the United States" beyond parody. The plain language of the statute simply does not authorize this "Land Is Waters" approach to federal jurisdiction.

In addition, the Act's use of the traditional phrase "navigable waters" (the defined term) further confirms that it confers jurisdiction only over relatively *permanent* bodies of water. The Act adopted that traditional term from its

---

[12] By describing "waters" as "relatively permanent," we do not necessarily exclude streams, rivers, or lakes that might dry up in extraordinary circumstances, such as drought. We also do not necessarily exclude seasonal rivers, which contain continuous flow during some months of the year but no flow during dry months such as the 290-day, continuously flowing stream postulated by Justice Stevens' dissent (hereinafter the dissent), *post,* at 15. Common sense and common usage distinguish between a wash and seasonal river.

Though scientifically precise distinctions between "perennial" and "intermittent" flows are no doubt available, *see, e.g.,* Dept. of Interior, U.S. Geological Survey, E. Hedman & W. Osterkamp, Streamflow Characteristics Related to Channel Geometry of Streams in Western United States 15 (1982) (Water-Supply Paper 2193), we have no occasion in this litigation to decide exactly when the drying-up of a stream bed is continuous and frequent enough to disqualify the channel as a "water of the United States." It suffices for present purposes that channels containing permanent flow are plainly within the definition, and that the dissent's "intermittent" and "ephemeral" streams, *post,* at 16 (opinion of Stevens, J.) that is, streams whose flow is "coming and going at intervals . . . broken, fitful," Webster's Second 1296, or "existing only, or no longer than, a day; diurnal . . . short-lived," *id.,* at 857 — are not.

[13] The principal definition of "stream" likewise includes reference to such permanent, geographically fixed bodies of water: "[a] current or course of water or other fluid, flowing on the earth, as a *river, brook, etc." Id.,* at 2493 (emphasis added). The other definitions of "stream" repeatedly emphasize the requirement of *continuous* flow: "[a] *steady flow,* as of water, air, gas, or the like"; "anything issuing or moving with *continued succession* of parts"; "[a] *continued current* or course; current; drift." *Ibid.* (emphases added). The definition of the verb form of "stream" contains a similar emphasis on continuity: "to issue or flow in a stream; to issue freely or move in a *continuous flow or course." Ibid.* (emphasis added). On these definitions, therefore, the Corps' phrases "intermittent streams," 33 CFR § 328.3(a)(3) (2004), and "ephemeral streams," 65 Fed. Reg. 12823 (2000), are — like Senator Bentsen's " 'flowing gullies,' " *post,* at 16, n. 11 (opinion of Stevens, J.) — useful oxymora. Properly speaking, such entities constitute extant "streams" only while they are "continuously flowing"; and the usually dry channels that contain them are never "streams." Justice Kennedy apparently concedes that "an intermittent flow can constitute a stream" only *"while it is flowing," post,* at 13 (emphasis added) — which would mean that the channel is a "water" covered by the Act only during those times when water flow actually occurs. But no one contends that federal jurisdiction appears and evaporates along with the water in such regularly dry channels.

predecessor statutes. See SWANCC, 531 U.S., at 180, 121 S. Ct. 675, 148 L. Ed. 2d 576 (STEVENS, J., dissenting). . . .

In sum, on its only plausible interpretation, the phrase "the waters of the United States" includes only those relatively permanent, standing or continuously flowing bodies of water "forming geographic features" that are described in ordinary parlance as "streams[,] . . . oceans, rivers, [and] lakes." See Webster's Second 2882. The phrase does not include channels through which water flows intermittently or ephemerally, or channels that periodically provide drainage for rainfall. The Corps' expansive interpretation of the "the waters of the United States" is thus not "based on a permissible construction of the statute." *Chevron U.S.A. Inc. v. NRDC*, 467 U.S. 837, 843, 104 S. Ct. 2778, 81 L. Ed. 2d 694 (1984).

IV

In *Carabell*, the Sixth Circuit held that the nearby ditch constituted a "tributary" and thus a "water of the United States" under 33 CFR § 328.3(a)(5) (2004). See 391 F.3d at 708 709. Likewise in *Rapanos*, the Sixth Circuit held that the nearby ditches were "tributaries" under § 328.3(a)(5). 376 F.3d at 643. But *Rapanos II* also stated that, even if the ditches were not "waters of the United States," the wetlands were "adjacent" to *remote* traditional navigable waters in virtue of the wetlands' "hydrological connection" to them. See *id.*, at 639 640. This statement reflects the practice of the Corps' district offices, which may "assert jurisdiction over a wetland without regulating the ditch connecting it to a water of the United States." GAO Report 23. We therefore address in this Part whether a wetland may be considered "adjacent to" remote "waters of the United States," because of a mere hydrologic connection to them.

[The Court again discussed *Riverside Bayview* and *SWANCC*.]

Therefore, *only* those wetlands with a continuous surface connection to bodies that are "waters of the United States" in their own right, so that there is no clear demarcation between "waters" and wetlands, are "adjacent to" such waters and covered by the Act. Wetlands with only an intermittent, physically remote hydrologic connection to "waters of the United States" do not implicate the boundary-drawing problem of *Riverside Bayview*, and thus lack the necessary connection to covered waters that we described as a "significant nexus" in *SWANCC*, 531 U.S., at 167, 121 S. Ct. 675, 148 L. Ed. 2d 576. Thus, establishing that wetlands such as those at the Rapanos and Carabell sites are covered by the Act requires two findings: First, that the adjacent channel contains a "water of the United States," (i.e., a relatively permanent body of water connected to traditional interstate navigable waters); and second, that the wetland has a continuous surface connection with that water, making it difficult to determine where the "water" ends and the "wetland" begins.

V

Respondents and their *amici* urge that such restrictions on the scope of "navigable waters" will frustrate enforcement against traditional water polluters under 33 U.S.C. §§ 1311 and 1342. Because the same definition of "navigable waters" applies to the entire statute, respondents contend that water polluters will be able to evade the permitting requirement of § 1342(a) simply by discharging their pollutants into noncovered intermittent watercourses that lie upstream of covered waters. See Tr. of Oral Arg. 74 75.

That is not so. Though we do not decide this issue, there is no reason to suppose that our construction today significantly affects the enforcement of § 1342, inasmuch as lower courts applying § 1342 have not characterized intermittent channels as "waters of the United States." The Act does not forbid the "addition of any pollutant *directly to* navigable waters from any point source," but rather the "addition of any pollutant to navigable waters." § 1362(12)(A) (emphasis added); § 1311(a). Thus, from the time of the CWA's enactment, lower courts have held that the discharge into intermittent channels of any pollutant *that naturally washes downstream* likely violates §§ 1311(a), even if the pollutants discharged from a point source do not emit "directly into" covered waters, but pass "through conveyances" in between. *United States Velsicol Chemical Corp.*, 438 F. Supp. 945, 946 947 (WD Tenn. 1976) (a municipal sewer system separated the "point source" and covered navigable waters). See also *Sierra Club v. El Paso Gold Mines, Inc.*, 421 F.3d 1133, 1137, 1141 (CA10 2005) (2.5 miles of tunnel separated the "point source" and "navigable waters").

[Remainder of plurality opinion, which comments on concurring and dissenting opinions, is omitted.]

We vacate the judgments of the Sixth Circuit in both No. 04-1034 and No. 04-1384, and remand both cases for further proceedings.

It is so ordered.

[CHIEF JUSTICE ROBERTS's concurring opinion omitted.]

JUSTICE KENNEDY, concurring in the judgment.

. . . .

I

. . . .

A

. . . .

The statutory term to be interpreted and applied in the two instant cases is the term "navigable waters." The outcome turns on whether that phrase reasonably describes certain Michigan wetlands the Corps seeks to regulate. Under the Act "the term 'navigable waters' means the waters of the United States, including the territorial seas." § 1362(7). In a regulation the Corps has construed the term "waters of the United States" to include not only waters susceptible to use in interstate commerce, the traditional understanding of the term "navigable waters of the United States," see, *e.g., United States v. Appalachian Elec. Power Co.*, 311 U.S. 377, 406 408, 61 S. Ct. 291, 85 L. Ed. 243 (1940); *The Daniel Ball*, 77 U.S. 557, 10 Wall. 557, 563 564, 19 L. Ed. 999 (1871) — but also tributaries of those waters and, of particular relevance here, wetlands adjacent to those waters or their tributaries. 33 CFR § 328.3(a)(1), (5), (7) (2005). The Corps views tributaries as within its jurisdiction if they carry a perceptible "ordinary high water mark." § 328.4(c); 65 Fed. Reg. 12823 (2000). An ordinary high-water mark is a "line on the shore established by the fluctuations of water and indicated by physical characteristics such as clear, natural line impressed on the bank, shelving, changes in the character of soil, destruction of terrestrial vegetation, the presence of litter and debris, or other appropriate means that consider the characteristics of the surrounding areas." 33 CFR § 328.3(e).

Contrary to the plurality's description, *ante*, at 2–3, 15, wetlands are not simply moist patches of earth. They are defined as "those areas that are inundated or saturated by surface or ground water at a frequency and duration sufficient to support, and that under normal circumstances do support, a prevalence of vegetation typically adapted for life in saturated soil conditions. Wetlands generally include swamps, marshes, bogs, and similar areas." § 328.3(b). The Corps' Wetlands Delineation Manual, including over 100 pages of technical guidance for Corps officers, interprets this definition of wetlands to require: (1) prevalence of plant species typically adapted to saturated soil conditions, determined in accordance with the United States Fish and Wildlife Service's National List of Plant Species that Occur in Wetlands; (2) hydric soil, meaning soil that is saturated, flooded, or ponded for sufficient time during the growing season to become anaerobic, or lacking in oxygen, in the upper part; and (3) wetland hydrology, a term generally requiring continuous inundation or saturation to the surface during at least five percent of the growing season in most years. See Wetlands Research Program Technical Report Y-87-1 (on-line edition), pp. 12–34 (Jan. 1987), www.saj.usace.army.mil/permit/documents/87manual.pdf (all Internet material as visited June 16, 2006, and available in Clerk of Court's case file). Under the Corps' regulations, wetlands are adjacent to tributaries, and thus covered by the Act, even if they are "separated from other waters of the United States by man-made dikes or barriers, natural river berms, beach dunes and the like." § 328.3(c). . . .

II

. . . .

A

The plurality's opinion begins from a correct premise. As the plurality points out, and as *Riverside Bayview* holds, in enacting the Clean Water Act Congress intended to regulate at least some waters that are not navigable in the traditional sense. *Ante*, at 12; *Riverside Bayview*, 474 U.S., at 133, 106 S. Ct. 455, 88 L. Ed. 2d 419; see also *SWANCC*, supra, at 167, 121 S. Ct. 675, 148 L. Ed. 2d 576. This conclusion is supported by "the evident breadth of congressional concern for protection of water quality and aquatic ecosystems." *Riverside Bayview*, supra, at 133, 106 S. Ct. 455, 88 L. Ed. 2d 419; see also *Milwaukee v. Illinois*, 451 U.S. 304,

318, 101 S. Ct. 1784, 68 L. Ed. 2d 114 (1981) (describing the Act as "an all-encompassing program of water pollution regulation"). It is further compelled by statutory text. . . .

B

. . . .

Consistent with SWANCC and *Riverside Bayview* and with the need to give the term "navigable" some meaning, the Corps' jurisdiction over wetlands depends upon the existence of a significant nexus between the wetlands in question and navigable waters in the traditional sense. The required nexus must be assessed in terms of the statute's goals and purposes. Congress enacted the law to "restore and maintain the chemical, physical, and biological integrity of the Nation's waters," 33 U.S.C. § 1251(a), and it pursued that objective by restricting dumping and filling in "navigable waters," § 1311(a), 1362(12). With respect to wetlands, the rationale for Clean Water Act regulation is, as the Corps has recognized, that wetlands can perform critical functions related to the integrity of other waters — functions such as pollutant trapping, flood control, and runoff storage. 33 CFR § 320.4(b)(2). Accordingly, wetlands possess the requisite nexus, and thus come within the statutory phrase "navigable waters," if the wetlands, either alone or in combination with similarly situated lands in the region, significantly affect the chemical, physical, and biological integrity of other covered waters more readily understood as "navigable." When, in contrast, wetlands' effects on water quality are speculative or insubstantial, they fall outside the zone fairly encompassed by the statutory term "navigable waters." . . .

As applied to wetlands adjacent to navigable-in-fact waters, the Corps' conclusive standard for jurisdiction rests upon a reasonable inference of ecologic interconnection, and the assertion of jurisdiction for those wetlands is sustainable under the Act by showing adjacency alone. That is the holding of *Riverside Bayview*. Furthermore, although the *Riverside Bayview* Court reserved the question of the Corps' authority over "wetlands that are not adjacent to bodies of open water," 474 U.S., at 131–132, n. 8, 106 S. Ct. 455, 88 L. Ed. 2d 419, and in any event addressed no factual situation other than wetlands adjacent to navigable-in-fact waters, it may well be the case that *Riverside Bayview's* reasoning — supporting jurisdiction without any inquiry beyond adjacency — could apply equally to wetlands adjacent to certain major tributaries. Through regulations or adjudication, the Corps may choose to identify categories of tributaries that, due to their volume of flow (either annually or on average), their proximity to navigable waters, or other relevant considerations, are significant enough that wetlands adjacent to them are likely, in the majority of cases, to perform important functions for an aquatic system incorporating navigable waters.

The Corps' existing standard for tributaries, however, provides no such assurance. As noted earlier, the Corps deems a water a tributary if it feeds into a traditional navigable water (or a tributary thereof) and possesses an ordinary high-water mark, defined as a "line on the shore established by the fluctuations of water and indicated by [certain] physical characteristics," § 328.3(e). *See supra*, at 3. This standard presumably provides a rough measure of the volume and regularity of flow. Assuming it is subject to reasonably consistent application, but see U.S. General Accounting Office, Report to the Chairman, Subcommittee on Energy Policy, Natural Resources and Regulating Affairs, Committee on Reform, House of Representatives, Waters and Wetlands: Corps of Engineers Needs to Evaluate Its District Office Practices in Determining Jurisdiction, GAO-04-297 pp. 3 –4 (Feb. 2004), www.gao.gov/new.items/d04297.pdf (noting variation in results among Corps district offices), it may well provide a reasonable measure of whether specific minor tributaries bear a sufficient nexus with other regulated waters to constitute "navigable waters" under the Act. Yet the breadth of this standard which seems to leave wide room for regulation of drains, ditches, and streams remote from any navigable-in-fact water and carrying only minor water-volumes towards it — precludes its adoption as the determinative measure of whether adjacent wetlands are likely to play an important role in the integrity of an aquatic system comprising navigable waters as traditionally understood. Indeed, in many cases wetlands adjacent to tributaries covered by this standard might appear little more related to navigable-in-fact waters than were the isolated ponds held to fall beyond the Act's scope in *SWANCC*. Cf. Leibowitz & Nadeau, Isolated Wetlands: State-of-the-Science and Future Directions, 23 Wetlands 663, 669 (2003) (noting that " 'isolated' is generally a matter of degree").

When the Corps seeks to regulate wetlands adjacent to navigable-in-fact waters, it may rely on adjacency to establish its jurisdiction. Absent more specific regulations, however, the Corps must establish a significant nexus on a case-by-case basis when it seeks to regulate wetlands based on adjacency to nonnavigable tributaries. Given the potential overbreadth of the Corps' regulations, this showing is necessary to avoid unreasonable applications of the statute. Where an adequate nexus is established for a particular wetland, it may be permissible, as a matter of administrative convenience or necessity, to presume covered status for other comparable wetlands in the region. That issue, however, is neither raised by these facts nor addressed by any agency regulation that accommodates the nexus requirement outlined here. . . .

[Remainder of opinion omitted.]

In these consolidated cases I would vacate the judgments of the Court of Appeals and remand for consideration whether the specific wetlands at issue possess a significant nexus with navigable waters.

JUSTICE STEVENS, with whom JUSTICE SOUTER, JUSTICE GINSBURG, and JUSTICE BREYER join, dissenting.

In 1972, Congress decided to "restore and maintain the chemical, physical, and biological integrity of the Nation's waters" by passing what we now call the Clean Water Act. 86 Stat. 816, as amended, 33 U.S.C. § 1251 *et seq.* The costs of achieving the Herculean goal of ending water pollution by 1985, see § 1251(a), persuaded President Nixon to veto its enactment, but both Houses of Congress voted to override that veto by overwhelming margins. To achieve its goal, Congress prohibited "the discharge of any pollutant" — defined to include "any addition of any pollutant to navigable waters from any point source" — without a permit issued by the Army Corps of Engineers (Army Corps or Corps) or the Environmental

Protection Agency (EPA). § 1311(a), 1362(12)(A). Congress further defined "navigable waters" to mean "the waters of the United States." § 1362(7).

The narrow question presented in No. 04-1034 is whether wetlands adjacent to tributaries of traditionally navigable waters are "waters of the United States" subject to the jurisdiction of the Army Corps; the question in No. 04-1384 is whether a manmade berm separating a wetland from the adjacent tributary makes a difference. The broader question is whether regulations that have protected the quality of our waters for decades, that were implicitly approved by Congress, and that have been repeatedly enforced in case after case, must now be revised in light of the creative criticisms voiced by the plurality and Justice Kennedy today. Rejecting more than 30 years of practice by the Army Corps, the plurality disregards the nature of the congressional delegation to the agency and the technical and complex character of the issues at stake. Justice Kennedy similarly fails to defer sufficiently to the Corps, though his approach is far more faithful to our precedents and to principles of statutory interpretation than is the plurality's.

In my view, the proper analysis is straightforward. The Army Corps has determined that wetlands adjacent to tributaries of traditionally navigable waters preserve the quality of our Nation's waters by, among other things, providing habitat for aquatic animals, keeping excessive sediment and toxic pollutants out of adjacent waters, and reducing downstream flooding by absorbing water at times of high flow. The Corps' resulting decision to treat these wetlands as encompassed within the term "waters of the United States" is a quintessential example of the Executive's reasonable interpretation of a statutory provision. See *Chevron U.S.A. Inc. v. NRDC*, 467 U.S. 837, 842 845, 104 S. Ct. 2778, 81 L. Ed. 2d 694 (1984).

Our unanimous decision in *United States v. Riverside Bayview Homes, Inc.*, 474 U.S. 121, 106 S. Ct. 455, 88 L. Ed. 2d 419 (1985), was faithful to our duty to respect the work product of the legislative and Executive Branches of our Government. Today's judicial amendment of the Clean Water Act is not.

[Remainder of dissent omitted.]

JUSTICE BREYER, dissenting.

In my view, the authority of the Army Corps of Engineers under the Clean Water Act extends to the limits of congressional power to regulate interstate commerce. See *Solid Waste Agency v. United States Army Corps of Eng'rs*, 531 U.S. 159, 181 182, 121 S. Ct. 675, 148 L. Ed. 2d 576 (2001) (*SWANCC*) (STEVENS, J., dissenting). I therefore have no difficulty finding that the wetlands at issue in these cases are within the Corps' jurisdiction, and I join Justice Stevens' dissenting opinion.

[Remainder of dissent omitted.]

NOTE

Postscript. After *Rapanos*, the EPA and COE issued a joint memorandum indicating each would determine CWA jurisdiction under either the Kennedy "significant nexus" test (assessed with reference to statutory goals and purposes) or the Scalia "continuous surface connection" test. The First and Third Circuits agreed with that approach. *United States v. Johnson,* 467 F.3d 56 (1st Cir. 2006); *United States v. Donovan,* 661 F.3d 174 (3d Cir. 2011). The Fourth, Seventh, Ninth, and Eleventh Circuits, however, have relied on the significant nexus test. *United States v. Gerke,* 464 F.3d 723 (7th Cir. 2006); *United States v. Robison,* 505 F.3d 1208 (11th Cir. 2007); *Northern California River Watch v. Healdsburg, Calif.,* 496 F.3d 993 (9th Cir. 2007); *Precon Development Co. v. U.S. Corps of Engineers,* 633 F.3d 278 (4th Cir. 2011). In 2011, the agencies issued a revised (nonbinding) draft Guidance Document indicating their intention to follow the significant nexus test.

Section 404 authorizes regulation of any "discharge of dredged or fill material into the navigable waters at specified disposal sites." We have already reviewed the question of what is a "discharge," in connection with point source regulation. See *supra.* But the same issue has arisen in the context of § 404.

NATIONAL MINING ASS'N v. U.S. ARMY CORPS OF ENGINEERS
145 F.3d 1399 (D.C. Cir. 1998)

WILLIAMS, CIRCUIT JUDGE:

. . . .

In 1986 the Corps issued a regulation defining the term "discharge of dredged material," as used in § 404, to mean "any addition of dredged material into the waters of the United States," but expressly excluding "*de minimis,* incidental soil movement occurring during normal dredging operations." 51 Fed. Reg. 41,206, 41,232 (Nov. 13, 1986). In 1993, responding to litigation, the Corps issued a new rule removing the *de minimis* exception and expanding the definition of discharge to cover "any addition of dredged material into, including any redeposit of dredged material within, the waters of the United States." 33 C.F.R. § 323.2(d)(1) (emphasis added). Redeposit occurs when material removed from the water is returned to it; when redeposit takes place in substantially the same spot as the initial removal, the parties refer to it as "fallback." In effect the new rule subjects to federal regulation virtually all excavation and dredging performed in wetlands.

The plaintiffs, various trade associations whose members engage in dredging and excavation, mounted a facial challenge to the 1993 regulation, claiming that it exceeded the scope of the Corps's regulatory authority under the Act by regulating fallback. The district court agreed and granted summary judgment for the plaintiffs. *American Mining Congress v. United States Army Corps of Engineers,* 951 F. Supp. 267 (D.D.C. 1997). The district court also entered an injunction prohibiting the Corps and the Environmental Protection Agency, who jointly administer § 404, from enforcing the regulation anywhere in the United States. *Id.* at 278. We affirm. . . .

In 1977 the Corps promulgated regulations that generally tracked the statutory language, defining "discharge of dredged material" as "any addition of dredged material into the waters of the United States," with a few limited exceptions. 42 Fed.

Reg. 37,145 (July 19, 1977). A new regulation issued in 1986 exempted from the permit requirement "*de minimis*, incidental soil movement occurring during normal dredging operations." 51 Fed. Reg. at 41,232. Although this regulation did not define "normal dredging operations," its preamble gave some guidance as to the exemption's coverage:

Section 404 clearly directs the Corps to regulate the discharge of dredged material, not the dredging itself.

Dredging operations cannot be performed without some fallback. However, if we were to define this fallback as a "discharge of dredged material," we would, in effect, be adding the regulation of dredging to section 404 which we do not believe was the intent of Congress. *Id.* at 41,210. The parties agree that the 1986 rule did, however, regulate "sidecasting," which involves placing removed soil in a wetland but at some distance from the point of removal (e.g., by the side of an excavated ditch). *See* 58 Fed. Reg. 45,008, 45,013/3 (Aug. 25, 1993) (noting that sidecasting has "always been regulated under Section 404.").

The 1993 rulemaking under challenge here was prompted by a lawsuit, *North Carolina Wildlife Federation v. Tulloch, Civ.* No. C90-713-CIV-5-BO (E.D. N.C. 1992), concerning a developer who sought to drain and clear 700 acres of wetlands in North Carolina. See 58 Fed. Reg. at 45,016. Because the developer's efforts involved only minimal incidental releases of soil and other dredged material, the Corps's field office personnel determined that, under the terms of the 1986 regulation, § 404's permit requirements did not apply. Environmental groups, concerned by what they viewed as the adverse effects of the developer's activities on the wetland, led an action seeking enforcement of the § 404 permit requirement. As part of the settlement of the *Tulloch* case (a settlement to which the developer was not a party), the two administering agencies agreed to propose stiffer rules governing the permit requirements for landclearing and excavation activities. The result — the regulation at issue here — has come to be called the "Tulloch Rule."

As mentioned above, the Tulloch Rule alters the preexisting regulatory framework primarily by removing the *de minimis* exception and by adding coverage of incidental fallback. Specifically, the rule defines "discharge of dredged material" to include "any addition, including any redeposit, of dredged material, including excavated material, into waters of the United States which is incidental to any activity, including mechanized landclearing, ditching, channelization, or other excavation." 33 C.F.R. § 323.2(d)(1)(iii) (emphasis added).

The Tulloch Rule does have its own *de minimis* exception, but it is framed in terms of the Act's overall goals. A permit is not required for "any incidental addition, including redeposit, of dredged material associated with any activity that does not have or would not have the effect of destroying or degrading an area of waters of the United States." 33 C.F.R § 323.2(d)(3)(I). Persons engaging in "mechanized landclearing, ditching, channelization, and other excavation activity," however, bear the burden of proving to the Corps that their activities would not have destructive or degrading effects. Id. Degradation is defined as any effect on the waters of the United States that is more than *de minimis* or inconsequential. *Id.* § 323.2(d)(5). Thus, whereas the 1986 rule exempted *de minimis* soil movement, the Tulloch Rule covers all discharges, however minuscule, unless the Corps is convinced that the activities with which they are associated have only minimal adverse effects. In promulgating the new rule the Corps "emphasized that the threshold of adverse effects for the *de minimis* exception is a very low one." 56 Fed. Reg. at 45,020.

It is undisputed that by requiring a permit for "any redeposit," 33 C.F.R. § 323.2(d)(1)(iii) (emphasis added), the Tulloch Rule covers incidental fallback. According to the agencies, incidental fallback occurs, for example, during dredging, "when a bucket used to excavate material from the bottom of a river, stream, or wetland is raised and soils or sediments fall from the bucket back into the water." Agencies' Br. at 13. (There is no indication that the rule would not also reach soils or sediments falling out of the bucket even before it emerged from the water.) Fallback and other redeposits also occur during mechanized land clearing, when bulldozers and loaders scrape or displace wetland soil, *see* 58 Fed. Reg. 45,017–18, as well as during ditching and channelization, when draglines or backhoes are dragged through soils and sediments. *See id.* at 45,018. Indeed, fallback is a practically inescapable by-product of all these activities. In the preamble to the Tulloch Rule the Corps noted that "it is virtually impossible to conduct mechanized landclearing, ditching, channelization or excavation in waters of the United States without causing incidental redeposition of dredged material (however small or temporary) in the process." *Id.* at 45,017. As a result, the Tulloch Rule effectively requires a permit for all those activities, subject to a limited exception for ones that the Corps in its discretion deems to produce no adverse effects on waters of the United States . . . .

The plaintiffs claim that the Tulloch Rule exceeds the Corps's statutory jurisdiction under § 404, which, as we have noted, extends only to "discharge," defined as the "addition of any pollutant to navigable waters." 33 U.S.C. § 1344, 1362(12). It argues that fallback, which returns dredged material virtually to the spot from which it came, cannot be said to constitute an addition of anything. Therefore, the plaintiffs contend, the Tulloch Rule conflicts with the statute's unambiguous terms and cannot survive even the deferential scrutiny called for by *Chevron U.S.A., Inc. v. NRDC*, 467 U.S. 837, 81 L. Ed. 2d 694, 104 S. Ct. 2778 (1984). The "jurisdictional" character of the issue has no effect on the level of deference, *Oklahoma Natural Gas Co. v. ERC*, 307 U.S. App. D.C. 414, 28 F.3d 1281, 1283 84 (D.C. Cir. 1994), as the plaintiffs seem to acknowledge by their silence on the subject.

The agencies argue that the terms of the Act in fact demonstrate that fallback may be classified as a discharge. The Act defines a discharge as the addition of any pollutant to navigable waters, 33 U.S.C. §§ 1362(12), and defines "pollutant" to include "dredged spoil," as well as "rock," "sand," and "cellar dirt." *Id.* §§ 1362(6). The Corps in turn defines "dredged material" as "material that is excavated or dredged from waters of the United States," 33 C.F.R. § 323.2(c), a definition that is not challenged here. Thus, according to the agencies, wetland soil, sediment, debris or other material in the waters of the United States undergoes a legal metamorphosis during the dredging process, becoming a "pollutant" for purposes of the Act. If a portion of the material being dredged then falls back into the water, there has been an addition of a pollutant to the waters of the United States. Indeed, according to appellants National Wildlife Federation et al. ("NWF"), who intervened as defendants below, this reasoning demonstrates that regulation of redeposit is actually required by the Act.

We agree with the plaintiffs, and with the district court, that the straightforward statutory term "addition" cannot reasonably be said to encompass the situation in which material is removed from the waters of the United States and a small portion of it happens to fall back. Because incidental fallback represents a net withdrawal, not an addition, of material, it cannot be a discharge. As we concluded recently in a related context, "the nearest evidence we have of definitional intent by Congress reflects, as might be expected, that the word 'discharge' contemplates the addition, not the withdrawal, of a substance or substances." *North Carolina v. FERC*, 112 F.3d 1175, 1187, 324 U.S. App. D.C. 209 (D.C. Cir. 1997). The agencies' primary counterargument — that fallback constitutes an "addition of any pollutant" because material becomes a pollutant only upon being dredged — is ingenious but unconvincing. Regardless of any legal metamorphosis that may occur at the moment of dredging, we fail to see how there can be an addition of dredged material when there is no addition of material. Although the Act includes "dredged spoil" in its list of pollutants, 33 U.S.C. § 1362(6), Congress could not have contemplated that the attempted removal of 100 tons of that substance could constitute an addition simply because only 99 tons of it were actually taken away.

[Remainder of opinion omitted.]

NOTES AND QUESTIONS

1. *Compare.* For a contrary view on this question of statutory interpretation, see *United States v. Deaton*, 209 F.3d 331, 335 (4th Cir. 2000):

> . . . the statute does not prohibit the addition of material; it prohibits "the addition of any pollutant." The idea that there could be an addition of a pollutant without an addition of material seems to us entirely unremarkable, at least when an activity transforms some material from a nonpollutant into a pollutant, as occurred here. In the course of digging a ditch across the [defendant's] property, the contractor removed earth and vegetable matter from the wetland. Once it was removed, that material became "dredged spoil," a statutory pollutant and a type of material that up until then was not present on the [defendant's] property. It is of no consequence that what is now dredged spoil was previously present on the same property in the less threatening form of dirt and vegetation in an undisturbed state. What is important is that once the material was excavated from the wetland, its redeposit in that same wetland added a pollutant where none had been before. *See* 33 U.S.C. § 1362(6), (12). Thus, even under the definition of "addition" (that is, "something added") . . . sidecasting adds a pollutant that was not present before.

2. *Regulations.* The EPA and Corps have issued regulations regarding incidental fallback, most recently in 2008. 40 C.F.R. § 232.2(2)(ii) (EPA definition); 33 U.S.C. § 323.2(2)(ii) (Corps definition).

3. *Mitigation; General Permits.* Wetlands permitting requirements call for minimizing adverse effects to aquatic ecosystems. If adverse impacts are foreseeable, § 404 permits typically require mitigation. Mitigation can take the form of restoration, enhancement of an existing wetland, or even creation of a new one. It can also mean payment of a fee to an environmental group or other third party to accomplish the same ends.

There are efforts in place to make the trek toward wetlands protection less onerous and unfriendly to landowners. In a great many cases, persons need not secure individual permits under § 404. The Corps of Engineers reported in 1996, for example, that 83% of its § 404 permits were approved under a general permit. The Corps has also issued "nationwide" permits to authorize and regulate activities affecting particularly small wetlands.

4.   *Exemptions.* Section 404 allows for two exemptions from the permitting requirement. Under § 404(f)(1), a permit is not required for either: (1) the discharge of dredged or fill material "from normal farming, silviculture, and ranching activities such a plowing, seeding, cultivating, minor drainage, harvesting for the production of food, fiber, and forest products, or upland soil and water conservation practices," 33 U.S.C. § 1344(f)(1)(A); or (2) the discharge of dredged or fill material "for the purpose of . . . the maintenance of drainage ditches." 33 U.S.C. § 1344(f)(1)(C).

Under COE and EPA regulations, the "normal farming activities" exemption is available only for discharges that are "part of an established (i.e., on-going) farming . . . operation." Thus, the exemption is unavailable either: (1) for "activities which bring an area into farming . . . use"; or (2) where "modifications to the hydrological regime are necessary to resume operations." 33 C.F.R. § 323.4(a)(1)(ii) (1993); 40 C.F.R. § 232.3(c)(1)(ii)(A), (B) (1993).

Even if § 404(f)(1) exempts a discharge from the permit requirement, the discharge may be "recaptured":

> Any discharge of dredged or fill material into the navigable waters incidental to any activity having as its purpose bringing an area of the navigable waters into a use to which it was not previously subject, where the flow or circulation of navigable waters may be impaired or the reach of such waters be reduced, shall be required to have a permit under this section.

Section 404(f)(2), 33 U.S.C. § 1344(f)(2). The regulations further provide that "[a] conversion of a section 404 wetland to a non-wetland is a change in use of an area of waters of the United States," 33 C.F.R. § 323.4(c), and states as an example, that "a permit will be required for the conversion of a cypress swamp to some other use . . . when there is a discharge of dredged or fill material into waters of the United Stated in conjunction with construction of . . . structures used to effect such conversion." *Id.*

5.   *Sections 404 and 306.* When the same discharge falls under both § 402 and § 404, the latter provision typically governs, because § 402 expressly yields to § 404 in that event. Section 402(a)(1), 33 U.S.C.A. § 1342(a)(1). In a recent case, however, the issue was § 404 as compared to § 306, 33 U.S.C.A. § 1316, the new source performance standards provision. *See supra.* Section 306 declares unlawful any discharge of pollutants, including fill material typically regulated under § 404, that fails to meet its performance standards. Section 306(e), 33 U.S.C.A. § 1316(e). But Section 306 fails to resolve how it should interplay with § 404. The question, therefore, was whether such discharges are free from new source performance standards. In other words, would the Corps of Engineers have the obligation of assuring compliance with EPA's § 306 performance standards even as it issued § 404 permits? EPA took the view that § 306 standards should be inapplicable: in its opinion, since § 402 is not relevant in these circumstances, nor should § 306 be relevant. The EPA interpretation was upheld 6-3 by the Supreme Court. *Coeur Alaska, Inc. v. Southeast Alaska Conservation Council*, 557 U.S. 261, 129 S. Ct. 2458 (2009).

6. ***State of Wetlands.*** According to EPA, there remain in the 48 lower states about 105 million acres of wetlands, an area about the size of California. This is down from 221 million acres in place in the 1700s. The Natural Resources Inventory, assembled by the EPA in conjunction with Iowa State University, has concluded as follows: between 1992 and 1997, the annual net loss of wetlands on non-federal land in the United States came to 28,000 acres per year (margin of error: 72%). Between 1997 and 2001, there was an annual net gain of 26,000 acres per year (margin of error: 82%). From 2001 to 2003, there was an additional net gain of 72,000 acres per year (margin of error: 90%). Natural Resources Conservation Service, 2003 NRI Wetlands Tables, www.nrcs.usda.gov/technical/land/nri03/table4.html. A more recent study found that wetlands increased by an average of 32,000 acres per year from 1998 to 2004. The amount of wetlands remains in 2011 essentially as it was between 2004 to 2009. Report to Congress, Status and Trends of Wetlands in the Conterminous United States, 2004–2009.

According to Secretary of the Interior Ken Salazar, "[W]etlands are at a tipping point. While we have made great strides in conserving and restoring wetlands since the 1950s when we were losing an area equal to half the size of Rhode Island each year, we remain on a downward trend that is alarming." Statement of Oct. 6, 2011. *See generally* http://water.epa.gov/type/wetlands/vital_status.cfm.

7. ***Ancillary Programs.*** By separate legislation, the federal government funds "water bank" programs and "wetland reserve" programs to encourage farmers to preserve, restore, and improve high priority wetlands. Landowners who agree to do this receive compensation from the Department of Agriculture.

Chapter 11

THE RESOURCE CONSERVATION AND RECOVERY ACT

"Don't blow it — good planets are hard to find." TIME Magazine (author unknown).

SYNOPSIS

A. INTRODUCTION

B. SUBCHAPTER IV — SOLID WASTE REGULATION

C. SUBCHAPTER III — HAZARDOUS WASTE REGULATION

   1. Applicability

   2. Regulatory Structure

   3. Hazardous and Solid Waste Amendments of 1984

      a. Land Disposal Restrictions

      b. Corrective Action

      c. Underground Storage Tanks

A. INTRODUCTION

It became clear after the enactments of the Clean Air Act in 1970 and the Clean Water Act in 1972 that land was becoming comparatively attractive as a medium for waste disposal. Not only was land largely unprotected by federal law, but with air and surface water off-limits, it was a logical default choice. Accordingly, the Resource Conservation and Recovery Act, or "RCRA" (usually pronounced "Ricra"), was enacted in 1976 as the last of the big three pollution control statutes. RCRA's purpose was to "close the loop," to protect land, in both its surface and its subterranean reaches, from pollution.

Congress's primary concern in enacting RCRA was to ensure that wastes would be managed safely. H.R. Rep. No. 1491, 94th Cong., 2d Sess. 3 (1976). As expressed in its statutory findings, Congress had come to the understanding that:

> the economic and population growth of our Nation, and the improvements in the standard of living enjoyed by our population, have required increased industrial production to meet our needs, and have made necessary the demolition of old buildings, the construction of new buildings, and the provision of highways and other avenues of transportation, which, together with related industrial, commercial, and agricultural operations, have resulted in a rising tide of scrap, discarded, and waste materials.

Section 1002(a), 42 U.S.C. § 6901(a). Thus, Congress wanted "to reduce the amount of waste and unsalvageable materials and to provide for proper and economical solid waste disposal practices," § 1002(a)(4), 42 U.S.C. § 6901(a)(4), thereby to ensure the protection of human health and the environment. Section 1003, 42 U.S.C. § 6902.

RCRA is divided into numerous subtitles, two of which establish major regulatory regimes. Subchapter IV deals with regulation of disposal of "solid waste." Section 1004(27) of the statute, 42 U.S.C. § 9603(27), gives the primary definition of "solid waste" and should be scrutinized. The definition, you will observe, contains exclusions; these exclusions play a large role in determining the reach of the statute. Subchapter III, which will receive the majority of our attention, regulates disposal of "hazardous waste." Note that hazardous wastes *are* solid wastes; they are merely solid wastes of a particular kind.

Since a solid or hazardous waste must first be a "waste," we begin there.

AMERICAN MINING CONGRESS v. U.S. ENVIRONMENTAL PROTECTION AGENCY ("*AMC I*")
824 F.2d 1177 (D.C. Cir. 1987)

STARR, CIRCUIT JUDGE:

These consolidated cases arise out of EPA's regulation of hazardous wastes under the Resource Conservation and Recovery Act of 1976 ("RCRA"), as amended, 42 U.S.C. §§ 6901 6933 (1982 & Supp. III 1985). Petitioners, trade associations representing mining and oil refining interests, challenge regulations promulgated by EPA that amend the definition of "solid waste" to establish and define the agency's authority to regulate secondary materials reused within an industry's ongoing production process. In plain English, petitioners maintain that EPA has exceeded its regulatory authority in seeking to bring materials that are not discarded or otherwise disposed of within the compass of "waste."

RCRA is a comprehensive environmental statute under which EPA is granted authority to regulate solid and hazardous wastes. RCRA was enacted in 1976, and amended in 1978, 1980, and 1984. See The Quiet Communities Act of 1978, Pub. L. No. 95-609, 92 Stat. 3081; The Solid Waste Disposal Act Amendments of 1980, Pub. L. No. 96-482, 94 Stat. 2334; Hazardous and Solid Waste Amendments of 1984, Pub. L. No. 98-616, 98 Stat. 3221. . . .

RCRA includes two major parts: one deals with non-hazardous solid waste management and the other with hazardous waste management. Under the latter, EPA is directed to promulgate regulations establishing a comprehensive management system. *Id.* § 6921. EPA's authority, however, extends only to the regulation of "hazardous waste." Because "hazardous waste" is defined as a subset of "solid waste," *id* § 6903(5), the scope of EPA's jurisdiction is limited to those materials that constitute "solid waste." That pivotal term is defined by RCRA as

> any garbage, refuse, sludge from a waste treatment plant, water supply treatment plant, or air pollution control facility and other discarded material, including solid, liquid, semisolid or contained gaseous material,

resulting from industrial, commercial, mining, and agricultural operations, and from community activities. . . .

42 U.S.C. § 6903(27) (emphasis added). As will become evident, this case turns on the meaning of the phrase, "and other discarded material," contained in the statute's definitional provisions.

EPA's interpretation of "solid waste" has evolved over time. . . .

After receiving extensive comments, EPA issued its final rule on January 4, 1985. 50 Fed. Reg. 614 (1985). Under the final rule, materials are considered "solid waste" if they are abandoned by being disposed of, burned, or incinerated; or stored, treated, or accumulated before or in lieu of those activities. In addition, certain recycling activities fall within EPA's definition. EPA determines whether a material is a RCRA solid waste when it is recycled by examining both the material or substance itself and the recycling of "secondary materials" (spent materials, sludges, by-products, commercial chemical products, and scrap metal). These "secondary materials" constitute "solid waste" when they are disposed of; burned for energy recovery or used to produce a fuel; reclaimed; or accumulated speculatively. *Id.* at 618–19, 664. Under the final rule, if a material constitutes "solid waste," it is subject to RCRA regulation unless it is directly reused as an ingredient or as an effective substitute for a commercial product, or is returned as a raw material substitute to its original manufacturing process. In the jargon of the trade, the latter category is known as the "closed-loop" exception. In either case, the material must not first be "reclaimed" (processed to recover a usable product or regenerated). EPA exempts these activities "because they are like ordinary usage of commercial products." *Id.* at 619. . . .

II

Petitioners, American Mining Congress ("AMC") and American Petroleum Institute ("API"), challenge the scope of EPA's final rule. Relying upon the statutory definition of "solid waste," petitioners contend that EPA's authority under RCRA is limited to controlling materials that are discarded or intended for discard. They argue that EPA's reuse and recycle rules, as applied to in-process secondary materials, regulate materials that have not been discarded, and therefore exceed EPA's jurisdiction. . . .

III

We observe at the outset of our inquiry that EPA's interpretation of the scope of its authority under RCRA has been unclear and unsteady. As previously recounted, EPA has shifted from its vague "sometimes discarded" approach of 1980 to a proposed exclusion from regulation of all materials used or reused as effective substitutes for raw materials in 1983, and finally, to a very narrow exclusion of essentially only materials processed within the meaning of the "closed-loop" exception under the final rule. We emphasize, therefore, that we are confronted with neither a consistent nor a long-standing agency interpretation. Under settled doctrine, "[a]n agency interpretation of a relevant provision which conflicts with the agency's earlier interpretation is 'entitled to considerably less deference' than a consistently held agency view." [citations omitted]. . . .

B

Guided by these principles, we turn to the statutory provision at issue here. Congress, it will be recalled, granted EPA power to regulate "solid waste." Congress specifically defined "solid waste" as "discarded material." EPA then defined "discarded material" to include materials destined for reuse in an industry's ongoing production processes. The challenge to EPA's jurisdictional reach is founded, again, on the proposition that in-process secondary materials are outside the bounds of EPA's lawful authority. Nothing has been discarded, the argument goes, and thus RCRA jurisdiction remains untriggered.

1

The first step in statutory interpretation is, of course, an analysis of the language itself. . . . Here, Congress defined "solid waste" as "discarded material." The ordinary, plain-English meaning of the word "discarded" is "disposed of," "thrown away" or "abandoned." Encompassing materials retained for immediate reuse within the scope of "discarded material" strains, to say the least, the everyday usage of that term. . . .

Although the "ordinary and obvious meaning of the [statutory] phrase is not to be lightly discounted," . . . [citation omitted] . . . , we are hesitant to attribute decisive significance to the ordinary meaning of statutory language. To be sure, our inquiry might well and wisely stop with the plain language of the statute, since it is the statute itself that Congress enacts and the President signs into law. But as the Supreme Court recently observed, the "more natural interpretation" (or plain meaning) is not necessarily determinative. . . . And it is not infrequently said, odd as it may seem in a society governed by codified and thus knowable rules, that a matter may be within the letter of a statute but not within its spirit. . . .

In short, a complete analysis of the statutory term "discarded" calls for more than resort to the ordinary, everyday meaning of the specific language at hand. For, "the sense in which [a term] is used in a statute must be determined by reference to the purpose of the particular legislation." . . .

As we previously recounted, the broad objectives of RCRA are "to promote the protection of health and the environment and to conserve valuable material and energy resources. . . ." 42 U.S.C. § 6902. But that goal is of majestic breadth, and it is dif cult . . . to pour meaning into a highly specific term by resort to grand purposes. Somewhat more specifically, we have seen that RCRA was enacted in response to Congressional findings that the "rising tide of scrap, discarded, and waste materials" generated by consumers and increased industrial production has presented heavily populated urban communities with "serious financial, manage-ment, intergovernmental, and technical problems in the disposal of solid wastes." *Id.* § 6901(a). In light of this problem, Congress determined that "federal action through financial and technical assistance and leadership in the development, demonstration, and application of new and improved methods and processes to reduce the amount of waste and unsalvageable materials and to provide for proper and economical solid waste disposal practices was necessary." *Id.* Also animating Congress were its findings that "disposal of solid and hazardous waste "without careful planning and management presents a danger to human health and the environment; that methods to "separate usable materials from solid waste" should be employed; and that usable energy can be produced from solid waste. *Id.* § 6901(b), (c), (d).

The question we face, then, is whether, in light of the National Legislature's expressly stated objectives and the underlying problems that motivated it to enact RCRA in the first instance, Congress was using the term "discarded" in its ordinary sense — "disposed of" or "abandoned" — or whether Congress was using it in a much more open-ended way, so as to encompass materials no longer useful in their original capacity though destined for immediate reuse in another phase of the industry's ongoing production process.

For the following reasons, we believe the former to be the case. RCRA was enacted, as the Congressional objectives and findings make clear, in an effort to help States deal with the ever-increasing problem of solid waste disposal by encouraging the search for and use of alternatives to existing methods of disposal (including recycling) and protecting health and the environment by regulating hazardous wastes. To fulfill these purposes, it seems clear that EPA need not regulate "spent" materials that are recycled and reused in an ongoing manufacturing or industrial process. These materials have not yet become part of the waste disposal problem; rather, they are destined for beneficial reuse or recycling in a continuous process by the generating industry itself. . . .

In sum, our analysis of the statute reveals clear Congressional intent to extend EPA's authority only to materials that are truly discarded, disposed of, thrown away, or abandoned. . . .

IV

We are constrained to conclude that, in light of the language and structure of RCRA, the problems animating Congress to enact it, and the relevant portions of the legislative history, Congress clearly and unambiguously expressed its intent that "solid waste" (and therefore EPA's regulatory authority) be limited to materials that are "discarded" by virtue of being disposed of, abandoned, or thrown away. While we do not lightly overturn an agency's reading of its own statute, we are persuaded that by regulating in-process secondary materials, EPA has acted in contravention of Congress' intent. Accordingly, the petition for review is *Granted.*

[Dissent by Mikva, Circuit Judge, omitted.]

NOTES

1. Additional Authority. *Accord Association of Battery Recyclers, Inc. v. U.S. Environmental Protection Agency*, 208 F.3d 1047 (D.C. Cir. 2000) (secondary materials stored and intended for reuse in another phase of an industrial process are not "discarded" for purposes of RCRA).

2. Compare:

(A) Owen Electric Steel Co. v. Browner, 37 F.3d 146, 149–50 (4th Cir. 1994). [In *Owen*, the issue was whether so-called "KO61" slag, left untouched for six months before sale to other entities, was a "waste" for purposes of RCRA.] Were *AMC I* the final case offering interpretation of the phrase "discarded material," Owen might be victorious here: because Owen's slag is eventually recycled, it cannot be said to have been discarded. Subsequent cases, however, have read *AMC I* narrowly. First, in *American Petroleum Institute v. EPA*, 906 F.2d 729, 285 U.S. App. D.C. 35 (D.C. Cir. 1990), the EPA asserted that the District of Columbia Circuit's holding in *AMC I* precluded it from regulating as waste hazardous slag that was delivered to a plant for metal reclamation. The court of appeals held otherwise, explaining:

> . . . The issue in *AMC [I]* was whether the EPA could, under the RCRA, treat as "solid wastes" "materials that are recycled and reused in an ongoing manufacturing or industrial process." [*AMC I*, 824F.2d at 1186.] We held that it could not because these materials have not yet become part of the waste disposal problem; rather, they are destined for beneficial reuse or recycling in a continuous process by the generating industry itself. *Id.* Materials subject to such a process were not "discarded" because they were never "disposed of, abandoned, or thrown away." *Id.* at 1193.

> *AMC [I]* is by no means dispositive of EPA's authority to regulate K061 slag. Unlike the materials in question in *AMC [I]*, K061 is indisputably "discarded" before being subject to metals reclamation. Consequently, it has "become part of the waste disposal problem . . ."

> [W]e glean that the fundamental inquiry in determining whether a by-product has been "discarded" is whether the by product is immediately recycled for use in the same industry; if not, then the by-product is justifiably seen as "part of the waste disposal problem," *AMC I*, 824 F.2d at 1186, and therefore as a "solid waste."

(B) Connecticut Coastal Fisherman Ass'n v. Remington Arms Co., 989 F.2d 1305 (2d Cir. 1993): Lead shot and clay targets accumulated in Long Island Sound constitute "discarded materials," and accordingly are solid wastes for purposes of RCRA, because they have accumulated "long enough." (The court declined to specify how long a time is necessary for materials to qualify as "stored.")

(C) American Mining Congress v. United States EPA, 907 F.2d 1179 (D.C. Cir. 1990) (" AMC II"). [In *AMC II*, petitioners, relying on *AMC I*, claimed that three hazardous substances were not wastes on the basis that "sludges [containing the substances] from wastewater that are stored in surface impoundments and that may at some time in the future be reclaimed are not 'discarded.' " *AMC II*, 907 F.2d at 1186. The court of appeals rejected petitioners' reading of *AMC I*, stating]:

> Petitioners read *AMC [I]* too broadly. *AMC [I]'* s holding concerned only materials that are "destined for immediate reuse in another phase of the industry's ongoing production process," *Id.* at 1185 (emphasis added), and that "have not yet become part of the waste disposal problem," *Id.* at 1186. Nothing in *AMC[I]* prevents the agency from treating as "discarded" the wastes at issue in this case, which are managed in land disposal units

that are part of wastewater treatment systems, which have therefore become "part of the waste disposal problem," and which are not part of the ongoing industrial processes.

Id. at 1186 (emphasis omitted).

(D) *United States v. ILCO, Inc.,* **996 F.2d 1126 (11th Cir. 1993).** [ILCO, Inc. ("ILCO") purchased spent batteries from various sources, subsequently recycling them. It contended the activity of recycling was inconsistent with discarding, and since the materials were not discarded, they were not solid waste. The Eleventh Circuit disagreed:]

> ILCO argues that it has never "discarded" the plates and groups [of the batteries] and, therefore, the material it recycles is not "solid waste" as defined in [section] 6903(27). The lead plates and groups are, no doubt, valuable feedstock for a smelting process. Nevertheless, EPA, with congressional authority, promulgated regulations that classify these materials as "discarded solid waste." Somebody has discarded the battery in which these components are found. This fact does not change just because are claimer has purchased or finds value in the components.

Id. at 1131.

3. *Even if it is a Solid Waste, is it? See, e.g., Connecticut Coastal Fishermen's Ass'n. v. Remington Arms Co.*, 989 F.2d 1305 (2d Cir. 1993):

> The RCRA regulations create a dichotomy in the definition of solid waste. The EPA distinguishes between RCRA's regulatory and remedial purposes and offers a different definition of solid waste depending upon the statutory context in which the term appears. In its amicus brief, the EPA tells us that the regulatory definition of solid waste — found at 40 C.F.R. § 261.2(a) — is narrower than its statutory counterpart. The regulations define solid waste as "any discarded material" and further define discarded material as that which is "abandoned." 40 C.F.R. § 261.2(a). Materials that are abandoned have been "disposed of." 40 C.F.R. § 261.2(b). According to RCRA regulations, this definition of solid waste "applies only to wastes that also are hazardous for purposes of the regulations implementing Subtitle C of RCRA." 40 C.F.R. § 261.1(b)(1). As previously noted, Subtitle C [Subchapter III] contains more stringent handling standards for hazardous waste, and hazardous waste is a subset of solid waste.

Id. at 1314.

The opinion then discusses EPA's regulatory decision to apply the broader definition with respect to both "imminent hazard" lawsuits brought under § 2003, 42 U.S.C. § 6973, and citizen suits, brought under § 7002, 42 U.S.C. § 6972:

> We recognize the anomaly of using different definitions for the term "solid waste" and that such view further complicates an already complex statute. Yet, we believe on balance that the EPA regulations reasonably interpret the statutory language. Hence, we defer to them. Dual definitions of solid waste are suggested by the structure and language of RCRA. Congress in Subchapter III isolated hazardous wastes for more stringent

regulatory treatment. Recognizing the serious responsibility that such regulations impose, Congress required that hazardous waste — a subset of solid waste as defined in the RCRA regulations — be clearly identified. The statute directs the EPA to develop specific "criteria" for the identification of hazardous wastes as well as to publish a list of particular hazardous wastes. 42 U.S.C. § 6921(a) & (b). By way of contrast, Subchapter IV that empowers the EPA to publish "guidelines" for the identification of problem solid waste pollution areas, does not require explanation beyond RCRA's statutory definition of what constitutes solid waste. *Id.* § 6942(a). Hence, the words of the statute contemplate that the EPA would refine and narrow the definition of solid waste for the sole purpose of Subchapter III regulation and enforcement.

Id. at 1315.

4. *Postscript.* EPA continues to tinker with the regulatory definition of "solid waste." At this writing, the regulation follows the lead of the above-discussed cases, characterizing as "discarded" materials that are "abandoned," "recycled," or "considered inherently waste-like." "Abandoned" materials are those disposed of, burned or incinerated, or accumulated, stored or treated before, or in lieu of, being abandoned. "Recycled" materials are those used in a manner constituting disposal, burned for energy recovery, reclaimed, or accumulated speculatively. Materials "inherently waste-like" are those so specified and determined by the Administrator as meeting a list of criteria. *See* 40 C.F.R. § 261.2. EPA has also specified a lengthy list of materials which shall not be considered as solid waste for purposes of RCRA. 40 C.F.R. § 261.4(a).

In June 2010, EPA reached a settlement agreement with the Sierra Club in which it promised to again revise the definition. *Sierra Club v. EPA*, 2010 U.S. App. LEXIS 12020 (D.C. Cir. June 10, 2010).

B. SUBCHAPTER IV — SOLID WASTE REGULATION

Solid wastes are routinely disposed in municipal solid waste landfills. Estimates are that over 220 million tons of solid waste materials were disposed in the year 2000 alone. RCRA-regulated solid waste landfills are discrete areas of land that receive household waste, and in some instances, commercial and industrial non-hazardous waste. They can be publicly or privately owned. Legally, they are distinguishable from other waste disposal units, such as land application units, surface impoundments, injection wells, and waste piles, which are regulated under the Clean Water Act and the Safe Drinking Water Act.

Solid waste disposal in landfills is regulated under Subchapter IV of RCRA. The Subchapter prohibits "open dumps" and requires the regulation of "sanitary landfills" by states or tribes, subject to EPA approval. Sections 4002 and 4003, 42 U.S.C. §§ 6942 and 6943. The EPA has established a set of requirements for construction and operation of these sanitary landfills. *See* 40 C.F.R. § 256.01 et seq. In the main, sanitary landfills must be operated in a manner designed to reduce or eliminate the formation of leachate and the release of leachate materials into groundwater.

EPA's regulations control sanitary landfills in six particulars:

- *location*: as a general matter, landfills must not be located near airports, flood plains, wetlands, fault areas, seismic impact zones, or unstable areas;

- *operation:* operators of municipal landfills may not receive hazardous waste and must set up a system, including inspections, record keeping, and personnel training, to detect hazardous wastes that might be mixed in with a drop-off load. To reduce or eliminate leachate, operators must cover disposed wastes with at least six inches of earthen material at the end of each working day. For the same reason, they must also prevent storm waters from running on to active parts of the landfill. Waters that do run off the landfill must be managed in compliance with the Clean Water Act. Operators must also control vectors, check for potentially explosive methane gas emissions, reduce air pollution from open burning, and restrict access by illegal dumpers and the public at large.

- *design:* new landfills (those that did not receive wastes before October 9, 1993) must be built to meet EPA's "Maximum Contaminant Levels" ("MCLs") (federal drinking water standards established under the Safe Drinking Water Act) at a "relevant point of compliance." This is a performance-based requirement that means that a landfill may not contaminate groundwater beyond a certain amount (the MCL) as measured at a pre-determined point, one no farther than 150 meters from the landfill's outer boundary and on the landfill property. Meeting this standard requires different actions at different sites. Meeting the standard gets expensive, for example, if soils are permeable and the climate is wet. In such circumstances, the landfill will likely need a composite liner, typically a flexible sheet of synthetic material set over a two-foot base of impermeable soil, and a leachate collection system to reduce amounts of leachate collecting over the liner to less than 30 centimeters.

Model of Landfill with Leachate Removal Capacity

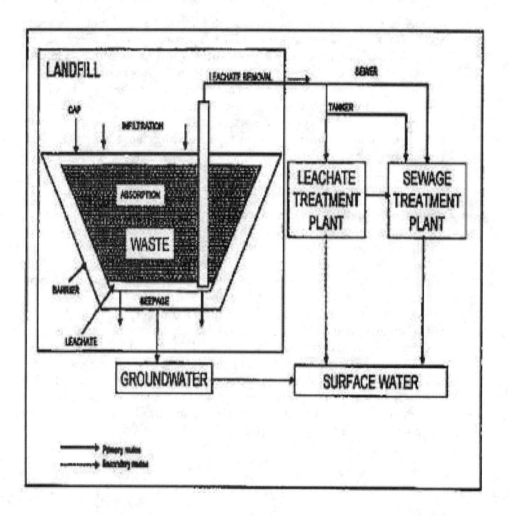

- *groundwater monitoring and corrective action:* monitoring systems allow for the sampling and analysis of groundwater in the immediate vicinity of the landfill to assess whether any leachate is making its way out of the impoundment. How extensive the system must be depends on geographic and climatic considerations, and the requirement can even be waived in some cases. If it is determined that groundwater has been contaminated by the landfill in violation of applicable standards, cleanup is required, by whatever appropriate methods.

- *closure and post-closure:* after disposal activity ceases, landfills must be "closed." A major closure requirement is the emplacement of an imperme-able "final cover" of at least 18 inches of earthen material and an additional erosion-control layer of at least another six inches of Earth capable of supporting foliage. Additionally, owners and operators must ensure the integrity of the landfill for 30 years thereafter. Deeds used to transfer title to the property in the future must note the land's prior use and must restrict future use appropriately.

- *financial assurance:* owners and operators must demonstrate sufficient financial strength to meet all of the construction, operation, closure, and post-closure requirements.

Small landfills, which comprise approximately 50% of all municipal landfills, may secure a partial exemption from these requirements for reasons of cost. Defined as landfills that dispose of less than 20 tons of municipal solid waste per day, averaged yearly, these facilities typically serve communities of fewer than 10,000 people. Owners and operators of small landfills may be exempted from design, monitoring, and corrective action requirements if there is no evidence of groundwater contamination, no practical waste management alternative, and the landfill is located in an area that receives less than 25 inches of precipitation per year, *or* if there is no evidence of groundwater contamination and the community endures an annual surface transportation interruption lasting at least three consecutive months (this latter exemption applies mainly to communities in difficult weather areas, such as in less developed reaches of Alaska).

Whether landfilling or recycling solid waste is preferable is a subject of debate. Some persons, maintaining that landfills are inherently not protective of human health, argue that recycling should be the national policy. Others argue that landfills are safe, are more economical than recycling, and can serve the nation's needs easily for at least the next one thousand years. For an interesting, if somewhat dated, article making the latter case, see John Tierney, *Recycling is Garbage*, N.Y. TIMES (MAG.), June 30, 1996.

While many municipalities have established voluntary recycling programs, some have gone beyond recycling wastes to a strategy of reducing the volume of such wastes. These municipalities would revolutionize the current system of solid waste disposal by using "unit-based pricing" systems, also known as "pay as you throw" programs. Unit-based pricing programs charge households by the bag, or by weight, or by container, for their wastes, thus creating an economic disincentive to waste generation. With such a system, individual payment amounts are better tailored to the landfill services each customer uses. Some concerns about unit-based pricing involve how to charge multi-family housing areas for trash removal, and how to allay increased financial burdens on large families (which generate relatively more waste) and poor families (which have less ability to pay for landfilling services).

NOTE

In 2009, the latest year for which information is available, Americans generated about 243 million tons of trash and they recycled and composted 82 million tons of this material, equivalent to a 33.8 percent recycling rate. Source: EPA.

C. SUBCHAPTER III[1] — HAZARDOUS WASTE REGULATION

1. Applicability

MOBIL OIL CORP. v. U.S. ENVIRONMENTAL PROTECTION AGENCY
35 F.3d 579 (D.C. Cir. 1994)

JUDGES: Before EDWARDS, BUCKLEY, and RANDOLPH, CIRCUIT JUDGES.

BUCKLEY, CIRCUIT JUDGE:

Petitioners raise numerous challenges to the "mixture" and "derived-from" rules promulgated by the Environmental Protection Agency under authority of Subtitle C of the Resource Conservation and Recovery Act of 1976 ("RCRA"), 42 U.S.C. §§ 6901-92k (1988 & Supp. IV 1992). We do not address these challenges, however, because we conclude that subsequent congressional action has rendered the dispute moot. Petitioners American Mining Congress and The Fertilizer Institute also challenge the so-called "Bevill mixture rule," promulgated under the same authority, which we vacate in part.

I. BACKGROUND

RCRA provides a comprehensive scheme for handling solid wastes. As part of this regime, Subchapter III, 42U.S.C. §§ 6921-6939b (1988 & Supp. IV 1992) ("Subtitle C"), subjects hazardous wastes to stringent cradle-to-grave regulation. The statute defines "hazardous waste" as a solid waste, or combination of solid wastes, which because of its quantity, concentration, or physical, chemical, or infectious characteristics may —

(A) cause, or significantly contribute to an increase in mortality or an increase in serious irreversible, or incapacitating reversible, illness; or

(B) pose a substantial present or potential hazard to human health or the environment when improperly treated, stored, transported, or disposed of, or otherwise managed.

42 U.S.C. § 6903(5) (1988). Subtitle C also established a two-step process for the identification of hazardous wastes: The EPA would first promulgate criteria for identifying the "characteristics" of hazardous waste, "taking into account toxicity, persistence, and degradability in nature, potential for accumulation in tissue, and other related factors such as flammability, corrosiveness, and other hazardous characteristics." *Id.* § 6921(a) (1988).Then, on the basis of those criteria, the EPA would "promulgate regulations identifying the characteristics of hazardous waste, and listing particular hazardous wastes (within the meaning of section 6903(5) of

---

[1] Subchapter III is often referred to as "Subtitle C."

this title), which shall be subject to the provisions of [Subtitle C]." *Id.* § 6921(b)(1).

Pursuant to this mandate, the EPA issued proposed rules in 1978. 43 Fed. Reg. 58,946 (1978). In that proposal, the EPA stated that it would identify hazardous wastes on the basis of the following characteristics: ignitability, corrosivity, reactivity and toxicity. 43 Fed. Reg. at 58,950, 58,955–57. Wastes displaying any of these characteristics were to be listed, as were wastes that independently satisfied the statutory definition of "hazardous waste" contained in 42 U.S.C. § 6903(5). 43 Fed. Reg. at 58,955, col. 2. A listed waste would remain subject to Subtitle C regulation until it was certified to the EPA that the waste was "non-hazardous according to the results of each characteristic or property tested." 43 Fed. Reg. at 58,953, col. 3.

The EPA issued its final rule on May 19, 1980, in which it published a list of some 400 hazardous wastes. 45 Fed. Reg. 33,084, 33,122 27 (1980). The final rule also promulgated the "mixture" and "derived-from" rules. The mixture rule provided that a solid waste would be treated as hazardous if "it is a mixture of solid waste and one or more [listed] hazardous wastes. . . ." *Id.* at 33,119, col.3. The derived-from rule provided that

> any solid waste generated from the treatment, storage, or disposal of a hazardous waste, including any sludge, spill residue, ash, emission control dust or leachate (but not including precipitation run-off) is a hazardous waste.

45 Fed. Reg. at 33,120, col. 1. Thus a substance that was mixed with a listed hazardous waste or derived from a hazardous waste was to be regulated as a hazardous waste regardless of whether the mixture or derivative actually "pose[d] a substantial present or potential hazard to human health or the environment. . . ." 42 U.S.C. § 6903(5). Any mixture or derived-from waste, however, could escape Subtitle C regulation through a "delisting" process. *See* 45 Fed. Reg. at 33,116, col. 3 (waste may be delisted if demonstrated that it is non-hazardous "based on the results of specific tests for each of the hazardous properties for which the waste was listed").

The initial promulgation of the mixture and derived-from rules was challenged on both substantive and procedural grounds. On December 6, 1991, we vacated both rules because the EPA had "entirely failed to comply with [the Administrative Procedure Act's ("APA")] notice-and-comment requirements. . . ." *Shell Oil Co. v. EPA*, 950 F.2d 741, 752, 292 U.S. App. D.C. 332 (D.C. Cir. 1991). As we disposed of the case on procedural grounds, we did not determine whether the EPA had exceeded its authority under RCRA in issuing the rules.

On March 3, 1992, the EPA issued an "interim final rule," reinstating the vacated mixture and derived-from rules under authority of the APA's "good cause" exception, 5 U.S.C. § 553(b)(3)(B), which permits the issuance of a rule without notice and prior opportunity for comment on a finding that such are "impractical, unnecessary, or contrary to the public interest." 57 Fed. Reg. 7,628, 7,628-29(1992). In doing so, the EPA sought to obtain "the time to sort through more fully the implications of alternative regulatory approaches and understand the scope and effect of current Subtitle C rules." 57 Fed. Reg. at 7,630, col. 3. The EPA promised to publish options for modifying or replacing the rules by April 28, 1992; and it included a provision terminating the interim final rules on April 28, 1993 ("sunset provision"). *Id.*

The promised revisions were issued on May 20, 1992. These included a "Hazardous Waste Identification Rule" ("HWIR") that would effect "modifications to the RCRA regulatory framework which will address over-regulatory situations created by the 'mixture' and 'derived-from' rules." 57 Fed. Reg. 21,450, 21,452, col. 1 (1992). In the HWIR, the EPA conceded that the mixture and derived-from rules were overinclusive, resulting in a regime where "millions of tons of mixtures and derived-from residuals that must be managed as hazardous waste [under Subtitle C] because of their history (i.e., what they were mixed with or derived-from) may actually pose quite low hazards." *Id.* at 21,451, col. 3.

Five months later, on October 6, 1992, Congress adopted an amendment to an EPA appropriations bill that reads as follows:

> EPA shall promulgate revisions to paragraphs (a)(2)(iv) [the mixture rule] and (c)(2)(I) [the derived-from rule] of 40 C.F.R. 261.3, as reissued on March 3, 1992, by October 1, 1993, but any revision to such paragraphs shall not be promulgated or become effective prior to October 1, 1994. Notwithstanding paragraph (e) of 40 C.F.R. 261.3 [the "sunset provision"], as reissued on March 3, 1992, paragraphs (a)(2)(iv) and (c)(2)(I) of such regulations shall not be terminated or withdrawn until revisions are promulgated and become effective in accordance with the preceding sentence. The deadline of October 1,1994 shall be enforceable under section 7002 of the Solid Waste Disposal Act.

Pub. L. No. 102-389, 106 Stat. 1571, 1602 (Oct. 6, 1992) ("Chafee Amendment"). The EPA contends that this amendment codifies the mixture and derived-from rules, mooting petitioners' challenges thereto.

Three weeks later, the EPA issued notices announcing its withdrawal of the HWIR proposal and rescission of the sunset provision. 57 Fed. Reg. 49,280, 49,280, col. 1 (1992) (withdrawing HWIR proposal); 57 Fed. Reg.49,278, 49,278, col. 1 (withdrawing the sunset provision). In both notices, the EPA announced its intent to promulgate revisions to the mixture and derived-from rules within 12 to 24 months. 57 Fed. Reg. at 49,278, col.2; 57 Fed. Reg. at 49,280, col. 3. We are also asked to review the EPA's treatment of wastes consisting of a mixture of a "Bevill waste" and one or more hazardous wastes. Bevill wastes are derived from the extraction, beneficiation, and processing of ores and minerals and are exempted from Subtitle C regulation by virtue of the Bevill Amendment to RCRA, 42U.S.C. § 6921(b)(3)(A)(ii) (1988). *See generally Horsehead Resource Dev. Co. v. Browner*, 16 F.3d 1246, 305 U.S. App. D.C. 35 (D.C. Cir. 1994). In 1989, the EPA promulgated regulations determining which mineral processing wastes qualified as Bevill wastes. At the same time, the agency issued what petitioners refer to as the "Bevill mixture rule." The "Bevill mixture rule" had two distinct provisions that are relevant here. One provision described how mixtures of Bevill wastes and characteristic wastes were to be treated, while the other declared that mixtures of Bevill wastes and listed wastes were governed by the Subtitle C mixture rule. 54 Fed. Reg. 36,592, 36,622 23, 36,641 (1989). The Bevill mixture rule was contested in *Solite Corp. v. EPA*, 952 F.2d473, 293 U.S. App. D.C. 117 (D.C. Cir. 1991), where we concluded that, because the EPA had assumed the validity of the Subtitle C mixture rule in "extending it to the Bevill content," our decision in *Shell Oil* vacating and remanding the Subtitle C mixture rule required us to vacate and remand the Bevill mixture rule as well. *Id.* at 493–94. In the interim final rule, the EPA repromulgated the characteristic waste provision of the Bevill mixture rule as well as the Subtitle C mixture and derived-from rules. 57 Fed. Reg. 7,628–32. Petitioners American Mining Congress and The Fertilizer Institute ("Bevill petitioners") challenge that action. . . .

III. Conclusion

We hold that petitioners' challenges to the Subtitle C mixture and derived-from rules, including the EPA's interpretation of the former to apply to mixtures of Bevill and listed wastes, are moot because the Chafee Amendment has enacted those rules as so interpreted into law. We vacate the provision of the Bevill mixture rule concerning Bevill/characteristic waste mixtures because the provision was reissued without compliance with the rulemaking requirements of the APA.

So ordered.

NOTES AND QUESTIONS

1. ***Regulations.*** The regulatory definition of "hazardous waste" may be found at 40 C.F.R. § 261.3. In addition to promulgating a regulatory definition, EPA has specified certain solid wastes which shall not be regulated as hazardous. 40 C.F.R. § 261.4(b). It has also exempted certain narrow subsets of hazardous wastes from regulation. 40 C.F.R. § 261.4(c). Section 261.3 also contains the most recent iteration of the mixture rule, *Id.* at § 261.3(a)(2)(iv), and the derived-from rule, *Id.* at § 261.3(c)(2)(i).

2. ***Effective Date of Mixture Rule.*** With *Shell* invalidating the mixture rule on administrative law grounds, what about the efficacy of the rule prior to the effective date of the Chafee Amendment? *See United States v. Goodner Brothers Aircraft, Inc.*, 966 F.2d 380 (8th Cir. 1992) (indicating that *Shell* stands for the principle that the mixture rule was void *ab initio* and accordingly was not in effect until established by the Chafee Amendment); *United States v. Bethlehem Steel Co.*, 38 F.3d 862 (7th Cir. 1994) ("we must reject the notion that the policy behind the mixture rule is 'embodied' as a general principle within the definition [of 'hazardous waste'] and that such a principle may operate to reach wastes that would have been covered by the mixture rule, but for its invalidation").

3. ***Contained-in Policy.*** Not to be lost in this discussion is EPA's "Contained-in Policy," explained in an EPA memorandum dated November 13, 1986. The policy stipulates that any combination of a listed hazardous waste and a non-solid waste (e.g., soil or groundwater) is a hazardous waste for purposes of regulation under Subchapter III of RCRA so long as it contains the listed hazardous waste. The policy was upheld in *Chemical Waste Mgmt., Inc. v. U.S. Environmental Protection Agency*, 869 F.2d 1526 (D.C. Cir. 1989).

2. Regulatory Structure

Subchapter III of RCRA divides the regulated community into three groups: generators (§ 3002, 42 U.S.C. § 6922); transporters (§ 3003, 42 U.S.C. § 6823); and owners and operators of hazardous waste treatment, storage, or disposal facilities ("TSDs" or "TSDFs") (§ 3004 05, 42 U.S.C. § 6824 25). The terms "generator," "transporter," and "owner and operator" are undefined in the statute. All of these entities are regulated with the overall purpose of tracking hazardous waste from "cradle to grave." This means that wastes are controlled from initial generation, through transport from the generation site, up to and including final treatment or other disposition. The regulatory structure is summarized in the following paragraphs.

• *Generators:* As set forth in § 3002 and implementing regulations, generators have the responsibility of identifying wastes and caring for them while on site. (Generators may accumulate hazardous waste on site for ninety days without taking on the status of a hazardous waste storage facility regulable under § 3004.) When the time comes to remove wastes, generators must prepare a "manifest," *see* § 1004(12), 42 U.S.C. § 6903(12), designate the facility to which the wastes shall be transported, and package and mark the wastes in accordance with the particularized standards of regulations of EPA and the Department of Transportation ("DOT"). Generators must also prepare biennial reports for EPA on their activities and their compliance with the regulatory requirements. The regulations carve out exceptions for farmers who use pesticides: there is no need to comply with § 3002 standards so long as the farmer triple-rinses pesticide containers and disposes of residues on the farm consistent with pesticide package labels. *See* 40 C.F.R. Part 262.

• *Transporters:* Transporters (other than generators and TSD operators transporting wastes on site) must meet regulatory requirements under § 3003 and implementing regulations. In important part, their major responsibility is to transport all wastes they receive to their ultimate resting place. To ensure this occurs, transporters must comply with the manifest system: they may not accept wastes for transport in the absence of a manifest, they must sign and date the manifest to indicate acceptance of wastes, and upon delivery they must secure the signature of the receiving party. Should an accidental discharge occur, transporters must take immediate action to protect the public health, must clean up the mess, and must notify the appropriate regulatory authorities. *See* 40 C.F.R. Part 263.

• *Owners and Operators of TSDFs:* The most detailed and intrusive standards are reserved for owners and operators of TSDFs. Authorized by § 3004 and accompanying regulations, these standards are implemented through a permit system established by § 3005. The § 3004 regulations require owners and operators of TSDFs, *inter alia*, to:

  • locate facilities in earthquake-safe areas, away from flood plains or other geologically risky areas;

  • construct TSDFs in accordance with rigid standards, including use of foundations and dikes as necessary, low permeability double-liners to avoid loss of materials to groundwater, provision for leachate collection and removal systems, and groundwater monitoring;

• secure the TSDF to limit human and livestock intrusion by fence or barrier and, if necessary, by 24-hour surveillance;

• prepare an emergency plan and supply such communication and other equipment as necessary to implement the plan should the need arise;

• prepare and have ready corrective action plans for use in the event of discharges of hazardous materials to the environment;

• inform generators in advance of willingness to accept wastes from that generator;

• ensure that wastes actually received are precisely those shipped by the generator;

• train workers in the proper handling of hazardous wastes;

• separate characteristic wastes as necessary, especially ignitable ones;

• treat, store, and dispose of hazardous wastes in accordance with rigorous standards;

• follow specific requirements for container use and maintenance, surface impoundments, waste piles, land treatment units, landfills, incinerators, drip pads, and miscellaneous units;

• conduct regular facility inspections to ensure smooth operation;

• provide for liability coverage in case of a major accident;

• provide for proper closure after receipt of wastes ceases;

• prepare and implement a post-closure plan designed to ensure no loss of hazardous materials for at least 30 years after closure; and

• provide assurance of financial capacity to correct any problems that might occur over the 30-year post-closure period.

See 40 C.F.R. Part 264.

Ten acres of black plastic covering a radioactive waste landfill at Oak Ridge, TN. The cap prevents gases from escaping and keeps precipitation from entering. U.S. Dept. of Energy Photograph, 1994.

A variety of treaters, storers, and disposers, especially those who fall under other regulatory regimes or those who do not resemble conventional TSDFs, are exempted from these requirements.

NOTE

Cooperative Federalism. Akin to the CAA and the CWA, RCRA provides for states to participate in regulatory efforts. State programs can operate in lieu of the federal program upon approval by EPA. To warrant approval, state programs must be "equivalent" to the federal program, "consistent" with federal or state programs applicable in other states, and provide for adequate enforcement. Section 3006(b), 42 U.S.C. § 6926(b).

Once a state program is approved, EPA shifts to standby mode. But EPA need not sit by idly while the state does the heavy lifting. Even if a state program is operating satisfactorily, the federal agency still can intercede in specific instances by filing civil or criminal enforcement actions. *See* § 3008, 42 U.S.C. § 6928. EPA is apt to do this when it believes a state has failed to enforce its laws against a specific polluter. As a legal matter, stepping in under these circumstances is uncontroversial.

What is more controversial is EPA's penchant to intercede even when a state is enforcing or has already enforced its laws against a specific polluter. This practice, known as "overfiling," results in two causes of action for the same allegedly illegal behavior, one in federal court (brought by EPA) and the other in state court (brought by the state enforcement agency). Courts had rejected the notion that enforcement by one entity barred enforcement by the other, *see, e.g., Wyckoff v.*

U.S. Environmental Protection Agency, 796 F.2d1197 (9th Cir. 1986), but a controversial 1999 decision ruled to the contrary. In *Harmon Industries, Inc. v. Browner*, 191 F.3d 894 (8th Cir. 1999), EPA had filed against a polluter in Missouri, a state with "primacy" (authority to run the federal program under auspices of state law). The state filed its own enforcement action eighteen months later. The issue in *Harmon* was whether the state's cause of action operated to terminate the ongoing federal suit. The *Harmon* court found that it did, on the theory that the state program operates "in lieu of" the federal program, and, therefore, duplicate enforcement actions are impermissible. EPA was extremely aggravated by the decision, for reasons of potential abuse: with the *Harmon* rule in place, a state could arrange a sweetheart deal with a polluter precisely to frustrate a vigorous federal enforcement effort.

Harmon, it turns out, was not the last word on this important enforcement question. Other cases have weighed in, some of which disagree with *Harmon*. *See, e.g., United States v. Power Eng'g Co.*, 303 F.3d 1232 (10th Cir. 2002) (opining that the "in lieu of" principle may extend to permitting functions, but not to enforcement), and others which choose to read *Harmon* narrowly. *See, e.g., United States v. Elias*, 269 F.3d 1003, 1011 (9th Cir. 2001) (" 'The position of the Eighth Circuit in [Harmon] is not that the federal government loses its civil enforcement power after a state program is authorized. The Eighth Circuit concludes only that the federal government loses its primary role in enforcing hazardous waste regulations.' [*quoting United States v. Flanagan*, 126 F. Supp. 2d 1284, 1289 (C.D. Cal. 2000)]. Thus understood, [*Harmon*] does not support Elias's contention that federal law is supplanted or that the United States lacks power to try him.").

3. Hazardous and Solid Waste Amendments of 1984

In 1984, Congress amended RCRA. The Hazardous and Solid Waste Amendments ("HSWA") of 1984 attempted to plug gaps in the regulatory structure of the 1976 RCRA as implemented by EPA. Some of the changes were in the nature of regulatory refinements. For one, the HSWA brought previously unregulated "small quantity generators," those which produce less than 1000 kilograms per month of hazardous waste, into the system. At present, small quantity generators are in the system unless they produce 100 kilograms per month or less of hazardous waste. The HSWA also imposed more rigorous design and operation standards for TSDFs and incinerators (these standards have already been incorporated in the discussion immediately above). The new legislation also conditioned permit receipt on satisfactory performance at all "solid waste management units" ("SWMUs"). A SWMU is defined as "any discernable unit at which solid wastes have been placed at any time, irrespective of whether the unit was intended for the management of solid or hazardous waste. Such units include any area at a facility at which solid wastes have been routinely and systematically released." 55 Fed. Reg. at 30,874 (July 27, 1990). And the HSWA broadened criminal penalties.

More important for our purposes, the 1984 legislation made several programmatic changes of enduring significance. First, it shifted the focus of hazardous waste regulation from disposal to treatment. Second, it introduced a "corrective action" program to cleanup leaks at TSDFs. And, third, it began a federal effort to rein in pollution from underground storage tanks, previously unregulated at the federal level. In the remainder of this chapter, we will discuss these three statutory innovations.

a.   Land Disposal Restrictions

Perhaps the most significant change worked by the HSWA is its renewed emphasis on treatment of hazardous wastes as contrasted with disposal. Before the HSWA, the preferred compliance method was land disposal: persons buried their hazardous wastes. Congress found this widespread practice to be unacceptable, declaring in the 1984 amendments that:

> [Certain] classes of land disposal facilities are not capable of assuring long-term containment of certain hazardous wastes, and to avoid substantial risk to human health and the environment, reliance on land disposal should be minimized or eliminated. . . . [Land] disposal . . . should be the least favored method for managing hazardous wastes.

Section 1002(b)(7), 42 U.S.C. § 6901(b)(7). Accordingly, Congress amended § 3004 to provide as follows:

> [T]he Administrator shall, after notice and opportunity for hearings . . . , promulgate regulations specifying those levels or methods of treatment, if any, which substantially diminish the toxicity of the waste or substantially reduce the likelihood of migration of hazardous constituents from the waste so that short-term and long-term threats to human health and the environment are minimized.

Section 3004(m)(1), 42 U.S.C. § 6924(m)(1).

Congress directed EPA to set waste treatment standards in accord with a strict timetable. Congress divided hazardous wastes into three groups (the first third, second third, and third third), identified other wastes as well, and specified the time frame for standard setting for each. Most significantly, it provided that, should EPA fail to enact treatment standards for any of the designated wastes as required by the Act, land disposal of those wastes must cease. These so-called "hammer" provisions come in two forms. A "soft hammer" drops if EPA fails to promulgate treatment standards by a specified date certain. In such a case, land disposal of the affected subclass of wastes is prohibited unless the disposal site complies with minimum technological design standards and the generator certifies the absence of practical waste treatment alternatives. *See, e.g.*, § 3004(g)(6)(A), 42 U.S.C. § 6924(g)(6)(A) (specifying the soft hammer for first third wastes). A "hard hammer," banning waste disposal for all purposes, drops if regulations remain unpromulgated by an even later date certain. *See, e.g.*, § 3004(g)(6)(C), 42 U.S.C. § 6924(g)(6)(C) (specifying the hard hammer for most hazardous wastes). The amended statute required EPA to enact regulations in accordance with the following dates:

Spent solvent and dioxin-containing wastes   November 8, 1986
California list wastes   July 8, 1987

First Third Wastes	August 8, 1988
Spent solvent, dioxin-containing, and California list soil and debris from CERCLA/RCRA Corrective Actions	November 8, 1988
Second Third Wastes	June 8, 1989
Third Third Wastes	May 8, 1990
Newly Identified Wastes	Within 6 months of identification as a hazardous waste

EPA moved on its mission with alacrity. As of May 1991, hard hammer deadlines had fallen only for California list cyanides and metals. The agency promulgated regulations requiring hazardous wastes to be treated to levels that are achievable by use of the "best demonstrated available technology" ("BDAT") or be treated by methods that constitute BDAT. *See* 40 C.F.R. Part 268, Subpart D. EPA decided not to engage in comparative risk assessment in determining BDAT, and was upheld in that determination. *American Petroleum Inst. v. EPA*, 906 F.2d 729 (D.C. Cir. 1990). EPA's preferred treatment method for most hazardous wastes is incineration.

Notably, these "land ban" provisions offer some flexibility. If the EPA determines, "to a reasonable degree of certainty, that there will be no migration of hazardous constituents from the disposal unit or injection zone for as long as the wastes remain hazardous," the prohibition on land disposal may be lifted. Section 3004(d), (e), (g), (m), 42 U.S.C. § 6924(d), (e), (g), (m). Additionally, once a waste has been treated to meet standards established by EPA pursuant to § 3004(m), 42 U.S.C. § 6924(m), it may be disposed of in land. EPA is authorized to grant exemptions upon a showing by an individual that a prohibition on land disposal is "not required in order to protect human health and the environment for as long as the waste remains hazardous." Section 3004(d)(1), 42 U.S.C. § 6924(d)(1).

CHEMICAL WASTE MANAGEMENT, INC. v. U.S. ENVIRONMENTAL PROTECTION AGENCY
976 F.2d 2 (D.C. Cir. 1992), *cert. denied*, 507 U.S. 1057, 113 S. Ct. 1961 (1993)

JUDGES: Before EDWARDS, BUCKLEY, and HENDERSON, CIRCUIT JUDGES.

OPINION PER CURIAM:

[This litigation involved a variety of challenges to EPA's "third-third" rule, in place to regulate land disposal of certain wastes deemed to be hazardous because of their defined characteristics. EPA's rule was challenged as allegedly going beyond the authority of the agency, for being arbitrary and capricious, and for improperly modifying regulations previously in place under the Clean Water Act and the Safe Drinking Water Act. These challenges are discussed in the body of the opinion, which follows]:

. . . .

II. Treatment Standards for Characteristic Wastes

[The first issue involved characteristic wastes. The reader will recall the four characteristics that may make wastes hazardous: ignitability, corrosivity, reactivity, and toxicity. The first three categories are often referred to collectively as "ICR wastes." The question was whether EPA's regulatory provisions governing both ICR and toxic wastes might require treatment to a level beyond which the materials would no longer qualify as hazardous, or whether alternatively RCRA authorized treatment to characteristic levels and no further. EPA argued it could require so-called "enhanced treatment" (i.e treatment beyond or "below") characteristic levels) based on § 3004(m). EPA nonetheless chose not to regulate to that level of stringency]:

While viewing its authority broadly, the EPA decided to exercise it sparingly:

> Today's rule reflects a decision to take limited, but nonetheless significant, steps within the point of generation framework. As a general matter, the Agency believes that the goals of [the program] may require application of standards which go beyond the characteristic level . . . in some future cases.

Id. at 22,654. The final regulations call for treatment below characteristic levels for only a handful of wastes. Among ICR wastes, ignitable liquids with high total organic carbons (a subset of the subcategory of ignitable liquids for which the proposed rule required treatment to below characteristic levels by technology), *see* Id. at 22,543 44, and reactive cyanides, *See id.* at 22,550c-51, would be subject to enhanced treatment. The Agency backed away from its original plan to mandate enhanced treatment for corrosive characteristic wastes.

The EPA determined that for most ICR wastes, treatment to characteristic levels would be sufficient. The Agency found upon review that

> the environmental concerns from the properties of ignitability, corrosivity, and reactivity are different from the environmental concern from E[xtration] P[rocedure] toxic wastes. Toxic constituents can pose a cumulative impact on land disposal even where waste is below the characteristic level. Where wastes pose an ascertainable toxicity concern . . . the Agency has developed treatment standards that address the toxicity concern and (in effect) require treatment below the characteristic level. . . . Otherwise, treatment that re-moves the properties of ignitability, corrosivity, and reactivity, fully addresses the environmental concern from the properties themselves.

Id. at 22,655.

The EPA also retreated from its emphasis on technology-based treatment in the final regulations, altering its position on the use of dilution as a method of treatment:

> In all cases, the Agency has determined that for non-toxic hazardous characteristic wastes, it should not matter how the characteristic property is removed so long as it is removed. Thus, dilution is an acceptable treatment method for such wastes.

Id. at 22,532. The Agency included dilution within the ambit of the "deactivation" treatment standard. The final rule defined the standard as "deactivation to remove the hazardous characteristics of a waste due to its ignitability, corrosivity, and/or reactivity." *Id.* at 22,693. As long as these characteristics are removed, any method can be employed under the final regulations. The EPA allowed full discretion among specified technological methods of treatment (such as neutralization or incineration) as well as dilution with water or other wastes. For toxic wastes, the prohibition on dilution remained. *See id.* at 22,656.

The Agency admitted that it

> believes the mixing of waste streams to eliminate certain characteristics is appropriate treatment for most wastes which are purely corrosive, or in some cases, reactive or ignitable. Asa general matter, these are properties which can effectively be removed by mixing.

Id. It further conceded that

> this approach does not fully address the potential problem of toxic constituents that may be present in such wastes, nor encourages minimization or recovery of non-toxic characteristic hazardous wastes. EPA has determined that these potential problems should be addressed, if at all, in other rulemakings . . . and are too difficult to resolve in this proceeding, given the extraordinary pressures and limited review time imposed by the May 8 [1990] statutory deadline.

Id. at 22,665 66. Only in three subcategories of ICR wastes did the EPA mandate the use of technological treatment: reactive sulfides, 57 Fed. Reg. 8,086, 8,089 (1992) (technical correction to third-third rule); reactive cyanides, 55 Fed. Reg. at 22,551; and ignitable liquid nonwastewater wastes containing more than ten percent total organic compounds, *id.* at 22,544. For all corrosive wastes, other ignitable liquid wastes (nonwastewaters with low total organic compounds and ignitable wastewaters), ignitable compressed gases, ignitable reactive wastes, explosive wastes, water reactives, and other reactives dilution would be acceptable. *Id.* at 22,543 53. . . .

D. Industry Petitioners' Challenge to the Treatment Standards

Industry petitioners contend that RCRA does not provide authority for the EPA to mandate treatment of characteristic wastes after their ignitability, corrosiveness, reactivity, or EP toxicity has been addressed. They make a straightforward argument: Subtitle C regulations attach to a waste only when it is hazardous. The moment a waste ceases to meet the regulatory definition of a hazardous waste, the EPA loses its authority to regulate further. Thus, in industry petitioners' view, RCRA's cradle-to-grave system covers waste only if it remains hazardous throughout its life and at the moment of its burial.

Industry petitioners point to a welter of provisions in RCRA where the words "hazardous waste" are used as proof that the statute applies only to waste defined as hazardous. Subtitle C, they explain, is entitled "Hazardous Waste Management," and the entire subtitle addresses that problem — the management of hazardous waste. They add that some statements by the EPA have suggested the same reading of the statute. *See, e.g.*, 54 Fed. Reg. 1,056, 1,093 (1989) (a waste that no longer exhibits a hazardous characteristic "is no longer subject to the requirements of Subtitle C of RCRA").

In their view, the 1984 Amendments did not change this boundary. . . .

. . . In *API [v. EPA*, 906 F.2d 729 (D.C. Cir. 1990)], we explained that "once a waste is listed or identified as hazardous, its subsequent management is regulated." *API*, 906 F.2d at 733. After the 1984 Amendments, we added, regulation of the waste included the prohibitions of section 3004. *Id.* In *Shell Oil*, we noted that the power to manage waste is created "at [the] point" a waste is defined as hazardous and discarded. *Shell Oil*, 950 F.2d at 754. Once in the system, we found that the power to manage hazardous waste provided by RCRA gave the EPA the authority to regulate waste until "it ceases to pose a hazard to the public." *Id.; see also* RCRA § 1004(7), 42 U.S.C. § 6903(7) (defining "hazardous waste management"). . . .

The 1984 Amendments also provide the EPA with the authority to mandate treatment past the point at which a characteristic is removed. Section 3004(g)(5) requires the Administrator to promulgate regulations prohibiting land disposal of hazardous wastes "except with respect to a hazardous waste which has complied with the pretreatment regulations promulgated under subsection(m) of this section." 42 U.S.C. § 6924(g)(5). Subsection (m)(1), in turn, calls on the Administrator to

> specify[ ]those levels or methods of treatment, if any, which substantially diminish the toxicity of the waste or substantially reduce the likelihood of migration of hazardous constituents from the waste so that short-term and long-term threats to human health and the environment are minimized.

RCRA § 3004(m)(1), 42 U.S.C. § 6924(m)(1). The requirement that treatment "substantially diminish the toxicity" or substantially reduce the likelihood of migration of hazardous constituents suggests concerns that go beyond the characteristics identified in 40 C.F.R. Part 261, subpart C. Similarly, in concluding that the EPA had the authority to require technologies that go beyond the elimination of hazardous characteristics, we have noted that "minimize" offers a broad mandate: "To 'minimize' something is, to quote the Oxford English Dictionary, to 'reduce [it] to the smallest possible amount, extent, or degree.' " HWTC III, 886 F.2d at 361. . . .

E. NRDC Petitioners' Challenge to Deactivation Treatment Standard

NRDC petitioners ask this court to vacate the deactivation treatment standard as applied to ICR wastes because it authorizes the dilution of these wastes to eliminate their ignitability, corrosiveness, or reactivity rather than mandating use of technological treatment. . . .

. . . In their view, the removal of these characteristics through dilution only affects the short-term risk that the waste will manifest that property; it does not address the threats posed by the hazardous organic and in organic constituents of those wastes. . . .

We believe that dilution can, in principle, constitute an acceptable form of treatment for ICR wastes. We do not read the 1984 Amendments as mandating the use of the best demonstrated available technologies ("BDAT") in all situations. . . .

We agree that [Section 3004(m)(1)] imposes an exacting standard: it requires that treatment prior to land disposal "substantially diminish the toxicity of the waste or substantially reduce the likelihood of migration of hazardous constituents from the waste so that short-term and long-term threats to human health and the environment are minimized." RCRA § 3004(m)(1), 42 U.S.C. § 6924(m)(1). But this provision does not bar dilution as a means of treating ICR wastes; instead, it defines the purposes that a method of treatment must achieve. Any treatment that meets those objectives is permissible. When read against RCRA's broad definition of treatment, we cannot say Congress clearly barred dilution as an acceptable methodology. . . .

[In applying this test, the court affirmed generally the agency's use of dilution as a treatment method for corrosive wastes, but objected to its use as treatment for ignitable or reactive waste.

Later in the opinion, the court addressed the impact, if any, of the RCRA third third rule on surface impoundments usually regulated under the Clean Water Act. These impoundments can accept characteristic wastes as part of their waste stream. Because surface impoundments constitute "land disposal" for RCRA purposes, the issue arose whether surface impoundments accepting such wastes should be subject to RCRA requirements, CWA requirements, or both. Held the court]:

We already have held that RCRA section 3004(m)(1) requires treatment both to remove the characteristic and to substantially reduce the toxicity of all hazardous constituents present in the characteristic waste. The treatment standards are the core of RCRA's hazardous waste management scheme, and nothing in RCRA or the CWA permits the EPA to establish different treatment standards when wastewaters are treated in CWA systems instead of facilities operated solely to RCRA standards. Nevertheless, Congress, when enacting RCRA, was cognizant of the substantial development of CWA systems, and, thus, permitted regulatory "accommodation" of RCRA and CWA systems. Thus, we agree with the EPA that, under RCRA, diluted formerly characteristic wastes may be placed in subtitle D surface impoundments which are part of an integrated CWA treatment train. However, in order for true "accommodation" to be accomplished, we find that RCRA treatment requirements cannot be ignored merely because CWA is implicated; that is, the CWA does not override RCRA. Thus, we hold that, whenever wastes are put in CWA surface impoundments before they have been treated pursuant to RCRA to reduce the toxicity of all hazardous constituents, these wastes must be so treated before exiting the CWA treatment facilities. In other words, CWA facilities handling characteristic wastes must remove the characteristic and decrease the toxicity of the waste's hazardous constituents to the same degree that treatment outside a CWA system would. . . .

. . . Congress, when enacting RCRA, recognized that prior environmental statutes, such as the Clean Water Act, would need to be accommodated.

The Administrator shall integrate all provisions of this chapter for purposes of administration and enforcement and shall avoid duplication, to

the maximum extent practicable, with the appropriate provisions of the . . .
Federal Water Pollution Control Act [and] the Safe Drinking Water Act
. . . , and such other Acts of Congress as grant regulatory authority to the
Administrator. Such integration shall be effected only to the extent that it
can be done in a manner consistent with the goals and policies expressed in
this chapter and in the other acts referred to in this subsection.

RCRA § 1006(b)(1), 42 U.S.C. § 6905(b)(1) (1988); *see* 55 Fed. Reg. at 22,654, 22,657.
The EPA's decision to permit "decharacterized" hazardous wastes to be deposited
in surface impoundments as part of continuing treatment is a reasonable accommodation.

We wish to make explicit the impact of our holding because we find merit in
significant parts of both parties' positions. First, where dilution to remove the
characteristic meets the definition of treatment under section 3004(m)(1), nothing
more is required. Second, where dilution removes the characteristic but does not
"treat" the waste by reducing the toxicity of hazardous constituents, then the
decharacterized waste may be placed in a surface impoundment if and only if the
resulting CWA treatment fully complies with RCRA § 3004(m)(1). In other words,
the material that comes out of CWA treatment facilities that employ surface
impoundments must remove the hazardous constituents to the same extent that any
other treatment facility that complies with RCRA does.[2]

. . . [T]his case differs from *API*, 906 F.2d 729. In that case, which considered
aspects of the first-third rule, several industry representatives challenged the EPA's
decision not to consider land treatment as a form of treatment for hazardous wastes
under section 3004(m)(1). The court affirmed the EPA's action, ruling that land
treatment was a form of land disposal and that "RCRA clearly specifies . . . that
hazardous wastes must be treated before being land disposed." *Id.* at 735. The *API*
court also noted that "pursuant to 42 U.S.C. § 6925(j)(11), Congress allowed surface
impoundments (a type of land disposal unit under § 6924(k)) to receive, on an
interim basis, hazardous wastes that have not been treated to meet § 6924(m)
standards" only so long as the impoundments met certain minimum technological
standards. *Id.* at 736; *see* RCRA § 3004(o)(1), 42 U.S.C. § 6924(o)(1) (1988)
(requiring double-lining, leachate collection and groundwater monitoring). Here,
however, the liquids, at the time they are placed in the surface impoundments, are
not technically "hazardous wastes," although they are fully subject to RCRA's
strictures because they were hazardous and have not yet met the treatment
requirements. Additionally, the liquids here are only placed in the surface impoundments temporarily; in API, the "land treatment" represented the final resting place
of the hazardous wastes. . . .

---

[2] To illustrate RCRA's focus on treatment of the hazardous constituents in a waste, consider a waste
stream hazardous by characteristic for cadmium. Both the characteristic and treatment levels for the
hazardous waste are 1.0 mg/l. Assume that a stream of 3.0 mg/l daily deposits 1000 liters into a treatment
facility. A RCRA treatment facility would remove at least 2000 mg of cadmium from the waste stream.
A CWA treatment facility must do the same — although to do so it will have to process at least three
times as much water (because dilution of 1000 liters of 3.0 mg/l to just below the characteristic level will
yield just over 3000 liters). Allowing dilution alone would decharacterize the waste, but it would not
reduce the total amount of cadmium entering the environment. One thousand liters of 3.0 mg/l cadmium
yields the same amount of hazardous constituent as 3000 liters of 1.0 mg/l cadmium.

B. Deep Injection Wells Regulated Under the Safe Drinking Water Act

1. Generally

. . . Consistent with our resolution of the Clean Water Act systems issue, we hold that dilution followed by injection into a deep well is permissible only where dilution itself fully meets section 3004(m)(1) standards or where the waste will subsequently meet section 3004(m)(1) standards. Because deep well injection is permanent land disposal, our holding in effect permits diluted decharacterized wastes to be deep well injected only when dilution meets the section 3004(m)(1) standard or where the deep well secures a no-migration variance. . . .

[Portions of the opinion dealing with issues of administrative law are omitted].

3. Should Rule 268.3(b) Include Listed Wastes for which the EPA has Developed Concentration-Based Treatment Standards?

[In discussing this question, the court held the rule to be adequate, in major part because of the difference between listed and characteristic wastes. Said the court: "listed wastes generally contain a certain substance that is per se harmful (such as arsenic). Dilution does nothing to remove that element from the waste stream and prevent it from entering the environment where it may reaccumulate. By contrast, some characteristic wastes may be altered permanently by dilution and, hence, it is reasonable to permit aggregation. In these cases, dilution and treatment are one and the same[.]"

[The remainder of the opinion is omitted].

NOTES

1. ***Rifle Shot Bill.*** On March 26, 1996, President Clinton signed into law the so-called "rifle shot bill," which revised RCRA by relaxing Subtitle C treatment standards for decharacterized hazardous wastes headed for disposal in facilities regulated under the Clean Water Act and the Safe Drinking Water Act. The law, a bipartisan effort, was an attempt to address regulatory problems that arise when more than one regulatory regime applies to a single set of circumstances (in a given case, for example, a single activity might be regulable as a point source under the CWA, as an injection well under the Safe Drinking Water Act (*see* Note 2, *infra*, and *Chemical Waste Management, supra*) and as a TSDF under RCRA). Certain holdings of *Chemical Waste Management* (not reproduced here) were overturned by Congress in that measure. The Act, formally titled the Land Disposal Program Flexibility Act of 1996, was codified as part of RCRA itself. The amendatory provisions regarding land disposal are found at RCRA § 3004(g)(7)–(11).

2. ***Safe Drinking Water Act.*** The Safe Drinking Water Act ("SDWA"), 42 U.S.C. § 300f et seq., is a federal statute that moves in the same circles as RCRA. The SDWA is divided into two parts. The first part deals with public water supplies, the entities that deliver drinking water to your faucet (Part B). The second part, of relevance to RCRA, deals with "underground injection" of "contaminants" which

"endanger[s]" "underground sources of drinking water" (Part C). Part C of the SDWA has traditionally been the legal control on injection into "wells" (at least where an "underground source of drinking water" is implicated). For that reason, RCRA has often taken a back seat when well injection is involved, even though it could be used: as you know, RCRA addresses all "disposal" of "solid wastes," even if by the mechanism of "injection." *See* § 1004(3), 42 U.S.C. § 6903(3) (defining "disposal" as including "injection").

In 1984, however, Congress added § 3004(f), 42 U.S.C. § 6924(f), to RCRA to deal with disposal of hazardous wastes into deep injection wells, and § 3020, 42 U.S.C. § 6939b, to deal with interim control of hazardous waste injection. These new provisions are broader in scope than the companion provisions in the SDWA, in that they protect from well injection groundwater resources not designated as underground sources of drinking water. The provisions in RCRA, as interpreted by EPA, prohibit all "migration of hazardous constituents from the disposal unit or injection zone for as long as the wastes remain hazardous." EPA determined that "wastes" means wastes that migrate outside the injection zone, that "migration" encompasses not only fluid migration, but also migration by molecular diffusion, and that an injector must demonstrate compliance with the no-migration standard for as long as the wastes remain hazardous, or for 10,000 years, whichever is shorter. These regulatory provisions were upheld on review. *Natural Resources Defense Council v. U.S. Environmental Protection Agency*, 907 F.2d 1146 (D.C. Cir. 1990).

3.   *Relative Health Hazard.* Since the enactment of RCRA in 1976, EPA has regulated hazardous waste disposal closely but has been less attentive to solid waste regulation. This is purportedly because hazardous waste poses the greater risk to public health. Given that hypothesis, it is notable that EPA commented, in an October 9, 1991, Federal Register notice, that available data "do not provide strong support for distinguishing the health and environmental threats" presented by solid waste disposal as compared to hazardous waste disposal.

b.   Corrective Action

As Congress considered its 1984 amendments to RCRA, it learned that the problem with hazardous waste facilities was not just about operation and maintenance. It was also about past performance. About 5,700 active RCRA-regulated hazardous waste facilities had already contaminated soils and groundwater, and a great deal of that contamination needed rectification. Indeed, the clean-up task was ominous: the cost of restoring privately owned RCRA Subchapter III sites alone had been projected at nearly $42 billion, and contamination from federal facilities likely would add millions to that figure.

The original RCRA, however, did not contain any provisions requiring clean-up at regulated TSDFs. Congress took care of that problem in the HSWA by creating a new program known as Corrective Action ("CA"). The major CA provisions are found in two short subsections, § 3004(u) and (v), 42 U.S.C. § 6924(u) and (v). Section 3004(u), the more significant of the two provisions, specifies that all RCRA permits issued after November 8, 1984, must contain requirements for "corrective action for all releases of hazardous wastes or hazardous constituents from any solid waste management unit" located at the permitted facility "regardless of the time at which waste was placed in the unit." Section 3004(v) expressly extends the corrective action requirement to pollution that has made its way beyond the boundaries of the affected facility.

These provisions are complemented by others. Section 3013, 42 U.S.C. § 6934, adopted originally in 1980, authorizes EPA to require owners and operators of TSDFs to monitor, test, and take other action to determine if environmental damage has occurred. If the required information is either not forthcoming or is unsatisfactory, EPA can do the investigation itself and seek cost reimbursement. Section 3013(d)(1), 42 U.S.C. § 6934(d)(1). *But see* § 3013(d)(2), 42 U.S.C. § 6934(d)(2). In addition, Section 3008(h), 42 U.S.C. § 6928(h), empowers EPA to issue corrective action orders for interim status facilities, and § 7003, 42 U.S.C. § 6973, part of the original 1976 statutory enactment but amended a couple of times thereafter, allows EPA to bring enforcement actions in cases presenting "imminent and substantial endangerment to health or the environment."

Under the terms of § 3004(u), all *releases of hazardous wastes or constituents from any solid waste management unit* at a TSD *facility seeking a permit* are now subject to corrective action requirements. Elaborating these requirements has been a daunting task for EPA: it took the agency six years to simply issue proposed rules to implement the section, and still only small portions of the overall program are underpromulgated regulations. Even though the July 27, 1990 regulation remains a proposal only, EPA uses it as guidance for its corrective action decisions.

In understanding this section, the relevant questions are: (1) which are the TSD facilities "seeking a permit"; (2) what is a "facility"; (3) what is a "solid waste management unit"; (4) what are "hazardous wastes or constituents"; and (5) what are "releases." Note that the meanings of these terms for CA purposes may differ from their meanings for other statutory purposes.

(1) *"Seeking a permit"*: Under RCRA § 3005, all owners and operators of an "existing facility or planning to construct a new facility for the treatment, storage, or disposal of hazardous waste . . . [must secure] . . . a permit." Clearly, then, when one submits a permit application, that TSDF becomes subject to the CA program. What do you project would be the result if a person violated § 3005 by receiving hazardous wastes without benefit of a permit? Would that person be free of CA requirements? *See* 40 C.F.R. § 264.101 (no).

Note in this regard that not all TSD facilities need a permit. Those that never fell within RCRA's regulatory reach are exempt. These are the sites where all treatment, storage, and disposal of hazardous wastes took place before November 19, 1980, the date EPA's initial Subchapter III regulations took effect. Sites which were regulated under RCRA but which obtained a "closure" certificate by January 26, 1983, are also exempt from CA requirements.

(2) *"Facility"*: Corrective action requirements apply to facilities, which have been defined by EPA in the July 27 Rulemaking as including "all contiguous property" under the control of a single owner or operator. *See* 55 Fed. Reg. 30808 (July 27, 1990).

(3) *"Solid Waste Management Unit"* or *"SWMU"*: EPA defined this term as:

> Any discernible unit at which solid wastes have been placed at any time, irrespective of whether the unit was intended for the management of solid or hazardous waste. Such units include any area at a facility at which solid wastes have been routinely and systematically released.

55 Fed. Reg. 30,808 (July 27, 1990).

What is a "discernible unit"? EPA explains the term as including units "typically" under RCRA, such as landfills and land treatment units, impoundments, waste piles, tanks, containers, container storage areas, wells, incinerators, waste recycle operations, and the like.

As the definition indicates, SWMUs are also areas "at which solid wastes have been routinely and systematically released." EPA includes in this category loading areas, where spillage can commonly occur, solvent washing areas, and even "kickback drippage" areas, which are storage places for pressure-treated wood and where substances applied to the wood might leak into soils.

Would a facility roadway traveled by trucks carrying hazardous wastes be such an area? What if a truck had an accident that resulted in a release? How about a sewer or a ditch which conveys wastes?

(4) *"Hazardous wastes or constituents"*: As we have seen in this chapter, hazardous wastes under RCRA are those listed specifically as hazardous or having hazardous characteristics. *See* § 3001, 42 U.S.C. § 6921. Also hazardous for RCRA CA purposes are wastes identified under the "derived-from" rule, the "mixture" rule, and the "contained-in" interpretation. *See supra*.

Materials subject to CA, however, also include solid wastes with hazardous constituents. This language means that a subset of solid wastes, those with hazardous constituents, fall under the CA program, even if those wastes do not rise to the level of hazardous wastes.

(5) *"Release"*: There must be a "release" to trigger CA responsibility. We will discuss "releases" in Chapter 12, *infra*.

c. Underground Storage Tanks

In contrast to the relatively few hazardous waste facilities, there currently exist about 595,000 underground storage tanks ("USTs") that store petroleum or hazardous substances. Source: EPA. The vast majority of USTs are made of bare steel and numerous of them are leaking because of corrosion, improper installation, overfilling, mechanical compromises caused by pressurization, and other reasons. Upon escape, leaking materials can contaminate groundwater. Since groundwater provides over 50% of the nation's drinking water, and as much as 99% in some rural areas, and since a single drop of gasoline can ruin a gallon of water, leaks can occasion serious consequences.

To address this problem, Congress in the Hazardous and Solid Waste Amendments of 1984 added Subchapter IX to RCRA. The Subchapter applies to "underground storage tanks" containing "regulated substances." "Underground storage tanks" are defined as:

any one or combination of tanks (including underground pipes connected thereto) which is used to contain an accumulation of regulated substances, and the volume of which (including the volume of the underground pipes connected thereto) is 10 per centum or more beneath the surface of the ground, but does not include any —

(A)   farm or residential tank of 1,100 gallons or less capacity used for storing motor fuel for non-commercial purposes,

(B)   tank used for storing heating oil for consumptive use on the premises where stored,

(C)   septic tank,

(D)   pipeline facility (including gathering lines) . . . ,

(E)   surface impoundment, pit, pond, or lagoon,

(F)   storm water or waste water collection system,

(G)   flow-through process tank,

(H)   liquid trap or associated gathering lines directly related to oil and gas production and gathering operations, or

(I)   storage tank situated in an underground area (such as a basement, cellar, mineworking, drift, shaft, or tunnel) if the storage tank is situated upon or above the surface of the floor.

Section 9001(1), 42 U.S.C. § 6991(1).

"Regulated substances" include petroleum and hazardous substances (as defined in CERCLA; *see* Chapter 12, *infra*), but not hazardous wastes regulated under Subchapter III. Section 9001(2), 42 U.S.C. § 6991(2). Of the regulated tanks, 49% are owned by gas stations and 47% are owned by other industries that store petroleum for their own purposes. Less than 5% of regulated tanks contain hazardous materials.

Subchapter IX is specifically directed to "owners and operators" of USTs. In a major sense, these terms are undefined: the statute characterizes owners as persons "who own" and operators as persons involved in daily "operation." Sections 9001(3)–(4), 42 U.S.C. § 6991(3)–(4). But the statute does draw some limits on the definitions. First, the definition of "owner" is divided into two parts. If the UST was in use on the effective date of the HSWA, or November 8, 1984, or brought into use thereafter, the "owner" subject to regulation is the current owner, that is, the person holding title at the time the lawsuit is brought. Section 9001(3), 42 U.S.C. § 6991(3). If the UST, however, was out of service before November 8, 1984, the "owner" is "any person who owned such tank immediately before the discontinuation of its use." Section 9001(4), 42 U.S.C. § 6991(4). While this definition allows for current and past owners to be liable, for the most part, the number of liable owners in any given case is limited to one. The definition of "operator" is not similarly bifurcated. An "operator" is "any person in control of, or having responsibility for, the daily operation of the underground storage tank." Section 9001(4), 42 U.S.C. § 6991(4). While this language would seem to reach present owners only, and exclude past operators, courts have held that past operators can be held liable for leakages, in their capacities as persons who dispose of solid or hazardous wastes into the environment. *See, e.g., United States v. Hill*, 1998 U.S. Dist. LEXIS 7894 (N.D.N.Y. May 20, 1998); *Singer v. Bulk Petroleum Corp.*, 9 F. Supp. 2d 916 (N.D. Ill. 1998). As with "owners," it seems that liability is largely limited to one operator per UST.

Subchapter IX establishes a comprehensive regulatory regime. First, § 9001a(a)(1), 42 U.S.C. § 6991a(a)(1), requires owners to notify state or local environmental agencies of the presence of their tanks, as well as information about their "age, size, type, location and uses." *Id.* Those agencies in turn are instructed to compile inventories of tanks and to supply that information to the EPA. Section 9001a(c), 42 U.S.C. § 6991a(c). EPA's obligation is to promulgate "release detection, prevention and correction regulations applicable to all owners and operators of underground storage tanks, as may be necessary to protect human health and the environment." Section 9003(a), 42 U.S.C. § 6991b(a). EPA's regulations, found at 40 C.F.R. § 280.60 et seq., impose automatic clean-up responsibility for leaks. 40 C.F.R. § 280.64(a). The regulations also establish requirements for spill and overfill control, corrosion protection, and release detection; procedural requirements for reporting, investigating, confirming, and recording release incidents; abatement measures, free product removal, and corrective action standards; standards for closure; and, added in 1989, financial requirements for owners and operators.

Should a leak be discovered, owners and operators must take immediate action to report the release, to prevent its continuation, and to mitigate fire, explosion, and vapor hazards. 40C.F.R. § 280.61. Initial abatement actions include removal of the regulated substance from the UST, prevention of further migration of the materials into soils and waters, and monitoring. 40 C.F.R. § 280.62. Depending on circumstances, permanent cleanup may need to accord with a corrective action plan. 40 C.F.R. § 280.66. Subject to limitations, the EPA is authorized to undertake cleanup of petroleum releases on its own if the action is necessary to protect human health and the environment. Section 9003(h)(2), 42 U.S.C. § 6991b(h)(2). *See generally* Candace C. Gauthier, *The Enforcement of Federal Underground Storage Tank Regulations*, 20 ENVTL. L. 261 (1990); Cyndy Day-Wilson, *Federal Environmental Issues in Commercial Leasing Transactions: A Practitioner's Guide*, 2 ENVTL. L. 597 (1996).

Just as RCRA calls for state participation in the overall regulatory effort (*see supra*), so also does it call for state participation in the UST program. Section 9004, 42 U.S.C. § 6991c.

Since RCRA does not allow for private parties to recover damages or cleanup costs, private parties seeking such relief typically must rely on common law. *See generally* Chapter 2, *supra*. In early leaking underground storage tank ("LUST") litigation, strict liability proved to be a useful tool on the theory that UST operation is abnormally dangerous activity. Acknowledging that USTs are very common and are valuable in comparison to the dangers they pose in the current day, courts hesitate to employ strict liability theories liberally. *See* Jason M. Basile, *Still No Remedy After All These Years: Plugging the Hole in the Law of Leaking Underground Storage Tanks*, 73 IND. L.J. 675 (1998). Still, the case can be made upon a showing that a tank is poorly situated, as, for example, if it is located near a well, *see, e.g., Yommer v. McKenzie*, 257 A.2d 138 (Md. 1969), or by a showing that the tank's size is uncommon or inappropriate, *see, e.g., City of Northglenn v. Chevron, Inc.*, 519 F. Supp. 515 (D. Colo. 1981). *See also* Alison Rittenhouse Hayward, *Common Law Remedies and the UST Regulations*, 21 B. C. ENVTL. AFF. L. REV. 619 (1994). In the absence of strict liability, plaintiffs must typically rely on conventional negligence, nuisance, and trespass theories, or on contract theories. For a more detailed discussion of common law actions in both tort and contract, see Michael J. Maher & Sheila Horan, *Lessons in L.U.S.T: The Complete Story of Liability for Leaking Underground Storage Tanks*, 16 N. ILL. U. L. REV. 581 (1996). On some occasions, state statutes may operate to preempt rights of plaintiffs to sue under common law theories. *See generally* Chapter 2 *supra*.

Recently controversial is the matter of methyl tertiary butyl ether ("MTBE") leakage from USTs. MTBE is a gasoline additive that increases octane in premium-grade fuel and helps improve air quality by reducing the concentration of ozone-forming compounds in tailpipe emissions. MTBE, however, is also an animal carcinogen that can, even in extremely small quantities, make water unfit for consumption. MTBE, moreover, is hydrophilic, or water-seeking; thus, upon escaping an UST, it travels quickly through soil and into groundwater. When this happens, lawsuits are sure to follow. Numerous MTBE lawsuits, for example, have been filed in California, Connecticut, Florida, New Jersey, and New York, alleging claims ranging from negligence and trespass to illegal and unfair business practices and even infliction of emotional distress. *See, e.g.*, Faulk, Berlanga et al., *Salem Revisited: Updating the MTBE Controversy*, SF97 ALI-ABA 949 (2001).

An ancillary dispute involves the question whether groundwater contamination lawsuits can be brought as class actions. *See, e.g., Sterling v. Velsicol Chemical Corp.*, 855 F.2d 1188 (6th Cir. 1988) (class action allowed); *Millett v. Atlantic Richfield Co.*, 760 A.2d 250 (Me. 2000) (class action not allowed).

Chapter 12

THE COMPREHENSIVE ENVIRONMENTAL RESPONSE, COMPENSATION AND LIABILITY ACT ("CERCLA")

"We abuse land because we regard it as a commodity belonging to us. When we see land as a community to which we belong, we may begin to use it with love and respect." ALDO LEOPOLD, A SAND COUNTY ALMANAC.

SYNOPSIS

A. INTRODUCTION

B. PERSONAL LIABILITY
    1. Prima Facie Liability
        a. Owners and Operators
        b. Arrangers
        c. Transporters
    2. Defenses

C. ISSUES OF LIABILITY AND DAMAGES

A. INTRODUCTION

As we have seen in the preceding three chapters, the goal of federal environmental law has been the elimination or curtailment of pollution. This approach is premised on the idea that once a pollution assault ends or eases, the receiving "media" (i.e., the ambient air or water) can get about the task of cleaning themselves by natural processes. In major measure, this approach has worked: ambient air is now cleaner nationally than it once was, and many stream segments are supporting aquatic life once again.

This convenient self-cleaning feature, however, has worked less well in the third medium of pollutant disposal — land. Rather than cleanse itself, land tends to hold pollution in place, often for many years. This unhappy geologic fact burst into public consciousness with the notorious episode at Love Canal, New York. The Hooker Chemical Company, it was learned at that time, had buried about 28,500 tons of hazardous chemicals in a 16-acre site in the Niagara Falls, New York area from 1942 to 1953. Using a deed which both disclosed the dumping activity and disclaimed future responsibility for it, the company sold the contaminated land to the local school board for a single dollar. As time passed, populations moved in and the site evolved into a residential community known as Love Canal.

In 1978, after a spate of heavy rains, Hooker's chemical mix leached into the yards and homes of many of Love Canal's residents. Spurred by the image of schoolchildren playing in toxic substances, these families were hastily evacuated, and what was an active neighborhood quickly became an eerie ghost town. Allegations of birth defects, miscarriages, skin irritations, and respiratory ailments soon followed, as did revelations of "other Love Canals," such as the infamous "Valley of the Drums" in Kentucky, and Meadowlands in New Jersey.[1]

The nation was horrified at all of this, and Congress reacted swiftly. In 1980, it enacted the Comprehensive Environmental Response, Compensation, and Liability Act ("CERCLA"), better known as "Superfund." CERCLA was to be the vehicle by which thousands of abandoned hazardous waste dumps would be cleaned. (CERCLA would be joined in 1984 by the Solid and Hazardous Waste Amendments to the Resource Conservation and Recovery Act, which established the corrective action program (*see* Chapter 11, *supra*) and in 1990 by the Oil Pollution Act ("OPA"), 33 U.S.C. § 2701 et seq., Congress's response to the Exxon Valdez oil spill in Alaskan waters. The OPA is aimed at the cleanup of contaminated waterways.)

CERCLA is the touchstone of this new era in environmental law. Unlike the CAA, CWA, and RCRA, CERCLA's purpose is not behavior modification. It does not protect the environment by telling persons how to conduct their pollution-causing activities. Its mission, rather, is the repair of environmental harms already done. CERCLA looks to restore damaged sites to pre-contamination, less unhealthful, condition.

---

[1] Hooker was later found to be negligent in the Love Canal case for failing to notify the board that chemicals were buried, often in shallow graves, in the central part of the school site; for failing to respond adequately when it learned that children were actually playing with and being harmed by the dumped material; and for failing to work harder to keep residents off the property. *See* BNA DAILY ENV'T REP., Item 3 (Mar. 18, 1994).

In succeeding years, the case remained active. In 1994, a federal court determined punitive damages were not called for in the case. *See* United States v. Hooker Chemicals and Plastics Corp., 850 F. Supp. 993 (W.D.N.Y. 1994): "Although Hooker's activities after the transfer [to the school board] were clearly unacceptable by present standards and at times violative of common sense, in general, given the state of scientific knowledge and the legal principles of that time, they did not exhibit the degree of recklessness which would warrant a punitive damages award." *Hooker*, 850 F. Supp. at 1068. The court noted that while information about the quantity and composition of chemicals was never revealed to the school board, still there was no effort to deliberately withhold that information. *Hooker*, 850 F. Supp. at 1068.

On June 21, 1994, the parties agreed to a settlement for an announced $120 million. United States v. Occidental Chemical Corp., No. 79-990C (W.D.N.Y. 1994). Under the settlement, the company agreed to pay New York $98 million over three years and undertake responsibility for operating and maintaining a remedial facility at Love Canal, at an estimated cost of $25 million over 30 years. It would also drop any claims it had made against the state. The state in return agreed to abandon all outstanding claims against Occidental, the successor in interest to Hooker, and agreed not to appeal the punitive damages decision mentioned above.

That left the claims of the United States and the City of Niagara Falls to be resolved. The United States settled its claims with Occidental in March 1996. Occidental agreed to pay for federal remediation of the contaminated site and the United States dropped its lawsuit. The liability issues between the City of Niagara Falls and Occidental were resolved by judicial decision in May 1997. The decree found both parties to be liable under CERCLA for remediation costs at the site. *United States v. Occidental Chemical Corp.*, 965 F. Supp. 408 (W.D.N.Y. 1997). The court did not decide the issue of damages.

The Love Canal-prompted interest in giving the land a good scrubbing produced a statute dramatically different in design than the pollution control measures that preceded it. CERCLA (a) looks backward, not forward; (b) directly addresses both environmental quality and public health protection; and (c) creates liability in the absence of conventional considerations of fault. It thereby gathers under its regulatory umbrella entire classes of persons previously unconcerned with and largely unaffected by "environmental law." It was truly a "sea change" in federal policy (some might say a "rude awakening"), and it took legal form despite a dearth of legislative debate and an almost complete unappreciation of the enormity of the problem. (Sound familiar?)

CERCLA was first enacted in 1980 and was amended in 1986 by the Superfund Amendments and Reauthorization Act ("SARA"). The statute was amended a second time by The Small Business Liability Relief and Brownfields Revitalization Act, Pub. L. No. 107-118 (2002).[2]

CERCLA is best understood as having four operative parts:

(1) First, CERCLA enables the federal government to compile information on the enormity and character of the abandoned dump site problem. It requires owners to tell EPA about their sites and to inform the agency of the materials buried at those sites.

(2) Second, CERCLA designates the Hazardous Substances Superfund, found in the Internal Revenue Code at 26 U.S.C. § 9507, as a funding mechanism to pay for site remediations. Section 111, 42 U.S.C. § 9611. The Superfund draws monies from general revenues, from violators of CERCLA, and in accordance with § 113 of the Superfund Revenue Act of 1986.

(3) Third, CERCLA empowers the federal government to clean sites as well as to take other action should a hazardous waste emergency occur. Section 104, 42 U.S.C. § 9604, authorizes the president to use Superfund money to respond to any threatened or actual release of any hazardous substance that may pose an imminent and substantial public health threat.[3]

The EPA decides which sites to cleanup by reference to the "National Priorities List" ("NPL"), the agency's tally of the most polluted sites in the nation. The List is compiled by use of a Hazard Ranking System ("HRS"), and includes about 1,300 sites. *See* 40 C.F.R. Part 300, Appendices A and B. When the EPA cleans a site, it must do so in accordance with the National Contingency Plan ("NCP"), 40 C.F.R. Part 300, promulgated by EPA in accordance with CERCLA § 105, 42 U.S.C. § 9605. The NCP sets forth "procedures and standards for responding to releases of hazardous substances, pollutants, and contaminants." *Id.* Once sites are cleaned, they may be deleted from the NPL. About 350 sites have been deleted.

---

[2] In these materials, the acronym "CERCLA" will be used for the statute as currently configured, unless otherwise specified.

[3] The president has delegated much of his authorities under CERCLA to the Administrator of the EPA. *See* Executive Order No. 12,580, 52 Fed. Reg. 2923 (Jan. 23, 1987), *reprinted in* 42 U.S.C. § 9615 App. at 168 72 (West Supp. 1989).

Section 107 of CERCLA, 42 U.S.C. § 9607, allows for recovery of governmental "response" costs from all persons liable for releases of hazardous substances at the location. The Agency prefers to see private money used to clean sites, and accordingly spends a good deal of time trying to identify those individuals or entities who might be tabbed to do the work.

(4) Last, the Act in § 107 identifies the array of potentially responsible parties ("PRPs") who may be liable for the costs of environmental repair. *See infra.*

The following pages demonstrate the mechanics of CERCLA in graphic form:

SITE DISCOVERY AND STUDY: FINDING THE MOST SERIOUS SITES

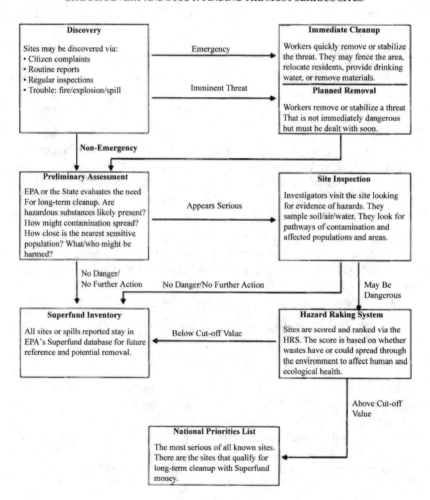

LONG-TERM CLEANUP: FIXING THE MOST SERIOUS SITES

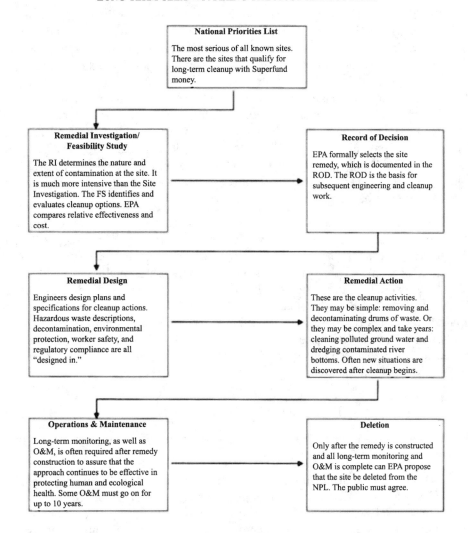

Both emergency and long-term cleanup work can be led either by EPA or by an individual state, or subject to their supervision, by parties responsible for the contamination. The public is afforded opportunities to participate throughout the process.

Following is EPA's description of the mechanics of this listing exercise.

ENVIRONMENTAL PROTECTION AGENCY, NATIONAL PRIORITIES LIST

http://www.epa.gov/superfund/sites/npl/p110916.htm#link3
(site visited Nov. 2011)

. . . .

C. What is the National Priorities List (NPL)?

The NPL is a list of national priorities among the known or threatened releases of hazardous substances, pollutants, or contaminants throughout the United States. The list, which is appendix B of the NCP (40 CFR part 300), was required under section 105(a)(8)(B) of CERCLA, as amended. Section 105(a)(8)(B) defines the NPL as a list of "releases" and the highest priority "facilities" and requires that the NPL be revised at least annually. The NPL is intended primarily to guide EPA in determining which sites warrant further investigation to assess the nature and extent of public health and environmental risks associated with a release of, pollutants or contaminants. The NPL is only of limited significance, however, as it does not assign liability to any party or to the owner of any specific property. Also, placing a site on the NPL does not mean that any remedial or removal action necessarily need be taken.

For purposes of listing, the NPL includes two sections, one of sites that are generally evaluated and cleaned up by EPA (the "General Superfund Section"), and one of sites that are owned or operated by other Federal agencies (the "Federal Facilities Section"). With respect to sites in the Federal Facilities Section, these sites are generally being addressed by other Federal agencies. Under Executive Order 12580 (52 FR 2923, January 29, 1987) and CERCLA section 120, each Federal agency is responsible for carrying out most response actions at facilities under its own jurisdiction, custody, or control, although EPA is responsible for preparing a Hazard Ranking System ("HRS") score and determining whether the facility is placed on the NPL.

D. How are sites listed on the NPL?

There are three mechanisms for placing sites on the NPL for possible remedial action (see 40 CFR 300.425(c) of the NCP):

1. A site may be included on the NPL if it scores sufficiently high on the HRS, which EPA promulgated as appendix A of the NCP (40 CFR part 300). The HRS serves as a screening tool to evaluate the relative potential of uncontrolled hazardous substances, pollutants or contaminants to pose a threat to human health or the environment. On December 14, 1990 (55 FR 51532), EPA promulgated revisions to the HRS partly in response to CERCLA section 105(c), added by SARA. The revised HRS evaluates four pathways: Ground water, surface water, soil exposure, and air. As a matter of Agency policy, those sites that score 28.50 or greater on the HRS are eligible for the NPL.

2. Pursuant to 42 U.S.C. 9605(a)(8)(B), each State may designate a single site as its top priority to be listed on the NPL, without any HRS score. This provision of CERCLA requires that, to the extent practicable, the NPL include one facility designated by each State as the greatest danger to public health, welfare, or the environment among known facilities in the State. This mechanism for listing is set out in the NCP at 40 CFR 300.425(c)(2).

3. The third mechanism for listing, included in the NCP at 40 CFR 300.425(c)(3), allows certain sites to be listed without any HRS score, if all of the following conditions are met:

- The Agency for Toxic Substances and Disease Registry (ATSDR) of the U.S. Public Health Service has issued a health advisory that recommends dissociation of individuals from the release.

- EPA determines that the release poses a significant threat to public health.

- EPA anticipates that it will be more cost-effective to use its remedial authority than to use its removal authority to respond to the release.

- EPA promulgated an original NPL of 406 sites on September 8, 1983 (48 FR 40658) and generally has updated it at least annually.

E. What happens to sites on the NPL?

A site may undergo remedial action financed by the Trust Fund established under CERCLA (commonly referred to as the "Superfund") only after it is placed on the NPL, as provided in the NCP at 40 CFR 300.425(b)(1). ("Remedial actions" are those "consistent with permanent remedy, taken instead of or in addition to removal actions. * * *" 42 U.S.C. 9601(24).) However, under 40 CFR 300.425(b)(2), placing a site on the NPL "does not imply that monies will be expended." EPA may pursue other appropriate authorities to respond to the releases, including enforcement action under CERCLA and other laws.

F. Does the NPL define the boundaries of sites?

The NPL does not describe releases in precise geographical terms; it would be neither feasible nor consistent with the limited purpose of the NPL (to identify releases that are priorities for further evaluation), for it to do so. Indeed, the precise nature and extent of the site are typically not known at the time of listing.

Although a CERCLA "facility" is broadly defined to include any area where a hazardous substance has "come to be located" (CERCLA section 101(9)), the listing process itself is not intended to define or reflect the boundaries of such facilities or releases. Of course, HRS data (if the HRS is used to list a site) upon which the NPL placement was based will, to some extent, describe the release(s) at issue. That is, the NPL site would include all releases evaluated as part of that HRS analysis.

When a site is listed, the approach generally used to describe the relevant release(s) is to delineate a geographical area (usually the area within an installation or plant boundaries) and identify the site by reference to that area. However, the NPL site is not necessarily coextensive with the boundaries of the installation or plant, and the boundaries of the installation or plant are not necessarily the "boundaries" of the site. Rather, the site consists of all contaminated areas within the area used to identify the site, as well as any other location where that contamination has come to be located, or from where that contamination came.

In other words, while geographic terms are often used to designate the site (e.g., the "Jones Co. plant site") in terms of the property owned by a particular party, the site, properly understood, is not limited to that property (*e.g.*, it may extend beyond the property due to contaminant migration), and conversely may not occupy the full extent of the property (*e.g.*, where there are uncontaminated parts of the identified property, they may not be, strictly speaking, part of the "site"). The "site" is thus neither equal to, nor confined by, the boundaries of any specific property that may give the site its name, and the name itself should not be read to imply that this site is coextensive with the entire area within the property boundary of the installation or plant. In addition, the site name is merely used to help identify the geographic location of the contamination and is not meant to constitute any determination of liability at a site. For example, the name "Jones Co. plant site," does not imply that the Jones company is responsible for the contamination located on the plant site.

EPA regulations provide that the Remedial Investigation ("RI") "is a process undertaken * * * to determine the nature and extent of the problem presented by the release" as more information is developed on site contamination, and which is generally performed in an interactive fashion with the Feasibility Study ("FS") (40 CFR 300.5). During the RI/FS process, the release may be found to be larger or smaller than was originally thought, as more is learned about the source(s) and the migration of the contamination. However, the HRS inquiry focuses on an evaluation of the threat posed and therefore the boundaries of the release need not be exactly defined. Moreover, it generally is impossible to discover the full extent of where the contamination "has come to be located" before all necessary studies and remedial work are completed at a site. Indeed, the known boundaries of the contamination can be expected to change over time. Thus, in most cases, it may be impossible to describe the boundaries of a release with absolute certainty.

Further, as noted above, NPL listing does not assign liability to any party or to the owner of any specific property. Thus, if a party does not believe it is liable for releases on discrete parcels of property, it can submit supporting information to the Agency at any time after it receives notice it is a potentially responsible party.

For these reasons, the NPL need not be amended as further research reveals more information about the location of the contamination or release.

G. How are sites removed from the NPL?

EPA may delete sites from the NPL where no further response is appropriate under Superfund, as explained in the NCP at 40 CFR 300.425(e). This section also provides that EPA shall consult with states on proposed deletions and shall consider whether any of the following criteria have been met:

    i. Responsible parties or other persons have implemented all appropriate response actions required;

    ii. All appropriate Superfund-financed response has been implemented and no further response action is required; or

    iii. The remedial investigation has shown the release poses no significant threat to public health or the environment, and taking of remedial measures is not appropriate.

H. May EPA delete portions of sites from the NPL as they are cleaned up?

In November 1995, EPA initiated a policy to delete portions of NPL sites where cleanup is complete (60 FR 55465, November 1, 1995). Total site cleanup may take many years, while portions of the site may have been cleaned up and made available for productive use.

I. What is the Construction Completion List (CCL)?

EPA also has developed an NPL construction completion list ("CCL") to simplify its system of categorizing sites and to better communicate the successful completion of cleanup activities (58 FR 12142, March 2, 1993). Inclusion of a site on the CCL has no legal significance.

Sites qualify for the CCL when:

1. Any necessary physical construction is complete, whether or not final cleanup levels or other requirements have been achieved;

2. EPA has determined that the response action should be limited to measures that do not involve construction (*e.g.*, institutional controls); or

3. the site qualifies for deletion from the NPL. . . .

NOTE ON ADMINISTRATIVE LAW #4[4]

The first Note on Administrative Law discussed how agencies must go about undertaking the actions they take, and the second and third Notes discussed how courts must go about assessing the legitimacy or illegitimacy of those actions. This last Note addresses a slightly different topic: what is to be done when an agency does nothing? Can persons go to court to require an agency to take an action it otherwise refuses to take?

On some occasions, the answer to this question is clearly no. For example, a court would not require an agency to undertake a prosecution of a putative lawbreaker, for the reason that decisions of this sort are peculiarly within the expertise of the agency, and a court would have no meaningful standard by which to assess the propriety of the agency's decision not to take action. *See, e.g., Heckler v. Chaney*, 470 U.S. 821, 830, 105 S. Ct. 1649, 1655 (1985) ("review is not to be had if the statute is drawn so that a court would have no meaningful standard against which to judge the agency's exercise of discretion").

On other occasions, however, the answer would seem to be yes. The primary reason is the federal Administrative Procedure Act, 5 U.S.C. § 551 et seq., which contemplates judicial review when agencies fail to take action. Section 702 of the APA calls for a right of review any time there exists an "agency action," and

---

[4] This is the fourth of four "Notes on Administrative Law" that appear at various points in this book. the material is inserted to assist students who have not learned administrative law. If you have already taken a course in this subject area, or have learned administrative law by some other mechanism, you should feel free to skip this Note. If you have not done so, however, you should both read this Note and resolve to master this important subject area at some future time.

§ 551(13) in turn defines "agency action" as including a "failure to act." And there is more. Section 706(1) of the APA directs reviewing courts to "compel agency action unlawfully withheld or unreasonably delayed."

Still, despite this statutory language, the right of review when agencies fail to act remains uncertain. In *Norton v. Southwest Utah Wilderness Alliance* ("*SUWA*"), 542 U.S. 55, 124 S. Ct. 2373 (2004), the United States Supreme Court held as a general matter that, despite the APA, review is available "only where a plaintiff asserts the agency failed to take a *discrete* action that it was required to take." *Id.* at 64, 124 S. Ct. at 2379 (emphasis in original). What this means is that APA § 706(1) does not have legal effect according to its terms. *SUWA* gives the provision a quite narrow reading.

One instance (of many) where the *SUWA* principle comes into play is with CERCLA. Suppose EPA chooses not to add a particular site to the NPL. Might an entity bring suit against EPA for this failure to act? *SUWA* would say no. Another occasion where *SUWA* might bar the door: the Endangered Species Act, *see* Chapter 7, *supra*, allows persons to petition the FWS and NMFS to secure the listing of species. After *SUWA*, the failure of those agencies to respond to such petitions could not be litigated, for the reason that the listing of a particular species is not a discrete action the agency is required to take. (Note that such a matter *would be* cognizable before the courts if an agency affirmatively denied such a petition, because the denial of a petition is an affirmative act, rather than a failure to act.) Another instance deals with planning issues. Suppose an agency promises in a national forest plan, for example, to undertake certain actions to promote environmental quality, and then fails to honor its promises. Might that be litigated? Again, *SUWA* would say no.

The basic proofs necessary to establish liability in a CERCLA case are as follows:

- The site involved in the dispute must be a "facility" or "vessel." Section 107(a), 42 U.S.C. § 9607(a). The term "facility" is defined broadly (*see* § 101(9), 42 U.S.C. § 9601(9)), but the definition expressly excludes "vessels" (defined at § 101(28), 42 U.S.C. § 9601(28)). EPA gives "facility" an even broader interpretation. For example, in *In re Port Authority of New York and New Jersey*, EPA EAB, No. 96-5 (5/30/01), the Environmental Appeals Board of the Agency ruled the ocean floor to be a facility because substances released from a vessel came to rest at a discrete place. (Thus, a facility was created *after* a release had occurred.) Had the dumped wastes dispersed over a large area, no new facility would have been created and the "vessel exclusion" would have controlled. Even a rocket engine, because it is "equipment," § 101(9), 42 U.S.C.A. § 9601(9), can be a facility. *American Int'l Speciality Lines Ins. Co. v. United States*, 2010 U.S. Dist. LEXIS 65590 (C.D. Cal. June 30, 2010).

- A "release" or "threatened release" of a "hazardous substance" from that facility or vessel must have occurred. Section 107(a)(4), 42 U.S.C. § 9607(a)(4). "Release" is defined extremely broadly in the statute (*see*

§ 101(22), 42 U.S.C. § 9601(22)), as is the term "hazardous substance." Section 101(14), 42 U.S.C. § 9601(14). Note that an abandonment of hazardous substances may qualify as a "release" under CERCLA. *See* § 101(22), 42 U.S.C. § 9601(22). EPA may declare an abandonment "when hazardous waste presents a serious, immediate threat and the waste's owner is not present to take control[.]" *A&W Smelter & Refiners, Inc. v. Clinton*, 146 F.3d 1107, 1112 (9th Cir. 1998). "Federally permitted releases" (defined at § 101(10), 42 U.S.C. § 9601(10)) are free of CERCLA regulation.

• The "release" or "threatened release" must have caused the plaintiff to incur "response costs." The term, "response," includes both removal and remedial actions. Section 101(25), 42 U.S.C. § 9601(25). Removal actions are immediate or interim responses, and remedial actions are more permanent responses. Response costs must be "necessary." In order to show that response costs were necessary under CERCLA, plaintiffs must demonstrate they were responding to a real, as distinct from a theoretical, threat to public health or the environment, and that the costs were necessary to meet the threat. *Carson Harbor Village v. Unocal Corp.*, 227 F.3d 1196 (9th Cir. 2000). In addition, response costs must be "not inconsistent with the national contingency plan." Section 107(a)(4)(A), 42 U.S.C. § 9607(a)(4)(A). (In a private cost recovery action, response costs must be "consistent with the national contingency plan." Section 107(a)(4)(B),) 42 U.S.C. § 9607(a)(4)(B).)

• The defendant is a member of at least one of four classes of persons subject to liability. Section 107(a), 42 U.S.C. § 9607(a). The classes are (a) current owners and operators; (b) certain past owners and operators; (c) arrangers (often, the generators of hazardous wastes); and (d) transporters.

The first three of these essential proofs goes to the nature of statutory liability, while the fourth is the mechanism by which liability may be affixed to individuals. The *Alcan* case that follows directs itself to the former issues; we will review issues of personal liability in Part B of this chapter.

UNITED STATES v. ALCAN ALUMINUM CORP.
964 F.2d 252 (3d Cir. 1992)

JUDGES: Before: GREENBERG and SCIRICA, CIRCUIT JUDGES, and DEBEVOISE, DISTRICT JUDGE.[5]

GREENBERG, CIRCUIT JUDGE:

[This case was on appeal from a summary judgment entered against Alcan, the only party among 20 defendants in the case which did not settle with the EPA. The release of hazardous substances for which EPA sought reimbursement of response

---

[5] HONORABLE DICKINSON R. DEBEVOISE, UNITED STATES DISTRICT JUDGE for the District of New Jersey, sitting by designation.

costs under CERCLA was one into the Susquehanna River via a system of underground tunnels, caverns, pools and waterways near Pittston, Pennsylvania. Wastes were deposited into the underground tunnel network through an entry point designated the "Borehole."]

Alcan did not respond to EPA's early settlement overtures. At trial, it maintained that the toxicity of its wastes was " . . . orders of magnitude below ambient or naturally occurring background levels. Moreover, the trace quantities of metal compounds in the emulsion [were] immobile. . . . " The government did not contest these assertions, arguing instead their irrelevance to the question of CERCLA liability.

On May 8, 1991, the district court entered judgment against Alcan in the amount of $473,790.18, which was the difference between the full response costs the Government had incurred in cleaning the Susquehanna River and the amount the Government had recovered from the defendants which settled with it. This court agreed with the reasoning of the district court, but vacated and remanded the district court judgment for further factual development on the scope of Alcan's liability.

. . . .

II. DISCUSSION

A. CERCLA Framework

. . . .

Reimbursement for response costs can be obtained in a variety of ways. For example, the Government can clean the sites itself using monies in the Hazardous Substance Response Trust Fund established by section 221of CERCLA, 42 U.S.C. § 9631 and now the Hazardous Substance Superfund or "Superfund" (see 26 U.S.C. § 9507); EPA can then seek reimbursement from responsible parties, as it has done in this case. In addition, section 106(a) permits EPA to request the Attorney General to "secure such relief as may be necessary to abate such danger or threat" by filing a civil action in federal district court. That section also permits EPA to issue administrative orders "as may be necessary to protect public health and welfare and the environment." . . .

Finally, and of great significance in this case, CERCLA imposes strict liability on responsible parties. 42 U.S.C. § 9601(32).

. . . .

B. CERCLA Contains No Quantitative Requirement in its Definition of "Hazardous Substance"

Alcan argues that it should not be held liable for response costs incurred by the Government in cleaning the Susquehanna River because the level of hazardous substances in its emulsion was below that which naturally occurs and thus could not have contributed to the environmental injury. It asserts that we must read a threshold concentration requirement into the definition of "hazardous substances" for the term "hazardous" to have any meaning. The United States Chamber of Commerce (the "Chamber") as amicus curiae agrees, observing that "Congress took pains to define 'hazardous substance'. . . . Congress clearly never intended to abandon altogether the requirement that the substance at issue be hazardous." Chamber Br. at 20–21 (footnote omitted). The Chamber further states that "the uncontested facts show that Alcan's waste contained less of these [hazardous] elements than can be found in clean dirt." Chamber Br. at 18. For these reasons it too claims that Alcan should not be held liable for any environmental injury to the Susquehanna River.

The Government responds that under a plain reading of the statute, there is no quantitative requirement in the definition of "hazardous substance." . . .

. . . [T]he district court in this case agreed with the Government. Quoting *Amoco Oil Co. v. Borden, Inc.*, 889 F.2d 664, 669 (5th Cir. 1989), the district court in *Alcan New York* observed, " 'the plain statutory language fails to impose any quantitative requirement on the term hazardous substance,' " 755 F. Supp. at 537, and concluded that "there is no principled basis upon which to deviate from the . . . rule that the mere listing of a substance by EPA renders that substance hazardous." *Id.* at 537–38. In response to Alcan's argument that virtually everything in the universe would constitute a hazardous substance under this reading of the statute, the court held:

> The corporate generator, a non-natural person, has added to what nature has already seen fit to provide for the continued existence of various life forms on this planet; that Congress has enacted laws to limit, and perhaps limit quite severely, additions to nature for the sake of the environment and of life on this planet seems eminently reasonable.

Id. at 538.

For the reasons that follow, we are satisfied that the court was correct in that conclusion. [The court then discusses the plain meaning of the statute, the legislative history (which in this case was unhelpful), and the wealth of jurisprudence indicating that liability does not depend on quantities of hazardous substances.]

. . . .

It may be that Congress did not intend such an all-encompassing definition of "hazardous substances," but this argument is best directed at Congress itself. If Congress had intended to impose a threshold requirement, it could easily have so indicated. We should not rewrite the statute simply because the definition of one of its terms is broad in scope.

. . . .

4. Environmental Policy

In Alcan's view, the district court's construction of the statute is at odds with environmental policy because it imposes liability on generators of allegedly "hazardous" substances although the substances pose no real threat to the environment. Alcan's argument, though superficially appealing, is awed. First, as noted above, the Government responds to "releases" that threaten environmental safety. Thus, it is the release alone that must justify the response costs, not the particular waste generated by one given defendant. Here, there is no question but that a release occurred. Second, the fact that a single generator's waste would not in itself justify a response is irrelevant in the multi-generator context, as this would permit a generator to escape liability where the amount of harm it engendered to the environment was minimal, though it was significant when added to other generators' waste. Accordingly, we find that the district court's construction of the statute furthers important environmental goals. . . .

D. Causation

Alcan maintains that, if we decline to construe the determination of "hazardous substance" to encompass a concentration threshold, we must at least require the Government to prove that Alcan's emulsion caused or contributed to the release or the Government's incurrence of response costs. The Government contends . . . that the statute imposes no such causation requirement, but rather requires that the plaintiff in a CERCLA proceeding establish that the release or threatened release caused the incurrence of response costs; it underscores the difficulty CERCLA plaintiffs would face in the multi-generator context if required to trace the cause of the response costs to each responsible party.

1. Plain Meaning

The plain meaning of the statute supports the Government's position. As noted above, section 107 imposes liability upon a generator of hazardous substances who contracts with another party to dispose of the hazardous substances at a facility "from which there is a release, or threatened release which causes the incurrence of response costs." 42 U.S.C. § 9607 (emphasis supplied). The statute does not, on its face, require the plaintiff to prove that the generator's hazardous substances themselves caused the release or caused the incurrence of response costs; rather, it requires the plaintiff to prove that the release or threatened release caused the incurrence of response costs, and that the defendant is a generator of hazardous substances at the facility.

2. Legislative History

The legislative history also supports the Government's position that CERCLA does not require the plaintiff to establish a specific causal relationship between a generator's waste and the release or the plaintiff's incurrence of response costs. It appears that the early House of Representatives' version of CERCLA imposed liability upon those persons who "caused or contributed to the release or threatened release." H.R. 7020, 96th Cong., 2d Sess. § 3071(a)(D), 126 Cong. Rec. 26,779. However, the version ultimately passed by Congress deleted the causation requirement and instead imposed liability upon a class of responsible persons without regard to whether the person specifically caused or contributed to the release and the resultant response costs. *See* 126 Cong. Rec.31,981-82. Moreover, Congress added three limited defenses to liability based on causation which are contained in 42 U.S.C. § 9607(b): acts of God, acts of war, and acts or omissions of a contractually unrelated third party when the defendant exercised due care and took appropriate responses. Imputing a specific causation requirement would render these defenses superfluous.

In sum, the legislative history indicates that Congress considered and rejected a requirement that the plaintiff establish that the defendant's waste caused or contributed to the release or the incurrence of response costs.

3. Jurisprudence

Further, virtually every court that has considered this question has held that a CERCLA plaintiff need not establish a direct causal connection between the defendant's hazardous substances and the release or the plaintiff's incurrence of response costs. . . . [citations omitted] . . . [*See, e.g.,*] *United States v. Wade*, 577 F. Supp. at 1333 ("the release which results in the incurrence of response costs and liability need only be of 'a' hazardous substance and not necessarily one contained in the defendant's waste. The only required nexus between the defendant and the site is that the defendant have dumped his waste there and that the hazardous substances found in the defendant's waste are also found at the site."). . . .

. . . Accordingly, we reject Alcan's argument that the Government must prove that Alcan's emulsion deposited in the Borehole caused the release or caused the Government to incur response costs. Rather, the Government must simply prove that the defendant's hazardous substances were deposited at the site from which there was a release and that the release caused the incurrence of response costs.

[The court then rejects Alcan's argument that its wastes fall within the "petroleum exclusion" of CERCLA section 101(14), 42 U.S.C. section 9601(14). The last portion of the case, dealing with joint and several liability, is omitted. The court remanded on this issue for a hearing on the divisibility of harm.]

NOTES AND QUESTIONS

1. *Nature of CERCLA Liability.* In the words of one highly placed EPA official, liability under CERCLA is joint, several, strict, retroactive, and perpetual. We will study the joint and several aspects of liability later in this chapter. "Perpetual" is self-explanatory. What about the others?

(A) *Strict.* Alcan removes the element of causation from the universe of necessary proofs for a plaintiff to prevail. The point was made as early as 1983, in *United States v. Wade*, 577 F. Supp. 1326, 1333 (E.D. Pa. 1983) (cited in *Alcan*):

> The government's experts have admitted that scientific technique has not advanced to a point that the identity of the generator of a specific quantity of waste can be stated with certainty. All that can be said is that a site contains the same kind of hazardous substances as are found in a generator's waste. Thus, to require a plaintiff under CERCLA to "finger-print" wastes is to eviscerate the statute. Given two possible constructions

of a statute, one which renders it useless should be rejected. Generators are adequately protected by requiring a plaintiff to prove that a defendant's waste was disposed of at a site and that the substances that make the defendant's waste hazardous are also present at the site.

(B) *Retroactive.* That CERCLA liability is retroactive means that persons may be liable even though they never violated an in-place legal standard. Are there constitutional problems with retroactive liability? *See, e.g., United States of America v. Northeastern Pharmaceutical & Chemical Co.*, 810 F.2d 726 (8th Cir. 1986) (justifying the retroactive liability scheme because of the remedial nature of the statute).

Even if retroactive application of statutes is constitutional, under what circumstances should a court conclude a statute in fact applies to pre-enactment behavior? Note that *Alcan* was decided before the decision in *Landgraf v. USI Film Products*, 511 U.S. 244, 114 S. Ct. 1483 (1994). In *Landgraf*, the Supreme Court found a presumption against retroactive application of statutes. *See also Eastern Enterprises v. Apfel*, 524 U.S. 498, 118 S. Ct. 2131 (1998). Following the *Landgraf* lead, a district court refused to find CERCLA liability where the releases of hazardous materials into the environment predated the 1980 enactment of CERCLA itself. *United States v. Olin Corp.*, 927 F. Supp. 1502 (S.D. Ala. 1996). The *Olin* court concluded CERCLA's failure to mention retroactive liability meant that the statute failed to overcome the *Landgraf* presumption.

The Eleventh Circuit promptly overruled the district court:

> Although the *Landgraf* Court reaffirmed the presumption against retroactive application of statutes, it emphasized that courts must effectuate congressional intent regarding retroactivity. *See Landgraf*, 511 U.S. at 272 74, 114 S. Ct. at 1501 (stating that "constitutional impediments to retroactive civil legislation are now modest"). The Court ruled that its approach simply was designed to "assure[] that Congress itself has affirmatively considered the potential unfairness of retroactive application and determined that it is an acceptable price to pay for the countervailing benefits." *Id.* As a result, we conclude that even absent explicit statutory language mandating retroactivity, laws may be applied retroactively if courts are able to discern "clear congressional intent favoring such a result."

United States v. Olin, 107 F.3d 1506, 1512 (11th Cir. 1997). The Circuit Court found the requisite congressional intent readily demonstrated by the statute's designation of past owners and operators as liable persons.

2.   *"Release."* Assume wooden logs are disposed into a body of still water. At the time of disposal, the logs are not hazardous, but as the forces of nature cause them to biodegrade, they attract microbes that in turn excrete hazardous substances such as ammonia and hydrogen sulfide which "come to be located" at the site. Under these circumstances, has a "release" of hazardous substances into a facility taken place? *See, e.g., Arkema, Inc. v. ASARCO*, 2007 U.S. Dist. LEXIS 45511 (W.D. Wash. June 22, 2007).

3. *Petroleum Exclusion.* The *Alcan* case makes mention of the express exclusion of petroleum from the definition of hazardous substances. Congress implemented the petroleum exclusion because it was considering, contemporaneous with its hasty deliberations of CERCLA, a companion statute going by the name of the "Oil Pollution Liability and Compensation Act" or "OPLCA." H.R. 85. The OPLCA passed the House but failed in the Senate. When CERCLA was enacted, the petroleum exclusion nonetheless remained in place.

B. PERSONAL LIABILITY

The critical legal question under CERCLA is upon whom does liability fall. Section 107(a), 42 U.S.C. § 9607(a), provides the answer by designating the persons and entities who are *prima facie* liable. Section 107(b), 42 U.S.C. § 9607(b), sets forth defenses to such liability. We will consider these matters in order.

1. Prima Facie Liability

a. Owners and Operators

CERCLA assesses liability on certain "owners and operators" of vessels and facilities. "Current" owners and operators, presumably persons who hold that status when an enforcement lawsuit is led, § 107(a)(1), 42 U.S.C. § 9607(a)(1), and "past" owners and operators, i.e., persons who hold that status "at the time of disposal," § 107(a)(2), 42 U.S.C. § 9607(a)(2), are *prima facie* liable for cleanup. The big questions are what is the meaning of "owner" and what is the meaning of "operator." Unfortunately, the statutory definitions of these terms found at § 101(20)(A), 42 U.S.C. § 9601(20)(A), are not helpful. (For that matter, much of CERCLA is poorly written. As stated by one court, "neither a logician nor a grammarian will find comfort in the world of CERCLA." *Pakootas v. Teck Cominco Metals, Ltd.,* 452 F.3d 1066, 1079 (9th Cir. 2006).) By default, the courts have undertaken the task of defining the terms. In these materials, we will first look to the meaning of "owner." Who, or what, is an "owner" for purposes of CERCLA? In partial answer to the question, we can rest assured that a person holding fee simple absolute title to real property would qualify. But would a holder in fee simple defeasible be an "owner"? A life tenant? A lessee for a term of years? Would it make any difference if a lessee for a term of years held a ninety-nine year lease as compared to a lease of three month's duration? What of a permittee or licensee?

CITY OF LOS ANGELES v. SAN PEDRO BOAT WORKS
635 F.3d 440 (9th Cir. 2011)

JUDGES: Before: RONALD M. GOULD and CARLOS T. BEA, CIRCUIT JUDGES, and DONALD W. MOLLOY, DISTRICT JUDGE.[6]

BEA, CIRCUIT JUDGE:

This case calls on us to determine, in the first instance, whether the holder of a revocable permit to use real property is an "owner" of that real property for purposes of imposing liability under the Comprehensive Environmental Response, Compensation, and Liability Act ("CERCLA") for the clean-up of hazardous substances disposed on that property by others. A common sense reading of the statute and existing state law persuade us that this permittee, as the holder of a possessory interest, cannot be such an "owner" under CERCLA, and we so hold.

The City of Los Angeles ("the City") appeals from the district court's grant of partial summary judgment in favor of BCI Coca-Cola Bottling Company of Los Angeles ("BCI Coca-Cola"). The City sued BCI Coca-Cola on ten counts arising from environmental contamination caused by operation of the San Pedro Boat Works located at Berth 44 in the Port of Los Angeles ("Berth 44"). The City seeks reimbursement for the expense of cleaning up hazardous substances disposed of at Berth 44. The parties do not dispute whether hazardous substances were released at Berth 44; they were. The disagreement is over who should pay the clean-up costs.

Under CERCLA, BCI Coca-Cola must pay if and only if it or its predecessor-in-interest — Pacific American[7] — was an "owner or operator" of the boatworks when the hazardous substances were disposed at Berth 44. See CERCLA, 42 U.S.C. §§ 9601-9675 (2006). In a separate decision, the district court held that Pacific American, and thus BCI Coca-Cola, was not an "operator" of the boatworks at Berth 44. The City, for reasons unexplained by the record, did not appeal the district court's ruling on "operator" liability. We therefore focus our analysis on the district court's determination that Pacific American, and thus BCI Coca-Cola, was not an owner of the boatworks for purposes of CERCLA.

Because the definitions Congress provides in CERCLA for "owners" and "operators" are mere tautologies, this court has looked to the common law — including the state law of the property's location — for guidance in other cases when imposing CERCLA liability on possessors and owners of various property interests. See Burlington N. & Santa Fe Ry. Co. v. United States, 129 S. Ct. 1870, 1881, 173 L. Ed. 2d 812 (2009) ("Congress intended the scope of liability to 'be determined

---

[6] The HONORABLE DONALD W. MOLLOY, UNITED STATES DISTRICT JUDGE for the District of Montana, sitting by designation.

[7] BCI Coca-Cola bought all of Pacific American's assets and assumed all of its liabilities in 1993. Hence, if Pacific American were liable under the law — including liability as an "owner" under CERCLA — BCI Coca-Cola would be so liable. The alleged disposal of hazardous substances occurred during Pacific American's tenure as permittee, so although BCI Coca-Cola is the named defendant for purposes of this appeal, all the relevant actions or omissions were those of its predecessor-in-interest, Pacific American.

from traditional and evolving principles of common law.' ") (quoting *United States v. Chem-Dyne Corp.*, 572 F. Supp. 802, 808 (S.D. Ohio 1983); *Long Beach Unified Sch. Dist. v. Dorothy B. Godwin Cal. Living Trust*, 32 F.3d 1364, 1368 (9th Cir. 1994) (looking to the common law, including California common law, to determine whether an easement holder is an "owner" under CERCLA). Under California law, the holder of a revocable permit, like the easement holder in *Long Beach*, has only a possessory interest in the real property governed by the permit, an interest "which exists as a result of possession, exclusive use, or a right to possession or exclusive use of land *unaccompanied by the ownership of a fee simple or life estate in the property." Bd. of Supervisors v. Archer*, 18 Cal. App. 3d 717, 96 Cal. Rptr. 379, 386 (Cal. App. 1971) (emphasis added). Given this common law distinction between ownership interests and possessory interests, and the juxtaposition of "owner" and "operator" in CERCLA — where "operator" liability has been construed expansively in this circuit and others — we conclude that Congress intended to give "owner" its common law meaning. We here hold that "owner" liability under CERCLA does not extend to holders of mere possessory interests in land, such as permittees, easement holders, or licensees, whose possessory interests have been conveyed to them by the owners of real property, which owners continued to retain power to control the permittee's use of the real property.

In conjunction with the more permissive "operator" liability, this narrow construction of "owner" liability furthers Congress's intent to hold liable both the passive fee title owner of real property who pollutes or acquiesces in another's discharge of harmful pollutants on his land, and the active (or negligent) operator of the facility who has only a possessory interest in the owner's real property. Under this construction, and in accordance with California common law, BCI Coca-Cola — as a permittee, subject to restrictions imposed by the landowner, City of Los Angeles, on BCI Coca-Cola's predecessor-in-interest — is not liable as an owner under CERCLA.

Further, the district court did not err in granting summary judgment to BCI Coca-Cola on the City's nuisance claims because the City did not raise a triable issue of fact that Pacific American ever had knowledge, or was put on notice, of the environmental contamination. Nor did the district court err in denying the City leave to amend its complaint to add a breach of contract claim against Pacific American. Therefore, we affirm.

I. Factual Background

Berth 44 is located within the Port of Los Angeles, which is itself part of the Los Angeles Harbor. It is owned by the City of Los Angeles and run by the Board of Harbor Commissioners. The Board of Harbor Commissioners "have the management, supervision and control . . . of all navigable waters and all tidelands and submerged lands . . . at Los Angeles Harbor." Charter of the City of Los Angeles ("Charter"), Art. XI § 138. The Board of Harbor Commissioners is responsible for issuing franchises, permits, and leases for use of the land at the Los Angeles Harbor. Charter, Art. XI § 140(c)-(d).

In 1965, the Board of Harbor Commissioners issued Revocable Permit 936 to the Los Angeles Harbor Marine Corporation ("L.A. Harbor Marine"), for the limited purpose of operating a boatworks — a facility for the repair, maintenance, and rebuilding of ships and boats — on Berth 44. The permit granted possession of roughly 3 acres of land and 1.6 acres of water at Berth 44. From 1965 to 1969, L.A. Harbor Marine operated a boatworks at Berth 44. During this time, Pacific American began negotiations with L.A. Harbor Marine to purchase the permit. While those negotiations were ongoing, Pacific American incorporated San Pedro Boat Works; it became a wholly owned subsidiary corporation of Pacific American. Pacific American and L.A. Harbor Marine agreed on the terms of the sale, and with the City's necessary and prior approval, Pacific American purchased the permit in an asset sale that closed in August 1969.

In the close of the 1969 asset sale, Pacific American conveyed all of its interest in L.A. Harbor Marine's physical assets, not including Revocable Permit 936, to its wholly-owned subsidiary corporation, San Pedro Boat Works, so that at no time did Pacific American ever own the boatworks assets. At closing, San Pedro Boat Works became the sole owner of the facilities and machinery at Berth 44.

Nevertheless, Pacific American's efforts to make San Pedro Boat Works wholly responsible for all things related to the boatworks on Berth 44 were not immediately successful. On August 4, 1969, Pacific American, not San Pedro Boat Works, accepted an assignment of Revocable Permit 936 from L.A. Harbor Marine. In April or May of 1970, Pacific American — not San Pedro Boat Works — obtained Revocable Permit 1076 from the Board of Harbor Commissioners to replace Revocable Permit 936. Not until June 1970 did Pacific American rid itself of its last direct connection to Berth 44 by assigning Revocable Permit 1076 to San Pedro Boat Works, which assignment was approved by the Board of Harbor Commissioners. Thus, Pacific American was the named permittee of Revocable Permits 936 and 1076 for operation of the boatworks for approximately ten months. The parties do not contest, however, that only San Pedro Boat Works operated the boatworks facility at all times, including during those ten months.

In 1974, Martin Vincent purchased the facilities and machinery of the San Pedro Boat Works. Although Pacific American remained the named permittee on Revocable Permit 1076, Vincent assumed San Pedro Boat Works's role as assignee of the permit upon his purchase of San Pedro Boat Works. In 1983, Vincent sold the assets of San Pedro Boat Works to Billfish, Incorporated, and Revocable Permit 1076 was assigned to Billfish. Subsequently, the City and Billfish entered into Revocable Permit 1737, replacing Revocable Permit 1076. In 1993, BCI Coca-Cola purchased Pacific American, including Pacific American's remaining assets and its liabilities. BCI Coca-Cola does not dispute that it acquired all of Pacific American's liabilities, and therefore stands in the shoes of Pacific American for the purposes of this case.

In 1995, the City first began to investigate the soil and groundwater at Berth 44. A variety of contaminants were discovered, including volatile organic compounds, petroleum hydrocarbons, polychlorinated biphenyls, polycyclic aromatic hydrocarbons, copper, lead, mercury, and chromium. In 2002 and 2003, subsea sediment samples collected by the City from the area surrounding Berth 44 revealed particularly high levels of copper and zinc. The City removed the contaminated sediments from the area in 2003 by dredging, which reduced contaminant concentrations to levels acceptable to a multi-agency Contaminated Sediments Task Force.

The City filed its initial complaint against BCI Coca-Cola, Pacific American, and San Pedro Boat Works, among others, on October 15, 2002, alleging the defendants were responsible for contamination of the soil, groundwater, and sediments at and around Berth 44, and thus were liable for the cleanup costs. In its Fourth Amended Complaint, the City alleged twelve claims against eight named defendants for site pollution at Berth 44. Relevant to this appeal, the City alleged three claims against BCI Coca-Cola under CERCLA, as well as claims for private and public nuisance under state law. The City also moved to add a claim for breach of contract in its Fourth Amended Complaint, but the district court denied this motion.

In its Fourth Amended Complaint, the City advanced four theories of CERCLA liability against BCI Coca-Cola based on Pacific American's relationship with Berth 44: The City alleged (1) Pacific American was a CERCLA "owner" because it held title to assets used at Berth 44, (2) Pacific American was a CERCLA "owner" because it held Revocable Permits from the City to do business at Berth 44, (3) Pacific American was derivatively liable as an "operator" because San Pedro Boat Works — Pacific American's wholly-owned subsidiary — was its alter-ego and San Pedro Boat Works was liable as an "operator" of the boatworks at Berth 44, and (4) Pacific American was itself an "operator" of the boatworks business at Berth 44.

II. CERCLA CLAIMS

The City contends on appeal that BCI Coca-Cola is liable for the clean-up of the Berth 44 boatworks because Pacific American possessed Revocable Permits from the City for ten months from 1969 to 1970, and was thus an "owner" of the physical assets of the Berth 44 boatworks when the pollution was discharged, and BCI Coca-Cola assumed Pacific American's CERCLA "owner" liability in the 1993 asset-liabilities purchase.

"CERCLA imposes the costs of the [environmental] cleanup on those responsible for the contamination." *Bestfoods*, 524 U.S. at 56 n.1 (quoting *Union Gas*, 491 U.S. at 7). "The remedy that Congress felt it needed in CERCLA is sweeping: *everyone* who is potentially responsible for hazardous-waste contamination may be forced to contribute to the costs of cleanup." *Id.*

Our court construes CERCLA liberally to effectuate the statute's two primary goals: "(1) to ensure the prompt and effective cleanup of waste disposal sites, and (2) to assure that parties responsible for hazardous substances [bear] the cost of remedying the conditions they created. *Carson Harbor Village, Ltd. v. Unocal Corp.*, 270 F.3d 863, 880 (9th Cir. 2001) (internal alterations omitted). However, in enacting CERCLA, Congress did not "intend[ ] to impose liability on everyone else who has any interest at all in land containing a toxic waste facility." *Long Beach*, 32 F.3d at 1369. Therefore, "we have cautioned that 'we must reject a construction that the statute on its face does not permit, and the legislative history does not support.' " *Carson*, 270 F.3d at 881 (quoting *3550 Stevens Creek Assocs. v. Barclays Bank of Cal.*, 915 F.2d 1355, 1363 (9th Cir. 1990)).

CERCLA imposes liability on "any person who at the time of disposal of any hazardous substance owned or operated any facility at which such hazardous substances were disposed of." 42 U.S.C. § 9607(a)(2). As a successor-in-interest to

Pacific American, BCI Coca-Cola is liable under CERCLA if Pacific American was an owner of the boatworks facility.

Congress did not clearly define the word "owner" in CERCLA. Instead, Congress defined the terms "owner and operator," to mean "in the case of an onshore facility or an offshore facility, any person owning or operating such facility." 42 U.S.C. § 9601(20)(A)(ii). In short, an "owner" is "any person owning a facility." The Supreme Court has recognized that this definition is entirely tautological, and thus useless. *Bestfoods*, 524 U.S. at 66.

Our court has examined the meaning of the term "owner" under CERCLA in just one case. *See Long Beach*, 32 F.3d at 1365. In *Long Beach*, the School District bought land from the Godwin Trust. The Godwin Trust had previously leased the land to the Schafer Brothers Transfer and Piano Moving Company ("Schafer"), which maintained a waste pit on the land. The School District sued the Godwin Trust and Schafer, both of which settled, and also Mobil Oil and Powerine Oil ("M & P"), which did not. The School District alleged M & P were liable under CERCLA as owners or operators because M & P held an easement to run a (non-polluting) pipeline across the land. The pipeline had no connection to the targeted waste pit. The district court granted M & P's motion to dismiss. *Id.* at 1366. We affirmed, holding that an easement for a non-polluting pipeline was not sufficient to show M & P were operators or owners under CERCLA. *Id.* at 1370. "Having an easement does not make one an 'owner' for purposes of CERCLA liability." *Id.*

First, we noted that because CERCLA did not provide a definition of "owner," we should read the statute as "incorporating the common law definitions of its terms." *Id.* at 1368. Looking to California law, we found a number of state law cases distinguishing easements — which convey only rights of and from *another* in or over the land — from ownership. *Id.* at 1368. *See, e.g., City of Hayward v. Mohr*, 160 Cal. App. 2d 427, 325 P.2d 209, 212 (Cal. App. 1958) (holding that although an easement is an "interest" in land, it is only "a limited use or enjoyment of the land in which the interest exists . . . it is not itself either land or an estate in land"); *Robinson v. Cuneo*, 137 Cal. App. 2d 573, 290 P.2d 656, 658 (Cal. App. 1955) (holding that an easement holder, unlike an owner, "owns no part of the land itself and has no right to exclude the owner from the use of any of the land"). From these state law cases, we determined that the common law definition of "owner" did not include an easement holder, and therefore, extending CERCLA owner liability to M & P was unwarranted. *Long Beach*, 32 F.3d at 1370.

Long Beach establishes the rule that this court should look to the common law — including the law of the state where the land at issue is located — in determining whether a party was an "owner" for purposes of CERCLA liability. *Id.* at 1368. Although the holding in *Long Beach* with regard to easement holders is not conclusive of the issue in this case, the case demonstrates that there is a relevant distinction, for purposes of CERCLA owner liability, between absolute title ownership to real property and less-than fee-title possessory interests in real property, conveyed by the holder of fee title.

However, not all courts have followed *Long Beach's* methodology of looking to the common law to determine whether a given holder of a property interest is an owner under CERCLA. Some district courts have determined CERCLA ownership liability by examining whether the holder of that interest (typically a lessee) possessed "site control" over the facility. *See United States v. South Carolina Recycling & Disposal, Inc.*, 653 F. Supp. 984 (D.S.C. 1984), *aff'd in part, vac'd in part sub nom. United States v. Monsanto Co.*, 858 F.2d 160 (4th Cir. 1988).

In *South Carolina Recycling*, the district court of South Carolina held that a lessee could be an owner under CERCLA. *Id.* at 999. There, the president of the lessee negotiated a verbal lease with the owners to use the site to store raw chemicals. Individuals associated with the lessee began storing waste at the site, but did not do so as employees of the lessee. Eventually, these individuals formed a new corporation to manage the waste operations. That entity assumed the lease two years after the verbal lease was formed. The entity continued to store hazardous waste on the property for six more years. The district court held the lessee was liable as an owner under CERCLA because it "maintained control over and responsibility for the use of property and, essentially, stood in the shoes of the property owners." *Id.* at 1003. The court explained that "site control is an important consideration in determining who qualifies as an 'owner' under [CERCLA]." *Id.*

In the only circuit court decision to address the liability of a lessee under CERCLA's owner provision, the Second Circuit held that lessees could be liable as owners only in the rare case where the lessee was a de facto owner, and expanded the site-control test into a five-factor test for determining de facto ownership. *Commander Oil Corp. v. Barlo Equip. Corp.*, 215 F.3d 321, 330–31 (2d Cir. 2000). In that case, Commander Oil bought two lots. Lot 1 was clean office space; Lot 2 was a polluted petrol depot. Commander Oil leased clean Lot 1 to Barlo Equipment and polluted Lot 2 to Pasley Solvents & Chemicals. A few years later, Commander Oil reorganized the leases, so that it leased both lots to Barlo and Barlo then sublet polluted Lot 2 to Pasley. The local Department of Health discovered the pollution on Lot 2 and ordered Commander Oil to clean that Lot. Commander Oil then sued Barlo and Pasley for contribution under CERCLA. The district court held Barlo was an "owner," by virtue of the consolidated lease, and ordered Barlo to pay one-fourth of the clean up costs. *Id.* at 325–26.

The Second Circuit reversed, holding owner liability applied only to lessees when the lessee was a de facto owner, such as in the case of "the proverbial 99-year lease." *Id.* at 330. The Second Circuit held Barlo "did not possess sufficient attributes of ownership" for owner liability. *Id.* at 331.

Commander Oil identified five factors to consider in determining *de facto* ownership:

> (1) whether the lease is for an extensive term and admits of no rights in the owner/lessor to determine how the property is used; (2) whether the lease cannot be terminated by the owner before it expires by its terms; (3) whether the lessee has the right to sublet all or some of the property without notifying the owner; (4) whether the lessee is responsible for payment of all taxes, assessments, insurance, and operation and maintenance costs; and (5) whether the lessee is responsible for making all structural and other repairs.

Id. at 330-31.

Instead of applying a nebulous and flexible analytical framework such as "site control" or *Commander Oil's* five-factor balancing test — tests which do not clearly call out what an investor in land can expect and which factors are themselves susceptible to endless manipulation in litigation — we follow our court's methodology in *Long Beach*. Looking to common law, including California common law, we find that the holder of a permit for specific use of real property is not the "owner" of that real property, where, as here, the fee title owner retained power to control the permittee's use of the real property. Instead, such a permittee holds merely a possessory interest in the land, comparable to the interest of a licensee or easement holder. As the California Court of Appeals has held, a "possessory interest [is] an interest in real property which exists as a result of possession, exclusive use, or a right to possession or exclusive use of land *unaccompanied by the ownership of a fee simple or life estate in the property*," which ownership interest is retained by the fee title owner of the real property. *Archer*, 96 Cal. Rptr. at 386 (emphasis added) (internal quotation marks, alterations, and citations omitted). Such a possessory interest "may be a leasehold interest or the interest of either an easement holder or a mere permittee or licensee," and "may exist as the result of a grant, among others, of a leasehold estate, a profit a prendre, or any other legal or equitable interest *of less than freehold. Id* (emphasis added).

California state courts have consistently distinguished between possessory interests, such as a revocable permit, and title ownership. As the Supreme Court of California recently reiterated with regard to a lease (which, as the facts of this case show, usually confers greater property interests than does a revocable permit):

> Notwithstanding the fact that a lease is a present possessory interest in land, there is no question that as a nonfreehold estate it is a different species of interest from a freehold estate in fee simple. . . . A lease-hold is not an *ownership* interest, unlike the possession of land in fee simple. . . . It is for that reason that common parlance refers to the "owner" of a freehold estate, encumbered or unencumbered, but to the "holder" of a lease; the freeholder is seised of land, whereas the leaseholder is not.

Auerbach v. Assessment Appeals Bd. No. 1., 39 Cal. 4th 153, 45 Cal. Rptr. 3d 774, 137 P.3d 951, 956 (Cal. 2006) (quoting *Pac. Sw. Realty Co. v. Cnty. of Los Angeles*, 1 Cal. 4th 155, 2 Cal. Rptr. 2d 536, 820 P.2d 1046, 1051 (Cal. 1991); *see also Dirs. of Fallbrook Irr. Dist. v. Abila*, 106 Cal. 355, 362, 39 P. 794 (1895) (" 'Owner,' in its general sense, means one who has full pro-prietorship in and dominion over property. In Bouvier's Law Dictionary it is said that: 'The word 'owner,' when used alone, imports an absolute owner.' ").

California is not alone in recognizing this distinction; other common law courts have held that a mere possessory interest in the use or enjoyment of real property, such as a permit, does not constitute "ownership." *See, e.g., Peoples Gas, Light, and Coke Co. v. Harrison Cent. Appraisal Dist.*, 270 S.W. 3d 208, 212 (Tex. App. 2008) ("Texas courts have generally defined taxable 'owner' as the individual or entity holding legal title to the property or holding an equitable right to obtain legal title."); *Stansbury v. MDR Dev., L.L.C.*, 161 Md. App. 594, 871 A.2d 612, 620 (Md. App. 2005) ("[T]he owner of land in fee holds all of the complex elements of a single right, a bundle of sticks, if you will, which include not only the right to use the surface, but so much of the superjacent airspace as he can use, as well as the subjacent reaches below.") (quoting *Macht v. Dep't of Assessments of Baltimore City*, 266 Md. 602, 605, 296 A.2d 162 (1972); *Mesa Verde Co. v. Montezuma Cnty. Bd. of Equalization*, 898 P.2d 1, 11 (Colo. 1995) (holding that the United States "owned" the real property at issue, while the permittees and lessees held only a "possessory interest" in the land); *Spanish River Resort Corp. v. Walker*, 497 So. 2d 1299, 1301 (Fla. App. 1986) (holding that an "owner enjoy[s] all of the sticks which constitute the bundle of rights that is fee owner-ship of real estate") (internal quotation omitted).

This interpretation of the term "owner" is particularly appropriate in the context of imposing CERCLA liability. After all, if Congress intended to impose no-fault, no-cause liability on the holder of a mere possessory interest in real property, the least it could do is speak clearly. In establishing "owner" liability, Congress did not say "de facto owner," or "possessor," or "person with some incidents or attributes of ownership," as it has in other legislation. *See, e.g.*, 26 U.S.C. § 2042(2) (stating that a life insurance policy can be included in the decedent's gross estate for estate tax purposes as if owned by the decedent, if the decedent possessed "incidents of ownership" in the insurance policy). Instead it used the unmodified term "owner" which, as the Supreme Court of California noted in *Abila*, "when used alone, imports an absolute owner." 106 Cal. at 362 (internal quotations omitted).

The logic of this well-recognized distinction between holders of possessory interests, in this case a permittee, and owners is made manifest by the narrow bundle of rights Pacific American in fact enjoyed during its ten-month possession of the revocable permits to operate the Berth 44 boatworks. . . .

Moreover, this construction of "owner" liability best serves Congress's intent in enacting CERCLA. Given the permissive "authority to control" standard for operator liability adopted by this circuit, "owner" liability need not be unduly expanded to resolve situations the other liability hook was intended to address. In conjunction with "operator" liability, the CERCLA framework holds liable both the passive *title* owner of real property who acquiesces in another's discharge of harmful pollutants on his real property or pollutes the land himself ("owner liability"), and the active (or negligent) operator of the facility who holds only a possessory interest in the real property but is in fact responsible for the discharge ("operator liability"). Congress struck this balance between two complementary forms of liability, and this court should uphold that legislative judgment. *See Virginian Ry. Co. v. Sys. Fed'n No. 40*, 300 U.S. 515, 551, 57 S. Ct. 592, 81 L. Ed. 789 (1937) (affirming that a court "cannot ignore the judgment of Congress, deliberately expressed in legislation.").

Thus, applying the methodology of *Long Beach*, we hold that Pacific American, as a holder of the revocable permits described, was not an "owner" of the boatworks at Berth 44 for the purposes of CERCLA liability. Accordingly, BCI Coca-Cola, which purchased Pacific American's assets and liabilities, is not liable to the City of Los Angeles — the fee title owner of Berth 44 at all relevant times — for the costs of the environmental cleanup under CERCLA.[8]

---

[8] We need not reach the broader question whether any other property interest less than absolute title

[Remainder of opinion omitted.]

Affirmed.

NOTES AND QUESTIONS

1. ***Trustees.*** Is a trustee an "owner" under CERCLA? *See, e.g., City of Phoenix v. Garbage Services Co.* 827 F. Supp. 600, 605 n.5 (D. Ariz. 1993):

> This court disagrees with the holding in [other] cases that these trustees are not "owners" of the trust property. "From the traditional point of view it would seem that the trustee is the legal owner of the trust property and is subject to the duties and responsibilities of an owner as far as the outer world is concerned." 2A Scott on Trusts § 265.4 (4th ed. 1988). However, a trustee's CERCLA liability in these situations is necessarily limited to the extent the trust is sufficient to indemnify him; under no circumstances could the trustee's personal assets be reached.

2. ***Passive Migration.*** Assume Person A is the owner of Blackacre at the time hazardous substances are dumped into a permeable lagoon on the property. A transfers title to B; during B's time of ownership, no hazardous substances are dumped. B transfers title to C. C is the "owner" at the time a lawsuit is brought under CERCLA. Who is *prima facie* liable under these facts? Certainly A and C are. What about B? B may be liable if the court subscribes to the theory of passive migration. The theory is that if wastes already in place migrated into the environment during B's tenure as owner (i.e., "passive migration"), then B is an owner "at the time of disposal" and is, therefore, liable under § 107(a)(2), 42 U.S.C. § 9607(a)(2).

The theory remains a matter of vigorous dispute among the circuit courts, some finding liability for "interim owners," others refusing to do so. *Compare Nurad, Inc. v. William Hooper & Sons Co.*, 966 F.2d 837, 844–46 (4th Cir. 1992) ("disposal" includes passive migration), *with United States v. 150 Acres of Land*, 204 F.3d 698, 705–06 (6th Cir. 2000) ("disposal" requires active human conduct); *ABB Indus. Sys. Inc. v. Prime Technology, Inc.*, 120 F.3d 351, 357–59 (2d Cir. 1997) (same); *United States v. CDMG Realty Co.*, 96 F.3d 706, 713–18 (3d Cir. 1996) (same). The debate

---

to real property — such as a lease — is sufficient to expose the holder of that interest to "owner" liability under CERCLA. We suggest, without deciding, that Congress intended to limit "owner" liability to those individuals possessing all of the proverbial "sticks in the bundle of rights," including fee title to the real property. For the reasons provided above, we believe Congress intended to apply this historical meaning despite some efforts to expand the traditional interpretation of ownership. *See, e.g., Pacific Coast Joint Stock Land Bank of San Francisco v. Roberts*, 16 Cal. 2d 800, 805, 108 P.2d 439 (1940) ("The term 'owner' is generic and being of general application is therefore frequently applied to one having an interest in or claim upon property less than the absolute and unqualified title."); *but see Auerbach*, 137 P.3d at 956 ("Notwithstanding the fact that a lease is a present possessory interest in land, there is no question that as a nonfreehold estate it is a different species of interest from a freehold estate in fee simple.")(quoting *Pacific Southwest*, 820 P.2d at 1051). However, we need not address the question of leases here because the revocable permits at issue conferred far fewer rights to the permittee than those granted to a typical lessee, such as those provided by the proverbial "99-year lease" at issue in *Commander Oil*. 215 F.3d at 330. As discussed *supra* at 3520, Pacific American's revocable permits vested fewer rights in the real property than did the lease in *Commander Oil*, and thus our result is not at odds with that of the Second Circuit.

centers on the meaning of "disposal." CERCLA declares the term shall have the meaning provided in RCRA. Seection 101(29), 42 U.S.C. § 9691(29). RCRA, in turn, defines "disposal" as "the discharge, deposit, injection, dumping, spilling, leaking, or placing of any solid waste or hazardous waste into or on any land or water so that such solid waste or hazardous waste or any constituent thereof may enter the environment or be emitted into the air or discharged into any waters, including ground waters." Section 1004(3), 42 U.S.C. § 6903(3).

Those who conclude this definition contemplates passive migration focus on the defining terms "discharge," "spill," or "leak," all of which can occur without human participation. They contend as well that a broad reading of "disposal" is warranted by the remedial nature of CERCLA and the statute's strict liability design. In that regard, they maintain an "active migration" reading would exempt from liability interim owners who knew of ongoing contamination and chose to do nothing about it.

Proponents of the active migration theory have arguments of their own. They contend the broad reading of these defining terms is unjustified because other modifiers in the same definition envision human participation. Moreover, in their view, the broad reading makes "disposal" synonymous with "release," even though the definition of "release" includes "disposing" as well as other terms such as "leaching" and "escaping." Section 101 (22), 42 U.S.C. § 9601 (22). Third, they argue Congress could have created liability for all owners "after introduction of wastes" into a facility had it wanted to do so; it would not have chosen the phrase "at time of disposal" if that were its intent. Last, they assert the passive migration reading effectively eviscerates the so-called "innocent landowner" defense. *See infra.*

As of this writing, the Supreme Court has not decided the question. Congress, however, has addressed the matter at least tangentially. In the Brownfields Revitalization and Environmental Restoration Act (P.L. 107-118, Jan. 2002), Congress added a new provision to CERCLA, § 107(q), 42 U.S.C. § 9607(q), which states that persons who own or operate "real property that is contiguous to or otherwise similarly situated with respect to, and that is or may be contaminated by a release or threatened release of a hazardous substance from real property that is not owned by that person shall not be considered to be an owner or operator" for purposes of CERCLA liability. To fall under this exclusion, persons must not have contributed to the release or threatened release of hazardous substances, and must otherwise be free of liability and have complied with applicable legal requirements.

UNITED STATES v. GURLEY
43 F.3d 1188 (8th Cir. 1994)

JUDGES: Before HANSEN, CIRCUIT JUDGE, FLOYD R. GIBSON, SENIOR CIRCUIT JUDGE, and KOPF, DISTRICT JUDGE.[9]

HANSEN, CIRCUIT JUDGE:

The Environmental Protection Agency (EPA), on behalf of the United States, brought this action to recover the costs of cleaning up a hazardous waste site near Edmondson, Arkansas. The district court entered judgment for the EPA, imposing liability for past costs ($1,786,502.92) and future costs (estimated at $6,000,000) on defendants Gurley Refining Company, Inc.; its principal shareholder and president, William Gurley; and an employee, Larry Gurley. These defendants appeal, raising several issues, the most significant of which are the argument that the present action is precluded by a prior action brought against the Gurley Refining Company, Inc., in 1983 and the argument that Larry Gurley's role in the company's disposal of hazardous waste was too tenuous to make him liable as an "operator" of a hazardous waste facility. We affirm in part and reverse in part.

I.

The facts of this case are well stated in the district court's memorandum order, *see United States v. Gurley Refining Co.*, 788 F. Supp. 1473, 1476 78 (E.D. Ark. 1992), and we will merely summarize them here. From 1970 to 1975, the Gurley Refining Company (GRC) rerefined used motor oil. GRC treated the used motor oil with sulfuric acid, mixed it with clay to absorb impurities, filtered out the clay, and sold the resulting rerefined oil. GRC then disposed of an acidic sludge and the spent clay in a borrow pit[10] it had leased from R. A. Caldwell pursuant to a permit issued for that purpose by the Arkansas Department of Pollution Control and Ecology (ADPCE). *Id.* The wastes of the rerefining process contained hazardous materials such as barium, lead, zinc, PCBs, and sulfuric acid. (Appellee's Br. at 4.)

In October, 1975, GRC discontinued its rerefining processes and stopped disposing of wastes at the pit. In 1978, the United States Fish and Wildlife Service discovered that contaminated water from the pit had spilled over and damaged nearby fish and waterfowl habitats. The Service reported this to the EPA, which performed some work on the pit to prevent future spillovers.

But in the spring of 1979, after heavy rains, the pit overflowed again, releasing about a half million gallons of oily water into the surrounding area. The EPA could not persuade Caldwell or GRC to clean up the pit, so later that year it again performed work on the site to contain and treat wastes. In 1983, the EPA brought

---

[9] The HONORABLE RICHARD G. KOPF, UNITED STATES DISTRICT JUDGE for the District of Nebraska, sitting by designation.

[10] A "borrow pit" is "an excavated area where material (as earth) has been borrowed to be used as fill at another location." Webster's Third New Int'l Dictionary 257 (1986).

an action against Caldwell and GRC under the Federal Water Pollution Control Act, also known as the Clean Water Act (CWA), 33 U.S.C. §§ 1251-1376, to recover the costs it had incurred in 1979. In 1985, the district court entered judgment in favor of the EPA and against Caldwell and GRC in the amount of $76,758.60. *See United States v. Caldwell*, J-C-83-399, slip op. at 9 (E.D. Ark. Oct. 30, 1985), *reprinted in* Appellant GRC's & William Gurley's Br. at A37 A45. GRC did not appeal.

Meanwhile, in 1983, the pit was listed on the EPA's National Priorities List. In 1985, an investigation conducted on behalf of the EPA revealed that the site was still contaminated. In 1986, a feasibility study proposed four alternative courses of remedial action. The EPA chose the third alternative, which called for stabilization of the soil and contaminates, disposal of the soil and contaminates in an on-site landfill, backfilling of the excavated area, construction of flood protection, on-site treatment of contaminated water, and annual groundwater monitoring. *Gurley Refining Co.*, 788 F. Supp. at 1477.

Then in 1987, the EPA brought this action to recover the costs, both past and future, of the remedial action it had adopted after the 1986 study. Before trial, defendant Betty Gurley was dismissed from the case, and defendant R. A. Caldwell settled with the EPA. *Id.* at 1476 n.2. The matter was tried to the court for eight days in June and September of 1990. The district court entered judgment for the EPA on March 27, 1992, concluding that GRC, William Gurley, and Larry Gurley should be jointly and severally liable for cleanup costs, with prejudgment interest from September 10, 1990. The district court also entered a declaratory judgment that those three defendants shall be liable for the costs of all remedial action taken by the EPA in the future. The three defendants appeal.

II.

In 1980, Congress passed the Comprehensive Environmental Response, Compensation, and Liability Act(CERCLA), 42 U.S.C. §§ 9601-9675. Under the Act, persons who are responsible for the release of hazardous substances may be liable for the costs of removing or remedying the contamination, the costs associated with damage to natural resources, and the costs to human health. *See id.* § 9607(a); *see also Dravo Corp. v. Zuber*, 13 F.3d1222, 1225 (8th Cir. 1994). The EPA may initiate a civil action to recover these costs. See 42 U.S.C. §§ 9607(a), 9613(h).

A.

Larry Gurley argues that he should not be held liable because, in short, he was merely an employee of GRC. . . .

1.

Liability for the release of hazardous substances may be imposed on "any person who at the time of disposal of any hazardous substance owned or operated any facility at which such hazardous substances were disposed of." 42 U.S.C. §§ 9607(a)(2) (emphasis added). The EPA does not contend that Larry Gurley had an ownership interest in either GRC or the site of the facility. Thus, he can be held liable only if he is an "operator." Larry Gurley argues specifically that the term "operator" should be limited to those individuals who had the "authority, responsibility, and capacity to control the corporate conduct in question." He contends that he did not have the authority to determine whether or how to dispose of hazardous wastes because he was not an officer, director, or shareholder in GRC and because his father, William Gurley, possessed nearly exclusive authority over GRC's operations.

CERCLA defines "owner or operator" simply as, "in the case of an onshore facility or an offshore facility, any person owning or operating such facility." *Id.* § 9601(20)(A)(ii). It is clear that the term "person" may include individuals, *See id.* § 9601(21), but it is not clear when an individual should be deemed to have "operated" a hazardous waste disposal facility. In *United States v. Northeastern Pharm.& Chem. Co.*, 810 F.2d 726 (8th Cir.1986) (*NEPACCO*), *cert. denied*, 484 U.S. 848, 108 S. Ct. 146, 98 L. Ed. 2d 102 (1987), we held that an individual could be held liable for the release of hazardous substances under a different subsection, which imposes liability on a person who "arranged for disposal or treatment . . . of hazardous substances owned or possessed by such person," *see* 42 U.S.C. § 9607(a)(3). We found that the individual defendant "possessed" the hazardous substances because he "had actual 'control' over the NEPACCO plant's hazardous substances." *NEPACCO*, 810 F.2d at 743.We also stated, "It is the authority to control the handling and disposal of hazardous substances that is critical under the statutory scheme." *Id.* Thus, we affirmed a finding that the individual had "possessed" hazardous substances on two closely related but distinct grounds: that the individual had "actual control" of the hazardous substances and that he had "authority to control" their disposal.

Federal courts have struggled with these two concepts when addressing the question of whether an individual may be found liable as an "operator" under § 9607(a)(2). In some circuits, a plaintiff must prove that an individual defendant had actual responsibility for, involvement in, or control over the disposal of hazardous waste at a facility. *See Sidney S. Arst Co. v. Pipefitters Welfare Educ. Fund*, 25 F.3d 417, 421 (7th Cir. 1994) (holding that plaintiff must allege that individual defendant "directly and personally engaged in conduct that led to the specific environmental damage at issue"); *Riverside Market Devel. Corp. v. International Bldg. Prods., Inc.*, 931 F.2d327, 330 (5th Cir.) (holding that proper focus is "the extent of [individual] defendant's personal participation in the alleged wrongful conduct"), *cert. denied*, 112 S. Ct. 636 (1991); *New York v. Shore Realty Corp.*, 759 F.2d 1032,1052 (1st Cir. 1985) (holding that individual defendant was "operator" because he was "in charge of the operation of the facility"); *see also Levin Metals Corp. v. Parr-Richmond Terminal Co.*, 781 F. Supp. 1454, 1457 (N.D. Cal. 1991) ("an individual cannot be liable as an 'operator' under CERCLA Section 107(a)(2) [42 U.S.C. § 9607(a)(2)] unless that individual actually participates in the operation of the facility at which hazardous substances are disposed of, exercised control over the company immediately responsible for the operation of that facility, or is otherwise intimately involved in that company's operations").

On the other hand, in one circuit, a plaintiff can succeed by proving less than that; an individual defendant " 'need not have exercised actual control in order to qualify as [an] operator under § 9607(a)(2), so long as the authority to control the facility was present.'" *United States v. Carolina Transformer Co.*, 978 F.2d 832, 836 -37 (4thCir. 1992) (emphasis added) (quoting *Nurad, Inc. v. Hooper & Sons Co.*, 966 F.2d 837, 842 (4th Cir.), *cert. denied*, 113S. Ct. 377 (1992)); *see also Northwestern Mut. Life Ins. Co. v. Atlantic Research Corp.*, 847 F. Supp. 389, 397 (E.D. Va. 1994) (holding that individual defendant may be liable if he has "the 'authority to control' activities on the facility"); *Robertshaw Controls Co. v. Watts Regulator Co.*, 807 F. Supp. 144, 152 53 (D. Me. 1992) (holding that liability is proper if individual defendant had authority such that he "could have prevented the hazardous waste discharge"); *cf. Kelley v. Thomas Solvent Co.*, 727 F. Supp. 1532,1543 44 (W.D. Mich. 1989) (stating that court should "weigh the factors of the corporate individual's degree of authority" but also should consider "evidence of responsibility undertaken and neglected").

An individual defendant who has actual control over the operation of a facility presumably also has authority to control the operation of the facility, with the possible exception of an individual acting ultra vires, a situation not present in this case or in the cases cited above. Thus, in reality, the two approaches differ in that one requires a plaintiff to prove that the defendant both had the authority to control the operation of the facility and actually exercised that authority, while the other requires a plaintiff to prove only that a defendant had the authority to control the operation of the facility.

We believe that the latter approach is inconsistent with the term "operator," whose common meaning is "one that produces a physical effect or engages himself in the mechanical aspect of any process or activity." Webster's Third New Int'l Dictionary 1581 (1986). Likewise, the verb "to operate" means "to perform a work or labor," to "exert power or influence," to "produce an effect," "to cause to occur," or to "bring about by or as if by the exertion of positive effort or influence." *Id.* at 1580–81. These definitions connote some type of action or affirmative conduct, an element not required by those courts that ask only whether a defendant had the authority to control the operation of the facility. We prefer not to interpret the statute in a manner that would produce the anomalous result of imposing CERCLA liability on an "operator" who in fact never "operated" a facility. Thus, we hold that an individual may not be held liable as an "operator" under § 9607(a)(2) unless he or she (1) had authority to determine whether hazardous wastes would be disposed of and to determine the method of disposal and (2) actually exercised that authority, either by personally performing the tasks necessary to dispose of the hazardous wastes or by directing others to perform those tasks. We believe that this rule is the wiser of the two choices reflected in the existing case law and is faithful to our closely analogous decision in *NEPACCO*.

The district court made oral findings that Larry Gurley "personally participated in the disposal of the hazardous substances in question in the pit that is involved in this litigation" and that he "had extensive authority in an effort to implement the policies and practices of the corporate entity, which included the disposal of these hazardous substances." (Trial Tr. at 210 11.) In fact, the district court found those facts to be "crystal clear." *Id.* These findings address both prongs of the standard we have set out above. We review the district court's findings for clear error. *See* Fed. R. Civ. P. 52(a).

[The court found no clear error. Although he was not an officer, manager or shareholder, Gurley undertook significant management responsibilities, including negotiations of leases, oversight of construction, and supervision of employees. He had authority for these purposes and he exercised his authority.]

[Remainder of opinion omitted.]

UNITED STATES v. BESTFOODS
524 U.S. 51, 118 S. Ct. 1876 (1998)

JUSTICE SOUTER delivered the opinion of the Court.

The United States brought this action for the costs of cleaning up industrial waste generated by a chemical plant. The issue before us, under the Comprehensive Environmental Response, Compensation, and Liability Act of 1980 (CERCLA), 94 Stat. 2767, as amended, 42 U.S.C. § 9601 et seq., is whether a parent corporation that actively participated in, and exercised control over, the operations of a subsidiary may, without more, be held liable as an operator of a polluting facility owned or operated by the subsidiary. We answer no, unless the corporate veil may be pierced. But a corporate parent that actively participated in, and exercised control over, the operations of the facility itself may be held directly liable in its own right as an operator of the facility.

I

In 1980, CERCLA was enacted in response to the serious environmental and health risks posed by industrial pollution. *See Exxon Corp. v. Hunt*, 475 U.S. 355, 358 359, 106 S. Ct. 1103, 89 L. Ed. 2d 364 (1986). "As its name implies, CERCLA is a comprehensive statute that grants the President broad power to command government agencies and private parties to clean up hazardous waste sites." *Key Tronic Corp. v. United States*, 511 U.S. 809, 814, 114 S. Ct. 1960, 128 L. Ed. 2d 797 (1994). If it satisfies certain statutory conditions, the United States may, for instance, use the "Hazardous Substance Superfund" to finance cleanup efforts, *see* 42 U.S.C. §§ 9601(11), 9604; 26 U.S.C. § 9507, which it may then replenish by suits brought under § 107 of the Act against, among others, "any person who at the time of disposal of any hazardous substance owned or operated any facility." 42 U.S.C. § 9607(a)(2). So, those actually "responsible for any damage, environmental harm, or injury from chemical poisons [may be tagged with] the cost of their actions," S. Rep. No. 96-848, p. 13 (1980). The term "person" is defined in CERCLA to include corporations and other business organizations, *see* 42 U.S.C. § 9601(21), and the term "facility" enjoys a broad and detailed definition as well, see § 9601(9). The phrase "owner or operator" is defined only by tautology, however, as "any person owning or operating" a facility, § 9601(20)(A)(ii), and it is this bit of circularity that prompts our review. *Cf. Exxon Corp. v. Hunt, supra*, at 363 (CERCLA, "unfortunately, is not a model of legislative draftsmanship").

II

In 1957, Ott Chemical Co. (Ott I) began manufacturing chemicals at a plant near Muskegon, Michigan, and its intentional and unintentional dumping of hazardous substances significantly polluted the soil and ground water at the site. In 1965, respondent CPC International Inc.[11] incorporated a wholly owned subsidiary to buy Ott I's assets in exchange for CPC stock. The new company, also dubbed Ott Chemical Co. (Ott II), continued chemical manufacturing at the site, and continued to pollute its surroundings. CPC kept the managers of Ott I, including its founder, president, and principal shareholder, Arnold Ott, on board as officers of Ott II. Arnold Ott and several other Ott II officers and directors were also given positions at CPC, and they performed duties for both corporations.

In 1972, CPC sold Ott II to Story Chemical Company, which operated the Muskegon plant until its bankruptcy in 1977. Shortly thereafter, when respondent Michigan Department of Natural Resources (MDNR) examined the site for environmental damage, it found the land littered with thousands of leaking and even exploding drums of waste, and the soil and water saturated with noxious chemicals. MDNR sought a buyer for the property who would be willing to contribute toward its cleanup, and after extensive negotiations, respondent Aerojet-General Corp. arranged for transfer of the site from the Story bankruptcy trustee in 1977. Aerojet created a wholly owned California subsidiary, Cordova Chemical Company (Cordova/California), to purchase the property, and Cordova/California in turn created a wholly owned Michigan subsidiary, Cordova Chemical Company of Michigan (Cordova/Michigan), which manufactured chemicals at the site until 1986.

By 1981, the federal Environmental Protection Agency had undertaken to see the site cleaned up, and its long-term remedial plan called for expenditures well into the tens of millions of dollars. To recover some of that money, the United States filed this action under § 107 in 1989, naming five defendants as responsible parties: CPC, Aerojet, Cordova/California, Cordova/Michigan, and Arnold Ott. (By that time, Ott I and Ott II were defunct.) After the parties (and MDNR) had launched a flurry of contribution claims, counterclaims, and cross-claims, the District Court consolidated the cases for trial in three phases: liability, remedy, and insurance coverage. So far, only the first phase has been completed; in 1991, the District Court held a 15-day bench trial on the issue of liability. Because the parties stipulated that the Muskegon plant was a "facility" within the meaning of 42 U.S.C. § 9601(9), that hazardous substances had been released at the facility, and that the United States had incurred reimbursable response costs to clean up the site, the trial focused on the issues of whether CPC and Aerojet, as the parent corporations of Ott II and the Cordova companies, had "owned or operated" the facility within the meaning of § 107(a)(2).

The District Court said that operator liability may attach to a parent corporation both directly, when the parent itself operates the facility, and indirectly, when the corporate veil can be pierced under state law. *See CPC Int'l, Inc. v. Aerojet-General Corp.*, 777 F. Supp. 549, 572 (WD Mich. 1991). The court explained that, while CERCLA imposes direct liability in situations in which the corporate veil cannot be

---

[11] CPC has [since] changed its name to Bestfoods . . . we use the name CPC herein.

pierced under traditional concepts of corporate law, "the statute and its legislative history do not suggest that CERCLA rejects entirely the crucial limits to liability that are inherent to corporate law." *Id.*, at 573. As the District Court put it,

> "a parent corporation is directly liable under section 107(a)(2) as an operator only when it has exerted power or influence over its subsidiary by actively participating in and exercising control over the subsidiary's business during a period of disposal of hazardous waste. A parent's actual participation in and control over a subsidiary's functions and decision-making creates 'operator' liability under CERCLA; a parent's mere oversight of a subsidiary's business in a manner appropriate and consistent with the investment relationship between a parent and its wholly owned subsidiary does not." *Ibid.*

Applying that test to the facts of this case, the District Court held both CPC and Aerojet liable under § 107(a)(2) as operators. As to CPC, the court found it particularly telling that CPC selected Ott II's board of directors and populated its executive ranks with CPC officials, and that a CPC official, G.R.D. Williams, played a significant role in shaping Ott II's environmental compliance policy.

After a divided panel of the Court of Appeals for the Sixth Circuit reversed in part, *United States v. Cordova/Michigan,* 59 F.3d 584, that court granted rehearing en banc and vacated the panel decision, 67 F.3d 586 (1995). This time, 7 judges to 6, the court again reversed the District Court in part. 113 F.3d 572 (1997). The majority remarked on the possibility that a parent company might be held directly liable as an operator of a facility owned by its subsidiary: "At least conceivably, a parent might independently operate the facility in the stead of its subsidiary; or, as a sort of joint venturer, actually operate the facility alongside its subsidiary." *Id.*, at 579. But the court refused to go any further and rejected the District Court's analysis with the explanation.

> "that where a parent corporation is sought to be held liable as an operator pursuant to 42 U.S.C. § 9607(a)(2) based upon the extent of its control of its subsidiary which owns the facility, the parent will be liable only when the requirements necessary to pierce the corporate veil [under state law] are met. In other words, . . . whether the parent will be liable as an operator depends upon whether the degree to which it controls its subsidiary and the extent and manner of its involvement with the facility, amount to the abuse of the corporate form that will warrant piercing the corporate veil and disregarding the separate corporate entities of the parent and subsidiary." *Id.*, at 580.

Applying Michigan veil-piercing law, the Court of Appeals decided that neither CPC nor Aerojet was liable for controlling the actions of its subsidiaries, since the parent and subsidiary corporations maintained separate personalities and the parents did not utilize the subsidiary corporate form to perpetrate fraud or subvert justice.

We granted certiorari, 522 U.S.[1024] (1997), to resolve a conflict among the Circuits over the extent to which parent corporations may be held liable under

CERCLA for operating facilities ostensibly under the control of their subsidiaries. We now vacate and remand.

III

It is a general principle of corporate law deeply "ingrained in our economic and legal systems" that a parent corporation (so-called because of control through ownership of another corporation's stock) is not liable for the acts of its subsidiaries . . . (citations omitted).

. . . .

. . . Thus it is hornbook law that "the exercise of the 'control' which stock ownership gives to the stockholders . . . will not create liability beyond the assets of the subsidiary. That 'control' includes the election of directors, the making of bylaws . . . and the doing of all other acts incident to the legal status of stockholders. Nor will a duplication of some or all of the directors or executive officers be fatal." Douglas 196 (footnotes omitted). Although this respect for corporate distinctions when the subsidiary is a polluter has been severely criticized in the literature, *see, e.g., Note, Liability of Parent Corporations for Hazardous Waste Cleanup and Damages*, 99 HARV. L. REV. 986 (1986), nothing in CERCLA purports to reject this bedrock principle, and against this venerable common-law backdrop, the congressional silence is audible. *Cf. Edmonds v. Compagnie Generale Transatlantique*, 443 U.S. 256, 266-267, 99 S. Ct. 2753, 61 L. Ed. 2d 521 (1979) ("silence is most eloquent, for such reticence while contemplating an important and controversial change in existing law is unlikely"). The Government has indeed made no claim that a corporate parent is liable as an owner or an operator under § 107 simply because its subsidiary is subject to liability for owning or operating a polluting facility.

But there is an equally fundamental principle of corporate law, applicable to the parent-subsidiary relationship as well as generally, that the corporate veil may be pierced and the shareholder held liable for the corporation's conduct when, *inter alia*, the corporate form would otherwise be misused to accomplish certain wrongful purposes, most notably fraud, on the shareholder's behalf . . . (citations omitted). . . . Nothing in CERCLA purports to rewrite this well-settled rule, either. CERCLA is thus like many another congressional enactment in giving no indication "that the entire corpus of state corporation law is to be replaced simply because a plaintiff's cause of action is based upon a federal statute," *Burks v. Lasker*, 441 U.S. 471, 478, 99 S. Ct. 1831, 60 L. Ed. 2d 404 (1979), and the failure of the statute to speak to a matter as fundamental as the liability implications of corporate ownership demands application of the rule that "in order to abrogate a common-law principle, the statute must speak directly to the question addressed by the common law," *United States v. Texas*, 507 U.S. 529, 534, 123 L. Ed. 2d 245, 113 S. Ct. 1631 (1993) (internal quotation marks omitted). The Court of Appeals was accordingly correct in holding that when (but only when) the corporate veil may be pierced,[12] may a parent corporation be charged with derivative CERCLA liability for its subsidiary's actions.

---

[12] There is significant disagreement among courts and commentators over whether, in enforcing

IV

A

If the act rested liability entirely on ownership of a polluting facility, this opinion might end here; but CERCLA liability may turn on operation as well as ownership, and nothing in the statute's terms bars a parent corporation from direct liability for its own actions in operating a facility owned by its subsidiary. As Justice (then-Professor) Douglas noted almost 70 years ago, derivative liability cases are to be distinguished from those in which "the alleged wrong can seemingly be traced to the parent through the conduit of its own personnel and management" and "the parent is directly a participant in the wrong complained of." Douglas 207, 208. n11. In such instances, the parent is directly liable for its own actions. *See* H. Henn & J. Alexander, Laws of Corporations 347 (3d ed. 1983) (hereinafter Henn & Alexander) ("Apart from corporation law principles, a shareholder, whether a natural person or a corporation, may be liable on the ground that such shareholder's activity resulted in the liability"). The fact that a corporate subsidiary happens to own a polluting facility operated by its parent does nothing, then, to displace the rule that the parent "corporation is [itself] responsible for the wrongs committed by its agents in the course of its business," *Mine Workers v. Coronado Coal Co.*, 259 U.S. 344, 395, 42 S. Ct. 570, 66 L. Ed. 975 (1922), and whereas the rules of veil-piercing limit derivative liability for the actions of another corporation, CERCLA's "operator" provision is concerned primarily with direct liability for one's own actions. *See, e.g., Sidney S. Arst Co. v. Pipefitters Welfare Ed. Fund*, 25 F.3d 417, 420 (CA7 1994) ("the direct, personal liability provided by CERCLA is distinct from the derivative liability that results from piercing the corporate veil") (internal quotation marks omitted). It is this direct liability that is properly seen as being at issue here.

CERCLA's indirect liability, courts should borrow state law, or instead apply a federal common law of veil piercing. *Compare, e.g.*, 113 F.3d at 584 585 (Merritt, J., concurring in part and dissenting in part) (arguing that federal common law should apply), *Lansford-Coaldale Joint Water Auth. v. Tonolli Corp.*, 4 F.3d at 1225 ("given the federal interest in uniformity in the application of CERCLA, it is federal common law, and not state law, which governs when corporate veil-piercing is justified under CERCLA"), and Aronovsky & Fuller, *Liability of Parent Corporations for Hazardous Substance Releases under* CERCLA, 24 U.S. F. L. REV. 421, 455 (1990) ("CERCLA enforcement should not be hampered by subordination of its goals to varying state law rules of alter ego theory"), *with, e.g.*, 113 F.3d at 580 ("Whether the circumstances in this case warrant a piercing of the corporate veil will be determined by state law"), *and* Dennis, *Liability of Officers, Directors and Stockholders under CERCLA: The Case for Adopting State Law*, 36 VILL. L. REV. 1367 (1991) (arguing that state law should apply). *Cf. In re Acushnet River & New Bedford Harbor Proceedings*, 675 F. Supp. 22, 33 (Mass. 1987) (noting that, since "federal common law draws upon state law for guidance, . . . the choice between state and federal [veil-piercing law] may in many cases present questions of academic interest, but little practical significance"). But cf. Note, Piercing the Corporate Law Veil: The Alter Ego Doctrine Under Federal Common Law, 95 HARV. L. REV. 853 (1982) (arguing that federal common law need not mirror state law, because "federal common law should look to federal statutory policy rather than to state corporate law when deciding whether to pierce the corporate veil"). Since none of the parties challenges the Sixth Circuit's holding that CPC and Aerojet incurred no derivative liability, the question is not presented in this case, and we do not address it further.

[Ed. note: the Sixth Circuit subsequently held that state common law should apply. Carter-Jones Lumber Co. v. LTV Steel Co., 237 F.3d 745 (6th Cir.), *cert. denied sub nom.* Dixie Distrib. Co. v. Carter-Jones Lumber Co., 121 S. Ct. 2244 (2001).]

Under the plain language of the statute, any person who operates a polluting facility is directly liable for the costs of cleaning up the pollution. *See* 42 U.S.C. § 9607(a)(2). This is so regardless of whether that person is the facility's owner, the owner's parent corporation or business partner, or even a saboteur who sneaks into the facility at night to discharge its poisons out of malice. If any such act of operating a corporate subsidiary's facility is done on behalf of a parent corporation, the existence of the parent-subsidiary relationship under state corporate law is simply irrelevant to the issue of direct liability. *See Riverside Market Dev. Corp. v. International Bldg. Prods.,Inc.*, 931 F.2d 327, 330 (CA5) ("CERCLA prevents individuals from hiding behind the corporate shield when, as 'operators,' they themselves actually participate in the wrongful conduct prohibited by the Act"), *cert. denied*, 502 U.S. 1004 (1991); *United States v. Kayser-Roth Corp.*, 910 F.2d 24, 26 (CA1 1990) ("a person who is an operator of a facility is not protected from liability by the legal structure of ownership").

This much is easy to say; the difficulty comes in defining actions sufficient to constitute direct parental "operation." Here of course we may again rue the uselessness of CERCLA's definition of a facility's "operator" as "any person . . . operating" the facility, 42 U.S.C. § 9601(20)(A)(ii), which leaves us to do the best we can to give the term its "ordinary or natural meaning." *Bailey v. United States*, 516 U.S. 137, 145, 116 S. Ct. 501, 133 L. Ed. 2d 472 (1995) (internal quotation marks omitted). In a mechanical sense, to "operate" ordinarily means "to control the functioning of; run: operate a sewing machine." American Heritage Dictionary 1268 (3d ed. 1992); *see also* Webster's New International Dictionary 1707 (2d ed. 1958) ("to work; as, to operate a machine"). And in the organizational sense more obviously intended by CERCLA, the word ordinarily means "to conduct the affairs of; manage: *operate a business*." American Heritage Dictionary, *supra*, at 1268; *see also* Webster's New International Dictionary, *supra*, at 1707 ("to manage"). So, under CERCLA, an operator is simply someone who directs the workings of, manages, or conducts the affairs of a facility. To sharpen the definition for purposes of CERCLA's concern with environmental contamination, an operator must manage, direct, or conduct operations specifically related to pollution, that is, operations having to do with the leakage or disposal of hazardous waste, or decisions about compliance with environmental regulations.

B

With this understanding, we are satisfied that the Court of Appeals correctly rejected the District Court's analysis of direct liability. But we also think that the appeals court erred in limiting direct liability under the statute to a parent's sole or joint venture operation, so as to eliminate any possible finding that CPC is liable as an operator on the facts of this case.

1

By emphasizing that "CPC is directly liable under section 107(a)(2) as an operator because CPC actively participated in and exerted significant control over Ott II's business and decision-making," 777 F. Supp. at 574, the District Court applied the "actual control" test of whether the parent "actually operated the business of its subsidiary," *id.*, at 573, as several Circuits have employed it, *see, e.g., United States v. Kayser-Roth Corp., supra,* at 27 (operator liability "requires active involvement in the affairs of the subsidiary"); *Jacksonville Elec. Auth. v. Bernuth Corp.*, 996 F.2d 1107, 1110 (CA11 1993) (parent is liable if it "actually exercised control over, or was otherwise intimately involved in the operations of, the [subsidiary] corporation immediately responsible for the operation of the facility" (internal quotation marks omitted)).

The well-taken objection to the actual control test, however, is its fusion of direct and indirect liability; the test is administered by asking a question about the relationship between the two corporations (an issue going to indirect liability) instead of a question about the parent's interaction with the subsidiary's facility (the source of any direct liability). If, however, direct liability for the parent's operation of the facility is to be kept distinct from derivative liability for the subsidiary's own operation, the focus of the enquiry must necessarily be different under the two tests. "The question is not whether the parent operates the subsidiary, but rather whether it operates the facility, and that operation is evidenced by participation in the activities of the facility, not the subsidiary. Control of the subsidiary, if extensive enough, gives rise to indirect liability under piercing doctrine, not direct liability under the statutory language." Oswald 269; *see also Schiavone v. Pearce,* 79 F.3d 248, 254 (CA2 1996) ("Any liabilities [the parent] may have as an operator, then, stem directly from its control over the plant"). The District Court was therefore mistaken to rest its analysis on CPC's relationship with Ott II, premising liability on little more than "CPC's 100-percent ownership of Ott II" and "CPC's active participation in, and at times majority control over, Ott II's board of directors." 777 F. Supp. at 575. The analysis should instead have rested on the relationship between CPC and the Muskegon facility itself.

In addition to (and perhaps as a reflection of) the erroneous focus on the relationship between CPC and Ott II, even those findings of the District Court that might be taken to speak to the extent of CPC's activity at the facility itself are flawed, for the District Court wrongly assumed that the actions of the joint officers and directors are necessarily attributable to CPC. The District Court emphasized the facts that CPC placed its own high-level officials on Ott II's board of directors and in key management positions at Ott II, and that those individuals made major policy decisions and conducted day-to-day operations at the facility: "Although Ott II corporate officers set the day-to-day operating policies for the company without any need to obtain formal approval from CPC, CPC actively participated in this decision-making because high-ranking CPC officers served in Ott II management positions." *Id.*, at 559; *see also id.*, at 575 (relying on "CPC's involvement in major decision-making and day-to-day operations through CPC officials who served within Ott II management, including the positions of president and chief executive officer," and on "the conduct of CPC officials with respect to Ott II affairs, particularly Arnold Ott"); *id.*, at 558 ("CPC actively participated in, and at times controlled, the policy-making decisions of its subsidiary thorough its representation on the Ott II board of directors"); *id.*, at 559 ("CPC also actively participated in and exercised control over day-to-day decision-making at Ott II through representation in the highest levels of the subsidiary's management"). In imposing direct liability on these grounds, the District Court failed to recognize that "it is entirely appropriate for directors of a parent corporation to serve as directors of its subsidiary, and that fact alone may not serve to expose the parent corporation to liability for its subsidiary's acts." *American Protein Corp. v. AB Volvo*, 844 F.2d 56, 57 (CA2), *cert. denied*, 488 U.S. 852, 102 L. Ed. 2d 109, 109 S. Ct. 136 (1988); *see also Kingston Dry Dock Co. v. Lake Champlain Transp. Co.*, 31 F.2d 265, 267 (CA2 1929) (L. Hand, J.) ("Control through the ownership of shares does not fuse the corporations, even when the directors are common to each"); Henn & Alexander 355 (noting that it is "normal" for a parent and subsidiary to "have identical directors and officers"). This recognition that the corporate personalities remain distinct has its corollary in the "well established principle [of corporate law] that directors and officers holding positions with a parent and its subsidiary can and do 'change hats' to represent the two corporations separately, despite their common ownership." *Lusk v. Foxmeyer Health Corp.*, 129 F.3d 773, 779 (CA5 1997); *see also Fisser v. International Bank*, 282 F.2d 231, 238 (CA2 1960). Since courts generally presume "that the directors are wearing their 'subsidiary hats' and not their 'parent hats' when acting for the subsidiary," P. Blumberg, Law of Corporate Groups: Procedural Problems in the Law of Parent and Subsidiary Corporations § 1.02.1, at 12 (1983); *see, e.g., United States v. Jon-T Chemicals, Inc.*, 768 F.2d 686, 691 (CA5 1985), *cert. denied*, 475 U.S. 1014, 89 L. Ed. 2d 309, 106 S. Ct. 1194 (1986), it cannot be enough to establish liability here that dual officers and directors made policy decisions and supervised activities at the facility. The Government would have to show that, despite the general presumption to the contrary, the officers and directors were acting in their capacities as CPC officers and directors, and not as Ott II officers and directors, when they committed those acts. The District Court made no such enquiry here, however, disregarding entirely this time-honored common law rule.

In sum, the District Court's focus on the relationship between parent and subsidiary (rather than parent and facility), combined with its automatic attribution of the actions of dual officers and directors to the corporate parent, erroneously, even if unintentionally, treated CERCLA as though it displaced or fundamentally altered common law standards of limited liability. Indeed, if the evidence of common corporate personnel acting at management and directorial levels were enough to support a finding of a parent corporation's direct operator liability under CERCLA, then the possibility of resort to veil piercing to establish indirect, derivative liability for the subsidiary's violations would be academic. There would in essence be a relaxed, CERCLA-specific rule of derivative liability that would banish traditional standards and expectations from the law of CERCLA liability. But, as we have said, such a rule does not arise from congressional silence, and CERCLA's silence is dispositive.

2

We accordingly agree with the Court of Appeals that a participation-and-control test looking to the parent's supervision over the subsidiary, especially one that assumes that dual officers always act on behalf of the parent, cannot be used to identify operation of a facility resulting in direct parental liability. Nonetheless, a return to the ordinary meaning of the word "operate" in the organizational sense will indicate why we think that the Sixth Circuit stopped short when it confined its examples of direct parental operation to exclusive or joint ventures, and declined to find at least the possibility of direct operation by CPC in this case.

In our enquiry into the meaning Congress presumably had in mind when it used the verb "to operate," we recognized that the statute obviously meant something more than mere mechanical activation of pumps and valves, and must be read to contemplate "operation" as including the exercise of direction over the facility's activities. *See supra*, at 13. The Court of Appeals recognized this by indicating that a parent can be held directly liable when the parent operates the facility in the stead of its subsidiary or alongside the subsidiary in some sort of a joint venture. *See* 113 F.3d at 579. We anticipated a further possibility above, however, when we observed that a dual officer or director might depart so far from the norms of parental influence exercised through dual office holding as to serve the parent, even when ostensibly acting on behalf of the subsidiary in operating the facility. Yet another possibility, suggested by the facts of this case, is that an agent of the parent with no hat to wear but the parent's hat might manage or direct activities at the facility. Identifying such an occurrence calls for line drawing yet again, since the acts of direct operation that give rise to parental liability must necessarily be distinguished from the interference that stems from the normal relationship between parent and subsidiary. Again norms of corporate behavior (undisturbed by any CERCLA provision) are crucial reference points. Just as we may look to such norms in identifying the limits of the presumption that a dual officeholder acts in his ostensible capacity, so here we may refer to them in distinguishing a parental officer's oversight of a subsidiary from such an officer's control over the operation of the subsidiary's facility. "Activities that involve the facility but which are consistent with the parent's investor status, such as monitoring of the subsidiary's performance, supervision of the subsidiary's finance and capital budget decisions, and articulation of general policies and procedures, should not give rise to direct liability." Oswald 282. The critical question is whether, in degree and detail, actions directed to the facility by an agent of the parent alone are eccentric under accepted norms of parental oversight of a subsidiary's facility. There is, in fact, some evidence that CPC engaged in just this type and degree of activity at the Muskegon plant. The District Court's opinion speaks of an agent of CPC alone who played a conspicuous part in dealing with the toxic risks emanating from the operation of the plant. G.R.D. Williams worked only for CPC; he was not an employee, officer, or director of Ott II, see Tr. of Oral Arg. 7, and thus, his actions were of necessity taken only on behalf of CPC. The District Court found that "CPC became directly involved in environmental and regulatory matters through the work of . . . Williams, CPC's governmental and environmental affairs director. Williams . . . became heavily involved in environmental issues at Ott II." 777 F. Supp. at 561. He "actively participated in and exerted control over a variety of Ott II environmental matters," *ibid.*, and he "issued directives regarding Ott II's responses to regulatory inquiries," *id.*, at 575. We think that these findings are enough to raise an issue of CPC's operation of the facility through Williams's actions, though we would draw no ultimate conclusion from these findings at this point. Not only would we be deciding in the first instance an issue on which the trial and appellate courts did not focus, but the very fact that the District Court did not see the case as we do suggests that there may be still more to be known about Williams's activities. Indeed, even as the factual findings stand, the trial court offered little in the way of concrete detail for its conclusions about Williams's role in Ott II's environmental affairs, and the parties vigorously dispute the extent of Williams's involvement. Prudence thus counsels us to remand, on the theory of direct operation set out here, for reevaluation of Williams's role, and of the role of any other CPC agent who might be said to have had a part in operating the Muskegon facility.

V

The judgment of the Court of Appeals for the Sixth Circuit is vacated, and the case is remanded with instructions to return it to the District Court for further proceedings consistent with this opinion.

It is so ordered.

NOTES AND QUESTIONS

1. ***Successor Corporations.*** *Bestfoods* deals with liability of parent corporations. What of successor corporations? On this matter, see *North Shore Gas Co. v. Salomon, Inc.*, 152 F.3d 642, 649–51 (7th Cir. 1998) (holding successor corporations to be liable under CERCLA):

> When Congress enacted CERCLA, it enabled the federal government to provide an efficacious response to environmental hazards and to assign the cost of that response to the parties who created or maintained the hazards. *See Anspec*, 922 F.2d at 1247. Accordingly, Congress was unlikely to leave a loophole that would enable corporations to die "paper deaths, only to rise phoenix-like from the ashes, transformed, but free of their former liabilities." *Mexico Feed*, 980 F.2d at 487; *see Betkoski*, 99 F.3d at 519. Moreover, there is no concern — at least theoretically — about punishing the successor for the acts (or omissions) of the predecessor; CERCLA is a remedial measure which is aimed only at correcting environmentally dangerous conditions. *See Smith Land*, 851 F.2d at 91. And holding the successor corporation liable for the cost of cleanup is not necessarily unfair, since the successor and its shareholders likely will have derived some benefit from the predecessor's use of the pollutant and the savings that resulted from the hazardous disposal methods. We therefore reach the same result as the other circuits that have considered this issue — that Congress intended the equitable doctrine of successor liability to apply under CERCLA. We note, however, that while CERCLA permits successor liability, it does not require it "unless justified by the facts of each case." *Carolina Transformer*, 978 F.2d at 837; *see also Chicago Truck Drivers, Helpers and Warehouse Workers Union Pension Fund v. Tasemkin, Inc.*, 59 F.3d48, 49 (7th Cir. 1995) ("Successor liability is an equitable doctrine, not an in flexible command.").

Most circuits which have construed CERCLA to incorporate successor liability have concluded that the parameters of the doctrine should be fashioned by federal common law. *See Betkoski*, 99 F.3d at 519; *Carolina Transformer*, 978 F.2d at 837 38; *Smith Land*, 851 F.2d at 92; *see also Mexico Feed*, 980 F.2d at 487 n.9 (declining to decide whether federal common law or state law supplied the rule of decision, but noting that the district court was probably correct in relying on federal common law). Of course, the mere fact that CERCLA is a federal statute does not dictate that "the federal courts should fashion a uniform federal rule," since "frequently state rules of decision will furnish an appropriate and convenient measure of the governing federal law." *Atchison, Topeka & Santa Fe Ry. Co. v. Brown & Bryant*, 132 F.3d 1295, 1299 (9th Cir. 1997). But most circuits have decided that resort to federal common law is warranted because of the need for national uniformity with respect to CERCLA, and the possibility that parties would frustrate the aims of CERCLA by choosing to merge or consolidate under the laws of states "which unduly restrict successor liability." *Smith Land*, 851 F.2d at 91.

Because CERCLA does not clearly indicate that Congress intended the judiciary to formulate federal common law, the three-part test established in *United States v. Kimbell Foods*, 440 U.S. 715, 99 S. Ct. 1448, 59 L. Ed. 2d 711 (1979), determines whether federal common law is appropriate. *Kimbell Foods* requires a court to decide (1) whether the issue requires "a nationally uniform body of law"; (2) "whether application of state law would frustrate specific objectives of the federal programs"; and (3) whether "application of a federal rule would disrupt commercial relationships predicated on state law." *Kimbell Foods*, 440 U.S. at 728-29.

At this writing, there remains disagreement among the circuits on the question whether state law or federal law should control these questions of successor corporate liability. *See, e.g., New York v. National Service Industries*, 352 F.3d 682 (2d Cir. 2003); *United States v. Davis*, 261 F.3d 1 (1st Cir. 2001).

   2. *Sovereign Immunity.* Is the federal government also at risk of liability under CERCLA or is it free from liability under the doctrine of sovereign immunity? *See* § 120(a), 42 U.S.C. § 9620 (waiving federal immunity). *See also East Bay Municipal Utility Dist. v. U.S. Department of Commerce*, 142 F.3d 479 (D.C. Cir. 1998) (holding the waiver of § 120 to be coextensive with the substantive liability standards of CERCLA).

A NOTE ON THE SPECIAL CASE OF LENDERS

A major issue since the enactment of CERCLA was how to treat lenders. It was long understood that lenders with security interests who foreclosed on real property, and thereby secured title to that property, would by that acquisition become "owners" for purposes of CERCLA and therefore liable for cleanup costs of contaminated lands. That unsavory consequence prompted many lenders to refuse to foreclose. That was the situation until some judicial decisions cut lenders a break. *See, e.g., United States v. McLamb*, 5 F.3d 69 (4th Cir. 1993) (holding that an entity which took title solely to protect a security interest and then promptly divested itself of ownership was not liable as an "owner" under CERCLA).

While decisions such as *McLamb* were helpful to lenders, they still faced potential operator liability. How? If a lender took an affirmative hand in running a facility or managing a property in which it held a security interest, it could by that fact assume operator status and become liable under CERCLA. *See, e.g., In re Bergsoe Metal Corp.*, 910 F.2d 668 (9th Cir. 1990) (lenders can be liable under CERCLA as operators if they exercise managerial authority). Lenders were unhappy enough with that prospect, but the worst was yet to come. In *United States v. Fleet Factors Corp.*, 901 F.2d 1550 (11th Cir. 1990), the Court of Appeals for the Eleventh Circuit held that lenders could be liable as operators even if they had not participated in the day-to-day management of the contaminated property:

> Under the standard we adopt today, a secured creditor may incur section 9607(a)(2) liability, without being an operator, by participating in the *financial* management of a facility to a degree indicating a capacity to influence the corporation's treatment of hazardous wastes. It is not necessary for the secured creditor actually to involve itself in the day-to-day operations of the facility in order to be liable — although such conduct will certainly lead to the loss of the protection of the statutory exemption. Nor is it necessary for the secured creditor to participate in management decisions relating to hazardous waste. Rather, a secured creditor will be liable *if its involvement with the management of the facility is sufficiently broad to support the inference that it could affect hazardous waste disposal decisions if it so chose.* . . .

Fleet Factors Corp., 901 F.2d at 1557–58 (emphasis added).

Fleet Factors engendered a spate of controversy, and a good many sleepless nights, within the banking community and in the federal government, which itself had been in the role of secured creditor with increasing frequency since the collapse of many savings and loan institutions in the late 1980s. The controversy prompted legislative efforts to protect lenders by amending CERCLA, but these initial efforts failed. *See, e.g.*, H.R. 4494, 101st Cong., 2d Sess. (1990), 136 Cong. Rec. H1505 (daily ed. Apr. 4). The EPA then instituted a rulemaking proceeding for the same purpose (*see* 56 Fed. Reg. 28,798 (1991)) but its final rule, promulgated in April 1992, was invalidated by the D.C. Circuit. *Kelley v. EPA*, 15 F.3d 1100 (D.C. Cir. 1994). Congress finally resolved the problem in the fall of 1996 by amending CERCLA. For the current state of the law, see § 101(20)(E)-(G), 42 U.S.C. § 9601(20)(E)–(G).

b. Arrangers

"Arrangers" for disposal or treatment, a group which usually captures generators of hazardous materials, are liable persons under CERCLA. They are persons:

> who by contract, agreement, or otherwise arranged for disposal or treatment, or arranged with a transporter for transport for disposal or treatment, of hazardous substances owned or possessed by such person, by any other party or entity, at any facility or incineration vessel owned or operated by another party or entity and containing such hazardous substances.

Section 107(a)(3), 42 U.S.C. § 9607(a)(3).

CERCLA does not define the terms "disposal" and "treatment," but instead incorporates the definitions of those terms as set forth in the Solid Waste Disposal Act ("SWDA"). *See* 42 U.S.C. § 9601(29). The SWDA defines "disposal" as "the discharge, deposit, injection, dumping, spilling, leaking, or placing of any solid waste or hazardous waste into or on any land or water so that such solid waste or hazardous waste or any constituent thereof may enter the environment or be emitted into the air or discharged into any waters, including ground waters." 42 U.S.C. § 6903(3). It defines "treatment" as "any method, technique, or process, including neutralization, designed to change the physical, chemical, or biological character or composition of any hazardous waste so as to neutralize such waste or so as to render such waste nonhazardous, safer for transport, amenable for recovery, amenable for storage, or reduced in volume. 42 U.S.C. § 6903(34).

Liability attaches upon (a) arrangement for disposal or treatment of hazardous wastes (b) at a facility which currently holds wastes of a similar type (c) from which a release has occurred and (d) for which response costs have been incurred. As the above recitation illustrates, CERCLA contemplates arranger liability (as distinct from owner or operator liability, *see supra*, or transporter liability, *see infra*) only if the disposal or treatment activity involves a "waste." By necessary inference, arranger liability does not attach if the hazardous substance is a "useful product," rather than a "waste." Thus dichotomy brought forth the "useful product doctrine." Useful products are non-waste materials typically the subject of a sale, rather than of a disposal or treatment.

BURLINGTON NORTHERN & SANTA FE RAILWAY CO. v. UNITED STATES
556 U.S. 599, 129 S. Ct. 1870 (2009)

STEVENS, J., delivered the opinion of the Court, in which ROBERTS, C. J., and SCALIA, KENNEDY, SOUTER, THOMAS, BREYER, and ALITO, JJ., joined. GINSBURG, J., filed a dissenting opinion.

[An agricultural and chemical distribution company, Brown and Bryant, Inc. ("B&B"), was in the business of purchasing pesticides and other chemical products from suppliers such as the Shell Oil. Co. ("Shell"). After storing these materials as necessary on its property, it would apply the materials, using its own equipment, to the farms of customers. During times of storage and transfer of the materials, spillages occurred on the surface of B&B's property. These spilled materials escaped into underlying groundwater.

Shell knew of the likelihood of spillage problems at the B&B site. Accordingly, it urged B&B to handle the materials safely, even going so far as to supply B&B with safety manuals and requiring it to undergo inspections by a qualified engineer, among other actions. Despite these efforts, the spillage problems at the site persisted. After B&B became insolvent, EPA added the B&B property to its NPL. Thereafter, EPA and certain state agencies brought this cause of action under CERCLA to secure a clean-up. EPA alleged that Shell was liable as an arranger for disposal and treatment. The 9th Circuit Court of Appeals determined Shell was indeed liable. It reasoned that Shell's knowledge that the disposal activity was a "foreseeable by-product" of its dealings with B&B was enough to establish such liability, even though the disposal activity was not the purpose of the dealings between Shell and B&B. In the 9th Circuit's view, arrangement for disposal could arise in the absence of any intent to dispose. Under this theory, liability can arise even if the purported arranger had done no more than transport a useful and previously unused product for purposes of sale.]

. . . It is plain from the language of the statute that CERCLA liability would attach under § 9607(a)(3) if an entity were to enter into a transaction for the sole purpose of discarding a used and no longer useful hazardous substance. It is similarly clear that an entity could not be held liable as an arranger merely for selling a new and useful product if the purchaser of that product later, and unbeknownst to the seller, disposed of the product in a way that led to contamination. See *Freeman* v. *Glaxo Wellcome, Inc.*, 189 F.3d 160, 164 (CA2 1999); *Florida Power & Light Co.* v. *Allis Chalmers Corp.*, 893 F.2d 1313, 1318 (CA11 1990). Less clear is the liability attaching to the many permutations of "arrangements" that fall between these two extremes — cases in which the seller has some knowledge of the buyers' planned disposal or whose motives for the "sale" of a hazardous substance are less than clear. In such cases, courts have concluded that the determination whether an entity is an arranger requires a fact-intensive inquiry that looks beyond the parties' characterization of the transaction as a "disposal" or a "sale" and seeks to discern whether the arrangement was one Congress intended to fall within the scope of CERCLA's strict-liability provisions. See *Freeman*, 189 F.3d, at 164; *Pneumo Abex Corp.* v. *High Point, Thomasville & Denton R. Co.*, 142 F.3d 769, 775 (CA4 1998) (" '[T]here is no bright line between a sale and a disposal under CERCLA. A party's responsibility . . . must by necessity turn on a fact-specific inquiry into the nature of the transaction' " (quoting *United States* v. *Petersen Sand & Gravel, Inc.*, 806 F. Supp. 1346, 1354 (ND Ill. 1992))); *Florida Power & Light Co.*, 893 F.2d, at 1318.

Although we agree that the question whether § 9607(a)(3) liability attaches is fact intensive and case specific, such liability may not extend beyond the limits of the statute itself. Because CERCLA does not specifically define what it means to "arrang[e] for" disposal of a hazardous substance, see, *e.g.*, *United States* v. *Cello-Foil Prods., Inc.*, 100 F.3d 1227, 1231 (CA6 1996); *Amcast Indus. Corp.* v. *Detrex Corp.*, 2 F.3d 746, 751 (CA7 1993); *Florida Power & Light Co.*, 893 F.2d, at 1317, we give the phrase its ordinary meaning. *Crawford* v. *Metro. Gov't of Nashville & Davidson County*, 555 U.S. 271, 129 S. Ct. 846, 172 L. Ed. 2d 650 (2009); *Perrin* v. *United States*, 444 U.S. 37, 42, 100 S. Ct. 311, 62 L. Ed. 2d 199 (1979). In common parlance, the word "arrange" implies action directed to a specific purpose. See Merriam-Webster's Collegiate Dictionary 64 (10th ed. 1993) (defining "arrange" as "to make preparations for: plan[;] . . . to bring about an agreement or understanding concerning"); see also *Amcast Indus. Corp.*, 2 F.3d, at 751 (words " 'arranged for' . . . imply intentional action"). Consequently, under the plain language of the statute, an entity may qualify as an arranger under § 9607(a)(3) when it takes intentional steps to dispose of a hazardous substance. See *Cello-Foil Prods., Inc.*, 100 F.3d, at 1231 ("[I]t would be error for us not to recognize the indispensable role that state of mind must play in determining whether a party has 'otherwise arranged for disposal . . . of hazardous substances' ").

The Governments do not deny that the statute requires an entity to "arrang[e] for" disposal; however, they interpret that phrase by reference to the statutory term "disposal," which the Act broadly defines as "the discharge, deposit, injection, dumping, spilling, leaking, or placing of any solid waste or hazardous waste into or on any land or water." 42 U.S.C. § 6903(3); see also § 9601(29) (adopting the definition of "disposal" contained in the Solid Waste Disposal Act). The Governments assert that by including unintentional acts such as "spilling" and "leaking" in the definition of disposal, Congress intended to impose liability on entities not only when they directly dispose of waste products but also when they engage in legitimate sales of hazardous substances knowing that some disposal may occur as a collateral consequence of the sale itself. Applying that reading of the statute, the Governments contend that Shell arranged for the disposal of D-D within the meaning of § 9607(a)(3) by shipping D-D to B&B under conditions it knew would result in the spilling of a portion of the hazardous substance by the purchaser or common carrier. See Brief for United States 24 ("Although the delivery of a useful product was the ultimate *purpose* of the arrangement, Shell's continued participation in the delivery, with knowledge that spills and leaks would result, was sufficient to establish Shell's intent to dispose of hazardous substances"). Because these spills resulted in wasted D-D, a result Shell anticipated, the Governments insist that Shell was properly found to have arranged for the disposal of D-D.

While it is true that in some instances an entity's knowledge that its product will be leaked, spilled, dumped, or otherwise discarded may provide evidence of the entity's intent to dispose of its hazardous wastes, knowledge alone is insufficient to prove that an entity "planned for" the disposal, particularly when the disposal occurs as a peripheral result of the legitimate sale of an unused, useful product. In order to qualify as an arranger, Shell must have entered into the sale of D-D with the intention that at least a portion of the product be disposed of during the transfer process by one or more of the methods described in § 6903(3). Here, the facts found by the District Court do not support such a conclusion.

Although the evidence adduced at trial showed that Shell was aware that minor, accidental spills occurred during the transfer of D-D from the common carrier to B&B's bulk storage tanks after the product had arrived at the Arvin facility and had come under B&B's stewardship, the evidence does not support an inference that Shell intended such spills to occur. To the contrary, the evidence revealed that Shell took numerous steps to encourage its distributors to *reduce* the likelihood of such spills, providing them with detailed safety manuals, requiring them to maintain adequate storage facilities, and providing discounts for those that took safety precautions. Although Shell's efforts were less than wholly successful, given these facts, Shell's mere knowledge that spills and leaks continued to occur is insufficient grounds for concluding that Shell "arranged for" the disposal of D-D within the meaning of § 9607(a)(3). Accordingly, we conclude that Shell was not liable as an arranger for the contamination that occurred at B&B's Arvin facility.

NOTES AND QUESTIONS

1. *Non-Arranging Arrangers?* Can the mere presence of unexercised authority to control the activities of an arranger under CERCLA create independent arranger liability in the non-acting party? *See, e.g., Concrete Sales and Services, Inc. v. Blue Bird Body Co.*, 211 F.3d 1333 (11th Cir. 2000) (no). Does an entity that causes a release of hazardous substances (by unknowingly damaging an underground methanol pipeline while installing an underground water pipeline) and fails to meet its obligation to investigate and control that release thereby take on arranger status under CERCLA? *Celanese Corp. v. Martin K. Eby Const. Co.*, 620

F.3d 529 (5th Cir. 2010) (no). Does a manufacturer which (a) designs a machine that purportedly makes disposal of hazardous substances by users of the machine inevitable and (b) fails to specifically warn users about proper disposal of such substances thereby take on arranger status under CERCLA ? *Team Enterprises LLC v. Western Investment Real Estate Trust*, 2011 U.S. App. LEXIS 19880 (9th Cir. 2011) (no). Does the sale of a foundry site for a significantly discounted price due to the presence on the site of electrical transformers containing PCBs constitute an "arrangement for disposal" of hazardous substances? *Sanford Street Local Development Corp. v. Textron, Inc.*, 768 F. Supp. 1218 (W.D. Mich. 1991) (yes).

2. ***Exemption for Recyclers.*** In 1999, Congress enacted the Superfund Recycling Equity Act, thereby amending § 127, 42 U.S.C. § 9627, to exempt certain persons who arrange for recycling from CERCLA liability. The idea underlying the statute was to encourage recycling: without the Act, many potential recyclers might choose to dispose of materials rather than assume the risk of CERCLA arranger liability. Recyclers could become liable as arrangers if parties down the chain of possession failed to handle the hazardous substances properly. The exemption is not available if the claimant had an "objectively reasonable basis" to believe the transferred substances would not be handled appropriately.

3. ***Exemption for Municipal Solid Waste.*** Title I of the Small Business Liability Protection Act established a municipal solid waste exemption long sought by advocates of CERCLA reform. The exemption removes arranger liability for residential landowners, small business entities (those employing fewer than 100 persons), and small non-profit organizations (those employing fewer than 100 persons) who generate municipal solid waste. Section 107(p), 42 U.S.C. § 9607(p). The exemption is unavailable if the waste in question contributes, or could contribute significantly, to the cost of cleanup, if the person has failed to comply with a governmental information request, or if the person has impeded a response or natural resource restoration action.

c.   Transporters

UNITED STATES v. WESTERN PROCESSING CO.
756 F. Supp. 1416 (W.D. Wash. 1991)

Walter T. McGovern, United States District Judge:

Transporter Defendants (Third-party defendants, Bayside Waste Hauling and Transfer, Inc.; Crosby & Overton, Inc.; National Transfer, Inc.; Pontius Trucking; and Widing Transportation, Inc.) move pursuant to Fed. R. Civ. P. 54(b) and 56 for dismissal of all claims against them based upon the Comprehensive Environmental Response, Compensation, and Liability Act (CERCLA), 42 U.S.C. § 9601 or Washington's Model Toxics Control Act (MTCA), RCW 70.105D.

The Transporter Defendants transported various wastes generated by others to the Western Processing site.

The Transporter Defendants argue, however, that they are not subject to liability under CERCLA or MTCA unless they selected the Western Processing site as the destination for the waste. Summary judgment should, therefore, be granted to all transporter defendants as to claims based on waste for which they did not select the Western Processing site.

Additionally, Transporter Defendants argue that under MTCA, regardless of who selected the site, there is no liability when the facility could legally receive the substances at the time of delivery.

Finally, Transporter Defendants argue that as to the four defendants who are common carriers, National Transfer, Pontius Trucking, Widing, and Bayside, rules imposing strict liability do not apply where the activity engaged in is required of the common carrier by virtue of its status as such.

Third-Party Plaintiffs The Boeing Company and American Tar Company, et al. (hereafter Boeing) oppose the motion in most of its aspects, but do concede others.

A. CERCLA Liability

1. CERCLA § 107(a)(4) Transporter Liability

CERCLA Section 107(a)(4) (42 U.S.C. § 9607(a)(4)) imposes liability on

> any person who accepts or accepted any hazardous substances for transport to disposal or treatment facilities, incineration vessels or sites selected by such person, from which there is a release, or threatened release which causes the incurrence of response costs, of a hazardous substance. . . .

Transporter Defendants argue that this language imposes liability against them only if they selected Western Processing as the disposal site. Boeing argues that the Transporters are misreading this section. . . .

The ambiguity of Section 107(a)(4) is resolved by reference to comments by Senators who played a role in drafting CERCLA, the view of the U.S. EPA, and by consideration of the Section in view of the CERCLA statutory scheme.

Senators Chafee and Randolph explained that as to lawsuits against transporters, selection of the disposal destination by the transporter was necessary before liability could be imposed upon him. *See* R.M. Eddy & D.T. Riendl, *Transporter Liability Under CERCLA*, 16 Envtl. L. Rep. 10244, 10251–52 (Sept. 1986).This comment was made in the context of the Senators introducing an amendment to the Resource Conservation and Recovery Act (RCRA) to limit possible citizen lawsuits against transporters and thus bring RCRA into accord with CERCLA, which, they stated requires site selection by the transporter. *Id.*;130 Cong. Rec. S9177 (daily ed. July 25, 1984).

The U.S. EPA takes the same view as the Senators. As a matter of EPA policy, transporters will not be sent notice letters nor have enforcement actions brought against them as potentially responsible parties until it has been determined that the transporter selected the disposal or treatment facility. . . .

To restrict transporter liability to those situations where transporters have selected the site for delivery of hazardous waste is equitable. "Site" in this context is used as a broad term that includes "facilities" for disposal and treatment of hazardous substances and incineration vessels. Also, the definition section of CERCLA, 42U.S.C. § 9601(9), broadly defines "facility" to include a "site" or "area." Thus, the terms are virtually interchangeable.

The terms being interchangeable, there can be little sense in holding the transporter liable for deliveries made to facilities designated by others, but holding him liable for deliveries to "sites" only if the transporter chose the site. An interpretation that this Section meant to hold transporters liable regardless of who selected the site conflicts with the Senators' view referenced above.

Moreover, transporters have a limited role in the activity surrounding hazardous substances. They neither create nor treat the material, but are responsible for its safe carriage between the point where it is generated and where it is left for disposal or treatment. If the transporter does not select the delivery site, the transporter's connection with the material is the most attenuated among potentially responsible parties. If the transporter does select the delivery site, the transporter's role becomes a less passive one. As one who actively selected a disposal site, the transporter may more equitably be subject to liability.

This analysis harmonizes with Section 107(a)(3) concerning "generator" liability where the site selection language is not present. A generator of hazardous substances may be liable for somehow arranging the disposal or treatment of the substances, or by arranging with a transporter for taking care of the material. Thus, whether a generator selected the site or not, the generator will be liable, and site selection language is unnecessary. *Accord*, Sever, *id.* at 6-143. This is appropriate owing to the generator's role in creating the hazardous material in the first place. The transporter, on the other hand, has had no role in the creation or treatment of the material. When the transporter finally does become involved with hazardous material, there will be two alternatives: either the transporter is directed where to take the material, or the choice is left to the transporter. In the latter case, the more active role generates potential liability.

Accordingly, the motion of Transporter Defendants for partial summary judgment as to those deliveries for which they did not select the site is GRANTED.

[The next portion of the opinion, which discusses generator liability, is omitted.]

3. Effect of Common Carrier Status

Four Transporter Defendants — National Transfer, Pontius Trucking, Widing, and Bayside — are common carriers licensed and regulated by the Interstate Commerce Commission and the Washington State Utilities and Transportation Commission. As such, they argue a separate and additional basis for this motion.

They argue that as common carriers, they must accept, carry, and deliver all goods offered to them for transport within the scope of the operating authority set forth in their permits. They cannot discriminate against customers nor refuse to accept commodities that may be dangerous for transport. Thus, courts have recognized a "public duty" exception to absolute or strict liability arising from the carriage of hazardous substances. While this argument may have been or could have been part of the rationale for requiring that a transporter select the site for delivering hazardous materials before liability may attach, this argument as a complete defense to liability is not well taken.

CERCLA's liability provision begins at Section 107(a):

> Notwithstanding any other provision or rule of law, and subject only to the defenses set forth in subsection (b) of this section. . . .

This Court has considered the availability of other defenses under this section and has concluded that this section precludes unenumerated defenses. *See United States v. Western Processing Co.*, 734 F. Supp. 930, 939 (W.D. Wash. 1990) (The better reasoned decisions and the majority of cases have held that the limited defenses of Section 107(b) are exclusive.) Therefore, since there are only three defenses under Section 107(b) — an act of God, and act of war, or an act or omission of a third party — and since the common carrier defense falls under none of these enumerated defenses, the Transporter Defendants may not raise it.

[The remainder of the opinion, dealing with defendants' liability under state law, and with procedural matters, is omitted.]

NOTE

More on Transporter Liability. A party may be liable as a transporter even if the material remains on the site, if the material is moved from one part of the site to another. *See, e.g., Kaiser Aluminum & Chem. Corp. v. Catellus Dev't Co.*, 976 F.2d 1338 (9th Cir. 1992). For a review of cases on CERCLA liability of transporters, see William B. Johnson, J.D., Annotation, *Transporter Liability Under § 107(a)(4) of the Comprehensive Environmental Response, Compensation, and Liability Act (CERCLA) (42 U.S.C.A. § 9607(a))*, 112 A.L.R. 49 (2001).

Title I of the Small Business Liability Protection Act added a provision establishing, as a general matter, a *de micromis* exemption from liability for arrangers or transporters whose total contribution to an NPL site is less than 110 gallons of liquid materials or less than 200 pounds of solid materials (or such lesser or greater amounts as the EPA shall determine). Section 107(o), 42 U.S.C. § 9607(o). The exemption is not available if the materials contributed significantly to costs of response or natural resource restoration actions, or if the otherwise liable party has failed to cooperate with an information request or enforcement activities or has been convicted criminally for the conduct to which the exemption would apply. Section 107(o)(2), 42 U.S.C. § 9607(o)(2). Such determinations are not judicially reviewable. Section 107(o)(3), 42 U.S.C. § 9607(o)(3).

2. Defenses

Once *prima facie* liability is established under § 107, the matter of defenses comes into play. Three of CERCLA's defenses are found in § 107(b), 42 U.S.C. § 9607(b). First is the "act of God" defense. Section 107(b)(1), 42 U.S.C. § 9607(b)(1). What is an act of God? For a definition, see § 101(1), 42 U.S.C. § 9601(1). Second is the "act of war" defense. Section 107(b)(2), 42 U.S.C. § 9607(b)(2). "Act of war" is undefined in CERCLA. For an at-length judicial discussion, see *United States v. Shell Oil Co.*, 841 F. Supp. 962 (C.D. Cal. 1993).

The third, and most important, of the § 107(b) defenses is the "third party defense." Section 107(b)(3), 42 U.S.C. § 9607(3). To understand this defense and its availability, it is necessary to review several statutory definitional sections, especially § 101(35), 42 U.S.C. § 9601(35), defining the term "contractual arrangement."

The fourth and final CERCLA defense is the bona fide prospective purchaser defense, which was added to the statute in January 2002, as part of the Small Business Liability Protection and Brownfields Revitalization Act, P.L. 107-118, 42 U.S.C. § 9607. That provision is described in the Notes following the *Westwood* case, *infra*. *Westwood* examines the third-party defense.

WESTWOOD PHARMACEUTICALS, INC. v. NATIONAL FUEL GAS DISTRIBUTION CORP.
964 F.2d 85 (2d Cir. 1992)

OPINION: TIMBERS, CIRCUIT JUDGE:

Appellant Westwood Pharmaceuticals, Inc. (Westwood) appeals from an order entered June 19, 1991 in the Western District of New York, John T. Curtin, District Judge, denying Westwood's motion for reconsideration of that portion of an order entered in the same court on May 21, 1990 denying Westwood's motion for summary judgment on its claim that appellee National Fuel Gas Distribution Corporation (National Fuel) is liable in Westwood's action brought pursuant to §§ 107(a)(2), 113(f) and 113(g) of the Comprehensive Environmental Response, Compensation and Liability Act (CERCLA), 42 U.S.C. §§ 9607(a), 9613(f) and 9613(g) (1988) as amended by the Superfund Amendments and Reauthorization Act, Pub. L. No. 99-499, 100 Stat. 1613 (1986).

On October 14, 1988, Westwood commenced this action against National Fuel seeking to recover costs incurred in investigating and remedying chemical contamination at certain premises in Buffalo it had purchased from National Fuel's predecessor in interest, Iroquois Gas Corporation (Iroquois). Westwood moved for partial summary judgment on the liability issues presented by its CERCLA action. After the district court denied Westwood's motion for summary judgment, Westwood moved for reconsideration of its order. The district court on June 19, 1991, denied Westwood's motion for reconsideration. On August 6, 1991, at the request of Westwood, the district court amended its order to include certification for an interlocutory appeal pursuant to 28 U.S.C. § 1292(b) (1988). On November 6, 1991, a panel of our Court granted Westwood's petition for leave to appeal pursuant to § 1292(b).

On appeal, Westwood contends (1) that the mere existence of a contractual relationship, without more, between it and National Fuel precludes National Fuel from invoking the third-party defense of CERCLA § 107(b)(3); and, alternatively, (2) that CERCLA § 101(35)(C), 42 U.S.C. § 9601(35)(c), precludes National Fuel from raising the third-party defense provided for in § 107(b)(3). For the reasons that follow, we affirm the order of the district court denying Westwood's motion for reconsideration of the district court's earlier order that denied Westwood's motion for summary judgment on the issue of National Fuel's liability under CERCLA.

I.

We shall summarize only those facts and prior proceedings believed necessary to an understanding of the issues raised on appeal.

The site which is the subject matter of this action was purchased in 1925 by Iroquois. Iroquois conducted gas manufacturing and storage operations on the land through 1951. For several years thereafter it continued to use the site for gas compression and storage. During these operations Iroquois placed or used various underground pipes and structures at the site. In 1968, Iroquois demolished certain structures on the northeast portion of the site, but left other structures on the site standing.

Iroquois sold the site to Westwood in 1972 for $60,100. Westwood demolished the remaining structures on the site and constructed a warehouse on the southern portion of the site. During these construction activities and associated soil testing, Westwood discovered various subsurface contaminants. In the instant action Westwood seeks to recover the response costs — the costs of cleaning up the contaminants — for which it claims National Fuel is liable. Westwood's complaint alleged claims pursuant to CERCLA as stated above, and related common law claims of public nuisance, private nuisance, and restitution. . . .

In its answer to Westwood's complaint, National Fuel alleged various affirmative defenses. In its order of May 21, 1990, 737 F. Supp. 1272 (W.D.N.Y. 1990), the district court, among other things, granted National Fuel's motion to dismiss Westwood's private nuisance and restitution claims; denied National Fuel's motion with respect to Westwood's CERCLA and public nuisance claims; and denied Westwood's motion for summary judgment which asserted that National Fuel was liable on its CERCLA claim.

The district court held that National Fuel had raised a triable issue of fact by contending that, under the "third-party defense" of CERCLA § 107(b)(3), it was not liable on Westwood's CERCLA claims. Section 107(b)(3) provides in relevant part:

> "There shall be no liability under subsection (a) of this section for a person otherwise liable who can establish by a preponderance of the evidence that the release or threat of release of a hazardous substance and the damages resulting therefrom were caused solely by — . . .

> "(3) an act or omission of a third party other than an employee or agent of the defendant, or than one whose act or omission occurs in connection with a contractual relationship, existing directly or indirectly, with the defendant . . . if the defendant establishes by a preponderance of the evidence that (a) he exercised due care with respect to the hazardous substance concerned, taking into consideration the characteristics of such hazardous substance, in light of all relevant facts and circumstances, and (b) he took precautions against foreseeable acts or omissions of any such third party and the consequences that could foreseeably result from such

acts or omissions. . . . " (emphasis added)

National Fuel did not dispute the fact that its 1972 sales contract with Westwood was a "contractual relationship", since CERCLA § 101(35)(A) provides that "the term 'contractual relationship', for the purpose of section 9607(b)(3) of this title includes, but is not limited to, land contracts, deeds or other instruments transferring title or possession. . . . " National Fuel asserted, however, that Westwood's construction activities were not undertaken by Westwood "in connection with" the contractual relationship between National Fuel and Westwood. Furthermore, National Fuel asserted that, if in fact it placed hazardous substances at the site it exercised due care with respect to such substances and took precautions against the foreseeable acts or omissions of third persons. Specifically, National Fuel asserted that any such substances that were not eventually removed from the premises for off-site use or disposal were left inside secure subsurface receptacles. Moreover, National Fuel asserted that the structural integrity of these subsurface receptacles left at the site would not have been breached and therefore hazardous substances would not have escaped but for the unforeseeable construction activities of Westwood.

The district court held that the phrase "in connection with" in § 107(b)(3) requires that there be some relationship between the disposal/releasing activity and the contract with the defendant for a defendant to be barred from raising the third-party defense. Since it held that National Fuel had raised a triable issue of fact by contending that Westwood was the sole cause of the release or threatened release of hazardous substances at the site, the court denied Westwood's motion for summary judgment which asserted that National Fuel was liable under CERCLA § 107(a)(2).

Westwood made a motion for reconsideration of the court's decision in light of CERCLA § 101(35)(C), which was added to CERCLA when Congress enacted § 101(f) of the Superfund Amendments and Reauthorization Act of 1986. Section 101(35)(A) and (B) establish what is known as the "innocent landowner exception", which protects landowners who acquire the property after the disposal or placement of hazardous substances on it and who do not know and have no reason to know that the hazardous substances are on the property. The first sentence of § 101(35)(C) provides that "nothing in this paragraph or in section 9607(b)(3) of this title shall diminish the liability of any previous owner or operator of such facility who would otherwise be liable under this chapter."

The district court, in its order of June 19, 1991, 767 F. Supp. 456 (W.D.N.Y. 1991), reaffirmed its holding that the mere existence of a contractual relationship does not preclude a former owner from invoking the third-party defense, and rejected Westwood's contention that § 101(35)(C) forecloses a prior owner like National Fuel from asserting the third-party defense provided for in § 107(b)(3). There followed the § 1292(b) certifications referred to above.

On the issues raised by Westwood's interlocutory appeal as stated above, we affirm the district court for the reasons set forth below.

II.

[Part II of the opinion, concluding that this interlocutory appeal should be entertained by the court, is omitted.]

III.

The district court held that the phrase "in connection with" requires that there be some relationship between the disposal/releasing activity and the contract with the defendant for the defendant to be barred from raising the third-party defense of § 107(b)(3). The court stated that to hold otherwise would render the language "in connection with" superfluous, a result generally at odds with an accepted principle of statutory construction. 737 F. Supp. at 1286 (citing *Ohio Power Co. v. Federal Energy Regulatory Comm'n*, 279 App. D.C. 327, 880 F.2d 1400,1406 (D.C. Cir.) (constructions rendering statutory language superfluous are disfavored), *reh'g and reh'g en banc denied*, 897 F.2d 540 (D.C. Cir. 1989), *rev'd on other grounds*, 111 S. Ct. 415 (1990); *National Ass'n of Recycling Indus., Inc. v. Interstate Commerce Comm'n.*, 212 App. D.C. 396, 660 F.2d 795, 799 (D.C. Cir. 1981) (same)).

Other cases considering this or similar questions also have indicated that something more than a mere contractual relationship is required. In *United States v. Hooker Chemicals & Plastics Corp.*, 680 F. Supp. 546 (W.D.N.Y. 1988), the court held that defendants' contractual relationship with the present landowner — defendants had deeded the land to the City precluded defendant from raising the third-party defense of § 107(b)(3) since "[defendant] was able to control the acts of these subsequent purchasers because of the nature of its relationship with these defendants in this case." *Id.* at 558. In *Shapiro v. Alexanderson*, 743 F. Supp. 268 (S.D.N.Y. 1990), the court held that the contractual relationship clause of § 107(b)(3) does not embrace "all acts by a third party with any contractual relationship with a defendant. Such a construction would render the language 'in connection with' mere surplusage." *Id.* at 271. "The act or omission must occur in a context so that there is a connection between the acts and the contractual relationship." *Id.* In *Shapiro*, the court described the "classic scenario" in which a landowner would be precluded from asserting a § 107(b)(3) defense: when the third party is operating a landfill pursuant to a contract with the owner. *Id.*

We agree with the district court that a landowner is precluded from raising the third-party defense only if the contract between the landowner and the third party somehow is connected with the handling of hazardous substances. The result would be the same if the contract allows the landowner to exert some control over the third party's actions so that the landowner fairly can be held liable for the release or threatened release of hazardous substances caused solely by the actions of the third party. The mere existence of a contractual relationship between the owner of land on which hazardous substances are or have been disposed and a third party whose act or omission was the sole cause of the release or threatened release of such hazardous substances into the environment does not foreclose the owner of the land from escaping liability, provided that the owner satisfies the additional requirements of § 107(b)(3)(a) and (b).

IV.

Section 101(35)(A) and (B) establish the "innocent landowner exception" (also referred to as the "innocent landowner defense" or the "innocent purchaser defense"). Section 101(35)(A) provides in relevant part:

"The term 'contractual relationship', for the purpose of section 9607(b)(3) of this title includes, but is not limited to, land contracts, deeds or other instruments transferring title or possession, unless the real property on which the facility concerned is located was acquired by the defendant after the disposal or placement of the hazardous substance on, in, or at the facility, and one or more of the circumstances described in clause (i), (ii), or (iii) is also established by the defendant by a preponderance of the evidence:

"(i) At the time the defendant acquired the facility the defendant did not know and had no reason to know that any hazardous substance which is the subject of the release or threatened release was disposed of on, in, or at the facility. . . .

"In addition to establishing the foregoing, the defendant must establish that he has satisfied the requirements of section 9607(b)(3)(a) and (b) of this title."

Section 101(35)(B) further provides that the "innocent landowner exception" is available only to defendants who make appropriate inquiry, at the time of acquisition, into the previous ownership and use of the property.

Section 101(35)(C) provides that:

"Nothing in this paragraph or in section 9607(b)(3) of this title shall diminish the liability of any previous owner or operator of such facility who would otherwise be liable under this chapter. Notwithstanding this paragraph, if the defendant obtained actual knowledge of the release or threatened release of a hazardous substance at such facility when the defendant owned the real property and then subsequently transferred ownership of the property to another person without disclosing such knowledge, such defendant shall be treated as liable under section 9607(a)(1) of this title and no defense under section 9607(b)(3) of this title shall be available to such defendant."

Westwood contends that the first sentence of § 101(35)(C) precludes National Fuel — indeed, all previous owners of property on which hazardous substances were disposed or placed — from invoking the third-party defense set forth in § 107(b)(3). The district court held Westwood's restrictive — though perhaps literal — reading of § 101(35)(C) to be untenable for several reasons. First, the court held that the second sentence of § 101(35)(C) makes it "abundantly clear" that, had Congress intended to place the defense provided for in § 107(b) beyond the reach of a particular class of defendants, it knew precisely how to do so. Second, it would be nonsensical for Congress virtually to bury in § 101(35)(C) a fundamental change in the scope of § 107(b)(3) rather than simply to amend the language of § 107(b)(3)itself. We hold both of these reasons to be persuasive. Logic suggests that

Congress intended § 101(35)(C) merely to circumscribe the parameters of the innocent landowner exception set forth in § 101(35)(A) and (B), and not to abrogate completely the right of previous owners to raise the third-party defense set forth in § 107(b)(3).

The district court suggested a third ground for its determination that the first sentence of § 101(35)(C) was not intended completely to bar § 107(a)(2) defendants — prior land owners — from asserting the third-party defense. The court stated that "the innocent-landowner" exception . . . provides an exemption from the 'in connection with' limitation: under certain circumstances, it will lift the extra burden normally placed on defendants who are contractually related to the allegedly responsible third party, thereby putting them in the same position as defendants who are not." 767 F. Supp. at 460. In other words, § 101(35) shields innocent landowners from liability for the release or threatened release of contaminants caused solely by the act or omission of a third party, even though the actor omission of the third party occurred "in connection with a contractual relationship" with the innocent landowner. The legislative history appears to support such a reading of the statute:

> "[Section 101(35)] is intended to clarify and confirm that under limited circumstances landowners who acquire property without knowing of any contamination at the site and without reason to know of any contamination (or as otherwise noted in the amendment) may have a defense to liability under section 107 and therefore should not be held liable for cleaning up the site if such persons satisfy the remaining requirements of section 107(b)(3). A person who acquires property through a land contract or deed or other instrument transferring title or possession that meets the requirements of this definition may assert that an act or omission of a third party should not be considered to have occurred in connection with a contractual relationship as identified in section 107(b) and therefore is not a bar to the defense."

H.R. Conf. Rep. No. 962, 99th Cong., 2d Sess. 186 87, reprinted in 1986 U.S. Code Cong. & Admin. News 3279 80.

Accordingly, an innocent purchaser subsequently may contract with a third party for the removal or disposal of hazardous wastes that he discovers on his property, without surrendering the third-party defense provided by § 107(b)(3). The first sentence of § 101(35)(C) is intended merely to emphasize that other § 107(a) defendants — those who are not "innocent" under § 101(35) — are denied such an exemption. For example, non-innocent landowners cannot invoke the third-party defense when they contract for the removal or disposal of hazardous substances on their property, even if a subsequent release or threatened release of hazardous substances is attributable solely to the acts or omissions of the party with whom they contracted.

Although we agree with the district court's ultimate conclusion that "the first sentence of § 101(35)(C) limits only the application of the innocent-landowner exception, rather than both the innocent-landowner exception and the balance of the third-party defense," we believe that the district court may have erred when it stated that the first sentence of § 101(35)(C) was intended "simply to underscore that the innocent-landowner exception was designed to apply only to current owners of property — that is, § 107(a)(1) defendants — who otherwise would not qualify for the § 107(b)(3) defense." 767 F. Supp. at 460-61.

The second sentence of § 101(35)(C) makes it clear that Congress intended the innocent landowner exception to allow innocent purchasers of property — i.e., purchasers who are unaware, despite appropriate inquiry, that hazardous substances have been placed or disposed of on the property — subsequently to sell the property without losing their exemption from liability caused solely by a third party "in connection with" such a sale. This is subject to several conditions: first, that such innocent purchasers either do not learn of the existence of such hazardous substances, or, if they do learn of their existence, they disclose such knowledge to the person to whom they subsequently transfer ownership of the property; second, that the innocent landowner fulfills the additional requirements of § 107(b)(3) (a) and (b) — i.e., the innocent landowner must exercise due care with respect to the hazardous substances he discovers on his property, and he must take precautions against the foreseeable acts or omissions of third parties. Indeed, the district court recognized (in apparent contradiction to its earlier statement) that "it would make little sense for Congress to provide a defense for an 'innocent' land purchaser but fail to provide corresponding protection for that same landowner when he or she becomes an 'innocent' seller. . . . " *Id.* at 462.

In short, we agree with the district court's holding that "nothing in either § 107(b)(3) or § 101(35) . . . precludes National Fuel as a matter of law from presenting its third-party defense." *Id.* at 463.

V.

To summarize:

We hold that the district court correctly held that the phrase "in connection with a contractual relationship" in CERCLA § 107(b)(3) requires more than the mere existence of a contractual relationship between the owner of land on which hazardous substances are or have been disposed of and a third party whose act or omission was the sole cause of the release or threatened release of such hazardous substances into the environment, for the landowner to be barred from raising the third-party defense provided for in that section. In order for the landowner to be barred from raising the third-party defense under such circumstances, the contract between the landowner and the third party must either relate to the hazardous substances or allow the landowner to exert some element of control over the third party's activities.

We also hold that the district court properly held that § 101(35)(C) does not entirely preclude previous landowners from invoking the third-party defense provided for in § 107(b)(3). The order of the district court denying Westwood's motion for reconsideration of its earlier order which denied its motion or summary judgment is affirmed.

Affirmed.

NOTES

1. ***Liability in Tort?*** Query whether an innocent landowner pursuant to CERCLA could be successfully sued under common law toxic tort theory. According to one commenter, the answer is no. Charles H. Sarlo, *A Comparative Analysis: The Affirmative Defense of an Innocent Landowner versus the Prima Facie Case of a Toxic Tort Plaintiff: Can CERCLA's Innocent Landowner Provision Be Used as a Defense in a Toxic Tort Suit?*, 16 Pace Envtl. L. Rev. 243, 269 (1999).

2. ***Reason to Know.*** While landowners have welcomed the innocent landowner exception, the difficulty in their view has been the "reason to know" limitation. The limitation specifies that, if a person had "reason to know" of any contamination on the property, he or she is disqualified as an innocent landowner. EPA has traditionally set a high bar on this determination. The agency considered a defendant to have had reason to know if the defendant did not find contamination but could have.

The Small Business Liability Protection and Brownfields Revitalization Act, P.L. 107-118, added to CERCLA in January 2002, lowered the bar on what it means to have had "reason to know." New § 101(35)(B) provides that a defendant had no reason to know if he or she made all "appropriate inquiries." Making an appropriate inquiry, in turn, means meeting "standards and practices" to be established by EPA in regulations. Significantly, however, "in the case of property for residential use or other similar use purchased by a nongovernmental or noncommercial entity, a facility inspection and title search that reveal no basis for further investigation shall be considered to satisfy the requirements of this paragraph." Section 101(35)(B)(v), 42 U.S.C. § 9601(B)(v).

A NOTE ON THE BONA FIDE PROSPECTIVE PURCHASER ("BFPP") DEFENSE

Title II of the Small Business Liability Protection and Brownfields Revitalization Act (P.L. 107-118, January 2002), added the fourth and final defense allowable under CERCLA. New § 107(r), 42 U.S.C. § 9607(r), entitled "Prospective Purchaser and Windfall Lien," stipulates that "bona fide prospective purchasers" of contaminated land "whose potential liability for a release or threatened release is based solely on the purchaser's being considered to be an owner or operator of a facility shall not be liable as long as the bona fide prospective purchaser does not impede the performance of a response action or natural resource restoration." This defense is akin to the innocent landowner exception to the contractual relationship limitation of the third-party defense, but stands separate from it. To qualify for this defense, a person must be a "bona fide prospective purchaser." The Act defines a BFPP as a person who acquired land after all disposal has taken place and who has made "appropriate inquiries." Section 101(40), 42 U.S.C. § 9601(40). "Appropriate inquiries," in turn, is defined in accordance with new § 101(35)(B). *See supra.* Moreover, as with the modification of the innocent landowner exception, "in the case of property in residential or other similar use at the time of purchase by a nongovernmental or noncommercial entity, a facility inspection and title search that reveal no basis for further investigation shall be considered to satisfy the requirements of this subparagraph." Section 101(40)(B)(iii), 42 U.S.C. § 9601(40)(B)(iii). Notably, the defense is not available for persons "affiliated with" other PRPs. Section 101(40)(H), 42 U.S.C. § 9601(40)(H). In September 2010, EPA issued guidance on what it means to be affiliated. *See "Enforcement Discretion Guidance Regarding the Affiliation Language of CERCLA's Bona Fide Prospective Purchaser and Contiguous Property Owner Liability Protections.* This guidance can be found on EPA's website, www.epa.gov.

Note the distinctions between the BFPP provision and the innocent landowner exception. First, this provision applies of its own force; it is not tied to another defense. Second, while either actual knowledge or having reason to know of contamination prior to purchase disqualifies one from the benefits of the innocent landowner exception, only having reason to know (by failing to make "appropriate inquiries") disqualifies one from using the BFPP defense. In other words, a BFPP may have *actual* knowledge of past contamination and still use the defense. Congress intended this result to help out with the brownfields problem. *See infra.*

As the title of new § 107(r) indicates, this defense is coupled with a windfall lien provision. Section 107(r)(2), 42 U.S.C. § 9607(r)(2). This provision allows the government to recoup response costs it may have paid out with respect to BFPP land. However, the government may not recoup more than the increase in market value, if any, directly attributable to the cleanup itself.

C.   ISSUES OF LIABILITY AND DAMAGES

When CERCLA became law in 1980, it authorized the federal government to proceed in two ways. It could do cleanup work itself under § 104, 96 U.S.C. § 9604, and thereafter seek reimbursement from liable persons for its expenditures, or it could require liable persons to do the work under § 106, 96 U.S.C. § 9606, and then secure from them its incidental expenses. These so-called cost recovery actions are authorized under § 107(a), 42 U.S.C. § 9607(a), which specifically allows for recovery of damages for:

(A) all costs of removal or remedial action incurred by the United States Government or a State or an Indian tribe not inconsistent with the national contingency plan;

(B) any other necessary costs of response incurred by any other person consistent with the national contingency plan;

(C) damages for injury to, destruction of, or loss of natural resources, including the reasonable costs of assessing such injury, destruction, or loss resulting from such a release; and

(D) the costs of any health assessment or health effects study carried out under section 9604(I) of this title.

(Note that cost recovery actions are available for private individuals as well. Section 107(a)(4)(B), 42 U.S.C. § 9607(a)(4)(B).)

That is how matters stood until CERCLA was amended by the Superfund Amendments and Reauthorization Act (SARA), 42 U.S.C. §§ 9601–9675, in 1986. As part of SARA, Congress added a new provision to the statute, § 113(f)(1), 42 U.S.C. § 9613(f)(1), which established an explicit right for contribution. Section 113(f)(1) provides that "[a]ny person may seek contribution from any other person who is liable or potentially liable under section 107(a) during or following any civil action under section 106 or under section 107(a)." Under § 113, "[a] person who has resolved its liability to the United States or a State for some or all of a response action or for some or all of the costs of such action in an administrative or judicially approved settlement" could bring a contribution action. Section 113(f)(3)(B), 42 U.S.C. § 9613(f)(3)(B).

The addition of § 113(f)(1) had an immediate effect. While non-PRP plaintiffs would remain limited to § 107 cost recovery actions, PRPs now, one might think, could seek either cost recovery under § 107 or contribution under § 113(f)(1). Why would non-PRPs be precluded from using § 113(f)(1)? The reason lies in the definition of "contribution." Contribution is defined as a "tortfeasor's right to collect from others responsible for the same tort after the tortfeasor has paid more than his or her proportionate share, the shares being determined as a percentage of fault." Black's Law Dictionary 353 (8th ed. 1999). Setting aside for the moment that CERCLA liability is statutory, not tortious, this definition would seem to restrict the universe of possible § 113(f)(1) plaintiffs to PRPs — one cannot seek contribution from liable persons unless one is himself or herself a member of the class of liable persons.

This reality brought to the fore a corollary question. If non-PRPs are limited to using § 107, was it Congress's implicit intention that PRPs should be limited to using § 113(f)(1) contribution actions? The issue was important because PRPs in some circumstances might prefer to seek cost recovery rather than contribution. For one thing, the statute of limitations for contribution actions (three years) is shorter than the statute of limitations for cost recovery actions (six years from initiation of on-site construction of remedy). Second, contribution actions may only be brought "during or following any civil action under section 106 or under section 107(a)." What this means is that PRPs who voluntarily clean a site may not seek contribution under § 113(f)(1). (This reality was brought home forcefully, if somewhat belatedly, by the Supreme Court in *Cooper Industries, Inc. v. Aviall Services, Inc.*, 543 U.S. 157, 125 S. Ct. 577 (2004). Interestingly, *Cooper Industries* adopted this reading of § 113(f)(1) despite the concluding sentence of the subsection, which provides that "nothing in this subsection shall diminish the right of any person to bring an action for contribution in the absence of a civil action under section 106 or section 107." The Court in *Cooper Industries* found this final sentence to relate only to causes of action in contribution that may exist independent of the one established in § 113 itself. *Id.* at 167, 125 S. Ct. at 584.) A third reason a PRP might choose a cost recovery action is § 113(f)(2), which limits the universe of potential defendants in contribution actions. Section 113(f)(2) provides that "a person who has resolved its liability to the United States or a State in an administrative or judicially approved settlement shall not be liable for claims for contribution regarding matters addressed in the settlement." There is no similar limitation with respect to § 107.

After SARA became law in 1986, the federal courts split on this question: some found a cause of action under § 107 for PRPs, while others did not. This split among the circuits has finally been resolved by the Supreme Court. In *United States v. Atlantic Research Corp.*, 551 U.S. 128, 127 S. Ct. 2331 (2007), the Court determined that PRPs have available to them both causes of action. Specifically, the Court reasoned that § 107(a)(4)(B), which allows for cost recovery actions by "any other person," means any person other than the three mentioned in § 107(a)(4)(A) (the United States government, any state, and any Indian tribe). So PRPs are in.

NOTES AND QUESTIONS

1. *Liability Shield.* Why would Congress add § 113(f)(2) to CERCLA?

2. *Fast Move?* Suppose a PRP defendant in a contribution action is required to pay monies to the plaintiff PRP. May the defendant then file an action under § 107 in hopes of getting back those same monies? The answer is no: Section 107 allows recovery only for "necessary costs of response." Contribution payments are not response costs. *See Cooper Industries, Inc. v. Aviall Services, Inc.*, 543 U.S. 157, 125 S. Ct. 577 (2004).

3. *Evisceration of § 113(f)(2)?* Suppose a PRP plaintiff who has assumed response costs cannot secure contribution from another PRP because the latter has settled with the government in accordance with § 113(f)(2). May the plaintiff PRP simply sue under § 107 and thereby render § 113(f)(2) effectively null and void? The answer is yes.

BELL PETROLEUM SERVICES, INC. v. U.S. ENVIRONMENTAL PROTECTION AGENCY
3 F.3d 889 (5th Cir. 1993)

JUDGES: Before JOLLY and DUHE, CIRCUIT JUDGES, and PARKER, DISTRICT JUDGE (Chief Judge of the Eastern District of Texas, sitting by designation)

OPINION: E. GRADY JOLLY, CIRCUIT JUDGE:

The Environmental Protection Agency (EPA) seeks to recover its response costs under the Comprehensive Environmental Response, Compensation and Liability Act (CERCLA) because of a discharge of chromium waste that contaminated a local water supply. . . . We REVERSE the portion of the judgment imposing joint and several liability, and REMAND for further proceedings. Our review of the administrative record has convinced us that the EPA's decision to provide an alternate water supply was arbitrary and capricious; accordingly, we REVERSE the portion of the district court's judgment allowing the EPA to recover the costs of designing and constructing that system, and REMAND for deletion of those amounts and recalculating prejudgment interest.

I

In 1978, a citizen in the Odessa, Texas area complained about discolored drinking water. The Texas Water Commission conducted an investigation. It ultimately focused on a chrome-plating shop that was operated successively from 1971 through 1977 by John Leigh, Western Pollution Control Corporation (hereinafter referred to as Bell), and Woolley Tool Division of Chromalloy American Corporation . . . [later merged into Sequa] . . . just outside the city limits of Odessa. The investigation showed that during the chrome-plating process, finished parts were rinsed, and the rinse water was pumped out of the building onto the ground.

In 1984, the EPA designated a 24-block area north of the . . . facility as a Superfund site — "Odessa Chromium I." It authorized a response action pursuant to its authority under CERCLA § 104, 42 U.S.C. § 9604, and entered into a cooperative agreement with the State of Texas. The State was to perform a remedial investigation, feasibility study, and remedial design work for the site, with the EPA reimbursing the State for ninety percent of the costs. The remedial investigation revealed that the Trinity Aquifer, the only source of groundwater in the area, contained elevated concentrations of chromium . . . [a hazardous substance under CERCLA. —Ed.].

A "focused" feasibility study (FFS) was undertaken to evaluate the need to provide an alternative water supply pending completion of the remaining portion of the feasibility study and implementation of final remedial action. The FFS concluded that the City of Odessa's water system should be extended to provide service in the Odessa Chromium I area. On September 8, 1986, the EPA Regional Administrator issued a Record of Decision (ROD), finding that city water service should be extended to the site. Pursuant to the cooperative agreement, the State, through its contractor, designed and constructed the system, which was completed in 1988.

II

In December 1988, the EPA filed a CERCLA cost-recovery action against Bell [et al] which was consolidated with an adversary proceeding the EPA had filed against Bell in Bell's bankruptcy case. The EPA sought to recover direct and indirect costs it incurred in studying, designing, and constructing the alternate water supply system.

In July 1989, the district court entered a case management order providing that the case would be decided in three phases: Phase I — liability, Phase II — recoverability of the EPA's response costs, and Phase III — "responsibility." In September 1989, the district court granted in part, and denied in part, the EPA's motion for summary judgment as to liability. In its memorandum opinion, it stated that the relative culpability of the parties and the "divisibility of liability" issues would be decided during Phase III. Although the district court ruled that CERCLA did not require the EPA to prove causation, it held an evidentiary hearing and made alternative findings and conclusions addressing causation, holding that "Leigh, Bell and Sequa caused the contamination." In March 1990, the district court granted the EPA's motion for clarification of the September 1989 summary judgment, holding that its previous opinion had provided that the defendants were jointly and severally liable. It also entered a declaratory judgment as to the defendants' liability for future response costs.

The Phase II proceeding on recoverability of response costs was handled through cross-motions for summary judgment. The district court held that the defendants had not met their burden of proving that the EPA's decision to implement an alternate water supply was arbitrary and capricious, and held that they were liable for the EPA's direct and indirect response costs, plus prejudgment interest from the date such costs were incurred.

[The District Court also granted a request for a hearing filed by Sequa and maintaining that Bell was not being required to pay its fair share of response costs. Thereafter, on July 24, 1990, the court denied relief to Sequa, holding "there was no method of dividing the liability among the defendants which would rise to any level above mere speculation, because each of the proposed apportionment methods involved a significant assumption factor, inasmuch as records had been lost, and because each of the apportionment methods differed significantly. In the alternative, it concluded that, based on equitable factors, responsibility should be divided as follows: Bell - 35%; Sequa - 35%; and Leigh - 30%."]

In December 1990, the district court entered an order approving another consent decree, pursuant to which the EPA settled its claims against Leigh for past and future costs — for $100,000. [EPA also settled with Bell for $1 million. —Ed.]

In sum, the district court held that Sequa is jointly and severally liable for $1,866,904.19, including the costs of studying, designing, and constructing the alternate water supply system. In addition, Sequa is jointly and severally liable for all future costs incurred by the EPA in studying, designing, and implementing a permanent remedy. . . .

IV

Joint and Several Liability

Since CERCLA's enactment, the federal courts have struggled to resolve the complicated, often confusing, questions posed by the concept of joint and several liability, and its application under a statute whose provisions are silent with respect to the scope of liability, but whose legislative history is clear that common law principles of joint and several liability may affect liability. The issue is one of first impression in this Circuit.

A

Common Law: The Restatement of Torts

Although joint and several liability is commonly imposed in CERCLA cases, it is not mandatory in all such cases. *United States v. Monsanto Co.*, 858 F.2d at 171. Instead, Congress intended that the federal courts determine the scope of liability in CERCLA cases under traditional and evolving common law principles, guided by the Restatement (Second) of Torts. . . . [citations omitted].

Section 433 of the Restatement provides that:

(1) Damages for harm are to be apportioned among two or more causes where

(a) there are distinct harms, or

(b) there is a reasonable basis for determining the contribution of each cause to a single harm.

(2) Damages for any other harm cannot be apportioned among two or more causes.

Restatement (Second) of Torts, § 433A.

The nature of the harm is the key factor in determining whether apportionment is appropriate. Distinct harms — e.g., where two defendants independently shoot the plaintiff at the same time, one wounding him in the arm and the other wounding him in the leg — are regarded as separate injuries. Although some of the elements of damages (such as lost wages or pain and suffering) may be difficult to apportion, "it is still possible, as a logical, reasonable, and practical matter, . . . to make a rough estimate which will fairly apportion such subsidiary elements of damages." *Id.*, comment b on subsection (1).

The Restatement also discusses "successive" harms, such as when "two defendants, independently operating the same plant, pollute a stream over successive periods of time." *Id.*, comment c on subsection (1). Apportionment is appropriate, because "it is clear that each has caused a separate amount of harm, limited in time, and that neither has any responsibility for the harm caused by the other." *Id.* xxx

The final situation discussed by the Restatement in which apportionment is available involves a single harm that is "divisible" — perhaps the most difficult type of harm to conceptualize. Such harm, "while not so clearly marked out as severable into distinct parts, [is] still capable of division upon a reasonable and rational basis, and of fair apportionment among the causes responsible. . . . Where such apportionment can be made without injustice to any of the parties, the court may require it to be made." *Id.*, comment d on subsection (1). Two examples of such harm are described in the comment. The first is where cattle owned by two or more persons trespass upon the plaintiff's land and destroy his crops. Although "the aggregate harm is a lost crop, . . . it may nevertheless be apportioned among the owners of the cattle, on the basis of the number owned by each, and the reasonable assumption that the respective harm done is proportionate to that number." *Id.* The second example involves pollution of a stream by two or more factories. There, "the interference with the plaintiff's use of the water may be treated as divisible in terms of degree, and may be apportioned among the owners of the factories, on the basis of evidence of the respective quantities of pollution discharged into the stream." *Id.*

Apportionment is inappropriate for other kinds of harm, which, "by their very nature, are normally incapable of any logical, reasonable, or practical division." *Id.*, comment on subsection (2). Examples of such harm are death, a single wound, the destruction of a house by fire, or the sinking of a barge. "Where two or more causes combine to produce such a single result, incapable of division on any logical or reasonable basis, and each is a substantial factor in bringing about the harm, the courts have refused to make an arbitrary apportionment for its own sake, and each of the causes is charged with responsibility for the entire harm." *Id.*

Apportionment is also inappropriate in what the Restatement describes as "exceptional" cases, "in which injustice to the plaintiff may result." *Id.*, comment h on subsection (1). For example, "one of two tortfeasors [maybe] so hopelessly insolvent that the plaintiff will never be able to collect from him the share of the damages allocated to him." *Id.* Where the court deems it unjust to require the innocent plaintiff to bear the risk of one of the tortfeasors' insolvency, it may refuse to apportion damages in such a case. *Id.*

In sum, the nature of the harm is the determining factor with respect to whether apportionment is appropriate. Ultimately, the decision whether to impose joint and several liability turns on whether there is a reasonable and just method for determining the amount of harm that was caused by each defendant (or, in some cases, by an innocent cause or by the fault of the plaintiff). The question whether the harm to the plaintiff is capable of apportionment among two or more causes is a question of law. Restatement (Second) of Torts, § 434(1)(b). Once it has been determined that the harm is capable of being apportioned among the various causes of it, the actual apportionment of damages is a question of fact. *Id.*, § 434(2)(b) & comment d. . . .

CERCLA is a strict liability statute, one of the purposes of which is to shift the cost of cleaning up environmental harm from the taxpayers to the parties who benefitted from the disposal of the wastes that caused the harm. *See, e.g., Chem-Dyne*, 572 F. Supp. at 805–06. "The improper disposal or release of hazardous substances is an enormous and complex problem of national magnitude involving uniquely federal interests." *Id.* at 808. Often, liability is imposed upon entities for conduct predating the enactment of CERCLA, and even for conduct that was not illegal, unethical, or immoral at the time it occurred. We recognize the importance of keeping these facts in mind when attempting to develop a uniform federal common law for CERCLA cases. We also recognize, however, that CERCLA, as a strict liability statute that will not listen to pleas of "no fault," can be terribly unfair in certain instances in which parties may be required to pay huge amounts for damages to which their acts did not contribute. Congress recognized such possibilities and left it to the courts to fashion some rules that will, in appropriate instances, ameliorate this harshness. Accordingly, Congress has suggested, and we agree, that common-law principles of tort liability set forth in the Restatement provide sound guidance. In applying those principles to this CERCLA case, we think that it will be helpful to examine briefly some of the relevant CERCLA jurisprudence. . . .

B

[At this point, the court discussed approaches taken by other federal courts to resolve questions of joint and several liability.]

Although these approaches are not entirely uniform, certain basic principles emerge. First, joint and several liability is not mandated under CERCLA; Congress intended that the federal courts impose joint and several liability only in appropriate cases, applying common-law principles. Second, all of the cases rely on the

Restatement in resolving the issues of joint and several liability. The major differences among the cases concern the timing of the resolution of the divisibility question, whether equitable factors should be considered, and whether a defendant can avoid liability for all, or only some portion, of the damages. Third, even where commingled wastes of unknown toxicity, migratory potential, and synergistic effect are present, defendants are allowed an opportunity to attempt to prove that there is a reasonable basis for apportionment (although they rarely succeed); where such factors are not present, volume may be a reasonable means of apportioning liability.

With respect to the timing of the "divisibility" inquiry, we believe that an early resolution is preferable. We agree with the Second Circuit, however, that this is a matter best left to the sound discretion of the district court. . . . We therefore conclude that . . . [Restatement principles shall control and that defendant, to avoid imposition of joint and several liability, must demonstrate the amount of harm its pollution has caused] . . . [w]e nevertheless recognize that the Restatement principles must be adapted, where necessary, to implement congressional intent with respect to liability under the unique statutory scheme of CERCLA.

C

Application of Joint & Several Liability

We now turn to consider the application of these traditional and evolving common law principles of joint and several liability to the facts of this case. . . .

Our review of the record convinces us that Sequa met its burden of proving that, as a matter of law, there is a reasonable basis for apportionment. This case is closely analogous to the Restatement's illustrations in which apportionment of liability is appropriate. For example, where cattle owned by two or more defendants destroy the plaintiff's crops, the damages are apportioned according to the number of cattle owned by each defendant, based on the reasonable assumption that the respective harm done is proportionate to that number. Thus, the Restatement suggests that apportionment is appropriate even though the evidence does not establish with certainty the specific amount of harm caused by each defendant's cattle, and even though there is a possibility that only one of the defendant's cattle caused all of the harm, while the other defendant's cattle idly stood by. Likewise, pollution of a stream by two or more factories may be treated as divisible in terms of degree, and apportioned among the defendants on the basis of evidence of the respective quantities of pollution discharged by each.

As is evident from our previous discussion of the jurisprudence, most CERCLA cost-recovery actions involve numerous, commingled hazardous substances with synergistic effects and unknown toxicity. In contrast, this case involves only one hazardous substance — chromium — and no synergistic effects. The chromium entered the groundwater as the result of similar operations by three parties who operated at mutually exclusive times. Here, it is reasonable to assume that the respective harm done by each of the defendants is proportionate to the volume of chromium-contaminated water each discharged into the environment.

Even though it is not possible to determine with absolute certainty the exact amount of chromium each defendant introduced into the groundwater, there is sufficient evidence from which a reasonable and rational approximation of each defendant's individual contribution to the contamination can be made. . . .

In sum, we conclude that the district court erred in imposing joint and several liability, because Sequa met its burden of proving that there is a reasonable basis for apportioning liability among the defendants on a volumetric basis. We therefore remand the case to the district court for apportionment.

V

Alternate Water Supply System

Sequa also challenges the EPA's decision to provide an alternate water supply (AWS) as an interim measure pending the completion of final remedial action. . . .

After thoroughly reviewing the administrative record, we conclude that the EPA's decision to furnish the AWS was arbitrary and capricious. In vain we have searched the over 5,000 pages of administrative record, and found not one shred of evidence that anyone in the area was actually drinking chromium-contaminated water. Amazingly, the EPA made no attempt to learn whether anyone was drinking the water, or whether anyone intended to utilize the AWS, until after it had made its decision to construct the AWS. One would think that surely such information was essential in order to reach an informed, rational decision as to whether an AWS was necessary, and whether it would reduce any significant threat to public health. . . .

VI

All Costs?

Having determined that the EPA's decision to implement the AWS was arbitrary and capricious, we must now decide whether the EPA nevertheless is entitled to recover its costs for designing and constructing the AWS.

The EPA takes the position that it is entitled to recover all costs — even if unreasonable or unnecessary — unless Sequa proves that such costs are inconsistent with the National Contingency Plan. The district court held that the EPA could recover all of its response costs, so long as they were not the product of "gross misconduct" by the agency.

Although we approve of the district court's attempt to impose some restraints on the EPA's ability to recover costs from private parties, we find no statutory basis for its "gross misconduct" limitation. Nevertheless, we are troubled by the implications of the EPA's position on this issue. Sequa contends that, under the EPA's interpretation, defendants will be liable even if the EPA allows a contractor to pay its officers and other employees unjustified millions and allows each of them a Rolls-Royce for transportation. Interestingly, the EPA did not attempt to refute Sequa's assertion, either in its appellate brief or at oral argument. Instead, the EPA asserts a policy reason to support its interpretation:

"By refusing to permit defendants to defend against cost recovery actions by engaging in detailed attacks on the 'reasonableness' of individual government cost items, Congress provided an incentive to those defendants to conduct the necessary response actions themselves. Where defendants refuse to conduct the appropriate response actions, CERCLA allows the Government to undertake the response actions it deems necessary and appropriate without being constrained by the possibility that each line item of the costs of these actions will be challenged in cost recovery."

In addition, the EPA asks us to take comfort in the fact that, through internal agency audits and other forms of self-policing, costs will be controlled.

Acceptance of the EPA's position would effectively prohibit judicial review of the EPA's expenditures. In short, we would give the EPA a blank check in conducting response actions. We seriously doubt that Congress intended to give the EPA such unrestrained spending discretion. Moreover, such unbridled discretion removes any restraint upon the conduct of the EPA in exercising its awesome powers; if the EPA knows there are no economic consequences to it, its decisions and conduct are likely to be less responsible.

We do not have to decide the question in this case, however, because the only costs Sequa challenges as unreasonable and unnecessary are those associated with implementation of the alternate water supply system, a decision that we have already concluded was arbitrary and capricious. . . . Because the decision to implement an AWS was arbitrary and capricious, it is inconsistent with the NCP. Accordingly, the EPA is not entitled to recover the costs of designing and constructing the AWS.

We realize that, as a result of our decision disallowing the EPA's costs for the AWS, those costs will have to be borne by the Superfund. Although regrettable, this is the inevitable result of arbitrary and capricious EPA decision making. Without knowing, or even attempting to learn, whether the AWS would serve to protect the safety and health of anyone, the EPA officiously ignored the comments of Bell and Sequa, and the results of its own remedial investigation, and stubbornly proceeded to spend over $300,000 to furnish a water supply system that was not needed, was not allowed to be used by the commercial establishments whose wells (according to the administrative record) were the only ones with chromium contamination in excess of the SDWA standards, and did very little — indeed, if anything — to reduce any perceived public health threat posed by the chromium-contaminated ground-water. We can only assume that the EPA was not concerned about the cost of the AWS, because it believed that it could recover whatever was spent from Sequa. Although the EPA's powers under CERCLA are indeed broad, Congress has not provided that private parties must pay for the consequences of arbitrary and capricious agency action. . . .

[The dissent by PARKER, DISTRICT JUDGE, is omitted.]

NOTES AND QUESTIONS

1. ***Divisible and Indivisible Harms.*** *Accord United States v. Monsanto Co.*, 858 F.2d 160 (4th Cir. 1988), *cert. denied*, 490 U.S. 1106 (1989). In *Monsanto*, the government was suing for response costs for cleaning a four-acre site which held over 7,000 large drums of highly dangerous chemical wastes. Citing *United States v. Chem-Dyne Corp.*, 572 F. Supp. 802 (S.D. Ohio 1983), for support, the court held, *inter alia*, that common law rules on joint and several liability were appropriate under CERCLA. Therefore:

> when two or more persons act independently to cause a single harm for which there is a reasonable basis of apportionment according to the contribution of each, each is held liable only for the portion of harm that he causes. . . . When such persons cause a single and indivisible harm, however, they are held liable jointly and severally for the entire harm.

Id. at 171–72. *See also United States v. Alcan Aluminum Corp.* *("Alcan-PAS")*, 990 F.2d 711, 722 (2d Cir. 1993) ("commingled" waste is not synonymous with "indivisible" harm); *United States v. Alcan Aluminum Corp.* *("Alcan-Butler")*, 964 F.2d 252, 270 n.29 (3d Cir. 1992) (same).

2. ***Liability in Bell.*** Bell indicated that Leigh settled for $100,000 in December 1990, and thereafter Sequa was found in the District Court to be liable for $1.8 million. Had this court affirmed the District Court result, could Sequa then have successfully demanded contribution from Leigh toward payment of the greater liability? (No.) Had the court found Leigh to be jointly and severally liable, could EPA then reopen its settlement as a matter of right to secure greater compensation from Leigh? (No.)

3. ***Proving Divisibility.*** How easy is it to prove that harms are divisible and thereby warrant an apportionment of damages? The conventional wisdom has been that it is definitely not easy. *See. e.g., O'Neil v. Picillo*, 883 F.2d 176, 178–79 (1st Cir. 1989), *cert. denied*, 493 U.S. 1071 (1990) ("The practical effect of placing the burden on defendants has been that responsible parties rarely escape joint and several liability, courts regularly finding that where wastes of varying (and unknown) degrees of toxicity and migratory potential commingle, it simply is impossible to determine the amount of environmental harm caused by each party.").

But this time-honored assessment is now in doubt. In *Burlington Northern & Santa Fe Railway Co. v. United States*, 556 U.S. 599, 129 S. Ct. 1870 (2009) (which case appears earlier in this chapter's coverage of arranger liability), the U.S. Supreme Court may have eased the burdens on defendants seeking to escape joint and several liability. In *Burlington*, the Court affirmed an apportionment of damages in a circumstance where commingled chemicals produced the need for site remediation. The District Court had established the liability of one party (collectively, the Railroads) at 9%, based on three factors. First, it calculated that the Railroads occupied 19% of the surface area of the site. Second, it observed that the Railroads had leased their parcel for 13 years, which was 45% of the total time during which contamination activities took place. Last, it found that the Railroads' releases had contributed to 66% of the contamination for which remediation was necessary (a finding for which there was "less support" in the record, according to the Supreme Court). Armed with these calculations, the District Court multiplied 0.19 by 0.45 by 0.66 and then rounded up. This produced a 6% liability share determination. Understanding the margin of error to be 50%, the court upped the Railroads' liability share to 9%.

The Supreme Court concluded this apportionment methodology enjoyed reasonable support in the record. Given the 50% margin of error adjustment, the Court was unworried about the relative lack of record support for the 66% calculation.

Whether *Burlington* will prove to be a watershed decision on the matter of CERCLA liability awaits its implementation by lower courts. Early returns tend to show the decision will be read narrowly.

4. *Equitable Allocation Among PRPs.* Even when PRPs are found to be jointly and severally liable, should not courts nonetheless attempt to apportion damages on an equitable basis? The answer is yes. *See, e.g., Hemingway Transport, Inc. v. Kahn*, 993 F.2d 915, 921 n.4 (1st Cir.1993):

> In a CERCLA contribution action among responsible parties who are jointly and severally liable, the burden of proof is less demanding, though the court nevertheless may undertake a comparable allocation of the relative responsibilities of the joint obligors. *See* 42 U.S.C. § 9613(f)(1) ("The court may allocate response costs among liable parties using such equitable factors as the court determines are appropriate."); *see also Smith Land & Improvement Corp. v. Celotex Corp.*, 851 F.2d 86, 90 (3d Cir. 1988), *cert. denied*, 488 U.S. 1029, 109 S. Ct. 837, 102 L. Ed. 2d 969 (1989). In approaching these divisibility and apportionment determinations, the courts have relied on various guideposts, including the legislative history in general, and the so-called "Gore Factors" in particular: (i) the ability of the parties to demonstrate that their contribution to a discharge, release or disposal of a hazardous waste can be distinguished; (ii) the amount of the hazardous waste involved; (iii) the degree of toxicity of the hazardous waste involved; (iv) the degree of involvement by the parties in the generation, transportation, treatment, storage, or disposal of the hazardous waste; (v) the degree of care exercised by the parties with respect to the hazardous waste concerned, taking into account the characteristics of such hazardous waste; and (vi) the degree of cooperation by the parties with Federal, State or local officials to prevent any harm to the public health or the environment. *Environmental Transp. Sys., Inc. v. Ensco, Inc.*, 969 F.2d 503, 508–09 (7th Cir. 1992) ("Gore factors" provide a nonexhaustive but valuable roster of equitable apportionment considerations) (quoting *United States v. A & F Materials Co., Inc.*, 578 F. Supp. 1249, 1256 (S.D. Ill. 1984)).

For its part, EPA has attempted to administratively allocate costs when it has the opportunity to do so. In 1993, it focused on *de minimis* parties, those who are technically liable but only for minuscule contributions of hazardous materials. Notably, Congress followed suit by subsequently adding to CERCLA subsection § 122(g)(7), 42 U.S.C. § 9622(g)(7). Entitled "De minimis settlements," the new provision allows for expedited settlements at reduced amounts for PRPs who have an inability or limited ability to pay response costs. By negotiating early and apportioned settlements, EPA claimed several years back to have removed 12,000 people from the system, persons who otherwise faced substantial financial ruin because of CERCLA liability. The agency similarly has focused on *de micromis* parties — those with even less culpability — promising to simply remove all liability from this set of technically liable persons. Last, it has undertaken the practice of volunteering an "orphan share." This share is EPA's contribution to a site cleanup; by volunteering to help out, the agency claims to expedite the settlement process among PRPs and eases the burdens on those persons as well. The problem for the EPA in this regard is budgetary: in the age of reduced governmental appropriations, there are fewer dollars available to contribute. Because of that budgetary difficulty, on some occasions, instead of contributing cash, the agency can opt to reduce its own oversight charges (a "tiered oversight" for those PRPs who can be trusted) or waive past EPA costs.

The agency also increased its use of alternative dispute resolution mechanisms.

5. *How Clean Is Clean?* In order to be reimbursable, remedial or removal activity must be justified by the National Contingency Plan. *See* CERCLA, § 105, 42 U.S.C. § 9605. The NCP establishes cleanup requirements, relying on the dictates of § 121, 42 U.S.C. § 9621. These cleanup standards, as a general matter, are designed to remove adverse impacts to human health and the environment. In determining the degree of cleanup that is required, the NCP refers to the level of cleanup mandated by other legislation, especially so-called "applicable or relevant and appropriate standards," or "ARARs." Section 121(d), 42 U.S.C. § 9621(d).

When EPA is a plaintiff, the cleanup must be "not inconsistent with" the NCP. When a private person is the plaintiff, however, the cleanup must be "consistent with" the NCP." Section 107, 42 U.S.C. § 9607. To be "consistent," one must be in "substantial" compliance with the standards set forth in the regulations, and must also accomplish a "CERCLA-quality clean-up." 40 C.F.R. § 300.700(c)(3)(i). (The 1985 version of the NCP required strict compliance. 40 C.F.R. § 300.71 (1988).) According to the 1990 NCP, having a "CERCLA-quality clean-up" means that remedial actions must be: protective of human health and the environment, implement permanent solutions and alternative treatment technologies to the maximum extent practicable, and be cost-effective; attain all ARARs; and provide meaningful public participation. 55 Fed. Reg. 8793 (3/8/90). *See also City of Detroit v. Miller*, 842 F. Supp. 957 (E.D. Mich. 1994). EPA cut plaintiffs some slack by stating that "an omission based on lack of experience with the Superfund program should not be grounds for defeating an otherwise valid cost recovery action, assuming the omission does not affect the quality of the clean-up." *Id.*

Consistency with the NCP is generally viewed to be a question of liability, not of damages. *Artesian Water Co. v. Government of New Castle County*, 659 F. Supp. 1269 (D. Del. 1987), *aff'd*, 851 F.2d 643 (3d Cir. 1988). Response actions carried out in compliance with the terms of an order issued by EPA pursuant to § 106, 42 U.S.C. § 9606, or a consent decree entered into pursuant to § 122, 42 U.S.C. § 9622, are irrebuttably presumed to be consistent with the NCP. 40 C.F.R. § 300.700(c)(3)(ii).

6. *Costs" Not Inconsistent With "the NCP.* In *Bell*, the court did not decide whether EPA could recover unreasonable, unnecessary, or excessive costs. The issue was whether these costs are "not inconsistent with" the NCP. In fact, EPA's policy argument regarding its "gross misconduct" standard has enjoyed support in the courts:

> In *United States v. Northeastern Pharmaceutical & Chemical Co., Inc.*, 810 F.2d 726 (8th Cir. 1986), the court noted that § 107(a)(4)(A) does not refer to "all reasonable costs" but simply to "all costs," and concluded that " 'all costs' incurred by the government that are not inconsistent with the NCP are conclusively presumed to be reasonable." *Id.* In *United States v. Hardage*, 982 F.2d 1436 (10th Cir. 1992), the court likewise stated that, "as long as the government's choice of response action is not inconsistent with the NCP, its costs are presumed to be reasonable and therefore recoverable." *Id.* at *1443. Cf. United States v. R. W. Meyer, Inc.*, 889 F.2d at 1504 (emphasis added) ("to the extent clean-up actions are necessary, . . . the statute contemplates that those responsible for hazardous waste at each site must bear the full cost of clean-up actions").

> Beyond that, most courts hold that defendants have the burden of proving that EPA's costs are inconsistent with the NCP. *E.g., Hardage*, 982 F.2d at 1442; *Northeastern*, 810 F.2d at 747; *Ottati & Goss*, 630 F. Supp. at 1395; *United States v. Conservation Chemical Co.*, 619 F. Supp. 162, 186 (W.D. Mo. 1985); *United States v. Ward*, 618 F. Supp. 884, 899 (E.D.N.C. 1985). In private cost recovery actions, however, under § 107(a)(4)(B), nongovernmental entities carry the burden of showing that their response costs are necessary and consistent with the NCP. *County Line Investment Co. v. Tinney*, 933 F.2d 1508, 1512 & n.8 (10th Cir. 1991); *Northeastern*, 810 F.2d at 726.

Bell, supra, at n.22, 23. xxx

7. *What Costs Are Recoverable Under CERCLA?* Direct response costs, such as costs of soil removal or contamination neutralization, are recoverable, of course. Direct costs also include the fees of contractors who design remedial action plans, the payroll and travel expenses of agency personnel, and enforcement costs and litigation expenses of the U.S. Department of Justice. Also recoverable are indirect costs. These can include the costs of on-site, rented office space for government officials as well as the *pro rata* portion of overall agency program costs attributable to a particular defendant. *See, e.g., United States v. R. W. Meyer, Inc.*, 889 F.2d 1497 (6th Cir. 1989). *But see United States v. Rohm & Haas*, 2 F.3d 1265 (3d Cir. 1993) (EPA may not recover damages under CERCLA for its oversight costs arising in association with a private party's remedial or removal actions); *Atlantic Richfield Co. v. American Airlines*, 98 F.3d 564 (10th Cir. 1996) (a private party's payment of EPA's oversight costs is recoverable in a subsequent contribution action).

Even though attorneys' fees are recoverable by the government, there is no similar right to recover attorney's fees in private cost recovery actions. *Key Tronic Corp. v. United States*, 511 U.S. 809, 114 S. Ct. 1960 (1994); *United States v. Chapman*, 146 F.3d 1166 (9th Cir. 1998) (on the theory that governmental attorneys' fees are a legitimate part of the government's "response" in that they relate to enforcement and their assessment can serve to encourage PRPs to take remedial action when requested to do so by the government).

In accordance with § 107(a)(4)(C), 42 U.S.C. § 9607(a)(4)(C), natural resource damages are recoverable in CERCLA actions. These are defined as "damages for injury to, destruction of, or loss of natural resources, including the reasonable costs of assessing such injury, destruction, or loss resulting from such a release." *Id.* In effect, this provision elevates the environment to the status of plaintiff. The federal government and the government of the state where the harmed resource is located are the entities designated to receive these damages awards on the environment's behalf. Section 107(f)(1), 42 U.S.C. § 9607(f)(1). As a procedural device, CERCLA calls for the appointment of a "trustee" to assess natural resource damages and recover them from liable parties, by filing legal action where necessary. Section 107(f)(2), 42 U.S.C. § 9607(f)(2). The difficulty here is computing the damages themselves. What is a chipmunk worth? *See, e.g., State of Ohio v. U.S. Department of Interior,* 880 F.2d. 432 (D.C. Cir. 1989); *National Association of Manufacturers v. U.S. Department of Interior,* 134 F.3d 1095 (D.C. Cir. 1998). *See also "Ask a Silly Question . . . ": Contingent Valuation of Natural Resources Damages,* 105 Harv. L. Rev. 1981 (1992).[13]

Relatively few natural resource damages claims have been made, in part because of the up-front costs of performing injury assessments to prove damages. A recent decision, however, may ease the burden by allowing plaintiffs to recover the costs of injury assessment as they are incurred, even before natural resource damages themselves are demonstrated. *Confederated Tribes and Bands of the Yakama Nation v. United States,* 616 F. Supp. 2d 1094 (E.D. Wash. 2007).

CERCLA does not allow recovery for loss of property value and loss of quality of life, but state law remedies might be available for these injuries. *See, e.g., Scribner v. Summers,* 84 F.3d 554 (2d Cir. 1996).

8. ***State Superfunds.*** Federal law is not alone in the hazardous waste cleanup effort. About 30 states have their own "superfunds" to both find potential cleanup sites and to effect removal and remedial actions at locations not on the federal NPL.

A NOTE ON CERCLA AND COMPREHENSIVE GENERAL LIABILITY INSURANCE

May a party liable under CERCLA nonetheless be saved by her or his comprehensive general liability ("CGL") insurance policy? (Note, of course, that the terms of an insurance policy cannot remove liability established by a sovereign enactment such as CERCLA; all it can do is transfer the liability as a matter of civil contract law to an insurer. A party found liable under § 107 remains so; insurance is just another way to meet the financial obligation.) Such CGL insurance

---

[13] Section 311 of the Clean Water Act, 33 U.S.C. § 1321, also authorizes federal and state officials to sue as public trustees to recover "any costs or expenses incurred by the Federal Government or any State government in the restoration or replacement of natural resources damaged or destroyed as a result of a discharge of oil or a hazardous substance" in navigable waters. CWA § 311(f)(4), 33 U.S.C. § 1321(f)(4). Trustees suing under § 311 of the Clean Water Act may use recovered funds "to restore, rehabilitate or acquire the equivalent of such natural resources." CWA § 311(f)(5), 33 U.S.C. § 1321(f)(5).

policies usually provide that "the Company will pay on behalf of the insured all sums which the insured shall become legally obligated to pay as damages because of bodily injury or property damage to which the insurance applies, cause by an occurrence."

In the early days of CERCLA, the question was whether response costs qualified as "damages" for purposes of these CGL policies. Some courts found that they did, on the notion that expectations of policyholders should govern interpretation of policies. *See, e.g., Avondale Industries, Inc. v. Travelers Indemnity Co.*, 887 F.2d 1200 (2d Cir. 1989); *Independent Petrochemical Corp. v. Aetna Casualty and Surety Co.*, 944 F.2d. 940 (D.C. Cir. 1991). Others held that response costs are not legally "damages" but are restitutive, and hence equitable, in nature. *See, e.g., Maryland Casualty Co. v. Armco*, 822 F.2d 1348 (4th Cir. 1987), *cert. denied*, 108 S. Ct. 703 (1988). This latter holding can be surprising for the legal initiate. As aptly put by counsel in *Aerojet-General Corp. v. San Mateo County Superior Court*, 211 Cal. App. 3d 216 (1989): "If a layman, having taken out a General Comprehensive Liability policy and paid the premiums, were told that he had to be wary of a distinction between law and equity, he or she would look at one in dumb amazement and say 'What's that, again?'" In some 60 case decisions on this matter, through June 1989, about three-fourths were decided in favor of policyholders, the remainder in favor of insurers.

The predictable result of this has been the insertion of new language in CGL policies to specifically include or exclude CERCLA-like liabilities. Having protected their flanks, insurers have now taken the offensive, offering individually "manuscripted" policies specifically taking on environmental risks, subject to due diligence and other requirements, and upon payment of hefty premiums. The policies can be useful in reducing risks associated with development of potentially contaminated properties.

ONE CLEANUP PROGRAM

As EPA views it, there are at least four federal programs in place to clean the environment. The overall CERCLA effort to address NPL sites is one, the attempt to reduce the proliferation of brownfields is another, the hazardous wastes program of RCRA is a third, and the concerted effort to remediate leaking underground storage tanks is a fourth. Each of these programs differs from each of the others in significant procedural and substantive ways. Not unexpectedly, these differences complicate the lives of entities subject to these programs. Compliance with regulatory requirements can be difficult in the absolute; that compliance is made all the more difficult when programmatic requirements are numerous, difficult to discern, and internally inconsistent.[14]

And that is just part of the problem. Add to these federal programs the motley array of state, tribal, and local initiatives of the same sort and you have a formidable regulatory challenge.

---

[14] This complexity can burden EPA as well. In many enforcement contexts, EPA must choose which regulatory program to use, and having done that, nonetheless assure satisfaction with all of the requirements of all applicable programs.

Not unexpectedly, the regulated community has chafed under this burden and has long pleaded for programmatic reform. Those entreaties were largely ignored until the advent of the One Cleanup Program. Initiated by EPA, this program is an administrative attempt to bring some semblance of order to all of this, and to do so within the auspices of the existing legislative framework. As stated on EPA's website:

> The nation's cleanup programs will work in harmony to achieve effective and efficient cleanups that protect human health and the environment, and support revitalization of communities. Cleanup programs will coordinate to promote sound and protective remedies, shared science and technical approaches, seamless public information systems, and the mutual acceptance of policies and results.

EPA otherwise characterizes the program as applying "cross-program, cross-agency thinking and planning to the universe of contaminated sites. It pools the best ideas, experiences and innovations from each program so that they can be applied to all programs. In this way, every cleanup project in every community can benefit." *Id.*

The One Cleanup Program may be a welcome effort, but it remains in its early stages. Still, EPA touts the program's virtues in one context, the cleaning of the Anacostia Watershed. The watershed, located near the nation's capital, is large (176 square miles) and suffers from numerous sources of contamination, the elimination of which is complicated by tidal flows. As part of its coordinated remediation effort, EPA convened the Anacostia Watershed Toxics Alliance, a coalition of 25 groups, agencies, and institutions. The idea was to bring together all the players who might accomplish change, and to pool technological and financial resources to that end. These resources might then be dedicated to solving this ecosystem-wide pollution problem in a process refreshingly free of judicial and administrative orders. EPA claims this effort has produced substantial gains already, including the repair of more than 6.5 miles of leaking storm sewers, the construction of sand filters to stem the flow of trash into the watershed, the installation of protective covers over 30 acres of land to reduce migration of contaminants, the removal of large amounts of coal tar, mercury, and petroleum, and the direct cleaning of more than 27,000 tons of contaminated soil and a million gallons of surface and groundwater. www.epa.gov/oswer/onecleanupprogram/anacostia.htm (site last visited November 2011).

Appendix One

ACRONYMS

AAPA	—	American Antiquities Preservation Act
AEA	—	Atomic Energy Act
AEC	—	Atomic Energy Commission
ALARA	—	as low as reasonably achievable
ALDF	—	Animal Legal Defense Fund
ANILCA	—	Alaska National Interest Lands Conservation Act
ANWR	—	Alaska National Wildlife Refuge
ARARS	—	applicable or relevant and appropriate standard
ASPCA	—	American Society for the Prevention of Cruelty to Animals
ATSDR	—	Agency for Toxic Substances and Disease Registry
AOC	—	Area of Concern
AOC	—	approximate original contour
APA	—	Administrative Procedure Act
AUM	—	animal unit month
AWS	—	alternative water supply
BACT	—	best available control technology
BANANA	—	build absolutely nothing anywhere near anything
BAT	—	best available technology economically achievable
BCF	—	bioconcentration factor
BCT	—	best conventional pollutant control technology
BDAT	—	best demonstrated available technology
BDT	—	best demonstrated technology
BFPP	—	bona fide prospective purchaser
BIA	—	Bureau of Indian Affairs
BLM	—	Bureau of Land Management
BMPs	—	best management practices
BO or BiOp	—	biological opinion
BOR	—	Bureau of Reclamation
BPT	—	best practicable control technology currently available
CA	—	corrective action
CAA	—	Clean Air Act
CAFE	—	corporate average fuel efficiency (standards)
CAMU	—	corrective action management unit
CCA	—	candidate conservation agreement
CCAA	—	candidate conservation agreement with assurances
CCL	—	Construction Completion List
CEMS	—	continuous emissions monitoring system
CEQ	—	Council on Environmental Quality

CERCLA	—	Comprehensive Environmental Response, Compensation, and Liability Act
CFCs	—	chlorofluorocarbons
CGL	—	comprehensive general liability (insurance)
CHD	—	critical habitat designation
CITES	—	Convention on International Trade in Endangered Species of Wild Fauna and Flora
CMA	—	Chemical Manufacturers Association
CMDB	—	combined metals data base
CO	—	carbon monoxide
CO_2	—	carbon dioxide
COE	—	Corps of Engineers
CWA	—	Clean Water Act
CZMA	—	Coastal Zone Management Act
DCC	—	Dormant Commerce Clause
DLA	—	Desert Lands Act
DOA	—	Department of Agriculture
DOD	—	Department of Defense
DOE	—	Department of Energy
DOI	—	Department of the Interior
DOJ	—	Department of Justice
DPS	—	distinct population segment
EA	—	environmental assessment
ECPA	—	Electric Consumers Protection Act
EEC	—	European Economic Community
EEZ	—	exclusive economic zone
EIS	—	environmental impact statement
EJ	—	environmental justice
EPA	—	Environmental Protection Agency
EPCRA	—	Emergency Planning and Community Right-to-Know Act
EO	—	Executive Order
ERDA	—	Energy Research and Development Administration
ERP	—	equipment replacement project
ESA	—	Endangered Species Act
ESC	—	Endangered Species Committee
ESU	—	evolutionarily significant unit
FAA	—	Federal Aviation Administration
FCLA	—	Federal Coal Leasing Amendments
FCLAA	—	Federal Coal Leasing Amendments Act
FCMA	—	Fishery Conservation and Management Act
FCZ	—	fishery conservation zone
FDA	—	Food and Drug Administration
FEA	—	Federal Energy Administration
FEMA	—	Federal Emergency Management Agency

FERC	—	Federal Energy Regulatory Commission
FIFRA	—	Federal Insecticide, Fungicide, and Rodenticide Act
FIP	—	federal implementation plan
FLPMA	—	Federal Land Policy and Management Act
FMP	—	fishery management plan
FOIA	—	Freedom of Information Act
FONSI	—	finding of no significant impact
FOOGLRA	—	Federal Onshore Oil and Gas Leasing Reform Act
FPA	—	Federal Power Act
FPC	—	Federal Power Commission
FRRRPA	—	Forest and Rangeland Renewable Resources Planning Act
FS	—	Forest Service
FTCA	—	Federal Tort Claims Act
FWCA	—	Fish and Wildlife Coordination Act
FWPCA	—	Federal Water Pollution Control Act (Clean Water Act)
FWS	—	Fish and Wildlife Service
GACT	—	Generally Achievable Control Technology
GAO	—	General Accounting Office
GATT	—	General Agreement on Tariffs and Trade
GFSZA	—	Gun-Free School Zones Act
GML	—	General Mining Law
GNP	—	gross national product
GPO	—	Government Printing Office
GSA	—	General Services Administration
H_2O	—	water
H_2SO_4	—	sulfuric acid
HAPs	—	hazardous air pollutants
HC	—	hydrocarbon
HCFCs	—	hydrochlorofluorocarbons
HCP	—	habitat conservation plan
HMTA	—	Hazardous Materials Transportation Act
HNO_3	—	nitric acid
HR	—	House of Representatives
HRS	—	Hazard Ranking System
HSUS	—	Humane Society of the United States
HSWA	—	Hazardous and Solid Waste Amendments
HWC	—	hazardous waste combustor
HWIR	—	Hazardous Waste Identification Rule
IBEs	—	Investment-backed expectations
IBLA	—	Interior Board of Land Appeals
ICC	—	Interstate Commerce Commission
ICR	—	ignitable, corrosive, reactive (hazardous wastes)
IMA	—	Intermunicipal agreement
IRM	—	interim remedial measure

IRS	—	Internal Revenue Service
ITP	—	incidental take permit
ITS	—	incidental take statement
LAER	—	lowest achievable emission rate
lb/MMBTU	—	pounds per million British Thermal Units
LDRs	—	land disposal restrictions
LLRWPA	—	Low-Level Radioactive Waste Policy Act
LNG	—	liquified natural gas
LOS	—	Law of the Sea
LRMP	—	land and resource management plan
LULU	—	locally unwanted land use
LUST	—	leaking underground storage tank
MACT	—	maximum achievable control technology
MBTA	—	Migratory Bird Treaty Act
MCL	—	maximum contaminant level
MFASAQHE	—	major federal action significantly affecting the quality of the human environment
mg/m^3	—	milligrams per cubic meter
MLA	—	Mineral Leasing Act
MMPA	—	Marine Mammals Protection Act
MMS	—	Minerals Management Service
MOA	—	memorandum of agreement
MOU	—	memorandum of understanding
MPRSA	—	Marine Protection, Research, and Sanctuaries Act
MSY	—	maximum sustainable yield
MTBE	—	methyl tertiary butyl ether
MUSYA	—	Multiple Use-Sustained Yield Act
NA	—	nonattainment
NAAQS	—	national ambient air quality standard
NAPAP	—	National Acid Precipitation Assessment Program
NAS	—	National Academy of Sciences
NASA	—	National Aeronautics and Space Administration
NCP	—	National Contingency Plan
NEA	—	National Energy Act
NEPA	—	National Environmental Policy Act
NESHAPs	—	national emission standards for hazardous air pollutants
NFMA	—	National Forest Management Act
NHPA	—	National Historic Preservation Act
NIMBY	—	not in my backyard
NMFS	—	National Marine Fisheries Service
NOAA	—	National Oceanic and Atmospheric Administration
NOx	—	nitrogen oxide
NPCA	—	National Park and Conservation Association
NPDES	—	National Pollutant Discharge Elimination System
NPL	—	National Priority List

NPS	—	National Park Service
NRA	—	national recreation area
NRC	—	Nuclear Regulatory Commission
NRDC	—	Natural Resources Defense Council
NSPS	—	new source performance standards
NSR	—	new source review
NWF	—	National Wildlife Federation
NWPA	—	Nuclear Waste Policy Act
NWRSIA	—	National Wildlife Refuge System Improvement Act
O_3	—	Ozone
OCS	—	outer continental shelf
OCSLA	—	Outer Continental Shelf Lands Act
OMB	—	Office of Management and Budget
OPEC	—	Organization of Petroleum Exporting Countries
ORVs	—	off-road vehicles
OSCLA	—	Outer Continental Shelf Lands Act
OSHA	—	Occupational, Safety, and Health Administration
OSM	—	Office of Surface Mining
OTA	—	Office of Technology Assessment
PA	—	preliminary assessment
PCBs	—	polycholorinated biphenyls
PETA	—	People for the Ethical Treatment of Animals
Pb	—	lead
PM	—	particulate matter
POTWs	—	publicly owned treatment works
PPA	—	prospective purchaser agreement
ppb	—	parts per billion
ppm	—	parts per million
ppq	—	parts per quadrillion
PRPs	—	potentially responsible parties
PSCs	—	public service commissions
PSD	—	prevention of significant deterioration
PSES	—	pretreatment standards for existing sources
PSNS	—	pretreatment standards for new sources
PUCs	—	public utility commissions
PUD	—	public utility district
PURPA	—	Public Utilities Regulatory Policies Act
RACM	—	reasonably available control measure
RACT	—	reasonably available control technology
RARE	—	Roadless Area Review and Evaluation
RCRA	—	Resource Conservation and Recovery Act
REA	—	Rural Electrification Administration
RFA	—	Regulatory Flexibility Act
RIA	—	regulatory impact analysis
RI/FS	—	remedial investigation/feasibility study

RMRR	—	routine maintenance, repair, and replacement
ROD	—	record of decision
ROP	—	rate of progress
RRA	—	Reclamation Reform Act of 1962
SARA	—	Superfund Amendments and Reauthorization Act
SCS	—	Soil Conservation Service
SDWA	—	Safe Drinking Water Act
SEC	—	Securities and Exchange Commission
SEPA	—	State environmental policy act
SHA	—	safe harbor agreement
SIH	—	substantial irreparable harm
SIP	—	state implementation plan
SLA	—	Submerged Lands Act
SMCRA	—	Surface Mining Control and Reclamation Act
SNUR	—	significant new use regulation
SO_2	—	sulfur dioxide
SO_4	—	sulfate
SPDES	—	state pollution discharge elimination system
SREA	—	Superfund Recycling Equity Act
SWDA	—	Solid Waste Disposal Act
SWMU	—	solid waste management unit
TCLP	—	toxicity characteristic leaching procedure
TDRs	—	transferable development rights
TGA	—	Taylor Grazing Act
TIP	—	tribal implementation plan
TMDL	—	total maximum daily load
TSCA	—	Toxic Substances Control Act
TSDFs	—	treatment, storage, and disposal facilities
TSS	—	total suspended solids
TTO	—	total toxic organics
TVA	—	Tennessee Valley Authority
UIC	—	underground injection control
UMTRCA	—	Uranium Mill Tailings Radiation Control Act (of 1978)
UNICEF	—	United Nations International Children's Fund
UMRA	—	Unfunded Mandates Reform Act
USTs	—	underground storage tanks
USGS	—	U.S. Geological Survey
UUD	—	unnecessary or undue degradation
VAWA	—	Violence Against Women Act
VMP	—	vessel management plan
VOCs	—	volatile organic compounds
WRP	—	Wetlands Reserve Program
WQS	—	water quality standard

Appendix Two

CANONS OF STATUTORY INTERPRETATION

LINGUISTIC CANONS (embodying no substantive preference)

- **the whole act rule:** courts should give meaning to the entire legislative enactment

- **inclusio unius** (i.e., *expressio unius est exclusio alterius*): the inclusion of one means the exclusion of the other

- **ejusdem generis** (as of the same kind or nature): a word appearing in isolation to have a broad meaning should be construed more narrowly when considered in its setting

- **noscitur a sociis:** a word takes its meaning "by its companion"

- **pari materia** ("of the same matter"): when more than one statute relates to a subject, the statutes must be considered together

- **plain meaning:** words should be accorded their usual common meaning

- **words and phrases shall be given their ordinary grammatical and dictionary meaning**

- **technical and legal terms and words with special meanings should be given an interpretation appropriate to the context of the statute**

- **words of gender, number, and tense should be read to include any other gender, number, or tense**

SUBSTANTIVE CANONS (embodying a substantive preference)

- **penal and tax statutes should be strictly interpreted**

- **it is presumed that a legislature does not enact legislation unless it intends to change the law**

- **all provisions within legislation are there for a purpose**

- **no provision should be construed to be entirely redundant**

- **specific provisions prevail over more general provisions**

- **when dealing with two pieces of legislation, later enactments prevail over earlier ones**

- **repeals are not implied**

- a repeal of an act that itself repealed legislation does not revive the earlier legislation

- statutes shall be interpreted to avoid constitutional problems

- **rule of lenity:** doubts about a criminal statute should be resolved in favor of a narrow construction

- statutes in derogation of the common law should be strictly construed

- federal statutes are presumed not to preempt state law regarding matters traditionally subject to state regulation

- remedial statutes should be read liberally to effect their remedial purposes

- an interpretation of a statute made contemporaneous with its enactment is a particularly valuable guide to statutory meaning

- an interpretation of a similar statute by another jurisdictions is a particularly valuable guide to statutory meaning

- (various specific presumptions)

*CLEAR STATEMENT RULES**

- there is a need for a clear statement to achieve a result that would raise a substantial constitutional question

- there is a need for a clear statement to warrant the extraterritorial application of American law

- there is a need for a clear statement to subject a state of the United States to suit in a federal court

---

* There are many of these, and an exhaustive list may be impossible. The idea is that in certain contexts, legislation should be read as achieving a particular result only if an explicit statement in the text so provides. Judges should hesitate to imply meaning from a statute's design.

TABLE OF CASES

[References are to pages]

[References are to pages]

[References are to pages]

[References are to pages]

[References are to pages]

[References are to pages]

N

[References are to pages]

[References are to pages]

[References are to pages]

Y

Z

INDEX

[References are to sections.]

A

AIR POLLUTION (See CLEAN AIR ACT)

B

BAT (See BEST AVAILABLE TECHNOLOGY (BAT))

BCT (See BEST CONVENTIONAL TECHNOLOGY (BCT))

BEST AVAILABLE TECHNOLOGY (BAT)
Clean Water Act . . . 10[C][1][b]

BEST CONVENTIONAL TECHNOLOGY (BCT)
Clean Water Act . . . 10[C][1][c]

BEST PRACTICABLE TECHNOLOGY (BPT)
Clean Water Act . . . 10[C][1][a]

BPT (See BEST PRACTICABLE TECHNOLOGY (BPT))

C

CERCLA (See COMPREHENSIVE ENVIRONMENTAL RESPONSE, COMPENSATION AND LIABILITY ACT (CERCLA))

CLEAN AIR ACT
Generally . . . 9[A]
Acid deposition control, 1990 amendments . . . 9[D][3]
Climate change . . . 9[E]
Criteria pollutants, 1970 Act regulation of
    Emissions limitations . . . 9[B][1][b]
    National Ambient Air Quality Standards . . . 9[B][1][a]
Hazardous air pollutants
    1970 Act . . . 9[B][3]
    1990 amendments . . . 9[D][2]
National Ambient Air Quality Standards, 1990 amendments . . . 9[D][1]
New source performance standards, 1970 Act
    Applicability . . . 9[B][2][a]
    Operation . . . 9[B][2][b]
1970 Act
    Criteria pollutants, regulation of
        Emissions limitations . . . 9[B][1][b]
        National Ambient Air Quality Standards . . . 9[B][1][a]
    Hazardous air pollutants . . . 9[B][3]
    New source performance standards
        Applicability . . . 9[B][2][a]
        Operation . . . 9[B][2][b]
1977 amendments
    Nonattainment . . . 9[C][1]
    Prevention of significant deterioration . . . 9[C][2]

CLEAN AIR ACT—Cont.
1990 amendments
    Generally . . . 9[D]
    Acid deposition control . . . 9[D][3]
    Hazardous air pollutants . . . 9[D][2]
    National Ambient Air Quality Standards . . . 9[D][1]
    Permits . . . 9[D][4]
    Stratospheric ozone protection . . . 9[D][5]
Nonattainment, 1977 amendments . . . 9[C][1]
Permits, 1990 amendments . . . 9[D][4]
Prevention of significant deterioration, 1977 amendments . . . 9[C][2]
Stratospheric ozone protection, 1990 amendments . . . 9[D][5]

CLEAN WATER ACT
Generally . . . 10[A]
Applicability, issues of . . . 10[B]
Certification, section 401 . . . 10[C][3]
Effluent limitations
    Best available technology (BAT) . . . 10[C][1][b]
    Best conventional technology (BCT) . . . 10[C][1][c]
    Best practicable technology (BPT) . . . 10[C][1][a]
Issues of applicability . . . 10[B]
National pollutant discharge elimination system . . . 10[C][4]
Nonpoint source regulation . . . 10[D]
Point source regulation
    Effluent Limitations (See subhead: Effluent limitations)
    National pollutant discharge elimination system . . . 10[C][4]
    Section 401 certification . . . 10[C][3]
    Water quality standards . . . 10[C][2]
Section 401 certification . . . 10[C][3]
Section 404 . . . 10[E]
Water quality standards . . . 10[C][2]

COMMON LAW CONSIDERATIONS
Generally . . . 2[A]
Conservation servitude . . . 2[B][2]
Nuisance, law of . . . 2[C]
Preservation servitude . . . 2[B][2]
Property law
    Conservation servitude . . . 2[B][2]
    Law of waste . . . 2[B][1]
    Preservation servitude . . . 2[B][2]
Tort law . . . 2[C]
Waste, law of . . . 2[B][1]

COMPREHENSIVE ENVIRONMENTAL RESPONSE, COMPENSATION AND LIABILITY ACT (CERCLA)
Generally . . . 12[A]
Damages, issues of . . . 12[C]
Defenses . . . 12[B][2]

I-1

[References are to sections.]

[References are to sections.]

[References are to sections.]